The SAGE
Handbook of

European
Studies

The SAGE
Handbook of

European
Studies

Edited by
Chris Rumford

Los Angeles • London • New Delhi • Singapore • Washington DC

First published 2009

SAGE Publications Ltd
1 Oliver's Yard
55 City Road
London EC1Y 1SP

SAGE Publications Inc.
2455 Teller Road
Thousand Oaks, California 91320

SAGE Publications India Pvt Ltd
B1/I 1, Mohan Cooperative Industrial Area
Mathura Road
New Delhi 110 044

SAGE Publications Asia-Pacific Pte Ltd
33 Pekin Street # 02-01
Far East Square, Singapore 048763

Library of Congress Control Number: 2008929505

British Library Cataloguing in Publication data

A catalogue record for this book is available from the British Library

ISBN 978-1-4129-3395-7

Typeset by CEPHA Imaging Pvt. Ltd., Bangalore, India
Printed in India by Replika Press Pvt Ltd
Printed on paper from sustainable resources

Contents

Acknowledgements

I am grateful to the following for their help in the preparation of this book, all of whom offered support and encouragement, or helped to solve a particular problem along the way: Dario Castiglione, Grace Davey, Gerard Delanty, Gavin Drewry and Sandra Halperin.

I would also like to single out the following contributors who demonstrated an unusual degree of flexibility or 'came on board' at a particularly opportune time: Faisal Devji, Effie Fokas and John Erik Fossum. I would also like to thank Chris Rojek and Jai Seaman at Sage.

"Sadly Charles Tilly died before the publication of this book. I knew Chuck only through our correspondence but he was generous in his support for the handbook and he has made a significant contribution to the volume."

Contributors

John Agnew is a Professor of Geography and Chair of the Global Studies Program at UCLA. He has interests in geopolitics and international political economy. For 2008-9 he is President of the Association of American Geographers. He is the author of several books including *Geopolitics: Re-Visioning World Politics* (Routledge, 2003) and *Hegemony: The New Shape of Global Power* (Temple University Press, 2005).

Barrie Axford is a Professor of Politics at Oxford Brookes University where he is also Head of the Department of International Relations, Politics and Sociology. His research interests include globalization theory, new media and politics and the whole area of transnational communication spaces. His publications include *The Global System: Economics, Politics and Culture* (1996), *Unity and Diversity in the New Europe* (with D. Berghahn and N. Hewlett) (2000), *New Media and Politics* (with R. Huggins) (2001) and 2 editions of *Politics: An Introduction* (with G K Browning, R Huggins and B Rosamond) (1997 and 2002). Currently he is completing a monograph *Theories of Globalization* (forthcoming 2010) and working on a manuscript, *Britain: Globalization in One Country* (due out in 2011).

Ulrich Beck is a Professor for Sociology at the University of Munich, and the British Journal of Sociology Visiting Centennial Professor at the London School of Economics and Sciences. He is founding-Director of Reflexive Modernization, a research centre at the University of Munich, financed since 1999 by the DFG (German Research Society). His books include *World Risk Society* (1998), *Power in the Global Age* (2006), *The Cosmopolitan Vision* (2006), *Cosmopolitan Sociology* (special issue BJS 2006) (edited with N. Sznaider), *The Cosmopolitan Europe* (2007) (with E. Grande), *World at Risk* (forthcoming). His books are translated into 35 languages.

Gurminder K. Bhambra is an Assistant Professor of Sociology at the University of Warwick. She has previously held appointments at the Universities of Sussex and Keele. Her research interests are in the area of historical sociology and she is also interested in the intersection of the social sciences with recent work in postcolonial studies. She has published in the areas of postcolonialism, nationalism, identity politics, and human rights. She is author of *Rethinking Modernity: Postcolonialism and the Sociological Imagination* (Palgrave, 2007) and co-editor of *Silencing Human Rights: Critical Engagements with a Contested Project* (Palgrave, 2009).

Neil Brenner is a Professor of Sociology and Metropolitan Studies, and Director of the Metropolitan Studies Program, at New York University. His writing and teaching focus on critical urban and regional studies, comparative geopolitical economy, state theory and sociospatial theory. Major research foci include processes of urban and regional restructuring; the generalization of capitalist urbanization; processes of state spatial restructuring and neoliberalization; and urban governance restructuring. Book-length publications include *Henri Lefebvre: State, Space, World* (co-edited with Stuart Elden) (University of Minnesota Press, forthcoming 2009), *The Global Cities Reader* (co-edited with Roger Keil) (Routledge, 2006), *New State Spaces: Urban Governance and the Rescaling of Statehood* (Oxford University Press, 2004), and *Spaces of Neoliberalism: Urban Restructuring in North America and Western Europe* (co-edited with Nik Theodore) (Blackwell, 2003). Brenner serves as Chief Editor for the book series, *Studies in Urban and Social Change* (SUSC), published by Blackwell-Wiley and affiliated with the *International Journal of Urban and Regional Research*. He is currently working on a new book, tentatively titled *The Urbanization of the World*, which explores the epistemological, methodological and theoretical challenges of studying the geohistory of capitalist urbanization.

Craig Calhoun is President of the Social Science Research Council and directs the new Institute for Public Knowledge at New York University, where is also University Professor of the Social Sciences. He received his doctorate from Oxford and has published widely in comparative and historical sociology and social and political theory. His most recent books include *Nations Matter: Culture, History, and the Cosmopolitan Dream* (Routledge 2007) and *Cosmopolitanism and Belonging* (Routledge forthcoming). He has also edited three recent collections, *Sociology in America* (Chicago 2007), *Lessons of Empire: Historical Contexts for Understanding America's Global Power* (with F. Cooper and K. Moore) (New Press, 2006) and *The Public Mission of the University* (with Diana Rhoten) (Columbia University Press, forthcoming).

Dimitris N. Chryssochoou is an Associate Professor of International Organization at the University of Crete. He has been Reader at the University of Exeter, Scientific Director of the Defence Analysis Institute in Athens, and has held visiting posts at the LSE, Cambridge, Columbia, Athens and Panteion universities, as well as at the Hellenic Centre for European Studies and the Centre for European Constitutional Law in Athens. His books include *Theorizing European Integration* (2nd edition, Routledge, 2009), *Theory and reform in the European Union* (2nd edition, Manchester University Press, 2003, with M. J. Tsinisizelis, S. Stavridis and K. Ifantis), *The emerging Euro-Mediterranean system* (Manchester University Press, 2001, with D. K. Xenakis), and *Democracy in the European Union* (I. B. Tauris, 1998).

Lisa Conant is an Associate Professor of Political Science at the University of Denver. Her research examines the impact of European Court of Justice decisions on politics in the European Union and its member states, the Europeanization of national judicial institutions, and transformations in "European" citizenship deriving from European Court of Justice and European Court of Human Rights case law.

Gerard Delanty is a Professor of Sociology and Social & Political Thought in the University of Sussex. He was previously a Professor of Sociology in the University of Liverpool, UK. He is editor of the *European Journal of Social Theory* and author of ten books and editor of five, including *Inventing Europe* (Macmillan 1995); *Social Science* (1997; new edition 2005); *Social Theory in a Changing World* (Polity Press 1998); *Modernity and Postmodernity* (Sage 2000); *Citizenship in a Global Age* (Open University Press 2000); *Challenging Knowledge: The University in the Knowledge Society* (Open University Press 2001); (with Patrick O' Mahony) *Nationalism and Social Theory* (Sage 2002); *Community* (Routledge 2003); *Rethinking Europe: Social Theory and the Implications of Europeanization* (Routledge 2005); and has edited *the Handbook of Contemporary European Social Theory* (Routledge 2005) and (with Krishan Kumar) *The Handbook of Nations and Nationalism* (Sage 2006). His most recent book is the *Cosmopolitan Imagination* (Cambridge University Press, 2009).

Donatella Della Porta is a Professor of Sociology in the Department of Political and Social Sciences at the European University Institute. Among her recent publications are: *Approaches and Methodologies in the Social Sciences* (with Michael Keating) (Cambridge University Press), *Voices from the Valley; Voices from the Street* (with Gianni Piazza) (Berghan, 2008), *The Global Justice Movement* (Paradigm, 2007), (with Massimiliano Andretta, Lorenzo Mosca and

Herbert Reiter) *Globalization from Below* (The University of Minnesota Press), (with Abby Peterson and Herbert Reiter), *The Policing Transnational Protest* (Ashgate, 2006), (with Manuela Caiani) *Quale Europa? Europeizzazione, Identità e Conflitti* (Il Mulino, 2006), (with Mario Diani) *Social Movements: An Introduction* (2nd edition) (Blackwell, 2006), (with Sidney Tarrow) *Transnational Protest and Global Activism* (Rowman and Littlefield, 2005), (with M. Diani) *Movimenti Senza Protesta?* (Bologna, Il Mulino, 2004), (with H. Reiter) *Polizia e Protesta* (Bologna, Il Mulino, 2003).

Faisal Devji is an Associate Professor of History at the New School in New York. He has held faculty positions at Yale University and the University of Chicago, from where he also received his PhD in Intellectual History. He is the author of *Landscapes of the Jihad: Militancy, Morality, Modernity* (2005) and *The Terrorist in Search of Humanity: Militant Islam and Global Politics* (2008).

Franck Düvell is a Senior Researcher at the Centre for Migration, Policy and Society (COMPAS), University of Oxford. From 2003-4, he was Jean Monnet Fellow at Robert-Schuman Centre for Advanced Studies, European University Institute (Florence), and from 1998-2003 he was Research Fellow at the University of Exeter. He has also been a Lecturer in Sociology, Political Science and in Geography at the University of Bremen, Germany. His research focus is on clandestine migration, mixed migration, European and international migration politics and on the ethics of migration control. His present projects concentrate on transit migration in Ukraine and Turkey and on quantitative methods in clandestine migration research. Amongst his publications are *Illegal Immigration in Europe* (Houndmills, 2006), *Migration. Boundaries of Equality and Justice* (Cambridge, 2003, with Bill Jordan), *Die Globalisierung des Migrationsregimes* (Berlin, 2003), and *Irregular Migration. Dilemmas of transnational mobility* (Cheltenham, 2002, with Bill Jordan).

Michelle Egan is an Associate Professor and Jean Monnet Chair in the School of International Service, American University. She has published on economic transition in Central and Eastern Europe, European integration, and business-government relations. She is author of *Constructing a European Market* (Oxford, 2001), editor of *Creating a Transatlantic Marketplace: Business Policies and Government Strategies* (Manchester University Press, 2005). She is co-editing *Future Agendas of the European Union* (Palgrave, Forthcoming 2009) and finalizing a book manuscript on *Single Markets: Economic Integration in Europe and United States* to be published by Oxford University Press.

Effie Fokas is director of the LSE Forum on Religion and visiting fellow at the LSE's European Institute. Previously she taught Theories of Nationalism in the Government Department of the LSE. Her research interests include the sociology of religion in a European perspective, with a special focus on Islam; religion and nationalism; and the politics and sociology of immigration in Greece and Europe in general. She is co-author (with Peter Berger and Grace Davie) of *Religious America, Secular Europe? A Theme and Variations* (Ashgate, 2008) and co-editor (with Aziz al-Azmeh) of *Islam in Europe: Diversity, Identity and Influence* (CUP, 2008).

John Erik Fossum is a Professor of Political Science at ARENA Centre for European Studies at the University of Oslo. He is substitute coordinator of the Commission-funded 6th framework integration program Reconstituting Democracy in Europe (RECON), and is co-editor (with Erik Eriksen) of the *Routledge Studies in Democratizing Europe*. He has published widely on democracy, constitutionalism, citizenship and identity in the EU and Canada. The most recent book is *The European Union and the Public Sphere* (Routledge: co-edited with Philip Schlesinger).

Susanne Fuchs is Deputy Managing Director of the Research Area "Civil Society, Conflict and Democracy" (ZKD). From January 2006 to September 2007, she was a research fellow in the research unit, "Transnational Conflicts and International Institutions" (TKI). Previously, she carried out research and instructed in the fields of social theory, theory of democracy, and political sociology at the Social Science Research Center Berlin (WZB), the Humboldt University of Berlin, the University of Leipzig and the New School University in New York City. She received her PhD from the University of Leipzig; her dissertation was on "The Loss of Clarity - An Approach to Reflexive Modernity with Georg Simmel" (Der Verlust der Eindeutigkeit - eine Annäherung an Individuum und Gesellschaft, Klett-Cotta, Stuttgart, 2007). Susanne Fuchs' most recent work, prior to taking up her present position focused on a state-of-the-art analysis and perspectives vis-à-vis a rapprochement between international relations and sociology.

Wyn Grant is a Professor of Politics at the University of Warwick and is a member of the Population and Diseases research group in the Department of Biological Sciences and teaches in the university's plant and environmental sciences department, Warwick HRI. He has written extensively on the Common Agricultural Policy and agricultural trade.

Martin Lawn is a Professorial Research Fellow at the Centre for Educational Sociology, University of Edinburgh; previously he was a Professor of Education at the University of Birmingham. He is an ex-Secretary General of the European Educational Research Association and a member of its Council. He works within the historical sociology of education and has published on the histories of education and educational sciences, and on European networking. He co-authored *Fabricating Europe-The Formation of an Education Space* [Kluwer 2002] and edited *An Atlantic Crossing? The Work of the International Examinations Inquiry; its Researchers, Methods and Influence* [Symposium Books 2008].

Jeffrey Lewis is an Associate Professor of Political Science at Cleveland State University. His research focuses on the institutions of the European Union, and, in particular, decision making in the Council system. His work has appeared in *International Organization, Comparative Political Studies*, the *Journal of Common Market Studies*, and the *Journal of European Public Policy*, as well as a number of book chapters, including most recently, "Strategic Bargaining, Norms and Deliberation," in Daniel Naurin and Helen Wallace (eds) *Unveiling the Council of the European Union: Games Governments Play in Brussels* (Palgrave Macmillan, 2008).

José M. Magone is a Professor of Global and Regional Governance at the Berlin School of Economics. Previously, he was Reader in European Politics at the University of Hull. His research interests include the relationship between global and regional governance, in particular the role of the EU in it, comparative European politics and sociology, in particular the countries of southern Europe. Among his most recent publications are: *The Politics of Southern Europe* (Praeger, 2003), *The Developing Place of Portugal in the European Union.* (Transaction, 2004), *The New World Architecture: The role of the European Union in the Making of Global Governance* (Transaction, 2006), and *Contemporary Spanish Politics* (extended 2nd edition) (Routledge, 2008).

Ian Manners is Head of the EU unit and Senior Researcher at the Danish Institute for International Studies, Copenhagen. He has previously been Associate Professor at Malmö University and the University of Kent at Canterbury. His research interests lie at the intersections of European integration, normative and critical theories. He is author of *Another Europe is Possible: Critical Perspectives on EU Politics* (Routledge, 2007), *Normative Power Europe: A Contradiction in Terms?* (JCMS, 2002), *Substance and Symbolism: An Anatomy of*

Cooperation in the New Europe (Ashgate, 2000), co-author of *The Danish Opt Outs from the EU* (DIIS, 2008), and co-editor of *Values and Principles in EU Foreign Policy* (Routledge, 2006) and *The Foreign Policies of EU Member States* (MUP, 2000).

John McCormick is a Professor of Political Science at the Indianapolis campus of Indiana University in the United States, and a Visiting Research Fellow at the University of Sussex. His academic interests focus on transatlantic relations, the meaning of Europe, and environmental policy. He is author of *Environmental Policy in the European Union* (Palgrave, 2001), *The European Superpower* (Palgrave, 2007), *The European Union: Politics and Policies* (Westview, 2008, 4th edition), and *Comparative Politics in Transition* (Wadsworth, 2009, 6th edition).

Francis McGowan is a Senior Lecturer in the Department of Politics and Contemporary European Studies, University of Sussex. His research and teaching interests are the policy making process in the EU, European political economy and the idea of Europe in historical perspective.

Stjepan G. Mestrovic is a Professor of Sociology at Texas A&M University. He has published extensively on genocide, the Balkans, and social theory, ranging from the classical thought of Emile Durkheim and Thorstein Veblen to Jean Baudrillard and postmodernism. His most recent books are *The Trials of Abu Ghraib: An Expert Witness Account of Shame and Honor* (Paradigm, 2007), *Heart of Stone: My Grandfather, Ivan Mestrovic* (Mozaik, 2007), and *Rules of Engagement? A Social Anatomy of an American War Crime: Operation Iron Triangle–Iraq* (Algora, 2008).

Philomena Murray is an Associate Professor in the School of Social and Political Sciences and Director of the Contemporary Europe Research Centre at the University of Melbourne. She holds Australia's only Personal Jean Monnet Chair (*ad personam*) awarded by the European Union. She received a national Carrick Citation for Outstanding Contribution to Student Learning for pioneering the first European Union curriculum in Australia and leadership in national and international curriculum development. She is a Visiting Professor in the International Relations and Diplomacy Studies Department at the College of Europe, Bruges. Her research interests are in EU-Australia relations; EU-Asia relations; EU governance and comparative regional integration. Recent books include *Australia and the European Superpower* (Melbourne University Press, 2005) and P. Murray (ed.) *Europe and Asia: Regions in Flux* (Palgrave Macmillan, 2008).

Claus Offe was (until his retirement in 2005) Professor of Political Science at Humboldt University, Berlin, where he has held a chair of Political Sociology and Social Policy. He earned his PhD (Dr rer. pol.) at the University of Frankfurt (1968) and his *Habilitation* at the University of Constance. Since 2006 he teaches on a part time basis at the Hertie School of Governance, a private professional school of public policy, where he holds a chair of Political Sociology. Previous positions include Professorships at the Universities of Bielefeld and Bremen, where he has served as Director of the Center of Social Policy Research. He has held research fellowships and visiting professorships in the US, Canada, Australia, Hungary, Poland, Austria, Italy, and the Netherlands. He was awarded an honorary degree by the Australian National University in 2007. His fields of research include democratic theory, transition studies, EU integration, and welfare state and labor market studies. He has published numerous articles and book chapters in these fields, a selection of which is recently reprinted as *Herausforderungen der Demokratie. Zur Integrations- und Leistungsfähigkeit politischer Institutionen* (2003). Book publications in English include *Varieties of Transition* (1996), *Modernity and the State: East and West* (1996), *Institutional Design in Post-Communist*

Societies (1998, with J. Elster and U. K. Preuss) and *Reflections on America. Tocqueville, Weber, und Adorno in the United States* (2006).

William Outhwaite is a Professor of Sociology at Newcastle University. He studied at the Universities of Oxford and Sussex, where he taught for many years. His recent publications include *The Future of Society* (Blackwell, 2006), *European Society* (Polity, 2008) and (with Larry Ray) *Social Theory and Postcommunism* (Blackwell, 2005). He is currently working on social and political change in Europe since 1989, supported by a Leverhulme Major Research Fellowship.

Anssi Paasi has been a Professor of Geography at the University of Oulu (Finland) since 1989. He is currently serving as an Academy Professor at the Academy of Finland (2008-2012). Paasi has published extensively on regional theory, regionalism and region building processes. He has also theorized and studied empirically political boundaries and spatial identities. He is the author of *Territories, Boundaries and Consciousness* (Wiley 1996).

Craig Parsons is an Associate Professor of Political Science at the University of Oregon. He is the author of *A Certain Idea of Europe* (Cornell University Press, 2003; winner of ISA Alger Prize), *How to Map Arguments in Political Science* (Oxford University Press, 2007, APSA Sartori Prize, Honorable Mention), co-editor of *With US or Against US: European Trends in American Perspective* (Oxford University Press, 2005) and *Immigration and the Transformation of Europe* (Cambridge University Press, 2006); and has published articles in *International Organization, Journal of Common Market Studies, European Journal of International Relations* and other journals. Previously he was founding director of the Maxwell EU Center and assistant professor at the Maxwell School of Syracuse University.

Ben Rosamond is a Professor of Politics and International Studies and Head of the Department of Politics and International Studies at the University of Warwick. His current research focuses on three areas: theories of European and international integration, the role of ideas in European political economy and applications of the sociology of knowledge and critical disciplinary history to the political sciences. His principal publications include *Theories of European Integration* (Macmillan, 2000) and *The Handbook of European Union Politics* (as co-editor) (Sage, 2007). He is also co-editor of the journal *Comparative European Politics*.

Victor Roudometof is an Assistant Professor of Sociology at the University of Cyprus. His research interests are in the areas of cultural sociology and sociology of religion. He is the author of two monographs and editor of several volumes on Americanization, nationalism, religious studies, and transnationalism. His most recent projects include editing a *Social Compass* issue on Church-State relations in Cyprus & the volume *Orthodox Christianity in 21st Century Greece* (Ashgate, 2009).

Chris Rumford is a Reader in Political Sociology and Global Politics at Royal Holloway, University of London where he is also co-Director of the Centre for Global and Transnational Politics. His research interests include globalization and cosmopolitanism, European transformations, and borders and bordering and he has published widely in these areas. He is the author of several books including *Cosmopolitan Spaces*: *Europe, Globalization, Theory* (Routledge, 2008), *Rethinking Europe: Social Theory and the Implications of Europeanization* (with Gerard Delanty) (Routledge, 2005), and *The European Union: A Political Sociology* (Blackwell, 2002). In addition he has edited *Cosmopolitanism and Europe* (Liverpool University Press, 2007) and *Citizens and Borderwork in Contemporary Europe* (Routledge, 2008).

Nick Stevenson is a Reader in Cultural Sociology in the School of Sociology and Social Policy at the University of Nottingham, UK. His work is mainly in the areas of media sociology, social theory, citizenship and education. He is the author of *David Bowie* (Polity, 2006), *Cultural Citizenship* (Open University Press, 2003), *Understanding Media Cultures* (Sage, 2003), *Culture and Citizenship* (Sage, 2002), *Making Sense of Men's Magazines* (Polity, 2001), *The Transformation of the Media* (Longman, 1999), and *Culture, Ideology and Socialism* (Avebury, 1995). He is currently writing a book on education, culture and citizenship.

Charles Tilly (1929–2008) worked in many fields but is perhaps best known for his historical sociologies of state formation, revolutions, democracy, and contentious politics. At the time of his death he was Joseph L. Buttenwieser Professor of Social Science, Columbia University. Professor Tilly published more than 50 books during his career. Recent titles include *The Politics of Collective Violence* (Cambridge University Press, 2003), *Contention and Democracy in Europe, 1650-2000* (Cambridge University Press, 2004), *Social Movements, 1768-2004* (Paradigm Press, 2004), and *Democracy* (Cambridge University Press, 2007).

Amy Verdun is a Professor of Political Science, Jean Monnet Chair and Director of the Jean Monnet Centre of Excellence at the University of Victoria, in Victoria BC, Canada where she has been since 1997. She holds a PhD in Political and Social Sciences from the European University Institute Florence Italy (1995). Her earlier appointments were at the University of Leiden (1991-1992) and at the University of Essex (1995-1996). She is author or editor of eleven books and has published in scholarly journals such as *Acta Politica, British Journal of Politics and International Relations, European Union Politics, International Studies Review, Journal of Common Market Studies, Journal of European Integration, Journal of European Public Policy, Journal of Public Policy* and *Review of International Political Economy*. Her most recent books include *Globalization, Development and Integration* (co-edited) (Basingstoke: Palgrave Macmillan 2009), *Innovative Governance: The Politics of Multilevel Policymaking* (co-edited) (Boulder: Lynne Rienner 2009), *The European Union in the Wake of Eastern Enlargement: Institutional and Policy-making Challenges* (co-edited) (Manchester University Press, 2005), *The Political Economy of European Integration: Theories and Analysis* (co-edited) (London/New York: Routledge 2005) and *European Responses to Globalization and Financial Market Integration. Perceptions of EMU in Britain, France and Germany*, (Basingstoke: Palgrave, 2000).

William Walters is an Associate Professor in the Departments of Political Science and Sociology/Anthropology at Carleton University, Canada. His current research concerns the geopolitical sociology of state borders, migration, citizenship and non-citizenship in Europe and North America. He is the co-editor of *Global Governmentality* (Routledge, 2004), the co-author of *Governing Europe: Discourse, Governmentality and European Integration* (Routledge 2005) and the author of *Unemployment and Government: Genealogies of the Social* (CUP 2000).

Introduction: The Stuff of European Studies

Chris Rumford

The introduction to book that calls itself a 'Handbook of European Studies' might be concerned with justifying its existence, explaining why European studies is important, and drawing attention to the ways in which the book illuminates the subject in an innovative way, redefines the field of study, or challenges some embedded orthodoxies. This would be a rather defensive and, I think, oversensitive approach to a subject that as Craig Calhoun pointed out a few years ago is 'always already there and still in formation' (Calhoun, 2003). European studies is neither in need of reinvention, nor does its existence need to be justified. What is required, it is argued – and this is the prime task of this handbook – is for it to achieve a greater degree of visibility and ultimately recognition. There is currently a certain 'invisibility' to European studies, assumed by some to be the poor relation of EU integration studies and by others to be constituted at the 'soft' end of multidisciplinary social science by a preference for questions of cultural identity and normative political visions.

The idea that European studies is 'always already there and still in formation' is a useful summary of the current state of affairs. It does exist in a fully constituted, robust, and purposeful form – but only if you know where to look for it. European studies does not possess the status, visibility, and profile that it deserves and this does limit the contribution that it can make to the study of contemporary Europe. That it is still in formation is fairly clear, given the low profile and lack of recognition that it enjoys. This should be seen as a strength rather than a weakness though because what is needed, I argue, is less a new orthodoxy for studying Europe, such as that represented by EU integration studies (Rumford and Murray, 2003), and more an openness toward studying European transformations and a continual questioning of how best to study Europe.

As a European studies text, the book has three core aims. The first is to explore the transformations that charecterize contemporary Europe. The second is to look at how we can best study Europe. The third is to bring under one roof, so to speak, some key resources in European studies in such a way as to provide a launch pad for future studies. This means that it is not another book on EU integration studies, although that subject is certainly represented within its 600-odd pages. It is a book about contemporary Europe and how we might study it, and the study of EU integration is situated in the context of Europe's transformations. This makes it a rather unusual book in relation to the majority of contemporary publication that take Europe as their theme. European integration is written about extensively and the vast majority of books published on 'Europe' are concerned in some way with charting, explaining or elucidating the progress of the integration processes. The predominance of this area of inquiry has resulted in a conflation between Europe and the European Union and the idea that that there is not much else to study in relation to Europe. It is possible that people will pick up this book assuming that it is another contribution to integration studies. After all, European studies is often used as a catch-all name for the study of EU integration, the institutions of the EU, and the public policy domains with which the EU is closely associated: agriculture, regional policy, the single market and so on, and indeed all things European. In such a situation what purpose is there in pursuing a different version of European studies?

MAPPING EUROPEAN STUDIES

In response to this question I can offer five good reasons why we need a healthy and robust European studies to sit alongside the more established integration studies (with the aim of enriching both). The first reason is that European studies offers multidisciplinarity, whereas integration studies tend to be dominated by political scientists and internatonal relations (IR) scholars. The broadening of the field to include geography, sociology, planning, and cultural studies is desirable for many reasons, not least of which is that research may coalesce around new, multidisciplinary agendas (but at the same time there is no guarantee that sociology, geography

and the rest are inherently more multidisciplinary than political science), and, perhaps most importantly, that many disciplines can engage in dialogue as equal partners. Too often, EU integration studies insists that if other disciplines wish to participate they must do so by following an agenda framed by political scientists. As things stand at present, there is much European studies-type work being carried out in many disciplines but academics in one discipline too rarely relate to work carried out by academics in another discipline. Political scientists do not read the work of geographers. IR scholars are not familiar with the agenda in sociology, and so on. European studies needs to become much more multidisciplinary in order to ensure that it studies Europe in the most effective way.

The second reason is that studying Europe should be seen as important as studying EU integration. What makes European studies distinctive is that it poses a range of questions about Europe which do not get posed in a more narrowly focused EU integration studies. European studies deals primarily with the transformation of Europe, of which EU integration is one part. European studies is centrally concerned with question of cultural identities, of Europe's relation to the rest of the world, of transnational communities, of cross-border mobilities and networks, of colonial legacies, and of the heritage of a multiplicity of European peoples. Jean Monnet is reputed to have said, when reflecting upon the creation of the original European communities, 'If I could start again I would start with culture.' If we could begin European studies again would we want to start with integration? Or should we too opt to start with culture, as Monnet suggested? Broadly the answer to the latter question is 'yes'. When we say that European studies should study Europe we are referring to the constructiveness of Europe, and its meaning to different people at different times and in different places. Upon further reflection though this might be anything but straightforward. Which construction of Europe should we study? Institutional Europe (of which there are in any case several constructions)? Cultural Europe (thereby taking Monnetliterally)? Geographical Europe? Political Europe? Social Europe? The answer has to be 'all of the above'. The point of studying Europe is to explore its multiple constructions, meanings, histories, and geographies. Europe is constantly changing in its geographical scope, self-identity, cultural heritage, and meaning to others. European studies needs to investigate the meanings attached to various constructions of Europe, how they have changed over time, and what is at stake when someone offers yet another construction of Europe. Europe is not a given and cannot be reduced to an institutional arrangement (the EU). European studies should be studying Europe, in the broadest and most inclusive sense possible; it should never presume to be able to answer the question 'What is Europe?' in definitive, once-and-for-all terms.

The third reason is that there is a wealth of literature which does not conform to the norms and expectations of EU studies but which makes a significant contribution to our understanding of Europe. This literature needs to be given more prominence, disseminated more widely between (and within) disciplines, and brought to a wider public. For this to happen European studies needs to be established on firmer intellectual foundations and the ongoing activity in different fields and different literatures needs to become 'joined-up' to form a more cohesive and substantial whole. Many authors and publishers would not, at this time, view their books as something contributing to European studies. This is a shame. Thus, an urgent project for European studies is to achieve the sort of collective identity which will only emerge if colleagues working in the field feel themselves to be part of a 'common pursuit', rather than working in isolation.

The fourth reason is that understanding Europe's changing role in world politics needs to be prioritized. Caricaturing EU studies we can say that it has been rather inward-looking and tends to see Europe as separate from the rest of the world. It has also not been good at studying the EU in relation to globalization. In contrast, European studies encourages approaches to studying Europe than place it within a global framework. European studies is concerned with exploring the transformations which have shaped and continue to shape Europe, both internally and in the wider world (assuming for the moment that it is meaningful to talk about Europe as separate and distinct from the world). This global framework acknowledges the interconnectedness of Europe with the rest of the world and embraces globalization theories in an attempt to understand the impact of global processes on Europe, and vice versa. Such an approach to understanding the relationship between Europe and globalization can be said to be a marker of European studies.

To assert the need for such a global framework in understanding Europe flies in the face of accepted wisdom in EU integration studies. Many accounts of integration make no reference to the impact of globalization on the EU (Wincott, 2000: 178–9). This is due in no small part to the nature of EU studies as an academic discipline: focusing on the internal dynamics of integration rather than the global environment, which is deemed external to the EU (Rosamond, 1999). Nevertheless, the EU cannot be fully understood without taking into account the impact of globalization on the transformation of post-war Europe and the project of European integration, and the role played by the EU in promoting globalization.

There have of course been many attempts to explain the relation between globalization and the EU (mainly from within European studies rather than EU studies). For example, Manuel Castells (2000: 348) writes that 'European integration is, at the same time, a reaction to the process of globalization and its most advanced expression.' This echoes a consensus view that the European Union was originally threatened by globalization, completed the single market and monetary union as a defensive reaction, following which the EU developed the capacities with which to shape globalization, both in Europe and the wider world.

However, Castells' account is problematic as it does not account for the complexity of the relationship between globalization and the EU. Several reservations can be noted. First, it assumes that globalization is primarily an economic process driven by international trade, capital flows, global markets, and multinational business organizations. This is an economistic interpretation of globalization which can be more productively thought of as multicausal and multidimensional. Second, it assumes that globalization is a relatively recent phenomenon. It does not acknowledge that processes of globalization (plural rather than singular) have a long history and can be traced back over a millennium or more (Robertson, 1992). In short, globalization existed long before the EU was around to shape it. Third, it views globalization as the increasing interconnectedness of nation-states. In doing so it ignores the more generalized interconnectedness which is characteristic of globalization, linking social movements, citizens, non-government organizations (NGOs), communities of interest, enterprises, and a range of other actors.

According to John W. Meyer (2001: 227), 'It is difficult to draw definite boundaries between Europe … and the wider world society.' However, studies of the EU and globalization tend to see the former as distinct from the rest of the world, more so as globalization is deemed to be leading toward the creation of regional economic trading blocs (NAFTA, MERCOSUR, ASEAN). Moreover, it is a mistake to conflate Europe and the EU (the EU does not comprise all European countries) and they are not necessarily driven by the same global dynamics. Globalization may act upon Europe in ways which bypass the EU, as for example in the case of global cities and regional autonomization (see the chapters by Brenner and Paasi in this book). Alternatively, global forces at work in Europe may increase the web of interconnectedness in which the EU operates. Citizenship would be one example. Citizenship became a formal part of

EU affairs with the Treaty on European Union (1993) and rests, in the main, on the model of citizen as worker and the 'four freedoms' at the heart of the single market (capital, goods, services, and persons). However, the institutionalization of citizenship by the EU accounts for only part of the broader transformation of citizenship for Europeans. In the post-war period, national citizenship rights have been recast as human rights (Soysal, 1994) and global discourses of personhood rights, sponsored by the UN, have become increasingly influential. One consequence of this has been the increased rights granted to non-national residents in a particular nation-state (such as, access to education, the labour market, welfare benefits, and even the entitlement to vote in local elections). As such, the advent of postnational rights is one effect of globalization, not an initiative of the EU.

The fifth reason, which follows on from the one above, is that European studies is much more concerned to study processes rather than institutions. The big question in EU studies has long been: 'What kind of state does the EU represent?' Much intellectual activity has been devoted to this question, with the underlying assumption that it must be *some* kind of state (see Delanty and Rumford, 2005, especially chapter 8 for an extended discussion). The 'governance turn' in EU studies has not changed the situation fundamentally, although now talk is about the possibility of a multilevel polity or a postnational polity. It can be argued that the processes of transformation which characterize Europe are much more rewarding to study, and European studies has an advantage in its focus on processes such as immigration, citizenship, and social movements.

HOW SHOULD WE STUDY EUROPE?

One recent book which I think captures the European studies spirit is not an academic book at all, and I think would be dismissed by many working on EU affairs and the study of Europe more generally as being too populist, certainly rather journalistic, and too superficial by half. Nevertheless, I do not hesitate to recommend to you *Did David Hasselhoff End the Cold War?* (Hartley, 2006). The author stakes out her approach to European studies in the introduction. As a university student she found 'Europe' a 'bafflingly dull course' full of details 'about bureaucracy and treaties' (Hartley, 2006: ix). She summarizes her experience of studying Europe in the following terms: 'The "Europe" course was a cul-de-sac ... it was baffling, jargon-filled and ultimately pointless' (Hartley, 2006: 31). Elsewhere she confesses that, 'I wanted to understand [Europe], but didn't really feel that I had the tools' (Hartley, 2006: ix). Her account of Europe aims to be all the things that her college course was not. Out go the architecture of European institutions, bureaucratic history, and the founding fathers. In return we are offered accounts of 'Europe's blood feuds, dungeons, piracy, food, gods or monsters' (Hartley, 2006: 30).

If the result is an imperfect stab at European studies it has the great merit of being lively and stimulating, and succeeds at something that most books on Europe do not even attempt. It brings together many different dimensions of Europe and the European experience and places them in a common frame: the desire to offer something 'interesting, amusing or useful about Europe' (Hartley, 2006: 30). Thus we are offered chapters on 'The European Union as empire' (Chapter 2), 'Why the EU makes things seem boring' (Chapter 8), and 'The role of Islam in making Europe' (Chapter 16). Such themes are central to European studies, I would argue, and many of the topics on which the 50 short chapters are written resonate with concerns in the more mainstream academic European studies literature. Students who enjoy Hartley's account of 'why the EU makes things dull' might just move on to John W. Meyer's penetrating analysis of why the EU is 'massively and deliberately boring ... gray men in gray Mercedes' discussing issues designed to be technical and mindbogglingly

uninteresting' (Meyer, 2001: 239) contained in his discussion of the relationship between the EU and the globalization of culture. Similarly, reading the chapter on the Islamic origins of Europe might lead the student to an engagement with the work of Jack Goody on the mutual histories of Islam and Europe. The chapter on the EU-as-empire could be served as an appetizer followed by a main course consisting of Jan Zielonka's *Europe as Empire* (Zielonka, 2007).[1] Hartley's *Did David Hasselhoff End the Cold War?*[2] serves at least two very useful functions. It juxtaposes different issues (economic, political, cultural, social, legal) in such a way as to make it a genuine European studies text, and it also flags up themes which resonate with core themes of European studies literature. As such, it represents a fine starting point for the European studies student.

I believe that European studies has been well served in recent years by a range of publications which have given expression to the idea that it is more important to study Europe, broadly conceived, than a narrow reading of integration. However, as mentioned above, the authors of such publications do not necessarily see themselves contributing to a common project. This is because they situate themselves primarily in relation to a disciplinary literature, particularly in those subjects for which European studies is a minority pursuit. This is certainly true in sociology, which does not have a strong tradition of contributing to EU integration studies, and where the study of Europe is generally pursued by those working at the social theory end of the sociological spectrum. This realization has caused some consternation amongst sociologists in recent times. For example, Guiraudon and Favell have voiced the concern that 'sociology in Europe is not dominated by empiricists but by social theorists' (Guiraudon and Favell, 2007: 4). They see as 'regretful' the identification of sociology with debates in social theory which, in their view, does not aid the development of an empirical sociology of European integration. The complaint that they lay at the door of social theory is formulated as follows (Guiraudon and Favell, 2007: 5–6):

> It is quite remarkable how little all the grand talk of contemporary social theory – about transnationalism, cosmopolitanism, mobilities, hybridity, identities, public spheres, governmentality, risk societies, modernity, postmodernity, reflexive modernization, or whatever – has to offer to studying contemporary Europe or the EU in empirical terms that have anything in common with how mainstream EU scholars approach the field.

There is more than whiff of panic in this critique. It makes no sense to lump together the 'grand talk of contemporary social theory' as if it were a coherent school of thought. Castells work on network Europe does not fit seamlessly alongside Meyer's cultural globalization approach to Europe's 'otherness', or Beck's work on the cosmopolitanization of Europe. Social theory approaches have given rise to a disparate body of work which shares few common reference points. More importantly, in their desire to fit sociology into the mainstream of EU studies Guiraudon and Favell miss the point that social theory approaches, on the whole, choose to study European transformations rather than EU integration. In other words, whereas Guiraudon and Favell wish to formulate a political sociology of EU integration, social theorists have turned their conceptual lens on a broader set of questions occasioned by European transformations, of which the integration process is but a part. Therefore, it makes perfect sense for social theorists to explore mobilities, hybridity, governmentality, risk society, the public sphere, post-national citizenship, Europeanization, and borderlands because this is the 'business end' of European transformation.

There are parallels between the situation sociologists find themselves in and developments within the field of European historical studies, where the EU studies/European studies division is reproduced. There are historians of European integration whose work is dedicated to understanding the origins and development of the EU's institutions, the motivations of its founding fathers, and the key turning points which shaped the process of integration (Dinan, 2004; Gillingham, 2003; Milward, 1993). The work of these historians is frequently annexed to the EU integration literature. Commentators on the development of the single market, institution building, and the development of public policy domains will rely upon the histories written by Dinan, Milward, and Gillingham because their field is EU history. At the same time there are many historians of modern Europe, many of them eminent in their field, whose work rarely, if ever, gets referred to by EU studies scholars, even though the work of these historians covers the same historical period and geographical scope, and they even devote chapters to the history of European integration. However, the work of Norman Davis, Tony Judt, and Harold James, to name but three, rarely get mentioned in political science accounts of European integration. See for yourself. Pick up an EU studies textbook and check the index and the bibliography; it is likely that you will find Dinan but not Davis, Milward but not Judt, Gillingham but not James.

When we read modern European history we have a choice. Either we want historical accounts which range across both Eastern and Western Europe, the processes that shaped the politics and society of the continent, and the unresolved tensions that 50 years of 'integration' have produced, or we are happy to work with solipsistic accounts of how the EU made itself and/or 'rescued the nation-state'. The resources for consolidating European studies are rich and abundant but to do so we must make a choice. There are political parallels. At the time of the Dutch and French electorates' rejection of the constitutional treaty there was a popular slogan, 'Not too much Europe; not enough social Europe', which can be read as an expression of concern that the EU had a preference for markets over welfare provisions. The institutional dominance of EI integration studies is our 'constitutional crisis' and our slogan should be, 'Not too much Europe; not enough European studies.'

DOES A EUROPEAN STUDIES LITERATURE EXIST AT PRESENT?

It will be useful to introduce some books published in the recent past which serve European studies well, and which endow it with both intellectual substance and a research momentum. In this section I will focus on three texts, all of which advance the European studies agenda, albeit in rather different ways. They do this because they are engaged with their chosen themes in a broader way than is dictated by their parent disciplines, and they are able to reflect upon the practice of studying Europe and in doing so acknowledge the need for broader research agenda and multidisciplinarity. The books in question are Jan Zielonka's *Europe as Empire* (2007), Walters and Haahr's *Governing Europe* (2005), and Jensen and Richardson's *Making European Space* (2004). The precise reasons for these selections will be detailed below, but they each advance a novel understanding of Europe, conceive Europe broadly, and, importantly, as something that requires explaining in terms other than those associated with integration, and offer new perspectives, disciplinary or methodological, on familiar issues.

Before moving on to consideration of these particular books it is necessary to situate them within the wider field of European studies publications which have emerged of late and which have begun to change the way we study Europe. Of particular note in this regard is the recent book by Ulrich Beck and Edgar Grande, *Cosmopolitan Europe*, which offers a rereading of integration, polity-building, Europeanization, enlargement, and Europe's relation to the wider world through the lens of 'cosmopolitan realism', and depicts the EU as an institutional arrangement which has long been inscribed with cosmopolitan values. Neil Brenner's *New State Spaces* (2004) provides an account of the 'post-national' spaces of European governance, particularly the way nation-states mobilize urban space to develop a competitive advantage in the global capitalist economy. William Outhwaite and Larry Ray's *Social Theory and Postcommunism* (2005) looks at the impact of the collapse of communist regimes on the whole of Europe, East and West. Delanty and Rumford's *Rethinking Europe* (2005) places the transformation of Europe within a global perspective, and offers a fresh approach to questions of the nature of the European state, society, and processes of Europeanization. A number of edited collections are also worthy of mention. Berezin and Schain's *Europe Without Borders* (2003) addresses themes such as the transnational foundations of Europe, the changing role of borders, and cosmopolitanism. In addition, it focuses on the often-neglected societal dimensions of integration: the public sphere, national versus European identity, and trans-border networks. More ambitious still is Gerard Delanty's *Europe and Asia Beyond East and West* (2006) which explores the relationship between Europe and Asia in a cosmopolitan and post-Western frame. Another edited collection, Rumford's *Cosmopolitanism and Europe* (2007), also contributes to the debate on the transformation of Europe.

Europe as Empire

I have chosen to look in detail at Jan Zielonka's *Europe as Empire* (2007) for several reasons. One is the commitment to recast Europe (as a neo-medieval empire) and thereby move the study of integration away from the familiar statist template. Another is the determination on the part of the author to challenge some assumptions dear to many political scientists who study the EU. A third is Zielonka's novel perspective on Europe which requires him to study the transformation of Europe through the lens of EU enlargement which he believes 'cannot be treated as a footnote to the study of European integration' (2006: 3). The argument is that enlargement renders the rise of a European state impossible (Zielonka, 2007: 9) and as a result EU scholars need to develop new paradigms with which to study integration: state-centric approaches being deemed insufficient.

While the origins of the book are in the traditions of political science, the author is concerned with challenging the accepted way of doing EU studies. 'The book is written as a polemical response to the mainstream literature on European integration' (Zielonka, 2007: 2). The argument advanced by Zielonka is simple. The EU is not becoming like a state but it is taking on the form of an empire. The empire-like qualities of the EU should not be understood in terms of imperial designs but rather in terms of its 'multiple and overlapping jurisdictions, striking cultural and economic heterogeneity, fuzzy borders, and divided sovereignty' (Zielonka, 2007: vii). In other words, its polycentric system of governance means that it can be likened to 'a neo-medieval empire' (Zielonka, 2007: vii).

But why should we be convinced by the idea that the enlarged EU resembles a neo-medieval empire? What, according to Zielonka, are the characteristics of the EU which make it more like an empire than a state? The EU is diverse, more so than ever after the recent enlargement. This diversity can be discerned in terms of economies and democratic institutions, as well as history and culture. National minorities and patterns of immigration also add to the diversity. In short, 'the current plurality of different forms of governance, legal structures, economic zones of transactions, and cultural identities is striking and bears a remarkable resemblance to the situation in medieval Europe' (Zielonka, 2007: 168). A second main reason why the EU is neo-medieval is the system of governance, particularly as it extends beyond the EU's borders ('soft borders in flux'). The EU has promoted EU governance in the near abroad in order to stabilize the region.

'Countries such as Bosnia and Kosovo are practically EU protectorates, and there is a long list of countries from Ukraine to Palestine which are following EU instructions on organizing economic governance' (Zielonka, 2007: 169).

Enlargement has increased the diversity of the EU, seen in terms of economic stability, levels of development, democratic sophistication, and cultural practices. Enlargement has made manifest a gradient of systemic differences between the EU 15 and the newer member states. However, the differences are not so large that the new member states are in a different category altogether: 'They clearly belong to the same broad category of states, economies, and societies' (Zielonka, 2007: 43). Similarly, the gap between the 12 newest members and the rest of postcommunist Europe is not dramatic. The argument is that the external boundaries of the EU are not marked by sharp differences in levels of economic and political development. The EU and non-EU countries form something like a continuum. These features reflect the neo-medieval nature of the EU; overlapping edges of the EU polity, softer distinctions between us and them, increased networking and connectivity, and polycentric governance regimes.

The idea of Europe-as-empire will not be to everyone's taste and it would be easy to take issue with the idea of Europe as neo-medieval, which in any case is in danger of becoming a rather 'tired' metaphor (Anderson, 1996). Nevertheless, the book is well placed to perform a useful service in EU studies, in the sense that it could become the launching pad for a fresh round of thinking on Europe and the EU which is not in thrall to the statist paradigm, which Zielonka is right to identify as a major fetter on EU scholarship. From a European studies perspective it is significant that an EU integration scholar has found the need to work against political science approaches to the EU. Where one leads others may well follow and *Europe as Empire* may prove to be a significant step in bringing integration studies and European studies closer together.

Governing Europe

Governing Europe (Walters and Haahr, 2005) is significant not least because it represents the most substantial effort to date to explore European governance and EU integration from the perspective of the governmentality approach inspired by the work of Michel Foucault (see also Barry, 2001; Huysmans, 2006). The book explores the processes which have shaped the way the EU governs in key areas (the common market, Schengenland, coal and steel) and, central to this, the ways in which Europe has been constructed as a domain which is amenable to governance. To do this the authors acknowledge that it is necessary to introduce new concepts into EU studies (e.g. ordoliberalism, governmentalization) (Walters and Haahr, 2005: 13). Interestingly this is another example of an attempt to approach the question of EU-as-state from a new and fresh perspective. Their project is 'to investigate the "how" of European government', 'how it is able to govern extended social and economic spaces without possessing anything like the administrative apparatus or financial capacity of a nation-state' (Walters and Haahr, 2005: 14).

Looking back to the origins of the EC/EU, Walters and Haahr explore the European Coal and Steel Community (ECSC) (dating from 1951), seeing it as an example of the approach to governance characteristic of 'high modernism'; that is, a statist project of societal modernization with a belief in scientific progress leading to satisfaction of human needs. High modernism is a name given to a certain approach to governance which was particularly prominent in the West by the middle of the twentieth century. Quoting Scott, they define it as a vision of 'how the benefits of technical and scientific progress might be applied – usually through the state – in every field of human activity (Scott, quoted by Walters and Haahr, 2005: 24). In relation to the early formation of the European Communities, Walters and Haahr identify 'a liberal version of high modernism because it

seeks to govern not in a totalizing fashion, but by enrolling and co-opting others' (Walters and Haahr, 2005: 29). Driven by the 'high modernist' vision of Jean Monnet, the ECSC adopted the technique of governing 'without controlling the decision-making apparatus' (Walters and Haahr, 2005: 30–1). The ECSC is an example of the rational planning, elitist decision-making, and social engineering typical of the 'high authority' associated with liberal high modernity. This 'high authority' is able to command a 'general view' of affairs; in the case of the ECSC the Monnet's European Community decision-makers (the 'High Authority', as it was termed) were able to 'see' an integrated Europe 'which member states alone were incapable of visualizing' (Walters and Haahr, 2005: 32–3). From this vantage point the High Authority was able to encourage and enlist others through this vision of Europe. The method was not heavy-handed state intervention (how could there be without a European state) but 'enrolling and co-opting others'. To this end the High Authority worked to constitute 'the coal and steel industries as a self-regulating domain populated by responsible economic actors' (Walters and Haahr, 2005: 34).

This is one example of the 'governmentalization of Europe' wherein social, ecomonic and political spaces are constituted as 'knowable domains' (Walters and Haahr, 2005: 137). The attainment of knowledge of these domains by a High Authority which is uniquely placed to do this is the means by which the European Commission 'governs' Europe. This leads Walters and Haahr to conclude that rather than talk about the EU as a state it is much more productive to talk about processes of governmentalization and the technologies of power that can be deployed by institutions of the EU.

There are three reasons why this book is a major contribution to European studies. One, it reframes the question of the EU-as-state emphasizing that 'European integration can be reframed in terms of the govenmentalization of Europe' (Walters and Haahr, 2005: 142).

Thus, rather than being fixated on the state we need to look more broadly at questions of governance (in the absence of a state). Two, it emphasizes that in order to govern Europe in this way Europe has to first be constituted as a governable entity. Thus, the authors focus on the ways in which a 'High Authority' was created so as to look at issues in a 'European way' and create European solutions to European problems (see also Delanty and Rumford, 2005, especially chapter 8). Third, Walters and Haahr introduce a new political science perspective to bear on issues at the heart of understanding contemporary Europe and in doing so throw fresh light on familiar territory.

Making European Space

Jensen and Richardson's *Making European Space* (2004) aims to add a much needed spatial dimension to thinking about Europe. At the centre of the book is the idea that central to the project of European integration is the 'making of a single European space', which the authors term a 'monotopia' (Jensen and Richardson, 2004: ix). The aim of the book is to 'reveal the discourse of 'Europe as a monotopia' as an organizing set of ideas that looks upon the European Union territory within a single, overarching rationality of making 'one space', made possible by seamless networks enabling frictionless mobility' (Jensen and Richardson, 2004: x) (the single market and single currency are also examples of a concerted attempt to create Europe as 'one space'). In other words, the EU is in the business of promoting a particular vision of European space as being unitary and interconnected. Such a space is associated with untrammelled mobility and a high degree of territorial cohesion. Jensen and Richardson are critical of this version of European space for being too simplistic and idealistic on one hand, and wilfully promoted on the other. The term monotopia is thus a critical response to what the authors see as the 'hegemonic vision of

EU space' (Jensen and Richardson, 2004: x). The authors deploy their critique of 'monotopic rationality' in order to explore the EU's attempts to advance spatial governance 'within the frame of seamless mobility' (Jensen and Richardson, 2004: 3).

According to Jensen and Richardson what has emerged in recent years is an 'official' vision of European space which aims to reconcile the drive for greater competitiveness with balanced geographical development, and promote a polycentric form of spatial organization in place of the long-standing centre-periphery imbalances which have characterized European patterns of growth. The key to this monotopic interpretation of European space is the idea of mobility, so central to the EU's self-image.

> Mobility has become a defining feature of contemporary Europe. The four freedoms at the heart of the European Treaties are based on the movement: of people, goods, capital, and services ... the European project seeks to break down the barriers to free movement: the great distances between the core cities and the peripheral dispersed communities, the natural barriers which are not crossed by high speed roads and railways, and the national borders across which transport systems do not mesh. (Jensen and Richardson, 2004: 5–6)

On this account, the challenge for Europe is infrastructural networks to enable 'frictionless mobility'. The Trans-European networks were one policy solution, casting national borders as a problem that could be rectified by enhanced mobility schemes which could link up separate national rail and road networks. The overall aim of the Trans-European Networks projects is to 'reorganise the dynamics between spaces, cities and regions, and to reframe the possibilities for transnational mobility. The core vision embodies the Europe of flows, relying on integrated networks, the reduction of peripherality, and the related polycentric spatial strategy' (Jensen and Richardson, 2004: 50). The Trans-European transport networks represent an attempt to forge a 'homogenous EU territory linked by a single transport network which seamlessly crosses the borders and natural barriers between member states' (Jensen and Richardson, 2004: 17).

Jensen and Richardson's book is significant because it places issues surrounding 'integration' in a very different context: the construction of European space. Their work contributes to the project of recasting the core concerns of EU integration studies, broadening them and developing a multidisciplinary approach. Their 'cultural sociology of space' combines elements of planning studies, human geography, sociology, cultural studies, and politics. The book encourages us to rethink questions of power and territorial identity through the lens of mobility. On Jensen and Richardson's account Europe is being imagined by EU policy-makers as a single, integrated space made possible by an unprecedented degree of connectivity. In this way, 'a Europe of global competitive flows has become hegemonic over the alternative idea of a Europe of places. Greater mobility is seen to be the answer to a range of social and economic problems – exclusion, peripherality, uncompetitiveness – and the key to the EU being a player in the global economy' (Jensen and Richardson, 2004: 223–4).

I have singled out these three recent books and held them up as exemplars of European studies because each of them performs (at least) three valuable services that deserve acknowledgement. Each offers a fresh perspective on a familiar theme in EU studies and each seeks to broaden the frame of reference in order to understand issues in integration within a wider framework of political and social transformation. With their ability to bring together core integration questions with wider perspectives on change in Europe these books are well placed to bring together disparate readerships. For example, Zielonka's book will be read by scholars of integration and by those who are keen to think the EU beyond the state. In this sense, European studies is multidisciplinary not just because authors choose to combine a range of disciplinary concerns or methodologies but also because it creates a new constituency

of readers for whom the focus is Europe rather than the EU.

The approach to studying Europe embodied in *Europe as Empire*, *Governing Europe*, and *Making European Space* is not representative of the literature on contemporary Europe as a whole, particularly the work which goes under the banner of EU studies. At the same time these books are not isolated examples. A growing proportion of work on Europe aims for multi- or trans-disciplinarity, seeks to broaden the focus beyond 'integration', and seeks to offer new perspectives on familiar problems and issues. The books surveyed above represent some of the best work in European studies, and hopefully will serve as an intellectual core around which more work will coalesce. This handbook aims to make this task somewhat easier, and to this end advances the view that the consolidation of European studies is not to be achieved on the basis of projections of what it might be or could be in a ideal world, but on the basis that European studies already has substance and a sense of purpose: what it does require however is a degree of recognition hitherto not evident.

WHY A HANDBOOK?

This handbook is designed to the showcase the best work representative of European studies. It is also designed as a resource that can assist scholars in producing work which focuses on the transformation of Europe rather than its institutional architecture, and which draws upon a range of perspectives and approaches. To this end the handbook takes seriously the question 'How should we study Europe?', a question to which the majority of chapters attempt to offer an answer. European studies is animated by a constant questioning of what Europe we are studying and how best we might go about it.

The handbook also aims to make the case for why it is important to study Europe broadly, rather than reproduce the more narrow focus on the EU. In outline the case is straightforward; there are many Europes, both institutionally (e.g. EU, Council of Europe, Schengen) and culturally. A concentration on institutional Europes tends to mark Europe off from the rest of the world, a study of cultural Europes draws attention to the connectivity of Europe with the rest of the world, the impossibility of delimiting Europe, and the global context within which Europe operates. Multidisciplinarity also points to the need to conceive Europe broadly; a combination of history, sociology, geography, and cultural studies will militate against a narrow and exclusive reading of Europe as the product of post-war 'integration'.

As has already been made clear the handbook is also centrally concerned with the need to bridge EU studies and European studies in such a way as to reduce the separation between the two that currently exists. One strategy for engendering this cross-over approach is to include in the handbook chapters by scholars recognized as leading authorities in EU studies side-by-side with chapters by authors whose concerns would not normally place them on the EU studies map. EU scholars may be drawn initially to the chapters by Ben Rosamond and Ian Manners on themes for which these authors are renowned, but will also be happy to make the short journey to Philomena Murray's critique of the concept of integration and Martin Lawn's account of the constitutive role of education in creating a European 'intellectual homeland'. The handbook also advances a distinctive European studies identity through the choice of 'themes and issues' covered in Section 3. These highlight the societal and spatial dimensions to thinking about contemporary Europe, in a way that embodies the multidisciplinarity of European studies. Thus the 18 chapters comprising this section deal with key European issues such as global governance, freedom and security, nationalism and transnationalism, migration, social movements, citizenship and democracy, the public sphere, religion, welfare, education, the information society,

urban politics, borders, and regions, and additionally address such 'core' EU studies concerns as global competitiveness, agricultural policy, and integration.

The bridge between EU studies and European studies is also evident in Section 2 which deals with issues of polity-building, institutionalization, and Europeanization. While the chapters focus on themes central to the EU studies agenda – markets, law and justice, the democratic deficit, enlargement – the treatment of these themes is anything but standard. Each of these chapters works to situate issues of EU governance within a broader European (and global) context, and each chapter in its ways addresses the question, 'How did institutional Europe come to be the way it is?' The chapters in this section also address the changing nature of Europe, viewing current institutional arrangements as 'always in motion' and the EU as an evolving polity, conditioned by wider European transformations at the same time as working to shape them.

The handbook does aim to be original in its approach to European studies, its coverage of core issues, and its choice of contributions. One feature worth drawing attention to is the way several key issues are studied from different perspectives. For example, the question of the place of religion in contemporary Europe is approached both from the possibility that we are living in a postsecular Europe (Chapter 23 by Effie Fokas) and from the challenge to (provincial) European liberalism posed by global Islam (Chapter 34 by Faisal Devji). Similarly, the democratic deficit characteristic of 'institutional Europe' (Chapter 10 by Dimitris Chryssochoou) frames the issue of democracy and Europe in very different terms from those staked out in John Erik Fossum's contribution (Chapter 20) on citizenship, democracy, and the public sphere which looks beyond institutionalized dimensions of democracy. What these examples point to is that for European studies there cannot be one single way of approaching any topic; it is necessary to admit different perspectives on a common theme.

The handbook also points up some interesting and novel directions in European studies research. These include Craig Parson's contribution on the role of ideas in shaping the project of European union, the chapter by José Magone on Europe's role in global governance, the idea of 'normative power Europe' advanced by Ian Manners, the cosmopolitan reality of Europe as formulated by Ulrich Beck, and the post-emotional interpretation of Europe advanced by Stjepan Mestrovic. The handbook aims to show that novel interpretations of Europe have a natural home in European studies, already demonstrated by the reception given to Zielonka's idea of Europe as a neo-medieval empire.

FINAL THOUGHTS

Craig Calhoun offers a useful characterization of European studies when he writes that it 'has never been simply the study of a region, but always complexly interwoven with ideas about modernity, the West, Christendom, democracy, and civilization itself' (Calhoun, 2003: 6). I think he is right in saying this and we could perhaps add to his list; European Studies is also interwoven with ideas about multiple modernities, post-Westernization, postsecularism, Empire, and cosmopolitanism. The list could of course be extended still further. But in characterizing European studies in this way are we not in danger of associating it with those things that scholars of integration studies most dislike, and are consequently reluctant to embrace European studies because of? Put another way, building bridges between EU integration studies and European studies may be made more difficult by portraying the latter as being preoccupied with 'modernity and civilization'. There are two possible answers. One is to emphasize the perceived gulf between a focus on institution-building and integration processes and the conceptual innovations associated with post-emotional Europe and multiple modernities and how

this might be responsible for promoting a 'never the twain' mentality. Thinking of this kind inspired Guiraudon and Favell's comments that an empirical sociology of the EU was losing ground to the abstractions of social theory. The other possible answer is to point to Zielonka's embrace of 'empire', the Prodi Commission's desire to talk about 'network Europe', or the widespread interest in the idea of Europeanization as strong indications that the gulf between integration studies and European studies is smaller than we might have been led to believe.

NOTES

1 With Beck and Grande's chapter 'Cosmopolitan Empire' as a side order (Beck and Grande, 2007).

2 The answer to the titular question is 'no'. He needed help from Frank Zappa.

REFERENCES

Anderson, J. (1996) 'The shifting stage of politics: new medieval and postmodern territorialities?', *Environment and Planning D: Society and Space*, 14 (2): 133–153.

Barry, A. (2001) *Political Machines: Governing a Technological Society*. London: The Athlone Press.

Beck, U. and Grande, E. (2007) *Cosmopolitan Europe*. Cambridge: Polity Press.

Berezin, M. and Schain, M. (eds) (2003) *Europe Without Borders: Remapping Territory, Citizenship and Identity in a Transnational Age*. Baltimore: Johns Hopkins University Press.

Brenner, N. (2004) *New State Spaces: Urban Governance and the Rescaling of Statehood*. Oxford: Oxford University Press.

Calhoun, C. (2003) 'European Studies: always already there and still in formation', *Comparative European Politics*, 1 (1): 5–20.

Castells, M. (2000) *End of Millennium: The Information Age: Economy, Society and Culture, Vol. 3* (2nd edn). Oxford: Blackwell.

Delanty, G. (2006) 'Introduction: the idea of a post-Western Europe', in G. Delanty (ed.) *Europe and Asia Beyond East and West*. London: Routledge, pp. 1–7.

Delanty, G. and Rumford, C. (2005) *Rethinking Europe: Social Theory and the Implications of Europeanization*. London: Routledge.

Dinan, D. (2004) *Europe Recast: A History of European Union*. Houndmills: Palgrave.

Gillingham, J. (2003) *European Integration 1950–2003: Superstate or New Market Economy?* Cambridge: Cambridge University Press.

Guiraudon, V. and Favell, A. (2007) *The Sociology of European Integration*. Paper presented at the EUSA Conference, Montreal.

Hartley, E. (2006) *Did David Hasselhoff End the Cold War? 50 Facts You Need To Know: Europe*. Cambridge: Icon Books.

Huysmans, J. (2006) *The Politics of Insecurity: Fear, Migration and Asylum in the EU*. London: Routledge.

Jensen, O. and Richardson, T. (2004) *Making European Space: Mobility, Power, and Territorial Identity*. London: Routledge.

Meyer, J.W. (2001) 'The European Union and the globalization of culture,' in S.V. Andersen (ed.) *Institutional Approaches to the European Union*. ARENA Report No 3/2001. Oslo: ARENA.

Milward, A. (1993) *The European Rescue of the Nation-State*. London: Routledge.

Outhwaite, W. and Ray, L. (2005) *Social Theory and Postcommunism*. Oxford: Blackwell.

Robertson, R. (1992) *Globalization: Social Theory and Global Culture*. London: Sage.

Rosamond, B. (1999) 'Discourses of globalization and the social construction of European identities', *Journal of European Public Policy*, 6 (4): 652–668.

Rumford, C. (2007) *Cosmopolitanism and Europe*. Liverpool: Liverpool University Press.

Rumford, C. and Murray, P. (2003) 'Do we need a core curriculum in European Union Studies?', *European Political Science*, 3 (1): 85–92.

Soysal, Y. (1994) *Limits of Citizenship: Migrants and Postnational Membership in Europe*. Chicago: Chicago University Press.

Walters, W. and Haahr, J. (2005) *Governing Europe: Discourse, Governmentality and European Integration*. London: Routledge.

Wincott, D. (2000) 'Globalization and European integration', in C. Hay and D. Marsh (eds) *Demystifying Globalization*. Houndmills: Palgrave.

Zielonka, J. (2007) *Europe as Empire: The Nature of the Enlarged European Union*. Oxford: Oxford University Press.

Contexts: History, Culture, Politics

Contexts: History, Culture, Politics

Europe Transformed, 1945–2000

Charles Tilly

Have you read Primo Levi's initially grim, but ultimately vivifying memoir, *The Reawakening*? The book recounts Levi's circuitous return from a Nazi concentration camp to his home in Turin. It begins in January 1945. Shortly after Russian troops arrived at the infirmary of the Buna-Monowitz camp in Poland's Auschwitz district, a liberated Russian–Jewish prisoner named Yankel started transporting sick inmates to a huge, improvised hospital camp in Auschwitz. Feverish Levi only half understood what was happening. Yankel's horse cart took its load of former prisoners through the Auschwitz gate with its fearsome motto *Arbeit macht frei:* work liberates. After sturdy Russian nurses grabbed, stripped, and bathed the ex-inmates:

> We were given a shirt and pants, and led to the Russian barber, so that our heads might be shaved for the last time in our careers. The barber was a dark-skinned giant, with wild and delirious eyes: he practised his art with uncouth violence, and for reasons unknown to me carried a sten-gun slung on his shoulder. 'Italiano Mussolini,' he said to me grimly; and to the Frenchmen 'Fransé Laval'; from which one sees how little general ideas help the understanding of individual cases. (Levi, 1995: 24)[1]

All Europeans and all students of Europe have become heirs of Auschwitz. We can easily make the entire period of European history since 1900 pivot on the Holocaust and World War II: before, during, and after the disaster. Across the world, the war killed something like 50 million people, the majority of them civilians.

The most lethal war in human history left a shattered Europe to rebuild, and finally to evolve into the fundamentally reshaped continent of our own time. This essay places European transformations since 1945 in historical perspective. While conceding the importance of individual cases, it challenges Levi's conclusion: without general ideas, we do not know what questions to ask of individual cases. It asks, among other things, to what extent and in what regards we can think of Europe's experience since World War II as, yes, a reawakening. It replies: Europe never slept. But the half-century's struggles and transformations certainly produced a Europe that would have been unrecognizable to the continent's residents and observers as World War II ended.

What was Europe before 1945? Atlases conventionally divide Eurasia into two continents: Europe and Asia, with Asia four times the size of Europe. At the extremes of the great Eurasian land mass, Europe and China occupy roughly equal amounts of territory. Over most of human history, furthermore, the European population has usually run around one-half to two-thirds of China's: 40 million versus 60 million a thousand years ago, 725 million versus 1.5 billion today. For more than two millennia, the world economy has typically centered on China and adjacent areas of the Western Pacific and South Asia rather than on Europe. Although the Atlantic economies unquestionably rose to world dominance after 1750, the 250 years since then have constituted little more than a blink in the eye of historical time. Today the economic and political rise of Eurasia's eastern half is restoring the customary historical balance.

Although Roman and Byzantine empires had earlier ruled significant portions of western and southern Europe, the European region only took shape as a distinctive, connected entity within the Eurasian complex after 1000 CE. It did so through intense interaction with Muslim territories to its south and east. Those territories controlled the western end of the world's greatest commercial system, which ran from eastern to western Asia while extending into northern and eastern Africa.

Between the millennium and 1500 CE, Europe and the Muslim world interacted triply in:

- a series of political struggles that realigned the boundary between territories controlled chiefly by Muslims and mainly by Christians;
- expansion of trade between Europe and Asia that stimulated a remarkable acceleration of Europe's economy;
- intensified exchanges of ideas and technologies between the Muslim and Judeo-Christian worlds.

After the year 1000, trade between Asia and Europe intensified dramatically. It increased interactions of European merchants with the Muslim merchants who predominated in western Asia, southeastern Europe,

and North Africa while generating commercial activity within Europe as well. Intensified trade also promoted the two other trends: political realignment and cultural exchange. In the course of these three processes, Europe moved from being a dull backwater of the great Eurasian commercial system to becoming an attractive target for Asian invaders. Mongols, who leaped Muslim territories to reach well into Muscovy and Central Europe starting in the thirteenth century, were simply the most successful of many conquerors from Asia. The Turks, whose descendants created the Ottoman Empire, had themselves started coming into Anatolia from Central Asia some time after 1000 CE.

After 1500, however, the balance began to shift. An expanding Ottoman Empire incorporated many of the Muslim territories that mediated trade between Europe and Asia. It became a major European power in its own right as it did so. But other Europeans created their own direct connections with eastern riches by navigating around Africa into the Indian and Pacific Oceans. They also began drawing coastal Africa into their own trading systems as they reached across the Atlantic to conquer and populate the Americas. European trade and conquest laid a base for industrial expansion, first through small shops and widely scattered cottage industry, then (from the eighteenth century onwards) by means of fossil-fuel-consuming factories.

During the nineteenth century, European powers (now including Russia) began to bypass and pick apart the mighty Ottoman force to their southeast. By the twentieth century, European settler regions, such as, Australia, Argentina, South Africa, Canada, and the United States had extended European influence across the world. Meanwhile, militarily backed forms of colonial control had brought much of the Caribbean, Oceania, Africa, and maritime Asia into the European web. As Europe approached 1945, its fate depended heavily on world trade and imperial extraction. After then, trade came to matter even more as European empires disintegrated. No postwar European power except Russia, for example, managed on its own to produce sufficient energy for its daily needs. All traded their own products for imported fuel.

Once historians conveniently divided history since 1914 into four lumps: World War I, an interwar period, World War II, and postwar. Now they increasingly see European history from 1914 to 1945 as a single, seething block extending from one world war to another. But they cut the postwar period into several slices. Volker Berghahn contrasts his own analysis of the period with two others, by Eric Hobsbawm and Mark Mazower. Hobsbawm treats the war-to-war era as an almost unmitigated catastrophe of religious conflict and intolerance followed by a temporary interval (1945 to 1973) of reconstruction and prosperity before the oil shock of the 1970s signaled a new time of uncertainty. Mazower (2000) portrays the twentieth century's first half as struggle and alternation between tolerance on one side, and racist extermination on the other. But for Mazower, the time after World War II offers greater hope that Europeans can come to terms with diversity, dissension, and a reduced place in the world.

By no means does Berghahn minimize the cruelty of European life before 1945. On the contrary, he centers his analysis of the century's first half on its violence. Yet for Berghahn, the postwar period has opened up the possibility of an alternative vision that had already started to crystallize earlier in the century:

> The alternative to the epoch of violence for the first time assumed more concrete shape in the decades before 1914. It was sidelined thereafter by horrendous wars and civil wars, except for a brief period in the mid-1920s. Only after 1945 did the alternative finally break through in Europe, leading to a period of peace and prosperity that the region basically enjoyed up to the 1970s and, pace Hobsbawm, even beyond until the late 1990s. The alternative I am thinking of is the model of an industrial society that, within a democratic-constitutional political framework, peacefully consumes the mass-produced goods that it has manufactured. (Berghahn, 2006: 3)

Berghahn adds that such a model takes much of its inspiration from the United States, and that European history since 1945 remains incomprehensible without considering American influence. As Berghahn reminds his readers repeatedly, European history between 1945 and 2000 lends itself easily to teleology. Did the postwar reconstruction of Europe and the rise of non-European power make something like a European Union inevitable? Did the state socialist regimes of the USSR and Yugoslavia leave World War II already stuffed with the seeds of their own destruction? Within capitalist Europe, did the surviving authoritarian regimes of Greece, Spain, and Portugal necessarily move toward democracy? Did globalization ineluctably dissolve boundaries separating European countries from each other and from the world outside of Europe? In each of these regards, any responsible analysis of Europe's postwar transformations must make three moves: (1) identify major changes in European life after World War II that require description and explanation; (2) consider what else could have happened, and why it did not; and (3) use the first two to sketch explanations of major European transformations between 1945 and 2000. This essay offers preliminary versions of the three moves.

WHAT'S TO EXPLAIN?

First, let us review the sorts of changes in European life that call for description and explanation. In a heroic feat of disciplined compression, Swedish sociologist Göran Therborn has documented European transformations between 1945 and 2000. He describes them as a parabola: ascent to the peak of modernity, followed by partial descent from that peak. Modernity, for Therborn, means 'a social period turned toward the future as a means of orienting the present, rather than to the past, or as opposed to gyrating in the present without a compass'

(Therborn, 1995: 355). In a survey drenched with facts and figures, Therborn makes the case that after World War II both Western and Eastern Europe headed broadly in the same directions. In his account, they both:

- experienced rapid economic growth up to the 1970s and slower but still positive growth thereafter;
- spread mass consumption despite great disparities in levels of living between East and West;
- secularized aggressively; and
- first increased then decreased the place of government-backed collective goods, such as, education and health services in everyday life.

Table 2.1 recasts a fragment of Therborn's evidence for his summary. I have used Therborn's data to compute annual average rates of growth in gross domestic product (GDP) for 20 European countries over three periods: 1938–1950, 1950–1965, and 1965–1990. The first twelve-year span includes the war and the first five years of postwar recovery. No European economy roared over those troubled years. Yet the countries scattered across a remarkable range, from net losses of GDP in Hungary, Spain, and (especially)

Table 2.1 Annual average rates of GDP growth for European Countries, 1938–1990

Country	1938–1950	1950–1965	1965–1990
Austria	0.5	5.4	3.3
Belgium	1.3	3.7	3.1
Bulgaria	2.8	6.7	—
Czechoslovakia	0.3	4.0	—
Denmark	2.4	4.2	2.4
Finland	1.7	4.9	3.6
West Germany	0.4	6.9	2.4
Greece	−2.2	6.6	3.9
Hungary	−0.4	4.4	—
Ireland	1.1	2.4	4.1
Italy	1.2	5.6	3.6
Netherlands	2.9	4.6	3.0
Norway	2.9	3.9	3.6
Portugal	2.5	4.8	4.2
Spain	−1.2	6.3	3.8
Sweden	3.1	4.0	2.3
Switzerland	2.1	4.8	2.2
United Kingdom	1.6	2.9	2.3
USSR	2.1	6.3	—
Yugoslavia	1.2	5.7	—

Source: computed from Therborn 1995, Table 7.1, p. 134

Greece to substantial postwar gains in Bulgaria, the Netherlands, Norway, and Sweden. The Bulgarian figures look suspicious, given the country's battering as an Axis partner during World War II and as a much-troubled Soviet satellite thereafter. The other relatively fast movers – the Netherlands, Norway, and Sweden – did begin rebuilding rapidly once the Germans (occupiers of the Netherlands and Norway, harassers of neutral Sweden) retreated and the war ended. Germany itself suffered widespread war damage, and had hardly started recovering by 1950.

The period from 1950 to 1965, in contrast, brought robust growth to most of the continent. Economic planners in the East and the West remember those golden years with nostalgia. By this time Germany, Bulgaria, and Greece led the pack, with the Soviet Union, Italy, Yugoslavia, and Austria not far behind. Statistical retrospect makes it easier to understand why many Europeans then saw state socialism as a viable economic competitor with the capitalism espoused by the US and its Western European beneficiaries. Although the Soviet Union's ham-fisted control of its Eastern European satellites became even more visible with its 1956 crushing of Hungarian liberalization, from the West it looked for a while as though the Warsaw Pact would bring off the combination of socialism, authoritarianism, and vigorous economic growth.

In 1956, intellectual cold warrior Shepard Stone gave a worried assessment to his sponsors at the Ford Foundation. As to Western Europe, even though 'the Soviet Union has abandoned hope to control' the region, efforts to influence it indirectly continued. For example, the Soviets would 'appeal to the youth of Europe by pointing to opportunities for talented young people in the Soviet Union to get to the top'. In short, having moderated its once aggressive rhetoric, Moscow 'will try to become the economic, ideological and cultural magnet for 200,000,000 Europeans'. Conversely, 'the Kremlin will continue to try to divide Europe within itself and to split Europe from the United States'. And he feared that the communists might well succeed: 'The economic and social structure of Europe is brittle. Europe's belief in its own future is fragile' (Berghahn, 2001: 183).

In 1957, after all, the Soviet Union launched the Sputnik satellite, impressing the entire world with its technological virtuosity. At that point, Eastern Europe was riding high. After 1965, growth slowed in both halves of Europe. Since communist powers became more secretive about their economic statistics, it is hard to detect which half slowed more. Of the reporting countries in Table 2.1, only Ireland accelerated its growth in the interval from 1965 to 1990. Nevertheless, along with Ireland, latecomers Portugal, Greece, Spain, and Finland joined oil-rich Norway with growth averages neighboring four per cent per year during that quarter-century.

Over the entire period, much of Europe industrialized, incomes rose widely, and mass consumption flourished. Industrialization also drew Europe out of the prewar period's still predominantly agrarian economy. Look, for example, at Therborn's data on changes in agricultural employment, which I have graphed from two complicated tables. Figure 2.1 shows that just before World War II the majority of European countries had 40 per cent or more of their working population in agriculture. Overwhelmingly, the most agrarian countries concentrated in eastern and southern Europe. The countries with their largest shares in agriculture – the USSR, Albania, Bulgaria, Lithuania, Romania, Yugoslavia, Poland, and Estonia – had all adopted (or been forced into adopting) one variety or another of state socialism by the 1940s.

By 1990, only Albania remained above the 40 per cent mark. In the vast majority of countries, the agricultural share had dropped to under 20 per cent. State socialist regimes, then breaking up, still retained significantly larger proportions in agriculture than capitalist and social democratic regimes, but differences were diminishing across the continent.

The shift promoted dramatic urbanization of national populations and vast rural–urban migration. Across the board, agriculture had become more mechanized, productive, and prosperous.

The continent's agricultural workers and their children moved into manufacturing and services, including government services. Up to the 1970s, European countries saw a rapid increase in the manufacturing labor force and a rise in the productivity and profitability of manufacturing. From that point on, manufacturing employment leveled off or declined, as services took up larger and larger shares of the labor force. Overall (unlike their American counterparts), European workers and their governments responded to rising productivity by shortening work weeks, hastening retirement, and expanding unemployment benefits. At first, a postwar fertility increase expanded the European labor force. By the 1980s, however, fertility was leveling off or declining over much of the continent.

Once urban services had absorbed a country's surplus rural population, international migration took over. Although nineteenth-century Europe retained a crazy, moving quilt of overlapping nationalities, World War I and its aftermath slowed its internal migration and homogenized its national populations:

> The tidier Europe that emerged, blinking, into the second half of the twentieth century had fewer loose ends. Thanks to war, occupation, boundary adjustments, expulsions and genocide, almost everybody now lived in their own country, among their own people. For forty years after World War Two Europeans in both halves of Europe lived in hermetic national enclaves where surviving religious or ethnic minorities – the Jews in France, for example – represented a tiny per centage of the population at large and were thoroughly integrated into its cultural and political mainstream. (Judt, 2005: 9)

Labor shortage and mass immigration changed all that. Immigrants arrived in two major streams: from former European colonies and from southeastern Europe including Turkey. As a result, countries that wartime ethnic cleansing, postwar repatriation, and

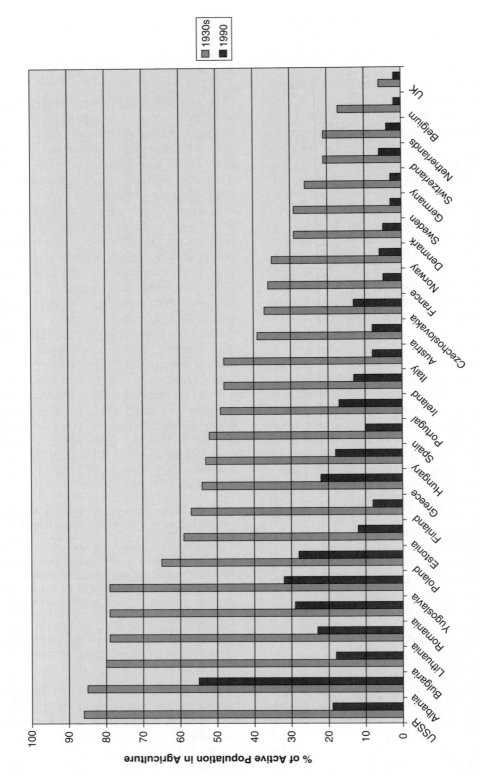

Figure 2.1 Agricultural employment in European countries, 1930s and 1990. (Source: Therbourn, 1995, 66–67.

border realignments of the peace settlements had homogenized with regard to language, religion, and culture again became ethnically heterogeneous. Absorption of culturally distinctive immigrants, long a hot political issue in such receiving countries as the United States, Australia, and Israel, became a matter of fierce contention in both Eastern and Western Europe. Whether recent arrivals of Muslims from North Africa and southeastern Europe have produced minorities more resistant to economic, political, and cultural integration than their non-Muslim predecessors remains a disputed matter among politicians and scholars alike. In my own view, the very processes by which long-distance migration occurs make it likely that Europe's Muslim immigrants will settle down at various positions in the range from rapid assimilation to uneasy accommodation (Tilly, 2000, 2007). Beyond the dispute, however, the richer parts of Europe are unquestionably becoming more diverse with respect to language, religion, and national origin.

Breakups of the Soviet Union and Yugoslavia accelerated the process, as internal controls over movement weakened and incentives to escape misery or lethal conflict increased. Major flows of migrants within the former USSR have run mainly toward the northeast, including the Baltic. Migrants from newly independent Warsaw Pact and Yugoslav states, however, have rejoined the centuries-old streams flowing from southeastern to northwestern Europe. Because long-distance migrants rarely abandon contacts with their places of origin, these mass migration streams are again knitting Europe together.

Therborn links these and related European transformations directly to the slash-and-burn effects of World War II:

> The way World War II ended radically restructured means, rights and opportunities, reshaped the political, economic and cultural space of the continent, and gave rise to new identities while discrediting others. It also generated grandiose efforts at social steering, East and West. The boom, which owed much to the war, accelerated the social and cultural dynamics of the Western European capitalisms and of the Eastern European socialisms, to the post-industrial, multicultural transformation of the former, to the erosion and dissolution of the latter (Therborn, 1995: 353).

Therborn sets a descriptive and explanatory agenda. Whatever else we do, we must trace the effects of World War II in Europe's two halves. We must also locate subsequent European experience in a changing world economy. Therborn establishes that the evidence exists both for sustained comparisons of countries and for detection of changes in politics, economics, culture, and social relations.

Still we must simplify. In this brief, preliminary treatment, we can't hope to account for all of Europe's social, cultural, political, and economic history between 1945 and 2000. Including only events that affected multiple countries and attracted international attention, Box 2.1 conveys the explanatory complexity that European political history alone presents. As compared with Therborn's comprehensive internal account, it calls attention to international institutions, US intervention, violent political struggles, and relations of Europe to the changing world economy.

The chronology traces a great series of political adventures (for sweeping surveys, see Calvocoressi, 2001: 213–378; and Judt, 2005). A shattered continent rebuilds, prospers, divides, returns to violent conflict, then makes significant strides toward internal coherence. Imperial connections largely disappear, but capitalist economies that had seemed exhausted come once again to occupy significant positions in the world economic system. However incompletely, democracy returns and even advances. A European Union that seemed a pious hope in 1945 not only intensifies relations among Western European countries, but begins integrating former members of the Soviet and Yugoslav state socialist systems.

Events in the chronology imply some remarkable shifts without pinpointing them precisely. Resistance to fascist forces during the war lent exceptional prestige to anti-fascists, especially communists, during the struggles for political control that roiled

---

Box 2.1   European political chronology, 1945–2000

1945	Defeat and surrender of Germany (January–May) and Japan (February–August); multiple peace conferences, 1945–1947
1945–46	Creation of United Nations, International Monetary Fund, World Bank, General Agreement on Tariffs and Trade (succeeded in 1990s by the World Trade Organization)
1945–54	European efforts to re-establish mandates and colonial control in Asia, Africa, the Middle East, and the Pacific often bloody, largely unsuccessful e.g. in India, Ceylon, Burma, Syria, Lebanon, Jordan, and Indochina
1946–49	Greek civil war
1947	Initiation of Marshall Plan and other US efforts to contain Soviet expansion in Western and Southern Europe
1948	Multiple Western European initiatives to coordinate recovery, including Organization for European Economic Cooperation
1949	Formation of Council for Mutual Economic Assistance to coordinate Soviet Bloc
1949	Formation of North Atlantic Treaty Organization as anti-Soviet military pact
1951	Formation of European Coal and Steel Community to coordinate Western European economies
1954–69	More colonial struggles and independence movements largely undoing European colonialism in Asia, Africa, and the Pacific; 53 newly independent states join the UN
1957	Creation of European Economic Community (= Common Market) among Western European continental powers (Britain not admitted until 1973)
1968	Major anti-regime mobilizations in Northern Ireland, France, West Germany, Poland, and Czechoslovakia
1974	Portuguese revolution, independence of Portugal's African colonies
1974	Fall of last Greek military regime, beginning of democratization
1975–78	Spain's dictator Franco dies, Juan Carlos becomes king, democratization ensues
1979	Soviet invasion of Afghanistan, spurring US attempts to check Soviet power in western Asia
1989–93	Disintegration of Yugoslavia, the USSR, and the Soviet Bloc, East and West Germany reunified, multiple civil wars, with 24 newly independent European states joining the UN, and another 4 mini-states (Andorra, Liechtenstein, Monaco, and San Marino) acquiring independent UN membership
1990	Schengen Agreement eliminates border controls among Belgium, France, Germany, the Netherlands, and Luxembourg
1992	Maastricht Treaty officially creates European Union, effective in 1993
1998–99	Serbian forces battle Kosovo Liberation Army, NATO bombs Serbs, international force occupies Kosovo

---

much of Europe between 1945 and 1950. As Gabriel Kolko puts it:

> In most of Europe the prewar ruling classes and dominant parties, having pursued varying degrees of collaborationist policies, sacrificed and lost their nationalist cachet and thereby endangered their purely class interests. The void to be filled was all the more ominous because the noncommunist socialist parties in many nations emerged from the war tainted with the stain of collaboration, and they failed to produce autonomous leaders who could articulated relevant responses to the burning issues each society and its people confronted. (Kolko, 1994: 263)

At the same time, participation in the war effort gave indigenous leaders of European colonies experience, contacts, and visibility that buttressed their bids to head independence movements.

The chronology also identifies several other parabolic trends that reshaped Europe:

sharpening division between capitalist and socialist blocs aligned, respectively with the US and the USSR, followed by disintegration of the socialist bloc after the 1980s; rising, then falling, influence of the socialist vision within the capitalist bloc; resurgence of independent national states in Western Europe, followed by their partial subordination to international institutions eventually including the European Union. A more mixed trajectory marks the history of European democracy during the same years: some decline in what remained of democratic traditions as state socialist and other authoritarian regimes rebuilt central state control, eventual democratization in such recalcitrant authoritarian regimes as Spain, Portugal, and Greece, splitting of former state socialist regimes into relatively democratic successors, such as, Estonia and Slovenia on one side, and increasingly undemocratic successors, such as, Russia and Belarus on the other.

At the risk of oversimplifying, we might divide postwar political history into four phases. First (roughly 1945–1950) comes a sweeping effort to repair the war's damage, including American and international agency support for Western European reconstruction, Soviet consolidation of control in the East, and the beginning of Cold War competition. Second (roughly 1950–1975), both East and West enter boom times and Westerners take their first steps toward economic integration as the Westerners lose their colonies and post-colonial immigration begins. During the same period, France and other Western regimes contain demands for radical democratization as well as their domestic communist parties. Third (perhaps 1975–1990), economic growth decelerates, the West's remaining authoritarian states democratize, and state socialist regimes stagnate. Finally (from 1990 onward), the same state socialist regimes disintegrate, long-distance migration transforms most European areas, and ethnically charged political conflict again becomes prevalent over much of the continent, while both the European Union and Russia become influential actors on the world's political and economic stages.

What do these demographic, economic, and political changes mean for Europe's culture and forms of solidarity? By 'culture', let us mean simply shared understandings and their representations in symbols and practices. By 'forms of solidarity' let us understand simply social ties on which people rely heavily when pursuing consequential collective enterprises. The two connect, since forms of solidarity, such as, kinship, friendship, and religion regularly shape people's shared understandings and representations (Tilly, 2005, 2006).

Changes in culture and forms of solidarity followed different schedules and trajectories in the East and West. In the East, much of life revolved around state-backed enterprises including factories and collective farms; benefits, obligations, and identities depended heavily on membership in such enterprises.

Citizens of the East long retained collective representations and commitments of their lives to state-backed enterprises even as they made up for the deficiencies of those enterprises by fashioning extensive (and often clandestine) networks of mutual aid (Alapuro and Lonkila, 2004; Castrén and Lonkila, 2004; Humphrey, 1999, 2001; Johnson et al., 1998; Ledeneva, 1998; Lonkila 1999a, 1999b; Volkov, 2002; Woodruff, 1999). With the economic slowdown of the 1980s and the shredding of state-sponsored safety nets thereafter, a culture of distrust for all but local and kinship-mediated solidarities grew more prevalent. At the same time, aspirations to the Western European style consumer culture became more salient; wealth occulted governmental and party connections in the acquisition of power, prestige, and comfort.

In the West, the immediate postwar period fostered a survivors' culture: pride in the sacrifice and solidarity that had helped people get through difficult times. Soon, however, a culture of consumption displaced the credit that people had received for their wartime sacrifices. It also challenged the disciplined redistribution of Western European socialism. Victoria de Grazia says it forcefully:

> By the 1980s Europe's old left did not have a consumer leg to stand on. Much had been said throughout the century about the false consciousness of false needs. But by the early 1990s it was clear that every movement to build 'insurmountable barriers against the invasion of false needs' had failed; the 'Maginot line of austerity' had been 'circumvented at the demand of consumers themselves'. Those who believed that new consumer advocacy movements could coalesce the 'dispersed interests' of consumers into a strong and effective political lobby were equally disillusioned. Acting in their interests as consumers, Europeans proved as agilely opportunistic as Americans, choosing exit, by going to another store or not buying at all; rather than voice, by mounting meaningful protests over the injuries of mass consumption. Well before the collapse of the Soviet bloc, there was a consensus, if a deeply disconsolate one, that with the exhaustion of 'alternative scenarios' the consumer society had to be recognized as 'our only future' (de Grazia, 2005: 465–6, quotations from Victor Scardigli and Michèle Ruffat; for the American model of the citizen consumer, see Cohen, 2003).

In the process, solidarities of religion, class, party, and nation that had emerged stronger from World War II began to lose their hold. Mass urbanization combined with long-distance migration to produce cities and suburbs sharply divided by national origin. Xenophobic politics like that of Italy's Northern League and France's National Front acquired widespread appeal in countries that had only recently turned away from organized anti-Semitism. Despite the economic and political unification promoted by mass consumption and the European Union, new parochial forms of culture and solidarity throve in late twentieth century Western Europe. In the East and West, the century's later decades brought a decline in the collective national visions of the early postwar years.

COUNTERFACTUAL EUROPES

What else could have happened? Aside from the Europe that actually emerged, what futures for Europe could close historical observers have plausibly predicted in 1945? Amid the ruins of World War II, close observers might have forecast a restored Europe, an authoritarian Europe, a socialist Europe, or an American Europe.

A restored Europe would have reconstituted the political, economic, and cultural map as of, say, 1920, with its striking contrasts of wealth, political organization, external connections, and lifestyles brought back into existence through mutual aid and (however wary) mutual respect. Replicas of the Bolshevik-dominated USSR, the precarious Weimar Republic, victorious but divided Britain, battered and likewise divided France and Italy, plus the Turkish remnant of the Ottoman Empire, would dominate their sections of the continent as they did before. Yet another European war would remain possible as these powers jockeyed for position.

An authoritarian Europe would have divided among different forms of top-down collectivism, with military regimes retaining

or recovering power in Greece, Iberia, and Germany as varieties of state socialism – from moderately to very authoritarian – became prevalent elsewhere. Eventually, in this scenario, we might expect war between the two types of authoritarian regimes, with the long-term victory and spread of militarily backed economic collectivism.

A socialist Europe would have given greater strength to the workers who fought and supplied World War II, fulfilling the Soviet program of solidarity among workers' organizations across the continent. Just as communist China wielded disproportionate influence among its neighbors without simply absorbing them, we might have expected the postwar USSR to create a large European web of clients, fellow travelers, and wary collaborators.

An American Europe would have subordinated Europe to the strength and the programs of a United States that World War II had lifted from economic crisis and brought to pre-eminence among world powers. With the USSR possibly surviving as a contained and impoverished enclave, most of Europe would have integrated into the American system of production, consumption, and distribution, with regional specializations resembling those of Canada, Mexico, and American states. The scenario implies domination by US military policy, which presumably would have centered on containing the Soviet Union and enhancing American power in South America and the Pacific.

Because none of these counterfactual Europes took shape, it is easy to raise objections against each and every scenario. Critics might claim, for example, that World War II's devastation made restoration of the prewar system utterly impossible. Let me offer two replies to that imagined criticism. First, elements of all four counterfactual scenarios did, in fact, come into being. As compared with the wholesale redrawing of boundaries that occurred at the end of World War I, for example, the settlements of World War II mostly restored the core territories and identities of states that had already existed during the 1920s. To some degree and in some places, furthermore, authoritarian survival, socialist expansion, and American influence did indeed occur.

Second, the point of the exercise is not to claim that these suppressed historical outcomes (in the phrase of Moore, 1978, chapter 11) had equal probabilities of realization with the history that actually transpired. Instead, it clarifies what an analysis of European trajectories since 1945 must explain. Explaining Europe's transformation since World War II entails specifying why a restored Europe, an authoritarian Europe, a socialist Europe, or an American Europe did not sweep the historical field.

Strictly speaking, the four scenarios do not qualify as counterfactuals (Hawthorn, 1991; Tetlock and Belkin, 1996). Some elements of each actually occurred. More important, partial realization and interaction of the four scenarios shaped Europe's historical transformations after 1945. Each one set limits for the others. Most obviously, American intervention contributed to the containment of state socialism, helped push Greece, Spain, and Portugal away from their previous authoritarian paths, and accelerated the disintegration of the Soviet Union. But influence also ran in the other direction: the vigorous viability of European socialism, for example, set serious obstacles in the way of the continent's thorough Americanization. Again, the vision of restored Europe that informed the peace settlements and the United Nations pitted national sovereignty against the consolidation of socialist states into a single seamless block.

The scenarios of restored Europe, authoritarian Europe, socialist Europe, and American Europe do not, however, exhaust the causes that transformed Europe after World War II. Remember Göran Therborn's description of the period as an approach to modernity – orientation of social life to the future – followed by substantial regression from that vision and organization of life. To the array suggested by the four scenarios, we must add at least these interrelated causal bundles:

- loss of overseas colonies;
- increased integration into the world economy;
- expansion of manufacturing employment, followed by shifts to services, leisure, and unemployment;
- rising then falling fertility, followed by population aging and mass immigration;
- urbanization, with concomitant contraction of the rural population.

In returning to description and explanation of what happened in Europe between 1945 and 2000, then, we must somehow integrate the causes implied by the four scenarios with these additional forces, which none of the scenarios entails directly.

WHY THIS EUROPE?

The largest process behind these complex changes has an ironic edge. It consists of Europe's increasing integration into the world capitalist system. The irony appears when we realize that Europeans invented and spread capitalism as a system well before encountering it as an external force. Whether appalled or enthused by Europe's capitalist integration, observers often think of it as Americanization. Yes, the US became the central power of world capitalism during the twentieth century. Yet that way of putting European experience since 1945 gets two things wrong. First, since World War II the world capitalist system has greatly internationalized, with Asian centers of manufacturing and finance increasingly crucial to its operation and a great deal of capital itself international in scope. Critics of globalization often have precisely the increasingly global reach of capital in mind. Second, Europe itself has played a crucial part in the creation of a genuinely worldwide capitalism. It has done so by participating in globe-spanning movements of capital, labor, and commodities as well as by creating many of the world's coordinating centers for capitalist production, consumption, distribution, and transfers of assets. The rise of European economic cooperation and finally of the European

Community has made European states and their capitalists major players in the world economy.

Take the case of multinational corporations. Arthur Alderson and Jason Beckfield provided an original and relevant perspective on the structure of world capitalism in 2000. They mapped head offices and branch locations of the world's 500 largest multinational firms (think Toyota, Microsoft, and Royal Dutch Shell) as a connected network. They then computed measures of centrality for individual cities. Their measure of 'betweenness', for example, gets at the extent to which possible connections among all cities pass through any particular city.

Let us call high scorers on that measure 'connectors.' The top 15 connector cities on the Alderson–Beckfield scale are given in Table 2.2, with their scores. The majority of the world's top connector cities – 9 of 15 – lie in Europe. The roster of cities changes somewhat with the measure of centrality. For instance, Tokyo heads the list of cities measured by the extent to which they maintain direct ties with all others ('outdegree'). But the proportion of European cities on the list remains high by all measures (Alderson and Beckfield, 2004: 830).

To be sure, multinational firms do not exhaust contemporary capitalism. Europe also

Table 2.2   The top 15 connector cities on the Alderson–Beckfield scale

City	Score
Paris	25.65
Tokyo	15.04
Düsseldorf	13.61
London	13.31
New York	10.01
San Francisco	7.29
Munich	4.89
Oslo	4.60
Vevey	4.46
Zurich	4.32
Beijing	4.23
Atlanta	4.22
Amsterdam	4.09
Stockholm	3.99
Osaka	3.98

figures significantly in world flows of energy. Here the former Soviet Union – not only Russia, but also Kazakhstan, Azerbaijan, and other energy-rich areas on the Asian side of the Asia-Europe border – looms much larger than on maps of multinationals and their subsidiaries. Consider the Putin government's arrest, prosecution, and imprisonment of Mikhail Khodokorsky, head of Yukos, the country's largest privatized energy company. It exemplified Putin's relentless campaign to recapture control over oil and gas supplies as a means of consolidating his personal political power and eliminating wildcat capitalist 'oligarchs' from his possible political opposition. Soon the state-controlled energy corporation became the world's largest producer of natural gas. With nearly a quarter of the world's known natural gas reserves, Putin's Russia is using its energy to buttress its international influence. As of 2006, Slovakia was importing 100 per cent of its gas from Russia, Bulgaria 94 per cent, Lithuania 84 per cent, Hungary 80 per cent, Austria 74 per cent, Germany 40 per cent, Italy 30 per cent, and France 25 per cent (Schmitt, 2006: 61). Clearly, the Russian state's monopolization of energy supplies was lending it tremendous clout both domestically and internationally. In a distinctive way, it was also making Russia a linchpin of world capitalism.

Russian experience underlines another crucial aspect of Europe's recent transformations. In 1945, many European and American leaders hoped that postwar reconstruction would block future varieties of totalitarianism by spreading democratic institutions and culture across the continent. To some extent they got their wish. Imperfect versions of democratic rule did become much more common in Europe between 1945 and 2000. Authoritarian regimes, such as, those of Spain, Portugal, and Greece moved into the democratic camp. More dramatically, the collapse of state socialism permitted partial democratization in Eastern Europe. Finally, the European Community's conditions for membership provide incentives for new members to take on the formal structure of democratic institutions, if not necessarily to build deep democracy.

To be sure, the EC itself incorporated a contradiction that haunts democratization wherever it occurs: the tension between popular voice, on one side, and executive authority sufficient to implement collective decisions, on the other. The creation of a European Parliament installed popular representation at a previously unimagined geographic scale. But the creation of technocratic bureaucracies to implement trans-European policies engaged EC leaders simultaneously in overriding local interests and negotiating with persistent national interests. Democratization therefore proceeded hesitantly at both the national and international scales.

In any case, democratization remained incomplete, and involved some U-turns. Freedom House can help us see what happened. For every independent country from 1973 onward, the New York democracy-monitoring organization produced annual ratings of political rights and civil liberties. In that dual scheme, countries run from 1 (high) to 7 (low) on each of the two. Ratings for rights emphasize the breadth, equality, and influence over governmental policy of citizens' voice, while ratings for liberties emphasize protection of citizens against governmental harassment. Change in the quantity (rights × liberties) therefore provides a rough measure of democratization (positive) and de-democratization (negative). Thus Freedom House rated Hungary 6 on rights and 6 on liberties in 1973, for a combined score of $6 \times 6 = 36$, while Hungary received 1 and 2 in 2001, for a $1 \times 2 = 2$, scoring an impressive $36 - 2 = 34$ for democratization between 1973 and 2001. Meanwhile, between 1991 and 2001 Russia (not rated separately before 1991) went from $3 \times 3 = 9$ to $5 \times 5 = 25$, for a resounding de-democratization score of −16.

In 2002, Freedom House classified every European country except Belarus, Bosnia-Herzegovina, and Yugoslavia – the three

regimes outlined in Figure 2.2 – as democratic. All but the three pariahs featured civilian governments competitively elected by general adult suffrage. But Freedom House's evaluators introduced much more variation into ratings of political rights and civil liberties. Figure 2.2 arrays the ratings for 43 European political units, from tiny to huge. Sixteen of them received the highest possible rating: 1 on political rights and 1 on civil liberties. Andorra, Austria, Greek Cyprus, Denmark, Finland, Iceland, Ireland, Liechtenstein, Luxembourg, Malta, the Netherlands, Norway, Portugal, San Marino, Sweden, and Switzerland all qualified for the highest possible grades on political rights and civil liberties. Fourteen otherwise democratic countries received ratings of 1, 2. All were experiencing major ethnic conflicts and/or visible political discrimination against minorities. In fact, they included all the larger democracies. They offered fairly broad, equal, and binding political rights, but faltered somewhat when it came to protection.

No European regime, according to Freedom House evaluations, quite traveled in the company of Afghanistan, Burma, Cuba, Iraq, North Korea, Libya, Saudi Arabia, Sudan, Syria, and Turkmenistan. All those non-European regimes scored at the bottom of the Freedom House scale: a bottom-scraping 7 for political rights, another abysmal 7 for civil liberties. But among European countries Belarus (6, 6) stood close to the bottom, while Moldova, Yugoslavia, Albania, Bosnia-Herzegovina, Macedonia, Ukraine, Turkey, and Russia all remained outside the privileged zone of regimes having extensive political rights and civil liberties.

Except for Turkey, as of 2001 all the low-ranking European countries had recently shed state socialist regimes. Among the regimes that had still styled themselves socialist or communist in 1989, the Czech Republic, Estonia, Hungary, Latvia, Lithuania, Poland, Slovakia, Slovenia, and – more dubiously – Croatia and Romania had as of 2001 moved away from their fellows by

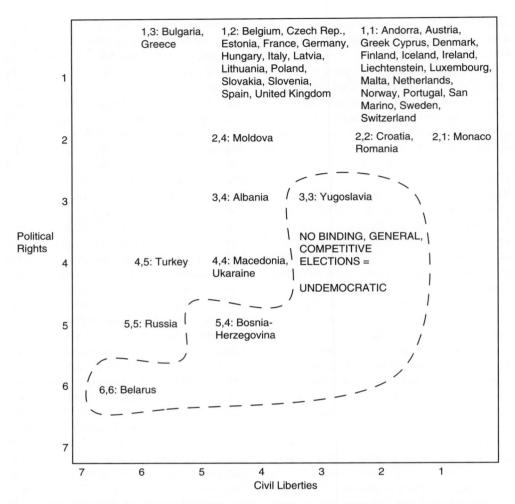

Figure 2.2   Freedom House ratings of European countries on political rights and civil liberties, 2001. (Source: compiled from Freedom House 2002).

installing ostensibly democratic institutions. The political problems of Belarus, Bosnia-Herzegovina, Macedonia, Ukraine, Yugoslavia, Moldova, and Russia did not stem, however, from too much socialism. They had all stuck with, or slid into, regimes ranging from petty tyranny to authoritarianism. Tyrants small and large blocked their ways to breadth, equality, protection, and citizen influence over government policy. Many of those tyrants had, of course, survived from socialist regimes. Yet their commitment to socialism did not hold back their

countries from democratization; their tyrannies did.

Once the Soviet regime collapsed, Russian nationalists within Russia (including the opportunistic nationalist Boris Yeltsin) faced a fierce dilemma. On the one hand, they claimed the right of Russians to rule the Russian Federation, which actually included millions of people from non-Russian minorities. Their claim supported the principle that titular nationalities should prevail throughout the former Soviet Union. On the other hand, they vigorously criticized the treatment of Russians outside the Russian federation as second-class minorities. Estonia, Lithuania, Ukraine, and Kazakhstan, for example, all numbered millions of self-identified Russians.

Those numerous Russians had suddenly become members of minorities – sometimes very large minorities – in newly independent countries. They faced choices among assimilation to the titular nationality, lesser forms of citizenship, and emigration. The Russian Federation posed as their protector. Unsurprisingly, newly independent neighbors often accused the Russian Federation's authorities of imperialism. Fairly soon, the great Western powers lined up together in a program of containing Russia and drawing its former satellites selectively into Western political and economic circuits. They tried to secure the enormous resources of former Soviet territories; for example, the huge oil reserves of Kazakhstan under and around the Caspian Sea. Led by the United States, the great powers unilaterally ended the Cold War. Outside of the Baltic, economies collapsed across the former Soviet Union, with output dropping about 60 per cent across the region as a whole between 1989 and 1998 (Campos and Coricelli, 2002: 794). At the same time, what remained of the Soviet Union's economic regulatory system fell to pieces.

Not all post-socialist regimes, by any means, then proceeded to democratize (Fish, 2001, 2005). Again using Freedom House measures, Figure 2.3 displays trajectories of four post-socialist countries from 1991 to 2001. (Freedom House only started treating Belarus, Croatia, Estonia, and Russia separately from the preceding socialist federations in 1991.) According to these ratings, every one passed through an early decline of political rights and/or civil liberties. But after its civil war ended, say the scores, Croatia took significant steps toward democracy. Estonia restricted political rights at first, but made a U-turn as civil liberties increased and then political rights expanded; the regime's discriminatory treatment of its substantial Russian minority accounts for Estonia's 2001 rating of 1, 2 – in the company of France, Germany, and the United Kingdom.

Meanwhile, Russia and (especially) Belarus headed downward toward fewer political rights and diminished civil liberties. In Russia, the Yeltsin–Putin wars in the Northern Caucasus and their silencing of opposition voices pulled back their country from the partial democratization Gorbachev had initiated. Yeltsin and Putin concentrated their energy on restoring the Russian state's internal capacity and external standing. They sacrificed civil liberties – or, more generally, protected consultation – as they did so. Inequalities of class and ethnicity became more salient in Russian public politics, Russian citizens disconnected their tattered trust networks even more definitively from public politics, and protection, breadth, equality, and bindingness of political participation diminished visibly.

Belarus President Aleksandr Lukashenka won his office in a 1994 popular election as an anti-corruption watchdog. But as soon as he had consolidated his hold on office, Lukashenka instituted censorship, smashed independent trade unions, fixed elections, and subjugated the legislature, thus compromising the country's small previous democratic gains.

Less than a year into his presidency, in April 1995, riot police acting on Lukashenka's orders beat up Popular Front deputies on the steps of the Supreme Council, in what was a first manifestation of regime violence. Ever since, the special interior ministry troops (OPMON) have become a most visible reminder of how Lukashenka prefers to deal with critics, being used against peaceful demonstrators with escalating brutality and frequency. In two years, the number of security forces is estimated to have risen to about 180,000, or double the size of the armed forces. (Mihalisko, 1997: 237)

The use of specialized military forces to establish political control drew on an old Eastern European repertoire. Post-socialist regimes that de-democratized after 1991 teetered between dictatorship and civil war. Nevertheless, as the Freedom House ratings illustrate, the majority of Europe's post-socialist regimes did move some distance

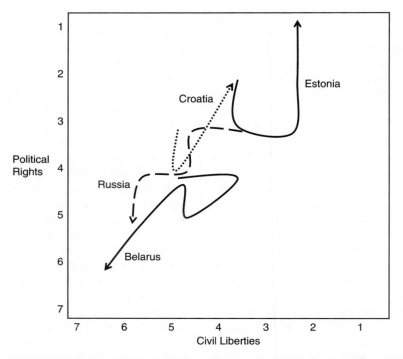

Figure 2.3   Trajectories of four post-socialist regimes, 1991–2001. (Source: compiled from Freedom House 2002).

toward democracy after 1991. That did not, of course, make them equally prosperous. Figure 2.4 underlines the wide income disparities among European countries at the twenty-first century's start. (Purchasing power parity adjusts national income differences for variation in the local cost of living.) In 2000, the range ran from $2,250 in desperate Moldova to $30,350 in wealthy Switzerland. Although greater income inequality in rich capitalist countries than in poor post-socialist countries makes per capita comparisons a bit misleading, the figures portray an average Moldovan as living on seven per cent of the purchasing power available to an average Swiss. By 2001, Slovenia had made it into the upper half of Europe's income distribution, but no other refugee from state socialism had yet arrived there. Except for Turkey, all the low-ranking countries had spent most of the postwar years under socialism. Since the majority of them have either joined the European Union or

have entered the Union's queue for eventual admission, the future portends the inclusion of many countries that missed the postwar prosperity of most present Union members.

Economists Alberto Alesina and Francesco Giavazzi, however, warn that even the currently prosperous European leaders face the prospect of economic decline *vis-à-vis* the rest of the world if they persist in their present policies. Alesina and Giavazzi do not recommend slavish European imitation of American models. For example, they deplore US health and welfare policies. But their comparison of industrial policies in Europe and the US lead them to the conclusion that anti-market actions are dragging Europe down:

Without serious, deep, and comprehensive reforms Europe will inexorably decline, both economically and politically. Absent profound change, in twenty or thirty years the share of Europe in the world economy will be significantly lower than it is today, and perhaps more important, its political influence will be much trimmed. Europeans seem to be living in the dream that their past splendor and

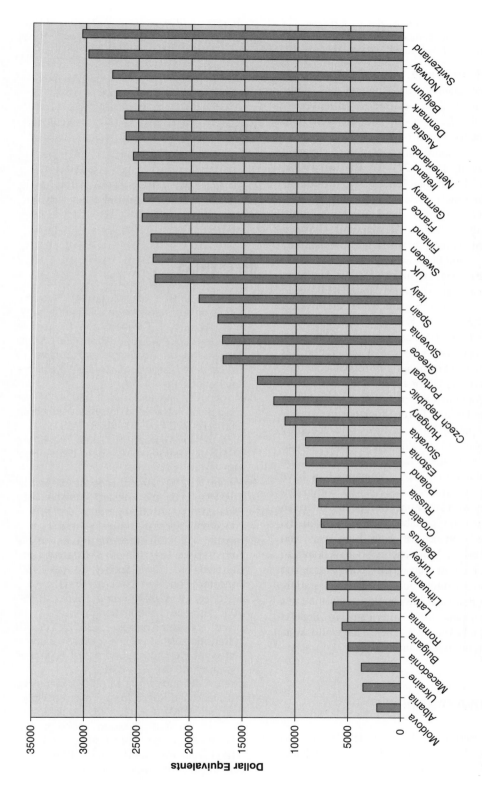

Figure 2.4 Gross national income per capita, purchasing power equivalents, European countries in 2000. (Source: World Bank 2001, Table 1).

their current prosperity cannot be lost. This is a mistake. A major European decline is indeed a serious possibility (Alesina and Giavazzi, 2006: 3–4).

Back in 1945, both American and European economic planners had thought that unrestricted markets had caused (or at least permitted) the Depression, and therefore that governments would have to cushion market effects with some forms of public planning (Hobsbawm, 1994: 271–2). By the 1990s, however, the US had turned away from market-cushioning policies while European governments generally held to them more steadfastly. Whether Alesina and Giavazzi have their grim prognosis right or wrong, they correctly point out how much farther from the neo-liberal ideal espoused by recent American governments even the most capitalist European economies have remained. If the overall transformations of Europe since 1945 have integrated the continent more firmly into the world capitalist system, that integration has fallen far short of making European countries replicas of the US or Japan. It always will.

The continued rise of Asia will nevertheless drive the US and Europe together in two different regards. First, as the world economy shifts back to its historical Asian center, Europe and America will lose some of the economic and political dominance they have enjoyed for two centuries. Second, within that changing world economy European–American exchange and collaboration will intensify. Increased reliance of both Europeans and Americans on Asian energy sources could, to be sure, increase transatlantic competition and compromise future attempts at collaboration. Even in that case, we should expect the fates of Europeans and Americans to depend increasingly on each other. The world knits together, but it knits unevenly.

ACKNOWLEDGEMENTS

Volker Berghahn, Victoria de Grazia, and Viviana Zelizer provided essential advice. I have adapted a few passages from my

Contention and Democracy in Europe, 1650–2000 (Cambridge University Press, 2004) and *Democracy* (Cambridge University Press, 2007).

NOTES

1 From THE REAWAKENING by Primo Levi. Translated by Stuart Woolf. English translation Copyright © 1965 by The Bodley Head. Reprinted by permission of Simon & Schuster Adult Publishing Group.

REFERENCES

Alapuro, R. and Lonkila, M. (2004) 'Russians' and Estonians' networks in a Tallinn factory', in R. Alapuro, I. Liikanen, and M. Lonkila (eds) *Beyond Post-Soviet Transition. Micro Perspectives on Challenge and Survival in Russia and Estonia*. Saarijärvi: Kikimora Publications, pp. 11–17.

Alderson, A.S. and Beckfield, J. (2004) 'Power and position in the world city system', *American Journal of Sociology*, 109 (4): 811–851.

Alesina, A. and Giavazzi, F. (2006) *The Future of Europe: Reform or Decline*. Cambridge: MIT Press.

Berghahn, V. (2001) *America and the Intellectual Cold Wars in Europe. Shepard Stone between Philanthropy, Academy, and Diplomacy*. Princeton: Princeton University Press.

Berghahn, V. (2006) *Europe in the Era of the Two World Wars. From Militarism and Genocide to Civil Society, 1900–1950*. Princeton: Princeton University Press.

Calvacoressi, P. (2001) *World Politics 1945–2000*, 8th edn. London: Longman.

Campos, N.F. and Coricelli, F. (2002) 'Growth in transition: What we know, what we don't, and what we should', *Journal of Economic Literature*, 40 (4): 793–836.

Castrén, A.-M. and Lonkila, M. (2004) 'Friendship in Finland and Russia from a micro perspective' in A.-M. Castrén, M. Lonkila and M. Peltonen (eds) *Between Sociology and History. Essays on Microhistory, Collective Action, and Nation-Building*. Helsinki: SKS/Finnish Literature Society, pp. 162–174.

Cohen, L. (2003) *A Consumers' Republic: The Politics of Mass Consumption in Postwar America*. New York: Vintage.

de Grazia, V. (2005) *Irresistible Empire. America's Advance through Twentieth-Century Europe*. Cambridge: Belknap Press of Harvard University Press.

Fish, M.S. (2001) 'The dynamics of democratic erosion', in R.D. Anderson, Jr. *et al.* (eds) *Postcommunism and the Theory of Democracy*. Princeton: Princeton University Press, pp. 54–95.

Fish, M.S. (2005) *Democracy Derailed in Russia. The Failure of Open Politics*. Cambridge: Cambridge University Press.

Freedom House (2002) 'Freedom in the World 2002: The Democracy Gap,' available at: www.freedomhouse.org/research/survey2002.htm, viewed 29 March 2002.

Hawthorn, G. (1991) *Plausible Worlds. Possibility and Understanding in History and the Social Sciences*. Cambridge: Cambridge University Press.

Hobsbawm, E. (1994) *The Age of Extremes. A History of the World, 1914–1991*. New York: Pantheon.

Humphrey, C. (1999) 'Traders, "Disorder" and Citizenship Regimes in Provincial Russia', in M. Burawoy and K. Verdery (eds) *Uncertain Transtion: Ethnographies of Change in the Postsocialist World*. Lanham, MA: Rowman & Littlefield, pp. 10–52.

Humphrey, C. (2001) 'Inequality and exclusion. A Russian case study of emotion in politics', *Anthropological Theory*, 1 (3): 331–353.

Johnson, S., Kaufman, D. and Ustenko, O. (1998) 'Formal employment and survival strategies after communism', in J.M. Nelson, C. Tilly and L. Walker (eds) *Transforming Post-Communist Political Economies*. Washington DC: National Academy Press, pp. 177–202.

Judt, T. (2005) *Postwar. A History of Europe Since 1945*. New York: Penguin.

Kolko, G. (1994) *Century of War. Politics, Conflict, and Society Since 1914*. New York: The New Press.

Ledeneva, A. (1998) *Russia's Economy of Favours. Blat, Networking, and Informal Exchange*. Cambridge: Cambridge University Press.

Levi, P. (1995) *The Reawakening*. New York: Simon & Schuster.

Lonkila, M. (1999a) *Social Networks in Post-Soviet Russia*. Helsinki: Kikimora Publications.

Lonkila, M. (1999b) 'Post-Soviet Russia: A society of networks?', in M. Kangaspuro, (ed.) *Russia: More Different than Most*. Helsinki: Kikimora Publications, pp. 99–112.

Mazower, M. (2000) *Dark Continent: Europe's Twentieth Century*. New York: Vintage.

Mihalisko, K.J. (1997) 'Belarus: Retreat to authoritarianism' in K. Dawisha and B. Parrott (eds) *Democratic Changes and Authoritairan Reactions in Russia, Ukraine, Belarus, and Moldova*. Cambridge: Cambridge University Press, pp. 223–281.

Moore, B., Jr. (1978) *Injustice. The Social Bases of Obedience and Revolt*. White Plains, NY: M.E. Sharpe.

Schmitt, G.J. (2006) 'Natural gas. The next energy crisis?' *Issues in Science and Technology*, Summer, 59–64.

Tetlock, P.E. and Belkin, A. (eds) (1996) *Counterfactual Thought Experiments in World Politics*. Princeton: Princeton University Press.

Therborn, G. (1995) *European Modernity and Beyond. The Trajectory of European Societies 1945–2000*. London: Sage.

Tilly, C. (2000) 'Chain migration and opportunity hoarding', in J.W. Dacyl and C. Westin (eds) *Governance of Cultural Diversity*. Stockholm: CEIFO [Centre for Research in International Migration and Ethnic Relations], pp. 62–86.

Tilly, C. (2005) *Trust and Rule*. Cambridge: Cambridge University Press.

Tilly, C. (2006) *Why?* Princeton: Princeton University Press.

Tilly, C. (2007) 'Trust networks in transnational migration,' *Sociological Forum*, 22 (1): 3–24.

Volkov, V. (2002) *Violent Entrepreneurs. The Use of Force in the Making of Russian Capitalism*. Ithaca: Cornell University Press.

Woodruff, D. (1999) *Money Unmade: Barter and the Fate of Russian Capitalism*. Ithaca: Cornell University Press.

3

The European Heritage: History, Memory, and Time

Gerard Delanty

To speak of the 'European heritage' is to refer to both a historical tradition and at the same time a consciousness of a tradition that is relevant to the self-understanding of the present. History considered in terms of what happened in the past and the knowledge of that history constitute the ground of heritage and memory. It is where a political community defines itself. That there is something called European history in the sense of the history of Europe is a point on which some agreement can be found, but to invoke the notion of a European heritage is a different and more contentious matter. What is at stake is a specific kind of time-consciousness in which the past is interpreted from the vantage point of the present and reflects its historical self-identity. Consciousness of a cultural heritage provides an orientation for the present in its relation to the past. This can take the form of a confrontation in which the past is repudiated and surmounted, a relation of continuity or one of revision and renewal.

In the movement from history to heritage there is an evaluation of the past in order for the present to judge what legacy it should derive from history. The debate about European heritage is very much a question of identifying the cultural resources that might be relevant to the current challenges of European societies. Thus, to speak of European heritage is to take up a position on European history that reflects the kind of self-understanding that has come into existence today.[1] It is a characteristic of present-day Europe that history has entered into the consciousness of a European identity that is not merely a political identity but also entails a cultural dimension. Collective identities generally do include a narrative of their genesis and often have a myth of origin. It is therefore not surprising that this consciousness of a shared past would enter into the articulation of a European identity. But the nature of this shared past is far from clear, for very often it is an invented past while for others it is one that has been distorted by violence against minorities and bears the legacy of colonialism. In short, it is not possible to speak of a European cultural heritage without considering alongside it its political meaning. For this reason the European cultural and political heritage cannot be separated. It is not possible, as is all too often the case in EU historiography, to see a political heritage emerging out of deeply rooted cultural orientations.

In this chapter these questions will be addressed, beginning with some remarks on memory and the cultural logic of the European heritage in terms of a mode of historical interpretation that is constitutive of current European self-understanding. The next section looks at some of the main expressions of European identity today in light of current developments. The third section provides a discussion of different contemporary readings of history.

MEMORY AND THE CULTURAL LOGIC OF HERITAGE

The question of the European heritage is inextricably connected with the problem of memory. In memory both experience and interpretation are played out. Since memory is always the memory of a subject, which can be a community, the interpretative dimension is unavoidable. Historical experience and historical interpretation provide a political community with a mode of historical self-knowledge that is more than collective memory, which assumes a basic continuity in the history of the community. The kind of memory that a cultural heritage encapsulates is one that includes the ruptures as well as the continuities of history. Viewed in such terms, European heritage cannot be defined in straightforward terms as narrative history or by reference to a foundational civilizational origin of which it is the history. As a history of ruptures, European heritage includes a relation with such discontinuities as major revolutions and periods of rebirth and renewal as well as controversies over the nature of authority as in religion doctrine and political ideologies, examples of which are the Renaissance, the Reformation, the wars of religion of the early modern period, and the French Revolution. All the great historical moments and events have led to a new relation with the past. Since 1492

the attempt to create a purely continental European empire was abandoned in favour of an aspiration to an overseas empire, first in the Americas and later in other parts of the world. This reorientation led to a separation of the idea of Europe and the idea of the West. Earlier the Great Schism of 1054 effectively severed the unity of a Christian civilization, which was divided furthermore with the Reformation. In the twentieth century, the end of the two world wars marked the end of an age. The year 1918 marked the end of the nineteenth century and the *ancien régime*, when it was finally abolished; 1945 marked the emergence of an American-led Western world and the end of the European age; and 1989 marked the final demise of the post-Second World War order, the 'short twentieth century,' as Eric Hobsbawn termed it.

So, major social transformations led to new expressions of historical time consciousness in which historical experience is subject to new interpretations. This has implications not merely for collective memory – of groups, nations, Europe itself – but also has direct political implications when it comes to commemoration. For how memory records the past is reflected in the ways in which the past is commemorated in the public sphere. In such cases we move from memory to the public recognition of a heritage. The cultural and political heritage of Europe is becoming increasingly difficult to commemorate in the ways nation-states have commemorated the past, ways which have mostly been connected with acts of liberation from an imperial power, wars against neighbouring countries or genocidal atrocities against minorities. Moreover, unlike most nation-states, which are based on a sense of peoplehood, there is no 'European people' as such and consequently commemoration cannot be the remembrance of a given people. This is one of the main differences between Europe and its nations. So the question of a European heritage cannot be so easily related to a specific people. What then might be the reference point for European heritage? One simple view is that the reference point is the vanquished or absent other. There is little doubt that Europe has been defined in this way at certain moments in its history, but this can lead to the dubious conclusion that a European self has been the result.

It is helpful to consider heritage not just only in terms of a collective memory of a given people. The memory that is established in a cultural heritage is both a matter of *what* memories and *whose* memories.[2] These do not translate into each other very easily: specific memories – what memories – often become not the memory of a collective actor but societal or historical memories and thus transcend a particular subject. In this respect, an important aspect of heritage is a memory conceived of as a mode of interpretation. The memories that are encapsulated in a heritage allow a society to interpret history and the relation of the present to history. To speak of heritage in such terms is to see it as a cultural model of interpretation. While this is pertinent to national traditions of memory and identity, it is highly relevant to the wider European context for the idea of a European heritage cannot be reduced to collective memories of a given people as such. Memory is central to any notion of a European heritage, but the memories of which it is the expression suggest more a mode of relating to the past that emphasizes the cognitive primacy of the *what*. Included in this will often be the range of previous interpretations such that a heritage may consist only of the memory of interpretations of a past that does not exist as history.

The body of traditions and the historical legacy that constitutes the European heritage has been interpreted by every age in light of the concerns of contemporaries. European heritage cannot be separated from these interpretations. It was not until the Renaissance that the consciousness emerged that there was a European heritage based on a relation to antiquity. With this came the view that there was a European heritage that was shaped in the relation of the present to the past. This relation could only be one of heritage rather than a direct history since the present age was seen as a new experience. The cultural logic that was at work in this had a cognitive dimension in the way history was organized into epochs: ancient, medieval, and modern. These were seen as ruptures – convenienced by regular episodes of forgetting out of which there can be no heritage – and history was discontinuous while at the same time constituting an underlying narrative of unity.

One of the problems that the very notion of a European heritage was faced with was that the principal voice of that tradition, Christianity, had repudiated the classical roots of Europe in the Graeco-Roman civilizations. Periodization in effect amounted to the secularization of history, which was no longer seen as fulfilling a divine plan, and the separation of human history and natural history. In a classic work, the French historian Paul Hazard (1953) referred to this development, which occurred in the late seventeenth century, as 'the crisis of the European mind'. Since the Enlightenment, this relation to the past constituted the basic dynamic of modernity which opened up new fields of interpretations. The European heritage itself constitutes the site of many of these interpretations. The European heritage was not just defined by reference to an archaic and classical past that was lost, but by reference to other worlds. In a sense the European self, the subjectivity of modern Europe, was defined by reference both to an Other (the non-European) and to its own Self (classical culture) which was experienced as distant and often irrecoverable. The secularization of Christianity and the emergence of modernity added to this sense of 'crisis'. Modernity replaced Christianity in much the same way Christianity had replaced antiquity. The resulting mood of uncertainty as to what Europe is as a political subjectivity translated into uncertainty as to what body of traditions constitute European culture and civilization.

By means of historicism – the view that each period in history and every expression of culture is historically unique – the European mind solved the problem of discontinuity.

Historicism, which triumphed in Germany, did not challenge the basic assumption of a civilizational foundation; it rather postulated different cultural expressions of European civilization, the universality of which was guaranteed by the diversity of its particular forms. The historicist position has been very influential in accounting for the alleged worldwide validity of European categories and modernity while denying some of the consequences, such as, self-government.

In the last two centuries or so there have been many attempts to define European heritage; some of these have reflected the ambivalence of Europe's historical self-identity, but others have been more self-confident. In the nineteenth century, the general preference was for a singular notion of civilization. But this very notion was itself in tension with heritage as culture: culture versus civilization offered two contrasting attitudes to the European heritage. Culture referred to the singularity of national culture, while civilization referred to a universal condition in which cultures participated. Since the Enlightenment the civilizational theme was often portrayed as the progress of the human mind or by reference to a notion of moral progress. There can be little doubt that it was often a racialized category (Goldberg, 2006).

Few accounts of European heritage are more famous than Max Weber's famous opening sentence to the *Protestant Ethic and the Spirit of Capitalism* ([1904–05] 1930):

> A Product of modern European civilization, studying any problem of universal history, is bound to ask himself to what combination of circumstances the fact should be attributed that in Western civilization, and in Western civilization only, cultural phenomena have appeared which (as we like to think) lie in a line of development having universal significance and value.

For Weber the uniqueness of Europe consisted of a cultural disposition towards disenchantment which had its origins in Christianity itself but which was a universal rationality even if it was more pronounced in Europe, especially since the confluence of Protestantism, capitalism, and the modern bureaucratic state

and legal domination. This suggests a view of the European heritage as one of ongoing disenchantment whereby a cultural logic of rationalism progressively undermines and transforms all forms of meaning, for Weber, who was a German cultural pessimist, to the point of eradicating all but an inner subjective meaning.

In the twentieth century, the emphasis shifted away from the unity of European civilization to a concern with culture and, more recently, the diversity of culture. In view of the catastrophes of the previous century and the undeniable link between colonial violence and European civilization, the very idea of a European heritage based on civilization has often been called into question. Julia Kristeva has commented on the theme of freedom, which she relates to the category of the self or subjectivity, and argues it was a crystallization of the intersection of Greek, Jewish, and Christian experience and constitutes the essence of European civilization (Kristeva, 2000: 117). The theme of freedom became one of the central ideas of the Enlightenment and was encapsulated in the philosophy of Immanuel Kant, who established the fundamental discord between the freedom of the moral will and the natural order.

According to the Czech philosopher Jan Patocka, writing in the 1970s, the basic continuity in European civilization is concerned with what he has called 'the care of the soul', a theme he associates with Plato and the centrality of the individual in European culture (Patocka, 2002).[3] There have been many attempts to postulate some such spirit that runs through European civilization guaranteeing an underlying meaning. Famous examples are Karl Jaspers's *The European Spirit* and the various works of the Swiss philosopher of European history, Daniel de Rougement. Jaspers, writing after the Second World War, aimed to offer an alternative to the pessimistic visions of the decline of the West, such as, Spengler's, that were dominant in the first half of the twentieth century. He defined Europe in positive terms as the spirit for freedom, which generates the will to history and to knowledge (Jaspers, 1947).[4] In a similar way, too, de Rougement in works, such as, *The Meaning of Europe* identified the spirit of a unity in diversity as the core of the European spirit, a spirit that he believed is exemplified in federalism as opposed to nation-states (de Rougement, 1965, 1966). A critic of both nationalism and an instrumentalized conception of Europe as a common market, he believed there was a higher ideal to be achieved and which was congruent with the European spirit. Before looking at some recent debates on readings of history, the next section will address the contemporary context of Europe as a cultural sphere of meaning in which new visions of European heritage are emerging.

EUROPE AS A CONTESTED CULTURAL FIELD

When the idea of a European identity emerged around the European Union over the past three decades or so the idea of a European heritage became a more politically significant matter. Until then the notion of a European heritage was second to national conceptions of the past, on the one side, and on the other a wider notion of Western civilization encapsulated the major cultural moments in Europe and modernity. In short, the idea of a European heritage was not directly linked with identity and memory. This is what has changed today as memory and identity have come to the fore along with the emergence of a European polity.

The first official accounts of European heritage in the post-1945 period emphasized its singular nature and the overall unity of Europe. The Congress of Europe in The Hague in 1948 marked the beginning of such interests (Dinan, 2006: 300). A much-cited example of a subsequent development was the 1973 Copenhagen 'Declaration of European Identity' when the then nine member states declared a notion of a 'European identity' in order to define Europe in its relation to the rest of the world. It referred to a 'common European civilization' based on a 'common heritage' and 'converging ways of life':

The diversity of cultures within the framework of common European civilization, the attachment to common values and principles, the increasing convergence of attitudes of life, the awareness of having specific interests in common and the determination to take part in the construction of a united Europe, all give the European identity its originality and its own dynamism.

At a time when the political identity of the EU, then the EEC, was little more than an inter-governmental organization the cultural identity indicated by this invocation of a European identity was not intended to be much more than a general appeal to the idea of the West and was, for the greater, not in tension with national identities. This, of course, was the height of the Cold War when capitalism and democracy were the taken-for-granted values of Europe.

Euro-federalists in contrast emphasized a stronger sense of a common European heritage in which the movement to 'ever closer union' was often read as the outcome of a long historical path from diversity to unity. The idea of a 'spirit of Europe' was frequently a theme in reflections on European heritage and the making of a European identity.[5] In such accounts the cultural and civilization foundations of political identity were emphasized.

Within the last twenty years the theme of the unity of the European heritage and an overarching 'European Identity' that transcends the diversity of cultures was slowly abandoned in place of an emphasis on a 'unity in diversity'. The Maastricht Treaty in 1992 announced a turn to diversity in the cultural policy of the EU: 'The Community shall contribute to the flowering of the cultures of the Member States, while respecting their national and regional diversity and at the same time bringing the common cultural heritage to the fore.' The emerging cultural policy of the EU moved the notion of a European heritage from a civilizational model of unity to one of regional diversity. This development clearly was a reflection of the political identity of the EU as a multi-tiered polity in which the regional, national, and supranational levels of governance interact (see Delanty and Rumford, 2005). Moreover, with many European countries embracing multiculturalism, a simple notion of the unity of the European heritage was inadequate.

While, for some, European heritage concerns issues of cultural protection, for others it is part of the intentional construction of a European identity. The annual 'European Heritage Day' was established by the Council of Europe in 1991, which has as its motto, 'Europe – a shared heritage'. What is invoked in this is a notion of a European consciousness that must be created through an active redefinition of the relation of the present to the past in the direction of a more inclusive cultural heritage. This is also borne out in developments in the representation of history in school textbooks and in a shift from monumental history to a new emphasis on the inclusion of the other in collective memories. The report commissioned by the President of the European Commission, 'The Spiritual and Cultural Dimension of Europe', defined a common European identity to be a 'task and a process', for Europe is of the present not of the past and there are no fixed boundaries or finality to it (Biedenkopf et al., 2004).

A striking feature of the late-twentieth century notion of a European heritage based on unity in diversity was a shift away from a universalistic frame of reference to what might be called a 'European republican consciousness'. The objective became less to define Europe in relation to the rest of the world, but rather to define the European project in relation to its national cultures. In the context of the post-Cold War situation in which Europe could not be any longer simply secure in its identity as the West or part of the American-led Western world, there was no clear Other that could present itself against which Europe could define itself (Friese, 2006; Stråth, 2002). With the increasing momentum of European integration between the Single European Act (1987) and the

Maastricht Treaty (1992) it became more expedient for Europe to define itself by reference to the national and the European, a relation that now included a rather vaguely defined notion of citizenship (Eder and Giesen, 2001). As the logic of Europeanization led to enlargement and the eventual incorporation of much of Central and Eastern Europe, the identity of the now quite large polity could no longer be posed in the terms of 1973, when nine relatively similar countries could appeal to a common Western civilizational heritage. The fact is that the EU had become a polity and the question of European cultural identity will have to be reconciled to the fact that Europe now exists in a political form.

The current situation is one in which any notion of the European heritage will have to balance diversity with unity. The notion of 'unity and diversity' must take into account the following: the diversity of regional and national cultures within Europe; the diversity of ethnic cultures arsing out of different traditions of migration and multiculturalism; and the wider diversity of popular culture due to globalization, which is not specially European but global. With the expansion of the European Union to include much of Central and Eastern Europe, along with the unresolved question of whether or not Turkey is part of the European heritage, there is the additional dimension to the cultural diversity of Europe, namely, civilizational diversity. While much of the unity and diversity debate relates to the internal diversity of national cultures on the one side, and on the other the diversity of the EU in terms of a plurality of nations, themselves already highly diverse, there is now the added civilizational diversity of Europe.

The dominant civilizational frame of reference until now was Europe as the West and it has often been claimed that the EU is a product of the Carolingian Empire in terms of a geopolitical area and a culture derived from Christianity. This assumption of a core Europe west of the Rhine can no longer be accepted simply because the reality is quite different. This 'Carolingian Europe' represents only one area in what is a wider and more polycentric European civilization. Any account of the European heritage will have to take into account a wider geopolitical area in which the West and East cannot be easily separated due to the interaction of its Jewish, Muslim, and Christian components. Embracing Western, Central, and Eastern Europe, the European Union is encroaching on societies whose routes to modernity have reflected different civilizational patterns. In view of the growing multicultural nature of Europe, relations with neighbouring Asian and North African countries, and the wider context of globalization, the identity of Europe cannot be defined in narrow terms as exclusively Western.

So in addition to the national and the regional diversity of Europe there is also a wider civilizational diversity. It is thus possible to speak of a plurality of 'Europes' to refer to the historical experiences of different geopolitical areas. One such example that is of continued relevance is *Mitteleuropa*, which had its origins in Pan-Germanism and was one of the most influential conceptions of German political and cultural identity in the early twentieth century. The concept took on different meanings in the post-1945 period when it became variously associated with Austria and the Habsburg tradition, on the one side, and on the other the civil society tradition associated with Central European countries under Soviet rule. In part a geopolitical term and in part a cultural term to designate a particular historical experience that is distinct from Western Europe, the idea of *Mitteleuropa* is a reminder of a different European heritage. It is hard not to agree with Milan Kundera (1984: 35) in his much-cited essay that 'Central Europe is not a state; it is a culture or a fate. Its borders are imaginary and must be drawn and redrawn with each new historical situation.' Like Europe itself, *Mitteleuropa* by definition lacks clear borders.

Any attempt to define Europe today must consider the fact that the term 'Western Europe' can no longer be used with the same self-confidence that it was used in the 1980s. Europe is not the West. It may be suggested

that a 'post-Western' kind of Europe is coming into focus today as Eastern and central Europe have entered the European political area as a result of the enlargement of the EU. The margins are becoming more important with a general shift to the East. The implications of this for an understanding of the European heritage are important. It suggests a general decline of the West as the overarching reference point for Europe (see Delanty, 2006).

The upshot of this is that the European heritage is largely a matter of how we define Europe. It is now becoming more and more evident that there are different concepts of Europe. In this context one only needs to consider the debate on such conceptions of Europe as 'Old Europe', 'New Europe', and 'Core Europe' for example (see Levy *et al.*, 2005). Such concepts of Europe can be seen as reflecting different models of modernity as well as different values and concepts of heritage. For present purposes it can be noted that the idea of Europe entails a diversity of civilizational routes to modernity and which have become more and more pronounced today as a result of the enlargement of the EU. In this wider, tendentially 'post-Western Europe', is the question of Islam in relation to the European heritage. There is now the reality of a European Islam as represented by some 12 million Muslims throughout European cities, most of whom are products of migration into Europe over the past four decades. However, the relation of Islam to Europe has a longer history, which we cannot explore here.[6] Viewed in the longer historical perspective migration into Europe in the last few decades can be seen in the context of diasporic movements of peoples that have occurred throughout history.

The question of Islam and Europe is, of course centrally too a question of Turkey as European. Such questions cannot be answered definitively since what is at issue is often the very terms of the debate. In this case the issue is not whether Turkey is European but whether the European heritage can be defined in a way that includes Islam. If it is plausible to argue that the European heritage has been largely created in debates about it, just as Europe is constructed in discourses about it, there is no reason why the European heritage excludes any one particular culture. Several centuries ago when the European heritage was being codified, what we today call Nordic Europe was not regarded as part of the European heritage. Clearly what is included in this is largely a matter of how Europe is defined. In this case an important consideration is the emergence of what might be called a hyphenated conception of Europe, for example, notions of the Euro-Mediterranean or the Euro-Balkans. The important point is that any consideration of 'European civilization' must include the interaction with the non-European and with margins. Implied in this plural notion of the European civilizational constellation is a strong emphasis on civilizational encounters and, in particular, a relation to the wider Asia context. This points to a hyphenated notion of civilizations as opposed to a singular notion of an enduring heritage. Thus, instead of a unitary notion of Western European civilization we can speak of a Graeco-Roman civilization, the Judeo-Christian civilization, Byzantine–Russian civilization. All of these civilizations are overlapping and formed out of a continuous process of interaction.[7]

In view of what appears to be a polycentric Europe consisting of not one centre but many – Massimo Cacciari (1997) speaks of Europe as an 'archipelago' – and the reality of ever-greater diversity, we can quite well ask the question whether there is any unity in the European heritage. Has diversity won the day? Before an attempt is made to answer this thorny question the next section looks at some of the main readings of history that are to be found in recent historical and philosophical scholarship.

CONTEMPORARY READINGS OF HISTORY

History considered as heritage and as an orientation for the present time is clearly

highly contested. Most positions on this question cannot be seen in terms of the nineteenth-century imperial discourse of the universality of European civilization and the received view of the 'rise of the West' has been subject to an exhaustive critical scrutiny that has had a major implication for any interpretation of European history. Joseph Fontana's (1995) interpretation of European history aimed to undermine the traditional wisdom of a common heritage by showing the adversarial logic to many of its achievement.[8] Many interpretations of European history avoid any direct political interpretation. Unlike earlier histories, which generally contained a 'grand narrative', contemporary readings of history generally avoid the search for meaning. Norman Davies (1996) in his major work on European history made no attempt to uncover a grand narrative in European history.[9] In *The Culture of the Europeans*, Donald Sassoon (2006) also avoids the search for an underlying 'spirit' that was a feature of earlier accounts. The intellectual historian J.G.A. Pocock denies the existence of such thing as European history, claiming that there are only different constructions of Europe which means many different things to many different people (Pocock, 1997, 2002). In his survey of post-war Europe, Tony Judt (2005) also avoided any single conclusion. Yet, the centrality of the Holocaust and the consequences of totalitarianism stand out in his narrative. But as he points out in the epilogue to his book the contemporary obsession with memory is a poor guide to the past. Post-war Europe was built on the forgetting of history, but since 1989 there has been a 'compensatory surplus of memory'. Judt does not venture further into the territory of what legacy of history should be and how we should view the European heritage in light of the catastrophes of the world wars of the previous century. This too is the case in Mazower's (1998) survey of twentieth-century Europe, *Dark Continent*.

The German historian Christian Meier (2005) addresses this question more directly in his book, *From Athens to Auschwitz*. He is struck by the 'absence of history', for in a sense history does not have a lot to tell us today. Despite its hagiography, the European Union is not as dependent on a history of its origins as most nations were in the past. This however does not mean we are living in a 'post-historical' era in which history does not matter. In his view it matters a lot for the present to situate itself with respect to history. For him the problem of history is the centrality of Auschwitz, as the symbolic term to refer to the Holocaust as a whole. What needs to be understood is how European civilization, from its origins in Athens, resulted in this event. Clearly it is not possible to explain the course of history by reference to an event that happened several centuries later and while Meier does not claim that the path of European history led inexorably to Auschwitz, he does contend that Auschwitz was the 'definitive end' of European history and must be taken into account in any assessment of the European legacy. Unlike Adorno and Horkheimer (1979) in an earlier and famous account of European modernity from Ancient Greece to Auschwitz as a dialectic whereby the Enlightenment itself became implicated in domination and genocide, Meier sees something to be rescued from history and the 'special path' of Europe has many dimensions.

If anything is common to recent approaches to the European heritage it is a differentiated view of history as a multilinear and open-ended process. The following discussion offers a summary of the main perspectives on European history as an orientation for the present. The first set of perspectives concern the revision of the 'rise of the West' thesis and leading on from this the idea of history as a learning process. From a slightly different perspective, deconstructive readings of history as a decentred process will be looked at before concluding the discussion with some remarks on the republican conception of history.

Although not explicitly addressed to the question of the European heritage as such, wide-ranging debates on the 'rise of the West' thesis among historians and historical sociologists offer important perspectives on European heritage. Against celebratory accounts of the European achievement that ignore the negative aspects, such as, imperialism and totalitarianism, a pronounced trend in recent scholarship is the problematizing of grand narratives in a more self-questioning account of history. S.N. Eisenstadt (2003) has stressed the multiple nature of modernity, which is not exclusively based on modern Europe but is plural and a reflection of different civilizational paths. This tendency to relative European modernity by stressing other models of modernity and diverse paths to modernity – some of which have not been directly connected to Europe – can be read in light of readings of history that aim to stress the internal pluralization of Europe. Jenö Szücs's (1988) well-known paper, originally published in Hungarian in 1981, on the three 'historical regions' of Europe stressed the internal pluralization of Europe. Szücs argued Europe consists of three geopolitical units, which were formed out of the East–West divide: a Western 'Carolingian' Europe, a Central Eastern Europe, and an Eastern Europe, which has been closely linked with Russia and has no clear-cut eastern frontier. The fate of Europe was determined by these three historical regions. There can be little doubt that it was the first one that was decisive in shaping the European legacy, which Szücs claimed was characterized by a synthesis of diverse elements that were assembled out of the prior disintegration of previous imperial structures. In line with the thesis of Maurice Bloch (1961: xx) that Europe was a creation of the Middle Ages, this is a view that sees Europe as shaped not in antiquity but from about 800 with the rise of the Carolingian Empire.[10] The characteristic features of the nascent European civilization were the separation of the church from the tutelage of the state and the drift towards urban centres.

This account can be read alongside Robert Bartlett's analysis of the making of medieval Europe as a process of what he has called internal colonization (Bartlett, 1993). Medieval Christendom, he argued, was an expanding world in which the edge of Europe was pushed in many directions through settlements and migratory movements: the Norman conquest of England, the English conquest of the Celtic world, German expansion in the Baltic region and in Eastern Europe, the Spanish reconquest. Europe was as much the product of conquest and colonization as, in later centuries, the initiator. The Europeans who later colonized much of the world were themselves products of societies that were themselves formed out of conquest and colonization over several centuries. But medieval conquest was different from later forms, for in the process of conquest and colonization medieval Christendom became increasingly homogenized while its outer regions were often divided and fragmented until a point has been reached when the centre established its power of the periphery and then a gradual process of cultural homogenization ensued. Any account of the Christian nature of European civilization must consider that this heritage divided as well as united Europe. Christianity, like Europe itself, did not lead to a single church.[11]

These accounts stress the tension between pluralization and homogenization. Other accounts of the European heritage emphasis the logic of cultural encounters with the non-European world prior to colonization. The frontiers of the Roman Empire are now viewed as tendentially open borderlands rather than closed lines and whose primary purpose was to expand rather than exclude (Whittaker, 1994). Recent scholarship has corrected a view of the Renaissance as a celebration of a narrow conception of humanism without due consideration of the fact that much of that heritage was based on an active engagement with the East.[12] While the Renaissance marked the beginning of European colonization of the Americas, it was a diffuse culture that was far from the unified culture it was often claimed to be. It is possible to read the Renaissance as neither an Italian movement preoccupied with antiquity nor a colonial movement, but a cosmopolitan

world view that was open to cultural influences from antiquity and from the wider world. This relation to the East can be seen in terms of a notion of cultural encounters or in terms of borrowings and cultural translations. In this context John Hobson (2004) has emphasized the 'eastern origins of European civilization.' In the view of Clarke (1997) and Osterhammel (1998), a relative openness to the East prevailed until the Enlightenment, which cannot be understood in the simple terms of 'orientalism'.

In an assessment of the 'rise of the West' thesis – by which he means the rise of a distinct civilization in Europe, the global supremacy of this civilization, and its diffusion throughout the non-Western world – Johann Arnason (2003) presents a general picture of the making of Europe that avoids the extremes of European exceptionalism and anti-orientalist polemics.[13] Rejecting a monocausal explanation of the 'great divergence' of Europe from the rest of the world in favour of a multi-dimensional account, he argues there are no grounds for crediting Europe with an inherent radical exceptionalism that was somehow generated out of itself. Moreover, there is no easily agreeable historical turning-point that would mark the beginning of Europe's irresistible ascent to supremacy, and there appears to be widespread agreement that the decisive edge that Europe gained over other civilizations was achieved at a later date than the received view would have it (Jones, 1987). His conclusion is that there were many reasons why Europe diverged from other Eurasian regions, but the overall dynamics of the process can only be understood in a global context of intercivilizational encounters, for Europe's rise and modernity was due in part to its interaction with other parts of the world and in part due its own internal advantages. So against the dichotomy of internalist or externalist accounts, the 'rise of the West' is best understood as an interactive process. The implications of this for an understanding of the European heritage suggest that neither the traditional view of the uniqueness of

Europe nor the orientalist critique offer a satisfactory account of European history.

Historical sociological work on history has not gone much further than offering a corrective to some of the more politicized positions on the European heritage. Political philosophers have ventured stronger accounts, with one prominent example being Habermas's notion of history as a learning process (Habermas, 1984, 1987a, 1987b). What this offers is a view of European history as seen through the lens of a particular interpretation of modernity in which different orders of rationality compete with each other. Habermas sees as one of the distinctive features of modernity in Europe to be the steady rise of communicative forms of rationality embodied in institutional processes as well as in forms of consciousness and collective action. The basic idea underlying Habermas's social theory, which informs his theory of history, is the constant contestation of power in communicative contexts. Drawing from the Hegelian–Marxist conception of history as an ongoing process driven by conflicting forces and the Weberian emphasis on the differentiation of modern values spheres – science, morality, religion, law – he has proposed a developmental theory of history that emphasizes the role of communicative processes in the contestation of power. This is a view of history that suggests an approach to the European heritage as one articulated through the communicative contestation of power rather than one that looks to the authority of tradition or the affirmative character of cultural traditions.

In a vast range of works, Habermas has given a comprehensive account of European modernity in terms of a conception of culture that problematizes truth claims as opposed to one that simply affirms the status quo or received views. So with modernity a new kind of culture has come into being in which a critical and self-problematizing rationality gains ground and steadily expands into many domains of life. One major expression of this is in public debates where a society engages in self-reflection and the critical scrutiny of

established wisdom and authority. With regard to the question of history, the so-called 'historians's dispute' in the early 1980s in Germany can be mentioned as a pertinent example of Habermas's view of the role of history (Habermas, 1989). In this debate he objected to the tendency to historicize the German Nazi past as if it were a thing of the past rather than connected to the present and integral to the self-understanding of post-war German identity as one that has learned to problematize its past. Habermas saw this capacity as being in danger of being neutralized by the tendency to 'normalize' the German past. Although this example has a particular German significance, it is of relevance to Europe more generally in that it illustrates the public use of history as a reflection on the past and an essential dimension of collective self-understanding. The capacity to learn from history is integral to modernity itself, according to Habermas. This argument is grounded in a conception of the European heritage that emphasizes precisely such learning mechanisms, as in the differentiation of value spheres, the constitutional and democratic state, human rights, and the integrity of the human person, civil society, and the critical reason associated with modern thought.

While Habermas argues that the European legacy consists of the critical capacity to be able to learn from history and to relativize truth claims in light of argumentative reason, various deconstructive readings of history suggest a related view of history. What is highlighted by such readings of history, as in the work of Jacques Derrida (1994) for instance, but as is also evident in Michel Foucault's genealogical approach, is a view of history as a decentred process and, especially with regard to Foucault, a perspective that privileges the view from the margins. Rejecting grand narratives – but not all kinds of narratives – the deconstructive reading of history offers an approach that emphasizes discontinuities as opposed to continuities, for example, a view of history in terms of the teleological idea of progress or an unbroken civilizational trajectory from antiquity to modernity. History itself contains no inherent pattern of meaning and cannot be viewed in holistic terms as constitutive of an overall unity or the expression of a subject. As an approach to European heritage the concrete implications of a deconstructive reading of history suggest an emphasis on those decentring events and moments where power is challenged.

One of the most important implications of deconstructive readings of history is the questioning of a foundational subjectivity, including an origin. While Habermas's approach does not posit the existence of such a subjectivity, placing instead the emphasis on developmental logics associated with learning processes and communicative competences, the deconstructive approach explicitly set out not only to reject the conventional notion of an origin linked to a foundational subject but also aims to offer an alternative approach. In place of history as the narrative of a subject, deconstruction draws attention to the constellation of social forces that create the illusion of a subject but also highlight alternatives to all kinds of essentialist readings of history.

This is an approach that has been reflected in Rémi Brague's account of European heritage as one articulated through a logic of distanciation from its own origins leading to a culture that can only see itself through the eyes of the other. So what distinguishes Europe is its mode of relating to itself, which is one of distance. Brague (2002) argues that because Europe borrowed everything from sources outside itself – which he associated with the Roman heritage – it is forever unable to see the present in terms of a narrative that can claim an origin of its own. European culture thus is a culture of what he calls 'secondarity'.

On this view, then, Europe's relation to its past is discontinuous. The past cannot be known, but it can be interpreted and reworked. For this reason, Eurocentrism is a myth, since one aspect of the European heritage has been the anti-Eurocentrism of modern thought and critique. In the terms of Dipesh Chakrabarty

(2000) such a reading of history can be termed a 'provencializing' of Europe. This does not involve rejecting European modernity, which has become an unavoidable heritage to engage with, but requires exploring how this heritage can be renewed from the margins.

The approaches discussed until now are characterized by largely critical and analytical dispositions and do not provide much in the direction of a political and normative orientation. To highlight one such approach, we can briefly consider the republican conception of the European heritage, which of course has also been closely linked to Habermas's political philosophy. With its origins in the classical Greek polis, the Roman *civitas*, and the Renaissance city state, the modern idea of republican citizenship was born with the Enlightenment and the ideas of the American and French Revolutions. It has been argued by several theorists, including Habermas, that republicanism is the defining aspect of the European political heritage (Van Gelderen and Skinner, 2002). The aspect of this that is highlighted is the notion of a self-governing political community based on autonomous individuals. The kind of subjectivity that is associated with this is not a foundational or essentialist subjectivity, but one that is formed in processes of self-constitution. As a political philosophy of Europe, it is highly relevant to a reading of the European political heritage (Friese and Wagner, 2002). It clearly makes more sense to see Europe as a polity than as a civilization but this does not mean that the civilizational heritage is no longer relevant. The republican heritage is clearly a strand that has a certain contemporary resonance given the movement towards a post-national European polity and the challenge to establish a transnational democratic order.

A problem, however, with the republican reading of European heritage is that the connection of republicanism with democracy can be misleading since republicanism preceded modern democracy and was often antithetical to it. Much of the republican tradition was hostile to democracy and its self-understanding was often based on an ideology of European exceptionalism.[14] A more pertinent consideration is whether the republican conception of political community can be reconciled with another trend in the European heritage, namely, cosmopolitanism, that is the open horizon of political community as inclusive of the other. It would be wrong to see a fundamental conflict in these orientations, but rather a creative tension between a vision of political community as the expression of a sovereign people and a vision of political community as an expression of an expanding universe of discourse. It would be beyond the scope of this chapter to explore this tension but it may be suggested in conclusion that there is ample evidence of how, for example, responses to globalization throughout history have led to cosmopolitan orientations in the self-understanding of societies. Hellenism led to the introduction of cosmopolitan sensibilities into the closed world of the Athenian polis; the Roman Empire was animated by both republican and cosmopolitan orientations; and the Christian civilization that developed in its wake was possible only by the incorporation of the culture of the outside.

CONCLUSION: REINTERPRETING EUROPEAN HERITAGE

Contemporary readings of history offer an interesting range of interpretations of European heritage as something that can be considered independently of national contexts. There are three broad approaches. There are positions that see Europe in terms of a certain uniqueness and which can be explained largely by reference to its internal institutional dynamics since the early Middle Ages. A second category of positions has been formed around conceptions of the European political heritage that stress a more limited range of orientations, such as, freedom or the democratic spirit. These two positions generally are cautious about universalistic claims but do not engage with the negative

aspects of European history. In opposition to such uncritical accounts, there have been a variety of interpretations that have stressed the adversarial relation to the rest of the world and a legacy of violence. Such critiques range from post-colonial approaches to positions akin to Adorno and Horkheimer's conception of civilization as a universalizing logic that requires the elimination of all particularisms.

When one looks at the construction of the European heritage in EU studies literature on the other hand there is little attempt to engage with the debates that have arisen in response to these positions. Europeanists, including its critics and those sympathetic to the European Union, tend on the whole to see European history only in internalist terms of a relation between nations and with the EU. In the EU historiography, the European cultural heritage is generally considered from the perspective of where one stands with respect to European integration. EU historiography tends to be divided between those who see the EU as a movement that tends towards the transnationalization of the nation-state and with a broadly federalist tendency and those who, following Alan Milward (1992), see the EU as an expression of the state tradition. The federalist school – as represented by such figures as Denis de Rougement (1965, 1966), Jean-Baptiste Duroselle (1990) and Hendrik Brugmans (1966, 1987) – has on the whole promoted a vision of the European heritage in a way that, in the view of Milward, amounts to an instrumentalization of history. In such approaches diversity and unity become increasingly reconciled with the progress of the European project.[15] European history since 800 is portrayed in quasi-teleological terms as a movement towards unity whereby conflict becomes a matter of diversity within an overall unity of purpose. The political developments are seen as the natural outcome of cultural orientations. Faced with such sweeping accounts it is difficult not to be sympathetic to Milward's dismissive account of the EU historiography. However, this leads to an unsatisfactory outcome in that we are simply left with a nation-centric account of European history.

This chapter has attempted to show that simplistic accounts of European history as a grand narrative or reductive accounts of the European heritage as essentialistic are as misleading as some of the conventional notions of the supremacy of the West or the universality of European civilization. Most interpretations no longer rely on univeralism and the universalism versus relativism dichotomy and there is a general recognition of the hybrid nature of European civilization. For reasons of space, only a few perspectives in historical sociology and social theory have been considered. A key point in the growing literature on the European heritage is that history must be interpreted through the categories of modernity rather than by reference to, for example, a notion of culture that can be invoked without considering its political conditions of creation and significance. This brings us to the key point with which we can conclude the chapter.

A defining tenet of European heritage is a cultural form which is also a political orientation that transforms both object and subject. The fact that no one culture or political structure has remained constant in European history suggests that the specificity of Europe might not be in such objective forms or in a unity that transcends the diversity of its expressions. No matter how hard we look, there is no European self or subjectivity that is self-positing. For the same reason it is arguably the case that there is no defining Other against which the self is formed. Culture is not to be equated with the identity of given people but is a mode of communication which includes evaluative standpoints and is always contested from within. For this reason culture, including the idea of a cultural heritage, cannot be equated with national or ethnic groups. So the diversity of culture is always more than questions about group boundaries. Culture entails the resources a society draws on to renew itself and it is inherently self-problematizing. For this reason cultural heritage is inevitably the site of conflicting interpretations of the world.

Those who stress the discontinuities and ruptures of history, on the one side, and on the other the diversity of European societies and histories, are wrong to dismiss any generalizable specificity to Europe simply because this cannot be attributed to an underlying unity associated with peoplehood. Rather this specificity, which could be said to be the source of its identity, is to be found in a cultural form of interpretation based on a self-understanding that incorporates the perspective of the Other. In this sense, Hans-Georg Gadamer is right when he argued against unity as the defining feature of the European heritage and a goal to be politically achieved: 'To participate with the other and to be a part of the other is the most and the best that we can strive to accomplish' (Gadamer, 1992: 235).

NOTES

1 See Morin (1987) and Stråth (2002).
2 This follows a distinction made by Paul Ricouer in his work on memory (Ricoeur, 2004).
3 See also Cerutti (2001).
4 On freedom as a European narrative, see also Heller (2006).
5 See Delanty (1995) and Pagden (2002).
6 On Europe and Islam see Goody (2004), Tibi (2001) and Delanty (2006).
7 The details of this conception of European civilization as a constellation of interacting civilizations is outlined in Delanty (2007).
8 For a similar reading of history, see Delanty (1995).
9 See also Davis (2006).
10 See also Le Goff (2005) for a more elaborated version of this thesis. The significance of this is explored by neither Bloch nor Le Goff, arguably the two most important medievalists, which is that the European legacy was shaped in the early medieval period and not, as is the traditional view, in antiquity. See also Geremek (1996).
11 For some recent interpretations on the question of Europe's cultural heritage, see Joas and Wiegandt (2007), O'Malley (2004), and Geremek (1996).
12 See Brotton (2002) and Jardine and Brotton (2000).
13 Examples of the latter include Frank (1998), Hobson (2004) and Pomerantz (2000), who argue that Europe was economically and culturally inferior to Asia until the nineteenth century.

14 For a critique, see Springborn (1992).

15 See Dinan (2006) for a discussion of the historiography of the EU. For a critique see Shore (2000: 56–60).

REFERENCES

Adorno, T.W. and Horkheimer, M. (1979) *Dialectic of Enlightenment*. London: Verso.

Arnason, J. (2003) *Civilizations in Dispute: Historical Questions and Theoretical Traditions*. Leiden: Brill.

Bartlett, R. (1993) *The Making of Europe: Conquest, Colonization and Cultural Change, 950–1350*. London: Allen Lane.

Biedenkopf, K., Geremek, B. and Michalski, K. (2004) *The Spiritual and Cultural Dimension of Europe*. Vienna: Institute for the Human Sciences.

Bloch, M. (1961) *Feudal Society*, Vol. 1. London: Routledge & Kegan Paul.

Brague, R. (2002) *Eccentric Culture: A Theory of Western Civilization*. South Bend, IN: St Augustine's Press.

Brotton, J. (2002) *The Renaissance Bazaar: From the Silk Road to Michelangelo*. Oxford: Oxford University Press.

Brugmans, H. (1966) *L'ideé Europeéne, 1918–1965*. Bruges: De Tempel.

Brugmans, H. (ed.) (1987) *Europe: Réve-Aventure-Réalité*. Brussels: Elsevier.

Cacciari, M. (1997) *L'Arcipelago*. Milan: Adephi.

Chakrabarty, D. (2000) *Deprovencializing Europe: Postcolonial Thought and Historical Difference*. Princeton: Princeton University Press.

Cerutti, C. (ed.) (2001) *A Soul for Europe: Vol. 1 A Reader*. Leuven: Peeters.

Clarke, J.J. (1997) *Oriental Enlightenment: The Encounter between Asian and Western Thought*. London: Routledge.

Davies, N. (1996) *Europe – A History*. Oxford: Oxford University Press.

Davies, N. (2006) *Europe East and West*. London: Jonathan Cape.

de Rougement, D. (1965) *The Meaning of Europe*. London: Sidgwick & Jackson.

de Rougement, D. (1966) *The Idea of Europe*. London: Macmillan.

Delanty, G. (1995) *Inventing Europe: Idea, Identity, Reality*. London: Macmillan.

Delanty, G. (ed.) (2006) *Europe and Asia Beyond East and West*. London: Routledge.

Delanty, G. (2007) 'The European civilizational constellation: a historical sociology', in *Encyclopaedia of Life Support Systems*. UNESCO. Available at: www.eolss.net.

Delanty, G. and Rumford, C. (2005) *Rethinking Europe: Social Theory and the Implications of Europeanization*. London: Routledge.

Derrida, J. (1994) *The Other Heading: Reflections on Today's Europe*. Bloomington: Indiana University Press.

Dinan, M. (2006) 'The historiography of the European Union', in *Origins and Evolution of the European Union*. Oxford: Oxford University Press.

Duroselle, J.-B. (1990) *Europe – A History of its Peoples*. London: Viking.

Eder, K. and Giesen, B. (eds) (2001) *European Citizenship: National Legacies and Transnational Projects*. Oxford: Oxford University Press.

Eisenstadt, S.N. (2003) *Comparative Civilizations and Multiple Modernities*, Vol. 1 and 2. Leiden: Brill.

Fontana, J. (1995) The Distorted Past: A Reinterpretation of European History. Oxford: Blackwell.

Frank, A.G. (1998) *Re-Orient: Global Economy in the Asian Age*. Berkeley: University of California Press.

Friese, H. (2006) 'Europe's otherness. Cosmopolitanism and the construction of cultural unities', in G. Delanty (ed.) *Europe Beyond East and West*. London: Routledge.

Friese, H. and Wagner, P. (2002) 'The nascent political philosophy of the European polity', *Journal of Political Philosophy*, 10 (3): 342–364.

Gadamer, H.-G. (1992) 'The diversity of Europe: Inheritance and future', in D. Misgeld and G. Nicholson (eds) *Applied Hermeneutics*. New York: SUNY.

Geremek, B. (1996) *The Common Roots of Europe*. London: Polity Press.

Goldberg, D.T. (2006) 'Racial Europeanization', *Ethnic and Racial Studies*, 29 (2): 331–364.

Goody, J. (2004) *Islam in Europe*. Cambridge: Polity Press.

Habermas, J. (1984) *The Theory of Communicative Action*, vol. 1. Cambridge: Polity Press.

Habermas, J. (1987a) *The Theory of Communicative Action*, vol. 2. Cambridge: Polity Press.

Habermas, J. (1987b) *The Philosophical Discourse of Modernity*. Cambridge. MIT Press.

Habermas, J. (1989) 'On the public use of history', in J. Habermas (ed.) *The New Conservatism: Cultural Criticism and the Historians's Debate*. Cambridge, MA: MIT Press.

Hazard, P. (1953) *The European Mind: The Critical Years, 1680–1715*. New Haven: Yale University Press.

Heller, A. (2006) 'European master narratives of freedom', in *Handbook of Contemporary European Social Theory*. London: Routledge.

Hobson, J. (2004) *The Eastern Origins of Western Civilization*. Cambridge: Cambridge.

Jardine, L. and Brotton, J. (2000) *Global Interests: Renaissance Art Between East and West*. London: Reaktion Books.

Jaspers, K. (1947) *Vom Europäischen Geist*. Munich: Piper.

Joas, H. and Wiegandt, K. (eds) (2007) *Europe's Cultural Values*. Liverpool: Liverpool University Press.

Jones, E. (1987) *The European Miracle: Environments, Economies and Geopolitics in the History of Europe and Asia*. Cambridge: Cambridge University Press.

Judt, T. (2005) *PostWar: A History of Europe since 1945*. London: William Heinemann.

Kristeva, J. (2000) *Crisis of the European Subject*. New York: Other Press.

Kundera, M. (1984) 'The tragedy of Central Europe', *New York Review of Books*, 26 (April): 33–8.

Le Goff, J. (2005) *The Birth of Europe*. Oxford: Blackwell.

Levy, D., Pensky, M., and Torpey, J. (eds) (2005) *Old Europe, New Europe, Core Europe: Transatlantic Relations after the Iraq War*. London: Verso.

Mazower, M. (1998) *Dark Continent: Europe's Twentieth Century*. London: Penguin.

Meier, C. (2005) *From Athens to Auschwitz: The Uses of History*. Cambridge, MA: Harvard University Press.

Milward, A. (1992/2000) *The European Rescue of the Nation-State*, 2nd edn. London: Routledge.

Morin, E. (1987) *Penser l'Europe*. Paris: Gallimard.

O'Malley, J. (2004) *Four Cultures of the West*. Cambridge, MA: Harvard University Press.

Osterhammel, J. (1998) *Die Entzauberung Asiens*. Munich: Beck.

Pagden, A. (ed.) (2002) *The Idea of Europe: From Antiquity to the European Union*. Cambridge: Cambridge University Press.

Patocka, J. (2002) *Plato and Europe*. Stanford: Stanford University Press.

Pocock, J.G.A. (1997) 'Deconstructing Europe', in P. Gowan and P. Anderson (eds) *The Question of Europe*. London: Verso.

Pocock, J.G.A. (2002) 'Some Europes in their history', in A. Pagden (ed.) *The Idea of Europe: From Antiquity to the European Union*. Cambridge: Cambridge University Press.

Pomerantz, K. (2000) *The Great Divergence: China, Europe and the Making of the World Economy*. Princeton: Princeton University Press.

Ricoeur, P. (2004) *Memory, History, Forgetting*. Chicago: University of Chicago Press.

Sassoon, D. (2006) *The Culture of the Europeans*. London: HarperCollins.

Shore, C. (2000) *Building Europe: The Cultural Politics of European Integration*. London: Routledge.

Springborn, P. (1992) *Western Republicanism and the Oriental Prince*. Austin: University of Texas Press.

Stråth, B. (2002) 'A European identity: To the historical limits of the concept', *European Journal of Social Theory*, 5 (4): 387–401.

Szücs, J. (1988) 'Three historical regions of Europe', in J. Keane (ed.) *Civil Society and the State*. London: Verso.

Tibi, B. (2001) *Islam between Culture and Politics*. London: Palgrave.

Van Gelderen, M. and Skinner, Q. (eds) (2002) *Republicanism: A Shared European Heritage*, vols 1 and 2. Cambridge: Cambridge University Press.

Weber, M. (1930) *The Protestant Ethic and the Spirit of Capitalism*. London: Allen & Unwin.

Whittaker, C. R. (1994) *Frontiers of the Roman Empire: A Social and Economic Study*. Baltimore: Johns Hopkins University Press.

4

Europe Beyond East and West

William Outhwaite

Europe is *between* east and west in an obvious geographical sense: between the Asian
continent, of which it forms a peninsula, and
the Europeanized societies of the Americas.[1]
Until recently, it was of course geopolitically
partitioned between East and West, as the
front line of, respectively, the Warsaw Pact
and NATO. Berlin, itself partitioned, was
both a Western metropolis and an Eastern
capital, with American GIs, off duty but in
uniform, strolling through the latter and the
odd Soviet sentry in the former. The residues
of the East/West partition of Europe are still
with us, not least in Berlin itself, though they
have again been overlaid, as they always
used to be, by other geographical and social
divisions. As Outhwaite and Ray (2005) put
it in their recent book, one can say that 'we
are all postcommunist now', not in the sense
of ideological demobilization or what
Habermas (1985) called 'the exhaustion of
utopian energies', but in the sense that Europe
as a whole, as well as the European Union,
has been radically transformed by what happened in and around 1989 in the communist
half of the continent. It now makes sense once
again, as it did for a year or two after World
War Two, to think of a political Europe which
in principle includes the whole sub-continent,

although East and West experienced radically
different trajectories over the second half of
the twentieth century.

Europe's eastern border will remain an
issue for the foreseeable future. At the time
of writing, the question of Turkey's membership of the EU is still not finally resolved.
Even if we take that proleptically as achieved,
along with the accession of the Western
Balkan states of former Yugoslavia and
Albania and of Ukraine and Belarus, there
remains the open question of Russia and the
rest of the Commonwealth of Independent
States. Many of the latter states, if they are
not unequivocally European, would certainly
pass the 'Turkish test' as substantially secularized and Westernized Muslim societies.
Whereas the western end of Europe is clearly
marked by the Atlantic Ocean, its eastern
edge is not just imprecise, but fundamentally
indeterminate, in the sense that any attempt
to fix it conceptually or politically generates
paradoxes which undermine the attempt. As
Liotta (2005: 69) puts it, 'In the broadest
sense, the "new" map of Greater Europe
includes Turkey, Ukraine, the Russian
Federation, and perhaps even Christian
Armenia and Georgia and Muslim Azerbaijan'
(see also Lavenex, 2004; Rumford, 2006).

Europe is however between East and West in a more interesting internal sense, with substantial populations in many parts of Europe identified with Asia in one way or another and/or with 'eastern' religions, such as, Islam, Hinduism, and Buddhism. This is, of course, true of North America or Australasia as well, but in Europe it is a much more prominent feature, with several prospective member-states of the EU predominantly Muslim by religion. Even excluding central Asia from consideration, we have Turkey, Bosnia-Herzegovina and Albania as prospective member-states with substantially Muslim populations.

To register these facts is to confront a Europe which is not so much between as beyond East and West (Delanty, 2006a; Wang Hui, 2005a, 2005b), just as much as hypermodern Dubai, Singapore or Hong Kong. At the same time, however, the internal East–West divide remains an important structuring feature, not just of Europe as a whole but of many European states and even many European cities, whose smart western suburbs are upwind of the central and eastern quarters. The East/West 'wall in the head'[2] is not confined to Berlin, nor more substantial walls to Jerusalem. Most fundamentally, the East/West divide has been shaped by ideologies of European (and, within Europe, Western) superiority which continue to influence such concrete issues as EU enlargement negotiations. As Étienne Balibar (2004: 24–5) has suggested, 'We should resist the illusion of believing ... that some national traditions are open, tolerant, and "universalist" by "nature" or on account of their "exceptionality", whereas others, still by virtue of their nature or historical specificity, are intolerant and "particularist".' Balibar was referring to national traditions and to their attitudes to foreigners, but the point has a more general application. Jan Nederveen Pieterse writes (2002: 141): 'A cultural analysis of Europe points towards traveling light, in the sense of leaving behind the heavy luggage of imperialism and colonialism, racism and chauvinism, nationalism and parochialism.'

EUROPE IN ITS PLACE

To think about Europe, then, at least the Europe of the last half-millennium, is to think, however sceptically and critically, about modernity, and this inflects the notion of the West. Since around half-way to two-thirds through the last millennium, Europe has come to see itself and portray itself to the rest of the world as 'Western' in an evaluative sense, and its neighbours and its own eastern or southern regions, and parts of its populations, as less Western or less than Western. This is an approach appropriately described and rightly condemned as Eurocentric in relation to the rest of the world and Western-centric or occidentocentric within Europe.[3] It is, of course, integrally linked to imperialism and to the processes, within Europe itself and its component states, of 'internal colonialism' (Hechter, 1966).[4] As Edward Said (2003) put it in one of his last articles:

> Think of the line that starts with Napoleon, continues with the rise of oriental studies and the takeover of North Africa, and goes on in similar undertakings in Vietnam, in Egypt, in Palestine and, during the entire 20th century, in the struggle over oil and strategic control in the Gulf, in Iraq, Syria, Palestine, and Afghanistan. Then think of the rise of anti-colonial nationalism, through the short period of liberal independence, the era of military coups, of insurgency, civil war, religious fanaticism, irrational struggle and uncompromising brutality against the latest bunch of 'natives'. Each of these phases and eras produces its own distorted knowledge of the other, each its own reductive images, its own disputatious polemics.

There are substantial disagreements about when a Eurocentric world-view becomes entrenched in Europe, to what extent it is counterbalanced by a more open and responsive, even admiring approach to the rest of the world, and to what extent it reflects genuine innovations and advances in Europe itself (Arnason, 2005, 2006a, 2006b, Delanty, 1995, 1996, 2006a, 2006b). Very briefly, one can distinguish between those who date the beginnings of European hegemony and a Europe-dominated world economy to around 1500 and those who would set the former much later and identify a Eurasian–African world economy at a much earlier date, when Europe was still pretty much a backwater. The second view seems clearly right in taking a global economic perspective, in which the world economy simply develops another growth node around the eighteenth century as a result of the much longer dominance of regions further east.

Unlike earlier economistic theories of modernization, however, modernity theory gives equal prominence to political, military and ideological or cultural aspects, and here the picture becomes more complicated. However much one might want to qualify the traditional view that there was something special about the European combination of small states and an over-arching ideological framework of Christianity and, for much of the region, Roman Law, or the gradual separation of political and religious authority and, with the protestant Reformation, the subordination of religion to the emergent national states (Bayly, 2004; Mann, 1986, 1993), it is clear that the French Revolution, for example, rapidly became, and remains, a major world-historical event. And although André Gunder Frank (1998) may be right that European beliefs in their superiority emerge in the late eighteenth and nineteenth century rather than in the middle of the millennium, it was still the case that Europeans, to the extent that they were Christians, believed not only in the unique truth of their religion (which is natural enough) but also, less plausibly, in its radical distinctiveness from Judaism and Islam. Islamic rule, as in the Ottoman Empire, was a good deal more tolerant of religious and cultural diversity than rule by Christians. Even today, when Christians have mostly abandoned their predilection for pogroms, the idea of an exclusively or predominantly Christian Europe continues to resonate in parts of the European Right.

Some contemporary writers argue that the term 'modernity' is irrevocably contaminated by Eurocentrism; Gurminder K. Bhambra's path-breaking book *Rethinking Modernity* (2007) is perhaps the best guide to and expression of this view. I take the more complacent

line that to replace 'Western' or 'European' with a more abstract notion of modernity and a complementary, more concrete notion of plural or multiple modern*ies* is a better, and even inescapable, way of thinking about these issues. (As I write the preceding sentence, Word suspiciously underlines the plural, but it is wrong to do so.) Modernity, to this way of thinking, is *contingently* European or Western in its first incarnation, but Europe has not retained a monopoly on modernity any more than Britain retained a monopoly on industrialization. As Gerard Delanty (2004: 176) puts it,

> Modernity ... is necessarily global in outlook; while it first emerged in western Europe, it is not Western, American, or European, but is an expression of world culture, which increasingly frames the local.

As for multiple modernities, Shmuel Eisenstadt (2000: 2–3), who pioneered this way of thinking, writes:

> The idea of multiple modernities presumes that the best way to understand the contemporary world – indeed to explain the history of modernity – is to see it as a story of continual constitution and reconstitution of a multiplicity of cultural programs ... One of the most important implications of the term 'multiple modernities' is that modernity and Westernization are not identical; Western patterns of modernity are not the only 'authentic' modernities, though they enjoy historical precedence and continue to be a basic reference point for others.[5]

Gerard Delanty and others have pointed out that there is a danger in proliferating modernities to excess. It makes perfect sense to talk about the differences between British and French culture, for example, but probably not between British and French modernity. On the other hand, one might want to say that East Asian or, say, Japanese modernity remains significantly different from European modernity. This is partly a matter of structural patterns, such as the form taken by industrialization and industrial employment, but also by the political and cultural ways in which these are framed. As Göran Therborn (1995: 14), suggests, summarizing one of the main themes of his brilliant book: 'Europe has been characterized, more than other areas of modernity, by a structuration of tasks, means and rights in terms of class, defined by clusters of economic tasks, and sustained by clusters of means and rights attached to groupings of economic tasks.'

Colin Crouch (1999, 2001) has written in similar terms of the importance of class in the European context. But there are also more long-lasting cultural differences of the kind emphasized by Eisenstadt which persist even when historical differences in class stratification and class politics between Europe and the rest of the world have evened out. In Therborn's formulation, 'The value patterns of European modernity are first of all those of Christian religion and its secularization, of the nation-state and citizenship, and of individualism and class' (Therborn, 1995: 272). It is at this level of historical differences in cultural traditions that theories of modernity can make a contribution, and it is also this level which counts in thinking about Europe in a cosmopolitan framework.

One way of framing this is in terms of the notion of a 'post-Western' Europe (Delanty, 2003, 2006a). Of the three principal civilizational constellations in Europe, those of Western Christendom and the Russian and Ottoman empires, the Western one has been dominant throughout the modern period, reinforced by twentieth century Atlanticism and a project of European integration which began in the west of the continent and initially roughly matched the contours of the Carolingian Empire. Further east, the Western referent becomes by definition more attenuated, as does the European one for, in particular, Turkey. The Europe of the early twenty-first century remains, of course, 'Western' in the sense of modernity and to some extent geopolitical attachment, while its centre of gravity has shifted east within Europe itself. What however remains uncertain is whether, or how long, Europe's representation of itself will continue to be shaped by the East/West polarity. The salience of these polarities can change, as illustrated by the no longer 'wild' west of the US or the no longer backward south of Germany.

EAST AND WEST, THEN AND NOW

This chapter is primarily concerned with contemporary Europe, but it is instructive to look at the way in which longstanding patterns, whether real or imagined, continue to shape perceptions of East/West differences. Stefan Auer, in his excellent book on Central European nationalism, rightly problematizes the common differentiation between 'Eastern' and 'Western' variants. A standard formulation is that by Anthony Smith (1997: 324):

> The Western model of the nation tended to emphasize the centrality of a national territory or homeland, a common system of laws and the importance of a mass, civic culture binding the citizens together. The Eastern model, by contrast, was more preoccupied with ethnic descent and cultural ties.

Smith stresses, 'The contrast between these two concepts of the nation should not be overdrawn, as we find elements of both at various times in several nationalisms in both Eastern and Western Europe.' Liah Greenfield, author of a influential book published in 1992, takes a similar line that despite such overlaps and mismatches (Greenfield, 1995: 18) one can distinguish between 'Western, less Western and anti-Western nationalism in Europe and elsewhere' (Greenfield, 1995: 22). Auer (2004, chapter 1) argues convincingly that such contortions are misleading, and reflect dubious dichotomies traced equally in relation to forms of transition (Vachudová and Snyder, 1997) and of political culture (Carpenter, 1997). The terms of the comparisons may vary, but in each case the contrasts simplify and overinterpret a more complex and unpredictable reality. The rapid transformation of Slovakia after 1998 from pariah to EU member state makes the point, whether or not one follows Auer's critical defence of what he calls liberal nationalism.[6] The east/west binary division was inescapable in the Cold War period, but it should be treated with caution in the post-communist context.

It remains a fact, however, that the mid-twentieth-century East/West division of Europe cut very deep. From the point of view of equalizing existing East/West divisions in Europe, it would, of course, have been better if the Red Army had liberated, and the Soviet Union colonized Western rather than Eastern Europe. (Whether, as an East German philosopher once assured me, state socialism in the West would have been incomparably more impressive than in the East because of the West's material advantages, is another question.) As it was, Soviet domination held back development in many parts of the bloc, notably East Germany and Czechoslovakia, and directed it in dubious directions in much of the rest. 'Eastern' Europe, the Europe east of what Churchill aptly baptized as the Iron Curtain, was largely cut off for 40 years, not, of course, from Europe, but from the mainstream of European development. This began with the Soviet ban on what came to be called the 'satellites' accepting Marshall aid. Whether or not the offer was seriously meant, it was at least on the table, and Czechoslovakia, in particular, was keen to accept and had at the time the political freedom to do so (Judt, 2005: 92).

Having been forced to reject aid from the original Marshall Plan, communist Europe in the 1990s missed out on a widely expected and badly needed, but never even seriously considered, second Marshall Plan. The rational response of the West to its sudden deliverance from the threat of attack from the Warsaw Pact would surely have been a massive shift of resources from defence to aid, comparable with that in the late 1940s. As it was, aid from individual Western states and from the EU was extremely limited, patchy and slow to arrive. Only in Germany was there a really significant transfer of resources, amounting to three trillion dollars over the decade, and here it took place in a context already sabotaged by the abrupt currency union of 1990 which, even if it was politically unavoidable as Kohl seemed to believe, rendered East Germany an economic disaster area. Elsewhere in the bloc, a serious aid program would undoubtedly have achieved far more, at far lower cost, than current EU

programs. To put it starkly, the four lost decades of communism in Central and Eastern Europe were followed by a further lost decade of postcommunist transition, when economic transformation was hampered by lack of resources, as well as, arguably, by the then fashionable neoliberal economic policies.

In retrospect it is surprising that this prodigious social dislocation produced so little violent disorder. Czechoslovakia and the Soviet Union split up peacefully, and Yugoslavia bloodily, but the widely expected break-up of the Russian Federation, with civil war as its likely accompaniment, did not take place, despite ongoing flashpoints in the Caususus and elsewhere. There was unpleasant street violence against foreigners, Roma and others, and a general increase in crime, but most of the pain of transition was borne by individuals. Suicide rates soared, especially for men, and in parts of the bloc, notably in Russia, life expectancy rates collapsed (Outhwaite and Ray, 2005: 50; Therborn, 1997: 376–7). At the other end of the prosperity gradient, in East Germany, people benefited as individuals, even if they lost their jobs, but the society was decimated (Spiegel, 2004). This German pattern, which ironically recalls Engels' remark that capitalism improved individual conditions at the cost of the human species, has a wider application in postcommunist Europe.

East/West divisions in contemporary Europe can best be examined in relation to three periods: (1) the *annus mirabilis* of 1989/90; (2) the long transition decade that followed and which culminated in (3) the EU enlargement of 2004 and its aftermath.

1989

If 1789 was, as I suggested earlier, one of the defining events of the modern political imagination, it remains to be seen what place will be given to the anticommunist revolutions of 1989. A number of commentators have stressed the absence of really new ideas in 1989, especially after the rapid eclipse of civil society movements like Solidarity in Poland or Civic Form in Czechoslovakia. Habermas (1990), for example, called it a 'catching-up' or 'rectifying' revolution: a return to democracy (and capitalism), and to the 'normal' path of post WWII European development. Perhaps the revolutionary period was just too fast and too peaceful to capture the world's imagination; by the end of 2001 many people in the West were giving similar prominence to an (admittedly spectacular) terrorist attack on the United States. Tocqueville (1971: 99) wrote in his *Recollections* of the 1848 revolution of the 'complete silence' regarding the former king. Within a few days he 'could not have been more out of the picture if he had been a member of the Merovingian dynasty'. Similarly, the former dictators and their associates were prominent only if and when they came to trial.

Transition

It is tempting to define postcommunist transition out of existence, suggesting that it is either essentially over, as many in east central Europe would argue is the case in the parts of their states which interest them, or not (yet) seriously begun, as jaundiced observers of points further east often say (Vachudová and Snyder, 1997). Either way, for this reductive view, the implications for the rest of Europe are seen as relatively limited and can be handled under the category of transitional arrangements, where 'transition', like 'convergence', now refers to the path to EU accession rather than the shift from totalitarian socialism to liberal capitalism. It is certainly true that the world-historical significance of the transition, rightly stressed by analysts like Andrew Arato, hardly seems to be reflected in the observable phenomena. Everything, so to speak, was tossed up into the air, but much of it fell down again into relatively familiar structures and patterns. But as I suggested in the introduction, it would be a mistake to play down the process

this way, as in the euphemistic language of transition invites.

The notion of transition is doubly problematic (Blokker, 2005a; Kennedy, 2002). It suggests a teleological movement from one state to another, driven by a technocratic and unpolitical ethos of 'There is no alternative' (TINA – see Grzymski, 2005) and the famous dentistry metaphor: 'If you don't visit the dentist for 40 years you can expect some extensive and painful treatment'. Second, the implication is that once the transition is over – a point which might be taken to coincide with, for example, EU accession, the postcommunist condition is essentially over, like the colonial history of the US. Although many citizens and political elites in the more fortunate parts of the postcommunist world would indeed take this view, it is probably wrong. The postcommunist condition is substantially shaped by the postcommunist state, in the sense of the state apparatus, and the postcommunist state, even in Germany, where it arrived ready-made, is a political structure of a particular kind. The philosopher and cultural theorist Boris Groys has brought this out very clearly. In a short but suggestive book, Groys (2006: 94) points out that the privatizing state is an activist state, no less than the communist nationalizing state: the establishment of capitalism is a political project. This left part of the region, at least for the transitional period, with 'capitalism without capitalists' (Eyal *et al.*, 1998), and a larger and less fortunate part with 'capitalists without capitalism', in other words, compradors of privatization oriented mainly to exporting their capital to more secure locations.

Enlargement

The EU enlargement of 2004 was striking for the mismatch between the enormous importance of what happened in May 2004 and the restricted form in which it was reflected both before and after the event. On the one hand there was the sense of a momentous transition, in which the European integration process finally embraced almost the whole of the sub-continent, including a majority of the European states excluded for 40 years not just from the European Community/Union but also from the postwar democratization process itself. As Étienne Balibar described the situation in 1991 (Balibar, 2004: 90), 'Following the disappearance of one of the two blocs, the struggle itself is vanishing, which in fact constitutes a great trial of truth: now or never is the moment for the dream to materialize, for Europe to rise up, renewed or revitalized. This is also the moment when the dream risks being smashed into pieces.'

On the other hand, there was an essentially technical and administrative process of harmonization and coordination. Hannah Arendt (1963) spoke (of course, in an entirely different context) of the banality of evil, and we might speak here of the banality or the banalization of enlargement. As Sobrina Edwards (2005) notes, the EU has oscillated in its public pronouncements between a position that this was just another accession and a more dramatic vocabulary of historic reconciliation.

Alongside all this, there was a further element, the constitutional convention, contingently related to the impending enlargement in that it could (and perhaps should) have taken place well before 1989, but intrinsically linked in its mission to make a larger Union viable and in the fact that the new members were fully represented in its deliberations. Although the convention failed to produce an acceptable constitution, in other respects it was quite an impressive deliberative assembly which may be remembered when more immediately successful ventures are forgotten (Norman, 2005). It was also one in which Old and New Europe met on relatively egalitarian and open terms. As Fraser Cameron (2004: 152) notes, 'It was difficult to distinguish speakers coming from existing or future member states,' though the research of Ruth Wodak and her collaborators suggests a rather more pessimistic assessment (see Krzyzanowski, 2005; Oberhuber, 2005). The dominant impression

of the 2004 enlargement remains that of a bureaucratic process managed in a bureaucratic manner, and tinged with arrogance on the part of the existing members. Like, some would say, the European Union itself.

What did this amount to in East–West terms? The Visegrad core of the 2004 accession states could, as their intellectuals had since the 1980s, invoke the idea of Central Europe. This had been an important ideological plank in their self-affirmation against a Soviet hegemon characterized as Asiatic, and could serve as a marker of their advanced place in the accession queue. In practice, the term more often used was East Central Europe or East and Central Europe (ECE). This had the advantage of accommodating Poland and the Baltic States, though it also obscured the more dramatic fact that in a sense Central Europe had ceased to exist. As Hans-Heinrich Nolte (1997, 2002) has pointed out, the Iron Curtain sealed the fate of a Central Europe already transformed by the loss of its Jewish and German populations – the former by persecution and genocide, the latter by voluntary or forced emigration westwards. Hungary, Czechoslovakia, and Poland became for 40 years the West of the East; EU accession has made them, for the moment, the East of the West (Nolte, 2002: 46).

One of the most prominent implications of this reshaping of East and West, of course, concerns migration. With Western Europe, now even including the Irish Republic, becoming a region of immigration, the flows are essentially from the south and east to the north-west. Many EC/EU enlargements have raised issues of this kind, notably the accession of Greece in 1981, the various non-accessions of Turkey over the past decades and the first eastern enlargement of 2004, which provoked considerable excitement about possible floods of Polish plumbers. All of this has the potential to ignite renewed anxieties around the EU's 'near abroad', which form part of the explanation for why 2004 came so late.

It is instructive to look back at some of the surveys conducted around the turn of the century, in which existing EU citizens warmly welcomed the idea of Swiss or Norwegian (and Maltese) accession but were more luke-warm or even negative about the ECE countries (CEC 2000) and emphatically negative in the case of Turkey. Political elites also often shared this view. For Jacques Attali, for example, writing in 1994 when he had only just left the post of President of the European Bank for Reconstruction and Development, there was a stark choice between widening and deepening the European Union: 'With twenty or twenty-two members, it would be impossible to move towards the single currency or establish common economic, social, judicial and foreign policies' (Attali, 1997: 349). Instead, he favoured a 'Continental Union' of which the EU would be a member and, 'with Russia, one of the essential motors' (Attali, 1997: 354). Such attitudes partly explain the EU's remarkably slow response to 1989, which provoked considerable resentment in Poland (Blazyca, 2002: 206–7, 212) and elsewhere in the region. Melinda Kovács (2001) neatly describes this response as 'putting down and putting off'. A more cosmopolitan union, one must conclude, would have been more responsive and understanding – not in the least since it had just emerged from a potentially lethal cold war. Beck and Grande (2004: 259) rightly point to a certain 'western European racism'. As Baldwin *et al.* write (1997: 168, quoted in Ingham and Ingham 2002: 15): 'Imagine how eager western Europe would have been in 1980 to pay ECU 18 billion a year in order to free central Europe from communism and remove Soviet troops from the region.'[7]

We should of course not forget the possibility of a very different scenario in which either the EU was even less welcoming to the East, or in which part or all of the East deliberately rejected full membership of the EU in favour of a looser attachment in the European Economic Area. On the latter question, however unlikely it may look at present, the prospect of an Eastern European Norway or Switzerland, deliberately rejecting the option of accession, should not be ruled out. More to

the point, as Böröcz and Sarkar (2005: 158–9) emphasize, full membership has been and is to be preceded by a long transitional period of dependency on EU regulations. 'For the entrants during the 2004 round of accessions (who will enjoy equal rights within the EU by 2011), this quasi-dependency status will have lasted for 18 years. For next-round members Bulgaria, Romania and Turkey – optimistically assuming only a five-year delay – it can be expected to be circa 23 years'. (On further impending accessions, see also, for example, Bechev and Andreev, 2005.)

If the ECE countries were treated for a decade somewhat like East Germans by their Western relatives, it is also true that their inhabitants tend for their part to have a more 'traditional' and positive ('pre-postcolonial') conception of Europe than Westerners. Very many Western Europeans, for example, belong to states which have had substantial colonial empires, and although they react to this past in very different ways (compare the generally positive and even nostalgic image of empire in the UK with the tendency to embarrassed denial in the Netherlands) it has perhaps given a more cosmopolitan and multicultural angle to their thinking about Europe. Habermas (2004: 51) emphasizes this effect of the experience of colonial rule and decolonization: 'With the growing distantiation from imperial rule and colonial history the European powers have had the chance *to take up a reflexive distance to themselves*'.[8] In the East, as noted earlier, 'Europe' in general and 'Central Europe' in particular have operated in part as tokens in a political strategy of distancation from the 'Asiatic' USSR, as in the East German Rudolf Bahro's now largely forgotten *Alternative* (Bahro, 1977). To put it bluntly, Easterners, even more than Westerners, often talk about the European heritage in upbeat language that can provoke hostility or embarrassment in parts of the West and the rest of the world.

The boot is perhaps on the other foot if one turns to a related issue, that of ethnocentric prejudice. The somewhat higher levels recorded in the east of Europe than in the west have generated something of a moral panic, starting with skinhead riots in the East German port of Rostock in 1992. Without wishing to belittle the unpleasant character of these manifestations, and the extremely serious levels of anti-Roma prejudice in particular, the pattern overall seems to be that such attitudes are driven by specific current crises rather than linked into nationalism and extreme-right ideology, as they have tended to be in the West (Hjerm, 2003). Very crudely, one might say that there is an intra-European cosmopolitan multicultural tradition in Eastern and Central Europe, historically tied to local empires, including of course the trans-European Russian empire (Sakwa, 2006), where the West has a more extra-European one more oriented to the Atlantic and the rest of the world via the Western European world empires. Both traditions, of course, are counterposed by explicit racism in the West and ethnic prejudice in the East, but the possibility of their fusion is one of the more optimistic scenarios in play here. As Paul Blokker (2005b: 10) argues, however, that populist nationalism is not a peculiarity of the East but 'inherent in modern societies as such'.

WHAT REMAINS?

We are confronted, then, with a Europe in which East–West divisions corresponding to the Iron Curtain remain extremely salient. This is in part a matter of historical memory. It is still possible, for instance, for Eastern public figures to be threatened by proof or rumours of past collaboration with the secret police, where their Western counterparts have only financial or sexual skeletons in their cupboards. The older generations are shaped by different historical events: the 1968 of the Prague Spring and its extinction is different from the 1968 of Western protest movements (Stockmann, 2005: 45; there is a fuller discussion of political generations in Germany in Blech (1995) and Arzheimer (2006)). Such East–West divisions are however

weakening in the face of countervailing forces. The first of these is of long standing – as long as the East–West division itself. It is that between North and South.

The North–South division is salient both in Europe as a whole and in a number of its component states – notably Germany, Italy and France. In all three it is historically more of an axis between a prosperous and advanced north-west and a more backward south-east. In the German stereotype, as expressed in a traditional song, southerners are 'hard-drinking, work-shy but loyal to the (Catholic) church' (Brückner, 1987: 13). Here, of course, part of the North became the East, bordered by the South. In Italy, the most extreme political expression of northern prejudice is in the early propaganda of the Lega Nord, contrasting a Germanic North with an African South. Modernization in the second half of the twentieth century substantially relativized this axis. Often the north-west lost out and became deindustrialized, while new technology thrived in the South, as in Germany, or in a number of provincial growth poles, as in France. In Italy, attempts to modernize the South were less successful, but not without effect.

A second trend which weakened the simple contrast between West (and North) and East (and South) is that, as in the French case, development became increasingly differentiated between high-tech cities and more backward hinterlaender. This has become even more striking in postcommunist Europe, with certain towns in, for example, Russia, heavily promoting themselves as sites for foreign investment (McCann, 2004, 2005). Here, the European case illustrates broader processes of the growth of world cities whose reference groups become one another rather than their respective rural surroundings.

Third, there is a more general eastward shift of some European investment in search of low wage costs; in Scandinavia, the move has, of course, been southwards to lower-cost regions of Western Europe as well as east-wards. Something which is still unclear is how far processes of this kind will modify the traditional image of a Europe whose productive core and consumption high-spots are located in the 'golden banana' running from south-east England through northern France and Germany to northern Italy. The EU itself remains, of course, heavily skewed to the west, with all its main institutions located in the original six member states; only if one takes the axis running from Portugal to Finland does the Brussels/Luxemburg/Strasbourg/Frankfurt institutional cluster appear like a natural centre. This may, of course, not matter, as long as the union overcomes its western bias and leaves behind the painful memories of a decade of relative neglect of the east, running into its grudging acceptance on western terms. The latter is, of course, a difficult area. Many of the aims of the strategy known as conditionality (see Pridham *et al.*, 1994) were laudable, such as, strengthening the independence of the judiciary, reducing corruption, and police brutality, and so on. But the circumstances under which it was done were uncomfortable, to say the least, and provoked resentments of a kind familiar from the history of German reunification.

It may be useful to take two more concrete cases cutting across East–West differences. Both are ambiguous and to some extent remain unpredictable. The first example is again that of Germany; the second is the longer-standing axis between state socialist Europe and Scandinavia. In Germany, of course, the internal borders were rapidly effaced, and 'Western' forms extended to the whole country. A massive transformation of technical infrastructure (roads, railways, electricity and communication cables) left much of the East more modern than the West. And yet, nearly 20 years on, there remain substantial objective and subjective differences, the latter neatly captured by the expression of the 'Mauer im Kopf' (the Wall in the head). A government report (Spiegel, 2004) traced a gloomy picture, where Chancellor Kohl at the time of reunification had predicted 'blooming landscapes'. The question whether 'we are *one people*' (Falter *et al.*, 2006) remains moot.

My second example was brilliantly marked out by Therborn (1995). In a wide-ranging survey entitled *European Modernity 1945–2000*, he noted the similarities in certain respects between the northern and central parts of communist Europe and their Scandinavian neighbours. Not only were welfare state *structures* comparably prominent, as was no surprise to anyone, but more interestingly, *attitudes* to a number of cultural and lifestyle issues showed substantial similarities compared with the more 'traditional' parts of Europe. Despite the currently fashionable discussion of postsecularism, Europe remains what Therborn (1995: 274) called 'the continent of secularization' and within Europe this is particularly strong in the Nordic countries and in Eastern Europe, particularly the non-Catholic regions. This is not just an effect of communist atheist propaganda; Poland in the early 1990s also scored highest in Europe for belief in God, even above the US, though elsewhere in the former communist bloc, belief was lower than anywhere in the West apart from Sweden. Taking a different issue, that of attitudes to parenting, Therborn's analysis, based on the World Values Survey, suggested not just a sharp cleavage between northern-central Europe and south-western Europe, as one might expect, but also within Eastern Europe. Respondents were asked, first, whether obedience or independence should be encouraged in children and, second, whether parents should sacrifice their interests to those of their children.

There are clearly two Europes, one more individualist than most of the world, and one not. But it is not the usual line-up. *Central Europe* (except Czechoslovakia and Poland but linking up with Bulgaria), *the Baltic and the North Atlantic areas* embrace child independence and are relatively restrained in demanding parental sacrifices. Denmark and West Germany and, on the eastern fringes, Latvia, Lithuania and Bulgaria have the strongest individualism.

The *south-west of Europe*, from Belgium to Portugal, including the British Isles, has a distinctively collectivist cast of family values. Portugal, France and Northern Ireland, in that order, also have a marked preference for obedience over independence (Therborn, 1995: 293).

Therborn's material derives of course from the beginning of the postcommunist 1990s, and it is, therefore, interesting to see how far these patterns have persisted. One particularly interesting area is that of attitudes to inequality. Survey evidence suggests a majority perception in eastern central Europe that there are 'strong' or 'very strong' conflicts between managers and workers and that income differentials are 'too great', and a relation between the perception of conflict and objective inequality as measured by Gini coefficient (Delhey, 2001: 203–5). Postcommunist electorates remain more egalitarian in their attitudes than Western Europeans, to a degree more closely related than in the West to the actual levels of inequality in their societies (Delhey, 2001). The traditional expression of egalitarian attitudes, in Europe and to some extent elsewhere, has been social democratic politics, but the scissor effect in the postcommunist countries of the local demise of socialist/communist political and economic policies and the general reorientation of social democracy into third way or 'new' politics has tended to restrict this development.

This returns us to questions of the interaction of long-term processes with more immediate events. Of the latter, the changing position of Eastern European states in what has aptly been called a regatta towards EU accession is a particularly good example. It is not long since Slovakia was seen as a remote possibility for accession in the foreseeable future; it is now a member. For a long time before their accession in 2007, the relative positions of Bulgaria and Romania remained shifting. In the postcommunist region, apparently open futures in 1989 rapidly solidified into fairly familiar 'Western' patterns, though with persisting differences sometimes reflecting long-term patterns, such as, the historical presence or absence of democratic traditions. The region displays, in a particularly interesting way, some of the difficulties of causal analysis in history and the other social

sciences, as I hope to show in future work, following a trail blazed by Reinhart Koselleck (1985, 2000) and most recently Jaroslav Krejčí (2004) and Charles Tilly (2006).

I have concentrated here on the divisions within Europe between East and West, and on the halting and partial way in which it is moving beyond them. But Europe as a whole remains inevitably in an intermediate *location* between Asia and America; how far this corresponds to an explicitly adopted *position* remains unclear. (Blech, 1995, draws this distinction between *Mittellage* and *Mittelstellung* in relation to Germany, but it can be extended to Europe as a whole.) In the short term, the Atlantic has grown a lot wider as a result of the adventurist power politics of President George W. Bush, but under future presidents it will no doubt narrow again somewhat, unless the US generates even more extreme regimes. For the moment, and despite this period of *froideur* (see Torpey, 2004), the EU and its close associates remain clearly part of what Martin Shaw (2000) has boldly called the global state: an emergent level of state power with its roots in North America, Europe, Australasia, Japan, and other parts of Asia. This is, of course, 'Western' only in the residual sense that it builds on the Atlantic Pact of the second half of the twentieth century and US hegemony over Japan.[9] The EU's internal configuration, in the sense of both its widening to new members and its deepening (or not) of the degree of integration, will, of course, affect its positioning in these respects, though perhaps not dramatically. The big enlargement of 2004 has made relatively little difference to the EU foreign policy, so far as it exists, despite US Defense Secretary Rumsfeld's crude attempt in 2003 to drive a wedge between 'old' and 'new' Europe. (Some 'new' elites followed the Anglo-Spanish line in supporting the attack on Iraq, but European *populations* were generally hostile, even in a somewhat 'Finlandized' United Kingdom.) More important, I think, is the need for the EU to develop itself as a democratic polity, against an unpromising background of neonationalism, 'Euroscepticism' and a slide towards what Crouch (2004) and others have aptly called 'postdemocracy'.[10] And the question remains whether a European Union which has become post-western in the trivial sense that it is no longer composed of Western and Central Europe (plus Greece) will also become post-western in a more interesting sense of multi-cultural cosmopolitanism. It is hard to predict the likely place of Europe at the end of this century, but I am inclined to follow Therborn's cautious prediction that it might well look like a macrocosm of Scandinavia: 'a nice, decent periphery of the world, with little power but some good ideas' (Therborn, 1997: 382).

CONCLUSION

What follows from all this for the practice of European studies? First, we should note that, like other forms of area studies, it must surely be interdisciplinary; intertemporal, in the sense of combining historical and contemporary concerns; and also geohistorical, locating European transformations in a broader context. All of this could of course be said of any other domain of area studies, but it takes on a particular importance in relation to Europe because of the historical conjuncture, in the later part of the last millennium, of European hegemony, modernity and imperialism. Second, these considerations determine the kind of social science of use to European studies. Most obviously, again, this is a Schengen space of border-free travel by social scientists who should not be required, and will most often not want, to display any disciplinary attachments they may have. Again however there is a specificity of the European situation: the peculiar form of the emergent European polity means that the relations between political, economic, cultural and other social processes are particularly fluid. Asking, for instance, whether there is something like a European society involves reference both to the history of Europe and its component national states and to the emergence of Europe-wide forms of interaction related

specifically to the EU as a political form. It therefore poses, in a particularly sharp light, broader issues about the relation between the social and the political which have shaped much recent social theory.

There used to be a fairly simple notion, in both Marxist and non-Marxist sociology, that there were things called societies or social formations, within which there had come to be things called states. Some people regretted the emergence of states (Clastres, 1974) or expected them to wither away (Marxism); for others, they were a permanent fixture, albeit secondary to broader social processes. Three things have happened to this simple model. Theda Skocpol and others powerfully restated the empirical and historical importance of the state apparatus, under the slogan of 'Bringing the State Back In'. Drawing on the work of Max Weber and Otto Hintze, and her own analysis of state collapse in the French, Russian, and Chinese revolutions, Skocpol's approach stimulated and legitimated a certain shift of emphasis from 'society-centred' to 'state-centred' explanations. Second, in social and political theory there was a parallel reaffirmation of the importance of political processes in the creation or 'institution' of societies, marked in very different ways by the work of Hannah Arendt and Cornelius Castoriadis. Putting the same issue in historical terms, Peter Wagner (2001) has traced the rise and fall of the concept of society and shown how sociology can be seen as offering a certain set of answers to questions of political philosophy, rather than transcending or relativizing them, as it had once claimed to do. Finally, globalization can be seen to have undermined or at least reconfigured the territorial state or society. As the editors of a recent volume write in their introduction, European integration is a test case for postnational conceptions of the state and an opportunity to extend our conceptions and theories to keep up with what is happening (Katenhausen and Lamping, 2003: 9).

The suggestions above may seem a rather predictable plea for the social scientific equivalent of motherhood and apple pie, but their context is the current malaise, as I see it, of much work in European Studies, polarized between slender if often stimulating essays on the one hand, and the 'normal science' of European integration studies on the other, dominated by specialists in politics and international relations, plus a few of the more interesting economists and lawyers. But Europe, like the particular case of its post-communist 'transition', is too important to be left to specialists, or to over-professionalized social scientists who draw a sharp sepration between social, political and cultural processes. A further handicap, persistent but temporary, is the tendency to discuss 'Western' and 'Eastern' Europe separately. This is partly a hangover from the availability of statistical sources, which is gradually being rectified. Comparisons are increasingly being framed in terms of the US, Japan and the Eurozone (which, of course, will gradually be extended to most if not all of the EU).

The good news is that in the past years there has been an explosion of theoretical perspectives which can contribute to the sort of developments for which I have argued the need. First, the revival of historical sociology (Delanty and Isin, 2003; Smith, 1991) and the rapprochement between the institutionally separated disciplines of sociology and international relations. Second, the emergence of postcolonial theory and the fore-grounding of the imperial relationship, both in its heyday and, by extension, in the expansion of the EU as a quasi-imperial polity. This has given rise to an impressive body of critical writing on contemporary Europe; see, for example, Bhambra (2007) and the work of Etienne Balibar (Balibar, 2004; Bojadžijev and Saint-Saëns, 2006) whose reflections on the internalization of European borders in discriminatory practices directed at different categories of European residents are highly relevant to the issues discussed here. Third, the related trend towards self-consciously cosmopolitan forms of theory (Beck and Grande, 2004; Delanty, 2005; Delanty and Rumford, 2005; Rumford, 2006; Wagner,

2005), drawing both on the internationalization process previously mentioned and on political movements oriented to cosmopolitan democracy in Europe and elsewhere. These three clusters of theory also bridge the gap between empirical and normative analysis, in a fusion of interdisciplinary and interterritorial cosmopolitanism. Together, they are beginning to provide an adequate social and political theory for and of contemporary Europe.

NOTES

1 Somewhat Eurocentrically referred to by Braudel (1963, 1987: 338) as 'les Europe d'Amérique qui en découlent directement'.

2 The expression was invented by Peter Schneider in 1982, in his classic novel *Der Mauerspringer*, in which he correctly predicted that it would take longer to demolish than the visible wall (Schneider, 1982: 117; see also Neller, 2006).

3 It should be noted that the term 'occidentalism' has an entirely different meaning. It is modelled on Said's concept of orientalism and has been used to refer to similar attitudes of suspicion and contempt, this time directed at the 'West' (see Buruma and Margalit, 2004; Carrier, 1995; Delanty, 2006b: 268).

4 Russia's land empire was, of course, a classic case of European 'internal colonialism', the securing of control over peripheries. The Soviet Union also presided over the last quasi-imperial structure in Europe, with the so-called 'Brezhnev doctrine' of the limited sovereignty of Warsaw Pact states. This differed from the 'normal' imperial relation in that here it was the hegemonic power which supplied its more developed client states with cheap energy and raw materials in exchange for relatively advanced consumer goods.

5 A shift of this kind this seems to have been important, for example, for 'Latin American' intellectuals. 'the concern with the 'West' fascinated 'Latin' American intellectuals for a long time. Only slowly did modernity become the focus of inquiry'(Dominguez, 2006: 391). Dominguez goes on to outline the way in which an analysis in terms of modernity gradually emancipated itself from an excessively abstract and (in either direction) value-loaded formulation.

6 For a related line of argument, made with special reference to the Spanish context, see Pollack (2001, 2002).

7 This figure was a current estimate of the likely cost of enlargement; the European Currency Unit (ECU) is of course the forerunner of the euro. See also Outhwaite (2006).

8 In a much more critical approach to this question, Böröcz and Sarkar (2005) see the EU as in some ways a continuation of Western European colonialism in another context.

9 Kees van der Pijl (2006a, 2006b) sets the EU firmly in the context of his longstanding analysis of the Atlantic ruling class (van der Pijl, 1984).

10 See also Wagner (2003). On the need for (Habermas, 2004: 69–70) and the existence of elements of deliberative democracy in the EU, see Eriksen and Fossum (2000).

REFERENCES

Arendt, H. (1963) *Eichmann in Jerusalem: a Report on the Banality of Evil.* London: Faber and Faber.

Arnason, J. (2005) 'East and West: From invidious dichotomy to incomplete deconstruction', in G. Delanty and E.F. Isin (eds) *Handbook of Historical Sociology.* London: Sage, pp. 220–234.

Arnason, J. (2006a) 'Civilizational analysis, social theory and comparative history', in G. Delanty (ed.) *Contemporary European Social Theory.* London: Routledge, pp. 230–241.

Arnason, J. (2006b) 'Contested divergence: rethinking the 'rise of the West'', in G. Delanty (ed.) *Europe and Asia Beyond East and West.* London: Routledge, pp. 77–91.

Arzheimer, K. (2006) 'Von 'Westalgie' und 'Zonenkindern': Die Rolle der jüngeren Generation im Prozess der Vereinigung', in J.W. Falter, O.W. Gabriel, H. Rattinger and H. Schoen (eds) *Sind wir ein Volk? Ost- und Westdeutschland im Vergleich.* Munich: Beck, pp. 212–234.

Attali, J. (1997) 'A continental architecture', in P. Gowan and P. Anderson (eds) *The Question of Europe.* London: Verso, pp. 345–356.

Auer, S. (2004) *Liberal Nationalism in Central Europe.* London: RoutledgeCurzon.

Bahro, R. (1977) *Die Alternative: zur Kritik des real existierenden Sozialismus.* Köln: Europäische Verlagsanstalt. [Trans. The alternative in Eastern Europe.] London: NLB.

Baldwin, R.E., François, J.F. and Portes, R. (1997) 'EU enlargement: small costs for the West, big gains for the East', *Economic Policy,* 12 (24): pp. 126–176.

Balibar, É. (2004) *We, The People of Europe? Reflections on Transnational Citizenship.* Princeton University Press.

Bayly, C.A. (2004) *The Birth of the Modern World, 1780–1914.* Oxford: Blackwell.

Bechev, D. and Andreev, S. (2005) 'Top-down vs bottom-up aspects of the EU institution-building strategies in the Western Balkans', Occasional Paper 3/05, South East European Studies Programme, European Studies Centre, St Anthony's College, Oxford.

Beck, U. and Grande, E. (2004) *Das kosmopolitische Europa.* Frankfurt: Suhrkamp. Trans. Cosmopolitan Europe Cambridge: Polity, 2007.

Bhambra, G.K. (2007) *Rethinking Modernity.* London: Palgrave.

Blazyca, G. (2002) 'EU accession: The Polish case', in H. Ingham and M. Ingham (eds) *EU Expansion to the East. Prospects and Problems.* Cheltenham: Edward Edgar, pp. 205–221.

Blech, K. (1995) 'Germany between East and West', *SAIS Review,* 15 (1): 23–38.

Blokker, P. (2005a) 'Post-communist modernization, transition studies, and diversity in Europe', *European Journal of Social Theory,* 8 (4): 503–525.

Blokker, P. (2005b) 'Populist nationalism, anti-Europeanism, post-nationalism, and the East-West distinction', *German Law Journal,* 6 (2): 371–389.

Bojadžijev, M. and Saint-Saëns, I. (2006) 'Borders, citizenship, war, class: a discussion with Étienne Balibar and Sandro Mezzadra', *New Formations* 58: 10–30.

Böröcz, J. and Sarkar, M. (2005) 'What is the EU?', *International Sociology,* 20 (2): 153–173.

Braudel, F. (1987) *L'Europe,* new edn. Paris: Arts et métiers graphiques (1st edn 1963).

Brückner, W. (1987) 'Nord und Süd im kulturellen Selbstverständnis der Deutschen', in *Nord-Süd in Deutschland?: Vorurteile und Tatsachen.* Redaktion: Hans-Georg Wehling. Stuttgart: W. Kohlhammer.

Buruma, I. and Margolit, A. (2004) *Occidentalism. The West in the Eyes of its Enemies.* London: Routledge.

Cameron, F. (ed.) (2004) *The Future of Europe. Integration and Enlargement.* London: Routledge.

Carpenter, M. (1997) 'Slovakia and the triumph of nationalist populism', *Communist and Post-Communist Studies* 30 (2): 205–220.

Carrier, J. (1995) *Occidentalism. Images of the West*. Oxford: Clarendon Press.

CEC (Commission of the European Communities) (2000) Eurobarometer 53: p. 54.

Clastres, P. (1974) *La Société contre l'etat*. Paris: Minuit. Oxford: Blackwell, 1977.

Crouch, C. (1999) *Social Change in Western Europe*. Oxford: Oxford University Press.

Crouch, C. (2001) 'Breaking open black boxes: The implications for sociological theory of European integration', in A. Menon and V. Wright (eds), *From the Nation State to Europe: Essays in Honour of Jack Hayward*. Oxford: Oxford University Press, pp. 195–213.

Crouch, C. (2004) *Postdemocracy*. Cambridge: Polity.

de Tocqueville, A. (1971) *Recollections*, J.P. Mayer and A.P. Kerr (eds). London: Macdonald.

Delanty, G. (1995) *Inventing Europe: Idea, Identity, Reality*. Basingstoke: Macmillan.

Delanty, G. (1996) 'The frontier and identities of exclusion in European history', *History of European Ideas*, 22 (2): 93–103.

Delanty, G. (2003) 'The making of a post-Western Europe: A civilizational analysis', *Thesis Eleven* 72: 8–24.

Delanty, G. (2004) 'Multiple modernities and globalization', *Protosociology*: pp. 165–85.

Delanty, G. (2005) 'Cultural translations and European modernity', in E. Ben-Rafael (ed.) *Comparing Modern Civilizations: Pluralism versus Homogeneity*. Leiden: Brill, pp. 443–460.

Delanty, G. (2006a) 'The idea of a post-Western Europe', in G. Delanty (ed.) *Europe and Asia Beyond East and West*. London: Routledge, pp. 1–5.

Delanty, G. (2006b) *Europe and Asia Beyond East and West*. London: Routledge.

Delanty, G. and Isin, E.F. (eds) (2003) *Handbook of Historial Sociology*. London: Sage.

Delanty, G. and Rumford, C. (2005) *Rethinking Europe: Social Theory and the Implications of Europeanization*. London: Routledge.

Delhey, J. (2001) *Osteuropa zwischen Marx und Markt: Soziale Ungleichheit und soziales Bewusstsein nach dem Kommunismus*. Hamburg: Krämer.

Dominguez, J.M. (2006) 'Social theory, "Latin" America and Modernity', in G. Delanty (ed.), *The Handbook of Contemporary European Social Theory*. London: Routledge, pp. 381–394.

Edwards, S. (2005) 'Explaining enlargement: space, identity and governance', unpublished paper for the UACES Conference, September 2005, University of Zagreb.

Eisenstadt, S.N. (2000) 'Multiple modernities', *Daedalus*, 129 (1): 1–29.

Eriksen, E.O. and Fossum, J.E. (eds) (2000) *Democracy in the European Union – Integration though Deliberation?* London: Routledge.

Eyal, G., Szelény, I. and Townsley, E. (1998) *Making Capitalism Without Capitalists*. London: Verso.

Falter, J.W., Gabriel, O.W., Rattinger, H. and Schoen, H. (eds) (2006) *Sind wir ein Volk? Ost- und Westdeutschland im Vergleich*. Munich: Beck.

Frank, A.G. (1998) *ReOrient: Global Economy in the Asian Age*. Berkeley: University of California Press.

Greenfield, L. (1995) 'Nationalism in Western and Eastern Europe compared', in S.E. Hanson and W. Spohn (eds) *Can Europe Work? Germany and the Reconstruction of Postcommunist Societies*. Seattle and London: University of Washington Press, pp. 15–23.

Groys, B. (2006) *Das kommunistische Postskriptum*. Frankfurt: Suhrkamp.

Grzymski, J. (2005) 'The story of TINA (There is no alternative)', unpublished conference paper.

Habermas, J. (1985) Die Krisis des Wohlfahrtsstaates und die Erschöpfung utopischer Energien', in *Die neue Unübersichtlichkeit*. Frankfurt: Suhrkamp, pp. 141–163. Trans. *The New Conservatism*. Cambridge: Polity, 1989.

Habermas, J. (1990) *Die nachholende Revolution*. Frankfurt: Suhrkamp.

Habermas, J. (2004) *Der Gespaltener Westen*. Frankfurt: Suhrkamp. Trans. *The Divided West*. Cambridge: Polity, 2006.

Hechter, M. (1966) *Internal Colonialism: The Celtic Fringe in British National Development, 1536–1966*. London: Routledge & Kegan Paul.

Hjerm, M. (2003) 'National sentiments in Eastern and Western Europe', *Nationalities Papers*, 31 (4): 413–429.

Ingham, H. and Ingham, M. (eds) (2002) *EU Expansion to the East. Prospects and Problems*. Cheltenham: Edward Edgar.

Judt, T. (2005) *Postwar: A History of Europe Since 1945*. London: Heinemann.

Katenhausen, I. and Lamping, W. (eds) (2003) *Demokratien in Europa. Der Einfluss der europäischen Integration auf Institutionenwandel und neue Konturen des demokratischen Verfassungsstaates*. Opladen: Leske + Budrich.

Kennedy, M. (2002) *Cultural Formations of Postcommunism. Emancipation, Transition, Nation, and War*. Minneapolis and London: University of Minnesota Press.

Koselleck, R. (1985) *Futures Past*. Cambridge, MA: MIT Press.

Koselleck, R. (2000) *Zeitgeschichten*. Frankfurt: Suhrkamp.

Kovács, M, (2001) 'Putting down and putting off: The EU's discursive strategies in the 1998 and 1999 follow-up reports', in J. Böröcz and M. Kovács, (eds) *Europe's New Clothes. Unveiling EU Enlargement*. Telford: Central European Review (http:www.ce-review.org/), pp. 196–234.

Krejčí, J. (2004) *The Paths of Civilization. Understanding the Currents of History*. Basingstoke: Palgrave.

Krzyzanowski, M. (2005) '"European Identity Wanted": On Discursive and Communicative Dimensions of the European Covention', in R. Wodak and P. Chilton (eds) *A New Agenda for Critical Discourse Analysis: Theory, Methodology, and Interdisciplinarity*. Amsterdam, Philadelphia: J. Benjamins, pp. 137–163.

Lavenex, S. (2004) 'EU external governance in "wider Europe"', *Journal of European Public Policy*, 11 (4): 680–700.

Liotta, P.H. (2005) 'Imagining Europe: Symbolic geography and the future', *Mediterranean Quarterly*, 16 (Summer): 67–85.

McCann, L. (ed.) (2004) *Russian Transformations: Challenging the Global Narrative*. London: RoutledgeCurzon.

McCann, L. (2005) *Economic Development in Tatarstan: Global Markets and a Russian Region*. London: RoutledgeCurzon.

Mann, M. (1986) *The Sources of Social Power, Vol. 1. A History of Power from the Beginnings to AD 1760*. Cambridge: Cambridge University Press.

Mann, M. (1993) *The Sources of Social Power, Vol. 2. The Rise of Classes and Nation-States, 1760–1914*. Cambridge: Cambridge University Press.

Neller, K. (2006) 'Getrennt vereint? Ost-West-Identitäten, Stereotypen und Fremdheitsgefühle nach 15 Jahren deutscher Einheit', in J.W. Falter, O.W. Gabriel, H. Rattinger and H. Schoen (eds) *Sind wir ein Volk? Ost- und Westdeutschland im Vergleich*. Munich: Beck, pp. 13–36.

Nederveen Pieterse, J. (2002) 'Europe, Traveling Light: Europeanization and Globalization', in M. Kempny and A. Jawlowska (eds) *Identity in Transformation. Postmodernity, Postcommunism, and Globalization*. Westport, Connecticut and London: Praeger, pp. 127–144.

Nolte, H.-H. (1997) *Europäische Innere Peripherien im 20. Jahrhundert*. Historische Mitteilungen; Beiheft 23. Stuttgart: Franz Steiner.

Nolte, H.-H., Bähre, K. (eds) (2002) *Innere Peripherien in Ost und West*. Historische Mitteilungen; Beiheft 42. Stuttgart: Franz Steiner Verlag.

Norman, P. (2005) *The Accidental Constitution: The Story of the European Convention*. Brussels: EuroComment.

Oberhuber, F. (2005) 'Deliberation or "mainstreaming"? Empiricially researching the European Convention', in R. Wodak and P. Chilton (eds) *A New Agenda for Critical Discourse Analysis: Theory, Methodology, and Interdisciplinarity*. Amsterdam, Philadelphia: J. Benjamins, pp. 165–187.

Outhwaite, W. (2006) 'Europe after the EU Enlargement: cosmopolitanism by small steps', in G. Delanty (ed.), *Europe and Asia Beyond East and West*. London: Routledge, pp. 193–202.

Outhwaite, W. and Ray, L. (2005) *Social Theory and Postcommunism*. Oxford: Blackwell.

Pollock, G. (2001) 'Civil society theory and Euro-nationalism', *Studies in Social and Political Thought*, 4 (March): pp. 31–56.

Pollock, G. (2002) *Civil Society and Nation*. PhD thesis, University of Sussex.

Pridham, G., Sanford, G. and Herring, E. (eds) (1994) *Building Democracy?: The International Dimension of Democratisation in Eastern Europe*. Basingstoke: Palgrave MacMillan.

Rumford, C. (2006) 'Borders and rebordering', in G. Delanty (ed.) *Europe and Asia Beyond East and West*. London: Routledge, pp. 181–192.

Said, E. (2003) 'A window on the world', *The Guardian*, 2 August 2003.

Sakwa, R. (2006) 'Russia as Eurasia', in G. Delanty (ed.) *Europe and Asia Beyond East and West*. London: Routledge.

Schneider, P. (1982) *Der Mauerspringer*. Neuwied: Luchterhand. trans. by Liegh Haffrey as *The Wall Jumper*. London: Penguin, 2005.

Shaw, M. (2001) *Theory of the Global State. Globality as Unfinished Revolution*. Cambridge: Cambridge University Press.

Smith, D. (1991) *The Rise of Historical Sociology*. Cambridge: Polity.

Spiegel (2004) 'Das Milliarden-Geständnis: warum der Aufbau-Ost scheitern musste', Nr. 15 (5.4.04), pp. 24–41.

Stockmann, U. (2005) 'Beobachtungen zu unterschiedlichen Politikkulturen im Europäischen Parlament', in R. Fikentscher (ed.) *Kultur in Europa. Einheit und Vielfalt*. Halle: Mitteldeutscher Verlag.

Therborn, G. (1995) *European Modernity and Beyond. The Trajectory of European Societies 1945–2000*. London: Sage.

Therborn, G. (1997) 'Europe in the twenty-first century: the world's Scandinavia?', in P. Gowan and P. Anderson (eds) (1997) *The Question of Europe*. London: Verso, pp. 357–384.

Tilly, C. (2006) *Why?* Princeton: Princeton University Press.

Vachudová, M. and Snyder, T. (1997) 'Aretransitions transitory? Two types of political change in Eastern Europe since 1989', *East European Politics and Societies*, 11 (1): 1–35.

van der Pijl, K. (1984) *The Making of an Atlantic Ruling Class*. London: Verso.

van der Pijl, K. (2006a) 'Lockean Europe?', *New Left Review*, 37 (Jan–Feb): pp. 9–37.

van der Pijl, K. (2006b) *Global Rivalries form the Cold War to Iraq*. London: Pluto.

Wagner, P. (2001) *A History and Theory of the Social Sciences: Not All That is Solid Melts into the Air*. London: Sage.

Wagner, P. (2003) 'Die westliche Demokratie und die Möglichkeit des Totalitarismus', in A. Grunenberg (ed.) *Totalitäre Herrschaft und republikanische Demokratie. Fünfzig Jahre* The Origins of Totalitarianism *von Hannah Arendt*. Frankfurt: Peter Lang, pp. 131–145.

Wagner, P. (2005) 'The political form of Europe, Europe as a political form', *Thesis Eleven*, 80 (Feb): 47–73.

Wang, H. (2005a) 'Imagining Asia: A Genealogical Analysis', available at: http://www.cscsban.org/html/Wang.

Wang, H. (2005b) 'Reclaiming Asia from the West: Rethinking Global History', available at: http://www.japanfocus.org/article.asp?id=226.

5

Postcolonial Europe, or Understanding Europe in Times of the Postcolonial

Gurminder K. Bhambra

INTRODUCTION

A line from Daljit Nagra's poem, 'The Man Who Would be English!', captures well the problem of identity in contemporary Europe, a Europe of dominant and minority voices: 'I was one of us, at ease, so long as I passed my voice into theirs' (2007: 15).

Defining Europe, as with any project of identity construction, is necessarily a political and contested exercise. From historical understandings of Europe as coterminous with Christendom, to later understandings emphasizing its secularization, to contemporary questions of European identity in the context of EU expansion and consolidation, culminating in anxieties regarding the integration of postcommunist Eastern Europe and secular Turkey with its predominantly Muslim population, Europe has typically been represented in terms of its internal solidarities as defined against the others from whom it seeks to distinguish itself. In consequence, Europe has often been understood in terms of being more

an idea than a place, with Hayden White, for example, asserting that '"Europe" has never existed anywhere except in discourse' (2000: 67). This is not to suggest that the discourse of Europe has no implication for a sense of place and who is 'in place'. This chapter takes these discourses seriously and examines the naturalized accounts of Europe from a postcolonial perspective that highlights the typical exclusion of non-European 'others'. As Stråth (2002) argues, it is difficult to conceive of Europe without also thinking of 'non-Europe'. Yet, as this chapter will demonstrate, the relationship of Europe to non-Europe (the 'non-Europe' *within*, as well as outside, 'Europe') is a relationship that is largely unacknowledged, even if it is regarded as integral.

Scholarship on the historical evolution of European integration and identity, for example, typically addresses what Hansen refers to as 'the most canonized frame of reference' (2002: 483); that is, the history of internecine rivalries among European countries, the role of the United States, and the bipolar division of the world order embodied in the Cold War. Alongside these well-established world historical events, however, Hansen also points to the curious omission of the simultaneous dismantling of another world order, that which 'had been structured on European colonialism and imperialism' (2002: 484). While European integration provided one avenue for former colonial powers to 'adjust to the changing political and economic circumstances brought about by decolonization', there has been very little work on the relationship between colonialism, the processes of decolonization, and European identity (Hansen, 2002: 493; see also Böröcz and Sarkar, 2005). Even a recent work by Delanty and Rumford (2005), providing an otherwise comprehensive overview of Europe and the implications of Europeanization, does not address the issues of colonialism and imperialism that are central to such undertakings.

In this chapter, four key aspects of Europe are addressed from this postcolonial perspective: first, typical representations of Europe as easily aligned to commonly recognizable geographical boundaries; second, the pervasive ascription of the term 'peaceful' to the postwar European project; third, wider hegemonic understandings of Europe as a 'world-historical' site of culture and civilization; and, finally, narratives of modernity as providing a form of universalizable legitimacy for the emerging European polity. In each section, I present the conventional understanding of Europe and then interrogate that understanding from a postcolonial perspective.

Postcolonial criticism bears witness not only to contemporary inequalities, but also to their historical conditions (Bhabha, 1992). By locating and establishing the centrality of experiences hitherto ignored within the dominant accounts of 'Europe', this chapter seeks to address the implications of their exclusion and reflect upon the future consequences of their inclusion. While there is increasing resonance within scholarly debate for claims, such as, Dirlik's (2002), that even voices critical of Europe subscribe to a form of Eurocentrism because of their continued focus on Europe, I suggest otherwise. To the

extent that there is widespread agreement on the significance of Europe within academic endeavours, it is necessary to deconstruct its claims to universalism through a recognition of its own particularity, as well as the particularity of others, and then to reconstruct frameworks of understanding on the basis of acknowledging wider interconnections and dynamics. As Said argues, it is necessary to make transparent the relationship between knowledge and politics 'in the specific context of … [a] study, the subject matter, and its historical circumstances' (1978: 15). It is by examining these wider interconnections that we are able to rethink current categories, and to rethink them from a perspective of the necessary provisionality of any claim (Holmwood and Stewart, 1991). This, I argue, provides a way of incorporating the experiences of 'others' without reducing their experiences to 'deviant' particularity or as mere supplements to existing categories.

Postcolonial approaches work 'backwards', in terms of reconstructing historical representations, as well as 'forwards' to the creation of future projects (see Bhambra, 2007). Colonialism is integral both to the story of European integration and to any understanding of our contemporary world. As Trouillot argues, the silencing of colonial encounters is one aspect of a wider narrative of global domination; a narrative that, he suggests, will persist as long as the history of the West – or, for our purposes, Europe – 'is not retold in ways that bring forward the perspective of the world' (1995: 107). Understanding Europe in times of the postcolonial, then, requires us to bring forward the perspective of the world – that is, to think of Europe from a global perspective – as well as bring forward other (non-European) perspectives on the world.

A BOUNDED EUROPE?

Defining the boundaries of Europe, both culturally and institutionally, is a necessary function of claiming a collective identity.

What European identity is differs according to the different proposals of where such boundaries are to be drawn (Eder, 2006; see also Delanty and Rumford, 2005; Lewis and Wigen, 1997). In this section, I address the typical construction of the boundaries of Europe and discuss the contested 'Eastern frontier' demarcating the limits of the European polity. While it is generally accepted that boundaries can often be 'messy', indeterminacy at the peripheries simply reinforces the substance of Europe at its centre. This is a substance, as I will argue in a subsequent section, that is itself contestable. Further, the idea of a clearly bounded Europe can only persist to the extent that the European dependencies and protectorates located across the world are excised from representations of Europe (as are colonial relationships within Europe; for example, Ireland and Poland historically). I will end this section with a discussion of the place of empire and colonialism, or, more usually, their *displacement*, in the emergence and construction of the idea of the European polity.

Starting with the question of boundaries, Outhwaite (2006), for example, suggests that while the linguistic, religious, and ethnic diversity of European societies contributes in one sense to 'messy' boundaries, there is something easily definable as Europe that underlies that messiness. He suggests that 'the conventionally defined borders of Europe are … as "natural" as they come' given that you can sail, for some of the year at least, around most of its circumference (2006: 109). These 'natural' boundaries, however, very quickly become compromised. It is, he continues, the landlocked 'Eastern frontier' that provokes the greatest cause for concern. Russia and Turkey – the two great geopolitical entities that stand in a relation of perpetual inclusion and exclusion with Europe 'proper' – have been part of the political system of Europe historically, even if they have not been recognized as culturally European (see also Yapp, 1992). Questions about their 'identity' constitute an ongoing aspect of European (and Muslim and Russian)

discussions about the nature and limits of Europe.[1] As the British politician David Owen has written, for example: 'You have to have clarity about where the boundaries of Europe are, and the boundaries of Europe are not on the Turkish–Iranian border' (cited in Hansen 2004: 50). There are similar anxieties regarding the inclusion, or not, of Russia and what would be the associated proposals for stretching the Eastern Front of Europe across the steppes to the Bering Straits.

The idea of a 'natural' border to the south, while typically demarcated by the waters of the Mediterranean is, nonetheless, conveniently forgetful of the enclaves of Ceuta and Melilla which stretch the frontiers of the EU into Africa. This is clearly indicated, as Hansen suggests, by the 'two parallel fences hedged off by barbed wire entanglements and equipped with electronic sensors and thermal cameras', floodlit at night to provide literal 'enlightenment' about where the 'frontiers of the EU lie in Africa' (2004: 55). Europe's 'messy' boundaries become 'messier' still when we begin to consider the geographical territories – the French Overseas Departments of Reunion, Guyana, Martinique, and Guadeloupe, for example – in which 'payments are made in euros and the inhabitants are "citizens of the EU"' (Hansen 2004: 55) and yet do not constitute any part of typical representations of the European Union. Their absence from the official discourses of the EU and from its territorial representations – that is, its maps – is reinforced by the failure of academics adequately to theorize the implications of EU borders that stretch into Africa, the Indian Ocean, the Pacific, South America, and the Caribbean. As Hansen has remarked, the invisibility of these borders further points to the European Union's 'disinclination to deal with the history and legacy of colonialism' (2004: 57), a history and legacy of which these borders are existing remnants.

If, as Eder (2006) argues, it is necessary to analyze the stories and the social relations that express shared experiences in order to make sense of the cognitive projects of constructing boundaries, then it is possible also to point to the boundaries as framing the very possibilities of particular stories being told or relationships acknowledged and legitimized (see also Rumford, 2006). The acknowledgement, or not, of Europe's colonial past, for example, continues to have implications for the inclusion and exclusion of countries and people in relation to the European Union today. For example, when Morocco applied to join in 1986 it was flatly rejected on the grounds that it was not a European country. Yet, Morocco has land borders, as well as cultural, linguistic, and other associations, with two territories claimed (and defended militarily) as European – Ceuta and Melilla (as well as Perejil/Leila and the other islands off the coast of Morocco, but claimed by Spain). Further, it shares a land border with Algeria which was unproblematically (as far as Europeans were concerned) a part of the integrated European polity until its independence from France in 1962.[2] Prior to this time, Algeria was considered to be co-extensive with France, which meant that 'more than 80 per cent of French territory was located in Africa' (Hansen 2004: 52), and not in the 'Europe' of commonly understood boundaries.

Indeed, four of the six original members of the European Economic Community held, at its inception in 1957, substantial territories outside the commonly represented borders of Europe. Alongside the French colonies and dependencies listed above, the Netherlands held Surinam in South America, and the Netherlands Antilles and Aruba in the Caribbean; Belgium had control over the Congo, Rwanda, and Burundi; and Somaliland, later known as Somalia, was under Italian administration.[3] While the European Union's borders receded to north of the Mediterranean by 1962, with the independence of most African countries from European rule, they returned once more to Africa with the accession of Spain in 1986 and the inclusion of its colonies of Ceuta and Melilla into the EU (Hansen, 2004). With the accession of the United Kingdom in 1973 the borders of the EU extended further to China and the Pacific Ocean, and, with Portugal's entry in 1986 and

its establishment of the Community of Portuguese Language Countries a decade later, further strengthened European associations with countries in South America and Africa. These territorial holdings belie the typical representations of the European Union as being congruent with the commonly perceived geographical borders of Europe.

While it could be argued that a few European countries did not have colonies, and so any focus on colonialism as central to the processes of European integration or constructions of European identity is misplaced, it has to be recognized that a key aspect contributing to the outbreak of the two world wars was the imperial conflict over territory in both Europe and the wider world. As Ruthner suggests, for example, the Austro-Hungarian Empire's expansion into the Balkans in the late nineteenth century 'can easily be seen as a foreign policy substitution for non-existent Austro-Hungarian colonies in Africa or Asia' (2002: 878). The official Austrian description of this expansion was as a 'peace-keeping' mission, but, as Ruthner argues, 'One could also ask what myth-laden clichés ... of the "wild" Balkans in need of civilization served as the narrative pretence for this policy – in a sense as Austria's minor version of Orientalism, which was intended as discursive justification of the occupation' (2002: 879). Moreover, as Böröcz and Sarkar note, over 90 per cent of European Union citizens in 2003 were citizens of former colonial powers and, as such, they suggest that it is not possible to decipher the EU's current reality without taking into account 'the historical impact of empire on today's world' (2005: 164). Considering these issues from the perspective of Britain, and its relation to processes of European integration, we see how significant Empire and its demise has been to its particular construction.

As Holmwood (2000) argues, in the immediate aftermath of war, other European countries were keen for Britain to play a central role in the reconstruction of a politically and economically integrated Europe; albeit facing a certain degree of scepticism and hostility from members, such as, de Gaulle in France. The postwar British governments, however, were less keen to be bound into tighter alliances with European countries given their significant interests in empire and the Commonwealth. Holmwood suggests that British policy towards Europe in the immediate postwar period, then, was characterized by 'ideas of maintaining distance and encouraging the formation of looser free-trade arrangements across a wider variety of countries' than the original six at the heart of European integration (2000: 464). It was only once it became clear that the various independence movements throughout the empire were undermining the significance of the Commonwealth trading bloc in comparison with the rapidly expanding European market, that Britain entered into serious negotiations with the EEC about its membership.

Further, as Hansen (2002) suggests, with European integration involving countries with colonies, once integrated, the issue of colonies becomes pertinent to all member countries. Whether specific countries were directly colonial powers themselves or not, they became indirect ones through processes of integration and, in particular, the pooling of colonial resources and markets. For example, there was a general expectation in the construction of the EEC that the *Union Française* (France's colonial empire) would simply be incorporated into the West European association of states. This remains the case for more than half of the world's de facto dependencies today (Böröcz and Sarkar, 2005). As Böröcz and Sarkar forcefully state, 'The political process of European identity construction tries to hide the corpse of colonialism while it continues … to partake of the material inheritance of the same colonialism' (2005: 167).

A PEACEABLE EUROPE?

The experience of imperialism, then, stands in contrast to the rhetoric most closely associated with the postwar European project; that is, the rhetoric of political integration leading to the establishment of peaceable relations among European states (see Eder 2006; Haller 2000). Habermas and Derrida, for example, in discussing the question of 'European identity', point to the postwar 'image of a peaceful, cooperative Europe, open towards other cultures and capable of dialogue' (2003: 293).[4] It is a Europe, they argue, that has learnt to pacify 'class conflicts within the welfare state' and limit 'state sovereignty within the framework of the EU', one in which, now, the 'threshold of tolerance for the use of force against persons lies relatively low' (2003: 294, 295).[5] The representation of an inclusive Europe, formed around a project of peace, effaces the history of domination in the past, as well as exclusions (of both territories and citizens) in the present. As Hansen (2002) argues, such an identification can only stand to the extent that violence in the European colonies is separated out as being of a different order to that occurring within the boundaries of Europe itself. He points, in particular, to the Algerian War of 1954–62, which resulted in the deaths of over a million people and engaged approximately half a million French troops. Hansen argues that 'not even a sizeable war fought *inside* the [European Economic] Community has been able to impinge on the notion of European integration as a symbol of peace' (2002: 488).

Indeed, the European Union's official website, Europa, starts its historical account of the Union with the following sentence: 'The historical roots of the European Union lie in the Second World War. Europeans are determined to prevent such killing and destruction ever happening again.'[6] While the Soviet Union's involvement in the disputes in Hungary in 1956 and in Czechoslovakia in 1968, together with the student riots and rebellions of that year, are all mentioned, the killing of over one million citizens of the newly formed European Economic Community in the Algerian War of Independence is not. Intellectuals such as Albert Camus believed freedom to be an absolute right of the Hungarians who, in their use of violence in 1956, were simply asserting their will 'to stand upright'. However, the violence of the Algerian Arabs, who thought that they were making the same claim, was regarded as 'inexcusable', thus demonstrating the moral double standards with regard to Europe and North Africa that were commonly in play at the time and subsequently (O'Brien, 1970). The displacement of this violence from the narrative of the emergence of the European polity is a consequence of a disjunctive translation of identity whereby France is seen to be European, Algeria is established as French, but it is not then recognized as European. This manoeuvre enables the violence in Algeria not to be recognized as occurring within the European polity even when the war is one of independence from France and, as such, from the European project. In the process, the fiction of European boundaries as congruent with a particular geographical representation are maintained, as is the fiction of the substance of Europe as peaceable.

The project of a peace-loving, cosmopolitan Europe, that is seen to emerge in the wake of the Second World War, is identified by scholars, such as, Beck (2003), as the political antithesis of the destructive nationalism that had culminated in the Holocaust. Europe, he suggests, was now to be 'motivated by clear ideas of inviolable human dignity, and of the moral duty to relieve the suffering of others' (Beck 2003: np). This duty appears not to apply, however, when those others exist outside of commonly acknowledged European frontiers, or commonly accepted understandings of 'being European', as the history of Jews, Gypsies, and long-standing immigrant communities testifies (see Ehrkamp and Leitner 2003; Weber, 1995). While the critique of Nazism is regarded as a key element in the reconstruction of Europe after the Second World War, this critique of oppression and domination does not usually extend to the contemporaneous colonial relationships of European states with other parts of the world. The killing of citizens in areas marked as colonies, then, is legitimized in any academic endeavour that seeks to establish the 'peaceable' character of Europe simply on the basis of them having refrained from killing other white Europeans.[7] Wagner is not unusual when he points to the period after the Second World War – the period of the Algerian War of Independence, the Mau Mau rebellions against British imperial rule, the Congo 'Crisis', and, more recently, the wars in Afghanistan and Iraq – as a period underlining 'the European commitment to *civic and political liberties*' (2005: 68).

This conception of Europe, then, is one that is shaped by an acknowledgement of the experience of Nazi Germany and the Holocaust, but is one which simultaneously elides the experience of imperial Germany, and imperial Europe, to horrors perpetrated *within* its borders; it typically fails to acknowledge the horrors perpetrated outwith those borders. As Stratton argues, however, in addressing the Holocaust it is necessary 'to demonstrate the historical continuity between German practices in Africa (and especially southwest Africa) and Poland' (2003: 516). For it was in southwest Africa that the 'total extermination of a people – or genocide – was espoused as official policy' for the first time providing 'a direct precursor to subsequent German policy in respect of the Jews' (2003: 517). Even in addressing the Holocaust directly, the link with colonialism cannot be ignored, for, as Stratton (2003) states, all Nazi death camps were in areas of German 'colonial' occupation, with six such camps in Poland and another in the Ukraine.

Acknowledging the centrality of colonialism and colonial practices to the Holocaust, then, points to a history of European-instigated genocide that Stratton argues 'is as central to modernity as the humanism for which the "West" likes to be known' (2003: 209). This Europe is not one that has learnt the lessons of decolonization (nor, now, of postcolonialism). Indeed, scholars as eminent as Habermas and Derrida continue to talk, in their joint statement, of the context of 'the *great* European nations' that had experienced 'the *bloom* of … imperial power' (2003: 297 [my italics]).

While many scholars accept the processes of imperialism and colonialism as aspects of any *history* of globalization, they seem much more reluctant to think through the implications of this history for contemporary social scientific engagements. Thus, Ross (1998) acknowledges imperialism as a key factor in globalization, and yet passes it over in his discussion of the impact of globalizing processes on the postwar integration of Europe. Even Nederveen Pieterse (1999), an otherwise sympathetic commentator on the necessity of addressing global interconnections, manages to discuss Europeanization and globalization, and the relationship between the two, with barely a mention of the globalizing processes of colonialism that accompanied (and were integral to) them. Instead, he suggests that any cultural analysis of Europe requires 'leaving behind the heavy luggage of imperialism and colonialism', while a political economy analysis points towards 'Europe reclaiming its social capitalism and social democratic character'. What is needed, he argues, is a forward-looking analysis that combines these agendas (1999: 14, 15). I would argue that it is not acceptable to 'look forward' on the basis of forgetting a constitutive aspect of the past, the forgetting of which has, in any case, already contributed to the perpetuation of long-standing injustices globally. As Mamdani has argued in the context of Africa (but, I suggest, no less relevant in the context of Europe), 'No matter how much we redraw boundaries, the political crisis will remain incomprehensible until we address the institutional–political legacy of colonial rule' (Mamdani 2001: 653).

EUROPE AS CULTURE AND CIVILIZATION?

In thinking about Europe, and European identity, discussions typically focus around four aspects: first, Europe as a national culture; second, as a civilization; third, as a construction; and finally, in terms of the deconstruction of European culture (Ifversen, 2002; see also Delanty and Rumford, 2005). What is remarkably similar in all four approaches is that the processes, components, markers, and so forth, identified as European are all regarded as unique to Europe, as distinctive, and unparalleled in the rest of the world. In this section, I address the constructions of Europe in these terms and the limitations to any discussion of Europe that does not take 'non-Europe' into consideration.

'European culture', the 'European spirit', the 'ethos of Europe', 'Europe's unique creativity' – these are all ways of identifying the deep rooted unity of Europe and pointing to a common destiny that emerges from the actions of Europe constructed as a singular subject (Sassatelli, 2002). As Burgess argues, for example, 'a long spiritual and cultural legacy is the red thread of European identity' (2002: 468). The spiritual or religious dimension of European identity is further emphasized by scholars, such as, Siedentop (2001) who claim a foundational basis for Christianity in determining the constitution of Europe. While Christendom, and then Christianity, has been seen as a key aspect of cultural unity for much of Europe through the centuries, this has occurred in the context of the largely unrecognized historical presence of a substantial number of non-Christian Europeans (Rodríguez-Salgado, 2005). Along with significant Jewish populations, it is necessary also to take into account the history of Spain, which had been Muslim for a number of centuries, as well as European Muslims in the Balkans, southeastern Europe and Turkey. Europe's longstanding religious plurality is complemented by its ethnic diversity which has similarly been erased from common depictions.[8]

The ascription of a religious identity to the European polity sits uneasily with claims that a key aspect of the specificity of modern Europe is its identification with the processes of secularization. Beck (2003), for example, suggests that representing the European

Union as a 'Christian club' is manifestly erroneous and that attempts to turn Europe back into a religion reverse the progress made through the project of the Enlightenment. Delanty, similarly, problematizes the association of Europe with Christianity, presenting an alternative argument that 'political equality and liberty in Europe were achieved by democratic struggles against Church and Throne rather than deriving unchanged from theological beliefs and feudal customs' (2003: 483). In contrast to Siedentop, then, scholars such as Delanty (2003) and Beck (2003) believe that it is the heritage of European secular civilization that is to be held up as an exemplar to the world, not the particularity of any specific religion active in its boundaries. Their disagreement over the priority to be given to the religious or the secular in understandings of Europe, however, turns on a common belief that Europe is to be held up as an exemplar to the world.

The focus on what unites Europe, or what Europe shares in common, often exists alongside calls for recognizing Europe's diversity, where cultural multiplicity is taken 'as the key feature of Europe' (Sassatelli, 2002: 439). Drawing on the work of Edgar Morin, Sassatelli argues that the idea of unity – and, indeed, uniqueness – in diversity is increasingly regarded as the most adequate way of theorizing European identity, where what is taken as distinctive is the combination, but not homogenization, of differences within it (2002: 439; see also Llobera, 2003). This solution of 'unity in diversity', however, as Sassatelli points out, has itself been criticized by Luisa Passerini among others, for being 'a *formal* solution with no substance' and one that risks falling into 'a new version of Eurocentric triumphalism' (2002: 440). The limitations of a narrowly defined cultural theory of the polity have led to scholars, such as Friese and Wagner, to think in terms of 'a European commonality that is larger and older than the national cultural–linguistic one'; one which they argue would be based on a 'broad cultural commonality … grounded on the observation of the diversity of Europe'

(2002: 351). In this way, Europe is no longer to be seen simply as a culture, but rather, a 'community of values', where the values believed to be quintessentially European include the concept of human rights, and the sense of history itself (Ifversen, 2002).

In identifying Europe as a civilization based on a 'broad cultural commonality', Ifversen suggests that it has been exceptional in leading the rest of the world in the areas of democracy, law, and science, among other things, further suggesting that Europe's destiny is one of universality and a universal humanity not bound to any particular community (2002: 10–11). It is this movement away from a notion of Europe as tied to a cultural core to defining Europe in terms of a civilization that allows European culture to be exported to the rest of the world. Llobera, for example, distinguishes between culture and civilization, suggesting that culture is 'the singularity, the subjectivity, the individuality, and the specificity of society', while civilization is 'cumulative and progressive … transmissible, objective and universal' (2003: 159). By distinguishing between culture and civilization in this way, it is possible to make culture that from which civilization emerges, and thus originary to that civilization. Civilization then becomes the mode of transmission of that culture to others. This further enables both the valorization of the particularity (and uniqueness of European culture), at the same time as enabling its universalization through the transmission of 'European civilization' to others. This latter occurs via the processes of imperialism, colonialism, and slavery; and is justified, ideologically, through the establishment of a narrative of cultural superiority and a teleological framework of modernity.

Whether Europe is defined in terms of culture or civilization, however, most scholars agree that what Europe is, is qualitatively different in the world, and whether implicitly, or more usually explicitly, it is thus seen as the 'leader' of the rest of the world. Concluding an article entitled 'Understanding the Real Europe', Beck, for example, writes that '[m]ore than anywhere else in the world, Europe *shows* ... Europe *teaches* ... Move over America – Europe is back' (2003: np; [my italics]). Perhaps what is needed, however, is for Europe to listen and to learn. The problems with identifying a specifically European 'community of values' is the erasure of the contributions of others from both historical events (and the idea of history itself), as will be discussed in more detail in the following section. Therborn (2002), for example, in discussing the formulation of the 1948 UN Declaration of Human Rights, attributes all agency to European and US actors and disregards the significant contribution of recently decolonized countries to these processes. However, 33 of the 48 signatories to the declaration were Latin American and non-Western countries meaning that Western countries accounted for less than one-third of the total signatories (see Morsink, 1999). Further, it was the predominance of newly decolonized countries within the United Nations that put matters of self-determination and discrimination firmly on the agenda together with issues of social and economic justice. These achievements, however, are presented by Therborn to be solely a consequence of 'the strivings of the European labour movement' (2002: 409), with no mention of the impact of the rest of world upon such processes.

While European projects of imperialism were often cast in the discourse of the civilizational superiority of Europe, imperialism itself was rarely understood as an aspect of civilization or, indeed, negating any claim to civilization. As Llobera writes, 'neither wars nor imperialisms, neither chauvinisms nor dictatorships have completely undermined democracy in Europe' (2003: 161); nor, it should be added, *the idea of Europe as democratic or civilized*. The increasingly common constructivist approach to Europe, whereby Europe can be anything Europeans claim it to be, also implies permanent deconstruction, whereby anything Europe has been can be dismantled and a new version established. Beck (2003), for example, identifies the project of a cosmopolitan Europe as the most recent incarnation replacing previously modern and postmodern conceptions of Europe. This cosmopolitan Europe, he suggests, is best understood in terms of being the institutionalization of the European tradition's own internal critique.

A thorough deconstruction of what Europe, or European identity, is about, however, would start, as Hansen suggests, with a discussion of 'the external as well as internal implications of an identity politics that extols "Europe" and the "European" without first reflecting on the fact that colonialism's crimes of genocide, slavery and exploitation were also carried out in the name of Europe and justified with reference to the racial and cultural superiority of Europeans' (2004: 57–8). The urgency for such reflection – and continued reflection – is made apparent in UK Prime Minister Blair's (2007) recent 'legacy' article in *Foreign Affairs*, where he suggests that the current war in Iraq, and the wider 'war on terror', is not about a clash *between* civilizations, but rather, a clash *about* civilization. He suggests that this struggle is one about values; values which he believes represent humanity's progress throughout the ages and which have had to be fought for and defended through those ages. Prime Minister Blair concludes by arguing that a new age is beckoning, one which requires 'us' to fight for those values again. The relationship of those values to what has also been perpetrated in their name – either historically or contemporaneously – is lost on the Prime Minister, but it will not be lost on those he seeks to persuade.[9]

EUROPE AS A PROJECT OF MODERNITY?

Along with contestations as to the boundaries of Europe, and European culture and civilization, then, there are also attempts to distinguish something specifically European from a wider notion of the West with which it has more usually been elided. As Therborn suggests, the popularity of phrases, such as, 'the West and the rest', or 'North and South', has meant that 'Europe' no longer has 'a major place in global consciousness, or in consciousness of the world' (2002: 406). This endeavour, to reclaim some significance for Europe, is perhaps best exemplified by Habermas's (2001, 2003) work on the question of the self-understanding of European modernity and could be attributed, in part at least, to the realignment of the global order in the wake of the Cold War and the fall of communism in Europe (on the latter, see Outhwaite and Ray, 2005). In this section, I examine the relationship of the European polity to processes of globalization and then discuss the typical narratives of modernity associated with its emergence before examining the implications of their general elision of imperialism and colonialism.

With the collapse of a bipolar world order, space opened up for a European identification differentiated from its common association with the United States as the hegemonic Western power, and was further substantiated by the increasing pace of EU integration. For many scholars, Europeanization is an integral aspect of the reordering of political and economic boundaries that are seen to be characteristic of the processes of globalization generally (Axtmann, 1998; Nederveen Pieterse, 1999; Rosamond, 1999). For some, a European polity is even considered a necessity in light of these global reorderings (see Friese and Wagner, 2002). Rosamond, for example, suggests that the concept of globalization has been used within the European Union 'to create cognitive allegiances to the idea of 'Europe/EU as a valid economic space' (1999: 666–7). This is not necessarily in a bid to define a territorial space, he continues, but rather, 'a legitimate policy space which is a deeply normative issue' (1999: 667). There is, nevertheless, a growing sense that the European Union needs to reimagine the idea of Europe – in terms of culture and identity – in order to provide a viable context for the development of the economic and

political union (see Stolcke, 1995; Sassatelli, 2002; Soysal 1994).

While the European Union and Europe are not coextensive, the project of European construction is being 'carried out in the name of Europe' and it is this 'that assures the *legitimacy* of the European Union' (Burgess, 2002: 476; see also Sassatelli, 2002). At the same time, however, any attempt to define a specifically European self-understanding has to take into consideration the variety and diversity of polities within Europe. While Delanty is ambivalent about the nature of the relationship between European national states and the EU, he does suggest that it is as a consequence of Europe being regarded as 'a motif of modernity' and as reflecting the transformations of modernity that it becomes a symbol that is appropriated by national discourses (2003: 478). As such, he sees current writing on Europe as 'part of the reflection on the continued transformation of modernity' (2003: 486). Wagner, similarly, acknowledges the diversity of Europe while suggesting nonetheless that 'it would make no sense to talk about European political modernity if there were not some common commitment that is specific to Europe' (2005: 69). As Friese and Wagner argue (2002), it is this 'common commitment' that is increasingly becoming the focus of analyses of the EU, shifting emphasis away from earlier work on the processes of integration to this 'spirit' of the Union itself.

Following Habermas, then, Wagner (2005) argues that European integration needs to be analysed in terms of the self-understanding of European modernity which, in turn, needs to be located in a complex concept of political modernity. He then addresses this by discussing the history of political Europe in terms of three, or, as he writes, possibly four familiar narratives. The *liberal* story of the extension of civic rights from the signing of the Magna Carta in 1215, to the French Declaration of Rights in 1789, followed by the United Nations Universal Declaration of Human Rights in 1948. This is a story, he suggests, 'of local European origins ... then a giant step towards universalization of the normative claims, followed by a long and difficult process of globalization, that is, the actual spreading of the claims around the world' (2005: 51). The second story that Wagner identifies is that of the development of the modern state system, which, he argues, starts with the elaboration of the concept of sovereignty in Bodin and Hobbes and in the political history inaugurated by the 1648 Treaty of Westphalia (2005: 52; see also Beck, 2003). The third is the rise of democracy, which he believes started in the Greek *polis*, was transformed in the Roman Republic, and again with the Florentine and Venetian Republics, to be reasserted in the eighteenth century with the American and French Revolutions. The final narrative, that of revolution, is implied in the earlier ones, he suggests, but is 'much less recognized as a constituent component of modernity' (2005: 53).

The connections between these stories, identified by Wagner, is that they all 'point to European origins of the political developments they emphasize' even if, as he suggests, 'none of them remains confined to the territory of Europe' (2005: 54). Further, they are stories which seek to demarcate a peculiarly European claim to a particular cultural heritage at the same time as they consolidate that European identity in the context of the post-war European project. Wagner argues that what is at stake in discussions of European political integration and identity is 'a form of engagement with others and with the world, that is a common European value and that, as such, is a value that goes beyond an instrumental relation to others and the world, as it is promoted globally from other positions today' (2005: 69). With this, Wagner suggests that it is possible to hold onto a belief in common European values separated from a European history of the violations of such values. He implicitly presents these values as solutions to the manifest problems of the world brought about by processes of modernity, but does not acknowledge their complicity in the generation and perpetuation of those problems, nor the involvement

of others in the creation of solutions through the production of new values. Ironically, the problems brought about by (European) modernity are coterminous with their solutions and no new values are seen to be necessary to solve the problems of modernity. While he suggests that any answers need to respond appropriately to the contemporary situation (2005: 68), he does not believe that, to be appropriate, they need involve non-European participants.

Despite the diversity of stories narrated briefly above, the one commonality, as noted at the end, is their European frame, at least in origin if not always over time. As I have argued elsewhere, however, the metanarrative of a specifically European provenance to such stories can no longer be regarded as adequate (see Bhambra, 2007). From scholarship on the slave revolutions of Haiti and elsewhere indicating a significant moment in the claiming of rights and political agency (see Buck-Morss, 2000; Dubois, 2004; Fischer, 2004; Grovogui, 1996; Shilliam, 2006; Trouillot, 1995); to an increasing recognition of the inadequacy of any attempt to understand the emergence of the modern state system independently of the encounters of colonialism and imperialism (see Barkawi and Laffey, 2002; Grovogui, 2001; Inayatullah and Blaney, 2004; Persaud and Walker, 2001); to an acknowledgement that while the word 'democracy' does indeed have Greek roots, coming as it does from the words *demos* and *kratia*, the concept itself is not the preserve of any one culture (see Markoff, 1999; Muhlberger and Paine, 1993; Thapar, 1966); such scholarship contests and undermines the received wisdom that all that is original and innovative occurred in Europe and from there was benignly disseminated to the rest of the world. Further, identifying 'revolution' (or in other words critique) with Europe has the additional consequence of making all opposition to Europe 'European'.

Not only is the inherent cultural superiority in such a claim in and of itself problematic, but most explanations of subsequent dissemination further elide the questions of colonialism and imperialism to a neutral process whereby European developments are said not to have remained confined to the territory of Europe, to have simply been spread around the world, with little discussion of the processes by which such dissemination occurred. The historian James Joll, for example, argues that it is generally accepted that it 'was through imperialism that European ideas became widely disseminated over the non-European world' (1980: 15), yet the central concepts of social science render that imperialism invisible, arguing for the abstract universality of foundational terms to be located outside of particular experiences. The innovations that can be most strongly associated with Europe – the modern forms of colonialism, imperialism, and slavery, for example – are, then, the very ones that are rarely mentioned in discussions of European cultural superiority. Instead, the only lesson seemingly to be learnt by Europeans from their experience of what Habermas and Derrida call the 'bloom' of imperialism is the ability to '*assume a reflexive distance from themselves*' (2003: 297), a distance which does not seem to provide reflections *upon* themselves.

CONCLUSION

While the idea of civilization provides a unified framework for the coexistence of different cultures within it, these different cultures are typically assumed to be different *European* cultures. The increasing multicultural and multiethnic composition of European states, however, as Amin suggests, problematizes any new appeal to the old idea of Europe based on 'nativist preconceptions of who has first call on the label "European"' (2004: 4).[10] The focus on cultural difference and distinction within Europe itself, he suggests, makes the old idea a blunt instrument for unity. Hansen similarly argues that any definition of the European Union, 'that is premised on ties to a European ancestral state, Christianity

and other ethno-cultural markers … ostracizes the millions of EU inhabitants who cannot lay claim to the ethno-cultural heritage in question' (2004: 50). While there have been few voices identifying a specifically 'postcolonial' Europe, there is an increasing focus on the diversity and hybridity of European cultural constellations (see Stevenson, 2006). This focus then prompts solutions to the post-Imperial order that have included, as Stevenson notes, the 'need to break with a Eurocentric imagination built upon the superiority of European values', a 'cultural politics that welcomes difference', as well as imagining 'new more convivial possibilities' (2006: 496, 497, 498; see also Gilroy, 2003). Amin similarly argues for the idea of European-ness today as resting on a notion of 'becoming European through active engagement with, and negotiation of, difference' (2004: 4).

It is, thus, partly in response to the identification of problems associated with an exclusivist identity, based on a past heritage, that scholars have begun to think about other ways of defining Europe. While these modes of understanding Europe would go some way beyond the definitions contested earlier, the question still arises of why we should imagine the 'negotiation of difference', for example, under the sign of Europe. Maintaining 'Europe' as the location of imagining 'newness' serves simply to reconfirm a traditional world view of Europe, and its place in the world, as opposed to contest or rethink it. The postcolonial challenge, I maintain, rests in calling into question the assumed connections between projects of identity formation that contest and remake relations and identities and such a charged signifier of identity as 'Europe'.

The privileging of Europe and the West in the context of a history of imperialism, colonialism, and slavery that covered almost the entirety of the globe is understandable. What is less understandable is the failure of most theorists, who privilege Europe and the West, to consider how the histories of imperialism, colonialism, and slavery enabled Europe and the West to achieve this dominance. As such, 'provincializing Europe', to use Chakrabarty's (2000) resonant phrase, is not only about bringing to the fore other histories and experiences, but also about recognizing and deconstructing – and then reconstructing – the scholarly positions that privilege particular narratives without any recognition of the other histories and experiences that have similarly contributed to the constitution of those narratives. Looking at Europe differently, as Dainotto argues, means not only changing perspectives and points of view, but also requires interrogating the very cultural categories on which ideas of Europe have been predicated (2006: 7). Addressing 'modern Europe' from the perspective of 'postcolonial' Europe, then, provides a more adequate understanding of both contemporary Europe and its decentred place in the world.

For some, such as, Featherstone and Venn, problematizing current understandings through an address of global histories and experiences requires 'both critique and the production of a different archive of knowledge'; an archive that, they suggest, would disrupt 'scholarly classifications, and usher in a declassificatory mood' (2006: 4, 5). New historical understandings cannot be added to pre-existing ones, however, without in some way calling into question the legitimacy and validity of the previously accepted parameters – both historical and ethical. As Keita (2002) argues, the 'regained voices' were not previously lost; they were voices associated with historical activities that were not seen as significant within dominant European accounts. As such, a more thorough-going critique is needed, one which goes beyond declassification to *re*-classification; a critique that calls into question European claims to knowledge inasmuch as it challenges any particular identity of Europe. In this sense, the reinterpretation of history is not just a different interpretation of the *same* facts (modern Europe) but the bringing into being of *new* facts (postcolonial Europe).

The problem that has been identified and addressed in this chapter is the problem of the exclusion of others from the narratives of Europe, European modernity, and European integration. In taking issue with the deeply embedded sets of assumptions within constructions of Europe – assumptions which have proved remarkably resilient over time – it has been necessary, first, to engage in a detailed critique of the emergence and development of both the boundaries of Europe and its self-proclaimed histories. This deconstruction, then, requires a reconstruction based on a process of learning (Holmwood and Stewart, 1991). In this chapter, I have sought to understand the typical narratives associated with the construction of Europe, deconstruct their universalist claims through a recognition of their particularity, and then point towards the necessity of a reconstruction of our understandings of Europe in a (post)colonial context.

Colonialism was intrinsic to the contemporary scene of European integration and yet the colonial is typically rendered unseen in most representations of Europe. Just as feminist scholarship has revealed the masculinist bias of thought presenting itself as universal (see, for example, Hartsock, 1984; Bordo, 1986), so postcolonial scholarship challenges the universals of European narratives constructed, as they are, on the basis of marginalizing and silencing other experiences and voices. The demise of colonialism as an explicit political formation has given rise to understandings of postcoloniality and, perhaps ironically, an increased recognition of the role of colonialism in the formation of understandings of Europe. In this context, then, it is insufficient to regard postcolonialism as simply implying new ways of understanding Europe for the future. The contribution of postcolonialism to reconstructing Europe's past(s) also needs to be acknowledged. To do this, however, further requires a reconstruction of the forms of understanding – concepts, categories, and methods – within which particular events are rendered apparently insignificant. In this way, Europe is placed in a frame of interconnections of networks of peoples and places that transcend the boundaries, both historical and geographical, established within dominant approaches and typical representations. It can be no more or less special than any other part of the world. To end with the words of Frantz Fanon: 'Come, then, comrades, the European game has finally ended; we must find something different' (1968 [1961]: 252).

ACKNOWLEDGEMENTS

I would like to thank John Holmwood, Mihnea Panu, Robbie Shilliam, Jeppe Strandsbjerg, and William Outhwaite for productive comments on this chapter.

NOTES

1 To the extent that Turkey, as with the Ottoman Empire before it, is constructed as a mirror with which to reflect an understanding of Europe back to itself (Yapp, 1992), so Arabs and others have used 'Europe' for similar purposes (Al-Azmeh, 1992; see also Raychaudhuri, 2002 [1988]). See Neumann (1996) for similar discussions in Russia about what Europe is and Russia's relation to Europe.

2 Ironically, however, the French settlers in Algeria – the *pied-noirs* – were only considered to be unproblematically French to the extent that they remained in Algeria. As soon as they decided to 'return' to France after Algerian independence in 1962, they were ostracized and regarded as foreigners. For further details see Haddour (2000).

3 Surinam gained independence from the Netherlands in 1975, although the Netherlands Antilles and Aruba in the Caribbean are still under Dutch control; the Belgian Congo gained independence in 1960, Rwanda and Burundi became independent in 1962; Somalia remained under Italian administration until 1960.

4 In the wake of global mass demonstrations against the US-led war in Iraq, Jacques Derrida and Jürgen Habermas co-signed an appeal and analysis seeking to determine 'new European political responsibilities beyond any Eurocentrism' (2003: 291). Their first move beyond Eurocentrism was to highlight the demonstrations in 'London and Rome, Madrid and Barcelona, Berlin and Paris' as indicating 'a sign of the birth of a European public sphere' (2003: 291) with no reference to the global nature, or implications, of these demonstrations.

5 This celebratory rhetoric, however, can be contrasted with the treatment imposed by European states upon their 'internal others'. 'Welfare pacification', as argued by Panu (2006), is often defined in racial, ethnic, economic, and gendered terms and implicitly sanctions the use of force by European states against these 'internal others'.

6 http://europa.eu/abc/history/1945-1959/index_en.htm.

7 The association of Jews as 'white', however, is contested and, as Boyarin notes, it is necessary to recognize the complexities of manoeuvre required in the incorporation of European Jews into whiteness (as cited in Stratton, 2003).

8 On the black African presence in Europe, for example, see Snowden (1970) and Van Sertima (1986) as well as the seminal text by Bernal (1987).

9 As was noted by Frantz Fanon almost half a century ago: 'That same Europe where they were never done talking of Man, and where they never stopped proclaiming that they were only anxious for the welfare of Man: today we know with what sufferings humanity has paid for every one of their triumphs of the mind' (1968 [1961]: 312).

10 As Stolcke argues, three criteria – descent, birthplace, and domicile (combined with various procedures of 'naturalization') – 'have usually been wielded to determine entitlement to nationality in the modern nation-states' (1995: 9).

REFERENCES

Al-Azmeh, A. (1992) 'Barbarians in Arab eyes', *Past and Present*, 134 (Feb): 3–18.

Amin, A. (2004) 'Multi-ethnicity and the idea of Europe', *Theory, Culture and Society*, 21 (2): 1–24.

Axtmann, R. (1998) (ed.) *Globalization and Europe: Theoretical and Empirical Investigations*. London: Pinter.

Barkawi, T. and Laffey, M. (2002) 'Retrieving the imperial: empire and international relations', *Millennium*, 31 (1): 109–127.

Beck, U. (2003) 'Understanding the Real Europe', *Dissent Magazine*, 50 (3): 32–38.

Bernal, M. (1987) *Black Athena: The Afroasiatic Roots of Classical Civilization Volume 1: The Fabrication of Ancient Greece 1785–1985*. London: Free Association Books.

Bhabha, H.K. (1992) 'Postcolonial criticism' in S. Greenblatt and G.B. Gunn (eds) *Redrawing the Boundaries: The Transformation of English and American Literary Studies*. New York: Modern Language Association of America, pp. 437–457.

Bhambra, G.K. (2007) *Rethinking Modernity: Postcolonialism and the Sociological Imagination*. Basingstoke: Palgrave MacMillan.

Blair, T. (2007) 'A Battle for Global Values', *Foreign Affairs* Jan/Feb. Available at: http://www.foreignaffairs.org/20070101faessay 86106-p0/tony-blair/a-battle-for-global-values.html, accessed 15 March 2007.

Bordo, S. (1986) 'The Cartesian masculinization of thought', *Signs*, 11 (3): 439–456.

Böröcz, J. and Sarkar, M. (2005) 'What is the EU?', *International Sociology*, 20 (2): 153–173.

Buck-Morss, S. (2000) 'Hegel and Haiti', *Critical Inquiry* 26 (Summer): 821–865.

Burgess, J.P. (2002) 'What's so European about the European Union? Legitimacy between institution and identity', *European Journal of Social Theory*, 5 (4): 467–481.

Chakrabarty, D. (2000) *Provincializing Europe: Postcolonial Thought and Historical Difference*. Princeton: Princeton University Press.

Dainotto, R.M. (2006) 'The discreet charm of the Arabist theory: Juan Andres, historicism, and the de-centring of Montesquieu's Europe', *European History Quarterly*, 36 (1): 7–29.

Delanty, G. (2003) 'Conceptions of Europe: A review of recent trends', *European Journal of Social Theory*, 6 (4): 471–488.

Delanty, G. and Rumford, C. (2005) *Rethinking Europe: Social Theory and the Implications of Europeanization*. London: Routledge.

Dirlik, A. (2002) 'History without a centre? Reflections on Eurocentrism', in E. Fuchs and B. Stuchtey (eds) *Across Cultural Borders: Historiography in Global Perspective*. New York: Rowman & Littlefield.

Dubois, L. (2004) *A Colony of Citizens: Revolution and Slave Emancipation in the French Caribbean, 1787–1804*. Chapel Hill: University of North Carolina Press.

Eder, K. (2006) 'Europe's borders: The narrative construction of the boundaries of Europe', *European Journal of Social Theory*, 9 (2): 255–271.

Ehrkamp, P. and Leitner, H. (2003) 'Beyond national citizenship: Turkish immigrants and the (re)construction of citizenship in Germany', *Urban Geography*, 24 (2): 127–146.

Fanon, F. (1968 [1961]) *The Wretched of the Earth*. Translated by Constance Farrington. New York: Grove Press.

Featherstone, M. and Venn, C. (2006) 'Problematizing global knowledge and the new encyclopaedia project: an introduction', *Theory, Culture, and Society*, 23 (2–3): 1–20.

Fischer, S. (2004) *Modernity Disavowed: Haiti and the Cultures of Slavery in the Age of Revolution*. London: Duke University Press.

Friese, H. and Wagner, P. (2002) 'Survey article: the nascent political philosophy of the European polity', *Journal of Political Philosophy*, 10 (3): 342–364.

Gilroy, P. (2003) 'Where ignorant armies clash by night': Homogenous community and the planetary aspect', *International Journal of Cultural Studies*, 6 (3): 261–276.

Grovogui, S. N'Z. (1996) *Sovereigns, Quasi Sovereigns, and Africans: Race and Self-Determination in International Law*. Minneapolis: University of Minnesota Press.

Grovogui, S. N'Z. (2001) 'Come to Africa: A hermeneutics of race in international theory', *Alternatives*, 26 (4): 425–448.

Habermas, J. (2001) *The Postnational Constellation: Political Essays*. Cambridge: MIT Press.

Habermas, J. (2003) 'Making sense of the EU: toward a cosmopolitan Europe', *Journal of Democracy*, 14 (4): 86–100.

Habermas, J. and Derrida, J. (2003) 'February 15, or what binds Europeans together: a plea for a common foreign policy, beginning in the core of Europe', *Constellations*, 10 (3): 291–297.

Haddour, A. (2000) *Colonial Myths: History and Narrative*. Manchester: Manchester University Press.

Haller, M. (2000) 'European integration and sociology: the difficult balance between the theoretical, empirical and critical approach', *European Societies*, 2 (4): 533–548.

Hansen, P. (2002) 'European integration, European identity and the colonial connection', *European Journal of Social Theory*, 5 (4): 483–498.

Hansen, P. (2004) 'In the name of Europe', *Race and Class*, 45 (3): 49–62.

Hartsock, N.C.M. (1984) 'The feminist standpoint: developing the ground for a specifically feminist historical materialism' in S. Harding (ed.) *Money, Sex and Power*. Boston: Northeastern University Press. Reprinted in S. Harding (ed.) (1987) Bloomington: Indiana University Press.

Holmwood, J. (2000) 'Europe and the "Americanization" of British social policy', *European Societies*, 2 (4): 453–482.

Holmwood, J. and Stewart, A. (1991) *Explanation and Social Theory*. London: Macmillan.

Ifversen, J. (2002) 'Europe and European culture – a conceptual analysis', *European Societies*, 4 (1): 1–26.

Inayatullah, N. and Blaney, D. (2004) *International Relations and the Problem of Difference*. London: Routledge.

Joll, J. (1980) 'Europe – an historian's view', *History of European Ideas*, 1 (1): 7–19.

Keita, M. (2002) 'Africa and the construction of a grand narrative in world history' in E. Fuchs and B. Stuchtey (eds) *Across Cultural Borders: Historiography in Global Perspective*. New York: Rowman & Littlefield Publishers.

Lewis, M.W. and Wigen, K.E. (1997) *The Myth of Continents: A Critique of Metageography*. Berkeley: University of California Press.

Llobera, J.R. (2003) 'The concept of Europe as an *idée-force*', *Critique of Anthropology*, 23 (2): 155–174.

Mamdani, M. (2001) 'Beyond settler and native as political identities: overcoming the political legacy of colonialism', *Society for the Comparative Study of Society and History*, 43 (4): 651–664.

Markoff, J. (1999) 'Where and when was democracy invented?', *Comparative Studies in Society and History* 41 (4): 660–690.

Morsink, J. (1999) *The Universal Declaration of Human Rights. Origins, Drafting, and Intent*. Philadelphia: University of Pennsylvania Press.

Muhlberger, S. and Paine, P. (1993) 'Democracy's place in world history', *Journal of World History* 4: 23–45.

Nagra, D. (2007) *Look We Have Coming to Dover!* London: Faber and Faber.

Nederveen Pieterse, J. (1999) 'Europe, travelling light: Europeanization and globalization', *The European Legacy*, 4 (3): 3–17.

Neumann, I.B. (1996) *Russia and the Idea of Europe: A Study in Identity and International Relations*. London: Routledge.

O'Brien, C.C. (1970) *Albert Camus: Of Europe and Africa*. New York: The Viking Press.

Outhwaite, W. (2006) *The Future of Society*. Oxford: Blackwell Publishing.

Outhwaite, W. and Ray, L. (2005) *Social Theory and Postcommunism*. Oxford: Blackwell Publishing.

Panu, M. (2006) *(Con)textualizing Health: An Analysis of Subject-Formation in Governmental Discourse*. PhD thesis, University of Birmingham.

Persaud, R.B. and Walker, R.B.J. (2001) 'Apertura: race in international relations', *Alternatives*, 26 (4): 373–376.

Raychaudhuri, T. (2002 [1988]) *Europe Reconsidered: Perceptions of the West in Nineteenth-Century Bengal*, 2nd edn. New Delhi: Oxford University Press.

Rodríguez-Salgado, M.J. (2005) 'Europe of the Mind' (Part I), BBC Radio 3 Sunday Feature, February 2005, repeated August 2005.

Rosamond, B. (1999) 'Discourses of Globalization and the Social Construction of European Identities', *Journal of European Public Policy*, 6 (4): 652–668.

Ross, G. (1998) 'European integration and globalization' in Roland Axtmann's (ed.) *Globalization and Europe: Theoretical and Empirical Investigations*. London: Pinter.

Rumford, C. (2006) 'Introduction: theorizing borders', *European Journal of Social Theory*, 9 (2): 155–169.

Ruthner, C. (2002) 'Central Europe goes post-colonial: new approaches to the Habsburg empire around 1900', *Cultural Studies*, 16 (6): 877–883.

Said, E.W. (1978) *Orientalism: Western Conceptions of the Orient*. London: Routledge and Kegan Paul Ltd.

Sassatelli, M. (2002) 'Imagined Europe: the shaping of a European cultural identity through EU cultural policy', *European Journal of Social Theory*, 5 (4): 435–451.

Siedentop, L. (2001) *Democracy in Europe*. London: Penguin Books.

Shilliam, R. (2006) 'What about Marcus Garvey? Race and the transformation of sovereignty debate', *Review of International Studies*, 32 (3): 379–400.

Snowden, F.M. (1970) *Blacks in Antiquity: Ethiopians in the Greco-Roman Experience*. Cambridge, MA: Harvard University Press.

Soysal, Y.N. (1994) *Limits of Citizenship: Migrants and Postnational Membership in Europe*. Chicago: University of Chicago Press.

Stevenson, N. (2006) 'European cosmopolitan solidarity: questions of citizenship, difference, and post-materialism', *European Journal of Social Theory*, 9 (4): 485–500.

Stolcke, V. (1995) 'Talking culture: new boundaries, new rhetorics of exclusion in Europe', *Current Anthropology*, 36 (1): 1–24.

Stråth, Bo (2002) 'A European identity: to the historical limits of a concept', *European Journal of Social Theory*, 5 (4): 387–401.

Stratton, J. (2003) 'It almost needn't have been the Germans': The state, colonial violence and the Holocaust', *European Journal of Cultural Studies*, 6 (4): 507–527.

Thapar, R. (1966) *A History of India: Volume One*. Middlesex: Penguin Books Ltd.

Therborn, G. (2002) 'The world's trader, the world's lawyer: Europe and global processes', *European Journal of Social Theory*, 5 (4): 403–417.

Trouillot, M.-R. (1995) *Silencing the Past: Power and the Production of History*. Boston: Beacon Press.

Van Sertima, I. (ed.) (1986) *African Presence in Early Europe*. Somerset, NJ: Transaction Publishers.

Wagner, P. (2005) 'The political form of Europe, Europe as a political form', *Thesis Eleven*, 80: 47–73.

Weber, B. (1995) 'Immigration and politics in Germany', *The Journal of the International Institute*, 2 (3). Available at: http://hdl.handle.net/2027/spo.4750978.0002.306, accessed 14 August 2008.

White, H. (2000) 'The discourse of Europe and the search for a European identity' in Bo Stråth (ed.) *Europe and the Other and Europe as the Other*. Oxford: P.I.E., Peter Lang.

Yapp, M.E. (1992) 'Europe in the Turkish mirror', *Past and Present: The Cultural and Political Construction of Europe*, 137 (Nov): 134–155.

Polity-Building: Institutionalization, Governance, Europeanization

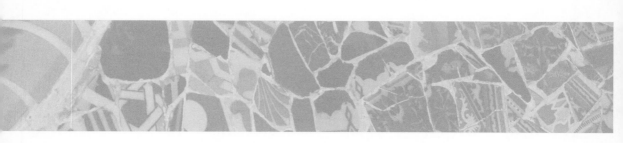

6

Supranational Governance

Ben Rosamond

This chapter concerns itself with the study of supranational governance in Europe. As such, its primary focus is the European Union (EU), or more precisely those scholarly literatures (signified hereafter by the shorthand term 'EU studies') which have ventured to understand that phenomenon. It is probably fair to say that the EU is most often treated as the benchmark case of supranational governance (although this should not be taken to imply that the EU harbours all of the significant post-national governance initiatives in contemporary Europe – Schimmelfennig, 2003; Wallace, 2001). Indeed, Stone Sweet and Sandholtz define supranational governance as a situation/condition that describes 'the competence of the European Community to make binding rules in any given policy domain' (1998: 1). Similarly, Keohane and Hoffmann (1991) use the term 'supranationality' to characterize the distinctive political process and style of decision-making that occurs within the EU. Early inductive studies of the Communities of the 1950s and 1960s (Haas, 1958, 1964) suggested that the creation of European-level institutions had created an environment in which its key participants (member-states) were no longer engaged in old-style diplomatic relations

characterized by the zero-sum exchange of national preferences. Instead, the new system was characterized by a culture of trust and an attendant tendency for states to refrain from the impulse to veto policy initiatives. Supranationality was about engaging in periodic compromises as part of a wider process by which common interests were upgraded. In these terms, supranationalism is a kind of collective action regime (Gruber, 2000), but it is one which departs from classical patterns of international cooperation where states seek to protect their (exogenously derived) interests. Under supranationalism interests are transformed and (re-)emerge endogenously in the context of novel institutional arrangements. For some, this internal dynamic was elemental to the transition of European international relations into a more federated system (Haas, 1958: 59).

Of course, this depiction of the particular qualities of the EU polity is open to contest. Most obviously a clutch of rival studies – generally labelled 'intergovernmentalist' – take fundamental issue with elements of the account developed by Ernst Haas and his followers (Hansen, 1969; Hoffmann, 1966; Moravcsik, 1998), emphasizing instead the prevailing logic of national interests and the (relatively trivial) role of EU-level institutions as mere 'agents' of member-state 'principals' (Pollack, 2003). Such work has significant problems with the description of the EU as 'supranational', not least because the term is suggestive of root and branch change to (as opposed to modification of) the basic structures and logics of international politics. Discussions of the EU can often get locked into a standoff between rival supranationalist and intergovernmentalist accounts of the growth of integration and European-level policy competence. While this debate clearly captures something important, it certainly does not exhaust the range of possible questions to be asked about European supranational governance. This chapter seeks to open up discussion of these questions as they have arisen within EU studies, while at the same time remembering the importance of connecting the inductive and 'localized' study of European governance patterns to broader debates that emerge from across the social sciences. There is a danger of using 'supranational governance' as a synonym for 'what the EU does', a problem exacerbated by the fact that almost all academic work on the subject takes place within EU studies. Thus it is important to think about how both EU studies as a scholarly community and 'supranational governance' as a topic emerge from, intersect with, and contribute to wider fields of social scientific enquiry.

STUDYING EUROPEAN SUPRANATIONAL GOVERNANCE

It follows that two questions are worth posing from the outset. The first concerns the disciplinary character of EU studies, and in particular those elements that concern themselves with supranational governance. The second is to query what exactly we might mean by 'supranational governance'.

The disciplinary character of EU studies

In response to the first of these questions, 'governance' is now a commonplace – if relatively recently established – research topic of political science in a number of its variants. The political science of EU studies is a major, well-established subfield that has spawned its own Handbook in this series (Jørgensen et al., 2007). There are at least six journals in English alone dealing predominantly with EU *politics* (which attract submissions almost exclusively from political scientists) and the there is some evidence that Anglophone EU studies is primarily the business of political scientists of various hues (Rosamond, 2007a). Of course, 'governance' (and certainly EU governance) is not the exclusive property of political science and there are numerous arguments as to why this should be so. This is not the place to get too bogged down in arguments about disciplinarity and interdisciplinarity in European/EU studies (Calhoun, 2003; Cini, 2006; Manners, 2003; Rosamond, 2007a; Rumford and Murray, 2003; Warleigh, 2004), other than to say that while this chapter's primary brief leads it – out of necessity – towards the output of the political science community of EU scholars, it does not neglect the contributions from a range of other cognate fields, notably law, sociology and history. Indeed, one of the core arguments advanced here is that some of the most important and productive work on European supranational governance has come from scholarship that keeps disciplinary borders avowedly open.

Furthermore, disciplinary location is perhaps less significant than the *type* of political science that is undertaken. Recent ferocious critiques of the general discipline (especially in the United States) have identified the complex emergence of disciplining moves that favour quantitative, rationalist and narrowly referential work at the expense of methodologically pluralist, ideographic and cross-disciplinary research (Monroe, 2005).

These tendencies and the debates they provoke reveal a struggle within political science over questions of admissibility (which work is considered of high quality/publishable/worthy of citation?), conduct (how should work be done and what standards of judgement should be applied to it?) and boundaries (what is the field and where do its limits reside?). These contentions are clearly visible within EU studies. Put crudely, there has evolved a distinction between work that locates itself clearly within the *mainstream* 'normal scientific' tendencies of US political science and that which inclines towards epistemological and methodological *pluralism* (Rosamond, 2007a, 2007b). We might be tempted to ignore these disputes as rarefied academic squabbles. In fact alternative ways of organizing and adjudicating the science of politics are profoundly important to the way in which knowledge about politics is structured (Kaufman-Osborn, 2006). As such, rival positions in the mainstreaming–pluralism debate alluded to above are constitutive of quite different understandings of EU politics (and thus of the character and significance of supranational governance). To return to our crude distinction, work that gravitates towards the mainstreaming/normal scientific pole tends to construe the EU as a polity like any other, in part because normal polities are the very objects of the standard and well-established technologies of mainstream political science. In contrast, work that emerges from more critical traditions of enquiry construes its field as much less bounded and as such tends to imagine the EU in rather more transformative and transcendent terms. This yields an epistemological loop that pretty much doubts the utility of mainstream political science on the simple grounds that its disciplinary conservatism prevents it from thinking otherwise about an unfamiliar political form such as the EU.

A further issue relates to the organization of EU studies. Quite strikingly, three recent attempts to classify the field (Hix, 2005; Hooghe, 2001; Pollack, 2005a, 2005b) each

identify governance as one of the key movements within a tripartite division of the study of EU politics. In Hix's (2005) classification, 'governance' captures a broad and loose coalition of sub-schools with varying epistemological commitments that acts as a residual category to two rather more tightly organized rationalist approaches to the study of the EU: liberal intergovernmentalism (LI) and rational choice institutionalism. Hooghe (2001) identifies a 'multi-level governance' (MLG) approach as a rival to LI and an updated version of neofunctionalism. Finally Pollack (2005a, 2005b) produces a more consistent and functionally equivalent classification which picks out scholarship on governance as one arena in the study of EU politics and policy-making, the others being the rationalist–constructivist debate (imported from IR) and work of various kinds that applies the insights of mainstream comparative political science to the EU. These classifications – although often very vague on what governance scholarship is – tend to reinforce the idea that 'governance' represents a rival to two sorts of academic narrative that have been commonplace in EU studies: mainstream IR and mainstream political science.

Supranational governance

The second preliminary question cannot be answered straightforwardly, in part because the descriptor 'supranational governance' hides within its derivation an animated debate about what is actually going on in the restructuring of European politics. 'Governance' has become one of the most used terms in recent social science, yet it is defined and used in numerous ways (see Treib *et al.*, 2007 for a very thorough and systematic overview). To simplify somewhat, it might be useful to think about two general uses of the term within the literatures of political science and IR. First, governance can be used as a general term to describe the methods through which order and coordination are delivered and from which rule-governed behaviour derives. As such, governance encompasses a range of possible modes, of which government (conventionally understood) is one. Indeed, government (formal rule-making through legitimate public authority) is placed at one end of a continuum of governance whose poles are 'hierarchy' and 'market'. This way of thinking provokes discussion not only about how societies' modes of governance may change and vary over time, but also about the extent to which governance is characterized by a predominant mode or co-existent modes in a particular period. Second, governance is often used to describe a particular, 'softer' variety of steering and coordination that departs from the command and control, hard law-making techniques of the centralized modern state. The 'softness' of this conception of governance refers to the dramatically reduced reliance upon the use of hierarchical methods of delivery, such as, law-making, together with the increased use of a variety of alternative techniques, such as, benchmarking against 'best practice'. A further feature of this second use of 'governance' is the perception of a move away from public actors as the sole players in the delivery of societal steering towards a much more variegated actor mix, where public authority gives way wholly or in part to a diverse set of private sites of authority.

The literature on governance (emerging from both of these broad meanings) has grown because of a generally understood need to capture conceptually the changing nature of authority and policy-making in the contemporary period. While huge portions of the resultant literature have been concerned with governance within nation-states (national, regional, local, urban), one of the key developments charted by the 'governance turn' has been not only spatial but also post-Westphalian. The literature on governance beyond national government tends to describe two shifts that are bound up with the declining authority and autonomy of national states.

The first is the advent of sites of public authority above the nation-state. The second is the emergence of private authority within the regional and global arenas. The EU is, of course, central to and embroiled within both of these discussions. First and most obviously, it represents a site of authority (a locus of authoritative and binding rules) that sits institutionally above its component 27 national governments. The governments involved have delegated or pooled elements of their formal juridical sovereignty in ways that suggest a significant reshuffle of authoritative capacity in contemporary Europe. At the same time, however, the EU is not a state, at least in terms of the conventional Weberian vocabulary that is so familiar to sociologists and political scientists. It deploys a variety of instruments and methods (modes of governance) to deliver its outputs and these often differ markedly in form and function from the methodologies of government associated with the modern nation-state.

The second shift – the shift from public to private authority – is often associated with the governing regime of neoliberalism that has broken decisively with the 'nationally centered, Fordist–Keynesian configuration of statehood' (Brenner, 2004: 7). Here supranational governance can be read as one way in which statehood has been transformed and rescaled to service an emergent market order. One such method is the creation (or perhaps reinvention) of institutions to entrench or 'constitutionalize' that market order via techniques that effectively 'depoliticize' policy-making or distance the exercise of authority from the gaze of democratic scrutiny. Here the key question about the EU is easily stated, but its implications are complex: to what degree is the EU a manifestation of this turn towards neoliberal governance mechanisms? Alternatively, and in contrast, we might consider the extent to which the EU represents some sort of collective response to these tendencies. The remainder of this chapter reviews scholarship on European supranational governance bearing in mind these two issues. It pays attention to three specific issues: the origins of European supranational governance, the dynamics of the evolution of governance and the question of whether there is a European model of supranational governance.

THE INSTITUTIONAL FORM OF EUROPEAN SUPRANATIONAL GOVERNANCE

To guide the discussion hereafter, it is possible to identify three key sub-questions that together have animated a huge proportion of scholarship on European integration over the course of the past half-century. The first is the question of the origins of supranational institutions. The second is the debate about the dynamics of supranational institutional evolution. The third is a set of issues about how best to characterize the EU model of governance.

The origins of supranational institutions

Why do supranational institutions appear in the first place? Theoretical work within IR has for long debated the reasons why states create international institutions. While there is obviously some intellectual mileage in exploring the utility of such theories, the EU offers a peculiar case of quite intensive institutionalization with few, if any, obvious comparators among the ranks of international organizations past or present. Classical realist theories see institutions as fragile and (thus) as temporary forms of inter-state cooperation. In Waltz's (1979) classic neorealist account, states – the epitome of unitary rational agents – draw their interests from their position within the international system and from time to time these may coincide with the interests of other states. Episodes of cooperation are more or less destined to fail because the gains from cooperation will be asymmetric.

As this logic of relative gains harms the interests of some states, they will seek to dissolve the cooperative institution they once helped to create. Cooperation is here modelled as a single play prisoners' dilemma game, where incentives to defect are compelling. Contemporary liberal IR (neoliberal institutionalism) disputes this account on two broad grounds. The first is the alteration of the basic condition of international society from anarchy to interdependence, an idea developed most persuasively in the work of Keohane and Nye in the 1970s (Keohane and Nye, 1977). The background condition of interdependence incentivizes ongoing cooperation. States may still create common cooperative institutions to resolve classical security dilemmas, and the full distinctiveness of the liberal contribution comes to the fore when it considers the effects of institutions. Thus second, cooperation is – in and of itself – a vehicle for the broadening of states' conceptions of their self-interest and the construction of mutual interests. The gains of cooperation are thus absolute rather than relative. Moreover, as Keohane (1984, 1989) argues, cooperative institutions and regimes also offer an enhanced degree of transparency to reduce mutual suspicion amongst states, significantly lessen costs for future cooperation and thus foster a widespread belief that cooperation will continue.

Not surprisingly, the study of European cooperation and institution-building has been fertile ground for scholarship in the liberal tradition. The so-called liberal idealist movement of the inter-war period mixed early IR scholarship with the propagation of schemes for the replacement of the war-prone European states system with some form of federation (Long and Wilson, 1995). The functionalist theories of David Mitrany (1966) that emerged most cogently in the mid-1940s were perhaps the most interesting products of this intellectual moment. Like many of his idealist contemporaries, Mitrany was ultimately exercized by the war-inducing pathologies of standard international politics.

Emphasizing the solution of human material welfare needs above the realization of ideological precepts, Mitrany proposed that human governance should be a matter for cool technocratic deliberation and that the state should not be taken as the ineluctable starting point for all discussion of how to improve institutional design. Institutional forms, many of which would be post-national in character, would take forms that were appropriate for their assigned function.

Mitrany's ideas differed in significant respects from those which drove the design of the European Communities inaugurated in the 1950s. For example, Mitrany's vision was much more flexible than that which came to prevail in post-war Europe. Indeed Mitrany was himself an outspoken critic of the organization of all post-national tasks along regionalist (European lines), suggesting that the state fixation had been replaced by a 'regional fallacy' that imposed boundaries upon institutional design and a 'federal fallacy' where institutional design was driven by political (rather than technocratic) purposes (Mitrany, 1965). That said, classical functionalism's emphasis on the technocratic drivers of supranational governance arrangements and its refusal to fall back upon idealistic criticisms of realist orthodoxy is shared with the work of the later neofunctionalists. Neofunctionalism's point of origin in the late 1950s and early 1960s coincided with the social sciences' growing interest in the operation of economically advanced, pluralistic, bureaucratized and technocratic societies (Bell, 1962). As such the neofunctionalists such as Haas (1958) and Lindberg (1963), echoing – yet significantly deepening – contemporaneous theories of international economic integration (Balassa, 1962), developed sophisticated accounts of how the haphazard interaction of self-interested socio-economic actors could, in the presence of certain specified conditions induce (a) an expanding range of governance tasks for region-level institutions, and (b) a process of 'loyalty transference' from national polities to the new European polity.

One of the most obvious problems with this take on the emergence of supranational governance was that it appeared to assume the pre-existence of some supranational institutions. Thus Lindberg's (1963) discussion of how a neofunctionalist system of governance emerges is premised on the presence of regional institutions with the clear capacity to initiate social and economic processes. More recently, the important work of Stone Sweet and Sandholtz (1998) revises neofunctionalist ideas to think about how demands for supranational governance are turned into concrete outcomes. They pay particular attention to the emergence of *de facto* transnational economic spaces that follow from the activities of economic agents (firms). Keen to reduce the uncertainties of their economic activity, these inhabitants of transnational society seek a rule-bound order. The Commission offers itself as a regulator capable of supplying such a regulatory environment. The growth of European supranational governance is, therefore, the product of strategic interaction between (a) private economic actors seeking to exploit their economic advantages, but needing to reduce chronic uncertainty to calculable risk and (b) purposive and opportunistic institutions tasked to ensure the growth of European governance. But both cases suggest that the most interesting and difficult question is being neglected. It might be that economic and political spillovers would occur when a purposive, task-oriented institution like the European Commission was in place. As noted below, there is plenty of empirical evidence showing how over time the Commission and the European Court have expanded their institutional remits and in so doing have enlarged the governance competences of the EU as a whole. But why are such institutions created in the first place? Why would states agree to the initiation of a new system of supranational governance where their own role would be heavily circumscribed?

This paradox poses particular challenges to state-centred accounts that deploy largely rational choice theories of agency (where an actor is unlikely to assent to an action where the evident costs outweigh the evident benefits). The literature has thrown up at least three types of answer. Each of these is consistent with the idea of states (or dominant states) exercising agency in the design of supranational governance arrangements. The first set of responses, favoured by liberal intergovernmentalists (Moravcsik, 1998), is to treat states (or perhaps more precisely national governments) as primary and central to the process, but to depart significantly from the realist view that institutions emerge from an outward-looking strategic calculus in which states preferences follow from a rational appreciation of their place within the structures of international security. Instead national preferences (primarily commercial – as opposed to 'hard' security – preferences) are taken to originate in processes of bargaining within the domestic polity. Following liberal IR assumptions, these preferences are bargained internationally in the context of positive sum expectations (absolute gains) before specific institutional choices are forged. Institutional choices can be traced back to the degree to which governments feel compelled to ensure the compliance of other governments. As a rule, governments cede power to supranational institutions in two situations: (a) where there is a relatively high risk of non-compliance by other governments (Moravcsik, 1999) and (b) where there is advantage to be secured in removing an issue or policy area from domestic political scrutiny (Moravcsik, 1993: 515). In any case, liberal intergovernmentalists doubt the utility of the descriptor 'supranational governance' to describe the resulting pattern of interaction because this suggests governance by supranational institutions. Instead, these institutions operate within the boundaries set by contracting governments.

The second set of responses alludes to the primary role of national executives in the design of supranational institutions, but leaves open the idea that acts of institutional design may provoke unintended consequences. 'Purer' versions of rationalism (such as LI) rely on a functionalist theory of institutional design where institutions are chosen to deliver collective efficiencies and are unencumbered by historical legacies. The most popular variant of the unintended consequences argument is that proffered by historical institutionalism (HI). HI reminds us that acts of institutional design occur within very specific sets of circumstances that set immediate imperatives upon decision-makers. These imperatives set the context for rational action at the time and yield institutional solutions geared to deal with those imperatives. Contexts change and imperatives change, but institutions are 'sticky' and lock-in. They do not simply act as a fix for context bound problems. New contexts and new problems are encountered through the lens of previous institutional choices and the descendents of the original institutional designers find themselves operating within a set of path-dependent institutional consequences that were not anticipated at the moment of design. The application of HI precepts to the case of European integration is fairly obvious (Pierson, 1998). By the normal standards of regional integration agreements, the bargains that founded the European Coal and Steel Community and its successors after 1951 produced a heavily institutionalized environment with a distinctive supranational-intergovernmental balance and a court with a mandate that would stretch to the assertion of the supremacy of Community law. What is striking is that the basic pattern of institutional design utilized in the early 1950s – Commission (initially the High Authority), the Court of Justice and the Parliament (initially the Assembly) – has been so durable, despite changing contexts, imperatives and, strikingly perhaps, preferences of institutional designers (member-state governments themselves). In line with HI logic, Pierson (1998) explains institutional survival in the EU via a combination of the limited time horizons of the designers and the emergent autonomy of the institutions themselves. In line with classical Weberian predictions, the latter become self-interested actors and these interests may diverge from those of member-state governments.

Following on, and deepening the argument considerably, is Rittberger's (2001) discussion of the precise institutional design of the early communities – a subject much neglected in the literature. In line with much recent work in EU studies, Rittberger refuses to set up a contest between rival rationalist and constructivist hypotheses. Rather he notes that both the normative and instrumental preferences for cooperation of the founding states of the European Coal and Steel Community can be translated into specific formulae for institutional design. He further argues that actors (in this case the founding 'six') have imperfect knowledge of the distributional consequences of their institutional choices. In this absence of clear rational logic, the institutional designers fall back on normative arguments to complete the institutional picture. This, maintains Rittberger, is how the European Parliament came into being; as an institutional solution to the normative problem of how to secure democratic accountability in the new supranational context (a point echoed by Pollack, 2003).

The third set of responses from political science utilizes the principal-agent (PA) framework of analysis. PA analysis is interested in those moments when significant actors ('principals' – in the EU context member-states) delegate tasks to subordinate institutions ('agents' – the Commission, the ECJ and the European Central Bank). Delegation occurs, according to Pollack (2003), because member-states are keen to reduce the heavy transaction costs of making policy and this in turn allows them to commit with a higher degree of credibility to international agreements. Moreover, agents are oftentimes better at performing certain tasks (such as monitoring the extent to which member states have complied with the rules they have set for one another) than principals. PA-informed research (e.g. Tallberg, 2003) has also tackled in great detail in the EU context the varying degrees to which various institutional agents have secured autonomy from the member-state principals.

Perhaps the most influential state-centred account of the origins of European supranationalism is found in the work of the economic historian Alan Milward (Milward, 1984, 2000, 2007; Milward et al., 1993). Milward's work revolves around the paradox mentioned above – why national governments should opt to cede a measure of their formal juridical sovereignty in an episode of supranational institutional creativity. In opposition to the idea that post-war Europe was governed by a federalist and post-national ideological atmosphere (an argument most associated with the work of Walter Lipgens (1985, 1986; Lipgens and Loth, 1988)), Milward insisted that the prevailing logic of post-war institution-building was that of national interests. European states chose integration and a supranational institutional design as a way of augmenting their own policy-making capacity and autonomy in the face of imperatives from the international economy and a potential overload of demands from their domestic publics. As such the design of what was to become the EU was perhaps the key factor in the 'rescue' of the European nation-state. While this approach locates the root of supranationalism a combination of domestic socio-economic developments and the evolution of the international political economy, it does not deny the immediate imperative of the ECSC's supranational design as a time bound 'fix' to the Franco-German security dilemma (on which see Gillingham, 1991).

We have already noted that other analysts do not buy into this type of explanation that emphasizes the role of material interests 'all the way down'. For instance, Parsons (2003) insists that brute rationalism (emphasizing either national commercial interest or security imperatives) cannot account for the particular institutional choices that have fashioned the modern EU, such as the important decisions to create a common agricultural policy or a supranational high authority. Instead, in a detailed examination of the French case, he emphasizes the crucial role of ideas and of particular elites as carriers of these ideas.

As the political science of EU studies continues to develop, rationalist state-centred accounts of the origins of supranationalism are likely to be confronted with more studies that emphasize ideational variables or speak the language of constructivism. As noted below, these are now commonplace in the study of EU governance. As such the traditional rival to intergovernmentalist explanations, neofunctionalism, might be thought of as largely residual to discussions of the origins of the supranational European system because (as intimated earlier), it is generally thought of as a theory which assumes (rather than explains) initial conditions. That said, recent scholarship on neofunctionalism (Börzel, 2006; Rosamond, 2005a) together with re-evaluations written by neofunctionalists themselves (Haas, 2001, 2004; Schmitter, 2004) reinspects the neofunctionalist legacy in an effort to go beyond standard textbook accounts of the theory. Looming large here is the neofunctionalists' long-standing interest in the necessary and sufficient 'background conditions' of regional integration projects. In this regard neofunctionalists were influenced by the earlier work on the formation of security communities conducted by Karl Deutsch and his research team (Deutsch *et al.*, 1957). For Deutsch, security communities (collections of states where the expectation of war is minimized) emerge in situations where there is a high level of communication and transaction between states and their component societies. While, it is never entirely clear how formal institution-building would emerge from high rates of mutual interaction (Puchala, 1981), this transactionalist approach asked interesting questions about the relationship between the sophistication of, levels of interdependence between, and the possibilities for collective institution building among component societies. It also offered another way into thinking about the significance of cognitive change for the establishment of European supranational order. Ideational explanations that emphasized the role of federal sentiments amongst elites and masses would give way to the study of mutual

expectations and common understandings as elemental building blocks of regional orders (Adler and Barnett, 1998). What Nye (1971) called 'perceptual background conditions' came to be added to a set of putative variables that neofunctionalists tabled as explanations for both the initiation and persistence of regional supranational orders. The roll call of independent variables included underlying rates of intersocietal transaction, the prevalence of bureaucratic styles of decision making within participating units, adaptive elite cultures, high levels of economic development and underlying societal pluralism (Haas, 1961; Haas and Schmitter, 1964). This in turn reflected the intellectual location of the early regional integration theorists of the sixties amidst debates around modernization, the end of ideology and pluralism as the political condition of modernity.

The dynamics of supranational institutional evolution

Neofunctionalists in turn had much to say about how a supranational order evolves after initiation (see Rosamond, 2000: 50–73). The idea of 'spillover' became very important in this analysis, describing as it did a number of interlinked phenomena which together would yield the deepening of economic and political integration. Spillover described the quasi-automatic functional pressures that would follow from the decision to integrate economic activity in one sector. These pressures would create cross-pressures to integrate cognate economic sectors, but would also induce impetus to deepen the scope and thus the institutional capacity of a regional scheme. This political science approach echoed the staged, teleological model of economic integration that was becoming dominant in the professional economics literature of the early 1960s. Lindberg (1963: 10) argued that spillover occurs because initial integrative goals can only be achieved via further actions, a process that seems – prima facie at least – to be evident in policy deliberations of the 1960s where movement towards monetary union was seen as a method of accelerating the achievement of the common market (Maes, 2006). Spillover could be better accomplished, as Haas (1961) observed, in scenarios where participating governments delegated a measure of initiative to an institution whose mission would be 'inherently expansive'. The consolidation and growth of supranationalism emerges through both the institutional effects of functional spillover and the pre-existence of institutional actors charged with bringing about 'more Europe'.

Many of the most cogent critiques of neofunctionalism pivoted on the observation that spillover was a localized phenomenon, specific to the European Communities for a quite particular phase of their evolution (Hansen, 1969; Hoffmann, 1966; and for oft-neglected neofunctionalist self-critique, Nye, 1971; Haas, 1975, 1976). Given that neofunctionalists had hoped to construct a set of generalizable propositions about integration from the inductive study of the early European experience, such critiques were attacking not only the empirical accuracy, but also the social scientific ambition of early EU studies.

From within the confines of orthodox political science, the most complete alternative account was realized in the work of Moravcsik (1998, 2005). Moravcsik claims to have produced a clearly specified theory with testable hypotheses that stand up to empirical scrutiny (1998: 10–13). The claim is not simply that his approach better captures the empirical reality of European integration, but that is also built upon more rigorous (and thus superior) social science (for intense critical scrutiny of these claims see Lieshout *et al.*, 2004). Moravcsik's liberal intergovernmentalism resuscitates the old theme of the persistent power of national governmental preferences as the key driver of integration outcomes. In so far as a supranational order evolves, then it does so through the interaction of national preferences (which emerge in domestic politics) in a heavily institutionalized environment. The evolution of the EU institutional can be mapped onto the development of the treaties, which reflect the balance of convergent national preferences at specific moments in the EU's history. But, as Pollack (2007: 48) remarks, this type of thinking tends to presume that the sources of change within the EU are ultimately exogenous. Changes in member-state preferences (which in turn impact upon the scope and shape of the EU order) are themselves reactions to structural changes in the global economy that impact upon national commercial interests.

The most powerful empirical critiques of liberal intergovernmentalism tend to cite endogenous institutional sources for the growth of supranational governance. Much of the important work here emerged from a productive dialogue between new institutionalist political science and legal studies (see Haltern, 2004; Wessel, 2007). On the face of it, this literature simply counters the standard intergovernmentalist–rationalist claim that compliance with European Community law is simply a matter of national interest (Garrett and Weingast, 1993) and that the independent role of the European Court of Justice needs to be factored into the analysis. However, this line of analysis runs deeper than simply offering up a rival to the intergovernmentalists' principal actor. The groundbreaking work of Weiler (1991) urged scholars to take seriously the activism of law and jurisprudence in the construction of the unique system of EU governance. In particular Weiler (1994) showed that while member-states had initiated the norms through which the EU was governed, the Court's judicial activism had been central to the creation of the compliance regime through which states came to be locked into a new normative order. Meanwhile political scientists began to criticize the intergovernmentalists' assumption of key change as resident in the 'history-making moments' of treaty change, instead choosing to show how informal day-to-day practices and interaction within the institutional environment of the Communities could be responsible for eventual treaty change. Thus, the growth of supranational policy competence could be shown to follow from the strategic use by the Commission of both ECJ judgements (Wincott, 1995) and the market-completion articles of the treaties. In terms of the latter, the growth of Community competence in areas such as social policy (Cram, 1997; Falkner, 1998; Leibfried, 2005; Leibfried and Pierson, 1995) and environmental protection (Jordan, 2000; Lenschow, 2005) occurred without direct treaty sanction. The Commission was able to argue for incursion into these domains with reference to the permissions granted to it by the treaties to innovate in ways conducive to the completion of the common market. One of the most striking findings from this type of work is that many of the key moments in the story of the growth of European supranationalism have taken place during times of intergovernmental stasis (Weiler, 1991).

Many of these debates were conducted in light of the observable acceleration in European integration that kicked off in the mid-1980s and culminated in 1986 with the signing of the first major revision to the founding treaties in the form of the Single European Act (SEA). To a large extent, these analyses tended to collapse discussion of the emergence/enhancement of supranational governance capacity into discussions about *integration*. In contrast, the work of Hix (1994, 1998, 2005, 2007) has consistently taken issue with the notion that the *problematique* of the political science of the EU should pivot on the question of integration. This is built around two key observations that tend also to caution against the overuse of governance terminology. First, the EU should be understood as a political system (a polity). The basic structure of its constitutional order is sufficiently stable, its politics consist of the interaction of interest-driven and resource-seeking actors and it is characterized by familiar processes such as interest intermediation, cleavage formation and struggles over the allocation of competences between different tiers of government. Second, because of this,

and notwithstanding its oddities as a political system, the tools of established, mainstream political science (comparative politics and public policy) should be used to analyse it (an idea first explored systematically by Lindberg and Scheingold, 1970). In one sense this posits the EU as a polity in some sort of equilibrium. Certain of its features – notably what Hix (2007) has come to call its 'upside-down' democratic quality – differentiate it from more orthodox political systems, but this does not prevent us from securing analytical leverage by studying the EU in terms of the classic categories of legislative, executive and judicial politics. A considerable body of scholarship on the EU polity conforms to the thrust of this agenda (for overviews, see Conant, 2007; McElroy, 2007; Tallberg, 2007). Indeed, the journal *European Union Politics* founded in 2000 is perhaps the best evidence of a sustained series of research program that (a) analytically place the study of the EU within the political science mainstream and (b) ontologically display reluctance to think about EU politics in terms of 'governance' questions (see Schneider *et al.*, 2000).

But the move away from thinking about the EU in terms of integration does not necessarily require the disposal of the idea of governance. If debates about integration involved competing claims about the extent to which statehood had become denationalized, then the literature on governance seeks to explore the extent to which politics and policy-making have been removed from the purview of the state (classically conceived) (Jessop, 2006). Governance accounts of the EU, according to Jachtenfuchs (2007), have the potential to inform where IR and comparative politics (CP) approaches are silent (see also Jachtenfuchs and Kohler-Koch, 2004). IR's emphasis on the EU as a complex international negotiating system and CP's starting assumption of the EU as a settled 'normal' political order together understate key elements of the distinctive and potentially transcendent character of the EU system. Contemporary governance approaches pay serious attention to the fact that the EU is not a state. This peculiar quality of EU 'stateness' means (a) that it is much more than the sum of its interacting component members, but (b) that it does not assume the domestic qualities associated with conventional (federal) states (see also Caporaso, 1996; Schmitter, 1996; Zürn and Leibfried, 2005). For example, the EU has a hierarchical legal system that ensures a degree of centralized authority, but it lacks the classic Weberian expectation of a monopoly of legitimate force and has no final authority in matters of taxation (Jachtenfuchs, 2007: 162–4). The vocabulary of 'governance', according to this view, is not just a useful term to capture the hybrid quality of the EU, but rather a route into think about how we might compare the multiple ways at a variety of levels in which ordered outcomes and policy outputs are secured. One example is Majone's well-known characterization of the EU as a 'regulatory state' (Majone, 1994, 1996, 2005). As noted below, this attribution, which emerges from the empirical claim that the EU is very prominent as regulator but weak in terms of redistribution, could be used simply as a way of identifying the dominant or characteristic mode of governance employed by the EU. Yet it also locates the EU within a much broader set of debates about the ways in which governance is being transformed across the advanced industrialized world. Majone's work pays particular attention to the affinities between the EU's regulatory order and that of the US, which is similarly deficient in terms of redistributive social policies. It is not just that the EU and the US are instances of the same phenomenon. Because the EU has become increasingly responsible for the economic governance of its member states, it follows that the growth of the supranational regime has been, over time, a source of pressure for the 'Americanization' of European social policy (Wincott, 2003).

If we assume that Majone's core observation is an empirically accurate depiction of the present equilibrium in EU governance (though see Robinson, 2007 and the next section),

then hugely important analytical and normative questions come to light. If anything, these reveal the importance of governance studies as a mechanism for connecting scholarship on the EU to broader patterns of social scientific thinking that reveal multiple readings of how the EU evolved into a regulatory (quasi-) state. One important and influential line of thinking takes issue with the Hixian view of the EU as, to all intents and purposes, a familiar polity. Jachtenfuchs (2007: 168), for example, identifies the lack of positive welfare governance as a function of the peculiarly weak democratic character of the EU. The absence of a supranational (redistributive) welfare regime deprives the EU of a major source of political legitimacy. This may be construed as a non-problem because the neoliberal choices (that culminate in the regulatory state) are made by rational governments with their own intact sources of domestic legitimacy (Moravcsik, 2002). Majone himself seems to regard the EU's regulatory equilibrium as technically sound, a position that betrays either an analytical/technocratic view of the inevitability of neoliberalism or a normative preference for a market order with minimal redistributive capacity (see Wincott, 2006 for a critique).

However, the EU's emphasis on negative integration (the creation of a market order via the removal of barriers to transaction) is often read from within political science as sub-optimal. In Scharpf's seminal formulation (Scharpf, 1988), the EU's decision rules (which tend to prefer unanimous rather than majoritarian decisions) created a so-called 'joint decision trap'. This means that there a complex pathology within the EU polity: (a) a tendency to deliver 'lowest common denominator' policy outcomes rather than yield positive policy programmes from which the EU could begin to secure public legitimacy and (b) an incapacity to reform common policies after initial agreement. Later application of the idea to other compound polities suggested that strongly equipped central governments could overcome these pathologies (Blom-Hansen, 1999), but in the EU case where the centralized threat of exit is weak, Scharpf's work explains both the gaps in and the relative stasis of the EU's governance regime.

Less mainstream lines of scholarship are less attached to the vocabulary of regulation (in Majone's sense), but are equally concerned with understanding the evident neoliberal emphasis of the EU. Three strands are worthy of mention. First, writers in the tradition of regulation theory locate the EU within an analysis of the changing state forms that accompany underlying shifts in regimes of capitalist accumulation such as Fordism and post-Fordism (Dannreuther, 2006; Jessop, 2006). From this vantage point, the EU's supranational regime evolved in two phases: the early integration into Fordist Atlantic capitalism and the more recent rescaling of statehood away from the Keynesian welfarist model. Second, scholars associated with the neo-Gramscian school of international political economy have developed a powerful analysis of the EU as a key site for the neoliberal restructuring of European states, itself a function of material changes in the pattern if production and the emergence of a transnational capitalist class (Bieler, 2006; Bieler and Morton, 2001; Cafruny and Ryner, 2003; van Apeldoorn, 2002). Gill (1998, 2003) has coined the phrase 'new constitutionalism' to capture the way in which neoliberal discipline has been embedded within European states via the project of economic and monetary union. Third, research influenced by Foucault's notion of governmentality has yielded a distinct and rich analysis of the ways in which 'Europe' has come to be imagined as a governable political and economic space on behalf of particular constellations of power (Barry, 1993, 2001; Walters and Haar, 2005).

The EU model of governance

Casual students of the EU might be surprised by the emphasis in the foregoing upon the regulatory character of European governance.

Classic textbook accounts of EU politics tend to be organized in the first instance around the institutional pattern that is formally laid out in the treaties. This institutional design, embodying the representation of both supranational/European and intergovernmental/national impulses into, respectively, the Commission and the Council and supplemented by the representative Parliament and the adjudicative Court of Justice does not simply offer a template through which EU decision-making is analysed. They also possess an evolving set of decision rules that explain the place of each institution within the policy process and specify how they should interact (for good introductory treatments see Cini, 2007; Nugent, 2006; Richardson, 2005).

There are at least three related reasons to be cautious about the description of this classic model with its in-built 'Community method' as *the* EU model of governance. The first, quite simply, is that the analysis of formal decision-making via the Community method does not at all capture the full range of informal political and policy-making processes that grow up around the formal template (Peters, 2006). The second reason is that treating the Community method as pre-eminent assumes a static and stable pattern of governance when there is considerable evidence of evolution. This can be thought about relatively simply as a matter of a changing balance of intergovernmental and supranational forces within the Community method over time or, in rather more complex vein, as evidence of the evolution of multiple and co-existent modes of governance within the EU (Wallace, 2005). A third reason follows from the likelihood that research on the Community method is likely to construe significant processes of EU governance as occurring at the EU level. More and more research now prefers to construe European governance in terms of a complex multi-level structure. The evolution of EU system of governance cannot be separated from the overall reorganization and redistribution of governmental and governance tasks across sub-national, national and supranational levels of action (Hooghe and Marks, 2001). These rationales for moving beyond the study of the Community method together build on the case – developed above – for thinking about the co-evolution of EU governance and patterns of governance more generally.

Wallace's work (2005; Wallace and Wallace, 2007) makes a very compelling case for organizing the study of day-to-day EU policy-making into the analysis of five policy-making or governance modes. The Community method is one of these, together with the EU's regulatory mode, its distributional mode (found especially in regional and agricultural policy), policy coordination and 'intensive transgovernmentalism'. These 'co-exist, vary over time and are not stable' (Wallace and Wallace, 2007: 341), functional policy areas may migrate from one to another over time and each is a domain for experimentation. One implication of such a reading is that it becomes very difficult, if not impossible, to construct a general set of propositions about the nature of EU governance in the preferred manner of some classical theories of integration. On the other hand, the study of EU policy-making is firmly connected to broader discussions of governance. For one thing, as we have seen, the importance of the regulatory mode of market-building is prima-facie evidence of the EU's association with modes of governance conducive to the securing of neoliberalism. The same might be said of the policy coordination mode, where the relatively 'soft' setting of best practice benchmarking standards (as opposed to 'hard', legally enforceable legislative acts) for the coordination of macro-economic policy and labour market policy is suggestive of a policy style long used by the OECD. In contrast, intensive transgovernmentalism – found most conspicuously in monetary governance and matters of internal and external security management – is used to describe a variety of ways in which national governments have sought to protect and enhance their involvement in the policy process beyond the gaze of formal supranational institutions, organized interests and domestic publics.

The net effects are varied, but they reveal a marked departure from traditional understandings of intergovernmental regime types with significant levels of intermeshing of ministerial and bureaucratic actors across national governments.

There are two further virtues of this type of approach to organizing knowledge about EU governance. First it facilitates the opening of discussion to consider questions of legitimacy and (particularly) democracy, and thus of the ethical quality of European governance (for an overview see Føllesdal, 2007). The question of the 'democratic deficit' has long been a question asked by students of the Community method. The evolution of the regulatory mode would seem to follow from a logic of technocratic efficiency rather than logics of either solidaristic-welfare or representative-democratic legitimacy. The transgovernmental mode might seem to follow a classic pattern through which member governments seek to insulate themselves from domestic (democratic) scrutiny. Interestingly, the EU's policy coordination mode – as exemplified by the open method of coordination (OMC) – has attracted supporters who find evidence of deliberation and positive learning within its operation (Sabel and Zeitlin, 2007; Nedergaard, 2006; see Citi and Rhodes, 2007, for a critique).

The second virtue of the Wallace classification is that it actively disallows sloppy discussions of *the* European model of governance – as if there were such a thing. This is especially important for the renewal of comparative analysis of regional integration projects, an enterprise that has for sometime held deep suspicions of the candidacy of the EU as a comparative case. In many ways the case against has been easy to make, especially if the oddly institutionalized character of the Community method (a project originating in quite specific temporal and spatial coordinates) is taken as representative of the EU model of governance. The possibilities for comparative analysis are strengthened considerably if the EU's experiences of regulation, policy coordination and transgovernmental exchange are taken into account. Rhetorical pronouncements about the EU model of governance premised upon the idea of the Community method are also open to scrutiny, particularly from constructivist scholarship interested in the role such discourse plays in the imagining of European political–economic space (Rosamond, 2005b).

Notwithstanding the value of deconstructing the Euro-polity in terms of its governance methodologies, other traditions of scholarship continue to seek an overall macro-classification of the EU mode of governance. Probably the most obvious candidate is the idea of multi-level governance (MLG). The terminology has its roots in discussions about the EU's distributional mode of governance, and structural or regional policy in particular. The key observation from the late 1980s and early 1990s was the appearance of a distributional politics in the EU where regions constituted themselves as resource-seeking actors in direct dialogue with the Commission, thereby bypassing the traditional 'gate-keeping function' of national governments (Hooghe and Marks, 1996; Marks, 1993, 1996; Marks *et al.*, 1996b). IR-based theories could not explain such developments so MLG was posited as a rival to resurgent intergovernmentalist literature on European integration (Hooghe and Marks, 2000; Marks *et al.*, 1996a; though for a state-centred critique see Bache, 1998). As scholarship has developed, so MLG has evolved from a description of a particular policy mode to a general depiction of the EU's governance system (Hooghe and Marks, 2001) and is now evolving into a fully fledged theory of governance in compound polities (Hooghe and Marks, 2003). As far as the EU is concerned MLG describes a governance system where authority is dispersed, where the state's control of both sub-national and supranational processes may be waning, where the number of significant actors has multiplied, where those actors may be mobile across different levels of political action and where actor constellations and patterns of policy making will vary from policy domain to policy domain. There is some affinity here

between MLG's depiction of the complex state of EU governance in terms of a series of multi-level policy networks and those who pay significant attention to the network properties of the EU polity (see Peterson, 2004). MLG scholarship has moved on to locate the EU within a broader analysis of the evolution of governance. The recent work of Hooghe and Marks (2003) makes a distinction between type I and type II MLG. The former is territorially fixed with a clear correspondence between jurisdictions and territorial scale. Type I MLG is thus hierarchical in terms of relationships between levels of the polity and the territorialized jurisdictions each comprise several functions. The obvious analogy is the federal polity. Type II MLG, of which the EU is an instance, is characterized by flexible institutional design and an emphasis on task-specific functional jurisdictions. Aside from developing a classification that allows comparison between different types of multi-level polity, this work also invites EU studies into ongoing discussions in fields such as public administration, IR, IPE and international law about (a) the various way political authority is being reconfigured and (b) the flexibility and variety of institutional design that is emergent across many scales of political action. One consequence is that it may become less and less helpful to think about the EU as a whole when looking for cases to use in comparative analysis.

CONCLUSIONS

A good deal of EU studies has concerned itself with the question of whether, how and why authoritative governance capacity has emerged above the level of European nation-states over the past half century. Much – perhaps the bulk – of the relevant scholarship accepts that there is something transcendent or profound about these developments (Delanty and Rumford, 2005: 137–54), but it has to be noted that a significant minority position cautions against overstating the transformative effects of European integration upon European governance. As we have seen, there are two variants of this position. In the first, the EU is treated as neither supranational nor an instance of governance. A position that follows from the precepts of mainstream liberal institutionalist IR wants to treat the EU as a sophisticated negotiated order involving a classic two-level game, whose outputs reflect the institutionalized interaction of national preferences, themselves rooted in traditional patterns of domestic political exchange. The second variant argues that the EU's polity bears all the hallmarks of a traditional political system, whose underlying logic is Laswellian ('who gets what, when, how' – Laswell, 1950). In so far as the EU is evolving, then its evolution would seem to correspond to the maturation of a domestic polity. These are powerful positions, not least because they emerge from the centre of and utilize the standard tools of mainstream US-style political science. An interesting subplot in the story of EU governance studies is the question of how opponents of these positions develop their critiques. A good deal of the work presented here does so from within the political science mainstream, either through the development of new ideas such as MLG in a standard political science way or by re-utilizing some older concepts or by connecting the study of EU politics to discussions going on elsewhere in the discipline about the changing nature and bases of authority. These moves offer good examples of what Warleigh (2004) has helpfully called 'intradisciplinarity', a term to denote a commitment to a wide and historically sensitive understanding of the broad discipline in contrast to a blinkered, 'normal science' approach. In addition, the contribution of legal scholarship in particular has been fundamental to understanding of the development and essence of the EU order. This suggests the importance of moving well beyond the formal disciplinary bounds of Anglophone political science, a task which remains relatively urgent (though see Delanty and Rumford, 2005; Favell, 2007).

From the foregoing it is possible to assemble numerous alternative readings of EU governance. It can be read as a complex and variable multi-level system, where the clear hierarchies that we associate with constitutionalized federal polities do not properly hold. Alternatively, this can be thought of as a venue for the practice of multiple, sometimes competing and sometimes overlapping modes of governance. It can be construed as a regulatory market-making order, whose poorly specified constitutionalism is integral to its pursuit of neoliberalism. These are active, ongoing, and vital debates even if they are conducted solely in terms of evaluation based upon functional or technical fit. But they become deeper and more urgent when they are attached to deeper normative questions about the EU's (non-) democratic character and the bases of its legitimacy. It is to these questions that the study of EU governance should now attend.

REFERENCES

Adler, E. and Barnett, M. (eds) (1998) *Security Communities*. Cambridge: Cambridge University Press.

Bache, I. (1998) *The Politics of European Union Regional Policy: Multi-Level Governance or Flexible Gatekeeping?* Sheffield: UACES/ Sheffield Academic Press.

Balassa, B. (1962) *The Theory of Economic Integration*. London: Allen and Unwin.

Barry, A. (1993) 'The European Community and European Government: Harmonization, Mobility and Space', *Economy and Society*, 22 (3): 314–326.

Barry, A. (2001) *Political Machines: Governing a Technological Society*. London: Athlone Press.

Bell, D. (1962) *The End of Ideology: On the Exhaustion of Political Ideas in the Fifties*. New York: Free Press.

Bieler, A. (2006) *The Struggle for Social Europe. Trade Unions and EMU in Times of Global Restructuring*. Manchester: Manchester University Press.

Bieler, A. and Morton, A.D. (eds) (2001) *Social Forces and the Making of the New Europe: The Restructuring of European Social Relations in the Global Political Economy*. Basingstoke: Palgrave.

Blom-Hansen, J. (1999) 'Avoiding the "joint-decision trap": Lessons from intergovernmental relations in Scandinavia', *European Journal of Political Research*, 35 (1): 35–67.

Brenner, N. (2004) *New State Spaces*. Oxford: Oxford University Press.

Börzel, T. (ed.) (2006) *The Disparity of European Integration: Essays in Honour of Ernst B. Haas*. London: Routledge.

Cafruny, A. and Ryner, M. (eds) (2003) *A Ruined Fortress? Neoliberal Hegemony and Transformation in Europe*. Lanham, MD: Rowman and Littlefield.

Calhoun, C. (2003) 'European studies: always already there and still in formation', *Comparative European Politics*, 1 (1): 5–20.

Caporaso, J. (1996) 'The European Union and forms of the State: Westphalian, regulatory, or post-modern?', *Journal of Common Market Studies*, 34 (1): 29–52.

Cini, M. (2006) 'The "state of the art" in EU studies: from politics to interdisciplinarity (and back again)', *Politics*, 26 (1): 25–31.

Cini, M. (ed.) (2007) *European Union Politics*, 2nd edn. Oxford: Oxford University Press.

Citi, M. and Rhodes, M. (2007) 'New modes of governance in the European Union: a critical survey and analysis', in K.E. Jørgensen, M.A. Pollack and B. Rosamond (eds) *Handbook of European Union Politics*. London: Sage, pp. 463–82.

Conant, L. (2007) 'Judicial politics', in K.E. Jørgensen, M.A. Pollack and B. Rosamond (eds) *Handbook of European Union Politics*. London: Sage, pp. 213–230.

Cram, L. (1997) *Policy-Making in the European Union*. London: Routledge.

Dannreuther, C. (2006) 'Regulation theory and the EU', *Competition and Change*, 10 (2): 180–199.

Delanty, G. and Rumford, C. (2005) *Rethinking Europe: Social Theory and the Implications of Europeanization*. London: Routledge.

Deutsch, K.W., Burrell, S.A., Kann, R.A., Lee, M., Lichterman, M., Lindgren, R.E., Loewenheim, F.L. and van Wangeren, R.W. (1957) *Political Community and the North Atlantic Area: International Organization in the Light of Historical Experience*. Princeton, NJ: Princeton University Press.

Falkner, G. (1998) *EU Social Policy in the 1990s: Towards a Corporatist Policy Community*. London: Routledge.

Favell, A. (2007) 'The sociology of EU politics', in K.E. Jørgensen, M.A. Pollack and B. Rosamond (eds) *Handbook of European Union Politics*. London: Sage, pp. 122–128.

Føllesdal, A. (2007) 'Normative political theory and the European Union', in K.E. Jørgensen, M.A. Pollack and B. Rosamond (eds) *Handbook of European Union Politics*. London: Sage, pp. 317–335.

Garrett, G. and Weingast, B.R. (1993) 'Ideas, interests, and institutions. Constructing the European Community's internal market', in J. Goldstein and R.O. Keohane, (eds) *Ideas and Foreign Policy. Beliefs, Institutions, and Political Change*. Ithaca, NY: Cornell University Press, pp. 173–206.

Gill, S. (1998) 'European governance and new constitutionalism: economic and monetary union and alternatives to disciplinary neoliberalism in Europe', *New Political Economy*, 3 (1): 5–26.

Gill, S. (2003) 'A neo-Gramscian approach to European integration', in A. Cafruny and M. Ryner (eds) *A Ruined Fortress? Neoliberal Hegemony and Transformation in Europe*. Lanham, MD: Rowman and Littlefield, pp. 47–70.

Gillingham, J. (1991) *Coal, Steel and the Rebirth of Europe, 1945–1955*. Cambridge: Cambridge University Press.

Gruber, L. (2000) *Ruling the World: Power Politics and the Rise of Supranational Institutions*. Princeton, NJ: Princeton University Press.

Haas, E.B. (1958) *The Uniting of Europe: Political, Social and Economic Forces, 1950–1957*. Stanford, CA: Stanford University Press.

Haas, E.B. (1961) 'International integration: the European and the universal process', *International Organization*, 15 (3): 366–392.

Haas, E.B. (1964) 'Technocracy, pluralism and the new Europe', in S.R. Graubard (ed.) *A New Europe?* Boston, MA: Houghton Mifflin, pp. 62–88.

Haas, E.B. (1975) 'The obsolescence of regional integration theory', working paper, Berkeley: Institute of International Studies.

Haas, E.B. (1976) 'Turbulent fields and the study of regional integration', *International Organization*, 30 (2): 173–212.

Haas, E.B. (2001) 'Does constructivism subsume neo-functionalism', in T. Christiansen, K.E. Jørgensen and A. Wiener (eds) *The Social Construction of Europe*. London: Sage, pp. 22–31.

Haas, E.B. (2004) 'Introduction: institutionalism or constructivism?', in *The Uniting of Europe: Political, Social and Economic Forces, 1950–1957*, 3rd edn. Notre Dame, IN: University of Notre Dame Press.

Haas, E.B. and Schmitter, P.C. (1964) 'Economics and differential patterns of integration; projections about unity in Latin America', *International Organization*, 18 (4): 705–737.

Haltern, U. (2004) 'Integration through law', in A. Wiener and T. Diez (eds) *European Integration Theory*. Oxford: Oxford University Press, pp. 177–196.

Hansen, R.D. (1969) 'European integration: reflections on a decade of theoretical efforts', *World Politics*, 21 (2): 242–271.

Hix, S. (1994) 'The study of the European Community: the challenge to comparative politics', *West European Politics*, 17 (1): 1–30.

Hix, S. (1998) 'The study of the European Union II: The 'new governance' agenda and its rival', *Journal of European Public Policy*, 5 (1): 38–65.

Hix, S. (2005) *The Political System of the European Union*, 2nd edn. Basingstoke: Palgrave Macmillan.

Hix, S. (2007) 'The European Union as a Polity (I)', in K.E. Jørgensen, M.A. Pollack and B. Rosamond (eds) *Handbook of European Union Politics*. London: Sage, pp. 141–158.

Hoffmann, S. (1966) 'Obstinate or obsolete? The fate of the nation-state and the case of Western Europe', *Daedalus*, 95 (3): 862–915.

Hooghe, L. (2001) *The European Commission and the Integration of Europe: Images of Governance*. Cambridge: Cambridge University Press.

Hooghe, L. and Marks, G. (1996) 'Europe with the regions: channels of subnational representation in the European Union', *Publius*, 26 (1): 73–92.

Hooghe, L. and Marks, G. (2000) 'Optimality and authority: a critique of neoclassical theory', *Journal of Common Market Studies*, 38 (5): 795–816.

Hooghe, L. and Marks, G. (2001) *Multi-Level Governance and European Integration*. Lanham, MD: Rowman and Littlefield.

Hooghe, L. and Marks, G. (2003) 'Unravelling the central state, but how? Types of multilevel governance', *American Political Science Review*, 97 (2): 233–43.

Jachtenfuchs, M. (2007) 'The European Union as a Polity (II)', in K.E. Jørgensen, M.A. Pollack and B. Rosamond (eds) *Handbook of European Union Politics*. London: Sage, pp. 159–174.

Jachtenfuchs, M. and Kohler-Koch, B. (2004) 'Governance and Institutional Development', in A. Wiener and T. Diez (eds) *European Integration Theory*. Oxford: Oxford University Press, pp. 97–116.

Jessop, B. (2006) 'The European Union and recent transformations in statehood', in S. Puntscher-Riekmann, M. Lazter and M. Mokre (eds) *The State of Europe: Transformations of Statehood from a European Perspective*. Frankfurt: Campus Verlag, pp. 75–94.

Jordan, A. (2000) *Environmental Policy in the European Union: Actors, Institutions and Processes*. London: Earthscan.

Jørgensen, K.E., Pollack, M.A. and Rosamond, B. (eds) (2007) *Handbook of European Union Politics*. London: Sage.

Kaufman-Osborn, T.V. (2006) 'Dividing the domain of political science: on the fetishism of subfields', *Polity*, 38 (1): 41–71.

Keohane, R.O. (1984) *After Hegemony: Cooperation and Discord in the World Political Economy*. Princeton, NJ: Princeton University Press.

Keohane, R.O. (1989) *International Institutions and State Power: Essays in International Relations Theory*. Boulder, CO: Westview.

Keohane, R.O. and Hoffmann, S. (1991) 'Institutional Change in Europe in the 1980s', in R.O. Keohane, R.O and S. Hoffmann, S. (eds) *The New European Community; Decisionmaking and Institutional Change*. Boulder, CO: Westview, pp. 1–39.

Keohane, R.O. and Nye, J.S. (1977) *Power and Interdependence: World Politics in Transition*. Boston, MA: Little, Brown and Co.

Laswell, H.D. (1950) *Politics: Who Gets What, When, How*. New York: Peter Smith.

Leibfried, S. (2005) 'Social policy: left to the judges and the markets?, in H. Wallace, W. Wallace and M.A. Pollack (eds)

Policy-Making in the European Union, 5th edn. Oxford: Oxford University Press, pp. 243–278.

Leibfried, S. and Pierson, P. (eds) (1995) *European Social Policy: Between Fragmentation and Integration*. Washington, DC: Brookings Institution.

Lenschow, A. (2005) 'Environmental policy: contending dynamics of policy change', in H. Wallace, W. Wallace and M.A. Pollack (eds) *Policy-Making in the European Union*, 5th edn. Oxford: Oxford University Press, pp. 305–327.

Lieshout, R.H., Segers, M.L.L. and van der Vleuten, A.M. (2004) 'De Gaulle, Moravcsik and the choice for Europe', *Journal of Cold War Studies*, 6 (4): 89–139.

Lindberg, L. (1963) *The Political Dynamics of European Economic Integration*. Stanford, CA: Stanford University Press.

Lindberg, L.N. and Scheingold, S.A. (1970) *Europe's Would-Be Polity: Patterns of Change in the European Community*. Englewood Cliffs, NJ: Prentice Hall.

Lipgens, W. (ed.) (1985) *Documents on the History of European Integration*, Vol. 1. Baden Baden: Nomos Verlag.

Lipgens, W. (ed.) (1986) *Documents on the History of European Integration*, Vol. 2. Baden Baden: Nomos Verlag.

Lipgens, W. and Loth, W. (eds) (1988) *Documents on the History of European Integration*, Vol. 3. Berlin: De Gruytes.

Long, D. and Wilson, P. (eds) (1995) *Thinkers of the Twenty Years' Crisis: Interwar Idealism Revisited*. Oxford: Clarendon Press.

Maes, I. (2006) 'The ascent of the European Commission as an actor in the monetary integration process in the 1960s', *Scottish Journal of Political Economy*, 53 (2): 222–241.

Majone, G. (1994) 'The rise of the regulatory state in Europe', *West European Politics*, 17 (3): 77–101.

Majone, G. (ed.) (1996) *Regulating Europe*. London: Routledge.

Majone (2005) *Dilemmas of European Integration: The Ambiguities and Pitfalls of Integration by Stealth*. Oxford: Oxford University Press.

Manners, I. (2003) 'Europaian studies', *Journal of Contemporary European Studies*, 11 (1): 67–83.

Marks, G. (1993) 'Structural policy in the European Community', in A.M. Sbragia, (ed.) *Euro-Politics*. Washington, DC: Brookings Institution.

Marks, G. (1996) 'Exploring and explaining variation in EU cohesion policy', in L. Hooghe (ed.) *European Integration and EU Cohesion Policy: Building Multilevel Governance*. Oxford: Oxford University Press, pp. 388–422.

Marks, G., Hooghe, L. and Blank, K. (1996a) 'European Integration from the 1980s: state-centric v. multi-level governance', *Journal of Common Market Studies*, 34 (3): 341–378.

Marks, G., Scharpf, F., Schmitter, P.C. and Streeck, W. (1996b) *Governance in the European Union*. London: Sage,

McElroy, G. (2007) 'Legislative politics', in K.E. Jørgensen, M.A. Pollack and B. Rosamond (eds) *Handbook of European Union Politics*. London: Sage, pp. 175–194.

Milward, A.S. (1984) *The Reconstruction of Western Europe, 1945–1951*. London: Methuen.

Milward, A.S. (2000) *The European Rescue of the Nation-State*, 2nd edn. London: Routledge.

Milward, A.S. (2007) 'History, political science and European integration', in K.E. Jørgensen, M.A Pollack and B. Rosamond (eds) *Handbook of European Union Politics*. London: Sage, pp. 99–103.

Milward, A.S., Lynch, F., Romero, F., Ranieri, R. and Sørensen, V. (1993) *The Frontier of National Sovereignty: History and Theory, 1945–1992*. London: Routledge.

Mitrany, D. (1965) 'The prospect of integration federal or functional?', *Journal of Common Market Studies*, 4 (2): 119–149.

Mitrany, D. (1966) *A Working Peace System*. Chicago: Quadrangle Books.

Monroe, K.R. (ed.) (2005) *Perestroika!: The Raucous Rebellion in Political Science*. New Haven, CT: Yale University Press.

Moravcsik, A. (1993) 'Preferences and power in the European community: a liberal intergovernmentalist approach' *Journal of Common Market Studies*, 31 (4): 473–524.

Moravcsik, A. (1998) *The Choice for Europe: Social Purpose and State Power from Messina to Maastricht*. Ithaca, NY: Cornell University Press.

Moravcsik, A. (1999) 'A new statecraft? Supranational entrepreneurs and international cooperation', *International Organization*, 53 (2): 267–306.

Moravcsik, A. (2002) 'In defence of the "democratic deficit": Reassessing legitimacy in the European Union, *Journal of Common Market Studies*, 40 (4): 603–624.

Moravcsik, A. (2005) 'The European Constitutional compromise and the neofunctionalist legacy', *Journal of European Public Policy*, 12 (2): 349–386.

Nedergaard, P. (2006) 'Policy learning in the EU: the case of the European employment strategy', *Policy Studies*, 27 (4): 311–323.

Nugent, N. (2006) *The Government and Politics of the European Union*, 6th edn. Basingstoke: Palgrave Macmillan.

Nye, J.S. (1971) 'Comparing common markets: a revised neofunctionalist model', in L.N. Lindberg, and S.A. Scheingold, (eds) (1971) *Regional Integration: Theory and Research*. Cambridge, MA: Harvard University Press, pp. 192–231.

Parsons, C. (2003) *A Certain Idea of Europe*. Ithaca, NY: Cornell University Press.

Peters, B.G. (2006) 'Forms of informality: identifying informal governance on the European Union', *Perspectives on European Politics and Society*, 7 (1): 25–40.

Peterson, J. (2004) 'Policy networks', in A. Wiener and T. Diez (eds) *European Integration Theory*. Oxford: Oxford University Press, pp. 117–136.

Pierson, P. (1996) 'The path to European integration: A historical institutionalist analysis', *Comparative Political Studies*, 29 (2): 123–163.

Pollack, M.A. (2003) *The Engines of Integration: Delegation, Agency and Agenda Setting in the European Union*. Oxford: Oxford University Press.

Pollack, M.A. (2005a) 'Theorizing EU policy-making', in H. Wallace, W. Wallace and M.A. Pollack (eds) *Policy-Making in the European Union*, 5th edn. Oxford: Oxford University Press, pp. 13–48.

Pollack, M.A. (2005b) 'Theorizing the European Union: international organization, domestic polity or experiment in new governance?', *Annual Review of Political Science*, 8: 357–398.

Pollack, M.A. (2007) 'Rational choice and EU Politics', in K.E. Jørgensen, M.A. Pollack and B. Rosamond (eds) *Handbook of European Union Politics*, London: Sage, pp. 31–55.

Puchala, D.J. (1981) 'Integration theory and the study of international relations', in R.W. Merritt

and B.M. Russett (eds) *From National Development to Global Community: Essays in Honour of Karl Deutsch*. London: George Allen and Unwin.

Richardson, J. (ed.) (2005) *European Union: Power and Policy-Making*, 3rd edn. London: Routledge.

Rittberger, B. (2001) 'Which institutions for post-war Europe? Explaining the institutional design of Europe's first community', *Journal of European Public Policy*, 8 (5): 673–708.

Robinson, N. (2007) 'More than a regulatory state: bringing expenditure (back) into EU research', *Comparative European Politics*, 5 (2): 179–204.

Rosamond, B. (2000) *Theories of European Integration*. Basingstoke and New York: Macmillan/St Martin's Press.

Rosamond, B. (2005a) 'The uniting of Europe and the foundation of EU studies: revisiting the neofunctionalism of Ernst B. Haas', *Journal of European Public Policy*, 12 (2): 237–254.

Rosamond, B. (2005b) 'Conceptualizing the EU mode of governance in world politics', *European Foreign Affairs Review*, 10 (4): 463–478.

Rosamond, B. (2007a) 'The political sciences of the European Union: disciplinary history and EU Studies', in K.E. Jørgensen, M.A. Pollack and B. Rosamond (eds) *Handbook of European Union Politics*. London: Sage, pp. 7–30.

Rosamond, B. (2007b) 'European integration and the social science of EU studies: the disciplinary politics of a subfield', *International Affairs*, 83 (2): 231–252.

Rumford, C. and Murray, P. (2003) 'Globalization and the limitations of European integration studies: interdisciplinary considerations', *Journal of Contemporary European Studies*, 11 (1): 85–93.

Sabel, C.F. and Zeitlin, J. (2007) 'Leaning from difference: the new architecture of experimentalist governance in the European Union', *European Governance Papers (EUROGOV)*, C-07-02. Available at: http://www.connex-network.org/eurogov/pdf/egp-connex-C-07-02.pdf, accessed 2 September 2007.

Scharpf, F. (1988) 'The joint decision trap: lessons from German federalism and European integration', *Public Administration*, 66 (3): 239–278.

Schimmelfennig, F. (2003) *The EU, NATO and the Integration of Europe: Rules and Rhetoric*. Cambridge: Cambridge University Press.

Schmitter, P.C. (1996) 'Imagining the Future of the Euro-Polity with the Help of New Concepts', in G. Marks, F. Scharpf, P.C. Schmitter and W. Streeck (eds) *Governance in the European Union*. London: Sage, pp. 121–151.

Schmitter, P.C. (2004) 'Neo-neo-functionalism?', in A. Wiener and T. Diez (eds) *European Integration Theory*. Oxford: Oxford University Press, pp. 45–74.

Schneider, G., Gabel, M. and Hix, S. (2000) 'European Union politics editorial statement', *European Union Politics*, 1 (1): 5–8.

Stone Sweet, A. and Sandholtz, W. (1998) 'Integration, supranational governance and the institutionalization of the European polity', in W. Sandholtz and A. Stone Sweet (eds) *European Integration and Supranational Governance*. Oxford: Oxford University Press, pp. 1–26.

Tallberg, J. (2003) *European Governance and Supranational Institutions: Making States Comply*. London: Routledge.

Tallberg, J. (2007) 'Executive politics', in K.E. Jørgensen, M.A. Pollack and B. Rosamond (eds) *Handbook of European Union Politics*. London: Sage, pp. 195–214.

Treib, O., Bähr, H. and Falkner, G. (2007) 'Modes of governance: towards a conceptual clarification', *Journal of European Public Policy*, 14 (1): 1–20.

van Apeldoorn, B. (2002) *Transnational Capital and the Struggle over European Integration*. London: Routledge.

Wallace, H. (ed.) (2001) *Interlocking Dimensions of European Integration*. Basingstoke: Palgrave.

Wallace, H. (2005) 'An institutional anatomy and five policy Modes', in H. Wallace, W. Wallace and M.A. Pollack (eds) *Policy-Making in the European Union*, 5th edn. Oxford: Oxford University Press, pp. 49–90.

Wallace, H. and Wallace, W. (2007) 'Overview: the European Union, politics and policy-making', in K.E. Jørgensen, M.A. Pollack and B. Rosamond, B. (eds) *Handbook of European Union Politics*. London: Sage, pp. 339–358.

Walters, W. and Haahr, J.H. (2005) *Governing Europe: Discourse, Governmentality and European Integration*. London: Routledge.

Waltz, K.W. (1979) *Theory of International Politics*. New York: McGraw Hill.

Warleigh, A. (2004) 'In defence of intra-disciplinarity: "European studies", the "new regionalism" and the issue of democratisation', *Cambridge Review of International Affairs*, 17 (2): 301–318.

Weiler, J.H.H. (1991) 'The transformation of Europe', *Yale Law Journal*, 100 (8): 2405–2083.

Weiler, J.H.H. (1994) 'The quiet revolution: the European Court of Justice and its interlocutors', *Comparative Political Studies*, 26 (4): 510–534.

Wessel, R. (2007) 'A legal approach to EU studies', in K.E. Jørgensen, M.A. Pollack, and B. Rosamond, B. (eds) *Handbook of European Union Politics*. London: Sage, pp. 104–113.

Wincott, D. (1995) 'Institutional interaction and European integration: Towards an 'everyday' critique of liberal intergovernmentalism', *Journal of Common Market Studies*, 33 (4): 587–609.

Wincott, D. (2003) 'The idea of the European social model: limits and paradoxes of Europeanization', in K. Featherstone and C. Radaelli (eds) *The Politics of Europeanization*. Oxford: Oxford University Press.

Wincott. D. (2006) 'European political development, regulatory governance, and the European social model: the challenge of substantive legitimacy', *European Law Journal*, 12 (6): 743–763.

Zürn, M. and Leibfried, S. (2005) 'Reconfiguring the national constellation', in S. Leibfried and M. Zürn (eds) *Transformations of the State*. Cambridge: Cambridge University Press, pp. 1–36.

7

National Interests

Jeffrey Lewis

The study of national interests in contemporary Europe is at the same time richly rewarding and terribly frustrating.[1] Rewarding because European states' postwar institutionalization among themselves and with the broader international arena has made the processes of interest formation fascinating to study. A now common observation, but with far-reaching implications for the study of interests, is that Europe represents the most advanced institutional setting of multilateralism to manage political and economic interdependence the modern world has ever seen. The willingness of European states, and in particular, the members of the European Union (EU), to 'pool' sovereignty and deepen collective policy-making competencies is what sets Europe apart from other regions and is unparalleled in today's international system. But frustration, too, is felt by those who try to study national interests in so dense an institutional environment – how do interests work in such a setting and how do we measure them using the conventional language of international relations and comparative politics?

This chapter examines the process of national interest formation and representation in Europe today, including how interests are formed, how international institutionalization tempers *and* safeguards what counts as an interest, and how competing interests are collectively legitimated within a deeply engrained value for consensus-based decisions. As the archetype of deeper regional integration, this chapter places emphasis on the way national interests work in the context of the EU but remains attentive to the broader transnational institutional setting in Europe and beyond in a globalizing world economy. Also important are the multifaceted relationships between members (new and old) and nonmembers in Europe's institutions and how this impacts national interests.

The chapter is organized into six parts. Section two establishes some initial parameters for how national interests are studied in contemporary Europe and the broad range of institutions, including but not limited to the EU, which bind and constitute the meaning of sovereign self-interested states in Europe today. Section three looks more closely at European states' postwar redefinition of sovereignty and connects the conceptual idea of 'pooled' sovereignty to the broader implications of how interests in such settings are calculated and pursued. In postwar Europe, the identity of the 'nation-state' became complexly entwined with that of 'member-state' (Sbragia, 1994). Europe's institutions, and especially the EU, are designed 'to reconcile the reflexes and ethos of the 'sovereign' national state with new modes of discourse and a new discipline of solidarity' (Weiler, 1991: 2480). This new understanding of sovereignty, it is argued, changes the meaning of what counts as 'the self,' and, along with it, what counts as 'self-interests.' Section four juxtaposes two ideal-typical ways to study interests: one based on a logic of consequences and instrumental reasoning and one based on a logic of appropriateness and internalized group-community standards.[2] While each logic offers distinctive predictions about self-interested behavior, there is growing doubt whether these are competing, opposed accounts. Europe today offers strong empirical support for such a 'both/and' view: national interests are safeguarded but within institutional rule-bound settings which temper how they operate (Checkel, 2007; Thomas, 2006; Youngs, 2004). Section five briefly summarizes the 'exogenous–endogeneous' interest debate, and makes a case for a more pluralistic conception of interest formation that is better attuned to interests being defined within an institutional environment of pooled, disaggregated sovereignty. Section six examines Europe's multilateral institutional context in further detail, looking in particular at how institutional environments can contextualize and give meaning to interests. Most distinctive here is the EU's informal and largely unwritten procedural code to solve problems and make joint decisions by consensus. Crucially, this section argues, the principled commitment to operate by consensus in Europe's most integrated club requires a certain institutional design to function and remain durable over time. Key attributes include shunning transparency and privileging insulation from domestic audiences to collectively legitimate individual claims through processes of deliberation. These characteristics, it is further argued, have imports beyond just the EU as well. If Europe's brand of regional integration is 'connected through a growing number of ties that invite, more than oblige, the submission of national power to the decisions of political

community' (Katzenstein, 2005: 74–5), then important ingredients in this formula include consensus-based decisions reached by insulated forms of deliberation. A brief concluding section follows this, reiterating the main findings and looking in greater detail at the case of Germany to illustrate how far the 'old' ways of determining national interests have evolved in Europe.

THE STUDY OF INTERESTS AND INSTITUTIONS IN EUROPE: THE EU AND BEYOND

This chapter begins with three basic observations about research on national interests in contemporary Europe. First, there is a growing body of empirical findings that challenge the conventional wisdom of how nation-states calculate and defend interests in a 'self-interested' way. That is to say, conventional approaches which assume instrumentalism and hard-nosed bargaining among boundedly rational egoists miss or misinterpret a range of national actor motivations and behavior in Europe today. This observation does not straw figure rational actor models. Later in the chapter we will return to the idea of rational actor models having 'first mover' advantages in establishing a baseline set of predictions about interest formation and interstate negotiation. The observation instead challenges those who hold steadfast to arguments that instrumentalism, individual rationality, and interest maximization are somehow *primordial* to understanding what makes up the calculus of interest in Europe (as everywhere else), without acknowledging the possibility that in some places at certain times, given the right institutional background conditions, this can indeed change. A now-classic statement of this argument was offered by Wayne Sandholtz (1993: 3) in his study of the then European Community's (EC) historic decision to create a single currency:

National interests are defined in the context of the EC. Membership in the EC has become part of the interest calculation for governments and societal groups ... the national interests of EC states do not have independent existence; they are not formed in a vacuum and then brought to Brussels. Those interests are defined and redefined in an international and institutional context that includes the EC. States define their interests in a different way as members of the EC than they would without it.

This brings us to our second introductory observation. While the above argument by Sandholtz refers specifically to the institutional context of the EU, the point has broader implications for Europe. On the one hand, the Europe outside the gates of the EU continues to shrink. Those who are not in and who do not seek eventual membership are a short list indeed, unified around fairly unique circumstances from oil reserves in Norway to neutrality and cantonal identities in Switzerland. The pull of the EU as a 'mighty magnet'[3] to nonmembers such as Turkey, parts of the Balkans, and even Russia's near abroad is a powerful inducement to mainstream with the political and economic interdependence so deeply implanted in the 'West' (Kelley 2004; Schimmelfenig, 2003). On the other hand, the EU is part of a much broader range of pluri- and multilateral settings into which Europe is embedded, including the North Atlantic Treaty Organization (NATO), the Council of Europe (CoE), the Organization for Security and Cooperation in Europe (OSCE), the European Space Agency (ESA), the OECD, the Nordic Council, the Western European Union (WEU), the Bank of International Settlements (BIS), and the G7/G8 to name just a few. It may well be impossible to study European politics without taking into account the EU, Europe's 'most important agent of change' in the words of some leading scholars (H. Wallace *et al.*, 2005: 3). But just studying the EU would miss the larger canvas. Europe embraces multilateral cooperation and complex interdependence more readily and more completely than any other region, and in turn participates in a much thicker web of institutional

commitments. In this institutional setting, the meaning of sovereignty and interest is different than in the past or elsewhere, such as in Asia (Pempel, 2005). 'Cooperation has become the sine qua non of a contemporary 'European' approach,' writes Stacia Zabusky, 'so much so that integration is often asserted as a value in itself' (1995: 5). Sharing this view is Peter Katzenstein who argues that 'porous regionalism in Europe is marked by multiple locations of governance, multiple dimensions of integration, and multiple modes of interaction' (2005: 28). Overall, including but not limited to the membership effects of the European Union, contemporary Europe pushes the envelope of multilateralism further than any other collection of states. What is important from this are not the nominal effects of multilateral memberships in Europe, but the *qualitative* effects of multilateralism which constitute 'certain principles of ordering relations among those states' (Ruggie 1993: 567). The basic arguments presented here about national interests and institutional environments thus apply to Europe beyond just the EU.

The third initial parameter is to acknowledge explicitly the need for research on interests to avoid overstating the effects of 'Europe' on national interests as if they were omnipresent. There are substantive issues (military commitments, fiscal and welfare state policies, culture and education to name a few) and both domestic and international settings where national interests are defined and defended in ways which the internal institutional mechanisms discussed in this chapter do not have much impact. The way Europe's institutions increasingly 'endogenize' the causal and constitutive processes of national interest formation (see below) still only account for a portion of national interest formation. Take the obvious case of Britain and France sitting on the UN Security Council with permanent *national* veto rights. Or European states' policies towards and obligations to former colonies (citizenship or immigration rights for instance) which are framed and acted out on a largely non-European stage and policy space. Or as Andrew Moravcsik finds in the case of the EU, which is arguably the 'thickest' conditioning mechanism on national interests for European states, there are still patterned omissions from what Brussels can regulate or does so only in the face of substantive, legal, fiscal, and procedural constraints, especially those that fall outside the remit of cross-border economic activity (Moravcsik, 2002) (but see Table 7.1 for the long-term trends).

This patchiness is one of the basic insights of the 'Europeanization' literature, summarized nicely by Johan Olsen:

European-level developments do not dictate specific forms of institutional adaptation but leave considerable discretion to domestic actors and institutions. There are significant impacts, yet the actual ability of the European level to penetrate domestic institutions is not perfect, universal or constant (2002: 936).

Researchers have traced systematic variation in 'Europeanization' effects depending

Table 7.1 Levels of authority in the European Union by issue-area

	1950	1957	1968	1970	1992	2001
Economic issues						
Goods/services	1	2	3	3	4	4
Agriculture	1	1	4	4	4	4
Capital flows	1	1	1	1	4	4
Persons/workers	1	1	2	2	3	4
Transportation	1	2	2	2	2	3
Energy	1	2	1	1	2	2
Communications	1	1	1	1	2	3
Environment	1	2	2	2	3	3
Regional development	1	1	1	1	3	3
Competition	1	2	2	2	3	3
Industry	1	2	2	2	2	3
Money/credit	1	1	2	2	2	4
Foreign exchange/loans	1	1	2	2	2	4
Revenue/taxes	1	1	2	2	2	3
Macroeconomic	1	1	2	3	2	4
Socio-cultural issues						
Work conditions	1	1	2	2	2	3
Health	1	1	1	1	2	2
Social welfare	1	2	2	2	2	2
Education and research	1	1	2	2	2	3
Labor-management relations	1	1	1	1	1	3
Political-constitutional issues						
Justice and property rights	1	1	1	2	3	4
Citizenship	1	1	1	1	2	3
Participation	1	1	1	1	2	2
Police and public order	1	1	1	1	1	2
International relations/external security issues						
Commercial negotiations	1	1	3	4	5	5
Economic–military assistance	1	1	1	1	2	4
Diplomacy	1	1	1	1	2	4
Defense and war	1	1	1	1	2	3

Key: 1 = All policy decisions at national level; 2 = only some policy decisions at EU level; 3 = policy decisions at both national and EU level; 4 = mostly policy decisions at EU level; 5 = all policy decisions at EU level.

Sources: Adapted from Pollack (2000: 522) and Schmitter (1996: 125–6); original categorization, key, and estimates to 1970 adapted from Lindberg and Scheingold (1970: 71).

on domestic political institutions and administrative traditions (Cowles *et al.*, 2001). Vivien Schmidt, for instance, argues that 'Europeanization' has more disruptive effects in 'simple national polities' such as Britain and France where 'power, access, and voice have traditionally been channeled through a single authority as a result of unitary institutional structures' compared to more 'compound polities' like Germany and Italy which have more diffuse channels 'through multiple authorities as a result of federal or regionalized structures, corporatist processes, and proportionate representation' (Schmidt, 2005: 412). In sum, the focus in the chapter is on the ways in which national interests are contributing to the transformation of Europe by engaging a qualitative form of multilateralism that changes the meanings of sovereignty, self, and interest. Adding the dimension of Europe's institutional contexts does not show us the complete picture, but it does allow us a richer and more complete explanation for how interests are formed and acted upon. The first step, and subject of the next section, is how Europe today increasingly resembles a 'post-Westphalian' place for state sovereignty.

THE MEANING OF SOVEREIGNTY IN POSTWAR EUROPE

International institutionalization has shaped contemporary Europe by changing Europe's understanding of sovereignty. The traditional conception of sovereignty, what Stephen Krasner (1999: 20) dubs 'Westphalian sovereignty' with the twin attributes of 'territoriality and the exclusion of external actors from domestic authority structures' no longer looks so neat and trim. Europe *by choice* has broken what Krasner calls the 'fundamental norm' of Westphalian sovereignty, namely, 'that states exist in specific territories, within which domestic political authorities are the sole arbiters of legitimate behavior' (Krasner, 1999: 20). From the 'novel legal order' administered by the EU's supranational European Court of Justice, or the policing of human rights and fundamental freedoms by the Council of Europe, to centralized monetary policy making for the 'eurozone', EU competition policy and external trade negotiations, and increasingly in areas of foreign policy covering security and defense, there exists a wide range of authority which no longer fits the Westphalian mold. In its place is a more malleable and relational conception of sovereignty, nicely captured in the phrase 'pooled sovereignty' (Keohane, 2002; Keohane and Hoffmann, 1991). As an inherently social construct, the meanings of sovereignty are 'neither fixed nor constant across time and space' (Biersteker, 2002: 157; Wendt, 1994) and Europe's states have evolved ideas of sovereignty since the 1950s in ever-widening clubs more, and more radically, than any other group of states in modernity.

There is no sign this is a harbinger of the demise of nation-states or national interests in Europe but, in this institutional context, the *meanings* of interest have changed quite considerably. As a 'distinctive model of internationalization,' Europe has 'transformed the exercise of political authority', writes Brigid Laffan, 'by embedding the national in the European and the European in the national' (1998: 250). Postwar Europe has reimagined sovereignty in a process of institutionalization that results in the collective expression of authority, influence, and legitimacy in a growing range of policy spheres. In Ole Waever's assessment, Europe has undergone 'a systematic and comprehensive collective redefinition of sovereignty' (1995: 418). Long ago, Hedley Bull (1977: 245) hypothesized such a possibility in his concept of 'a new medievalism' based on a 'system of overlapping authority and multiple loyalty' but he was elusive on what would happen to sovereign states. In Bull's 'new medievalism' sovereign states 'might disappear' (Bull, 1977: 245). But he goes on to conceptualize a more contingent and more intriguing 'intermediate stage':

> It is possible that the process of integration might arrive at the stage where, while one could not

speak of a European state, there was real doubt both in theory and in reality as to whether sovereignty lay with the national governments or with the organs of the 'community' (Bull 1977: 256).

As a 'part-formed' polity of 'post-sovereign' policy making (W. Wallace, 2005), Europe has arrived at just such an 'intermediate' form. The image of Bull's 'intermediate' form is also an appropriate reminder that in a setting of overlapping authority, national interests can still be pursued, defined, realized, etc. in purely domestic contexts and/or in other bilateral, plurilateral, and multilateral settings. The institutional context of 'Europe' does not exhaust or subsume nation-state interests. At the same time, it is important to underline the binding, cumulative nature of international institutionalization in Europe's institutions and how the sovereignty redefinitions in this brand of multilateralism impact interest formation generally. A classic formulation of this trend in the case of the European Union is Lindberg and Scheingold's (1970: 66–75) scale for the 'locus' of decision-making authority in the European integration process which has seen subsequent updating by a number of EU experts (see Table 7.1).

In the aggregate, Table 7.1 nicely depicts the long-term pattern: by the turn of the century, no major issue area is made in a purely national context without a 'Europe' component. What issues and interests European states (especially EU members) subject to international scrutiny is unmatched in other comparative regional and global contexts among modern 'Westphalian' nation-states. While research on contemporary Europe is increasingly cognizant to how sovereignty meanings have evolved, there is far less clarity on how this affects processes of national interest definition (or 'preference formation') and articulation. The overall significance of this development is eloquently summed up by Robert Keohane (2002: 744):

The conception that a state must have control of its external policies and be free of external authority structures is an essentially European invention, dating from the sixteenth and seventeenth centuries. For over 300 years such external sovereignty has been associated with political success.

A major historic accomplishment of the EU is that it has ended this association between sovereignty and success. The EU has begun to institutionalize a conception of limited and pooled sovereignty, while at the same time successfully pursuing relatively autonomous policies, exercizing influence in world politics, and maintaining very decent conditions of life for its citizens. Europe's emerging conception of pooled sovereignty affects all aspects of European life, from criminal justice to foreign policy.

While not the focus of his article, Keohane is less concerned with how the institutionalization of pooled sovereignty affects interests. Building on the insightful concept of pooled sovereignty, this chapter will explore in more detail how pooling affects the institutional context in which interests are formed and given meaning. One important caveat however. 'Pooling' as used here does not imply a zero-sum conception of sovereignty. We are not attempting to measure the extent of sovereignty 'transfers' (which implies zero-sumness) since that would overlook completely a range of informal arrangements (more on this later) and the way in which pooling involves the collective redefinition of what individuality and authority means. When meanings of legitimate political authority change, so too do meanings of interest and even more basically, *what counts* as an individual/national interest. To pose a few illustrative questions: what counts as a national interest in eurozone macroeconomic policy making, or in a European Council summit dinner with Russian President Vladimir Putin to discuss Europe's energy needs,[4] or the Doha round trade talks, or combating cross-border crime and terrorism, coordinating corporate tax rates or immigration policy? The overall argument offered here is that where meanings of sovereignty change – become pooled and relational – meanings of interest change as well.

In short, European states' new self-understandings of sovereignty have significant implications on how interests work; and crucially, *not just* the cost–benefit calculations of interests. Rational actor models can and do offer sophisticated accounts for much of the 'thick' cooperation taking place in Europe's institutions: long time horizons, seeking to accommodate rather than outvote, diffuse understandings of reciprocity, even empathetic interests to help a colleague in need (Scharpf, 2006). Perhaps only 'vulgar' rationalists[5] – hardcore realists? – would expect national officials to maximize utility to the point of driving each other to the wall every time to eek out every last ounce of concession and gain left on the bargaining table within a continuous negotiation and institutional 'lock in' system such as we find in Europe today. For example, one of the very first lessons EU newcomers learn is that no one can be a *demandeur* too often and expect others to listen.[6] A hard bargaining utility maximizer would not thrive in such a setting, nor accumulate much social influence regardless of relative size, preference intensity or voting power. In such an institutional environment, rational actor models would expect to see an enlightened sense of self-interest practiced. But, and here we return to the crucial point, all rational actor models will hold that where we do see such patterns of cooperation prevail, they ultimately hinge on favorable cost–benefit calculations which might include 'diffuse' considerations such as social capital, reputation, and/or status. In this view, as Ian Hurd nicely summarizes, 'any loyalty by actors to the system or its rules is contingent on the system providing a positive stream of benefit ... actors do not value the relation itself, only the benefits accruing from it' (1999: 387).

Yet some hold the instrumental interpretation of self-interest, and the calculative reasoning expected to accompany norm-adhering behavior is too limited. Instead, they emphasize how sovereignty redefinitions reach further into the configuration of basic actor properties. Some argue that sovereignty redefinitions have triggered constitutive changes in how European nation-states conceptualize their identities, or the very boundaries of the 'self'. Thomas Risse describes this as 'the incorporation of 'Europe' into their self-descriptions' (2003: 498). John

Ruggie labels the EU the modern era's first 'multiperspectival polity' whereby 'it is increasingly difficult to visualize the conduct of international politics among community members, and to a considerable measure even domestic politics, as though it took place from a starting point of [25] separate, single, fixed viewpoints ... the identity of each ... increasingly endogenizes the collectivity they comprise' (1998: 195). Likewise, James Caporaso contemplates the idea of a 'post-modern' form of state in Europe, where 'elements of politics and governance occupy different sites (Basle, Brussels, the national capitals, Luxembourg, bilateral meetings among economic and finance ministries), and these sites can change ... the state becomes ... a set of spatially detached activities, diffused across the Member States' (1996: 45). It thus appears that Hedley Bull's prescient insight of 'intermediate' types of overlapping authority and identity have come to fruition, at least in Europe, and the implications of changes in the meaning of sovereignty affects how we study interests. As the next section will explore, the challenge for researchers today is building more complexity and nuance into models to account for *both* the utilitarian and rule-following calculus in European self-interests.

WHAT DIFFERENCE DO INSTITUTIONS MAKE? THE LOGICS OF CONSEQUENCES AND APPROPRIATENESS

There is a wide range of approaches to studying national interests, which generally cluster into two traditions. The first tradition, rationalism, tends to focus on an instrumental conception of interest, individual rationality, and the 'logic of consequences' engrained in various institutional settings. In a 'logic of consequences' mode, interests are the product of calculated costs and anticipated benefits. In this instrumental conception, institutions alter costs and/or create (dis)incentives for certain courses of action. The second tradition, constructivism, emphasizes a more expansive conception of interest (and the self) based on collective, social rationalities and expectations for norm-adhering behavior based on the 'logic of appropriateness' which can become institutionalized under certain background (scope) conditions. In a 'logic of appropriateness' mode, interests are not merely based on expected utility but also derive from internalized rules, norms, roles, and values which prescribe and proscribe certain actions in a given situation. Under certain background (scope) conditions such as intense, long-term face-to-face negotiations or in a highly specialized 'epistemic community' of like-minded individuals, this can include a sense of obligation, and/or responsibility to act or restrain from acting in certain ways.

Studying interests in Europe is also a field of methodological pluralism, ranging from 'large N' quantitative studies of voting behavior, public opinion, and the like, to 'small N' qualitative studies employing case study and interviewing techniques. The current state-of-the-art does not favor the emergence of a clear victor leading to a definitive approach to studying national interests; rather, a pluralistic range of approaches is likely to continue. Furthermore, it remains doggedly uncertain whether many of these seemingly opposed approaches – rationalism *versus* constructivism – are actually incommensurable, or whether they can and should be treated as more complementary ways of conducting research (Fearon and Wendt, 2002; Jupille *et al.*, 2003; Pollack, 2007).

As ideal-types the logics of consequences and appropriateness are conceptually quite distinct. But there is good reason to doubt their separability in the real world, as March and Olsen have long emphasized. In their own words: 'The two logics are not mutually exclusive … political actors … calculate consequences and follow rules, and the relationship between the two is often subtle' (March and Olsen 1998: 952). While not ruling out the potential for 'first mover' bias,[7] it is fruitful to consider whether a more

expansive rationalist framework could take into account appropriateness logics and the endogeneity effects of Europe's institutional environment on interests. One advantage of this approach is avoiding an oversocialized view since Europe's institutional environment is *conditioning,* not determining, on interests. Europe's states, even those inside the EU, still also pursue a range of interests outside of the EU, and accounts of national interest must stay sensitive to the differential impacts of such variegated institutional settings (see later).

An expansive rationalist framework (what some call 'soft' rationalism) can help us develop more nuanced and arguably realistic accounts for the subtle blending of calculative and rule-following behavior in different institutional environments. Miles Kahler argues in favor of just such an approach where he discusses the prospects for a 'modified rational choice framework' (1998: 933). Jeffrey Checkel advocates the potential theory payoffs for more of a thin rationalist–constructivist synthesis based on 'bridge building consistent with the empirical evidence' (2005: 819). Two other brief mentions are worth singling out here as exemplars of what a bridge-building approach might look like. First, Fritz Scharpf uses rational choice modeling to show how 'relationally defined preferences' might arise under different 'transformation rules' which vary how 'ego interprets the relationship with alter' (1997: 84–5). Between individualism, 'the standard assumption of self-interest maximization of neoclassical economics and conventional rational-choice approaches', and altruism are a range of what Scharpf calls 'intermediate' forms, which are 'a softened version of the individualistic orientation in which ego gives some small weight to the interests of alter' (1997: fn. 22, 96). A second exemplar in this vein is research by David Stasavage (2004, 2006) using rational choice to predict institutional design choices by states to 'shun' transparency. In documenting the extent of *in-camera* negotiations within Europe's institutions, he finds a powerful motivation is the perceived benefit of deliberative-based negotiation and using group-community standards behind closed doors to assess individual arguments. In such an institutional environment, secrecy rather than public debate is essential since it may result in national representatives who 'take positions that deviate from the prior views of their constituents about policy' (Stasavage 2006: 7) (see later). For European states who participate inside the thick webs of transnational institutions which embed contemporary Europe's political economy, national interests undergo filtering and framing processes which inform their content in substantive and nontrivial ways. Hardcore rationalism with axiomatic reliance on assumptions of interest maximization (an unrestrained 'logic of consequences') will be of little help in understanding this development, but a softer version of rationalism can indeed lead to a fuller and more accurate account of the context of national interest formation in modern Europe.

The most fruitful way forward is to not treat logics of action as 'either/or' accounts but to better specify models which can account for both dynamics when they occur. This view finds favor with Checkel's take on studying Europe: 'The point is not to make all theoretical schools happy; rather, it is to bring our models closer to the empirical reality we observe on a daily basis, where social actors in Europe are not only strategic and instrumental, *but also* deliberative and other-regarding' (2001: 243). An important first step, the next section argues, is to develop a more pluralistic conception of interest formation that can account for Europe's institutional setting of pooled, disaggregated sovereignty.

WHERE DO INTERESTS COME FROM? TWO VIEWS

Many researchers begin from the premise that national interests are exogenous to

international institutional contexts found in Europe. That is, states first figure out what they want domestically, within the bounds of the achievable and under conditions of bounded rationality, and then bargain internationally for maximal gains and minimal losses. A particularly sophisticated version of this is found in liberal intergovernmental (LI) theory, most clearly articulated by Andrew Moravcsik (see also Milner, 1999). The great strength of this model is the ability to account for the domestic politics in national interest formation, clearly linked to a set of micro-foundations anchored in a pluralist view of state–society relations. In Moravcsik's (1993: 481) words, 'National interests ... emerge through domestic political conflict as societal groups compete for political influence, national and transnational coalitions form, and new policy alternatives are recognized by governments.' In effect, this is a two-stage theory of national preference formation, or what Jeffrey Legro (1996) calls the 'rationalist two-step'. Again in Moravcsik's (1993: 481) words, 'Governments first define a set of interests, then bargain among themselves in an effort to realize those interests.' This account of domestic interests and the 'supply side' of underlying societal factors – such as the convergence of macroeconomic policy preferences that led to interest in the Single European Market in the mid-1980s (Moravcsik, 1998) – is a powerful explanatory model.

However, doubts remain whether this is a complete account. Some argue treating interests as exogenous to Europe's international institutional context truncate our understanding of national interest formation (Eising, 2002; Niemann, 2004; Lewis, 2005). In particular, the LI insistence that international institutional environments do not have independent causal effects on the constitutive processes of interest formation leaves some researchers unconvinced. The two-step logic that states first figure out their preferences and then act on them in a separate, subsequent stage of interstate negotiation is potentially very constraining. Moravcsik's sophisticated LI model does recognize the possibility for 'second image reversed' effects, but note his insistence: 'To the extent that international factors, such as economic interdependence or external threats to national security influence preference formation, they must pass through the domestic polity' (1993: fn. 9, 483).

To address this constraint, some researchers have begun to endogenize Europe's interaction context by beginning from the idea that institutional memberships and the 'lock in' effects that accompany them not only exert instrumental effects on interests but causal and even constitutive ones. Causal effects would include what negotiation theorists like Lax and Sebenius call an 'expansive conception' of interests such as 'process,' 'relationship,' and 'principled' interests (1986: 64–74). Process interests are 'intrinsic interests in the character of the negotiation process itself' (Lax and Sebenius 1986: 72). Relationship interests place value in the relationship itself and can develop into 'an almost transcendent status' (i.e. a taken-for-granted quality) including concern with the 'well-being' of others and even 'the collegiality of the process' (Lax and Sebenius, 1986: 64–5). Principled interests are those based on shared undertandings of fairness, 'equal division,' or proportionality (Lax and Sebenius, 1986: 73). Participating in Europe's institutions *causally* affects how interests are informed by introducing noninstrumental process, relationship, and principled interests in achieving certain kinds of outcomes (say, for example, consensus-based compromise).

Constitutive effects operate at a deeper level, affecting basic actor properties – the self – ('Who am I in this context'?) and are driven through micro-processes of socialization and the internalization of norms, rules, and principles of collective decision making (Checkel, 2005). As meanings of sovereignty have changed so too have national conceptions of the self and self-interest. In particular, the sovereignty implications for interests problematize assumptions of unitary states pursuing single-peaked preferences defined domestically and negotiated internationally as found in the exogenous account. First, Europe goes further than anywhere in evolving 'disaggregated' state sovereignty. Once sovereignty is disaggregated, the idea of the state thinking and acting in unitary ways is potentially very misleading. As Anne-Marie Slaughter argues, a benefit of viewing the state in disaggregated terms is that it allows us to see sovereignty as 'relational rather than insular' which 'describes a capacity to engage rather than a right to resist' (Slaughter, 2004: 268). Disaggregated state sovereignty challenges 'the fiction of a unitary will and capacity for action' (Slaughter. 2004: 12). Second, disaggregated states make exogenous interests harder to defend as a conceptual choice in theorizing how interest formation works. The national actors who make up the disaggregated state are engaged in international institutional contexts that shape, inform, and give meaning to what national interests *are* in increasingly significant ways. There are learning curves for newcomers to this institutional context, such as the Central and Eastern European states joining the EU and undergoing socialization to the 'culture of compromise' which prevails. As one senior diplomat from Poland described to me in an interview:

> Membership in the EU will have a very positive experience for our internal [national political] system ... because of [our] historical experience, [compromise] is a symbol of weakness. There is a saying in Poland of a 'rotten compromise' where a man of compromise equals a weak character. We are learning to change. (Author's interview, Brussels, 23 May 2003).

But those looking for one-off transfers of sovereignty or the formal accretion of supranational competencies away from national authorities as a test of this argument miss the significance of disaggregated, pooled sovereignty. Pooling and disaggregating sovereignty can occur through informal processes of collective decision making. A clear empirical example from the context of the EU is Michael Smith's (2004) careful process-tracing of foreign policy cooperation from the 'intergovernmental' days of European Political Cooperation in the 1970s to the formal addition of the Common Foreign and Security Policy (CFSP) in the 1990s. Before CFSP ever existed, an informally institutionalized system of collective consultation and consensus-building became deeply engrained in European foreign ministries' policy-making calculus. A concrete empirical example is the so-called *cotumier* (or 'custom'), a cumulative and politically binding 'soft law' of foreign policy experience, defined by Smith as 'a compilation of all formal and informal working procedures which became the 'bible of EPC' for all European correspondents in foreign ministries' (1998: 318). A key finding of this research is how member-states over time learned to cooperate and consult one another (Smith calls this the development of a 'consultation reflex') and how this led to increased institutionalization and collective preference formation. EU members still (mostly) pursued foreign policy interests outside the scope of EU institutions, yet nonetheless, these institutional frames conditioned how interests were framed and gradually socialized national foreign policy actors to internalize appropriateness standards for consultation and consensus-based outcomes.

Disaggregated sovereignty in Europe has promoted a policy-making model of relatively autonomous specialist networks who develop intensive, long-term collaborative relationships while enjoying differential patterns of insulation from domestic audiences (a point returned to in the next section). Assuming interests are defined in a domestic vacuum then carried to the international setting for negotiation is suspect in such a multilateral context of disaggregated, pooled sovereignty. As the next section will show, there is also a strong correlation between deliberative styles of negotiation, where individual arguments are collectively weighed and judged through processes of communicative rationality, and insulated European institutional settings out of the camera's eye. Deliberative negotiation relies less on formal rules and procedures than informal understandings and, crucially, communicative rationality in assessing individual arguments. National interest claims in such settings are subject to a kind of 'peer review' process (Heisenberg 2006: 4). Taken

all the way down to the microlevel, we see empirical evidence of national officials operating in institutional environments which require a 'double hatting' identity configuration to be successful at their jobs (Laffan, 2004; Lewis, 2005). Newcomers to such institutional environments find themselves inducted into the culture of rules, roles, and norms through a process of socialization (Checkel, 2005: 804–5).

Disaggregation creates a tendency for networks of what Helen Wallace (2005: 87–8) calls 'intensive transgovernmentalism' to form, based on 'a distinct circle of key national policy-makers'. In such settings, a group of, say, military planners, or cross-border crime specialists may have more in common and identify with each other more than with their own national colleagues within or across ministerial lines back home in the national capital. National officials may engage in 'collective plotting' to sell agreements back home, even helping each other with arguments to use to sell results or fake group outrage to underline opposition to an isolated or outlier position deemed unacceptable by the group (Lewis, 2003, 2005). Disaggregated, pooled sovereignty in Europe generally, and most pervasively among the EU member states, promotes an intensive type of interstate interaction which can blur the boundaries of the 'national' and the 'European'. March and Olsen (1998: 967) note:

> The number of meetings in the context of the EU, together with meetings in the context of other international institutions, during some periods actually make ministers, bureaucrats, and experts interact as much with colleagues from other countries as with their domestic colleagues.

The EU goes furthest in such boundary blurring but is not alone. Two examples of this from the context of the EU and one from the Council of Europe can illustrate the point further. First, the 13 EU 'eurozone' finance ministers have forged a tightly knit community of macroeconomic policy coordination which relies heavily on insulation and informal methods of deliberation (Puetter, 2006).

Puetter (2007: 4) argues that 'EU finance minsters have always acted as an independently minded group often being at odds with cabinet colleagues in the national capitals'. Second, justice and interior ministries have taken advantage of the new burst of EU activism in the field of Justice and Home Affairs (JHA) since the late 1990s to insulate 'collective decisions from parliamentary and judicial review at both national and EU levels' (Den Boer and Wallace, 2000: 518; Guiraudon, 2003). But as late as 1995–1996, Brussels insiders would talk about JHA officials as 'the men in grey suits who trust no one'; one official at an EU permanent representation described the lack of mutual trust in the following way:

> [The Justice and Interior ministries] are still terrible, they are not results oriented. They are not aware of their common interests and sharing their competencies and authority. This is not helped by the legal and institutional framework, because they are not obligated to share national competencies. Their mentalities are not geared to results … But what many people forget is that this was the same for people in 1950 in economic competencies. (Author's interview, Brussels, 21 May 1996).

Since the 1990s, the net effect has been to create a much more tightly coupled transnational judicial-law enforcement policy network among like-minded national actors in a field traditionally guarded by states as an 'off-limits' area of national sovereignty. Third, and finally, the Council of Europe (CoE) has an extensive specialist committee network promoting citizenship rights that blur the traditional boundaries of 'national' and 'European' in areas as diverse as 'greater tolerance for the cultural rights of minorities (especially in the linguistic and educational realms), more standardized procedures for speeding the process of immigrant integration, and greater tolerance of dual nationality' (Checkel, 2003: 215). As Checkel's research on the CoE finds, 'Judges and committee experts often see themselves as part of social networks that are both European and national in orientation' (Checkel, 2003: 216).

Substantively, however, it is important to stress that disaggregated, pooled sovereignty is quite issue-specific (monetary but not fiscal policy in the eurozone for example) and is thus patchy, not linear or complete. Since only some national interests are subject to the endogenity effects of Europe's institutions, it is important to avoid pushing the endogenity argument too far. Even in such densely knit normative institutional environments as we find in Europe, European states protect and promote national interests, some of which are formed in textbook 'exogenous' ways. In addition to this, there are a range of institutional safeguards to protect national interests even in issue-areas where disaggregated, pooled sovereignty applies. Indeed it is difficult to image such *voluntary* deeper integration in Europe without safeguards to cushion members from being forced to adopt policies with disproportionate costs or domestic politicization effects. One does not have to search far in current headlines to find examples of national interests trumping European ones or collective action problems resulting in suboptimal outcomes. Economic nationalism still regularly prevails. Despite the convincing market liberalization logic, if the French want to maintain a national postal monopoly they can resist cross-border competition. Irrespective of the functional logic for a Single European Market, national tax authorities and banking regulators jealously guard national autonomy even in the face of convincing evidence of 'tax poaching' and staffing redundancies in Europe's banking sector. Or in another recent headline case, despite the zero-sum nature for the EU as a whole, 11 European cities have made competitive bids to host the European Satellite System ('Galileo') Headquarters while work on the project itself slips further behind schedule due to disputes over common financing.

Thus, while Europe's institutions temper and limit national claims, national interests retain numerous safeguards. As Calleo puts it, 'Europe's institutions aim not only to concert policies around general shared interests, but also to protect the rights of individual states' (2004: 34). Some safeguards are formal, such as voting weights or unanimity decision rules. Others are informal, such as working by consensus or the ability to use arguments and principled reasoning ('fairness' or 'nondiscrimination') to persuade others to change their position or at least remain open to compromise. Another safeguard is gatekeeping: carefully controlling who is allowed into the club, on what terms, and with what conditions attached (Sperling, 1999). The EU, NATO, and the CoE use 'partnership' and 'association' agreements as a way to offer probationary status to those who wish to join and/or internalize the established *acquis* (Adler, 1998: 133–4; Jacoby 2004). EU membership has the most far-reaching conditionality – the EU *acquis communitaire* (i.e., cumulative body of law) is estimated at some 95,000 pages – and increasingly EU members leverage conditions on those who only seek more limited partnership or market access. A good example of the latter is the EU's new 'European Neighborhood Policy' (ENP) for border states who do not have eventual membership prospects but are offered tiered incentives for policy reform. According to Kelley (2006: 36), 'The countries that push more shared values will get priority in financial support, greater and speedier access to the internal market.' Within Europe's institutions, as the next section will document, two design features stand out for their ability to simultaneously safeguard *and* condition national interests and how states pursue them: insulation from domestic politics and deliberative methods of negotiation.

INSULATION AND DELIBERATION: SHUNNING TRANSPARENCY TO MAKE CONSENSUS-BASED POLICY

Recent research on decision making within the European Union, confirms empirically what had long been known to Brussels insiders – there is a principled interest among members to make decisions by consensus.

Since the early 1990s when voting records were made public, we know that votes occur in fewer than 25 percent of the cases where formal voting is allowed. And in cases of contested votes, they tend to cluster in certain issue areas (nearly half involve agriculture and fisheries), frequently involve the use of 'abstentions'[8] rather than 'no' votes, and only rarely involve two or more dissatisfied states (well short of a 'blocking minority') (Hayes-Renshaw and Wallace, 2006: 279–86). This pattern of consensus-seeking imprints other important institutions in Europe as well including the European Central Bank (whose Governing Council never votes), NATO's North Atlantic Council, the Council of Europe's Committee of Ministers, the European Space Agency, and the OSCE.

The durability of consensus-based decision making in Europe's dense institutional environment relies heavily on two features: insulation and deliberation. Insulation from domestic constituencies and a deliberative style of negotiation promote the kind of intensive transgovernmentalism discussed above and helps maintain a high output of legislation under the demanding requirements of consensus-based decision making. Compared to other regions and institutional environments, the design of insulated deliberation is one of Europe's most distinctive institutional characteristics. This style of decision making is what sets Europe as a region apart and has a big impact on how national interests are contributing to the transformation of European politics.

First, *insulation* from domestic audiences is extensively relied on in Europe's institutional settings. Without insulation, negotiations would be subject to more bargaining breakdowns. The reason, as David Stasavage explains, is that 'uncertainty about disagreement payoffs can create an incentive for representatives to "posture" by adopting uncompromising bargaining positions. These uncompromising positions may be adopted to convince the public that representatives are not caving in to opposition demands because they are biased' (2004: 670). Insulation reinforces the deliberative process by relying on a host of informal mechanisms to 'oil' or 'lubricate' negotiations. Restricted sessions and lunches are often used to discuss sensitive issues in highly insulated settings. In the EU, for example, informal Council meetings have expanded widely – from the European Council summits of heads of government and state to the foreign ministers, finance ministers, and other sectoral formations – which indicates the growing reliance on intensive exchanges of views in more intimate, in-camera settings. One obvious negative implication of this design, however, is the growing disquiet over Europe's 'democratic deficit' or lack of accountability to citizens with important national policy being made in opaque, technocratic forums.

Second, *deliberation* fosters consensus-seeking rules that retain legitimacy without explicit formalization. Indeed the informal yet durable character of consensus norms is perhaps their most striking feature across Europe's institutional settings. Without such informality, there would be more reliance on formal rules, and voting and relative power resources would factor more importantly and be *more publicly visible* in outcomes. The informal character of consensus norms helps explain why rationalist theories often miss the significance and weight of group-community standards in deliberative decision making. They have a very difficult time explaining why delegations practice self-restraint in dropping demands or requesting concessions that the group fails to accept under those conditions when a formal decision rule of unanimity applies and the recourse to the veto is available (Lewis, 2005).

In general, Jürgen Neyer argues that deliberative methods of consensus-based arguing are an intentional design feature to thwart strategic instrumental bargaining. What is critical is this deliberative process is different than bargaining. As Neyer (2003: 691) explains, 'While bargaining relies on the use of promises and threats … arguing rests on claims of factual truth and/or

normative validity.' In the OSCE, for example, consensus-based decisions are used to promote political binding decisions whose 'compliance pull' does not derive from enforceable law as in the EU but exhibits similar deliberative standards for legitimate, acceptable member-state behavior. As Adler explains, consensus-based decision making 'generates the need to persuade other members, thereby promoting socialization and learning processes. According to Marton Krasznai, a Hungarian ambassador to the OSCE, 'the consensus practice works because of the existence of "a unique political culture within the OSCE community"' (1998: 137).

To restate in slightly different terms, insulation and deliberation are important scope conditions for interstate bargaining in Europe's institutions. The two are highly interrelated and mutually reinforcing, but by no means 'natural' or inevitable. Although something of a chicken-and-egg puzzle, which environmental conditioning variable came first – insulation or deliberation – is a relevant question. One might hypothesize insulation is a deeper background condition, enabling deliberative methods of negotiation to become institutionalized through trust and mutual responsiveness to create shared expectations about its use. Insulation helps promote deliberation, since 'the presence of an audience may make officials more reluctant to retreat from initial claims when faced with superior evidence' (Stasavage, 2004: 668). The rotating EU presidency, for example, employs discursive resources to validate or reject arguments on legitimacy grounds, using group standards of fairness and at the crucial stage of derogation discussions, determining whose domestic context or special circumstances warrant abrogation or opt-out. A particularly interesting finding from a recent comparative study of EU presidencies is the ability of a president to show partiality, towards an emerging majority viewpoint, in order to persuade isolated delegations to compromise and/or drop reserves (Elgström, 2003: 44–5). In a deliberative environment, this can act as a mechanism for determining the legitimacy of arguments. In another institutional setting, the Council of Europe, Checkel finds evidence of committee and working party participants who acquire reputations for their 'powers of persuasion' (such as Austrian Ambassador Ulrich Hack) to be able to change people's minds through the use of discursive resources (Checkel, 2003: 222).

In summary, Europe's institutional environment was designed to soften hard bargaining among rational, egoistic states. Both insulation and deliberation are key background conditions for European states' 'tamed' national interests. Much of this environment can be captured within a rational actor framework: the need to moderate demands, conform to informal rules and norms, display sympathy and mutual responsiveness to others who find themselves in need of special consideration, and so on. Yet at the same time there is a certain irreducible element of collective community standards which do not follow an instrumental logic based on cost–benefit calculations but instead track a noninstrumental appropriateness logic where certain behavior is considered the 'right thing to do' in that institutional setting.

CONCLUSION

This chapter has not argued that an integrating and globalizing Europe dilutes the weight of national interests. To do so assigns a narrow zero-sum quality to the boundary between 'the national' and 'the European' which the blurring argument of disaggregated, pooled sovereignty rejects. Rather, 'by exercising sovereignty together', Calleo tells us that European states seek 'to enhance their control over the environment in which they live' (2004: 35–6). National interests are contributing to the transformation of Europe by embracing complex multilateralism and molding individual conceptions of sovereignty (including what is subject to international scrutiny). The molding process extends

beyond just Europe's institutional centers – Brussels, Strasbourg, Paris, Basle, Frankfurt, and so on – and changes, at a more basic level, how European states act internationally as well. There is evidence, for example, that an increasingly integrated Europe votes together in the UN General Assembly, including newcomers such as Malta and Cyprus who used to line up votes with the G77 but now align themselves with an EU block.[9] Another intriguing line of development is how Europe now looks to 'export' aspects of its own 'Europeanization' with the intention of influencing international relations. This includes, as Peter Katzenstein points out, 'a different calibration of the requirements of economic efficiency with social justice, resistance to treating culture as a commodity, stronger opposition to the death penalty, more self-conscious commitment to environmental causes, and insistence on the primacy of international law and multilateral international organizations in world affairs' (2005: 74). In diverse policy areas such as product standards, consumer protection, antitrust, financial regulation, and corporate governance, Europe is emerging as an influential global rulemaker.

Nor has this chapter presented evidence that European states fail to act in self-interested ways. Altruism has not trumped egoism. However, there is reason to question whether the rational actor models commonly employed by integration theorists, and in international relations more generally, give us a complete picture about how interests are formed and how nation-states in Europe configure their interests in different institutional settings. The reason, as sketched in this chapter, is at a deeper level of basic actor properties – at the level of social identities and roles – what counts as 'the self' has altered the causal and constitutive processes of how interests are conceptualized, articulated, and defended. The focus of this chapter has been how the institutional framework of contemporary Europe impacts national interests and how researchers study the process of national interest formation. If theories of international relations 'are generally uncomfortable evoking the language of community to understand international politics' (Adler and Barnett, 1998: 3), then Europe today offers ample grounds to reconsider when and how this might change. Europe has forged a different kind of sovereignty, and in the process, a different kind of nation-state and a different kind of national interest. The identity of 'nation-state' has become inextricably intertwined with that of 'member-state' (Laffan, 1998; Sbragia, 1994). Whether we label this an enlightened sense of self-interest based on internalized appropriateness standards, or identification with collective decision making, or soft rationalism, or something else, the implications are far reaching for how we study and conceptualize national interests in this institutional environment. Not all brands of multilateralism are alike, and Europe's version clearly illustrates how a nominal definition would miss deeper and more basic constitutive effects on members.

Europe's brand of multilateralism fits nicely the interpretation offered by Kratochwil (1993: 444): 'Multilateralism is constituted by distinct normative principles possessing a generative logic of its own.' Echoing this view is Katzenstein's argument that institutions 'offer a normative context that constitutes actors and provides a set of norms in which the reputation of actors acquires meaning and value' (1997: 12–13). Perhaps the leading example of this in both observable behavior and in stark contrast to the past, is postwar Germany. Peter Katzenstein's labels for postwar Germany as a 'semi-sovereign' state (Katzenstein, 1987) and a 'tamed power' (Katzenstein, 1997) are apt in this regard. As an identity marker, Europe's true Other is not Turkey, radical Islam, or American culture, but as Thomas Risse has argued, 'Europe's "other" became Germany's own past' (2003: 498). European nationalism has cognitively evolved, and postwar integration has had what Joseph Weiler calls a 'civilizing effect on intra-European statal intercourse' (1992: 38).

In resolving the 'German problem,' Germany became an exemplar of Europe's new sovereignty understandings, and the degree of internalization of membership norms and appropriateness standards runs deeper and across a wider section of elite attitudes than perhaps anywhere in Europe today. In a recent article on Germany's new national assertiveness under the grand coalition government led by Chancellor Angela Merkel, Charles Grant is cited as observing: 'There has been a secular trend over the last 15 years for German political leaders to be less dewy-eyed about Europe, but there remains a deep-rooted view that greater European unity in Germany's national interest.'[10]

As diehards to Europe's brand of multilateralism Germany offers leadership by example for others to follow. German self-definitions of interest include an intangible commitment to Europe, an empirical fact that crosses all possible partisan, public-private, subnational (Länder), and temporal (Cold War, post-Cold War) lines (Pond, 1996; Risse and Englemann-Martin, 2002). Jeffrey Anderson calls this Germany's 'reflexive support for an exaggerated multilateralism' (1997: 85). And as Risse puts it, 'to be a "good German" meant to be a "good European" and to wholeheartedly support European integration efforts' (2003: 498). Seen from this perspective, we gain a richer understanding of Germany's leadership role in Europe and the European Union in particular. Rather than simplistically assume Germany is Europe's regional hegemon,[11] the interpretation offered here helps us understand the legitimacy underlying Germany's regional role. Germany leads by example utilizing a 'culture of restraint' (Katzenstein, 1997: 2). Germany's commitment to the euro is all but impossible to account for in instrumental terms; it is only by accounting for Germany's self-definition of identity and the collective macroeconomic policy environment that we can understanding the creation of the eurozone (Kaelbaerer, 2005). Another unambiguous example is Germany's accepted, yet domestically controversial, role as the paymaster to the EU's budget. Why has Germany restrained from either pushing for a British-style rebate or ending Britain's 'right' to a permanent rebate? Does Berlin calculate that such demands would not work or would carry other unacceptable costs? Or does Berlin deem such behavior as inappropriate given Germany's role in the EU and Europe? The answer is a British reputation as 'awkward partner' would have more than just reputational costs for Germany, it would be inconsistent with the Germany's own understanding of the 'self'. According to Anderson, 'preserving multilateralism meant satisfying partners' expectations about appropriate German conduct, which included footing the bill with little regard for the net return' (1997: 85). Germany's motivation for such self-sacrifice is undoubtably a blend of both reputational calculations and appropriateness standards which brings us full circle to the research challenges of studying interests in so dense an institutional environment as Europe today. There is a growing appreciation among scholars who study Europe, mirroring a wider trend in IR, to move away from 'either/or' theories towards 'both/and' research designs. In Peter Katzenstein's words, 'We can adequately understand the world of power and interest in Europe only when we see power and interest not simply as attributes of distinctive actors, Germany *and* Europe, but as aspects of relationships that place Germany *in* Europe, through institutions that tame power' (1997: 6). The remarkable postar reconstruction of European states in a voluntary process of deeper integration reinvented meanings of sovereignty, and in the process, the meanings of the self and interest.

NOTES

1 For comments on earlier drafts, I thank Chris Rumford and David R. Elkins.

2 The widely used distinction between a logic of consequences and a logic of appropriateness was originally developed by March and Olsen (1989, 1998).

3 *The Economist*, 'Europe After Communism: Ten Years Since the Wall Fell,' November 1999: 22.

4 *Financial Times*, 'EU Invitation to Putin a Blunder, Diplomats Say,' October 16, 2006.

5 I borrow the 'vulgar' rationalist imagery from Andrew Moravcsik (2001: 228) where he argues that critics of rationalism often target a straw figure rather than a 'sophisticated rationalist alternative' (ibid.: 239).

6 Nor is this diplomatic convention unique to the EU's institutions; on the European Space Agency, see Zabusky (1995) and on NATO, including the development of a 'NATO spirit', see Zartman and Berman (1982).

7 See Jupille *et al.* (2003: 27–8) for a discussion of how 'paradigmatic privileging' 'tilts the playing field in favor of the theoretical first mover'.

8 Abstentions are a political gesture to signal dissatisfaction with some aspect of a proposal without casting a 'no' vote.

9 The *Financial Times*, 31 January 2003, London Edition.

10 *Financial Times*, 'Germany's EU Fatigue Ruffles Feathers Among Brussels Elite,' September 21, 2006.

11 For example, Mattli portrays Germany as the EU's 'undisputed leader' (1999: 56; cf. pp. 100–5). For a more nuanced view of leadership in the EU, see W. Wallace (2005: 492–93).

REFERENCES

Adler, E. (1998) 'Seeds of peaceful change: The OSCE's Security Community-Building Model', in E. Adler and M. Barnett (eds) *Security Communities*. Cambridge: Cambridge University Press, pp. 119–160.

Adler, E. and Barnett, M. (1998) 'Security communities in theoretical perspective', in E. Adler and M. Barnett (eds) *Security Communities*. Cambridge: Cambridge University Press, pp. 3–28.

Anderson, J. (1997) 'Hard interests, soft power, and Germany's changing role in Europe', in P. Katzenstein (ed.) *Tamed Power: Germany in Europe*. Ithaca, NY: Cornell University Press, pp. 80–107.

Biersteker, T. (2002) 'State, sovereignty and territory', in W. Carlsnaes, T. Risse and B. Simmons (eds) *Handbook of International Relations*. London: Sage, pp. 157–176.

Bull, H. (1977/2002) *The Anarchical Society: A Study of Order in World Politics*, 3rd edn. New York: Columbia University Press.

Calleo, D. (2004) 'The broken west', *Survival*, 46 (3): 29–38.

Caporaso, J. (1996) 'The European Union and forms of state: westphalian, regulatory, or post-modern?', *Journal of Common Market Studies*, 34 (1): 29–52.

Checkel, J. (2001) 'From meta- to substantive theory? Social constructivism and the study of Europe', in J. Checkel and A. Moravcsik, A. 'Forum section: a constructivist research program in EU studies?', *European Union Politics*, 2 (2): 219–249.

Checkel, J. (2003) '"Going native" in Europe? Theorizing social interaction in European institutions', *Comparative Political Studies*, 36 (1–2): 209–231.

Checkel, J. (2005) 'International institutions and socialization in Europe: Introduction and framework', *International Organization*, 59 (4): 801–826.

Checkel, J. (ed.) (2007) *International Institutions and Socialization in Europe*. Cambridge: Cambridge University Press.

Cowles, M., Caporaso, J. and Risse, T. (eds) (2001) *Transforming Europe: Europeanization and Domestic Change*. Ithaca, NY: Cornell University Press.

Den Boer, M. and Wallace, W. (2000) 'Justice and home affairs: integration through incrementalism?', in H. Wallace and W. Wallace (eds) *Policy-Making in the European Union*, 3th edn. Oxford: Oxford University Press, pp. 493–519.

Eising, R. (2002) 'Policy learning in embedded negotiations: explaining EU electricity liberalization', *International Organization*, 56 (1): 85–120.

Elgström, O. (2003) 'The honest broker? The presidency as mediator', in O. Elgström (ed.) *European Union Council Presidencies: A Comparative Perspective*. London: Routledge, pp. 38–53.

Fearon, J. and Wendt, A. (2002) 'Rationalism v. constructivism: a skeptical view', in W. Carlsnaes *et al.* (eds) *Handbook of International Relations*. London: Sage, pp. 52–72.

Guiraudon, V. (2003) 'The constitution of a European immigration policy domain: a political sociology approach', *Journal of European Public Policy*, 10 (2): 263–282.

Hayes-Renshaw, F. and Wallace, H. (2006) *The Council of Ministers*, 2nd edn. New York: Palgrave Macmillan.

Heisenberg, D. (2006) 'Informal Bargaining meets formal modeling in the Council of Ministers', Discussion paper for the workshop *Who Governs in the Council of Ministers*, Robert Schuman Centre for Advanced Studies, Florence, 19–20 May 2006.

Hurd, I. (1999) 'Legitimacy and authority in international politics', *International Organization*, 53 (2): 379–408.

Jacoby, W. (2004) *The Enlargement of the European Union and NATO: Ordering from the Menu in Central Europe*. Cambridge: Cambridge University Press.

Jupille, J., Caporaso, J., and Checkel, J. (2003) 'Integrating institutions: rationalism, constructivism, and the study of the European Union', *Comparative Political Studies*, 36 (1/2): 7–41.

Kaelberer, M. (2005) 'Deutschemark nationalism and Europeanized identity: exploring identity aspects of Germany's adoption of the euro', *German Politics*, 14 (3): 283–296.

Kahler, M. (1998) 'Rationality in international relations', *International Organization*, 52 (4): 919–941.

Katzenstein, P. (1987) *Policy and Politics in West Germany: The Growth of a Semisovereign State*. Philadelphia, PA: Tempel University Press.

Katzenstein, P. (1997) *Tamed Power: Germany in Europe*. Ithaca, NY: Cornell University Press.

Katzenstein, P. (2005) *A World of Regions: Asia and Europe in the American Imperium*. Ithaca, NY: Cornell University Press.

Kelley, J. (2004) 'International actors on the domestic scene: membership conditionality and socialization by international institutions', *International Organization*, 58 (3): 425–458.

Kelley, J. (2006) 'New wine in old wineskins: promoting political reforms through the new European neighbourhood policy', *Journal of Common Market Studies*, 44 (1): 29–55.

Keohane, R. (2002) 'Ironies of sovereignty: the European Union and the United States', *Journal of Common Market Studies*, 40 (4): 743–765.

Keohane, R. and Hoffmann, S. (1991) 'Institutional change in Europe in the 1980s', in R. Keohane and S. Hoffmann (eds) *The New European Community: Decisionmaking and Institutional Change*. Boulder: Westview Press, pp. 1–39.

Krasner, S. (1999) *Sovereignty: Organized Hypocrisy*. Princeton, NJ: Princeton University Press.

Kratochwil, F. (1993) 'Norms versus numbers: multilateralism and the rationalist and reflexivist approaches to institutions – a unilateral plea for communicative rationality', in J. Ruggie (ed.) *Multilateralism Matters: The Theory and Praxis of an Institutional Form*. New York: Columbia University Press, pp. 443–474.

Laffan, B. (1998) 'The European Union: a distinctive model of internationalization', *Journal of European Public Policy*, 5 (2): 235–253.

Laffan, B. (2004) 'The European Union and its institutions as "identity builders"', in R. Herrmann, T. Risse and M. Brewer (eds) *Transnational Identities: Becoming European in the EU*. Lanham, MD: Rowman and Littlefield, pp. 75–96.

Lax, D. and Sebenius, J. (1986) *The Manager as Negotiator: Bargaining for Cooperation and Competitive Gain*. New York: Free Press.

Legro, J. (1996) 'Culture and preferences in the international cooperation two-step', *American Political Science Review*, 90 (1): 118–137.

Lewis, J. (2003) 'Informal integration and the supranational construction of the council', *Journal of European Public Policy*, 10 (6): 996–1019.

Lewis, J. (2005) 'The Janus face of Brussels: socialization and everyday decision making in the European Union', *International Organization*, 59 (4): 937–971.

Lindberg, L. and Scheingold, S. (1970) *Europe's Would-Be Polity: Patterns of Change in the European Community*. Englewood Cliffs, NJ: Prentice-Hall.

March, J. and Olsen, J. (1989) *Rediscovering Institutions: The Organizational Basis of Politics*. New York: Free Press.

March, J. and Olsen, J. (1998) 'The institutional dynamics of international political orders', *International Organization*, 52 (4): 943–969.

Mattli, W. (1999) *The Logic of Regional Integration: Europe and Beyond*. Cambridge: Cambridge University Press.

Milner, H. (1999) *Interests, Institutions, and Information: Domestic Politics and International Relations*. Princeton, NJ: Princeton University Press.

Moravcsik, A. (1993) 'Preferences and power in the European Community: a liberal intergovernmentalist approach', *Journal of Common Market Studies*, 31 (4): 473–523.

Moravcsik, A. (1998) *The Choice for Europe: Social Purpose and State Power From Messina to Maastricht*. Ithaca, NY: Cornell University Press.

Moravcsik, A. (2001) 'Bringing constructivist integration theory out of the clouds: has it landed yet?' in J. Checkel and A. Moravcsik 'Forum section: a constructivist research program in EU studies?', *European Union Politics*, 2 (2): 219–249.

Moravcsik, A. (2002) 'In defence of the 'democratic deficit': reassessing legitimacy in the European Union', *Journal of Common Market Studies*, 40 (4): 603–624.

Neyer, J. (2003) 'Discourse and order in the EU: A deliberative approach to multi-level governance', *Journal of Common Market Studies*, 41 (4): 687–706.

Niemann, A. (2004) 'Between communicative action and strategic action: The Article 113 Committee and the negotiations on the WTO Basic Telecommunications Services Agreement', *Journal of European Public Policy*, 11 (3): 379–407.

Olsen, J. (2002) 'The many faces of Europeanization', *Journal of Common Market Studies*, 40 (5): 921–952.

Pempel, T.J. (ed.) (2005) *Remapping East Asia: The Construction of a Region*. Ithaca, NY: Cornell University Press.

Pollack, M. (2000) 'The end of creeping competence? EU policy-making since Maastricht', *Journal of Common Market Studies*, 38 (3): 519–538.

Pollack, M. (2007) 'Rational choice and EU politics', in K. Jørgensen, M. Pollack, and B. Rosamond (eds) *The Handbook of European Union Politics*. New York: Sage. Pages refer to the ARENA Working Paper version, No. 12, October 2006.

Pond, E. (1996) 'Germany finds its niche as a regional power'. *Washington Quarterly*, 19 (1): 25–44.

Puetter, U. (2006) *The Eurogroup: How a Secretive Group of Finance Ministers Shape European Economic Governance*. Manchester: Manchester University Press.

Puetter, U. (2007) 'Intervening from outside: the role of EU finance ministers in the constitutional politics', *Journal of European Public Policy*, 14 (8): 1293–1310.

Risse, T. (2003) 'The euro between national and European identity', *Journal of European Public Policy*, 10 (4): 487–505.

Risse, T. and Engelmann-Martin, D. (2002) 'Identity politics and European integration: the case of Germany', in A. Pagden (ed.) *The Idea of Europe: From Antiquity to the European Union*. Cambridge: Cambridge University Press, pp. 287–316.

Ruggie, J. (1998) *Constructing the World Polity: Essays on International Institutionalization*. New York: Routledge.

Ruggie, J. (1993) 'Multilateralism: the anatomy of an institution', *International Organization*, 46 (2): 561–598.

Sandholtz, W. (1993) 'Choosing union: monetary politics and Maastricht', *International Organization*, 47 (1): 1–39.

Sbragia, A. (1994) 'From 'nation-state' to 'member-state': the evolution of the European Community', In P. Lützeler (ed.) *Europe After Maastricht: American and European Perspectives*. Providence, RI: Berghahn Books, pp. 69–87.

Scharpf, F. (1997) *Games Real Actors Play: Actor-Centered Institutionalism in Policy Research*. Boulder, CO: Westview Press.

Scharpf, F. (2006) 'The joint-decision trap revisited', *Journal of Common Market Studies*, 44 (4): 845–864.

Schimmelfennig, F. (2003) *The EU, NATO and the Integration of Europe: Rules and Rhetoric*. Cambridge: Cambridge University Press.

Schmidt, V. (2005) 'The EU 'polity' and the Europeanization of national polities', in N. Jabko and C. Parsons (eds) *The State of the European Union: With US or Against US? European Trends in American Perspective*, vol. 7. Oxford: Oxford University Press, pp. 411–438.

Schmitter, P. (1996) 'Imagining the future of the Euro-polity with the help of new concepts', in G. Marks, F. Scharpf, F., P. Schmitter, and W. Streeck (eds) *Governance in the European Union*. London: Sage, pp. 121–150.

Slaughter, A-M. (2004) *A New World Order*. Princeton, NJ: Princeton University Press.

Smith, M. (2004) *Europe's Foreign and Security Policy: The Institutions of Cooperation*. Cambridge: Cambridge University Press.

Smith, M. (1998) 'Rules, transgovernmentalism, and the expansion of European political cooperation', in W. Sandholtz and A. Stone Sweet (eds) *European Integration and Supranational Governance*. Oxford: Oxford University Press, pp. 304–333.

Sperling, J. (ed.) (1999) *Two Tiers or Two Speeds? The European Security Order and the Enlargement of the European Union and NATO*. Manchester: Manchester University Press.

Stasavage, D. (2004) 'Open-door or closed door? Transparency in domestic and international bargaining', *International Organization*, 58 (2): 667–703.

Stasavage, D. (2006) 'Does transparency make a difference? The example of the Council of Ministers', in D. Heald and C. Hood, C. (eds) *Transparency, The Key To Better Governance?* New York: Oxford University Press).

Thomas, D. (2006) 'The negotiated construction of EU foreign policy and external relations', Paper prepared for the conference *The Negotiation of EU External Relations: From Divergent Preferences to Common Policies?*, University of Pittsburgh, 25–27 January 2007.

Waever, O. (1995) 'Identity, integration and security: solving the sovereignty puzzle in EU Studies', *Journal of International Affairs*, 48 (2): 389–431.

Wallace, H. (2005) 'An institutional anatomy and five policy modes', in H. Wallace, W. Wallace, and M. Pollack (2005) *Policy-Making in the European Union*, 5th edn. Oxford: Oxford University Press, pp. 49–90.

Wallace, H., Wallace, W., and Pollack, M. (2005) *Policy-Making in the European Union*, 5th edn. Oxford: Oxford University Press.

Wallace, W. (2005) 'Post-sovereign governance: The EU as a partial polity', in H. Wallace, W. Wallace and M. Pollack (2005) *Policy-Making in the European Union*, 5th edn. Oxford: Oxford University Press, pp. 483–503.

Weiler, J. (1991) 'The transformation of Europe', *Yale Law Journal*, 100 (2): 2403–2483.

Weiler, J. (1992) 'After Maastricht: community legitimacy in post-1992 Europe', in W.J. Adams (ed.) *Singular Europe: Economy and Polity of the European Community After 1992*. Ann Arbor: University of Michigan Press.

Wendt, A. (1994) 'Collective identity formation and the international state', *American Political Science Review*, 88 (2): 384–396.

Youngs, R. (2004) 'Normative dynamics and strategic interests in the EU's external identity', *Journal of Common Market Studies*, 42 (2): 415–432.

Zabusky, S. (1995) *Launching Europe: An Ethnography of European Cooperation in Space Science*. Princeton, NJ: Princeton University Press.

Zartman, I. and Berman, M. (1982) *The Practical Negotiator*. New Haven: Yale University Press.

8

Markets

Michelle Egan

In the comparative political economy of Europe, there is scarcely a topic more contested or controversial than the extent to which ongoing processes of integration and globalization have eroded the boundaries of market and state (Berger and Dore, 1996; Weiss, 1998). Efforts to reform markets in Europe have been ubiquitous. Even where there have been crucial needs to enhance state capacity, consolidate democracy and rule of law, and improve the functioning of public institutions, there has also been a focus on ensuring the performance and operation of the market as well. Although there has been a huge literature on the market in different disciplines, drawing on a range of methods and tools, there has been a sharp distinction between those who focus on understanding the development and efficiency of different types of political–economic system and those who focus on the normative implications of specific political–economic institutions and policies. In the former, scholars use the techniques of economic analysis to understand the phenomena of market systems (Downs, 1957; Olsen, 1965). In the latter, scholars focus on understanding the norms and practices of market institutions, and emphasize the role of social relations and institutions in markets (Duina, 2006;

Swedberg, 1994). Since markets represent an important economic institution in society, the focus of this chapter is to understand the complexity of changes in markets in contemporary Europe, aided by the seminal work of Karl Polanyi. In doing so, the chapter follows his argument that markets cannot be construed as self-regulating: they are always constituted by framework conditions that cannot be set by the markets themselves (Polanyi, 1944).

The chapter begins with a discussion of the construction of markets, and emphasizes the extensive institutional support that structures market relations. It then highlights how the process of state building and market building are interlinked, before providing a comprehensive analysis of different market developments in Europe. As the nineties were the decade of market-making both in Eastern and Western Europe, this means focusing on economic adjustment underway in Central and Eastern Europe, and the economic adjustment in Western Europe in response to pressures of integration and globalization that have reduced the policy autonomy of nation-states (Mosley, 2003). Attention is given to the organizational and institutional innovations in markets and the remaking of states in order to constitute, preserve, and maintain market capitalism. Yet even as countries experience endogenous and exogenous pressures, there are variations in state responses to pressures for economic modernization and change. It is essential to examine distinctive national economic responses to internationalization of markets forces rendered by globalization, as well as the processes of European integration that have played a crucial role in providing the legal base, organizational structure and political inducements towards closer economic cooperation. The chapter then draws attention to the contestation surrounding markets, and concludes with some suggested directions for future research.

MARKETS AS INSTITUTIONS

Sociologists, political scientists and economists have developed different approaches to markets, to the role that institutions play in the economic process, to what is typically regulated in a market, and to the rules and social relations that underpin markets (Swedberg and Nee, 2005). Yet markets remains ambiguous, and are often discussed in many different conceptual forms, and analyzed by different theories, concepts, and models. Markets can be understood to consist of interconnected economies that include both formal and informal markets, as well as different forms such as labor, goods, capital, and service markets. Yet, consistent with the early foundations of the field, states and markets are part of the overall process of governance, and thus we cannot separate the public domain of politics and the private domain of markets in Europe (Underhill, 2003). The promotion of economic growth and development, the organizational activities and architecture of markets (Fligstein, 1990, 2002; the relationship between states, regimes, and markets (Haggard 2000; Strange, 1988); and the structural power relations within and across states (Gill, 1995) are central issues in European political economy.

The argument throughout this chapter is that markets are social institutions, created and sustained by political authority. Markets are always constituted by framework conditions that cannot be set by the markets themselves. Not only has 'the market' been perceived and represented differently in different epochs; it has also been experienced differently, brought into being within dissimilar political and social settings, generating new political economic structures to govern markets in Europe.

That the state plays a key role in structuring markets is a key theme in many political, sociological, and historical studies. Globalization may limit the boundaries of state action, but this does not necessarily mean that there will not be a role for states to play in structuring markets. Following Polanyi, 'markets' have specific attributes, which can be manipulated by government mechanisms in order to regulate economic activities, and particularly to maintain trust and legitimacy in the economic system. These develop-ments can be grouped under the heading of 'market-creating', 'market-facilitating', 'market-regulating' and 'market-replacing' activities in which European governments at local, state, and international level have sought to respond to a variety of challenges that must be met to sustain efficient and equitable markets. Here, issues of market regulation are considered to be inseparable from the broader context of governance, with an appreciation of the role of the government in achieving these goals.[1] For much of the postwar period the state in Europe has served as the primary mechanism for resource allocation. Across Europe, government has played a critical role in investment in infrastructure and human capital, ensuring property rights, maintaining entry for new participants or competitors, directly owning and operated enterprises to ensure public goods, and has increasingly sought to secure or maintain entry into all aspects of economic life for market citizens.

ECONOMIC REFORM AND CHANGE IN WESTERN EUROPE

Following the tradition of political economy in sociology and political science, the most prominent approach to understanding markets in Europe has focused on the different models of market organization and economic governance in Europe. By far the most influential early analysis was Shonfield's *Modern Capitalism* in which he drew attention to the different economic paths taken by advanced industrial states. Subsequently, Schmitter focused attention in the 1970s on the different organized relations between state, business, and labor under corporatism (Schmitter, 1979), as did Katzenstein in *Small States and World Markets* in the 1980s where he linked such domestic economic policies and practices to external economic forces and the global economic system. While this earlier period focused on the pursuit of state- and corporatist-led development, policy shifts over the ensuing 20 years towards more market-oriented reforms meant that the different styles of capitalism that were initially characterized by increased rates of growth, modernization of economies, and interventionism in economic policy (Shonfield, 1965) have changed dramatically. The work of Andrew Shonfield linking different postwar economic strategies to economic performance is still relevant today although the regulation and characteristics of those markets has changed.

In the earlier era the implied commitment to a free market economy, stressing the virtues of competition and greater efficiencies, was balanced by a widespread acceptance of dirigisme and intervention. Across Western Europe, the legitimacy of democratic capitalism was maintained through the explicit compromise between markets and social protection (Polanyi, 1944).[2] A key factor in generating political support and legitimacy for economic policies was the pursuit of an acceptable distribution of tangible benefits through different welfare regimes

(Esping-Anderson, 1993). By supplying important collective goods, promoting wage bargaining, and stable exchange rates, many corporatist economies were considered able to overcome problems of social unrest and enhance productivity (Katzenstein, 1985; Scharpf, 1991). By supplying selective credit, economic planning, and industrial policy, many state-led economies were considered crucial in promoting economic development and modernization. By remaining detached from business, emphasizing self-regulation and voluntary coordination, many liberal models tended to emphasize shareholder value and private financial capital without the corresponding investment in technology or human resources (Hall, 1986).

However, as the favorable Keynesian policy-environment that characterized many European economies collapsed in the mid-1970s and 1980s, demand style economic management was replaced by supply-side measures. Even while international economic changes drove the movement towards a free market orientation, national solutions had domestic political, social, and electoral logics of their own. Pressures from global and domestic socioeconomic change prompted major policy and coalitional shifts in party politics (Heinisch, 2005; Jones, forthcoming) Yet the recurrent oil-price shocks, and the ensuing debt crisis, which aggravated the tensions of the postwar order of finance, trade, and Fordist production, generated a reorganization of production and capital (Goldthorpe, 1984). Many states in Europe clustered around a common set of changes that included fixed exchange rates and monetary stability, privatization of state-owned enterprises, and financial and trade liberalization. Since states could no longer use trade policy, competitive devaluations, and monetary policy to adjust, the liberalization of financial systems and the opening of the domestic market created major economic opportunities for competitive firms. Across Europe economies privatized, market mechanisms were adopted, and trade and financial regimes were deregulated, giving credence to the conventional wisdom that market forces have been on the rise during the last two decades (Mistral, 2006; Pontusson, 2005; Schmidt, 2002). Cross-border goods and service liberalization, import penetration, and capital mobility have all served as a catalyst for neoliberal values, undermining traditional concerns for social cohesion and reducing the role of labor market organizations (Heinisch, 2000). Focusing on economic growth dynamics, the changing role of the state, and welfare and labor reform enables us to consider a number of significant changes in the organization and operation of markets in Europe.

ECONOMIC GROWTH DYNAMICS

Over the past decade, the strong connection between institutions (including those of government) and economic performance has been a central issue, particularly as economic growth has been sluggish over the past 25 years in comparison to the postwar golden era (Pontusson, 2005: 1). Some European states are in better shape, having demonstrated greater ability to reform and meet the challenges of globalization. Varying national performances led scholars to study the impact and effects of integration and globalization on the sustainability of different national models of capitalism.[3] Known as the 'varieties of capitalism' debate (e.g. Berger and Dore, 1996; Crouch and Streeck, 1997; Hollingsworth and Boyer, 1997; Hall and Soskice, 2001; cf. Kitschelt et al., 1999), this research outlines the institutional and social structure of the economy in industrial countries, focusing on explaining the resilience of distinctive national models based on economic performance, state capacity, and institutional embeddedness (Zysman, 1994). These scholars point to macro-level differences in wage bargaining institutions, corporate governance, tax and welfare regimes, financial markets and production regimes to explain the continued variation in national

economic systems (see e.g. Soskice, 1999; Thelan, 2004). They also highlight the micro-level variations in terms of social capital and interpersonal trust to explain different economic outcomes (Putnam, 1993).

Based on the new economics of organization, this literature develops a distinction between two modes of coordination, one based on competitive markets and the other on strategic interaction (Hall and Soskice, 2001). In the former, the liberal market economy (LME) operates through competitive markets and formal contracts. In the latter, the coordinated market economy (CME) produces strategic interaction between firms and other actors. LMEs have high stock market capitalization, low employment protection, and high levels of income inequality, with the market as the main instrument of economic coordination. CMEs, by contrast, have high rates of employment protection, greater emphasis on bank capital, and view non-market relationships as crucial for economic coordination.

As a result, national case studies emphasize whether the character of economic challenges faced such as the shift from manufacturing to services, technological change, and economic liberalization, are best dealt with under different institutional configurations (Hall and Soskice, 2001; Schmidt, 2001, 2002). LME typically respond through market prices and wage adjustments, as well as mobile capital flight, while CME will focus on assets, skills, and productivity in response to pressures. These models rest on institutional complementarities among different spheres of political economy. Yet they tend to focus on equilibrium rather than change, pay less attention to institutional innovation, and may in fact ignore different types of state provision that may constitute alternative models of capitalism (Schmidt, 2003; Wilks, 1996). Models of capitalism enable us to think about what explains different national outcomes in the process of state reshaping, focusing on the political incentives, institutional constraints, and economic influences that affect resource allocation and welfare distribution.

ROLE OF THE STATE

For most of the postwar era, the state has served as the primary mechanism for resource allocation. The changing role of the state in the economy is one of the central shifts in Europe over the past two decades, as fiscal crises, ideological shifts, and economic pressures compelled states to reconsider the role of states. After the oil shocks and recession of the 1970s, losses of state-owned enterprises increased, forcing governments to continue to invest resources and bail out state-owned industries. State owned industries were viewed as core elements of economic policy in which they provided substantial employment opportunities and were considered part of the key public and distributive goods supplied by the state (*services publique*).

Nationalization in Western Europe was the dominant form of public regulation, and so the process of privatization was an ideological shift (Vogel, 1996). Fiscal need served also as a justification for the wave of privatization of public and semi-public enterprises across Europe. Reorganization of public monopolies was designed to increase efficiency, productivity, and competitiveness, create a larger role for market forces, and provide the foundation for increasing competition and technological development (Smith, 2005). Yet privatization also has important political dimensions, and was designed to depoliticize the state sector so that state-owned companies could no longer be used for political patronage and party support, as had been the case in Italy, France, and elsewhere. As the public sector was increasingly subordinated to the logic of market dynamics, the processes of privatization were often contested. The pattern of privatization varied, as states placed different restrictions on foreign ownership, provided substantial financial support for productive restructuring and allowed debt write-offs (Schmidt, 2003). From a form of 'popular capitalism' as in Britain, to the '*noyau dur*' model in France or

voucher privatization as in Eastern Europe (Manzetti, 1999; Neumann and Egan, 1999; Schmidt, 2002), privatization represented a major shift in the interventionist strategies and role of the state.

Yet this does not mean that the state withdraws itself from the economy, as regulation remains an important feature of European economic policy-making. Instead we have seen the emergence of non-majoritarian institutions such as central banks, regulatory agencies, anti-trust authorities, and courts which have become more prominent in the postwar period, most notably in the area of economic management (Majone, 1996; Sbragia, 2003). These institutions which play key roles in the economy operate on the assumption that power should be shared, dispersed, limited, and delegated to experts, transforming traditional patterns of policy-making. Throughout Europe non-majoritarian practices have become more widely used in Western democracies, as majoritarian rule has declined (Anderson, 1999). The functional similarities between delegation in domestic and EU settings suggest that political insulation of certain decisions is the product of compelling political reasons. Such delegation is designed to provide greater efficiency and expertise, and can afford insulation from the more politicized decision-making process, where government policy has often been subject to regulatory capture.

Another change has been the interconnections between state organizations and the organizations of civil society, especially market actors. The growth of such public–private networks can be viewed as a reaction to the limited efficiency of governmental regulation, which is diminishing even further in the face of globalization. Such societal coordination provides alternative mechanisms of economic coordination based on cooperation, mutual interest, and accommodation. It reflects the reality that economic management increasingly is an activity that must involve a range of actors, both public and private, and that economic decision-making is the product of involvement, not imposition, as the authority and monopoly of the state is now challenged on several fronts. Just as decentralization and devolution have delegated power downwards, so the processes embodied by globalization have highlighted the importance of non-state actors (Rossenau, 1992). The resulting blurring of functions between public and private has meant that decisions, such as wage bargaining, environmental protocols and accords, and corporate governance practices, involve networks of interests and actors that regulate market practices and business behavior. The shift from command and control to alternative approaches to regulate markets across Europe means that a variety of private and semi-public institutions and organizations can create their own rules and establish both formal and informal market norms and practices, unencumbered by more formal and procedural regulatory requirements. Such interorganizational networks play in economic development both at the national and the global levels. The notion of 'network' as a form of social organization between the state and the market offers a concept that is able to capture such changes in political organization that in effect coordinates markets (Castells, 1996).

WELFARE AND LABOR REFORM

Welfare state retrenchment has generated a vast literature over the past decade (Pierson, 2001). While European welfare states are adapting to globalization and other shocks, the different types of adaptation and reforms reflect different political and welfare institutions. Across Europe, states face strong constraints on their welfare budgets due to the maturation of commitments, and their fiscal problems appear similar even if their welfare regimes are structured differently. Part of that fiscal burden is the result of debt undertaken in the 1970s and 1980s, and the heavy borrowing undertaken by governments means that

they must now service that debt. As a result, Flora's analysis in the 1980s about *Growth to Limits* was borne out (Flora, 1986). Many states are embracing both labor market and welfare reform, using different mechanisms to facilitate adjustment. Many involved tightening of eligibility requirements, shifting from passive to active labor market measures, promoting part-time employment, fostering a variety of training and placement programs, and shifting benefits between different beneficiaries (Levy, 1999). Such a strategy is not without political cost.

Although seeking to address sluggish or even stagnant growth and high levels of structural unemployment, many welfare regimes suffer from insider–outsider cleavages, and face severe fiscal pressures resulting from wage-based contributions. At the national level, anxiety about employment, sustaining employment relations systems and protecting social protection run extremely high (Taylor-Gooby, 1982, 1986). Yet part of the problem of social reform in Europe has focused on the so-called service economy trilemma, or the incompatibility of having simultaneously balanced budgets, low levels of economic inequality and high levels of employment (Iversen and Wren, 1998). The result has been a heterogeneity of welfare state reforms in the 1990s to tackle distinctive welfare regime problems (Zeitlan and Trubek, 2003). However, in welfare policy, state intervention has been critically important in shaping reform outcomes. In this policy area, the state is not constrained by the kinds of legal impediments that it faces in labor-market policy (Hemerijck and Vail, 2005).

Corporatist institutions which were once widely celebrated as models of economic success are now viewed as part of the problem. Despite differences in size and economic performance, social partnerships characterize many Northern economies and have been routinely described as corporatist models (Heinisch, 2000; Katzenstein, 1978; Jones, forthcoming). While the overall framework is determined primarily by consensus, corporatist response strategies to greater pressures for economic modernization, liberalization, and integration vary significantly among states. While Germany, whose economic system underwent a major crisis in the 1990s, has found it difficult to maintain its market position under conditions of high wage costs and limited mobility, Austria has managed to maintain decentralized bargaining and substantial welfare policies, consolidate advantages through macro-level economic coordination, such as, organized decentralization, flexibilization, and a corresponding incomes policy (Heinisch, 2005: 21). Compounded by the pressures of reunification, Germany has also seen a decline in collective bargaining arrangements, growing fragmentation among labor organizations, and the logic of the market increasingly shaping outcomes. Sweden, by contrast, facing fiscal crises in the 1990s, opted for fiscal policy stimulation and wage restraint, and was able to expand the public sector. To the extent that change became unavoidable, the public clearly preferred it to be channeled through the established mechanisms of interest representation and conflict resolution. Important differences in organization, strategies, and objectives between states have played a role in the extent to which social partners have secured a stake in effecting their traditional role in income policy and effective wage coordination. Across Europe, labor relations systems have undergone dramatic changes throughout the 1990s, resulting in what Rhodes has called 'competitive corporatism' (Rhodes, 2001).

Thus small European states that follow corporatist patterns have sought to bring flexibility to both labor markets and the welfare state by specialized production strategies, negotiating among social partners, and maintaining large welfare states to redistributive and alleviate adjustment costs. However, surprisingly, Portugal, Italy, Spain, and Ireland also adopted a similar strategy, by introducing social pacts and negotiated bargaining introducing flexible hiring and firing practices in the private sector (flexicurity) to improve market competition and economic growth (Perez, 2000), and they have promoted changes in fiscal policy and patterns of foreign direct investment. The effect is both convergence in macro-economic policy under a single currency and social contracts, but with continued divergence in labor market regulation, corporate governance, and other domestically protected sectors, which affects their ability to adjust different policy areas.

A final but by no means insignificant change in the postwar period has been the organization of production. Changing modes of production have been associated with the work on 'flexible production' (e.g. Piore and Sabel, 1984). This has focused attention on the role and existence of industrial districts and the decentralizing impact of some new technologies and production practices. Such practices have primarily been associated with the most vibrant parts of the Italian and German economies, where industrial districts with specialized firms engage in a fairly radical decentralization of production, operating on the basis of informal enforcement and sharing norms that are based on reciprocity and trust (Farrell, 2005). Here market relationships are based on flexibility and cooperation where norms of trust and reciprocity supplement more formal organizational rules and practices (Farrell and Knight, 2003).

Cultural factors have often been a key explanation in determining the context in which such forms of cooperation evolve (Trigglia, 1986). As alternative patterns of industrialization have evolved in Europe, the centrality of regional networks and supporting institutions have led to debate about the role played in economic growth by the shift from mass production to 'flexible specialization' (Locke, 1995; Piore and Sabel, 1984). Critics argue that these new patterns of capitalist development, in which production is increasingly reorganized into small-scale, decentralized and more flexible economic units, has (and is still) associated with the informalization of employment relations and atypical employment thereby undermining traditional models of labor solidarity.

ECONOMIC REFORM AND CHANGE IN CENTRAL AND EASTERN EUROPE

In the former socialist countries, the disintegration of state socialism in the 1990s left an ambiguous political and economic order. The major simultaneous changes of democratic and market transition meant that postcommunist states disengaged themselves from the state socialist path of modernization and entered the road of market economy and capitalist transformations. Much of the literature on Central and Eastern Europe has focused on the transformation from a planned to a market economy, and the political effects of market transition and economic reform (Appel, 2004; Hellman, 1998; Orrenstein, 1996; Murrell, 1992; Schamis, 2001; Stark and Bruszt, 1998; World Bank, 1996).

Specifically, it has focused on the politics of economic adjustment, with debate centered initially among economists on the optimal speed of reform, and specifically whether shock therapy or more gradual reform worked better in prompting market capitalism (Sachs, 1984). Shock therapy advocates were associated with international institutions promoted rapid liberalization, privatization, and stabilization, while more evolutionary advocates argued that specific institutions such as legal and regulatory agencies were critical for a functioning market economy (Murrell, 1992). While the former highlight the pressure of international markets, and subjected firms to massive exogenous shocks, the latter emphasized the effect of domestic institutions that makes change less automatic due to ongoing transaction costs and path dependence.

The main perspective was that the state should reduce its role within the economy and economic activity should be freed from state intervention. Across Central Europe, this process of liberalization has proceeded via many routes with the institution of private

property being crucial (Lane 2006; Schamis, 2001). The process of privatization was designed to reduce the role of the state and accelerate corporate ownership and remove restrictions on foreign direct investment. Yet the privatization process, as well as the divergent forms of governance that emerged, reflect weak property rights and legal protections. While market reforms generated heterogeneity in ownership structures and corporate strategies, the process resulted in a struggle over the allocation of wealth and income played an entirely negative role in the process of economic reform. Such predatory groups make corruption a central problem in postcommunist states.

After nearly a decade of transition, the process has not produced the market reform and competition expected. In many instances, privatization in Central and Eastern Europe has meant continuous state control over partially privatized firms (McDermott, 2002). Instead of creating a functioning market order, state institutions fail to provide collective public goods as they tend to institutionalize past patterns and practices that may in fact elevate particularistic interests (Schamis, 2001). Because of sucsh partial reforms, states have not fully adopted the necessary legal and regulatory framework to preserve and create a functioning market economy. In emphasizing market reform, the fragility of the rule of law figures centrally in the Central and East European literature (Hellman, 1998). While constitutional debates focused mainly on questions related to political legitimacy and institutional design, in some cases the new constitutions weakened state capacity to create and preserve a stable market order (Bruszt, 2000).

As such, attention has now focused on recreating the state to maintain the rule of law, enforce contracts, and ensure effective regulation of economic behavior (Bruszt, 2002). Since the results expected from economic policy reform in transition economies, such as sustained economic growth, widespread prosperity, and democratic reforms have proved elusive in some cases, there has been increased attention to fostering strong public sector organizations. State weakness has contributed to the reform problems, and so the economic transformation undertaken in the context of accession negotiations has focused on creating states with strong administrative capacities to preserve and regulate markets. Economic transformations undertaken in Eastern and Central Europe mostly under the banner of 'Europeanization' has increased focused on the process of adopting, implementing, and sustaining economic reform initiatives (Vachudova, 2005). The result is substantial variation among postsocialist states with the Visegrad states having more market-oriented sectors and a substantial private sector, whereas the transition laggards of Bulgaria and Romania have maintained statist economies rife with corruption (Vachudova, 2005). Just as in Western Europe, there are different models of capitalism due to variation in firm ownership and control, interfirm relations, patterns of production and innovation and the role of the state in the economy varies. In each case, choices are heavily constrained by the institutional and historical context, and so the trajectories of economic development, market reform, and social contracts have been different (Fligstein, 2002; Grabbe, 1998; Stark and Bruszt, 1998). Yet socialist states with their different forms of coordination and ownership than Western societies have also been subject to strong convergent pressures as a result of European integration (Grabbe, 1998; Zysman, 1994).

Despite the significance of international institutions – notably the European Union – as a major source of policy prescriptions and financial redistribution, the emphasis on social justice and redistribution differs in CEE from that of the West European social contract. And here the impact of the welfare state can play a role as the degree of universality and coverage can have a substantial impact in reducing the incentives for a large informal economy in Western Europe whereas resistance to state control generated a significant second economy in Eastern Europe

(Stark, 1989). In Central and Eastern Europe, the process of structural adjustment was also associated with an expansion of employment in the informal economy. The new reality in transition economies is that the informal sector has grown, as social protection systems have receded, unemployment has risen and labor force participation has declined. The informal sector is a critical component of many economies of the Eastern Europe and the former Soviet Union, yet little attention has been given to the market challenges that this poses to newly admitted EU member states. One of the main questions is whether European membership can credibly provide the social and political basis of market economy which continues to be undermined by the rise of the informal economy, state capture, and social marginalization (Brusis, 2005).

EUROPEAN INTEGRATION: CREATING A COMMON MARKET

Scholars have argued extensively about the relationship between Europeanization and globalization (Verdier and Breen, 2001). Some argue that the two are synonymous as they comprise a set of ideas centered around liberalization, deregulation, and privatization which have altered social relations, and generated increased market integration (Katzenstein and Shirashi, 2005; Scharpf, 2002). Others argue that their effects mitigate each other, as regionalism has sought to adapt to and shape the acceleration and transformation of the global economy, and as the erosion of national autonomy has been compensated by closer regional cooperation (Verdier and Breen, 1999; Wallace, 2000). This is very evident in the European case where the European Union has effectively shaped markets both within Europe and beyond through its effort to remove barriers to trade between countries, which are the product of domestic regulations which, intentionally or not, serve as sources of trade friction and stifle market access (Egan, 2001; Young, 2000). But while the European Union has served as a conduit for global forces, by opening member states up to international markets and trade; it has also served as a shield against them, by reducing member-state vulnerability to global economic forces through monetary integration and the single market. The single market has thus been used to promote new principles and norms across a range of policy sectors from competition policy, to environmental sustainability to product and process standards (Egan, 2001; Jones, 2006). Policy areas that were traditionally within the national domain – such as environmental and consumer protection, transportation regimes, telecommunication regulation, regional equality and research – have shifted to the European level. Sociologists focus on the institutions necessary to make markets, and the relational and network features that define relations of competition and cooperation in different settings (Fligstein, 1990). Economists point to such economic coordination as a means of addressing negative externalities, promoting economies of scale and greater contestability of markets (Pelkmans, 2006) whereas political scientists focus on issues of governance and the implications for national systems of an integrated European market and less than integrated European polity. This has led to discussions in law and economics about the trade-offs in promoting market efficiencies and policies promoting social protection and equality given the systemic bias towards negative integration in Europe (Scharpf, 1999).

The economic rationale underlying European integration plays a central role in how the EU functions (Jones, forthcoming). Within Europe itself, the deepening of market integration has continued dramatically over the past two decades, drawing on the legal foundations of the treaties as well as changing perspectives about the role and dynamics of markets, with pro-competitive logics of market liberalization replacing state-led economic development and intervention (Egan, 2001; Hooghe and Marks, 1997).

Such deepening of market integration has not only transformed the structure and organization of industry, through promoting economies of scale, reduced transaction costs, and consolidation and mergers, but has also constrained the regulatory and interventionist tools that member states had utilized in the past (Pelkmans, 2006: 3). Intra-European trade has risen dramatically and foreign direct investment has accelerated. However, the operation of the European market was not left unfettered. The market needed protection not only against private transactions that threatened the fair operation of market processes but also against the abuse of public power with regard to resource allocation, monopolies, and protectionism (Egan, forthcoming). Thus negative and positive integration worked together in this process in which the removal of national barriers to trade required the introduction of new community rules (Scharpf, 1999).

The favorable starting conditions for the European trade liberalization effort in the 1950s and 1960s occurred against the backdrop of the mixed economy and welfare state, which were central components of the postwar settlement (Tsoukalis, 1997). One manifestation of this resurgence of postwar European integration was the rise of so-called intra-industry trade (Grubel and Lloyd, 1975). Yet even with these national policies, it has been politically necessary to provide some sort of fiscal transfers at the European level to ease the effects of competition. These measures include basic investment in underdeveloped regions, suppression of large-scale unemployment, and the coordination of economic policies (see Hooghe, 1998). Most prominently, the absence of market pressures and welfare transfers occurred in agriculture, where the sustained high price support and subsidies that emerged internally were at odds with broader trade liberalization. Trade barriers are indeed extensive, although they are tempered by a variety of preference schemes which give more favorable access terms to developing countries which links trade and development goals, albeit creating discriminatory market practices.

While such economic policies succeeded in promoting national economic growth in the decades immediate following WWII, the tools of national politics were ultimately unable to cope with changes in the international economy. By the 1970s, neocorporatist class compromises and consensual incomes policies, which underpinned Keynesian economic policy, were under immense pressure as government capacity to manage the economy failed (Egan, forthcoming). Such a situation drove subsequent institutional reforms and treaty changes from the mid-1980s onwards, transforming the statist postwar system to a neoliberal project that converged with domestic preferences (cf. Hooghe and Marks, 1997). The framework that has emerged in the European context is one which Gill has argued 'promotes the power of capital through extension and deepening of market values and disciplines' (Gill, 1995).

Much research has focused on the factors promoting market integration and the establishment of an ambitious single market program in which optimistic expectations of the perceived economic benefits of market integration were widely touted. Economists focused on the dynamic and static welfare gains, as well as the impact of more contestable markets on growth and innovation (Pelkmans, 2006). However, attention has now turned to making the single market deliver which has led scholars in public administration to focus on the constraints of decision rules and decision styles that hamper economic coordination. The record shows, however, that creating a single market with free trade in goods, capital, labor, and service markets in which separate national economies has not been easy (Sandholtz and Zysman, 1989). According to Shapiro, the early efforts to establish the common market were essentially driven by negative constitutional law, using the treaty provisions to tackle national laws of the member states that were barriers to free trade (Egan, 2001; Shapiro, 1997). Legal research on the basic relationship between law and the economy has generated significant research on legal norms and decisions, as European case law has opened up opportunities, reducing much of the cost of innovation and entrepreneurship by shifting the focus towards creating the context for open markets and competition. As Conant argues (this volume) law can play a critical role in enabling the economy because economic integration involves a substantive legal and political project that has drawn state and local laws under its purview, while also determining the economic relationship between public intervention and the market and the political relationship between member states and the union (Egan, 2001).

However, across Europe, rules governing markets vary in their precision, formality, and authority (Shapiro, 2000). While earlier research focused on issues of policy formation, greater attention is now given to issues of implementation and compliance in relation to the single market (Falkner *et al.*, 2005; Taalberg, 2002). This focuses on the fit between administrative and regulatory traditions at the national level with that of European policies, the emphasis on compliance, with enforcement and implementation also brings into play the role of administrative law in implementing the regulatory statutes the European Union has enacted. Compliance is further ensured by a range of legal remedies in the European context, with use of both coercive and soft mechanisms to promote European market norms (Berman and Pistor, 2004). Countries facing accession in the Balkans have to organize market and production activities so that local standards and regulations meet EU procedures. In Eastern and Central Europe, reforms of both local government and administrative institutions were crucial given the importance of administrative performance to overarching goals of economic development and transition (Goertz, 2001).

The simultaneous process of deepening and widening of regional integration has fostered both dynamic market development as well as the creation of political institutions (Katzenstein and Shirashi, 2005). Creating a single market is thus an exercise in institutional design in which new governance structures and new patterns of juridification through transnational networks and regimes are emerging (Slaughter, 2004). These alterative modes of governance are explained in part by the challenges of managing production and distribution that followed from the shift from local markets to national and international markets. On the one hand, there has been a greater emphasis on delegation as part of the new public management movement that has sought to foster independent regulatory agencies to administer or implement certain government policies (Radaelli, 2004). Much attention has been given to European agencies, for instance, which have begun to proliferate in recent years, to deal with areas such as social and risk regulation (Chiti, 2002; Gilardi, 2005). This transformation towards a statutory model of regulation is part of a wider phenomenon of delegation to autonomous agencies to enhance the efficiency of outcomes given the complexities of economic governance (Coen and Thatcher, 2005: 1; Majone, 1996).

On the other hand, the delegation to private networks to promote rule enforcement, joint development of rules with public authorities, and voluntary coordination of business practices illustrates the myriad of practices across Europe. As the increasing fragmentation of public authority continues across Europe, both horizontally and vertically, new modes of regulatory governance have emerged in areas that were previously immune from European intervention, including telecommunication, energy, postal services, and railways (Smith, 2005). Industries that were once the domain of public sectors have been privatized, and in many instances open to competition. Internal market rules and competition policy have increasingly encouraged greater competitive pressures, although this has not extended to the remaining services barriers within the European Union (Smith, 2005).

Frustration with low growth and poor economic performance has fostered rising efforts to tackle declining productivity through an integrated approach to competitiveness (Lisbon Agenda, 2000; Sapir, 2006). The Lisbon Agenda is about comprehensive economic reforms and has dominated debates in Europe. As Polanyi anticipated, market considerations are given a very strong hearing in any kind of policy conflict which pits the market against other claims, whether social or environmental rights (Sbragia, 2003). Deepening the internal market, limiting distortions and protectionist behavior, and reducing the regulatory burden on business are all indications that there is no systematic policy reversal with regard to markets. On the one hand, critics argue that the political and legal reforms in the European context are designed to ensure commitment to a specific market order in which economic and political mechanisms are separate, so that economic governance institutionalizes a framework of constraints that promotes the disciplinary power of market forces (Gill, 2002). On the other hand, Sbragia argues that there has been a shift in the role of the state from 'provider of benefits' to 'builder of markets'. Although the ability of national governments to provide welfare benefits and public goods may be diminishing, the regulatory role of the EU in creating and sustaining rules for a functioning market economy has not eroded or diminished (Sbragia, 2001). European integration thus reflects 'an effort to regain some measure of political control over processes of economic globalization that have curtailed national policy instruments' (Oman, 1994: 11, 35; quoted in Katzenstein, 2005).

This development has generated considerable debate about the most appropriate way to govern European markets, with different views about the most efficient and effective regulatory instruments, and their legal rationale and legitimacy (de Búrca, 2003; Dehousse, 2002). Yet the terms of integration reflect contested identities and values. Building popular support is as important as other factors that promote market integration, and economic governance has to deal with politically entrenched and staunchly defended economic practices, sometimes making cooperation difficult. In the current contentious and politicized context, the European Union is still seeking to promote market deepening where serious restrictions and barriers remain. In the end, the European Union has opted for both binding market norms such as liberalization of factor and product markets, price stability and broad economic policy guidelines, while allowing for flexibility in tackling social coordination and unemployment through the open method of coordination that eschews common rules or principles (Zeitlin, 2005). The traditional model of growth promotion within the European Union, based on lowered barriers to trade and intensified competition, has been complemented by promoting structural reforms through benchmarking, innovation, and best practice. This has changed the economic mode towards research, technology, and innovation, and the policy method towards prescription rather than specific actions, rules, and constraints (Erixson, 2005: 255–6).

While the European experience does not represent a template, it highlights the potential and problems of integration (Egan, forthcoming a). The political processes and institutions that evolve – or not – in support of the growth of a single market play an equally important role in the economic successes of the European Union. In other parts of the world, regional economic integration is proceeding, but political integration is either not desired or so limited that many debates about territoriality, sovereignty, and governance have not yet been addressed (Sbragia, 2003). Yet the capacity of governance structures in Europe, both in terms of its substantive and institutional focus, will remain crucial as market pressures will ensure that scholarship focuses on making the single market deliver, and will reinvigorate organizational studies on state capacity and transformation of public administration, as attempts to change basic economic rules by liberalizing public enterprises and marketizing social provisions will ensure that political economy approaches will continue to focus on distributional considerations. It will also open up

research on the impact of the acceleration and broadening of the economic reform process and how it differentially affects a member state and applicant states, given the instruments – both national and European – used to promote macro-economic stabilization, micro-economic structuring and the design of institutions.

CORE ISSUES AND CONCERNS: CONTESTED MARKETS IN EUROPE

Throughout the postwar period, the political and social organization of markets has generated contrasting economic visions and understandings of how markets work, reinforcing the interaction between economic interdependence and institutional context which characterizes the recent effort depicted in the varieties of capitalism literature (Hall and Soskice, 2001; Hay 2004; Kornai, 1992; Shonfield, 1965). The characteristics of these markets differ considerably from one country to another, as well as across different sectors, but they all face pressure to sustain competitive advantage, maintain and deliver collective goods, enhance flexibility and improve productivity, and maintain social peace and partnership in the during process of economic modernization or reform.

Thus while many forms of governance and production regimes remain intact in Western Europe, demonstrating the resilience of existing institutional structures, specific processes of change have undermined the 'embedded liberalism' where countries benefited from the protective barriers of capital exchange controls, fixed but adjustable exchange rates, and variable barriers to trade (Ruggie, 1982). Although much attention has been given to the transformation of embedded liberalism as a result of liberalization, privatization, and deregulation, the overall capacity of states to constitute and maintain market order and enforce competition and market orientation remains crucial (Bruszt, 2002: 54). The relationship between firms and the state and the role of the state in coordinating and monitoring market behavior requires careful attention to the various governance mechanisms to preserve markets. Clearly the nature and intensity of state intervention has changed over the past five decades, but the range of tools and policies that encompass both national and European levels (such as risk capital and venture funds, competition policies) are illustrative of efforts to promote competition and regulation that are profoundly market-oriented (Pelkmans, 2006). The contestation surrounding markets centers on how effective and appropriate is the role of the state in resource allocation and redistribution, and in financing and monitoring industry in a market economy (McDermott, 2002). Thus the state takes many different conceptual forms in Western Europe, even though some of its activities appear to be receding, its value lies in bringing together and influencing society and economy, both in terms of regulatory authority and distributive outcomes (Various, 1994).

That said, preserving the functions of the state remains critical in shaping the Central and East European market context in the postcommunist era. Efforts to uphold property rights, enforce laws, and regulate economic transactions all focus on the state-making role in Central and Eastern Europe. With postcommunist countries making a transition to market capitalism, it was politically expedient for CEE policymakers to claim to be emulating Western models given the influence of international financial institutions and foreign governments that were keen to promote neoliberal economic orthodoxy in CEE (Grabbe, 2000; Orrenstein, 1996). The new policies assumed that markets are essentially the same and yield parallel benefits everywhere without regard for the underlying societies and the characteristics and achievements of the states in need of reform (Portes and Cento, 2003: 24). However, past legacies and industrial networks play a role on economic modernization efforts upon East European markets, and it is debatable whether emerging models

of capitalism are even comparable with advanced economies at all, given the diversity of institutional solutions adopted during postcommunist transition (Stark and Bruszt, 1998). As such, the abandonment of communism in Central and Eastern Europe has not generated convergence around any specific forms of economic exchange, industrial production, or model of capitalism as predicted and supported initially by early writings on postcommunist political economy (Grabbe, 2000; Stark and Bruszt, 1998). Instead, the capacity to foster a strong economic environment through a broad program of privatization has led to differential impacts and distributional consequences and emphasized the relative power of specific economic and political groups (nomenklatura) in society (Aslund, 2001; Neumann and Egan, 1999).

Any analysis of the responsibility of European governments for creating and sustaining markets; that is, of nurturing individual economic choice and of creating a supportive environment for enterprise will find, as the economic historian Douglass North has observed, competent public administration and governance are critical for well-functioning markets since they provide an environment of known, stable, and enforceable rules. Thus, the elements of functioning markets are dependent on the characteristics of the state which means that we need to pay attention to state capacity as government is responsible for overall economic management and performance (Bruszt, 2002). Although globalization is widely viewed as reducing the parameters of economic choice in contemporary Europe, Sbragia argues that the rule of law and well-defined legal and judicial mechanism for resolving conflicts among parties are critical for a market economy (Sbragia 2000, 245). We should not just view the study of markets as being governed by economic incentives and driven solely by mechanisms to reduce transaction costs and increase efficiencies, but rather link the economy with the polity.

At least as important as the regulative capacity of states to ensure economic transactions, is the allocative and distributive capacity of states to deal with problems of social and economic development. The need to assure an acceptable distribution of benefits among states and classes has led European states to consider the social impact of their respective economic development.[4] In Western Europe, such efforts to modify market outcomes to correct market failures and carry out various forms of redistribution generated a substantial welfare state. Subsequent welfare retrenchment has undermined the post war social contract, and placed greater emphasize on market discourse and practices. As a result, social discontent has tended to be aggravated by the arrival of privatization and market liberalization, as privatization reduces public employment which, until now, has been a central component in many models of capitalism in Europe. In Eastern Europe, the welfare state and its restructuring have generated less benefits and narrower entitlements than their Western counterparts. (Bohle and Greskovits, 2004). With higher unemployment, lower wages and low union density, the socioeconomic foundations of the European social model have not emerged in Eastern Europe (Bohle and Greskovits, 2004). At the same time, the mechanism of regulatory competition among European states generated by the internal market further challenges the autonomy of states in the pursuit of traditional functions of governance, such as those inherent in regulatory and redistributive policies (Maduro, 2002; Scharpf, 1999). Yet European integration with its emphasis on market freedom and economic rights has not been compensated by the development of a European welfare state. Thus the 'reliance on markets to solve political and social problems is a savage attack on the principles of citizenship'.(Sassen, 2003). As such, the emphasis on markets has endangered the welfare state, which is viewed by many as an important component of social citizenship (Marshall, 1950), and while states can guarantee the conditions for effective markets to function, the specific mode in which the state carries out this function can vary cross-nationally.

Whether we choose to study the recent transformation of European markets under pressure of globalization or regionalism, or the study of the diverse forms of economic governance and the related diversity in economic and social performance, we need to acknowledge that states are experimenting with organizational and strategic changes nationally and internationally in order to respond to a networked economy and polity (Castells, 1996). In this context, it is important to consider the implications of new governance structures that have emerged in response to liberalization and integration, both at the national and European levels. Deregulation and privatization have not eliminated the tasks and functions of states. Instead they have been accompanied by the emergence of regulatory instruments as a new form of public intervention. The redefinition of the role of the state has in fact resulted in the emergence of the regulatory state across Europe, which has transformed the organization of the economy and (re) embedded the European market through regulation (Levi-Faur, 2005; Majone, 1994; see Grand, this volume).

Against this background, privatization has typically been accompanied by an extraordinarily intensive degree of reregulation and creation of independent regulatory agencies. Most governments have set up independent regulatory agencies and have sought to insulate them from political control through delegation. While independent regulatory agencies have long existed in the United States, the delegation to nonmajoritarian institutions has evolved across Europe into a common institutional model. From monetary policy to utility regulation, European polities rely on the technical expertise of autonomous or insulated agencies that are removed from electoral competition and oversight. While such delegation is inevitable in managing risk in market societies, it generates concerns in terms of accountability and democracy. A similar concern exists in terms of the growing role of self-regulation or delegation of economic tasks to the private sector.

Due to the discrepancy of preferences, concerns about asymmetries of economic and informational power, the 'delegation' of regulatory tasks to non-governmental actors or independent regulatory agencies is accompanied by new concerns with the social responsibility of the economy, its performance and the legitimacy of its governance structures. While the core principles of the EU are market liberalization and economic growth, such efforts to coordinate markets has strengthened the resort to private governance regimes on the transnational level (Egan, forthcoming) This raises questions about the legitimacy of new private forms of juridification in regulating markets, the balance between public and private, and the relationship between states and markets in conditions of complex economic interdependence.

After two decades of seeking to liberate markets, and reduce the role of the state, there is now resistance to these policies based on their actual consequences. Underlying these concerns with governing is the sense that global competition has made societies more aware of their differences in economic performance, and the difficult process of maintaining low unemployment, welfare benefits, and reasonable economic growth. The new political and economic realities, including the collapse of the planned economies in Central and Eastern Europe, the extension of the single European market, and the populist backlash against neoliberal public discourse, has heightened anxiety about the capacity to deal with internal and external pressures.

FUTURE RESEARCH

The discussion about markets is closely associated with another key concept in the literature: governance. Both are concerned with the challenges to the capacity of state autonomy and authority as globalization appears to circumscribe political and economic choices by reducing the impact of territoriality.

While there is general agreement that emerging governance regimes blur the boundaries between public and private authority, the governability debate masks the continued importance of state capacity to preserve, create, and maintain markets. Strong institutions ensuring the rule of law, contract enforcement and the protection of property rights (North, 1990; Schamis, 2001; Bruszt, 2002/3) are central to a well-functioning economy.

The recent interest in governance and markets, and the debate about the nature of the state, reflects a fundamental shift in thinking about the political economy of market relations in Europe. The simultaneity of democratic transition and market capitalism, the advent and extension of the single market, and the internationalization of market forces have drawn attention to tradeoffs and tensions between promoting growth and efficiency, and dealing with equity and distributional impacts.

The discussion to this point should make it clear that an analysis of markets is both empirical and normative. One the one hand, empirically, there are some common trajectories, variable patterns, and divergent outcomes with regard to European markets (Hay, 2004; Schmidt, 2002). This invokes the current debate in political economy between those who see a process of convergence between national policies and institutions and those who see a process of sustained diversity (Berger and Dore, 1996). On the other hand, the discourse about markets reflect concerns about a whole new set of issues and priorities which are the product of global competition and challenge patterns of domestic political–economic organization. Such concerns center around the extent to which market competition and international economic pressure diminishes the capacity of states to achieve democratically legitimate political goals to mitigate the effects of the market (Scharpf, 1999: chapter 1). This closing section highlights four topics that are emerging as research areas of concern. While not directly linked, all four focus on the impact and effect of the *institutionalization of markets* on both the polity and the economy.

The first essential task in studying markets is analyzing and evaluating the processes of economic modernization and change. Despite efforts to import institutions, it is apparent in the Central and East European context, where there has been a simultaneous transition with the creation of both capital and democratic institutions, that many past forms of economic exchange and industrial production have proved to be resilient (Appel, 2004: 1466). The challenge of building capitalist institutions and market order has also been shaped by the role of conditionality which is much more extensive and concentrated in CEE (Vachudova, 2005). This serves as an effective mechanism to transmit certain economic preferences, not only by reducing the impact of conventional means of governance such as subsidies and state aids, and fiscal and trade preferences, but also in providing a blueprint (ACQUIS) for implementing the single market program. Yet in looking at economic reform and market transition, the old debates under modernization concerning corruption and collusion have returned as patterns of privatization, liberalization, and market reforms have focused attention on the politics of structural adjustment. However, research on the impact of European integration on accession members has primarily focused on meeting entry requirements whereas closer attention needs to be paid to the consistency and credibility of reform success and tie the recent focus in EU studies on implementation and compliance, regulation and control, accountability, and transparency to issues of distributional politics, market power, and corruption since this effects the capacity of the state to promote the development of the market economy (Schamis, 2006).

A second set of implications relates to governance and private regimes (Schepel, 2005). Most of this governance literature has highlighted the diffusion of authority in which private actors play an increasing role in shaping economic transactions through a variety of mechanisms. This might include self-regulation, corporate codes of conduct, or corporatist intermediary bargaining. Yet in many cases such practices rely heavily on legal contractual arrangements or the continued importance of the state in creating the conditions for such negotiations. However, any semblance of delegation of decisions to either private bodies or independent regulatory agencies raises concerns about the impact on representation, constitutionalism and legitimacy. The immediate questions that follow from this are whether such delegation is ultimately the best means to govern markets, how such patterns of interaction emerge, and under what conditions the rules of economic governance are best served in such a system.

A third issue centers around the multiplicity of markets, and the need to consider both formal and informal markets. Informal market institutions continue to persist across Europe, often by choice, as part of the overall dynamics and features of the economy. Whether it is barter, payment systems in some states, circumventing traditional state authority to regulate and tax economic transactions, notably in Russia and Eastern Europe (Woodruff, 1999), or the organizational networks that play a key role in economic development by providing effective economic and social resources in Italy, such informal market arrangements continue to persist (Locke, 1995; Trigilia, 1986). Although the vast informal sector is often associated with the failure of state policies, there has been limited attention to this issue in the European context, despite the fact that the informal sectors of the economy leads in turn to the weakening of state institutions and the rule of law (Castells and Portes, 1989; Centeno and Portes 2006; Portes and Sassen, 1987). This challenges us to pay more attention to certain market practices and their effects on economic development as informal practices continue to undermine legally governed contractual relations, and to reinforce social inequality. Across Europe, a growing share of the workforce is no longer in stable protected employment, as markets have become more flexible, and the informal economy has emerged in new guises that relate to the nature of employment. Yet research on informal markets could be further tied to ethnicity and the economy, or women and the economy, where in fact much of the pattern of informal market relationships tends to occur (Emigh and Szelenki, 2001).

A final issue relates to Europeanization and the consequences of domestic changes induced by European market making. While European political economy has moved in a market-oriented direction, systematic adjustment efforts to cope with the single market project have focused on the impact both on the sustainability of different national models of capitalism, and the 'goodness of fit' between European and national level governance (Cowles *et al.* 2001; Schmidt, 2006). Though the widespread view is that no distinct European regulatory model is emerging, the focus of research has been on the relationship between economic governance and economic performance at the national level (see e.g. Della Salla, 2004 Heinisch, 2005; Schmidt, 2006). Yet less attention has been given to the respective roles of regional and local factors in shaping the trajectories of different regional economies across Europe. The impact of Europeanization on regional politics has been the source of significant research (Hooghe, 1998). However it has focused primarily on understanding the impact of multi-level governance rather than the impact of greater market integration on economic performance in both core growth regions and peripheral areas (Perroux, 1955). Rather than treat national economies as monolithic economic structures, as is often the case with the 'varieties of capitalism literature, we need to understand how regions with very distinct trajectories of economic history will respond differently to Europeanization. The recent work of urban economists and geographers in focusing on the spatial relationships between economic regions and cities, as well as the earlier work of development economists (such as, Myrdal, Hirschman) recognizes the importance of

comparative advantage and geographical location as a determinant of economic growth (Krugman, 1990; Venables, forthcoming). Thus the impact of economic globalization on the territoriality of states needs to focus on subnational variation. To date, however, the literature on regional industrial governance has tended to focus on regionally embedded institutions and networks without taking into account the impact of European economic governance.

CONCLUSION

The chapter has highlighted the transformation of some of the key processes, rules and outcomes of one of the central institutions coordinating modern economic and social life in Europe. The organization of economic transactions is influenced by a variety of institutions and instruments as well as by different levels of government. The phenomena of the market is one that is both complex and contested, as markets assume a variety of patterns and interact with states and societies in multiple ways. European market economies face a complex set of rules and regulations that shape their structure and operation. Even though markets are politically and social constructed entities, subject to intense ideological debates about their operation and organization, markets do not receive the same kind of attention as traditional political institutions such as parties, legislatures, courts, and bureaucracies. Despite the linkages between governments and markets, the main emphasis in recent scholarship has been on freeing markets, which involves removing government barriers to private exchange through deregulation and privatization with much less attention given to facilitating markets which involves creating or permitting a particular market through specific state or legal interventions (Egan, 2001; Patashnik, 2000). Of course, there is more to European postwar transformation than economic governance. Still, issues of economic performance and growth, and the attendant political and institutional relations that govern markets, are of central importance in Europe. However, the challenge is to move beyond economic analysis which has paid particular attention to explaining how a market economy functions in order to pay more attention to explaining how a market economy is transformed. It is in this context that a detailed examination of marketization in Europe highlights the prominent role that European integration has played, triggering vast processes of institutional change, whose scope and nature point to the central role of public authorities in shaping the wave of liberalization policies over the past two decades. Though the processes leading to, and the political effects of market reform have been the center of debates in European integration, the institutional changes challenge the notion that economic integration leads to a shrinking of the state since European integration has reorganized macroeconomic institutions, privatized public sector firms, and enhanced regulatory capacity. Both, at the national and the European level the institutional effects of privatization, deregulation, liberalization has in fact transferred assets and allocation processes to the market – while allowing the state to retain redistributive functions – and also creating new norms, rules, and organizational practices to govern and regulate markets.

As Polanyi argued, markets are not 'natural propensities', and are 'kept open by an increase in continuous, centrally organized, and controlled interventionism' (Polanyi, 1944). However, the nature and visibility of that intervention has changed in Europe in subsequent decades in response to the challenges of globalization, by shifting to modes of flexible production, liberalization of markets, and privatization of state enterprises. Making economic adjustments is challenging, and often involves conflict. Yet states help make stable markets possible by, for example, establishing the rule of law, regulating firm behavior, and fostering wage moderation. Creating competitive markets has not reduced the role of the state in the economy

but has altered the boundaries of state activity across Europe. Because institutional configurations may vary across national, regional or sectoral level, states will respond to economic pressures and interdependence depending on different patterns of state–market relations. Whether states follow informal or formal modes of economic production, engage in collaborative state–private sector collaboration, or cushion the social consequences of market competition have implications for both comparative and international political economy. These institutions are part of the long-term state building process that affects the design, operation and structure of markets. By focusing on the interactions between formal and informal state and market institutions in Europe, research on political economy can link both domestic polities and societies by embedding them in the larger international system.

NOTES

1 This has also been a prominent theme of legal realism, in which modern economies require the state to play a role to protect individual rights in a market economy.

2 See Polanyi's 'double movement' in *The Great Transformation*.

3 Weber in *Economy and Society* talks about different types of capitalism – rational, political and traditional – although this is not the categorization used here, it points to the importance of classics in political economy to understand contemporary capitalism and market developments in Europe.

4 See the account in Karl Polanyi's *The Great Transformation* about the re-embedding of the market system.

REFERENCES

Anderson, J. (1999) 'European integration and political convergence since Maastricht: The view from the member states', *Proceedings of the European Union Studies Association (EUSA) Biennial Conference*, June 2–5 1999, Pittsburgh University.

Appel, H. (2004) 'Institutional continuity and change in postcommunist economies', *Review of International Political Economy*, 11 (2): 424–437.

Aslund, A. (2001) *Building Capitalism: The Transformation of the Former Soviet Bloc*. Cambridge: Cambridge University Press, 2001.

Berger, S. and Dore, R. (1996) *National Diversity and Global Capitalism*. Ithaca: Cornell University Press.

Berman, G. and Pistor, K. (2004) *Law and Governance in an Enlarged European Union*. Oxford: Hart Publishing.

Bohle, D. and Greskovits, B. (2004) 'Capital, labor, and the prospects of the European social model', Working paper no. 58, The East Center for European Studies, Harvard.

Brusis, M. (2005) 'Assessing democracy, market economy and political management', Working paper, Center for Applied Policy Research, Munich.

Bruszt, L. (2002a) 'Making markets and Eastern enlargement: diverging convergence?' in P. Mair and J. Zielonka (eds) *The Enlarged European Union: Diversity and Adaptation*. London: Frank Cass, pp. 121–141

Bruszt, L. (2002b) 'Market making as state making: constitutions and economic development in postcommunist Eastern Europe', *Constitutional Political Economy*, 15: 53–72.

Castells, M. (1996) *The Information Age: Economy, Society and Culture, The Rise of the Network Society*. Oxford: Blackwell Publishers.

Castells, M. and Portes, A. (1989) 'World underneath: the origins, dynamics, and effects of the informal economy' in Portes, A. *et al*. (eds) *The Informal Economy: Studies in Advanced and Less Developed Countries*. Baltimore: John Hopkins University Press, pp. 11–37.

Centeno, M. A and Portes, A. (2006) 'The state and the informal economy' in P. Fernandez-Kelly (ed.) *Out of the Shadows*. Pittsburgh: Penn State Press.

Chiti, E. (2002) 'Decentralised integration as a new model of joint exercise of community functions? A legal analysis of European agencies', Arena Working Paper WP 02/3, Arena, Oslo.

Coen, D. and Thatcher, M. (2005) 'The new governance of markets and non-majoritarian regulators', *Governance: An International Journal of Policy, Administration and Institutions*, 18 (3): 329–346.

Cowles, M., Caporaso, J. and Risse, R. *et al*. (2001) *Transforming Europe: Europeanization and Domestic Change*. New York: Cornell University Press.

Crouch C. and Streeck W. (eds) (1997) *Political Economy of Modern Capitalism: Mapping Convergence and Diversity*. London: Sage.

de Búrca, G. (2003) 'The constitutional challenge of new governance in the European Union', *European Law Review*, 28 (6): 814–839.

Dehousse, R. (2002) 'Misfits: EU Law and the evolution of European governance,' in C. Joerges and R. Dehousse (eds) *Good Governance in Europe's Integrated Market*. Oxford: Oxford University Press.

Della Salla, V. (2004) 'The Italian model of capitalism: on the road between globalization and Europeanization?', *Journal of European Public Policy*, 11 (6): 1041–1057.

Downs, A. (1957) *An Economic Theory of Democracy*. New York: Harper.

Duina, F. (2006) *The Social Construction of Free Trade: The European Union, NAFTA, and Mercosur*. Princeton: Princeton University Press.

Egan, M. (2001) *Constructing a European Market*. Oxford University Press, Oxford.

Egan, M. (forthcoming a) *Single Markets: Economic Integration in Europe and US*. Oxford: Oxford University Press.

Egan, M. (forthcoming b) 'Single market' in M. Cini (ed.) *European Politics*. Oxford: Oxford University Press.

Egan, M. (forthcoming c) 'Governing the single market: from coordination to regulation' in A. Verdun and I. Toemmel (eds) *Governance of the EU*. Boulder: Lynne Rienner Publishers.

Emigh, R.J. and Szelenki, I. (2001) *Poverty, Ethnicity and Gender in Eastern Europe During the Market Transition*. Westport: Praeger.

Erikson, F. (2005) 'Transatlantic and global dimensions to the Lisbon agenda' in D. Hamilton and J. Quinlan (eds) *Deep Integration*. Washington: Brookings Press.

Esping-Anderson, G. (1990) *The Three Worlds of Welfare Capitalism*. Princeton: Princeton University Press.

Farrell, H. (2005) 'Trust and political economy: comparing the effects of institutions on inter-firm cooperation', *Comparative Political Studies*, 38 (5): 459–483.

Farrell, H. and Knight, J. (2003) 'Trust, institutions and institutional evolution: industrial districts and the social capital hypothesis', *Politics and Society*, 31 (4): 537–556.

Fligstein, N. (1990) *The Transformation of Corporate Control*. Cambridge: Harvard University Press.

Fligstein, N. (2002) *The Architecture of Markets: An Economic Sociology of Twenty-First-Century Capitalist Societies*. Princeton: Princeton University Press.

Flora, P. (1986) *Growth to Limits: The Western European Welfare States Since World War II*. Berlin: de Gruyter.

Gilardi, F. (2005) 'The institutional foundations of regulatory capitalism: the diffusion of independent regulatory agencies in Western Europe', *Annals of The American Academy of Political and Social Science*, 598 (1): 84–101.

Gill, S. (1995) 'Globalisation, market civilization, and disciplinary neoliberalism', *Millennium*, 23 (3): 399–423.

Goertz, K. (2001) 'Making Sense of post-communist central administration: modernization, Europeanization, or Latinization?', *Journal of European Public Policy*, 8: 132–151.

Goldthorpe, J.H. (ed.) (1984) 'Order and conflict in contemporary capitalism: studies', in *Political Economy of Western European Nations*. Clarendon: Clarendon Press.

Grabbe, H. (1998) 'A partnership for accession? The implication of EU conditionalitiy for the Central and East European applicants', Working Paper, Robert Schuman Centre, San Domenico di Fiesole.

Grabbe, H. (2000) 'European integration and corporate governance in central europe: trajectories of institutional change', unpublished paper, University of Birmingham.

Grubel, H. and Lloyd, P.J. (1975) *Intra-Industry Trade*. New York: John Wiley & Sons.

Haggard S. (2000) 'Interests, institutions and policy reform' in A. Krueger (ed.) *Economic Policy Reform: Second Stage*. Chicago: University of Chicago Press.

Hall, P. (1986) *Governing the Economy: The Politics of State Intervention in Britain and France*. Oxford: Oxford University Press.

Hall, P.A. and Soskice, D. (2001) *Varieties of Capitalism. The Institutional Foundations of Comparative Advantage*. Oxford: Oxford University Press.

Hay, C. (2004) Common trajectories, variable paces, divergent outcomes? Models of European capitalism under conditions of complex economic interdependence', *Review of International Political Economy*, 11 (2): 231–262.

Heinisch, R. (2000) 'Coping with economic integration: corporatist strategies in Germany and Austria in the 1990s', *West European Politics*, 23 (3): 67–96.

Heinisch, R. (2005) 'Change and continuity: the adaptation of Austrian consociationalism to new realities', *Proceedings of the European Union Studies Association (EUSA) Biennial Conference*, March 31–April 2 2005, Pittsburgh, Pittsburgh University.

Hellman, J. (1998) 'Winners take all: the politics of partial reform in postcommunist transitions,' *World Politics*, 50 (2): 203–234.

Hemerijck, A.C. and Vail, I. M. (2005) 'The forgotten center: the state as dynamic actor in corporatist political economies' in J.D. Levy (ed.) *The State after Statism: New State Activities in the Age of Globalization and Liberalization*. Cambridge, MA: Harvard University Press.

Hollingsworth, J.R. and Boyer, R. (1997) *Contemporary Capitalism: The Embeddedness of Institutions*. New York: Cambridge University Press.

Hooghe, L. (1998) 'EU cohesion policy and competing models of European capitalism', *Journal of Common Market Studies*, 36 (4): 457–477.

Hooghe, L. and Marks, G. (1997) 'The making of a polity: the struggle over European integration', *European Integration Online Papers (EIoP)*, 1 (4).

Iversen, T. and Wren, A. (1998) 'Equality, employment, and budgetary restraint: the trilemma of the service economy', *World Politics*, 50 (4): 507–546.

Jones, E. (2005) 'Economic adjustments and political transformation in small states', Unpublished draft, August 2005. Available at: http://www.jhubc.it/facultypages/ejones/Jones-EAPTSS.pdf.

Jones, E. (forthcoming) 'European economic governance,' in R. Tiersky and E. Jones (eds)

Europe Today. Lanham: Rowan and Littlefield Publishers.

Katzenstein, P. and Shirashi, T. (eds) (2005) *A World of Regions: Asia and Europe in the American Imperium*. Ithaca: Cornell University Press.

Katzenstein, P. (1978*) Between Power and Plenty: Foreign Economic Policies of Advanced Industrial States*. Madison: University of Wisconsin Press.

Katzenstein, P. (1985) *Small States in World Markets. Industrial Policy in Europe*. Ithaca: Cornell University Press.

Kitschelt, H., Lange, P., Marks, G. and Stephens, J.D. (eds) (1999) *Continuity and Change in Contemporary Capitalism*. Cambridge: Cambridge University Press.

Kornai, J. (1992) *The Socialist System: The Political Economy of Communism*. Princeton University Press, Princeton.

Krugman, P. (1990) *Geography and Trade*. Cambridge: MIT Press.

Lane, D. (2006) *Varieties of Capitalism in Post-Communist Countries*. New York: Palgrave.

Levi-Faur, D. (2005) 'The global diffusion of regulatory capitalism', *Annals of the American Academy of Political and Social Science*, 598 (1): 12–32.

Levy, J. (1999) 'Vice into virtue? Progressive politics and welfare reform in continental Europe', *Politics and Society*, 27 (2): 239–273.

Locke, R.M. (1995) *Remaking the Italian Economy*. Ithaca: Cornell University Press.

McDermott, G. (2002) *Embedded Politics: Industrial Networks and Institution Building in Post-Communism*. Ann Arbor: University of Michigan Press.

Maduro, M. (2002) 'Where to look for legitimacy', in E.O. Eriksen, J.E. Fossum and A. J. Menendez (eds) *Constitution Making and Democracy*. Arena Report no. 5, Arena, Oslo, pp: 81–91.

Majone, G. (1994) ,The rise of the regulatory state in Europe', *West European. Politics*, 17: 77–101.

Majone, G. (ed.) (1996) *Regulating Europe*. London: Routledge.

Marshall T.H. (1950) *Citizenship and Social Class and Other Essays*. Cambridge: Cambridge University Press.

Manzetti, L. (1999) *Privatization South American Style*. New York: Oxford University Press.

Mistral, J. (2006) 'Market forces and fair institutions: the political economy of Europe and the U.S. reconsidered', CES Working Papers Series, no. 138, Harvard University.

Mosley, L. (2003) *Global Capital and National Governments*. New York: Cambridge University Press.

Murrell, P. (1992) 'Evolutionary and radical approaches to economic reform', *Economics of Planning*, 25 (1): 79–95.

North, D. (1990) *Institutions, Institutional Change, and Economic Performance*. New York: Cambridge University Press.

Neumann, S. and Egan, M. (1999) 'Between German and Anglo-Saxon capitalism: The Czech financial markets in transition', *New Political Economy*, 4 (2): 173–195.

Olson, M., Jr. (1965) *The Logic of Collective Action*. Cambridge: Harvard University Press.

Orrenstein, M. (1996) Out of the Red: *Building Capitalism and Democracy in Postcommunist Europe*. Ann Arbor: University of Michigan Press.

Pastanick, E. (2000) *Political Science and the Study of 'the Market': The Role of Market Forces in American Politics and Government*. American Political Science Association, September 2000.

Pelkmans, J. (2006) 'The internal market: an economic perspective', College of Europe, Bruges, unpublished paper.

Perroux F. (1955) Note sur la Notion de Pole de Croissance. *Economic Appliquee*, 7: 307–320.

Pierson, P. (ed.) (2001) *The New Politics of the Welfare State*. Oxford: Oxford University Press.

Piore, M. and Sabel, C. (1984) *The Second Industrial Divide: Possibilities for Prosperity*. New York: Basic Books.

Polanyi, K. (1944) *The Great Transformation, The Political and Economic Origins of Our Time*. Boston: Beacon Hill.

Pontusson, J. (2005) *Inequality versus Prosperity: Social Europe versus Liberal America*. Ithaca: Cornell University Press.

Portes, A. and Sassen, S. (1987) 'The informal sector: comparative materials on Western market economies' *American Journal of Sociology*, 93 (1): 30–61.

Putnam, R. (1993) *Making Democracy Work: Civic Traditions in Modern Italy*. Princeton: Princeton University Press.

Rhodes, M. (2001) The political economy of social pacts: competitive corporatism and European welfare reform', in P. Pierson (ed.) *The New Politics of the Welfare State*. Oxford: Oxford University Press, pp. 165–194.

Rossenau, J.N. (1992) 'Governance, order and change in world politics', in J.N. Rossenau and E.O. Czempiel (eds) *Governance Without Government: Order and Change in World Politics*. Cambridge: Cambridge University Press, pp. 1–29.

Ruggie, J. (1982) 'International regimes, transactions, and change: embedded liberalism in the postwar economic order', *International Organization*, 36 (2): 379–415.

Sachs, J. (1984) *Poland's Jump to the Market Economy*. Cambridge: MIT Press.

Sapir, A. (2006) 'Globalization and the reform of European social models', *Journal of Common Market Studies*, 44 (2): 369–390.

Sassen, S. (2003)'The repositioning of citizenship', *The New Centennial Review*, 3 (2): 41–66.

Sbragia, A. (2000) 'Governance, the state and the market: what is going on?', *Governance*, 13 (2): 243–250.

Sbragia, A. (2003) 'Post-national democracy: a challenge to political science?', Paper delivered as the Introductory Presentation, Convegno Nazionale Della Societa Italiana di Scienza Politica (SISP), Universita degli Studi di Trento.

Schamis, H.E. (2001) *Re-Forming the State: The Politics of Privatization in Latin America and Europe*. Michigan: University of Michigan Press.

Scharpf, F.W. (1991) *Crisis and Choice in European Social Democracy*. Ithaca: Cornell University Press.

Scharpf, F.W. (1999) *Governing in Europe. Democratic and Efficient?* Oxford: Oxford University Press.

Scharpf, F.W. (2002) 'The European Social Model: Coping with Diversity', *Journal of Common Market Studies*, 40 (4): 645–670.

Schepel, H. (2005) *The Constitution of Private Governance: Product Standards in the Regulation of Integrating Markets*. Oxford: Oregon: Hart Publishing, 2005.

Schmidt, V. (2001) 'Europeanization and the mechanics of economic policy adjustment', *European Integration online Papers (EIoP)*, 5 (6).

Schmidt, V. (2002) *Varieties of Capitalism*. Oxford: Oxford University Press.

Schmidt, V. (2003) 'French capitalism transformed, yet still a third variety of capitalism', *Economy and Society*, 32 (4): 526–554.

Schmidt, V. (2006) 'Procedural democracy in the EU: The Europeanization of national and sectoral policymaking processes', *Journal of European Public Policy*, 13 (5): 670–691.

Schmitter, P.C. (1979) 'Still the century of corporatism?' in P.C. Schmitter and G. Lehmbruch (eds) *Trends Toward Corporatist Intermediation*. Beverly Hills: Sage, pp. 7–52.

Shapiro, M. (2000) 'The institutionalization of administrative space', MS #2000-09, Center for Culture, Organization and Politics, University of California Berkeley.

Shonfield, A. (1965) *Modern Capitalism. The Changing Balance of Public and Private Power*. Oxford: Oxford University Press.

Slaughter, A.M. (2004) 'Disaggregated sovereignty: towards the public accountability of global government networks', *Government and Opposition*, 39 (2): 336–391.

Smith, M. (2005) *States of Liberalization*. New York: SUNY Press.

Soskice, D. (1999) 'Divergent production regimes: coordinated and uncoordinated market economies in the 1980s and the 1990s', in H. Kitschelt, P. Lange, G. Marks and J.D. Stephens (eds) *Continuity and Change in Contemporary Capitalism*. Cambridge: Cambridge University Press.

Stark, D. (1989) 'Bending the bars of the iron cage: bureaucratization and informalization under capitalism and socialism', *Sociological Forum*, 4 (4): 637–664.

Stark, D. (1996) 'Recombinant property in East European capitalism', *American Journal of Sociology*, 101 (4): 993–1027.

Stark, D. and Bruszt, L. (1998) *Postsocialist Pathways: Transforming Politics and Property in Eastern Europe*. Cambridge: Cambridge University Press.

Strange, S. (1988) *States and Markets: An Introduction*. London: London Pinter.

Swedberg, R. (1994) 'Markets as social structures', in N. Smelser and R. Swedberg (eds) *Handbook of Economic Sociology*. New York and Princeton: Russell Sage Foundation and Princeton University Press, pp. 255–282.

Swedberg, R. and Nee, V. (2005) *The Economic Sociology of Capitalism*. Princeton: Princeton University Press.

Taylor-Gooby, P. (1982) 'Two cheers for the welfare state', *Journal of Public Policy*, 2 (4): 319–346.

Taylor-Gooby, P. (1986) 'Consumption cleavages and welfare politics', *Political Studies*, 34 (4): 592–606.

Thelen, K.(2004) *How Institutions Evolve: The Political Economy of Skills in Germany, Britain, the US and Japan*. New York: Cambridge University Press.

Trigilia, C. (1986) 'Small-firm development and political subcultures in Italy', *European Sociological Review*, 2 (3): 161–175.

Underhill, G.R.D. (2003) 'States, markets, and governance for emerging market economies: private interests, the public good, and the legitimacy of the development process', *International Affairs*, 79 (4): 755–781.

Vachudova, M. (2005) *Europe Undivided Democracy, Leverage, and Integration after Communism*. Oxford: Oxford University Press.

Various (1994) Special edition on 'Reshaping the State in Western Europe. *West European Politics*, 17 (3).

Venables, A. Economic geography: spatial interactions in the world economy. Paper prepared for *Oxford Handbook of Political Economy*, forthcoming.

Verdier, D. and Breen, R. (2001) 'Europeanization and globalization: politics against markets in the European Union', *Comparative Political Studies*, 34 (4): 227–262.

Vogel, S.K. (1996) *Freer Markets, More Rules: Regulatory Reform in Advanced Industrial Countries*. Cornell University Press: Ithaca.

Wallace, H. (2000) 'Europeanisation and globalisation: complementary or contradictory trends?', *New Political Economy*, 5 (3): 369–381.

Weber, M. *Economy and Society* (1978) Berkeley: University of California Press.

Weiss, L. (1998) *The Myth of the Powerless State*. New York: Cornell University Press.

Wilks, S. (1996) 'Regulatory compliance and capitalist diversity in Europe', *Journal of European Public Policy*, 3 (4): 536–559.

Woodruff, D. (1999) *Money Unmade: Barter and the Fate of Russian Capitalism*. Ithaca: Cornell University Press.

World Bank (1996) *From Plan to Market*. Washington: World Bank.

Young, A. (2000) 'The adaptation of European foreign economic policy: from Rome to Seattle', *Journal of Common Market Studies*, 38 (1): 93–116.

Zeitlan, J. (2005) *The Open Method of Coordination in Action: The European Employment and Social Inclusion Strategies*. Brussels: Presses Interuniversitaires, PE Lang.

Zeitlan, J. and Trubek, D. (eds) (2003) *Governing Work and Welfare in a New Economy: European and American Experiments*. Oxford: Oxford University Press.

Zysman, J. (1994) 'How institutions create historically rooted trajectories of growth', *Industrial and Corporate Change*, 3 (1): 243–283.

9

Law and Justice

Lisa Conant

In the postwar era, the institutions of law and justice have come to play a prominent role in European politics. The expanding influence of courts is evident in domestic politics, the supranational European Union (EU) and Council of Europe (CE), and international human rights and trade regimes. The literature on European law and justice contributes to debates in comparative and international politics on the expansion of judicial power, politics of legal integration, and globalization of law. While legal scholarship chronicles domestic, supranational, and international jurisprudence, interest among political scientists has concentrated on transformations within states and the EU. Most observers agree that legalization in Europe has progressed tremendously since the end of the Second World War, and particularly since the 1980s, but scholars disagree about the impact of this development. Substantial gaps in our empirical knowledge about the effects of legalization and the interaction of legal systems at different levels suggest a wealth of opportunities for future research, but render normative assessments of legal transformations difficult. Because changes are so recent, many discussions develop descriptive accounts of single institutions within one country or international venue and focus on

debates within political science subfields. Future scholarship might build a more comprehensive understanding of European legal transformations by (1) studying the interaction of institutions in a context of competing domestic, supranational, and international jurisdictions; and (2) learning from broader theoretical literatures on judicial politics in settings where it is more developed.

The chapter proceeds in three sections. The first surveys scholarship that identifies the empowerment of courts and politicization of the law within domestic settings in postwar Europe. The second addresses select debates on judicial politics within supranational venues. The third explores research on the interaction between international and European systems of law and justice. The chapter concludes by discussing the extent to which legalization has emerged simultaneously at all three levels and is likely to depend on cooperation to function effectively.

TOWARD A GOVERNMENT OF JUDGES?

One of the most dramatic transformations is the demise of legislative supremacy.

Doctrines of separation of powers on the continent and parliamentary sovereignty in the United Kingdom (UK) historically relegated the judiciary to a subsidiary role in politics. According to conventional understandings, judges applied the law written by legislatures, but they did not make laws through inventive interpretation or overturn laws adopted by legislatures on the grounds of 'higher law' constitutions. The idea that all law exists in codes and legislation was always an exaggeration since judges necessarily engage in supplementary lawmaking when they clarify ambiguities and fill in gaps as they resolve disputes (Shapiro, 1981). Yet postwar institutional changes expanded the courts' power and destroyed any pretense that their rulings play little role in the evolution of laws.

The postwar adoption of constitutions that created specialized courts to review legislation fundamentally altered European politics, enhancing the authority of courts. Before the Second World War, constitutional review powers existed only in Denmark, Ireland, the Weimar Republic, and countries that broke away from empires including Austria, Czechoslovakia, Greece, and Romania. While these courts rarely invoked their review powers in the interwar period and soon lost authority as constitutional democracy gave way to Nazi occupation or authoritarian regimes, the constitutional courts of the postwar era have reviewed laws for their compatibility with constitutions and sustained their authority in nearly all cases. Furthermore, even the judiciaries of several European countries that lack constitutional courts and formal powers of constitutional review experienced empowerment in recent decades as well.

A burgeoning literature chronicles the rise of courts as central actors in domestic politics. Beginning in the 1990s, comparative politics scholars investigated the expansion of judicial power in Western Europe and debunked the prevailing myth that the US was exceptional in the degree to which judicial review affected politics. Although forms of judicial review vary across countries, yet the use of constitutional review to make public policy was no longer a US monopoly (Shapiro and Stone, 1994; Tate, 1992; Tate and Vallinder, 1995; Volcansek, 1992). This expansion in judicial power has been conceptualized as a 'judicialization of politics' characterized by (1) the increasing role that courts play in the making of public policy previously made by legislatures and executives; and (2) process by which formerly 'political' forums become dominated by legalistic rules and procedures and engage in quasi-judicial argumentation (Stone 1992a; Tate 1995: 28). While this early research describes the ways in which courts influence politics, preliminary efforts to identify causes of judicialization suggest a number of contributing factors. Tate views the following factors as conducive to judicialization: presence of democracy, separation of powers, politics of rights, interest groups, opposition aware of legal strategies, weak parties or fragile governing coalitions leading to policy deadlock, and delegation of authority to courts. He also argues that judicialization requires that judges decide that they *should* participate in policymaking and actually substitute their own policy solutions for those provided by other institutions (1995: 33). Among possible other causes, Shapiro and Stone (now Stone Sweet) attribute judicialization to the proliferation of levels of government, decreasing confidence in technocratic government, liberalization and democratization of formerly authoritarian polities, and expansion in pressure groups (1994: 402).

Judicialization and regime change

The most extensive powers of constitutional review emerged in countries emerging from colonial (Ireland), fascist (Germany and Italy), authoritarian (Spain and Portugal), or communist domination (Central and Eastern Europe) as newly democratic regimes sought to entrench commitments to individual rights and freedoms. Administrative law traditionally offered citizens procedural guarantees and protections from abusive state power across Western Europe prior to the postwar constitutionalization process, but the perversion of the German Rechtsstaat (rule of law) by the Nazis inspired new commitments to entrenched human rights and higher order constitutional protections (Ziller, 2003). Most observers consider Germany to have the most active and powerful constitutional court in Europe: the Federal Constitutional Court, which has the ability to (1) engage in concrete and abstract review (testing the constitutionality of bills and legislation in force); and (2) take cases arising from legislators' challenges, courts' references, and individual complaints, giving it a wealth of opportunities to intervene in politics (Blankenburg, 1996; Stone Sweet, 2000). Kommers demonstrates that Germany's Federal Constitutional Court has regularly been at the center of controversies, successfully laying down guidelines to govern the legislature's behavior. Enjoying prestige and support from the public and legal community alike, this court is heralded as the principal architect of the 'constitutional patriotism' that has characterized postwar German political identity (Kommers, 1994, 1997). Stone Sweet concurs, arguing that the German Federal Constitutional Court does far more than act as a negative legislator, rejecting legislative provisions. He argues that this court has engaged in 'coordinate construction' where sustained judicial–political interaction determines outcomes as judges recast policymaking to encourage certain legislative solutions, dictate the precise terms of provisions, and compel other actors to debate constitutionality in judicial terms (Stone, 1994). Although Landfried agrees with these analyses, she argues that judicialization endangers representative democracy because it has reduced the number of viable political alternatives, preventing political reforms in areas, such as, abortion (1988, 1992, 1995). Yet in-depth analysis of implementation also illustrates the limits of the court's ability to determine practical outcomes. In this particular case, abortion has been more readily available in

Länder controlled by parties that support legalized abortion than in Länder controlled by parties that support most prohibitions of abortion, despite a uniform constitutional and criminal prohibition on abortion in prescribed circumstances (Prützel-Thomas, 1993).

Like Germany, Italy's post-fascist constitution conferred the power of judicial review on a new, specialized constitutional court to safeguard civil liberties and democratic government. Insulated from direct access by citizens with complaints, Italy's court receives fewer opportunities to influence politics than Germany's court (Stone Sweet, 2000). Observers also characterize the Italian constitutional court as more deferential to majorities in parliament and hesitant to challenge the central government in disputes over regional autonomy. Yet it has protected rights that were threatened by Fascist-era laws, gutting provisions governing church–state relations, and actively scrutinizing referendums. Along with the regular magistrates, the constitutional court is among the few institutions to maintain popular legitimacy in the aftermath of wide-ranging investigations of corruption and Mafia association among Italy's governing elites (De Franciscis and Zannini 1992; Volcansek 1994). Some scholars consider the prosecution of corruption by the Italian magistrates corps of prosecutor judges to mark the most significant transformation of Italian politics since the turn to fascism (Tate and Vallinder, 1995). Others paint a darker picture of an extraordinarily independent magistrates corps that has become factionalized, irresponsible, uncontrollable, self-serving, and ultimately threatening to the freedoms of Italian citizens (Di Federico, 1995; Guarnieri, 1995; Zannotti, 1995). Meanwhile, Michael Mandel (1995) echoes Landfried's concern about Germany in his observation that despite a political environment with a persistently strong political left, judicialization in Italy has not encouraged progressive policy.

The instability of Fourth Republic governments in postwar France inspired the first French constitutional review process in the country historically most suspicious of a 'government of judges'. Inspired by the idea that statute law is an expression of the general will, the historic French *principe de légalité* included an explicitly democratic ideal that has been less compatible with vigorous judicial review procedures. Nonetheless, despite its separation from the normal judiciary, the supreme administrative tribunal, the Council of State, has traditionally protected individuals from abuse by the administration (such as its annulment of the establishment of special military tribunals to try suspected terrorists during the Algerian War (Provine, 1996: 189; Ziller, 2003)). Charles de Gaulle supported the creation of a specialized Constitutional Council for the 1958 Fifth Republic to strengthen the executive relative to the legislature. A handful of elites originally controlled challenges because only the president of the republic or presidents of either house of the legislature could bring suspect bills to the Constitutional Council. Because de Gaulle's party presided over governing majorities while he was president, few measures faced scrutiny. A constitutional amendment in 1974, however, empowered either 60 senators or 60 deputies to challenge bills, which transformed constitutional review into a meaningful constraint and offered minorities in the legislature a means to dilute majority reforms (Provine, 1996). According to Stone Sweet, the French Constitutional Council became the equivalent of a 'third legislative chamber,' issuing the final word on all important pending legislation, foreclosing particular options by constitutionalizing legal principles, and prescribing the precise terms of legislation (Stone 1992a, 1992b, 1994). The French government is extraordinarily insulated from the constitutional grievances of its citizens, however, in comparison to Germany and Italy. While Germans can directly access the Federal Constitutional Court and request references to it from other German courts, and Italians can request references from the regular courts, French citizens enjoy no direct or indirect access to the French Constitutional

Council. As a result, it is not surprising that many observers characterize judicialization in France as substantially weaker than the cases of Germany and Italy (Lafon, 1995).

The post-Cold War transitions to democracy in Central and Eastern Europe, while newer and still works-in-progress in some states, ushered in another wave of judicialization. Poland established a constitutional tribunal in 1986, preceding its transition to democracy, and most other postcommunist democracies soon followed. These new constitutional courts have enjoyed successes in patrolling the division of power and gaining respect for their rulings, although most have not yet acted boldly to protect the rights of unpopular minorities such as the Roma. The success of courts has corresponded with popular commitments to democratization: courts in Bulgaria, Russia, and Slovakia defended themselves against political attacks and ultimately contributed to democratization, but judicial efforts to check political power resulted in the abolition of the constitutional court in Kazakhstan, the suspension of the constitution and its court for a year and a half in Russia, and judicial failures to uphold democracy in Albania, Armenia, Belarus, and Romania (Schwartz, 2000). Courts that did function independently have become popular: the approval rating for the Hungarian Constitutional Court reached 90 per cent during the 1990s, and the Russian Constitutional Court receives 15,000 petitions a year from citizens (Scheppele, 2003). Judicial protection of the role of religion in public life is an emerging area for rights claims in postcommunist democracies (Arjomand, 2003; Richardson, 2006).

Incremental judicialization in established democracies

The judiciaries of many established democracies lack extensive review powers but experienced empowerment in the postwar era nonetheless. For example, the UK lacks a constitution in the form of a single document, and its judges lack the authority to overturn legislation on the ground that it is unconstitutional. The Netherlands also forbids its courts from considering the constitutionality of legislation, and Belgium formally limits judicial review to consideration of the federal distribution of powers. Switzerland allows its Federal Supreme Court to strike down legislation adopted by the cantons, but not the federal parliament. Finally, while judicial review has long been institutionally available in Denmark, Finland, Norway, and Sweden, the judiciaries in these countries avoided exercising judicial review to intervene in political controversies until recently.

Courts in the UK historically contributed more overtly to lawmaking than courts in continental European countries since the development of precedents in the common law was long a primary source of law (Drewry, 1992). The judge-made common law develops gradually and incrementally, however, and has always remained subordinate to legislated statutes, which began to dominate UK lawmaking by the twentieth century. Although the common law developed procedural and substantive controls on the administration for over 350 years (Craig, 2003), concern about bureaucratic power from the mid-twentieth century inspired reforms to emphasize legality. The 1958 Tribunals and Inquiries Act began the process of demanding greater legal accountability from British bureaucracy (Sterett, 1992). From the 1960s, commentators noted an increase in the exercise of 'judicial review' of government action for conformity with laws passed by parliament. Although UK courts cannot review parliamentary statute itself, their review of public acts nonetheless can serve as a constraint on government practice (Kritzer, 1996). By the 1980s Drewry and Sterett argue that the expansion in recourse to judicial review proceedings increasingly held government officials accountable in controversial areas such as local government financing, local government discretion over schools, and immigration. The Thatcher government felt sufficiently burdened by the

rise in judicial review to publish a document warning administrators to take care of 'the judge over your shoulder' (Drewry, 1992; Sterett, 1994, 1997). As 'new public management' reforms created alternative modes of delivering public services, hybrid relationships between public and private bodies presented British judges with new challenges in their efforts to control state power and become more accessible to citizens contesting public authority (Drewry, 2003). Epp (1998) demonstrates that a modest UK 'rights revolution' improved the rights of criminal defendants and prisoners and promoted sex equality, and he attributes this to the diversification of the legal profession, expansion in legal aid, and emergence of state-funded enforcement agencies, such as, the Equal Opportunities Commission. While Sunkin agrees that judicialization has progressed in the UK with the growing pressure to instill court-like procedures into administrative decision-making, he is less convinced that the expansion of judicial review has provided citizens with a check on administrative discretion because judicial review continues to affect a small range of subject areas, impinges on a tiny fraction of government decisions, and often results in the approval of officials' decisions (Sunkin, 1992, 1995). J.A.G. Griffith, another skeptic, argues that courts in the UK consistently support conventional and established interests (1997).

Judicialization has also progressed in other long-established European democracies without traditions of active judicial review. Although the traditional French separation of powers doctrines influenced the Netherlands and Belgium, judicial empowerment has proceeded in both countries. Van Koppen shows that the Dutch Supreme Court began to shift from a traditional focus on a strict application of statutes to a role that involves the development of the law through broad interpretation as early as 1919. This trend continued and contemporary observers consider the development of law to be the Supreme Court's most important function, with some dubbing it a 'deputy legislator'.

Van Koppen attributes this transformation to a political structure that had to reconcile competing demands within coalition governments, which prevented parliament from producing clear legislation on many controversial issues. With some questions left undecided, and others addressed in ambiguous compromises, courts were left to fill in the gaps (Van Koppen, 1992). Dutch citizens and corporations have also driven the process of judicialization by challenging official acts in administrative courts (ten Kate and van Koppen, 1995). In Belgium, courts in the normal judiciary have also begun to interpret laws creatively, although they have tended to mirror prevailing views in society and have inspired little controversy as a result. The institution of a quasi-constitutional court accompanied the Belgian transition to a federal regime, and while federal statutes are equal to those of communities and regions, the national constitution itself is the supreme arbiter when national and subnational legislatures enact incompatible legislation (Verougstraete, 1992).

Finally, judicialization has proceeded more gradually and incompletely in countries where judicial review has long been possible but not common. Rothmayr (2001) identifies a moderate trend toward judicialization in Switzerland, where the jurisdiction of the Federal Supreme Court is formally limited to striking down laws at the cantonal level. Although the court applies federal laws that violate rights guaranteed by the federal constitution, it nonetheless interprets federal laws, defines their meaning, and criticizes them. Furthermore, it exercized decisive influence over federal policy-making in the case of assisted reproductive technologies, when it ruled against restrictive laws adopted by a number of cantons. While this instance represents an exception rather than the rule, Rothmayr evaluates it as part of a trend toward judicialization in Swiss politics. Meanwhile in Sweden, the broadening acceptance of judicial review and the discovery of courts by interest groups has increased judicial power in policy-making areas previously dominated by majoritarian institutions. The second form of judicialization, however, has retreated as the use of judicial procedures in the historically legalized Swedish administration has declined in recent years (Holmström, 1995). Similar to other critics, Selle and Osterud (2006) argue that the judicialization of politics in Norway has strengthened the legal system and weakened the autonomy of local democracy in ways that privilege short-term action groups with immediate concerns over long-term organizations and parties pursuing more comprehensive agendas. Along with the expansion of market forces, these transformations threaten citizen participation and put a strain on the Norwegian social contract.

Legalization or European politics as usual?

Despite this expansion in the role of law and courts, Kagan remains skeptical that European politics has been infected with the adversarial legalism that pervades US politics. Far from a criticism of European approaches, Kagan argues that the more bureaucratic policy process of West European democracies balances accountability, efficiency, and fairness better than its more legalized US counterpart, and is more likely to address the needs of ordinary individuals. By contrast, Kagan argues that the US remains exceptional in the degree to which its political culture features legally framed, complex, litigant-driven adversarial contestation. Assessing this approach as more costly than comparable bureaucratic approaches, Kagan also observes that it provides disproportionate benefits to actors with the resources to mobilize legal venues. Kagan (2001) attributes American adversarial legalism to the US state's unusual incapacity to respond programmatically to the public's demands for reform and reformers' consequent reliance on judicially mandated changes.

Although Kagan acknowledges European and global trends toward legalization, he does not equate increasing litigation with adversarial legalism. He considers legalization to be coincident with dynamics of modernization that do not necessarily transform politics in Europe. Instead Kagan argues that six entrenched differences between Europe and the US are likely to limit any Americanization of the European relationship between law and politics. These six differences include the politicized nature and strong remedial powers of US judiciaries; high levels of adversarial contestation in the US regulatory process; uniquely threatening US tort laws and practices; limited rights to social and labor protections in US law; less demanding obligations of US tax law; and a US criminal system characterized by more punitive sanctions, permissive gun laws, and reliance on adversarial legalism in criminal adjudication and police accountability. Kagan concludes that national legal cultures and political structures in Europe will be tenacious in rejecting these features (Kagan, 2006).

Epp lauds the scope of Kagan's research, but contests its thesis by arguing that a significant degree of convergence has emerged as most advanced economies experienced a growth of legal oversight and the US experienced an increase in bureaucratic discretion. As countries face similar social problems, Epp observes that they adopt similar strategies to handle these challenges. Rather than finding dramatic distinctions between the US and UK, Epp demonstrates that growth in prison populations and pervasive racial disparities in criminal justice systems characterize both countries. Moreover, he disputes the idea that Americans are particularly litigious by showing that (1) litigation remains rare in the US; and (2) rates of legal claims and legal representation vary across issue areas in different countries, with some societies boasting more litigation in particular areas of law. Epp points to liberalizing standing doctrines as providing the impetus for the entry of interest groups into legal venues, and observes that concerns about a 'compensation culture' have emerged in the UK as groups mobilized in areas including

employment law and torts (Epp, 2003). Sarat and Scheingold (2001) also tracked an expansion in politically motivated 'cause lawyering' as evidence of the growing use of adversarial legal procedures around the world.

SUPRANATIONAL LAW AND THE END OF SOVEREIGNTY?

As many states in Europe restructured to allow for constitutional review, they also laid the foundations for two European systems of law and justice within the contexts of the EU and CE's Convention for the Protection of Human Rights and Fundamental Freedoms (hereafter, the Convention). Scholarship by social scientists has focused overwhelmingly on the EU legal system, even though both European venues have become successful supranational institutions that have eroded state sovereignty. A large international relations literature debates the relative power of member states and EU institutions such as the European Court of Justice (ECJ), and a growing literature evaluates EU judicial politics within the framework of comparative politics, where the ECJ is an authoritative institution constrained only by the forces that limit domestic courts. For a survey of this literature, see the judicial politics chapter in the Handbook of European Union Politics (Conant, 2007). In this chapter I will focus on the extent to which supranational legal venues contribute to judicialization in Europe and the 'Europeanization' of law and politics.

The supranational judicialization of politics in Europe

Both supranational venues advance judicialization because both systems offer national courts the opportunity to overturn domestic provisions. EU member states never intended the EU legal system to function in this way, but the ECJ's declarations that EU law is supreme and directly effective combined with the preliminary ruling mechanism whereby national courts refer questions of EU law to the ECJ nonetheless created a system by which individuals challenge national law on the grounds of its incompatibility with EU law (Alter, 2001; Burley and Mattli, 1993; Stein, 1981; Weiler, 1991). Meanwhile, Moravcsik (2000) demonstrates that the European Court of Human Rights' (ECHR) power to declare violations of the Convention, whose resolution often requires changes in domestic law and practices, was intentionally created by newly established postwar democracies that wanted to 'lock-in' commitments to liberal democratic institutions. Conventional accounts tend to be more dismissive of the transformative power of the ECHR in comparison with the ECJ because the Convention is characterized as imposing the obligations of international law rather than constitutional law (even though 'constitutionalization' was entirely a judicial invention in the EU case), so that the CE must compel compliance with ECHR judgments by persuading 'sovereign' states to obey. This claim appears to be of decreasing relevance given the ECHR's (1) proclamations that the Convention is a 'constitutional instrument of European public order' (Wildhaber, 2005); and (2) recent efforts to forge a relationship with national courts that encourages them to enforce the Convention and ECHR case law directly (Nicol, 2001a). In practice, Shapiro and Stone Sweet (2002) observe that the ECHR 'has rendered enough judgments that have caused enough changes in state practices so that it can be counted to a rather high degree as a constitutional judicial review court'. And Helfer and Slaughter (1997) argue that both the ECJ and ECHR have effectively transformed classic public international legal systems into supranational systems that make their judgments as effective as those of national rulings.

European judicial review merely provides a new venue for legal challenges in countries that already adopted constitutional review, but it restructures domestic politics more fundamentally in countries that have continued to

reject judicial review of national legislation such as the UK, Netherlands, and Switzerland. Chalmers' research on UK judgments from 1973 to 1998 demonstrates that British judges have rarely utilized EU opportunities to engage in judicial review of national law (2000), although this power is available to them. By contrast, the domestic incorporation of the Convention via the 1998 Human Rights Act formally prohibits British judges from overturning laws that they deem to be incompatible with the Convention (Nicol, 2001b). Judicial declarations of incompatibility put the burden of reform on government and parliament, who remain in control of the precise content of any changes unless litigants are willing to appeal to the ECHR. In the case of Switzerland, Rothmyr shows that the Federal Supreme Court has started to refuse to apply federal laws that violate the Convention even though it still applies federal laws that violate the federal constitution. As a result, the ECHR has successfully forced Switzerland to revise its judicial procedures, improve the protection of the rights of the accused and prisoners, and expand the right of all individuals to have their cases reviewed by an independent court (Rothmayr, 2001).

Both supranational venues have also contributed to judicialization by inspiring the use of politically motivated litigation from business and civil society actors. Kelemen argues that the adversarial legal style that Kagan considers to be distinctively American is spreading to Europe through EU institutions. In this account, the EU's pursuit of economic liberalization and its fragmentation of political power create functional pressures and political incentives to shift toward the US legal style. Kelemen identifies an increase in adversarial legal strategies in environmental and securities regulation, antidiscrimination measures, and consumer protection within the EU (Kelemen, 2006; Kelemen and Sibbitt, 2004). Cichowski (2007) argues that both the EU and CE legal venues have created new opportunities for the participation of civil society in international governance, tracing the mobilization of activists promoting gender equality and environmental protection in the EU, and the explosion of litigation concerning civil rights under the Convention (Cichowski, 2006), Cichowski considers the two supranational courts to be significant sources of support for democratic constitutionalism within Europe. Although economic enterprises and civil society groups promoting the causes of middle-to-upper income groups still dominate European litigation (Alter and Meunier, 1994; Börzel, 2006; Conant, 2002, 2003; Harlow and Rawlings, 1992), recent case law also indicates that even the most disadvantaged individuals – including foreign welfare recipients – have begun to claim social rights by invoking both EU and Convention law (Conant, 2006).

The Europeanization of law through supranational venues

In addition to contributing to judicialization, supranational legal institutions encourage a Europeanization of law where legal norms increasingly converge across member states in the EU and CE. Research on Europeanization uncovers variations in the extent to which domestic institutions are changing in response to pressures from supranational venues. Doctrinal analyses indicate that it took decades for many national courts to accept the ECJ's case law on the direct effect and supremacy of EU law (Slaughter, et al., 1998), and that a number of constitutional courts justified EU legal supremacy in their own terms to maintain opportunities to reassert control (Alter, 2001). The overwhelming majority of national court decisions on EU law are independent decisions that involve no references to the ECJ for preliminary rulings and no citation of ECJ case law (Conant, 2002), and case studies of particular areas of law indicate that national courts do not necessarily refer cases that involve uncertainty about the interpretation of EU law or follow ECJ principles in areas where established case law exists (Chalmers, 2000; Conant, 2002; Golub, 1996; Schwarze, 1996).

The record of Europeanization appears similarly mixed in the Convention system, where national courts vary within and across states in their propensity to use the Convention to challenge national laws and practices and incorporate the principles developed in ECHR case law when they do apply the Convention directly (Blackburn and Polakiewicz, 2001; Dembour, 2004; Jarmul, 1995; Keller, 2005; Limbach, 2000; Mahoney et al., 2000; Nay, 2005; Pache, 2004; Papier, 2005; Romboli and Passaglia, 2005; Sauer 2005).

Finally, the existence of two supranational courts that claim to be the constitutional courts of Europe creates a convergence challenge at the supranational level as well. The ECJ has long invoked the Convention, and more recently cited ECHR interpretations directly, to protect human rights within the EU legal order. Comparative analysis of the case law of the two jurisdictions indicates that although the ECJ explicitly refers to and follows ECHR case law in some instances, in others it avoids addressing human rights claims that arise and decides differently from the ECHR. While some scholars see such divergence, parallel to the divergence between national and European case law, as useful for the evolution of rights protection, others increasingly worry about the coherence and consistency of rights protection (Robert, 1994; Scheeck, 2005; Spielmann, 1999). Debates concerning the possible accession of the EU to the Convention and the adoption of a legally binding EU charter of fundamental rights inspired reflections on the relationship between EU and CE institutions. Some observers press for EU accession to the Convention as the best means to assure more comprehensive rights protection (Drzemczewski, 2001; Krüger and Polakiewicz, 2001). By contrast, A.G. Toth (1997) supports the incorporation of all Convention rights into the EU treaties and a withdrawal of EU member states from the Convention, which transfers all human rights adjudication to the ECJ. Others see ongoing joint responsibility for rights protection (de Witte, 1999) or the situating of the ECJ in a similar position to national constitutional courts, under the ECHR, as viable approaches (Weiler, 1996).

More systematic research on Europeanization is necessary to improve our understanding of factors that affect interactions between jurisdictions. Sociological variables, including networking and secondments to supranational institutions, appear to promote cooperation (Burley and Mattli, 1993, Slaughter, 2004), and the mobilization of civil society and development of institutional support structures for litigation seem crucial to generating a stream of opportunities for judges to engage European law (Alter and Meunier, 1994; Alter and Vargas, 2000; Conant, 2001, 2002; Moravcsik, 1995). Meanwhile, concerns about retaining control can lead to competition and resistance (Alter, 2001). Too much of the existing empirical research on Europeanization remains anecdotal, focused exclusively on finding instances of cooperation, and idiosyncratically organized to explore one country with little effort to make findings comparable across cases. Systematic comparative research on Europeanization is challenging since it requires fluency in multiple languages and ultimately a team of researchers committed to testing the same sets of hypotheses with the same types of data. Comparable data on case law is particularly problematic since the legal systems of larger states generate millions of decisions a year, only a fraction of which are archived in electronic databases. Electronic databases vary in the extent to which they (1) cover court decisions at different levels of the judiciary; and (2) allow for analytical legal basis searching that enables researchers to isolate cases engaging particular areas of law.

INTERNATIONAL LAW AND THE CREATION OF A LIBERAL ORDER?

As the courts emerged as forces in the European politics, institutions of law, and justice also proliferated in the postwar international arena. Inspired by efforts to liberalize the international order after the atrocities of the Second World War and protectionism of the interwar period, international tribunals of regional and global jurisdiction overwhelmingly concentrate on enforcing human rights and trade regimes (Breining-Kaufmann, 2005; Thürer, 2005). European states and supranational institutions have often been involved in the internationalization of law as supporters of multilateralism and sources of doctrinal inspiration to less established tribunals. Judging has also been globalizing in recent decades, as judges in both domestic and supranational venues explore and incorporate legal principles from other jurisdictions.

The internationalization of law and European exceptionalism

Although the internationalization of law began to increase in the early postwar period, the most dramatic gains began recently. Alter's research demonstrates that 19 of today's 26 international courts were created since 1990, and that 70 per cent of all international judicial activity has come in the past 14 years (2006: 22–3). In analyzing this legalization of world politics, Keohane, Moravcsik, and Slaughter distinguish between interstate and transnational dispute resolution in order to understand why the behavior and impact of different international tribunals has been so divergent. Transnational dispute resolution, which is characterized by international courts that are (1) highly independent; (2) accessible to private litigants, and; (3) embedded within domestic structures of compliance through linkages to domestic courts, tends to generate (1) more litigation; (2) case law more independent of national interests; and (3) an additional source of pressure for compliance relative to interstate dispute resolution, which is characterized by tribunals that enjoy a lower degree of independence and embeddedness and restrict standing to states. The 80 per cent compliance rate achieved by the late 1980s in the dispute resolution panels of the General Agreement on Trade and Tariffs (GATT) and successor World Trade Organization (WTO) demonstrate that interstate dispute resolution can be effective despite its reliance on state decisions. Yet the only courts that fit under the category of transnational dispute resolution – the ECJ and ECHR – achieve even higher compliance rates (Keohane *et al.*, 2000). Furthermore, the ECHR is the strongest international human rights regime in terms of offering individual access to address grievances and achieving compliance (Thürer, 2005).

European exceptionalism is even more pronounced in terms of the volume of litigation: while judgments exceeded 17,000 from the ECJ and EU's Court of First Instance by 2004 and numbered over 4,000 from the ECHR by 2003, the Court of Justice of the Cartagena Agreement (Andean Pact) ranks a distant third with 850 decisions. The only other international tribunals whose judgments have exceeded 100 include the GATT/WTO system (operational since 1953), the International Court of Justice (operational since in 1946), and the Inter-American Court of Human Rights (operational since 1979). Alter concludes that private litigants have yet to exploit opportunities to bring rights claims to international tribunals outside of Europe, and notes that the few who have are overwhelmingly international corporate actors pursuing intellectual property rights in the Andean system (Alter, 2006: 26–7).

What drives this proliferation of institutions of law and justice at the international level remains contested. Alter (2006) attributes the growth in international tribunals to an effort to extend the juridical checks available at the domestic level to the international level. By contrast, Jacobson (2003) argues that international 'judicialism' threatens checks and balances in government because transnational judging is not effectively checked by transnational executives or legislatures. In his view, delegating authority to elitist, democratically unaccountable legal institutions threatens republican values of self-government. He attributes European

enthusiasm for international law to a project of political and intellectual classes who hold postnational, even postdemocratic, values. In the case of war crimes tribunals, Rudolph argues that expanding liberal norms explain the growing number of tribunals but that realist factors have dominated the politics of war crimes adjudication. For example, permanent members of the United Nations (UN) Security Council have insisted on controlling who is prosecuted in the International Criminal Court to avoid 'frivolous' suits in cases of 'legitimate' military intervention that serve the 'collective good'. Moreover, he accounts for the existence of tribunals in some cases of atrocities but not in others in terms of the strategic interest of great powers, where establishing a war crimes tribunal in an area of low strategic interest allows states to respond to public demands to 'do something' without committing to costly military intervention (Rudolph, 2001).

The globalization of judging

A globalization of judging has also emerged alongside the progression of judicialization. As the number of politically powerful courts has increased, judges from diverse jurisdictions have begun to interact as they resolve disputes related to similar challenges. Slaughter (2004) argues that a 'new world order' operates through networks of government officials who exchange information and coordinate activity to address contemporary problems. Judges increasingly participate in these networks by attending judicial summits, meeting their counterparts abroad, reading each other's case law, and communicating with modern information technologies. A growing number of courts translate their judgments into English to facilitate dialogue, and electronic databases of case law have begun to add foreign and international collections.

In her typology of transjudicial communication, Slaughter (1995) observes that the globalization of judging requires that participants enjoy autonomy, rely on persuasive authority, and feel a sense of common identity and enterprise. The ability to attract adherence through persuasive authority is particularly important since few judges consider the decisions of other jurisdictions as binding precedents within their own legal systems. Antonio Cassese illustrates the significance of persuasive authority in his research on the International Criminal Tribunal for the former Yugoslavia, which did not consider itself bound by the Convention or the ECHR but nonetheless followed their criteria in establishing what constituted a fair trial, appropriate standards of treatment for those in detention, and the lawfulness of detention. The ECHR was ultimately more influential than the UN's own International Covenant on Civil and Political Rights, which was the focus of the human rights set out in the statute creating the Yugoslav tribunal (Cassese, 2000).

Slaughter distinguishes between horizontal, vertical, and hybrid forms of communication. In horizontal communication, courts with a similar status and no binding connections to each other nonetheless begin to follow each other's case law. This often takes the form of a monologue where newer courts seek guidance from the respected case law of an established court, such as the adoption of the ECHR's reasoning and methodologies by the Inter-American Court of Human Rights and the United Nations Human Rights Committee and the flow of ideas from the US Supreme Court to courts around the world. Yet horizontal communication has also taken the form of a dialogue in Europe, where judges from constitutional courts meet in a triennial conference. Vertical communication, by contrast, occurs between supranational and national courts that are institutionally linked to each other through treaties and conventions. Most developed in the EU context, a direct dialogue takes place between national judges who refer questions concerning EU law to the ECJ via the preliminary ruling mechanism. The ECHR acts more hierarchically as an 'appeals' court that lacks a direct channel of communication to national courts because cases reach the ECHR after individuals exhaust domestic remedies. National courts, however, have also begun to refer to the Convention and cite ECHR judgments in a manner that parallels the usage of EU law by national courts in the vast majority of EU related disputes that they resolve without a formal reference to the ECJ. Finally, a hybrid form of communication proceeds as supranational courts serve as the conduit for horizontal links between national courts. As the ECHR develops legal principles, sometimes borrowing from a national system, it contributes to the diffusion of legal principles among national systems both within the Convention system and even without as judges on newer courts seek guidance (Slaughter, 1995).

An emerging globalization of judging is evident, but it remains unclear how prevalent this dynamic has become across legal jurisdictions. While the Canadian and South African Supreme Courts appear to be among the most active participants in the global dialogue along with Europeans, the US Supreme Court has remained largely tuned out. Even within Europe, where transnational dialogue has been most intense, the Europeanization literature reveals variations across national courts and even specialized court systems within individual countries. At the international level, Thürer (2005) argues that the various international human rights regimes remain relatively isolated from each other, operating autonomously most of the time.

Interactions among legal systems across levels of governance

Scholarship on the relationship between the various international, regional, and domestic legal systems also reveals incoherence and resistance. Cazala observes that the proliferation of international conventions with dispute resolution mechanisms implies the potential for disagreements over competence. More specifically, he argues that the ECJ's competence to resolve disputes concerning the external relations of the EU and its member states is not yet clearly established. The intellectual property and trade in services provisions under the WTO pose particular problems of jurisdiction, which became evident when the US sued the EU, the UK, and Ireland regarding domestic legislation that implemented EU legislation (Cazala, 2004). The ECJ's own position on WTO law generates ambiguities and gaps in legal protection. It has held that GATT 1947 is hierarchically superior to EC secondary legislation and that WTO law is an integral part of the EU legal order, obligating courts to interpret EU legislation in a manner that is consistent with WTO agreements to the extent that this is possible. However, it typically accepts the EU legislature's assertion that EU legislation is WTO-compatible, presuming consistency rather than examining it. And, while the ECJ has used WTO law as an aid in interpreting EU legal instruments related to anti-dumping measures, it has refused to use it to interpret state aids. Most important, the ECJ has consistently held that WTO law does not have direct effect, which prevents private parties from relying on GATT and WTO agreements to challenge EU secondary legislation before national courts (De Mey and Colomo 2006; Snyder, 2003). Arguing that the ECJ does not want to compromise the EU's negotiating position with a unilateral acceptance of direct effect (the US explicitly rejects the direct effect of WTO law), Snyder (2003) concludes that the ECJ supports the premise that the executive and legislature remain the dominant actors in international trade policy rather than courts, administrators, and private actors.

Adding a further complication to the international web, Breining-Kaufmann demonstrates that overlaps between the legal systems of the EU, WTO, and CE are possible in disputes regarding public morals and order. Although she finds conflicts between the EU and WTO and between the EU and CE to be the most prevalent, she documents how the complaint that Caroline of Monaco lodged concerning publication of family photos in newspapers pitted WTO decisions on the import and export of media against ECHR case law on privacy and family life (Breining-Kaufmann, 2005). The potential authoritative reach of the Convention remains contested as well. Although Costa (2003) has stated that the Convention has no jurisdiction beyond the territories of its member states, Wilde's analysis of ECHR case law suggests that the Convention can apply to the actions of member states outside the boundaries of the CE when they exercise control over either individuals or territory. This conclusion, if it bears itself out in future disputes, could have implications for member states' military interventions abroad because it defies the British position that the Convention does not apply to its activities in Iraq (Wilde, 2005).

The cooperation of domestic institutions is crucial to the practical implementation of international law. Wilde (2005) observed that the British High Court chose to apply ECHR case law that denied extraterritoriality in a recent dispute, ignoring the conflicting ECHR case law that implied extraterritorial jurisdiction when states exercise control outside the CE region. Research on the impact of war crimes tribunals reflects a similar dynamic. O'Shea (1995) demonstrates that state cooperation is necessary to transfer suspects to the international criminal court, which usually requires a reduction in extradition requirements. Although many states in Europe have adopted the requisite reforms, other liberal democracies including Australia, New Zealand, and the US maintain their right to refuse transfer requests. Variations also persist in the extent to which states pass legislation to implement requirements under Security Council resolutions for ad hoc tribunals (O'Shea, 1995). John Hagan and Sanja Kutnjak Ivkovic argue that local support for the International Criminal Tribunal for the Former Yugoslavia (ICTY) remains important for its legitimacy. They observe that skepticism about the independence and neutrality of the ICTY typically grows overtime: Serbians and eventually Bosnians preferred local national courts as venues to try suspected war crimes offenders, while only Kosovars – whose experience with atrocities was more recent – preferred ICTY jurisdiction (Hagan and Kutnjak Ivkovic, 2006).

International systems of law and justice depend heavily on the cooperation of domestic institutions for coherence and effectiveness, and tensions are evident within international legal regimes related to trade and human rights. As a result, the relationship between institutions of law and justice across the domestic, regional, and international levels deserves more systematic attention in future research.

CONCLUSION

Europe has been a key site of a 'global expansion of judicial power', whether this is measured in terms of the legalization of politics at the domestic, European, or international level. One of the strongest forces behind the rise of institutions of law and justice appears to be transitions to democracy after the fall of illiberal regimes. Postwar distrust in unfettered democratic institutions promoted constitutional transformations in these states, and along with broader interests in the liberalization of trade and protection of human rights, simultaneously gave rise to supranational and international systems of law and justice. While judicialization has proceeded more gradually in established European democracies, demands for greater protection of individual rights and the evolution of supranational authority have challenged legislative supremacy and elevated the position of courts in these states as well. A wealth of scholarship chronicles these developments, with most observers assuming that judicialization has improved democratic politics by solidifying the rule of law and the protection of individual rights and freedoms. A smaller group of scholars express doubts, arguing that courts often protect established

interests and suppress progressive causes. The most common image that emerges from the literature on courts in Europe is one of an imperious judiciary, whether it is acting for the common good or not. Courts seem to rule their countries, and increasingly, supranational courts seem to rule states.

Yet nuanced case studies in some European research, and a fairly dominant consensus of the US judicial politics literature, suggest that even courts that do play an authoritative role do not necessarily enjoy the last word in disputes and usually rely on the cooperation of other institutions to exert much impact. Normative assessments of the judicialization of European politics may be premature before we understand more about why and how courts exercise influence in political controversies. One aspect of this influence operates through the linkages courts have with each other across the increasingly multilayered jurisdictions of law and justice. Future research could fruitfully explore how different political and societal actors interact with courts across the domestic, supranational, and international levels, tracing the ultimate impact of what appear to be innovative and audacious rulings.

REFERENCES

Alter, K. (2001) *Establishing the Supremacy of European Law*. New York: Oxford University Press.

Alter, K. (2006) 'Private litigants and the new international courts', *Comparative Political Studies*, 39 (1): 22–49.

Alter, K., and Meunier, S. (1994) 'Judicial politics in the European Community', *Comparative Political Studies*, 26 (4): 535–561.

Alter, K., and Vargas, J. (2000) 'Explaining variation in the use of European litigation strategies', *Comparative Political Studies*, 33 (4): 452–482.

Arjomand, S. (2003) 'Law, political reconstruction, and constitutional politics', *International Sociology* 18 (1): 7–32.

Blackburn, R. and Polakiewicz, J. (eds) (2001) *Fundamental Rights in Europe*. Oxford: Oxford University Press.

Blankenburg, E. (1996) 'Changes in political regimes and continuity of the rule of law in Germany', in H. Jacob *et al.* (eds) *Courts, Law and Politics in Comparative Perspective*. New Haven, CT: Yale University Press, pp. 249–314.

Börzel, T. (2006) 'Empowering citizens in post-decisional politics?', *Comparative Political Studies*, 39 (1): 128–152.

Breining-Kaufmann, C. (2005) 'Europas Grundrechte und die WTO', *Zeitschrift für Schweizerisches Recht*, 124 (II): 73–96.

Burley, A.M., and Mattli, W. (1993) 'Europe before the Court', *International Organization*, 47 (1): 41–76.

Cassese, A. (2000) 'The impact of the European Convention on Human Rights on the International Criminal Tribunal for the former Yugoslavia', in P. Mahoney *et al.* (eds) *Protecting Human Rights*. Köln: Carl Heymans Verlag, pp. 213–236.

Cazala, J. (2004) 'La contestation de la competence exclusive de la Cour de justice des Communautés Européennes', *Revue Trimestrielle de Droit Européen*, 40 (3): 505–532.

Chalmers, D. (2000) 'The much ado about judicial politics in the United Kingdom', Harvard Jean Monnet Working Paper 1/100.

Cichowski, R. (2006) 'Courts, rights, and democratic participation', *Comparative Political Studies*, 39 (1): 50–75.

Cichowski, R. (2007) *The European Court and Civil Society*. Cambridge: Cambridge University Press.

Conant. L. (2001) 'Europeanization and the courts', in M. Green Cowles, J. Caporaso, and T. Risse (eds), *Transforming Europe*. Ithaca, NY: Cornell University Press, pp. 97–115.

Conant, L. (2002) *Justice Contained*. Ithaca, NY: Cornell University Press.

Conant. L. (2003) 'Europe's no fly zone?', in T. Börzel and R. Cichowski (eds) *The State of the European Union*, 6. New York, NY: Oxford University Press, pp. 235–254.

Conant, L. (2007) 'Judicial politics', in K.E. Jørgensen, M. Pollack, and B. Rosamond (eds) *Handbook of European Union Politics*. London: Sage, 213–229.

Conant, L. (2006) 'Individuals, courts, and the development of European social rights', *Comparative Political Studies*, 39 (1): 76–100.

Costa, J.P. (2003) 'The European Court of Human Rights and its recent case law', *Texas International Law Journal* 38: 455–471.

Craig, P. (2003) 'Administrative law in the Anglo-American tradition', in B.G. Peters and J. Pierre (eds) *Handbook of Public Administration*. London: Sage, pp. 269–278.

De Franciscis, M. and Zannini, R. (1992) 'Judicial policy-making in Italy', *West European Politics*, 15 (3): 68–79.

Dembour, M. (2004) 'Ten years on', *European Human Rights Law Review*, 4: 400–423.

De Mey, D. and Ibáñez Colomo, P. (2006) 'Recent developments on the invocability of WTO law in the EC', *European Foreign Affairs Review*, 11 (1): 63–86.

de Witte, B. (1999) 'The past and future role of the European Court of Justice in the protection of human rights', in P. Alston (ed.) *The European Union and Human Rights*. Oxford: Oxford University Press, pp. 859–897.

Di Federico, G. (1995) 'Italy', in C.N. Tate and T. Vallinder (eds) *The Global Expansion of Judicial Power*. New York, NY: New York University Press, pp. 233–242.

Drewry, G. (1992) 'Judicial politics in Britain', *West European Politics*, 15 (3): 9–28.

Drewry, G. (2003) 'Law and administration', in B.G. Peters and J. Pierre (eds) *Handbook of Public Administration*. London: Sage.

Drzemczewski, P. (2001) 'The Council of Europe's position with respect to the EU Charter of Fundamental Rights', *Human Rights Law Journal*, 22 (1–4): 14–31.

Epp, C. (1998) *The Rights Revolution*. Chicago: University of Chicago Press.

Epp, C. (2003) 'The judge over your shoulder', *Law and Social Inquiry* 28 (3): 743–770.

Golub, J. (1996) 'The politics of judicial discretion', *West European Politics*, 19 (2): 360–385.

Griffith, J.A.G. (1997) *The Politics of the Judiciary*, 5th edn. London: Fontana.

Guarnieri, C. (1995) 'Judicial independence and policy-making in Italy', in C.N. Tate and T. Vallinder (eds), *The Global Expansion of Judicial Power*. New York: New York University Press, pp. 243–260.

Hagan, J. and Kutnjak Ivkovic, S. (2006) 'War crimes, democracy, and the rule of law in Belgrade, the Former Yugoslavia, and beyond', *Annals of the American Academy of Political and Social Science*, 605 (1): 130–151.

Harlow, C. and Rawlings, R. (1992) *Pressure Through Law*. New York: Routledge.

Helfer, L., and Slaughter, A.M. (1997) 'Toward a theory of effective supranational adjudication', *Yale Law Journal*, 107 (2): 273.

Holmström, B. (1995) 'Sweden', in C.N. Tate and T. Vallinder (eds) *The Global Expansion of Judicial Power*. New York: New York University Press, pp. 345–368.

Jacobson, D. (2003) 'Europe's post democracy?', *Society*, 40 (2): 70–76.

Jarmul, H. (1995) 'Effects of decisions of regional human rights tribunals on national courts', in T. Franck and G. Fox (eds) *International Law Decisions in National Courts*. Irvington, NY: Transnational Publishers.

Kagan, R. (2001) *Adversarial Legalism*. Cambridge, MA: Harvard University Press.

Kagan, R. (2006) 'American and European ways of law', Paper presented at the Annual Meeting of the American Political Science Association, 31 August–3 September, Philadelphia.

Kelemen, R.D. (2006) 'Suing for Europe', *Comparative Political Studies*, 39 (1): 101–127.

Kelemen, R.D., and Sibbitt, E. (2004) 'The globalization of American law', *International Organization*, 58 (1): 103–136.

Keller, H. (2005) 'Reception of the European Convention for the Protection of Human Rights and Fundamental Freedoms in Poland and Switzerland', *Zeitschrift für Ausländisches Öffentliches Recht und Völkerrecht*, 65 (2): 284–349.

Keohane, R., Moravcsik, A., and Slaughter, A.M. (2000) 'Legalized dispute resolution', *International Organization*, 54 (1): 457–488.

Kommers, D. (1994) 'The federal constitutional court in the German political system', *Comparative Political Studies*, 26 (4): 470–491.

Kommers, D. (1997) *The Constitutional Jurisprudence of the Federal Republic of Germany*, 2nd edn. Durham, NC: Duke University Press.

Kritzer, H. (1996) 'Courts, justice and politics in England', in H. Jacob *et al.* (eds) *Courts, Law and Politics in Comparative Perspective*. New Haven: Yale University Press, pp. 81–176.

Krüger, H. and Polakiewicz, J. (2001) 'Proposals for a coherent human rights protection system in Europe', *Human Rights Law Journal*, 22 (1–4): 1–13.

Lafon, J. (1995) 'France', in C.N. Tate and T. Vallinder (eds) *The Global Expansion of Judicial Power*. New York: New York University Press, pp. 289–305.

Landfried, C. (1988) 'Constitutional review and legislation in the Federal Republic of Germany', in C. Landfried (ed.) *Constitutional Review and Legislation: An International Comparison*. Baden-Baden: Nomos.

Landfried, C. (1992) 'Judicial policy-making in Germany', *West European Politics*, 15 (3): 50–67.

Landfried, C. (1995) 'Germany', in C.N. Tate and T. Vallinder (eds) *The Global Expansion of Judicial Power*. New York, NY: New York University Press, pp. 307–324.

Limbach, J. (2000) 'Inter-jurisdictional cooperation within the future scheme of protection of fundamental rights in Europe', *Human Rights Law Journal*, 21 (9–12): 333–336.

Mahoney, P., Matscher, F., Petzold, H., and Wildhaber, L (eds) (2000) *Protecting Human Rights*. Köln: Carl Heymanns Verlag.

Mandel, M. (1995) 'Legal politics Italian style', in C.N. Tate and T. Vallinder (eds) *The Global Expansion of Judicial Power*. New York: New York University Press, pp. 261–286.

Moravcsik, A. (1995) 'Explaining international human rights regimes', *European Journal of International Relations*, 1 (2): 157–189.

Moravcsik, A. (2000) 'The origins of human rights regimes', *International Organization*, 54 (2): 217–252.

Nay, G. (2005) 'Koordination des Grundrechtsschutz in Europa', *Zeitschrift für Schweizerisches Recht*, 124 (II): 97–112.

Nicol, D. (2001a) 'Lessons from Luxembourg', *European Law Review*, 26 (supplement)

Nicol, D. (2001b) *EC Membership and the Judicialization of British Politics*. Oxford: Oxford University Press.

O'Shea, S. (1995) 'Interaction between international criminal tribunals and national legal systems', in T. Franck and G. Fox (eds), *International Law Decisions in National*

Courts. Irvington, NY: Transnational Publishers, pp. 285–333.

Pache, E. (2004) 'Die Europäische Menschenrechtskonvention und die deutsche Rechtsordnung', *Europarecht*, 39 (3): 393–415.

Papier, H.J. (2005) 'Koordination des Grundrechtsschutz in Europa', *Zeitschrift für Schweizerisches Recht*, 124 (II): 113–128.

Provine, D.M. (1996) 'Courts in the political process in France', in H. Jacob *et al.* (eds) *Courts, Law and Politics in Comparative Perspective*. New Haven, CT: Yale University Press, pp. 177–248.

Prützel-Thomas, M. (1993) 'The abortion issue and the federal constitutional court', *German Politics*, 2 (3): 467–484.

Richardson, J. (2006) 'Religion, constitutional courts, and democracy in former communist countries', *Annals of the American Academy of Political and Social Science*, 603 (1): 129–138.

Robert, J. (1994) 'Constitutional and international protection of human rights', *Human Rights Law Journal*, 15 (1–2): 1–22.

Romboli, R. and Passaglia, P. (2005) ' La coordination de la protection des droits fondamentaux en Europe – Rapport italien', *Zeitschrift für Schweizerisches Recht*, 124 (II): 129–156.

Rothmayr, C. (2001) 'Towards the judicialisation of Swiss politics?', *West European Politics*, 24 (2): 77–94.

Rudolph, C. (2001) 'Constructing an atrocities regime', *International Organization* 55 (3): 655–691.

Sarat, A. and Scheingold, S. (2001) *Cause Lawyering and the State in a Global Era*. New York: Oxford University Press.

Sauer, H. (2005) 'Die neue Schlagkraft der gemeineuropäischen Grundrechthtsjudikatur', *Zeitschrift für Ausländisches Öffentliches Recht und Völkerrecht*, 65 (1): 35–69.

Scheeck, L. (2005) 'The relationship between the European Courts and integration through human rights', *Zeitschrift für Ausländisches Öffentliches Recht und Völkerrecht*, 65 (4): 837–885.

Scheppele, K. (2003) 'Constitutional negotiations', *International Sociology* 18: 219–238.

Schwarze, J. (ed.) (1996) *Administrative Law under European Influence*. Baden, Baden: Nomos.

Schwartz, H. (2000) *The Struggle for Constitutional Justice in Post-Communist Europe*. Chicago: University of Chicago Press.

Selle, P. and Osterud, O. (2006) 'The eroding of representative democracy in Norway', *Journal of European Public Policy* 13 (4): 551–568.

Shapiro, M. (1981) *Courts*. Chicago: University of Chicago Press.

Shapiro, M. and Stone, A. (1994) 'The new constitutional politics of Europe', *Comparative Political Studies* 26 (4): 397–420.

Shapiro, M. and Stone Sweet, A. (2002) *On Law, Politics, and Judicialization*. Oxford: Oxford University Press.

Slaughter, A.M. (1995) 'Typology of transjudicial communication', in T. Franck and G. Fox (eds) *International Law Decisions in National Courts*. Irvington, NY: Transnational Publishers, pp. 37–69.

Slaughter, A.M. (2004) *A New World Order*. Princeton, NJ: Princeton University Press.

Slaughter, A., Stone Sweet, A. and Weiler, J. (eds) (1998) *The European Court and the National Courts – Doctrine and Jurisprudence*. Oxford: Hart.

Snyder, F. (2003) 'The gatekeepers', *Common Market Law Review*, 40 (2): 313–367.

Spielmann, D. (1999) 'Human rights case law in the Strasbourg and Luxembourg courts', in P. Alston (ed.) *The European Union and Human Rights*. Oxford: Oxford University Press, pp. 757–780.

Stein, E. (1981) 'Lawyers, judges, and the making of a transnational constitution', *American Journal of International Law*, 75 (1): 1–27.

Sterett, S. (1992) 'Legality in administration in Britain and the United States', *Comparative Political Studies*, 25 (2): 195–228.

Sterett, S. (1994) 'Judicial review in Britain', *Comparative Political Studies*, 26 (4): 421–442.

Sterett, S. (1997) *Creating Constitutionalism*. Ann Arbor, MI: University of Michigan Press.

Stone, A. (1992a) *The Birth of Judicial Politics in France*. New York: Oxford University Press.

Stone, A. (1992b) 'Where judicial politics are legislative politics', *West European Politics*, 15 (3): 29–49.

Stone, A. (1994) 'Judging socialist reform', *Comparative Political Studies*, 26 (4): 443–469.

Stone Sweet, A. (2000) *Governing With Judges*. New York: Oxford University Press.

Sunkin, M. (1992) 'The incidence and effect of judicial review procedures against central government in the United Kingdom', in D. Jackson and C.N. Tate (eds) *Comparative Judicial Review and Public Policy*. Westport, CT: Greenwood, pp. 143–156.

Sunkin, M. (1995) 'The United Kingdom', in C.N. Tate and T. Vallinder (eds) *The Global Expansion of Judicial Power*. New York, NY: New York University Press, pp. 67–78.

Tate, C.N. (1992) 'Comparative judicial review and public policy', in D. Jackson and C.N. Tate (eds) *Comparative Judicial Review and Public Policy*. Westport, CT: Greenwood, pp. 3–13.

Tate, C.N. (1995) 'Why the expansion in judicial power?', in C.N. Tate and T. Vallinder (eds) *The Global Expansion of Judicial Power*. New York, NY: New York University Press, pp. 27–37.

Tate, C.N. and Vallinder, T. (eds) (1995) *The Global Expansion of Judicial Power*. New York: New York University Press.

ten Kate, J. and van Koppen, P. (1995) 'The Netherlands. In C.N. Tate and T. Vallinder (eds) *The Global Expansion of Judicial Power*. New York: New York University Press, pp. 369–380.

Thürer, D. (2005) 'Grundrechtsschutz in Europa – Globale Perspektive', *Zeitschrift für Schweizerisches Recht*, 124 (II): 51–71.

Toth, A.G. (1997) 'The European Union and human rights', *Common Market Law Review* 34 (3): 491.

Van Koppen, P. (1992) 'Judicial policy-making in the Netherlands', *West European Politics*, 15 (3): 80–92.

Verougstraete, I. (1992) 'Judicial politics in Belgium', *West European Politics*, 15 (3): 93–107.

Volcansek, M. (1992) 'Judges, courts, and policy-making in Western Europe', *West European Politics*, 15 (3): 1–7.

Volcansek, M. (1994) 'Political power and judicial review in Italy', *Comparative Political Studies*, 26 (4): 492–509.

Weiler, J. (1991) 'The transformation of Europe', *Yale Law Journal*, 100 (8): 2403–2483.

Weiler, J. (1996) 'European citizenship and human rights', in J. Winter *et al.* (eds) *Reforming the Treaty on European Union*. The Hague: Kluwer Law International.

Wilde, R. (2005) 'The 'legal space' or 'espace juridique' of the European Convention on Human Rights', *European Human Rights Law Review*, 2: 115–124.

Wildhaber, L. (2005) 'The coordination of the protection of fundamental rights in Europe', *Zeitschrift für Schweizerisches Recht*, 124 (II): 43–50.

Zannotti, F. (1995) 'The judicialization of judicial salary policy in Italy and the United States', in C.N. Tate and T. Vallinder (eds) *The Global Expansion of Judicial Power*. New York: New York University Press. pp. 181–204.

Ziller, J. (2003) 'The continental system of administrative legality', in B.G. Peters and J. Pierre (eds) *Handbook of Public Administration*. London: Sage, pp. 260–268.

10

Institutionalizing Democracy: Facing up to a Common Future

Dimitris N. Chryssochoou

Recent developments in the European Union (EU) raise the question of what kind of Europe we want or, indeed, need. Underlying this ever-topical issue is how to transform the present-day EU into a political community of free and equal citizens, thus bringing about a dynamic equilibrium between the parallel demands for 'unity in diversity' or for 'synarchy in heterarchy'. All this occurs against the background of a profound political crisis, created by the rejection of the constitutional treaty by the French and Dutch electorates. Although the addition of 'reform' to the title of any EU-related analysis makes the work appear more relevant, any attempt at sketching out a comprehensive reform package for the EU should strive towards creating a new 'civic contract' between decision-makers and decision-receivers. Such a civic-minded process of reforming the general system implies a move towards a 'democentric' form of union and captures the dialectic between the viability of national public spheres and the making of a mixed sovereignty regime: a 'synarchy' of states and demoi, in the sense of a densely institutionalized system of sovereignty-sharing among highly interrelated polities.

But, in the absence of a formal European Constitution and a fully-fledged European demos to legitimize it socially, there is an urgent need for a substantive restructuring of democratization strategies based on a new concept for Europe that would assign new meaning to the practice of democratic politics in an era characterized by the emergence of new forms of postnational governance.

INTRODUCTORY COMMENTS

Half a century since its inception as a rather limited community of Western European democracies, the 'EU order' is now taken to denote a composite polity structure that combines unity and multiplicity, and is capable of producing publicly binding decisions, as well as allocating values to European society. It is thus possible to capture its endemic complexity through the lens of new conceptual schemes, with the view to developing a series of novel understandings of polyarchical governance in Europe during these early stages of the twenty-first century. Namely, we can create a system of institutionalized shared-rule among multiple state and non-state actors that diffuses political authority and encourages all segments in European society to engage themselves in an open democratic dialogue about their future vocation. The point to make here is that public debate can become the medium through which a polity constitutes itself from the lower level upwards. This chimes well with the 'new governance' debate in political science, implying a transcendence of hierarchical and territorial forms of power distribution, where different notions of legitimacy and representation are capable of producing novel accounts of postnational politics. A new democratic concept for Europe should, in that regard, entail a balanced mix of social and political forces that share in the emerging sovereignty of the larger political association. Within the latter, public authority should not reside in a single decision-making centre, but should be diffused among different governance levels and forms of social, political, and cultural contention that can combine territorial with substantive public issues.

At the same time, one could argue that recent changes in the workings of the EU political system have not affected its character. It remains an essentially state-centric project, preserving a balance between state sovereignty and a relatively moderate (yet easily discernible) deepening of integration, by means of producing a system of political co-determination; what in other words makes for a new form of synarchy between states and demoi – an ensemble *sui generis* of highly interdependent political systems, whose structural and functional interaction results in a multilevel system of entangled sovereignties (Chryssochoou, 2009). The EU still remains a treaty-constituted political body, as it is not the creation of a unilateral act by a single and undifferentiated demos. Also, it does not derive its political authority from its citizens directly and has not – as yet – created a complete fusion among different levels of public authority. Moreover, its constitutive units, in the form of historically constituted

nation-states, are free to dissociate themselves from the larger association if and when they so wish. Finally, its emerging yet nebulous (and even controversial) constitutional identity rests heavily upon the domestic orders of states, although the EU already ensures the locking together of democratic states when it comes to the joint use of fundamental political and economic powers. Arguably, all the above offer the key to understanding the changing conventions of state sovereignty, which might now be interpreted as the right to be involved in the joint exercise of competences with other states.

But what is urgently needed is a new blueprint for reform that would guarantee a sense of process towards a more democentric polity. In that regard, European citizenship carries an undisputed political weight, whose democratic potential appears to be threefold: first, it sets up a transnational system of rights giving access and voice to the constituent publics; second, it induces integrative sentiments by motivating greater civic participation in the affairs of the larger polity; and third, it strengthens the bonds of belonging to an 'active polity' by means of facilitating the process of positive EU awareness-formation at the grassroots. The crucial question, however, remains: Does the EU simply entail a rearrangement of existing rights and civic entitlements, or does it amount to a shared European civicness and hence to a new political subject? From that perspective, the aim is for the EU to allocate authoritatively, and not merely derivatively, the rights and values within European political society. Taking the argument further, the outcome would not resemble the creation of a 'community of fate', but rather a new democratic design, whose civic value exists independently of national public spheres, but whose 'politics' extends to both EU and national civic arenas. This would signal a shift in legitimation from a functionalist-driven process of polity-building to a community of free and equal citizens based on the more inclusionary virtues of belonging to a transnational political community. However, as recent treaty reforms failed to produce a common democratic vision, a new concept for Europe is needed to face the challenges of the new era.

The question of democracy in the EU and, more precisely, its largely deficient nature, points to a negative side-effect of European integration as a whole, namely the growing dissonance between the requirements of contemporary democratic rule and the actual – both functional and structural – conditions upon which the political and institutional management of EU affairs is largely based. Arguably, to be more specific than that is to pre-empt the discussion below, which stresses the contested nature of the so-called 'democratic deficit' of the EU. Not only does the debate revolve around the question of how to resolve the deficit in question, but it also concerns its nature and often its future evolution. In that regard, the crucial distinction concerns an institutional and a sociopsychological perspective. Whereas the former focuses more on power-sharing and on institutional reform as a solution to the actual or perceived problems of democracy in the EU, the latter is concerned with questions of European identity (especially multiple identity-holding) and the formation of a composite, yet distinct, European civic demos. As the current debate raises fundamental questions about the future form of the EU as a composite polity of highly interrelated states and demoi – what was termed above as a 'synarchy of entangled sovereignties' – the conclusion to be drawn is that recent reforms, including the constitutional treaty of which ratification is pending, failed to enhance the democratic properties of the general system, leaving the EU as a system of democracies and not a democratic system in its own right.

When the integration process began in the late 1950s, no one gave much thought to its democratic credentials. For decades since, the European Community (as was) was resting on a 'permissive consensus', that is to say the tacit agreement of the member state citizens. Indeed, its political legitimacy came from elsewhere: the peace and prosperity that integration would bring to Western Europe, rather than from its aspirations to becoming a democratic political system like any other (Newman, 2001: 358). But since the early 1990s, especially since the ratification crisis of the Treaty on European Union (1993), such a modest consensus is said to have broken down. In its place has arisen new 'polity discourses' which offer conflicting solutions to the problem of democratizing the political system of the EU. Especially in a period when transnational political and economic pressures are challenging both intra- and inter-state relations, it may no longer be enough to confine democracy within the territorial boundaries of the nation-state to deal effectively with the implications of new forms of polity.

This general understanding raises new questions, such as, how it might be possible for citizens to hold transnational decision-makers to account. Questions of this kind reflect substantive democratic concerns that have grown as the integrative process has evolved, and moved away from acting merely as an interstate diplomatic forum and towards a fully-fledged European 'polityhood'. This development, otherwise known as a 'normative turn' in EU studies, has led to scholarly interest in the idea that the present-day EU might one day transform itself into a democratic political system. While there is some measure of agreement that the EU is not democratic, there is no consensus as to how it might become so. Indeed, there are two different understandings of what the EU's democratic deficit is all about. The first focuses, in large measure, on institutional properties by arguing that the problem of democracy in the EU is tied to the flawed interinstitutional interactions that characterize the functioning of a non-state polity like the EU. In this context, proposals for further reform speak of the EU's 'institutional imbalance', and of the need to enhance the public accountability as well as the representative nature of EU policy-makers and decision-takers. The second understanding of the deficit in question focuses on sociopsychological factors and makes the case for a new sense of European 'demos-hood'. In particular, it argues that the EU's present democratic pathology occurs, in large measure, because of the absence of a European civic demos. As a consequence, this second perspective on the democratic deficit is more interested in European civic and (more broadly) political identity, and the extent to which there is 'a feeling of community' among Europeans. Acknowledging that the absence of a European civic demos – and, by implication, assuming that a legal or economic demos already exists, either through European Court of Justice (ECJ) rulings or through participation to a common currency area – is a barrier to the making of a democratic European polity, proposals for further reform tend to suggest paths to transnational demos-formation based on a common European civicness. Taken together, these notions of plural citizenship in a non-state polity give rise to the idea of multiple national citizenries being turned into what can be described as a 'republic of Europeans'.

DEMOCRACY OR 'DEMOS-CRACY'?

The term 'democratic deficit' first appeared in a European Parliament report in 1984 and has been in inflationary use ever since, to the extent that one can legitimately refer to a voluminous 'democratic deficit *acquis*' in EU studies. In general terms, the orthodox view of the deficit holds that the transfer of legislative powers from member-state legislatures to common institutions of governance, and particularly to the state-controlled Council of Ministers (the EU's *de facto* legislator), has not created a corresponding degree of democratic accountability or an effective democratic legislature, in the form of the European Parliament, the only directly elected institution of the EU. This has emerged as the dominant view of the 'democratic deficit *acquis*' since the first European

Parliament elections of 1979, and one which has become even more convincing since the implementation of the Single European Act (1987). The latter extended the scope of European competences, as well as the use of qualified majority voting (QMV) in the Council, albeit in areas relevant to the completion of the single market. This made it possible for member states (and hence for a national demos) to be outvoted in a process of joint decision-making. Although greater majority rule has, overall, increased the decision-taking efficiency of the general system – as it speeded up the process of adopting common legislative acts – it has exacerbated further the already marginal role that national parliaments enjoy within the integration process. This is due to the fact there is no substantive institutional guarantee that the scrutiny of national parliaments will matter, when national governments and, by extension, sovereign populations, may be outvoted in the various Councils. The orthodox view also brings together two forms of institutional deficiencies. The first refers to the gradual 'de-parliamentarization' of national political systems and the growing influence of the executive branches of government; a process related to the notion of 'postparliamentary governance'. The second focuses on the transfer of decision-making authority away from the national (or subnational) level of governance to the supranational level. This weakens the already problematic link between the electorate and *de facto* legislators that enjoy proper democratic legitimacy at the state level. Shifting control of the integration process from national governments from the civil servants who support them, and from the unelected EU institutions (especially the European Commission, which remains the sole initiator of European legislation), provides an obvious, yet partial, solution to the deficit in question. Thus, the core argument in defence of the orthodox view is that a loss of national democratic control must be compensated for by the parliamentarization (along federalist lines) of the EU. Accordingly, the European

Parliament must be granted greater legislative and controlling powers if it is to perform functions that are equivalent to a 'proper' parliament. This usually implies a move towards a federally inspired bicameralism: a mixed system of direct, popular representation within the European Parliament and indirect, territorial representation within the Council.

Yet the European Parliament, and others who make the case for an extension of the parliamentary model to the EU recognize that the European Parliament's gains have not entirely compensated for democratic losses at national level, and that the integration process remains controlled by the executive branches of national governments and their counterparts at EU level. As a consequence, measures to extend further the European Parliament's involvement in both the legislative process and in scrutinizing the executive have been proposed; for example, in the form of an extension of the co-decision procedure so as all provisions falling under its jurisdiction also operate on the basis of QMV in the Council, and in extending the European Parliament's involvement in the appointment of the Commission, especially its president. But there is also growing support for greater involvement of national parliaments in EU affairs. National MPs already have an important role to play in scrutinizing EU legislation, though in practice they are more often than not unable to perform that function effectively. Since the Treaty of Nice (2001), there has been a renewed interest in giving national legislatures more of a formal say in EU legislative processes. One suggestion is that they should be granted a role over whether EU legislation has been made on the basis of the subsidiarity principle. This would entail them deciding whether decisions are being taken at the most appropriate level. Others have sought to reinstate national parliamentary assizes, by adding a second chamber to the European Parliament (critics of this approach assert that a similar experiment was attempted in the early 1990s with little success).

In general terms, the political agenda of those who favour a greater role for national parliaments in EU legislative processes often stretches to support for the *de facto* 'renationalization' of EU policies. For this group, arguments about the democratic deficit may mask a more general hostility to the integrative project. Alternatively, they may assume that the EU political system is incapable of promoting substantive democratic reforms and that the only viable solution to its democratic (as well as legitimation) deficits is for the common institutions to play much less of a role in domestic politics and for the EU to become more state-centric that it currently is.

As the process of integration is said to privilege executives at the expense of directly elected legislatures, the criticism is not just that national parliaments do not possess sufficient powers, but that non-elected bodies possess too many. In this line of reasoning, many in the past have attacked the Commission for being the archetypal undemocratic institution, in that it is a civil service composed of appointed members that possess substantive agenda-setting and policy making, if not legislative, powers. There are various possible perspectives on such criticisms. Perhaps the most relevant has been that this issue is really about accountability and institutional autonomy, namely the extent to which the Commission, as an executive body, is accountable to the collective body of European citizens or the degree to which it has been able to break free from the control of national institutions, and to act in an independent fashion, thereby directly influencing policy and integrative outcomes. While there has clearly been an extension to the scrutiny role of the European Parliament over the Commission in the successive treaty revisions of the mid-1980s and throughout the 1990s, the Commission has retained a sufficient degree of discretion – both functional and political – over how it performs its initiative function. But whether this is undemocratic or not remains an open-ended and disputed question.

It is not only the Commission that is subject to criticism of this kind. The ECJ – and, more explicitly, its oft-quoted political activism – has also been attacked for their teleological pro-integrationist bias. While the court has an obligation to interpret the treaties, and has also been instrumental in pushing out the boundaries of European law, there is once again little agreement on the extent to which the ECJ really plays an autonomous role in the EU policy process. Inventive as it may be, the role played by the ECJ is, by and large, in line with the spirit of the treaties that it was set up to interpret. Also, criticisms of the Council usually refer to the fact that it is the Council rather than the European Parliament (or, for that matter, the member-state legislatures) that has the final say in legislative matters – or at least on issues of vital importance to national governments. One reason why this criticism is deemed credible is that the Council is a somewhat arcane body, operating under conditions of secrecy rather than transparency; its legislative decisions being taken behind closed doors.

Underpinning arguments that the non-elected EU bodies need to become more open and accountable to European citizens is a more general point – that the EU has traditionally been a technocratic body, which has valued expertise and policy effectiveness much more than representation and civic participation. Since the early 1990s, the democracy debate within the EU has been extended, so that even when it remains institutionally orientated, it has become inextricably linked with issues both of public participation in the EU policy process and of social legitimacy regarding the level of popular support in the EU. Thus, democratizing the European polity is not just about rejigging the institutional balance of the EU system to give certain institutions more of a policy role, and nor is it solely reliant on the representative role of parliaments. It is also about bringing Europe closer to citizens, ensuring that the integration process is no longer an elite-driven process or a states-led project that is distant or even irrelevant for the vast majority of European citizens. There are various dimensions to these arguments, ranging from the idea of strengthening the representation of regions and localities in the EU (as favoured by the multilevel governance approach) to increasing transparency and simplification. In the latter case, democracy is said to be facilitated through greater openness and visibility, such as the availability of Council minutes or enhanced public consultation by the Commission at prelegislative stage.

The problem associated with institutional approaches to the democratic deficit is that they leave the equally crucial sociopsychological dimension largely unexplored. Such a dimension shifts the emphasis from the question, 'Who governs and how?' to the more demanding question, 'Who is governed?', thereby focusing more on the treatment of the disease than on its symptoms. The starting-point is that at the heart of the democratic deficit lies the absence of a composite European demos and hence of 'civic we-ness' or a commonly shared civic identity among Europeans (Chryssochoou, 1998). This normative democratic perspective builds on the wider assumption that political democracy, in the form of representative and responsible government, pre-supposes a popular infrastructure upon which certain basic properties, such as, adherence to and acceptance of majority rule, apply in any given political community. A transnational civic demos can be defined as a composite citizen body whose members share an active interest in the democratic governance of the larger polity to which they also belong, and who can direct their democratic claims to and via the central institutions. Put differently, it is this notion of a composite demos that endows the European polity with the necessary level of social legitimacy. It also follows that the qualitative transformation of the EU 'from democracies to democracy' requires the positive feelings of the member state demoi to be stronger to offset any politically divisive issues that may arise as the process of integration proceeds.

As Cohen argues, 'there can be no larger part unless the larger part and the smaller parts are indeed parts of one whole' (Cohen, 1971: 46).

The more the EU relies on democratic credentials, the more important it is for citizens to have feelings of belonging to an 'inclusive' polity. In this context, the emergence of a European civic identity out of the varied democratic traditions that currently exist in the EU is imperative, not only for the political viability of democratic shared-rule in a composite polity like the EU, but also if the democratic integrity of the constituent publics is to be respected, and for cultural variation and multiple identity-holding to be fostered. For a European demos to exist, its members must recognize their collective existence as such. Merely being granted citizenship rights is far from adequate. This is a question of a change in the way citizens think about themselves and their view of the communities to which they belong. As the EU cannot be detached from its constituent identities, transnational demos formation does not imply a melting-pot type of society in which pre-existing (mainly territorial) identities are assimilated into a new supranational identity. Rather, it projects an image of a pluralist political system – a 'sympolity' of states and demoi in the sense of a 'polity of polities' – within which the civic demos emerges as the unchallenged unit of transnational authority and the ultimate focus of political purpose within the larger association. In that sense, 'many people, one demos', rather than 'many demoi, one people', epitomizes the normative equivalent of a European 'demos-cracy'. This implies 'a many turned into one without ceasing to be many'. A European civic demos can be said to exist when the member publics see themselves as part of a larger democratic unit and are given the institutional means to mark their impact in the affairs of the EU, even though they retain their constituent identities. It is possible to identify the following properties as necessary for European demos-formation: (a) the democratic self-consciousness of citizens; (b) adherence to shared democratic values; (c) public awareness of the transnational polity; and (d) a desire to shape democratically the future, so as to build a plurality of interrelated demoi, without endangering the very essence of that plurality – its diversity.

REINVENTING THE CIVIC

Linking the question of the EU polity with different democratic perspectives helps us confront some of the central puzzles of integration theory today. One such example that merits our attention is neorepublican theory, in that new normative understandings of shared democratic rule have sought to both revive, and nurture a paradigm of social and political organization for the EU, defined as a mixed and composite polity and founded upon novel forms of civicness. In its basic conception, a *res publica* aims at three primary objectives which, taken together, capture the imagination of a virtue-centred life: (a) justice through the rule of law; (b) the common good through a mixed and balanced constitution; and (c) liberty through active citizenship. From a macrohistorical perspective, more than 2,500 years since the founding of the Roman republic, an anniversary that passed largely unnoticed by present-day Europeans, the above features still constitute the *raison d'être* of an idealized notion of *res publica*, marking their impact in the search for 'the good polity' (Schwarzmantel, 2003).

Reviving a republican tradition constitutes a rather complex enterprise. We are dealing with clusters of internally coherent arguments, values, and concepts that facilitate reflection on present political arrangements (Skinner, 1998: 101–20). As Lavdas (2001) argues, liberty and civic participation have been interpreted and combined in a number of ways, yet the challenge for today's republican scholarship is to develop a pluralist rather than a populist republicanism, in which tolerance would be guaranteed in diverse, multicultural societies. This refurbishment of

republican thinking reflects a wider democratic concern with the construction of a
socially legitimated political ordering
founded upon the notion of 'balanced government' and 'undominated' (or quality)
choice. But it is not the latter that causes
liberty, as liberty is constituted by the legal
institutions of the polity – namely, the republican state (Pettit, 1997: 106–9). As Brugger
(1999: 7) explains, 'Whereas the liberal sees
liberty as essentially pre-social, the republican sees liberty as constituted by the law
which transforms customs and creates citizens.' Accordingly, civic participation should
not be taken as a democratic end in itself, but
rather as a means of ensuring a dispensation
of nondomination by others (or nonarbitrary
rule). In short, the rule of law, opposition to
arbitrariness and the republican constitution
are constitutive of civic freedom itself.

The notion of 'balanced government' is
also central to republicanism. It is forged in
two related ways: negatively, by associating
the constitution of 'a proper institutional
balance' with the prevention of tyranny; and
positively, by ensuring a deliberative mode of
civic rule, whereby 'the different 'constituencies' which make up civil society are encouraged to treat their preferences not simply as
givens, but rather as choices which were
open to debate and alteration' (Craig, 1997:
114). Liberty was expected to be best preserved under a mixed form of polity through
certain constitutional guarantees, with no
single branch of government being privileged
over the others. Here, republicanism strikes a
balance between civic participation and the
attainment of the public good, by allowing
for 'a stable form of political ordering in a
society which contains different interests or
constituencies' (Craig, 1997: 116). A republican form of European governance refers,
first and foremost, to the range of normative
qualities embodying the construction of an
extended civic space, where citizens share
among themselves a sense of a 'sphere of
spheres' (as a component of civic virtue that
is a valuable resource for the polity) and a
regard for good governance (as a training

ground for civic learning), at the same time
as they take part in different public spheres.
A republican account of liberty and mixed
government can thus contribute in a constructive manner to constructing a European
polity. In particular, with reference to the
ongoing debate on the incorporation of
the Charter of Fundamental Rights into the
formal treaty framework, it has been shown
that the discussion is pregnant with frustrated
potentialities, indicating the need for a more
extensive, if thin, institutional public space,
through which civic competence can be
expanded and citizens can enter into a European
demos (Lavdas and Chryssochoou, 2006).

Given the absence of an engaging European
civic demos, republicanism has the potential
to disentangle 'the issue of participation in
an emerging polity from the cultural and
emotional dimensions of citizenship as pre-
existing affinity and a confirmation of belonging' (Lavdas, 2001: 4). The point is that
'some elements of the real and symbolic *res
publica*, may sustain a degree of political
motivation *vis-à-vis* the EU and its relevance
for peoples' lives while also allowing for
other and more intense forms of motivation
and involvement at other levels of participation' (Lavdas, 2001: 5). But given the lack of
organic unity among the member state demoi,
the challenge facing republican ideals is to
institutionalize respect for difference and
group rights while sustaining 'a shared sense
of the public good' (Bellamy, 1999: 190).
This is more likely to emerge through Pettit's
third (structural) concept of freedom as 'nondomination', as it combines 'the recognition
of the significance of the pluralism of cultural possibilities for meaningful choice and
a framework based on a minimal set of
shared political values' (Lavdas, 2001: 6). To
the extent that the EU political system cannot
motivate extensive public engagement
through emotions and sentiments of community, the making of a European demos calls
for a different approach. The question is how
to disentangle the issue of civic participation
from its cultural and emotional dimensions
that are based on pre-existing affinity and

confirmations of belonging. From a different angle, Eriksen (2000: 51) prompts us to 'decouple citizenship and nationhood' from the prism of the discourse–theoretical concept of deliberative democracy and to view the constitution as 'a system for accommodating difference' (Lavdas, 2001). But since most aspects of active citizenship can be reduced to either 'emotional citizenship' or the expression of rational and deliberative capacities, the question is how to strengthen the latter in a context where the weakness of the former presents both opportunities and constraints: one expects various asymmetries to have developed between the member state polities with different state traditions, constitutional, cultures, and historical patterns of multicultural or monocultural legitimations of political authority (Lavdas, 2001).

This civic conception of Europe contributes to the making of a large-scale political order, steered by an active community of citizens belonging to different nations but sharing a genuine interest in their common future. Here, the emphasis is not on the crystallization of liberal–democratic norms in Europe's emerging political constitution, but rather on the search for an inclusive civic space, and the belief that democratic reform is not really the cause, but rather the consequence of popular aspirations to democratic rule: a desire to participate in a socially legitimized polity. From this view, a European *res publica* requires deliberative political decisions to promote certain public goods, the relevance of which extend far beyond the politics of democratic elections. Put differently, a republican polity should not be seen as representing any kind of constitutional union set up 'for narrowly instrumental purposes', but rather as a civic association based on virtue-centred practices to serve the common good, where freedom and, more accurately, civic liberty come first. Indeed, by pointing at a mixed sovereignty regime – a synarchy of highly interrelated states and demoi – new republican theorizing effectively makes the point that the polity that is currently emerging in Europe rests upon a on

a political and not a judicial constitution, and that the notion of republican citizenship could foster a shared sense of civic identity among the constituent publics. In that sense also, new republican thinking seems to be better equipped to offer a plausible answer to the question of whether the present-day European formation can be seen as 'a community united in a common argument about the meaning, extent and scope of liberty' (Ignatieff, 2000: 265).

REVISITING INTEGRATION

After half a century of theorizing about the democratic qualities and deficiencies of the integration process, it seems that the study of this uniquely observed political formation has reached a high *plateau*. This is not to imply that integration scholarship should start looking for new democratic experiments of a comparable potential; the idea is that the challenges facing the future of democracy in an post-statist polity like the EU should not take place in a theoretical vacuum, but should strive at a balancing act between explanation and understanding, or between first- and second-order theorizing. Legitimately, though, one asks whether Puchala's (1984: 198) cynical prophesy that the study of the EU will amount to 'a rather long but not very prominent footnote in the intellectual history of twentieth century social science' will prove as accurate as the author would have us believe.

A first response from a normative standpoint is that theory – and, in particular, democratic theory – matters, for familiarity with theory helps to test our analytical tools and appreciate their relevance in real-life situations, leading 'to unique insights which are valid starting points for the purpose of comparison and evaluation' (Taylor, 1971: i). This view is shared by the likes of Church (1996: 8), who argues that 'awareness of theory is a necessary ground-clearing measure'; Rosamond (2000: 5), who states that 'theorizing intellectualizes perceptions'; Groom (1990: 3), in his notion of theory as 'an intellectual mapping exercise which tells us where we are now, from where we have come and to where we might go'; and Unger (1975: 12), in arguing that theorizing links 'the order of ideas' (as conceptual entities) with 'the order of events' (as actual occurrences). The aim is to transcend purely descriptive approaches to EU democracy and to tackle fundamental ontological and even post-ontological issues facing a historically unprecedented polity, whose democratic potential remains subject to diverse interpretation. This, in turn, requires 'structured ways of understanding changing patterns of interaction' (Church, 1996: 8), free from the fragmented boundaries of microanalysis. In other words, we should aim to project a macroscopic view of the relationship between democracy and integration based on a systematic conceptual explanation. Church (1996: 8) notes: 'We need to be aware of the conceptions we use since they determine our perception of things'. Similarly, Hamlyn (1995: 31) asserts, 'One cannot get at reality except from within some system of concepts.'

This methodological pathway allows a heightened access to reality or offers the basis from which 'a hierarchy of realities' might emerge (Taylor, 1971: 149). The hypothesis in here is that a continuum of accessible knowledge domains might bridge the distance between the study of specialized issue-areas within collective political conduct, and the exercise of specific institutional choices. Important links will, thus, be established between knowledge acquisition and knowledge evaluation. Integration theory may, thus, be seen as the systematic study of links between wholes and parts, or between universals (totalities) and particulars (substructures). But there exists some variation in the way scholars ascribe different meanings to concepts whose examination is crucial to furthering our understanding of complex social and political phenomena. Also, there are those who are interested in the larger picture (the hierarchy); others who aim at

capturing part of the overall image (a particular reality); others who focus on the relationship of different realities; and others who focus on the art of theorizing. As Rosamond (2000: 4) notes: 'Theories are necessary if we are to produce ordered observations of social phenomena.' In Stoker's (1995: 17; quoted in Rosamond, 2000: 4) words: 'Theories are of value precisely because they structure all observations.'

The validity of the above is justified further when identifying the common values of distinct polities and the emergence of new ones; when throwing light on the union between an interactive society of states and new sources of democratic legitimacy; and when assessing the allegedly *sui generis* nature of a polity based on interlocking and overlapping authority structures. But theory also helps to assess the changing conditions of sovereignty and its implications for states: sovereignty has not been surrendered to a statist regional 'centre'; rather, the delegation of competences to common institutions passes through the capacity of states to control the depth and range of the regional process. Hence the corresponding need to place sovereignty within a context that accounts for the consensus-seeking norms embodied in joint decisions, which in turn affect state behaviour in ways that promote synergy and even co-operation, not conflict and contestation. These norms promote neither the retreat of the European nation state nor do they enhance its capacities at the expense of an overarching federal authority. A symbiotic relationship has thus emerged, where the growth of central competences is not seen as a direct challenge to sovereign statehood and its assorted notions of polity-building. As Taylor (1996: 97) put it: 'Any assertion of the former was likely, in the pattern of the historical evolution of the latter, to be accompanied by its countervailing force.'

A primary scholarly challenge for contemporary integration theorists is to assess an ever-expanding corpus of literature dealing with a rich kaleidoscope of relations, whose study often defies the categories of conventional thinking about such processes as transnational polity-building, multiple identity-holding and large-scale demos formation; while trying to make sense of:

- the future of the European state system itself
- the political viability of democracy both within and across national boundaries
- novel forms of plural citizenship and multiple loyalty-holding
- complex processes of 'meta-rule-making' in a non-state polity
- formal and informal interactions between the functional scope, territorial scale and integrative level of the regional process
- the institutionalization of new avenues of political communication across a plurality of national demoi.

'And yet,' Pentland (1973: 189) notes, 'we need not be routed by the apparent diversity and chaos of the field'. In this light, whatever lessons we draw from the current state of play regarding integration in the early 2000s both as a project and a process, this essay argues that the ordering of relations among the subunits amounts to a new politics of co-determination and, from a normative institutional standpoint, co-constitution. The question this raises is whether the EU strikes a balance between it becoming the main locus of decision-making for a plurality of the demoi, as well as the dominant focus of citizen identification within an extended European civic space.

Arguably, it takes no specialist in international theory – and, in particular, in normative theorizing – to understand that, to a greater extent than any other international organization, the present-day EU has installed a cooperative ethos in both the political and administrative workings of the constituent units. This amounts to a complex but enduring learning process of peaceful social change, combined with a remarkable degree of systemic political stability. Elements of this enduring capacity for governance offer the intellectual and cognitive capital needed to capture the dynamics of change 'from a diplomatic to a domestic arena', 'from policy to polity' and, as noted above, 'from democracies to democracy'. Although no shortage of available theory exists that might be used to guide EU scholarship, the field is still embroiled in theoretical controversy, compounded by conceptual complexity and a propensity to adopt the logic of methodological individualism. In some interpretations, the political system of the EU is described as complex, not because it is seen as a polity mix of multiple states, non-state actors and institutions, but because it defies any easy notions as to how it is organized in relation to other polities. Hence the question of whether existing theories of integration are in a position to reconcile the preservation of segmental autonomy and a multilevel regional order, two apparently contradictory principles. In that regard, the challenge to integration scholarship is to capture the dynamics of two complementary objectives: strengthening the viability of separate domestic orders (as opposed to idealized notions of the Westphalian sovereignty regime) through the institutionalization of joint sovereignty, such as through novel forms of synarchy that are capable of transcending the sovereignty of states, without subsuming it into a federal political authority or, to quote from recent EU parlance, into a European super-state.

The problem associated with this ambitious task rests in the different treatment of such 'general concepts' as sovereignty and integration, democracy and diplomacy, policy and polity, order and fragmentation and, crucially, unity and diversity. But which of the many interpretations these concepts entail ought we to utilize for deepening our understanding of EU polity? All the more so, given its capacity for institutional self-renewal, which is of importance when employing different lines of theoretical inquiry? Whatever the mixture of evidence and the method embedded in the existing models of integration, whether their emphasis is on conflict or equilibrium, and irrespective of their preference for the familiar (concrete) or the unique (unidentified) in prescribing a more or less democratic end-point, it is fair to suggest that their systematic examination becomes a prime theoretical requisite for the crossing of a qualitative research threshold. Many discourses on EU polity-building lead 'to an unhelpful focus on the formal characteristics of the actors at the expense of the processes which characterize, and flow from, their interactions, making the latter entirely dependent on the former' (Branch and Øhgaard, 1999: 124). Also, competing approaches tend to disagree on background conditions and process variables, the need for more or less integration, the impact of informal structures on integrative policy outcomes, and the feasibility or even desirability of ascribing a political *telos* to an otherwise common enterprise. This 'battle' of theories has often in the past of EU politics, led to zero-sum notions coupled with unjustified confidence in how the system 'actually' works and towards what it is developing into. The 'elephant' though, to recall Puchala's (1972) colourful metaphor, is not easy to manipulate in theoretical terms: it often turns into a 'chameleon', adjusting itself to the requirements of any given day. Thus, it may not only be that integration theorists are aware of having access to only a limited picture of this elusive political animal with nebulous democratic characteristics, but also that the creature itself changes so rapidly and even profoundly as to render its study an exercise that is ultimately misleading.

While the EU remains, to a large degree, an unresolved social-scientific puzzle, it does represents a novel form of regionalism that, 'more than any other form of deep regionalism … has displayed the potential to alter the relative congruence between territory, identity and function which characterized the nation state' (Laffan, 1998: 238). All the above defining properties of contemporary sovereign statehood are being subjected to change: territories are gradually but steadily embedded within wider sociopolitical spaces, if not also constitutional orders; identity displays the potential to contain multiple loyalties and affiliations; while traditional statist functions are influenced by a dramatic

increase in the levels of interdependence and internationalization (Laffan *et al.*, 1999). It logically follows that 'the EU is more than an expression of modified interstate politics: it is the focus for processes that bring together new varieties of identity and need' (Laffan *et al.*, 1999). These issues are compounded further by the fact that although the EU is taken to imply something more than the mere aggregate of its parts, sovereignty, the ultimate responsibility, remains removed from the new regional 'centre', thus becoming a systemic property of the general system. The EU is neither an international organization proper, nor is it developing into an ordinary state with a monopoly (or a delegated panoply) of law-making and law-enforcing powers. Equally puzzling remains its legal nature; for some, still resting on a dynamic system of international treaty-based rules, while others prefer the conceptual analogy of a metaconstitutional system, which is rule-driven by procedural innovation and political aspirations akin, but not identical, to statist forms of order-building.

All that we can say with a fair degree of confidence is that the EU's final vocation – presuming there will be one – is yet to become discernible in political and institutional terms. Even taking into account the series of neologisms invented over the last decades to capture its elusive political and legal ontology, to simply argue that the EU of today is yet another political formation *sui generis*, which should thus be examined only through the lens of new conceptual paradigms, runs the danger of complying with undisciplined formulations. Yet there is the danger of perpetuating its present stance in the grey area of 'normal interstate' and 'normal intrastate relations' as the two extremes which polities are conventionally located (Forsyth, 1981). Herein lies a major scholarly challenge, which may be crucial for the future development of the institutionalist aspects of EU studies: to focus on the study of more likely intermediate institutional outcomes, the format of which may differ from 'the forms of political domination that we are used to dealing with' (Schmitter, 1996:14). The aim, in other words, is to conceptualize 'the transient results of an ongoing process, rather than the [imagined] definitive product of a [presumed] stable equilibrium' (Schmitter, 1996: 106). What is more likely to emerge from this unique exercise in large-scale polity-building will differ markedly both from the constitutional properties attributed to a conventional federal state and the type of policy competences delegated to an average international organization. As to the oft-raised question of what kind of political terminology can be employed in order to arrive at a more realistic image of the EU, a plausible answer lies in that fact that real-life events outstrip theoretical constructs: 'as language precedes grammar, so politics precedes political theory' (Hallstein quoted in Pentland, 1973: 106). Wessels (1997: 292) makes the point well, linking the EU's conceptual conundrum with Tocqueville's insightful description of the United States in the nineteenth century: 'The human mind invents things more easily than words; that is why many improper terms and inadequate expressions gain currency ... Hence a form of government has been found which is neither precisely national or federal; ... and the new word to express this new thing does not yet exist'.

CONSTITUTIONAL REGRESSION

In a high-stakes public campaign the French and Dutch publics rejected in May and June 2005, respectively, the constitutional treaty, even though it had previously been approved by EU Heads of States and Government on 29 October 2004 in Rome. These two major blows to the ratification process threw the EU into a profound but not entirely unexpected political crisis. Interestingly enough, the constitutional treaty, to be replaced by a reform treaty after the decision of the Brussels European Council in June 2007, was viewed by many as a relatively modest step towards

the full constitutionalization of the treaties. Most analysts have asserted that the constitutional project would contribute to a more functional, viable and balanced form of decision-making in an enlarged EU of 27 members, coupled by a strengthening of the EU's institutional capacity to act in a more coherent and co-ordinated manner in its external relations (mainly through a European Foreign Affairs Minister, who would also to serve as a member of the Commission, even though this provision was not included in the exact wording in the new reform mandate).

Despite being discernable, the voting block that defeated the treaty was ideologically incoherent, largely being created by divergent national causes. This is not to imply that greater democracy in the EU can only be an outcome of integration, as the respective publics exercised their equally democratic right to oppose the acceptance of a major treaty reform, in the drafting of which they had little input. Be that as it may, even if the treaty had been ratified by all its signatories, the fact would remain that the EU's institutions would have continued to be based on an international treaty or (at best) a quasi-constitutional system of checks and balances designed to organize political authority in a non-state polity. This was not a constitution 'proper'. Yet, by virtue of its integrative and symbolic nature, the constitutional treaty aimed at a new constitutional order, albeit of a much less federalist kind than a formal constitutional settlement. At this point, the following questions are in order: Did the innovative Convention on the Future of Europe act as a 'constituent assembly'? Has the outcome of deliberating on the constitutional treaty been legitimized by European public opinion? Would the envisaged 'constitution' take the whole system further down the road to federalization?

Arguably, the answer to these questions is closer to a 'no', for three reasons. First, the whole drafting process was characterized by the lack of a European constituent power; let us immediately recall that the Convention was composed of appointed delegates, albeit drawn from a wider sociopolitical spectrum than has previously been the case in the history of EU treaty-making. Second, the outcome of the Convention was liable to amendments by an Intergovernmental Conference (IGC), which retained the right of states to a final say over the end product through the classical forms of interstate bargaining; a good case in point is the final voting arrangement, where QMV requires the support of 55 percent of (at least 15) participating states and 65 percent of the population. Third, following the argument about the lack of a genuine European constituent power, the reform process failed to produce a kind of European *Grundgezetz* that derives its social and, by extension, democratic legitimacy directly from a European demos.

Given the above, the general assessment may well be that the agonizing search for a new constitutional ordering in Europe comes in direct contrast to the democratic means available for creating it. Statecentrism seems to have been the order of the day, as was the case with previous treaty reforms, when it came to bestowing the EU with 'basic law' provisions. Nor does the integrative nature of a constitutional treaty suffice to transform a constellation of democracies into a democratic polity in its own right. The constitutional treaty would have to be based as much on the constitutional orders of states as on a new kind of political ordering for the EU to retain its character as a mixed and balanced association of states and demoi. At best, the outcome of constitutionalizing (but not necessarily federalizing) the treaties can follow the logic of constitutional engineering –as opposed to formal constitution-making – which has been part and parcel of the EU's *acquis conferencielle*. It thus emerges that the general direction of EU constitutionalism follows the previous path of sovereignty-conscious states wishing to bring about a moderate reordering of the existing treaties, which may well lead to a new and perhaps more viable and democratic constitutional equilibrium. But this does not amount to a substantive transformation of the EU's constitutional order.

It also follows from the above that the constitutional treaty was not meant to endow the EU with 'a new base of sovereignty' which would be able to transcend the sovereignty of its parts, contrary to early federalist predictions during the first stages of drafting. Instead, Article 5(1) of the treaty states: 'The Union shall respect the national identities of its Member States, inherent in the fundamental structures, political or constitutional … It shall respect their essential State functions, including those of ensuring the territorial integrity of the State, and for maintaining law and order and safeguarding internal security.' This provision epitomizes the dynamic yet unstable interplay between coordinated interdependencies and diffused political authority, suggesting that the EU is not inevitably developing towards a certain federal end. Rather, it is about the preservation of those state qualities that allow the member units to survive as distinct polities, whilst engaging themselves in a polity-building exercise that transforms their traditional patterns of interaction. Although this allows for the transformation of a community of states into the most advanced scheme of voluntary regional integration the world has ever witnessed, it should not carry with it the assumption of the end of the European nation-state.

The EU has not thus taken us 'beyond the nation-state' and towards a postnational state. Whether its logic of power-sharing can be explained through a theory of institutional delegation based on the principle of conferral, the most compelling evidence for the lack of a European sovereignty *per se* is that EU citizens are still taken to be 'sovereign' only within their national context. Thus the set of constitutional arrangements advanced by the constitutional treaty were confronted with the same old challenge: the level of support the EU would enjoy from the public and the means through which its institutions would open up new participatory opportunities for citizens. In that regard, effective governance for managing an integrated political order based on output legitimacy is but a poor substitute for the democratic norms of governance in relation to a demos. What is needed is a deliberative and civic-minded process of union as a platform from which a European constituent power can emerge. Title IV of the constitutional treaty on 'The Democratic Life of the Union' enlists a set of principles to guide the EU, such as democratic equality, representative and participatory democracy. The latter is an interesting addition, since it states that central institutions should 'give citizens and representative associations the opportunity to make known and publicly exchange their views on all areas of Union action'. An 'open, transparent and regular dialogue' is envisaged between the EU, representative associations and civil society, coupled by a citizen's initiative, used to respond to the Commission's invitation 'to submit any appropriate proposal on matters where citizens consider that a legal act of the Union is required for the purpose of implementing the Constitution'. These provisions, however, do not amount to a constitutional democratic order, although a shift in emphasis has taken place from the more traditional forms of representation, where expression mainly occurred through parliamentary channels of political deliberation and contestation, to a framework of politics which allowed for a greater and more active public engagement in EU affairs.

At a time when the EU retains its character as a *via media* between different forms of polity, governance and representation, the initial prospects for a smooth and uncontroversial ratification of the constitutional treaty raised the expectations of endowing a fragmented European demos with a common civic identity that would nurture a sense of 'demoshood'. Such aspirations did not in the end prove realistic. Instead, the nebulous and rather unceremonious outcome of Europe's constitutional project revealed that the exclusion of citizens from the drafting stages of the process, namely the absence of a participatory method of EU constitution-making, had

ensured that their status was not elevated and they continued to lack the ability to act as system-steering agents. The whole enterprise has thus been detrimental to efforts to better equip citizens to become the decisive agents of civic change and enhance further their horizontal integration within a nascent pluralist order composed of entangled arenas for action. Anything less would perpetuate a predominantly elite-based operation that is detrimental to legitimate forms of polity. It would also prevent the EU from acquiring a distinct political subject, where civic identity exists independently of national public spheres and extends to both EU and national civic arenas, signalling a shift in the basis of legitimation to a European demos. Even the new dialectic between sovereignty and integration, carrying the implication of an explicit right to political co-determination, failed to produce a credible commitment to democratizing the EU. As in previous treaty reforms, the outcome of the process, far from representing a *cause célèbre* for a democratic Europe, amounted to a cautiously negotiated deal of 'partial offsets' to key democratic problems facing the future of the EU. Not only did these forms fail to product a common democratic vision, but they also generated a belief that such a vision remains beyond reach, at least for the foreseeable future. This is justified further by understanding the outcome of treaty reforms as the product of a predominantly utilitarian calculus among the divergent preferences and expectations of the dominant national political elites.

Such trends were also evident in the June 2007 European Council in Brussels, where a decision was taken for the setting up of a new IGC to prepare a reform treaty by the end of 2007 (so it could have been ratified by 2009). The new mandate included some pro-integrationist elements like the further extension of QMV to some 40 new instances, a strengthening of the European Parliament's co-legislative rights through co-decision making, an enhanced role for national parliaments in their dealings with the Commission, and the retention of measures previously evident in the constitutional treaty on the EU's democratic life. Once again though, instead of politicization becoming a weapon in the strategic arsenal of pro-integrationist forces, the June 2007 Brussels European Council resulted in a compromised structure that accommodated the demands of the more sceptical actors (in particular Britain and Poland), thus making it difficult to achieve a democratic equilibrium between the EU and 'the civic'. Too many reservations, opt-outs, references to the retention of states' prerogatives in relation to competences and reform practices, along with a considerable delay in the application of the double majority system of the constitutional treaty, prevented the EU from consolidating its political identity, thus failing to signal a shift in the basis of legitimation from managerial forms of executive elite governance to a transnational civic demos founded on more active and inclusionary virtues of belonging.

True, for a polity that was founded and is still based on a system of international treaty-based rules, and whose incipient but fragmented demos still lacks effective civic competence, the transition 'from democracies to democracy' and, by extension, from an aggregative to a deliberative model of governance, is neither easy nor linear, let alone automatic. Yet, recent trends in EU treaty reform seem to give credit to those who argue that the general system is closer to a state-centric form of governance than to a demo-centric form of polity. This is far from an ideal state, as it hinders the emergence of a European demos. In other words, political pragmatism, if not cynicism, as the June 2007 Brussels Summit showed, seems to have had its day at the expense of a visionary project to reignite the public's interest in EU affairs. Like any other polity that aspires to becoming a democracy, the EU has to engage itself in a constitutive process to bring about a new framework of participatory politics by inventing and, where necessary, reinventing, a sense of *res publica*. Hence, it is increasingly

important for the EU to address issues of democracy and to ensure that its decisions are informed by a principled public discourse. This is because the EU will continue to be confronted with the reality of multiple polities and demoi, as well as by the fact that its present structure invests more in accommodationist reforms than in fundamental constitutional reorderings.

FUTURE PROSPECTS

Given the remarkable profusion of theories aiding the study of the EU and the level of mutual incomprehension that often pervades amongst them, especially on how democracy might work in such a composite, non-state polity, scholars should aim at rediscovering a sense of process (and purpose) to enable them to rethink the archetypal 'laboratory' of concepts and ideas within which novelunderstandings of democracy draw. Normative theory, drawing from the likes of new republican thinking, constitute an appropriate point of departure with far-reaching intellectual possibilities for the study of the EU as a new type of political constellation concerned with the quality of its own democracy. The EU has thus to associate itself closely with the formation of a European civic space which could act as the equivalent of a polis whose politeia reflects its essential purpose. This approach accords with the EU's nature as a synarchy of democratic polities, or a mixed commonwealth of states and demoi, as well as with the view that the making of a new political ordering in Europe should be a condition for uniting the member publics and their respective public spheres into a polycultural and polycentric res publica (Lavdas and Chryssochoou, 2006, 2007). Thus, 'many peoples, one demos' captures the imagination of a 'republic of Europeans' based on a certain notion of democratic *civitas* that stems from a rich intellectual tradition of European political thought. Admittedly, this is much less of a concrete strategy for future developments, but offers more than a democratic wish for the shape of things to come. Yet, it is a virtuous cause that that would assign meaning to a new vision of politics that would still be part of a great democratic tradition.

REFERENCES

Bellamy, R. (1999) *Liberalism and Pluralism: Towards a Politics of Compromise*. London: Routledge.

Branch A.P. and Øhgaard, J.C. (1999) 'Trapped in the supranational-intergovernmental dichotomy: a response to Stone Sweet and Sandholtz', *Journal of European Public Policy*, 6 (1): 123–143.

Brugger, B. (1999) *Republican Theory in Political Thought: Virtuous or Virtual?* London: Macmillan.

Chryssochoou, D.N. (1998) *Democracy in the European Union*. London: I.B. Tauris.

Chryssochoou, D.N. (2009) *Theorizing European Integration*. London and New York: Routledge.

Church, C.H. (1996) *European Integration Theory in the 1990s*. European Dossier Series, No. 33, University of North London.

Cohen, C. (1971) *Democracy*. Athens: The Georgia University Press.

Craig, P.P. (1997) 'Democracy and rule-making within the EC: An empirical and normative assessment', *European Law Journal*, 3 (2): pp. 105–130.

Eriksen, E.O. (2000) 'Deliberative supranationalism in the EU', in E.O. Eriksen and J.E. Fossum (eds) *Democracy in the European Union*. London: Routledge, pp. 42–64.

Forsyth, M. (1981) *Unions of States: The Theory and Practice of Confederation*. Leicester: Leicester University Press.

Groom, A.J.R. (1990) 'The setting in world society', in A.J.R. Groom and P. Taylor (eds) *Frameworks for International Co-operation*. London: Pinter

Hamlyn, D.W. (1995) *Metaphysics*. Cambridge: Cambridge University Press.

Ignatieff, M. (2000) 'Republicanism, ethnicity and nationalism', in C. McKinnon and I. Hampsher-Monk (eds), *The Demands of Citizenship*. London: Continuum, pp. 257–266.

Laffan, B. *et al.* (1999) *Europe's Experimental Union: Rethinking Integration*. London: Routledge.

Laffan, B. (1998) 'The European Union: a distinctive model of internationalization', *Journal of European Public Policy*, 5 (2): 235–253.

Lavdas, K.A. (2001) 'Republican Europe and multicultural citizenship', *Politics*, 21 (1): 1–10.

Lavdas, K.A. and Chryssochoou, D.N. (2006), 'Public spheres and civic competence in the European polity: a case of liberal republicanism?', in I. Honohan and J. Jennings (eds) *Republicanism in Theory and Practice*. London: Routledge, pp. 154–169.

Lavdas, K.A. and Chryssochoou, D.N. (2007), 'A republic of Europeans: civic unity in polycultural diversity', in M. Mascia (ed.) *Intercultural Dialogue and Citizenship: Translating Values into Actions*. Venice: Marsilio, pp. 207–227.

Newman, M. (2001) 'Democracy and accountability in the EU', in J. Richardson (ed)., *European Union: Power and Policy Making*. London: Routledge, pp. 357–354.

Pentland, C. (1973) *International Theory and European Integration*. London: Faber and Faber.

Pettit, P. (1997) *Republicanism: A Theory of Freedom and Government*. Oxford: Clarendon Press.

Puchala, D.J. (1984) 'The integration theorists and the study of international relations', in C.W. Kegley and E. Wittkopf (eds) *The Global Agenda: Issues and Perspectives*.New York: Random House, pp. 336–351.

Puchala, D.J. (1972) 'Of blind men, elephants and international integration', *Journal of Common Market Studies*, 10 (3): 267–284.

Rosamond, B. (2000) *Theories of European Integration*. London: Macmillan.

Schmitter, P.C. (1996) 'Examining the present euro-polity with the help of past theories', in G. Marks *et al.* (eds) *Governance in the European Union*. London: Sage, pp. 1–14.

Schwarzmantel, J. (2003) *Citizenship and Identity: Towards A New Republic*. London: Routledge.

Skinner, Q. (1998) *Liberty before Liberalism*. Cambridge: Cambridge University Press.

Stoker, G. (1995) 'Introduction', in D. Marsh and G. Stoker (eds) *Theory and Method in Political Science*. Basingstoke: Macmillan, pp. 1–17.

Taylor, P. (1996) *The European Union in the 1990s*. Oxford: Oxford University Press.

Taylor, P. (1971) *International Co-operation Today: the European and the Universal Patterns*. London: Elek.

Unger, R.M. (1975) *Knowledge and Politics*. New York: Free Press.

Wessels, W. (1997), 'An ever closer fusion? A dynamic macropolitical view on integration processes', *Journal of Common Market Studies*, 35 (2): 267–299.

11

Competing Visions of European Union

Craig Parsons

The rise and institutionalization of the supra-national European Union is often seen as the most novel transformation in postwar European politics. The only development that can rival it for broad importance on the postwar scene – the fall of communism and the reintegration of East and West – fits more comfortably in fairly traditional narratives of the ebb and flow of ideologies and empires. The EU, by contrast, is generally perceived as marking an explicit departure from long-standing historical patterns. Its federalizing project has recast the locus and major principles of political authority across the continent and shifted the distribution of a large volume of tangible resources. At a global level, these changes have typically been seen not only as departures from European norms but as the most significant formal break in any region from the main organizing lines of the modern world. Along with these shifts on the ground we have seen corresponding evolutions in academic focus. Scholars of European domestic politics and law have increasingly found that they need EU expertise to understand their historically separate national bailiwicks (among many, Dyson and

Goetz, 2003; Pierson, 1996; Wessels *et al.*, 2003). Students of international relations, both inside Europe and in other regions, have found themselves drawn out of diplomatic studies and into discussions of the boundary-crossing dynamics of 'multi-level govern-ance' (Cowles *et al.*, 2001; Marks *et al.*, 1996).

Yet if few now dispute the transformative nature of the EU, people continue to hold very different basic visions of what the project is about (or should be about). Such contestation goes on at two levels. Among political actors, normative variants of the anti-supranationality of de Gaulle and Thatcher are still a force on the European stage. Since the 1990s they and other objections to the EU have broadened beyond the elite circles that contained them for several decades, bringing a new level of public contestation about the EU's legitimacy. Among academics, lively analytic debates play on about the core logic by which the EU appeared, became institutionalized, and continues to evolve. To date, however, these two kinds of contestation have been largely separate. For most academics, capturing the

EU phenomenon analytically does not require us to discuss Europeans' normative visions of European institution-building. They have argued about how much the EU reflects structural or institutional imperatives, not battles over interpretation, legitimacy and meaning. Such analytic visions acknowledge that pro- and anti-EU actors employ normative rhetoric and engage in symbolic politics, of course, but cast them as decorative flourishes on more tangible underlying processes of political change.

This chapter argues, however, that these two kinds of contestation are intimately related. To capture the core analytical story of how the EU became institutionalized we must pay close attention to the normative visions of European institution-building around which people have mobilized. Recognition of this link will allow scholarship to catch up with the pervasive sense of transformation that the EU evokes among real Europeans (and non-Europeans as well). The causal heart of EU history is about how a scattered elite minority managed to institutionalize their contested vision of the organization of the continent.

COMPETING ANALYTICAL VISIONS OF THE EU PROJECT

To understand how most academics have thought about the EU project, it is helpful to consider briefly how most academics have thought about politics in general. Most social-science work since the nineteenth century explains what people do as fairly rational responses to some sort of unambiguous obstacle course. Political action varies not with different interpretive 'visions' of the world but with the resources people hold and the positions they inhabit in arenas like markets, security competitions, or contests for domestic political power. The most classic versions of such thinking are materialist – Marxism, economic liberalism, realism – where the obstacle course is presented as a set of structural givens. Such approaches gain dynamism from exogenous mechanisms of structural change, like new technology or macro-level evolutions in economic patterns. The obstacle course shifts, and patterns of political action shift in response. More recent, but now very well established, is institutionalist work that emphasizes man-made organizational aspects of the obstacle course. Its focus on a man-made environment leads to emphasis on feedback and 'path dependence,' gaining dynamism from the notion that institution-building at one point creates unforeseen resources or incentives for certain actions at later points. Otherwise its core logic shares some features of structural materialism. Both rest on the expectation that the main patterns of politics will follow from groups of people who share positioning (and so clear 'interests') in an objective landscape. The most salient debates in postwar political science have been about the shape of the obstacle course, which positions dictate which actions, and which position–action logics predominate where (Parsons, 2007).

The two main views of EU history are ideal-typical examples of these traditions. One is Andrew Moravcsik's 'liberal intergovernmentalist' (LI) theory, which became the obligatory point of departure for theoretical work on the EU by the 1990s (Moravcsik, 1998). LI explains the EU institutions as a function of economic–liberal-style structure and an exogenously given territorial patchwork of sovereign states. Its foundations are domestic economic interest groups who derive their main preferences from positions in markets (domestic and international). A pluralistic domestic process informs state policies: 'Groups formulate preferences; governments aggregate them' (Moravcsik, 1993: 483). Demands for integration thus come from domestic actors who stand to gain economically from new international arrangements. States are reluctant to delegate their sovereignty, but will carefully bargain with other states to the extent that cooperation is necessary to realize their domestic lobbies' policy preferences. Larger and more powerful states get more of what they want in bargaining. The substantive shape of these deals in turn determines the delegation of power to European-level institutions. The more international commitments raise problems of defection, the more governments will give up policy control and sovereignty to binding institutions that render the policy commitments more credible. Overall, we should see the best-developed EU responsibilities where high interdependence in sectors with substantial state intervention[1] produces strong domestic preferences in larger states for European policies, but where some divergence in state preferences requires institutionalization to minimize defection in the long term. The EU's Common Agricultural Policy (CAP) and Economic and Monetary Union (EMU) ostensibly epitomize these conditions and their integrative consequences.

The other major approach is institutional work that follows from the early 'neofunctionalist' theory of Ernst Haas (Haas, 1958). In its clearest and most ambitious codification (Sandholtz and Stone Sweet, 1998), it too begins from economic–liberal structural thinking. Haas used interest groups as 'the building blocks of a theory of politics', and many later institutionalists argue that Haas 'got it right' on this score (Burley and Mattli, 1993: 54; Haas, 1964: 30–50; Sandholtz and Stone Sweet, 1998: 5). Growing transnational exchange creates societal actors 'who need supranational governance' to further their (mainly economic) interests (Sandholtz and Stone Sweet, 1998: 11). Unlike LI, however, institutionalists allow that interest-group demands can be realized in a variety of ways, and that state or supranational actors have their own agendas and use their institutional positions to craft certain interest-group coalitions. Supranational agents in particular persuade or outmaneuver reluctant national governments to meet interest-group demands in ways that expand supranational rules and policies. Such extensions prove difficult to reverse, notably because backward movement in EU policy-making usually requires member-state unanimity. Thus a combination of transnational mobilization, supranational

actors, and 'sticky' institutional rules engenders a 'self-sustaining dynamic' (Sandholtz and Stone Sweet, 1998: 4–5). New supranational rules feed back to encourage further mobilization of societal actors at the European level. The largely unintended effects of supranational institutionalization 'gradually, but inevitably, reduce the capacity of the member-states to control outcomes' (Sandholtz and Stone Sweet, 1998: 4).

Political actors' visions of the EU receive little attention in a literature dominated by debate between these two approaches. After early atheoretical accounts stressed the importance of Europeanist ideology in initial postwar institution-building (Aron and Lerner, 1957; Brugmans, 1965; Lipgens, 1977), ideas and ideology fell out of the discussion. As a result these schools of thought developed in debates that were limited to competing positional claims. Historians debated whether it was mainly economic or geopolitical positioning that dictated the EU outcome (Hitchcock, 1998; Milward, 1992). Moravcsik confronted similar debates between realists and neoliberals in international relations (IR) theory, and combined them by boiling down the EU story to a clever combination of interest groups reacting to economic positions and states reacting to positions in a distribution of power. Institutionalists focused mainly on showing that this nationally framed aggregation of positions failed to capture what happened when early institution-building steps altered the shape of the positional obstacle course. They argued that aggregation of positions came out differently given some supranational rules and institutional actors (who followed their own organizational interests in fostering more supranational power). Several scholars in an institutionalist vein gave at least some attention to ideas and visions in the 1990s, arguing that the European Commission played a deeply transformative role in 'framing' the 'Single Market 1992' program and EMU. Yet their core narratives still portrayed Commission officials who acted largely out of organizational power-maximization and affected developments by cleverly 'trading off the interests of important state and corporate actors' (Fligstein and Mara-Drita, 1996; Jabko, 1999). Other theorists seemed to touch on competing visions in emphasizing the complexity and unforeseen consequences of the emerging EU policy (Marks *et al.*, 1996; Pierson, 1996). But even this thrust was largely about the messiness and unpredictability of the overall EU process, not the notion that major political actors were fighting over distinct normative visions of Europe.

In sum, practically none of the academic literature on the EU suggests that Europe's national political leaders have intentionally pursued European institution-building in 'visionary' ways, without being forced by domestic interest groups or cajoled by cleverly entrepreneurial supranational agents. This may seem peculiar to less academic observers. Many national leaders – from Robert Schuman to François Mitterrand in France, from Konrad Adenauer to Helmut Kohl and Joschka Fischer in Germany, and many others across Europe – have constantly proclaimed their European ideology. Journalists and non-academic writers have often described the champions of the EU's major treaty deals as ideologically committed to supranational integration. Critics of the project, from Charles de Gaulle to Margaret Thatcher to today's Kaczynsky brothers in Poland, have denounced them in similar terms. Certainly the tendency of academics to dismiss ideological rhetoric as 'cheap talk' is a healthy reflex. Cheap talk about the EU has never been in short supply. But a closer look at political patterns in the construction of the EU, and more serious consideration of its rhetoric, leads to another analytic vision that places competing normative visions (and the institutionalization of one of them) at the heart of the story.

WHY FOCUS OUR ANALYTIC VISION ON NORMATIVE ONES?

This section summarizes a broad argument about EU history that I document in detail

elsewhere (Parsons, 2003). Its point of departure is the claim that most scholarship on the EU overlooks a rather striking pattern of debate. Though it is now common among political-party experts to observe that current debates over the EU cross-cut political right and left across Europe (Hix and Lord, 1997; Hooghe and Marks, 2001; Taggart and Szczerbiak, 2006; Van der Eijs and Franklin, 2004), research on the dynamics of EU history has largely dismissed this possibility. Instead structurally and institutionally minded scholars have focused their attention on political conflict between national and supranational organizations, and have generally conceived of the domestic landscapes underneath these organizations as arenas of competition between discrete, fairly cohesive interest groups and political parties. Had scholars thought to look for debate and conflict inside organizations at all these levels – in parties, interest groups, state bureaucracies, and the EU organizations themselves – they would have found that the main patterns of political conflict around proposals for EU institution-building have divided coalitions, parties, regions, sectors, and bureaucratic organizations in many member-states to a remarkable degree. This makes it very difficult to argue that certain choices in these debates reflect the clear positional 'interests' of groups or organizations. Instead it suggests that EU history has featured a battle of ideas with considerable autonomy from underlying positioning in any sort of obstacle course. No pre-existing constellation of clear organizational interests dictated which of several ideas would come to define the shape of twenty-first century Europe. Competing visions – and the fairly contingent victory and institutionalization of one of them over time – form the core of the EU story.[2]

Even a general overview of cross-cutting debates over the 50 years of the EU project and all its member-states would be too large a task for a short chapter. Instead let me begin with a brief summary of the main visions of European institution-building that have competed in the postwar period.

Then I set out one line of argument why we should see these visions as the critical animating forces of the EU project, as opposed to simply being a range of options from which structural or institutional processes determined one outcome. This section focuses on the construction of the main lines of today's EU, taking the consolidation of the basic EU architecture in the 1990s as its endpoint. The following sections consider the role of these ideas in more recent EU developments, and their implications for the broader study of European politics.

It is common to chart debates over European integration along a spectrum from nationalist opponents of supranational institutions to 'federalist' advocates of a 'United States of Europe'. This dimension captures the most central and longstanding disagreements over the EU project and its alternatives. But especially in the first postwar decades – before the early steps to the EU organized political conflict into a fight mainly for or against its version of Europe – Europeans' regional proposals were more varied. They reflected three major organizational formats that I call the 'community', 'confederal', and 'traditional' models.

Community-model thinking is familiar, since it largely informed the proposals that won the competition and defined today's landscape. In the early postwar years, its proponents argued that a new program had to be found to break the cycle of nationalist violence that drove (in their view) the Franco-Prussian War and two world wars. In particular, Germany needed to be tied into some new structure to mute its atavistic inclinations (and many Germans agreed). Together with observations about the imperative for European 'integration' to match the scale and power of the American and Soviet superpowers, and with calls for commitments to open international trade in the wake of the Great Depression, these points were drawn together into plans for bindingly 'supranational' regional institutions. In explicit contrast to standard international contracts between states, these institutions would have their own independent powers and legal authority. They would oversee the Germans, police open markets, and generally tie all Europeans into a long-term agenda of cooperation. With time they might displace everyone's national loyalties, develop their centralized responsibilities, and give rise to a federal 'United States of Europe' as powerful and prosperous as the US. As we know, this rhetoric informed Jean Monnet's plan (advanced by, and named for, French Foreign Minister Robert Schuman) for the European Coal and Steel Community (ECSC) in 1950, its expansion into the much broader European Economic Community (EEC) in 1958, and has featured prominently in the development of the EU through the Single European Act (SEA) of 1986 and the Maastricht Treaty of 1991.

But early skeptics of a community Europe were not simply nationalist defenders of the status quo. Except at the communist and far-right political extremes, few postwar European elites denied that new plans were necessary to solve the 'German problem', to encourage economic integration, and to rally together Europeans dwarfed by the superpowers. Many elites simply took issue with the notion that supranational institutions offered the best solution to all these problems. A large group argued for 'confederal' alternatives, picturing Europe organized in a multilateral but not supranational framework. They saw independent supranational institutions as unfamiliar, hard to predict, and illegitimate in an arena of democratic nation-states. Rather than using a new level of government to tie down the Germans and encourage cooperation, they proposed that a loose continental framework presided by the two main liberal powers – France and Britain – would most safely and effectively respond to political and economic challenges. They went on to propose several successful organizations on this format: the 16-member Organization for European Economic Cooperation (OEEC, later expanded into today's Organization for Economic Development and Cooperation, OECD), the originally 10-member Council of Europe (now with 46 members), and in the mid-1950s the Western European Union (WEU, the first substantial European organization focused on security and defense – absorbed into the EU in the 1990s).

Other mainstream elites across Europe were skeptical that any single multilateral framework was the right way to deal with Europeans' many problems. They shared confederalists' dislike for uncontrollable supranational institutions, but also suspected that even a more standard multilateral framework would be unwieldy and ineffective. Some politicians in Germany or the many smaller countries disliked the likelihood of Franco-British dominance in a confederal format; some French disliked the possibility of British dominance, and vice versa. They argued that the various pressures for political and economic cooperation could best be managed in a flexible network of traditional intergovernmental contracts. They also pointed out that Europe's security landscape was different from its conditions in industrial trade, agriculture, or monetary affairs. While such thinkers usually did not contest that European interdependence was high and rising, they questioned why governments needed an additional level of personnel and bureaucracy to bargain out such arrangements. Europeans could pursue all sorts of more intense cooperation within a traditional framework of intergovernmental contracts, without risking sovereignty and adaptability in uncontrollable international organizations. This organizational model had the added virtue of being the default format as of the late 1940s. Trade was expanding rapidly in a web of bilateral contracts and partial multilateral deals (Milward, 1984). Such arrangements would continue to proliferate across the postwar period. In addition to salient deals like the extensive package of Franco-German cooperation negotiated in 1954 or the Franco-German Treaty of the Elysée of 1963, European countries long maintained a complex network of specific bilateral arrangements (and still do in many areas).

Though these strategies focused first in the 1940s on the 'German problem,' their key difference was not anti- or pro-Germanism. Some traditionalists soon proved quite willing to deal bilaterally with the new West Germany. Some individuals arrived at confederal or community strategies out of visceral fear of Germany unfettered. Instead, the fundamental distinctions concerned the appropriate principles linking the various European nation-states themselves to their European environment. Their views paralleled an emerging intellectual debate between realists, liberals, and functionalists. The traditional model located the enduring structures of power and legitimacy solely in the nation-state. Arrangements other than time-honored intergovernmental ties would place unpredictable and illegitimate constraints on sovereignty. Confederalists also saw nation-states as lasting realities, but tempered their absoluteness with explicitly liberal, usually Anglophilic, pragmatism. New international structures were desirable to support practical (mostly economic) cooperation, as long as Franco-British leadership balanced the illiberal Germans and sacrifices of national control were minimized. Community advocates drew a more radical conclusion from the world wars and rising economic interdependence. Legitimacy followed welfare functions; to maximize the Europeans' long-term security and prosperity, their fractious nation-states had to be modified. Not only would supranational institutions control the Germans, they would allow all Europeans to pursue welfare-enhancing relationships free from ossified national structures.

That Europeans made these various arguments is not really a subject of debate. No one disputes that Charles de Gaulle consistently employed the rhetoric of a traditional Europe, that Ludwig Erhard favored the language of a confederal format, or that Robert Schuman and later François Mitterrand and Helmut Kohl made most of their arguments in a community vocabulary. For the vast majority of scholarship on EU history, however, it is positioning in structural or institutional obstacle courses that explains exactly who advanced these models. These discursive models were just rhetorical elaborations on underlying 'interests': the most straightforward strategies that objectively benefited people in certain positions in the real world. To the extent that certain groups or organizations ever appeared to have trouble connecting their clear positional interests to certain institutional projects, this was just a normal process of vetting alternatives in a complex situation before settling on the best choice.

As I suggested above, however, the problem with most of this literature is that it is generally wrong about these underlying patterns of mobilization. EU history has been riddled with cross-cutting debates, in which governments, political parties, bureaucracies, interest groups, and territorial units have disagreed about which institutional format best served their positional interests. Today's community-style EU was not selected from these alternatives by a straightforward aggregation of structural interests or powerful institutional path dependence, but through a much more contingent and indirect political mechanism. Since European debates have generally cross-cut the right–left and other political cleavages around which domestic elections and coalition-building operate, national politicians have enjoyed considerable autonomy to follow their personal views among the alternative visions. They have consistently achieved national power on the basis of their positions on other issues, and confronted fragmented domestic arenas from which weak support could be assembled for a variety of different European strategies. In the words of Hubert Védrine, who advised French President François Mitterrand for 15 years and later served as foreign minister, today's EU is 'the pure product of a process of enlightened despotism' (Védrine, 1996: 298). This is not to say that the EU project has been *anti*-democratic. Just as there were no widely perceived structural or institutional imperatives to this ideational vision, so there was no clear majority for an alternative.

Rather it is a story of *a*-democratic elite action in a new, fragmented battle of ideas.

Again, this chapter is too short to even summarize these claims across time and the European countries. But we can obtain a good deal of support for this basic vision of EU history by focusing on snapshots of French policy-making. Scholars of all theoretical persuasions agree that European institution-building took the shape it did in the 1950s – the institutionally supranational, geographically limited EEC – above all because the French government demanded it. The preferences of the other main governments (Germany, Britain, Benelux) summed to favor broader and less supranational institutional options. In the 1980s, the French led the charge to strengthen the supranationality of the EEC institutions over British opposition and German hesitation. From the 1970s to the 1990s, the French championed progressively stronger delegations of monetary sovereignty, again over British and German reticence. At each step, all historical accounts agree that other institutional deals (or the status quo) were available had the French chosen non-community strategies. Thus certain French strategies were necessary causes of a wide range of European outcomes. If we can show a cross-cutting debate of visions in France and explain its (partial) resolution with today's EU, we can capture a necessary major thread of the EU outcome. I also strongly suspect that further research on other countries – most importantly Germany, the other half of the 'Franco-German engine' of the EU project – will unearth similar dynamics.[3]

Let me turn to the French story, then, with the understanding that in my view France simply presents the most central and clearly-visible battlefield in a war of ideas across the European theater. New disagreements over European-level institutional projects began to emerge in the late 1940s. Initial French postwar plans called for rebuilding France while blocking a German revival through occupation and anti-German alliances. By 1948, however, the emergence of the Cold

War undercut these plans. The Americans were intent on rebuilding West Germany into an ally against the Soviets; in addition to simply forcing this on the French, they offered Marshall Plan funds as an incentive. In the face of this pressure, French parties, ministries, regions, and sectors fragmented in a debate around the three potential strategies described above. They ultimately agreed that extensive European cooperation was unavoidable, but favored very different formats. Traditionalists called for a minor modification of earlier plans. Some direct controls on Germany could still be salvaged; military and economic alliances with other powers could still be sought; if necessary, bilateral deals could even be struck with the Germans themselves. These steps would uphold a balance of power, and support technical cooperation in standard bilateralism, without risking French sovereignty. Confederalists shared this concern for sovereignty, but felt that Franco-British direction of a multilateral Europe would best prevent German dominance and foster technical cooperation. Community advocates, lastly, argued that only a new sort of strong European institutions could control the Germans and bring prosperity on an American scale. Since most British abhorred supranationality, this meant forsaking the Franco-British counterweight to Germany. But the result would be real 'integration', perhaps leading to a powerful 'United States of Europe'.

From this observation about early postwar debates, four claims summarize the core of the EU story. First, international bargains and French domestic support for all three strategies were available – not just in the 1950s, but across EU history. I will sketch two examples here: the approaches to the foundational EEC deal of 1957, and to the EMU deal of 1991 that marked the greatest expansion of European institutional authority. In the mid-1950s, almost all French elites saw rising structural incentives to more European cooperation in industrial trade, agricultural trade, and the new realm of atomic energy. Internationally, France's partners were not

pushing it into a community format. In industrial trade, the British, Germans, and most Benelux elites favored extending the currently dominant format for cooperation: the confederal, Franco-British-dominated Organization for European Economic Cooperation (OEEC). In agriculture, all but the Dutch preferred the traditional status quo of bilateral export contracts. In atomic energy, the Germans, Benelux, and Italy prioritized ties with the advanced British, all favoring a confederal OEEC plan. Domestically – contrary to most accounts – French business preferred bilateral or confederal OEEC deals to a more binding 'community' framework.[4] French agriculture was also 'suspiciously antagonistic of anything more complicated [than bilateral contracts]' (Milward, 1992: 293). Most French nuclear officials favored either OEEC cooperation or independence (Scheinman, 1965). Most support for a supranational 'community' deal came from politicians – though even here, fairly even thirds of parliamentarians scattered across right, left, and center favored traditional, confederal, and community formats.

Consider next the approach to EMU. In the late 1980s, almost all French elites saw rising structural and institutional pressures toward new monetary cooperation. Increasing capital mobility, and the asymmetric constraints of earlier monetary deals in the European Monetary System (EMS, which forced the French to shadow German interest rates), made some change desirable (Sandholtz, 1993). Unlike in 1955, there was no question about the basic framework for cooperation: the EC and its EMS appendage were widely accepted. But within this partly institutionalized arena, further steps could still take several formats. Internationally, again France's partners were not pushing the strongly community-style option of wholesale delegation of power to a supranational central bank (full EMU). If German Chancellor Helmut Kohl was open to full EMU, broader German reluctance meant that at most Kohl could accept, not demand, this project (Heisenberg, 1999; Kaltenthaler, 1998). The British favored the status quo, but would accept either stronger links among national banks without new institutions (a traditional-style solution), or possibly an intermediate 'common currency' plan (along confederal lines).[5] Domestically, 'there [was] no evidence of strong private sector preferences in favor of or against EMU' in France (de Boissieu and Pisani-Ferry, 1998: 82). Finance officials mostly favored either more national-bank coordination or the 'common currency'. Successive Finance Ministers Édouard Balladur (Gaullist) and Pierre Bérégovoy (Socialist) strongly favored the confederal-style common currency – not just in initial discussions, but through the EMU negotiations (Aeschimann and Riché, 1996; Bauchard, 1994).[6] Again, parties on right and left were divided.

In both the EEC and EMU cases, then, alternative international deals and domestic coalitions were clearly available. Why did the French government demand 'community' deals? My second claim is that top French leaders[7] have consistently been elected on cleavages that cross-cut these European debates. This gave them the autonomy to pursue their personal preferences over European strategies. Each deal we see with hindsight as leading to the EU emerged when 'pro-community' leaders reached power through support on other issues. After engaging France in treaty deals, they used payoffs on other issues and party and coalitional discipline to assemble one of several potential majorities for ratification. EEC negotiator Guy Mollet (socialist) became premier in 1956 at the head of a coalition built on social policies, and led electorally by anti-EEC centrist Pierre Mendès France.[8] Rather than being lobbied by interest groups or parties to pursue EEC, Mollet earnestly lobbied *them* to accept it. Support for his unrelated policies in Algeria helped deliver ratification. EMU champion François Mitterrand (also a socialist) surprised his own advisors in demanding the full, dated EMU commitment at Maastricht. He had no electoral mandate to do so; not only did his referendum to ratify

win by the slimmest of margins (50.9 percent), but the victory was 'built on the votes of his opponents in the UDF and RPR' (Appleton, 1992: 14). A clear majority of Mitterrand's 1988 voters opposed ratification. A majority of his socialist parliamentarians voted to ratify 'without really knowing why', due to presidential and party pressure (Criddle, 1993: 238). France pursued these community deals, over radically different alternatives, because leaders enjoyed the autonomy to assemble support behind their personal ideas in a fragmented 'multidimensional issue space'.

My third claim explains why the ideational battle narrowed over time. For the purposes of the 'institutionalization' theme of this section of the volume, this is the critical step. While elections on other cleavages cycled power erratically between community, confederal, and traditional leaders, French policies in Europe (and elite debates about them) displayed decreasing variation as the EU arose. Each community-style deal erected a further set of explicit constraints on subsequent policies (which is, of course, what institution-building treaties are for). The original ECSC plan did so the least; it was a narrow arrangement in sectors of decreasing importance. But the much more broadly framed EEC treaty expanded constraints across the entire foreign economic relations of France and its partners. The European Monetary System (EMS) deal of 1979 added monetary constraints; the SEA of 1986 brought changes across the domestic economy; and the Maastricht Treaty of 1991 extended these steps and set them in a more thoroughly supranational framework. After each deal, it became more difficult for anti-community leaders to shift French strategies and European bargains back to the alternatives they had previously preferred. This did not mean that traditionalists or confederalists were 'converted' to community zeal. At each new step the competition between the visions occurred again, and the community project only moved forward when pro-community leaders reacquired control of policy-making. But each round of the debate concerned a narrower range of active policy options. After each community-style deal, confederal or traditional leaders who came into power explicitly considered defection or renegotiation, but in each case decided that the costs of undoing elaborate institutional arrangements were too high.[9] By the late 1990s, the debate was so narrow that extremists on right and left denounced '*la pensée unique*' (uniform thinking) of mainstream politicians. Over the course of the 1980s and especially the 1990s, longtime EU skeptics (like French President Jacques Chirac) forgot about their opposition, reluctantly rationalizing the supranational EU as 'in French interests'. As Chirac said in the wake of the Maastricht Treaty – under pressure from some of his pro-community domestic allies – he would support its ratification 'without enthusiasm, but without soul-searching'. All but the most extreme traditionalists had reluctantly accepted a community Europe as the lay of the land.

My fourth claim addresses a final obvious question: why did community ideas gradually win this battle? What prevented confederal or traditional leaders like Charles de Gaulle, Georges Pompidou, and Chirac from better institutionalizing their different views when in power? Though I believe the answer must recognize historical contingency – nothing made the community victory inevitable – two factors favored this outcome. The first lay in the nature of community ideas themselves. The ideology of the community model emphasized that strong, binding, elaborate new institutions would solve a whole host of European problems. The competing ideas of confederalists or traditionalists centered on *avoiding* binding institutional relationships. Thus each pro-community leader left a legacy of new institutional constraints to his successor, whereas confederal and traditional leaders did not. This was not due to passivity; Europe is littered with the weak husks of confederal and traditional projects (OECD, Council of Europe, Western European Union, Franco-German Treaty, and so on.).

But in a world where binding institutions matter, ideas that change them matter more than those that do not. The second factor was that community ideas connected fortuitously to other powerful European norms. The clearest such connection was law: enshrining community projects in elaborate legal arrangements (which confederal or traditional projects avoided) made them particularly difficult to undo. In no way did law *per se* require supranational institutions, but basing such institutions in law – and especially in their own elaborate system of courts, crowned by the European Court of Justice – gave them a long-term advantage (Alter, 1997; Burley and Mattli, 1993; Weiler, 1991). Later community projects (EMS, EMU) connected to the newer norm of monetarism. Again, monetarism did not dictate EMU (as many economists argued), but its broad legitimacy as of the 1980s gave power to simplistic arguments for EMU in public debates. The institutional activism of community ideas, together with connections to broader norms, allowed them to progressively crowd out their competitors.

If we take as endpoint the basic consolidation of the current EU architecture in the 1990s, then the visions of French elites were demonstrably distinct, necessary causes of this outcome across an immense range of possibilities. The range of debate between viable French community, confederal, and traditional strategies – and the range of active, well-supported alternatives in European bargaining over the decades – extended from construction of the most centralized and authoritative international institutions ever built to retention of a loosely organized diplomatic space much like what prevailed everywhere else in the twentieth century. Only because the elite advocates of the community project episodically obtained democratic power on other issues, and because their visionary blueprint led to binding institution-building, was Europe transformed into the sole formal, powerful, well-established instance of politics 'beyond the nation-state' (Haas, 1964).

COMPETING VISIONS IN RECENT AND FUTURE EU DEVELOPMENTS

Today's EU is certainly not a purely 'community' Europe. Although community-minded leaders led the major treaty revisions that built the EU, they did so in difficult domestic and international negotiations with opponents of supranationality, and their agenda control has been episodic. Nor did 'community-minded leaders' always want as much supranationality as they could possibly get. Like in any complex ideological debate, the positions in battles over the EU institutions are relative rather than absolute. A normative democrat, for example, is not someone who wants unlimited bottom-up input to every conceivable decision to the exclusion of all other considerations. She just wants a model of decision-making that incorporates more popular input than the models of a normative autocrat, technocrat, or royalist. Similarly, Schuman, Adenuaer, Mollet, Mitterrand, or Kohl did not argue for anything close to simple abdication of national sovereignty. They often expressed concern for retaining sovereignty in certain areas, especially some which other longstanding norms identified as especially important to sovereignty. The most obvious examples are the policy areas of the EU's 'second and third pillars', where supranational influence was explicitly limited: foreign and security policy and justice, policing, and border control. While community-minded leaders have demonstrably differed from their compatriots in committing energy and resources to push for relatively supranational institutions, the institutions they built reflect many important reservations of national power.

As the EU institutions took on concrete authority, they have also become effective vehicles for the advance and institutionalization of other norms and agendas. One example is human rights. The clearest organizational source of a human rights agenda in the European context is the Council of Europe – one of the confederal-model 'losers' of the battle over the regional political architecture. It became the seat of the European Convention on Human Rights (ECHR) and has actively promoted such concerns across the postwar era. Yet it has never taken any steps at all toward the kind of political power and resources that the EU gradually accumulated. Direct Council efforts at human rights promotion have been important in their own right, but the institutionalization of such rights inside and outside of Europe has advanced most where the EU has taken up this agenda. The most obvious instances arise in the recent and ongoing processes of EU accession, where the conditionality of EU membership has exerted massive leverage for domestic change. Not only does today's EU reflect a partial and negotiated implementation of the community model, then, but it also incorporates principles from sources other than community ideology.

If the EU is not purely a community construct in its institutional structure and principles, it is even less so in the views of the political actors who inhabit it today. Mainstream non-community thinkers across Europe who opposed past steps in the construction of the EU have rationalized its basic architecture as acceptable, but few seem to have internalized community-style views. Chirac, for example, explicitly opposed the SEA and EMU projects as they were negotiated. He reluctantly accepted to work within these arrangements upon reaching power, and has at points adopted rhetoric that incorporates much of the basic community discourse. But no close observer would mistake him for a serious proponent of *more* supranationality. More broadly, not only is there not growing support for more supranationalization among elites and citizens – as Monnet hoped and neofunctionalists predicted there should be – there is less.

It is not hard to see several reasons why the visionary advance of European integration may have reached its end. First, as the progressive narrowing of French debates over the EU suggests, recent discussions of

EU institution-building have taken place in an arena fundamentally unlike the backdrop to past steps. Until the consolidation of the EEC the basic institutional format of postwar Europe was wide open, allowing for a real contest between alternative visions. From Rome in 1957 to Maastricht in 1991, the institutional space for this contest was progressively narrowed. The subsequent treaty modifications at Amsterdam (1997) and Nice (2000) changed the resultant framework in relatively minor ways. Today, would-be European visionaries (of whatever persuasion) confront a complex, highly institutionalized set of practices and distribution of resources which are even harder to change than most national constitutional orders.

One aspect of this narrowing institutionalization (and one foreshadowed, if vastly exaggerated, in the early neofunctionalist literature: Haas, 1958) is the mobilization of broader participation on EU issues. If leaders' past autonomy in European policies was largely rooted in fragmented elite positions, it also benefited from widespread public ignorance and passivity. But since the Maastricht Treaty and the high-profile shift to the euro – and even more so with the rise and fall of the EU Constitution – publics across Europe are more likely to scrutinize major EU plans. A poll shortly before the French referendum of 29 May 2005 that rejected the EU Constitution found that an astounding 80 percent of citizens had recently discussed the issue privately. This increased mobilization broadly coincided, however, with a steep fall in public support for the EU across the 1990s. The proportion of Europeans who saw EU membership as a 'good thing' peaked at 72 percent in 1991, between the SEA and Maastricht, but then fell steadily to a low of 46 percent in 1997. It has since hovered around the 50 percent mark. These numbers partly reflected an economic downturn in the early 1990s, but they were also widely interpreted as representing the replacement of the EU's longstanding 'permissive consensus' in public opinion with a new level of public scrutiny. A more active

and hostile public will tend to favor incremental EU change over grand initiatives in any direction.

Another reason to expect less visionary leadership and more incremental evolution is the passing of the postwar generation. One of the most surprising discoveries of my interview and archival research (to me) was the remarkable depth and consistency of the personal European views that French elites adopted in the debates of the late 1940s and early 1950s. Being 'present at the creation' and participating in the initial battle of ideas wedded individuals strongly to a certain ideational model. The baby-boomers and subsequent generations appear to have weaker commitments. They have grown up mostly within a community-format Europe. Polls show that they support the EU more consistently than their elders, but journalistic accounts frequently observe that leaders like Gerhard Schröder, Lionel Jospin, and Tony Blair feel little of the European urgency (pro- or anti-community) of postwar figures. Jacques Chirac, who entered politics in the 1960s as an aide to Georges Pompidou and is two years younger than Helmut Kohl, is the last active politician who might remember the early debates around the EEC.

Moreover, the EU project has simultaneously reached the end of its blueprint and run into unforeseen challenges. The completion of the Single Market program and the inauguration of the euro realized the furthest substantive ambitions of the postwar founding fathers. Even younger Europeans who do feel strongly connected to a supranational project are generally uncertain about what they might next propose. Some see a European security and defense policy as the 'next big idea' (Medley, 1999), but the debacle of intra-European disagreements over Iraq (and above all Tony Blair's hard-to-explain personal engagement alongside the US) has made proposals in that direction especially complicated. The concurrent disappearance of communism and ensuing process of Eastern EU enlargement have also occupied the union's energies with a task that a great many West European elites resent but feel unable to reject. Pro-community figures in Western Europe conceived of the EU to strengthen their own economies and role in the world, not as a device to leverage westernizing change in Eastern Europe, the Balkans, and Turkey. Most pro-EU politicians find it difficult to argue strongly against conditional enlargement – especially publicly – because they do want to see such changes on the edges of Europe, and because they fear what the applicant states would do if they were clearly rejected. Yet it is also increasingly difficult to contest that the continued process of 'widening' the Union is making 'deepening' of federal-style integration more difficult. The fall of the EU constitution, in which opposition to Eastern enlargement and its consequences played a role, suggests that major steps in deepening may already have been rendered impossible. For the moment, at least, it is hard to imagine any EU treaty amendment of any ambition at all achieving ratification across all 27 member-states.

While this chapter cannot fit in a careful tracing of major EU developments since the 1990s, they appear to correspond well to this image of an institutionalized, 'post-visionary' EU. There have been fewer leaders who would be inclined to stand out from their domestic support to champion new EU projects; the few that are so inclined have been unsure of substantive steps to propose; they have faced more intractable institutional inertia and more mobilized opposition; and the EU as an organization has been preoccupied with the difficult task of adapting to a much larger and more heterogeneous membership. The two treaty modifications that followed Maastricht, the Treaty of Amsterdam in 1997, and the Treaty of Nice in 2000, were presented mainly as efforts to clean up issues left unresolved at Maastricht and to prepare for Eastern enlargement (Moravcsik and Nicolaidis, 1999). The Nice negotiations in particular were seen as devoid of leadership and vision, with the final institutional accommodations for enlargement decided by 'late

night horse trading rather than any mathematical or demographic formula' (Norman, 2003). The widespread sense of unresolved issues, together with the growing sense of public dissatisfaction with the EU more broadly, led to the 'Convention on the Future of Europe' that eventually produced the draft EU Constitution. But if the eventual Constitution text modified some of the internal rules in ways that mattered to insiders – extending and altering majority voting in the Council of Ministers, creating a European Foreign Minister, incorporating a Charter for Fundamental Rights – it included little (if anything) that could be called a 'visionary' modification to how EU policy-making relates to its citizens or the broader environment. Not only did it not offer a new substantive aspiration like the earlier 'Single Market 1992' plan or the euro, but it was difficult to see how the Constitution would make any real difference on the themes of 'democracy, transparency, and effectiveness' which had formed the Convention's original mandate. Legal commentaries generally found that the Constitution brought 'no relevant structural change' to the EU order (Pfersmann, 2005; Weiler, 2005). The potential gains in effectiveness from more majority voting were mitigated by new majority-voting principles that made majoritarian decisions harder to reach. The new EU Foreign Minister would only represent a slight centralization of authority in that field. Overall, the Constitution codified already-institutionalized EU rules much more than it changed them.

Unfortunately for the EU, this grandiose declaration of a 'constitutional' discussion around a largely unchanged EU architecture mobilized opposition more than support. Many Europhiles were lukewarm about a treaty modification that contained no new substantive ambitions and did little to address the announced goals of transparency, democracy, and efficiency. Making a case for a 'pro-European no' was neither difficult nor uncommon (Milner, 2006). Critics, by contrast, leapt at the opportunity to complain about many different aspects of the union.

Tellingly, they focused practically all their attention on broader EU features – market liberalization, openness to Eastern European competition and immigration, questionable accountability – that the constitutional text itself did nothing to alter (Aarts and Van der Kolk 2006; Perrineau, 2005). It amounted to a referendum on the earlier EU vision and its unintended expansion to Eastern Europe, not on the arcane modifications in the new treaty. The 'no' votes by substantial French and Dutch majorities (54.7 percent and 61.6 percent, respectively) brought an end to the EU's constitutional episode – and perhaps to the 50-year period of visionary institution-building at the European level.

COMPETING VISIONS AND THE STUDY OF EUROPE

The core story of the EU, in short, is that all Europeans have been progressively bound into the ideational model advocated by a dispersed elite minority. Most Europeans did not spontaneously see this EU as the best response to structural conditions or institutional pressures. Other historically active, technically and political viable models of European cooperation have been gradually crowded out and forgotten. A once-contested vision has been deeply institutionalized. Whether we see this process as heroic and visionary, or as illegitimately separate from democracy and participation, depends on our own normative views of the outcome.

What does this account suggest about how to study contemporary Europe? Two implications stand out. First, it recasts the relationship between change in postwar Europe and change elsewhere in the world. Most of the literature on the EU (and especially the best-known theoretical work from Moravcsik) presents the EU story as an advanced instance of global processes of rising interdependence, liberalization, and international institution-building. This view of the EU fits well with a large amount of scholarship that sees

similar changes driven by globalization at the national level (Frieden, 1991; Frieden and Rogowski, 1996; Giddens, 2000; Hiscox, 2001; Milner, 1988; Ohmae, 1990; Webb, 1991). Yet this chapter bolsters the contrasting arguments, usually from institutionalists, that see less globalizing change and more distinct national or regional trajectories in contemporary Europe (Berger and Dore, 1996; Hall and Soskice, 2001; Katzenstein, 1985; Pierson, 1994; Steinmo et al., 1992; Thelen and van Wijnbergen, 2003; Vogel, 1996). An emphasis on the role of ideational models in the EU suggests that important strands of the story are unique to Europe. A community-model Europe was certainly *a* response to rising interdependence to some degree, but it has never been *the* obvious response for a large number of Europeans. If it was not the obvious way forward even for most Europeans who experienced all the precise conditions that textbooks tell us pointed to the EU – the cycle of war, a search for economic dynamism, a concern with bolstering the role of a group of small- and medium-sized states in the world, and so on – it seems unlikely that anything much like this ideational model would spontaneously appear elsewhere in the world. Of course the EU project has inspired a good deal of partial imitation in other regions: MERCOSUR, a variety of African organizations, and even NAFTA to some degree. But no powerful actors in any of these organizations have seriously advocated major supranationalization. As the worldwide fascination with the 'postmodern' EU underscores, it is much more about a European *divergence* from global processes than any sort of universal pattern.

Second, this version of EU history suggests that students of contemporary Europe must pay more attention to networks, ideas, and mobilization that do not correspond to familiar patterns of organizational or material positioning. I have argued that today's EU does not reflect a straightforward aggregation – or even a less straightforward institutionally steered one – of pre-existing national interests. The relationship between

the EU and national politics is more complicated. The EU project has advanced not
when clear national or transnational social
groups gave leaders a mandate for supranationalization, but when national leaders
gained the *autonomy* to push a highly contested agenda. This implies that the study of
power, representation, and policy-making in
Europe's quasi-federalized arena forces us to
consider not just a logic of 'two-level games'
but the complex interaction of cross-cutting
battles within them (Parsons, 2000; Putnam,
1988). Not only may political mobilization
on certain issues cut across material and
organizational positioning, but power and
authority gained on one issue may be decisive for action on another.

Even beyond Europe, this EU story hints
that social scientists more generally should
pay more attention to the potential for such
cross-cutting politics. Past studies of the EU,
of other aspects of European politics, and in
all of political science have tended to posit a
fairly clear world of competing positional
'interests'. They have gone looking for coherent groups and organizations with clear
notions of what they want and how to get it.
The problem with this mindset is not that it is
systematically wrong, but that it can gloss
over patterns of action that cut across organizational lines or ideas that do not trace to
positioning in simple ways. The consequences of such oversights on other issues
may not be as dramatic as in scholarship
on EU history, where an especially strong
pattern of cross-cutting ideas left traditional
theorists with unusually large empirical gaps
in their arguments. But Europe's main political lines – like those in other arenas around
the world – are also at least partly cross-cut
by mobilization around several other important issues like immigration, protectionism,
and religious identity. From a superficial
look, none of these issues seems to cross-
cut Europe's right/left and other party-
organization lines as strongly as EU debates.
Especially in immigration and protectionism,
the cross-cutting pattern more often looks
like a convergent rejectionism on the

political extremes than a continuous cleavage
that bisects other issues. Still, just how far
these cross-cutting issues go is an empirical
question that we can not afford to overlook.
Any research into complex political phenomena must allow that competing visions may
stretch across material and organizational
lines, and may carry the concrete dynamics
of politics with them.

NOTES

1 In sectors without much state intervention,
strong demands for integration just lead to 'negative'
integration (erasing barriers) that may not require
major new central institutions.

2 I use 'visions' as interchangeable with 'ideas',
just for rhetorical variation. Ideas are semi-related
packages of causal and normative assumptions that
sketch possible strategies of action and assign costs
and benefits to them (Parsons, 2003: 8).

3 For work on Germany that hints in these
directions, see Kaltenthaler (1998), Küsters (1986),
Heisenberg (1999), and Wurm (1995).

4 Thus, for example, the business representatives
in the French Economic and Social Council voted
unanimously in July 1956 to relocate the early EEC
talks to the OEEC (Mahant, 1969; Szokolóczy-
Syllaba, 1965).

5 The common currency would be emitted by a
European bank alongside national currencies, rather
than in place of them. My larger study shows
that the common currency plan shared the same
justifications as earlier confederal projects, and was
supported by many of the same people in France.

6 Given German skepticism of the 'common
currency,' it probably was not a potential outcome.
Had the French pushed for it and refused full EMU
(as Balladur and Bérégovoy wanted), the outcome
would have defaulted to traditional-style national-
bank coordination (which both Balladur and
Bérégovoy preferred to full EMU).

7 Prime Ministers under the Fourth Republic;
presidents under the Fifth.

8 Everyone expected Mendès France to become
premier; conservative President René Coty chose
Mollet instead, partly because Mollet promised a
tougher policy against Algerian independence.

9 Only de Gaulle actually tried (but failed) to rene-
gotiate a community deal, in the 'open chair' crisis of
1965. Parts of Mitterrand's government argued for
leaving the European Monetary System in the early
1980s; Prime Minister Jacques Chirac considered
non-ratification of the Single European Act in 1986;

and Prime Minister Edouard Balladur and President Chirac explicitly considered slowing or stopping progress toward economic and monetary union in the early 1990s (Parsons, 2003).

REFERENCES

Aarts, K. and van der Kolk, H. (2006) 'Understanding the Dutch "No"', *PS: Political Science and Politics*, 39 (2): 243–246.

Aeschimann, E. and Riché, P. (1996) *La Guerre de Sept Ans*. Paris: Calmann-Lévy.

Alter, K. (1997) 'European governments and the European Court of Justice', *International Organization*, 52 (1): 121–147.

Appleton, A. (1992) 'Maastricht and the French party system: domestic implications of the treaty referendum', *French Politics and Society*, 10 (4): 1–18.

Aron, R. and Lerner, D. (eds) (1957) *France Defeats EDC*. New York: Praeger.

Bauchard, P. (1994) *Deux Ministres Trop Tranquilles*. Paris: Belfond.

Berger, S. and Dore, R. (eds) (1996) *National Diversity and Global Capitalism*. Ithaca: Cornell University Press.

Brugmans, H. (1965) *L'idée Européenne, 1918–1965*. Bruges: De Tempel.

Burley, A.M. and Mattli, W. (1993) 'Europe before the court: a political theory of legal integration', *International Organization*, 47 (1): 41–76.

Cowles, M., Caporaso, J., and Risse, T. (eds) (2001) *Transforming Europe: Europeanization and Domestic Change*. Ithaca, NY: Cornell University Press.

Criddle, B. (1993) 'The French referendum on the Maastricht Treaty', *Parliamentary Affairs*, 46 (2): 228–239.

de Boissieu, C. and Pisani-Ferry, J. (1998) 'The political economy of French economic policy in the perspective of EMU', in B. Eichengreen and J. Frieden (eds) *Forging an Integrated Europe*. Ann Arbor: University of Michigan Press, pp. 49–90.

Dyson, K. and Goetz, K. (eds) (2003) *Germany, Europe and the Politics of Constraint*. Oxford: Oxford University Press.

Fligstein, N. and Mara-Drita, I. (1996) 'How to make a market: reflections on the attempt to create a single market in the European Union', *American Journal of Sociology*, 102 (1): 1–33.

Frieden, J. (1991) 'Invested interests: the politics of national economic policies in a world of global finance', *International Organization* 45 (4): 425–451.

Frieden, J. and Rogowski, R. (1996) 'The impact of the international economy on national policies: an analytical overview,' in R. Keohane and H. Milner (eds) *Internationalization and Domestic Politics*. New York: Cambridge University Press, pp. 25–47.

Giddens, A. (2000) *Runaway World: How Globalization is Reshaping Our Lives*. New York: Routledge.

Haas, E. (1958) *The Uniting of Europe: Political, Social and Economic Forces, 1950–1957*. Stanford, CA: Stanford University Press.

Haas, E. (1964) *Beyond the Nation-State: Functionalism and International Organization*. Stanford, CA: Stanford University Press.

Hall, P. and Soskice, D. (eds) (2001) *Varieties of Capitalism: The Institutional Foundations of Comparative Advantage*. New York: Oxford University Press.

Heisenberg, D. (1999) *The Mark of the Bundesbank: Germany's Role in European Monetary Cooperation*. Boulder, CO: Lynne Rienner.

Hiscox, M. (2001) 'Class versus industry cleavages: inter-industry factor mobility and the politics of trade', *International Organization*, 55 (1): 1–46.

Hitchcock, W. (1998) *France Restored: Cold War Diplomacy and the Quest for Leadership in Europe, 1944–1954*. Chapel Hill, NC: University of North Carolina Press.

Hix, S. and Lord, C. (1997) *Political Parties in the European Union*. New York: St Martin's.

Hooghe, L. and Marks, G. (2001) *Multi-Level Governance and European Integration*. Lanham, MD: Rowman and Littlefield.

Hooghe, L. and Marks, G. (2006) 'Europe's blues: theoretical soul-searching after the rejection of the European Constitution', *PS: Political Science and Politics*, 39: 2: 247–250.

Jabko, N. (1999) 'In the name of the market: how the European commission paved the way for monetary union', *Journal of European Public Policy*, 6 (3): 475–495.

Kaltenthaler, K. (1998) *Germany and the Politics of Europe's Money*. Durham, NC: Duke University Press.

Katzenstein, P. (1985) *Small States in World Markets: Industrial Policy in Europe*. Ithaca: Cornell University Press.

Küsters, H. J.. (1986) *Les Fondements de la Communauté Économique Européenne*. Brussels: Official Publications of the European Communities.

Lipgens, W. (1977) *Die Anfänge der Europäischen Einigungspolitik, 1945–1950*. Stuttgart: Klett.

Magnette, P. and Nicolaidis, M. (2004) 'The European Convention: bargaining in the shadow of rhetoric', *West European Politics*, 27 (3): 381–405.

Mahant, E. (1969) *French and German Attitudes to the Negotiations About the European Economic Community, 1955–1957*. Unpublished dissertation, Politics, London University.

Marks, G., Hooghe, L., and Blank, K. (1996) 'European integration since the 1980s. state-centric versus multi-level governance', *Journal of Common Market Studies*, 34 (3): 343–378.

Medley, R. (1999) 'Europe's next big idea: strategy and economics point to a European military', *Foreign Affairs*, 78 (5): 18–22.

Milner, H. (1988) *Resisting Protectionism: Global Industries and the Politics of International Trade*. Princeton: Princeton University Press.

Milner, H. (2006) 'Some reflections on France's rejection of the EU Constitution', *PS: Political Science and Politics*, 39 (2): 257–260.

Milward, A. (1984) *The Reconstruction of Western Europe, 1945–1951*. London: Methuen.

Milward, A. (1992) *The European Rescue of the Nation-State*. Berkeley, CA: University of California Press.

Moravcsik, A. (1993) 'Preferences and power in the European Community: a liberal intergovernmentalist approach', *Journal of Common Market Studies*, 31 (4): 473–524.

Moravcsik, A. (1998) *The Choice for Europe: Social Purpose and State Power from Messina to Maastricht*. Ithaca, NY: Cornell University Press.

Moravcsik, A. and Nicolaidis, K. (1999) 'Explaining the Treaty of Amsterdam: interests, influence, institutions', *Journal of Common Market Studies*, 37 (1): 59–85.

Norman, P. (2003) *The Accidental Constitution: The Story of the European Convention*. Brussels, Eurocomment.

Ohmae, K. (1990) *The Borderless World*. New York: Harper Collins.

Parsons, C. (2000) 'Domestic interests, ideas, and integration: lessons from the French case', *Journal of Common Market Studies*, 38 (1): 45–70.

Parsons, C. (2003) *A Certain Idea of Europe*. Ithaca, NY: Cornell University Press.

Parsons, C. (2007) *How to Map Arguments in Political Science*. New York: Oxford University Press.

Perrineau, P. (ed.) (2005) *Le Vote Européen 2004–2005: De l'élargissement au Référendum Français*. Paris: Presses de Sciences-Po.

Pfersmann, O. (2005) 'The new revision of the old constitution', *International Journal of Constitutional Law*, 3 (2): 383–404.

Pierson, P. (1994) *Dismantling the Welfare State? Reagan, Thatcher, and the Politics of Retrenchment*. New York: Cambridge University Press.

Pierson, P. (1996) 'The path to European integration: a historical institutionalist analysis,' *Comparative Political Studies*, 29 (2): 123–163.

Putnam, R. (1988) 'Diplomacy and domestic politics: the logic of two-level games', *International Organization*, 42 (3): 427–460.

Sandholtz, W. (1993) 'Choosing union: monetary politics and Maastricht', *International Organization*, 47 (1): 1–39.

Sandholtz, W. and Stone Sweet, A. (eds) (1998) *European Integration and Supranational Governance*. New York: Oxford University Press.

Scheinman, L. (1965) *Atomic Energy Policy in France Under the Fourth Republic*. Princeton: Princeton University Press.

Steinmo, S., Thelen, K., and Longstreth, F. (eds) (1992) *Structuring Politics: Historical Institutionalism in Comparative Perspective*. New York: Cambridge University Press.

Szokolóczy-Syllaba, J. (1965) *Les Organisations Professionnelles Françaises et le Marché Commun*. Paris: Armand Colin.

Taggart, P. and Szczerbiak, A. (eds) (2006) *Opposing Europe? The Comparative Party Politics of Euroscepticism*. Oxford: Oxford University Press.

Thelen, K. and van Wijnbergen, C. (2003) 'The paradox of globalization: labor relations in Germany and beyond', *Comparative Political Studies*, 36 (8): 859–880.

Van der Eijs, C. and Franklin, M. (2004) 'Potential for contestation on European matters at national elections in Europe', in G. Marks and M. Steenbergen (eds). *European Integration and Political Conflict*. New York: Cambridge University Press, pp. 32–50.

Védrine, H. (1996) *Les Mondes de François Mitterrand*. Paris: Seuil.

Vogel, S. (1996) *Freer Markets, More Rules: Regulatory Reform in Advanced Industrial Countries*. Ithaca: Cornell University Press.

Webb, M. (1991) 'International economic structures, government interests, and international coordination of macroeconomic adjustment policies', *International Organization*, 45 (3): 309–342.

Weiler, J. (1991) 'The transformation of Europe', *Yale Law Journal*, 100: 2403–2483.

Weiler, J. (2005) 'On the power of the word: Europe's constitutional iconography', *International Journal of Constitutional Law*, 3 (2): 173–190.

Wessels, W., Maurer, A., and Mittag, J. (eds) (2003) *Fifteen into One? The European Union and its Member States*. Manchester: Manchester University Press.

Wurm, C. (ed.) (1995) *Western Europe and Germany: The Beginnings of European Integration, 1945–1960*. Washington DC: Berg.

12

Enlargement and the Meaning of Europe

John McCormick

Few developments have been more funda-mental to shaping the identity both of Europe and of the European Union than enlarge-ment. In the broader sweep of history, and on the wider international stage, the growth of the EU has been one of the most dramatic political and economic enterprises of recent decades, changing both the internal character and the external identity of the EU. Changes to the treaties may have been at the core of debates about the personality and work of the EU, the agenda of integration was for many years topped by the single market and the single currency, and the expansion of policy responsibilities has altered the goals and the reach of the EU. Nothing, however, has more vitally altered the political, economic, social and even psychological dynamics of contem-porary Europe than the widening borders of the EU.

For EU member states, enlargement has been at the heart of an ongoing debate about the purposes and meaning of European integration, and about its wider global sig-nificance. There has seldom been a time since the 1950s when a membership applica-tion has not been pending, or when there has not been discussion about the acceptability of applications, or when accession negotiations have not been in progress, or when new

members have not been settling in (Nugent, 2004: 1). Existing members have been chal-lenged to think about the implications of enlargement, to ponder their willingness to share the economic opportunities that inte-gration has helped create, and to adjust to the new diversity that has come with enlarge-ment: a core concern has been how much the EU can accommodate before its durability is adversely impacted (Preston, 1997: 3). They have wondered how enlargement might change the relationship among the member states, with particular attention paid to the once-dominating role of France and Germany. They have worried about the impact that a bigger EU might have on the unity of Europe, given the many opt-outs, transition periods, trade-offs, exceptions, and extended timeta-bles that have been the legacy of membership negotiations. And they have had to adjust to the decline of the old East–West distinctions of the Cold War era, and to acknowledge that – with enlargement – Europe and the European Union have come close to the point where they are synonymous.

For non-member states, even those (like the Ukraine and Belarus) for whom member-ship of the EU is more a long-term possibil-ity than a short-term probability, the prospect of joining the EU remains the benchmark against which many other political and economic options must be measured. Enlargement has always been part of the historic mission of European integration, the assumption of Monnet, Schuman, and others being that it had implications for the whole of Europe. The gravitational pull of integration may have been weak at first, but as the original experiment revealed its possibilities, so the attractions of Europe proved irresistible. But the doubts about the details of EU membership have always lingered. If the concept of Europe has any real meaning, then why have so many conditions been attached to the membership terms of Eastern European states? Why were so many uncertainties allowed to linger over the process of Eastern enlargement in the mid-1990s, with the EU being unclear about which countries it wanted to admit, unwilling to set a timetable, and generally leaving aspirant members feeling more like supplicants than applicants (Rumford, 2002: 263–6)?

As Europe and the EU have been redefined, so enlargement has attracted the attention of growing numbers of scholars, journalists and political leaders. This has been particularly true since the mid-1990s, when attention turned from expansion within Western Europe to a new focus on the prospects of enlargement to the east, a development that gave new meaning to the significance of integration. After many years in the background, enlargement finally moved to the forefront of debates about Europe, with two issues in particular attracting the most attention: the manner in which enlargement was changing the role of the EU as a global actor, and the troubling question of when enough was enough – when would 'enlargement fatigue' become a problem, when would the EU reach its 'absorption capacity', and what danger would enlargement pose to the EU's decision-making systems?

As enlargement has attracted new attention, new questions have arisen. Central among them has been the implications for the meaning of Europe, where the search for answers has been complicated by the contrasting perceptions of Europeans; as Wallace (2002: 79) puts it, 'What Europe you see depends on where you live.' Another question relates to the implications of enlargement for the EU's relationship with other parts of the world, and most centrally with the United States. Europeans and Americans were brought together in common cause during the Cold War by their opposition to the Soviet threat, but that threat is now gone, and the differences between a larger and more confident Europe and an America with declining international credibility have become more visible and pronounced. What impact will this have on the meaning of the West? Enlargement has been with us since the first wave of new arrivals in 1973, but in some ways the debate about its implications has only just begun.

THE STORY SO FAR

Membership of the European Coal and Steel Community was open to all European states, but only France, West Germany, Italy, and the three Benelux countries participated, and European integration in its earliest iteration was a western, democratic, capitalist affair. The founding members agreed on the need to promote democratic stability and free markets, and to side with the United States in the struggle against communism, but on little else. When the era of enlargement began in 1973, 21 years after the signing of the Treaty of Paris, it was to be a piecemeal affair, proceeding more on the basis of disjointed incrementalism than on the basis of a fully worked out grand plan (Hill, 2002: 96); it was a 'journey to an unknown destination' (Shonfield, 1974). But with each stage of growth, there were changes in the relationship among the new members, adjustments to the institutional character and policy agenda of the Community/EU, and alterations to its international role and standing, all of which forced a reassessment of the goals of integration.

Most conspicuous by its absence from early discussions was Britain, still the major power in Europe and the state whose membership of the European Economic Community (EEC) was widely regarded as most essential. But Britain's primary foreign policy and trade interests lay outside Europe, focused particularly on what remained of the British Empire, and on the 'special relationship' with the United States (Milward, 2002: 75). It was only at Suez in 1956 that Britain finally awoke to the realization that it was no longer a great power, and that it needed to pay more attention to Europe. Its initial response was to champion the European Free Trade Association (EFTA), a loose intergovernmental body focused on free trade rather than economic and political integration. But when it became clear that the EEC seemed to be working, and that the US opposed the emergence of competing free trade blocs (Dinan, 2004: 91–3), Britain changed its mind and made its first application to the Community in 1961. It was joined by Denmark (most of whose agricultural exports went to Britain), by Ireland (which wanted a boost for its industrial development plans, and saw the EEC membership as an opportunity to reduce its reliance both on Britain and on agriculture), and Norway (which also recognized the importance of EEC markets). Britain was twice turned down by the de Gaulle administration, which viewed Britain as a rival to French influence and as a channel for American influence in the Community, and resented Britain's lack of enthusiasm for the first steps on integration. But in January 1973, with de Gaulle gone, Britain, Denmark and Ireland finally joined the EEC; Norway would have joined as well, but a public referendum in September 1972 narrowly went against membership.

This first enlargement did not much change the political, economic and social variety of the Community. The overall per capita GDP of the Community was reduced slightly, but the new states found themselves able to adjust quickly to the demands of membership (which were more modest than they were to become for later arrivals), and to absorb new initiatives in the fields of regional and fisheries policy. Risks of a different order were taken in the 1980s with the so-called 'Mediterranean enlargement' to Greece in 1981 and to Spain and Portugal in 1986. These were states that had only recently freed themselves from authoritarian regimes (Portugal and Greece in 1974, and Spain in 1975), and whose democratic credentials and administrative structures were weaker. Although the Treaty of Rome stipulated that 'any European State' could apply to join the Community, democracy was – in practice – a basic precondition. The three countries were also relatively poor, with a per capita GDP that was less than two-thirds the average in the nine existing member states. The chances of the graft succeeding were less than they had been with the accession of Britain, Ireland and Denmark, but the potential political and economic benefits of enlargement for the new members – and for the EEC – were substantial.

The doubling of its population and membership between 1973 and 1986 (see Table 12.1) meant new global influence for the Community (which was now the largest capitalist economic bloc in the world), but it also complicated the Community's decision-making processes; the relative closeness of the six was replaced by the greater diversity of the twelve. The influence of France and Germany was reduced, and the internal economic balance was altered, leading to a debate on the relative merits of deepening versus widening, which some saw as competing tensions and others saw as two sides of the same coin. Deepeners argued that the Community should develop closer internal ties before it took on new members, while wideners argued that membership should be opened to other states immediately, but for different reasons: Eurosceptics hoped to slow down the process of integration, while pragmatists feared an outbreak of ethnic rivalries in Eastern Europe, and saw enlargement as a possible preventative response. Controversially, East Germany joined the

Community in October 1990 through the back door of German reunification, and while West Germany may have agreed to foot the bill for reunification, the economic and social costs of reintegrating the two Germanies heightened the concerns of the deepeners.

With 12 members now on board, the focus moved to deepening the 1987 Single European Act, being the first new treaty initiative since 1957. The Single Market negotiations raised concerns among several EFTA members that they might be excluded from that market (Dinan, 2004: 223), which led in 1994 to the creation of the European Economic Area (EEA). This provided EFTA members with access to the Single European Market, in return for which they agreed to accept the rules of the Single Market. But the game quickly changed when four members of the EEA – Austria, Finland, Norway and Sweden – applied for Community membership. The rules for enlargement had been clarified in 1993 when the European Council – meeting in Copenhagen – agreed a formal set of requirements for membership of the EU: an applicant state should be democratic (with respect for human rights and the rule of law), should have a functioning free-market economy (and the capacity to cope with the competitive pressures of capitalism), and should be able to take on the obligations of the acquis communitaire. Negotiations with the new applicants were completed in 1994, referendums were held in each country, and all but Norway (where once again the vote went against membership) joined the EU in January 1995. These were three democratic and wealthy countries, with a per capita GDP that was slightly larger than that of the 12 existing members, and so the so-called 'EFTA enlargement' was relatively painless and uncontroversial.

The integration of Western Europe was now all but complete: only Norway, Switzerland, and Iceland remained outside the club, but through their participation in EFTA, the EEA, and/or the open-border Schengen Agreement (signed in 1985), they

Table 12.1 Growth of the European Union

Year	Member States	Cumulative population
1952	Belgium, France, Italy, Luxembourg, Netherlands, West Germany	160 million
1973	Britain, Denmark, Ireland	233 million
1981	Greece	249 million
1986	Portugal, Spain	322 million
1990	East Germany (via German reunification)	339 million
1995	Austria, Finland, Sweden	379 million
2004	Cyprus, Czech Republic, Estonia, Hungary, Latvia, Lithuania, Malta, Poland, Slovakia, Slovenia	459 million
2007	Bulgaria and Romania	489 million

had close ties with the EU, and adjusted domestic law and policy accordingly. Expanding into Eastern Europe was bound to be a challenge of a different order: it might help former Soviet Bloc countries complete their transition to capitalism and democracy, it offered the promise of new investment opportunities, and it might pull Eastern Europe into a strategic relationship with the West that could be useful if problems in (or with) Russia worsened. However, the task of integrating poorer states whose recent experience with free markets and competitive elections was relatively modest – at least in the cases of eight of the ten – posed a stronger set of challenges. The EU was slow to respond to the end of the Cold War, argues Grabbe (2002: 67), and its approach to Eastern enlargement was symptomatic of the hesitancy: it was too preoccupied with completing the Single Market, and foreign and security policy was still very much in the hands of the member states. But most EU leaders soon began to appreciate that, with the end of the Cold War, Eastern enlargement was inevitable. The EU had long proclaimed its inclusiveness, and for the Eastern states, 'membership in the EU was a badge of honour, a stamp of political approval, and a path to prosperity' (Dinan, 2004: 268–9).

The EU's commitment to expand to the east came quickly, and between 1991 and 1996 Association Agreements were signed with ten Eastern European countries, allowing for the gradual expansion of free trade, and encouraging preparations for an eventual EU membership (for details, see Avery and Cameron, 1998). (Agreements had already been signed with Malta (1970) and Cyprus (1972).) In 1997, the Agenda 2000 programme listed the measures that needed to be agreed in order to clear the way for eastward expansion; these included agricultural reform, simplifying legislation, and financial aid. In 1998–2000, negotiations on membership opened with 12 new states: Bulgaria, Cyprus, the Czech Republic, Estonia, Hungary, Latvia, Lithuania, Malta, Poland, Romania, Slovakia and Slovenia. All but Bulgaria and Romania were invited to join in a first round, which they did in May 2004: membership of the EU expanded from 15 to 25, the borders of the EU moved 600 km (400 miles) to the east, and – for the first time – former Soviet republics (Estonia, Latvia, Lithuania) became part of the European Union. Following the completion of remaining preparations, Bulgaria and Romania joined in January 2007, an event widely seen less as a new enlargement than as a second stage of the 2004 enlargement. Membership of the EU had now reached the maximum of 27 members for which institutional plans had been made under the terms of the 2001 Treaty of Nice.

With the 2004–2007 enlargements, the population of the EU grew by more than 29 per cent, but its economic wealth grew by less than 6 per cent; the per capita GDP of the new EU-12 was less than half the average per capita GDP of the existing EU-15. There was greater public and political misgiving in the West about Eastern enlargement, which has indeed had its teething troubles: the (sometimes unrealistic) expectations for membership have not always lived up to reality, the quality of life in Eastern Europe has not improved as quickly as some once expected, and concerns about second-class citizenship remain. Under the terms negotiated for membership, the new members do not have equal access to EU subsidies, and

there are restrictions on the movement of workers to most Western states. Meanwhile, average wage levels remain lower in the East than those in the West. But EU institutions have continued to function, economic growth in most new member states has been healthy, foreign direct investment flows into the new members remain high, and most barriers to trade have gone. And Eastern enlargement has also challenged the rhetoric of European unity: how could Europe be complete without a return to the historical identity and borders of the subcontinent? For true Europeanists, Eastern enlargement has always been an essential part of the reconstruction of 'Europe'.

The process has not ended. Three Western European states (Iceland, Norway, and Switzerland) remain outside the EU. All three do most of their trade with the EU, and have preferential trade agreements with the EU through EFTA and (except Switzerland) the EEA. Norway and Iceland have adopted the bulk of the *acquis*, and there are strong prospects for both countries eventually joining the EU. Switzerland too is unavoidably impacted by the *acquis*, but it may remain the hole in the EU doughnut for many years to come. The Swiss applied for Community membership in 1992, but rejected the EEA in 1992, and heavily rejected the prospect of EU membership in a March 2001 referendum; the anti-EU views of many voters have also been reflected in the gains made by right-wing Swiss political parties at recent elections.

Meanwhile, to the east, there is the (variable) prospect of EU membership for at least a dozen more states (see Table 12.2). Croatia, Macedonia and Turkey are considered candidate countries, and the EU has signed – or has been in negotiations about – stabilization and association agreements with Albania, Bosnia, Montenegro and Serbia. These are designed to pave the way for eventual EU membership through a mix of trade concessions, economic and financial assistance aimed at reconstruction, and institutional/ legal development. For most of these countries, the EU is the single biggest trading partner and the biggest source of investment or development aid, but more progress is needed on dealing with corruption and organized crime, and on strengthening the judiciary, and Serbia's prospects have been blocked because of its failure to capture senior war criminals. Further afield, agreements have also been signed with Armenia, Azerbaijan, Georgia, Moldova, and the Ukraine, encouraging trade liberalization and economic cooperation.

Aside from enlargement itself, the EU has become more conscious in recent years of the importance of reaching out to neighbouring non-member states and building a 'circle of friends'. The launch in 1995 of the Barcelona process, designed to strengthen ties between the EU and 12 Mediterranean states, was one step in the process. More recently, the EU in 2003–2004 launched a European Neighbourhood Policy under which more financial assistance is offered, along with more cross-border cooperation, increased trade, and cooperation on a range of policies, including energy, the environment, transport, and research and development. Sixteen Eastern European, Middle Eastern, and North African states are now involved. For Dannreuther (2004: 1), this engagement with its immediate neighbours is the most distinctive and dynamic feature of Europe's foreign and security policy, and is the development that most clearly differentiates current policy from Cold War-era policy. It has not just regional implications, argues Aliboni, but also global geopolitical implications, impacting relations between the EU and the Arab world, Russia, and the United States (Aliboni, 2005).

No EU membership application has been more controversial than that from Turkey. The Community agreed as long ago as 1963 that membership was possible for Turkish but the waters have been muddied by Turkey's poor (albeit improving) record on human rights, and by concerns about its size and its relative poverty, which raises the twin spectre of increased immigration of Turkish workers into Western Europe and the diversion of EU structural funds into Turkey. There are also

Table 12.2 Prospects for future members

Albania	Potential candidate. Stabilization and association agreement signed with EU 2006.
Armenia	Partnership and cooperation agreement since 1999. Participates in European Neighbourhood Policy (ENP).
Azerbaijan	Partnership and cooperation agreement since 1994. Participates in ENP.
Belarus	Serious economic and political barriers to EU membership. Participates in ENP.
Bosnia and Herzegovina	Potential candidate. Stabilization and association agreement since 2008.
Croatia	Candidate. Applied 2003, candidate country 2004, negotiations opened 2005.
Georgia	Partnership and cooperation agreement since 1994. Participates in ENP.
Iceland	Free-trade agreement with EEC in 1972, member of EEA since 1994, and of Schengen Agreement since 2000.
Kosovo	Potential candidate. Currently under UN administration. EU membership dependent upon how member states deal with independence from Serbia.
Macedonia	Candidate. Applied 2004, candidate country 2005, negotiations not yet started.
Moldova	Partnership and cooperation agreement since 1994. Participates in ENP.
Montenegro	Potential candidate. Stabilization and association agreement since 2007.
Norway	Twice accepted for membership, twice turned it down. Member of EEA since 1994, and of Schengen Agreement since 2001.
Serbia	Potential candidate. Stabilization and association agreement since 2008.
Switzerland	Applied 1992, 2001 referendum rejected membership. Multiple bilateral agreements with EU. 2005 referendum ratified membership of Schengen.
Turkey	Candidate. Applied 1987, candidate country 1999, negotiations started 2005, but many problems have arisen.
Ukraine	EU membership aspirations; 2015 discussed as target date. Participates in ENP.

concerns about the social impact of absorbing nearly 73 million Muslims into the EU, portrayed by many of its supporters as a Christian union. In 1963, Turkey became an associate member of the EEC; in 1987, it applied for full membership; in 1995, an EU–Turkey customs union came into force; in 1999, it was formally recognized as a candidate country; and in, 2005 negotiations on a membership procedure began. For its champions in the EU, Turkish membership would have important strategic implications. For its detractors, it would bring too many economic and social problems in its wake. The waters have been muddied by disputes over Turkish–Cypriot relations, and over slow progress by Turkey on changing its laws to fit with the *acquis*. Estimates of how long it will take to achieve Turkish entry currently range between 10 and 20 years.

THE DEBATE OVER ENLARGEMENT

Opinion on the merits of enlargement is divided. On the public front, no more than half of EU citizens in recent years have been in favour, while opposition in several countries has been substantial. In 2000, the Eurobarometer survey research service found that 44 percent of those polled in the EU-15 were in favour while 35 percent were opposed, and only 39 percent were in favour of expansion to the countries with which negotiations were then under way. Opposition was strongest in Austria and France, which were both 50 per cent opposed (Eurobarometer 54, April 2001). By 2002, support for enlargement in the EU-15 had risen to 52 per cent and opposition had fallen to 30 per cent (Eurobarometer 58, March 2003). But by 2006, when the polling covered the EU-25 for the first time, only 45 per cent were in favour of further enlargement, while 42 per cent were opposed. Support was strongest in Mediterranean and Eastern European member states, and opposition was greatest in Austria, Finland, France, Germany, and Luxembourg,

where approximately 60 percent of respondents were hostile to further growth (Eurobarometer 65, July 2006).

On the political front, it is easier to find voices of caution and doubt than of outright support. In 2004, enlargement commissioner Günter Verheugen warned that the EU was not politically prepared for Eastern enlargement. In 2005, German Chancellor Angela Merkel suggested that the EU had reached the limits of its capacity to integrate, while then French Interior Minister Nikolas Sarkozy argued that further enlargement should be suspended. In the same year, the French and Dutch governments suggested that enlargement was a key reason why their voters had rejected the proposed European constitution. In September 2006, Commission President José Manuel Barosso called for a pause in plans for further enlargement, suggesting that it would not be wise to proceed without a resolution of the constitutional issue.

The debate about enlargement is increasingly driven by terms such as 'enlargement fatigue', 'absorption capacity' (the French prefer 'assimilation capacity'), and 'functioning capacity' (a term mooted by the Commission, referring to the ability of EU institutions to absorb new members). The flurry of code words reflects a mix of public and political doubt, questions about the economic costs of integrating poorer member states, and concern over the practical considerations of absorbing new members into an EU whose decision-making procedures have – in the eyes of many – not kept up with needs. The arguments against enlargement include the following:

- Opening up the European labour market will lead to the movement of workers from poorer states to richer states, reducing the workforce in source countries, taking jobs from workers in target countries, increasing the load on Western welfare systems, potentially exacerbating social stresses, and perhaps leading to a worsening of crime rates. Concerns about immigration have already fed in to the rise of anti-immigration political parties in the West. The European Commission estimated that there would be 70,000–150,000 migrants per year throughout the EU after the 2004 enlargement; in fact, the UK alone (which took a more liberal position on opening up its borders) received nearly 450,000 applications to work in the UK from the Eastern European states in the period 2004–2006 (Home Office, 2006), with government estimates that the number of new arrivals was as high as 600,000 if self-employed workers were included.

- Businesses in wealthier countries will be inclined to relocate to poorer states with lower labour costs, lower levels of social protection, and weaker regulations.
- Bringing in poorer states will divert the flows of EU structural funds away from the wealthier states, and will increase the overall demands on those funds.
- The bigger the EU becomes, the greater will be the difficulties of deepening the effects of integration; in other words, widening will conflict with deepening, complicating attempts to reach agreement on policy (particularly foreign and defence policy), and undermining attempts to achieve 'ever closer union'.
- The bigger the membership, the more varied will be the population of the EU, making it more difficult to agree on the values and norms that Europe represents.
- There have been concerns about the ability of new members – especially Bulgaria and Romania – to follow through on the economic, legal and bureaucratic reforms required of EU membership. There are also concerns about the demands that EU membership impose on the transformation of the political systems, economic policies, laws, institutions, and even cultures of new member states.
- There have been concerns about inflationary pressures, with growth expected in particular in the prices of food and imported products, and the danger of a growth in consumer credit and spending.

Conversely, the arguments in favour of enlargement include the following:

- Because aspirant members must be stable democracies with strong records on human rights, support for the rule of law, and the protection of minorities, enlargement encourages democratic change through the democratization of institutions, processes and political culture. By being bound more closely into the political structure of the West, security and stability are enhanced in the East.
- Immigration can help drive economic growth, and remittances sent home to their families by foreign workers can help build wealth and opportunity at home. And because new members must adopt the *acquis*, enlargement can help deal with crime and social problems by strengthening domestic institutions and legal systems, and by promoting cross-border cooperation on crime, drugs and illegal immigration.
- Cheaper labour is good for the economies of wealthier European states, and if companies are going to relocate, better that they do it to poorer parts of the EU than to China or India.
- Because new members must have a functioning free market, enlargement supports economic liberalization by opening markets in goods and services, stimulating economic growth and offering new trading opportunities. By thus encouraging political stability and economic prosperity, and by helping build the role of the EU as a trading superpower, integration gives Europe more weight on the world stage.
- The possible negative impact on integration may be overstated. The population of the EEC/EU more than doubled in size before the 2004–2007 enlargements, and there was – by most analyses – no lessening of progress on deepening. In spite of worries about the impact on decision-making, and in spite of the nostalgic reflections of senior bureaucrats and government officials that the once clubby atmosphere of EU institutions has gone, the EU continues to function at roughly the same levels of efficiency with 27 members as it once did with 15. (It is instructive to read today the many predictions of institutional paralysis made before Eastern enlargement, and to wonder how the authors must now feel about their misplaced pessimism.)
- Enlargement is helping reunite a continent that still feels the residual effects of Cold War divisions, and is helping build a stronger sense of the identity and meaning of Europe. The increased diversity of the EU, rather than complicating the decision-making process, has brought new ideas to the table, has reinvigorated the debate about the meaning of Europe, and has encouraged Europeans to take more inclusive positions on public policy.
- For those who have worried about the influential role in the EU of the Franco-German axis,

or indeed of any of the larger member states, enlargement has already reduced their powers, and will continue so to do.

- The addition of poorer states with substantial potential for economic growth might help inject new energy into a European Union where growth is often sluggish, and where labour markets are often in need of reform. Pessimists often charge that the EU faces a demographic crisis as birth rates fall, populations age, and the balance between workers and retirees changes. These pressures will be eased as new and younger member states join.
- Western Europeans who have long focused their attention on their own immediate neighbourhoods are being reminded that there is more to Europe than the core members of NATO or the OECD, and are being encouraged to continue the process of reaching out to Eastern Europe that began with the end of the Cold War.

In spite of the doubts and warnings of the pessimists, there has been an inevitability to enlargement, and the EU has made the necessary adjustments, which will continue with the arrangements agreed under the Lisbon Treaty. Bringing in poorer states was always going to have more visible effects than if the EU had remained a club for Western capitalist members, but access to new markets and labour, the role of enlargement in promoting consumerism and political growth in the East, and the impact of enlargement on redefining the regional and global role of the EU held out greater promise of gains than of losses.

THE TRANSFORMATION OF EUROPE

Until the end of the Cold War, there were at least three Europes: the European Community, Western European states outside the Community, and Eastern European states behind the iron curtain. The first two pursued democracy and capitalism, their interests dominated by those of the Atlantic Alliance. The latter pursued state socialism, their interests dominated by the relationship with the Soviet Union. But since the end of the

Cold War – bringing in developments in the Balkans, the introduction of the euro, the fallout over Iraq, and Eastern enlargement in 2004–2007 – the continent has been transformed, in at least five different ways.

First, enlargement has altered relationships among the states of Europe. Barely two generations ago, Europe was dominated by the nation-state, national governments pursued national interests rather than European interests, and individual Europeans were reminded of their differences whenever they crossed internal borders. With those borders largely removed, and with the near complete freedom of movement of people, money, goods and services now achieved (at least among Schengen states), the governments and citizens of EU member states relate to each other in a fundamentally different fashion; the nation-state is on the decline, and European interests vie for attention with national interests. As membership of the EU has grown, the dimensions of European interests have broadened, and the voices and opinions added to the debate over the meaning of Europe have become more diverse.

Second, enlargement has increased the size and reach of the European single market. The original six member states were home to 160 million consumers, living in states still recovering from the war and working to redefine their relationships with each other and with third parties. Today, the EU is the biggest capitalist marketplace in the world, with nearly half a billion consumers, most of them living in some of the wealthiest states in the world. In terms of collective gross national product, the EU lead over the US has grown, and the 27 states also work and act together on trade issues: they account for approximately 40–45 per cent of world trade, and have been able to translate their collective strength into enormous influence over bilateral and international trade negotiations (see discussion in McCormick, 2007: chapter 4).

Third, integration has helped remodel the European economy. The postwar reconstruction of the six founding members was underpinned by the opportunities provided by access to a larger market. Then, while the accession of Britain and Ireland lowered the overall per capita GDP of the Community, it drew new attention to the imbalance created by regional economic differences, and helped generate the decision to create the European Regional Development Fund. This was followed by the European Social Fund, and by the Cohesion Fund. Together, the structural funds have become the second biggest item on the EU budget, and currently channel nearly €45 billion annually into helping close the economic gap between the richer and the poorer parts of the EU.

The economic record of Ireland since joining the Community exemplifies the possibilities. In 1973, it was one of the poorest countries in Western Europe, with a per capita GDP barely half that of West Germany. But by the 1990s it was enjoying double-digit annual economic growth, record low unemployment, booming exports, reduced rates of income, corporate and capital gains tax, and a flood of foreign investment, much of it headed for the high technology and financial sectors (OECD, 2004). Membership of the Community was not alone in bringing about the change: Ireland's growth did not begin until the mid-1980s, and the structural funds were not able to achieve similar results in other member states (Powell, 2003). The reduction of corporate tax rates also played its part, as did the reduced role of the state in the marketplace, and Ireland also had the advantage of an English-speaking workforce, attractive to American investors. Eastern European states would do well to appreciate the importance of a combination of sensible economic policies and the opportunities afforded by integration.

Fourth, enlargement has transformed the global role of the European Union. Where once there was small cluster of Western European states, dominated by their relationship with the United States, divided from their eastern neighbours by differences over policy and political culture, and pursuing occasionally competing views of the role that Europe might play in the international system, there is today a European superpower, whose political and economic presence has global implications. Enlargement has also strengthened ties between the EU and other regions of the world. When Britain joined, the EEC had to build a new association with the Commonwealth, and had to redefine its relationship with the Third World; one of the results was the creation of the African, Caribbean, and Pacific (ACP) program. When Greece, Spain, and Portugal joined, ties between the Community and Latin America and the rest of the Mediterranean were strengthened, and expansion to Austria, Sweden and Finland helped shift the EU's geographic priorities eastward (van den Hoven, 2004). And when the EU finally moved eastward in 2004–2007, Western European member states had to broaden both their perspectives on the world and their definition of the idea of Europe.

Finally, and perhaps most importantly, enlargement has allowed the European Union to become the most compelling force for the promotion of democracy and capitalism in the world. The US – particularly during the Clinton and Bush administrations – has made much of its role in promoting democracy, but has tended to rely upon a mixture of diplomacy, coercion and the use of military force (as in Iraq). Europe, by contrast, has chosen not to pursue the military path to democratic change, and has instead relied upon soft power and 'Europeanizing', or encouraging prospective members to adopt its norms and methods (Grabbe, 2005; see also discussion in McCormick, 2007: 124–30). The impact of integration on democracy was revealed early by the contribution it made to the internal stabilization of the six founding member states: in the cases of Germany and Italy, the ravages of war might have promoted instability and dysfunction, but instead the two countries enjoyed democratic reform and economic growth in the postwar years, much credit for which must go to the effects of integration. Enlargement to Greece, Spain, and Portugal, in turn, helped these countries strengthen their fledgling democracies, and provided them with improved access to the major international organizations. Most recently, Eastern enlargement has helped complete the changes that began with the end of the Cold War: membership has compelled the new states to reform their bureaucracies, coordinate their laws and policies with those of the rest of the EU, and open up their markets.

CURRENT AND FUTURE DEBATES

Enlargement has long been a topic of scholarly analysis and debate, but the volume has risen in recent years for two main reasons. First, there has been a new level of appreciation for the implications of enlargement, which has itself been driven by a new level of appreciation for the implications of European integration. As recently as the 1980s, integration was relatively low on the list of academic, political and public interests, but the revival of the single market programme combined with preparations for the single currency, institutional reforms, and the extension of EU responsibilities into new policy areas to draw more attention to integration, and to the related significance of the prospects for further enlargement. As Sjursen (2006) argues, however, enlargement has been seen as a series of isolated episodes, there have been few systematic studies of its broader significance, and the debate over enlargement has so far shed less light on the EU and Europe than it might.

Second, the extension of the borders of the EU into Eastern Europe had an entirely different set of implications from those of previous enlargements, and this has been reflected in the wider and deeper levels of discourse and analysis. There have been many studies published in recent years on enlargement broadly defined (see e.g. Baun, 2000; Croft *et al.*, 1999; Mair and Zielonka, 2002; Nugent, 2004; Preston, 1997; Steunenberg, 2002; and Hamilton, 2005), but the implications of Eastern enlargement have attracted

more attention than all previous rounds of expansion combined (see e.g. Artis *et al.*, 2006; Charezma and Strzala, 2002; Dabrowski and Rostowski, 2001; Dannreuther, 2004; Dimitrova, 2004; Hughes *et al.*, 2004; Ingham and Ingham, 2002; O'Brennan, 2006; Poole, 2003; Pridham, 2005; and Schimmelfennig and Sedelmeier, 2005). The bulk of the analysis has focused on the potential problems of Eastern enlargement, with worried investigation of the impact of migration on labour markets, of potential strains on the EU decision-making process, of the impact of expansion on the identity of Europe, and of the challenges faced by the new members, which have had to undergo rapid modernization, making – in the space of a few years – the kinds of changes that evolved over a much greater length of time in Western European states.

Some elements of the debate have been studied more thoroughly than others, resulting in a particularly healthy volume of new research on the economic implications of Eastern enlargement (see Dabrowski and Rostowski, 2001; Landesmann and Rosati, 2004; Manzocchi, 2003; Piazolo, 2001). This is hardly surprising given concerns about the adjustments demanded by integrating ten relatively poor and recently state socialist regimes into a grouping of relatively wealthy and capitalist states, with the prospects of more to come. But other policy implications have not been forgotten, and there have been studies of the impact of enlargement on trade policy (Karadeloglou, 2002), agricultural policy (Münch, 2002), health policy (McKee *et al.*, 2004), and environmental policy (Carmin and Vandeveer, 2005). It should be noted, though, that much of the debate looks at the impact of the EU on the new member states, rather than vice versa. One exception is the study of social policy by Vaughan-Whitehead (2003), which – ahead of enlargement – contemplated the potential dangers of unfair competition and social dumping, asked whether existing member states might reduce their own social provisions in order to be able to compete with the newcomers, and

considered the possible impact of enlargement on the European social model.

The richest seams of current and future
analysis of enlargement lie in two key areas,
one internal to Europe and the other external.
Internally, there is the crucial question of the
impact of enlargement on the political and
economic meaning of Europe. Cameron
(2004: 14) notes that the shift away from an
initial focus on markets towards the high
politics of money, justice, and foreign and
defence policy has made more critical the
need for 'government', but what sort and by
whom? What impact has enlargement had –
or will it have in the future – on the competing visions of a united states of Europe
versus a Europe of the nations, and what
impact will it have on the meaning of 'ever
closer union'? The Community – and then
the EU – has always occupied a position
somewhere between an intergovernmental
organization and a supranational superstate;
has enlargement pushed it further along the
spectrum towards the latter, and what does
this mean for the ongoing debate about federalism and sovereignty? Stretching the issue
still further, has enlargement meant that the
EU has gone beyond being a superstate, and
instead – as Zielonka (2006) suggests –
acquired some of the characteristics of a
neo-Medieval empire? Enlargement has
watered-down the strength of the member
states; when there were just six members, it
was relatively easy to achieve a consensus in
which the views of all six might be represented, but with 27 competing sets of national
interests, the collective views of the other 26
have come to matter much more.

On a related matter, what impact has
enlargement had on the cultural or psychological meaning of Europe? Grabbe (2002:
69) argues that the Cold War created 'the
strong feeling that the countries of central
Europe had "lost" their European identity
and that they needed to "return to Europe" in
order to regain that identity'. Eastern enlargement not only provided final and emphatic
confirmation of the end of the Cold War division of Europe, but it also helped redefine the
meaning of Europe. Until 2004 the 'European'
Union had ultimately been a 'Western'
European Union, and the absence of its
Eastern neighbours reflected the remaining
political, economic and social divisions of
the continent. Between May 2004 and
January 2007 almost all of Europe was
finally brought together under the aegis of
the European Union, and three out of four
Europeans now live within its borders, with
the prospect that the political and economic
pressures and opportunities of integration
will have much the same effect on countries
such as Poland, Romania and the Baltic
states as they once did on Greece, Portugal,
and Spain. But many questions remain
unanswered.

On another related matter, there is the
challenge of establishing the frontiers of
Europe. It is widely assumed that Europe
needs such frontiers, whether to allow institutional progress (Zielonka, 1998), or to
more clearly define the nature of the European
superstate, or to control the ingress into the
EU of 'undesirables'. But an alternative view
offered by Maier (2002) holds that many
negatives are associated with frontiers and
their defence, that place and territory no
longer encourage forward-looking aspirations, and that the idea of Europe might be
associated with a principle of community or
association rather than with lines on a map.

On the external front, there is the challenge of clarifying the effect of enlargement
on the global role of the EU. Clearly, the
extension of its borders has changed the
shape of Europe on the radar of international
relations. Some recent studies of the strategic
and geopolitical implications of enlargement
have taken a pessimistic view, asking whether
the kinds of divisions previously found
among existing member states would be
exacerbated by expansion to the east (see
Brimmer and Fröhlich, 2005 and Armstrong
and Anderson, 2006). Others have tied
enlargement to an expansion of the EU's
global significance, the most extravagant
statement of this view being offered by
Leonard, who writes of a 'Eurosphere'

stretching to cover 109 countries and two billion people. Including the EU, the former Soviet Republics, the western Balkans, and virtually all of the Middle East and Africa, this is – he argues – a 'zone of influence which is gradually being transformed by the European project and adopting European ways of doing things' (Leonard, 2005: 53–5 and 145–6).

A more focused issue is the impact of enlargement on transatlantic relations. Since 1945, the US has supported both the idea of integration and the EU's efforts to expand, regarding the notions of European unity and an extended US commitment to Europe as both compatible and complementary (Serfaty, 2004: 136). The transatlantic relationship was far from being an easy one, with differences of opinion over policy and over the pursuit of the Cold War (Lundestad, 2003); it was uncertain whether the Community would evolve as a counterpart of American power or as a counterweight to US leadership (Serfaty, 2004: 138). During the Cold War, Western European states were loath to publicly express their misgivings about US power and policy, because they needed the US security guarantee and US investments. But recent years have seen a combination of declining US credibility on the world stage, greater willingness by EU states to assert their differences with the US, and questions about the future of the Atlantic Alliance (see McCormick, 2007, for further discussion).

Eastern enlargement increased the number of EU governments that took pro-American foreign policy positions (see discussion in Leiven, 2002), but it also increased the economic power of the EU, as well as its political and social reach. As the differentials between the EU and Europe decline, so – inevitably – the transatlantic relationship must change. Some (e.g. Ikenberry, 2004; and Wohlforth, 2004), argue that there is no prospect of an increasingly competitive transatlantic relationship, but others (e.g. Calleo, 2004; Kupchan, 2002: 67–8; and Moïsi, 2003) see the rise of an assertive Europe and wonder whether 'the West' still even exists.

The response to Islamic fundamentalism, international terrorism and weapons of mass destruction has not had the same unifying effect as the Soviet threat, Moïsi concludes, because the EU and the US differ over how to respond. But they do not need to think the same way; they need to better understand each other's way of doing things.

Transatlantic relations have been impacted not only by EU enlargement but also by NATO enlargement. There is an emerging literature on this topic (see Jacoby, 2004; Leech, 2002; and McAllister and Dannreuther, 2002), with a particular interest in what the twin enlargements might mean for European security and for the consolidation of democracy in Eastern Europe. There has been one suggestion that the EU had better prospects for the latter than for the former (Smith and Timmins, 2000: 167–71), and another that while Europe has become EU-centric economically and NATO-centric in the field of security, the gains can only be consolidated through a fundamental redesign of both institutions (Trenin, 2003: 2). Sperling (2000) predicted that while NATO enlargement had been relatively swift and painless, because there were no compelling reasons not to proceed, EU enlargement was likely to be a more challenging process with an uncertain outcome. In fact, the opposite has been true. EU enlargement has been more successful than most of the sceptics would have predicted, while searching questions are now being asked about the value and purpose of NATO. Conventional wisdom argues that Europe needs NATO because it does not have its own significant security capacity, but there are indications that several EU member states prefer to commit themselves to UN operations rather than NATO operations, in large part because of disquiet about US foreign policy.

Finally, what impact has enlargement had on the development of the EU's foreign policy? Hill (2002: 95–6) makes the point that enlargement *is* foreign policy, and that it raises fundamental questions about where the EU is headed, and about the consequences of its actions. The geopolitical impact of enlargement, he argues, depends both upon the pace of enlargement and the eventual size of the EU, which raises questions about whether the EU of the future will be large and loose, or large and tight, whether its end state (whatever that is) will be quickly or slowly achieved, and whether it will experience progressive supranationalism or will stall along the way.

CONCLUSIONS: CHALLENGE OR OPPORTUNITY?

Fraser Cameron (2004: ix) notes that we are not always aware that we are living through major historical changes. It is often only with the benefit of hindsight that we can fully understand the broader implications of the changes that we have recently witnessed. This is certainly true of the enlargement of the European Union. We can follow the different stages in the process (1973, 1981–1986, 1990, 1995, and 2004–2007), and we can identify the institutional changes that were made as a result. We can draw conclusions about the earlier stages (because we have the benefit of hindsight), and can also make some estimates about the economic implications of enlargement, because we have numbers that can shed light on the changes (although, as we know, even economists struggle to prove that particular actions result in particular consequences). But when we start to consider the effects of enlargement on the shaping of Europe, on its political and social transformation, on its cultural dynamics, or on its place in the world, it is more difficult to reach a consensus. Commentaries on the evolution of the EU have been heavily influenced over the years by pessimism, and yet many of the forecasts of failure have not come to pass, and indeed it is difficult – unless, of course, one is opposed to the very concept of European integration – to conclude that enlargement has not been a positive force in the history of postwar Europe.

Just what it will mean for Europe over the longer term remains to be seen. It is easy to become diverted by immediate political, economic, and social concerns, and to lose sight of the bigger picture. Each phase in enlargement has generated its own debates and concerns, but each phase was completed and has been absorbed into our understanding of European integration. Significant question marks now hover over the prospects of being able to absorb Turkey, not because it is poor (like many recent or aspirant Eastern European states), but because it is *large* and poor and Muslim. No prospective new member has raised more fundamental questions about the meaning of Europe, and much of what Europe will come to represent in the future will depend on how the EU deals with the Turkish question. Less debatable, meanwhile, is the prospect of enlargement to the rest of the Balkans, or the pressures that must lead to the kind of economic and political changes that will eventually bring Belarus and Ukraine into the equation. Meanwhile, we have only just begun to understand the effects of past and prospective enlargement on the meaning of Europe.

REFERENCES

Aliboni, R. (2005) 'The geopolitical implications of the European neighbourhood policy', *European Foreign Affairs Review*, 10 (1): 1–16.

Armstrong, W. and Anderson, J. (eds) (2006) *The Geopolitics of European Union Enlargement*. London: Routledge.

Artis, M., Banerjee, A., and Marcellino, M. (eds) (2006) *The Central and Eastern European Countries and the European Union*. Cambridge: Cambridge University Press.

Avery, G. and Cameron, F. (1998) *The Enlargement of the European Union*. Sheffield: Sheffield Academic Press.

Baun, M.J. (2000) *A Wider Europe: The Process and Politics of European Union Enlargement*. Lanham: Rowman and Littlefield.

Brimmer, E. and Fröhlich, S. (eds) (2005) *The Strategic Implications Of European Union Enlargement*. Baltimore: Center for

Transatlantic Relations, Johns Hopkins University.

Calleo, D. (2004) 'The broken West', *Survival*, 46 (3): 29–38.

Cameron, F. (2004) 'Widening and deepening', in F. Cameron (ed.) *The Future of Europe: Integration and Enlargement*. London: Routledge, pp. 1–17.

Carmin, J., and Vandeveer, S.D. (eds) (2005) *EU Enlargement and the Environment: Institutional Change and Environmental Policy in Central and Eastern Europe*. London: Routledge.

Charezma, W. and Strzala, K. (eds) (2002) *East European Transition and EU Enlargement*. Physica-Verlag, Heidelberg.

Croft, S., Redmond, J., Rees, G.W., and Webber, M. (1999) *The Enlargement of Europe*. Manchester: Manchester University Press.

Dabrowski, M. and Rostowski, J. (eds) (2001) *The Eastern Enlargement of the EU*. Dordrecht: Kluwer Academic.

Dannreuther, R. (ed.) (2004) *European Union Foreign and Security Policy: Towards a Neighbourhood Strategy*. London: Routledge.

Dimitrova, A. (ed.) (2004) *Driven to Change: The European Union's Enlargement Viewed from the East*. Manchester: Manchester University Press.

Dinan, D. (2004) *Europe Recast: A History of European Union*. Basingstoke: Palgrave Macmillan.

Grabbe, H. (2002) 'Challenges of EU enlargement' in A. Lieven and D. Trenin (eds) *Ambivalent Neighbors: The EU, NATO, and the Price of Membership*. Washington DC: Carnegie Endowment for International Peace, pp. 67–89.

Grabbe, H. (2005) *The EU's Transformative power: Europeanization through Conditionality in Central and Eastern Europe*. Basingstoke: Palgrave Macmillan.

Hamilton, D.S. (ed.) (2005) *New Frontiers of Europe: The Enlargement of the European Union, Implications and Consequences*. Baltimore: Center for Transatlantic Relations, Johns Hopkins University.

Hill, C. (2002) 'The geopolitical implications of enlargement', in J. Zielonka (ed.) *Europe Unbound: Enlarging and Reshaping the Boundaries of the European Union*. London: Routledge, pp. 95–116.

Home Office (2006) *Accession Monitoring Report May 2006–June 2006*. Published online 22 August 2006.

Hughes, J., Sasse, G., and Gordon, C. (2004) *Europeanization and Regionalization in the EU's Enlargement to Central and Eastern Europe: The Myth of Conditionality*. Basingstoke: Palgrave Macmillan.

Ikenberry, G.J. (2004) 'Liberal hegemony or empire? American power in the age of uni-polarity', in D. Held and M. Koenig-Archibugi (eds) *American Power in the 21st Century*. Cambridge: Polity Press, pp. 83–113.

Ingham, H. and Ingham, M. (eds) (2002) *EU Expansion to the East: Prospects and Problems*. Cheltenham: Edward Elgar.

Jacoby, W. (2004) *The Enlargement of the European Union and NATO: Ordering from the Menu in Central Europe*. Cambridge: Cambridge University Press, Cambridge.

Karadeloglou, P. (ed.) (2002) *Enlarging the EU: The Trade Balance Effects*. Basingstoke: Palgrave Macmillan.

Kupchan, C.A. (2002) 'The end of the West', *Atlantic Monthly*, 290 (4): 42–4.

Landesmann, M.A. and Rosati, D.K. (eds) (2004) *Shaping the New Europe: Economic Policy Challenges of European Union Enlargement*. Basingstoke: Palgrave Macmillan.

Leech, J. (2002) *Whole and Free: NATO, EU Enlargement and Transatlantic Relations*. London: Federal Trust.

Leonard, L. (2005) *Why Europe Will Run the 21st Century*. London: Fourth Estate.

Lieven, A. (2002) 'Conclusions: The pangs of disappointed love? A divided west and its multiple peripheries', in A. Lieven and D. Trenin (eds) *Ambivalent Neighbors: The EU, NATO, and the Price of Membership*. Washington DC: Carnegie Endowment for International Peace, pp. 295–312.

Lundestad, G. (2003) *The United States and Western Europe Since 1945*. Oxford: Oxford University Press.

Maier, C.S. (2002) 'Does Europe need a frontier? From territorial to redistributive community', in J. Zielonka (ed.) *Europe Unbound: Enlarging and Reshaping the Boundaries of the European Union*. London: Routledge, pp. 17–37.

Mair, P. and Zielonka, J. (eds) (2002) *The Enlarged European Union: Unity and Diversity*. London: Routledge.

Manzocchi, S. (2003) *The Economics of Enlargement*. Basingstoke: Palgrave Macmillan.

McAllister, R. and Dannreuther, R. (2002) *EU and NATO Enlargement*. London: Routledge.

McCormick, J. (2007) *The European Superpower*. Basingstoke: Palgrave Macmillan.

McKee, M., MacLehose, L. and Nolte, E. (eds) (2004) *Health Policy and European Union Enlargement*. Maidenhead: Open University Press.

Milward, A. (2002) *The UK and the European Community, Vol. 1: The Rise and Fall of a National Strategy, 1945–1963*. London: Whitehall History Publishing.

Moïsi, D. (2003) 'Reinventing the west', *Foreign Affairs*, 82 (6): 67–73.

Münch, W. (2002) *Effects of EU Enlargement to the Central European Countries on Agricultural Markets*. Frankfurt: Peter Lang.

Nugent, N. (ed.) (2004) *European Union Enlargement*. Basingstoke: Palgrave Macmillan.

O'Brennan, J. (2006) *The Eastern Enlargement of the European Union*. London: Routledge.

Organization for Economic Cooperation and Development (OECD) (2004) *Economic Survey: Ireland 2003*. Paris: OECD.

Piazolo, D. (2001) *The Integration Process Between Eastern and Western Europe*. Berlin: Springer-Verlag.

Poole, P.A. (2003) *Europe Unites: The EU's Eastern Enlargement*. Westport: Praeger.

Powell, B. (2003) 'Economic freedom and growth: the case of the Celtic Tiger', *Cato Journal*, 22 (3): 431–448.

Preston, C. (1997) *Enlargement and Integration in the European Union*. London: Routledge.

Pridham, G. (2005) *Designing Democracy: EU Enlargement and Regime Change in Post-Communist Europe*. Basingstoke: Palgrave Macmillan.

Rumford, C. (2002) *The European Union: A Political Sociology*. Oxford: Blackwell.

Schimmelfennig, F. and Sedelmeier, U. (eds) (2005) *The Politics of European Union Enlargement: Theoretical Approaches*. London: Routledge.

Serfaty, S. (2004) 'The transatlantic dimension', in F. Cameron (ed.) *The Future of Europe: Integration and Enlargement*. London: Routledge, pp. 135–148.

Shonfield, A. (1974) *Journey to an Unknown Destination*. London: Royal Institute of International Affairs.

Sjursen, H. (2006) *Questioning EU Enlargement*. London: Routledge.

Smith, M.A. and Timmins, G. (2000) *Building a Bigger Europe: EU and NATO Enlargement in Comparative Perspective*. Aldershot: Ashgate.

Sperling, J. (ed.) (2000) *Two Tiers or Two Speeds? The European Security Order and the Enlargement of the European Union and NATO*. Manchester: Manchester University Press.

Steunenberg, B. (ed.) (2002) *Widening the European Union: The Politics of Institutional Change and Reform*. London: Routledge.

Trenin, D. (2002) 'Introduction: the grand redesign' in A. Lieven and D. Trenin (eds) *Ambivalent Neighbors: The EU, NATO, and the Price of Membership*. Washington DC: Carnegie Endowment for International Peace.

van den Hoven, A. (2004) 'The European Union as an international economic actor', in N. Nugent (ed.) *European Union Enlargement*. Basingstoke: Palgrave Macmillan.

Vaughan-Whitehead, D.C. (2003) *EU Enlargement Versus Social Europe: The Uncertain Future of the European Social Model*. Cheltenham: Edward Elgar.

Wallace, W. (2002) 'Where does Europe end? Dilemmas of inclusion and exclusion', in J. Zielonka (ed.) *Europe Unbound: Enlarging and Reshaping the Boundaries of the European Union*. London: Routledge.

Wohlforth, W.C. (2004) 'The transatlantic dimension' in R. Dannreuther (ed.), *European Union Foreign and Security Policy: Towards a Neighbourhood Strategy*. London: Routledge, pp. 186–201.

Zielonka, J. (1998) 'Policies without strategy: the EU's record in Eastern Europe', in Jan Zielonka (ed.), *Paradoxes of European Foreign Policy*. The Hague: Kluwer Law International, pp. 131–146.

Zielonka, J. (2006) *Europe As Empire: The Nature of the Enlarged European Union*. Oxford: Oxford University Press.

Themes and Issues

13

Uses and Abuses of the Concept of Integration

Philomena Murray

A reassessment of the European Union (EU) studies in recent years has seen an increasing interplay among disciplines, resulting in increased breadth and depth of conceptual development. The need for sustained dialogue between EU studies and international relations (IR) has been persuasively argued by scholars, such as, Warleigh (2006), while the need to break down the barriers between disciplines and subdisciplines and particularly what Peterson regards as phoney wars between IR and comparative politics (CP) has, for some time, been a theme in the examination of the state of the study of the EU (Hix, 1999; Peterson, 2001; Pollack, 2001; Rumford and Murray, 2003a). In addition, the study of the EU has often been confined to the study of European integration (EI). European Studies is now becoming more broad and therefore, should include more than EI studies. In particular, it should be more interdisciplinary.

This chapter examines the ways in which the concept of integration has been utilized and politically misused by scholars and the EU alike. As long as the term 'integration' is utilized to mean a political objective, a theoretical model, a policy process, a set of theories

and a paradigm for regional bodies, then overuse of the term will take place. European integration has become increasingly contested as both a concept and a process and it is incumbent upon scholars to subject the EU to analytical treatment that does justice to its contemporary complexity of governance and its evolving nature (Murray, 2000).

The chapter argues that the core issues of power and of the direction of the EU's integration project remain unclear. In particular, it examines how newer and fresher perspectives on 'integration' can assist us in understanding the transformation of Europe. It seeks a clear differentiation of studies of the nation state from those that seek to move us forward conceptually in our understanding of the EU's transformative role in – and impact on – the nation state and in the international arena. It calls for caution in attempts to utilize terms of the past in our study of the present and in forming our pathways to future research.

The study of integration theory is not only about EI and the EU but also concerns comparative regionalism and inter-regionalism for example (Breslin and Higgott, 2003;

Hettne and Soberbaum, 2000; Murray 2004a, 2008a). Further, if the study of the EU is to be an intrinsic part of IR, the transformation of the EU and, in turn, its transformative impact on the state require finer analysis.

The study of the EU can be introspective, with respect to the EU's internal process and conflicts, for example. Examinations of the EU in an international context often tend to deal with its relations with individual countries and, occasionally, regions, such as the Association of South East Asian Nations (ASEAN) or Mercosur, the Common Market of South America. From outside the EU, some analyses portray the EU as a rather successful economic entity but do not necessarily understand the transformative nature of the EU in political or normative terms. For example, Jachtenfuchs (2001: 256) has argued that 'the most exciting and most important aspect of European integration – namely the transformation of traditional nation-states into constituent units of a new transnational political system that is not going to become a state – is largely overlooked from the outside'.

The EU's project of cooperation has always contained the means to radically alter international and national politics. While the EU's current agenda is very different from its origins, its current problems and crises are in part due to the distinctiveness of those very origins. This chapter surveys the existing literature on the topic of integration in an interdisciplinary manner and attempts to offer a critical and informed reading of the current debates on integration, the integration project and approaches to examining the EU.

A key challenge is that the term 'integration' is not always clearly defined. It is used in scholarly enterprise and EU pronouncements in a number of distinctive ways. For instance, it can be used to mean the construction of a pan-European political edifice, as in French and Italian language scholarly analysis, or an objective which has a clear meaning that does not require explanation, as in many academic articles and EU speeches. Some scholars take integration as a given, and do not analyse it, consistently referring to the process of integration without actually defining it.

The chapter now examines how integration is presented in the scholarly literature, and to an extent by the EU itself, under a number of themes. These can be grouped as integration as process, integration as polity-making, integration as end-goal and integration as international influence.

INTEGRATION AS A PROCESS

Integration has often denoted a process. For example, in the past, while she did not explicitly use the term 'integration', Hannah Arendt regarded the 'European Project' both as a process and a goal, shaped and impelled by socio-cultural and economic modernization, resulting in a pan-European identity (Rensmann, 2006). This linking of identity with EI is a recurrent characteristic in the literature regarding the EU. In this way, integration is portrayed as a process involving identity-building or identity-formation (Sbragia, 2005). Bátora (2005: 25) expressly evaluates the EU as not constituting a state, but as developing a legal personality, and participating in the diplomatic system based on a particular logic of appropriateness where the EU fulfils roles on a par with the roles fulfilled by the states.

A further theme of 'integration as process' is the growing interconnectedness of domestic administrative systems of member states, whereby sector-specific policies are coordinated across national borders without involving diplomats (Bátora, 2005). Arrangements such as mutual recognition allow entities operating in one state to be regulated by laws of another state. The EU has been described as 'a system in which authority structures over different policy areas are not geographically coterminous' (Krasner, 1995: 119–20, quoted in Batora, 2005). This transnationalism and the interdependence of EU and of national administrative and governance systems form an important part of the expanding literature on Europeanization, which can perhaps be regarded as a new means of examining the EU that does not focus exclusively on integration. Green Cowles *et al.* (2001: 3, 217) define Europeanization as involving the 'evolutions of new layers of politics that interact with older ones'. This may refer to the transformation of the nation state and of policy domains, and, as such, Europeanization can be juxtaposed with globalization as a transforming influence on the state.

The view of integration as a process is more dynamic, multifaceted and multidisciplinary than other approaches. For example, Börzel (2005) regards integration as the transfer or evolution of responsibilities, competencies and decision-making from state to European level and the development of a new supranational framework, albeit with defined limitations. This is based on the purpose and achievements of successive treaties, such as Rome, Maastricht, and the three-pillar structure. Borzel is careful however to point out that 'while the achieved level of integration is rather similar, the scope of integration differs significantly', as, for example, while justice and home affairs now fall largely under the EU's first, Community, pillar, common foreign and security policy and defence policy, remain firmly inter-governmental. She regards this disparity between what she calls the level and scope of European integration as posing a serious theoretical challenge to scholars (Börzel, 2005: 217).

This leads to a further theme in analysis of integration as process – that of defining *types* of integration. It is certainly both useful and necessary to define types of 'integration' and to differentiate periods, actor, achievements and failures. Sbragia (1993) has discussed what she calls asymmetrical integration, whereby legal integration advanced more rapidly than did other types. In much of the contemporary analysis, political integration is regarded as distinctive from, and somehow separated from, economic or other forms of integration. Börzel regards EI as presenting a major empirical puzzle: on the one hand, the *acquis communautaire* represents a unique degree of political integration beyond the nation state, while on the other hand, political integration in other sectors has lagged behind. This is based upon two assumptions. The first is that there is an optimal type of achievement in political integration and the second that economic integration has somehow achieved some measure of excellence in performance whilst political integration has not. While writers such as Börzel are at pains to illustrate the use of terms such as 'scope and level' of integration,[1] the fact remains that many scholars imply the existence of a pathway to an optimal level of supranational political integration. This can, in turn, encourage a teleological approach to the study of the EU (Bourlanges, 1997; Vigo, 1998) – an approach that has not been helpful due to its occasional normative tone.

The study of integration as process is further evident in examinations of EU enlargement. Boucher (2005), for example, regards integration as the process of enlargement, underpinned by the commitment of member states to shared principles: human rights, democratic institutions and the rule of law, principles at the core of EU enlargement, in the Copenhagen criteria. Enlargement has been regarded as a means of advancing European integration and the expansion of the EU's policy scope and norm impact and influence. Zielonka (2006: 2) is critical of the fact that the EU's 2004 Eastern enlargement is often regarded as a 'routine institutional operation that is unlikely to change the course of European integration'. Rather, he correctly argues that it is an unprecedented historical event that cannot be accurately reflected only in the adoption of the *acquis communautaire*. Joerges (2005) regards the 2004 enlargement as 'the most visible new challenge to the technocratic and economic potential of the Union'. He does not only see it in those terms, however, as he regards it, significantly, as a challenge to the 'historical bases for and the aspirations of the integration project', because the accession states did not participate in the postwar settlement. For this reason, he regards the EI project as challenged by the need to harmonize the post-Cold War motivations of the accession states with those of the founding post-World War II settlement.

We can see that the study of EI as a process contains many dynamic elements and an understanding of the historical underpinnings of the ways that interstate cooperation has developed over time. Despite all these pertinent approaches to the study of EI as process, the core issues of power and of the direction of the EU's integration project remain undefined. Newer and fresher perspectives on integration can assist us in understanding how best to study the transformation of Europe (Zielonka, 2006: 3). This requires a clear delineation of studies of the state from those perspectives that seek to advance conceptualizations and comprehension of the EU's transformative role, both on the nation state and in the international arena. The state is the central component and key actor in all of the EU apparatus, but state-centric approaches are not appropriate to the study of the EU.

Scholars need to move to an understanding of its transformation not just *by* the EU but also the transformation *of* the EU by the member states. This is not a simple symmetry of approaches. It requires a study of transformation that is not only involved with transition studies, as in Eastern and Central Europe. In order to rethink the state and reassess how we understand power in the EU, we need also to re-examine our concepts. It is perhaps in this context that the study of the many facets of Europeanization can be advanced – and perhaps even supplant the centrality of the term 'integration'. Europeanization has both EU-to-member-state and member-state-to-EU level dynamics. Its external, extra-territorial, impact also merits broader scholarly attention.

Caution is required when utilizing terms of the past, however much they may be justified, whether 'state', 'Europe as Empire' (Zielonka, 2006) or *condominio* (Schmitter, 2000) when studying the present or hypothesizing the future. Terms harking back several decades or centuries are not necessarily useful to describe a highly sophisticated

system of power, decision-making, identity-formation and transformative process such as the EU. This is particularly the case for pre-democratic eras, which had little experience of the structures that characterize the EU.

Egeberg examines the process involving the transformation of actors, institutions and policy processes, suggesting that these are best understood using organizational theory, which provides 'a yardstick for the degree of overall system integration' (Egeberg, 2004: 199). For Egeberg,

> the extent to which sub-territories are politically integrated into a larger system is reflected in the extent to which the interests of these sub-territories are expressed organizationally at the centre. Thus, in a highly integrated political system, non-territorial principles of organizational specialization have taken clear precedence over the territorial principle at the centre (Egeberg 2004: 206).

Egeberg illustrates the meanings and measures of integration among different schools of analysis by regarding neofunctionalism as useful to assess the degree of integration and governance transformation by considering how many, and which, government functions or issue areas are dealt with at the EU level, while others emphasize the amount of 'interwovenness', 'multi-levelness' or 'fusion' and a further group presents the 'EU polity' as loosely coupled and open-ended.

This serves to illustrate the difficulties in EI analysis if degrees of development and achievement are utilized as benchmarks of success. Further, while it is indeed tempting to regard the EU as open-ended, and so not committing to a single form of integration, therein also lies the attraction of seeing the EU as unfinished and somehow being in need of an end point. Discussion as to whether the EU is finished or unfinished is not particularly useful. It is however important to recognize that it is an entity that is in a constant state of flux, or what has been referred to as a moving target (Cram, 1996) and therefore a challenge to scholars.

The 'EI as process' approach also is evident in the approach of Fabbrini (2005: 189), who regards EI as a process of federation. He compares the EU to the federation of the United States:

> The US and the EU are different species of a common genus of democratic model, which might be called 'compound democracy', distinguished by: the fact that it embodies both consensual and competitive models ...); the (statist) nature of its cleavages; the (separated) structure of its institutions, and the (anti-majoritarian) logic of its functioning. Compound democracies are based on territorial or state cleavages and necessarily function without a government.

For Majone, integration (especially economic integration) is a 'two fold process', with 'partial intermeshing of nation states'. He continues by stating that Europe has 'overstretched itself' (Everson, 2005: 405). He points to the (unsuccessful) recreation of a (nation-state like) polity and the creation of a supranational constitutional order (Majone, 2006: 607). This sense of process leading to a polity forms part of the 'integration as process' approach to the study of the EU. The next section therefore examines the idea of EI as creating or building a polity.

INTEGRATION AS POLITY-BUILDING

As early as 1970, Lindberg and Scheingold (1970) suggested that the European Community, the precursor to the EU, was a polity in the making. While there has been considerable academic output on understanding integration as a type of governance in the case of the EU, or as leading to polity and polity-building (Laffan, 1997; Marks *et al.*, 1996), there are nevertheless reasons for concern. The emphasis on the expansion of both EU membership and the scope of EU activities has not led to adequate critical awareness of the outcomes and characteristics of the integration process, or its theoretical underpinnings.

Further, an element of teleology is often evident in governance and particularly polity debates. Does integration lead to polity?

Successive developments in the European Community (EC) and EU since the 1950s, such as enlargement of its membership, extension of the scope of its activities and the Europeanization of public power and policy, all have contributed to the development of a sophisticated system of governance. Increasingly, it is being suggested that the EU is now in a position to play the role of a polity or government – a role traditionally ascribed to the nation state.

Bátora, for example, regards integration as a process of 'institutional development of the European polity' (Bátora, 2005: 44). Janssens regards integration as a 'process' which 'can be seen as an attempt to found a polity that is in many ways unprecedented in scope and ambition'. Sbragia refers to integration as a process leading to a polity. Since at least the early 1990s, polity has been the focus of literature on the EU, including analysis of the original ideal of 'European Union'. The development of new governance tasks and the interplay of economics and politics led some scholars to examine the EU as a possible polity and to examine its changing governance structures and practices (Hix, 1999; Marks *et al.*, 1996; Sandoltz and Stone Sweet, 1998; Traxler and Schmitter, 1995). Hix (1999: xvii) suggests that since the 1990s there has been a 'huge increase in the number of political scientists trying to approach the EU as an emerging "political system"'. Yet caution is required in analysis of polity. The EC's distinctive origins led to a body of ambitious literature which envisaged an undermining of nationalism and promoted the new idea of 'European Union', interpreted as a supranational European governance or even a European government (Haas, 1964, 1968; Lindberg and Scheingold, 1970). It has been argued that the very nature of governance transformation leads us to surmise that the system of interdependence of the member state and the EU means that we cannot apply the model of one (the state) to understand the other (the EU). That is, the EU in part comprises the nation state in its structure – a nation state undergoing transformation to member-state status in its public policy sphere (Murray, 2004b). State-influenced approaches are limited in understanding the EU. Yet the use of the term 'polity' is widespread in the scholarly literature, necessitating reassessment as it is becoming as overused and ill-defined in much the same way as the term 'integration'.

One way of dealing with the idea of the EU as a 'polity' is to regard it as in a state of in-betweenness (Laffan *et al.*, 2000) or as under construction (Bretherton and Vogler, 2006). According to Elmar Brok, Chairperson of the European Parliament's Committee on Foreign Affairs, 'The European Union is a state under construction.' This assumes that the EU is on its way to being something defined, moving towards an end point. Such teleology, however unintended, is not useful. This chapter is critical of the idea of the EU as being under construction. Although the EU is constantly changing, this does not mean that we cannot attempt to advance our understanding of it by drawing on archival sources, interviews and official documents and engaging critically with the literature on the EU and interdisciplinary research. Some current international relations literature does not fully understand the EU's political *persona* in its historical context and it is only in recent years that there has been sustained analysis of the practice and development of EU actorness and power (e.g. Manners, 2006).

INTEGRATION AS END GOAL

Integration has been expressed as the ultimate objective of the EU and its precursor, the European Community. This has sometimes meant that the end goal of integration is referred to but not clearly defined. The term 'integration' is utilized to explain many of the considerable changes and process that have taken place in Europe, regardless of whether it is part of the EU or because of the EU. Not everything that takes place within the EU is due to transformations wrought by

the EU (Rumford and Murray, 2003b). There have been transformations and synergies that have taken place on a number of levels and in transnational contexts. Many people in the EU live in comparatively blissful ignorance as to the effects – positive or negative – of the EU on their lives and their nation state. In 1999 a warning was issued by Coombes:

> Assuming that the end of the process (or even more so the process itself) is an integrated (or integrating) system, in the sense of a harmonious uniform whole, is a dangerous trap, allowing one to interpret anything and everything that serves the maintenance of the 'system' can be justified as integration.

There is growing agreement among many scholars that there is no clear end goal for EU integration. Bowman (2006) suggests there is no clear model of integration, and no end goal. He suggests that this is due to the democratic deficit and due to the many differing approaches and views of federalists, sceptics and revisionists. Other scholars suggest that there is some sort of objective to be achieved. Habermas, for example, believes that European integration consists of 'political and economic integration' with an end goal of a 'post-national public sphere' and 'legally mediated solidarity' with influence on 'a postnational identity in Europe' and on social policy (Habermas, 1999; Murphy, 2005: 143; Murray, 2008b). For Habermas, what is required is the development of a postnational form of social policy as a crucial component of future solidarity construction.

Many scholars have regarded the EI process as having an ultimate end goal of political union, often interpreted as polity, as expressed in accounts that were explicitly in favour of continued advances in integration and deterministic goals. Debates on polity and EU objectives often contain a set of promissory assumptions, which are not always explicit. European integration analysis is thus challenged by concepts expressed in teleological terms, which may express a desire to advance towards an undefined end-point of integration. It is imperative that social scientists do not feel tempted to conflate the contemporary

EU to the status of a polity without carrying out a methodologically sound endeavour to clarify the meanings of integration and whether or not to utilize the term at all (Murray, 2004b). For Borzel, integration is problematic because both the end goal and logic have changed.

While the EU today is a relative success story of economic integration, its inception was about peace and security rather than economic wealth. In other words, initial attempts of European integration after the Second World War started in the area of high politics. For Börzel, the failure in the 1950s to establish a political community, to unite the European Coal and Steel Company (ECSC) with a European defence community ensured that successful integration would have to follow a functionalist rather than federalist logic (Börzel, 2005: 219).

This again is part of the double bind of integration – that economic and political integration have not kept pace with each other and that there is often a sense of disappointment in some scholars' accounts in this regard, not unlike pronouncements of EU actors.

Some scholars (e.g. Egeberg, 2004: 199) seem to imply that integration is a process towards an end goal, whose progress can be measured using, for example, organizational theory as a 'yardstick for the degree of overall system integration'. This 'end goal' is not defined by most scholars.

The end goal of integration is often presented as a polity, as we have seen. This is defined in a number of different ways. For example, Fabbrini (2005: 197) regards it as a compound democracy or federal European state. In his comparison with the US, he makes the point that the US was subject to a systemic imperative to promote an anti-hegemonic order, and that this was also the case for the EU, due to the asymmetry of powers between its member states. He concludes that because of the anti-hierarchical structure which supports it, an anti-hegemonic order is weak in terms of decision-making capacity.

The alleged need for a polity was accepted, without questioning, as the EC's ultimate, if ill-defined aim. The EC goals of increased integration, the creation of economic and monetary union or a common foreign and security policy, were foregrounded as 'logical' consequences of earlier attempts at integration. A problem in discussing integration as goal is that there is no agreed consensus on what the end state would be. That in itself is not a problem – rather, the problem arises when the shape of an end state or EU polity is taken as given, in particular in normative or polemic accounts.

Moreau Defarges (1985: 5) suggested that, for the founders of the ECSC in the 1950s, the goal and methods of European construction were clearly defined: building a federation, a 'United States of Europe', by the multiplicity of interdependencies. Writing in 1985, he posited that the EC's three aims had been both half-achieved and half-altered: first, the integrated area was not fully transparent; second, it does not have an efficient industrial system; and, third, it had little legitimacy. This changing agenda of integration has been a characteristic of the EU since its inception. It is noteworthy that the term European (Political) Union (EPU) – like integration – has been imprecise, although it possesses some identifiable features in EU discourse. Second, EPU has not been achieved, although it remains a goal of many federalist activists. Third, the realization of EI, however defined, continues to constitute a threat to the nation state (Murray, 2004b).

The recognition of the problems inherent in the term integration – as a political end goal – is not a recent one. Bieber *et al.* (1985: 7), in their analysis of the Spinelli draft treaty on European Union, saw this clearly:

> The term European Union is delightfully ambiguous; it has been used as the ideological underpinning and justification for almost all proposals designed to forward the process of European integration. The most disparate visions and strategies – the draft Act for European Union (the Genscher–Colombo proposal) on the one hand and the Draft Treaty itself on the other, to give but two recent examples – make reference to European Union. Empirically one might as well abandon any hope of arriving at a common meaning of the term.

The term EU, as utilized in the pre-Maastricht era, was both an ideal type (Bieber *et al.*, 1985: 7) and something that covered a multitude of structures and modalities changing over time – which meant that it did not have 'a single authentic meaning' (Bieber *et al.*, 1985: 8). This ideal of integration, as expressed in the literature which is in favour of European political union, encompassed: an aspiration for a constitutional governance or government; democratic institutions; increased use of majority voting in the Council; joint legislative and budgetary (co-decision) powers of the European Parliament and Council; common foreign and security policy; economic and monetary union; subsidiarity; and European citizenship.

Wallace (1983) has been critical in the past of what he called the unilinear assumptions about European integration, which have altered immeasurably and asserted that European unification had achieved no final form. This highlights the requirement for contemporary analysts of the EU to reassess European integration, utilizing a broader conceptual space. This requires a shift beyond statements with elements of teleology, such as: 'European unification does not make me sad. I do not join those post-Maastricht mourners. Political union will come about; it is only a matter of time; 25, 30 years'.[2]

The idea of integration as a long-term objective and end-goal is expressed in comments, such as, those of Romano Prodi, while European Commission president:

The time has come to build a political Europe. By redefining the European project and making our objectives quite clear, we can ensure that Europeans take charge of Europe. I do not yet wish to discuss the final form which the Union should take; I merely wish to outline the projects for which it should exist and what we hope to achieve together. In this sense I share the opinion expressed yesterday by the French Prime Minister, Lionel Jospin: 'Europe is first and foremost a political project'. Before any further institutional negotiations, we must first of all define our objectives. Once our objectives have been clearly defined, we can acquire the means of action commensurate with out ambitions. Then we must consolidate our shared democracy.[3]

More recently, current Commission President Jose Manuel Barroso has spoken of the EI process as moving forward: 'European integration is a dynamic process which necessarily gives rise to some resistance. But meeting resistance does not mean that the process is not moving forward. Problems are only to be expected in such a highly complex process'.[4]

This perspective is not limited to commissioners. In 2005, the then German minister for Europe stated: 'The EU Constitution is the birth certificate of the United States of Europe. The Constitution is not the end point of integration, but the framework for – as it says in the preamble – an ever closer union'[5]. The controversial view of Guy Verhofstadt, the Belgian prime minister, was that 'the Constitution was the capstone of a European Federal State' (*Financial Times*, 21 June 2004). Some years earlier, the EU was regarded as a path or a journey, with comments such as 'A signal must be sent that a single market and a single currency is not the end of the EU journey.'[6] This sense of paths, of step-by-step gradualism to a goal of increased 'integration' is seen also in the statement that 'monetary union is a federative project that needs to be accompanied and followed by other steps'.[7]

INTEGRATION AS END GOAL: THE EU'S FOUNDING MOMENT AND THE ROLE OF MEMORY

Discussions of the EU's end goal, while somewhat under-defined, often refer to the EU's distinctive origins. Duverger (1997: 139) has regarded integration as a process that dominates today's collective and personal memories in Europe. This interpretation may well be generational with reference to World War II. Certainly, many writings in several languages and disciplines, especially history, political science and law, examine the role of memory. The study of the role of memory in identity-building and identity-formation may yield even more fruitful research in the future (Judt, 2002; Nora, 1992). In particular the politics of post-World War II are considered as essential to understanding the contemporary EU. The desire for reconciliation forms the basis of the postwar integration project. Many continue to regard the EU's original agenda and major achievement as the transformation from a continent torn by violence into one of the world's most prosperous and peaceful regions. This has, in turn, shaped the development of Europe's nation states. Thus for many scholars and EU actors, the foundation of the ECSC and the European Economic Community remains the 'constitutionalizing moment' of the postwar EI project. In the words of Joerges (2005), 'The sum of the atrocities of the 20th century in general, and the persecution and extermination of European Jews in particular' and the dignity of this response is what gives the EU its strength and legitimacy. This dignity was a characteristic of the leadership of this project of elites in the 1950s, and the beginning of the evolution of a permissive consensus towards the EI process.

Yet memory has changed considerably since then. Generational changes are evident as the EU of Western Europe has transformed into an EU of 27 member states of considerable diversity. Memories of the Cold War and its aftermath are now at least as vivid, if not more so, than memories of the post-World War II reconstruction.

The EU is advancing agendas that are very different from its origins, while at the same time its current problems and challenges are in part due to the distinctiveness of those very origins – the creation of a number of supranational institutions and devices and the originality of some leadership approaches. The problems of the EU are not mirrored in the experiences of nation states. New conceptualizations are often required. The EU continues to be described by some scholars and EU leaders as *sui generis*, unique and hence exceptional, distinctive and not directly comparable, as it did not conform to traditional concepts and roles of

nation states. However, many analysts have successfully argued against the use of the term *sui generis* in defining the EU as this limits comparison. The current crises of the EU are in part a legacy of a system designed for distinctive power structures and international systems that no longer pertain. This chapter concurs with Joerges (2005) that the aspirations of the 'integration' project have altered, given that newer member states did not take part in the 'postwar settlement'. It advances a need to understand transformations of power in this context too. Memory and transformation need to be examined more closely. The role of the memory of World War II remains a pivotal dimension of the EU process. Memory is generational and based on personal and national experiences – and can be highly selective. Different actors have different prominent memories, such as the break-up of Yugoslavia and subsequent intervention in the early 1990s. There is more to the EU's development over the last 55 years than milestones such as the Single Market or Maastricht. Even the fact that 2007 was the year to commemorate a half-century of 'Europe' denotes that the EU's economic imperatives and achievements are more important than those of the ECSC and its attempts at supranationalism and institution building and the end to interstate rivalries.

Further, the EU's failures over time are just as important as its recent successes and crises. The apparent success of the 2004 and 2007 enlargements sit awkwardly alongside the failure of the ratification process of the constitutional treaty and the problems related to the ratification of the Lisbon Reform Treaty more recently. So the knowledge of a more comprehensive history of the EU, including its visions and reflections on its meaning and actors, remains pivotal to the study of the EU.

Similarly, the role of transformation – of the EU and of its nation states – did not commence with the end of the Cold War. The transformation of the nation state has occurred since the early 1950s (Milward, 1992). Yet many past debates have regarded it as a means to fight out intergovernmentalism versus supranationalism slogans and shibboleths. Others saw it as a means to argue about IR versus comparative politics approaches to the study of the EU. The EU has transformed the nation state and the constituent nation states have transformed the EU over time. In effect there has been Europeanization. Transformation is not only that of states, but also of the public sphere, of subnational regions, of governance and participation, and even identity. Hence the important debates in the EU on democracy, legitimacy and the democratic deficit.

The early decades of the history of the EU were characterized by an elite consensus. The contemporary EU is characterized by elements of direct democracy such as referenda and debates regarding the possible creation of a public sphere. There is increased awareness among EU elites of the need for EU outcomes to be based on the participation in many important decisions of the citizens of the EU as well as European political elites and leaders. This relates to the debate on salience and relevance of EI to the citizens. Hobolt suggests that 'the salience of the issue of European integration affects attitudes and reception of élite cues and, in turn, influences patterns of voting behaviour in referendums' (Hobolt 2006: 155). The debate on direct democracy in the EU and its relationship with democratic legitimacy and accountability is an ongoing and relevant one, particularly when many scholars already define the EU as a polity or as one in the making.

The original purpose of integration has changed, according to Majone (2006: 607), who argues: 'The institutional system established by the founding fathers was not designed for effective policy-making, but largely to pursue objectives of negative integration'. The desire for reconciliation forms the basis of the postwar integration project, seeking to merge sovereignty rather than to continue tensions. There has been a remarkable transformation from a continent torn by violence into one of the world's most prosperous and peaceful regions. This has been accompanied by a transformation of the nation state.

There have been bitter divisions, including amongst those with a long memory or deep knowledge of the original battles regarding the political development of the incipient European Community and its institutions and the role of the state. These cleavages have suffused the original development of the EU as much as they have suffused many EI studies. In Navari's terms, battle lines were formed among the creators of the postwar reconstruction projects and these are still evident in part today. There has been the battle between the supranationalist and intergovernmentalist perspectives. There have been the underlying economic imperatives of reconstruction alongside the major ideological struggles (Navari, 1996).

Yet transformation has been a feature of the EU since its origins. This is evident in the expansion and transformation of membership, scope, goals, institutional architecture, policy concerns and international impact. It is apparent in the interaction between the nation states that have been altered, which has led to altered dynamics of international diplomacy, trade relations, and the role of global actors. It is apparent in the ways that the EU has partly rewritten the international rule book for negotiations as it becomes an increasingly influential actor in global and multilateral forums, in trade aid and in its attempts to be a manager of globalization and a norms entrepreneur and norms exporter. This has been a significant transformation of sovereignty, as the EU rewrites the rulebook of international diplomacy, international negotiations, regional integration and the EU role therein.

The EU has considerable external impact and extraterritorial influence and this warrants more attention from scholars than has occurred to date. The EU is developing its global agenda, which is based on factors such as its history and memory of war and peace, its constitutionalizing milestones, its economic might, its influence in the World Trade Organization (WTO) and its efforts at international peace-promotion. This global dimension to the EU has not led to fulsome praise and admiration throughout the world. There remains a perception of the EU as a 'fortress Europe' in some parts of the globe (Murray, 2008c).

Just as EU's policy reach is not confined to Europe, neither are the influences upon it confined to its member states. The EU is not immune to the forces of globalization – and this understanding must be increasingly embedded in the study of the EU (Rumford and Murray, 2003a). The EU is not simply the symbol of a reconciliation of a difficult past. It is also regarded by many in Europe as the substantial power of the future and it will advance its policies in a manner that some outside of Europe may well find extraordinary. Yet there remain problems of legitimacy and democracy and there are many who oppose the continued expansion of EU policy domains, its constitutional structure and territorial membership.

Majone (2006: 607) has suggested that the legitimacy problem of the EU can be solved by limiting, rather than continuously expanding, the competences of its supranational institutions. There are those who see the EU as not fulfilling the role of a body politic. Manent concurs: he regards integration as the 'construction of Europe' which 'while coeval with the deconstruction of the sovereign nation-states, is also an attempt to define a new body politic'. He points out that the EU is plagued by an incapacity to define itself. This means that 'construction' becomes 'indefinite expansion'. According to Manent, 'Europe has failed so far either to find or to produce a new body politic, and its attitude regarding this requirement has been markedly ambiguous. It seems to point in the direction of "an enormous Nation" or perhaps even a new version of the empire as a political form.'

Among the many obstacles on this path, Manent considers the absence of a unified European people as most prominent. Europe – in his eyes – appears to be incapable of defining itself politically, of constituting a body politic: 'The problem of the Europeans is that they don't know what things to put in common.' He sees the EU as ushering in a new, depoliticized 'realm of civilization', the most blatant sign of which is the seemingly interminable process of territorial expansion through the acceptance of new member states. This ambiguity has resulted in Europe becoming politically paralysed and caught up in a dynamic of indefinite extension (Janssens, 2006).

THE INTERNATIONAL INFLUENCE OF 'INTEGRATION'

This is an exciting period for scholars, who are in the midst of a revolution of the use of conceptual and analytical tools, rethinking assumptions regarding the dynamics of international politics. Analysts are re-examining the transformation of the state. These central questions possess a multiplicity of answers contingent upon historical period, country, length and experience of membership of the EU, and attitude to membership. States, integration and the EU need to be reconceptualized. This movement has already begun. The EU has been examined as possible regional state (Schmidt, 2004), a superpower (Leonard, 2005), a civilian, or, more recently, normative, power (Duchene, 1972; Manners, 2002, 2006), a soft power and a metrosexual superpower (Khanna, 2004), and with pertinent questions as to the nature of EU power (e.g. Sjursens, 2006).

The EU's significant economic and political weight has led to an increasing transformative affect on international agendas; for example, through its ability to vote *en bloc* in international and multilateral forums. This has lead to a re-evaluation of many of the norms governing international relations. Of particular importance is the EU's extraterritorial influence. With the exception of the transatlantic relationship, the influence of the EU and European integration – and Europeanization – on third countries has been somewhat neglected by scholars until recently. Yet many aspects of international relations have been affected and influenced by EU developments.

It has been argued that the EU and its integration have affected diplomacy on several levels. Bátora (2005: 44) suggests three levels: the intra-European bilateral relations; the multilateral setting of the council; and the emerging capacity of the EU to conduct external diplomatic relations with third states. To this can be added the impact of the EU's deregulation and regulations and what one non-EU diplomat referred to as 'pre-regulation', which he esteemed to have negative impacts on some third countries. Thus the EU can be regarded as an unbound Prometheus or Leviathan which is unleashing its regulations and protectionism on the world stage and is unstoppable in its advance (Murray, 2005).

Within the EU, there has been change in the scope and nature of foreign policy implementation and decision-making. This has occurred since the early days of information-sharing under European Political Cooperation's incipient coordination of foreign policy positions and the European Correspondence system. Bátora (2005: 50) suggests that the 'process of European integration features a set of tendencies and developments that may challenge the logic of appropriateness upon which diplomacy as an institution is based'. He sees this process as leading to a possible metamorphosis, described as 'a change in the standards of appropriateness, at the level of bilateral diplomatic relations within the EU' (Bátora, 2005: 53, 55) with interstate relations characterized by a three-dimensional aspect, of intra-European, the more traditional national and the transnational aspects of national diplomacy.

This transformation of diplomacy is part of a broader transformation of the Westphalian system of nation states. Majone (2005: 195) regards the EU as 'transcending and mutating the Westphalian system of states':

> The experience of the EU shows that a rule-based system of cooperation and dispute resolution can not only civilize relations among sovereign states

by eliminating the excesses of narrowly conceived national interests but by protecting the rights of citizens even against their own governments, such a system strengthens the foundations of liberal democracy that have been eroded by decades of discretionary executive power.

Polity building and the creation of an international order based on new principles of international cooperation remain firm themes of much integration analysis. Morgan refers to the 'the project of constructing a politically integrated federal polity and a new post-Westphalian international order', contrasting two dominant models of international order, namely liberal Kantian (prominent in Europe) and Hobbesian realist (prominent in the US), arguing that the latter provides a superior understanding of European political integration (Morgan, 2005: 199, 207). He argues that the need for the EU to play an important international role necessitates an integrated federal polity similar to the US.

Risse (2005: 291) refers to the double puzzle of European integration, which he defines as:

> The persistent balance in the EU's constitution-building between supranational and intergovernmental institutions on the one hand, and the lagging behind of foreign/defence affairs in European integration on the other. If national processes and collective understandings are crucial to understanding the Europeanization of national identities, this will lead to uneven and varied degrees to which Europe can be embedded in collective identities. Federal states with respective constitutional traditions change their collective understandings more easily to include Europe and orientations toward supra-nationalism than unitary and centralized states.

Thus we see that Europeanization, like integration, can sometimes be associated with the different distinctions regarding types of integration, especially types of political integration. It is also associated with debates on the role of European identities.

Habermas views the process of European integration as an 'inescapable response to the pitfalls of globalization and the shortcomings of nation-state bounded welfare systems' (Murphy, 2005: 143). The response to globalization of many citizens throughout Europe, in many cases, is also framed in terms of a fear of loss of identity, with evidence that in referenda and opinion polls in the member states there is an identification of the EU with the process of globalization, thereby undermining national or microregional identity. For example, the referenda in France and the Netherlands both featured this fear regarding loss of sovereignty and identity. Rensmann (2006: 139) suggests that Europeanism (expressed as integration and identity) is 'often intimately linked to mobilizations of widely spread fears of global sociocultural and economic modernization'.

Former Commission President Jacques Santer stated in 1999: 'It is now up to us to see that we embark on the next stage leading to political unity, which I think is the consequence of economic unity, so that Europe can in the future also play a political role on the international stage, leading even as far as a common defence policy.'[8] There is a need to further examine the ways the EU has positioned itself as an international political actor and to assess its impact, whether in its broad foreign policy agenda or its role in global trade or as a development aid provider or as a norms exporter.

NO SINGLE INTEGRATION, NO SINGLE CONCEPT, NO SINGLE THEORY, NO SINGLE MODEL

It is increasingly an accepted fact that there is no single theory of the EU or of European integration and that the study of the EU is broader than the study of European integration. It is less accepted that there is no single concept of integration. The phoney wars and skirmishes of different theoretical concepts have been superseded by round table debates on the appropriate conceptual or theoretical framework for various issues or events and by more sophisticated conceptualization (Jachtenfuchs, 2001). Peterson (2001: 313) has suggested that 'EU scholars need to stop

fighting phoney theoretical wars, make choices about what they want to explain, and make the European Union a touchstone in the more general effort of political science to synthesize insights from comparative politics, international relations and public policy'. Egeberg (2004: 199) argues that 'no single theory can adequately account for everything in this area'.

There are many ways to approach the study of the EU, beyond integration. Its depth and breadth prohibit it from exclusively belonging to one academic discipline or subdiscipline alone. The extension of the EU's policy remit, territory and tasks has encouraged the multiplicity of approaches and concepts and theories. This has enriched the study of the EU, integration and international affairs in a number of positive ways. This task-expansion was a term utilized by Haas in *The Uniting of Europe* in an attempt to explain European integration (Börzel, 2005). It has been associated with the neofunctionalist approach as an evolutionary process, characterized by spillover (Cini, 2006: 39). The assumption of task expansion was brought into question by inter-governmentalists. A historical understanding of the EU is critical to the contemporary comprehending of the 27-member EU, whether it is characterized as hybrid, mixed or postnationalist (Chalmers, 2006). However, the contemporary EU is a significantly different and more important actor than in the 1950s, as reflected in the divergent approaches and increased multidisciplinarity in contemporary EU studies.

While many of the early works on the EU focused on the apparently remarkable individuals involved in its creation, the motivations of these actors remain an important element of European Union studies. While an organizational approach focuses on individual actors' organizational context in order to account for their behaviour, interests and identities (Egeberg, 2004), many institutionalists focus on how EU institutions shape and reshape individual actors' preferences and sense of belonging. A distinctive approach that is increasingly popular is that of constructivism (Pollack, 2001). The difference of emphasis and interpretation are worthy of increased analysis.

There have been divisions among analysts of the EU, as we see very clearly in this volume. It is important to explore the relationship between the EU and globalization, and between European Union studies and the study of globalization and comparative regionalism. Investigating the relationship between globalization and the EU provides an opportunity for EI studies to challenge the dominant view that globalization has been responsible for impelling 'ever closer union'. The contradictory and differential impact of globalization on the EU also needs to be acknowledged. So too does the impact of the EU on globalization and on regional and multilateral agendas. The predominant view of globalization in many European integration studies has been to present it as being compatible with economic integration. Delanty (1998) describes it thus: 'Globalization is the condition which has replaced the need for peace in the justification of European integration today'. (Rumford and Murray, 2003a).

Many commentators (Cameron, 2003; Manners, 2002, 2006) urge the EU to advance its international agenda – often with a teleological imperative. They believe that the EU needs a more robust foreign policy as part of an evolution towards a powerful EU better able to face global challenges and threats as a united agency. There are proposals to impose some kind of order in an anarchic system. Some even campaign for an EU hegemon to balance the US hegemon (Cameron, 2003; Knodt and Princen, 2005: 3).

Finally, the EU experience of 'integration' has been regarded as a useful paradigm for other parts of the world, in particular the ASEAN and ASEAN Plus Three (China, Japan, South Korea) region. Just as the term 'integration' is overused within EU analysis, there is a danger that this tendency will be replicated in non-EU contexts too, as the EU is often admired as a model of regional integration. A further, worrying aspect of this issue is the self-conscious efforts by some EU actors to advance the EU as a model not just of economic integration but also as a European social model and as the manager of globalization and prototypical example of good governance – both global governance and EU governance norms and values (Murray, 2004b).

The EU experience of cooperation, institutionalization and economic and monetary development is also regarded as exportable to other parts of the world. For example, then Commissioner Chris Patten regarded the EU experience as exportable to a world in need of new paradigms. This issue is one that merits caution. A number of research questions forms part of the debate on the EU as a putative paradigm. For example, what types of understandings are there of the EU outside of its orbit? What aspects of the EU's experience might be useful in a comparative context for other regions? How might we compare interstate bargaining in the different regional groupings throughout the globe? Are some parts of the EU more useful to examine than others? Which type of 'integration' is relevant – economic, financial or other? How might community be defined and assessed? Might an integration paradigm necessarily encompass governance? Is a security community the most or least appropriate type of community-building? Increased research is required regarding which factors influence choices of states and regions in attempting regionalism. Who are the important actors? What are the drivers of integration in the regionalizing states? What role is accorded to civil society? This issue has been the subject of a number of studies in recent years (Fort and Webber, 2006; Moon and Andreosso, 2005; Murray, 2008a) and the pertinent issue is that there is no single EU model.

CONCLUSION

This chapter has argued that the study of the EU is now at a stage where the use of the term 'integration' is becoming increasingly redundant – and this is a positive development, as EU studies are broadening and becoming more interdisciplinary. In the past, the term 'integration' has appeared to have meanings as diverse as process, end-goal and Europeanization, for example. The study of the EU has seen a remarkable increase in theories and concepts, and for this reason the once-pivotal place occupied by 'integration' in EU discourse and analysis has been supplanted – and not by one term of means of analysis but by several. The rise of both studies of governance and of Europeanization – although neither of these terms should be conflated as 'integration' has been – has undoubtedly been a positive development in this regard. Scholars increasingly engage with EU studies rather than EI studies.

The study of the EU has long remained within a closed context of area studies and EI studies. This has been recognized by seeking to move beyond the comparative politics versus international relations debates; the supranationalism versus intergovernmentalism debates, and the studies of individual policies. Phoney wars are ending but still there are many assumptions that tend towards normative or moralistic approaches. There is still too close a relationship with the European Commission, which has a capacity to fund research on European integration, which the Commission defines in its *vademecum* for applicants for funding, as issued in 2003, as follows: 'The term European integration studies is taken to mean the study of the construction of the European Community and the institutional, legal, political, economic and social developments related to this process'.

Vibrant debate on power (civilian, soft, normative ethical, smart) is increasingly a focus of studies of the EU – and this is a positive step. In an international context, for example, it encompasses normative power and the EU as a new type of international global actor and superpower. As integration studies become more flexible, so too has the EU become more flexible, with innovations such as the open method of coordination, variable geometry and multispeed Europe. The crisis of the constitutional treaty and Lisbon Treaty and the challenges of recent enlargements render the study of the EU more fascinating.

Scholars are becoming increasingly comparative in the analysis of integration. We are examining EU external relations and its extra-territorial impact in greater detail, although this dimension requires further research and analysis. There are many transnational research projects and conferences that are rich and varied and the European Consortium for Political Research is one of many fruitful examples. Increasing numbers of disciplines are becoming involved in the study of the EU, from anthropology to cultural studies to linguistic studies. This is enriching our understanding of a complex entity.

Examining the EU as simply a package comprising the study of institutions, theories and policies is largely moribund. The desire for a streamlined approach to the study of the EU – and for a core curriculum – must be resisted (Rumford and Murray, 2003b). Normative overtones and moralistic approaches should be avoided. The study of the EU can benefit from more critiques of the EU as a putative polity, a global actor, a negotiator, a creator of a public sphere on its own – and especially the Commission's own – terms. We should examine the EU's achievements and failures and the implications of the EU's actions and failures to act. We should examine opposition to the EU and the ways in which the EU has transformed public and international discourses and international agendas.

Rejecting the simple approach of seeing the study of the EU as the study of integration promotes valuable debate on other key terms and concepts. Intellectual barriers, strictly national perceptions and scholarly cul-de-sacs can also be productively dismantled. Only with this open, flexible and innovative approach can we transcend scholarly borders, respect good scholarly traditions of exploration and original research and avoid the pitfalls of only admiring the deity of European integration studies.

A fresh consideration and understanding is needed regarding the transformative aspects of the EU's expansion and transformation of membership, goals, institutional architecture and policies. We need to examine the EU's transformative power in an international context, which has rewritten, and is continuing to rewrite, international negotiations and engagements. A new conception of the EU, its norms and influence, is required. Further, transformation has been evident in the enlargement project; for example, in its challenge to the established norms of integration practices of Western Europe and to its historical basis. Finally, this chapter concurs with Joerges (2005) that the aspirations of the 'integration' project have altered. There is a need to understand transformations of power in this broader context too. A move away from a dependence on integration as a focal point can only be beneficial in our search for fresh understanding of the EU.

NOTES

1 The idea of scope and level (locus) were developed by Lindberg and Scheingold (1970: 67–71). Börzel explains that, while scope relates to the initial expansion of the EU authority to new policy areas, locus stresses 'the relative importance of Community decision-making processes as compared with national processes' (Börzel: 219).

2 Sicco Mansholt, former EC Commissioner, NCR Handelsblad, 12 June 1993, quoted in *Eurinfo*, newsletter of the Brussels Office of the EC Commission, no. 178, September 1993.

3 Romano Prodi, Speech to Sciences-Po 2001: http://europa.eu/constitution/futurum/documents/speech/sp290501_en.pdf, p.3.

4 Jose Manuel Barroso, 'Strengthening the Citizens Europe' 8 May 2006,

5 Hans Martin Bury, German Minister for Europe, Debate in the Bundestag, reported in *Die Welt*, 25 February 2005.

6 Victor Klima, Chancellor of Austria, Poertschach, Austria, 24 October 24 1998.

7 Giscard d'Estaing and Helmut Schmidt, quoted in *International Herald Tribune*, 14 October 1997.

8 Jacques Santer, then president of the European Commission, *The Daily Telegraph*, 1 January 1999.

REFERENCES

Bátora, J. (2005) 'Does the European Union transform the institution of diplomacy?', *Journal of European Public Policy*, 12 (1): 44–66.

Bieber, R., Jacque, J.P. and Weiler, J. (1985) 'Introduction', in R. Bieber, J.P. Jacque and J. Weiler (eds) *An Ever Closer Union*. Luxembourg: Commission of the European Communities.

Börzel, T.A. (2005) 'Mind the gap! European integration between level and scope', *Journal of European Public Policy*, 12 (2): 217–236.

Boucher, D. (2005) 'The rule of law in the modern European state: Oakeshott and the enlargement of Europe', *European Journal of Political Theory*, 4 (1): 81–107.

Bourlanges, J.-L. (1997) 'Qui a peur d'une Europe federale', *Societal*, 6 (Mars): 13–18.

Bowman, J. (2006) 'The European Union democratic deficit. Federalists, skeptics, and revisionists', *European Journal of Political Research*, 5 (2): 191–212.

Breslin, S, and Higgott, R. (2003) 'New regionalism(s) in the global political economy. Conceptual understanding in historical perspective', *Asia Europe Journal*, 1 (2): 167–182.

Bretherton, C. and Vogler, J. (2006) *The European Union as a Global Actor*. London: Routledge.

Cameron, F. (2003) 'The European Union and global governance', European Policy Centre, Working Paper 7, Brussels. Available at: http://www.theepc.be/en.

Chalmers, A. (2006) 'Reconfiguring the European Union's historical dimension', *European Journal of Political Theory*, 5 (4): 437–454.

Cini, M. (2006) 'The 'state of the art' in EU studies: From politics to interdisciplinarity (and back again?)', *Politics*, 26 (1): 38–46.

Coombes, D. (1999) *Seven Theorems in Search of the European Parliament*. London: Federal Trust.

Cram, L. (1996) 'Integration theory and the study of the European policy process', in J. Richardson (ed.) *European Union: Power and Policy Making*. London: Routledge.

Delanty, G. (1998) 'Social theory and European transformation: is there a European society?', *Sociological Research Online*, 3 (1).

Duchene, F. (1972) 'Europe's role in world peace', in R.J. Mayne (ed.) *Europe Tomorrow: Sixteen Europeans Look Ahead*. London: Fontana.

Duverger, M. (1997) 'Reflections: the political system of the European Union', *European Journal of Political Research*, 31 (1–2): 125–146.

Egeberg, M. (2004) 'An organisational approach to European integration: Outline of a complementary perspective', *European Journal of Political Research*, 43 (2): 199–219.

Everson, M. (2005) 'Majone's Europe', *European Political Science*, 4 (4): 395–406.

Fabbrini, S. (2005) 'Madison in Brussels: the EU and the US as compound democracies', *European Political Science*, 4 (2): 188–198.

Fort, B. and Webber, D. (2006) *Regional Integration in East Sia and Europe- Convergence or Divergence?* London: Routledge.

Green Cowles, M., Caporaso, J. and Risse, T. (eds) (2001) *Transforming Europe*. Ithaca and London: Cornell University Press.

Haas, E. (1964) *Beyond the Nation State*. Stanford: Stanford University Press.

Haas, E. (1968) *The Uniting of Europe*. Stanford: Stanford University Press.

Habermas, J. (1999) 'The European nation-state and the pressures of globalization', *New Left Review*, 235: 46–59.

Hettne, B. and Soberbaum, F. (2000) 'Theorising the rise of regionness', *New Political Economy*, November 5, p. 3.

Hix, S. (1999) *The Political System of the European Union*. London, Macmillan.

Hobolt, S.B. (2006) 'Direct democracy and European integration', *Journal of European Public Policy*, 13 (1): 153–166.

Jachtenfuchs, M. (2001) 'The governance approach to European integration', *Journal of Common Market Studies*, 39 (2): 245–264.

Janssens, D. (2006). 'Habeas corpus? Pierre Manent and the politics of Europe', *European Journal of Political Research*, 5 (2): 171–190.

Joerges, C. (2005) 'Introduction to the Special Issue: Confronting Memories: European "Bitter Experiences" and the Constitutionalization

Process', *German Law Journal*, 6 (2): 245–254.

Khanna, P. (2004) 'The metrosexual superpower', *Foreign Policy*, July/August. Available at: http://www.foreignpolicy.com/story/files/story2583.php.

Knodt, M. and Princen, S. (2003) *Understanding the European Union's External Relations*. London: Routledge.

Krasner, S. (1995) 'Compromising Westphalia', *International Security*, 20 (3): 115–151.

Laffan, B. (1997) 'The European Union: A Distinctive Model of Internationalisation?' *European Integration online Papers (EIoP)*, 1 (18). Available at: http://eiop.or.at/eiop/texte/1997-018a.htm

Laffan, B., O'Donnell, R. and Smith, M. (2000) *Europe's Experimental Union: Rethinking Integration*. London, Routledge.

Leonard, M. (2005) *Why Europe Will Run the 21st Century*. London and New York: Fourth Estate.

Lindberg., L. and Scheingold, S. (1970) *Europe's Would-Be Polity: Patterns of Change in the European Community*. New Jersey: Prentice Hall.

Majone, G. (2005) *Dilemma's of European Integration: The Ambiguities and Pitfalls of Integration by Stealth*. Oxford: Oxford University Press.

Majone, G. (2006) 'The common sense of European integration', *Journal of European Public Policy*, 13 (5): 607–626.

Manners, I. (2002) 'Normative power Europe: a contradiction in terms?', *Journal of Common Market Studies*, 40 (2): 235–258.

Manners, I. (2006) 'Normative power Europe reconsidered: beyond the crossroads', *Journal of European Public Policy*, 13 (2): 182–199.

Marks, G., Scharpf, F., Schmitter, P. and Streek, W. (1996) *Governance in the European Union*. London: Sage.

Milward A. (1992) *The European Rescue of the Nation State*. London, Routledge.

Moon, W. and Andreosso-O'Callaghan, B. (2005) *Regional Integration – Europe and Asia Compared*. Aldershot: Ashgate.

Moreau Defarges, P. (1985) 'Les trois circles de la Construction Europeene', *Revue Francaise de Science Politique*, 35 (1):

Morgan, G. (2005) 'Realism and European political integration: the lessons of the United States', *European Political Science*, 4 (2): 199–208.

Murphy, M. (2005) 'Between facts, norms and a post-national constellation: Habermas, law and European social policy', *Journal of European Public Policy*, 12 (1): 143–156.

Murray, P. (2000) 'European integration studies: the search for synthesis', *Contemporary Politics*, 6 (1): 19–28.

Murray, P. (2004a) 'Towards a research agenda on the European Union as a Model of Regional Integration', *Asia Pacific Journal of EU Studies*, 2 (1): 33–51.

Murray, P. (2004b) 'The clash of integrations? Recasting the European Union Bargain', Jean Monnet Working Papers Series, Jean Monnet Lecture Series 2003, Dipartimento di Sociologia e Ricerca Sociale, Facoltà di Sociologia, (Department of Sociology and Social Research, Faculty of Sociology), University of Trento, Jean Monnet Lecture Series, JML No. 4. Available at: http://193.205.192.18:8080/poloEuropeo/content/e57/e130/e353/JML4.pdf.

Murray, P. (2005) *Australia and the European Superpower: Engaging with the European Union*. Melbourne, Melbourne University Press.

Murray, P. (ed.) (2008a) *Europe and Asia: Regions in Flux*. Basingstoke: Palgrave, pp. 1–22.

Murray, P. (2008b) 'Exporting a new public space? Reflections on the EU integration experience as a paradigm', *European Political Science*, 264–272.

Murray, P. (2008) 'What Australians think about the EU: National Interests in an international setting', in Natalia Chabar and Martin Holland eds., *The European Union and the Asia Pacific: Media, Public and the elite perceptions of the EU*, Abingdon, Routledge, pp. 164–183.

Navari C. (1996) 'Functionalism versus federalism: alternative visions of European unity', in P. Murray and P. Rich (eds) *Visions of European Unity*. Colorado: Westview Press.

Peterson, J. (2001) 'The choice for EU theorists: establishing a common framework for analysis,' *European Journal of Political Research*, 39 (3).

Pollack, M. (2001) 'International relations theory and European integration', *Journal of Common Market Studies*, 39 (2): 221–224.

Rensmann, L. (2006) 'Europeanism and Americanism in the age of globalization: Hannah Arendt's reflections on Europe and America and implications for a post-national identity of the EU polity', *European Journal of Political Research*, 5 (2): 139–170.

Risse, T. (2005) 'Neofunctionalism, European identity, and the puzzles of European integration', *Journal of European Public Policy*, 12 (2): 291–309.

Rumford, C. and Murray, P. (2003a) 'Globalization and the limitations of European integration studies: interdisciplinary considerations', *Journal of Contemporary European Studies*, 11 (1): 85–93.

Rumford, C. and Murray P. (2003b) 'Do we need a core curriculum in European Union studies?', *European Political Science*, 3 (1): 85–92.

Sandoltz, W. and Stone Sweet, A. (eds) (1998) *European Integration and Supranational Governance*. Oxford: Oxford University Press.

Sbragia, A. (1993) 'Asymmetrical integration in the European community', in D. Smith and J. Ray (eds) *The 1992 Project and the Future of Integration in Europe*. New York: Armonk.

Sbragia, A. (2005) 'Seeing the European Union through American Eyes: the EU as a Reflection of the American Experience', *European Political Science*, 4 (2): 179–187.

Schmidt, V. (2004) 'The European Union: democratic legitimacy in a regional state?', *Journal of Common Market Studies*, 42 (5): 975–997.

Schmitter, P. (2000) *How to Democratise the European Union, and Why Bother?* Oxford: Rowman and Littlefied.

Sjursens, H. (2006) 'What kind of power', *Journal of European Public Policy*, 13 (2): 169–181.

Traxler, F. and Schmitter, P. (1995) 'The emerging euro-polity and organized interests', *European Journal of International Relations*, 1 (1): 191–218.

Vigo, G. (1998) 'A profile of European integration', *The Federalist*, XL: 2.

Wallace, W. (1983) 'Political cooperation: integration through intergovernmentalism', paper presented at the *Seminar on the International Relations of the EEC*, European University Institute, Florence.

Warleigh, A. (2006) 'Learning from Europe? EU studies and the re-thinking of "international relations"', *European Journal of International Relations*, 12 (1): 31–51.

Zielonka, J. (2006) *Europe as Empire: The Nature of the Enlarged European Union*. Oxford: Oxford University Press.

14

Economic Growth and Global Competitiveness: From Rome to Maastricht to Lisbon

Amy Verdun

Member states of the European Union have gone through a remarkable transformation since the end of the Second World War. From a time in which member states were narrowly focused on their own economic growth and national strategies they have moved towards securing competitiveness in the global economy. The European Community and later the European Union have been used to strengthen those ambitions. This chapter looks at the way in which European countries have sought to deal with economic growth and global competitiveness from the start of the European integration after the Second World War until today.

In the early postwar days, many countries were still developing their welfare states. Some countries developed stronger ones than others. Most of these economies had carved out a strong role for the state, also in providing social services and labour protection to citizens. Goods, services, labour and capital did not move freely and many industries were owned by the state. As the years progressed,

European countries removed barriers to trade, opened up their economies, privatized, deregulated, and relied more than before on market principles for steering the economy. These trends were in part triggered by global changes, and in part by the internal dynamics of European integration.

During the second half of the twentieth century, various West European member states showed mixed economic performance. They experienced booming economic conditions in the 1950s and 1960s, much less growth (at times even economic stagnation) in the 1970s and 1980s, and low or moderate growth since. As a result, many observers and critics have pointed to the European model as in need of restructuring. Comparisons are made with the growth of the US during the same period, and then the question is posed why, for most of the past two decades, Europe has been 'lagging behind'.

Central and Eastern European member states have witnessed different conditions altogether. Having rid themselves of Soviet domination in 1989, these countries have had to adjust to becoming liberal market economies, and hence go through a major restructuring of their economies. These countries went through difficult years in the 1990s but have since created a market economy that typically performed better than their Western European counterparts, at least in terms of economic growth as a percentage of gross domestic product (GDP) per capita. Yet, they face challenges as well, as they are still, on average, less wealthy than West European countries.

The structure of the chapter is as follows. The first section provides an historical overview of the stages of developments in this area. The second section reviews recent literature on this topic by examining a number of leading field journals of European integration which draw on academic research in various disciplines (political science, economics, business, law and others), as well as other literature and textbooks published in the same period. The third section discusses a number of criticisms of EU member states and the EU as a whole, regarding why they might be losing global competitiveness and discusses if these are fair criticisms. The fourth section looks at what strategies the European Union member states are developing to address them. The final section concludes and offers some avenues for future research.

HISTORY OF EUROPEAN INTEGRATION ON ECONOMIC GROWTH AND COMPETITIVENESS

European countries have been centre-stage of global trade and prosperity for many centuries. They have taken turns in being global leaders and in relative prosperity. Cities such as Genoa, countries such as Portugal, Spain, the Low Countries, and England all experienced times with high levels of economic prosperity, most of which was generated by their active international trade but also colonial exploitation. The Industrial Revolution, first in the United

Kingdom and later in Germany and Italy, enabled these countries to increase their national wealth. The late nineteenth and early twentieth centuries, however, were fraught with military developments. These developments included the signing of pacts and alliances, but also the presence of wars. Today, European countries live in a world in which none of them individually or collectively is a superpower; they are neither the most prosperous, nor among the fastest-growing economies. They are based on a continent that has embarked on a project of integration that includes many aspects of state building (economic, political and judicial, and to some extent even military). Much of this process is triggered by a desire to increase economic prosperity among them. In order to understand this, let us turn to review the historical developments that took place in Europe from 1945 to the present time.

After the devastation of the two world wars, a number of countries in Western Europe took the brave step forward to cooperate rather than to fight each other. Assisted by the aid of the US (the Marshall Plan), they developed plans first to integrate among themselves the production and sales of coal and steel, an aim known as the European Coal and Steel Community (ECSC). The ECSC lay the foundation of the present EU in creating institutions that were the predecessor of those found in the EU today (Commission, Council, Court of Justice, Parliament). By creating the ECSC the two primary elements of war machinery – coal and steel – were put under joint supervision. The choice to focus on a 'functional' aspect of protecting peace and promoting prosperity was not accidental (see Haas, 1958, 1964). It was the vision of Jean Monnet not to focus on politically sensitive matters, but rather to target smaller, functional depoliticized collaboration (Duchêne, 1994). Rather than seeking to make explicit steps to move towards a federal Europe, his vision was to find ways in which progress in collaboration could be made that focused on welfare-increasing factors. In these early years, a distinction was often made between 'low' and 'high' politics (Hoffmann, 1966). Hoffmann responded to Haas' work on the origins of the European Community with an analysis that integration of 'low politics' was easier than in areas of 'high politics'. High politics was seen as more politically sensitive, touching upon the very essence of state sovereignty (such as foreign affairs, monetary policy and defence). Low politics were considered those areas in which one could make welfare gains by integration, which also would be politically less crucial to state sovereignty, such as social policy, education, environment and agriculture. This differentiation between 'low' and 'high' politics has been discredited as the separation between the two is not analytically clear, nor did the original prediction hold that integration the policy-making areas of low politics would be more easy than policy making in areas of high politics (see Ojanen, 2002; Verdun, 2000: 36–7, 196–7 for Haas' response see Haas (1968).).

The next two communities were the Euratom (European Atomic Energy Community) and subsequently, the European Economic Community (EEC). The latter aimed at creating an economic market among the participating member states. At the core of the EEC was the idea to create a customs union: an area in which the barriers to trade among participating member states (the Benelux countries, France, Italy and West Germany) are removed and which features a common external tariff for goods coming into the EEC from so-called 'third countries' (countries outside the customs union). The basic idea was to increase trade among the partners. The choice of the six original member states to move towards a customs union was inspired by the idea that a customs union further integrates the economies, as opposed to settling for a free-trade area, in which each member can have its own external tariff for products from outside the free-trade area.

In 1960, the European Free Trade Association (EFTA) set up among some West European countries who were not members of the EEC. At this time the members of EFTA were: Austria, Denmark, Ireland, Norway, Portugal, Switzerland, Sweden and the United Kingdom. Again, the aim was free trade, although with less far-reaching implications.[1] The creation of the customs union was achieved ahead of time in 1968. Part of the success of this period can be traced back to high levels of economic growth, stability of exchange rates (through the Bretton Woods system of fixed exchange rates), the growth of the welfare state, and stable relations between member states. Of course within the European Community there were some difficulties, for example, the UK wanting to join the EC, which was initially not possible, largely because French President Charles de Gaulle did not support the UK application. European member states' government strategies towards economic prosperity and growth still showed a mixed strategy, relying both on domestic national objectives and policies as well as using European collaboration to increase their economic performance.

In the area of agriculture considerable progress was made. The Common Agricultural Policy was created to offer an integrated Community policy on agricultural production. However this policy was based on price subsidies and protectionism, and in due course would lead to problems related to overproduction, cost increase and environmental concerns (Hennis, 2001). Once the customs union was completed in the EC, its member states were searching for new initiatives to strengthen further the process of integration. Inspired by writers such as Balassa (1961) and Tinbergen (1965), the thinking of EC member states was that deeper economic integration could produce welfare gains and improve the rate of economic growth in these countries. By the late 1960s, it became clear that currency matters were becoming more of a problem, especially since exchange rates were under pressure (Strange, 1976). The Common Agricultural Policy (based on price subsidies) required fixed exchange rates, or at least an accounting system that dealt with the fluctuations in currency (Tsoukalis, 1977). At this time the Bretton Woods system of fixed exchange rates was slowly showing signs of deterioration, so a plan to create an economic and monetary union in the EC became attractive (Werner Report, 1970). At the same time three Western European countries – Denmark, Ireland and the UK – had prepared to join the EC.[2]

By 1971 the then US President Richard Nixon unilaterally abandoned the gold-standard by taking the dollar off gold. In the turbulent period that followed, the various EC member states had a difficult time coordinating their efforts, and each of the member state governments looked to develop their own strategies to deal with the difficulties. There were further problems for EC member states during the 1970s as the price of oil inflated, causing a recession and increasing unemployment. They were confronted for the first time with the phenomenon termed 'stagflation', to which the member states had differing responses (Tsoukalis, 1977; Kruse, 1980). Some of the member states allowed more inflation and concentrated on a strong role for the state (e.g. France and Italy). Others were more concentrated on keeping inflation more under control and towards the end of the 1970s sought more openness as a strategy for facing the global challenges (e.g. Netherlands, United Kingdom and West Germany). By the late 1970s and early 1980s the EC member states did not have much confidence that the EC was a very useful tool to deal with global challenges.

However, by 1979 and under Franco-German leadership, the European Monetary System was set up (Ludlow, 1982). Its modest aim was to incorporate a system of fixed exchange rates among EC member states that had had moderate success in its predecessor, the so-called 'snake'. The 'snake' was the name of a system of 'fixed but adjustable exchange rates' that was set up after the Bretton Woods system of fixed exchange rates collapsed. Currencies were to stay stable around at an agreed parity (and would not be allowed to fluctuate more than 2.25 per cent above or below this level). Initially it was intended to contain the currencies of all the EC member states, but as the decade unfolded

only West Germany and some small countries were stable members. In many ways the EMS followed the design of the snake (for example, 2.25 per cent fluctuation) but its relaunch was aimed at including countries, such as France and Italy, that had dropped out of the snake in previous years. Not much was expected from the EMS, so in 1983 it was still in its trial phase. It was at this point in time that an important turnaround occurred in Western Europe. Many of the countries of the EC came to the conclusion that their policies of focusing on national industries and protectionism, and seeking to increase economic wealth and prosperity through state intervention, were not delivering the desired results (Gourevitch, 1986). The choice was made to anchor monetary policies to those of West Germany and also to keep wages low, so as to become more competitive *vis-à-vis* the most successful economy, West Germany. In France the turnaround was sudden (as is documented in Hall, 1986), with then Finance Minister Jacques Delors suggesting to French President François Mitterrand that a more market-oriented approach to economic policies would be successful. A similar awareness developed in Italy and Belgium, countries that also came to realize the importance of pegging their currencies more closely to the other EMS currencies, and realizing the importance of keeping prices and wages low to maintain competitiveness (Maes and Quaglia, 2003). Italy was not immediately successful in executing its policies, and thus still opted for repeated devaluations.

By this time a group of industrialists, under the leadership of Philips Chairman Wisse Dekker, sought to promote the idea of completing the internal market as opposed to concentrating on protectionism (Cowles, 1995; Dekker, 1984). The idea caught on and eventually was transformed into the Single European Act (SEA), which enabled more laws to be passed by qualified majority vote (QMV) as (decreasing the number of policy areas where the national veto could be used), and seeks to complete the single market.

This change in the legislative procedure was even favoured by the otherwise Eurosceptic British Prime Minister, Margaret Thatcher, who liked the prospect of being able to outvote those with a national interest to block the further development of the single market.

The period from 1986 to 1992 was characterized by Europhoria. The drive to 'complete the internal market by 31 December 1992' becomes a powerful slogan throughout the late 1980s, leading to a rise in European optimism. Suddenly, member states and citizens felt that European global competitiveness might be saved through this new environment of increased competitiveness in the internal market. This heightened sense of looming prosperity and success was further fuelled by influential reports that argued for the possible economic benefits that would be derived from the completion of the internal market (Cecchini, 1988; Padoa-Schioppa, 1987). The Padoa-Schioppa Report suggests that successful European integration would be built on the completion of the internal market, a successful monetary regime, and an increased EU budget to bring about greater economic and social cohesion. The Cecchini Report in turn calculates the likely benefits from completing the single market (which were shown in retrospect to have been somewhat exaggerated).

The SEA envisaged revisiting the creation of Economic and Monetary Union (EMU), something that has been shelved for more than a decade. The idea of integrating further in the monetary domain is based on a desire for a more complete internal market, even a liberalized capital market, and as such would create a more market-friendly economic environment. It also builds on a relatively well-performing EMS that has managed to keep exchange rates stable, in particular in the latter part of the 1980s.

Exchange rates globally were turbulent in the late 1980s. The US, Japan and West Germany sought to discuss exchange rate cooperation in the so-called Plaza (1985) and Louvre (1987) accords, but without much success (Funabashi, 1989). When EMU came back onto the agenda by 1989 it was a European attempt to deal more generally with global challenges (Verdun, 2000). By this time, an important change had occurred in economic philosophy, and in particular about what causes growth and the role that monetary policy could play in producing growth. At this time the idea has become accepted among central bankers and ministries of finance, as well as other monetary and financial experts, that stable exchange rates and stable inflation rates were a necessary precondition for European member states to integrate further (McNamara, 1998; Verdun, 2000). Furthermore, governments draw the conclusion that deeper European integration was the right solution to halting the economic malaise that Europe had witnessed in the 1970s and first part of the 1980s.

The Maastricht Treaty (1992) incorporated EMU as well as many other changes that deepened economic integration and extended the so-called Community method into other areas of policy-making not previously spelt out in the EEC Treaty. It changed the name of the European Communities to the European Union, and incorporated the previous EC treaties into the same document. All these developments followed on the heels of a major economic, political and social transformation that was occurring in Central and Eastern Europe (CEE), when Eastern Bloc countries escaped Soviet domination, and adopted liberal democracy and market mechanisms. Joining the new EU was an attractive prospect for these CEE countries: to obtain democracy, to secure liberal values and to ensure prosperity. Thus, a number of them applied for membership. The EU took some time to decide how to respond, but by 1993 the EU had formulated conditions under which these countries might join (the so-called Copenhagen criteria) (Friis and Murphy, 1999; Verdun 2005).

Meanwhile, in 1992, the countries of Central and Eastern Europe themselves already established the Central Eastern Free Trade Agreement (CEFTA) which originally contained Czechoslovakia, Hungary and Poland;

most other accession states joined later. Again, the aim was to capitalize on the opportunities of liberalizing trade amongst participating members, in anticipation of having to wait a considerable number of years before being able to join the EU (Dangerfield, 2006). CEFTA was set up as an arrangement for the transition period, but eventually it took on a life of its own, with more and more neighbourhood countries joining (but also leaving as countries joined the EU).

The Maastricht Treaty was but the first of a series of major treaty changes that occurred in the 1990s. The Maastricht Treaty was not as well received as some Euro-enthusiasts had hoped. After the initial economic boom derived from German reunification, Western Europe experienced a recession; the restructuring of the economies of Central and Eastern Europe was proving to be more more costly in terms of productive destruction (without simultaneous new industry creation) than had been anticipated; and Scandinavian countries were going through very difficult times as well. The mid-to-late 1990s saw a focus on using European integration as a method for regaining lost terrain in global competitiveness. At this time the EU also embarked on major liberalization and privatization activities, a trend that originated in the UK in the 1980s. A number of traditionally state-dominated sectors, such as electricity, telecommunications, railways, and so on, were sold off and opened up to competition (Eberlein and Grande, 2005; Eising, 2002; Lehmkuhl, 1999).

The treaty changes in the 1990s were not based on a new philosophy – most of these principles had been part of the basic idea underlying the completion of the single market. Increasingly, EU competition and industrial policy has sought to prevent national governments protecting industries for seemingly arbitrary reasons (Sauter, 1998). The treaty changes (Amsterdam, 1997; and Nice, 2001) aimed to streamline the TEU and prepare it for enlargement. During these years it seemed that every major treaty change was followed by a declaration of the need to make another major treaty change. After Nice, the Laeken declaration suggested that further changes would be necessary (eventually that process would lead to the drafting of a treaty establishing a constitution for Europe – for a discussion of this process see Crum, 2005).

The Lisbon agenda was both a practical marker and an important symbol of Europe's realization that it was still struggling with global competitiveness. By 2000, under the Lisbon presidency, EU member states sought to find a way to deal with high unemployment, low growth, and loss of competitiveness of European economies *vis-à-vis* the rest of the world. The Lisbon strategy boldly stated that it aimed to have Europe as the most competitive economy in the world by 2010 (European Council, 2000). Though an almost laughable aim, the Lisbon agenda focused attention on a number of areas of policy-making that were seen as strategic to increase the likelihood of success in becoming more competitive. The focus was on developing the knowledge economy, strengthening market principles, investing in research and development, as well as in higher education.

The commencement of EMU is another major achievement during these years – initially with eleven countries, but soon after with twelve member states. Exchange rates are irrevocably fixed in 1999, and the euro was introduced into financial markets from 1 January 1999; banknotes and coins started to circulate in 2002. The introduction of the euro, it was argued, would increase trade, efficiency and specialization – however, it has also been claimed that these benefits would be relatively small (less than one per cent of growth of gross domestic product) (De Grauwe, 2005). Nevertheless, there was a real buzz in the air when the new currency was introduced.

Shortly afterwards, however, the economies of the EU member states, and even the applicant countries, started to show signs of an economic downturn. A recession took hold in Western Europe, and in 2003 the governments of many EU member states are once again considering what strategies to pursue to increase their economic performance. With the euro in place in many EU member states, a currency devaluation was no longer an option (especially not for the Italians, who had used that particular policy instrument in the past). The countries were, once again forced to turn to domestic solutions: reform of the labour market, reconsidering social spending, possibly tax reform, and improving the opportunities for small and medium-sized businesses.

At the time of the mid-term review of the Lisbon agenda (2005) it had become clear that the EU was still far from becoming the most competitive economy in the world. Even the ten new member states that had joined the EU on 1 May 2004 were not doing as well as had expected (Johnson, 2004). However, there are a few countries that have performed very well in these early years of the new millennium. They include some of the countries that were previously known as 'cohesion countries', but who, having joined the EMU, and are now performing better than average. These include Ireland and Spain (Grimwade, 2004). Other countries that are performing well, somewhat ironically, are Denmark, Sweden and the United Kingdom – in other words, those who stayed outside EMU (Verdun, 2006a), even though the larger economies of the euro area were performing better again in 2006 (Verdun, 2007).

The most recent years have seen an upswing in the economic situation of Europe (2006) and generally a more positive attitude about the years to come. At the same time, European countries are more than ever before aware that the wellbeing of Europe and its countries is directly related to the prosperity of the other major economic players of the world. The attacks of 11 September 2001 created an awareness that events in other parts of the world affect the economies and political systems of the Europeans (through, for example, the effect on air travel, security, economic transactions, judicial change, and consumer confidence). Also, the rise in the economic power of China and India has

meant steeply increasing competition in many traditional strongholds of European industry, such as textiles and shoe manufacturing. The European member states are more than ever before aware that global pressures are permanently present, and that responses to these challenges must be based on the strengths of European member states and the group of countries as a whole that form the European Union.

Within the EU, the question that keeps re-emerging is whether Europe's social model has a future. Are the various European welfare states sustainable in the long-run? Some argue that a couple of the European member states' models are outdated and unable to address current challenges such as an ageing population, a declining birth rate, and the need for a flexible labour market to deal with global competition (Sapir, 2006). Others argue that the fear of the necessary retreat of the state as was anticipated in the 1990s (see Pierson, 1994) was overdrawn, and that there is still plenty of space for individual social models to thrive (Bolukbasi, 2007; Martin and Ross, 2004; Pierson, 2001; Scharpf and Schmidt, 2001; Starke, 2006). According to these authors, the welfare state serves both to protect those who are 'victims' of restructuring, but also to increase the possibility that change can occur. Contrary to what was feared in the mid-1990s, the welfare state can also offer a safety net against opposition to reform. Furthermore, the welfare state offers a financial buffer related to changes in macroeconomic policy that enables the economy to bounce back after periods of low economic growth, stagnation or decline. The other leg of the European social model includes labour protection through labour law. This element of national policy-making has also been revisited, and in the second half of the first decade of the twenty-first century is seen to provide stability, as well as the potential flexibility needed for reform. In some countries a two-tier labour market has developed offering some in the labour market full protection; others are on temporary contracts and do not have access to the same rights.

REVIEW OF RECENT LITERATURE

In recent years there has been considerable debate about whether Europe can deal with competitiveness or not. Perhaps one of the more eye-catching reports was first issued in 2003, and written by André Sapir and others: 'An Agenda for a Growing Europe' (also known as the Sapir Report) (Sapir *et al.*, 2004). The report was commissioned by the then president of the European Commission, Romano Prodi, and was prepared and written by high-ranking academics (mostly economists but also a political scientist). The report studied 'the consequences of seeking to reach by 2010 two economic goals, namely (1) to become the most competitive sustainable and dynamic knowledge-based economy with sustainable economic growth and social cohesion (the 'Lisbon agenda'); and (2) to make a success of the (then) pending enlargement by rapidly raising living standards in the new Member States.' (Sapir *et al.*, 2003: 3).

The report stressed that the major problem Europe was facing is its relative lack of economic growth and prosperity *vis-à-vis* the US, in particular its steady decline since the early 1980s and stagnation at 70 per cent of the US per capita GDP. The concern of the report is that without stronger economic growth a number of European 'models' will be no longer sustainable. The Sapir Report calls for six changes: (1) to make the Single Market more dynamic; (2) to boost the investment in knowledge; (3) to improve the macroeconomic policy-framework for EMU; (4) to redress policies for convergence and restructuring; (5) to achieve effectiveness in decision-making and regulation; and (6) to refocus the EU budget (Sapir *et al.*, 2003: 4).

In response to the Sapir Report, policy-makers and politicians concentrated on the need to enhance growth and developed many strategies to do so. It became clear, however, that there might well be a potential clash between those who do not want change in Europe and those who realize that the message of the Sapir Report was that change was imminent. Those who were against the kind of change the Sapir Report proposed included those who were benefiting from the distribution of the EU's budget up until that time (e.g., French farmers). Others who were reluctant included those who favoured leaving the British rebate untouched. It was obvious that the Sapir recommendations would reorient the funds of the European Union.

In March 2004, the European Council asked a group of experts under the chairmanship of former Dutch Prime Minister Wim Kok to review the Lisbon agenda (Kok *et al.*, 2004). The eventual report did not receive as much coverage as the Sapir Report had done, but still drew considerable attention. In its findings it was critical about how little had been achieved. It gave a good analysis of what rigidities were causing the lack of growth (such as 'an overloaded agenda, poor co-ordination and conflicting priorities') and blamed member state government for not showing sufficient political will (see Bongardt and Torres, 2006; Verdun, 2006b). The Kok Report was however weaker on offering inspiring, clear new strategies to deal with the difficulties. The recommendations made in the report echoed many of those made in the earlier Sapir Report.[3] Scholars were divided in their assessment of the Lisbon Agenda, with some being considerably more critical of a lack of achievement of its goals (Groenendijk, 2006; Pochet, 2006; Schelkle, 2006); others were more willing to give Lisbon the benefit of the doubt, as it has reopened the debate and triggered initiatives (Bongardt and Torres, 2006; Smith, 2006).

Meanwhile the academic literature on economic growth and global competitiveness of the European Union has many different faces. Most of the work that deals with (lack of) economic growth typically focuses on many different aspects of the development of policies in the EU. It ranges from examining the labour market, social policy, industrial and competition policy, and global trade, to the role of micro- and macroeconomic policies in generating a favourable environment for growth. Reviewing merely the past five years of articles in selected field journals of

European integration,[4] that publish work from a variety of disciplines, as well as some leading monographs and textbooks that came out at this same time, reveals a multifaceted analysis.

Padoan and Mariani (2006) look at the effects of financial innovation on economic growth. They argue that although financial and technological integration might be necessary, it is by no means the sole condition to create growth and thereby move closer to the Lisbon Agenda. Their formal model incorporates various economic indicators and circumstances that would facilitate economic growth of countries (both EU and non-EU countries) and such as stable macroeconomic conditions, financial and monetary environment. Using cluster analysis they find three groups of countries and different structural characteristics. The effect of financial innovation is not the same on all three groups of countries. In an earlier study on liberalization of the single market, Mitchell Smith (2001) had also found that the success of liberalization in selected sectors depended on the strength of incentives of private sector actors, government preferences and domestic institutions. His study did showcase success in liberalization in the three cases he studied; cases in which private sectors actors had success in legal proceedings against government practices that restricted competition, thereby further opening up the market (and further 'completing' the single market).

André Sapir (2006) concentrates on the question of whether the four European social models he identifies – Nordic, Anglo-Saxon, Continental and Mediterranean – are sustainable over the long run in light of the challenges of globalization. As already alluded to above, he is not convinced that there is room for four types of European social models in the coming years. He argues that in particular the continental and Mediterranean models are inefficient and unsustainable in the long run. He is also critical of the Anglo-Saxon model as it fails to balance equity with efficiency. He does not advocate the creation of a 'European' (read: EU) model, as it is most

efficient that these developments stay the responsibility of member state governments. There would be a role for the EU, but merely to provide a more productive economic environment (e.g. ensure product and capital market reform, but more generally to complete the single market, in particular in the area of services).

Cappelen *et al.* (2003) examined the effects of regional policy on economic development in the weaker areas of the EU. They find that the funds provided by the EU to these areas are successful in increasing growth. However they also find that in recent years the discrepancies within countries (the difference between the economic growth rates in weaker regions *vis-à-vis* the stronger regions within countries) have not decreased. This was true in the 1980s, but since that time it is no longer the case. However, countries as a whole have done better (see the example of Spain mentioned already above, but they also point to the case of Poland). Finally, they find that regional policies of late have been most successful in developed areas, which suggests the positive effect flanking policies have a on the economic performance of these regions.

Alasdair Young (2004) examines the EU role in world trade. He argues that the EU's policies in this area in the international arena are characterized by contradictions. On the one hand, through its trade policy, it is usually quite liberal. Yet on the other hand, it still has difficulties complying with World Trade Organization (WTO) judgments. His analysis suggests that these contradictions are due to the internal dynamics of European policymaking. In the areas in which member governments have made strong domestic rules (when governments are risk averse) the subsequent EU rules can gravitate to the most risk-averse national rule. This strict rules (or as he calls it 'regulatory peak') will often clash with international ones (such as common agricultural policy – food safety measures and so on). His analysis suggests that enlargement will increase rather than decrease this trend and, in so doing, make Europe seem more like a fortress than the image it has tried to portray in the past. A similar argument is made by Erik Jones (2006) who claimed that the EU has not been very successful in transforming the single market to the global level.[5] Reflecting on that insight, he suggests that global trade liberalization should focus on what is called a 'shallow agenda of economic issues'; meaning that market, social and environmental concerns should remain off the global agenda.

BIG ISSUES IN ECONOMIC GROWTH AND COMPETITIVENESS

In reviewing the history of Europe's strategy towards economic growth and competitiveness, and the reviews of what road to take to deal with global challenges, one can easily discern a number of key criticisms that one often hears regarding Europe, European states and the EU about why it lacks competitiveness and thus, ultimately, growth.

The first is that *Europe's growth is lagging behind* vis-à-vis *the US*. As was mentioned above, the comparison is often made between growth rates in the US and in Europe. However, *The Economist* of 19 June 2004 suggests that, excluding Germany, GDP per capita essentially grew at the same rate in Europe as in the US between 1994 and 2003. Employment grew slightly less in Europe than in the US, and productivity per worker hour grew slightly faster in Europe. In other words, besides Germany, aggregate growth in Europe and the US over the last decade has been essentially equal.

The second is that *Europe does not work enough and Europe is not productive enough*. It is an interesting observation that European workers do not work the same number of hours as their US American counterparts. Also, as was already mentioned above, European income per capita is only about 70 per cent of the US average. Olivier Blanchard's seminal piece on this subject shows that per capita income is lower in Europe not because

workers are less productive – output per worker hour in Europe and the US are almost the same – but because Europeans work fewer hours. This is not due primarily to higher unemployment or lower labour market participation, but to a shorter working week, longer vacations, and earlier retirement. During their lives, US Americans work 40 per cent more hours than do Europeans. Blanchard (2004) also finds that over the last 30 years, productivity growth has been much higher in Europe than in the US. The result is that productivity levels are now roughly similar in the EU and in the US. Europe has used some of the increase in productivity to increase leisure rather than income, while the US has done the opposite.

The third is that *Europe lacks a business environment*. It is true that it is often stressed that for a small firm to start up in the US costs quite a bit less time than it would in Europe. Another point often raised is that Europeans are less mobile and thus labour is less likely to move to where the jobs are. Finally the question is sometimes raised about whether outcomes would be altered if Europeans has the same access to support from venture capitalists as do US Americans. However, there are few firm conclusions on this issue. The developments of recent years, especially the changes in the single market and EMU have improved business climate.

The fourth is that *Europe has too rigid labour markets and social protection*. Traditionally, labour markets are less mobile in Europe compared to the US due to lower labour mobility (even intra-EU country mobility is lower than intra-state mobility in the US), but also because of secure labour market protection. As a result of liberalization and deregulation processes, these labour markets have become considerably less rigid than was the case before. Germany, for example, increasingly has a two-tiered labour market (*Financial Times*, 26 October 2006). One part of the labour market has jobs for life, social security and pensions in part paid for by the employer, and have jobs from which one can almost not be dismissed. The other part of the labour market is based on temporary, freelance and flexible jobs, based on short-term contracts and lacking social security and pensions premiums paid for by the employer and so on. These developments stand in stark contrast with what one often thinks of when considering the 'European social model'.

The fifth is that the *Euro Area and the European Cental Bank (ECB) are not geared towards growth*. The European Central Bank has as its primary objective to keep inflation at or just below two per cent of GDP over the medium term. Without doing injustice to the first objective, it should also be seeking to promote the general objectives of the EU that includes economic growth and employment. The conventional wisdom on the relationship between inflation rate and economic growth has changed over the years. But in recent decades the financial elites in central banks, ministries of finance, major international financial institutions (International Monetary Fund, World Bank, etc). The current view of economists is that there is no long-term trade-off between inflation and unemployment. In other words, it does not 'pay-off' to have inflation in order to seek to achieve employment. The sea change in economic thought since the late 1970s is that a stable money supply is a necessary condition for growth. In addition to the interest rate not being an instrument to improve employment figures, recent research also suggests that many of the long-term or mass unemployment problems should be dealt with very locally with incentive schemes rather than with macro tools, such as interest rates or exchange rates.

Sixth, *the 'rest of the world' is overtaking Europe*. One of the difficulties of recent years has been to explain why the euro-area countries have not kept up with the average world growth, US growth, or at least that of the EU member states that are not in the euro area. As mentioned above, it depends a little how one looks at the statistics, but it is clear that one could still make aggregate comparisons

and point to the weakness of, in particular, Germany, France and Italy over the past four years. These three countries have needed to embrace reform to deal with low birth rate, an ageing population, and social security protection that does not offer sufficient incentives to create a flexible labour market. If we take those countries out of the equation, the situation is less gloomy. There are of course many other countries growing much stronger, such as China and India, but it is standard knowledge in international development and international trade literature to expect some developing countries to experience stronger-than-average periods of growth.

Seventh, *Europe's internal market is still incomplete*. As was made clear in the review above, it is true that Europe's single market is not yet complete. In particular in the area of financial services, and services more generally, Europe is still working at reducing barriers and increasing access. In recent years some very high-profile cases have appeared before the Court of Justice about trans-border investments, such as the Marks and Spencer case (see O'Brien, 2007). Another high-visibility case was a Dutch bank trying to penetrate the Italian banking market. At the same time, recent years have seen the development of a European system of accounting standards (Elliot, 2007), and an attempt at creating a services directive (also known as the Bolkenstein Directive). These developments, combined with the Lisbon Agenda, might suggest that, although it might take time, Europe is on the right track.

CONCLUSIONS

European responses to economic growth and global competitiveness have increasingly been based on a two-track approach. On the one hand, countries seek to promote their own interests, focus on their own preferences, secure their own aims, and protect their own traditions. On the other hand, European countries are increasingly using

European integration and European collaboration in their attempt to increase competitiveness in the global market place. Today's European model includes a number of the above changes, such as liberalization of the labour market, reforms in social policy and having to deal with reforms due to the ageing population. Some of these cooperative/coordinated solutions focus not so much on centralization or transferring sovereignty over these policy areas to the supranational level, but rather on informal policy coordination (some things include changes totally unrelated to the EU policies such as Bologna process of higher education) (Bache, 2006; Haskel, 2009).

European countries, both EU and non-EU, are firmly committed to globalization (in some form or other), even though they do not all conceptualize the process in the same way. Overall, they typically welcome relying on market principles for economic processes and expanding the areas in which international trade flow freely. At the same time, they are not willing to give up all protection just yet (see chapter in this volume by Wyn Grant on CAP, etc.). Of course, given their sizable agricultural sectors and their on average lower per capital GDP, new entrants to the European Union are keen to keep much of the CAP in tact. As we have seen, the EU is a leader in low-key international economic trade matters, but issues that require more regulation typically have not been dealt with at the global level but instead at the EU level. As a result of these and other factors, the discussions in the so-called Doha round stalled repeatedly – most recently in Potsdam in 2007.

Although the EU is seeking to complete the internal market and focus on deregulation, privatization and liberalization, Europe at times still finds the solution to be intervention in the market (regional or cohesion policy) or even just focusing on investment in large projects (Airbus, big infrastructural projects, EU grants for large callaborative research projects, etc.).

The EU countries have taken the relationship between it and the rest of the world to mean different things at different times. They take a different role when relating to accession states (posing conditions and eventually letting them join), but in other areas the influence is more indirect. On the world stage their focus is mainly on seeking to protect a free-trade regime, albeit with large exceptions.

All in all Europe still faces some challenges to economic growth rates, many of which may have possible local, regional, national, European and global solutions. The European countries still have a long way to go to optimize their situation. But taken together the situation in Europe might not at all be as gloomy as people sometimes make it out to be.

The avenues for further research are many. It is interesting to focus on challenges to European competitiveness and to what extent they are related to changes in the world economy. With China and India offering increasingly high-quality goods at low labour costs, other countries in the world have to reassess their comparative advantage and find their niche. How do different European countries cope with this insight? What choices do they make? What strategies do they adopt? Do most EU member states seek to compete on better high quality (service) jobs rather than industry (manual labour) oriented jobs? Next, what level of social security, welfare spending and labour market protection is optimal to offer a solid basis for a healthy economy? It will be interesting to follow the choices made by those who have an Anglo-Saxon, Nordic, Continental or Mediterranean model to see how they balance the need for security, equality, efficiency and equity in the economy with keeping costs under control and seeking to avoid creating disincentives to labour mobility. Finally, it will be interesting to follow the choices Europeans have made in keeping a balance between global trade liberalization (through global multilateral institutions) and a still-resilient conservatism to protect some sectors and rules (as, for example, agriculture and food standards). How will that tension play out? There are many more avenues for interesting research. The above are just some of the ones that will remain of interest in the years to come, as European countries find their way in the global economy amidst a unique set of specific European regional multilateral rules, regulations, institutions and governance structures, which we call the EU.

NOTES

1 Today, many of the EFTA members have joined the EU, and thus there are very few members left: Iceland, Liechtenstein, Norway and Switzerland. Furthermore, three of the four EFTA states (all but Switzerland) joined a new arrangement: the European Economic Area (EEA) – signed in 1992; entered into force in 1994. It created a large free trade area that included the three above-mentioned EFTA states, the European Community and its member states. Switzerland decided not to join the EEA following a popular referendum that showed a majority against joining the EEA.

2 By joining the EC in 1973 Denmark and the UK left EFTA. Ireland had not been a member of EFTA, but was part of the Anglo-Irish Free Trade Agreement that was signed in 1965 after its application for EEC membership was declined which came into effect in 1966. It phased out tariffs on most industrial products over ten years. For details on Ireland's approach to the EEC and Anglo-Irish relations, see also Fitzgerald (2006).

3 Complete the internal market (particularly in services); improve the climate for entrepreneurs; build an adaptable and inclusive labour market; focus on an environmentally sustainable future, and so on.

4 The two journals reviewed are *Journal of Common Market Studies* and *Journal of European Public Policy* in the period 2001–2006.

5 See also Meunier and Nicolaïdis (2006) who analyse how the EU tries to influence labour and social standards through trade – which they find to be of only limited success.

REFERENCES

Bache, I. (2006) 'The Europeanization of Higher Education: Markets, Politics or Learning?', *JCMS: Journal of Common Market Studies*, 44 (2): 231–248.

Balassa, B. (1961) *The Theory of Economic Integration*. London: Allen and Unwin.

Blanchard, O.J. (2004) 'The economic future of Europe', *Journal of Economic Perspectives* 8 (4): 3–26.

Bolukbasi, H.T. (2007) 'Plus ça change … ? The European social model between 'economic governance' and 'social Europe' from the Maastricht Treaty to the European Constitution', *Current Politics and Economics of Europe*, 18 (2): 149–179.

Bongardt, A. and Torres, F. (2006) 'Is Lisbon not delivering?' *EUSA Review*, Fall.

Cappelen, A., Castellacci, F., Fagerberg, J. and Verspagen, B. (2003) 'The impact of EU regional support on growth and convergence in the European Union', *Journal of Common Market Studies*, 41 (4): 621–644.

Cecchini, P. (1989) *Alles op Alles voor Europa: de Uitdaging 1992*. Amsterdam and Brussels.

Cowles, G.M. (1995) 'Setting the agenda for a New Europe: The ERT and EC 1992', *Journal of Common Market Studies*, 33 (4): 501–526.

Crum, B. (2005) 'Towards finality? An assessment of the achievements of the European Convention', in A. Verdun and O. Croci (eds) *The European Union in the Wake of Eastern Enlargement: Institutional and Policy-making Challenges*. Manchester: Manchester University Press/Vancouver: UBC Press/New York: Palgrave, pp. 200–217.

Dangerfield, M. (2006) 'Subregional integration and EU enlargement: where next for CEFTA?', *JCMS: Journal of Common Market Studies*, 44 (2): 305–324.

De Grauwe, P. (2005) *Economics of Monetary Union*, 6th edn. Oxford: Oxford University Press.

Dekker, W. (1984) 'Europa 1990', Lecture at the Centre for European Policy Studies, 13 November, Brussels.

Duchêne, F. (1994) *Jean Monnet: the First Statesman of Interdependence*. New York: Norton.

Eberlein, B. and Grande, E. (2005) 'Beyond delegation: transnational regulatory regimes and the EU regulatory state', *Journal of European Public Policy*, 12 (1): 89–112.

Eising, R. (2002) 'Policy learning in embedded negotiations: explaining EU electricity liberalization', *International Organization*, 56 (1): 85–120.

European Council (2000) 'Lisbon European Council, 23 and 24 March 2000, Presidency Conclusions'. Available at: http://www.

europarl.europa.eu/summits/lis1_en.htm, accessed 30 October 2006.

Fitzgerald, M. (2006) 'Ceart go leor – Ireland, the UK, the Sterling area and EMU', in F. Torres, A. Verdun and H. Zimmerman (eds) *EMU Rule: The Political and Economic Consequences of European Monetary Integration*. Baden-Baden: Nomos, pp. 245–260.

Friis, L. and Murphy, A. (1999) 'The European Union and Central and Eastern Europe: Governance and Boundaries', *Journal of Common Market Studies*, 37 (2): 211–232.

Funabashi, Y. (1989) *Managing the Dollar: from the Plaza to the Louvre*. Washington, DC: Institute for International Economics.

Gourevitch, P.A. (1986) *Politics in Hard Times: Comparative Responses to International Economic Crises*. Ithaca: Cornell University Press.

Grimwade, N. (2004) 'Developments in the economies of the European Union', *Journal of Common Market Studies*, 42 (Suppl. 1): 169–185.

Groenendijk, N. (2006) 'The revised Lisbon Agenda: flawed but not yet failed' *EUSA Review*.

Haas, E.B. (1958) *The Uniting of Europe*, 1st edn. London: Stevens.

Haas, E.B. (1964) *Beyond the Nation State. Political, Social, and Economic Forces 1950– 1957*. Stanford: Stanford University Press.

Haas, E.B. (1968) *The Uniting of Europe*, 2nd eds. Stanford: Stanford University Press.

Hall, Peter A. (1986) Governing the Economy: *The Politics of State Intervention in Britain and France*. New York: Oxford University Press.

Haskel, B. (2009) Weak Process, Strong Results: Cooperation in European Higher Education, in Tömmel, I. and Verdun, A. (eds) *Innovative Governance in the European Union: The Politics of Multilevel Policymaking*, Boulder, Col: Lynne Rienner, pp. 273–288.

Hennis,M. (2001) 'Europeanization and globalization: The missing link', *Journal of Common Market Studies*, 39 (5): 829–850.

Hoffmann, S. (1966) 'Obstinate or obsolete? The fate of the nation-state and the case of Western Europe', *Daedalus*, 95 (3): 862–916.

Johnson, D. (2004) 'Developments in the economies of the applicant states', *Journal of Common Market Studies*, 42 (Suppl. 1): 187–202.

Jones, E. (2006) 'Europe's market liberalization is a bad model for a global trade agenda', *Journal of European Public Policy*, 13 (6): 943–957.

Kok, W. (ed.) (2004) 'Facing the challenge: the Lisbon strategy for growth and employment', Report for the High-Level Group, November.

Kruse, D.C. (1980) *Monetary Integration in Western Europe: EMU, EMS and Beyond*. London and Boston: Butterworth.

Lehmkuhl, D. (1999) *The Importance of Small Differences. The Impact of European Integration on Road Haulage Associations in Germany and the Netherlands*. Thela Thesis, Amsterdam.

Ludlow, P. (1982) *The Making of the European Monetary System: A Case Study of the Politics of the European Community*. London: Butterworth Scientific.

McNamara, K.R. (1998) *The Currency of Ideas: Monetary Politics in the European Union*. Ithaca: Cornell University Press.

Maes, I. and Quaglia, L. (2003) 'The process of European monetary integration: a comparison of the Belgian and Italian approaches', *Banca Nazionale del Lavoro Quarterly Review*, 224: 451–478.

Martin, A. and Ross, G. (2004) *Euros and Europeans: Monetary Integration and the European Model of Society*. Cambridge: Cambridge University Press.

Meunier, S. and Nicolaïdis, K. (2006) 'The European Union as a conflicted trade power', *Journal of European Public Policy*, 13 (6): 906–925.

O'Brien, M. (2006) 'Direct taxation, the ECJ and implications for member state budgets', *Current Politics and Economics of Europe*, 18 (2): 307–333.

Ojanen, H. (2002) 'Theories at a loss? EU-NATO fusion and the 'low-politicisation' of security and defence in European integration', UPI Working Paper 35/2002.

Padoan, P.C. and Mariani, F. (2006) 'Growth and finance, European integration and the Lisbon strategy', *Journal of Common Market Studies*, 44 (1): 77–112.

Padoa-Schioppa, T. (1987) *Efficiency Stability and Equity, A Strategy for the Evolution of the Economic System of the European Community ('Padoa-Schioppa-Report')*. Oxford: Oxford University Press.

Pierson, P. (1994) *Dismantling the Welfare State? Reagan, Thatcher and the Politics of Retrenchment*. Cambridge: Cambridge University Press.

Pierson, P. (ed.) (2001) *The New Politics of the Welfare State*. Oxford: Oxford University Press.

Pochet, P. (2006) 'Lisbon and the Open Method of Coordination: Political Alliances and an Unclear Future', *EUSA Review*, Fall 2006.

Posner, E. (2007) "Financial Transformed in the European Union", in McNamara, K. and Meunier, S. (eds) *Making History: European Integration and Institutional Change at Fifty* (State of European Union, Volume 8), Oxford: Oxford University Press, pp. 175–193.

Sapir, A. (2006) 'Globalization and the reform of European social models', *Journal of Common Market Studies*, 44 (2): 369–390.

Sapir, A., Aghion, P., Bertola, G. *et al.* (2003) *An Agenda for a Growing Europe*. Available at: http://www.euractiv.com/ndbtext/innovation/sapirreport.pdf.

Sapir, A., Aghion, P., Bertola, G. *et al.* (2004) *An Agenda for a Growing Europe*. Oxford: Oxford University Press.

Sauter, W. (1988) *Competition Law and Industrial Policy in the EU*. Oxford: Oxford University Press.

Scharpf, F.W. and Schmidt, V.A. (eds) (2001) *Welfare and Work in the Open Economy. Volume I: From Vulnerability to Competitiveness*. Oxford: Oxford University Press.

Schelkle, W. (2006) 'Structural reform and fiscal consolidation: how compatible are the Lisbon and Maastricht Agendas?' *EUSA Review*, Fall 2006.

Smith, M.P. (2001) 'In pursuit of selective liberalization: single market competition and its limits', *Journal of European Public Policy*, 8 (4): 519–540.

Smith, M.P. (2006) 'Lisbon lives: institutional embedding of the competitiveness objective', *EUSA Review,* Fall 2006.

Starke, P. (2006) 'The politics of welfare state retrenchment: A literature review', *Social Policy and Administration*, 40 (1): 104–120.

Strange, S. (1976) 'International monetary relations. Vol 2', in A. Shonfield (ed.) *International Economic Relations of the Western World 1959–1971*. London, New York and Toronto: OUP for RIIA.

Tinbergen, J. (1965) *International Economic Integration*, 2nd revised edn. Amsterdam, London and New York.

Tsoukalis, L. (1977) *The Politics and Economics of European Monetary Integration*. London: Allen and Unwin.

Verdun, A. (2000) *European to Globalization and Financial Market Integration. Perceptions of EMU in Britain, France and Germany*. Basingstoke: Palgrave-Macmillan/New York: St. Martin's Press/Palgrave.

Verdun, A. (2005) 'The Challenges of European Union – where are we today, how did we get there, and what lies ahead?', in A. Verdun and O. Croci (eds) *The European Union in the Wake of Eastern Enlargement: Institutional and Policy-making Challenges*. Manchester: Manchester University Press/Vancouver: UBC Press/New York: Palgrave, pp. 9–22.

Verdun, A. (2006a) 'Economic developments in the euro area' *Journal of Common Market Studies*, 44 (September): 199–212.

Verdun, A. (2006b) 'Taking stock of the Lisbon Agenda: Is Lisbon flawed, necessary, window-dressing, or all of the above?', *EUSA Review*, Fall 2006. 19 (4): p. 1.

Verdun, A. (2007) 'Economic developments in the euro area', *Journal of Common Market Studies*, 45 (September): 213–230.

Werner Report (1970) 'Report to the Council and the Commission on the Realization by Stages of Economic and Monetary Union in the Community'. Council and Commission of the EC, Bulletin of the EC, Supplement 11, Doc 16.956/11/70, 8 October.

Young, A.R. (2004) 'The incidental fortress: The single European market and world trade', *Journal of Common Market Studies*, 42 (2): 393–414.

15

Agricultural Policy and Protectionism

Wyn Grant

The story of European agriculture in the period since the end of the Second World War is one of a transformation from shortage to abundance, from being a major importer of food to a major exporter. This transformation was driven in part by major technological changes and in part by the policies of the European Economic Community (EEC), later the European Union (EU). The EEC instituted policies of protection and subsidy that provided relatively risk-free markets for European farmers with surplus products being dumped onto the world market to the detriment of producers in the global South. It should be noted that countries that chose to remain outside the EU, notably Iceland, Norway and Switzerland, provided even higher levels of subsidy and protection to their farmers. Policy in the early postwar decades emphasized the maximization of production and little attention was paid to the substantial environmental impacts of agriculture. By the 1990s, there was a new emphasis on the environmental costs of intensive agriculture, while there was an attempt to shift to a more general rural policy rather than privileging agriculture as one of a number of economic activities in rural areas.

THE IMPORTANCE OF TECHNOLOGICAL CHANGE

The land war fought in continental Europe in 1944 and 1945 disrupted agriculture and the food supply chain with agricultural production in France falling to two-thirds of its pre-war level (Tracy, 1989: 216). Tracy notes (1989: 217): 'When hostilities finally ceased, food supplies were woefully inadequate, especially in Germany itself, and agriculture's productive capacity was seriously depleted.' However, recovery was relatively rapid, assisted by funding provided under the American Marshall Plan.

What is often overlooked in accounts that focus on the policy process is the role of technology in fostering a transformation towards a more intensive form of farming. Intensive farming seeks to maximize production from a given area of land, making as effective as possible use of developments in science and technology. The move towards more intensive farming initially developed slowly, with the use of artificial fertilizers developing at a modest pace after their invention in 1850. However, the trend towards more technologically intensive farming accelerated in Europe after the Second World War, although recently there has been something of a consumer backlash against it with encouragement for more extensive forms of farming, including organic farming. These technological developments had two main dimensions, mechanization and the use of the discoveries of chemistry (and more recently biology) in farming.

Mechanization has brought about a transformation in European farming. In 1955 there were 4.4 million horses in the EC-6 and only 1.06 million tractors (there were already more tractors than horses in the UK). By 1970 the picture had been reversed with 1.4 million horses and 3.5 million tractors. Tractors per 1,000 farm workers in the EC-6 increased from 59 in 1955 to 364 in 1970 and reached 806 in 1986 (figures derived from Johnson, 1991: 64). The tractor is the most basic piece of farm kit and over time the equipment available has become more and more sophisticated. A modern plough or combine harvester is an elaborate piece of machinery which will use a global positioning system in conjunction with an on-board computer to decide, for example, how fertilizer applications should be changed in different parts of a field. In livestock farming, milking by hand has been replaced by increasing sophisticated parlours, for example, using a revolving rotary design with a computer receiving information triggered by microchips in each cow. All these developments have made farming a much more capital intensive activity, leading to larger farms and a considerable displacement of labour.

However, these developments have not been uniform across Europe. Poland has large numbers of semi-subsistence farmers, usually selling only into local markets. Travel through the countryside of Romania, shortly to become an EU member state, at harvest time and you will see people carrying bundles on their shoulders with horses being used extensively for transport purposes and even to plough the fields. People sell berries or small quantities of vegetables by the roadside.

In both Poland and Romania, workers displaced from industry eke out a living on the land.

Agriculture was also transformed by 'chemical farming' involving the extensive and systematic use of fertilizers and of crop protection chemicals produced by agrochemical companies. Very substantial increases in yields were obtained as a result. Veterinary medicines supplied by pharmaceutical companies have enabled the effective treatment of a wide range of livestock diseases, although these treatments were often expensive. It is also important to note that the quality of seeds was substantially improved by the use of methods of hybridization with hybrid seed first being developed in maize in the 1920s. However, chemical farming is not the technological frontier that it once was and the number of active ingredients available for pesticides in the EU has fallen sharply, in part as a consequence of regulation, in part because of commercial decisions. The discovery of the structure of DNA in 1953 increased the importance of biological knowledge in relation to agriculture. One consequence was the development of genetically modified crops. These are used extensively in North and South America and in China, but have encountered considerable resistance from environmentalists and consumers in Europe and are only grown commercially in Romania and Spain.

The implications of the technological revolution in agriculture were underestimated by the devisers of the Common Agricultural Policy (CAP). One of the objectives they set for the CAP was an improvement in agricultural productivity, but this would have been attained without state intervention of the kind created by the CAP, although agricultural extension services were important in diffusing knowledge and understanding of new techniques to farmers. The consequence of the combination of technological change and CAP policies which ensured that all produce could be sold at least above the marginal cost of its production meant that supply increased so as to produce structural surpluses. For example, in the 20 years to 1997 there was about a 20 per cent increase in the total volume index of production in the EU (Keane and Lucey, 1997: 231). However, demand was relatively static, given the limited capacity of the human stomach. In the immediate postwar decades, the population of Europe increased rapidly, but the demographic trend is now towards smaller families with population increases (leaving aside immigration) falling below the net replacement ratio. An ageing population eats less food.

THE EMERGENCE AND DEVELOPMENT OF THE CAP

Agriculture had to be included in the common market because it was so important to the economies and societies of the founding member states, but it was also a subject on which there were many tensions which could have undermined the negotiations. In broad terms there was a broad division between the export-oriented countries (France, Italy and the Netherlands) and the food importers (Federal Germany, Belgium and Luxembourg):

> The exporters (dominated by France) argued most forcefully for community preference and were generally in favour of guaranteed minimum prices but at low levels … The importers dominated by the FRG … were in favour of high minimum prices, but less in favour of community preference (Wilson and Wilson, 2001: 79).

France had the strongest interest in the subject as it 'produced 40 per cent of all agricultural commodities in the EEC6 in 1957' (Wilson and Wilson, 2001: 71) and was already a significant agricultural exporter. French politicians and French people generally, then as now, had a strong symbolic and emotional attachment to the French countryside. Agriculture was particularly important in certain areas of the country such as the Midi and Brittany, while the grain barons of the Paris Basin assumed a greater influence on policy, particularly in Brussels, with the passage of time. 'French farmers appear less

committed than in other member states to a particular party or doctrine. Thus, they constitute an effective body of floating voters who are accorded political attention far in excess of their relative importance in the French economy' (Fearne, 1997: 22).

Germany had lost its main arable producing areas in the east to the German Democratic Republic (DDR) when the country was split after the Second World War. Federal Germany had an agriculture riddled with structural inefficiencies with too many small-scale farmers although, as the economy expanded, many of them became part-time, with the classic example being the farmer who made Volkswagen cars by day and tended his fields at the weekend. Even in the late 1990s, 'Thirty-seven per cent of German farmers had some other employment, the highest figure for any member state' (Grant, 1997: 57). Of course, as in France, many smaller farmers left farming altogether, symbolized by the scene in the German film *Heimat* where the main character gets rid of her only cow in response to the pressures of modernity represented by the prospect of a holiday in Florida. More generally, 'There were well-grounded fears that the structural deficiencies of FRG agriculture would be exposed in an expanded and more open agricultural market' (Wilson and Wilson, 2001: 79).

Italy was largely quiescent in the formation of the CAP and the subsequent negotiations on its development. This was largely because of the structure of Italian agriculture and the country's lack of a major interest in the proposals outside of fruit and vegetables. In addition, 'Italian agricultural politics was not really institutionally equipped to pursue an active foreign agricultural policy' (Knudsen, 2001: 147). Belgian agriculture 'produced at relatively high costs and was much less efficient than the Dutch sector' (Knudsen, 2001: 105).

In the absence of Britain in the negotiations, the Netherlands was the country most likely to push for an agricultural policy that favoured commercially oriented, efficient farming. 'Dutch agricultural activity may be characterised as the most modern, efficient agricultural production in western Europe, with a high level productivity' (Knudsen, 2001: 104). The Dutch interest was in being able to import raw materials as cheaply as possible, process them in its food manufacturing industry and export into the German market. The Dutch government did argue against what turned out to be some of the most objectionable features of the CAP, such as excessively high support prices. However, the Dutch had other interests to consider. The expansion of economic activity and trade in the Community would favour their ports, notably Rotterdam. Their priority was obtaining export markets for the dairy sector and they were prepared to concede higher prices on imports of grain, on which they were short, if they could secure market access for their largest sector, dairying. (Fearne, 1997: 26–7).

Given all these difficulties, discussions on agriculture were postponed so that other issues could be got out of the way first. 'Hence, it was not until seven weeks in the negotiations following the Messina summit in June 1955 that the subject of agriculture was raised at all' (Knudsen, 2001: 87). Once the Treaty of Rome came into force, a conference had to be convened which include delegations from the farmers' organizations and also from the food industry. This was convened at Stresa in Italy in July 1958 and 'the final resolution presented a much more coherent view of the Common Agricultural Policy than can be found in the Treaty' (Neville-Rolfe, 1984: 195). A guiding influence at the conference was the agriculture commissioner, Sicco Mansholt, formerly the Dutch minister of agriculture, who held the post until 1972.

The eventual achievement of agreement is often presented as a Franco-German compromise with France seeking to protect and gain additional markets for her farm produce and Germany eager to secure markets for its manufactured products. Knudsen (2001: 10) challenges the conventional wisdom, pointing out: 'The Franco-German explanation cannot explain why the CAP is there, and it is even less effective in explaining why the CAP turned out to be so massively dominant in the EU in less than a decade.' The reality is undoubtedly more complex, although Knudsen accepts (2001: 9) that the Franco-German trade-off scenario 'is not completely wrong'. Part of the explanation is that German agricultural interests were both vulnerable and influential and pushed very hard to defend their interests which moved the German government closer to the French position (Fearne, 1997: 29). 'The views of the farmers apparently prevailed on the government, despite the overall German interest in developing trade' (Tracy, 1989: 253). There was also a general commitment to the successful launch of a common market. 'In the end a desire to compromise over agriculture seems also to have prevailed among the four countries which did hold strong views about it' (Neville-Rolfe, 1984: 194), although the views of the Netherlands were probably more strongly held and of more importance than those of Belgium.

Comecon

Countries in Eastern Europe during this period were organized in Comecon which was an Eastern Bloc equivalent of the EEC, but organized in terms of the allocation of production rather than as a market. The experiences of individual countries differed to some extent. In Hungary, which had elements of a legal and illegal market economy, 'the dominance of the state in the food industry was sometimes diluted by imaginative circumventions of state directives and a substantial degree of competition emerged'. (OECD, 1994: 11).

Nevertheless, three generalizations can be made about Comecon countries. First, subsidies were paid to consumers rather than producers so that the cost of staple foods in the shops was subsidized. When these countries joined the EU, there was no history of substantial producer subsidies to contend with. Second, efforts were made to collectivize farming in large state-owned farms. Strictly speaking, there was a distinction on Soviet lines between state *(sovkhoz)* and collective *(kolkhoz)* farms, but in practice this made little difference. 'Collective and state farms occupied and cultivated about 90 per cent of Hungarian farm land.' (OECD, 1994: 40). In contrast 'Poland in the 1950s aborted its collectivization programme and opted for the continuation of small-scale private farming, circumscribed by centrally planned targets for compulsory deliveries' (Répassy and Symes, 1993: 83). Third, although communism was supposed to promote mechanization and other forms of capital investment, in practice this was often slow and patchy and the machinery less effective than that produced in the West. The author recalls visiting a food processing plant in Hungary where a Dutch computer controlled plant processing salami was next to a room where workers were preparing meat by hand. Replacing the old systems in agriculture during the transition period after the end of the Cold War was not easy, not least because of a lack of clarity about land ownership.

The objectives of the CAP

The objectives for agricultural policy set out in the Treaty of Rome have been unchanged ever since and they bear a remarkable similarity to those of the German Agricultural Act of 1955 (Fennell, 1997: 9, 14). The first objective was to increase agricultural productivity by promoting technical progress but, as noted earlier, technological and market forces were pushing in that direction anyway, although the provision of subsidies underwrote the substitution of labour by capital. 'Between 1973 and 1998, EU15 cereals production grew at an average of 2 per cent a year' (Ackrill, 2000: 193). This represented an even larger increase in yields of around 2.5 per cent a year, given that the land falling to cereals was falling by at least 0.37 per cent a year.

The second objective was to ensure a fair standard of living for the agricultural community and there is no doubt that there was great political concern about the gap between urban and rural incomes. Knudsen (2001: 202) takes the view:

[T]here was an informal hierarchy of goals in the CAP The relative improvement of farm income stood above that of stabilizing markets, as well as above reasonable prices to the consumers and the promise in the Treaty to work for harmonic development of world trade.

Knudsen argues that 'post-war agricultural policies have to be seen within the welfare state framework, rooted in the ideas of government social security in the inter-war period' (2001: 46; see also Sheingate, 2001). The CAP can be defended as a social and welfare policy (Rieger, 2000) although it is important to note that if it is, it has been a remarkably inefficient one, with most of the benefits going to larger-scale farmers. The decision-makers in the 1950s were not so much guided by a belief in distributive equity as concerns about the explosive political potential of an impoverished peasantry. 'Policy-makers were aware that a dissatisfied peasantry had played a considerable part in Hitler's rise to power. Unrest in rural areas and the emergence of right-wing radicalism had to be avoided at all costs' (Hendriks, 1991: 40). However, there was also a concern in relation to France and Italy that small farmers might form a basis of support for the then large communist parties in those countries.

The third objective, to stabilize markets, reflects the fact that it is difficult to obtain a supply and demand equilibrium in agricultural markets. Even under conditions of modern agricultural production, with all the knowledge and techniques of agronomy that are available, weather conditions can produce surpluses or shortages of a particular product. However, there might be means of dealing with this problem other than an elaborate structure of intervention and protection, for example through the insurance of risk.

The fourth objective, to ensure the security of supplies, reflected the recent experience of severe shortages at the end of the Second

World War and the concerns about the security environment at the height of the Cold War. These concerns were intensified by the Hungarian uprising of 1956. Although it was not actually spelt out 'in the Treaty of Rome, or anywhere else, the objective was the achievement of self-sufficiency – the provision of as much as possible of the food supply [from European farmers], with minimal dependence on the outside world' (Gardner, 1996: 17). This had profound implications for countries that had been suppliers of food to Europe, the 'third countries' as they were referred to in the jargon, even though special arrangements were made for the (largely) former colonies making up the African, Caribbean and Pacific (ACP) countries for special access to the European market. Limiting imports served another objective as supporting agricultural production was also seen as a means of easing balance-of-payments deficits against the background of a fixed exchange rate regime in which currency crises could rapidly run down a country's reserves. As Fennell notes (1997: 3), 'The balance-of-payments argument for supporting domestic agriculture continued to be used long after its relevance has diminished.' Outside the EEC, it was very influential under the UK Labour government of 1964–1970 giving that reducing the balance-of-payments deficit was a key economic policy goal.

The fifth objective, ensuring that supplies reach consumer at reasonable prices, was honoured as much as the breach as in the observance, particularly given that a reasonable price was never defined. The apparatus of protection and intervention erected by the EEC naturally maintained European prices above world prices, although it has to be remembered that the removal of these subsidies and protections would drive European farmers out of business to the extent that world prices would rise. Farmers would also point out that food has fallen as a share of the average family budget, not just because of growing prosperity, but also because food prices have not risen as fast as other prices.

Establishing the CAP

The treaty objectives then had to be translated into a series of operational principles which were not adopted until July 1962 which could be treated as the official start of the CAP. The three principles were:

- market unity – a single agricultural market with free internal trade and common pricing;
- community preference – ensuring that third country imports were priced so that they did not undermine Community producers;
- financial solidarity – expenses to be jointly met by member states through the Community and income generated, for example, from import levies, to form part of the funds available to the Community.

The first principle was breached once the system of 'green money' developed. This originally emerged in 1969 to cope with parity changes in France and Germany but soon developed into a high complex system that in effect allowed member states to pursue national pricing policies and to ensure that farmers received more generous subsidies than appeared to be the case, particularly after the introduction of the so-called 'switchover' mechanism in 1984 which increased the complexity of the policy. As a consequence, 'common' agricultural support prices were allowed to diverge in the member states, so much that the gap between them at times was larger than what existed before the common EC price regime.' Governments were able to manipulate the green rates to suit domestic policy objectives such as restraining inflation or to increase or decrease the amounts their farmers received in national currencies. The integrative character of the CAP was thus undermined (see Grant, 1997: 83–98 for a full discussion).

It is also worth noting that the second and third principles 'were major victories for France, since they, in effect, committed other European producers to provide markets for French produce and to contribute jointly to the cost of doing so' (Atkin, 1993: 54). What became the real focus of controversy was 'the level at which the common price for grains should be fixed. Because grains are at the centre of the food chain, grain prices usually determine the prices for practically all other agricultural products' (Knudsen, 2006: 196). The disputes between France and Germany over setting the grain price, only resolved when France threatened to walk out, were a harbinger of what was to come.

What was seen as the cornerstone of the EEC, as its only effective working policy, also tilted the common market in a particular direction. The proposals issued by the Commission initially in November 1959 and then in a final form in June 1960 were afterwards referred to as 'the Bible … because they so much resemble the final policy that was to dominate the EU for the next four decades' (Knudsen, 2001: 420). Yet at least one of those present at the creation, Commissioner Mansholt, the sagacious former colonial tobacco grower, resistance fighter, farmer and socialist, had warned at Stresa 'that the combination of family farms and an open-ended price support system would lead to surplus production, inefficient agriculture and ever-increasing costs' (Fearne, 1997: 33). What then followed was a series of attempts to reform the CAP which had achieved only partial success by the first decade of the twenty-first century, an example of path dependency if there ever was. As Kay (2003: 411) notes, 'The history of the CAP is an illustration of early developments becoming deeply embedded in a particular political environment, which has modified the incentive structure and hence affected economic and political behaviour.'

THE LONG JOURNEY TOWARDS REFORM

Commissioner Mansholt knew that European agriculture was fundamentally flawed and that in particular it had too many small farms that could not be viable in the longer run. His solution was to tackle the structural problems of European agriculture by providing incentives for early retirement and the amalgamation of holdings. There was nothing wrong with his diagnosis or his prescriptions; it was just that they were politically unacceptable. His plan 'had something unacceptable in it for almost everybody directly concerned: ministers, national governments, and farmers' organisations' (Neville-Rolfe, 1984: 300). It did lead to three directives on structural reform, but they were relatively limited in their impact.

The CAP was taking up two-thirds or more of Community expenditure in the 1970s and 1980s, peaking at 75 per cent in 1985. Prices were supposedly determined by a so-called 'objective' method, but even if it was a method, it was not particularly objective particularly in terms of its analysis of the supply and demand situation (see Ackrill, 2000: 53–4). There was continuous upward pressure on support prices which reached crisis levels in the 1980s. Guarantee expenditure 'jumped by 20 per cent in 1983 and 10 per cent in 1984' (Tangermann, 1998: 14). In the period between 1980 and 1986, spending doubled 'largely because of increasing costs for market intervention, storage and surplus disposal' (Moyer and Josling, 1990: 24). The CAP was threatening to bankrupt the European Community.

The crisis in the dairy sector

The crisis was particularly acute in the dairy sector where a structural surplus of milk had to be bought into intervention in the form of dairy products and eventually got rid of by whatever means possible; for example, the sale of 'ageing butter' to Soviet consumers. The solution adopted was the restriction of production through the use of milk quotas. In principle, this meant that each country and each farm (although there were variations by country in the method of administration) had a largely historically determined amount of milk they could produce with penalties for production beyond the permitted level. This was effective in halting any further growth in the structural surplus of milk, but it stored up serious problems for the future.

First, it tended to ossify the structure of milk production in the EU, making it harder to compete with lower-cost producers elsewhere in the world. Some countries permitted the trading of quota between farmers, but it could not be traded across member state boundaries as an internal market might imply. Second, it gave farmers a windfall capital gain which meant that new entrants to the sector had to acquire quota, generally sold with the farm (leaving aside some very limited new-entrant schemes). This made it more difficult for new and innovative farmers to enter the sector, leaving an ageing farmer population that was happy to carry on producing even if the returns were often not very good.

The continuing budgetary crisis

In any case, the introduction of milk quotas did not solve the budgetary crisis of the CAP. Unless the EC could cut its expenditure on the CAP, it would simply run out of funds. 'Under the balanced budget rule, the EC had been technically bankrupt from 1983 to 1985' (Ackrill, 2000: 88). In 1988 the EC introduced a system of budgetary stabilizers, triggered by production exceeding a specified level, to keep agricultural commodity programmes within budgetary targets. The intention was to make risk free production for intervention less attractive in its own right and to restore its original function as a cushion against short-term fluctuations. In fact the budgetary stabilizers were not very effective, in part because they were not as draconian as was initially claimed and in part because they were undermined by the green currency system which in effect lifted prices in line with the strongest currency in the European Monetary System, the DM, a situation that was not rectified until the introduction of the euro. The budget position was helped in the short run by an improvement in the market situation in 1988 and 1989, but overspending pressures soon re-emerged in the early 1990s.

The more general point is that 'there is a limit … to the efficiency impetus created by a budget crisis. As soon as enough resources have been saved to deal with the crisis, pressure is removed to take any further action.' (Moyer and Josling, 1990: 201–11). Given the complexity of the CAP, and the fact that it is understood by very few outsiders, it is very easy to 'fudge' a budget-driven reform so that it appears to be more thorough than it actually is. CAP expenditure has decreased over time as a percentage of the EU budget because spending on other policies has increased rather than because assistance to farmers has been cut back. In order to provide a real impetus to reform, actors external to the agricultural policy community had to be brought into play and this is what happened when agriculture was brought into trade policy with the 1986 Uruguay Round of trade talks.

The MacSharry reforms

It is generally agreed that 'in May 1992, the EC enacted the most far-reaching agricultural policy reforms in its history' (Daugbjerg, 1999: 415). The so-called MacSharry reforms, named after the then agriculture commissioner, Ray MacSharry, did not abolish intervention or subsidy. But they did set the CAP on a new path which influenced all subsequent reforms. Although the reforms were principally focused on the arable sector, they introduced a new policy instrument that was later to be used in relation to other commodities. Intervention prices were cut substantially and in compensation farmers were given a direct (and rather generously calculated) subsidy based on the area of land farmed. In EU jargon this was known as 'decoupling' as it meant that farmers no longer had to overproduce in order to claim their subsidy through sales of product into intervention stores as they would receive the subsidy provided that they cultivated the land or had permission to leave it fallow ('set aside'). The decoupling was, of course, only partial as the payment was still linked to the area of land farmed.

There is disagreement about how far these reforms were driven by the continuing budgetary crisis and how far they were a response to the need to find agreement in the Uruguay Round of trade talks. There are two schools of thought on this point:

[One] argues that the 1992 CAP reform occurred largely independently of the simultaneous international negotiations. Internal domestic problems related to budgetary constraints and over-supply of some commodities forced political leaders to consider fundamental reforms of the CAP. The second hypothesis does not deny the importance of these domestic problems. It postulates, however, that the timing of CAP reform and the very logic of the reforms introduced represent direct responses to international pressures emanating from GATT negotiations (Coleman and Tangermann, 1999: 386).

The view taken here was that the international trade negotiations were the most important factor in bringing about change. With a few exceptions, agriculture had largely been excluded from the General Agreement on Tariffs and Trade (GATT) because it was mutually convenient for both the US and the EU. However, the cost of agricultural support had risen sharply in the US in the 1980s, contributing to the budget deficit, while corporate agribusiness interests in the US pressed for freer agricultural trade from which they though they could benefit. Hence, agriculture was brought within the ambit of the Uruguay Round, eventually leading to the conclusion of an Agreement on Agriculture. This brought a much broader range of actors into the relatively closed world of agricultural policy-making, including trade ministers and ultimately heads of government. When the impasse over agriculture threatened to derail the whole round, German manufacturing interests put pressure on their chancellor to intervene. It was not easy to accommodate French concerns and the original Blair House agreement between the EU and the US on agriculture had to be supplemented by further discussions known as Blair House 2 or Breydel to secure French agreement.

Although interpretations again differ, it is also evident that the European Commission's directorate-general for agriculture, DGVI, was playing a very sophisticated game in relation to the Uruguay Round and the reform of the CAP. In essence, the breakdown of trade negotiations at the 1990 Heysel conference suited the Commission reform strategy:

MacSharry perhaps calculated that the best way to get CAP reform was to come close to reaching a GATT agreement at Heysel, then break off the talks. This would show the Heads of EC governments that a GATT agreement was possible, and lead them to apply pressure on their agricultural ministers to make the necessary changes in the CAP (Moyer and Josling, 2002: 109).

This is not to say that budgetary pressures were unimportant, and if there had been no Uruguay Round, there would have had to have been further changes to the CAP. However, they would have been made within the existing paradigm rather than introducing a new paradigm, albeit at the level of policy instruments rather than objectives. One consequence of not linking payments to farmers to production was to raise the possibility of whether they should be made at all. Even more important in the medium term was a shift away from a productionist paradigm which emphasized the maximization of output regardless of the environmental consequences. A new multi-functional paradigm emerged that justified financial support in terms of the public goods produced by farmers. In particular, a new emphasis was placed on the contribution that farmers could make to the environment and maintaining cherished landscapes. There was also a new emphasis on a broader rural strategy in which farming would be just one of the contributors to a more diversified rural economy.

Franz Fischler became Commissioner for Agriculture on 1 January 1995 and remained in office for two full five-year terms, surviving the collapse of the Santer commission. He had a clear strategic vision for the future of European agriculture which he was able in large part to accomplish because he was a wily tactician. The first challenge he faced was the impact of the enlargement of the EU to the east on the CAP. What he was clear about from the beginning was that the new member states would not need agricultural subsidies to expand their agriculture, but structural assistance to improve their infrastructure. He also recommended that there should be a long transition period for the new member states. These principles formed the basis of the eventual enlargement settlement in agriculture.

THE BROADENING OF THE DEBATE

The period since the late 1990s has seen a substantial broadening of the debate about agricultural policy. It is no longer focused on production and the financial rewards of the producers, but on a broader policy frame (rural policy), a concern with negative externalities (environmental policy), a concern with the wellbeing of consumers (food safety) and with the impact of the CAP on those living in poverty outside the EU.

Rural policy

A conference convened by the Commission at Cork in November 1996 was, in the view of agriculture commissioner Franz Fischler, explicitly concerned with the creation of a 'common rural development policy' to run in parallel with the CAP and to be funded by reduced expenditure on intervention and storage. The conference produced the so-called Cork Declaration which called for sustainable rural development to be top of the EU agenda. In particular, policies must protect and sustain the quality of rural landscapes. The European farm organization, COPA-COGECA, argued that rural policy concerned with 'secondary' activities such as farm crafts and agri-tourism must not substitute or replace the promotion of agriculture as an economic activity. They suspected that the Cork Declaration was a Commission plant containing 'the framework of a pre-established rural policy' with the conference used as

'a mere instrument for its legitimation' (*Agra Europe*, 6 December 2005: 5). Divisions on the subject became evident at the November Farm Council:

> Some member states such as Germany, the Netherlands and Spain, had reservations about the Declarations, fearing that they might have a negative impact on the future of the CAP. Other member states, such as the UK, Sweden and Denmark, welcomed the declarations on apparently precisely the same grounds, seeing them as way of implementing further CAP reforms (*Agra Europe*, 22 November 1996: E/7).

More trouble followed at the European Council meeting at Dublin. The Irish presidency 'tried to include in the official conclusions of the Dublin summit a statement which committed the Commission to draw up a proposal or a discussion paper based on the Cork Declaration. However, the move was blocked by the French and German delegations who said it went "too far"' (*Agra Europe*, 20 December 1996: E/5). 'The timing was bad: EU policy makers were at that stage deeply caught up in the BSE crisis, with little time or inclination to come to grips with a common rural policy for the EU' (Moyer and Josling, 2002: 178). Fischler now had to back-pedal 'to rescue his now floundering strategy and to allay the opposition of agriculture ministries, Fischler then sought to detach the promotion of rural policy from the question of CAP reform: the two, he argued, should proceed in parallel but separately.' (Lowe *et al*., 2002: 2). Although tactically necessary, this step may have ended any chances of the CAP being transformed into at least a Common Agricultural and Rural Policy in which there was some intention to secure equivalence between the two strands. Instead, rural policy became a supplement to the CAP.

Admittedly, the 1999 Agenda 2000 reforms did introduce a rural development regulation which struck 'an uneasy balance between continuity and change' (Lowe *et al*., 2002: 4). In fact, only one of the measures incorporated in it was new, although it was arguably more innovative in terms of procedures based on decentralization and partnership and the requirement for member states to draw up seven-year rural development programmes. However, the so-called 'second pillar' of the CAP has always been dwarfed by the amount spent on more traditional forms of farm support in the 'first pillar', even if they have become subject to 'cross-compliance' with environmental and other requirements. In the difficult 2005 budget settlement, the amount available for rural development was sharply cut back. The Commission had originally suggested that €88.7 billion should be made available; a compromise proposal had been €74 billion; and the amount eventually arrived at was €69.25 billion. This meant that pillar 2 accounted for just over 19 per cent of all agricultural spending, although member states could voluntarily increase the rate of modulation (budgetary transfers from pillar 1 to pillar 2) up to a maximum of 20 per cent (*Agra Europe*, 23 November 2005: EP/2-EP/3).

Environmental policy

Since the passage of the rural development regulation, there has been an effort to integrate agri-environmental and rural development measures. From the 1980s onwards there was concern that European agricultural policies might be generating significant negative environmental externalities. 'Environmental NGOs, the media and independent voices were central in constructing an environmentalist critique of the CAP, while environment ministries in most European countries remained cautious in confronting often larger and more influential agricultural ministries' (Lowe and Baldock, 2000: 39). The MacSharry reforms introduced an agri-environmental regulation which set up agri-environmental schemes which 'provide a means whereby government provide farmers with an incentive to adopt practices which are more sensitive environmentally' (Lowe and Baldock, 2000: 45).

Environmental policy has impacted agriculture through a series of more general directives such as the Birds Directive (1979),

the Drinking Water Directive (1980), the Nitrates Directive (1991), The Registration of Plant Products (Pesticides) Directive (1991) and the Habitats Directive (1992). These directives have not necessarily been implemented quickly or thoroughly in all member states and there is still controversy about their precise impact. Nevertheless, directives relating to water quality are particularly important given that agriculture is the major diffuse source of pollution in rivers and watercourses. The EU Water Framework Directive aims to restore inland water quality levels to 'good' by 2015 and governments have until 2009 to implement plans to overcome water management problems. The rural advisory service ADAS suggest that, given low levels of rainfall in the intensively farmed area of East Anglia, as much as half of the cultivated arable land there would have to be converted to unfertilized grassland or forest by 2015 (*Agra Europe*, 21 April 2006: N/1). These figures were not universally accepted, but even if ten per cent of the land area had to be converted, the impact on production would be substantial.

Food safety

Food safety regulation has a long history in the member states and was originally concerned with adulteration of food. However, concerns about the link between food consumption and health have grown, reinforced by the debate about obesity. Pesticide residues on food were one of the first issues to attract attention, reinforced by concerns about pollution of groundwater. Change was generally incremental and piecemeal, however, although an impetus to harmonization of national legislation was given by the 1987 Single European Act which gave the EU responsibility for 'the attainment of a high level of health protection' and the 'strengthening of consumer protection'. 'The European Community's ban from 1989 onward of hormone-fed beef production and imports was a response to heightened consumer concerns in the early and mid-1980s regarding the use of growth hormones to produce meat'. (Skogstad, 2001: 491). Food additives and their possible link with hyperactivity in children were another area of concern, particularly among mothers with young children.

Nevertheless, food safety issues remained relatively technical and were driven by a complex of variety of factors. This was shown by the controversy over bovine Somatotropin (bST) in the early 1990s. This was a naturally occurring protein hormone which it was possible to reproduce synthetically using recombinant bST technology to boost milk output per cow. It was introduced commercially in the US, being produced by firms such as Monsanto, but its commercial use was prohibited in the EU. Part of this concern was driven by public health concerns, but also by animal health concerns, with suggestions that the incidence of mastitis in cows could increase. However, of at least equal concern was the fact that increasing the productivity of cows could further disturb the supply–demand imbalance for milk in the EU, particularly if it came to be perceived as a less 'natural' product.

The debate over food safety was transformed in 1996 into a matter of high politics by the discovery of a link between a disease of the brains of cattle, bovine spongiform encephalopathy (BSE) that was first identified in 1986, and a new variant of a similar human illness, Creutzfeld-Jakob disease (NVCJD). Although the number of people that have died from NVCJD is not as great as initially feared, probably because a genetic predisposition to the disease is required, the numbers were still substantial (1,132 in the UK up to March 2006) and the fatalities occurred preponderantly among young, otherwise healthy individuals. The European Commission was threatened with a no-confidence vote from the European Parliament over its failure to protect consumers, and 'the then new Commission President, Romano Prodi, made the introduction of new and comprehensive food safety legislation the Commission's first priority' (Skogstad, 2001: 49).

Responsibility for food safety had been scattered across five directorates-general of the Commission, but was consolidated in one, the Directorate-General for Health and Consumer Protection, known as SANCO. However, 'in general, Member States are responsible for the enforcement of EU legislation and this results in wide variations across countries in how EU/EC food safety legislation has been implemented and enforced' (Skogstad, 2001: 490). A European Food Safety Authority was established, although it was beset by arguments about where it should be located and what constituted an adequate budget. 'The structure of the EFSA reflects unease about transferring national competences to an unaccountable supranational agency, so its role is restricted to strategic overview, policy advice and risk assessment, and it has no regulation and enforcement powers' (Greer, 2005: 39–40).

No food issue has caused more difficulty for the EU in recent years than that of genetically modified (GM) crops. The principal objections to their use are environmental rather than food safety related, but the idea of 'Frankstein Foods' became embedded in public perceptions, while the issue was vigorously pursued by a number of environmental non-governmental organizations. The EU instituted a *de facto* moratorium on the approval of new varieties for the EU, but this was successfully challenged by the US and other countries through the Disputes Settlement Mechanism of the World Trade Organization (WTO). A limited number of approvals have been made, but dissenting member states continue to ban GM seeds because of concerns that they might cross-fertilize with traditional crops. There are also issues about producer liability, as well as continuing disagreements on the need for laws to regulate their co-existence with organic crops, that may effectively halt their wider introduction in the EU.

Organic farming has secured an important niche within the EU food market, although because organic products are usually more expensive, they are more likely to be bought by more prosperous consumers. There is also considerable variation in the size of the organic market between EU member states with Germany having the largest market (Coleman *et al.*, 2004: 63–4). Organic farming has been portrayed by the Commission as 'a solution to a number of problems within the CAP' (Lynggaard, 2005: 240). Organic farming was institutionalized within the CAP:

> as a solution to consumer demands for the protection of the environment and as contributing to the objectives of the CAP to protect the environment and maintain the countryside. However, after the late 1990s, it was also acceptable within the CAP to refer to organic farming as a solution to problems related to food safety, the diversity of food products, food quality and animal welfare (Lynggaard, 2005: 267).

The development of a policy on organic agriculture might be seen as part of an implicit attempt to develop a two-tier approach to agriculture in the EU. Some areas would continue to be areas of intensive production, with reduced subsidies and protection, but yet competitive internationally such as the Paris Basin in France or East Anglia. Other more marginal and peripheral areas would rely more heavily on a rural policy that would stress a range of 'multifunctional' and mutually reinforcing activities such as maintaining landscapes, organic agriculture, niche production of high value added products such as specialist cheeses or ice creams and agritourism.

Impact on the Global South

Farmers in the Global South are affected by the three pillars of EU agricultural policy: export subsidies, market access barriers and domestic support. It should be remembered that most poverty in the Global South is rural poverty. Even in 2015 it is estimated that 622 million people in developing countries will be existing on incomes of less than one dollar a day (Anderson and Martin, 2006: 19).

Export subsidies are particularly damaging as they lead to the dumping of product in countries to the Global South to the detriment of local farmers. In Jamaica, import tariffs on milk powder were reduced and subsidies for local dairy farmers abolished as a result of conditions attached to a World Bank loan. This led to a quadrupling of milk powder imports into Jamaica, mostly from the EU. 'With cheap imported milk powder easily available, Jamaican food companies have been turning their backs on Jamaican fresh milk. In particular they have been cutting back on purchasing from the smallest farmers based in rural areas' (Green and Griffith, 2002: 9). In the Dominican Republic, 'the price of EU milk powder imports systematically undercuts the price of local fresh milk by 25 per cent – at least partly because of the level of EU export subsidies ... Around 10,000 farmers are thought to have been forced out of business in the past two decades' (Oxfam, 2002: 19).

Export subsidies are supposed to be phased out by 2013 if the provisional agreements made in the Doha Round trade talks are eventually ratified. However, 'Subsidy disciplines are important, but increased market access in agriculture is crucial.' (Anderson and Martin, 2006: 12). Tariffs for some agricultural products are at the three figure level in percentage terms, but even double figure tariffs effectively close the European market. The EU does have a preferential regime, embodied in the Cotonou Agreement of 2000 which replaced the earlier Lomé Convention, which offers special treatment, largely to former colonies in Africa, the Caribbean and the Pacific. This agreement 'is not WTO-compatible, but has survived under a GATT waiver, expires on January 1, 2008 and must be replaced if preferential treatment is to continue' (Bouët *et al.*, 2006: 165). Indeed, arrangements for preferential access for Caribbean bananas to the European market, particularly from the Windward Islands, were successfully challenged by the US through the WTO Disputes Settlement Mechanism, although that decision did not eliminate preferential access.

The EU's Everything But Arms initiative does allow duty- and quota-free market access for Least Developed Countries from 2009. The EU's notorious sugar regime, which sustained

European beet sugar against more competitive tropical cane sugar, underwent a fundamental reform in 2005. However, greater liberalization of international trade sugar may not benefit less developed countries like Jamaica, Mauritius or Mozambique, but more competitive producers like Brazil. These emerging countries are also able to exert greater influence in international trade negotiations. However, there is no doubt that the debate about CAP reform in recent years has been increasingly shaped by concerns about its impact on the Global South, stimulated by research-based advocacy by Third World NGOs like Oxfam and Cafod.

REFORM FOR THE TWENTY-FIRST CENTURY

The failure of Agenda 2000

Agenda 2000, agreed in 1999, was supposed to set the CAP up for Eastern enlargement, but resulted was a weak and disappointing reform. The political context was not helpful:

> Complicating factors were a weakened Commission following the resignation of Jacques Santer's team, a French President (Jacques Chirac, an ex-minister of agriculture) well versed in the intricacies of the CAP and unconvinced of the need for reform, and an inexperienced German Presidency … unwilling or unable to push France too far (Swinbank and Daugbjerg, 2006: 51).

The Farm Council at the beginning of March was delayed for two days while the German farm minister Karl-Heinz Funke and his French counterpart Jean Glavanay sought to reach agreement culminating in a working lunch in Cologne. Germany then tabled a new paper reflecting the Franco-German entente which meant that all the existing compromise papers had to be torn up with the proposed price cuts reduced. The agreement was then further diluted at the Berlin Summit with dairy reform delayed until 2005/2006. Britain's potential influence in these discussions was weakened by its preoccupation

with protecting subsidies to its large farmers. All this weak reform did was to allow the EU to keep within agreed spending limits, but it was evident that more would have to be done if it was to have a credible position in the next round of international trade talks.

The 2003 or Fischler reform

This reform was preceded by an agreement between President Chirac of France and Chancellor Schroeder of Germany at the Brussels summit in November 2002 that agreed that the overall ceiling for CAP market support expenditure (thus excluding rural development spending) would rise by no more than 1 per cent per annum between 2006 and 2013. This addressed German concerns about the budgetary cost of the CAP, but also ensured the CAP would remain intact throughout this period, limiting Prime Minister Blair's room for manoeuvre in the 2005 budget discussions.

The centrepiece of the 2003 reform was the 'decoupling' of the bulk of subsidies from January 2005 through a single farm payment which can be based on historic payments or a regional per hectare payment. 'Modulation' will start at a rate of 3 per cent in 2005, rising to 5 per cent by 2007 which by then would transfer €1.2 billion a year in funds to the second pillar. Receipt of the single payment is dependent on 'cross-compliance' with statutory environmental, food safety, animal and plant health as well as animal welfare standards.

However, member states were given considerable discretion in the way in which they implemented these changes in terms of how payments were made, the existence of 'national envelopes' or additional payments, and the option to retain an element of 'coupling' for some payments. 'In effect the CAP had undergone an element of renationalization' (Swinbank and Daugbjerg, 2006: 56). An element of this had always been retained; for example, lower fuel duties for 'red diesel' in Britain or VAT concessions in Germany.

Indeed, 'such national income supports often turned out to be more important to the marginal level of farm income than the product prices' (Knudsen, 2006: 197). Hence, one is left with a CAP 'that is increasingly less common, and second that is no longer simply about agriculture' (Greer, 2005: 202).

Tony Blair was unsuccessful in obtaining major changes in the CAP during the budget discussions of 2006 and the review to be undertaken during 2008–2009 during the 2007–2013 budgetary period is likely to be limited in scope and effect, if only because of the Chirac–Schroeder agreement which preserves the basic budgetary parameters of the CAP. However, if the Doha Round does reach a conclusion, and export subsidies are phased out, this will put increasing pressure on domestic subsidies. The run up to 2013 therefore looks like being a crucial period for the future of CAP during which some fundamental decisions about its shape and content may have to be taken.

CONCLUSIONS

European agriculture has undergone an economic, social and technological transformation, although this has been more marked in Western than in Eastern Europe where small-scale semi-subsistence farming still survives to a significant extent in some countries. With some difficulty the CAP has been reshaped to be more responsive to market forces and the concerns of consumers and more sensitive to environmental considerations. We are still, however, far short of a policy which forms an integrated social policy addressing the special needs of rural areas of which agriculture forms just one part. Farmers, of course, have grown accustomed to a subsidy regime and would argue that they have difficult in getting a fair return from the market with power shifting up the food chain to increasingly dominant retailers. There has always been an analytical case for converting subsidies into a capital bond

which a specified life which could either be used as an income supplement or sold to provide capital for expansion or diversification, but achieving political support for that policy is always more difficult (Swinbank and Tranter, 2004).

The period since the late 1990s has seen the emergence of a European model of agriculture that 'brings together a number of assumptions about the nature of rural space and the central role of agriculture in defining and producing that space' (Potter, 2004: 16). In particular, multifunctionality 'has become the "European model of agriculture"' (Landau, 2001: 915). European policy-makers have favoured an interpretation 'that joint production of agricultural and environmental goods is widespread throughout the EU, but that the broad multifunctionality to which this gives rise is vulnerable to market liberalization, justifying continued safety-net state aids and a system of support designed to keep farmers on the land' (Potter, 2004: 17). This justification for continued European 'exceptionalism' plays well within Europe, but less well outside it, despite attempts to form a group of 'friends of multifunctionality' within the WTO that attracted support from countries like Japan who wish to maintain existing systems of agriculture.

The greatest damage that is done by CAP is to Europe's image in the wider world (and many of the European countries outside the EU are, if anything, more protectionist). The EU's subsidy and protection of agriculture causes tensions in its relationship with the US and agricultural exporters such as Brazil and Australia, but above all it is seen as disadvantaging the least developed countries in the Global South and the poorest segments of their populations. The CAP thus conveys an image of a Europe that is protectionist, sclerotic, over-regulated and slow to change. In some ways, this is an unfair picture as much of European agriculture is technologically advanced, dynamic in its deployment of new and more environmentally friendly methods of cultivation, responsive to changing patterns of consumer demand and capable of diversifying into new activities. Europe's large food industry is made up of a mix of large international firms and smaller niche producers and is highly innovative in terms of products and processes. It is the politics of European agriculture which is its most backward aspect and which in many respects is holding back European agriculture and damaging international understandings of Europe.

REFERENCES

Ackrill, R. (2000) *The Common Agricultural Policy*. Sheffield: Sheffield University Press.

Anderson, K. and Martin, W. (2006) 'Agriculture, trade reform and the Doha Agenda' in K. Anderson and W. Martin (eds) *Agricultural Trade Reform and the Doha Development Agenda*. Basingstoke: Palgrave Macmillan, pp. 3–35.

Atkin, M. (1993) *Snouts in the Trough: European Farmers, the Common Agricultural Policy and the Public Purse*. Abington: Woodhead Publishing.

Bouët, A., Fontagné, L. and Sébastien, J. (2006) 'Is erosion of tariff preferences a serious concern?' in K. Anderson and W. Martin (eds) *Agricultural Trade Reform and the Doha Development Agenda*. Basingstoke: Palgrave Macmillan, pp. 161–192.

Coleman, W., Grant, W. and Josling, T. (2004) *Agriculture in the New Global Economy*. Cheltenham: Edward Elgar.

Coleman, W.D. and Tangermann, S. (1999) 'The 1992 CAP reform, the Uruguay round and the commission: Conceptualizing linked policy games', *Journal of Common Market Studies*, 37 (3): 385–405.

Daugbjerg, C. (1999) 'Reforming the CAP: Policy networks and broader institutional structures', *Journal of Common Market Studies*, 37 (3): 407–428.

Fearne, A. (1997) 'The history and development of the CAP, 1945–1960' in C. Ritson and D. Harvey (eds) *The Common Agricultural Policy*, 2nd edn. Wallingford: CAB International, pp. 11–55.

Fennell, R. (1997) *The Common Agricultural Policy*. Oxford: Clarendon Press.

Gardner, B. (1996) *European Agriculture*. London: Routledge.

Grant, W. (1997) *The Common Agricultural Policy*. Basingstoke: Macmillan.

Green, D. and Griffith, M. (2002) *Dumping on the Poor*. London: Cafod.

Greer, A. (2005) *Agricultural Policy in Europe*. Manchester: Manchester University Press.

Hendriks, G. (1991) *Germany and European Integration*. Oxford: Berg.

Johnson, D.G. (1991) *World Agriculture in Disarray*, 2nd edn. Basingstoke: Macmillan.

Kay, A. (2003), 'Path dependency and the CAP', *Journal of European Public Policy*, 10 (3): 405–420.

Keane, M. and Lucy, D. (1997) 'The CAP and the farmer' in C. Ritson and D. Harvey (eds) *The Common Agricultural Policy*, 2nd edn. Wallingford: CAB International, pp. 227–239.

Knudsen, A.-C. (2001) *Defining the Policies of the Common Agricultural Policy. A Historical Study*. PhD thesis, European University Instititute.

Knudsen, A.-C. (2006) 'European integration in the image and the shadow of agriculture' in D. Dinan (ed.) *Origins and Evolution of the European Union*. Oxford: Oxford University Press, pp. 191–217.

Landau, A. (2001) 'The agricultural negotiations in the WTO: The same old story?', *Journal of Common Market Studies*, 39 (5): 913–925.

Lowe, P. and Baldock, D. (2000) 'Integration of environmental objectives into agricultural policy-making' in F. Brouwer and P. Lowe (eds) *CAP Regimes and the European Countryside*. Wallingford: CABI Publsihing, pp. 31–52.

Lowe, P., Buller, H. and Ward, N. (2002) 'Setting the next agenda? British and French approaches to the second pillar of the Common Agricultural Policy', *Journal of Rural Studies*, 18: 1–17.

Lynggaard, K. (2005) *The Common Agricultural Policy and the Dynamics of Institutional Change: Illustrations from Organic Farming in the European Union*. Odense: University Press of Southern Denmark.

Moyer, H.W. and Josling, T.E. (1990) *Agricultural policy reform: Politics and Process in the EC and USA*. Hemel Hempstead: Harvester Wheatsheaf.

Moyer, W. and Josling. T. (2002) *Agricultural Policy Reform: Politics and Process in the EU and US in the 1990s*. Aldershot: Ashgate.

Neville-Rolfe, E. (1984) *The Politics of Agriculture in the European Community*. London: Policy Studies Institute.

OECD (1994) *Review of Agricultural Policies: Hungary*. Paris: Organisation for Economic Cooperation and Development.

Oxfam (2002) 'Milking the CAP', Oxfam Briefing Paper 34, London.

Potter, C. (2004) 'Multifunctionality as an agricultural and rural policy concept' in F. Brouwer (ed.) *Sustaining Agriculture and the Rural Environment*. Cheltenham: Edward Elgar, pp. 15–35.

Répassy, H. and Symes, D. (1993) 'Perspectives on Agrarian reform in East–Central Europe', *Sociologia Ruralis*, 33: 81–91.

Rieger, E. (2000) 'The Common Agricultural policy' in H. Wallace and W. Wallace (eds) *Policy-Making in the European Union*, 4th edn. Oxford: Oxford University Press, pp. 179–210.

Sheingate, A.D. (2001) *The Rise of the Agricultural Welfare State*. Princeton: Princeton University Press.

Skogstad, G. (2001) 'The WTO and food safety regulatory policy innovation in the European Union', *Journal of Common Market Studies*, 30 (3): 485–505.

Swinbamk, A. and Daugbjerg, C. (2006) 'The 2003 CAP reform: Accommodating WTO pressures', *Comparative European Politics*, 4 (1): 47–64.

Swinbank, A. and Tranter, R. (eds) (2004) *A Bond Scheme for Common Agricultural Policy Reform*. Wallingford: CABI Publishing.

Tangermann, S. (1998) 'An ex-post review of the 1992 MacSharry Reform' in K.A. Ingersent, A.J. Rayner and R.C. Hine (eds) *The Reform of the Common Agricultural Policy*. Basingstoke: Macmillan, pp. 12–35.

Tracy, M. (1989) *Government and Agriculture in Western Europe 1880–1988*, 3rd edn. Hemel Hempstead: Harvester Wheatsheaf.

Wilson, G.A. and Wilson, O.J. (2001) *German Agriculture in Transition*. Basingstoke: Palgrave.

16

Europe and Global Governance

José M. Magone

The developments in European political, economic, social and cultural spaces in the past 50 years have been of utmost importance to the emergence of many aspects of the global governance agenda. However, it has been just one among many such continental and regional expressions of this kind. In terms of definition, we must avoid conflating the concept of Europe as a multiple space in which actors shape a multilayered governance system, with the supranational organization, the European Union. There are different dimensions of Europe which create different organizational configurations. In turn, these are interconnected and feed off each other. On one hand, this multilayered, multilevel and multidimensional conceptualization of Europe has to be regarded as one of the strengths of the continent. It is wise to speak of 'multiple Europes' in order to show that the continent is not a single entity (Rumford, 2002: 271–2). The different identities produced in this way are not exclusive, but complement, making it possible to see this intertwined political, economic, social and cultural European space as the most advanced regional expression of interconnectedness and global governance. As a result, the European model of capitalism, based on social protection and high standards in environmental protection has been presented

as a model that should be expanded worldwide (Teló, 2006: 152–171). The so-called European social model was and remains a powerful ideological construct to change the nature of world capitalism towards one of sustainable development and a 'non-hegemonic culture of global relations'. Additionally, the model is employed by those arguing for a move from unilaterialism to multilaterialism (Lamy and Laidi, 2002: 9–12; Laidi, 2006).

However, whilst Göran Therborn characterized Europe as the 'Scandinavia of the world' (Therborn, 1997), research into the relationship between European and global governance would be well advised to avoid such analysis, as it would simplify and ignore the wide range of diversity within Europe and globally (on this tendency, see Ágh, 2006: 193–4). There is a continuing learning process ongoing between Europe and other regions of the world, as methods of global governance are passed on. At the centre of this is the potential to, in the long-term, overcome nationalism. As a consequence, the multiplicity of Europes are moving away from the narrow national identities that have previously defined them, and towards a more open, cosmopolitan world society (Boon and Delanty, 2007: 19). It follows that European studies must reorient future research away from narrow 'methodological nationalism' towards an open 'methodological cosmopolitanism' without being caught out by a nationally inspired 'methodological Europeanism' (Beck, 2007: 46). European studies provides the ideal research area to explore the relationship between localism and cosmopolitanism, and it's the latter's expression of European identities that are both endogenous and exogenous. It means that at the centre of research in European studies should be the interaction between the regional governance created by the 'multiplicity of Europes' and global governance in the context of an emerging world society.

In this chapter, we intend to look at different approaches that the growing interaction of the different Europes and global governance has stimulated. Clearly, such an endeavour first requires us to discuss the term global governance and arrive at an effective definition. This task is undertaken in the next section of this chapter. This is followed by a section which discusses the different dimensions of 'European governance'. Although many of these dimensions are overlapping and shape each other, for analytical purposes we differentiate between approaches dealing with the political, security, economy and the social/cultural dimensions of European governance in relation to global governance. The next section of this chapter consists of a discussion of how the European Union is engaging with global institutions and other regions, and creating a dialogue between the emerging European model of governance in global politics. Finally, the chapter ends with some conclusions.

GLOBAL GOVERNANCE AND REGIONAL GOVERNANCE

Although they are interlinked, there are major differences between government and governance. James N. Rosenau differentiates government from governance as follows:

[G]overnance is not synonymous with government. Both refer to purposive behaviour, to goal-oriented activities, to systems of rule; but government suggests activities that are backed by formal authority, by police powers to insure the implementation of duly constituted policies, whereas governance refers to activities backed by shared goals that may or may not derive from legal and formally prescribed responsibilities and that do not necessarily rely on police powers to overcome defiance and attain compliance. Governance, in other words, is a more encompassing phenomenon than government. It embraces governmental institutions, but it also subsumes informal, non-governmental mechanisms whereby those persons and organizations within its purview move ahead, satisfy their needs, and fulfil their wants (Rosenau, 2000: 4).

One can locate the beginning of transition from thinking about government to governance in the mid-1970s, the high days of the welfare state in most Western democracies. The emergence of the philosophy new public management (NPM) created the conditions for the emergence of governance as a third form of coordination and organization besides hierarchies (government) and markets (economy). Governance has elements of both, and as such is deemed a more efficient way of delivering public and private services, but it is definitely oriented towards flat hierarchy and horizontal structures (Sbragia, 2000).

The rigid structures of government until the 1970s began to be replaced by more flexible forms of policy decision making. In particular, this involved the use of public–private partnerships in the delivery of public goods. The use of public–private partnerships by the British government under Prime Minister Margaret Thatcher, and the US government under Ronald Reagan in the 1980s contributed to a blurring of the boundaries between government and the economy. Moreover, the growing importance of civil society organizations played a major role in creating a triangle of relationships that contributed to the transformation of policy-making globally. This triangle included public actors (government or public institutions), private actors (enterprises, regulatory agencies), and civil society actors (non-governmental organizations, political parties and interest groups). Governance can be characterized as an interactive network of interactions of these public, private and civil society actors and their respective action rationales(political, economic and civic), which allow for more dynamic mixed structures and processes to emerge, which are inter-organisational, self-organising and aim at solving concrete problems (Aberbach, 2003; Rhodes, 1997).

NPM is now used at all levels of global politics. The OECD countries set the pace of the reform in relation to the developing and less developed countries. Governance is referred to in the publications of international institutions, such as the World Bank and the International Monetary Fund, who see it as a positive measure to create market mechanisms and move countries towards democracy. Good governance entails a virtuous cycle towards successful reform of economies in the developing and less developed world. A wider definition also includes respect for human rights, democratic accountability and transparency.

One of the major transformations of world politics has been the emergence of what has been labelled 'global governance'. This concept is widely used in the institutions of the United Nations and implies the growing importance of a complex web of coordinating policy tasks undertaken at the global level. Examples of such coordinating tasks include the fundraising, organization and distribution of aid to catastrophe and war victims; the monitoring and control of infectious diseases; the negotiation and implementation of trade agreements; and the monitoring and control of global climate change.

What we are experiencing is the transition from an 'international society of states', which shared common rules of the game and a culture of behaviour, towards a 'global society of states and non-state actors'. Global governance does acknowledge the important role that states still play in the world system, but recognizes that reality has become more complex due to the emergence of new actors, such as non-governmental organizations, stronger international organizations, transnational corporations,

and private and public regulatory agencies. According to Fulvio Attinà, we can already speak of a global political system, even if it is incomplete and still emerging (Attinà, 2003). Naturally, there are different regimes of governance related to the different policy areas. Economic governance will deal with issues of economic and monetary stability. The Asian crisis of 1998 is a good example of how international organizations and the G8 tried to halt the collapse in the region's economies. In international conflicts, political governance related to diplomatic negotiations, decisions on the deployment of troops, and monitoring of agreements have become a more complex process with many tools accumulated over decades of practice. Probably the most urgent example comes from environmental governance, in which the International Panel for Global Climate Change (IPCC) interacts with United Nations organizations, non-governmental organizations, and states to achieve policy solutions to the problem. In this sense, what is labelled as 'global governance' consists of many fragmented policy regimes, some of them exclusively involving public or private actors, and some a mix of both (Elliott, 2002: 58–60). Global governance precludes a restructuring of the world architecture between states, supranational, intergovernmental and subnational institutions, all of them increasingly integrated in continental regional and transcontinental subsystems of governance, although this vision exists as a heuristic theoretical device with which to analyse current events in long-term perspective. This chapter tries to shed some light on the contribution that actors in the European space have made to global governance. In the end the picture remains incomplete and the chapter can merely provide some avenues for prospective future research.

The growth in complexity induced by the spatiotemporal rhythm of global capitalism through the processes of globalization is creating pressures upon states to denationalize certain functions and policies, and transfer them to shared sovereignty regimes. Such shared sovereignty regimes – for example, environmental policy, police cooperation, immigration control, trade liberalization and global economic stability – enhance global governance. This interaction among different actors in different policy regimes does not happen only at global level. Global governance has to be conceptualized as a multilevel system that includes the global, the supranational and intergovernmental, regional, national and subnational. Interactions between all these levels are contributing to the expansion of the global governance system. The density of these interactions in partial regimes of governance is uneven, meaning that in certain areas one can already find sophisticated, well-coordinated networks that lead to successful solutions being found to policy problems. In other cases though, regimes are still in their infancy. According to Michael Zürn, we are experiencing a societal denationalization. He describes a society as denationalized 'when transactions within national borders are no denser than transnational transactions' (Zürn, 2002: 237). Global governance has, therefore, to be conceptualized functionally by concentrating on partial policy regimes, and territorially by looking at the interactions between global, supranational and intergovernmental, transnational, national, regional, transregional, and subnational levels. In most cases, the functional and territorial levels are intrinsically linked. According to Dirk Messner, such relationships between global and regional governance structures are an important condition for successful world politics (Messner, 2002: 59).

THE DIFFERENT DIMENSIONS OF GOVERNANCE IN EUROPE: THE CENTRALITY OF THE COUNCIL OF EUROPE

The political dimension: a community of democratic states

European political integration has been one of the main areas of European studies research.

In this respect, the experience of organizational Europes, particularly the European Union and the Council of Europe, is of great relevance for the study of global governance, especially since the EU has expanded to have 27 members. Regardless of its advanced complexity of governance, the EU itself is characterized by different levels of integration. At the core are the 15 countries of the Eurozone. There are member states that have opted out of other arrangements; for example, Ireland and the UK from the Schengen Agreement and the UK, Sweden and Denmark from Economic and Monetary Union. However, there are also differences between these countries. While the UK and Sweden are not part of the exchange rate mechanism, the Danish krone is pegged to the euro. Despite these exceptions, the European Union has achieved the highest level of integration of any regional actor. This becomes quite visible in World Trade Organization (WTO) negotiations in which the EU negotiates on behalf of its member states, as well as Iceland, Norway and Liechtenstein, all members of the European Economic Area (EEA). Although the EU has expanded considerably in the past 30 years, it would be a mistake to conflate it with Europe. Organizationally, Europe is quite diverse and is a multilayered space. Other organizational layers such as the Council of Europe (CoE), the Organization for Security and Cooperation in Europe (OSCE), the North Atlantic Treaty Organization (NATO), and the Organization for Economic Cooperation and Development (OECD) cooperate with the EU, but also contribute to the organizational diversity and complexity of Europe. Furthermore, in recent decades Europe has experienced a boom of organizations working at the subnational level. This is partly to aid lobbying for EU structural funds, as well as the EU's regional policies, but it also reflects a rise in awareness of subnational regions. Among such organizations one can cite the Association of European Regions (AER), the European Association of Border Regions (AEBR), the Conference of Peripheral and Maritime Regions (CPMR), and the Association of Regions of Industrial Tradition (ARIT). This has reinforced the importance of subnational-level institutions to both national and supra-national decision making (Balme, 1999). One also speaks of a parallel foreign policy, also known as 'paradiplomacy', of the more self-conscious regions such as Scotland, Catalonia, and Baden-Württemberg (Aldecoa and Keating, 1999). The programmes of the European Union such as the INTERREG (to foster development between EU border regions and those of third countries) allow for a stronger engagement of the regions with different levels of the European governance system. This includes engagement at the supranational level through the Committee of the Regions and Local Authorities (CoR) and other channels. Although the CoR has only consultative powers, it allows for the presence of the subnational level within the decision-making process (Muñoa, 1999). Similarly, the CoE established the Congress of Regional and Local Authorities, which meets once a year in Strasbourg, and consists of 344 members, so as to include the input of subnational entities into their resolution. Traditional state sovereignty is being eroded from above and below (Christiansen and Jorgensen, 2000). This means that the national state has to restructure its political system to accommo-date a growing awareness of its subnational entities and increasing pressure to communi-tarize policies, such as immigration, police cooperation, competition policy and regional policy. The consequence of this is the building of what Wallace calls 'shared sovereignty' (1999) or most recently 'post-sovereignty' (2005). Marks links the emergence of EU multilevel governance (MLG) to this upgrading of regional policy (1993: 401).

In another study, Marks and his team have shown that regions used the new structure of opportunities to open up multiple channels for lobbying and influence. This 'multiple crack' strategy is most visible in Brussels, where regions from different countries have established offices of representation (Marks *et al.*, 1996). A recent study by Marks *et al.* shows that the influence of these offices is quite different from country to country and that levels of funding plays a major role in allowing for a stronger protagonism. This confirms the uneven development of this multilevel, multilayered European governance system (Marks *et al.*, 2002).

The actor-centred MLG approach has cer-tainly advanced our understanding of the European Union. Slowly, the approach is also being used to understand the relationship between regional and global governance sys-tems (Magone, 2006; Smith, 2004a; Teló, 2006). Nevertheless, the MLG approach has still not attempted to link other expressions of organizational Europe, such as the Council of Europe and the Organization for Security and Cooperation in Europe (OSCE). The main reason may be the role that national sover-eignty plays in these organizations. While the European Union has characteristics of post-sovereign governance, there are other European organizations that still work intergovernmen-tally and where sovereignty matters. Probably the most important organization in terms of membership is the Council of Europe, which was founded on 5 May 1949 in London and predates the European Union. It consists of 47 members from a wider Europe, including countries from the Caucasus. Its intergovern-mental nature has allowed for considerable enlargement. In comparison with the European Union, which has a budget of about €100 bil-lion, the European Council is disadvantaged with a mere €180.5 million. Nevertheless, one has to acknowledge that the Council of Europe is an extremely important forum, acting as a European zone of democratic peace. Due to its intergovernmental nature, resolutions and decisions can take quite a long time, but they establish important principles for democratic life in the member states. The CoE has also become an antechamber to join-ing the European Union. If a country does not comply with the minimal requirements of the Council of Europe, it is not able to join the EU. Human rights, pluralist liberal democracy and the rule of law are important areas in which the Council of Europe intervenes and shapes national legislation. The European

Court of Human Rights (ECHR), which is part of the Council of Europe, and remains the last instance of appeal for European countries after all national appeal procedures have been exhausted. The ECHR was dormant between the 1950s and 1970s, but since then has gained an important new role in an integrated Europe. It also shows the multilayered nature of European governance (Storey, 1995: 141–2). The ECHR is linked to courts at the global level; for example, the International Court of Justice and the new International Criminal Court. There are also strong links to the European Union. The whole policy of human rights of the European Union is shaped by long-standing policies of the Council of Europe. Several human rights and democracy enhancement projects are being implemented in the former Yugoslavian and Soviet republics, most notably Bosnia-Herzegovina, Russia and the Ukraine.

The crucial document of the ECHR is the Convention for the Protection of Human Rights and Fundamental Freedoms which was adopted in 1953. Since then, 13 Protocols were added to the Convention, including the right of individuals to appeal directly to the Court (Protocol 9). The Convention and the follow-up protocols are based on the 1948 United Nations Universal Declaration of Human Rights, demonstrating its strong linkage to the policies of the United Nations (Council of Europe, 2006). The Council of Europe has been an important watchdog of developments towards democracy in many countries. For example, the Council of Europe condemned the violation of human rights and the lack of democracy in Belarus, which is still going on and still closely monitored by this intergovernmental organisation.

Moreover, the secret rendition flights of the American Central Intelligence Agency (CIA) were first investigated by the Parliamentary Assembly of the Council of Europe and led to a critical report by the Swiss politician Dick Marty, in which such practices were condemned (*Financial Times*, 25 January 2006: 9). Due to its intergovernmental structure and lack of resources, the Council of Europe and

particularly the ECHR act more as a moral and ethical instance above the national concerns of member states in Europe and indirectly across the world.

The security dimension: the politics of democratic peace

The most important security organization in Europe is NATO, which was founded in 1949 in order to contain the communist threat. NATO was a product of the Cold War and had as its counterpart the Warsaw Pact coalition, which consisted of all Central and Eastern European countries and the Soviet Union. Since the fall of the Berlin Wall in 1989, NATO has struggled to find a new mission. Slowly, it has become clear that the aftermath of the Cold War has created instabilities in many of these Central and Eastern European countries. In 1991, NATO developed a new strategic concept which identified these new instabilities in the Central and Eastern European countries as the danger to peace in Europe. NATO has developed a new role, acting as a regional security organization for the United Nations and the OSCE. It began to play an important role in the Balkans: Bosnia-Herzegovina since 1995, and Kosovo since 1999 being probably the most important deployments. NATO's bombardment of Serbia during the Kosovo War was an important milestone in the development of this new role (Lepgold, 2001: 231–2). In terms of European governance, NATO was an important antechamber for democratization of the Central and Eastern European Countriess. Although NATO is a military organization, all the Central and Eastern European countries were keen to join as soon as possible. After decades under Soviet occupation and dominance, these new democracies regarded NATO as a way to protect themselves from such situations in the future. The expansion of NATO was not seen positively by the new Russian Federation. The Partnership for Peace (PfP) was devised to include Russia in the new European security architecture. It was also quite difficult for the European Union to overcome NATO. The members of NATO do not coincide with the members of the European Union. Moreover, some neutrals, such as Austria, Sweden, Finland and Ireland, are unwilling to join NATO. Turkey was a member of NATO but not of the European Union. The compromise reached was that NATO would remain a central pillar of the European security architecture. Simultaneously, the European Union was allowed to develop its own coordinating political–military structures and foreign policy. The Amsterdam and Nice Treaty established the High Representative of Common Foreign and Security Policy, attached to the Council of Ministers, which led to the appointment of Javier Solana from Spain. There should not be any overlap of deployments, and the EU and NATO should complement each other. EU peacekeeping forces have now been deployed in Macedonia in order to prevent violence between Macedonians and the Albanian minority, and in the Democratic Republic of Congo (Schimmelfennig, 2003; Smith, 2004b).

Most recently, NATO has deployed peacekeeping and combat troops in Afghanistan; their main task is to help rebuild the country and fight against the Taliban. It is part of the 'war on terrorism' announced by the American administration after the 11 September 2001 attacks on the Twin Towers by Al-Qaeda. NATO is also involved in the training of security forces in Iraq and provides logistical support to the African Union mission in Darfur. Moreover, it provided assistance during the Southeast Asian tsunami of early 2005, Hurricane Katrina in the US, and the earthquake in Pakistan. This expansion of NATO to non-European arenas is, on the one hand, making this organization integrated in security aspects of global governance, but, on the other hand, it is overstretching its human and material resources. There are now plans to expand membership of NATO to Australia, Japan, and New Zealand (Daalder and Goldgeier, 2006). Ivo Daalder and James Goldgeier (2006) have therefore called it 'global NATO' to highlight the potential

transformation of this transatlantic regional organization into a global one.

The European security architecture is complemented by the OSCE. Over the past three decades, this organization has contributed massively to the establishment of a democratic peace zone. The fall of the Berlin Wall in 1989 strengthened the position of the OSCE in the overall European security architecture. In terms of membership, the organization is quite diverse, stretching over three continents: North America, Europe, and Asia. Nevertheless, it acts an important forum to build common purposes and alliances in order to deal with the major problems of security in the European continent, which now are more likely to involve combating criminal activities, such as drug running, illegal immigration, and arms trafficking. The OSCE also fulfils important election observation missions and contributes to the monitoring of peace-building measures. The OSCE has been quite critical of elections in Russia, Ukraine, Belarus, and other countries in the Caucasus. There was also a deployment of election observers in Afghanistan, showing the expanding role of the organization (Barry, 2004). It is an important watchdog which works closely with the European Union, Council of Europe and United Nations organizations.

The new European security architecture after the Cold War created a democratic peace space which has enlarged outwards through cooperation policies, such as the European Neighbourhood Policy of the EU. The objective is to expand democratic peace beyond the European space, making it part of global governance. This is certainly a policy that converges with those of international organizations (Flynn and Farrell, 1999; Geeraerts and Stouthuysen, 1999).

The economic dimension of Europe: the politics of the Single European Market

The most visible expression of the global reach of the European Union is the Single

Market Project and the Lisbon Strategy. All European countries and neighbouring regions are still adjusting to these developments. The EU directives and recommendations mainly target the Single European Market (SEM). Regardless of the introduction of the euro in 2002, the SEM is far from being a reality. The division in national markets is still one of the main characteristics of the European economy. One of the reasons for pushing forward the SEM was the need to enhance European competitiveness compared with the US and Japan (Cecchini, 1988). In the long term, it is expected that greater economies of scale will emerge in the European continent. The number of mergers and acquisitions within the EU, and between the EU and other regions has increased considerably. There is still a low level of mobility among the labour force in Europe, and some areas, such as the services sector, are still too compartmentalized and protected by national markets. There is a danger that the European Union will lose out, as it will be unable to achieve greater efficiency in this emerging economic space. The rise of China and India are major pressures for the European Union to develop in this direction (Piening, 1998: 203).These changes will also enshrine the need to continue on the path of economic reform in many European countries, most notably Germany, France, Italy, Belgium, Poland, Spain and Portugal (Magone, 2006: 188–91).

According to Manuel Castells, Europe, which has at its centre the European Union, has become one of the three main centres of the world economy, along with North America and the Asian Pacific. These three core economic regions of informational capitalism each have a respective hinterland. North America has Latin America, Europe dominates Russia and the Southern Mediterranean, and Japan and the Asian Pacific rule economically over the rest of Asia, as well as Australia and New Zealand, and maybe the Russian Pacific, Eastern Siberia and Kazakhstan. Moreover, Castells argues that Africa and the Middle East are also integrated

into this structure through, respectively, neocolonial networks and global energy supply networks. Nevertheless, he is also aware that the new world economy is characterized by a combination of enduring architecture and variable geometry (Castells, 2000: 145–6).

As already mentioned, the OECD fulfils an important function by setting best practice benchmarks across Europe. Although the majority of its members are European, it is an international organization containing all the developed nations of world. This means that OECD benchmarking and best practice examples condition all developing regions globally. In summary, the economic dimension is a crucial aspect of the relationship between Europe and global governance. The ambition of the European Union and subjacent areas to become one of the most competitive and dynamic regions of the world by 2010 is unrealistic. Nevertheless, the thrust towards economic integration will remain an important factor in this context and may lead to the increasing importance of Europe in the global economy.

The social and cultural dimension: towards a world society?

Some decades ago John Burton developed the concept of world society to characterize the growing global multilayered integration of different dimensions (Burton, 1972). Burton's general idea was taken over by one of the most important German sociologists: Niklas Luhmann. The Luhmanite concept of *Weltgesellschaft* has led to the establishment of a school of thought at the University of Bielefeld which uses his vast social theoretical writings to undertake empirical research. The 'world society' concept of Niklas Luhmann goes beyond Burton's meaning of it, because it clearly argues that we are moving towards a global integration of local,national, regional social living forms both diachronically and synchronically. All of these social experiences are no longer nationally compartmentalized but shared by the whole world. This world society is char-acterized by an autopoietic development, meaning that it organizes itself. We are all part of this world society and it is difficult for us to escape from it. Luhmann clearly shows that European society is already part of a larger whole world society due to its accu-mulated sociology of knowledge. European society in a restrictive sense does not exist anymore. Due to the communicative integra-tion of the world, all regional societies are only expressions of world society when we take a historical long-term perspective (Luhmann, 1998: 145–71). Richard Münch also makes us aware of the growing integra-tion of the world through the new communi-cation technologies. This is leading to a marketization of culture, and the increased dominance of Western culture over other regions. He presents the main consequences of the transition from the industrial to what he calls the 'communication society', and clearly links the sociological interpretation to the impact of the modern world system as defined by Immanuel Wallerstein (Münch, 1991, 1993). Most recently, Chris Rumford linked the EU to the globalization paradigm. In his *European Union. A Political Sociology* he reads the European integration process through the lens of global processes. In contrast to the sociological–economic approach of Manuel Castells, he advocates a multidimensional approach towards understanding the making and development of the European Union. Rumford is also quite critical of the tendency among scholars to conflate the European Union with Europe. He speaks of 'different Europes', which are multilayered and inte-grated in different arrangements (Rumford, 2002: see chapter 2; 271–2). These approaches look beyond a mere European perspective and offer quite advanced interpretations of Europe as an expression of global governance.

More settled empirical studies on the con-vergence of regional societies have been pub-lished since the late 1980s. Among them is that of the historian Hartmut Kaeble who, in his comparative study of Japan, USA, Soviet Union and Europe, identified key patterns towards a European society in the making. He clearly outlines the main differences of European society in relation to American, the Soviet (as was) and Japanese societies. Among the main distinctive features of European Society noted is the low level of social mobility and of inequality (Kaeble, 1987: 75–6; Kaeble, 1997; Kaeble, 2005).

Further studies on the convergence of national societies towards a European one have been undertaken by Stefan Hradil, Stefan Immerfall, and Göran Therborn. These studies confirm that there is a growing con-vergence between European national socie-ties, but that diversity continues to persist, particularly in relation to cultural differences, inequalities and quality of life. This work is all contextualized in the transition from industrial to post-industrial society (Hradil and Immerfall, 1997: 20–22; Immerfall, 1995; Therborn, 1995).

In a very interesting contribution Göran Therborn characterized Europe as the 'Scandinavia of the world', showing that in all major development indicators European countries mostly have positive figures – this despite the persistence of intraregional dif-ferences (Therborn, 1997). Most recently, Gerard Delanty and Chris Rumford put forward the thesis that we have to embrace a multilay-ered diverse Europe and change our mindset to a cosmopolitan way of thinking. They predict the emergence of a cosmopolitan Europe, which is different from just a distinc-tive European society (Delanty and Rumford, 2005: 194). While Kaeble *et al.* provide us with hard facts about the convergence of national patterns of behaviour diachronically, Delanty and Rumford show that cosmopoli-tanism is slowly becoming part of the identity of the different Europes. There is a danger that Therborn's characterization of Europe as being the 'Scandinavia of the world' could be used as a justification to impose it on other parts of the world (see also Inglehart and Welzel, 2005). This is certainly the wrong approach in a system of global governance that should celebrate a diversity of demo-cratic expressions.

While Gerard Delanty and Chris Rumford are sceptical about the midterm creation of a European *demos*, which is distinctive from national populations, Cris Shore's anthropological study *Building Europe* sees many similarities between the process of nation-building and the European integration process. Influenced by Benedict Anderson's *Imagined Communities*, Shore allocates the European political elites and its growing administrative structures an important role in symbolic production and interaction in order to create a cultural framework for the populations of the European Union (Shore, 2000: 32–7).

Parallel to the discussion about global civil society, there has been also an intensive discussion about European civil society. This is comprised of all the different interest groups that are engaged in shaping and influencing policy-making in the EU and intergovernmentally in the other European forums. Meanwhile, the Economic and Social Committee of the European Union has developed the concept of 'organized European civil society', that comprises all Eurogroups represented at supranational level and have to register with the main institutions, particularly the European Commission and the European Parliament. The comitology of the European Commission allows interest groups to send representatives, who may then shape consultation processes related to new policy initiatives. Meanwhile, there are over 2,000 interest groups (including lobbying firms) and 10,000 lobbyists working in Brussels. During the European Convention of 2002–2003 (which was in charge of drafting the European Constitution) involved 547 interest groups and produced 1,251 contributions (Greenwood, 2003; Magone, 2006: 172–85). European civil society is regarded as a means to democratize the highly technocratic approach of European Union institutions, nevertheless there is still a long way to go in order to speak of a complementary European citizenship that would take part in such organized civil society (Mascia, 2004). Organized civil society interest groups are also integrated into the Council of Europe. They have several regular meetings and take part in joint projects concerned with the enhancement of democracy and human rights in Europe. The Council of Europe also plays an important role highlighting violation of the rights of minorities (Council of Europe, 2006).

In summary, the attractiveness of Europe for other regions of the world, and ultimately as a possible structure of global governance, remains quite strong. It is its multilayered, multilevel, complex system of interorganizational networks that makes its example so worth looking at. Transformations are taking place in political, security, economic, and social–cultural dimensions, although analytically differentiated, they are naturally interlinked and feed off each other. This will certainly remain a central area of research for European studies.

EUROPE AS A GLOBAL ACTOR

The most efficient global actor in Europe is the European Union. Therefore, this section will discuss the impact of the EU on global governance institutions such as the United Nations and the WTO. One should keep in mind that other European organizations are also engaged in managing conflicts and processes of global governance. We have already mentioned the engagement of the OSCE in Afghanistan and many Central Asian countries, and the possibility of NATO becoming an organization with global reach. Japan is the main country that is interested in taking part in both in NATO and OSCE. The OECD is dominated by European countries, but comprises the richest economies across the world, including the US and Japan. Moreover, the Council of Europe has five observers, four of them being from other continents: The Holy See, the US, Canada, Mexico and Japan (Council of Europe, 2006). In the next pages we will discuss the impact of the EU on international organizations, particularly the United Nations and WTO. Thereafter, the inter-regional cooperation with other parts of the world is highlighted.

The European Union and the institutions of global governance

The fall of the Berlin Wall in 1989 and the subsequent end of the Cold War between the US and the Soviet Union was an important liberating moment for the European Community (only renamed as the European Union in 1993). In the 1990s, the European Union had to deal with this new situation, to develop global policies, and become a global actor. The growing importance of the EU at global level had spill over effects on the other European organizations. The EU has always sought to establish synergies, due to the very limited resources at its disposal. A major effort to redefine the policies of the European Union came at the end of the 1990s and continued into the new millennium. The White Paper on European Governance issued in 2001 has to be regarded as an important milestone in this process of policy formulation. The European Union clearly decided upon a multilateralist policy in which the United Nations would be at the centre. The European Commission defined the relationship between the European Union and global governance as follows:

The objectives of peace, growth, employment and social justice pursued within the Union must also be promoted outside for them to be effectively attained at European and global level. This responds to citizens' expectations for a powerful Union on the world stage. Successful international action reinforces European identity and the importance of shared values within the European Union (European Commission, 2001: 26–7)

In *The European Union and the United Nations: The Choice of Multilateralism*, which was published two years later, the European Commission goes even further and emphasizes that there is no alternative to multilateralism; if multilateralism fails, this will lead to an international catastrophe. It means that the European Union is regarded as a regional expression of the global policies of the United Nations and most international organizations. The main task of a European

foreign policy is to push forward the institutionalization of global governance by restructuring and reforming its institutions towards more inclusion and democratization (European Commission, 2003: 5).

In financial terms, the rhetoric has been followed by generous acts. In 2006, the EU Member States together contributed to 38 percent of the regular UN budget, 40 percent of deployment costs of UN peacekeeping forces, and contributes to about 50 percent of all voluntary contributions. (United Nations, 2006: 8); this becomes even more important when the US is lagging behind in the payment of its contributions (1st of March 2008: $2.4 billion in arrears). The European Union has been also quite active in UN peacekeeping operations across the world. The coordination of common positions within the United Nations has proved to be more difficult. Although there are mechanisms to articulate the positions, France and the UK, two larger member states who are also permanent members of the Security Council, can create considerable splits among the other member-states. The 2003 Iraq War was a good example of an event where the credibility of the European Union suffered immensely because of the split between the UK and Spain, who advocated an intervention without a second resolution; and France and Germany, who wanted to wait for the inspection work of the United Nations team to be completed before making a decision. However, European foreign policy has found other areas where consensus was easier to reach. According to Sophie Meunier and Kalypso Nicolaidis, 95 per cent of all decisions are taken in common in the United Nations General Assembly votes (Meunier and Nicolaidis, 2005: 254).

Several authors, therefore, refer to the European Union as a 'civilian' or 'normative power'. This means that the EU's policies of multilateralism related to democratic peace, human rights, and global governance are becoming norms of world politics. It also means that the European Union is a force for good (see Manners, 2006; Sjursen, 2006; Teló, 2006) As Chris Hill highlights, there are still problems and a mismatch between expectations and capabilities (Hill, 1998), but the overall thrust has become clearer and better structured over time, such as the policy on human rights and the rejection of capital punishment (Lerch and Schwellnus, 2006; Smith, 2004a: 98–120). The latter is a significant problem due to the sensitivities within the Commission of Human Rights of the United Nations, which includes members with an appalling record of human rights. The recent discussion also included the proposal to introduce an Ombudsman for Human Rights comparable to that within other organizations such as the Council of Europe (Hoffman and Mégret, 2005).

The European Union has been also an important agent in the WTO. The European Commission, through its trade commissioner, is able to negotiate worldwide deals on behalf of its member states. This has probably been the most successful aspect of the European Union acting with one voice. In spite of this unity in trade negotiations the decision-making process is still difficult. The reform of the Common Agricultural Policy (CAP) undertaken by several commissioners has so far been very limited. The most recent reform, negotiated and implemented by former commissioner Franz Fischler, has introduced a phasing out of part of the subsidies by 2013, but France, Spain, Italy, Germany and Greece still have strong interests in preserving this protection for their farmers. This lack of progress may condemn European preferences towards civilianization of the global governance system to end in failure. A non-hegemonic culture of global politics also means economic and social solidarity with concerns of the southern hemisphere.

This naturally complicates the negotiating parameters for the trade commissioner in charge. Two negotiating rounds (Doha 2001 and Caucun 2003) failed because the richer countries were not able to agree on reducing their subsidies and allowing the products of developing countries to enter their markets. According to Alasdair Young and John Peterson, a so-called 'new trade politics' has emerged after the Uruguay Round of the 1980s and 1990s. Apart from the fact that the European Union and the US changed their priorities in terms of areas, new actors emerged such as non-governmental organizations which have made the whole process more complex and difficult. Moreover, the balance of power shifted towards the developing world, which created a G20 group to counteract the dominance of the northern partners. The European Union is clearly operating in a new context (Young and Peterson, 2006).

This is reinforced by the fact that the European Union is the second largest economy in the world. Indeed, by some measure, it comes first. As a result, the EU has a strong responsibility for the stability of the world economy. The successful introduction of the euro, the world's second most important currency in 2002 led to a 25 per cent share of the global currency market. Sophie Meunier and Kalypso Nicolaidis argue that the European Union is becoming a power *through* trade. The very flexible approach towards the establishment of preferential and inter-regionalist approaches enhances its role as a 'civilian' or 'normative power' (Meunier and Nicolaidis, 2005: 265–6). Similarly, to these two institutions one can observe a growing coordination of the EU and the euro-zone in the International Monetary Fund and the World Bank.

The European Union and inter-regional cooperation

European Union is engaged in many regions in the world, in some cases endeavouring towards a minimalist cooperation through regular meetings, in other cases pushing forward regional integration projects, that are, according to Pascal Lamy, 'euromorphous', meaning similar to or emulating the European Union project (Lamy, 2002).

Probably the most important inter-regional cooperation is with Russia and the Community of Independent States. Russia wants to have a special relationship with the European Union and can not be put in a basket with other smaller countries. This means that Russia is not happy with only having a relationship within the broader European Neighbourhood Policy of the EU. Since 1994 the EU has advocated a strategic partnership with Russia that would focus predominantly on aspects of security and regional stability. A common strategy on Russia was issued in 1999 that acknowledged the importance of a partnership for the preservation of security in multiple areas, such as weapons of mass destruction, illegal immigration and organized crime. This EU common strategy has been reciprocated by Russia's medium-term strategy for relations between the Russian Federation and the European Union. The EU is engaged in technical assistance in Russia and several CIS members through the TACIS programme, which deals with human rights, democracy, but also nuclear safety and economic projects. The EU and Russia also work together in security forums like the Quartet in the Middle East and the Contact group in the Balkans. However, despite this complex network of linkages, the EU, the Council of Europe and the OSCE have been critical of irregularities in elections in Russia and other members of CIS (Marsh and Mackenstein, 2005: 195–203).

The relations to the United States of America and the North American Free Trade Area have been more longstanding. The Cold War created a close relationship between the US and the European Union. Nevertheless, the 1990s allowed the EU to become more liberated and to pursue policies distinct from the main hegemonic power in the world system. The Iraq War in 2003 clearly showed that in terms of security and allegiance there is a cleavage emerging between Atlanticists, advocating a close relationship to the US, and Europeanists, who want a more independent foreign policy. This tension will not go away and will continue to shape the relationship with the US. Apart from the security dimension, the EU is intrinsically linked to the US through the high level of economic interdependence created over the past five decades. The framework of cooperation includes both EU–US summits for soft security and NATO summits for hard security issues. This is followed up by regular transgovernmental and transnational cooperation mechanisms in the political, economic and security fields. The crucial agreements organizing this transatlantic cooperation are the Transatlantic Declaration of 1990 and the New Transatlantic Agenda of 1995 (Smith and Steffenson, 2005: 353–4; see also Pollack and Shaffer, 2001). Beyond this formalized cooperation, the relationship between the US and EU is probably among the best of all the institutionalized relationships. The cooperation in other areas such as the 'war on terrorism', the fight against criminal organizations, and all forms of trafficking is very well established. One could maybe argue that the powers wielded between the US and EU complement each other effectively. According to Joseph Nye, the US is strong on *hard* military power, but has a much reduced *soft* power capacity related to diplomacy and influence through other non-military mechanisms. The EU is regarded as having too much soft power, but very limited hard power, being dependent for most of the time on US military support (Nye, 2004: 75–83; 142–147).

Latin America has become an important partner for the European Union. The attempts from within Latin America to create economic communities in different parts of the region led to a growing interest from the European Union to establish general systems of preferences and far-reaching free trade agreements. Probably the EUs most important partner is Mercosur, which consists of Brazil, Argentina, Paraguay, Uruguay and Venezuela. Bolivia and Chile are also associated members. Although it is inter-governmental, Mercosur tries to emulate many of the policies of the European Union. Moreover, it wants to be an alternative to US attempts to dominate the region. The EU is also providing Mercosur with funding to strengthen its institutions; the objective being to create a transatlantic free-trade area between the EU and Mercosur. This is regarded as a way to moderate the dominance of the US in the region and develop the project of a free-trade area for the Americas (FTAA) (Hoffmann, 2003; Philipps, 2003). The EU also cooperates with the Andean Community (*Comunidad Andina* – CAN), which was founded in 1969 and consists of Bolivia, Colombia, Ecuador and Peru. Venezuela was also a member but left to join Mercosur, while Chile withdrew its membership in 1973. The EU has also established a free-trade agreement with Mexico. In the long term, the Latin American region may gain in importance if its democracies become more consolidated, inequalities within countries diminish, political corruption is tackled, and political violence replaced by non-violent means of conflict resolution (Magone, 2006: 279–98).

The replacement of the Organization of African Unity (OAU) by the African Union in 2002 documents this growing importance of the European Union as a model for other regions. The new African Union is still too young, so a detailed assessment of its capabilities is not yet possible. As already mentioned, the budget is too small. Nevertheless, it was the European Union–Africa meeting during the Portuguese presidency of the European Union in 2000 that led to this thrust towards a 'euromorphous' organization. The AU has a 15,000 strong Standby Peacekeeping force in order to intervene in African conflicts. Peacekeeping forces have been deployed in Darfur (although it seems with limited impact – the region continues to be quite unstable and the refugees still threatened by the Arab militia allegedly created by the Sudanese government). The European Union is also engaged in promoting subregional integration by cooperating with the Economic Community of West African States (ECOWAS), which comprises 15 members; the Central African Economic and Monetary Union (CEMAC) which consists of 7 members; and the South African Development Community (SADC) which consists of 14 members. Cooperation with the latter goes back to 1986 and intensified after the end of apartheid in South Africa. All this is overarched by the ACP (African, Caribbean and Pacific) Group, which was established in 1973 and consists of 79 members. This organization clearly retains postcolonial links with countries across the globe. The ACP is mainly a development community and as such is also part of the development policy of the European Union, which is being more and more articulated with the member states (de Flers and Regelsberger, 2005: 324; Mayall, 2005).

One of the most original cooperation frameworks has been the Euro-Mediterranean Partnership, which started in 1995 after a conference in Barcelona during the Spanish presidency. Consisting of the EU member states and the Southern Mediterranean countries, its main objective is to create a Mediterranean free-trade area by 2010. This huge task comprises of three cooperation arenas, similar to the Conference of Cooperation and Security in Europe (CSCE): political, economic and social–cultural. In spite of a decade of efforts by institutions, non-governmental organizations and other actors, the overall success has been quite meagre. Several evaluations show that there are problems of corruption related to the nature of the neo-patrimonial democracies of the Maghreb and the Mashreq. The Israeli–Palestinian conflict has been a major obstacle for substantial improvement of the living conditions of the Middle Eastern populations, and the war in Iraq further complicated the cooperation. Notwithstanding the problems, the mere presence of the EU in the region, the continuing cooperation, and the slow but substantive progress in democratization in some countries such as Morocco or Jordan, may contribute to a change of mentality towards more postmodern, transparent and accountable forms of governance. In this context, the time factor is crucial (Gillespie, 1997; Magone, 2006: 267–71).

Last but not least, the EU's relationship to Asian countries has improved considerably in the past decade. One of the main reasons is that Asia is also moving slowly towards regionalist integration. A crucial formal channel of communication is the biennial Asia–Europe meetings (ASEM), of which there have been six since 1996. ASEM includes the EU member states, the European Commission and 13 Asian states. Moreover, the EU also meets regularly with the ASEAN and the South Asian Association for Regional Cooperation (SAARC) (de Flers and Regelsberger, 2005: 331–3). Tensions have arisen due to human rights violations in some countries, such as Burma/Myanmar, particularly in the ASEM forum. Nevertheless, the EU recognizes that the Asia-Pacific is one of the fastest expanding regions economically and it has to be present there. The EU's relationship with China has been particularly longstanding: the EU has kept an open channel with China since 1975 and there have been regular annual meetings since 1998. The growing importance of China as a world power makes it essential to keep a receptive dialogue. Nevertheless, human rights violations have led to tensions in this relationship. Moreover, the recent trade disputes between EU and China have also shown the problems that the Single European Market faces in the immediate future. In contrast, Japan is much better integrated into the European and global networks (e.g. the OECD, the OSCE, the Council of Europe, and G8) (Marsh and Mackenstein, 2005: 203–9; Youngs, 2001).

In conclusion, the European Union has considerably expanded its engagement with all regions of the world. Overall, the pattern is one of a diversity of relations in a multilayered global governance system. The proactive engagement allows for an interactive transformation of European identities towards cosmopolitanism.

CONCLUSIONS: EUROPE IN GLOBAL GOVERNANCE

After 1989, Europe began to assert itself as an actor of global governance; this happened during an increase in interconnectedness between the different regions of the world in political, economic, security, social and cultural terms. What emerged are different Europes that are interconnected and feed off

each other. They are multilayered and multi-level. Europe is an expression of the emerging multilevel global governance system and as such assists the global institutions in pushing forward the respect for human rights, quality of democracy, and peaceful solutions to conflicts. Many authors have labelled the European Union as a 'civilian' or 'normative power' or a 'force for good'. The overarching political and social culture of Europe is laid out by the Council of Europe, which is the most comprehensive organization in the European continent. Although the European Union is not able to export the model to other regions of the world, it plays an important role of assisting regional integration projects in order to strengthen and expand the principles of global governance. As such, it retains its role as a *primus inter pares* in pushing the boundaries of cosmopolitanism and contributing to the transition towards a global governance regime.

REFERENCES

Ágh, Attila (2006) *Eastern Enlargement and the Future of the EU27:EU Foreign Policy in a Global World*. Budapest:'Together Europe' Research Centre of the Hungarian Academy of Sciences.

Aldecoa, F. and Keating, M. (eds) (1999) 'Paradiplomacy. The foreign relations of sub-national governments', *Regional and Federal Studies*, 9 (1):

Attinà, F. (2003) *Il Sistema Politico Globale. Introduzione Alle Relazioni internazionali*. Bari: Editori Laterza.

Aberbach, J.D. (2003) 'The U.S. Federal Executive in an era of change', *Governance*, 16 (3): 373–399.

Balme, R. (1999) 'Las condiciones de las acción colectiva regional', in F. Letamendia (ed.) *Nacionalidades y Regiones en la Unión Europea*. Madrid: Fundamentos, pp. 69–91.

Barry, R.L. (2004) Afghanistan votes. The OSCE breaks new ground in a partner country. *OSCE Magazine* (December), 6–15.

Beck, U. (2007) '*Reinventing Europe – a cosmopolitan view*', in C. Rumford (ed.)

Cosmopolitanism and Europe. Liverpool: Liverpool University Press, pp. 39–50.

Boon,V. and Delanty, G. (2007) '*Cosmopolitanism and Europe: historical considerations and contemporary applications*', C. Rumford (ed.) *Cosmopolitanism and Europe*. Liverpool: Liverpool University Press, pp. 19–38.

Burton, J.W. (1972) *World Society*. Cambridge: Cambridge University Press.

Castells, M. (2000) *The Rise of the Network Society, vol. I: Information Age:Economy, Society and Culture*. London: Blackwell.

Cecchini, P.M., Catinat, M. and Jacquemin, A. (1988) *The European Challenge 1992: The Benefits of a Single Market*. Aldershot: Wildwood House.

Christiansen, T. and Jorgensen, K. (2000) 'Transnational governance 'above' and 'below' the state:the changing nature of borders in the new Europe', *Regional and Federal Studies*, 10 (2): 62–77.

Council of Europe (2006). Available at http://www.coe.int, accessed 8 September 2006.

Daalder, I. and Goldgeier, J. (2006) 'Global NATO', *Foreign Affairs*, 85 (5), 105–113.

Delanty, G. and Rumford, C. (2005) *Rethinking Europe. Social Theory and the Implications of Europeanization*. London: Routledge.

de Flers, N.A. and Regelsberger, E. (2005) 'The EU and inter-regional cooperation', in C. Hill and M. Smith (eds) *International Relations and the European Union*. Oxford: Oxford University Press, pp. 317–42.

European Commission (2001) *White Paper on European Governance*. Brussels, 25 July 2001.

European Commission (2003) 'The European Union and the United Nations:the choice of multilateralism', Communication of the Commission to the Council and the European Parliament, Brussels, 10 September 2003.

Elliott, L. (2002) 'Global environmental governance', in R. Wilkinson and S. Hughes (eds) *Global Governance. Critical Perspectives*. London: Routledge, pp. 57–74.

Flynn, G. and Farrell, H. (1999) 'Piecing together the democratic peace: The CSCE, norms, and the 'construction' of security in post-Cold War Europe', *International Organizations*, 53 (3): 505–535.

Geeraerts, G. and Stouthuysen, P. (eds) (1999) *Democratic Peace in Europe*. Brussels: VUB University Press.

Gillespie, R. (ed.)(1997) *The Euro-Mediterranean Partnership. Political and Economic Perspectives*. London: Frank Cass.

Greenwood, J. (2003) *Representing Interests in the European Union*. Basingstroke: Palgrave.

Hill, C. (1998) 'Closing the capabilities-expectations gap?', in J. Peterson and H. Sjursen (eds) *A Common Foreign Policy for Europe?* London: Routledge, pp. 18–38.

Hoffmann, A.R. (2003) *Foreign Policy of the European Union towards Latin American Southern Cone States (1980–2000)*. Frankfurt: Peter Lang.

Hoffman, F. and Mégret, F. (2005) Fostering human rights accountability:an ombudsman for the United Nations?', *Global Governance*, 11: 43–63.

Hradil, S. and Immerfall, S. (1997) 'Modernisierung und Vielfalt in Europa', in S. Hradil and S. Immerfall (eds) *Die westeuropäischen Gesellschaften in Vergleich*. Opladen: Leske+Budrich, pp. 11–25.

Immerfall, S. (1995) *Einführung in den Europäischen Gesellschaftsvergleich. Ansätze, Problemstellungen, Befunde*. Passau: Rothe.

Inglehart, R. and Welzel, C. (2005) *Modernization, Cultural Change and Democracy. The Human Development Sequence*. Cambridge: Cambridge University Press.

Kaeble, H. (1987) *Auf dem Weg zu Einer Europäischen Gesellschaft*. Muenchen: C.H. Beck.

Kaeble, H. (1997) 'Europaische Vielfalt und der Weg zu einer europäischen Gesell-schaft', in S. Hradil and S. Immerfall(eds), *Die Westeuropäischen Gesellschaften im Vergleich*. Opladen: Leske + Budrich, pp. 27–68.

Kaeble,H. (2005), *Sozialgeschichte Europas. 1945 bis zur Gegenwart*. München: C.H. Beck.

Kaldor, M. (2003) *Global Civil Society. An Answer to War*. Cambridge: Polity.

Laidi, Z. (2006) 'Are European Preferences Shared by Others?', Keynote speech given at the *Are European Preferences Shared by Others?* conference sponsored by CERI, Centre d'Etudes Européennes de Sciences Po, Paris, 23–24 June 2006. Available at: http://www.laidi.fr, accessed on 2 July 2007.

Lamy, P. (2002) 'Mercosur hacia modelo "euro-morfo"', Available at: http://www.mercosur. com, accessed on 18 March 2002.

Lamy, P. and Laidi, Z. (2002) 'A European approach to global governance', *Progressive Politics*, 1 (1): 1–12.

Lepgold, J. (2001) 'NATO's Post-Cold war collective action problem', in P.F. Diehl (ed.) *The Politics of Global Governance. International Organizations in an Interdependent World*. Boulder, London: Lynne Rienner Publishers, pp. 229–260.

Lerch, M. and Schwellnus, G. (2006) 'Normative by nature? The role of the coherence in justifying the EU's human rights policy', *Journal of European Public Policy*, 13 (2): 304–321.

Luhmann, N. (1998), *Gesellschaft der Gesellschaft. 2 vols*.Frankfurt: Suhrkamp.

Magone, J.M. (2006) *The New World Architecture. The Role of the European Union in the Making of Global Governance*. New Brunswick: Transaction.

Manners, I. (2006) 'Normative power Europe reconsidered: beyond the crossroads', *Journal of European Public Policy*, 13 (2): 182–199.

Marks, G. (1993) 'Structural policy and multi-level governance in the EC', in A.W. Cafruny and G.G. Rosenthal (eds) *The State of the European Community.Vol.2: The Maastricht Debates and Beyond*. London: Longman-Lynne Rienner Publishers, pp. 391–411.

Marks, G., Nielsen, F., Ray, L. and Salk, J. (1996) 'Competencies, cracks and conflicts: regional mobilization in the European Union', in G. Marks, F.W. Scharpf, P.C. Schmitter and W. Streeck (eds) *Governance in the European Union*. London: Sage, pp. 40–63.

Marks, G., Haesly, R. and Mbaye, H.A.D. (2002) 'What do subnational offices think they are doing in Brussels?', *Regional and Federal Studies*, 12 (3): pp. 1–23.

Marsh, S. and Mackenstein, H. (2005) *The International Relations of the European Union*. London: Longman.

Mascia, M. (2004) *La Societá Civile nell'Unione Europea. Nuovo Orizzonte Democratico*. Venezia: Marsilio.

Mayall, J. (2005) 'The shadow of empire: The EU and the former colonial world', in C. Hill and M. Smith (eds) *International Relations and the European Union*. Oxford: Oxford University Press, pp. 292–316.

Meunier, S. and Nicolaidis, K. (2005) 'The European Union as a trade power', in C. Hill and M. Smith (eds) *International Relations and the European Union*. Oxford: Oxford University Press, pp. 247–269.

Messner, D. (2002) 'World society – structures and trends', in P. Kennedy, D. Messner and F. Nuscheler (eds), *Global Trends and Global Governance*. London: Pluto Press, pp. 22–64.

Muñoa, J.M. (1999) 'El Comité de las Regiones y la Democracia Regional y Local in Europa', in F. Letamendia (ed.) *Nacionalidades y Regiones en la Unión Europea*. Madrid: Editorial Fundamentos, pp. 51–68.

Münch, R. (1991) *Dialektik der Kommunikationsgesellschaft*. Frankfurt: Suhrkamp.

Münch, R. (1993) *Das Projekt Europa. Zwischen Nationalstaat, regionaler Autonomie und Weltgesellschaft*. Frankfurt: Suhrkamp.

Nye, J.S. Jr. (2004) *Soft Power. The Means to Success in World Politics*. New York: Public Affairs.

Philipps, N. (2003) 'Hemispheric integration and subregionalism in the Americas', *International Affairs*, 79 (2): 327–349.

Piening, C. (1998) *Global Europe. The European Union in World Politics*. Boulder: Lynne Rienner.

Pollack, M.A. and Shaffer, G.C. (2001) 'Transatlantic governance in historical and theoretical perspective', in M.A. Pollack and G.C. Shaffer (eds) *Transatlantic Governance in the Global Economy*. Lanham: Rowman and Littlefield, pp. 3–42.

Rhodes, R.A.W. (1997) *Understanding Governance. Policy Networks, Governance, Reflexivity and Accountability*. Buckingham: Open University Press.

Rosenau, J.N. (2000) 'Governance, order, and change in world politics', in: *Governance Without Government:Order and Change in World Politics*. Cambridge: Cambridge University Press, pp. 1–30.

Rosenau, J.N. (2004) 'Strong demand, huge supply; governance in an emerging epoch', in I. Bache and M. Flinders (eds) *Multi-level Governance*. Oxford: Oxford University Press.

Rumford, C. (2002) *The European Union. A Political Sociology*. London: Blackwell.

Sbragia, A.M. (2000) 'Governance, the state and the market; what's going on?',

Governance: An International Journal of Policy and Administration, 13(2): 243–250.

Schimmelpfennig, F. (2003) *The EU, NATO, and the Integration of Europe. Rules and Rhetoric*. Cambridge: Cambridge University Press.

Shore, C. (2000) *Building Europe. The Cultural Politics of European Integration*. London: Routledge.

Sjursen, H.S. (2006) 'The EU as a 'normative power': how can this be?', *Journal of European Public Policy*, 13(2): 235–251.

Smith, K.E. (2004a) *European Union Foreign Policy in a Changing World*. Cambridge: Polity.

Smith, M.E. (2004b) *Europe's Foreign and Security Policy. The Institutionalization of Cooperation*. Cambridge: Cambridge University Press.

Smith, M. and Steffenson, K.(2005) 'The EU and the United States', in C. Hill and M. Smith (eds) *International Relations and the European Union*. Oxford: Oxford University Press, pp. 343–363.

Storey, H. (1995) 'Human rights and the new Europe: experience and experiment', *Political Studies*, XLIII: 131–151.

Teló, M. (2006) *Europe: A Civilian Power? European Union, Global Governance, World Order*. Basingstoke: Palgrave.

Therborn, G. (1995) *European Modernity and Beyond. The Trajectory of European Societies 1945–2000*. London: Sage.

Therborn, G. (1997) 'Europas künftige Stellung-Das Skandinavien der Welt?', in S. Hradil and S. Immerfall (eds) *Die westeuropäischen Gesellschaften im Vergleich*. Opladen: Leske+Budrich, pp. 573–598.

United Nations (2006) *The partnership between the UN and the EU. The United Nations and the European Commission working together in Development and Humanitarian Cooperation*. Brussels: United Nations System in Brussels.

Young, A.R. and Peterson, J. (2006) 'The EU and new trade politics', *Journal of European Public Policy*, 13 (6): 795–814.

Youngs, R. (2001) *The European Union and the Promotion of Democracy. Europe's Mediterranean and Asian Politics*. Oxford: Oxford University Press.

Wallace, W. (1999) 'The sharing of sovereignty: The European paradox', *Political Studies*, XLVII: 503–521.

Wallace, W. (2005) 'Post-sovereign governance: The EU as a partial polity', in H. Wallace, W. Wallace and M.A. Pollack (eds) *Policy-Making in the European Union*. Oxford: Oxford University Press, pp. 483–503.

Zürn, M. (2002) 'From Inderdependence to Globalization', in W. Carlnaes, T. Risse, B.A. Simmons (eds) *Handbook of International Relations*. London: Sage, pp. 235–254.

17

The Geopolitics of European Freedom and Security

John Agnew

Ever since the fall of the Roman Empire someone or other has longed to recreate an overarching political organization for Europe as a whole, often using that empire as a model. The fact that the Roman Empire at its height was Mediterranean rather than European in geographical scope has been lost to modern political consciousness. From Charlemagne to Napoleon and Hitler, to name just a few of the most famous, numerous despots have, taken the making of a new Roman *imperium* as at least their initial goal. Of course, the ancient Romans have inspired democrats as much as despots, and not just in Europe. They had their own romance with republic, although that was before they became an empire. Today, the idea that European unity and peace are totally intertwined is an article of faith among all 'pro-Europeans'. This is the idea of a *Pax Europa*. Perhaps not coincidently, it is in those places that were once parts of Charlemagne's empire – France, Germany, Italy, the Netherlands – that the most recent drive to European political unity had its origins. Elsewhere, particularly in Britain and Scandinavia, political fragmentation has never been seen as necessarily inimical to

peace. Perhaps it has something to do with their geographical marginality or collective belief in the virtues of balance of power. Be that as it may, many European politicians and historians now take as self-evident the idea that constantly moving towards political unity and away from the territorial fragmentation of the Europe of nation-states is a *sine qua non* for a 'Europe' that can both guarantee peace within its borders and compete effectively with other states/regional blocs in the world political economy. Crucial to both goals is defining what Europe is and establishing a strategy that goes beyond the geopolitical imperatives inherited from the Cold War era when Europe was the geographic focus for conflict between the US and the Soviet Union rather than a plausible geopolitical 'actor' in its own right.

Yet, as the political project for making the European Union more constitutionally integrated seems to have stalled and with increasing 'fatigue' over further enlargement, the residual institutional influence of the Cold War years has reasserted itself. This has occurred in part through a revived security reliance on NATO rather than a new EU security apparatus, along with the re-emergence of Russia as a threat or menace under the presidency of Vladimir Putin, rather than an opportunity for further realizing a widening of the 'European vision'. Of course, 'Europe' (either as the EU or the larger geographical area) is neither as alone in the world nor as capable of directing events as those of a conspiratorial cast of mind tend to suppose. The EU and European national governments have had to respond to political and economic pressures from the US, even as US governments have become less consultative in their relations with putative allies, and to deal, among other things, with conflicts over increasingly needed Russian gas supplies and the socioeconomic impacts, in terms particularly of refugees and terrorism, emanating from wars, despotic regimes, and the rise of militant Islam in the Middle East, Europe, and Africa. Power is not simply pooled up in Washington, Brussels, Paris or London. Others have political agency too. Indeed, in a world of increasingly successful asymmetric warfare and nuclear proliferation, as well as economic globalization, it is less and less useful to think of 'big' territory as if this were equivalent to being more politically and economically effective. But this logic of territorial power tends to be the one driving the thinking about European integration (as it is equally in *realpolitik* (e.g. Mearsheimer, 2002) and capital-determinist (e.g. Gowan, 1999; Harvey, 2003) thinking about world politics in general): that the economies of scale associated with a bigger Europe will bring enhanced political freedom and military security for those within its borders, even if at the necessary expense of those outside. Approaching these issues in a more dialectical fashion, I subscribe to the view that while the ideals of geographical expansion and institutional integration remain powerful, increasingly there are questions about both the material possibility and desirability of their achievement.

This perspective raises a number of implications about how to study 'Europe' in terms of the geopolitics of security and freedom.

One is to maintain a clear distinction between Europe and the European Union. Many countries in Europe are not members of the EU and attempts to use the idea of Europe to underpin the EU project are, as we shall see, fraught with difficulties. Another implication is the importance of historical geopolitics, particularly the historic significance of certain Western European states such as France and Britain, in defining the parameters of 'Europeanness'. For every core it seems there must also be a periphery. Though the enlargement of NATO and the EU has brought many countries from Central–Eastern Europe into full political–economic engagement with Western Europe, there is still a lingering divide through Europe that is only slowly being erased. This is as much psychological as material, in that it represents the lingering after-effects of the different political–economic systems that were embedded in Western and Eastern Europe over the period 1945–1990 and a long previous history of cultural and economic differences between polities in the two Europes (Berend, 2005). Of course, Western Europe has not always been the beacon of democracy it is now seen as representing: from the infamous examples of Nazi Germany and Fascist Italy to the very recent cases of dictatorship, only ending in the mid-1970s, in Spain, Portugal, and Greece. A third implication is that the modern geopolitical imagination has always privileged the territorial state as the exclusive actor in guaranteeing security and in claiming to underwrite social and political freedom, but the precise nature of the EU as a political form is as yet unclear. Though the EU does not conform at all to the modern 'state' as we have usually imagined it, nevertheless many of the actual states of Europe must adapt to an institutional setting in which they share their security roles with emerging supranational power centres of which the most important is the EU. The EU is a new type of 'political subject' which is probably not best regarded as just a 'scaled-up' state. Finally, the world has actually been more 'peaceful' with respect to major conflicts since the end of the Cold War than many of us perceive it to have been. This is partly because during the Cold War many of the most violent conflicts took place in poor countries distant from Europe and North America. Now the threat of global terrorism is directly on 'home' ground so to speak, and rolling 24-hour news alerts us almost instantaneously to the fruits of violence whenever it occurs and on whatever scale (Stephens, 2006a). In this context of a changed meaning to security, the most important areas for EU security policy will be those problems states either cannot or have not developed the capacity to deal with (terrorism, controlling access to weapons of mass destruction, immigration, environmental risks, etc.) but which are of increasing global significance relative to conventional 'great power' war or wars between their surrogates. Even though success in 'high policy' areas such as presenting a common policy on Iran's nuclear processing program and brokering a truce in Lebanon may augur well for developing a common EU foreign policy, the past track record advises looking instead to 'creeping integration' in new policy areas as a more successful long-term strategy.

In this chapter, I begin with a discussion of how a unified European political space has been envisaged and recently put into effect. The discussion includes particular attention to the geographical limits of Europe, the question of 'common norms' among member states, and examples that test notions of geographical destiny and common norms in recent Balkan conflicts. I then turn to the Cold War inheritance, particularly that of NATO, and the possibility of a purely European security compact. The main focus is on how the Yalta Agreement (1945), the Marshall Plan (1947), and NATO (1949) split Europe into competing parts and how the lingering impact of these still divides Europe. At the same time, NATO has become a strange sort of 'half-way house' between estrangement and full membership in the EU in part of East-Central Europe and the main mechanism, more generally, for European

military interventionism beyond European shores. I then turn to the critical issue of US–European relations and whether or not there can ever be a return to 'business-as-usual' after the disastrous US adventure (with British connivance) in Iraq. I emphasize that at the same time the EU has adopted many of the neoliberal policies encouraged elsewhere, if not always practiced, by US governments and business, the US–Europe security relationship has entered into crisis for a complex set of reasons often reduced to sound bites ('The US is from Mars and Europe from Venus,' etc.) that fail to do justice to a messier world. Finally, I raise the spectre of the increased tension between the security agendas of member states, on the one hand, and the security goals of European unification, on the other. The primary point is that the EU is still an organization of states, even though much of the dominant discourse of European unity envisages some new institutional entity that certainly does not yet exist, and shows as yet only a few weak signs of existing, at least in relation to security and military affairs. In the conclusion I suggest that controversy over the idea of a 'separate' political Europe, US–European tensions, and the difficulty of establishing new superpowers set real limits to the goal of a new European enterprise in the imperial Roman mould. Democracy remains a choice to be made.

EUROPE AS POLITICAL SPACE

'Europe' is a concept that floats between geographical, cultural, and political definitional poles (Hay, 1968; Wilson and van der Dussen, 1995). First, it is a geographical term. Unfortunately, its location is difficult to fix; its heartland is as hard to demarcate as are its notoriously shifting borders. Pocock (1997, 2002) claims that the ancient Greeks located 'Europa' in the lands west of the Bosphorus; in what we would today call the Balkans; an area has had much difficulty being accepted recently as European by many people to its north and west. But there has never been a definitive geographical measure of how to divide Europe from Asia. Definitions such as 'from the Atlantic to the Ural Mountains' may sound definitive but they are just mere conventions. The eastern border has been variously defined, with Russia and Turkey, for example, neither fully inside nor outside the continent. Even so, the geographic category of the continent has acquired an elemental status in organizing and understanding how the world works (Connery, 2004). However vague, it provides a template onto which other criteria are projected.

By extension, then, the indeterminacy is not only geographic. The European 'idea' is cultural more than anything else. Most typically in this usage, Europe is merely the modern designation for Christendom as defined by the medieval Popes. In fact, as Pagden (2002) reminds us, Christianity's roots are entirely Asian. The religion spread to Europe from somewhere else. Admittedly, the Latin (Roman) church did originally constitute the nexus for a supra-European organization after the collapse of the Roman Empire. Again, however, this raises doubts about the 'European' bona fides of much of Eastern Europe. If Turkey is easily excluded on this criterion, as many opponents of Turkey's entry into the EU see as foundational, and Albania and Bosnia because of their Muslim majorities, what to make of Orthodox Christian Russia, Romania, Bulgaria, Serbia, Greece or the Ukraine (Neumann 1999; Wolff 1994)? Politically, the supremacy of Western Europe and Christianity in this understanding suggests something about who has been doing the defining. Partly to justify their national projects but also, in some cases, to give a civilizational veneer to their imperial designs beyond European shores, it has been Western European elites who have been most exercised about and most capable of establishing the meaning of Europe (Heffernan, 1998). This has been the case since the medieval knights, clerics, and peasants of Latin Europe expanded into the edges of Europe, thus laying the groundwork for a more

homogeneous cultural sphere well beyond their initial territory of occupation (Bartlett, 1993). But it has been especially so since Western Europeans, such as, the Spanish, Portuguese, Dutch, British, and French began creating their extra-European empires in the sixteenth century. They looked in teleological self-justification to where they came from (a Europe that was special, creative, innovative, free, and more adventurous than other places) to explain their success in doing so (Wickham, 1994). European intellectuals have continued these efforts by invoking 'special' environmental and cultural conditions that set Europe apart. In tying together colonization within Europe with that outside, Bartlett (1993: 314), makes the vital point: 'Europe, the initiator of one of the world's major processes of conquest, colonization and cultural transformation, was also the product of one.'

Unavoidable as it is, defining the meaning of Europe is invariably problematic. As a result, some commentators have urged a focus solely on how 'Europe' is used as a discursive category and how it crops up in debate over 'Europeanness': the cultural and political form institutionalized by states and supranational organizations (including, but not limited to, the EU). From this viewpoint, images of an emerging European order must be related to the longer history of nation-statehood and how state elites in Europe have long traded in using ideas about Europe (links back to the classical Greeks and Romans, special environmental conditions, etc.) to legitimize their European and global roles (Agnew, 2007; Herzfeld, 2002; Malmborg and Stråth, 2002). After World War II and the Holocaust, however, any European claim to be an uncontaminated seat of high culture or civilization, the land of Goethe and Beethoven, had to come to terms with the reality of an industrialized mass extermination based on religious affiliation. After that time, barbarism now obviously existed at home and not just beyond Europe's borders. Beginning in the 1970s, though having obviously older roots, 'Europe' (wherever *it* was thought to begin or ended) began to compete with the states in an explicit and officially endorsed discourse about 'European identity' (Passerini, 1998). This was one of the main purposes of the Copenhagen Summit of the EC (as the future EU was then called) in 1973, which laid down a set of norms promoting a (Western) European identity: (1) the unity of the then nine members; (2) responsibility to the rest of the world, moving outwards from those European states not yet members, through the countries of the Mediterranean, the Middle East, and Africa, to the US (based on 'equality and the spirit of friendship'), then to Japan and Canada, détente with the Soviet Union and Eastern Europe and, finally, to China and Latin America; (3) the dynamic nature of the construction of a political Europe. While emphasizing as a central theme the struggle against underdevelopment in general, what is most interesting about the list of regions under the second criterion is that the Middle East ranked higher than the US. This was, after all, the year following the collapse of the dollar and the year of the OPEC oil-price shock associated in the popular mind with the major Middle Eastern oil producers. Often taken as the founding moment of the era of 'globalization,' the massively important if unintended outcome of these events (see, e.g. Agnew, 2005), the early 1970s was also a time of economic crisis in the EC as the growth momentum of the member states faltered and the accession of Britain promised increasing dissent over supranational policies (Gillingham, 2003). So, 'the utopian dream of a common identity was mobilized precisely at this moment when the cohesion of the European Community was conspicuous by its absence. "Integration" was the concept of the 1950s and 1960s which was used in the cold war to conjure up images of European unity and for translating Europe into a political project. When integration failed as an instrument of mobilization, identity was promoted in its place' (Malmborg and Stråth, 2002: 12). This is how 'Europe' has become completely intertwined in official discourse, and much academic writing, with the political project now associated with the EU.

Though it is easy to show with Eurobarometer surveys and other data that a European identity, in the Copenhagen sense, is still relatively weak relative to national ones across Europe, not least because it privileged the old standard Western Europe, there is a sense in which the EU and other institutions with European member states (such as the Council of Europe, OSCE, NATO, etc.) have developed common norms that imply, in an institutional context at least, that there may be an emerging European political space. This has been thought about in three ways. One is with respect to how the 'soft borders' that serve to direct the institutionalization of the EU and its policies on immigration, human rights, product liability, antitrust, and so on, have increasingly taken 'hard' forms in which Europe is mobilized as a set of stories about what can and cannot be done *where* that gain increasing circulation and currency across Europe (and into adjacent regions) (Eder, 2006; Sedelmeier, 2006). In this way, at the very minimum, 'Europe may be presented as a cognitive project of constructing a collective identity carried by elites' (Eder, 2006: 257; see also Berg and Ehin 2006; Giesen, 1998). Second, within given policy areas, there is convergence in norms and expectations across member states such that common 'cultures' develop among practitioners and bureaucrats. Thus, Meyer (2005), for example, finds strong evidence, though in the face of some counter evidence (e.g. Rynning, 2003), of increasingly common strategic norms in relation to national security and defence policies in Europe with respect to international authorization of force, preferred modes of cooperation, and goals for the use of force (see also, for example, for a Nordic case study, Rieker, 2004). The actual content of the common norms, however, is not directly European, but often reflects the pre-existing norms of a dominant state. As Ruttley (2002) has established for the EU overall, the two defeated European Axis powers of World War II, Germany and Italy, were unable to provide leadership and given the relative weakness of the other founding members, such as Belgium and the Netherlands, it has been the French government and its administrative models that have channelled the course of European identity. As late joiners to what later became the EU, the British, for example, have thus faced something of a *fait accompli* in many areas where they would like to be more influential. A common view is that, in response, they block proposals or opt out of policies rather than participate in establishing common norms, thus weakening the overall European project. Finally, various philosophers, from Habermas and Derrida to Balibar and Cacciari, have proposed rethinking Europe precisely as a borderland or incongruous zone whose identity should be that of challenging 'binary distinctions' (Derrida, 2004: 3). Alternatively, Europe might serve as a 'mediator' (Balibar) because the region has not and cannot have an absolute identity distinct from those around it (Bialasiewicz and Minca, 2005). In this construction, as the world economy is seen as operating increasingly as a set of flows through networks that resist traditional bordering, the possibility of territorializing a separate 'European' identity makes less and less sense if only because of the massive violence (and thus self-evident barbarism) it would now take to impose it (e.g. Agnew, 2005; Luke, 1996). Geo-philosophy *ex-cathedra* and powerful economic practices thus mutually reinforce an evolving image of Europe as no longer capable of adequate representation as a singular culturally homogeneous territorial space.

The bloody conflicts that sprang up in the Balkans with the collapse of communism in the early 1990s presented a serious challenge to the discourse of European identity in general, and the security norms for using force (even if claimed as humanitarian) in particular. If one aspect to this was how these conflicts would spill over into the Europe of the EU (with refugees, collateral violence, etc.), another was that these conflicts were on Europe's very doorstep, if not actually 'inside' it, more broadly speaking. The Balkans provided a critical 'test' for the peace and security aspirations of the 'new' Europe. Long associated

with the Turkish attempt at conquering Europe, leaving behind a residue of indigenous Muslims and cultural forms that came about in 400-odd years of Ottoman Turkish occupation, the Balkans had long taken on a connotation in Western Europe as a borderland or in-between zone signifying intermixing, chaos and despotism. This image owes much to the European great powers' long-term meddling in the region and the imposition of their model of statehood as necessarily mapping directly onto nations (pre-existing or made by ethnic cleansing). The Turks may not be blameless (*pace* Žižek, 2006: 377) but they certainly bear much less immediate responsibility for what became of the Balkans after they left. There is more than a hint of geographical irony in all this. As noted previously, the etymology of the term Europe says something about its historic expropriation, given that the ancient Greeks first applied it to the region now known as the Balkans. As Pocock (2002: 67) succinctly puts it, 'The lands originally called "Europa" are those in which "Europe" experiences a continuing problem in defining itself.' Eventually, of course, 'Europe', under US prompting, in the form of NATO and not the EU, did intervene militarily in the Balkans and has since provided, if now under EU auspices, in Bosnia and Kosovo in particular, a reticent form of imperial rule. Throughout the Balkans region, the main political goal, notwithstanding continuing enmity with immediate ethnic neighbors, is to join the EU and thus become 'part' of Europe.

COLD WAR INHERITANCE

The downing of the Berlin Wall in November 1989 has become something of a 'clean break' in the conventional history of contemporary Europe. Rather like the doubtful US Bush administration claim that 'everything' changed after 11 September 2001, the end of the Cold War which had dominated European geopolitics for the previous 40 years has proved to be somewhat less than cataclysmic. In fact, a number of its most important features have not only lived on, so to speak, but have even undergone revival. One is the continuing East–West divide in Europe, not just in terms of standards of living and economic development but also in terms of world views and cultural expectations. Eased somewhat with the invocation in the immediate aftermath of the communist collapse by locals of the designation of much of former communist Eastern Europe as Central (and thus less distant from the Western heartland) (Hagen, 2003; Neumann, 1999, chapter 5), and by the EU strategy of admitting some states preferentially because of their greater conformity to Western political and economic 'norms', there is nevertheless a continuing sense of difference on both sides, so to speak, going back many years but reinforced by the drawing of US and Soviet spheres of influence at the Yalta Conference in 1945 and the subsequent administration of the Marshall Plan solely in Western Europe, with the creation of the Pan-Atlantic NATO in 1949, and the arrival of the Soviet-sponsored Warsaw Pact in 1955 administering the *coup de grâce*. Verdery (1996: 4), for example, argues that the division of Europe in the 1940s shaped the subsequent 'cognitive organization of the world'. Even today, therefore, and on both sides of the divide, assumptions about attitudes to work, conceptions of the state, understandings of history, valuation of US foreign policy, and opinions about other ethnic groups and nationalities are held to differ profoundly (Kuus, 2004).

Eastern Europe is often seen in the West as occupying a 'waiting room of history', in Chakrabarty's (2000) evocative phrase, as the West makes history. The distinction that US conservative politicians have made between an 'old Europe' in the West going its own way and an Eastern, or 'new Europe,' supportive of US imperialism, plays off precisely this division, if with opposite meanings as to which is superior to the other (see, e.g. Bialasiewicz and Minca, 2005; Jacoby, 2004). If, on objective criteria such as GDP per capita and conformity to EU norms, there are significant differences between, say, Bulgaria and Albania on the one hand, and Slovenia and Estonia on the other, there is still a reluctance to acknowledge such distinctions in much popular discourse in Western Europe about 'the East'. By way of illustration, in Western Europe, the fear of a flood of immigrants from the East affected relations before and after the accession of a number of East-Central European countries into the EU in 2004 (only Britain, Sweden, and Ireland of existing members did not impose immigration restrictions). A stereotypical 'Polish plumber' arriving from the East and undercutting the wages of his French colleagues was the dominant symbol of the French 'No' campaign against the EU Constitution in 2005. The dangers of organized crime and sex trafficking alike are seen as further justifying such restrictions on immigration (Berman, 2003).

At first sight, the most surprising inheritance from the Cold War is that of NATO. Plausibly regarded as an organization without a role at the end of the Cold War after the disappearance of its primary foe, the Soviet Union, it has undergone something of a revival. This suggests not only that international institutions have staying power even when *raison d'état* might suggest otherwise but can invent new stories for themselves in order to stay in business (Williams and Neumann, 2000). The revival of NATO seems to have happened for several reasons. One is that it has been an instrument for bringing East-Central Europe into the European fold in anticipation of later accession to the EU (e.g. Gheciu, 2005; Kuus, 2002). Eastward enlargement of NATO has thus anticipated the enlargement of the EU. Much of this has depended on picturing Russia in particular as either a lingering or a possible future threat to European security. The Clinton administration in the US was particularly anxious to paint this sort of picture when Boris Yeltsin was still Russia's president (Albright, 1997). There was much anxiety about a Russian 'collapse' (Dean, 1997). Local pressure was added to this. Given the recent history of Russian military and political dominance in Eastern Europe, East European scepticism about Russian motivations is not very surprising. This has undoubtedly been enhanced by Russian intransigence in conflicts in the Caucasus (above all in Chechnya), explicit Russian involvement in challenging unwanted political change in such places as Georgia and the Ukraine, the more recent reassertion of central government control over the Russian economy by President Putin, and latterly by the explicit use of Russian gas and oil supplies to Europe as a geopolitical weapon (Ash *et al.*, 2006; Lieven, 2008). Putin, however, is hard to characterize in simple anti-Western terms and he has undoubtedly tried to respond reasonably to the approach of NATO to Russia's immediate borders and to amazingly hostile rhetoric from US politicians such as Vice-President Dick Cheney (e.g. Lieven, 2006; O'Loughlin *et al.*, 2004). So, when West European governments insist that Russia should behave as if it were an applicant to the EU even though neither entry into it nor into NATO is on offer, they cannot expect anything but a chilly reception (Lieven, 2006).

Another reason for NATO's revival is that since the mid-1990s the organization has become committed to 'humanitarian interventions', initially in the Balkans but now more widely (the idea of a 'global' NATO is not entirely recent; see Sandler and Hartley, 1999, for example; but has been further stimulated by the US declared worldwide 'war on terror'; see Daalder and Goldgeier, 2006). The stimulus here lies partly in US military overstretch, particularly in Iraq, but also in the US attempt to have Europe share more of the burden of nation-building and peacekeeping around the world. So far, the major intervention has been in Afghanistan, fighting against the Taliban that was ousted from Kabul in 2001 but which is now back as a significant insurgent force in the southern and eastern parts of the country. This is the first time that NATO has been active beyond the conventional limits of Europe. Although the EU, as such, as become involved in peacekeeping missions abroad

(for example, in the DR Congo and under UN auspices in Lebanon from summer 2006), there has been limited development of a European security apparatus outside of the confines of NATO. Partly this is the result of US and British opposition but it is also because of the inherent difficulties of coordinating the foreign policies of member states as illustrated most dramatically in the disarray in 2003 at the time the US invaded Iraq with France and Germany adamantly opposed and Britain, Spain, and Italy, for example, giving various levels of support. A number of EU members do not belong to NATO (Ireland, Sweden, Finland and Austria) and, of course, the US, Canada, Iceland, Norway, and Turkey are non-EU members and some countries were still en route to EU membership (Bulgaria, Romania) when admitted. This lack of overlap makes for serious complication in seeing NATO as the security arm of Europe.

Much scepticism has been expressed about NATO's capacity to deliver on military commitment so far from home. The lack of collective agreement about foreign policy goals across the Atlantic Alliance makes it unlikely that further missions beyond that in Afghanistan will ever take place. If the intervention in Afghanistan goes badly, as seems likely given current circumstances, then NATO may well have finally reached the end of its road (e.g. Bereuter 2006; Carpenter, 2004; Fidler and Morarjee, 2006; *Economist*, 10 June 2006; *Financial Times*, 31 August 2006; but on the continuing power of the industrial/military symbiosis across the Atlantic supporting the NATO connection; see Rosecrance, 2003). Then, there may well be no other choice than to establish some sort of purely European security apparatus but for use in the immediate neighbourhood rather than on the other side of the world.

THE US VERSUS EUROPE

Beyond these specific legacies, perhaps the major inheritance of the Cold War is the continuing political and security relationship across the Atlantic with the United States. Through NATO, the US obviously has a continuing alliance with many European states. But this relationship has come under enormous strain over the past five years, in large part because of the post-September 11 obsession of the US Bush Administration with Iraq and the questioning by some European leaders (particularly President Chirac of France and Chancellor Schroeder of Germany) of the purported intelligence about 'weapons of mass destruction' and an Iraq–terrorism connection that the US government used to justify the invasion and occupation of Iraq in 2003. Of course, some European leaders, such as Tony Blair in Britain (following the fabled 'special relationship' with the US), Silvio Berlusconi in Italy, José Manuel Barroso in Portugal, and José Maria Aznar in Spain, opted to support the US policy, which illustrates how difficult constructing an EU foreign policy will be. Subsequent revelations about the fabrication of much of the intelligence and the disastrous course of the occupation, not to mention the repeated use of inaccurate analogies to World War II and the dangers of appeasement, have made many European governments increasingly wary of following the lead of the US (shown, for example, in relation to policy towards Iran and the Israeli invasion of Lebanon in summer 2006) in the face of widespread public opposition across Europe to US Bush administration policies. At the same time, however, the US Bush administration view of NATO shows signs of being shoe-horned into the religious-based, Manichean view of the world it adopted after 11 September 2001. This involves moving away from an Atlantic partnership towards a global alliance in which other member countries, no longer limited to North America and Europe, will take a subsidiary role to the US in a worldwide 'war on terror' against 'Islamic fascism' (Rhodes, 2004). Europe, in this construction, has lost its centrality to US foreign policy as the Middle East (because of oil and terrorism) and East Asia (because of trade and credit) have risen in importance.

US military unilateralism, particularly in relation to what Saul Cohen (2005) calls the 'Eurasian Convergence Zone' (from the Baltic to the Black Sea through Central Asia to Korea), has introduced a new disequilibrium into world politics that threatens the geopolitical status quo. This explicit US devaluation of Europe's role in NATO, however, is just the tip of a veritable iceberg of differences between the two. The approval of most European states (both directly and through the EU) on the one hand, and the opposition of the United States, on the other, to the International Criminal Court (ICC), the Kyoto Protocol on climate change, the ban on anti-personnel land mines, the biodiversity treaty, and the verification procedures for the Biological Weapons Control Treaty are some examples. During the Cold War, Western European governments often deferred to US governments even as they were seriously consulted by them. In one perspective, with the Cold War's end and the increased political–economic strength of the EU relative to the US, plus the everyday familiarity with negotiation and compromise that the EU requires, Europeans have continued to engage in multilateral approaches to global problems such as terrorism, environmental risks, and drug trafficking, just as the US, in a fit of religiously inspired imperial hubris, has become increasingly unilateral (e.g. Matthews, 2001).

From another perspective, however, something more structural is afoot. This is the decline of American supremacy and the possible rise of Europe (or China) as a challenger (e.g. Kupchan, 2002; Layne, 2003; Wallerstein, 2006). In brief, the US is running down both its economic and ideological credits to support an overstretched military budget as it alienates what allies it has left. This is a formula for decline, not for successful empire. Of course, many American commentators do not see things this way. They see Europe as 'weak' militarily and, hence, as unthreatening. The US has no military peer (in spending, at least) and the demography of the US, experiencing more immigrants and higher relative fertility, gives it greater potential 'boots on the ground' (the new euphemism for 'cannon fodder') and a better prospect for paying the costs of pensions and health care as baby-boomers retire than the countries of Europe (*Economist*, 24 August 2002). Although implicit in such demographic discourse is not only an old-fashioned view of war potential but also the hidden implication that, if absolute population size translates into geopolitical destiny, then China has already won.

To Robert Kagan (2003), for example, the most famous American pundit on the differences between the US and Europe, Europe 'is not really capable of constraining the United States'. As a result of reacting against its own martial past, a 'Kantian' Europe, devoted to negotiation and diplomacy, distances itself from a muscular American militarism. This reduces to banalities opinions such as Kagan's that just as Europe follows Immanuel Kant, the US follows Thomas Hobbes; hardly doing justice to the richness of these luminaries' political thought. 'Obvious' as all this may be to many American conservatives, however, it suffers from some serious errors. For one thing, the US is not nearly as powerful militarily or in other respects that this viewpoint assumes. The military and political failure in Iraq speaks volumes. If the invasion was easy, occupation has proved impossible both because of the difficulties inherent in occupying other countries and the almost unbelievable incompetence with which the US government prepared for and prosecuted this occupation (see Chandrasekaran, 2006; Fallows, 2006; Ricks 2006). The economic vulnerability of the US because of its need to import vast amounts of credit to fund current private and government spending also needs underlining (Calleo, 2003). Though the EU may suffer by comparison in military spending and organization, the EU shows few signs of wanting to assert military supremacy anywhere. The European preference for 'soft' power, a trail once blazed by the US, by enrolling others in one's projects, fits better the contemporary world than does the direct application of military force. It is the entire

basis to the negotiation process associated with EU enlargement; both enticing and coercing applicants in equal measure. In a world experiencing the proliferation of nuclear weapons, not least because of US 'blind eyes' towards a nuclear-armed Israel and support for India's nuclear weapons program (even though India has never signed up to the Nuclear Non-Proliferation Treaty), and whose possession inevitably put limits on the use of conventional forces, military superpower faces real operational constraints (Calleo, 2003: 13). This is why states such as Iran and North Korea seek nuclear weapons and, once they have them, refuse to give them up (D. Smith, 2006). The growth of non-state actors as powerful agents in world politics, from shadowy terrorist networks pushing this or that cause to global corporations with limited national loyalties, also means that foreign policies directed solely at other states are sorely lacking in strategic grasp. Increased global economic interdependence between states likewise reduces the possibility of translating territorial resource control into geopolitical clout. The 'escalator model' of hegemonic succession, which posits the inevitable rise of a new superpower as the old one fades away, does not seem to fit contemporary conditions, notwithstanding its manifest popularity (e.g. Reid, 2004; Leonard, 2006). Thus, Europe, the US, and other putative 'great powers' such as China, now must adjust to a world in which the prospects for singular-state hegemony have been much reduced (Agnew, 2005).

Ironically, the mutual disenchantment of Europe and the United States over security comes at a time when the EU has moved towards a more American-style economic liberalism in its economic policy orientation that was previously much more balanced by an emphasis on redistributive and welfare policies, the so-called European social model. Since the Single Market was agreed to in 1986, and in response to the perception that globalization entails adopting neo-liberal policies (the infamous There Is No Alternative), the EU has been on a more 'neoliberal' track, encouraging deregulation of markets, privatization of state assets, and limits on redistributive policies. This ideology is premised on the 'emancipation' of the economy from the state. With clear intellectual connections to the contemporary victory within academic economics of neoclassical thought (Van der Pijl, 2006), this approach to economic management has much deeper cultural origins in US economic history and in the US engagement with the world economy (Agnew, 2005; Van der Pijl, 2006). It shows both how important hegemonic packages are in ordering the world and how limiting a focus on foreign relations as coercion truly is. Appealing to the release of entrepreneurial energies, the bundles of policies referred to by the term 'neoliberalism' are, however, often given greater coherence than they deserve and their top-down imposition is frequently exaggerated (Barnett, 2005). Thus the Lisbon Agenda of 2000, emphasizing making Europe's economy 'more competitive', was the result of negotiation among governments not of imposition of a centralized agenda agreed in advance by a neoliberal Committee of Public Safety. Yet, it seems clear that the popular perception of an EU on a neoliberal course, and the view that the proposed Constitution would enshrine it, led to some of the opposition to the Constitution in the French and Dutch referenda of 2004. The battle over the adoption of the various tenets of neoliberalism, therefore, is still engaged.

Returning to the status quo ante (a favourite phrase of US Secretary of State, Condoleezza Rice, referring to refusing to go back to Israel–Lebanon relations as they were before summer 2006) in Europe–US relations seems unlikely after the disruptions and contention focused on the war in Iraq. The parting of ways does not appear to be simply contingent on a series of policy disagreements but based on a much more profound geopolitical alienation (e.g. Habermas, 2006; Kashmeri, 2006). This has roots in now competing cultures of diplomacy and statecraft as well as in very different adaptations to the post-Cold War world. Opinion surveys report increased differences in popular attitudes between the two

sides of the Atlantic about, for example, general cultural values relating to personal freedom and government control over behaviour and provision of goods and services, the desirability of the spread of American customs relating to food and consumption, American ideas about religious belief and democracy, and the US government as a threat to world peace (e.g. *Economist*, 4 January 2003; Peel, 2006). If in the US the predominant sense of victory in the Cold War has encouraged a triumphal attitude towards hitherto valued allies, in Europe the Cold War is seen as having ended because of the exhaustion of the Soviet model (and its failure to enchant those it conquered) and leads to a sceptical view of all imperialisms, whether in rhetorically democratic or in other guise (although there is now a developing European subgenre (e.g. Münkler, 2005) of a popular American brand claiming the 'necessity' for empire in 'barbarian' parts of the world).

STATES VERSUS EU

This does not mean that the sense of purpose of the EU or Europe-in-the-world has become any clearer. The failure to move forward in reorganizing the EU after the victory for the 'no' vote in the French and Dutch referenda of 2005 and renewed failure on a watered down version of constitutional reform in Ireland in 2008 suggests a serious crisis in the European political project. This is certainly not the first such predicament but because it involves how the EU works and relates to member states (now totalling 27), it may be the most serious (Gillingham, 2003; Cohen-Tanugi, 2005). In particular, many aspects of the Lisbon Agenda (such as the services directive) have stalled within the EU Council of Ministers because of public opposition. This is an indication of how European integration by 'stealth', the long-favoured approach through which elite agreement is then presented to the public as a *fait accompli*, is no longer possible, after the referendum exposé of the Constitution's institutionalization of many policies popularly judged as mistaken. Democratic responsibility is now centre stage. This may make further enlargement that includes many Balkan states and Turkey increasingly difficult. Yet, in so doing, it will also reduce the leverage that the EU has come to exercise over states waiting to join. This has been one of the most important collective powers exercised by the EU beyond its borders. At the same time, insecurity over opening markets has driven voters in many member states into renewed enthusiasm for their national governments as the EU is condemned both as an agent of globalization and as a barrier to its effectiveness in answering economic woes. But optimists can point to the fact that the EU does at least now have an official common foreign policy position and that the desire, if not much by way of ability to carry this out, remains in place (e.g. Hill, 2004; M.E. Smith, 2004). As Alan Milward (2005: 100) rightly says: 'Even when these policies amount only to declarations, they remind us that it would be very difficult to find anything comparable in Europe's long history.' Unfortunately, there is as yet an absence of effective leadership and institutional reorganization to push this forward. As a result, tensions and conflicts between particular states have come to dominate debate over Europe's future political shape. The 'reassertion of the states' pushes 'Europe' into the background.

With respect to the common foreign policy, for example, though there is a Commissioner for Foreign Affairs and a Common Foreign and Security Policy (CFSP), the office is beholden to the decisions of member states without much reference to its operation. If in other areas, such as agricultural and antitrust policies, there may be multiple 'veto points' *within* European institutions, in security and foreign affairs policy making is still largely in the hands of the individual member states. From the start, foreign and security policy was regarded as 'the most unpropitious area for institutional co-operation' (Milward, 2005: 100). As a result, national governments

still jealously guard their foreign policy imperatives. They will not be surrendered until the EU itself is reformed to make it both more democratic and more decisive. John Gillingham's (2003: 484) conclusion that 'Common defense and security policy will go nowhere until European taxpayers are willing to foot the bill for it; it lies in the distant future' seems largely correct. Although 'de-Europeanization' of foreign and security policy can be seen as operating in numerous countries (in Germany, for example; see Hellmann, 2006), Franco-British differences have been central to this impasse. What is most striking is how differences over their foreign policies reflect longstanding conventional wisdom in the two countries. As Philip Stephens (2006b) cogently argues, following their common debacle in the Suez Crisis of 1956, political elites in the two countries drew different conclusions about where to go next. If the French decided to use Europe as a counterweight to the US, the British opted for the American 'connection'. Neither has worked out as planned. But they will both have to bury the hatchet if Europe is to effectively develop its own foreign policies. This is not on the horizon:

> It is not only the French, with their efforts to build the Maginot line against globalization, who refuse to reclaim the future from the past. Driving in London the other day I saw a large official hoarding that heralded a weekend of celebrations to mark Wellington's victory against Napoleon at Waterloo in 1815. 'Celebrate one European win they can never take away,' the hoarding proudly declared (Stephens 2006b: 13).

France and Britain are also Europe's two nuclear powers and the two countries with the continent's largest military–industrial complexes (excluding Russia). These factors have undoubtedly worked against a meeting of minds on foreign policy. In France the first has remained closely associated with the office of the president and thus with the 'prestige' of the country. At key moments French presidents invoke the 'force de frappe' to emphasize France's 'great power' status, even as the defense of 'Europe' is also symbolically evoked. President Chirac's speech on 19 January 2006 about using nuclear weapons against states sheltering 'terrorists' was of this genre (Munchau, 2006). Chirac neglected to say how 'Europe' might go about launching a nuclear weapon. In Britain, its 'independent' nuclear force is dependent on US designs. Quite what either force adds to European security remains far from clear. Defence industries, however, suggest a somewhat more intricate impact. There is now considerable collaboration between European defence firms, including French and British ones, to the extent that some write about the growth of an incipient 'European security–industrial complex' (Athwal, 2006; Jones, 2006). But this view is more a reflection of the existence of an official EU Security Research Program (ESRP) and growing collaborative ventures between firms in different countries since the end of the Cold War rather than a *fait accompli* with a common industrial base that has a multinational character. Indeed, there is much evidence that not only are some major actors, such as BAE Systems (from Britain) more interested in breaking into the US market than expanding in Europe (Boxell, 2006), consolidation across national borders has been restricted with cross-border links mainly limited to joint ventures (*Economist*, 15 April 2006). Cross-border consolidation would help individual countries make the most of their defence budgets, avoid the high costs of government-sponsored collaboration, and match the US competition. It would help if European governments then ordered what was on offer. If the English Channel may still be particularly wide when it comes to defence industry consolidation, other European borders also continue to interfere with the creation of anything equivalent to the US military–industrial complex with its five major groups.

Countervailing pressure against the tendency of states to undermine the CFSP comes from more humble concerns such as those over immigration, home-grown terrorism, environmental risks, human trafficking, and policing. These seem likely to be the areas that ultimately encourage greater communality in security policy than traditional diplomacy and statecraft (Hill, 2004). The EU may ultimately pioneer in foreign policy 'from below'. Though these areas are as yet also still fraught with tensions over 'national sovereignty' in relation to traditions of criminal justice and the practicalities of how to manage immigration (e.g. on the former, see Laitner, 2006; on the latter, see Laitner and Schmid, 2006). The problem of undocumented or illegal immigrants is a particularly urgent one. For example, in the first half of 2006 alone 15,500 undocumented immigrants landed in the Canary Islands from Africa – three times the number for the whole of 2005 – and boatloads also arrived in Andalusia, Malta, and the Italian island of Lampedusa (around 12,000 on Lampedusa in the first half of 2006) (Dombey and Giles, 2006; Pérez and Robles, 2006; Repubblica, 2006). In the face of this influx, governments have actually called for help from the EU. Frontex, an EU organization, uses military equipment and personnel from all over Europe to help meet this challenge to the 'gate keeping' states such as Spain and Italy. But deciding who should and who should not have access to Europe cannot be solved militarily, however humanitarian that task is defined. Given the reduction of barriers to movement within Europe, it will have to be the EU and not the member states that ultimately must develop a common policy on immigration as on other issues such as police work across borders and limiting human trafficking. The threat from home-grown terrorism, particularly of disenchanted Muslim immigrants and converts, also seems likely to stimulate cross-border collaboration on policing. Finally, environmental risks, from global climate change and epidemics of flu and HIV/AIDS to the threats to the food chain from industrialized farming, will increasingly require policies that do not stop at international borders. As states, particularly the large ones with histories of global grandeur, disagree over 'high' foreign policy, possibly the only way the EU will be bolstered will be by the need to address problems that the states alone either cannot or will not address.

CONCLUSION

Europe cannot be reduced to the EU in the way that part of North America can be to the US. A fundamental element in the official rhetoric of the EU is to make the confusion between them as if the organizational and the geographical Europe map neatly onto each other. The issue is not the question of whether membership must cover all European states but, more profoundly, which ideas of Europe underpin the attempt to unify it. This is important geopolitically because confusing Europe with the EU presents a more homogeneous subject for discussion about the prospects for global presence than the truly variegated and contested EU ever could. Yet, this geographical inheritance is more contestable than self-evident. While many of the largest states, particularly, Britain and France, continue to harbour delusions of grandeur as independent operators, the EU is only likely to develop an effective common security framework by building from such relatively humble security policy arenas as terrorism, immigration, and environmental risks. Overall, however, in terms of securing a common European space, a separate 'political' Europe is still more incipient than accomplished. Even if it does develop its collaborative and coordinating roles, it is not clear that a 'scaled-up' state will ever replace the existing ones as many scenarios about 'Europe' as a future superpower contend. A crucial issue in developing the basis for a collaborative security policy is the degree to which this Europe will remain entangled with an American foreign policy and a security apparatus – that of NATO – which seem increasingly at odds in method and geographical scope with the original Atlantic compact. Strangely, at the moment when it seems least adapted to European goals, it has undergone a revival.

This paradox may not last long if NATO's intervention in Afghanistan goes badly. A change of US administration in 2009 could bring greater parallelism between US and European security goals. Of course, that change would also depend on how much the division between many EU states and the US government over the Middle East in general and Iraq, in particular, could be transcended, and the extent to which the American 'war on terror' is exacerbated by new events. The profligacy of the US Bush administration in spending its vast resources of political capital around the world after 9/11 will also not readily be undone. Even as the US faces the real possibility of hegemonic decline, however, 'Europe' is neither ready – because Europe and the EU are not the same thing – nor capable, in current world conditions (as American baseball parlance would have it) 'to step up to the plate'.

ACKNOWLEDGMENTS

I would like to thank Ivan Berend, Felicity Nussbaum, and Chris Rumford for helpful comments and suggestions on previous drafts of the chapter. Of course, they are not responsible for what I have finally produced.

REFERENCES

Agnew, J.A. (2005) *Hegemony: The New Shape of Global Power*. Philadephia: Temple University Press.

Agnew, J.A. (2007) 'No borders, no nations: making Greece in Macedonia', *Annals of the Association of American Geographers*, 97 (2): 398–422.

Albright, M. (1997) 'Enlarging NATO: why bigger is better', *Economist*, 15 February.

Athwal, H. (2006) 'The emergence of a European security-industrial complex', *IRR News*. Available at: www.irr.org.uk/2006/may/ha000016.html, accessed 20 May 2006.

Ash, T.G., Moisi, D., and Smolar, A. (2006) 'Europe must not trade its principles for Russian gas', *Financial Times*, 10 July.

Barnett, C. (2005) 'The consolations of "neo-liberalism"', *Geoforum*, 36: 7–12.

Bartlett, R. (1993) *The Making of Europe: Conquest, Colonization and Cultural Change.* London: Penguin.

Berend, I.T. (2005) 'What is Central and Eastern Europe?', *European Journal of Social Theory*, 8: 401–416.

Berg, E. and Ehin, P. (2006) 'What kind of border regime is in the making?', *Cooperation and Conflict*, 41: 53–71.

Berman, J. (2003) '(Un)popular strangers and crises (un)bounded: discourses of sex trafficking, the European political community and the panicked state of the modern state', *European Journal of International Relations*, 9: 37–86.

Bereuter, D. (2006) 'NATO must try harder in its Afghan mission', *Financial Times*, 29 June, p. 15.

Bialasiewicz, L. and Minca, C. (2005) 'Old Europe, new Europe: for a geopolitics of translation', *Area*, 37: 365–372.

Boxell, J. (2006) 'BAE Systems pursues its Atlantic devotion', *Financial Times*, 30 August, p. 19.

Calleo, D.P. (2003) 'Power, wealth and wisdom: the United States and Europe after Iraq', *The National Interest*, 72: 5–15.

Carpenter, T.G. (2004) 'Outside view: NATO – a troubled marriage', UPI. Available at www.washingtontimes.com/upi-breaking/20040623-102730-7970r.htm, accessed 20 May 2006.

Chakrabarty, D. (2000) *Provincializing Europe: Postcolonial Thought and Historical Difference.* Princeton: Princeton University Press.

Chandrasekaran, R. (2006) *Imperial Life in the Emerald City: Inside Iraq's Green Zone.* New York: Vintage.

Cohen, S. (2005) 'The Eurasian convergence zone: gateway or shatterbelt?', *Eurasian Geography and Economics*, 46: 1–22.

Cohen-Tanugi, L. (2005) 'The end of Europe?', *Foreign Affairs*, 84 (November/December): 55–67.

Connery, C. (2004) 'Ideologies of land and sea: Alfred Thayer Mahan, Carl Schmitt, and the shaping of global myth elements', *Boundary 2*, 28 (2): 173–201.

Daalder, I. and Goldgeier, J. (2006) 'Global NATO', *Foreign Affairs*, 85 (September/October): 105–113.

Dean, J. (1997) 'The NATO mistake: expansion for all the wrong reasons', *Washington Monthly*, 7: 7–12.

Derrida, J. (2004) *Une Europe de l'espoir.* Paris: Flammarion.

Dombey, D. and Giles, C. (2006) 'The price of prosperity: why Fortress Europe needs to lower the drawbridge', *Financial Times*, 18 May, p. 9.

Economist (24 August 2002) 'Half a billion Americans?', 20–22.

Economist (4 January 2003) 'Living with a superpower', 18–20.

Economist (15 April 2006) 'Not in formation', 62–65.

Economist (10 June 2006) 'The Taliban resurgent', 37–38.

Eder, K. (2006) 'Europe's borders: the narrative construction of the boundaries of Europe', *European Journal of Social Theory*, 9: 255–271.

Fallows, J. (2006) *Blind into Baghdad: America's War in Iraq.* New York: Vintage.

Fidler, S. and Morarjee, R. (2006) 'Mission impossible? Why stabilizing Afghanistan will be a stiff test for NATO', *Financial Times*, 31 July, p. 9.

Financial Times (2006) 'Allies wary of backing UK force in Afghanistan', 31 August, p. 1.

Gheciu, A. (2005) *NATO in the 'New Europe'.* Stanford CA: Stanford University Press.

Giesen, B. (1998) *The Intellectuals and the Nation: Collective Identity in the German Axial Age.* Cambridge: Cambridge University Press.

Gillingham, J. (2003) *European Integration, 1950–2003: Superstate or New Market Economy?* Cambridge: Cambridge University Press.

Gowan, P. (1999) *The Global Gamble: Washington's Faustian Bid for Global Dominance.* London: Verso.

Habermas, J. (2006) *The Divided West.* Cambridge: Polity.

Hagen, J. (2003) 'Redrawing the imagined map of Europe: the rise and fall of the "center"', *Political Geography*, 22: 489–517.

Harvey, D. (2003) *The New Imperialism.* Oxford: Oxford University Press.

Hay, D. (1968) *Europe: The Emergence of an Idea*, revised edn. Edinburgh: Edinburgh University Press.

Heffernan, M. (1998) *The Meaning of Europe: Geography and Geopolitics*. London: Arnold.

Hellmann, G. (ed.) (2006) *Germany's EU Policy on Asylum and Defense: De- Europeanization by Default?* New York: Palgrave Macmillan.

Herzfeld, M. (2002) 'The European self: rethinking an attitude', in A. Pagden (ed.) *The Idea of Europe: From Antiquity to the European Union*. Cambridge: Cambridge University Press, pp. 139–70.

Hill, C. (2004) 'Renationalizing or regrouping? EU foreign policy since 11 September', *Journal of Common Market Studies*, 42: 143–163.

Jacoby, W. (2004) *The Enlargement of the European Union and NATO: Ordering from the Menu in Central Europe*. New York: Cambridge University Press.

Jones, S.G. (2006) 'The rise of a European defense', *Political Science Quarterly*, 121: 241–267.

Kagan, R. (2003) *Paradise and Power: America and Europe in the New World Order*. New York: Knopf.

Kashmeri, S. (2006) *America and Europe after 9/11 and Iraq: The Great Divide*. Westport CT: Praeger.

Kupchan, C. (2002) *The End of the American Era*. New York: Basic Books.

Kuus, M. (2002) 'Toward cooperative security? International integration and the construction of security in Estonia', *Millennium*, 31 (1): 1–20.

Kuus, M. (2004) 'Europe's eastern expansion and the reinscription of Otherness in East-Central Europe', *Progress in Human Geography*, 28: 472–489.

Laitner, S. (2006) 'EU plan to fight terror in tatters', *Financial Times*, 23/24 September, p. 2.

Laitner, S. and Schmid, F. (2006) 'EU ministers challenge Madrid's policy on migrants', *Financial Times*, 22 September, p. 3.

Layne, C. (2003) 'America as European hegemon', *The National Interest*, 72: 17–29.

Leonard, M. (2006) *Why Europe will Run the 21st Century*. New York: Public Affairs.

Lieven, A. (2006) 'A hypocritical approach to Russia', *Financial Times*, 31 May, p. 11.

Lieven, A. (2008) 'The West shares the blame for Georgia', *Financial Times*, 14 August, p. 9.

Luke, T. W. (1996) 'Governmentality and contragovernmentality: rethinking sovereignty and territoriality after the Cold War', *Political Geography*, 15: 491–507.

Malmborg, M. af and Stråth, B. (2002) 'Introduction: the national meanings of Europe', in M. af Malmborg and B. Stråth (eds) *The Meaning of Europe*. Oxford: Berg.

Matthews, J. (2001) 'Estranged partners', *Foreign Policy*, (November/December): 5–9.

Mearsheimer, J.J. (2002) *The Tragedy of Great Power Politics*. New York: Norton.

Meyer, C.O. (2005) 'Convergence towards a European strategic culture? A constructivist framework for explaining changing norms', *European Journal of International Relations*, 11: 523–549.

Milward, A. (2005) 'Review article: the European Union as a superstate', *International History Review*, 27: 90–105.

Munchau, W. (2006) 'Chirac's vain threat is a strategic mess', *Financial Times*, 23 January, p. 15.

Münkler, H. (2005) *Imperien: Die Logic der Weltherrschaft – vom Alten Rom bis zu den Vereinigten Staaten*. Berlin: Rowohlt.

Neumann, I.B. (1999) *Uses of the Other: 'The East' in European Identity Formation*. Minneapolis: University of Minnesota Press.

O'Loughlin, J., Ó Tuathail, G. and Kolossov, V. (2004) 'A risky westward turn? Putin's 9-11 script and ordinary Russians', *Europe-Asia Studies*, 56: 3–34.

Pagden, A. (2002) 'Conceptualizing a continent', in A. Pagden (ed.) *The Idea of Europe: From Antiquity to the European Union*. Cambridge: Cambridge University Press, pp. 33–54.

Passerini, L. (ed.) (1998) *Identità culturale Europea: Idée, sentimenti, relazioni*. Florence: La Nuova Italia.

Peel, Q. (2006) 'Old Europe continues to lose enthusiasm for US', *Financial Times*, 16 June, p. 13.

Pérez, F.S. and Robles, E.S. (2006) *L'Immigration Illégale en Europe: Le cas d'Espagne*. Paris: Fondation Robert Schuman.

Pocock, J.G.A. (1997) 'What do we mean by Europe?', *Wilson Quarterly*, 21(Winter): 12–29.

Pocock, J.G.A. (2002) 'Some Europes in their history', in A. Pagden (ed.) *The Idea of Europe: From Antiquity to the European Union*. Cambridge: Cambridge University Press, pp. 55–71.

Reid, T.R. (2004) *The United States of Europe: The New Superpower and the End of American Supremacy*. London: Penguin.

Repubblica, La (2006) 'Lampedusa, bloccati 260 clandestini', 14 August.

Rhodes, E. (2004) 'The good, the bad, and the righteous: understanding the Bush vision of a New NATO Partnership', *Millennium*, 33: 123–143.

Ricks, T.R. (2006) *Fiasco: The American Military Adventure in Iraq*. New York: Penguin.

Rieker, P. (2004) 'Europeanization of Nordic security: The European Union and the changing security identities of the Nordic states', *Cooperation and Conflict*, 39: 369–392.

Rosecrance, R. (2003) 'Croesus and Caesar: the essential transatlantic relationship', *The National Interest*, 72: 31–34.

Ruttley, P. (2002) 'The long road to unity: the contribution of law to the process of European integration since 1945', in A. Pagden (ed.) *The Idea of Europe: From Antiquity to the European Union*. Cambridge: Cambridge University Press, pp. 228–259.

Rynning, S. (2003) 'The European Union: towards a strategic culture?' *Security Dialogue*, 34: 481.

Sandler, T. and Hartley, K. (1999) *The Political Economy of NATO: Past, Present and into the 21st Century*. Cambridge: Cambridge University Press.

Sedelmeier, U. (2006) *Constructing the Path to Eastern Enlargement: The Uneven Policy Impact of EU Identity*. New York: Palgrave Macmillan.

Smith, D. (2006) *Deterring America: Rogue States and the Proliferation of Weapons of Mass Destruction*. Cambridge: Cambridge University Press.

Smith, M.E. (2004) *Europe's Foreign and Security Policy: The Institutionalization of Cooperation*. New York: Cambridge University Press.

Stephens, P. (2006a) 'The paradox of being insecure in a more peaceful world', *Financial Times*, 15 September, p. 15.

Stephens, P. (2006b) 'Chirac and Blair reach the end of the road from Suez to Iraq', *Financial Times*, 9 June, p. 13.

Van der Pijl, K. (2006) 'Lockean Europe?', *New Left Review, Second Series*, 37: 9–37.

Verdery, K. (1996) *What was Socialism and What Comes Next?* Princeton NJ: Princeton University Press.

Wallerstein, I. (2006) 'The curve of US power', *New Left Review, Second Series*, 40: 77–94.

Wickham, C. (1994) 'Making Europes', *New Left Review*, 208: 133–143.

Williams, M.C. and Neumann, I.B. (2000) 'From alliance to security community: NATO, Russia, and the power of identity', *Millennium*, 29: 357–387.

Wilson, K. and van der Dussen, J. (eds) (1995) *The History of the Idea of Europe*. London: Routledge.

Wolff, L. (1994) *Inventing Eastern Europe: The Map of Civilization in the Mind of the Enlightenment*. Stanford CA: Stanford University Press.

Žižek, S. (2006) *The Parallax View*. Cambridge MA: MIT Press.

18

Nationalism and Transnationalism

Victor Roudometof

This chapter discusses both nationalism and transnationalism and focuses on the dynamic interplay between the two. While attention is paid to the global evolution of these concepts, emphasis is placed in the historical patterns of the New (post-1945 and post-1989) Europe. By way of introduction, the chapter discusses the different disciplinary conventions that have shaped our understandings of 'national' and 'transnational'. Taking the current transnationalization of individual life-worlds throughout Europe as its departure point, it poses the question whether the nation-state is becoming a relic of the past, and whether post-World War II European developments offer sufficient support for such a postnational thesis. By the term 'post-national' I refer to these theoretical and policy-making perspectives that have suggested that the world (and Europe, in particular,) has moved beyond the historical phase of nationalism as a popular form of legitimacy and sovereignty. Accordingly, in the post-1989 New World Order the principles of democracy, rule of law, human rights and so on are (or should be) applied universally without them being mediated, filtered, reinterpreted and restricted by the nation state. However, a brief overview of recent policy trends suggests that there is insufficient support for such a thesis: while postnationalism was a major popular theme in the 1990s, the post-9/11 international environment has significantly curtailed its appeal both in Europe and worldwide.

But this does not mean that Europe remains hostage to nationalism. Rather, as the next section of this chapter argues, European institutions have rather successfully developed a formal and informal culture of compromise whereby nationalist disputes are managed through various institutions. Europeans have been able to put their nationalisms into good use, so to speak, and the strength and progress of the EU is largely dependent upon the local national images of a future united Europe. Lastly, while the cross-cultural flows of people, ideas, and media products have led to the transnationalization of everyday life throughout Europe, the same does not apply to various regimes governing the movement of 'Third Countries nationals' (TCNs) into the common EU space. With regard to immigrant transnationalism, several different modes of incorporation have been developed, ranging from immigrant assimilation to interactive pluralism. European societies are not likely to adopt a uniform regime or mode of incorporation with regard to TCNs. On the contrary, it is far more likely that each society will develop its own context-specific regime.

UNDERSTANDING THE 'NATIONAL' AND THE 'TRANSNATIONAL': CROSS-DISCIPLINARY FORMULATIONS AND RESEARCH AGENDAS

The terms 'national' and 'transnational' are used in several different disciplines, each with its own research agenda and its own conventions. Traditionally, the 'national' was an area of sociological inquiry and historical introspection, while the 'international' was sharply separated from it and was constructed as a separate field addressing the interaction among states. This division of intellectual work was reconfigured after World War II as the term 'transnational' gradually gained currency in different discourses.

The concept of the 'national' and its related terms (such as, nationalism, the nation, and so on) have been traditionally viewed as expressions of European modernity and modernization processes (Gellner, 1983; Hobsbawm, 1990). Smith, for example, makes it abundantly clear that for him 'the key to an understanding of nations and nationalism as general phenomena of the modern world lies more with the persisting frameworks and legacies of historical cultures and ethnic ties than with the consequences of global interdependence' (1995: viii). Such a view of the 'global' entails an implicit understanding of global interconnectedness as fairly recent and congruent with post-World War II increases in mass communication. More historically oriented views of globalization suggest that the nation-state is not the conceptual adversary of globalization. Rather, its existence in the long duree of world history was shaped by globalization, while its presence continues to be fuelled by transnational processes

(see Anderson, 1991; Holton, 1998; Short, 2001; Walby, 2003). Echoing these new intellectual currents, the perspective adopted in the discussion in this chapter is closer to that of Delanty and O'Mahoney (2002: 3), who view modernity (and the nation) as emerging out of historical globalization. To push this argument further, I suggest that both the 'national' and the 'transnational' are mutually constructed expressions of the 'global'. That is, if nationalism is said to be a motivational force behind nation formation, the transnationalization of individual life-worlds is but the inescapable consequence of successfully concluding the nation-formation process. To put it differently, it takes a world of nations for transnational experiences to exist.

Initially, the 'transnational' was used to designate the movement of corporations outside their original bases of operation. Whether such enterprises ought to be considered multinational or transnational was the subject of an early debate in economic sociology and economics. The label migrated into the discipline of international relations (IR) in the early 1970s, whereby, the argument was originally made that transnational forces were altering the foundations of IR (Keohane and Nye, 1971). Instead of relations among states (e.g. inter-national), researchers had to conceptualize their field as being shaped by a multitude of non-state actors – ranging from NGOs to social movements – that intervened into the very nature of relations among states and altered the foundations of global politics. Over the last three decades, James Rosenau (1990, 2003) emerged as a key figure in this research agenda and his influence extended beyond the IR literature. Rosenau has been one of the progenitors of what came to be known as globalization theory in the 1990s (see Waters, 1995).

In the 1990s, the label 'transnational' migrated to anthropology, political science and sociology and its employment reflected the research agendas of each discipline and the conventions of each particular field (for reviews and comparisons of different research foci, see Mahler, 2000; Morawska, 2003;

Vetrovec, 2003). To this day, the IR defini- tion of 'transnational' activities and similar definitions of it in social theory remain looser than sociologically oriented defini- tions (e.g. Portes, 2001), whereby the terms 'international', 'multinational' and 'transna- tional' are sharply distinguished from each other. Portes (2001) maintains that the 'tran- snational' should be reserved for activities initiated and sustained by non-institutional actors, whether these are organized groups of networks of individuals across borders.

However, in addition to its application to the field of international migration, the concept of the 'transnational' has been applied since the early 1990s in several other fields – such as cross-border activism, religious communities, social movements, family, the study of the state, and class analysis (for examples, see Chamberlain and Leyedsdorff, 2004; Keck and Sikkink, 1998; Kennedy and Roudometof, 2002; Smith *et al.*, 1997; Robinson, 2001; Sklair, 2001; van der Veer, 2002). In a review of the trends in the field, Portes (2003) insists that the concept of transnationalism should remain connected to movement of peoples without extending into its application to cross-cultural flows and communities of taste or profession. In contrast, cosmopolitan the- orists, such as, Beck (2005) have used the notion of transnationalization or the transna- tional ways of life as indicators that the expe- rience of social life is changing, leading to the possible emergence of a cosmopolitan society.

Hence, current academic discourse suggests that there are at least two ways to interpret the 'transnational'. First, there is a 'narrow' interpretation, whereby the 'transnational' is restricted to activities of actors across borders. Second, there is a broader and loose sense of the 'transnational' as a designation that can refer to a broader range of biographical expe- riences (such as, the metaphorical crossing of borders through Internet communication) and/or cultural and institutional trends. This second interpretation of the 'transnational' is closely connected to a major shift in the under- standing and interpretation of the 'national'. Sociologists have grown increasingly aware

that looking upon the social world as consist- ing of 'national societies' which are 'contained' within nation states is a highly distorted image of reality, one that no longer provides an accurate representation of social realities and perhaps it never did (Albrow, 1997; Touraine, 2003). Transcending or overthrowing meth- odological nationalism (Wimmer and Glick Schiller, 2004) has become a new gospel that aims at reconceptualizing social relations through the development of conceptual frameworks that do not reify national borders (see Urry, 2000).

In light of the above, then, it is reasonable to distinguish between the broader cultural experience of the 'transnational' and the nar- rower concept of immigrant transnationalism. This distinction is relevant for understanding the specificity of the European condition. The construction and operation of the EU's free and unrestricted zones of cultural, politi- cal and economic activities and a wealth of Commission directives and other actions (such as, for example, the Schengen Treaty) have led to the strengthening and routiniza- tion of transnational ways of life in EU's member states. This is particularly true for the pre-2004 EU member states (the so-called EU-15). But the sheer generation of transna- tional forms of broadcasting, media, residency, leisure, sports (e.g. Champions League) and so on does not necessarily imply that the EU has successfully dealt with immigrant tran- snationalism as a reality. On the contrary, even EU citizens display relatively limited (in comparison to the US) desire to work and live outside their nation-state. It is important to stress that, as a matter of law, the right to work and live anywhere in the EU is a reality for the citizens of the EU member states (at least for the EU-15, but increasingly for the EU-25 as well). In this regard, the EU-sponsored policy of fostering develop- ment toward its less developed regions has a nationalist impulse: it sharply reduces the necessity for transnational mobility within an integrated Europe. Over the post-1970 period, the decline of southern European immigration toward Germany and other northern European countries is an apt illustration of this paradoxical situation. The realization of this paradox, whereby Europeans lack the motivation to exercise their right to work throughout the EU, has led the EU to sponsor student mobility (in the form of the SOCRATES program and other similar schemes), in an effort to prompt the socialization of youth with other cultures, which in turn might provide an incentive for transnational mobility.

As the above example illustrates, constructions of European transnational space are not necessarily all-inclusive. To cite another relevant example, religion (Protestantism and Catholicism) was employed as a means of defining 'Europe' in terms of a shared cultural space (see, for example, Delanty, 1995: 48–58; Gemerek 1996). This use of transnational religion for the purposes of EU membership was popular in the 1980s and 1990s throughout Catholic and Protestant Eastern European countries, and was in large part based upon the earlier and popular Russophobia in the region (see, for example, Kundera, 1984; for further discussion, see Schopflin and Wood, 1989). Such a use of transnational religion amounted to a new civilizational division of Europe along religious lines, with the Central (Catholic and Protestant) Europeans having a legitimate claim to EU membership to the detriment of Eastern Orthodox countries. Its most blunt expression has been Huntington's (1996) 'clash of civilizations' thesis, where Orthodox Eastern European countries were altogether excluded from membership to the 'West'.

The limited and short-lived appeal of such a vision became apparent fairly quickly. In the 1990s, the EU's strategy of pursuing its 2004 East European enlargement without a social profile or social convergence sparked fear in large segments of the European public. Its reactions are fairly well known: support for xenophobic parties or for right-wing regionalism, a negative vote in the referenda for the EU Constitution in France and the Netherlands, and widespread negative attitudes regarding the possibility of Turkey's ascent to the EU. European enlargement and efforts toward integration have been thus haunted by the prospects of EU enlargement into geographical zones traditionally viewed as 'exotic' and 'dangerous' (Todorova, 1997). In turn, delaying or postponing the expansion of full membership benefits to the new post-2004 East European EU member states was greeted with hostile remarks that such strategies of exclusion are to a degree anti-European, or that they pave the way toward a segmentation of European unity. It is not accidental that East European reaction to the Habermas-Derrida 'Core Europe' proposal (see Levy et al., 2005) centred precisely on this issue |of Eastern Europeans being made to feel second-class citizens.

Underneath it all, of course, lies the deep-seated fear that EU enlargement is detrimental to the welfare state, that further participation and strengthening of EU breeds the lowering of the living standards and the disappearance of the social welfare system that took over a century to construct. Fear of job losses is but an aspect of this attitude – and it remains widespread in countries whose economies have had considerable difficulties and where unemployment remains high. It is within this reality in mind, then, that the 'transnationalization' of European life-worlds has provided the means to argue that twenty-first century European nations now open up their 'national containers' to the 'world' and become cosmopolitan in nature (Beck, 2000). A critical component of this interpretation concerns the extent to which European nationalisms have been superseded by more inclusive and broader loyalties. To put it differently, do we live in a postnational Europe?

EUROPEAN DEVELOPMENTS IN GLOBAL PERSPECTIVE: TOWARD A POST-NATIONAL EUROPE?

In the nineteenth century and up to 1945, nationalism served as a mainstream idea for the construction of homogeneous national societies around the globe, while transnational people were often viewed as anomalies within the international system of nation states (Mayall, 1990; Musgrave, 1997). It is important to stress that, while this image of European homogeneous national societies does not conform to the historical reality of the pre-1945 era (see Sassen, 1998; Thaller, 2001), it nonetheless provided the *modus operandi* during the modern era of European nation-state building. This particular world-view lies underneath the great catastrophes of European history – such as the Holocaust, various cases of ethnic cleansing in Eastern Europe, the two world wars, and so on (Hobsbawm, 1990; see Vardy and Tooley, 2003).

During the post-1945 period, the growth of transnational institutions, the construction of a world culture (Lechner and Boli, 2005), the proliferation of major economic alliances (NAFTA, EU), the multiplication of international treaties, the emergence of an international post-World War II regime of international law, rules, and conventions have significantly circumscribed state sovereignty. The aforementioned developments have provided the backdrop for the argument that the era of the nation state is now over and that state sovereignty no longer provides the foundational cornerstone for international politics and interstate relations (for discussions, see Held, 1995; McGrew and Lewis, 1992; Ohmae, 1995). Europe provides perhaps the most suitable example of this interpretation. With the rise of the EU over the second half of the twentieth century, elements of state sovereignty have been transferred at the supranational or subnational levels, thereby making the state less directly engulfed by nationalism. Additionally, the expressed desire of the post-World War II generation to construct institutions that would in effect make impossible a return to the nationalist policies of the pre-World War II era contributed greatly to the EU's post-World War II economic and political success. The very success of the new institutions (the EU, the Council of Europe, the ECHR, etc.) has fostered the image of a post-national Europe, whereby nationalism has become obsolete and transnationalization

contributes to the construction of a broader regional identity.

This new cosmopolitan internationalism looks upon the age-old principle of state sovereignty as a remnant of the 1648 Westphalian regime – a regime that is disintegrating rapidly in the post-Cold War 'New World Order'. The 1990–1991 Iraq War and, later on, the international interventions in the former Yugoslavia offered good test cases to plausibly argue that the world was now operating under a very different set of rules than in the Cold War era. The 1999 'Kosovo crisis' provided the paradigmatic case of international intervention to circumscribe the effects of local Serb nationalism. The decision to forcefully alter Serb policy in the area and to transform Kosovo into an international protectorate under UN control owed much to the strength of the US-sponsored globalist thinking of the 1990s (for a critique, see Chomsky, 1999). In many respects, it provided a tangible application of discussions about nationalism (and internationalism or cosmopolitanism) in the mid-1990s (see Neusbawm, 1996). The theme already explored in the mid-1990s concerned the degree to which a new form of cosmopolitan society was now emerging and which, if any, was the place of nationalism (or patriotism) in the 'New World Order'.

The US experience is not exceptional. On the other side of the Atlantic, a similar agenda was pursued in the 1990s. In the aftermath of the Amsterdam (1997) and Maastricht (1992) treaties and the evolution of the 'European Community' (EC) into the 'European Union' (EU), it looked as if a future united European state would be a tangible project that could supersede local European nationalisms. The EU logo 'unity in diversity' was therefore tilted toward the first of the two components. Signs that indicated the limited inclusion of immigrants into the body politic of the European states were halted as a sign of a move toward the 'postnational' membership to a state (Soysal, 1994). That is, immigrants who were hitherto excluded from the benefits of formal citizenship could find informal or semiformalized ways to participate into the national or local politics of their host countries, thereby eroding the exclusive nature of citizenship.

Contrary to such an optimistic scenario, Sassen (1996) argued that immigration did not bring about the denationalization of national politics, but rather it promoted the renationalization of the political body by strengthening xenophobia, racism and ethnocentrism. Her argument was cast as a compromise solution between those who viewed a more open, cosmopolitan future of a borderless world and those who expressed considerable scepticism toward such a vision. The ongoing discussion on cosmopolitanism as an expression of a European world-view is in many respects the latest twist on long-standing efforts to transcend local European nationalisms in favour of a larger European identity (see Beck, 2005; Delanty, 1995; Delanty and Rumford, 2005).

All of the above represent trends popular in the post-1989 period among the scholarly community but also in discussions in the press and the public. The tenor of such debates did not always coincide with contemporary developments. For example, when the Austrian ultra-right-wing conservatives won the 1999 national elections, the general European and American reaction was that of surprise and great effort was placed to explain Austrian exceptionalism from shared European standards. In addition, the EU reacted by enforcing an effective and persistent embargo against the new government and that action quickly led to a different coalition government in Austria. If Austria could be 'explained away' as a somewhat anomalous case in 1999, the post-9/11 shifts in the cultural landscapes of North America and Western Europe cast grave doubts upon the possibility of treating nationalism as a remnant of the past – as Hobsbawm did in the last chapter of his *Nations and Nationalism* (1990). In the US, the 9/11 tragedy was quickly 'nationalized' and the 'war on terrorism' soon assumed the characteristics of a national crusade to vindicate American patriotism. In the EU, popular opinion also shifted toward localism amid

fears of terrorist attacks and through the rejection of the EU Constitution in France and the Netherlands, and widely expressed fears of a future Turkish membership into EU (which provides a good template upon which to register resentment against immigration or simply xenophobic sentiments). Irrespectively of whether 'nationalism is the enemy of Europe's nations' – as Beck and Giddens (2005) declared – at least in the foreseeable future the notion of a postnational Europe does not represent a popular trend in European societies.

FACING NATIONALISM IN THE NEW EUROPE

But while the death of European nationalisms might have been somewhat prematurely announced, it does not necessarily mean that twenty-first century Europe is still hostage to its bloody history of ethnic and national antagonisms. On the contrary, over the post-1945 period, Europeans, through a variety of institutions, have developed particularly successful institutional means to face up to the nationalism of their respective nation states. In fact, it is the very success of the post-1945 European developments that has provided the foundation for contemplating a postnational future. That is, as already discussed in the previous section, in post-1945 Europe the devolution of sovereignty both in supranational and subnational units, as well as the web of agreements, associations and treaties into which most European states are parties has meant a considerable curtailment in the ability of the European states to act as the principle carriers of nationalism.

Consequently, contemporary European nationalisms are no longer neatly connected with particular states. This is particularly evident when one looks at the two main expressions of the post-1945 nationalism in the continent, that is (a) the 'peripheral' nationalisms within predominantly Western European states; and (b) the nationalisms of the East European 'nations without states', which dominated Europe's political land-scape over the 1990s. Let us briefly review both these categories of nationalism. First come the 'peripheral' nationalisms observed in the heart of the so-called 'Old Europe' (Spain, Britain, France); that is, in nation states that, for the most part and with some exceptions (such as, Italy, for example) can boast a long and continuous history of state building. Such nationalist movements were observed in Italy (through the creation of Northern League), in Spain (through the Basque and Catalan movements), in France, and of course in Great Britain (through the Welsh and Scottish national movements). In the post-1945 period, these peripheral national movements have challenged the authority of the centralized state. In so doing, such move-ments did not hesitate to use the EU as a supranational agent that could legitimize their aspirations. The EU often sought to capitalize on such developments by fostering the construction of the 'Europe of the regions', thereby, suggesting that subnational units could find a place into a united Europe, and use the EU as a mechanism that would allow them greater autonomy from the national centre. It became thus possible to think of 'nations without states' – such as the cases of Catalonia or Scotland (Giordano and Roller, 2002; Guibernau, 1999; Nairn, 1977).

The second instance of local nationalisms comes from the experience of the Eastern European 'nations without states' which, in the post-1989 period, sought to formalize their national status by seeking formal inde-pendence. In Eastern Europe, three multieth-nic or multinational units disappeared from the map (the USSR, Yugoslavia and Czechoslovakia). While in the USSR and in Czechoslovakia statesmen were able to find amicable ways for their 'velvet divorce' with their former partners, in Yugoslavia this type of minority nationalism paved the way for the bloody warfare in Croatia and Bosnia (Cohen, 1993; Hayden, 1999). In spite of their differ-ences in terms of the peaceful or confron-tational dissolution of these disputes, all these cases deserve to be treated differently from their Western European counterparts.

All Eastern European societies share the experi-ence of communism as a constitutive compo-nent of their post-1945 history. Of course, communist regimes were neither monolithic nor uniform and they adopted themselves to local national conditions with an almost chameleon-like ability. In Romania, FYR-Macedonia and Albania, for example, commu-nist regimes did not hesitate to use extensively nationalism as a means for gaining legitimacy; in effect, leading to a continuation of past nationalization tendencies within these regions. In contrast, in the People's Republic of Ukraine or in Tito's Yugoslavia, the communist regimes effectively excluded nationalism from their rhetoric and viewed it as their arch-rival.

But in practical terms and irrespective of the policy pursued by local communist parties, the communist regimes throughout Eastern Europe contributed greatly to the tacit accept-ance of national sovereignty. They did so by providing a territorial reference point for several nations-without-states by creating state structures that were meant to be under the control of the Communist Party. This pat-tern is observed both in the former USSR as well as in the former Yugoslavia. When, in the aftermath of the 1989–1990 revolutions, the communist regimes collapsed, the abstract statehood of the various People's Republics was quickly seized by local politicians and used as a means for obtaining their formal recognition as sovereign, independent states. The challenge involved in this transformation pertained to the artificiality of the new borders, which were originally meant to be 'internal' borders within the context of a larger federa-tion (such as, in Czechoslovakia, Yugoslavia and the former USSR). These borders were not drawn as external, international borders among sovereign states. The logic followed by the communists in constructing them served purposes completely different from circumscribing the boundaries of a nation-state – the inclusion of the Crimea within the People's Republic of Ukraine is an apt exam-ple of past communist practices. It was quite predictable, then, that border disputes and national rivalries would emerge (or in some cases, re-emerge) in a forceful manner.

Brubaker (1996) has provided perhaps the most insightful analysis of the East European imbroglio. In his interpretation, Brubaker has pointed out that catastrophic outcomes – such as the Yugoslav wars of the 1990s – are typically borne out of an institutional interplay among three units. First, there are nationalizing states set on assimilating minorities into their mainstream; second, there are national minorities that identify with nation-states other than the ones they are located; and third, there exist external national homelands that can be construed as these minorities' desired or 'natural' places of belonging. In the 1990s, the ethnic rivalry between Romania and Hungary (and Romania and Moldova) provided another tangible application of Brubaker's model; yet, these states were able to deal with the situation more constructively than the former Yugoslavia.

Following the collapse of communism in Eastern Europe, then, it might be more fruitful to view the nationalisms developed in the two parts of the continent not on the basis of divisions that no longer exist (such as, East and West), but rather in terms of the strategies pursued within the context of the emerging twenty-first century Europe. Csergo and Goldgeier (2004) point out that these strategies are shaped to a considerable degree by whether the EU is viewed as an alliance of states or as a union of nations. The former option provides both for the pursuit of a traditional nationalism and that of a protectionist nationalism. Traditional nationalism maintains its state-centred focus and seeks to unite a people with a national homeland. In addition to the Irish Catholics in Northern Ireland, many newly independent states, such as, Croatia, Estonia, Latvia, Lithuania, and Slovakia, as well as some older states such as Bulgaria and Romania, provide solid examples that this old-fashioned form of nationalism persists. Protectionist nationalism is most often found in Western European states (Austria, Belgium, France), although instances exist (such as, the Czech policy toward the Roma) where Eastern European states also act in a similar fashion.

The latter option (e.g. viewing the EU as a union of nations) can provide both for

substate nationalism (which has already been discussed above) and trans-sovereign nationalism. Trans-sovereign nationalism can be observed in Romania's policy toward the Romanians in the Republic of Moldova or Hungary's policy toward its minorities in neighbouring countries or in Greece's policy toward Albania's Greeks. In this case, the home country is seeking to develop specific policies that co-opt and integrate a minority beyond its borders within its nation. Most often, the pursuit of such policies does lead to extensive and protracted disputes among neighbouring states. Perhaps the most destructive example of such conflict is the Serbian policy pursued during the reign of Slobodan Milosevic toward the Serb minorities in Kosovo, Bosnia, and Croatia. The persistent crises of the 1990s were in large part fuelled by the confrontation between the traditional nationalist strategy of the former Yugoslav 'nations without states' and the Serb trans-sovereign nationalism.

Generally, the EU has been relatively powerless and/or unwilling to intervene in the Balkans. Both in Bosnia and in Kosovo, it was the US that assumed the leading role in military intervention. If the EU was not able to formulate a coherent foreign policy with regard to direct intervention, however, its impact upon the development of broader strategies for managing and negotiating nationalist tensions and assisting regional stability has been considerable. The Council of Europe's 1995 Framework Convention and its preceding treaties and agreements codified a new legal framework on minority protection, whereby not only individual rights were guaranteed but also a limited degree of collective rights (Tesser, 2003: 485–6). Using the promise of eventual EU entrance, the EU has been successful in engaging most of the Balkan nation states into a policy of alignment of their legislation and their policies with EU norms (Kavalski, 2006). The reversal of Bulgarian policies toward its Turkish and Muslim minorities and changes in Romanian legislation dealing with religion and minorities are good examples of changes instigated through such a policy of engagement.

Furthermore, in Poland, Hungary, Slovakia and the Czech Republic, EU pressure to adopt European standards did impact post-1989 minority policy (for a review, see Tesser, 2003). However, a somewhat unexpected outcome of such pressure was the growing tension between formal acceptance of legislation and the practical acceptance of minority rights in everyday life. A major factor that hinders full implementation is memory of the pre-1945 conflicts associated with minority rights – and it is this memory that 'explains why a tension exists between European standards on minority protections and local understandings of the nation' (Tesser, 2003: 531).

In regions such as the Balkans where the cultural logic of nation-state building has promoted the view of minorities as 'untrustworthy' subjects whose loyalty to the state is doubtful, the end result has been the failure of strategies of inclusion and the pursuit of secessionist visions (Roudometof, 1996). In contrast, in Western European regions, power devolution has promoted the development of substate nationalisms. However, whether Western European de-evolution policy is sufficient to defuse nationalist tensions in the long run is doubtful. For a viable long-term solution, it might be necessary for substate regions to develop their own institutional representation at the EU level – a development that is bound to pose considerable challenges to EU's governance structure (Csergo and Goldgeier, 2004: 21–2).

More ambitious efforts in a similar direction included the creation of the European Court for Human Rights (ECHR) and the International Criminal Court (ICC). Both institutions have provided mechanisms for peaceful conflict resolution of national and international disputes – albeit their track record and overall success has been quite different. Empowered by the EU, the ECHR has assumed the task of monitoring and addressing grievances among the public in EU states. Thanks to its successful institutionalization in the context of the EU, the ECHR has been able to address such poisonous topics like restitution of property confiscated during World War II

or after 1945; or appeals made by minority groups with respect to their cultural rights; or appeals made on behalf of persons denied their property rights, and so on. By providing an institutional forum for negotiation and arbitration of such matters at a personal level, the ECHR offers a tangible means for preventing the transformation of such grievances into issues of national concern, and hence into issues of inter-national rivalry among member states.

In contrast to the ECHR, the ICC track record has been mixed by all accounts – for its limited success of providing a legal means for a catharsis of the crimes of the Yugoslav wars has circumscribed its clout. However, it is not the efficacy of these institutions that is always the goal. Rather, their sheer operation shows the ability of Europeans to deal with practical aspects of disputes in a manner that acts pre-emptively, by refusing to allow such disputes from achieving the status of pre-1945 national claims and counterclaims. Through these institutions Europe (and the EU) attempts to exert its influence across the globe by providing non-European societies with a practical example for dealing with international conflicts. They provide an important aspect of the 'European dream' (Rifkin, 2005) or European model of social relations, a model based on faith in legal regimes and commitment to EU's famous 'culture of compromise'. Overall, then, the European record in terms of dealing with new expressions of nationalism shows that European institutions are not just passive recipients of post-World War II developments; they are also able to develop the means for constructive solutions of potentially global applicability.

IMMIGRANT TRANSNATIONALISM AND EUROPE

While the transnationalization of European lifeworlds is a growing reality across the continent, the issue of immigrant transnationalism provides a major challenge for European institutions. Given the widespread misgivings expressed about the 2004 EU enlargement, it is hard to underestimate the difficulties of developing 'modes of incorporation' (Alexander, 2001) that would face up to the increasing diversity of Europe *vis-à-vis* the transnational communities of the TCNs. In their review of the common European legislative trends, Hansen and Weil (2001: 10) note that there is a broad European convergence with respect to the granting of citizenship to second-generation migrants, while legislative responses to dual citizenship remain contradictory. Furthermore, there is a marked polarization between a northern European trend of liberalizing their naturalization requirements versus a southern European trend toward restriction. While the EU does extend EU rights to citizens of its member states, it does not generally extend such rights to TCNs – while it has also attempted to develop hard borders between its territory and surrounding states (Geddes, 2003: 197; for a review see Geddes, 2000: 43–66). However, immigrant transnationalism in Europe concerns precisely the over 11 million of TCNs who do not posses any guarantees of work or residency like the ones enjoyed by the citizens of the EU member states. With Article 13 of the Amsterdam Treaty the EU has extended its guarantees of non-discrimination even toward TCNs. This anti-discrimination agenda focuses on combating discrimination on the basis of nationality, ethnic origin, gender and race. The choice of anti-discrimination legislation versus full citizenship for TCNs reveals the limits of EU-driven policies (for a discussion, see Geddes, 2003:143–6 and Geddes, 2000). In Italian for example, there is even a new word (*excommunitari*) for these foreigners, which aptly registers the new post-Schengen reality even at a linguistic level, as Debeljak (2003: 158) reports.

Although the formation of transnational communities is a feature of advanced industrial societies around the globe, yet there are still considerable differences in the manner the newly acquired heterogeneity is dealt with in specific national contexts. In the US as well as in the other non-European postcolonial democracies (Canada, Australia), immigration was always part of the national mythology. Glazer's (1997) famous statement, 'We are all multiculturalists now,' simply codifies a stance popular in immigrant-based, mostly British, postcolonial societies. The legendary march to the West, the cult of the explorer, and the other forms of cultivating a frontier mentality provided, of course, the ideological infrastructure of negating Indian habitation in North America or of simply dismissing the Australian aboriginals (who were not legally citizens of Australia until the 1960s).

But, while these mythologies certainly allowed the appropriation of land and resources for the settlers and their descendants, they also provided a culture of inclusion that differed in important ways from the continental European attitude on such matters. Nativism has never achieved the same strength in countries of immigration as in nations where attachment to the soil forms the very backbone of their own self-image. Religion, ethnicity and racial politics persist in shaping the image of Europeans. For example, negating the presence of ethnic and racial minorities in the UK is often based on an intertwining of nationalism and racialization. This trend has been famously inscribed in the title of Gilroy's (1991) classic monograph *There Ain't No Black in the Union Jack*. But Britain is not exceptional – especially when it comes to religion. Many European societies have based their self-image on some form of semi-secularized religiosity, which in turn becomes an essential component of belonging and an indispensable identity marker. As such, 'Muslims are now emerging as the critical "other" in various nationalist discourses and in definitions of Europe in western Europe' (Modood, 1997: 2). Even in the Scandinavian countries, the furthest of any in Europe from Muslim territories, where there is hardly any historical encounter with Muslims, extreme right-wing discourse constructs racialized images of Muslims as 'the invaders' (Bjorgo, 1997). The racialization of

Bosnian Muslims in the context of the recent Yugoslav conflicts provides another more familiar example of the same tendency.

Consequently, the 'politics of recognition' are quite different in continental societies. Most importantly, the very notion of such politics is predicated on a clear-cut separation between religion and the state as well as a notion of liberalism that has been charged with being inherently anti-Islamic (see Modood, 1997: 3). Therefore, in order to develop their own response to the challenges of increasingly diversified European societies, Continental European theorists have felt the necessity to critique and revise considerably Taylor's (1994) original formulation of the 'politics of recognition'. Habermas' (1994) critique is exemplary of a different continental view, whereby claims of immigrants and those of national and ethnic minority groups (or of feminists) are sharply differentiated from one another. Contemporary scholarship points to the considerable variation that different states develop in order to come to terms with multiculturalism as an actually existing condition (see, for example, Cornwall and Stoddard, 2001). Alexander (2001) has referred to different 'modes of incorporation' in order to highlight the fact that current realities around the globe go far beyond a simplistic juxtaposition between monoculturalism and multiculturalism.

Going a step further, Hartmann and Gerteis (2005) have suggested the existence of four conceptual alternatives that can provide for different modes of incorporation. First, there is the assimilationist option. While it is possible to advocate a return to old style assimilationism or monoculturalism of the past (see, for example, Schesinger, 1991), this type of a romantic proposal is far from being the most attractive or even realistically feasible option. On the contrary, researchers have suggested that even past assimilationism was far more flexible than conventionally assumed. Alba and Nee (2003), for example, have argued that assimilation continues to exert an influence upon the contemporary US by providing a means of incorporating successive generations of immigrants. In this respect, the new mainstream constructed in the course of the twentieth century is quite different from the WASP-dominated society that confronted the European immigrants of the 1870–1925 period. The new mainstream is more middle class, 'white' (in a sense quite different from that of the nineteenth century), and actually more 'multicultural'. Brubaker (2001) has also provided evidence from several European states suggesting that such a flexible or civic-minded notion of assimilation is also popular in Europe, where its pursuit registers an attempt to effectively combat the popularity of more extreme nationalist parties that capitalize on xenophobic sentiments.

Second, there is a cosmopolitan response, whereby maintenance of difference rests upon the individual who often assumes a flexible or symbolic appropriation of his or her ethnic or racial descent. In the US, for example, white ethnic Americans exemplify this pattern of eclectic or cosmopolitan diversity whereby ethnicity is symbolically maintained (see Alba 1990; Gans, 1979; Waters, 1990). While the traditional line of interpretation is that symbolic ethnicity represents a pattern of assimilation whereby difference survives only to a minimal (e.g. symbolic) degree, this interpretation is by no means the only one. Conzen et al. (1992: 4–5) suggest that the immigrants and their descendants are engaged in an actual invention of ethnicity 'which incorporates, adapts and amplifies pre-existing communal solidarities, cultural attributes, and historical memories'. While the US provides a paradigmatic case for considering this 'mode of incorporation', it should be noted that similar examples are found in other societies around the globe. Some of the older or traditional diasporic communities in Europe (such Jews or Armenians) provide good examples of this mode of incorporation – and in due course, this pattern could also be emulated by some of the most recent arrivals in the continent.

Third, there is the model of fragmented pluralism, which 'focuses on the existence of a variety of distinctive and relatively self-contained communities as a social reality, but also as a necessity and strength' (Hartmann and Gerteis, 2005: 229). Under such conditions, ethnic enclaves might be formed, group identity remains strong, and there is a minimum of integration or assimilation. In addition to the US, where ethnic enclaves have been a feature of public life for over a century, it is important to stress that fragmented pluralism is also characteristic of the situation of many diasporic communities in Europe and other countries around the globe. Several European cities – from London to Berlin – have their own Arabic or Indian or Pakistani or Turkish ethnic enclaves.

Finally, there is interactive pluralism, which, while acknowledging the preservation of group identity as essential for a community, goes a step further: 'It posits the need to cultivate common understanding across these differences through their mutual recognition and ongoing interaction' (Hartmann and Gerteis, 2005: 231). Such a vision comes closer to the normative notion of multiculturalism. Outside the US, the EU provides a good example of such a normative vision, for it posits itself as a union of nations, and it explicitly rejects claims that it views national identity as its rival. On the contrary, it seeks a vision of 'unity in diversity', whereby national identities can be preserved under the rubric of an emergent European identity (see Delanty and Rumford, 2005).

Yalcin-Heckmann's (1997) comparison between the effects of the different modes of incorporation is instructive of the differences between different forms of pluralism and assimilation. In a comparison between the experiences of Turkish communities living in a French and a German city, the contrast between the two modes is striking. On the one hand, in the German town, it was initially taken for granted that Turks were not German citizens and that they did not belong in Germany. In contrast, in the French town, multiculturalism was fostered by a strong grassroots movement, but with no state backing. Still, the Turkish community is more marginalized in the French town than in the German town. Since the 2005 urban riots in France, immigrant marginalization has been dramatically publicized. Moreover, the existence of different modes of incorporation and the ability to assess the success of these modes in different states around the globe suggest that states will eventually develop their own choices with regard to their own particular mode of incorporation. That is, the models that will be eventually applied in specific states cannot be decided without taking into account the specificity of each national context.

The above responses might be revised in the future – as political theorists and philosophers are developing more complex and sophisticated normative models for multicultural states and societies around the globe (see Benhabib, 2002; Parekh, 2000). But what these different responses point toward is that uniformity is perhaps the most unlikely outcome, as each country might feel the need to articulate its own response according to local demands. In a quantitative analysis of European attitudes toward immigration, Luedtke (2005: 85) argues that the EU's failure to develop a unified immigration policy is attributed to a clash between historically rooted national identities and the proposed supranationalization of immigration policy. In their overview of European legislative trends with regard to immigration and citizenship, Hansen and Weil concur: 'What is clear is that the extension to permanent residents and new migrants of the rights of citizenship will occur, or be impeded, at the national level' (2001: 19).

Given the persistence of national identities throughout Europe, it might be quite doubtful, then, to expect a consistent or Europe-wide common policy with respect to responding successfully to immigrant transnationalism (for a brief synopsis of past policies see Geddes, 2000, 2003: 126–42). Rather, the most likely outcome is that of bricolage: while the lowest common denominator might be pursued at the EU level, each European country is likely to develop its own institutional and cultural means in order to realize the form of multicultural inclusion that is most suitable to each local setting. Whether such an approach is too feeble to allow Europe to meet both its growing labour needs and the necessity for maintaining its safety net over the majority of its public or whether this approach might provide a winning strategy remains an issue of passionate debate among European policy makers.

CONCLUSION

In this chapter nationalism and transnationalism were treated as a pair. With regard to the former, it has been suggested that despite the success of the EC/EU over the post-1945 period, nationalism has not become obsolete and that postnationalism is still a vision rather than a reality for twenty-first century Europe. Nevertheless, post-1945 Europe has been able to develop a wide range of institutions and formal and informal mechanisms that have contributed greatly to the containment of national antagonisms among nation states. Consequently, dealing with national antagonisms has become a routine of ongoing European affairs. The engulfment of most European nation states into a web of treaties and associations (such as the various treaties that constitute the EU and the related *acquis communicateur*) has diminished their ability to act solely on the basis of parochial national sentiment.

In fact, the majority of post-1945 national movements in Europe have been connected either with substate units (such as Catalonia or Northern Italy) or with the Eastern European 'nations without states'. Substate nationalisms exist in an interactive symbiotic relationship with EU institutions – for it is in the benefit of both sides to foster the development of the 'Europe of the regions'. In contrast, post-1989 Eastern European nationalisms aimed at transforming the fictitious sovereignty granted to various state units in the context of broader communist-controlled federal units into truly existing national sovereignty. Post-1989 nationalisms in Europe

have adapted to EU by developing different responses based on whether the EU is viewed as an association of states or as a union of nations. This development suggests that the future interplay between local nationalisms and EU institutions might be of considerable significance for the shape, direction and prowess of various nationalisms in Europe. It also suggests that the future shape of European institutions will be in part developed by the manner in which various local European nationalisms will develop – and whether the vision that will carry the day among them will be that of a Europe of nations or that of a loose association of states.

In contrast to this symbiotic relationship between the EU and local nationalisms, the experience of contemporary transnationalism poses deeper and fundamental challenges for European states. While the 'transnationalization of European life-worlds' refers to the reality of experiencing mobile cultures in everyday life, 'immigrant transnationalism' remains a term typically associated with the modes of incorporation developed in contemporary societies in their efforts to absorb and accommodate waves of international immigrants. In Europe, this transnationalization of everyday life is a reality enshrined through numerous means, such as the unified labour market for EU nationals and other formal and informal means devised to accomplish the EU-sponsored project of European integration.

Immigrant transnationalism, however, poses a fundamental challenge to traditional conceptions of European nationalism. In this chapter's final section, several modes of immigrant incorporation were reviewed and their applicability to different European states briefly contemplated. Given societal variation within the EU, it is likely that EU policy in this area will be confined to the lowest possible denomination, with different states allowed to develop further the mode of incorporation that fits mostly with local cultural traditions and societal conceptions of national membership. Whether this particular response is sufficient for Europe to accomplish the task of successfully recruiting and incorporating enough immigrants to maintain both its competitive edge worldwide but also its social welfare systems is an issue of critical importance for the future. Perhaps the real challenge of twenty-first century Europe is not to push aside the remnants of European nationalisms, but rather to develop those modes of incorporation that would help sustain its economic success and diversify its heritage in order to become a truly multicultural constellation.

REFERENCES

Alba, R. (1990) *Ethnic Identity: The Transformation of White America*. New Haven, CT: Yale University Press.

Alba, R. and Nee, V. (2003) *Remaking the American Mainstream: Assimilation and Contemporary Immigration*. Cambridge: Harvard University Press.

Albrow, M. (1997) *The Global Age*. Stanford: Stanford University Press.

Alexander, J. (2001) 'Theorizing the "modes of incorporation"', *Sociological Theory*, 19 (3): 237–249.

Anderson, B. (1991) *Imagined Communities*, 2nd edn. London: Verso.

Beck, U. (2000) *What is Globalization?* Oxford: Polity.

Beck, U. (2005) *The Cosmopolitan Vision*. Oxford: Polity.

Beck, U. and Giddens, A. (2005) 'Nationalism has now become the enemy of Europe's nations', *The Guardian*, October 4.

Benhabib, S. (2002) *The Claims of Culture: Equality and Diversity in the Global Era*. Princeton, NJ: Princeton University Press.

Bjorgo, T. (1997) '"the invaders", "the traitors" and "the resistance movement": the extreme right's conceptualisation of opponents and self in Scandinavia', in T. Modood and P. Werbner (eds) *The Politics of Multiculturalism in the New Europe: Racism, Identity and Community*. London: Zed Books, pp. 54–72.

Brubaker, R. (1996) *Nationalism Reframed*. Cambridge: Cambridge University Press.

Brubaker, R. (2001) 'The return of assimilation? Changing perspectives on immigration and its sequels in France, Germany and the United States', *Ethnic and Racial Studies*, 24 (July): 531–548.

Chamberlain, M. and Leydesdorff, S. (eds) (2004) 'Transnational families: memories and narratives', *Global Networks*, 4 (3): 227–334.

Chomsky, N. (1999) *The New Military Humanism: Lessons from Kosovo*. Vancouver: New Star Books.

Cohen, L.K. (1993) *Broken Bonds: The Disintegration of Yugoslavia*. Boulder: Westview Press.

Conzen, K., Gerber, D., Morawska, E., Pozzetta, G. and Vecoli, R. Jr (1992) 'The invention of ethnicity: a perspective from the US', *Journal of American Ethnic History* 12: 3–41.

Cornwell, G.H. and Stoddard, E.W. (eds) (2001) *Global Multiculturalism: Comparative Perspectives on Ethnicity, Race and Nation*. Lanham, MD: Rowman and Littlefield.

Csergo, Z. and Goldgeier, J.M. (2004) 'Nationalist strategies and European Integration', *Perspectives on Politics*, 2 (1): 21–37.

Debeljak, A. (2003) 'European forms of belonging', *East European Politics and Societies*, 17 (2): 151–165.

Delanty, G. (1995) *Inventing Europe: Idea, Identity, Reality*. Houndmills, Basingstoke: Macmillan.

Delanty, G. and O'Mahoney, P. (2002) *Nationalism and Social Theory: Modernity and the Recalcitrance of the Nation*. London: Sage.

Delanty, G. and Rumford, C. (2005) *Rethinking Europe: Social Theory and the Implications of Europeanisation*. London: Routledge.

Gans, H. (1979) 'Symbolic ethnicity: the future of ethnic groups and cultures in America', *Ethnic and Racial Studies* 2: 1–20.

Geddes, A. (2000) *Immigration and European Integration: Towards Fortress Europe?* Manchester: Manchester University Press.

Geddes, A. (2003) *The Politics of Migration and Immigration in Europe*. London: Sage.

Gellner, E. (1983) *Nations and Nationalism*. Ithaca: Cornell University Press.

Gemerek, B. (1996) *The Idea of Europe*. Cambridge: Polity.

Gilroy, P. (1991) *'There ain't no black in the Union Jack': The Cultural Politics of Race and Nation*. Chicago, IL: University of Chicago Press.

Giordano, B. and Roller, E. (2002) 'Catalonia and the 'idea of Europe': Competing strategies and discourses within Catalan party politics', *European Urban and Regional Studies*, 9 (2): 99–113.

Glazer, N. (1997) *We Are All Multiculturalists Now*. Cambridge: Harvard University Press.

Guibernau, M.M. (1999) *Nations Without States: Political Communities in a Global Age*. Oxford, MA: Basil Blackwell.

Habermas, J. (1994) 'Struggles for recognition in the democratic constitutional state', in C. Taylor, K.A. Appiah, J. Habermas, S.C. Rockefeller, M. Walzer and S. Wolf (eds) *Multiculturalism: Examining the Politics of Recognition*. Princeton, NJ: Princeton University Press, pp. 107–148.

Hansen, R. and Weil, P. (2001) 'Introduction: citizenship, immigration and nationality: toward a convergence in Europe?' in R. Hansen and P. Weil (eds) *Towards a European Nationality: Citizenship, Immigration and Nationality Law in the EU*. London: Palgrave, pp. 1–23.

Hartmann, D. and Gerteis, J. (2005) 'Dealing with diversity: mapping multiculturalism in sociological terms', *Sociological Theory*, 23 (2): 218–240.

Hayden, R. (1999) *Blueprints for a House Divided: The Constitutional Logic of the Yugoslav Conflicts*. Ann Arbor: University of Michigan Press.

Hobsbawm, E.J. (1990) *Nations and Nationalism Since 1780*. Cambridge: Cambridge University Press.

Held, D. (1995) *Democracy and the Global Order: From the Modern State to Cosmopolitan Governance*. Stanford, CA: Stanford University Press.

Holton, R. (1998) *Globalization and the Nation-State*. New York: St Matrin's Press.

Huntington, S.P. (1996) *The Clash of Civilizations and the Remaking of World Order*. New York: Simon and Schuster.

Kavalski, E. (2006) 'Divide and reward: maintaining EU's deterrence in the Balkans after the 2004 enlargement', *Journal of Political and Military Sociology*, 34 (2): 289–299.

Keck, M. and Sikkink, K. (1998) *Activists Beyond Borders: Advocacy Networks in International Politics*. Ithaca, NY: Cornell University Press.

Kennedy, P. and Roudometof, V. (eds) (2002) *Communities Across Borders: New Immigrants and Transnational Cultures*. London: Routledge.

Keohane, R. and Nye, J. (eds) (1971) *Transnational Relations and World Politics*. Cambridge, MA: Harvard University Press.

Kundera, M. (1984) 'The tragedy of Central Europe', *New York Review of Books*, 26 (April).

Lechner, F. and Boli, J. (2005) *World Culture: Origins and Consequences*. Oxford: Basil Blackwell.

Levy, D., Pensky, M. and Torpey, J. (eds) (2005) *Old Europe, New Europe, Core Europe: Transatlantic Relations after the Iraqi War*. London: Verso.

Luedtke, A. (2005) 'European integration, public opinion and immigration policy: Testing the impact of national identity', *European Union Politics*, 6 (1): 83–112.

Mahler, S.J. (2000) 'Constructing international relations: the role of transnational migrants and other non-state actors', *Identities: Global Studies in Culture and Power*, 7 (2): 197–232.

Mayall, J. (1990) *Nationalism and International Society*. Cambridge: Cambridge University Press.

McGrew, A. and Lewis, P. (1992) *Global Politics: Globalisation and the Nation-State*. Cambridge: Polity.

Modood, T. (1997) 'Introduction: The politics of multiculturalism in the New Europe', in T. Modood and P. Werbner (eds) *The Politics of Multiculturalism in the New Europe: Racism, Identity and Community*. London: Zed Books, pp. 1–26.

Morawska, E. (2003) 'Disciplinary agendas and analytic strategies of research on immigrant transnationalism: challenges of interdisciplinary knowledge', *International Migration Review*, 37 (3): 611–640.

Musgrave, Th. D. (1997) *Self-Determination and National Minorities*. Oxford: Clarendon Press.

Nairn, T. (1997) *The Break Up of Britain*. London: New Left Books.

Nussbawm, M. (ed.) (1996) *For Love or Country*. Boston: Beacon.

Ohmae, K. (1995) *The End of the Nation-State: The Rise of Regional Economies*. New York: Free Press.

Parekh, B. (2000) *Rethinking Multiculturalism: Cultural Diversity and Political Theory*. London: Macmillan.

Portes, A. (2001) 'Introduction: The debates and significance of immigrant transnationalism', *Global Networks*, 1: 181–194.

Portes A. (2003) 'Conclusion: theoretical convergencies and empirical evidence in the study of immigrant transnationalism', *International Migration Review*, 37 (3): 874–893.

Rifkin, J. (2005) *The European Dream*. New York: Penguin.

Robinson, W. (2001) 'Social theory and globalisation: the rise of a transnational state', *Theory and Society*, 30: 157–200.

Rosenau, J.N. (1990) *Turbulence in World Politics*. Princeton, NJ: Princeton University Press.

Rosenau, J.N. (2003) *Distant Proximities: Dynamics Beyond Globalisation*. Princeton, NJ: Princeton University Press.

Roudometof, V. (1996) 'The consolidation of national minorities in Southeastern Europe', *Journal of Political and Military Sociology*, 24 (2): 189–207.

Schlesinger, A. Jr. (1991) *The Disuniting of America: Reflections on a Multicultural Society*. New York: W.W. Norton.

Sassen, S. (1996) *Losing Control? Sovereignty in an Age of Globalisation*. New York: Columbia University Press.

Sassen, S. (1998) *Guests and Aliens*. New York: New Press.

Schopflin, G. and N. Wood (eds) (1989) *In Search of Central Europe*. Cambridge: Polity.

Short, J.R. (2001) *Global Dimensions: Space, Place and the Contemporary World*. London: Reaktion Books.

Sklair, L. (2001) *The Transnational Capitalist Class*. Oxford: Basil Blackwell.

Smith, A.D. (1995) *Nations and Nationalism in a Global Era*. London: Polity Press.

Smith, J., Chaterfield, C. and Pagnucco, R. (eds) (1997) *Transnational Social Movements and Global Politics*. Syracuse NY: Syracuse State University Press.

Soysal, Y.N. (1994) *The Limits of Citizenship: Migrants and Post-national Membership in Europe*. Chicago: University of Chicago Press.

Taylor, C. (1994) 'The politics of recognition' in C. Taylor, K.A. Appiah, J. Habermas, S.C. Rockefeller, M. Walzer and S. Wolf (eds) *Multiculturalism: Examining the Politics of Recognition*. Princeton, NJ: Princeton University Press, pp. 25–74.

Tesser, L.M. (2003) 'The geopolitics of tolerance: minority rights under EU Expansion in East-Central Europe', *East European Politics and Societies*, 17 (3): 483–532.

Thaller, P. (2001) 'Fluid identities in Central European borderlands', *European History Quarterly*, 31 (4): 519–548.

Todorova, M. (1997) *Imagining the Balkans*. Cambridge: Cambridge University Press.

Touraine, A. (2003) 'Sociology without societies', *Current Sociology*, 51 (2): 123–131.

Urry, J. (2000) *Sociology Beyond Societies*. London: Routledge.

van der Veer, P. (2002) 'Transnational religion: Hindu and Muslim movements', *Global Networks*, 2 (2): 95–109.

Vardy, S.B. and Tooley, H. (eds) (2003) *Ethnic Cleansing in Twentieth-Century Europe*. Boulder: East European Monographs.

Vetrovec, S. (2003) 'Migration and other modes of transnationalism: towards conceptual cross-fertilization', *International Migration Review*, 37 (3): 641–665.

Yalcin-Heckmann, L. (1997) 'The perils of ethnic associational life in Europe: Turkish migrants in Germany and France', in T. Modood and P. Werbner (eds) *The Politics of Multiculturalism in the New Europe: Racism, Identity and Community*. London: Zed Books, pp. 95–110.

Walby, S. (2003) 'The myth of the nation-state: theorizing societies and polities in a global era', *Sociology*, 37 (3): 529–546.

Waters, M. (1995) *Globalization*. London: Routledge.

Waters, M. (1990) *Ethnic Options: Choosing Identities in America*. Berkeley: University of California Press.

Wimmer, A. and Glick Schiller, N. (2004) 'Methodological nationalism and beyond: nation-state building, migration and the social sciences', *Global Networks*, 2 (4): 301–334.

19

Migration, Minorities and Marginality: New Directions in Europe Migration Research

Franck Düvell

'Migration is one of the key factors which shape [and change] the world in which we live, ... [it] plays a central role in current global processes of social, economic and political change' (IMI, 2006: 1)[1]. Migration links neighboring or distant countries and their economies and cultures and facilitates the exchange of its people and their culture (Hoerder, 2003). Migration changes size, ethnicity and age structure of populations; it alters the cultural, religious and linguistic composition of societies; and it enriches or deprives a society's social and economic fabric (Castles, 2000). Finally, migration affects both the migrants' and their hosts' national, cultural and individual identities (Triandafyllidou, 2001). Vice versa, changing social, political and economic environments and conditions lead to ever-changing migration patterns. For instance, an unfolding conflict or war, an economic crisis, or new migration policies (new recruitment schemes or the introduction of visa) impact on the behavior of people and trigger or disrupt migration networks and migration systems. Furthermore, processes of political integration or disintegration – e.g. through Europeanization

and globalization or through the dissolution of states – ensues reinterpretation of borders, boundaries and membership regimes. Both these processes bring about new coordinates for migration. Not only does the cause and composition of migration continuously change, but so does the direction and scale of movement (Düvell, 2006a). Countries that have previously not had net emigration may become a source of migrants, and countries that have long been providing migrant workers to their neighbors could end up becoming immigration countries themselves. Thus, all European countries undergo a migration transition (e.g. Venturini, 2004; also see Zelinski, 1971) and either swing from one characteristic to another or display more than one characteristic; in fact, most countries are simultaneously sending, receiving and transit countries (GCIM, 2005). In short, migration is both cause and consequence of constant social transformation. It refers to an extremely dynamic process, which has occasionally been described as turbulence (Papastergiadis, 2000). Migration is neither predictable, as most attempts to forecast migration have exposed themselves to ridicule (as most recently in the case of EU accession-related migration);[2] nor can the impact of policy measures be reliably forecasted. In any case, migration will be 'a permanent part of our future' as it was a permanent part of our past. However, Europe is only now 'waking up to reality' (Spencer, 2003: 2).

Migration has significant social and political implications. It affects the core sovereignty of a state, controlling its borders and access of non-citizens to its territory (Joppke, 1998). But because regional and global economic integration and the increasing mobility of people has undermined states' authority to control its territorial borders, in Europe sovereignty shifts towards controlling access to its social systems (e.g. labor markets, welfare systems, public services – see Schierup *et al.*, 2006). Continuing and deepening European integration, namely expanding the right of freedom of movement to another twelve countries, has added another factor to the political dimension of migration. The arrival of newcomers in either large numbers or from different ethnic, cultural, religious or linguistic backgrounds often irritates citizens and residents of the receiving state. Thus, migration has become a major policy concern, and is as emotionalized and politicized as it is polarized and disputed. Policy responses often lag behind actual migration processes and are sometimes ill-informed, ad hoc and ill-prepared. Migration and its consequences trigger processes and discourses which often bring about a variety of stereotypes and negative and misconceived perceptions, and create open hostility which becomes a part of the social reality. Most commonly, migration is conceptualized negatively, and as a deviation from the settled norm. Thus, it is seen as a social and political problem (Düvell, 2006a), a crisis (Weiner, 1995), or even a threat (Kicinger, 2004) and leads to moral panic (Pijpers, 2006). It is only recently that the benefits of migration – its positive effect on economic growth, the crucial role of remittances in the development of sending countries and exchange of cultural knowledge – have been acknowledged (GCIM, 2005).

Governing migration and managing integration and diversity, in other words managing change whilst maintaining social cohesion, poses a huge challenge to modern societies. In highly regulated societies such as in Europe, *laissez-faire* approaches, as practiced in the US, seem to be no option. The ideal, as declared by scholars and institutions alike, is to manage migration for the benefits of all and to create a win–win–win situation where all actors, sending and receiving societies, and the migrants can gain from migration. Often however, this is no more than a euphemism for migration restrictions (Düvell, 2005). Unfortunately, the preconditions for management are not ideal owing to significant knowledge gaps, the chaotic character of migration, the relative autonomy of migrants, and the emotionalized and politicized nature of the subject, all of which often impede a rational and reasoned political approach (Spencer, 2003).

Finally, and as a consequence, research is characterized by a whole range of problems. These are (1) ignorance and failures related to the social, political and legal construction of the subject and its politicization; (2) biased concepts and perspectives which lead to negligence of various phenomena, such as migration in minor, sending and non-urban regions, non- and post-working age migration, non-international migration and return migration; (3) simple and simplifying models; (4) incomplete research agendas and ahistorical approaches; (5) the ever-changing subject and the time lag between phenomenon, research and publication; and (6) the lack of commonly agreed and plausible definitions, and, as a result, incomplete and incomparable figures. As a consequence, the issue of migration is as intricate as it is blurred, and it is as contested as politicized. None is particularly helpful, and distortions, confusions, misinterpretations, simplifications and knowledge gaps are plentiful. This contribution instead encourages studies which aim at keeping pace with the metamorphosis of its subject and which are prepared to undergo a metamorphosis themselves (see also Joly, 2004).

MIGRATION IN EUROPE – NEW DEFINITIONS, NEW FIGURES, NEW PATTERNS

At the outset of any analysis of migration stands the definition of migration. Three conditions are identified which determine migration. First, migration is understood as international geographic mobility, hence the movement of people across the borders of a nation state and into another. In contrast, movements within a country are not usually understood as migration but as mobility. Second, migration is understood to mean a significant stay in a country, hence the definitions of temporarily staying in another country for at least three months (temporary migration) or taking residence in another country for more than twelve months (immigration) (UN, 1998). Third, purposes such as employment, family reunification or asylum are commonly understood as migration. On the other hand, taking residence in another state for the purpose of education is sometimes not (King and Ruiz-Gelices, 2003). Nor is moving for the purpose of retirement (Williams *et al.*, 2000) or recreation (Düvell, 2006a). Thus, migration is a political, legal and social construct, meaning that 'definitions of migration are highly varied in nature' (Castles, quoted in IOM, 2003: 8) and tend to display severe limitations.

The first problem has to do with the political construction of migration as the crossing of the borders of a nation state. However, the character of the political borders of Europe,[3] the borders of the Schengen countries, the borders of the European Union, and the borders of those European countries which are outside the European Union, are of very different character and meaning and entail different control mechanisms. Further to these differences, borders are subject to constant changes. New borders are introduced, as between Czech Republic and Slovakia; other borders change their meaning, as has occurred with the external EU border between Greece and Bulgaria, which in January 2007 became an internal border of the European Union.

Sometimes borders vanish completely, as did that between East and West Germany in 1989. As a consequence, movements between Belgium and the Netherlands can hardly be understood as international migration but as a version of internal mobility within the European Union. Movements within the EU are free according to EU law and can no longer be limited, thus states' sovereignty is significantly weakened. On the other hand, the new external EU border running between Poland, Slovakia and its neighbor Ukraine is more strictly controlled than ever. As a consequence, the once visa-free entry from Ukraine to Poland has now turned into illegal immigration into the EU. Thus, a scale of geographic mobility ranging from internal mobility to diverse versions of international migration can be identified. Accordingly, migration can be entirely free, subject to some controls, or it can be illegal. It creates something of a paradox that internal European mobility, even though it is free, is low, with the exception of the new eastern and southeastern member states, whilst migration from non-EU countries is significantly higher but also often illegal. Indeed, illegal migration has been identified one of the fastest growing types of migration (OECD, 2001).

The second problem has to do with the time dimension of migration under conditions of increased mobility and flexibility. First, in an integrating world, transportation is cheap, easy and regular. Second, there are cross-border markets for services and labor, coinciding with short-term contracts, flexible delivery arrangements and working times. Third, trends have been observed toward multiple homes, multiple jobs and online communication enabling staff to work from home. Thus, conditions are set which enable self-employed service providers and labor migrants alike to develop increasingly flexible commuting and migration strategies. The patterns emerging might not necessarily match official definitions of migration. Phenomena such as daily or weekly cross-border commuting are not understood as migration. Nor are repeated stays of less than three months each, even if they add up to several months in total over the course of a twelve-month period. New mobility patterns, such as British buying homes in France, commuting to work in London, or German doctors flying into London for a weekend shift could be dubbed 'Eurostar' or 'EasyJet migrants'. As a result, temporary migration is continuously rising (OECD, 2002).

The third problem is related to those purposes that are defined as migration. Probably the largest version of human geographic mobility is tourism; recently international tourist arrivals to Europe passed the 400 million mark (World Tourism Organization, 2005). Tourism and migration are intertwined in a complex manner: tourists might be disguised irregular immigrant workers; tourists might attend language courses; they might engage in occasional work and stay for more than three months; tourism might lead to marriage migration, and frequent visitors might turn into immigrants, for example after retirement. Tourism also opens up new links and transportation between countries which then facilitate migration. Hitherto, the study of tourism and the study of migration have existed in entirely separate spheres, and the interaction between both has largely been ignored.

Mostly for political and administrative reasons migration categories are constructed in order to register mobile people accordingly. Registered are border crossings, passenger arrivals (but not always departure), (net) migration flows and stocks. These are characterized by a range of uncertainties. Distinctions between ethnic minorities, naturalized aliens, immigrants, foreign born and in-country-born 'Ausländer' are unclear. Usually, more attention is paid to inflow than to outflow and departure records are rarely kept. Emigrants or returnees might not bother about deregistration, irregular movements can only be estimated or guessed at. Often cases instead of individuals are registered, hence the number of dependants goes unregistered or several entries might in fact refer to only one individual. Unfortunately, each country applies its own practices and definitions, and no

common European method has been agreed so far; therefore, national figures are difficult to compare. Finally, certain figures have been taken for granted and were repeated over long periods of time, as an alleged arrival of 500,000 irregular arrivals annually in the EU (Widgren, 2000). However, this figure is not only out of date, but even when new was essentially a 'best guess', lacking any scientific evidence. Recent publications instead refer to apprehensions on the border, a number in the region of 100,000 cases (UNODC, 2006). For the reasons listed here, official and other European figures have to be treated with some reservation.

Migration patterns constantly change. Initially, large-scale immigration was recorded during the 1960s and mostly involved northern countries (UK, Germany, Austria, France, the Netherlands and Belgium) (Castles and Miller, 2003). Post-war migration to Europe has often been associated with migration systems.[4] These were either related to ties between former empires and their colonies; for example, France and francophone Africa; the UK, the Indian subcontinent and the Caribbean; and the Netherlands and Indonesia; or to recruitment schemes introducing new systems, as occurred between Germany and Turkey. During the 1980s and 1990s, southern European countries too (Portugal, Spain, Italy and Greece) became major destination countries. Meanwhile, immigration is also recorded in Central and Eastern Europe (Hungary, Czech Republic and Poland). Even Romania has recently noted vacancies which cannot be filled by indigenous workers and which attract migrants from Moldova and Ukraine (Ilie, 2006). Vice versa, the once major 'sending' countries of Portugal, Spain, Italy, Greece, Yugoslavia and Turkey have been replaced by Albania, Romania, Moldova, Poland, Ukraine, Armenia and Georgia, with only Morocco and Algeria retaining their character as important 'sending' countries. Meanwhile, European integration has changed the political and legal character of migration. Initially, migration from communist Central and Eastern Europe was barred by the Iron

Curtain and the only migrants were refugees. Once the East opened its borders, strict controls borders were implemented by the West. In the meantime, freedom of movement was granted to all citizens of the accession countries. As a consequence, those who were often perceived as illegal immigrants have now become citizens of an EU member state and are free to move. It could be hypothesized that other nationals, probably Ukrainians and Moldavians, will fill the vacancies of the shadow economy. Finally, during the 1980s and 1990s several million refugees from many parts to the world arrived in Europe; many remained and contributed to the diversification of the profile of the immigrant population. But because of severe restrictions, refugee migration has meanwhile decreased, some scholars even referring to the 'end of asylum' (Van Hear, 2005).

Meanwhile, new arrivals not previously recorded have recently been observed in many countries, such as the migration of large numbers of Ukrainians to Portugal, Spain and Italy; the emergence of Romanian communities in Ireland; and the migration of Portuguese agricultural workers to the UK. Additionally, the emergence of Chinese communities in Italy and Romania; of Algerians, Moroccans and Brazilians in London; Georgians in the Netherlands; Nigerians in Odessa; and Turks in Moscow (to list just a few examples) illustrate a multiplication of migration patterns. As a result, migrants from approximately 200 countries are currently residing in Germany; London prides itself to be host to the world; and even Ukraine hosts migrants from around 50 countries. In the course of globalization, traditional migration systems have been supplemented, if not replaced, by new regional and global migration systems linking together countries and people in ways that had not previously been the case. Thus the combined effect of changing economic and political environments brings about new migration systems and new migration patterns. To sum up, migration has become super-directional (Düvell, 2006e), and, accordingly, European

societies have become super-diverse (Vertovec, 2006).

It is true, however, that the parameters for migration to Europe will fundamentally change again over the coming decades. China, Russia, India and Brazil will become the economic powerhouses of future global growth (Daley, 2007). At the same time, most European and CIS countries will experience ageing and decreasing populations (some countries, namely Russia, to an even greater extent than EU countries) (Heleniak, 2002). The situation will become more complex when the one-child policy ensures that China's population starts to age dramatically too (United Nations, 2005). Even Turkey, the most important sender of immigrants in Europe, is already undergoing population transition – ageing set in during the 1980s – and its population will decrease from around 2050 (Icduygu, 2006). Sources of future migration will be Arab countries, South East Asia, the Pacific and some parts of Africa (GCIM, 2005). The EU is already competing with the US over highly skilled migrants and it seems plausible to assume that soon the EU will also be competing with Russia over migrant workers and replacement populations. Finally, climate change will lead to the loss of currently habitable land. These changes are expected to lead to up to 50 million 'environmental refugees'; some of them will certainly resettle in Europe (United Nations University, 2005).

THEORIZING MIGRATION – TOWARDS EUROPEAN MIGRATION STUDIES

Until the mid-1940s migration was largely explained as a quasi-natural phenomenon, hence frequent references to 'pressure', 'floods' and 'waves'. The 1940s to 1970s were dominated by economic thinking, which can be identified with the 'push and pull factor' model. Accordingly, individuals were thought of as reacting to macro-economic forces, such as supply and demand structures, employment levels and wage differentials (Borjas, 1989). This has been refined by some micro-economic and behavioral approaches, which study individual and collective decision-making processes within given opportunity structures (Stark, 1991). The 1970s and 1980s, however, saw a continuously rising interest of sociology and anthropology in migration. Lately, various non-economic theories have been made fruitful, such as network theory, system theory (Kritz *et al.*, 1992) and transnationalism (Glick-Schiller *et al.*, 1992). Last but not least, political science developed an interest in how politics shaped migration flows, addressing such issues as migration and integration, and policy responses to migration (Hollifield, 1992).

American analysis has been particular productive and often took the lead in analyzing and theorizing migration. This is perhaps not surprising, given the country's history as an immigrant country. There is, however, a danger that generalizing from what are ultimately case studies can produce misleading results. The US American case is a rather special example for a number of reasons. It is a separate continent; it has a long established national identity as a liberal immigration country; its dominance of the global economy makes it an attractive destination country; and it has extremely diverse migration patterns. In contrast, Europe, has a particular geography characterized by being an annex to the Asian landmass and by its proximity to Africa; a distinctive history (spanning from colonialism, crumbling empires, two world wars and inherent massive destructions and loss of populations to the Iron Curtain and subsequently its economic and political integration); unique political philosophies and institutional cultures, a specific social model; an ageing and decreasing population; and it is made up of diverse national identities which have often produced xenophobic trends. This provides for a very different case. Processes of Europeanization have been associated, amongst others, with the emergence of Eurocities, linked together through distinct transportation systems (for example,

high-speed trains and low-budget airlines). These shape specific European migration patterns (Favell, 2003), which take the form of a distinctive and comprehensive European migration space (Morawska 2001; Morokvasic and Rudolph, 1994). Finally, a specifically 'European dilemma' dealing with migration and welfare, nationhood and citizenship has been identified (Schierup *et al.*, 2006).

To illustrate the scientific implications three examples shall be given. First, studies of large-scale Mexican migration – because of the specific profile of Mexican migrants as low-educated and low-skilled rural Catholic people – can hardly produce theories that are then applicable to large-scale migration or integration of much better-educated urban Poles or rural (but Muslim) Turks and Moroccans. Second, geographic and labor market mobility of US citizens is considerably higher than that of their European counterparts. As a result, Americans are more likely to respond to changes in the supply–demand structure for labor, and move to where the vacancies exist. As a result, local demand for labor is more likely to be filled by resident workers. Europeans are less mobile, so vacancies are more difficult to fill with resident workers, and hence a demand for mobile workers is far more likely to be met by those who come from outside the European Union. Third, according to different migration experiences and national identities, specific political models addressing the inclusion of immigrants have been developed. The concept of segregation was related to the analysis of the exclusion of black Americans. In contrast, the assimilation model is based upon the analysis of European immigration to the US and believes that European migrants display few traces of their cultural heritage. The 'melting pot' concept reflects the US's *laissez-faire* attitude to the incorporation of immigrants. Meanwhile, the model of multiculturalism, based on diversity, social equality, and participation, and an emphasis on social integration has been practiced successfully in major immigration countries such as Canada, Australia, the US and to some extent in the UK and Sweden. Continental Europe instead tends to rely on models of assimilation (as in France), based on formal equality or integration (for example Germany and the Netherlands) based on participation and adaptation to a host society. In the meantime, multiculturalism is alleged to be in crisis, especially in the UK, which has led to the concept of social cohesion gaining some level of popularity. Alternatively, interculturalism has gained prominence in some new immigration countries (Italy, Spain and Ireland). It goes beyond both integration and multiculturalism, and emphasizes the obligations and the need for change of the host society (NCCRI, 2005; Rodriguez-Garcia, 2005). Thus, because these are specifically European conditions, processes and politics, there are grounds for specific European research agendas, theories and migration typologies.

Research on European migration has added considerable value to network theory (Bleahu, 2005), system theory (Bommes, 1999) and transnationalism theory (Faist, 2000; Vertovec, 1999), as refined by notions of transregionalism and translocalism (Garbin, 2002). European scholars have also introduced several typologies to the nomenclature of migration. For instance, the concept of 'ethnic migration' has been effectively used to analyze the movements of ethnic Germans, Turks and Greeks, and of movements on the Balkan and in post-Soviet countries. Migration associated with the fall of the Iron Curtain, the re-emergence of a European migration space and the emergence of new migration path from the East into Western Europe has been dubbed 'new migration' (Koser and Lutz, 1998). Related to this are typologies of pendulum migration, shuttle migration and cross-border commuting which are derived from European case studies (e.g. Morokvasic, 1994). Additionally, transit migration represents movement through a range of countries until a final destination is reached is derived from processes observed within the context of immigration to Europe and in response to the restrictions found in this part of the world (Düvell, 2006b).

Equally, politics and political concepts can be identified which have a specific European touch. For example, the politics of large-scale 'guestworker' immigration is, with the exception of the short-lived US 'bracero' program, a distinctly European concept. It reflected beliefs held during the 1960s and 1970s that European countries are not immigration countries and that the required additional migrant labor can therefore be admitted on temporary basis only. Furthermore, the integration of Europe has encouraged joint efforts to tackle migration and facilitated some policy convergence which has been conceptualized as the Europeanization of migration politics (Geddes, 2003). Most recently, the expansion towards non-EU countries, labeled the internationalization, externalization or globalization of EU migration policy has been noted (Düvell, 2005). Another typically European issue is the challenges of migration to the unique European model of the welfare state (Bommes and Geddes, 2001) and concerns over the balance of immigrants' contributions versus their claims. And concepts such as denizenship as developed by Hammar (1990) argue that the practice of granting social and economic rights to immigrants whilst withholding citizenship is a largely European conceptualization. However, the idea of transnational citizenship (Bauböck, 1994) can be seen as an attempt to reconcile citizenship with human geographic mobility, and is thus a product of European liberal thinking.

CHALLENGING CONVENTIONAL CONCEPTS, FRAMES AND BIASES

It is not always easy to make a distinction between concepts as analytical tools and concepts as expressions of some normative biases or as social and political constructs. This section addresses and challenges various conventional beliefs, which have in the past guided as well as distorted European migration studies. Methodological nationalism, ethnocentrism, urban centrism, sectorcentrism, fragmentism, ahistorism, Eurocentrism and numerous cases of simplifications have all considerably distorted academic discourse on the subject.

European migration studies take the nation state for granted, because it is the dominant social and political form in which humanity is organized, and thus the chief shaper of migration. Thereafter, people move from one 'container' to the other and because this involves the crossing of the borders of nation states this is perceived both socially and politically relevant. This world order then serves as a template for the research and creates the conceptualization of human geographic mobility. It is assumed that the nation state is the prime unit of research. As a consequence, movements which do not affect the nation state, because they occur within its borders, raise much less attention, are less researched and rarely provoke political intervention. Equally, migration processes that involve more than two countries are rarely fully understood, and only recently migration chains have been acknowledged where large-scale emigration results in some scarcities which are then filled with migrants from a third country (Lutz, 2002). But specifically the various processes in-between and beyond nation states, namely transnational processes, have long been overlooked. The shortcomings this practice creates has been criticized as 'methodological nationalism (Wimmer and Glick-Schiller, 2002) which is reflected, for example, in the 'prevalence of national case studies' (Zincone and Caponi, 2006: 291). Consequently, Hoerder (2002: 140) argues that 'in order to analyze migration processes, socio-economic regions are much more suitable than states with their often arbitrarily drawn borders'.

Indeed, the very research question focusing on why and how people migrate reflects a certain bias. Obviously, people can be sedentary or mobile, and they can be mobile to very different extents in terms of time, space and purpose. The question constructed, however, focuses on mobility only, and only on some aspects, but turns a blind eye to

sedentarism. It can be found that the question 'why people do not migrate' has rarely been asked (Fischer and Straubhaar, 1994) and even less researched. This is the more surprising as populations experiencing relatively poor living standards and high levels of unemployment, as in the south of Spain and Italy or the north of Germany, remain relatively immobile. Indeed, the lack of mobility of European workers (with the exception of the UK) compared with mobility in the US is low, and has become a policy concern (OECD, 1999) with numerous initiatives being sought to address barriers to mobility. Forced immobility due to migration restrictions and its social consequences has (with maybe the sole exception of Carling, 2002) never been studied. And in the case of Russia, where sizeable parts of society have suffered from the negative consequences of transformation processes, large-scale emigration to the West has been expected. This, however, has never materialized. Instead, only small numbers of wealthy Russians have chosen to settle in Prague or London. The poor rarely move west for work. Whereas non-migration under adverse conditions seems to contradict most commonly shared assumptions, and points to economic and behavioral inconsistencies, it has hardly ever been researched. Hence, the *explanandum* chosen is of rather selective nature and requires some elaboration. First, it seems that as some normative assumptions – how things ought to be – guide migration research, and because people are assumed to be sedentary, only the exemption from the norm – namely migration – is studied. Second, sociology in general (and this seems particularly true for the study of migration) concentrates on the study of social problems, thus where there are no problems, either real or perceived, research is unlikely to be conducted.

It is often assumed that migrants of the same nationality, similar color, culture and religion represent a distinct social group. This is most commonly constructed on the basis of ethnicity and often aspects of otherness are attached to such groups. These classifications however are not necessarily reflected in reality. Research has shown that ethnic solidarity cannot be taken for granted. Instead, Poles often mistrust co-nationals (Jordan and Düvell, 2002) and amongst Turks in Germany adverse relationships have been noted. Instead it is often family relations, locality within either country of origin or the host country, or simple market interaction that play the prime role in structuring social relations. Furthermore, ethnicity is intertwined with disadvantages, such as poverty and class. However, because ethnicity has become such a dominant concept, other analytical frameworks have become secondary. Social problems which affect immigrants or their offspring tend to be studied in terms of ethnicity rather than social class or neighborhood (Wimmer, 2004). It is equally telling that ethnic groups associated with some 'otherness', and specifically when 'otherness' is associated with problems, as is the case with Muslims, are more frequently researched than groups that are perceived to be less different or problematic. For instance, studies of German immigrants to the UK, the third largest group of recent immigrants, or studies of Australian and New Zealand migrants to the UK are basically unknown.

A frequently occurring mismatch has been observed between legal, political or sociological classification by the host countries institutions, by academics or by the self-identification of migrants (Düvell and Vogel, 2006). Politics and law aim to distinguish between labor migrants, who are dealt with according to economic concerns; visitors, who are appreciated for reasons of international relations and economics; and refugees and family members, who are both accepted in accordance with international law and obligations. In reality, however, 'persecution and violent conflict often overlap with, or may be provoked or aggravated by, economic marginalization, population pressure, environmental degradation or poor governance' (Loescher, 2003). As a result, the line between forced and voluntary migration is difficult to draw. A migrant worker identified as Polish and therefore

subject to certain immigration restrictions might describe himself as European and thereby claims some belonging to his host society; an illegal immigrant might portray himself as a worker who is contributing to the economy thereby justifying his or her stay; and a labor migrant might apply for refugee status simply because there is no other legal status available. These examples demonstrate why it is not advisable to blindly accept legal or political categories but to look behind the scenes of the obvious and ask for hidden agendas and identities. Recently, efforts have been made to escape the shortcomings of conventional categorizations through introducing broader concepts such as 'mixed flows' of economic migrants, asylum seekers and irregular migrants (UNHCR, 2006). It remains to be seen whether this offers anything helpful to the researcher.

European migration studies usually focus on immigration to urban areas, in particular to capitals or other major cities, and on integration matters. Towns, or indeed rural areas, which provide for some very different economics and social structures, are rarely chosen; therefore, recent Polish arrivals in Banbury (Oxfordshire, UK), Vietnamese in Hoya (Lower Saxon, Germany) or Romanians in Viterbo (Lazio, Italy) never make it onto the European research agenda. This is more disturbing as around half of all new immigrants to UK, to take just one example, are found in rural areas. In a similar manner, the research design often focuses on labor markets and only on those some industries that absorb significant numbers of migrants. Whereas in the past, industries identified with male labor migrants (such as, heavy industry and automobile industry) raised the most interest, more recently the domestic sector has become heavily studied. In contrast, migrant staff in white collar industries and on senior levels only occasionally make it onto the research agenda. This practice indicates a certain bias revealing that groups that are not perceived as a 'problem' are of little interest to the research community. Another group that is underresearched are agricultural migrant workers.

The reason for this seems to be their relative (i.e. to city-based researchers) invisibility. In other words, there seems to be a hierarchy of research interests, which to some extent reflects a hierarchy of migration (Bauman, 1998). Those at the top neither raise much political concern nor research interest, and vice versa those at the bottom raise both political and research interests.

Migration studies like to focus on dichotomies, such as, legal and illegal migration, voluntary and forced migration, tourism and migration, permanent and temporary migration and highly and low skilled migration. Often, a close look reveals that reality is far more complex; the cases found rarely match any of the two categories but fall somewhere in between. For example, migration is often thought of as pairs of sending and receiving countries, such as Turkey and Germany, Algeria and France, or Romania and Italy. Research has found that sending countries are most often also receiving countries, such as Poland, which send millions of workers to Western European countries whilst simultaneously receiving hundreds of thousands of Ukrainian migrant workers. Other studies show that the majority of illegal migrants enter and stay legally but engage in irregular working (Jordan and Düvell, 2002). Semi-compliance with immigration law (Ruhs and Anderson, 2006) seems a more adequate description of their experience. With respect to voluntary migration, a synonym for any non-refugee movement, the question is how voluntary, for instance, labor migration is in cases where economic conditions do not enable sufficient standards of living (Bade, 2002a). Equally unconvincing are characterizations of migration on the basis of skills as highly skilled migrants often experience some deskilling and a shop manager may well become a cleaner, or a teacher a domestic worker. One possible consequence would be to abstain from dichotomies altogether and instead turn to scaling phenomena.

Related to this problem of migration dichotomies are views suggesting that the direction of European migration is predominantly east–west and south–north, from Poland and Ukraine west to Germany, the UK and Italy, and from Morocco and Algeria north to Spain, France and Italy. This necessitate a blind eye being turned to south–south movements (from Turkey to Saudi Arabia, or from Mali to Libya), to east–east migrations (such as Ukraine to Russia), to east–south migration (as from Moldova to Turkey) and to south–east movements (for example Turkey to Poland and Russia). Equally neglected are movements from north to south, as occurs when post-employment-age Dutch, British or Germans move to France, Spain, Portugal or Italy. Even Turkey and Bulgaria are increasingly becoming destinations for sunshine or retirement migration. These movements, if taken into account, would significantly impact on the calculation of the net balance of migration and put into perspective the often held northern perception that 'half the world' is heading north when, in fact, 'half the north' probably dreams of a retirement home under Mediterranean sun. West–east movements too fall victim to this thinking and are left under-researched. Though admittedly small in numbers, it has been hypothesized the migration of Western experts, managers and entrepreneurs from the old EU into the new EU countries has a considerable 'qualitative impact' on political and economic transformation of these countries (Iglicka, 2003: 47).

Just as much of the public conscience is startlingly blind to history, so too is European migration studies, where migration processes are analyzed within relatively short periods, resulting only in the production of 'snapshots' (IMI, 2006: 9). Whilst case studies allow the identification of patterns of migration, they fail to understand the meaning and dynamics of migration processes within the time dimension. For example, European migration studies usually take the end of World War II as a significant point of reference for the calculation of net migration, which produces positive figures and thus the conclusion is reached that Europe is an immigration continent. That, however, is only half the truth. Alternatively, the point of reference could be set at the outset of European migration, in, for example, 1820, which would produce a completely different picture, as around 50–65 million Europeans emigrated between 1820 and 1930 (Hoerder and Knauf, 1992); large-scale immigration only started to occur after 1950, with at present around 45 million immigrants and their offspring settled in Europe. Thus, the net balance is actually a minus figure. Equally, so-called new migration from East to West after the fall of the Iron Curtain can hardly be called 'new' from an historical perspective since East–West movements have been ongoing throughout history. Even recent history is sometimes either ignored or under-researched, in a combination of historical blindness and politically driven negligence. As a result, pre-1989 migration in Central and Eastern Europe is largely unknown to Western scholars. The conventional separation of historical and sociological migration studies is problematic; instead history should be consulted before the present is interpreted.

European migration studies are largely fragmented, thus studies cluster around specific themes, patterns, types and locations but neglect others. Accordingly, trends and even fashions can be identified. For example, studies in transnationalism became popular during the late 1990s. Research of female migrants in domestic work has become prominent too, firstly detailing Philippine workers, but then moving onto other nationalities. Until the late 1990s, irregular migration was a topic too hot to be touched. Now, shelves can be filled with publications. All this must certainly be welcomed in its own right because once-overlooked patterns have been acknowledged, gender-ignorant practices overcome and research taboos eliminated. What is problematic though is that it is sometimes concluded that because a phenomenon has entered the research agenda at a certain time it has only emerged at that time. For example, several authors claim a 'feminization' of migration during the 1980s and 1990s, even though historians have recorded independent migration

of women in earlier periods too (Bade, 2002b). In reality, migration has not been feminised, but the research agenda has been. Another downside of such research trends is that other patterns are left neglected, and consequently a lot more is left to be done, as shown in this chapter.

In political terms (and because migration has been perceived as a problem) both policy and research concentration has focused on how to address migration. Rarely has it been asked whether the problem might be with the structure of the political organization of humanity, of its membership regimes, labor markets and systems of redistribution, which are ill-prepared to accommodate mobile populations. Here it is suggested that there must be a reframing of migration policy research which addresses the structural shortcomings of analysis rooted in the nation state system (see also Düvell, 2006d: 231).

Eurocentrism and EU-centrism, overemphasizing the experience of a few northwestern countries, is particularly detrimental and contributes to European studies' failure to consider the migration experience in non-EU or non-European countries. As a result, immigration to Russia is widely ignored, and not much is known about migration to Hungary and Romania. The latter recalls the absence of studies into immigration to Italy, Spain and Portugal, a field of research that only gained pace some 20 years after immigration set in. One explanation appears to be that the northwestern EU countries are perceived as the major attraction to international migrants, therefore it has long been overlooked that first Southern and subsequently Central and Eastern European countries (in other words middle-income countries) have become destinations for migration. As yet, non-EU European migration systems in the East also remain largely unresearched.

Further difficulty is added by oversimplification, derived from popular models and myths which are loaded with ideology (Sriskandarajah, 2005). This applies to the concept of 'brain drain', and its supplementary concepts, the brain gain and brain exchange.

The idea that developmental policies can reduce migration has certainly been proven wrong, as has the fear that immigrants displace indigenous workers or that irregular migrant workers represent unfair competition to regular workers (Düvell, 2006d).

MIGRATION, POLITICS AND SCIENCE

The relation between migration, politics and science is multifaceted and tense. Politics responds to migration and migrants respond to politics, science informs politics and politics impact on science. It is really only possible, within the context of this article, to highlight a few key issues that impact on this relationship.

Often, public and media perception is shaped by images, such as queues of hundreds of Roma asylum seekers outside German registration offices for refugees in 1989, the arrival of thousands of Albanians on board a cargo ship in Italy in 1991, or poorly dressed sub-Saharan Africans climbing the fences of the Spanish exclave of Ceuta in 2005. Rhetoric and evocative phrases such as 'bogus asylum seekers', 'welfare scroungers', 'the Polish plumber' and more recently the 'Muslim bomber' capture as much as they fuel public fear. Such images often create a sense of crisis and panic over irregular immigration (Jordan and Düvell, 2002), asylum (Loescher, 2003) and mass immigration, and contribute to a 'politics of fear' (Sparks, 2003). Concepts, such as, 'sending and receiving countries', 'illegal migration', 'transit migration' and 'human trafficking' have developed enormous political power and even become a sort of 'war cry' (Düvell, 2006b). Countries labeled accordingly face enormous pressure from the EU to address that feature. Polarization over migration does not only produce images of 'bad migrants', but also the image of 'good migrants', who might be highly skilled, a successful foreign businessman, a much-needed seasonal worker or a needy, but well-integrated refugee.

Unfortunately, governments frequently fail to facilitate a balanced public debate and instead fuel tensions (Spencer, 2003).

Politics aims to reassure public confidence and occasionally develops hectic responses. Efforts are made to (a) return and remove unwanted migrants, (b) to enhance control of paths and entry points, (c) to manage migration of wanted migrants and (d) to address what is dubbed the 'root causes' through, for example, development policies. Some of this, as research has shown, is impractical, uneconomic, ethically questionable and will have unintended negative effects. For instance, as a consequence of recruitment stops issued during the 1970s 'guest workers' could no longer come and go as it was previously possible; they were deprived of their mobile strategy and instead had to decide whether to stay or to return permanently. As a consequence, once temporary labour migrants were effectively 'locked in' by their host countries became immigrants instead (Hansen, 2003: 26). And also immigration restrictions that are aimed at turning away unwanted migrants instead often drive these underground or towards alternative paths (Düvell, 2006d). Some policies will be challenged by court rulings or by civil society activism, and both limit policy implementation to an extent that 'policy gaps' are arising (Cornelius et al., 1994). Unfortunately, scientific evidence is not always appreciated, instead migration policy tends to act in a knowledge-free space, as some critics have argued.

The Europeanization of migration politics has brought about a specific terminology, such as 'third countries', 'family reunification' and 'border management'. First and foremost, these terms are invented to facilitate international communication between policy makers and administrations. Furthermore, they have developed under specific historic circumstances and political power relations within the European Union. Finally, they inherit a specific connotation, reflect specific thinking, a specific culture and are loaded with normative assumptions. Yet, such technical terms and jargon frequently enter academic discourse.

Thus, political terms quickly become conflated with scholarly language. Thereby, academic attempts to achieve distance and critical analysis is further complicated. Instead, scientists need to develop their own analytical tools including an appropriate terminology.

CHANGEABLE SUBJECT AND LIMITED RESEARCH DESIGNS

Migration appears to be of a non-linear, dynamic and non-predictable nature. Any attempt to present a snapshot which reflects a rather static picture of a situation at a given point in time inevitable misses the dynamic and process-based nature of migration. Accordingly, migration research must develop adequate and equally dynamic and flexible methods that are geared up to catch and grasp the phenomenon. Suggested are longitudinal research designs and ethnosurveys (Massey, 1987), social drama analysis (Wimmer, 2004), and chaos theory (Papastergiadis, 2000).

Four forces shape migration processes: economics, politics, climate and human agency. Research into the latter two approaches, but especially human agency, are grossly underdeveloped and partially absent from the research agenda or often simply ignored. Sometimes, this is due to some unpopularity of post-Marxist approaches, which would focus on the antagonism between social groups and state or capital. Therefore, efforts should be made to: (1) study 'human agency' (Rodriguez, 1996), (2) analyse the 'tug-of-war' between institutions and individuals (Shresta, 1987), (3) carve out the 'autonomy' in migration processes (Mezzadra, 2004), and (4) to understand the political meaning of migration.

Another setback lies in the separation of Anglophone, Francophone and Russophone research communities. English scholars know little about migration from Francophone Africa, French scholars did not engage in Anglo-Saxon discourses on the ethics of migration, and Russian migration studies are

basically inaccessible to most Western scientists. The latter is a particular challenge as Russia is now a top recipient of international migrants. This problem is, in part, the product of simple language barriers, but also due to a lack of interest in migration occurring in the other cultural spheres.

Knowledge production is enormous; unfortunately, many products never make it onto the stage of books and journal articles. Recent research is increasingly found in grey literature, such as working papers, conference papers, project reports and graduation theses. This is because of funding limitations, the politics of research or for career-related reasons. Today's migration researchers must therefore be prepared to spend hours surveying the Internet for such outputs.

MIGRATION, EXCLUSION, MARGINALITY

Immigrants in Europe principally suffer from four types of marginalization: (1) deprivation of political rights, (2) economic marginalization, (3) social exclusion and (4) spatial segregation.

In classic immigration countries, naturalization is taken for granted. In contrast, most European countries restrict access to citizenship and, to some extent, exclude migrants from full political membership, even in their second and third generation (see Bauböck et al., 2006). Some countries (Germany, Greece, Spain, Portugal, Italy and Turkey) favor specific groups, such as ethnic migrants, over others and thereby display some racial logic in their immigration policy. Complex immigration legislation has created equally complex hierarchies of immigrants, ranging from citizens, denizens, refugees, dependants, contract workers, asylum seekers and undocumented migrants. Anti-discrimination legislation indirectly favors some groups over others, as in the UK; in other cases, as for instance in Germany, established communities (e.g. Turks) are well represented in civil and political society, whilst recently emerging communities (e.g. immigrants of African origin) are side-lined. Meanwhile, comparisons between legal conditions, institutional practices and related identity processes across Europe and access to civic participation remain major gaps in existing research.

By and large, numerous country studies illustrate that Europe's immigrants are over-represented in specific entrepreneurial and labor market sectors, and in specific profes-sions; they are also over-represented in socially disadvantaged groups such as low-paid, unemployed, welfare recipients. Geographically, they are concentrated in deprived neighbor-hoods and in substandard housing.[5] Trends, however, vary greatly across time, countries, ethnicity and gender; in some cases immigrants perform better even than indigenous popula-tions, while some groups do not display great differences, whereas others suffer from con-siderable marginalization.

During the 1960s and 1970s, migrants to the north have been over-represented in manufacturing industries, usually the least modern. These did not withstand international competition and subsequent deindustrializa-tion, technological change and restructuring ultimately led to higher than average unem-ployment amongst migrant workers, who, con-trary to political expectations, did not return but instead invited their families to join them in the host country. The first generation of migrants, but even more so the second genera-tion, suffer from sustained economic exclusion due to the combined effect of their low skill levels, language deficiencies, the educational failure of the second generation, and dis-crimination. For many, self-employment has become a problem-solving strategy and immi-grant entrepreneurs have been crucial in reviving entire sectors and areas (Klosterman and Rath, 2004). Meanwhile, new opportuni-ties for new immigrants have arisen, specifi-cally in agriculture and food processing, in the service sector and in domestic work. Migrants to the south, arriving since the 1980s, tend to work in domestic service, tourism, construc-tion and agriculture, as well as increasingly in small and medium-sized manufacturing

(Calavita, 2005). Deskilling, skills waste and brain waste of otherwise skilled migrant workers occur to different degrees dependent on gender, nationality and the category of migrant, as has been observed frequently in Europe (Brandi, 2001; Gächter, 2006). This is either explained with a mismatch of skills and labor market demand, or the institutional (and often discriminating) barriers to skills recognition practices. Accordingly, pay dif-ferentials are considerable and commonplace (Taran, 2006). Much of new labor migration occurs on a *laissez-faire* basis, and leads to a rise in irregular immigration. However, more recent trends favor a return to managed guest worker or 'temporary labor migrant (TLM)' schemes (Ruhs, 2005). This signals that, once again, it is workers that are wanted, not people. It is striking that 'economic issues have not been the centerpiece of migration research' in Europe (Bommes and Kolb, 2006: 99). Notably the impact of immigra-tion on the economy and on indigenous workers often remains based on assumptions rather than evidence-based knowledge.

Instead, social marginality has attracted much more attention (Asselin *et al.*, 2006). Recently, integration and multiculturalism are perceived to be in crisis. This crisis is identified with alleged segregation, parallel live worlds, alienation and radicalization of ethnic minority (specifically, Muslim) youth. A close look however shows that residential segregation is nowhere near the US level (Lucassen, 2004); therefore, clustering seems a more adequate description for residential patterns of Europe's immigrants and ethnic minorities. Youth radicalization takes either the form of mass street violence, though only on occasions (as in the UK in 2001 and in France in 2005), and political murder (as in the Netherlands in 2004) or terrorism (as in Spain in 2004 and the UK in 2005 and 2006), involves only small numbers of indi-viduals. Public discourse is quick to link and explain immigrants' and ethnic minority pro-tests and terrorism to immigration, ethnicity and religion. Accordingly, policy responses frequently refer to immigration policies (controls and deportation) and to measures specifically addressing the immigration aspect of the target group. Alternatively, it is suggested it would be useful to also analyze radicalization, political violence and terrorism as a political movement and youth protest, and to compare it with similar forms of domestic social movements, radicalization processes and terrorism during the 1960s to 1980s.

Marginalization and failure of integration is either blamed on immigrants and their refusal and failure, or on the host society and on institutional failure, hostile public discourses (xenophobia and Islamophobia), discrimination and racism. Both explanations are often presented as being mutually exclusive. The truth is possibly found somewhere in between. Failing integration is instead due to a complex interaction between host societies, which only reluctantly admit immigrants, and migrants who are unwilling or unable to adapt to their new environments.

CONCLUSION

European migration studies suffer from poor data, outdated assumptions, politicized concepts, lack of theory, binary thinking and distorted analyses. First, diverging national statistical and political practices result in largely incomparable data. Second, migration studies suffer from the absence of a coherent theory and most scholars seem to have given up on the idea of creating one. Third, numerous biases confuse rational dealing with migration. Fourth, too many concepts are taken for granted for reasons of convention and convenience. Fifth, migration studies are fragmented, with research clustering in some areas and lack of research on other aspects of migration. Finally, politics creates perceptions rather than knowledge. Future scholars must address all these issues. First of all, it is advisable to adopt an integrated approach to migration studies, as, for example, suggested by migration system theory,

and to study the many types of movements, for many purpose, and across history to fully understand the interaction, inter-relations and dynamics of migration. Second, efforts are required to develop a coherent migration theory which integrates all existing elements. Third, conventional concepts must be put to the test, so as their validity can be assessed and terminology revised accordingly. Fourth, researchers should take into account the specific historical and political circumstances under which a concept or typology became popular and separate its political meaning from its potential scientific use. Fifth, fashion and taboos distracting researchers need to be identified and challenged. Sixth, types and categories have often been identified through comparison, even though underlying cases might have changed, or a feature or pattern has disappeared. As a consequence, fresh cross-country, cross-regional, cross-city and cross-ethnicity comparison is required to generate fresh results. Seventh, researchers should abstain from simple models such as forced/voluntary or sending/receiving country, and instead analyze the scales, hence the relationship between emigration and immigration, and the proportion of choice and coercion in migration decision-making.

NOTES

1 Because of word limits only a selection of references can be given.

2 British government sources estimated the immigration of no more than 15,000 annually, but during the period May 2004 to December 2005, 345,000 A8 nationals registered for work with the Workers Registration Scheme. In contrast, German sources estimated a maximum of 400,000 A8 immigrants in 2004 and 2005, instead the net flow was negative (see Düvell, 2006c for both examples).

3 There are also cultural and geographic borders and boundaries, such as, between distinct culturally, linguistically or religiously defined regions. These too have implications for the mobility of people but because the borders are of only national administrative and not of international meaning their crossing is of little interest to migration research.

4 Migration systems link together regions and states historically, culturally, linguistically, economically, politically and socially. Within such systems there are simultaneous flows of information, capital, goods and people of any kind, for any purpose and in any direction (see Kritz *et al.*, 1992).

5 For case studies see diverse country reports compiled for the EU funded POLITIS project, http://www.uni-oldenburg.de/politis-Europe/.

REFERENCES

Asselin, O., Dureau, F., Fonseca, L. *et al.* (2006) 'Social integration of immigrants with spezial reference to the local and spatial dimension', in R. Penninx, M. Berger and K. Kraal (eds) *The Dynamics of International Migration and Settlement in Europe*. Amsterdam: Amsterdam University Press, pp. 133–170.

Bade, K. (2002a) Historische Migrationsforschung', *IMIS-Beiträge*, 20: 21–43.

Bade, K. (2002b) *Europa in Bewegung*. Munich: Beck.

Bauböck, R. (1994) *Transnational Citizenship: Membership and Rights in International Migration*. Aldershot: Edward Elgar.

Bauböck, R., Ersboll, E., Groenendijk, Kees and Waldrauch, H. (eds) (2006) *Acquisition and Loss of Nationality. Policies and Trends in 15 European States*. Amsterdam: Amsterdam University Press.

Bauman, Z. (1998) *Globalization*. Cambridge: Polity.

Bleahu, A. (2005) 'Romanian migration to Spain. Motivation, networks and strategies', in Public Policy Centre (CENPO) (ed.) *New Patterns of Labour Migration in Central and Eastern Europe*. Cluj Napoca: CENPO, pp. 21–35.

Bommes, M. (1999) *Migration und nationaler Wohlfahrtsstaat. Ein differenzierungstheoretischer Entwurf*. Wiesbaden: Opladen.

Bommes, M. and Kolb, H. (2006) ‚Migrant's work, entrepreneurship and economic integration', in R. Penninx, M. Berger and K. Kraal (eds) *The Dynamics of International Migration and Settlement in Europe*. Amsterdam: Amsterdam University Press, pp. 99–132.

Bommes, M. and Geddes, A. (eds) (2001) *Immigration and Welfare*. London: Routledge.

Brandi, C. (2001) 'Skilled immigrants in Rome', *International Migration*, 39 (4): 101–131.

Borjas, G.J. (1989) 'Economic theory and international migration', *International Migration Review*, 23 (3): 457–485.

Calavita, K. (2005) *Immigrants at the Margins*. Cambridge: Campbridge University Press.

Carling, J. (2002) 'Migration in the age of involuntary immobility: theoretical reflections and Cape Verdean experiences', *Journal of Ethnic and Migration Studies*, 28 (1): 5–42.

Castles, S. and Miller, M. (2003) *The Age of Migration*. Houndmills: Palgrave Macmillan.

Castles, S. (2000) *Ethnicity and Globalization*. New York and London: Sage.

Cornelius, W., Martin, P. and Hollifield J.F. (eds) (1994) *Controlling Immigration: Aglobal Perspective*. Stanford: Stanford University Press.

Daley, J. (2007) 'Four developing markets set to dominate the world', *The Independent*, 24 February.

Düvell, F. (2005) 'Globalisation of migration control. A tug-war between restrictionists and the human agency?' in H. Henke (ed.) *Crossing Over: Comparing Recent Migration in Europe and the United States*. New York: Lexington Books, pp. 23–46.

Düvell, F. (2006a) *Europäische und Internationale Migration*. Hamburg: Lit.

Düvell, F. (2006b) 'Crossing the fringes of Europe: Transit migration in the EU's neighbourhood', Working paper 06-33, Centre on Migration, Policy and Society, Oxford.

Düvell, F. (2006c) 'Entwicklung der Migration nach der EU-Osterweiterung', in M. Bommes and W. Schiffauer (eds) *Migrationsreport 2006*. Frankfurt: Campus, pp. 63–112.

Düvell, F. (2006d) *Illegal Immigration in Europe*. Houndmills: Palgrave Macmillan.

Düvell, F. (2006e) 'Questioning convenient concepts: the sending country/receiving country dichotomy', paper presented to COMPAS Seminar Series, 26 October.

Düvell, F. and Vogel, D. (2006) 'Polish migrants: tensions between sociological typologies and state categories', in A. Triandafyllidou (ed), *Contemporary Polish Migration in Europe. Complex Patterns of Movement and Settlement*, Lewiston, NY: Edwin Mellen Press, pp.. 267–289.

Faist, T. (2000) *The Volume and Dynamics of International Migration and Transnational Social Spaces*. Oxford: Oxford University Press.

Favell, A. (2003) 'Eurostars and Eurocities: towards a sociology of free moving professionals in

Western Europe', Working paper 61, Centre for Comparative Immigration Studies, San Diego.

Fischer, A.F. and Straubhaar, T. (1994) *Ökonomische Integration und Migration in einem gemeinsamen Markt*. Stuttgart: Verlag Paul Haupt.

Gächter, A. (2006) *Migration and the Austrian Labour Market in an Enlarging European Union*. Vienna: Zentrum für Soziale Innovation.

Garbin, D. (2002) 'From transnational to trans-local: Migration, space and power', paper presented at the conference on *The European City in Transition: Urbanism and Globalization*, Weimar, 8–9 November.

Geddes, A. (2003) *The Politics of Migration and Integration in Europe*. London: Sage.

Glick Schiller, N., Basch, L. and Blanc-Szanton, C. (eds) (1992) *Towards a Transnational Perspective on Migration: Race, Class, Ethnicity, and Nationalism Reconsidered*. New York: New York Academy of Sciences.

GCIM (Global Commission on International Migration) (2005) *Migration in an Interconnected World: New Directions for Action*. Geneva: GCIM.

Hammar, T. (1990) *Democracy and the Nation State: Aliens, Denizens and Citizens in a World of International Migration*. Aldershot: Avebury.

Hansen, R. (2003) 'Migration to Europe since 1945: its history and its lesson', in S. Spencer (ed.) *The Politics of Migration in Europe*. Oxford: Blackwell, pp. 25–38.

Heleniak, T. (2002) 'Russia beckons, but diaspora wary', Migration Information Source, 1 October 2002. Available at: www.migrationinformation.org/feature/print.cfm?ID=56.

Hoerder, D. (2002) 'Europäische Migrationsgeschichte und Weltgeschichte der Migration: Epochenzäsuren und Methodenprobleme', *IMIS-Beiträge*, 20: 135–168.

Hoerder, D. (2003) *Cultures in Contact. World Migrations in the Second Millennium*. Durham and London: Duke University Press.

Hoerder, D. and Knauf, D. (eds) (1992) *Fame, Fortune and Sweet Liberty. The Great European Emigration*. Bremen: Temmen.

Hollifield, J.F. (1992) *Immigration, Markets and States*. Cambridge, MA: Havard University Press.

Icduygu, A. (2006) 'Migration from and to Turkey. Past trends and prospects', paper presented to IMISCOE Workshop, 10–12 March, Istanbul.

Iglicka, K. (2003) 'The foreign labour market in Poland', in I. Iglicka (ed.) *Migration and Labour Markets in Poland and Ukraine*. Warsaw: Institute of Public Affairs, pp. 40–50.

Ilie, L. (2006) 'Romanian industries turn to foreign workers', *Kathimerini*, English edition, 28 December.

IMI (2006) *Towards a New Agenda for International Migration Research*. Oxford: International Migration Institute.

International Organization for Migration (IOM) (2003) *World Migration Report*. Geneva: IOM.

Joly, D (ed.) (2004) *International Migration in the New Millennium: Global Movement and Settlement*. Aldershot: Ashgate.

Joppke, C. (1998) (ed.) *Challenge to the Nation State. Immigration in Western Europe and the United States*. Oxford: Oxford University Press.

Jordan, B. and Düvell, F. (2002) *Irregular Migration: Dilemmas of Transnational Mobility*. Cheltenham: Edward Elgar.

Kicinger, A. (2004) 'International migration as a non-traditional security threat and the EU responses to this phenomenon', Working paper, Central European Forum for Migration Researc, Warsaw.

King, R. and Ruiz-Gelices, E. (2003) 'International student migration and the European "year abroad": effects on European identity and subsequent migration behaviour', *International Journal of Population Geography*, 9 (3): 229–252.

Klosterman, R. and Rath, J. (eds) (2004) *Immigrant Entrepreneurs. Venturing Abroad in the Age of Globalisation*. Oxford: Berg.

Koser, K. and Lutz, H. (1998) 'The new migration in Europe: Contexts, constructions and realities', in K. Koser and H. Lutz (eds) *The New Migration in Europe. Social Cosntructions and Social Realities*. Macmillan: London, pp. 1–17.

Kritz, M., Lim, L.L. and Zlotnik, H. (eds) (1992) *International Migration Systems: a Global Approach*. Oxford: Clarendon Press.

Loescher, G. (2003) 'Asylum crisis in the UK and Europe', Open Democracy, 22 May. Available at: www.opendemocracy.org.

Lucassen, L. (2004) 'Old wine in new bottles? Turks and Poles in Germany and the importance of historical comparisons', paper presented at the Workshop on the Integration of Immigrants from Turkey in Austria, Germany and Holland, Bogazici University, 27–28 February, Istanbul.

Lutz, H. (2002) 'At your service madam! The globalisation of domestic service', *Feminist Review*, 70: 1–16.

Massey, D. (1987) 'The ethnosurvey in theory and practice', *International Migration Review*, 21 (4): 1498–1522.

Mezzadra, S. (ed.) (2004) *I confini della libertà. Per un'analisi politica delle migrazioni contemporanee*. Rome: DeriveApprodi.

Morawska, E. (2001) 'Structuring migration: The case of Polish income-seeking travellers to the West', *Theory and Society*, 31: 47–80.

Morokvasic, M. (1994) Pendeln statt Auswandern. Das Beispiel Polen', in M. Morokvasic and H. Rudolph (eds) *Wanderungsraum Europa. Menschen und Grenzen in Bewegung*. Berlin: Sigma, pp. 166–187.

Morocvasic, M. and Rudolf, H. (eds) (1994) *Wanderungsraum Europa. Menschen und Grenzen in Bewegung*. Berlin: Edition Sigma.

National Consultative Committee on Racism and Interculturalism (NCCRI) (2005) *Changing Ireland*. Dublin: NCCRI.

OECD (1999) ,Getting European workers moving', OECD Observer, no. 217/218.

OECD (2001) *SOPEMI. Trends in International Migration*. Annual Report 2000. Paris: OECD.

OECD (2002) International Mobility of the Highly Skilled. Paris: OECD.

Papastergiadis, N. (2000) *The Turbulence of Migration*. Cambridge: Polity.

Pijpers, R. (2006) 'Help! The Poles are coming': Narrating a contemporary moral panic', *Geografiska Annaler, Series B, Human Geography*, 88 (1): 91–103.

Rodriguez, N. (1996) 'The battle for the border: Notes on autonomous migration, transnational communities and the state', *Social Justice*, 23 (3): 21–37.

Rodríguez-García, D. (2005) From emigration to immigration: changing trends in international migration in Europe and the case of Spain', seminar paper, presented in Toronto, Centre of Excellence for Research on Immigration and Settlement. Available at: http://ceris.metropolis.net/events/seminars/2005/January/Jan05_Dan.htm.

Ruhs, M. (2005) *The Potential of Temporary Migration Programmes in Future International Migration Policy*. Geneva: Global Commission on International Migration (GCIM).

Ruhs, M. and Anderson, B. (2006) 'Semi-compliance in the migrant labour market', Working paper 06-30. Oxford: COMPAS.

Schierup, C.U., Hansen, P. and Castles, S. (2006) *Migration, Citizenship, and the European Welfare State. A European Dilemma*. Oxford: Oxford University Press.

Shrestha, N.R. (1987) 'International policies and migration behaviour: a selective review', *World Development*, 15 (3): 329–345.

Sparks, C. (2003) 'Liberalism, terrorism and the politics of fear', *Politics*, 23 (2): 200–206.

Spencer, S (ed.) (2003) *The Politics of Migration in Europe*. Oxford: Blackwell.

Sriskandarajah, D. (2005) 'Migration and development: a new research and policy agenda', *World Economics*, 6 (2): 141–146.

Stark, O. (1991) *The Migration of Labour*. Oxford: Blackwell.

Taran, P.A. (2006) 'Imperatives and options for combating discrimination against migrants in the age of globalization', in International Labor Organization (ed.) *Thematic Discussion on Globalization and Racism, Intergovernmental Working Group on the Effective Implementation of the Durban Declaration and Program if Action*. Geneva: ILO.

Triandafyllidou, A. (2001) *Immigrants and National Identity in Europe*. London: Routledge.

United Nations (1998) 'Department of Economic and Social Affairs Statistics Division 1998, Recommendations on statistics of international migration', *Statistical Papers Series M*, No. 58, Rev. 1. New York: United Nations.

United Nations (2005) *World Population Prospects: the 2004 Revision Population Database*. New York: United Nations.

UNHCR (2006) *Addressing Mixed Migratory Movements: A 10-Point Plan of Action*. Geneva: UNHCR.

United Nations Office on Drugs and Crime (UNODC) (2006) *Organized Crime and Irregular Migration from Africa to Europe*. New York: UNODC.

United Nations University (2005) 'Environmental refugees to top 50 million in 5 years', News release, 11 October. Available at: http://news.mongabay.com/2005/1011-unu.html.

Van Hear, N. (2005) 'The end of asylum?', talk given at UN Association, Oxford, 29 November.

Venturini, A. (2004) *Postwar Migration in Southern Europe, 1950–2000*. Cambridge: Cambridge University Press.

Vertovec, S. (1999) 'Conceiving and researching transnationalism', *Ethnic and Racial Studies*, 22 (2): 447–462.

Vertovec, S. (2006) 'The emergence of super-diversity in Britain', Working paper 25, Centre on Migration, Policy and Society, Oxford.

Weiner, M. (1995) *The Global Migration Crisis. Challenges to States and Human Rights*. New York: Harper Collins.

Widgren, J. (2000) Statement presented at 10th UN Congress on the Prevention of Crime and Treatment of Offenders, 10–17 April, Vienna.

Williams, A.M., King, R., Warnes, A.M. and Patterson, G. (2000) 'Tourism and international retirement migration: new forms of an old relationship in southern Europe', *Tourism Geographies*, 2 (1): 28–49.

Wimmer A. (2004) 'Does ethnicity matter? Everyday group formation in three Swiss immigrant neighbourhoods', *Ethnic and Racial Studies*, 27 (1): 1–36.

Wimmer, A. and Glick-Schiller, N. (2002) 'Methodological nationalism and beyond: nation-state building, migration and the social sciences', *Global Networks*, 2 (4): 301–334.

World Tourism Organization (2005) 'International tourism obtains its best results in 20 years. News release. Geneva: WTO. Available at: http://www.world-tourism.org/newsroom/Releases/2005/january/2004 numbers.htm.

Zelinski, W. (1971) 'The hypothesis of the mobility transition', *Geographical Review*, 61: 219–249.

Zincone, G. and Caponio, T. (2006) 'The multi-level governance of migration', R. Penninx, M. Berger and K. Kraal (eds) *The Dynamics of International Migration and Settlement in Europe*. Amsterdam: Amsterdam University Press, pp. 269–304.

20

Citizenship, Democracy and the Public Sphere

John Erik Fossum

Modern democracy has been intrinsically linked to the democratic nation-state. No account of democracy in contemporary Europe can ignore the close association that has existed for centuries in Europe between the state as an organizational form, the nation as a mode of community, and democracy. (Western) Europe is the cradle of the modern nation state and the system of states (which is often referred to as the Westphalian system, from the Treaty of Westphalia in 1648). As such, there is no question that the modern configuration of nation-state-based democracy can trace much of its lineage back to Europe. Even the American democratic revolution, and the central role played by the US in the development of modern nation-state-based democracy were orientated in relation to, and took intellectual nourishment from, Europe. Europe has projected its ideals, its institutions and its modes of belonging onto the world, through peaceful promotion of European ideas and civilization, and through colonial domination and military conquest.

Europe has over the centuries and often in the name of some noble purpose, inflicted its conflicts upon the world, helped to spark conflicts outside of Europe, and involved itself in conflicts going on outside of Europe. In that connection it is also important to recognize that the contemporary situation of democracy across much of the terrain we normally associate with Europe could not have come about without the ideas, the convictions, the support, and the sacrifice of non-Europeans. Hence, when addressing the broad theme of democracy in Europe, it is necessary to keep in mind that European developments are deeply imbricated in global ones. There has been an (uneven) dialectic between democratization within Europe and democratization outside of Europe. At some points, developments internal to Europe have spurred democratization in Europe; at other points, developments external to Europe have spurred democratization in Europe. It is only really in the last two decades, with the demise of the Soviet empire, that the external and the internal democratization thrusts have appeared to play in harmony (albeit whether this is really the case is disputed, as is how long it will last).

This chapter focuses on the question of democracy, citizenship, and public sphere in Europe. Each of these topics has spawned comprehensive, multilingual, and multidisciplinary debates. The debates do not unfold along clearly defined faultlines in democratic theory, such as communitarian versus liberal, or participatory versus elite-based democracy. Neither is the debate on the democratic character of the European Union particularly well connected with mainstream debates in political theory. One major reason is that globalization and Europeanization raise questions about the continued relevance of the mainstay of democracy, the nation state. To clarify the role of democracy in contemporary Europe it is therefore necessary to shed light on these changes.

My argument is that contemporary Europe grapples with profound changes in the macroscopic nation-state-based context surrounding democracy. But these changes are far from uniform, neither do they cover all of Europe, certainly not to the same extent or degree. Examining the depth and breadth of such changes across Europe forms a necessary backdrop for a closer examination of contemporary forms and shapes of democracy, citizenship, and public sphere in Europe.

FORMS AND THEORIES OF DEMOCRACY

Democracy in ordinary parlance is generally couched as an organizational form, and is associated with such labels as parliamentary or presidential democracy. The essence of democracy, from the vantage point of deliberative democratic theory, is that of a principle of justification: only norms that have been consented to by those affected in open discourse can be considered as legitimate (Habermas, 1996). This principle nevertheless has to be entrenched in legal–organizational form to be effective.

Democracy is a normative concept; it comes with explicit presuppositions for how human beings should relate to each other, and how they should address problems and issues that concern them all, individually and collectively. Democracy is thus associated with a conception of the relevant community, or *demos*; there are therefore also associated presuppositions of membership (and citizenship); that is, of who are part of the community and of how and in what sense they are part; of identity (people need to identify with the community for this to make up a community in the first place); and of legitimacy, as people must believe that the community's basic norms are just and valid for this to make up a democracy. Such additional presuppositions are necessary, for at the core of democracy there is a fundamental ambiguity: democracy cannot itself determine the *demos*; that is, spell out precisely who the people shall be.

Democracy thus depends on as well as places particular democratic requirements on identity, membership status (citizenship) in a given community, and legitimacy. Modern democracy's essence as a justification principle entails that all the criteria for establishing the demos have to be open to constant contestation; hence a central precondition for a democratic order is a viable public sphere – namely, a communicative space (or spaces) in which relatively unconstrained debate, analysis and criticism of the political order can take place (Habermas 1989[1962]). The public sphere has a *triadic* character, with a speaker, an addressee, and a listener. It presupposes that citizens have rights that they can exercise against the state, which again implies that decision makers face the need to justify their decisions and to gain support in public. In such a setting, power cannot be legitimated solely by reference to divine law or traditional authority. Within this framework, it is clear that particular institutions or concrete persons cannot guarantee the legitimacy of the law. Only public debate in itself has norm-giving power (Eriksen and Weigård, 2003).

Modern systems of political rule are of such a scale, scope and complexity that democracy cannot operate in a wholly deliberative or in a fully participatory manner; for its operation it requires representative arrangements, wherein citizens elect delegates who stand for them, and through whom the popular will is articulated and carried out. The rulers must be effectively controlled by the ruled for the system to be democratically accountable; and the rulers need to be able to exercise effective rule, lest accountability will amount to nothing.

Given that democracy at its core is a principle of justification, it follows that representative arrangements cannot simply be understood as aggregators of fixed preferences but also as integrators, and transformers of preferences. This has implications for how we understand the public sphere. *Formally* organized institutions within the political system also figure as 'publics'. Nancy Fraser initially captured this added complexity in a key distinction between 'strong' and 'weak' publics. Strong publics are spaces of institutionalized deliberation 'whose discourse encompasses both opinion formation and decision making', and weak publics are spaces 'whose deliberative practice consists exclusively in opinion formation and does not also encompass decision making' (Fraser 1992: 134). From these brief comments we see that a proper examination of the nature and status of democracy in contemporary Europe requires attention to the ideas that inform the practice of democratic self-government; the vocabulary that is used to describe this; the criteria for establishing membership, and so on; the ways in which ideas and interests are articulated, aggregated and formed into collective decisions; whether these are effectively carried out; and how decisions and political systems are legitimated.

IS THERE A CHANGING MACROSCOPIC CONTEXT FOR DEMOCRACY IN EUROPE?

Since the nineteenth century, Europe has spawned relatively homogeneous and powerful nation states that have territorially confined democracy, together with principles, doctrines and arrangements associated with cosmopolitanism, such as human rights and the rule of law, which are universal in their orientation. These seemingly opposite developments were in Europe long sustained through the combined nationalization and democratization of European states. This led to the emergence of a distinctive category of national citizenship: 'a legal and social status which combines some form of collectively shared identity with the entitlement to social and economic benefits and the privileges of political membership through the exercise of democratic rights' (Benhabib 2007: 19). National citizenship thus makes up a particular configuration of membership status, rights and identity. But nationalization need not entail democratization; neither need democratization entail nationalization. When these two developments part ways, the particular configuration that makes up national citizenship will also unravel.

The de-linking of two of the central presuppositions underlying nation-state-based democracy is one of the core challenges facing contemporary Europe. What does this entail for democracy? Addressing this from an analytical perspective entails looking for: (a) new terminology for describing, new doctrines for justifying, and new modes for co-existence that replace or greatly modify the mode of community that is associated with nationalism; (b) the establishment of new organizational forms that replace or greatly modify state-based hierarchical rule, with implications for membership and for individual, collective and territorial conditions for exit/entry; and/or (c) the development of new ways of thinking and practising democratic self-rule. The former two speak to constitutive changes to the nation-state context, which are relevant here insofar as they have direct bearings on democracy.

Europe as a political space is complex and composite, and not clearly delineated; hence there might not be one single overarching trend or pattern of democratic transformation. I will here focus on three sets of developments that all bear on democracy, citizenship and the public sphere. One is globalization (along economic, cultural and political lines), combined with the emergence of a global system of rights, both of which impinge on states' sovereignty. State sovereignty is rendered increasingly vulnerable to economic and other developments outside of state control; state sovereignty is also to some extent made conditional on individual sovereignty. The second is the development of regional supranational and trans-national arrangements that may transform core democratic nation-state tenets. The development of such arrangements is often considered as taking place in conjunction with internal regionalization, so that the nation state is hollowed out through some form of a combined top-down and bottom-up process (MacCormick, 1999). The most important – and Europe-specific – supranational entity in today's world is the European Union.The third development is the decline of the Soviet Empire, and the subsequent development/ reassertion of (democratic) nation states from the previous Warsaw Pact and Eastern and Central Europe.

GLOBALIZATION: COSMOPOLITANISM VERSUS STATE WITHERING

Globalization has spawned elements of a new vocabulary of political association, new (revamped) political doctrines, and legal–organizational arrangements that carry these. These conceptions take as their point of departure that globalization has profound democratic implications, as 'states, increasingly *ensnared* in the interdependencies of a global economy and society, forfeit their capacities for autonomous action as well as their democratic substance' (Habermas 2003: 89).

Proponents of cosmopolitan democracy speak to the need for a new global political order:[1]

Cosmopolitan democracy is based on the assumption that important objectives – control of the use of force,

respect for human rights, self-determination – will be obtained only through the extension and development of democracy. It differs from the general approach to cosmopolitanism in that it does not merely call for global responsibility but actually attempts to apply the principles of democracy internationally' (Archibugi 2003: 7).

Cosmopolitans also note that there are important legal developments that underpin the case for a global system of public law. Institutionally speaking this is at least partly carried by the UN (and regional arrangements and entities, such as, the ECHR and the EU), and accompanying institutions that have rendered state sovereignty at least somewhat conditioned on compliance with citizen's sovereignty. The cosmopolitan thesis is that in a globalized world, democracy cannot stand for a national 'community of fate' that autonomously governs itself. The rise of cosmopolitan norms has also had citizenship implications, as a result of liberalized access to membership, universalized rights and the severing of the link between membership and identity, so that in some locations 'membership in the state no longer connotes a specific identity' (Joppke, 2007: 39).

These developments are however far from uniform across the globe. In overall terms, they have been carried further in Europe than anywhere else. This applies to the European Convention of Human Rights (ECHR) of November 4, 1950 and to European Union Law (the two converge in the field of human rights). The ECHR permits citizens to initiate proceedings against their own governments. The Court is outside of the jurisdiction of the states, and its judgments are *de facto* legally binding on the states. 'Within this framework, states are no longer free to treat their own citizens as they think fit … The European Convention on Human Rights is most explicit in connecting democracy with state legitimacy, as is the statute of the Council of Europe, which makes a commitment to democracy a condition of membership' (Held *et al.*, 2000: 68–9). The most explicit curtailments of state sovereignty have occurred in Western Europe, where the greatest transformations of international law have taken place. Here these are bolstered and sustained by a supranational structure of governance.

Another somewhat overlapping interpretation of ongoing developments is to see these as part of the emergence of a global system of transnational governance, marked by a proliferation of organizations, where no single organizing principle dominates and where no single actor wields supreme control of a given territory. One of the hallmarks of transnational governance is the shifting loci of authority, which may converge, overlap or diverge. Governance is not political rule through responsible institutions, such as parliament and bureaucracy – which amounts to government – but innovative practices of networks or horizontal forms of interaction, and represents a configuration of political, legal, economic and social factors distinctly different from a government-based system. If transnational governance becomes the global pattern we could talk about the *withering* of the states system.

There is no consensus on the democratic effects of these developments. There are still many who see democracy as exclusively linked to the nation state; hence both globalization and transnationalization/state withering are held up as threatening to democracy, as both would undercut national democracy's core notion of an identifiable democratic people. Cosmopolitans and transnational governance scholars on their side underline the democratic potentials in their respective scenarios. Some cosmopolitans, such as, David Held (1993, 1995, 2000) and Daniele Archibugi (1998, 2003), see cosmopolitanism democracy as compatible with the state form; but in greatly modified form, and as made compatible with a global system. Transnationalists, such as, Joshua Cohen and Charles Sabel (1997 and more recent works) speak of the democratic merits of a transnational, experimental *mode of governance*, based in directly deliberative polyarchy, whereas Jim Bohman (2007) argues for the need to rethink core tenets of democracy; no longer as a singular *demos* but

rather as rule by plural *demoi* across national boundaries.

The events of September 2001, and notably how they have been framed in the US and in a number of other countries (as a clash of civilizations and of religions), have weakened the cosmopolitan thrust, as states have strengthened their systems of control and surveillance, have introduced measures to incarcerate persons that violate the principle of *habeas corpus*, and have introduced more restrictive regimes for admitting immigrants and asylum seekers. On balance, Europe more often responds than initiates, and state resurgence is neither uniform nor equally strong. Joppke (2007: 45) further notes that 'the exclusionary impulse is more often couched in the language of liberalism, in terms of the notion that the liberal state is for liberal people only'. This rather paradoxical situation shows that the factors that drove the cosmopolitan thrust have altered the terms of justification, which could mean that there is a limit to state resurgence and a possibility of reversing it.

EUROPEANIZATION AND DEMOCRACY

The second transformation revolves around the European Union (EU). A central objective in establishing the EU was to preserve peace through legally binding co-operation among formerly warring parties. The founders of the EU were acutely aware of the excesses of nationalism after having gone through two devastating world wars. Hence, an intrinsic rationale for the EU was to develop new forms of political association that would render war among the former enemies unthinkable. Jean Monnet and Altiero Spinnelli, two of the most influential figures in the movement towards European unity, envisaged the formation of a political system that built upon, albeit transformed and transcended the nation state.

Precisely how novel and distinct the EU should be has been a major bone of contention since the very outset. Monnet saw the EU as an experiment and was not very clear on the nature of the resultant entity, whereas Spinelli envisaged a European federation (Holland 1996: 102). Murray and Rich note, 'The fascinating character of European unity ideals has … been the fact that the theories and actual programmes in, for example, the EC, often were interrelated.' The process of European integration has thus been marked by a close interaction between the development of theories of integration and the development of strategies of integration (Wallace, cited in Murray and Rich 1996: 4). The dominant integrationist ones are functionalism, federalism and neofunctionalism. At the same time, critics of these theories – notably realists, or in EU-parlance, intergovernmentalists, have highlighted not only theoretical defects within the functionalist argumentation, but have also constantly underlined how the EU as a polity falls short of federation. Thus, what at some instances poses as a theoretical debate also takes on an explicit ontological hue, as the theoretical debates become sparring matches over what type of entity the EU is *and should be*. This has not been overly democratically clarifying as none of these theories are set up to properly address the issue of democracy. Most of the intellectual energies have been expended on explaining what causes integration, rather than clarifying the relationship between integration and democratization. It was only really in the early 1990s, after the Maastricht Treaty when the issue of the EU's democratic deficit was highlighted, that a broad and multifaceted debate on democracy within the multilevel constellation that makes up the EU started to unfold. This debate is still quite inchoate: some, notably Euro-sceptics, see the EU as a threat to national democracy; others see it as a vehicle to rescue the nation state and by implication, national democracy; others yet, see it as a vehicle to rescue democracy in Europe because the nation states can no longer be relied upon to sustain democracy.

There is no agreement among analysts on the need to apply democratic standards to the EU level. Those that agree on the need to apply democratic standards to the EU level still disagree on whether state-based standards are required.[2] A major reason for this is disagreement on the type of entity the EU is, and whether EU democracy should emanate from somehow 'uploading' national democracy to the EU level or whether the EU needs to develop new modes of thinking about democracy, such as transnational or regional–cosmopolitan ones.

NEW MODES OF ASSOCIATION AND JUSTIFICATIONS FOR COMMUNITY

The debate on democracy in the EU has not been helped much by EU decision-makers and participants, who have refrained from committing themselves to a clear vision of the EU.[3] Jacques Delors even designated the EU an *objet politique nonidentifié* (cf. Schmitter, 2000: 2). The general principles that the EU has appealed to, in particular post-Maastricht, are democracy, the rule of law, solidarity, subsidiarity, tolerance and respect for difference and diversity. These principles are universal in orientation and thus leave considerable room for institutional and even polity choice. But whereas there is disagreement on whether the EU should have a democratic vocation or confine itself to assisting in the continued effective operation of member-state-based democracy, there is agreement that EU cooperation should be legally based, and further that respect for difference and diversity is a central tenet of the EU. This latter recognition is also recently amplified through a shift in the Union's credo: from the 'ever closer Union' of the Rome and Maastricht Treaties to Laeken's 'united in diversity'. Offe and Preuss argue that 'the European Union is the first – by definition voluntary – federation in the history of mankind that recognizes the dissimilarity of its constituent parties. The EU is a political body which is committed to respecting the distinctive national identities of its member states and citizens, yet at the same time subjects them in many significant areas to the jurisdiction of a common government' (Offe and Preuss, 2006: 194). Offe and Preuss, in my view, overstate the uniqueness of the EU here. Canada shares important traits with the EU, notably on the commitment to respect for difference/diversity, and is as the EU an essentially contested entity (cf. Fossum, 2005), but the EU is far more culturally and institutionally diverse than Canada.

The EU is set up with an onus on accommodating difference and diversity at a scale far greater than that of any nation state. We see in Europe today a process of ransacking of vocabulary of association that may be similar to that which took place with the emergence of the modern European state, but now the search is for terms that can adequately capture the complex, composite and diverse social entity that the EU has become. Some analysts still resort to the vocabulary of federalism, such as cooperative confederation (Bulmer, 1996), or quasi-federal entity (Sbragia, 1992) but modify it. A decade ago Ulrich Preuss underscored the unique character of the EU's institutional–constitutional structure: dynamism, complementarity with the member states' constitutions, polycentricity, and a dual legitimacy basis. These are clearly features that set the EU apart from the nation state. They are used to underline the EU's need to accommodate a much greater degree of complexity and diversity than would any state. Preuss' argument can be construed as a plea for prioritizing federalism over statism, and for developing a new combination of federalism and democracy in a non-state entity (Preuss, 1996).

Other analysts see the EU as a system of multilevel governance, such as a multilevel polity (Hooghe and Marks, 2003; Marks *et al.*, 1996), a new kind of commonwealth (MacCormick, 1999: 191), or a mixed commonwealth (Bellamy and Castiglione, 1997), or *condominio, consortio* (Schmitter, 1992, 1996, 2000). Others think of it as some form of transition such as partial polity (Wallace, 1993: 101), postnational entity (Curtin, 1997;

Habermas, 1998, 2001) or postmodern entity (Ruggie, 1993). Others still think of it in globalist terms, such as cosmopolitanism (Archibugi, 1998; Delanty and Rumford 2005; Held, 1993, 1995; Held *et al.*, 2000; Linklater, 1996, 1998). Many of these are new terms whose common denominator is to envisage a more complex and less definite relation between territory and identity. Old pre-nation principles have also been redesigned to try to capture the institutionally complex and asymmetrical nature of this multilevel entity, such as *subsidiarity* (cf. Føllesdal, 1998; Schmitter, 1996).

The sheer wealth of designations, most of which are only tangentially related to democracy, underlines the essentially contested character of the EU. That there is such a search is testimony to the reflexive character of the integration process. Why is this important to democracy? First is because the EU today affects the member states so much and so directly that the democratic quality of the member states cannot be established without taking the EU directly into account (Beetham and Lord, 1998; Eriksen and Fossum, 2007; Offe and Preuss, 2006). The issue of European democracy is no longer a matter of the sum total of Europe's states, but is foremost a matter of the democratic quality of the multilevel constellation that makes up the EU.

Second is that the EU's leaders have systematically shirked away from declaring what kind of polity and political project the EU is. This ambiguity pertains not only to the type of entity, but also to the appropriate normative-democratic standards that should be used to assess it. This would not have been such a pressing problem had it not been for three further aspects. One is somewhat ironically that the EU appeals to and clothes itself in normative principles, the most notable among which are those designative of the democratic constitutional state. But if there is no commitment to set the EU up as a democratic constitutional state, what status should these principles have in a normative-democratic assessment of the EU? When it is not clear what institutional form or even polity type that the EU is and aspires to be, there will always be uncertainty regarding which democratic standard should be chosen to evaluate it.

The other aspect is that the EU has not only embraced democracy as the applicable standard, but also applies democratic criteria as entrance requirements for applicants. The institutions at the EU level not only assert that all future members must comply with these standards (and as such reciprocally assert that these are the standards that the EU's own institutions must comply with), but also actively seek to enforce these.[4] One issue is the credibility of EU enforcement: if the EU does not comply with the standards, can it credibly enforce these on others? The other issue is that of the EU as a democratic role model.

The final aspect is seen in the so-called Lisbon Treaty, which is intended to replace the now defunct treaty establishing a constitution for the European Union (TEC). The former has *retained* much of the substance of the TEC, but has dropped any reference to constitution (and state-type symbols). The Lisbon Treaty will thus sustain the unfortunate mix of an EU made up of formally speaking an amalgam of international treaties; but where the European Court of Justice and most legal analysts see the EU's legal order not as an international treaty but as a material constitution (based as it is on the principles of supremacy and direct effect). How credible is the EU's commitment to European-level democracy when this cannot be entrenched in a self-professed constitutional arrangement? In this situation the EU can easily be relegated to an expedient instrument that national political leaders can use to undertake unpopular common tasks *without their having to admit to the effects this will have on national sovereignty*. It is in this context not helpful that the EU's main executive, the Commission, lacks an explicit political mandate from the EU's citizens. Such a mandate could have served as a safeguard against national leaders who simply want to offload the odium of unpopular decisions to the EU.

The debate on EU democracy has focused on all relevant dimensions of citizenship. The debate has also taken heed of the EU's complex and contested character; hence has brought to the fore alternative configurations of identity, membership and rights. I shall focus on two such here: constitutional patriotism and deep diversity.

CONSTITUTIONAL PATRIOTISM

Constitutional patriotism has been widely promoted as the answer to two central components of the EU's democratic deficit, namely the absence of a European demos and the absence of a European identity and 'we' feeling. Constitutional patriotism has been held up as a particularly promising doctrine because it is not saddled with the homogenizing thrust that we normally associate with the nation and national allegiance. In Habermas' version, notably, it elicits a more inclusive, thinner, *postnational* and rights-based type of allegiance, one that is not derived from pre-political values and attachments steeped in a culture, tradition or a way of life, but rather from a set of principles and values that are universal in their orientation, albeit contextualized (Habermas, 1994, 1996). Individual rights are based on a notion of reciprocal recognition that ensures personal autonomy, which is intrinsic to the medium of law. Legal relations highlight the general and universalizable aspect of the recognition relationship, so that what is recognized is the person as a holder of rights, not the particular personality traits or attributes of the person.

Constitutional patriotism is seen to elicit support and emotional attachment, because universalistic principles are *embedded in a particular context*. People's attachments are then seen to be derived from the manner in which a set of universal principles are interpreted and entrenched within a particular institutional setting. The principles are fused with a set of values that are steeped in a particular geographical setting, and embedded in a particular set of traditions. The universal principles help entrench a set of procedures that, when made to operate within a particular context, render this self-reflective and hence responsive to change.

The clearest effort to foster constitutional patriotism in the EU is through the Charter of Fundamental Rights of the European Union. The Charter, proclaimed at Nice but not part of the ratified treaties (although incorporated in the 2007 Lisbon Treaty, with some opt-outs, notably for the UK and Poland), is the most explicit commitment to individual rights ever presented by the European Union. The Charter holds provisions on civil, political, social and economic rights – to ensure the dignity of the person, to safeguard essential freedoms, to ensure equality, to foster solidarity, to provide a European citizenship, and to provide for justice. Its provisions are similar to most charters and bills of rights, and it is also more updated than most such.

The Charter's approach to constitutional patriotism is 'rooted' in ethical content, in particular through the commitment to social rights and social solidarity, as part of the Communities' socioeconomic structure. In my previous assessment of the Charter's basic philosophy I noted that this makes it appear thicker than that of a classical liberal statement of fundamental rights and freedoms (Fossum, 2003). This commitment may not amount to that much, however, given the limited competence the EU has in the social policy area (Menéndez, 2003). This latter point has a strong bearing on how pervasive the EU's embrace of constitutional patriotism can be, given that the Charter's provisions will be steeped in the particular legal–institutional context that makes up the Union (and the Charter will only apply to the EU level). The Charter reflects the *weakly* developed citizenship rights of the EU, a set of rights that fail to offer citizens the political participatory rights that constitutional patriotism requires. The most important limitation here is the fact that what Rainer Bauböck labels as 'SCNs' (second-country nationals) do not have the right to vote in regional and national elections and referenda (and the provisions for obtaining such rights vary greatly in Europe, although the scope of variation has been reduced as a consequence of Europeanization). In other words, there is not in the EU, as in federal states, a set of procedures to ensure that the deliberations of those living within a particular setting are reflected in the decisions of the institutions that operate over that body of citizens.[5] A similar argument can be made for the EU level, due largely to the EU's pillar structure. It is only within the first pillar that the entire populace of the EU can conceive of itself as a lawmaker. Within pillars two and three the citizens are represented by their respective national representative systems and here decisions are reached by unanimity. Although there has been a gradual move of policy areas from pillars two and three to one, the ECJ is excluded from pillars two and three, and the European Parliament's role is merely consultative.[6]

The prospects for constitutional patriotism in the EU therefore hinge on the Union's overall development *as a political entity*. The sheer diversity of the EU renders any effort to instill constitutional patriotism difficult. One obvious risk facing Europe is that the integration process unleashes identitarian struggles without at the same time being able to ensure that these are subjected to a constitutional *working arrangement* that helps ensure agreement on basic rights and mutually respectful procedures of communication and interaction. This problem likely remains even if the Lisbon Treaty is ratified. Further, if the decision to remove the constitutional designation of the EU legal order also precludes further moves in a constitutional direction, then the problem may become more rather than less pressing.

DEEP DIVERSITY

The discussion of constitutional patriotism has revealed that the problem of ensuring allegiance is particularly acute in the EU.

This is partly due to the EU's sheer diversity. In the EU there is no single language, ethnic group or nation that can command majority support. There is no overarching European identity (although there are numerous efforts to create such). The European Union at present consists of 27 member states (4 are federal or quasi-federal), it has 23 official and working languages, numerous minority nationalisms and ethnic minorities (some of which cross state bounds), and regional movements.

But the problem of ensuring allegiance in the EU is also partly due to *how* the EU ends up addressing pluralism, difference and diversity. An important source is national identitarian opposition to the EU. Can these traits be cast in terms of a doctrine of allegiance with distinct citizenship features? Charles Taylor has coined the term 'deep diversity' as a way to capture a situation where a 'plurality of ways of belonging ... (are) ... acknowledged and accepted' (Taylor, 1993: 183) within the same state or polity.[7] Acceptance entails that special political–legal and even constitutional measures have been devised to preserve and promote it.[8] This position, which draws on Taylor's particular liberal spin on communitarianism, underlines that rights and constitutional arrangements are inadequate as means of fostering a sense of community and belonging. The law and rights are always steeped in a particular cultural setting that provides people with deep-seated cues as to who they are and what is good and valuable.[9] In the EU there is a plethora of such communities: national, regional, linguistic, ethnic, and so on.

Deep diversity acknowledges the existence of separate national popular wills, but establishes a set of common institutions and principles which need not be entrenched in a fully fledged constitution. The society contains *several and different* collective conceptions of its cultural or national or linguistic or ethnic make-up, and there is thus *no overarching agreement on what the country (or polity) is for*. Further, the existence of different collective goals is not only an acknowledged and accepted fact, but also something that is accommodated through differentiated citizenship, and other means, through which collectives try to maintain their sense of difference. Deep diversity presumes that a group's sense of belonging to the overarching entity *passes through* its belonging to another smaller and more integrated community. Citizenship in the overarching entity is thus differentiated, because it must reflect the nature of this relation and the character of the smaller and more integrated community.

European citizenship is based on citizenship in a member state. Member states have different national incorporation rules, and also vary in terms of rights and duties; in this sense European citizenship takes on a differentiated character. But the strong horizontal dimension of European citizenship can be understood as a means to *weaken* the scope for national coding of European citizenship. European citizenship 'is not so much a relation of the individual *vis-à-vis* Community institutions, but rather a particular legal status *vis-à-vis* national member states, which have to learn how to cope with the fact that persons who are physically and socially their citizens are acquiring a kind of legal citizenship by means of European citizenship without being their nationals' (Preuss, 1998: 147) European citizenship reflects the *explicit inclusion of non-nationals* into the operations of every member state. This applies foremost to SCNs (and somewhat less to 'FCNs' – first country nationals), but to some extent also to 'TCNs' (third country nationals, who are not EU citizens). TCNs also hold more extensive rights within the EU than what is implied in the notion of deep diversity. Terms such as 'postnational membership'[10] and 'denizenship' have been used to depict the role of TCNs in Europe.

Neither constitutional patriotism nor deep diversity adequately captures the pluralist character of European citizenship, which represents a complex mixture of *four* categories: FCNs (EU citizens who reside in their country of nationality), SCNs, TCNs, and EEUCs (external EU citizens residing in third countries) (Bauböck, 2007: 468). In overall terms, constitutional patriotism is the best doctrine to depict what the EU *seeks*, whereas deep diversity is a better descriptor of what the EU *is*.

PUBLIC SPHERE

The complex character of the EU has forced analysts to reconsider how they conceive of the public sphere, within a European context. For one, the sheer presence of the EU has made clear that the nation state is based in a distinct public sphere configuration. The EU will not be able to emulate this configuration, certainly not in the foreseeable future. It is quite clear that any effort to conceive of a European public sphere must start from the notion of a multitude of overlapping communicative spaces rather than one, single, overarching public sphere. Further, we need to consider the role of institutionalized discourses (such as, strong publics), how they interact with general publics, and the vital role of media as conveyers.

Today, the EU is still foremost a collection of quite segmented nationally based publics.[11] Particular publics (of experts and of issue communities) have emerged within the numerous transnational networks that have been fostered by the EU. There are also strong publics at the EU level, the most entrenched being the European Parliament (and this is linked to national parliaments through such bodies as COSAC), and the EU also avails itself of temporary measures with semi-strong public character, such as, Conventions (Charter and Constitutional). The presence of such institutions raises the prospects for greater overlapping, convergence and mutuality among the still nationally oriented publics, although a Union of multiple, overlapping publics remains a prospect only (Fossum and Schlesinger, 2007).

To sum up thus far, the EU is emblematic of a major transformation in Western Europe, in that its unprecedented system of law,

supranational institutions and border-transcending/eliminating arrangements tie the member states (and affiliated states) up and weaken or undermine their sovereignty. The Union propounds a *postnational* type of allegiance that is thinner than that of nationalism. It seeks to navigate a course of constitutional patriotism, but is constantly pulled back to a line of deep diversity by recalcitrant member states and collectives, bent on protecting their identities. It is tempting to conclude with Gerard Delanty that

> [t]he question of Europe is now a central dimension of the wider societal transformation of modernity, the reflection on which is also a reflection on the meaning of Europe. It is thus difficult to be specific on what we are talking about, for 'Europeanization' is not leading to a society, a state, a cultural or a geographical entity that can be specified with precision, but a process. (Delanty, 2003: 472).

One source of such dynamism emanates from enlargement which adds diversity. But democracy requires us to go beyond process. Even if we acknowledge that there is in Europe today a reflexive search for new ways of configuring the polity, we need reference to basic polity parameters (to establish membership, governing conditions etc.), lest we lose sight of the democratic quality of this endeavour. The EU clearly strains the democratic imagination, and the integration process has proceeded so far as to force theorists and practitioners of democracy to rethink basic categories. But it is possible to develop apt standards to assess this entity.[12]

THE EU – SPEARHEAD FOR DEMOCRATIZATION WITHIN AND BEYOND EUROPE?

The EU is made up of democracies only; it harbours a commitment to democracy at the EU level; it has contributed to consolidate democracy within the new member states, from the very onset (initially notably Germany and Italy and later also Greece,

Spain and Portugal, and the twelve recent entrants from East and Central Europe); and it contributes to the transformation of national democracy and citizenship. We have seen that these processes take place by means of an EU that itself harbours democratic defects.

In sofaras the EU seeks to develop a more inclusive notion of democracy than marks the nation state, it is interesting to clarify how far this extends. The most inclusive democratic approach would be a postnational version that transforms the states system in a cosmopolitan direction. If so, we should expect a consistent pursuit of democracy, not only in the EU's internal arrangements and dealings, but also with regard to its external orientations and dealings. Three dimensions of the EU's external orientation merit special attention: (1) enlargement or the formal inclusion of new members and citizens; (2) structured relations through association agreements; and (3) what the EU contributes to international relations.

Enlargement or the formal inclusion of new members and citizens

One dimension is 'internalization of the external relation' through adoption of new members. Knowing what drives this tells us a lot about the EU's democratic vocation. Has this process been driven mainly by economic or security considerations, or is it driven by concerns with solidarity/justice? Frank Schimmelfennig argues that neither egoistic self-interest (and patterns of state power), nor solidaristic norms, is an adequate explanation. Instead, he introduces the notion of 'rhetorical entrapment' to underline how recalcitrant actors who were concerned with their reputation found themselves entrapped within the prevailing norm set, and thus felt compelled to embrace enlargement (Schimmelfennig, 2001). Helene Sjursen has studied the justifications for enlargement and finds that very different arguments were used in relation to the East European states as opposed to Turkey (Sjursen, 2002). With regard to the former, there was a kind of kinship-based

duty, ultimately anchored in a common sense of identity, whereas with regard to the latter, strategic considerations weighed more heavily. This debate over what drives enlargement has a broader theoretical aim, namely to clarify what are the drivers of human action, self-interest calculations, common identities, or norms of justice and fairness.

EU enlargement is not simply a process of widening of membership. The EU is a constitutional entity; hence any major change in composition should be understood as a process of *reconstitution* (Eriksen *et al.*, 2005). The EU does not admit members through a two-way process of mutual adaptation; this is better understood as a process of unilateral adaptation on the part of the applicant to the EU, where the EU monitors compliance with a set of criteria (including democracy) throughout the process. The quality of the resultant EU democracy therefore actually to a large extent hinges on the EU undertaking a proper monitoring and control there.

Notably because the process is so tightly steered by the EU, enlargement should be expected to place a strong onus on the EU to keep its own democratic house in order: it cannot credibly command compliance with democratic norms from applicants and would-be members unless it upholds democratic norms itself: 'Imagine for a moment what would happen if the European Union applied for membership in the European Union. Its application would be flatly rejected. Why? Because the European Union doesn't live up to its own criteria of democracy' (Beck, 2003: 32).

The EU's actual democratizing thrust will however hinge on many factors, such as the quality of EU-level democracy, the democratic disposition of the EU's member states and their commitment to EU-level democracy. From this we may conjecture that the democratic thrust of the EU will be the greatest the better entrenched democracy is at the EU level, the greater the proportion of democratically stable member states, and the greater their commitment to EU-level democracy. In this case we can anticipate a positive democratizing spiral. Significant tensions or conflicts could arise between these factors. But if all three move in a negative direction, then the overall result will be a downward, de-democratizing spiral.

Structured relations through association agreements

The EU affects non-EU European states through most of the remaining non-EU states seeking membership in the EU. But there are states that are associated with the EU without becoming members. The most obvious case is the European Economic Area (EEA). This was set up as an agreement between EFTA and the EU. As the bulk of the remaining EFTA countries joined the EU, the present EEA consists of Norway, Iceland and Lichtenstein. The EEA has proven to be a highly dynamic agreement, premised as it is on a common market. More and more issues have come under its sway, and since the EU seeks legal homogeneity within the entire EFTA area (the EU and the EEA included), the EFTA Court, which oversees the arrangement, echoes the EU Court of Justice. The net effect has been a strong Norwegian, Icelandic and Lichtensteinian integration in the EU, with the political authorities (parliament) of the non-EU EEA members frequently taking on the role of rubber-stamper of legislation, rather than of legislator proper (Claes, 2003). EU legislation today covers a much wider range of issue-areas than was initially envisaged. Norway and Iceland also joined the Schengen Agreement, which locates them *within* the EU's border. Hence, whereas the EEA may be considered as a formalized agreement with the EU for states that were bent on not seeking membership for political reasons, in practice these states are deeply integrated in the EU, *with minimal influence*. A very large proportion of their legislation emanates from the EU, and the democratic quality of the decisions that their national parliaments are embracing thus hinges on the quality of EU-level democracy.

Civilian or normative power EU?

The third and most controversial external dimension pertains to the claim that the EU, by virtue of its progressive civilian power, or distinctive character as a normative power, contributes to transform international relations. François Duchêne (1972, 1973) dubbed it a Civilian Power Union which was long on economic and short on military power; relied on diplomacy in the handling of international conflicts and problems; and was willing to submit to legally binding supranational institutions. Ian Manners, in recent work (2002, 2006), has labelled the EU a normative power: 'The central component of normative power Europe is that it exists as being different to pre-existing political forms, and that this particular difference predisposes it to act in a normative way' (Manners, 2002: 242; 2006). To Manners, this normative propensity stems from the particular historical context within which it was forged, which highlighted the need to entrench *peace* and move beyond aggressive nationalism; the EU's hybrid and less bounded and more permeable post-Westphalian form; and its legal constitution, which highlights human rights. The presumption is that the EU as organization is such set up as to be able to change norms in the international system. Further, it implies that it actually also acts to change such; and finally that it *should* act in this manner. A key intention has been to try to solve the problems at the source, and to do so in a manner consistent with global cosmopolitan norms.

The notion of normative power Europe is contested.[13] Robert Kagan (2003) argued instead that it was the EU's weakness that compelled it to seek rule-based cooperation; further, the EU's multilateralism and trust in international institutions ultimately depended on US power. The European project in its internal and external dimensions has a stronger cosmopolitan – law-based – orientation than is the case with present-day US. But this does not reduce to power differentials. The US played a central role in framing the global legal system; it played a vital role in establishing the EU; and there is more that binds Europeans and Americans than sets them apart. Further, some analysts (notably Fabbrini, 2007) argue that through European integration, the EU 'differs more from the institutional and political organization of its member states than it does from that of America'. We should however beware of over-stating such institutional convergence, because the US talk of empire notwithstanding, it is a state with a national vocation, whereas the EU is a non-state, postnational construct. How salient this difference is hinges on European developments, on global developments, and on the third and final development to be discussed here.

POST-SOVIET DEMOCRATIZATION

The rapid decline of the Soviet empire from the latter part of the 1980s onwards heralded in a major wave of regime changes in Central and Eastern Europe. This process which spawned both new democracies and rein-statement of previous democratic regimes nevertheless cannot in itself be couched as a major experiment in democratic governance, although the region formed 'an ideal laboratory for comparative inquiry' (Bunce, 2003: 169), and important lessons for democratic transitions can be learnt (Bunce, 2003; King, 2000; McFaul, 2002). The rhetoric is quite reveal-ing as these states were seen to be 'returning to Europe'; that is, they finally were able to become like their Western European breth-ren. When we consider the vocabulary and the doctrines that they appealed to the gen-eral impression is that state socialism was replaced with nation-state democracy. Offe and Preuss (2006: 186) note that 'in spite of all the rhetoric of "returning to Europe", what these countries are eager to return to is the condition of their own nationhood, with joining the EU being largely perceived as a tribute to eco-nomic expediency, not to political aspiration'.

What is further clear is that this so-called fourth wave of democratization was everything

but a uniform process. As Michael McFaul (2002: 213) has noted, '[D]ecommunization triggered a fourth wave of regime change – to democracy *and* dictatorship.' McFaul distin-guishes between three sets of regimes: democracies (Croatia, Czech Republic, Estonia, Hungary, Latvia, Lithuania, Poland, Slovakia, Slovenia, Bulgaria, Mongolia, and Romania); partial democracies (Armenia, Bosnia-Herzegovina, Georgia, Moldova, Russia, Ukraine, Albania, Azerbaijan, Macedonia, and Yugoslavia/Serbia); and dictatorships (Tajikistan, Belarus, Kazakstan, Kyrgyzstan, Turkmenistan, and Uzbekistan). What appears clear from this list is that there is a clear correlation between distance from the West and regime type, in the sense that those regimes closest to the West were the most likely to make successful transitions to democracy (Kopstein and Reilly, 2000; McFaul, 2002; Rupnik, 2007: 22).

But a once successful transition to democ-racy does not necessarily imply that a country will remain a workable democracy; there are cases of backsliding (Rupnik, 2007), such as the fact that in both Poland and Slovakia, ruling coalitions which included extreme-nationalist parties were formed after EU accession. The Eurobarometer Survey of December 2006 also reveals that in postcom-munist states, the trust in democratic institu-tions is far lower than in Western Europe. Informal legacies from the communist era, combined with weak civic culture and the lack of truly independent media also contribute to weaken the democratic regimes. Mungiu-Pippidi makes the interesting observation that 'the problems for democracy stem from elites, not voters' (2007: 11).

The important point for democracy in Europe is how the postcommunist democra-cies' incorporation in the EU shapes the EU's overall democratic vocation. It is clear that many of the new members take a critical stance towards a strong EU; they have recently won their freedom from an involuntary union and are loath to renege on it to another. As such, they can join forces with the integration-sceptical old members and push the EU in a more intergovernmental direction. Doing so today may come with a higher democratic cost because of the dangers of backsliding. This could happen in new as well as old members, but the higher the ratio of unstable democracies, the potentially greater the effects of such backsliding. A democratically committed and equipped EU thus appears more important now than before the last two rounds of enlargement.

CONCLUSION

I have discussed the question of democracy, citizenship and public sphere in contemporary Europe by focusing on major transformations in the doctrines, justifications and organizational foundations. The main argument is that there is a major transformation going on. This resonates with global cosmopolitan developments. But whereas there are non-European sources, this is first and foremost a (Western) European democratic experiment. Europe is a vanguard. It is not alone – there are parallels in other parts of the West, notably in North America – but it is in Europe that the greatest *confluence* of transformative forces is found.

The core of the democratic experiment is in *Western* Europe. Both globalization and enlargement will obviously affect the character of this democratic experiment. *If* there is a further general process of state resurgence, and the EU embarks on further enlargement, we should expect a double-pronged intergovernmentalist thrust in and on the EU.

Further large-scale enlargement could overexert the EU's democratizing ability. The EU, if it is to retain its democratizing thrust, needs to consolidate before taking on new members. The last two rounds of enlargement greatly affected the EU's composition, so much so that the current situation is unique in the ratio of new as opposed to established democracies. The new democracies must digest the EU, and EU democracy must work on stabilizing these. Here we see

a particularly important aspect of further democratization at the EU level: more than before this has to work as a safeguard for member-state-based democracy.

The EU's experience shows that there is a difficult balance to strike between democratization through expansion in membership, and democratization through polity formation and regime building. In democratic terms it is easy to think of this as a trade-off between widening and deepening. But this hinges on global developments: we might conjecture that the more prominent the factors that propel a cosmopolitan–democratic thrust, the easier it will be for the EU to stabilize democracy on the European continent, as a regional–cosmopolitan democratic arrangement.

Seeing Europe as an experiment in democracy beyond the nation state has implications for the character of social science research. First is that we can take less for granted than before and must make explicit our assumptions pertaining to polity and standard of democracy. We, therefore, need to be more willing to 'go all the way up and all the way down' within any one single study. When we study democracy in Europe, we need to ensure that we use the most appropriate terminology, that this is anchored in appropriate and relevant normative standards, and that the empirical analysis is calibrated to terminology and normative standards. The European research scene has become more specialized, making such endeavours even more difficult. Such specialization is inevitable and has its own merits, but what is desirable is to try to organize our research in such a manner as to permit us to 'go all the way up and down'.

Second, we need to be more critical about the concepts and the kind of vocabulary we rely on. We have been socialized into thinking from a 'nation statist' perspective, with a nation-state-based democratic vocabulary. The European experience forces us to self-critically examine the continued relevance of these terms and the 'grammar of democratic politics' that they add up to. It is necessary to bring democratic theory more directly into the study of integration and Europeanization, so that we become clear on the democratic status and implications of new concepts, doctrines, justifications and organizational arrangements. What is also important is to critically assess the *relationship* between integration and democratization. Are the two processes mutually reinforcing or are they conflicting? Is there a clear one-on-one relationship, or does it vary with circumstances? If so, how?

NOTES

1 See notably, Archibugi, 2003; Archibugi *et al.*, 1998; Held, 1993; Held *et al.*, 2000; Delanty and Rumford, 2005, for different versions of this. This trend naturally coincides with renewed interest in Kant's work, see notably Bohman and Lutz-Bachmann, 1997.

2 For a brief selection of different positions here, see Beetham and Lord, 1998; Eriksen and Fossum, 2000; Lord, 2004; Schmidt, 2006; Schmitter, 2000; Siedentop, 2000; Weale and Nentwich, 1998.

3 '(T)here has never been a basic template or "structural ideal".' (Walker, 2003: 373).

4 See Eriksen *et al.*, 2005 for further details.

5 Bauböck (2007) lists a number of traits of EU citizenship that deviate from the equality required by constitutional patriotism.

6 Citizens' protective rights can thus be weakened in the sense that and insofar as persons are not able to appeal to the ECJ when their rights are infringed upon. The ECJ has only jurisdiction on what regards articles TEU 35 and 40 as specifically provided in Article TEU 35, Section 1 and Article TEU 40, Section 4, second paragraph.

7 For an application of this notion to the EU context, see Fossum (2003).

8 This has some affinity to Weiler's notion of constitutional tolerance (2001, 2002), but deep diversity is more of a doctrine on positive allegiance and is also not confined to national allegiance, as Weiler's appears to be.

9 See Taylor (1989). This is a standard communitarian argument.

10 For the definition of this term and how it differs from the conventional model of citizenship, see Soysal (1994).

11 See the contributions in Fossum and Schlesinger (2007).

12 We have within the context of the integrated project Reconstituting Democracy in Europe (RECON) come up with three such revised notions labeled as audit democracy, multinational federal democracy,

and cosmopolitan democracy, respectively (Eriksen and Fossum, 2007).

13 See the contributions to Sjursen (2007) for different positions on this.

REFERENCES

Archibugi, D., Held, D., and Kohler, M. (eds) (1998) *Re-imagining Political Community.* Cambridge: Polity Press.

Archibugi, D. (2003) *Debating Cosmopolitics.* London: Verso.

Bauböck, R. (2007) 'Why European citizenship? Normative approaches to supranational union', *Theoretical Inquiries in Law*, 8 (2): 453–488.

Beck, U. (2003) 'Understanding the real Europe', *Dissent Magazine*, summer. Available at: http://dissentmagazine.org/article/? article=483.

Beetham, D. and Lord, C. (1998) *Legitimacy in the European Union.* London: Longman.

Bellamy, R. and Castiglione, D. (1997) 'Building the union: The nature of sovereignty in the political architecture of Europe', *Law and Philosophy* 16 (4): pp. 421–445.

Benhabib, S. (2007) 'Twilight of sovereignty or the emergence of cosmopolitan norms? Rethinking citizenship in volatile times', *Citizenship Studies*, 11 (1): 19–36.

Bohman, J. and Lutz-Bachmann, M. (eds) (1997) *Perpetual Peace. Essays on Kant's Cosmopolitan Ideal.* Cambridge, MA: MIT Press.

Bohman, J. (2007) *Democracy Across Borders: From Demos to Demoi.* Cambridge, MA: MIT Press.

Bulmer, S.J. (1996) 'The European Council and the Council of the European Union: Shapers of a European Confederation', *Publius*, 26 (4): 17–42.

Bunce, V. (2003) 'Rethinking recent democratization: lessons from the postcommunist experience', *World Politics*, 55 (2): 167–192.

Claes, D.-H. (2003) 'EØS-avtalen – mellom diplomati og demokrati', *Internasjonal Politikk*, 3: pp. 275–302.

Cohen, J. and Sabel, C.F. (1997) 'Directly-deliberative polyarchy', *European Law Journal*, 3 (4): 313–342.

Curtin, D. (1997) *Postnational Democracy: The European Union in Search of a Political Philosophy.* The Hague: Kluwer Law.

Delanty, G. (2003) 'Conceptions of Europe: a review of recent trends', *European Journal of Social Theory*, 6 (4): 471–488.

Delanty, G. and Rumford, C. (2005) *Rethinking Europe*. London: Routledge.

Duchêne, F. (1972) 'Europe's role in world peace', in R. Mayne (ed.) *Europe Tomorrow: Sixteen Europeans Look Ahead*. London: Fontana.

Eriksen, E.O. and Fossum, J.E. (eds) (2000) *Democracy in the European Union: Integration Through Deliberation?* London: Routledge.

Eriksen, E.O. and Fossum, J.E. (2007) 'Europe in transformation – how to reconstitute democracy?', RECON Working Paper Series 1/07. Available at: http://www.reconproject.eu/main.php/RECON_wp_0701.pdf?fileitem=5456091.

Eriksen, E.O. and Weigård, J. (2003) *Understanding Habermas*. London: Continuum.

Eriksen, E.O., Fossum, J.E., and Sjursen, H. (2005) 'Widening or reconstituting the EU?', in Eriksen, E.O. (ed.) *Making the European Polity – Reflexive Integration in Europe*. London: Routledge.

Fabbrini, S. (2007) *Compound Democracies: Why the United States and Europe Are Becoming Similar*. Oxford: Oxford University Press.

Føllesdal, A. (1998) 'Subsidiarity', *Journal of Political Philosophy*, 6 (2): 190–218.

Fossum, J.E. (2003) 'The European Union – in search of an identity', *European Journal of Political Theory*, 2 (3): 319–340.

Fossum, J.E. (ed.) (2005) 'Constitutional processes in Canada and the EU compared', ARENA Report 8/2005.

Fossum, J.E. and Schlesinger, P.R. (eds) (2007) *The European Union and the Public Sphere: A Communicative Space in the Making?* London: Routledge.

Fraser, N. (1992) 'Rethinking the public sphere. A contribution to the critique of actually existing democracy', in C. Calhoun (ed.) *Habermas and the Public Sphere*. Cambridge, MA: MIT Press, pp. 109–42.

Habermas, J. (1989) [1962]. *The Structural Transformation of the Public Sphere*. Cambridge, MA: MIT Press.

Habermas, J. (1994) 'Struggles for recognition in the democratic constitutional state', in C. Taylor and A. Gutmann (eds) *Multiculturalism*. Princeton, NJ: Princeton University Press.

Habermas, J. (1996) *Between Facts and Norms: Contributions to a Discourse Theory of Law and Democracy*. Cambridge, MA: MIT Press.

Habermas, J. (1998) *The Inclusion of the Other – Studies in Political Theory*. Cambridge: Polity Press.

Habermas, J. (2001) *The Postnational Constellation: Political Essays*. Cambridge: Polity Press.

Habermas, J. (2003) 'Toward a cosmopolitan Europe', *Journal of Democracy*, 14 (3): 86–100.

Held, D. (1993) 'Democracy: from city-states to a cosmopolitan order?', in D. Held (ed.) *Prospects for Democracy: North, South, East, West*. Cambridge: Polity Press, pp. 13–52.

Held, D. (1995) *Democracy and the Global Order*. Cambridge: Polity Press.

Held, D., McGrew, A., Goldblatt, D. and Perraton, J. (2000) *Global Transformations*. Cambridge: Polity Press.

Holland, M. (1996) 'Jean Monnet and the federal functionalist approach to European unity', in P. Murray and P. Rich (eds) *Visions of European Unity*. Boulder, Colorado: Westview Press.

Hooghe, L. and Marks, G. (2003) 'Unraveling the central state, but how? Types of multi-level governance', *American Political Science Review*, 97 (2): 233–243.

Joppke, C. (2007) 'Transformation of citizenship: status, rights, identity', *Citizenship Studies*, 11 (1): 37–48.

Kagan R. (2003) *Paradise and Power: America and Europe in the New World Order*. New York: Knopf.

King, C. (2000) 'Post-communism: transition, comparison, and the end of "Eastern Europe"', *World Politics*, 53 (1): 143–172.

Kopstein, J.S. and Reilly, D.A. (2000) 'Geographic diffusion and the transformation of the post-communist world', *World Politics*, 53 (1): 1–37.

Linklater, A. (1996) 'Citizenship and sovereignty in the post-Westphalian state', *European Journal of International Relations*, 2 (1): 77–103.

Linklater, A. (1998) *The Transformation of Political Community*. Cambridge: Polity Press.

Lord, C. (2004) *A Democratic Audit of the European Union*. Basingstoke: Palgrave Macmillan.

MacCormick, N. (1999) *Questioning Sovereignty*. Oxford: Oxford University Press.

Manners, I. (2002) 'Normative power Europe – a contradiction in terms?', *Journal of Common Market Studies*, 40 (2): 235–258.

Manners, I. (2006) 'Normative power Europe reconsidered: beyond the crossroads', *Journal of European Public Policy*, 13 (2): 182–199.

Marks, G., Scharpf, F., Schmitter, P.C. and Streeck, W. (eds) (1996) *Governance in the European Union*. London: Sage.

McFaul, M. (2002) 'The fourth wave of democracy and dictatorship: non-cooperative transitions in the postcommunist world', *World Politics*, 54 (2): 212–244.

Menéndez, A.J. (2003) '"Rights to solidarity": Balancing Solidarity and Economic Freedoms', in E.O. Eriksen, J.E. Fossum and A.J. Menéndez (eds) *The Chartering of Europe*. Baden-Baden: Nomos.

Mungiu-Pippidi, A. (2007) 'Is East-Central Europe backsliding? EU accession is no "End of History"', *Journal of Democracy*, 18 (4): 8–16.

Murray, P. and Rich, P. (eds) (1996) *Visions of European Unity*. Boulder: Westview Press.

Offe, C. and Preuss, U.K. (2006) 'The problem of legitimacy in the European polity: is democratization the answer?' in C. Crouch and W. Streeck (eds) *The Diversity of Democracy: Corporatism, Social Order and Political Conflict*. Cheltenham, UK and Northampton, MA: Edward Elgar.

Preuss, U. (1996) 'Prospects of a constitution for Europe', *Constellations*, 3 (2): 209–224.

Preuss, U. (1998) 'Citizenship in the European Union; a paradigm for transnational democracy?', in D. Archibugi, D. Held and M. Køhler (eds) *Re-imagining Political Community*. Cambridge: Polity Press.

Ruggie, J.G. (1993) 'Territoriality and beyond: problematizing modernity in international relations', *International Organization*, 47 (1): 139–174.

Rupnik, J. (2007) 'Is East-Central Europe backsliding? From democracy fatigue to populist backlash', *Journal of Democracy*, 18 (4): 17–25.

Sbragia, A. (ed.) (1992) *Euro Politics: Institutions and Policymaking in the 'New' European Community*. Washington DC: Brookings Institution.

Schimmelfennig, F. (2001) 'The community trap: liberal norms, rhetorical action, and the eastern enlargement of the European Union', *International Organization*, 55 (1): 47–80.

Schmitter, P. (1992) 'Representation and the future Euro-polity', *Staatswissenschaft und Staatspraxis*, III (3): 379–405.

Schmitter, P. (1996) 'Imagining the future of the Euro-polity with the help of new concepts', in G. Marks, F.W. Scharpf, P.C. Schmitter and W. Streeck (eds) *Governance in the European Union*. London: Sage, pp.121–150.

Schmitter, P. (2000) *How to Democratize the European Union ... And Why Bother?* Lanham: Rowman and Littlefield.

Siedentop, L. (2000) *Democracy in Europe*. London: Penguin.

Sjursen, H. (2002) 'Why expand? The question of legitimacy and justification in the EU's enlargement policy', *Journal of Common Market Studies*, 40 (3): 491–513.

Sjursen, H. (ed.) (2007) *Civilian or Military Power?* London: Routledge.

Soysal, Y. (1994) *Limits of Citizenship – Migrants and Postnational Membership in Europe*. Chicago: University of Chicago Press.

Taylor, C. (1989) *Sources of the Self: The Making of the Modern Identity*. Cambridge, MA: Harvard University Press.

Taylor, C. (1993) *Reconciling the Solitudes: Essays on Canadian Federalism and Nationalism*. Montreal and Kingston: McGill-Queen's University Press.

Walker, N. (2003) 'Constitutionalising enlargement, enlarging constitutionalism', *European Law Journal*, 9 (3): 365–385.

Wallace, H. (1993) 'Deepening and widening: problems of legitimacy for the EC', in S. Garcia (ed.) *European Identity and the Search for Legitimacy*. London: Pinter, pp. 95–105.

Weale, A. and Nentwich, M. (eds) (1998) *Political Theory and the European Union. Legitimacy, Constitutional Choice and Citizenship*. London and New York: Routledge.

Weiler, J.H.H. (2001) 'European democracy and the principle of toleration: The soul of Europe', in F. Cerutti and E. Rudolph (eds) *A Soul for Europe*, vol. 1. Peeters: Leuven.

Weiler, J.H.H. (2002) 'A constitution for Europe: some hard choices?', *Journal of Common Market Studies*, 40 (4): 563–580.

21

Social Movements

Donatella della Porta

In Europe, as in the rest of the Western world, scholarly interest in social movements developed with the wave of protest that, in the late sixties, shook confidence in the 'end of ideology' and the pacification of postwar societies. Since then, first in sociology and then in political science, research on social movements has grown steadily, expanding especially during intense waves of protest, but also surviving the low ebb of mobilization. By the 1980s, social movements had already attracted much attention among European sociologists, sharing Alain Touraine's belief that 'social movements are not a marginal rejection of order, they are the central forces fighting one against the other to control the production of society by itself and the action of classes for the shaping of historicity' (Touraine, 1981: 29). Later, political scientists also started to extend their analysis to social movements, now considered important actors in the political process (Neidhardt and Rucht, 1993).

In this chapter, in addressing the issue of European studies on social movements, I do not aim at either reviewing the broad social science research in the field, or developing an original cross-national comparison of social movements in Europe. Rather, I shall sketch some main trends in European approaches to social movements, selectively develop some main dimensions of cross-national comparison, and, finally, address the issue of the Europeanization of social movements.

EUROPEAN SOCIAL SCIENCE AND SOCIAL MOVEMENTS

In contrast to the United States, where research on social movements had developed within a collective behaviour approach stressing its pathologies (or at least its anomalies) *vis-à-vis* conventional forms of participation, in Europe Marxism had offered the main frame to deal with social movements prior to the 1960s. Attention focused upon the labour movement, considered as the expression of the main conflict in capitalist societies. Given the difficulties in dealing with the late-sixties wave of protest that, among other things, challenged the centrality of the capital–labour conflict, European studies on contentious politics in the seventies and early eighties were characterized by a critique of Marxism and the (open or implicit) stress upon the differences between 'new social movements' and the labour movement of the past. Criticism of Marxism addressed not only the 'institutionalization' of industrial conflict, but also the deterministic assumption behind its interpretation of collective action.

Beyond singling out the characteristics of the collective actors that had to substitute for the working class, the new approaches also rejected the deterministic element of the Marxist tradition; that is, its understanding that social and political conflicts were largely determined by the level of development of the forces of production. Departing often from a Marxist background, scholars associated with the so-called 'new social movements' approach reflected upon the innovation in the forms and contents of contemporary movements (della Porta and Diani, 2006: chapter 1).

If 'new social movement' scholars agreed on the diminishing relevance of industrial conflict, they differed on the possibility of identifying a new central conflict that would characterize the model of the emerging society, variously defined as 'post-industrial', 'post-Fordist', 'technocratic' or 'programmed'. This search for a new actor was central in the influential contribution of Alain Touraine. For him, the category of social movement fulfils a fundamental task, both in defining the rules by which society functions and in determining the specific goal of sociology: 'The sociology of social movements', writes Touraine (1981: 30), 'cannot be separated from a representation of society as a system of social forces competing for control of a cultural field'. As within the Marxist approach, the way in which each society functions reflects the struggle between two antagonistic actors who fight for control – not of the material instruments of production, but of the core cultural concerns which, in turn, determine the type of transforming action that a society exercises upon itself (Touraine, 1977: 95f). The main conflicts develop around the control of what Touraine calls 'historicité', defined by the interweaving of a system of knowledge, a type of accumulation and a cultural model, along with the social classes that accompany them. In contrast with Marxism, therefore, classes are defined not only in relation to the system of production; action is 'guided by

cultural orientations and set within social relations defined by an unequal connection with the social control of these orientations' (Touraine, 1981: 61).

According to Touraine, social movements struggle to influence the cultural sphere, seen as the main arena for the exercise of social domination (Girling, 2004). A particular trait of the *programmed society* – which, for Touraine, substitutes for the industrial one – is the 'production of symbolic goods which model or transform our representation of human nature and the external world' (Touraine *et al.*, 1987: 127; Touraine, 1985). The principal source of social power is the control of information, and conflicts tend to shift from the workplace to areas such as research and development, the elaboration of information, biomedical and technical sciences, and the mass media. The central actors in social conflict are no longer classes linked to industrial production, but groups with opposing visions concerning the use and destination of cognitive and symbolic resources (see della Porta and Diani, 2006, for a critical review).

With different nuances and less focus on the search for the new central actor, Italian sociologist Alberto Melucci (1982, 1989, 1996) located the action by social movements in contemporary societies, defined as composed of highly differentiated systems and characterized by a tension between increasing individual autonomy and the requirement of closer integration. In this view, new social movements emerged from opposition to the intrusion of state and market into social life, and reclaim the right to determine private life against the omnipresent and comprehensive manipulation of the system. Unlike the labour movement, new social movements do not ask for an increase in state intervention and welfare provisions, but especially defend personal autonomy, resisting the expansion of political–administrative intervention in daily life.

Changes in the nature of the conflict are also reflected in the characteristics of the new actors. In contrast with the labour movement, social movements develop a fundamental, metapolitical critique of the social order and representative democracy, challenging institutional assumptions regarding conventional ways of 'doing politics', in the name of a radical democracy (Offe, 1985). Among the principal innovations, in contrast with the workers' movement, are a critical ideology in relation to modernism and progress; decentralized and participatory organizational structures; defence of interpersonal solidarity against state and corporate bureaucracies; and the reclamation of autonomous spaces, rather than material advantages.

Inspired by Pierre Bourdieu, European sociologists also engaged in the analysis of cultural habits (or the cultural predispositions produced by processes of socialization) as well as their structural determinants. Attention has been paid to the cultural meanings (or habitus) within the specific fields of social action to which individuals belong: 'Going beyond economic interests, some scholars explained indeed social movement activism as following needs and desires that derive from values and norms that are typical of specific cultures (or fields)' (della Porta and Diani, 2006).

New social movements' approaches have been criticized on various grounds. First – looking especially at the evolution of the environmental or women's movements – the very concept of 'new social movement' tended to be constructed around historically contingent characteristics (such as informal organization or a focus on non-material issues) taken as general defining traits of social movements (della Porta and Diani, 2006: chapter 1). Moreover, focusing on the structural and cultural determinants of social conflicts, new social movement scholars paid little attention to the transformation of grievances, interest or identities in collective mobilizations, or to the evolution of movement strategies and repertoires of action in the interaction with their changing environment.

These limitations notwithstanding, a focus on the origins of the conflict and the culture of the new conflictual actors remained important in European studies and influential in other continents, both in developing and Anglo-Saxon cultures. The attention to the construction of collective identities resonated with a growing interest in so-called neo-Marxian approaches, but also among cultural sociologists all over the world. Interest in the cultural dimensions of social movements is, for instance, well developed in the works of Scandinavian sociologists such as Ron Eyerman (1994) and Abby Peterson (2001), as well as in the journal *Social Movement Studies*. In addition, the focus on the cultural habitus of different movement communities remains relevant for those researching social movements as agents of communication (Neveu, 2000). Attention to the development of alternative codes was even revitalized after the emergence of the recent wave of protest against neoliberal globalization (della Porta, 2007a; della Porta *et al.*, 2006).

The specificity of the European approach to social movements was to a certain extent challenged by the encounters between European and American scholars that has become particularly intense since the second half of the 1980s. In 1986, a conference in Amsterdam started to bridge the gap between Europe and the US (Klandermans *et al.*, 1988), creating a loosely-linked international network of social movement scholars who met several times in the years to come, helping to develop the agenda for social movement research (della Porta and Tarrow, 2004; della Porta *et al.*, 1999; Diani and McAdam, 2003; Klandermans *et al.*, 1988; McAdam *et al.*, 1996). In this context, European scholars' attention to the structural bases but also the cultural dynamics of social movements met with the Americans' focus upon the process of mobilization and its organizational bases.

With the increasing interest in social movement by political scientists as well, European scholars started to use in cross-country research projects the concept of political opportunities, central in the so-called political process approach developed by American scholars such as Charles Tilly (1978), Sidney Tarrow (1989) and Doug McAdam (1982).

Alexis de Tocqueville's famous contrast between a 'weak' American government and a 'strong' French one is usually an implicit or explicit starting point for analyses linking institutional factors – or 'regimes' in Tilly's definition (1978) – with social movement development (Kriesi, 2004: 71). Suggesting an opposition between state and civil society, Tocqueville considered that a system in which the state was weak and civil society strong (e.g. the US) would face a constant but peaceful flux of protest from below. Where the state was strong and civil society weak (e.g. France), episodic and violent revolt would result. Sidney Tarrow (1994: 62–5) has convincingly nuanced this hypothesis, claiming that Tocqueville's analysis was partial even with respect to the historical situation to which the author referred.

The idea that states' strength or weakness influences social movement strategies remains central to the literature on collective action in general, and on revolutions in particular. Especially in Europe, this approach 'à la Tocqueville' resonated with political science's focus on the cross-national comparison of different types of European democracies, based upon different institutional assets and cultural traditions. Many case studies operationalized on the power of the central executive, using categories that refer to the 'power of the state'. In general, a system has been considered more open (and less repressive) the more political decisions are dispersed. The prevalent belief is that the greater the number of actors who share political power (the greater the checks and balances), the greater the chance that social movements will gain access to the system. However, while a weak executive may ease access to the decision-making process, it will have little hope of implementing policies to meet social movement demands.

Beyond the comparison of different institutions, the political process approach also stressed the role of institutional allies for social movements. A more dynamic set of variables – susceptible to change in the short term and the object of pressure from social movements – included aspects such as electoral instability or elite divisions (see, for example, Jenkins, 1985; Piven and Cloward, 1977; Tarrow, 1983, 1989). Attention to allies such as unions and parties also resonated with the relevance assigned to these actors by European political science and sociology. In fact, European scholars soon imported and adapted those concerns, developing new concepts more apt to address cross-national comparisons within Europe. In a comparative analysis of social movements in France, Germany, the Netherlands and Switzerland, Hanspeter Kriesi *et al.* (1995) addressed what they called *configuration of power* – that is, the distribution of power among the various actors operating within the party or interest group system which interacts with social movements (Kriesi, 1989). In a comparison of Italy and Germany, Donatella della Porta and Dieter Rucht (1995) paid particular attention to the field of action within which social movements move, distinguishing an *alliance structure* composed of those political actors who support them, and an *opposition structure* composed of those who oppose them. These and other similar concepts have been used within several cross-national comparative projects that – as we shall discuss in the next paragraph – have facilitated interactions among European scholars.

COMPARING EUROPEAN SOCIAL MOVEMENTS CROSS-NATIONALLY

One of the reasons for the spread of the political opportunity approach in Europe may have been the interest, well developed in European political science and sociology, in infra-European cross-national comparison. Especially in the nineties, this interest produced large comparative research projects, singling out and exploiting different dimensions of comparison among European countries.

A first dimension mirrored the traditional comparison between consensual and majoritarian democracy, stressing centralization versus decentralization of power (Kitschelt, 1986: 61–4; Kriesi, 1995; Rucht, 1994: 303–12). A set of hypotheses concerns *territorial decentralization*, with the basic suggestion that the more power is distributed to the periphery (local or regional government, component states within a federal structure), the greater the possibility for social movements to access the decision-making process. Following the same logic, federal states are considered more open than centralized ones (see, for example, Giugni, 1996; Kitschelt, 1986; Kriesi, 1995). Regarding the *functional separation of powers*, political opportunities are considered more open the greater the division of tasks among legislature, executive and judiciary. The openness of the system to pressure from below should increase the power of elected organs and the autonomy and powers of the judiciary.

In this comparative line, federalist states with high functional separation of power, such as Switzerland and Germany, have been contrasted with more centralized ones, such as France or the Netherlands (Kriesi *et al.*, 1995). It has frequently been observed that in decentralized states, challengers can rely on a variety of actors to penetrate the system. For example, concerning the anti-nuclear movement, Nelkin and Pollack (1981: 179) stated that the 'German decentralised decision-making context has provided ecologists with greater political opportunity, because they can play one administration against the other'. Unlike their counterparts in other countries, the German environmentalists were also successful in using the quite independent judicial system. While the centralized system in France, for example, favoured political control by the government, in Germany the wide distribution of power 'allowed some courts to take a very powerful and independent role in nuclear disputes' (Nelkin and Pollack, 1981: 159).

However, decentralization of power does not always work in social movements' favour: the dispersal of power increases the chances of access, not just for social movements but also for *all* political actors, including counter-movements. Additionally, it reduces the

implementation capacity of central governments. In his comparison of the French, German, Swedish and American anti-nuclear movements, Herbert Kitschelt (1986: 61–4) distinguished between the conditions that influence demands entering the political system and those influencing its output in terms of public policies. On the input side, a large number of political parties, the capacity of the legislature to develop and control policy independently of the executive, pluralist patterns of mediation between interest groups and the executive branch, and the possibility of building policy coalitions are indicators of openness. On the output side, however, the capacity of the political system to implement policies is increased by a centralized state apparatus, government control over the market and a low level of judicial independence from the other arms of the state.

Institutional variables have a stronger influence on the *strategies* adopted by social movements however. Social movements, in fact, tend to use the channels of access made available to them by 'weak' states. According to a comparative research project based upon newspaper data, in Switzerland, where there is a strong tradition of referendum, 195 per thousand inhabitants were mobilized in forms of action involving the use of direct democracy, compared with only 4 per thousand in Germany and none in France and the Netherlands (Kriesi *et al.*, 1995: 45). Additionally, protest is more widespread but also more moderate in 'weak' states than in 'strong' ones (Kriesi *et al.*, 1995: 45).

Social movements have also been compared cross-nationally with reference to the relatively stable characteristics of *national political cultures* (Kitschelt, 1985: 302f) – another dimension that resonates with attention to consociationalism, quite familiar to European political science. Looking at those aspects of political culture relevant to interaction between social movements and institutions, Hanspeter Kriesi has emphasized the importance of prevailing strategies, referring in particular to the procedures used by members of a system when dealing with 'challengers': 'national strategies set the informal and formal rules of the game for the conflict between new social movements and their adversaries' (Kriesi, 1989: 295). According to this hypothesis, countries with a strategy of exclusion (i.e. repression of conflict) will tend to experience polarization of conflict with opponents, whereas a strategy of inclusion (co-optation of emergent demands) would produce a moderation of conflict. As Kriesi *et al.* (1995) have noted in their comparison of France, Germany, Switzerland and the Netherlands, consociational national traditions are reflected in the moderate participatory repertoires of the Dutch and Swiss protest. These (self-reproducing) prevailing strategies influenced the way in which the conflict between labour and capital was confronted, leading to exclusion in certain cases and integration in others (Kriesi, 1989). Initially elaborated in response to trade unionism, these strategies developed their own self-perpetuating logic through political socialization and interaction. In fact, it has been argued that in each country, new social movements have 'inherited' consequences from the reactions originally reserved for the labour movement.

Again resonating with an interest in cross-national comparison in the development of democratic regimes in European political science, social movement research also addressed the influence of a country's *democratic history*, remarking that past authoritarianism often re-emerges in times of turmoil. Young democracies tend to fear political protest and to have police forces that remain steeped in the authoritarian values of the preceding regime (Flam, 1994a: 348; on Italy, see della Porta and Reiter, 2004; Reiter, 1998). In a cross-national comparison of the anti-nuclear movement, for example, Helena Flam noted that

the speedy and substantial responses came in the nation-states whose political and bureaucratic state elites have either long ago (Sweden, Norway) or immediately after the Second World War, if not earlier (Austria, the Netherlands, West Germany) learnt to recognize as legitimate and even formalized interest groups representation and the influence that trade unions and employers exert over governmental decision making (Flam, 1994b: 309).

The elites in these countries tend to recognize the legitimacy of interests lying outside the party system, knowing that the movement of today may be the interest group of tomorrow.

National democratic history has also been seen to influence protest through its impact on protest policing (della Porta and Reiter, 1998a, 1998b). With regard to traditional police styles, the 'civilized' British 'bobby' – unarmed, integrated in the community and tendentially autonomous from political power – has been contrasted with the militarized continental police, who live in barracks and are dependent on political power. On the continent, police action against challengers seemed to aim at defending not only a general system of power, but a concrete government. The *protest policing styles* traditionally dominant on the continent were more 'brutal', more repressive, more confrontational and more rigid than in England. Prevailing strategies and protest policing styles are seen to influence the repertoires of protest, which tend to be more conventional in traditionally assimilative countries. In a comparison of political repression in nineteenth-century Europe, for example, it has been noted that 'those countries that were consistently the most repressive, brutal, and obstinate in dealing with the consequences of modernization and developing working-class dissidence reaped the harvest by producing opposition that was just as rigid, brutal, and obstinate' (Goldstein, 1983: 340; see also della Porta and Reiter, 1998a).

Another dimension of cross-national comparison locates social movements within broader organizational fields that include their allies, among them two actors that have occupied a central role in European political science and sociology: unions and political parties. In Europe, the *trade unions* have often been an important ally for emerging actors such as the student movement or the women's movement. With a broad social base and very often privileged channels of access to institutional decision-makers (both directly through the public administration and indirectly through the political parties), trade unions can increase the mobilization capacities and chances of success for social movements with which they ally. In general, the most radical ideologies and strategies have developed in countries characterized by low parlamentarization and the political isolation of the labour movement (Bartolini, 2000: 565–66). In contrast, the institutionalization of collective bargaining contributed to depoliticizing conflicts on social inequality by constraining them within industrial relations (Gallie, 1989). In fact, 'repression stimulated working-class radicalism; whilst political relaxation and a structure of free collective bargaining encourages reformism' (Geary, 1981: 179). In Mediterranean Europe, France and Germany, absolutism and the late introduction of universal suffrage led to a divided and radicalized labour movement. In the smaller, open-market countries in Great Britain and Scandinavia, on the other hand, where there was no experience of absolutism and universal suffrage was introduced early, inclusive strategies produced a united and moderate labour movement (Marks, 1989: 14–15, passim).

Within this attention to the labour movement, cross-national comparisons have taken into account the prevailing *model of industrial relations*. A main hypothesis is that the more influential the interest groups, the smaller the space for relatively unorganized movements because 'a well-resourced, coherently structured, and professionalized system of interest groups may also be able to prevent outside challengers from having access to the state. Moreover, highly institutionalized, encompassing arrangements of policy negotiations between the public administration and private interest associations will be both quite inaccessible to challengers and able to act' (Kriesi *et al.*, 1995: 31). *Neocorporatism* – that is, a model of interest representation with monopolistic, centralized interest organizations (Schmitter, 1974) that participate in public decision-making (Lehmbruch, 1977) – would reduce the incidence of protest. Access to the institutional system of public decision-making

would facilitate agreement between different social groups and the state without the need for non-institutional forms of collective action. Both control over the formation of social demand (Schmitter, 1981) and the capacity to satisfy that demand (Nollert, 1995) would have the effect of discouraging protest. On the other hand, neocorporatism could just as easily create a tendency to incorporate emerging groups within the structure of concerted policy-making. A comparison between the American and German antinuclear movements revealed that the American system, with its multiple points of access and traditionally weak executive, favoured legal strategies and pragmatic movements. The initial closure of the German state (traditionally assertive of its supremacy over civil society) to interests that cut across its corporatist outlook favoured strategies of direct action (Joppke, 1993). However, 'once new issues and interests pass the high hurdles of party and parliament, the German polity firmly institutionalizes them' (Joppke, 1993: 201). In contrast, in Italy, continuously repressed unions were more eager to support mass protests, even of the most disruptive types (della Porta, 1996; Tarrow, 1989).

Where social movement allies are concerned, attention has mainly focused the *political parties*, especially in Europe. Social movements' relationship with parties has evolved over time: from articulating party positions to permeating parties in order to try to influence them; from co-optation to independence (Hanagan, 1998). Movements have often developed special links with a given political party or party family: the labour movements arose from or gave birth to socialist parties; ethnic movements often refer to regionalist parties for support; ecologists tend to vote for the Greens. So strict have been their reciprocal relations that 'indeed in the United States and Europe, political parties and social movements have become overlapping, mutually dependent actors in shaping politics' (Goldstone, 2003: 4). Past research has especially focused on new social movements, which have seen, although with tensions, the Left as an ally

(Kriesi, 1989: 296). Indeed, the programs and membership of the institutional left, whether British Labour, German Social Democrats, French Socialists or Italian communists, have all been altered by their interactions with social movements (i.e. Duyvendak, 1995; Koelble, 1991; Koopmans, 1995; Maguire, 1995).

The alliance of the parties of the left has been considered as particularly important for social movements in southern Europe. In a comparative analysis of Italy, Spain, Greece and Portugal, della Porta *et al.* (forthcoming) suggested that, although the women's movements were strongly influenced by the left political parties in all countries, the improvement in women's conditions followed different paths in different countries: in Italy, a semi-autonomous women's movement allied with an old left who was always in the opposition; in Greece, feminism was associated with leftist parties as well as a PASOK-driven state feminism; in Spain, 'pressure groups feminism' developed with few direct contacts with a state feminist machinery directly controlled by the PSOE; and in Portugal, state feminist institutions played a role in the creation of women's non-governmental organizations.

Attention to the configuration of parties on the left has re-emerged with research on the movement that developed around issues of global justice – variously referred to as alter-globalist, anti-neoliberal, new global or no-global, but defined here as the Global Justice Movement (GJM). Here, a comparative analysis of France, Italy and Spain, on the one hand, and Germany, Switzerland and the UK on the other, has pointed at the presence of two different constellations (della Porta, 2007a). In the first, disruptive protest dynamics appear as more dominant; networks are denser and more decentralized, with participation of both informal groups and formal associations; and the issue of global justice is linked with a struggle against neoliberalism at home within a global discourse and a conception of radical participatory democracy. This is the case in Spain, where a frame of radical democracy spread together with

appeal to direct action, as well as in France, where social issues play a central role (Jimenez and Calle, 2006; Sommier and Combes, 2006). In Italy, the metaframe of global justice contributed to bringing together a dense network of rank-and-file unions (and later more traditional unions as well), religious groups, squatted youth centres, ecologists and peace activists.

In all of these cases, although more traditional NGOs were also present, the transnational network developed as activist based and protest oriented (della Porta *et al.*, 2006). In this constellation, unions are (more) present in the mobilization, both in the form of the 'critical unions' that emerged in an already fragmented system of industrial relations and in the left-wing component of the traditional unions: especially in Italy and France, rank-and-file unions have been involved in the transnational wave of protest since its inception. Political opportunities appear as closed in terms of access to government but open in terms of potential allies; and the GJM is stronger its capacity to mobilize in the street. In Spain, the socialists of the PSOE are more open towards the GJM when opposing a right-wing PP government (Jimenez and Calle, 2006); In Italy, the movement gained enormous mobilization capacity during Berlusconi's government, but also developed from a critique of the party system (Reiter *et al.*, 2006).

In the second constellation, collective action relies largely on lobbying and media campaigns; strong associations and NGOs are more visible, although not unchallenged; global justice issues are framed especially, although not exclusively, in terms of solidarity with the south; and associational conceptions of democracy prevail. In Germany as well as Britain, the GJM is supported by well-endowed NGOs, among which protest is 'rehabilitated' thanks to the frustrating results of more moderate techniques (Rootes and Saunders, 2006; Rucht *et al.*, 2006). Similarly in Switzerland, notwithstanding the presence of a more radical wing and a remobilization of the unions, the GJM relies widely on the already existing, rich organizations coming from the new social movements (especially on environmental and solidarity issues) of the 1970s, while the weakness of the class cleavage reduces support by the old left (Eggert and Giugni, 2006). In this second constellation, with more institutionalized systems of industrial relations, critical unions are weak or nonexistent, and traditional unions, involved in neocorporatist agreements, remain more distant from the movement (with the exception of the public sector and metalworkers' unions). With more open political opportunities, the movement tends to rely less on street mobilization and more on lobbying and information campaigns. However, also in these countries, the movement has often taken to the street.

A recent trend in comparative studies has also been the attempt to specify political opportunities for specific movements. In this sense, in an attempt to link specific institutional opportunities to specific movements, differences in the characteristics of national citizenship regimes have been considered as related with the forms and intensity of conflicts around immigration politics (Koopmans and Statham, 1999) and national welfare regimes in the contentious politics of unemployment (Berclaz et al., 2004).

SOCIAL MOVEMENTS AND EUROPEANIZATION

All of these studies on European social movements confirm the relevance of national political traditions and contingent opportunities. The wave of transnational protest impacted, however, on national movement families. In a process of downward scale-shift (Tarrow and McAdam, 2004), cosmopolitan activists who had been involved in transnational countersummits and protest campaigns contributed to bringing the conflict back home. In Europe, this process focused attention on the potential for and paths of Europeanization of social movements. By the nineties, two streams of research addressed these issues.

Protest event analysis has repeatedly concluded that concerns about EU decisions have been mainly expressed at the national level, where elected political institutions are considered more accountable to the citizen-electors. Using data on protest collected mainly from newspaper sources, these studies stress the paucity of protests directly targeting European institutions. Relying upon Reuters World News Service and the Reuters Textline, Doug Imig and Sidney Tarrow (2001) found a very limited number of such protests. Similarly for Germany, Dieter Rucht (2002) observed a low (and declining) proportion of protests aimed at the international level (with the high point coming in 1960–1964), including EU institutions, and/or whose actions were organized cross-nationally. Giugni and Passy (2002) as well as Koopmans (2004) noted how rarely protests on migrant rights targeted the EU, notwithstanding the increasing Europeanization of decisions on migration at least in terms of quotas of access and border controls. Even environmental action only very rarely turns on Brussels: a cross-national research project on environmental movements revealed that protest events with EU targets ranged from 0.8 per cent of total protest on environmental issues in Italy to 4.6 per cent in Germany in the last decade, with no discernible increasing trend (Rootes, 2002).

The low presence of protest at the European level was explained by the political opportunities available at various territorial levels of government (della Porta and Kriesi, 1999). Social movement studies have in fact stressed that protest grows when not only grievances, but also resources and opportunities are present – that is, when protesters believe their actions could have an impact upon decision makers (see above). Taking this hypothesis forward, the limited number of protests to turn on the institutions of the EU could be explained by the undeniable deficit in representative democracy: if protesters could produce disagreements and criticisms, these would be difficult to mobilize against an unaccountable and opaque target. Besides the weak electoral accountability of EU representative political institutions, the difficulties in building a European public sphere has been emphasized (by, among others, Gerhards, 1993; Le Toree *et al.*, 2001). If more recent research has pointed at more complex results, revealing an increasing Europeanization of national public discourses (see Eder and Trenz, 2003; Seidendorf, 2003), the participation of civil society actors in the mass-mediatic debate on Europe remains limited.

In a cross-national research project on the Europeanization of the public sphere (Koopmans and Statham, 2002) in France, Germany, Italy, the Netherlands, Spain, Switzerland and the UK, similar results emerged for claim-making (i.e. the analysis of the demands by different actors published in newspapers or other mass media) on seven issues: ever more than the public discourse on domestic issues, the public discourse on Europe is dominated by institutional actors (Koopmans, 2004). Social movements and NGOs are the collective actors least present in mass-mediatic debates Europeanized policy fields, showing less capacity to frame issues in European terms (della Porta and Caiani, 2004 and 2005). When looking at the scope of the *claimant* who enters the public sphere, in all countries, European actors account for a moderate proportion of claims (from 6.6 per cent of European claimants in Britain to 19.9 per cent in Spain), which drops even more when focusing on transnational European civil society associations (no more than 2 per cent in all the countries). Looking at the choice of European institutions as the *target* of claims, in all our countries, although national (and subnational) actors are still the main target of call or appeal, the role of European actors and institutions is relevant (from 15.4 per cent of European targets in the British public sphere to 32.8 per cent in the French). Here as well, however, the presence of social movements and NGOs declines when the target shifts from the national to the EU level (from 3.4 per cent of claims targeting the EU made by social movements in Britain to 12 per cent in France). When looking

at the scope of the *object* of claim-making, this research found a similar picture, with a significant presence of European objects/interests in the public debates of all countries in general, but a sharp decline when focusing on social movements and NGOs. Finally, in the debates of the European countries under study, about one-fourth of all claims are framed with a specific reference to Europe; once again, the European reference remains less important in the claims presented in the printed public sphere by social movements and NGOs (della Porta and Caiani, 2007c, 2007e).

The weakness of the European public sphere explains why the target of social movements continues to be predominantly national governments. In particular, movements that want to put pressure on the EU in favour of national interests, in direct competition with other national interests represented in the EU, tend to choose a two-level game (Putman, 1983: 434) – pushing the national governments that, in turn, can try to negotiate better arrangements at supranational levels. In their analysis of protest in Europe, Doug Imig and Sidney Tarrow (2001) indeed stressed that most EU-related events (406 out of 490) were cases of *domestication*. This was confirmed in the mentioned research on the Europeanization of the public sphere, where in fact domestication (operationalized as the claims with a European object addressed by national actors to their national governments) covered about one-third of the claims of all actors, but more than half of the claims made by social movement organizations (della Porta and Caiani, 2007a, 2007f). This protest targets EU decisions, but runs at the national level: domestic actors target their national governments, pushing them to address the EU institutions. Domestication characterizes in particular many mobilizations of European farmers (Bush and Simi, 2001).

Such paths of mobilization might be seen as proof of the persistent relevance of the nation state as target for protest, as well as the permanent weakness of the EU institutions. However, national protests against

EU-induced policies indicate also a potential for transnationalization of protest and the emergence of a transnational public sphere. In fact, in the course of these campaigns, innovations develop both in the organizational structure and in the frames of the protest, with the development of European networks and European identities, as indicated by an analysis of the protest of dairy farmers against EU milk quotas in Italy in the mid-1990s (della Porta, 2007b).

If the 'milk quota' campaign tended to remain mainly national, it also indicated also the limits of 'domestication', which in fact works only to the extent that national governments retain large autonomous power, and for actors that are better protected at the national than at the supranational level. The organization of a march of the Italian farmers (with their 'live' symbol, a cow called *Mucca Carolina*) in Brussels confirms the perception of the need to address the EU level as well. In fact, not only did the Italian farmers protest in Brussels, they also met other groups with similar concerns from other countries. The march in Brussels as well as the mobilization of European farmers against WTO-supported policies indicate the capacity of collective actors that emerge and act mainly at the domestic level to overcome national borders, framing their concerns within a broader social agenda. Especially after the shift in agricultural policies (with Agenda 2000) from subsidies to market liberalization and WTO-supported policies of competition, the Confederation Paysanne Européenne mobilized at the EU level against what they defined as neoliberal stances (Delorme, 2002), developing a European identity while criticizing the specific policies of reduction of regulations on the use of hormones, genetically modified organisms, pesticides and the like. Concluding, domestication is often the strategy that allows protesters to overcome the weak democratic accountability of EU institutions, meanwhile producing European structures and frames.

If domestication emerges as a frequent path of Europeanization of social movements,

the EU institutions are also seen as an additional arena for the mobilization of resources that may then be used at the national level. In this case, there is a strategy of *externalization* (Chabanet, 2002) – defined as the mobilization of national actors targeting the EU in attempts to put pressure on their own governments. In these cases, actors who feel weak at home try to mobilize allies at the supranational level; their protest addresses EU institutions, pushing them to intervene upon domestic governments. This is the case, for instance, with environmental campaigns (Rootes 2002) as well for as the 1997 Eurostrike of Spanish, French and Belgian workers, who accused Renault of disregarding the right to consultation with the workers' representative that was imposed by European legislation (Lefébure and Lagneau, 2002).

Focusing on the action of social movement organizations another trend of research addressed the presence and activities of social movement organizations at the EU level. For those organizations, influencing the EU was not easy,[1] In contrast to business organizations, movements active at the EU level – such as the Platform of the European Social NGOs, the European Anti-Poverty Network, the Human Rights Contact Group, the European Migrant Forum, United (against racism), and the European Network of Women – are usually loose and poorly staffed. EU-level environmental movement organizations are, for the most part, little more than transnational alliances of various national groups with only very limited resources (Rootes, 2002: 382). Inclusion has also been selective: only the organizations that adapt to the 'rules of the game' obtain routine access, though usually of an informal nature, to EU institutions (Guiraudon, 2001; Marks and McAdam, 1999). Moreover, the more important EU institutions become, the more structured and less accessible they seem to be for weakly organized interests (Rootes, 2002).

Nevertheless, some changes in the European institutions facilitated access by movement organizations. First, if the building of the

European institutions as oriented to the creation of a common market explains the dominance of producers' interests, with the progression of market-making legislation (from the European Commission, the Council, but also the Court) there was also an increase in demand for market-correcting policies (with mobilizations of consumers, environmentalists, and so on). Moreover, in recent times, the debate about good governance and the democratic deficit induced the Commission to reflect about the involvement of civil society (starting with Delors and the 'Social Dialogue') and, especially after Maastricht, to look for broader social acceptance of EU policies (e.g. the White Paper on Governance) as well as for allies in the power-play with the Council. In fact, (some) social movement organizations have recently been granted increased participation in return for expertise and legitimacy. The Commission has biannual meetings with all NGOs involved in the social platform and holds weekly meetings with the environmental 'group of eight', plus various groups of experts. The largest environmental groups of the so-called 'gang of four' – Greenpeace, WWF, Friends of the Earth and the EEB – have close relationships with the then DG XI (now DG ENV), which gives all but Greenpeace financial support (Rootes, 2002). So strong was the support of the European Union (especially the former DG V, now DG EMPL) for the European Trade Union Confederation that the Europeanization of trade unions has been described as 'a story of interactions between European institutions seeking to stimulate Euro-level interest representation, a small number of unionists who perceived Europe as important, and the growing significance of European integration itself' (Martin and Ross, 2001: 57; see also Branch, 2002). The European Parliament has worked as a main channel of access to various organizations, especially in areas where parliamentary committees are more active (for instance environmental issues) and movement organizations relations' with the Commission more difficult. Feminists, environmentalists

and unions have also been able to obtain favourable decisions from the Court of Justice, especially with the increasing competence of the EU on environmental and social policies (Balme and Chabanet, 2002; Mazey, 2002). Although access remained unequal, some formal and informal opportunities for influencing the EU institutions have been opening up and tested by social movement organizations (Ruzza 2004). Beyond their varying degrees of success, initiatives at the EU level have facilitated networking among social movement organizations of different countries, focusing their attention on the European dimension of multilevel governance.

The Europeanization of protest also followed a third, broader trend of *transnationalization* that contributed to the development of the global justice movement. At the turn of the millennium, international summits were often accompanied by counter-summits and protest demonstrations that sometimes received wider press coverage than the official agenda (Pianta and Marchetti, 2006). Transnational mobilizations of this type have also targeted European institutions. One of the first European mobilization was the European marches against unemployment, insecurity and exclusion, which addressed the Amsterdam summit in 1997; two years later, 30,000 mobilized on the same issues at the EU summit in Cologne (Chabanet, 2002; Balme and Chabanet, 2002 and 2008). These marches played an important role in the emergence of the European wave of protest that became visible in the July 2001 anti-G8 demonstrations in Genoa (della Porta and Mosca, 2004). In fact, since Amsterdam and Cologne, counter-summits have contested all of the main EU summits. In Nice, Gothenburg, Barcelona and Copenhagen, tens of thousands marched during EU summits to protest EU decisions.

Since 2002, protesters have also met yearly in European Social Forums to debate Europeanization and its limits. The European construction was at the core of the first European Social Forum in Florence in

November 2002, followed by a second one in Paris in 2003, a third in London in 2004 and a fourth in Athens in May 2006. The large success of the first European forum – with 60,000 activists from all over Europe participating in three days of debate, and between 500,000 and 1,000,000 activists in the closing march – was the result of networking among groups and individuals with different political and social backgrounds that continued in the following years (della Porta *et al.*, 2006).

The platform of the first European Social Forum presented it as the first step in the construction of a critical public sphere for the discussion of the European Convention and its limits. Together with the democratization of the European institutions, it demanded a charter of social rights that would go beyond the commitments made in the Treaty of Nice. The policies of the EU are criticized as essentially neoliberal, advocating the privatization of public services and the flexibility of the work market, with resulting increases in work insecurity. Under the banner 'another Europe is possible', more social policies were demanded, including taxation of capital and of financial transactions. There were also claims for the reduction of indirect taxes and public intervention to help the weakest social groups, as well as the strengthening of public services like school and health. On these issues, European social democracy was criticized as supporting economic policies of privatization and deregulation of a neoliberal type (della Porta 2009).

Similar claims were presented by the social movement organizations interviewed within the Europub project (della Porta and Caiani, 2005, 2009). The research, based upon claims analysis, indicates that social movements tend to be marginally present in the debate on European integration, but also more critical than more institutional actors of the decisions taken by European institutions (della Porta and Caiani, 2006a, 2006b, 2007a, 2007f). These interviews confirmed, however, that the emerging critique is not of 'too much' Europe, but of not enough social Europe.

A (stigmatized) 'Europe of the market' is contrasted with the (desired) Europe of the citizens. In particular, those movement organizations active on issues of immigration specifically criticize the lack of recognition of migrants' political and social rights. In these circumstances, the consequences of Europeanization are described as dangerous for solidarity, while on migration issues the EU is accused of 'building a fortress'. In addition to the critiques of specific policies, social movement organizations, although perceiving at the European level an opportunity to move towards a politics 'from below', express a general criticism of the perceived democratic deficit. In this view, a strengthening of the European Parliament is perceived as a main step towards participation and electoral accountability, facilitating responsiveness to demands 'from below'.

Although critical of the European institutions, social movement organizations do address those institutions and even promote a European identity. The same research based upon interviews confirms that social movement organizations share a tendency to coordinate their action at the cross-national level and to address (especially via lobbying) the European institutions. Social movements reveal a greater tendency to direct claims to the European level than what emerged from the mass-mediated debate (della Porta and Caiani, 2004, 2005). Overall, they very often address European targets (about two-thirds addressed at least one EU target in the last year) as do the other powerful actors (della Porta and Caiani, 2007c, 2007e). They are also particularly well connected transnationally, even slightly more so than the general trend of all actors considered. Some social movement organizations have European offices, but even the others often act at the European level through European partners. European institutions, beyond being the target of an increasingly Europeanized public discourse, provide occasions for the creation of supranational networks and identities through continuous and contentious interactions of various political and social actors around

EU institutions (Imig and Tarrow, 2001a: 23; della Porta and Caiani, 2005, 2007b, 2007d, on the Italian case). The building of European networks and identity is also related to the belief that the process of European integration has had and continues to have a strong impact on civil society organizations.

Despite criticisms – even the most radical, levelled at the 'Europe of markets' – most of the social movement organizations in the mentioned research interviewed expressed support for the construction of 'a different Europe'. These organizations present themselves as belonging to 'a European movement'. The discourse 'from below' on Europe appears in fact to be more oriented to social and political rights than to territorial politics. This position is illustrated in the words of a representative of the Italian pacifist organization Beati i Costruttori di Pace, who expressed that 'our wish is for the European level to become always more important. The European Social Forums, for example, are opportunities for this. One of the fundamental points of the first European Social Forum in Florence was to bring civil society from European countries together' (quoted in della Porta, 2006). Nevertheless, the social movement organizations are, in the words of an activist of the Spanish organization Red con Voz, not 'unconditional Europeanists, but Europeanists conditioned to the fulfillment of the social part in which there is presently a deficit. If this is fulfilled we will be with Europe' (quoted in della Porta, 2006).

The development of these critical voices can be related to the politicization of the debate on Europe, in response to the (perceived and real) growth in EU competences. The fact that national actors have held the integration process responsible for economic policies or rigorous environmental policies has contributed to increased worries about the consequences of European integration. In this situation, contrasting demands are addressed to the European Union, which is perceived as a relevant level of governance.

A similar image of 'critical Europeanists' emerges if we look at the attitudes of the activists of the global justice movement. According to a survey at the European Social Forum in Florence, activists from different countries express strong criticisms of the actual politics and policies of the European Union (della Porta, 2006). There is consensus among activists that the EU strengthens neoliberal globalization, with a shared mistrust in the capacity of the EU to mitigate the negative effects of globalization and safeguard a different social model of welfare: less than 10 per cent believe that the EU attempts to safeguard a social model other than the neoliberal one; 19 per cent believe that it mitigates some of the worst effects of globalization, and 88 per cent believe that it strengthens neoliberal globalization. The ESF survey also indicates mistrust in the EU institutions, with only a tiny minority (about 10 per cent) expressing high levels of trust in them.

In order to complete this picture, however, we have to add that the activists of the European Social Forum express both a high affective identification with Europe and a certain level of support for the building of a European level of governance. First, about half of the activists feel enough or strong attachment to Europe. Moreover, only a few express support for a strengthening of national governments (19 per cent agree much or very much), while 33 per cent support a strengthening of the EU and macro-regional institutions and as many as 70 per cent would welcome the building of new institutions of world governance. The mix of dissatisfaction with the existing EU and support for the building of 'another Europe' is confimed by the results of a 2005 survey carried out at a demonstration in Rome against the EU Bolkestein Directive: although only 11 per cent of the activists disagreed with the statement that the EU constitutional treaty would endanger the national welfare state and social policies, as many as 80 per cent agreed (64 per cent of them strongly) that 'an alternative model of European integration is necessary in order to resist neoliberal globalization'. In this sense, social movement activists represent a 'social capital' of committed citizens that, although critical, might represent an important source for the building of a European citizenship. As with the construction of the nation state, for European institution-building the presence of critical citizens works as a challenge and a resource (della Porta, 2007b).

Support or opposition to Europe are positions usually considered as pertaining to territorial identity, pitting nationalists against Europeanists – or intergovernmentalists against federalists. However, it should be added that at various points in time and on various policies, national actors have symbolically intertwined their positions on Europe with those held on other issues, some using their veto powers, other fashioning themselves as Europe's 'entrepreneurs'. This complex process of symbolic appropriation of Europe as a theme has also brought about an extension of the definition of the 'conflict over Europe', layering various other cleavages over the original territorial ones (concerned with the boundaries of the *polity*). As in the formation of the nation state, the territorial issue is articulated alongside others: support for Europe is linked to different images of Europe as built by different actors. Support and opposition thus tend to refer not only to (or not very much to) the integration process itself.

CONCLUSION

Concluding, research on social movements is no longer a marginal field in European studies. As for the theoretical approaches, the field of social movement studies is quite pluralistic. Departing from an approach that emphasized the structural bases of new conflicts, it has extended to include an interest in social movements as political actors as well as producers of new cultural codes. Although influenced by the American-born resource mobilization approach, research on social movements in Europe has also maintained its distinctive focus on the social and cultural

bases for the development of contentious forms of political participation.

In addition, cross-national comparison has represented a growing interest in European studies. Sensitivity to the effects of national institutions and political culture on the development of social movements resonates with the relevant attention to comparativism in European social sciences. Several studies on the ecologist movement, the women's movement and the peace movement have developed hypotheses about the role of democratic history, political institutions and policing models as well as interactions with potential allies such as trade unions and political parties in explaining degrees and forms of collective mobilization. In this process, European scholars working on social movements have interacted with other streams in the social sciences, using concepts developed in comparative research on party systems, industrial relations, political culture and, more in general, on the typologies and trends of European nation states.

This research still appears as central for European studies on social movements, which have stressed, especially since the 1980s, the evolution of social movements into important actors for 'normal politics', well-endowed public interest groups, efficient voluntary organizations involved in a growing 'third sector', active between the state and the market. Nevertheless, quite unexpectedly, at the turn of the millennium a new wave of protest brought citizens back into the streets, challenging not only the picture of 'institutionalization' of movement politics but also some of the established approaches in social movement research. In fact (one might say, as with all other actors in the European political system), social movements have also Europeanized. Slowly but steadily, they have increased their attention on European institutions, perceived now as opponents, now as potential allies. In this process, social movements have also intensified both trans-European structural ties – via cross-national or EU level organizations and coordinations – and the use of European frames of reference. More than 'Eurosceptic', social movements have grown into 'critical Europeanists'.

As with the construction of the nation state, the focusing of protest at the national level followed the centralization of decisional power (Tilly, 1978). Then, as now, social and political actors moved on more territorial levels: alliances with *state-builders* targeted local governors, but there were also alliances with the periphery against the centre (Tarrow, 2005). The construction of the nation state has been a conflictual process: citizens' rights are the result of social struggles (Bendix, 1964; Marshall, 1976 [1950]). Democracy emerged with the contestation of public decisions; criticism of national governments contributed to legitimizing the state as the main decisional level. Similarly, it is not the agreement upon borders, ideologies and values, but the public debate about them that indicates the existence of a European public sphere (Risse, 2003: 6–7; also Risse, 2000; Habermas, 1981).

NOTES

1 In 1991, in fact, there were at the EU level 583 business associations, as compared to 112 of workers, artisans, professionals and consumers (Rucht, 2002: 170). According to other sources, 67 per cent of EU pressure groups represent sectors of economic interests, 9.6 per cent the organized interests of professions, business and labour and only 23 per cent public interests (Balme and Chabanet, 2002: 59).

REFERENCES

Balme, R. and Chabanet, D. (2002) 'Introduction. Action collective et gouvernance de l'Union Européenne', in R. Balme and D. Chabanet (eds, *L'action Collective en Europe*. Paris: Presses de Sciences Po, pp. 21–120.

Balme, R. and Chabanet, d. (2008) *European Governance and Democracy*. Lanham: Rowman and Littlefield.

Bartolini, S. (2000) *The Political Mobilization of the European Left, 1860–1980. The Class Cleavage*. Cambridge: Cambridge University Press.

Bendix, R. (1964) *Nation Building and Citizenship*. New York: Wiley & Sons.

Berclaz, M., Fueglister, K. and Giugni, M. (2004) 'Etats-providence, opportunités politiques et mobilisation des chômeurs. Une approche néo-institutionnaliste', *Revue Suisse de Sociologie*, 30: 421–440.

Branch, A.P. (2002) 'The impact of the European Union on the trade union movement', in R. Balme, D. Chabanet and V. Wright (ed.), *L'action Collective en Europe*. Paris: Presses de Sciences Po, pp. 279–312.

Bush, E. and Simi, P. (2001) 'European farmers and their protests', in D. Imig and S. Tarrow (eds) *Contentious Europeans. Protest and Politics in an Emerging Polity*. Lanham: Rowman & Littlefield, pp. 97–121.

Chabanet, D. (2002) 'Les marches européennes contre le chômage, la précarité et les exclusions,' in R. Balme, D. Chabanet and V. Wright (ed.), *L'action Collective en Europe*. Paris: Presses de Sciences Po, pp. ???–???

della Porta, D. (1996) *Movimenti Collettivi e Sistema Politico in Italia, 1960–1995*. Bari: Laterza.

della Porta, D, (2007a) 'The global justice movement: An introduction', in D. della Porta (ed.) *The Global Justice Movement: Cross-national and Transnational Perspectives*. Boulder Co.: Paradigm.

della Porta, D. (2007b) 'The Europeanization of protest: a typology and empirical evidence', in B. Kohler-Koch and B. Rittberger (eds) *Debating the Democratic Legitimacy of the European Union*. Lanham: Rowman and Littlefield, pp. 189–208.

della Porta, D. (ed.) (2009) *Another Europe*. London: Routledge.

della Porta, D., Andretta, M., Mosca, L. and Reiter, H. (2006) *Globalization from Below. Transnational Activists and Protest Networks*. Minnesota: University of Minnesota Press.

della Porta, D. and Caiani, M. (2004) 'L'Europeizzazione della sfera pubblica in Italia: Un processo top-down?', *Rivista Italiana di Scienza Politica*, 34: 459–489.

della Porta, D. and Caiani, M. (2005) 'Di cosa si parla quando si parla d'Europa', *Il Mulino*, 56 (421): 937–948.

della Porta, D. and Caiani, M. (2006a) *Quale Europa? Europeizzazione, identita e conflitti*. Bologna: Il Mulino.

della Porta, D. and Caiani, M. (2006b) 'The Europeanization of public discourse in Italy:

a top-down process?', *European Union Politics*, 7 (1): 77–112.

della Porta, D. and Caiani, M. (2007a) 'Eurosceptics or critical Europeanists? Civil society actors and Europe', in R. Koopmans and P. Statham, forthcoming.

della Porta, D. and Caiani, M. (2007b) 'Addressing Europe: How domestic actors perceive European institutions and how they try to influence them', in J. Lacroix and R. Coman (eds) *Les Résistances à l'Europe/ Resisting Europe*. Bruxelles: Editions de l'Université de Bruxelles, forthcoming.

della Porta, D. and Caiani, M. (2007c) 'Social movements and multilevel governance', in O. Jarren, D. Lachenmeier and A. Steiner (eds) *Entgrentze Demokratie? Herausforderung fuer die politische Interessenvermittlung*. Baden-Baden: Nomos, pp. 163–180.

della Porta, D. and Caiani, M. (2007d) 'Talking Europe in the Italian public sphere', *South European Society and Politics*, 12 (1): forthcoming.

della Porta, D. and Caiani, M. (2007e) 'Europeanization from below? Social movements and Europe', *Mobilization*, forthcoming.

della Porta, D. and Caiani, M. (2007f) 'Eurosceptics or critical Europeanists? Civil society actors and Europe', in R. Koopmans and P. Statham (eds), forthcoming.

della Porta, D. and caiani, M. (2009) *Europeanization and Social Movements*. Oxford: Oxford University Press.

della Porta, D. and Diani, M. (2006) *Social Movements. An Introduction*. Malden, MA, Oxford: Blackwell Publishing.

della Porta, D. and Kriesi, H. (1999) 'Social movements in a globalizing world. An introduction', in D. della Porta, H. Kriesi, and D. Rucht (eds) *Social Movements in a Globalizing World*. New York, London: Macmillan, pp. 3–22.

della Porta, D., Kriesi, H. and Rucht, D. (eds) (1999) *Social Movements in a Globalizing World*. New York: Macmillan.

della Porta, D. and Mosca. L. (2004) ' Global-net for global movements? A network of networks for a movement of movement', *Journal of Public Policy*, 25: 165–190.

della Porta, D. and Reiter, H. (1998a) 'Introduction. The policing of protest in Western democracies', in D. della Porta and H. Reiter (eds) *Policing Protest. The Control of Mass Demonstrations in Western Democracies*. Minneapolis: University of Minneapolis Press, pp. 1–32.

della Porta, D. and Reiter, H. (1998b) *Policing Protest. The Control of Mass Demonstrations in Western Democracies*. Minneapolis: The University of Minneapolis Press.

della Porta, D. and Reiter, H. (2004) *Polizia e Protesta*. Bologna: Il Mulino.

della Porta, D. and Rucht, D. (1995) 'Left-libertarian movements in context. Comparing Italy and West Germany, 1965–1990', in C.J. Jenkins and B. Klandermans (eds) *The Politics of Social Protest. Comparative Perspectives on States and Social Movements*. Minneapolis: University of Minnesota Press, pp. 229–272.

della Porta, D. and Tarrow, S. (2004) *Transnational Protest and Global Activism*. Lanham: Rowman & Littlefield.

della Porta, D., Valiente, C. and Kousis, M. (forthcoming) 'Women and democratisation. The women's movement and their outcomes in Italy, Greece, Portugal, and Spain', in N. Diamantouros, R. Gunther, and H.-J. Puhle (eds) *Democratic Consolidation in Southern Europe*. Washington DC: The John Hopkins University Press.

Delorme, H. (2002) 'Les agriculteurs et les institutions communautaires: du corporatisme agricole au lobbyisme agro-alimentaire', in R. Balme and D. Chabanet (eds), *L'action Collective en Europe*. Paris, Presses de Sciences Po, pp. 313–375.

Diani, M. (2003) 'Networks and social movements: A research program', in M. Diani and D. McAdam (eds) *Social Movements and Networks*. Oxford, New York: Oxford University Press, pp. 299–318.

Diani, M. and McAdam, D. (eds) (2003) *Social Movements and Networks*. New York: Oxford University Press.

Duyvendak, J.-W. (1995) *The Power of Politics. New Social Movements in an Old Polity. France 1965–1989*. Boulder, CO: Westview Press.

Eder, K. and Trenz, H.J. (2003) 'Transnational resonance structures. Searching for the Link between National Governance and European policy-making. The Case of Justice and Home Affairs.' in B. Kohler-Koch (ed.) *Linking EU and National Governance*. Oxford: Oxford University Press, pp. 111–134.

Eggert, N. and Giugni, M. (2006) 'The Global Justice Movement in Switzerland: The heritage of the new social movements', in D. della Porta (ed.) *The Global Justice*

Movement: Cross-national and Transnational Perspectives. Boulder, CO: Paradigm.

Eyerman, R. (1994) *Between Culture and Politics. Intellectuals and Modern Society.* Cambridge: Polity Press.

Flam, H. (1994a) 'Political responses to the antinuclear challenge. Democratic experiences and the use of force', in H. Flam (ed.) *States and Antinuclear Movements.* Edinburgh: Edinburgh University Press, pp. 329–54.

Flam, H. (1994b) 'Political responses to the antinuclear challenge. Standard deliberative and decision-making settings.' in H. Flam (ed.) *States and Antinuclear Movements.* Edinburgh: Edinburgh University Press, pp. 299–328.

Gallie, D. (1989) *Social Inequalities and Class Radicalism in France and Britain.* Cambridge: Cambridge University Press.

Geary, D. (1981) *European Labour Protest 1848–1939.* New York: St Martin's Press.

Gerhards, J. (1993) Westeuropaeische Integration und die Schwierigkeiten der Entstehung einer europaeischen Oeffentlichkeit', *Zeitschrift fuer Soziologie,* 22: 96–110.

Girling, J.L.S. (2004) *Social Movements and Symbolic Power. Radicalism, reform and the Trial of Democracy in France.* Basingstoke: Palgrave MacMillan.

Giugni, M. (1996) 'Federalismo e movimenti sociali', *Rivista Italiana di Scienza Politica,* 26: 147–171.

Giugni, M. and Passy, F. (2002) 'Le champ politique de l'immigration en Europe: opportunités, mobilisations et héritage de l'Etat national', in R. Balme and D. Chabanet (eds) *L'action Collective en Europe.* Paris: Presses de Sciences Po, pp. 433–460.

Goldstein, R.J. (1983) *Political Repression in 19th Century Europe.* London: Croom Helm.

Goldstone, J.A. (2003) 'Introduction. Bridging institutionalized and noninstitutionalized politics', in J.A. Goldstone (ed.) *States, Parties and Social Movements.* New York: Cambridge University Press, pp. 1–25.

Guiraudon, V. (2001) 'Weak weapons of the weak? Transnational mobilization around migration in the European Union', in D. Imig and S. Tarrow (eds) *Contentious Europeans. Protest and Politics in an Emerging Polity.* Lanham: Rowman & Littlefield, pp. 163–183.

Habermas, J. (1981) *Theorie des kommunikativen Handeln.* Frankfurt am Main: Suhrkamp.

Hanagan, M. (1998) 'Social movements. Incorporation, disengagement, and opportunities – a long view,' in M. Giugni, D. McAdam and C. Tilly (eds) *From Contention to Democracy.* Lanham, MD: Rowman & Littlefield, pp. 3–31.

Imig, D. and Tarrow, S. (2001) *Contentious Europeans. Protest and Politics in an Emerging Polity.* Lanham, MD: Rowman & Littlefield.

Jenkins, C.J. (1985) *The Politics of Insurgency. The Farm Worker Movement in the 1960s.* New York: Columbia University Press.

Jiménez M. and Calle, Á. (2006) 'The Global Justice Movement in Spain', in D. della Porta (ed.) *The Global Justice Movement: Cross-national and Transnational Perspectives.* Boulder: Paradigm.

Joppke, C. (1993) *Mobilizing against Nuclear Energy. A Comparison of Germany and the United States.* Berkeley, Los Angeles: University of California Press.

Kitschelt, H. (1985) 'New social movements in West Germany and the United States', *Political Power and Social Theory,* 5: 273–342.

Kitschelt, H. (1986) 'Political opportunity structures and political protest. Anti-nuclear movements in four democracies', *British Journal of Political Science* 16: 57–85.

Klandermans, B., Kriesi, H. and Tarrow, S. (1988) *From Structure to Action. Comparing Social Movement Research across Cultures.* Greenwich, CT: JAI Press.

Koelble, T.A. (1991) *The Left Unraveled: Social Democracy and the New Left Challenge in Britain.* Durham: Duke University Press.

Koopmans, R. (1995) *Democracy from Below. New Social Movements and the Political System in West Germany.* Boulder, CO: Westview Press.

Koopmans, R. (2004) *The Transformation of Political Mobilisation and Communication in European Public Spheres. Integrated Report. Cross-national, Cross-issue, Cross-time.* Report on Work Package 2. Europub, research project.

Koopmans, R. and Statham, P. (1999) 'Ethnic and civic conceptions of nationhood and the differential success of the extreme right in Germany and Italy', in M. Giugni, D. McAdam, and C. Tilly (ed.) *How Movements Matter.* Minneapolis: The University of Minneapolis Press, pp. 225–252.

Koopmans, R. and Statham, P. (2002) *The Transformation of Political Mobilization and Communication in European Public Spheres.* A Research Outline, EUROPU.COM Research Project. Available at: http://europub. wz-berlin.de.

Kriesi, H. (1989) 'The political opportunity structure of the Dutch peace movement', *West European Politics* 12: 295–312.

Kriesi, H. (1995) 'Political opportunity structure of new social movements. Its impact on their mobilization.' in C.J. Jenkins and B. Klandermans (eds) *The Politics of Social Protest. Comparative Perspectives on States and Social Movements*. Minneapolis: University of Minnesota Press, pp. 167–198.

Kriesi, H. (2004) 'Political context and opportunity', in D.A. Snow, S.H. Soule, and H. Kriesi (eds) *The Blackwell Companion to Social Movements*. Oxford: Blackwell, pp. 67–90.

Kriesi, H., Koopmans, R., Duyvendak, J.-W. and Giugni, M. (1995) *New Social Movements in Western Europe*. Minneapolis, London: The University of Minnesota Press/UCL Press.

Lefébure, P. and Lagneau, E. (2002) 'Le moment Volvorde: action protestataire et espace publique européen', in R. Balme and D. Chabanet (eds) *L'action Collective en Europe*. Paris: Presses de Sciences Po, pp. 495–529.

Le Torrec, V., Blanchard, P., Garcia, G. and Patou, C. (2001) *Framing Europe. News Coverage and Legitimacy of the European Union in Five Countries*. Madison: European Community Studies Association.

Lehmbruch, G. (1977) 'Liberal corporatism and party government', *Comparative Political Studies*, 10: 91–126.

McAdam, D. (1982) *Political Process and the Development of Black Insurgency. 1930–1970*. Chicago: University of Chicago Press.

McAdam, D., McCarthy, J.D. and Zald, M.N. (1996) *Comparative Perspectives on Social Movements. Political Opportunities, Mobilizing Structures, and Cultural Framing*. Cambidge, New York: Cambridge University Press.

Maguire, D. (1995) 'Opposition movements and opposition parties. Equal partners or dependent relations in the struggle for power and reform?', in C.J. Jenkins and B. Klandermans (eds). *The Politics of Social Protest. Comparative Perspectives on States and Social Movements*. Minneapolis: University of Minnesota Press.

Marks, G. (1989) *Union in Politics. Britain, Germany and the United States in the Nineteenth and Early Twentieth Century*. Princeton: Princeton University Press.

Marks, G. and McAdam, D. (1999) 'On the relationship of the political opportunities to the form of collective action', in D. della Porta, H. Kriesi, and D. Rucht (eds) *Social Movements in a Globalizing World*. New York: Macmillan, pp. 97–111.

Marshall, T.H. (1976) [1950]. 'Citizenship and social class.' in T.H. Marshall. *Citizenship and Social Class*. London: Pluto Press, pp. 3–51.

Martin, A. and Ross, G. (2001) Trade union organizing at the European Level: The dilemma of borrowed resources', in D. Imig and S. Tarrow (eds) *Contentious Europeans. Protest and Politics in an Emerging Polity*. Lanham: Rowman & Littlefield, pp. 53–76.

Mazey, S. (2002) 'L'Union Européenne et les droits des femmes: de l'européanisation des agendas nationaux à la nationalisation d'un agenda européen?', in R. Balme and D. Chabanet (eds), *L'action Collective en Europe*. Paris, Presses de Sciences Po, pp. 405–432.

Melucci, A. (1982) *L'Invenzione del Presente. Movimenti, Identità, Bisogni Individuali*. Bologna: Il Mulino.

Melucci, A. (1989) Nomads of the Present. Social Movements and Individual Needs in Contemporary Society. London: Hutchinson Radius.

Melucci, A. (1996) *Challenging Codes. Collective Action in the Information Age*. Cambridge, New York: Cambridge University Press.

Neidhardt, F. and Rucht, D. (1993) 'Auf dem Weg in die 'Bewegungsgesellschaft'? Über die Stabilisierbarkeit sozialer Bewegungen', *Soziale Welt*, 44: 305–326.

Nelkin, D. and Pollack, M. (1981) *The Atom Besieged. Extraparliamentary Dissent in France and Germany*. Cambridge, MA: MIT Press.

Neveu, E. (2000) *Sociologie des Mouvements Sociaux*. Paris: La découverte.

Nollert, M. (1995) 'Neocorporatism and Political protest in the Western democracies. A cross-national analysis.' in C.J. Jenkins and B. Klandermans (eds) *The Politics of Social Protest. Comparative Perspectives on States and Social Movements*. Minneapolis: University of Minnesota Press, pp. 138–164.

Offe, C. (1985) 'New social movements. Challenging the boundaries of institutional politics', *Social Research* 52: 817–890.

Peterson, A. (2001) *Contemporary Political Protest. Essays on Political Militancy*. Aldershot: Ashgate.

Pianta, M. and Marchetti, R. (2006) 'The Transnational Dimension of Global Justice Movements', in D. della Porta (ed.) *The*

Global Justice Movements: A Cross National and Transnational Perspective. Boulder Co: Paradigm Publishers.

Piven, F.F. and Cloward, R.A. (1977) *Poor People's Movements*. New York: Pantheon.

Putnam, R.D. (1988) 'Diplomacy and domestic politics: the logic of two-level games', *International Organization*, 42 (3): 427–460.

Reiter, H. (1998) 'Police and public order in Italy, 1944–1948. The case of Florence', in D. della Porta and H. Reiter (eds), *Policing Protest. The Control of Mass Demonstrations in Western Democracies*, Minneapolis: The University of Minnesota Press, pp.43–65.

Reiter, H, Andretta, M., della Porta, D. and Mosca, L. (2006) 'The Global Justice Movement in Italy', in D. della Porta (ed.) *The Global Justice Movement: A Cross-national and Transnational Perspective*. Boulder Co.:Paradigm, Boulder (CO).

Risse, T. (2000) '"Let's Argue!" Communicative Action in International Relations', *International Organization* 54: 1–39.

Risse, T. (2003) 'An emerging European public sphere? Theoretical clarifications and empirical indicators.' in Annual Meeting of the European Union Studies Association (EUSA), Nashville.

Rootes, C.A. (2002) 'The Europeanisation of Environmentalism', in R. Balme and D. Chabanet (eds), *L'action Collective en Europe*. Paris: Presses de Sciences Po, pp. 377–404.

Rootes, C. and Saunders, C. (2006) 'The Global Justice Movement in Britain', in D. della Porta (ed.) *The Global Justice Movement: Cross-national and Transnational Perspectives*. Boulder, CO: Paradigm.

Rucht, D. (1994) *Modernisierung und Soziale Bewegungen. Deutschland, Frankreich und USA im Vergleich*. Frankfurt am Main: Campus.

Rucht, D. (2002) 'The EU as a target of political mobilization: Is there a Europeanisation of conflict', in R. Balme and D. Chabanet (eds), *L'action Collective en Europe*. Paris: Presses de Sciences Po, pp. 163–194.

Rucht, D., Teune, S. and Yang, M. (2006) 'The Global Justice Movement in Germany', in D. della Porta (ed.) *The Global Justice Movement: Cross-national and Transnational Perspectives*. Boulder, CO: Paradigm.

Ruzza, C. (2004) Europe and Civil Society. Manchester: Manchester University Press.

Schmitter, P.C. (1974) 'Still a century of corporatism?' *Review of Politics*, 36: 85–131.

Schmitter, P.C. (1981) 'Interest intermediation and regime governability in contemporary Western Europe and North America.' in S. Berger (ed.) *Organized Interests in Western Europe. Pluralism, Corporatism, and the Transformation of Politics*. Cambridge, New York: Cambridge University Press, pp. 287–327.

Seidendorf, S. (2003) 'Europeanization of national identity discourses? Comparing French and German print media', ECPR Joint Sessions, March 28–April 2, Edinburgh.

Sommier, I. and Combes, H. (2006) 'The Global Justice Movement in France', in D. della Porta (ed.) *The Global Justice Movement: Cross-national and Transnational Perspectives*. Boulder, CO: Paradigm.

Tarrow, S. (1983) *Struggling to Reform. Social Movements and Policy Change during Cycles of Protest*. Ithaca, NY: Cornell University.

Tarrow, S. (1989) *Democracy and Disorder. Protest and Politics in Italy, 1965–1975*. Oxford, New York: Oxford University Press.

Tarrow, S. (1994) *Power in Movement. Social Movements, Collective Action and Politics*. New York, Cambridge: Cambridge University Press.

Tarrow, S. (2005) *The New Transnational Contention*. New York, Cambridge: Cambridge University Press.

Tarrow, S. and McAdam, D. (2004) 'Scale shift in transnational contention', in D. della Porta and S. Tarrow (eds) *Transnational Protest and Global Activism*. Lanham: Rowman & Littlefield, pp. 121–149.

Tilly, C. (1978) *From Mobilization to Revolution*. Reading, MA: Addison-Wesley.

Touraine, A. (1977) *The Self-Production of Society*. Chicago: Chicago University Press.

Touraine, A. (1981) *The Voice and the Eye. An Analysis of Social Movements*. Cambridge: Cambridge University Press.

Touraine, A. (1985) 'An introduction to the study of social movements', *Social Research*, 52: 749–788.

Touraine, A., Wieviorka, M. and Dubet, F. (1987) *The Workers' Movement*. New York: Cambridge University Press.

22

Multiculturalism and Public Culture: A Historical Critique

Nick Stevenson

The idea of the public sphere in the European context has historically been underpinned by a normative concern with human rights, democracy and pluralism. In the shadow of the threat of a twentieth century totalitarian Europe this has been a considerable achievement. However that these publics are currently dominated by the cultural legacies of superiority and race hatred is case enough for continued concern. European publics then are rightly viewed as places of ambivalence given the continued co-existence of democratic pluralism and racist exclusion. These features are, however, inevitably complex and demand forms of understanding that are able to do justice to the complex histories of barbarism, progress and resistance.

As we shall see, central to the development of European cultural identities and ideas of the public has been the notion of 'civilization'. The idea of civilization in the European context is essentially an ambivalent construction. First, ideas of the public sphere require associated cultures of dialogue, discussion and disagreement. This much is central to Europe's democratic heritage. The idea of a 'civil' society depends upon the minimization

of violence and the public use of reason on shared issues of concern. Relatively peaceful and self-reflective zones of civility are central to any relatively emancipated society and have an important place within European history. However, these ideals had to emerge historically and culturally in settings where they were threatened by the colonization of capitalism, nationalism, imperialism and racism. More specifically the threat of totalitarian governments during the twentieth century and imperialist foreign policies risked undermining any sense of plural public space. However, many social movements argued that the public sphere remained overly exclusive in its construction, repressing the voices and interests of the masses in favour of the privileged. The attempt to build more inclusive public spheres has also been the concern of feminism, social democracy, peace movements, civic initiatives and movements more explicitly concerned with multiculturalism and racial justice. Especially since the 1960s there has developed a desire to push liberal societies into recognizing and respecting a more explicitly multicultural range of identities. Here we could argue that the public is 'civilized' the extent to which it is able to accommodate the voice of the Other. Second, the idea of civilization has another history whereby Europeans have sought to impress the cultural standards and preferences of elites on subordinate classes and groups assumed to be barbarous. In this, the politics of the public sphere has built into it a form of symbolic violence whereby cultural hierarchies built upon class, race, gender and other features can become normalized as part of the taken-for-granted rules of public interaction. The struggle for an inclusive public realm is then no longer simply a matter of pluralism but concerns more complex problems of recognition and respect. This arguably makes the struggle for a genuinely multicultural Europe less a matter of historical achievement and more an ongoing social and cultural struggle without end. Finally, the idea of civilization in the European context is used to refer to high culture or more generally intellectual or artistic pursuits. As Francis Mulhern (2000) has argued, the idea of civilization here is connected to the perception of cultural values being under threat or in danger of being diluted. These arguments usually trade upon the distinction between a literary and a mass culture that continues to have a resonance within wider publics despite the impact of postmodernism in the arts and criticism more generally.

THE IDEA OF CULTURE

In 1851 Mathew Arnold, a respected English poet and cultural critic, had been appointed as an inspector of schools and was later to become a passionate advocate of popular forms of education. It is perhaps in this context we might consider his best-known work *Culture and Anarchy* originally published in 1869. Indeed this title might have been called *Culture or Anarchy* for the way in which Arnold opposes the possibility of the cultivation of our best selves through an engagement with the finest works of culture, or the destructive and potentially disorderly cultures of

individual liberty. Culture then is concerned with the perfection of the self and the development of a common humanity. In essence, to concern the self with culture is to be concerned with 'becoming something rather than in having something' (Arnold, 1869/1987: 208). In particular Arnold is keen to defend the value of culture against those who would argue that – unlike the accumulation of wealth or the development of industrialism – it has little worth. For Arnold, those who think that wealth is the best measure of us have little understanding of the spiritual or moral development of the self. For Arnold (1869/1987: 222) culture offers 'increased sweetness, increased light, increased life, increased sympathy'. If culture suggests the possibility of learning and personal transformation, unbridled liberalism simply offers the idea of the free-choosing individual. The market-driven individual is then the best chooser of his or her own personal destiny and interests. Yet the emphasis upon 'an Englishman's right to do what he likes' ends in violence and the domination of commerce (Arnold 1869/1987: 231). If culture offers the idea of perfecting our best selves through the practices of reading, thinking and educating the self, liberalism insists upon our right to be ignorant. What Arnold feared was not only that liberalism's emphasis upon freedom of choice could lead people to reject cultures of education and learning, but by emphasizing individual freedom it masked the dominance of a culture driven by money and technology. The 'men' of culture whom Arnold sought to represent were not themselves the dominant culture but were part of the Romantic tradition seeking to protest against abrasive, mean-spirited capitalism. In short, whereas liberalism looks as though it is democratic it is actually reaffirming the dominant values of greed and instrumentality.

If we move to our own time, many of those seeking to defend a more multicultural public culture are making similar arguments. Charles Taylor (1992) has argued that by making 'culture' a matter of choice simply reaffirms the linguistic, artistic and cultural practices of the dominant. Without the support of the state he fears that 'minority' cultures will either turn inwards or split away, seeking to form their own separate state. This he suggests is an argument for the granting of cultural rights for 'minorities'. It is then notable that after more than a century, Arnold's concerns about the cultural indifference of liberalism are being reinvented in more contemporary discussions. If in Arnold's time liberalism was overly concerned with 'abstract' freedoms, today its excessive concern with freedom and choice inscribe its cultural insensitivity. Liberalism under the guise of neutrality supports a dominant culture which is inadequate to the wider cultural needs of modern publics.

Raymond Williams (1970/1980) comments that the anarchy of Arnold's title directly related to the battle in and over London's Hyde Park. In the 1860s the Reform League had been pressing for the extension of the vote to working-class men. This had culminated in many frustrated protestors on 23 July 1866 gaining entry to Hyde Park, only for the troops to be called out to restore order. 'Culture' was urgently required to civilize the passion of the Hyde Park rioters. Not surprisingly, many have written off Arnold's views on 'culture' as a conservative attempt to quell more passionate forms of rebellion. Yet Williams's essay is careful not simply to tread this particular path. What Williams (1970/1980: 5) recognizes within Arnold is the idea that culture represents something more than an obsession with the economy. However Edward Said (1993) has argued that these debates about culture in the context of a European imperial society should not be reduced to purely national questions of education and class identity. In 1865, the then Govenor of Jamaica ordered the massacre of colonial subjects which caused considerable debate amongst notable public figures like Arnold and John Ruskin, who defended the action, and John Stuart Mill, who had opposed. The preservation of 'culture' then should also be seen in a colonial context where 'the best' of our cultural traditions needs to be defended against the barbarians both at home and abroad.

Despite the complexities of Arnold's views on culture he remains tied to a European imperialist tradition where his culture was indeed the only culture. If Arnold sought to defend a view of the cultural which was principally concerned with questions of learning and educated debate he did so in such a way that inscribed the domination of the educated middle and upper classes of the metropolitan centre. Arnold's ideas of civilization would need to be connected to nineteeth-century imperialism and racialized thinking that sought to quell the barbarism of the working-classes as well as the natives (Young, 1995). These features, as we shall see, continue to have implications for the ways in which we connect culture to European publics in a global context.

CULTURES OF THE PUBLIC

Questions of culture matter because they help to define the very process of learning and self-transformation within contemporary society. Arnold then remains worth reading through a defence of the way that 'culture' can become the site of self-reflection and critique. As Martin Ryle and Kate Soper (2002) have reminded us, an idea of the self-reflective subject capable of learning, development and autonomy is part of the legacy that can be traced – albeit problematically – back to Arnold's initial reflections. This tradition not only seeks to question the increasing dominance of market-place forms of rationality, but also potentially helps us link issues of culture to the public sphere.

Habermas (1989) famously traces the historical emergence of a critical domain that upholds the principle of open public discussion on matters of universal concern. In seventeenth- and eighteenth-century Europe there emerged coffee houses and salons where male members of the bourgeoisie met to discuss works of literature. The initial development of the public sphere in the European setting was concerned with specifically locally organized forums for discussion that would later include museums, meeting houses, theatres and lecture halls. The relatively disorganized character of these debates were soon to turn to matters of politics and current affairs. Indeed Habermas continues to claim that despite the exclusive character of these conversations they continue to have a normative relevance. Yet the tragedy of the bourgeois public sphere was that the very social forces that brought it into being would eventually lead to its decline and destruction. The instituted dialogue of the salons and coffee houses would give way as communication became increasingly organized through large commercial concerns. The progressive institutional elimination of communicative individuals coming into conversation in the public sphere emphasized an increasing separation between public and private life. From around the 1870s the public sphere was increasingly replaced by a commercial culture consumed in private, requiring no further debate or discussion.

This process accelerated during the twentieth century as unlike the print culture of the discursive bourgeois salons, much of the new media (television, film and radio) disallowed the possibility of talking back and taking part. Along with the 'privatization' of culture, Habermas adds, there has also been a corresponding trivialization of cultural products in order to gain a larger share of the market. The idea of citizens coming together to freely discuss and deliberate issues of common concern is central to the self-identity of societies that wish to consider themselves democratic. The idea of the public sphere, then, is normative while also having an active purchase upon reality. Indeed it is hard to see how any critical theory more generally can live without the idea of public space that is capable of raising critical questions, fostering debate among its citizens and challenging previously held views and positions. Public space then remains educative space in the broadest possible sense.

At this point in the argument, Habermas's idea of the kinds of public sphere that developed within Europe is in need of some revision.

Geoff Eley (1992) has argued that Habermas largely ignores the existence of more plebian public spheres that became connected to the rise of the labour movement in the nineteenth and twentieth centuries. In other words, Habermas neglects the idea that there might be competing and contested versions of the public. The radical historian E.P. Thompson (1965) describes how a variety of cultural influences from Thomas Paine to John Bunyan and from religion to the idea of village rights helped construct a radical working-class culture in England during the 1830s. Indeed Thompson describes the subaltern public sphere constructed by this movement as the 'most distinguished popular culture England has known' (Thompson, 1965: 914). Further, if the idea of a liberal public sphere was held in distinction to more submerged working-class public spheres it was also built upon the idea of 'public man'. While Habermas is aware that the early public sphere excluded women, he neglects to analyse the ways in which it was constituted through ideas of masculinity and femininity. Whereas the speech of rational, disinterested masculinity was welcome, competing languages of play, pleasure and artifice were deemed as feminine and relegated to the private sphere. Women then were seen as the Other to a male-dominated world of power, property and politics. In other words, Habermas fails to consider the ways in which public domains can be constituted through the marginalization of groups who were not male and propertied (Fraser, 1997).

Despite the need to talk of competing publics and these various exclusions it remains the case that ideas of a critical public sphere are as important as ever. The idea of the public remains key as a site of cultural exchange and discussion. Without a shared understanding of the value of critical forms of debate and reflection there would be no possibility of citizens learning through common forms of debate and discussion. Yet Habermas's original representation of the public is overly constructed through a narrative of rise and fall, thereby remaining trapped in a similar form of cultural pessimism to that of the early Frankfurt school. The tale of the public sphere is the progressive cancelling of mostly elite conversations for the eventual triumph of mass culture. Yet if the early Frankfurt school looks to modernist art for a utopian critique of instrumental reason, Habermas discovers within bourgeois salon society the possibility of a more democratic and public project. While Habermas mostly steers clear of high cultural pessimism he remains trapped within the shortcomings of the mass culture debate. Further, his neglect of more aesthetic concerns tends to mean that the public sphere becomes constructed in overly 'rationalistic' terms. Habermas's original narrative lacks a more subtle appreciation of how different cultural institutions and cultural forms (like literature, education, broadcasting, popular culture and art) help constitute overlapping ideas of the public. If the public sphere is valued through its ability to open up critical questions, offer new experiences or challenging works of art and culture, then Habermas's idea of it seems locked into a rational conversation where we calmly exchange reasons.

Here I continue to think that Raymond Williams's ideas concerning the historical development of a learning and communicating society continues to have a more contemporary resonance. First, Williams's account of the development of public spaces is alive to processes of contestation and aesthetics largely overlooked by Habermas. For example, Williams (1962) notes that cultural conservatives during his own time continued to argue that the state should preserve high culture both against democratic tendencies and the market. Williams noted that such features had a great deal in common with the commercial culture that it was meant to oppose. The strict separation between an elite high culture and the more populist concerns of the market divides 'our culture into separate areas with no bridges between them' (Williams 1962: 108).

Further, like Habermas, Williams was concerned about what happens to cultural

forms once they become overly commodified. There is an important distinction to be made between different forms of cultural production that aim to educate, inform and provoke and those that simply aim to make money. If Habermas (1982) expresses this as the functional separation between democracy and capitalism, Williams is more explicitly concerned to struggle for a culturally complex society where citizens feel empowered to become cultural producers. Williams then more explicitly asks the question as to what kinds of institutions would be required to create the possibility of a democratic public culture. More explicitly he argues for an educative and above all publicly informed culture that can only be sustained through the eventual abolition of capitalism. Williams reasoned that capitalism could never allow the learning and creative potential of all of its citizens to flourish as it requires both hierarchy, commodification and educational failure. In this sense Williams passionately argued that the labour movement should not settle for the undoubted historical achievements of social democracy, but should seek to create a genuinely democratic culture in common.

For Williams (1989) a culture in common had several aspects, but overall it was an instituted culture of dialogue rather than agreement. To be able to talk of a culture in common meant rejecting the choice between either atomized privatization or cultural communalism. However it did mean the development of democratic public spaces of engagement built upon a shared education system that had broken with the class bound logic of the past. The *common* element of Williams's argument concerns the ability of ordinary people – not just paid professionals – to contribute, criticize and reinterpret aspects of their culture. Within this process the meanings of 'high' or indeed 'popular' culture are not fixed in stone but require open criticism by members of the community. Notably, Williams's work also provides a defence of the ability of literature and drama to ask critical questions of both historical and more contemporary societies. In this respect, complex works of art and criticism did not belong to the dominant class, but could be potentially commented on by everyone. A culture in common requires the provision of institutions that transmit the knowledge, skills and resources that allow for full participation. This was no longer the Arnoldian project of simply transmitting the best works of civilization, but of enabling citizens to realize their critical potential.

The guiding aspect of a democratic culture in common is its ability to be able to promote dialogue across a number of cultural divides and enclaves while developing a common capacity to become a cultural producer and critic. Similarly Bhikhu Parekh (2000) argues that a multicultural society needs a shared common culture fashioned out of diversity. In a multicultural society diverse cultures constantly encounter one another and change owing to the presence of the other. Unless we are content to live in a society of cultural apartheid and fragmentation then institutional conditions must be created to foster intercultural dialogue. While a 'common culture' cannot be engineered, the opportunities for a common dialogue need to be politically created. Just as Williams argued that the 'national culture' needs to be extended and criticized by working-class voices so Parekh argues that similar privileges need to be extended to 'minorities'. Within this process both Williams and Parekh highlight the centrality of cultural and educational institutions. They are both critical of monocultural institutions which aim to impose a collective conformist culture. Yet the insistence on multiculturalism necessarily moves the analysis on from the culturally 'bounded' national society and cultural nationalism that is assumed by much of Williams's writing. For Parekh, any attempt to introduce more multicultural forms of public space would necessitate a sustained critique of Eurocentrism. This would include the need to interrogate ideologies of 'Western supremacy' that can be detected in both high as well as more popular forms of culture (Said, 1993).

EUROPEAN COLONIAL CULTURES

The main problem with the proceeding argument is the nationalist assumption that notions of the public are constituted by exclusively national public spaces. It presents an image of publics emerging inside of exclusively national borders. Such a view is of course not without a certain resonance; however, it is blind to the ways in which cultures and publics can be said to cross over borders. Indeed this 'internal' account of European histories and cultures serves to prevent any recognition or memory of European imperialism and colonialism. Racism then is not simply incidental to the development of European ideas about culture and the public but lies at its heart. Here the argument is that such features have long and complex histories, including the encounter between Europeans and non-Europeans. The European expansion into the Americas during the fifteenth century not only involved the destruction and segregation of Native Americans but the deportation of enslaved Africans. This established the basis of the Atlantic economy and the imperial system that was built upon both economic exploitation and the dehumanization of non-Europeans. European modernity, then, is formed through the crossing of colonialism and capitalism. For Hannah Arendt (1986) imperial domination required both the racialized understandings of inferior peoples as well as bureaucratic forms of administration. This resulted in the European domination of the globe which by 1914 ruled over approximately half the land and a third of its people (West, 1993).

The institution of European rule helped to promote ideologies and practices that were built upon the assumed inferiority of non-Europeans. According to Albert Memmi (2003) the European colonists were initially lured by stories of privilege and adventure. This allowed even the most 'mediocre' citizens to indulge in fantasies of superiority and authority that would have been unavailable back home. Hence within the European imperial project the word 'race', like that of 'culture', was concerned with distinguishing between the primitive and the civilized. However what these racialized and imperial-driven projections continually fail to appreciate is that what passes for European culture is more often than not a product of cultural inter-mixing and hybridity. Pieterse (1999) argues that the contact between Christendom and Islam was not only about the Crusades but involved the adoption of a number of Turkish artefacts by Europeans including coffee, honey and certain plants including the tulip. Yet if Europe can to some extent be described as a place of learning and interaction prior to 1800, after this time different patterns built upon domination and subordination begin to emerge.

Before the 1850s the racialized dominance of the Europeans was based upon the ideology of scientific racism. This depended upon the idea that all races could be traced back to Adam in the Old Testament. In this respect, the extent to which they were corrupted depended upon how far they had strayed from their 'original' source. Races were assumed to have been perverted by dwelling in different climates. The competing idea was that races did not so much have a singular source but are classifiable and have plural places of origin and creation. These features were eventually to give way to evolutionary theory that more explicitly sought to rank races through explicit forms of measurement. However ideologies of European dominance would take a crucial turn in 1851 with the World Exhibition at Crystal Palace in London. According to Anne McClintock (1995) this event converted imperialism into a commodified spectacle. The exhibition 'offered the illusion of marshalling all of the globe's cultures into a single, visual pedigree of world time' (McClintock 1995: 58). It offered the idea of progress and technological superiority to a mass audience for the first time. The superiority of European civilization was no longer simply a matter for scientific measurement but could be purchased for immediate consumption. In other words, unlike scientific racism which had largely been confined

to the literate classes, the development of commodity racism offered the masses a sense of national and European superiority to the popular classes. The advertising of consumer items as 'imperial kitsch' served to domesticate the accomplishments of empire amongst a broader public. Despite the ending of direct forms of European colonial control in the Third World through the impact of nationalist struggles for decolonization, there is a widespread concern that the legacies of European dominance continue to live on through the advent of contemporary racism. Here the cultural and political task suggested by this history is poorly captured by liberal ideas of tolerence and rational exchange in the public sphere, but requires the decolonization of the imagination (Thiong'o, 1986).

Similar to imperialism, totalitarian thought and practice works with a model of substandard humanity that needs to be eliminated. Totalitarian language depends upon the idea of perfectable humanity and dehumanized others who stand in the way of progress. As the European histories of facism and communism demonstrate, there is no place for otherness in a society understood through metaphors of war and conquest. In this respect, totalitarianism is the opposite of democracy or multiculturalism as the world becomes divided between the 'us' who must prevail and the 'them' who are to be slaughtered (Todorov, 2003). The rise of Nazism and Stalinism lead to the deaths of millions of people (many of whom belonged to 'minority' groups such as Jews, Gypsies and homosexuals) which in turn secured the definition of crimes against humanity found in the Nuremberg Charter. Indeed for Ulrich Beck (2006) it is the legacy of the Holocaust that has led Europeans to seek to institutionalize cosmopolitanism through the introduction of human rights and law beyond the national polity. Yet the cultural legacies of venomous nationalism and racism remain a disturbing feature of European public spheres. To oppose ideas of national cultural purity seemingly requires more concerted forms of deconstruction that includes legal forms of protection as well as the questioning of stereotypes and formulaic thinking.

EUROPEAN PUBLIC CULTURE

The idea of the public is historically mediated by the prevailing culture and politics of the time. The struggle for a more 'inclusive' public realm in the European setting is intimately bound up during the nineteenth and twentieth century with the struggle for socialism. The critical idea here was that a public sphere and culture dominated by capitalism would both promote competitive forms of individualism and exclude the voices and perspectives of working-class people. Notably many liberals during the nineteenth century had been hostile to the extension of the franchise for the fear that the working classes would lack the education to understand the workings of liberal democracy. The fear here is that the newly enfranchised working-class would use the power of the ballot box against the bourgeoisie (Bobbio, 1979). Further, the struggle for socialism also sought to change the ethos of the public sphere by building a society based upon cooperation rather than individualized competition. The development of Left political parties across Europe after 1850 meant an enhanced questioning of a society built upon the power of private property and the inequalities of social class (Eley 2002; Sassoon, 1996). These struggles sought to question the idea as to how a genuinely inclusive public realm could be achieved in a class-based society. This was a time when the politics of class rather than gender, race, sexuality or age was the main public concern. Notably such features all too rarely become connected to the attempt to create more cosmopolitan, less nationally orientated public spaces.

The struggle for democratic socialism spurned two competing traditions. The first sought to expand democracy, establish social rights through the setting up of national welfare states while seeking to regulate the labour market. The other was more revolutionary in intention with a vanguard acting on behalf of the popular masses. Initially, however, these traditions converged through their attempts to defeat capitalism. Yet the impact of the First World War, the revolution in Russia and the rise of nationalist and fascist movements across Europe would break up these shared goals. The split between reformist social democratic and communist parties in Europe and the rise of the far right would polarize in Europe's public sphere during the interwar years. The historical tragedy of the socialist traditions and movements were that they were unable to offer an alternative to the nationalism and imperialism of the 1914–1918 war.

The idea of a democratic Europe based upon nation states after the catastrophe of the First World War led to the break up of multiethnic empires and thereby, created national minorities. This partially helped create the idea of ethnically pure nation-states despite the signing of minority rights treaties by Poland, Hungry and Romania. That these treaties were imposed upon new states was a cause of considerable resentment given that Europe's colonial empires refused to grant the colonized equal rights (Mazower, 1998).

From the end of the Second World War until the beginning of the 1970s national social democratic politics became dominant. Western European societies developed public cultures built upon attempts to distribute wealth fairly, full employment, the empowerment of trade unions and the development of the social rights of the welfare state. These features had a tremendous impact upon the character of the public sphere. Gerassimos Moschonas (2002: 28) comments that the major achievement of postwar social democracy was the establishment of working-class people as 'a central political–social actor of modernity'. During this period social democratic parties helped establish a 'plebian public sphere' thereby establishing a foothold in the 'official public sphere' for many people outside the dominant classes. Despite the decline in working-class membership of social democratic parties during the 1950s and 1960s, such parties helped create the conditions for a decent life for ordinary people until the early 1970s. However if Europe was divided between facism and democracy in the early part of the century this became replaced in the postwar period by the logics of the Cold War. The divisions of the Cold War meant not only a dividing line between capitalism and state socialism but also that the democratic forces within civil society were constantly curtailed. In the Eastern Europe any sense of an emergence of a relatively independent civil society was closely monitored by the state whereas in the West socialists and peace activists were often seen as agents of communism in disguise. This polarized logic would only become widely contested due to the development of the peace movement in the West and civic initiatives like Charter 77 in the East during the 1980s (Kaldor, 1991).

The culture of social democracy itself was dependent upon a progressive alliance between the middle and the working classes. Central here was an idea of self and collective improvement. The idea of the welfare state was built upon ideas of collective solidarity and notions of moral 'advance' through education, welfare and the eradication of poverty.

The British cultural critic Richard Hoggart's (1958) *Uses of Literacy* is a key cultural work of this period. Notably, Francis Mulhern (2000) would later describe Hoggart as the British labour movement's Mathew Arnold. Hoggart's classic text tells an often-painful story of a man born into the working-class culture of 'us' and 'them' before becoming a lecturer in English literature. The autobiographical tone of this work tells not only of an erosion of working-class culture by American commercialism, but also a story of earnest self-improvement and the desire to become educated. Throughout Hoggart's life he sought to defend liberal public institutions such as the BBC, comprehensive education and the Arts Council. Notably however Hoggart has been criticized by many for trying to separate 'good' culture from 'bad' culture without appreciating the ways in which this could exclude other cultural experiences. In particular, many critics such as Carolyn Steedman (1986) and Dick Hebdige (1979) have criticized both Hoggart's maleness and his inability to appreciate the cultural difference evident within postwar working-class life.

The 'progressive' way in which social democracy sought to order public life was to become increasingly open to question. Many who wrote enthusiastically about the emergence of youth cultures in postwar society began to investigate how cultures were structured by different relations of power. In this process, dominant cultures, and here we would have to include the culture of self-improvement that came along with social democracy, sought to represent themselves as 'the culture'. The affluent society during of the late 1950s and 1960s developed cultural styles through music and leisure that sought to transform the public sphere. These emergent public spheres from below, through different subcultures, could be seen as collective attempts to 'win space for the young' (Clarke *et al.*, 1976: 45). The invention of specifically youth cultures unsettled the cultural supremacy of the dominant culture of deference, an industrious work ethic and emotional restraint; and they are poorly understood through the rubric of Americanization so beloved of cultural critics at the time.

However, the stylistic youth cultures of this period can be said to cut a number of ways. First, they helped to create relatively autonomous public spheres where young people could explore issues related to identity and more specifically pose reflexive cultural questions such as, 'What counts as normal?' However, they also simultaneously promoted a culture of consumer-based permissiveness, hedonism and consumption rather than thrift that capitalism would find so central to its reinvigoration during the 1970s and 1980s. The experimentation in lifestyles in the 1960s not only opened up a number of questions related to youth identity, but also for women and ethnic minorities. The political development of feminism and black politics was communicated to mass populations not simply through organized meetings but through a genuinely mass media. It is through the inter-action of new social movements and cultural forms that feminism, anticolonial struggle and lifestyle revolts more generally expanded the literacy of the public realm.

Further, it is also notable that despite the emancipatory achievements of social democ-racy, few intellectuals connected to the labour movement managed to link the struggle for justice at home to that within the colonies. Perhaps most evident amongst those who resisted this general intellectual trend are George Orwell and Jean Paul Sartre. Despite Orwell's well-documented cultural nationalism, his travellings and reflections also turned him into a critic of the British Empire. For instance, Orwell (1939/1970) was a stern critic of the argument that the Second World War could be simply represented as conflict between democracy and facism thereby forgetting the continued existence of the British and French empires. On the other hand, Jean Paul Sartre's (2006) critique of French colonialism and public support of the FLN's violent campaign to end French colonial rule in Algeria similarly sought to articulate a sense of public respon-sibility in an age of violence and war. The voices of Orwell and Sartre further remind us that any consideration of European publics during the heyday of social democracy also needs to concern itself with the question of borders in respect of where Europe in an age of colonial domination could be said to begin and end.

CRITICAL MULTICULTURALISM AND THE PUBLIC

If the 1960s had witnessed a rethinking of the relation between culture and the public, it had initially done so through an idea of the possibilities of creating a more democratic public realm. The elitism of the traditional art world came under question as the impact of increasingly diverse forms of popular culture

sought to unsettle established ways of valuing culture. Notably the 1960s saw the emergence of more subaltern public spheres amongst the black community through public forms of political protest against racism, but also through alternative mediums such as music. Indeed Paul Gilroy (1996) argues that the culture and society tradition represented by figures such as Hoggart and Williams sys-tematically marginalized any discussion of 'race' in their construction of the relationship between culture and the public. Here, Gilroy explicitly seeks to criticize the way that nationalism, class and social democracy have determined the contours of the debate. Any attempt to appreciate the multicultural char-acter of the public would mean repositioning the nation state in a broader set of coordinates that included a discussion of both colonialism and the postcolonial world that had been defined by the Cold War. In this respect, Edward Said (1993) has insisted that if national publics have largely sought to insist upon their own identities then new initiatives are required to look at the ways in which human identities are a far more hybrid achieve-ment than most national institutions allow.

For Gilroy, many ethnic minorities have created subaltern cultural public spheres through explicitly commercial forms of musi-cal expression. The circulation of music amongst the black community has provided a critical commentary on questions of justice and democracy for blacks living in Europe, North America and the Caribbean. These aes-thetic forms operate as global publics providing a sense of interconnection for black peoples across the planet. Here we should also add that the globalization of musical genres such as rap and hip hop have been reinvented within the Paris suburbs to give voice to the frustrations of predominately poor white and French Arab communities. Much of this music, like that of their black American counterparts, acts as a critique of a world of violence, pov-erty and hopelessness (Prevos, 1996). It was widely reported during the rioting in France during 2005 that hip hop had played a key role in affirming a sense of identity for the

French underclass. These examples suggest that if we are to consider the construction of educative public spheres under modern conditions we need to be able to move creatively across a number of national, cultural and commercial borders.

Similarly, Europe's Muslim population has discovered through the practices of culture a similar sense of diasporic interconnection. It is estimated that there are currently 15 million Muslims living within Europe. Despite the challenge of fundamentalism we must be careful not to 'essentialize' the different communities and traditions represented by Muslims in Europe. Bassam Tibi (2002) argues that European Muslims are largely constituted through three main groups: Turkish and Kurdish Muslims mostly settled in Germany; Maghrebis resident within France; and South Asians mainly found within Britain. However, in terms of the relations with the 'official' nationally constituted public sphere Soysal (2000) notes that Muslims are increasingly likely to pursue their claims to recognition through discourses of human rights. Despite the continued power and authority of national forms of citizenship Muslims are most likely to mobilize their claims for recognition through a universalistic language. Here the right to have certain cultural practices recognized within public institutions (such as dress or the provision of schools) is located through a defence of personal integrity. Human rights then are interpreted as rights to personhood and as the 'natural' right of individuals to pursue their own culture. It is for Muslim communities, then, that the language of rights (rather than say, religious duty) that has linked them to a wider sense of the public sphere.

Despite these findings it remains the case that some liberal Muslim scholars have been pressing the need for European Muslims to develop a wider European civic identity. Tariq Ramadan (1999) argues against Muslim fundamentalists who suggest that European constitutional democracy is intrinsically anti-Muslim. However Europe needs to go much further in extending basic forms of respect and recognition to Muslim communities, while Muslims themselves should be encouraged to develop more civic political forums. This would imply a Muslim identity that neither retreated into the certitude of fundamentalism, but sought to develop more intercultural forms of dialogue. The desire here is to build an educative public sphere through the interrogation of difference. However, as Roshi Naidoo (2006) has argued, the need to attend to negotiation of difference should not disregard questions of sameness. A public culture that only approached issues of ethnic identity through difference would also need to be open to what we need for common forms of life. Racism not only works by denying critical space for the Other, but also by denying that we share a number of needs necessary for a dignified life.

An appreciation of the extent to which public spheres under contemporary conditions have both been pluralized and globalized remains central to our argument. Despite the undoubted importance of more diasporic and transnational forms of identity and politics the nation-state continues to be powerful as a place for the organization of identities and publics. While some overstate the power of the nation at this level it remains the case that its dominance of the public through the organization of education, media and other cultural systems continues to frame much of what passes as politics in the context of everyday life (Shore, 2004). These features are especially evident in the way that national cultures have sought to impose loyalty and citizenship tests upon immigrant communities (Kofman, 2005).

Much of the important cultural work done by multiculturalism has sought to unsettle and ask disturbing questions about the construction of identity at the national level. It is specifically national memories, habits and customs as well as the wider language of civilizations that has been multiculturalism's main preoccupation (Hall, 2000). Despite the widespread recognition of the European cultural achievement of liberal freedoms such as religious tolerance and the freedom of speech, neither have necessarily ensured the construction of public spheres built through difference rather than homogeneity. Europe's imagined national communities, especially since the 1960s, have become increasingly challenged by 'minority cultures' pressing for cultural rights of recognition. This has included the demand to move within public cultures that have banished stereotypical images, that recognizes a diversity of cultural forms of production in respect of identity, and allows for people to experience their identities as fluid and overlapping. Europe's nationally constituted public spheres have had to increasingly encounter the demand that difference and sameness should be constantly renegotiated. Despite the impact of identity politics in European societies after the 1960s this should not be allowed to cancel the claim that much of this cultural struggle is about the way that we view history.

The powerful nostalgic appeal of a 'pure' white past as opposed to the confusions of the multicultural present undoubtedly seeks to banish memories of colonialism (Gilroy, 2004). Further as Omer Bartov (2000) has argued, both Germany and France sought to adapt ideas of victimhood as a way of remembering their shared collective suffering as a result of two world wars. Such self-understandings however have the function of displacing their mutual (if not equal) responsibility for the annihilation of the Jews. The organized mass killing of Jews was made possible by ideologies that polarized the world between good and evil and friend and enemy. The often neglected writing of Franz Fanon (2001) serves to remind Europeans that Nazism was actually an attempt to subject fellow Europeans to similar forms of barbaric violence to that which had existed (and continued to exist) in respect of Europe's colonial adventures. Indeed Europeans have had trouble facing the horror of the Holocaust with the more self-critical 'new left' narratives only beginning to be written during the 1960s (Levy and Sznaider, 2002). It is notable that facing the barbarism of Europe's own past is often displaced behind a more pleasing self-image of European values and achievement. Indeed if, as Fanon (2001) suggests, that there is a connection between the histories of colonialism and fascism, then Europe's continued tolerance of public cultures of racism is deeply troubling. The rise of right-wing anti-immigration and anti-asylum parties along with a nationalist revival that demands the undivided loyalty of all of its subjects will be the focus of much public controversy for years to come. Within this context the danger is that Europeaness will continue to be defined in overtly exclusive terms. Such features can be discerned in the resistance to accept Turkey into the European Union, the construction of a fortress Europe in relation to the Global South and the continuing unblemished rhetoric of European civilized values (Hansen, 2004). Here the struggle for more multicultural futures needs to become attentive to the ways in which collective memory can be sterilized.

EUROPEAN COSMOPOLITAN PUBLICS

The idea of the public depends upon a politics of contestation and languages and practices that aim to educate and engage modern citizens. Along with the decline of social democracy and the triumph of neoliberalism has come the erosion of the left/right divide. The displacement of the language of progressive development that accompanied the rise of European social democracy has lead many to abandon the idea of culture as being an educative project. If the language of the market still prefers to reduce education to the language of strategic advantage and market opportunity and to treat ideas of the public as the place of choice then more critical notions of the public sphere should insist upon the role of publics as places of potential learning and self-criticism. Notions of the public then hold out the possibility of us becoming critical citizens and of building a more informed and educated curiosity about the shared worlds within which we move.

In this context Habermas's (1994) notion of constitutional patriotism has been seen by many as holding out the possibility of building upon Europe's democratic rather than colonial heritage. Here collective loyalty is consolidated within a commitment to the language of citizen's rights and responsibilities rather than the ethnos of national identities. Similarly Craig Calhoun (2001) argues that rather than engaging in the languages of civilization such a model aims to build a shared sense of European solidarity through public forms of communication. European identity then is constituted through overlapping and multiple forms of dialogue and identification. However in Habermas's agnostic view of identity he fails to answer the case that multiculturalism makes in terms of the public sphere being constituted through languages of power. The question then becomes whether some citizens are deserving of special forms of protection through access to cultural rights, or whether such a move would simply reify the expression of identity and encourage the developments of cultural enclaves rather like the still-powerful nationalisms.

Habermas's (2003) work aims to give the European project a sense of utopia and unfulfilled destiny after the decline of communism. If the Marxist dream for Europe was of a world built upon the educated and emancipated labour of workers then a cosmopolitan Europe will be built through the constraint of nationalism and capitalism so that we are able to build public spaces built on the principles of pluralism, democracy and social solidarity beyond the nation state. Like Marx, Habermas seeks to imagine a European society that has moved beyond nationalist hatred. For Habermas without the careful construction of a federal European state the idea of Europe is likely to be dominated by a neoliberal race to the bottom, racist border controls and nationalist forms of regression. In this respect, the European Union's ability to secure an institutional basis for human rights and democracy announces the beginning of Europe's progressive project and not its end point.

The European Union itself has sought to institute a transnational public sphere in order to foster a sense of shared identification among its citizens. These efforts have included educational projects, cultural and artistic events (including the European City of Culture) and communications policies in addition to other initiatives. The main problem here is that despite the impact of globalization and the fragmentation of identity much public conversation remains organized through specifically national cultures. Despite these drawbacks, both Habermas and the European Union have consistently argued for a composite sense of identity that does not necessarily compete with national identity, but recognizes the possibility of having both local and global identities. The aim here being to both integrate national identities into an inclusive framework and thereby potentially domesticating nationalist hostility. In more cultural terms the European Union has funded a number of educational projects that have aimed to facilitate the teaching of European languages, exchange programmes such as Erasmus and Socrates and developed the idea of the European City of Culture to promote an inclusive European cultural identity. It is widely felt within the European Union that unless the idea of Europe is able to mobilize an affective identity among European citizens then the European Parliament will be unable to legitimate itself as a political forum.

Ulrich Beck's (2006) idea of cosmopolitan Europe has marked similarities to that of Habermas in his argument that Europe is being cosmopolitanized from the inside. What then becomes distinctive about the cosmopolitan nature of modern European public spheres is an increasing awareness of their own internal complexity and that they can no longer assume the national homogeneity of the past. A cosmopolitan Europe becomes constructed through a struggle to confront the traditions that stem from aggressive nationalism, genocide and colonialism. Yet the reflexive project of a Europe of self-criticism is threatened by the continuation of nationalism. This is the idea that democracy could become recentred within the nation state at some later point. Here, Beck agrees with Habermas that such a project is wholly unrealistic in a world being reconstituted through the global flows of money, knowledge and people.

Such views however are only partially correct. What is more to the point is how European public cultures can become a place of European learning. Here it seems to me that Habermas and Beck have an overly enhanced faith in the ability of Europe's liberal traditions to contradict the cultural hierarchies that remain in evidence within European public spheres. Undoubtedly there have been considerable advances in tackling some of the most overt forms of racism evident in public cultures. Further collective memories of fascistic masculine warrior values that sought to dominate Europe partially explain widespread resistance to the 'war on terror' pursued by the US. However the hysterical reaction to asylum seekers, continued racist violence and hostility against so-called 'political correctness' suggests that liberalism can actually co-exist with the continuation of racism. The critical question then is not about the contradictions within Europe but about the ability of European societies to instigate self-critical cultures of public debate and reflection. Despite the optimistic sounding rhetoric of cosmopolitan Europe the divisive languages of a Europe torn apart by a 'clash of civilization' has served to argue that multiculturalism in all its variety as a project is finished. The idea of tolerant European societies currently besieged by a fundamentalist Islam, illegal asylum seekers and economic migrants has sought to inform popular understandings. The rise of right-wing anti-immigration political parties across a resurgent nationalist Europe should be reason enough to halt a European self-congratulatory language that prefers to perceive some realities rather than others. For a genuinely grassroots cosmopolitan Europe to emerge it will require a number of critical cultural initiatives that cut across civil society, popular culture, education and national borders. Such features would also need to include an understanding of how a neoliberal Europe through the promotion of economic inequality and uncertainty can itself be connected to a politics of fear and concerns about the alienness of the Other.

If the idea of Europe is indeed to provide an alternative cultural and political space to the world's only superpower then given its downsizing of social democracy and the return of some of the barbaric languages of the past it would seem to have some way to go in this process. As George Steiner (1965/1984: 232) put it some time ago the idea of the cosmopolitan is to 'show that whereas trees have roots, men have legs and are each other's guests'. The Other then can never finally be dispelled from our midst but forms part of our common collective multicultural and European futures. However if the Other is to find a place within a hospitable European home it will only do so in the context of a wider politics of solidarity and dialogue. If the European crimes of nationalist aggression, genocide and colonialism teach us anything it is that when citizens are indifferent to the practice of educated dialogue and the fate of the Other then violence and hatred are likely to threaten to take hold. Europe needs to be sceptical of the languages of civilization given their entanglements with the racialized politics of the past. Instead Europeans might learn to consider its project as 'the interpreter of the world' (Balibar, 2004: 235). Here Europeanness becomes constituted through the ways in which ideas of culture and the public connect through the ability to move between different lanaguages while seeking to convert social anatagonism into dialogue. These features require a European-wide 'civilized' cultural politics that simultaneously connect to plural publics.

REFERENCES

Arnold, M. (1869/1987) 'Culture and anarchy' in P.J. Keating (ed.) *Matthew Arnold: Selected Prose*. London: Penguin, pp. 202–300.

Arendt, H. (1986) *The Origins of Totalitarianism*. London: Andre Deutsch.

Balibar, E. (2004) *We, The People of Europe? Reflections on Transnational Citizenship*. Princeton and Oxford: Princeton University Press.

Bartov, O (2000) *Mirrors of Destruction*. Oxford: Oxford University Press.

Beck, U. (2006) *Cosmopolitan Vision*. Cambridge: Polity Press.

Bobbio, N. (1979) *Liberalism and Democracy*. London: Verso.

Calhoun, C. (2001) 'Europe divided: politics, ethics, religion' in L.-E. Cederman (ed.) *Constructing Europe's Identity: The External Dimension*. London: Lynne Reinner Publishers.

Clarke, J. Hall, S. Jefferson, T. and Roberts, B. (1976) Subcultures, cultures and class', in *Resistance Through Rituals: Youth Subcultures in Post-War Britain*. London: Hutchinson.

Eley, G. (1992) 'Nation, publics and political cultures: placing Habermas in the nineteenth century', in G. Eley (ed.) *Habermas and the Public Sphere*. Cambridge, MA: MIT Press, pp. 289–339.

Eley, G. (2002) *Forging Democracy: The History of the Left in Europe 1850–2000*. Oxford: Oxford University Press.

Fanon, F. (2001) *The Wretched of the Earth*. London: Penguin.

Fraser, N. (1997) *Justice Interruptus*. London: Routledge.

Gilroy, P. (1996) 'British cultural studies and the pitfalls of identity' in H.A. Baker Jr. M. Diawara, and R.H. Lindeborg (eds) *Black British Cultural Studies: A Reader*. Chicago and London: University of Chicago Press, pp. 223–246.

Gilroy, P. (2004) *After Empire: Melancholia Or Convivial Culture*. London, Routledge.

Habermas, J. (1982) *The Theory of Communicative Action, volume 2: The Critique of Functionalist Reason*. Cambridge: Polity Press.

Habermas, J. (1989) *The Structural Transformation of the Public Sphere*. Cambridge: Polity Press.

Habermas, J.(1994) 'Citizenship and national identity', in Steenbergen, B.V. (ed.) *The Condition of Citizenship*. London: Sage, pp. 20–35.

Habermas, J. (2003) 'Toward a cosmopolitan Europe', *Journal of Democracy*, 14 (4): 86–100.

Hall, S. (2000) 'Conclusion: the multicultural question', in B. Hesse (ed.) *Un/settled Multiculturalisms: Diasporas, Entanglements, Transruptions*. London: Zed Books, pp. 209–240.

Hansen, P. (2004) 'In the name of Europe', *Race and Class*, 45 (3): 49–62.

Hebdige, R. (1979) *Subcultures: The Meaning of Style*. London: Methuen.

Hoggart, R. (1958) *The Uses of Literacy*. Harmondsworth: Penguin.

Kaldor, M. (1991) *The Imaginary War*. Oxford: Blackwell.

Kofman, E. (2005) 'Citizenship, migration and the reassertion of national identity', *Citizenship Studies*, 9 (5): 453–467.

Levy, D. and Sznaider, D. (2002) 'Memory unbound: The Holocaust and the formation of cosmopolitan memory', *European Journal of Social Theory*, 5 (1): 87–106.

McClintock, A. (1995) *Imperial Leather: Race, Gender and Sexuality in the Colonial Contest*. London: Routledge.

Mazower, M. (1998) *Dark Continent*. London: Penguin.

Memmi, A. (2003) *The Coloniser and the Colonised*. London: Earthscan Press.

Moschonas, G. (2002) *In The Name of Social Democracy: The Great Transformation: 1945 to the Present*. London: Verso.

Mulhern, F. (2000) *Culture/Metaculture*. London, Routledge.

Naidoo, R. (2006) 'Fear of difference/fear of sameness: the road to conviviality' *Soundings*, 33: 24–33.

Orwell, G. (1939/1970) 'Not counting niggers', in *The Collected Essays, Journalism and Letters of George Orwell, Volume 1, An Age Like This*. London: Penguin, pp. 434–438.

Parekh, B. (2000) *Rethinking Multiculturalism: Cultural Diversity and Political Theory*. London: Macmillan.

Prevos, A.J.M. (1996) 'The evolution of French rap music and hip hop culture in the 1980s and 1990s', *The French Review*, 69 (5): 713–725.

Pieterse, J.N. (1999) 'UnPacking the West: How European is Europe?', in A. Rattansi and S. Westwood (eds) *Racism, Modernity and Europe on the Western Front*. Cambridge: Polity Press.

Ramadan, T. (1999) *To Be A European Muslim*. Leicester: The Islamic Foundation.

Ryle, M. and Soper, K. (2002) *To Relish the Sublime? Culture and Self-Realisation in Postmodern Times*. London: Verso.

Said, E. (1993) *Culture and Imperialism*. London: Chatto and Windus.

Sartre, J.P. (2006) *Colonialism and Neocolonialism*. London: Routledge.

Sassoon, D. (1996) *One Hundred Years of Socialism: The West European Left in the Twentieth Century*. London: I.B. Tauris.

Shore, C. (2004) 'Whither European citizenship? Eros and civilisation revisited', *European Journal of Social Theory*, 7 (1): 27–44.

Soysal, Y.N. (2000) 'Citizenship and identity: living in diasporas in post-war Europe?', *Ethnic and Racial Studies*, 22 (1): 1–15.

Steedman, C. (1986) *Landscape for a Good Woman: A Story of Two Lives*. London: Virago.

Steiner, G. (1965/1984) *A Kind of Survivor, George Steiner: A Reader*. London, Pelican.

Taylor, C.(1992) *Multiculturalism and 'the Politics of Recognition'*. Princeton: Princeton University Press.

Thompson, E.P. (1965) *The Making of the English Working Class*. London: Pelican.

Thiong'o, N. (1986) *Decolonising the Mind*. London: Heinemann.

Tibi, B. (2002) 'Muslim migrants in Europe' in W. Alsayyad and M. Castells (2002) (eds) *Muslim Europe or Euro-Islam*. Oxford, Lexington Books.

Todorov, T. (2003) *Hope and Memory*. London: Atlantic Books.

West, C. (1993) 'The new cultural politics of difference', in S. During (ed.) *The Cultural Studies Reader*. London: Routledge, pp. 256–267.

Williams, R. (1962) *Communications*. Harmondsworth: Penguin.

Williams, R. (1970/1980) '*A Hundred Years of Culture and Anarchy' in Culture and Materialism*. London: Verso.

Williams, R. (1989) *Resources of Hope*. London: Verso.

Young, J.C. (1995) *Colonial Desire: Hybridity in Theory, Culture and Race*. London: Routledge.

23

Religion: Towards a Postsecular Europe?

Effie Fokas

These are strange times we are living in Europe in so far as religion is concerned. Europe is meant to be the last bastion, the remaining thread, of the secularization thesis, the continent where God was declared dead. From this perspective it may seem ironic that today there are many high-profile developments related – if only superficially – to religion. One such development, indicative of the peculiar nature of religion's presence in the European public debate, is that related to the British Airways regulations on the wearing of religious symbols: when a British Airways employee was told in 2006 that she could not wear an exposed symbol of her Christian faith (a cross as a necklace), whereas turbans and headscarves are allowed. A high-profile legal battle was circumvented only when the airline agreed to reconsider its policy, notably following the intervention of the Archbishop of Canterbury in the form of threats to withdraw the Church of England's investment in the airline. Each part of that story seems incredulous from a certain perspective, not least the fact of a 'high profile' *anything* to do with religion in Europe.

An additional peculiar example is the recent publication of two particular texts on

religion in Europe, co-authored by somewhat unlikely pairs. The most recent of these is a collaboration between Jürgen Habermas and Joseph Ratzinger, entitled *The Dialectics of Secularization: On Reason and Religion* (Habermas and Ratzinger, 2006). Here the 'methodological atheist' German philosopher and the current Pope question whether secular reason provides sufficient grounds for a democratic constitutional state. The second book reflects the exchange between Marcello Pera – a philosopher of science and a professed unbeliever – and the then Cardinal Ratzinger. Entitled *Without Roots: Europe, Relativism, Christianity and Islam* (Ratzinger and Pera, 2004), the text becomes a meeting ground for the two in their opposition to relativism as a force undermining Europe's Christian identity. Relativism, they argue, has led to a void left by Christianity which is now being filled by Islam. Pera's suggestion is the adaptation of a Christian-based civil religion for Europe.

Indeed these are strange times we are living in in Europe and, as these examples illustrate, there are developments seemingly moving in opposite directions: one removing and the other reintroducing religion. In many cases, Islam is the catalyst for such developments, through debates arising mainly around the 'new' Muslim presence in Europe (that following mass postwar immigration). However, our subject is much broader and wide-reaching than Islam, and in recent years has seen the development of intense debates regarding the proper place of religion in the European public sphere.

In order to fully appreciate the significance of these debates, some insight into the *longue durée* of Europe's religious trajectory is helpful. Europe is the setting of an extraordinary story of a continent's identification with Christianity and subsequent division along finer religious lines. The story continues with its breeding of both secularist and nationalist ideology, and the ensuing love–hate relationships between religions and states, many of which continue today. Throughout, religion has maintained a strong presence, if only through its cultural embeddedness, or through its particular relationship (whether 'positive', as in the Greek case, or 'negative', as in the French case) with national identity. In the pages that follow, brief attention will be given to this general narrative, as a backdrop against which to understand the diverse religious patterns to be found at the national level in Europe today. These patterns will be addressed in a second section.

Increasingly, developments related to religion at the national level are exposed to influence by membership, or potential membership, of the European Union. Thus, an exploration of trends at the supranational level is useful in understanding the European situation as a whole. The EU is also a significant factor in migration from Eastern to Western Europe and, whether directly or indirectly, in immigration to Europe from beyond the EU. The changes to the European religious landscape resulting from this mobility will be addressed in a fourth section. Finally, a fifth section picks up the threads of debates touched upon throughout the chapter and shows how these debates are culminating in discussions of a postsecular Europe.

SETTING THE STAGE: THE HISTORICAL BACKDROP

The identification of Europe with Christendom is a familiar narrative, with the crowning of Charlemagne as the Holy Roman Emperor a conspicuous landmark. Conceptions of a Christian Europe are also reflected in the great historiographies of Europe, including those of Denis de Rougement, Jean-Baptiste Duroselle, Denys Hay, and Christopher Dawson. With approaches ranging from descriptive to prescriptive, historians of Europe have focused on religion as fundamental to European identity. The line between Christianity and Islam was the central marker (Rodinson, 1987). In time, the further divisions between eastern and western Christianity, and within each, left their mark on notions of European identity and on national identities in Europe. Historical maps of Europe trace these divisions. As David Martin explains, 'Religion is one reason why older maps exist like older paintings underneath contemporary configurations' (Martin, 1994: 14).

Thus, religion has acted as a factor for both unification and division of Europe, and historically it has fluctuated between these two roles. Meanwhile, conceptions of Christianity as constitutive of European identity have underpinned (substantively or superficially) many a European unification movement, including the Christian Democracy-led integration project which materialized in the form of the contemporary European Union.

Intimately intertwined with the narrative identifying Europe with Christianity is that which links Europe with secularization, secularism and secularity.[1] Trends beginning with the French Revolution in particular and the Enlightenment in its various manifestations were in time embedded in the 'theory of secularization' (or the secularization thesis, depending on one's perspective), which in broad terms suggests that modernity is linked in inverted proportion to the decline of religion. What is meant by 'decline' and by 'religion' in the many versions of secularization theory varies.

Decline may be interpreted as privatization or as a weakening of faith. Meanwhile, some scholars focus on religious institutions in their study of religion's decline, whilst others trace individual faith and practices.[2]

Secularization theory may be traced back to the writings of Henri Saint-Simon and Auguste Comte. In its early versions, this 'grand master narrative' was based on observation of trends in Europe and posited that increased modernization inevitably led to secularization, in Europe as it would elsewhere (Gorski, 2003). It is expressed more recently by scholars such as Brian Wilson, Karel Dobbelaere and Steve Bruce. The latter posits that secularization is intrinsically linked to the general processes of modernization, because the rationalization that comes with modernization leads to a decline in the societal significance of religious institutions which, in turn, leads to a decline of religious beliefs and practices (Bruce, 2002).

One of the most influential articulations of secularization theory came from Peter Berger in his *The Sacred Canopy* (1967; published in the UK in 1969 under the title *The Social Reality of Religion*). Here he describes religion's role as a kind of 'canopy', a social construction which projected a sacred cosmos and in so doing served to shelter individuals and society from a seemingly meaningless existence. This canopy began to fall apart with modernization, which brought secularization in a dialectical relationship with pluralism. Put simply, modernization led to the increased exposure to different religious creeds than one's own which, in turn, undermined exclusive truth claims and, ultimately, faith itself.

David Martin made a seminal contribution to the understanding of secularization with his 1978 *General Theory of Secularization*. Martin focuses on the distinctions within Europe in terms of the pace and nature of secularization across different cultural contexts. He describes a set of 'universal processes' of secularization which 'tend to occur other things being equal'. 'But things are not equal', he continues '– ever' (Martin, 1978:3);

Martin thus lays the groundwork for extensive consideration of the variables influencing differentiation in secularization patterns.

A central concept in secularization theory is that secularization, like modernization, is a process that is born in Europe and spreads outward, though with certain mutations. In this narrative, the US is considered an exceptional case in the persisting relatively high levels of religiosity, in spite of the advanced stage of modernity. A body of theory developed to explain the 'American exception'.[3]

But a series of events provoked questioning of the secularization thesis. This includes the Iranian revolution in 1979; the rise of the Solidarity movement in Poland and the Catholic Church's role in the eventual fall of communism there; the role of Catholicism in the Sandinista Revolution, and in other political conflicts throughout Latin America; and the public re-emergence of Protestant fundamentalism as a force in American politics (embodied for many in the person of Jerry Falwell). Increasingly, discussion turned from the American exception to the European exception: (Western) Europe was the exception to the secularization thesis and to what was otherwise, in Berger's words, a 'furiously religious world'. Berger famously confessed that he (and other secularizationalist scholars) had been wrong: 'The world today is massively religious, is *anything but* the secularized world that had been predicted (whether joyfully or despondently) by so many analysts of modernity' (1999: 9). Since his 'turn-around' in the early 1990s, Berger's work is characterized more by the perspective that (in his own words) 'to say the least, the relation between religion and modernity is rather complicated' (1999: 3).

Indeed, the fate of religion could not be so simply linked to modernity, particularly at a time when increasingly the 'multiple modernities' approach was taking root (Davie, 2007). Today, social scientists are largely divided into two camps: those who would like to scrap secularization theory altogether, and those who seek to preserve parts of it (After Secularization, 2006: 5). The staunchest remaining supporters of the secularization thesis are Karel Dobbelaere and Steve Bruce; a main tool of this camp is the quantitative data produced by such surveys as the World Values Survey and European Values Survey.

The opposing camp tends to offer more nuanced approaches to the study of religious practice. For example, David Martin focuses on the adaptability of Christianity to secularism: 'Christianity embodies a dialectic of the religious and the secular that more easily generates secular mutations of faith than straightforward replacements and displacements' (2006: 68).[4] Within this context, religion in Europe does not function as a separate channel of culture but as a distinctive current which 'mingles in the mainstream, sometimes with the flow, sometimes against'. The result is that religious forms and moulds are often reflected in secular analogues. With reference to the quantitative data supporting the secularization thesis, Martin argues that 'counting matters, but one needs some account of religion as a mode of social consciousness and identity rooted in history and geography, time and place'. This, according to Martin, is how Christianity has functions in Europe, as a flexible repertoire of images and as a code which adjusts to changing circumstances (2006: 68). As an extension of this fact, Christianity maintains a distinctly strong presence in Europe through culture and tradition (e.g. church weddings, baptisms and funerals), as well as through architecture and town planning (Martin, 2005).

For her part, Danièle Hervieu-Léger focuses on the limitation in secularization theory entailed by its assumption that the decline in religious practice is an indicator of a retreat in religious belief (Hervieu-Léger, 2006b). Christianity maintains a presence through what she calls a 'chain of memory', linking individuals to a community through memory of a shared past, with religion deeply rooted in tradition which persists in the (otherwise secular) present. Hervieu-Léger's critique is based in the fact that theories of European secularization tend to take into account only the historic religions as

representing religion in the full sense of the term; they thus are missing a lot of 'where religion is, actually'. In fact, through a process of 'bricolage' (or 'tinkering'), we see how religion in Europe is no longer simply embedded in the culture in a taken-for-granted manner, but rather becomes an object of individual choices (Hervieu-Léger, 2000). The major religions are less and less 'codes of meaning' imposed on individuals from above, and they are less and less 'natural communities' through which successive generations inherit religious identity. Rather, increasingly, religious identity is a matter of personal choice, with Europeans choosing either as pilgrims, in their own spiritual journeys, or as converts (Hervieu-Léger, 2006a: 47–8).

Meanwhile, Grace Davie has argued that people in Europe *believe*, but in different ways which are not necessarily traceable through affiliation with traditional religious institutions; rather, many in Europe 'believe without belonging' (1994). The opposite is also the case in certain contexts: many Europeans feel a strong sense of belonging to their traditional religious institutions, demonstrating fairly high levels of loyalty, in spite of relatively (compared to America) low levels of belief as can be measured through empirical surveys (e.g. a belief in the tenets of their particular religious tradition; claimed belief in God and in an afterlife, etc.).

Many in Europe also experience religion 'vicariously', and they expect their religious institutions to offer certain services and play certain roles, regardless of whether they are regular recipients of these services (Davie, 2000). Such 'vicarious religion' as Davie describes is of course difficult to trace: it entails religion performed by an active minority but on behalf of the wider population who understand, approve of and *anticipate* (if not demand, in the case of their expectations of religious leaders) what the minority is doing. The notion includes popular attitudes towards the activities of the majority churches, as well as the ways in which these churches often serve as spaces for debate of 'unresolved issues' in modern societies (e.g. homosexuality).

'Vicarious religion' also refers to the fact that churches and sacred spaces are expected to be available as spaces for celebration, and especially for mourning, such as was the case following the sinking of the Estonia ship off the shores of Sweden in 1994; in the 'religious reaction' to 9/11; and in Archbishop Rowan Williams' (and others religious leaders') engagement with the public through declarations following the devastating tsunami in Southeast Asia in 2005. In other words, in Davie's words, 'If you really want to understand the patterns of religion in modern Europe, you need to look through quite sensitive glasses' (Pew Forum, 2005).

NUANCING THE NARRATIVE: RELIGION AT THE NATIONAL LEVEL

A sensitive approach is also needed to understand patterns of religion at the national level: identifications with Christianity and levels of secularity carry a very specific character from one national case to another. There are differences to consider at practically every level, including the constitutional status of religion (with varying degrees of establishment or privilege for most majority churches); practices in provision, or compulsion, of religious education; policies on religious symbols; political mobilization of religious groups; treatment of religious minorities; and regulation of the religious market. And within each of these categories in each national case, there are significant differences between the *de jure* and *de facto* situations (Madeley and Enyedi, 2003).

To a large extent, the national variations are based on two interrelated factors: the particular relationship between religion and national identity in each case, and the relationship between church and state. Across Europe we find interesting and complex patterns in these relationships. Simply for indicative purposes, the cases of the Netherlands, France and Greece will be considered. Each case is easily identified with its hallmark

attributes of pillarization, *laïcité*, and accommodation, respectively. And in each case, these hallmark attributes have been challenged in recent years, introducing a state of flux on matters related to religion.

The system of pillarization entails a segmentation of society on the basis of different religious of philosophical views. The Netherlands offers one noteworthy manifestation, representing a very particular approach to religion whose roots go back to the seventeenth century. Dutch pillarization is perhaps best understood through the prism of the education system. An 1806 law on primary education dictated that all pupils should be educated in 'all social and Christian virtues'. The idea was for *all* Christian virtues to be prioritized and to avoid preferential treatment of any one faith. Implicitly, a separation of church and state is maintained in the Education Act of 1806, but not of religion and state (ter Avest, 2007: 203).

Dissatisfaction arose amongst certain Protestant groups who found this Christian education insufficient: they sought a seamless socialization into a particular church community which began at home and was continued in school. Privately financed denominational schools began to materialize (in some cases without state approval), but discontent mounted again in the late eighteenth/early nineteenth centuries over the lack of public financing for these schools. Parents began pressing the state for equal financial treatment for the denominational schools. The so-called 'school struggle' ended with the Pacification Act of 1917, which allowed for pillarization of the education system whereby each religious group (at the time, Roman Catholics and various Protestant denominations) could run its own state-funded school. The 1917 Pacification gave an extra and, according to some historians, *the* impetus for the process of societal pillarization (i.e., the denominational segregation of public life in the Netherlands). It resulted in a fragmentation of almost all societal institutions and groups along denominational lines. Thus pillarization spread from the education domain into all of public and political life in society that became organized along segregational lines: universities, political parties, trade-unions, welfare work, hospitals, elderly homes, and so on (ter Avest, 2007: 204).

The other, positive side of the coin is the image of the proverbial Dutch tolerance of religious beliefs, whatever they may be. This made Dutch social life conducive to an advanced form of multiculturalism. The two concepts of tolerance and multiculturalism have developed into fundamental aspects and symbols of Dutch national identity. The image (and reality) of both were, however, seriously challenged through a series of events, especially the murders of Pim Fortuyn and Theo van Gogh – a subject which is revisited later in this chapter.

French and Dutch society share similar levels of secularity (Norris and Inglehart, 2005: 85), but the French state's approach to religion is somewhat different. *Laïcité* is essentially an untranslatable term (Chelini-Pont, 2005: 611), both literally and metaphorically as it applies exclusively to the French case.[5] The term represents something of a mixture of secularism and secularity, each in their French specificity – a mixture of ideology and description of reality on the ground, in terms of the absence of religion from the public sphere.

Jean Baubérot, a principal authority on *laïcité*, revealingly describes French secularity as 'a particular way of embodying shared values' – the key assumption under which is an exclusion of religion because of its lack of universality. Like Dutch pillarization, it emanates from a long historical process beginning with the French Revolution, followed by a robust struggle between opposing views of French national identity (in simplified terms, between clericalists and anti-clericalists), and by the Dreyfus Affair, which led to the law of 1905, formally separating church and state.

The 1905 law enjoys 'iconic status' in France: 'It symbolizes the moment when "church" finally gives way to "state" as the dominant institution in French society'

(Davie, 2007: 162). It is also a significant symbolic reference point in French national identity, not least because of the aforementioned major milestones in French national history which presaged it.

If tolerance and multiculturalism are markers of Dutch national identity, in the French case assimilation and anti-*communautarisme* are the relevant coordinates. This much is evident through attention to the *affaire du foulard*, from its 1980s beginning to its ultimate culmination in the Stasi Commission report and its subsequent formulation into French policy in 2004 (banning the wearing of headscarves and all conspicuous religious symbols in schools).

Catherine Audard (2007) unhesitatingly describes the entire affair as a crisis of French national identity above all else. Similarly, Talal Asad describes the dominant position in the debate as an assumption that, in a conflict over constitutional principles, the state's right to defend its personality trumps all other rights. In this case, the headscarf was considered a religious sign conflicting with the secular personality of the French Republic (Asad, 2006: 95). 'Political hysteria' is how Emmanuel Terray explains the issue and its resolution – hysteria craftily used to obscure material realities. 'Of course, this is precisely what *laïcité* is', claims Asad; 'Its overriding concern is with transcendent values (neutrality of the state, the separation of "religion" from politics, "sacredness" of the republican compact, etc.) and not with immanent materialities' (2006: 103). In short, the issue was very much about identities, with the antipathy, and hostilities, evoked throughout indicative of what it means to be a secular Frenchman or Frenchwoman (2006: 103).

If one could simply replace certain words and concepts, then the same structure and framework could apply well to the Greek case, but only with the opposite foundations: the passions and hostilities aroused in relation to religion tend to be those identifying the Greek identity with (rather than against) orthodoxy, especially in the face of a perceived threat to Greek national identity.

In this case, *laïcité* would not be replaced with 'establishment' or 'religiosity' but, rather, with an emphasis on *accommodation* between church and state. And this accommodation rests on strong links between religion and national identity embedded in the Greek national imagination (and carefully presented in history schoolbooks).[6] Furthermore, it is maintained through staunch efforts on the part of the church leadership (this varies of course depending on the leader but most certainly applies to the current archbishopric), and through the activities of many politicians who stand to gain from it in a given situation. The most recent context for one such struggle on the part of the church was the 'identity card issue' (beginning in May 2000), when the church leadership challenged the government's decision to remove reference to religion from national identity cards (Molokotos-Liederman, 2003, 2007). At root, the struggle on the part of the church leadership entailed a negotiation of power relations *vis-à-vis* the state – a negotiation which the church ultimately lost.[7]

Danièle Hervieu-Léger refers to both the Dutch and French cases to illustrate how Europeans' shared religious identity is expressed today through the advent of a spiritual individualism that 'overturns established structures for the transmission of religious identity' (2006a: 48–9). The Greek case is the example *par excellence* of a national church fighting against just that trend. It represents what one scholar calls a collectivistic Christianity which has as a central element the notion of *belonging*: the belonging is specific, historically embedded, it exists independently from believing, is rarely private, and rarely de-institutionalized (Jakelić, 2006: 137).

In the Greek case, as in the Dutch and French cases, this state of affairs evolved through a very particular historical experience. A first significant milestone in this history is the experience of the Orthodox Church under the Ottoman millet system, through which it enjoyed significant privileges and grew to a position of relative strength.

A second factor – albeit fabricated (or at least considerably embellished for children's schoolbooks) – is the concept of the church as a hero in the revolution against the Ottomans, having led the country to freedom. A third marker is the establishment of the autocephalous church, quite soon after the establishment of the modern Greek state, in a revolutionary act (breaking away from the Ecumenical Patriarchate in Constantinople without the latter's approval) which signified the full expression of national autonomy. It is this historical period to which the current church leadership in Greece most frequently refers when making its claim to representation of the Greek nation. All these references are echoed in the Greek education system, hence they find resonance amongst the population at large, and hence again the church's ability to mobilize much of the Greek public on issues relating to Greek national identity.

In each of these national cases we have seen very particular patterns of religion–nation, church–state relations, patterns influenced by historical and cultural factors which must be taken into account in order to understand current developments related to religion. As Asad puts it:

> Varieties of remembered religious history, of perceived political threat and opportunity, define the sensibilities underpinning secular citizenship and national belonging in a modern state. The sensibilities are not always secure, they are rarely free of contradictions, and they are sometimes fragile. But they made for qualitatively different forms of secularism (2006: 101).

What the three cases have in common is a state of flux through challenges (though of different types) to the status quo in terms of the place of religion in politics and society.

RELIGION IN THE EUROPEAN INTEGRATION PROJECT

Challenges in the religious domain have also arisen at the supranational level of the European Union. Two issues in particular have carried religion to a space of prominence in relation to the EU: notions (and accusations) of the EU as a 'Christian Club' in its exclusion of Turkey; and the debates on reference to religion in the preamble to the Union's draft Constitutional Treaty. Appreciating the full significance of these issues requires a broader perspective on the role of religion in the construction of the European Union.

Where one begins narrating this history is largely revealing of his or her perspective on the nature of the European Union. For some, the EU represents a continuation – albeit with periods of interruption – of a European identity which began to take shape in antiquity. For such individuals, a strong unification of Europe is a logical result of a long historical process. For others, the history of the integration project begins in the aftermath of WWII, with the establishment of the first institution to which we can draw clear and direct lineage from the current European Union. Each narrative comes with different perspectives on the role of religion: the first harkens back to the Holy Roman Empire as the golden age of European unity, and the second to the strength of postwar Christian Democracy in the face of the (atheistic) communist threat in Europe.

Certainly the central role played by Christian Democrats in the postwar integration project – including Jean Monnet, Robert Schuman, Konrad Adenauer and Alcide de Gasperi – is conspicuous (although this says nothing of any religious, *per se*, content in their political activities). In recent years, scholars have paid increasing attention to the relatively strong levels of support for the integration project from within the ranks of Christian Democracy (Marks and Wilson, 2000); and from within the Roman Catholic faith, as compared with other faith groups (Nelsen *et al.*, 2001).

Another important element in the role of religion in the European integration project is the adoption of the 'Communiqué on European identity' at the 1973 Copenhagen Summit. The aim to create a European identity was then embedded in the Maastricht Treaty, through a chapter in the treaty (Title IX, article 128) devoted to culture: Article 128, paragraph 1 of the Maastricht Treaty claims that the Community shall contribute to the flowering of the cultures of the member states *while* respecting their national and regional diversity; and, at the same time, it shall bring the common heritage to the fore. The question naturally arises whether culture, in the case of European identity, can be detached from religion and, if not, what the implications might be for religious minorities within Europe or non-Christian (perhaps even non-Western Christian – i.e., Christian Orthodox) countries wishing to join.

A third significant factor is the explicit policy approaches to communication of the European Commission with religious (and humanist) groups. These were spearheaded mainly by Jacques Delors, whose words in 1992 communicate a sense of urgency: 'If in the next ten years we haven't managed to give a Soul to Europe, to give it spirituality and meaning the game will be up' (cited in Massignon, 2007). The first formal relations between the European Commission and religious groups began under Jacques Delors' second term of office. Significantly, the 'Soul for Europe' initiative (established in 1994), offers funding for ecumenical or inter-religious seminars for the discussion of the meaning of European integration. Religious groups have strengthened their presence in Brussels since then and, together with humanist groups, actively lobby on issues of concern to them (Massignon, 2007).

In principle, the EU is neutral on matters of religion, and in this domain strictly applies the principle of subsidiarity – itself a religious (Roman Catholic) concept. However, there are significant tensions between this foundational principle of the EU, and another – namely, that of pluralism. And it is in the context of these tensions that we see certain *de facto/de jure* distinctions:

On the one hand, by way of respect to national specificity, the principle of subsidiarity indicates that issues which can be effectively addressed at the national level should be addressed there, without EU intervention. On the other hand, the EU claims to be religiously and philosophically neutral, but devoted to the principle of pluralism. Accordingly, it aims to influence member states in such a way as to create environments conducive to the flourishing of diversity and pluralism. Intimately related to the latter aim is protection of religious freedoms. These two interests – subsidiarity and pluralism – often come into conflict in particular cases, such as when the handling of religious matters in certain member states is not conducive to the flourishing of pluralism, but rather quite the opposite.

Thus in practice, the EU *does* influence national religious affairs, at least indirectly through the European Convention on Human Rights (ECHR) and the European Court of Human Rights (ECtHR) mainly in protection of individual religious liberties.[8] In terms of direct influence, though, the principle of subsidiarity is indeed respected and there are no EU directives, legislations or treaty provisions on religion (Ferrari, 2006: 13). However, there is unpredictable potential for influence through the (somewhat unclear, and openended,) *acquis communautaire*, mainly via provisions on human rights and religious freedom. Through the *acquis*, beyond any legislation directly produced by the EU institutions, two other sets of legal provisions come into play: the laws of member states and international law. In the domain of human rights, the rights recognized by the EU and enforceable in its legal system are those deriving from EU legal provisions, the European Convention on Human Rights, *and* the constitutional traditions common to the EU member states. The same applies to religious freedom, although there is some distinction between collective and individual rights: the *acquis* encompasses both, but there is greater emphasis on the constitutional traditions of the member states (rather than on EU and ECHR provisions) when it comes to collective religious rights (Ferrari, 2006: 10–11).

The influence of the *acquis communautaire* has been especially controversial in relation to Turkey's protracted accession process, with Turkish protests against moving goalposts through the vague nature of the *acquis*. Suspicions that religious prejudice underlies the delays on the part of the EU are old and rampant (but certainly the 'Christian Club' has also been used by some Turks as a reason for Turkish resistance to European integration, particularly by Turkish Islamists in the 1980s and 1990s (Ayata 1999; Cakir, 1990, 1999)). Such suspicions are naturally heightened through declarations along these lines by many EU leading figures – most notably, through comments by Giscard d'Estaing and Angela Merkel.

The case of Turkish–EU relations is a highly complex situation, evident in mixed messages relating to matters of religion emanating from the European Union. On the one hand, and especially in a post 9-11 environment, the EU seeks to support Turkey in resisting any developments of Islamic radicalism within its borders. At the same time, in its commitment to pluralism and the protection of freedoms of religious practice and expression, the EU chastises the Turkish state for developments limiting the latter (more specifically, for the military's role seeking to limit Turkish Islamism).

One example of mixed messages relates to the bill on reforms to the Higher Education Board (YOK) proposed in 2004, which was designed to allow equal opportunity amongst students of *all* subjects and vocations, including graduates of religious (imam-hatip) schools, to enter into university.[9] Here, the Turkish military's intervention in the matter warranted a negative reaction from the European Union. At the same time, other statements emanating from EU Commissioner Verheugen's office declared that the Higher Education Board issue is an entirely *national* issue (implementing subsidiarity), and one which does not concern the EU. The case of Turkey's troubled path to EU membership continues.

In contrast, the debates on references to God in the preamble to the Constitutional

Treaty in many ways seem far off, particularly after being overshadowed by the precarious fate of the Treaty as a whole with the French and Dutch 'No's in their respective referenda. The Constitutional Treaty itself remains an open issue, but the question of reference to religion was 'resolved' after protracted deliberations: religious heritage could appear on a par with cultural and humanist heritage, but God could not be invoked; nor would Christianity serve as a reference point.[10]

Perhaps more important than the outcome were the debates themselves. And certainly beyond the content of the preamble, these debates have left their mark on public thinking on the role of religion in the EU. They mobilized both religious and secular groups, and gave rise to otherwise unlikely alliances between particular groups in their lobbying efforts in Brussels, where a 'European compromise between immanence and transcendence is being forged' (Massignon, 2007). They also provided a context for popular and public discussion of religion at the European level – a discussion which attracted a surprising level of participation.

MOBILITY AND THE CHANGING RELIGIOUS LANDSCAPE

To a large extent, increased attention to religion in European public debates is based upon, or is at least sharpened by, the 'new' Muslim presence in Europe – that is, the Muslim presence in Europe following patterns of mass immigration in the postwar period. Certainly the influx and local growth of Muslim groupings within Europe has introduced the most conspicuous change to the European religious landscape – in so far as public attention to it is concerned. On the ground, however, a number of factors contribute to the changing religious landscape of Europe and, in some cases, the Muslim presence is the least influential at the local level.[11]

Mobility in general is a major source of change in the religious domain, with the three main factors being immigration of Muslims from the Middle East and Africa; immigration of Christians from Africa; and migration westwards of practicing Christians in Eastern Europe. But it is of course the Muslim presence that is most often portrayed as the greater challenge to the religious status quo in Europe: it challenges both notions of a Christian European identity, and conceptions of a secular Europe. A number of factors concur to 'sensationalize' the Muslim presence. First, its size: even taking into account the great discrepancy between statistical data, Islam is clearly Europe's 'second religion', and in many cases Muslims make up sizeable proportions of the overall population (8–9 per cent in France and 3.6 per cent in Germany by some measures), and quite large proportions in particular areas (35 per cent in the Ile-de-France, for example). Meanwhile, the Muslim presence is particularly young (i.e., if nothing else, bears far greater potential for its own 'chain of memory'), and is characterized by high birth rates (strikingly so as compared to Europe's especially low birth rates).

Alasdair Crockett and David Voas study mobility and demography in order to get a sense of the future of religion in Britain. They identify two potential modulators of religious decline in Britain: immigration of people who are more religious than the existing population, and higher fertility rates among the religiously active population. They suggest that only immigration plays some role, as fertility rates tend to converge with the European norm with successive generations, and rates of intergenerational religious decline are similar for native and immigrant populations (Crockett and Voas, 2006).

In fact, mobility and demography have become domains for extended debate on the secularization thesis as applied in Europe. Demographics are used to radically different scholarly ends. Eric Kauffman uses them to question European secularization and asks: 'Do we see the end of religion, or its rebirth?

The evidence supports the latter' (Kaufmann, 2007: 2). Bat Y'eor, meanwhile, warns of the trend Europe is taking towards becoming Eurabia, while George Weigel worries about Notre Dame becoming an 'Hagia Sophia on the Seine' in his *The Cube and the Cathedral*. Significantly, such perspectives are reflected in right-winged political trends in Europe and by large sectors of the media (Al-Azmeh 2007; Fokas, 2007). In *God's Continent*, Philip Jenkins seeks to allay such scaremongering, suggesting that secularization is affecting young Muslims in Europe similarly as it is young Christians. However, as became clear in a recent public debate on demography and secularization in Europe, this is a very delicate area in which conflicting statistical evidence can be found to support each direction of the argument.[12]

As for the potential influence of a westward-migrating, religiously active East European population, it is still too early to make sound predictions, but scholars have voiced their opposing perspectives on the matter. The core thesis of a recent book on *Religion in an Expanding Europe* is that eastward EU enlargement is 'infusing renewed religious vitality into Europe's political and social life, thus chipping away at its exceptional secularism' (Katzenstein, 2006: 2). Studies from various national contexts of Catholic, Orthodox and Muslim traditions are employed in the text to substantiate this claim. Conversely, Peter Berger describes a 'massively secular Euro-culture' which has spread especially from north to south in Europe and suggests 'it is not fanciful to predict that there will be similar developments [to Western European secularization] in Eastern Europe, precisely to the degree that these countries too will be integrated into the new Europe' (2000: 44). His focus, therefore, is on religious trends in the home countries, and his expectation is that European secularization is contagious and will spread with European enlargement (and, presumably, with the mobility it entails).

What about those individuals migrating to Western European countries? Might their levels of religiosity be different from both their host and their home countries? Further research on the religiosities of successive generations of Eastern European immigrants is necessary, as predictions based on other diaspora communities are insufficient in this case (given their relatively high rates of mobility between host and home countries). However, one scholar argues emphatically that integration into Europe by countries such as Poland, Bulgaria and Serbia will not serve to waver the religiosities of their populations, specifically because these are collectivistic Christianities wherein religion is a constitutive element in people's collective memory. The belonging of these individuals is 'shaped by religious identification that is ascribed to individuals rather than chosen by them, and experienced as fixed rather than as changeable' (Jakelić, 2006: 136). Thus from this perspective, Europe should brace itself for a significant wind of change as increasing encounters will take place between secular Europeans and collectivistic Christians.

The changes to the European religious landscape are diverse, thus defying generalization. They are also very much in a state of flux, a *process*. It is therefore difficult to grasp the likely outcomes for religion in Europe in the longer term. What is clear, though, is that few Europeans remain unaffected by these changes: the daily lives of Europeans are increasingly influenced in some way by the growing plurality, or by the influx of new religious ideas, resulting from mobility and immigration. The conspicuous presence of religion resulting from this mobility and immigration has itself become a significant factor in the debates on European secularity and the proper place of religion in the European public sphere.

RELIGION IN EUROPEAN PUBLIC DEBATE

At a number of different levels, then, religion has a more conspicuous presence in European public debate. The stimuli are many, but perhaps the most influential have to do with certain developments that are in some way related to Islam or to the Muslim presence in Europe – developments which have significantly challenged optimisms regarding a potentially peaceful coexistence between Muslims and non-Muslims. This is due not least to the mediatic attention to a few events and the under-representation, underestimation and lack of knowledge regarding the great majority of Muslims in Europe. Regardless, the effects have been intense.

One such development is the murder of Theo van Gogh (2004), following his collaboration with Hirsi Ali on the film *Submission*. This development was shocking at many levels. First, it took place in the Netherlands, the home of multiculturalism and tolerance. Second, the victim was a film director (not a politician) who – in the opinion of many – was carrying out important work that encourages the liberation of Muslim women from oppression that they might be experiencing. (Of course, the alternative perspective was one which saw an artist antagonistically criticizing Islam). Third, the brutality through which the murder was perpetrated was shocking. And finally, the murder came so soon after that of Pim Fortuyn (2002). In other words, it took place in a context of already heightened sense of shock and danger. Debates developed around the notion that Europeans were not free 'on their own soil' to express themselves, mainly due to a threat from their Muslim cohabitants.

Two other developments carried the same message: challenges to freedom of speech by the Muslim population in Europe. The first is the aftermath of the printing, in the Danish *Jyllands-Posten* and subsequently in countless other publications, of caricatures of the prophet Mohammed. The sheer volume of the wave of protests, in addition to the nature of the protests (e.g., placards carrying messages of hate and warnings of violence), were formidable. The second development is the aftermath of Pope Benedict XVI's speech in

Regensburg, through which he offended Muslims worldwide (and for which he failed to offer an apology for the statements he made). Here, as in the period following the Mohammed cartoon publication, the strength of the reaction amongst Muslims across the globe was impressive. And, much like the case of the two murders in the Netherlands, the temporal proximity of these last two developments made them all the more powerful in the imagination of Europeans – Muslim and non-Muslim alike.[13]

Each of these three developments had their starting points in particular European cities, but their ripple effects were felt globally and they fuelled debates about the compatibility of Muslim and non-Muslim values. When one adds to this the series of bombings in European cities (failed and successful) perpetrated by individuals claiming to act in the name of Islam, the picture is indeed bleak.

Meanwhile, book-length explorations of this 'picture' have been pitched to reach the popularity rate of best-selling novels, including Lawrence Wright's *Looming Tower*, Melanie Phillips' *Londonistan*, Bruce Bawer's *While Europe Slept*, Ian Buruma's *Murder in Amsterdam*, and Philip Jenkins' *God's Continent*. The context is the same but the content vastly varied, with some authors heralding the death of Christian Europe and the Muslim 'invasion', and others desperately reaching into memory banks and history books to draw parallels with other times and contexts and to overcome generalizations about Islam.

Beyond the aforementioned localized events that led to worldwide debates, a host of other debates have spread in different parts of Europe, each arising within particular local and national contexts. Islam may have been a catalyst in each case, but the debates have grown much broader. The most obvious case in this type of debate is focused on the Muslim headscarf. Debates on the headscarf have, at various periods, been especially pronounced in France, in the UK, in Germany and elsewhere in Europe. These debates may be understood as part of (or a stimulant for) a wider debate on religious symbols in general, and on places where they are or are not appropriate: for example, the Christian cross hanging on walls in Bavarian schools, or the cross as a necklace for an airline company employee, and the question of which rules should apply to students and/or to teachers. In other words, these raise broader theoretical questions about the proper place of religion in the public sphere. And they overflow into such areas as the celebration of religious feasts; for example, the debates surrounding Birmingham Council's proposal in the late 1990s to use the term 'Winterval' for winter (including Christmas-time) festivities.

Another type of debate experienced in different forms in different parts of Europe has to do with religious education and its public funding. Most of these discussions may have been sparked by demands for public-funded Muslim schools, but they have prompted more general debates on whether segregation along religious lines in the school system is desirable, and on the potential long-term repercussions of such segregation in the given society.

One clear effect of all of the above is that debates about the place of religion in the European public sphere have reached the popular level, with mass attention to and engagement in the questioning of various national approaches to religion and religious difference – whether questionings of the assimilationist model after the French riots in Paris in 2005, or of multiculturalism after the London bombings in the UK and the murder of Van Gogh in the Netherlands. What these developments have in common is their reactive nature; indeed, Europe finds itself at a critical juncture in its relationship to religion, but currently we experience an unhealthy situation in which definitions of this relationship are being drawn on a *reactive* basis, in a climate of frequent, attention-grabbing 'events'. Debates about free speech followed *threats* to free speech felt in the aftermath of particular developments.

In response to this state of affairs, certain scholars have sought to address the problem and have identified as central to it the secularist assumptions which reign in Europe – the strict secular neutrality claimed and (theoretically) maintained in Europe. Assumptions of a strictly secular Europe, the argument goes, impede us from engaging in a healthy way with what, in reality, is a complex religious landscape in need of delicate handling. As a result of Europeans' philosophical attachment to the *knowledge regime* of secularism, there is a sense that Europeans lack the proper tools for dealing with this complex reality of many open questions to do with religion.

José Casanova makes this statement boldly. In his view, secularist assumptions turn religion into a problem, thus precluding the resolution of religion-related challenges in a pragmatic manner. Criticizing what he describes as a European preference to hold on to the idea of a single, secular modernity emerging out of the Enlightenment, Casanova paints a picture of European secular neutrality as anything but neutral:

> Thus, the secularist paradox, that in the name of freedom, individual autonomy, tolerance, and cultural pluralism, religious people – Christian, Jewish, and Muslim – are being asked to keep their religious beliefs, identities and norms 'private' so that they do not disturb the project of a modern, secular, enlightened Europe (2006b: 67).

Continuing his analysis of European societies, he argues that 'to guarantee equal access to the European public sphere and undistorted communication, the European Union would need to become not only post-Christian but also post-secular' (2006a: 39).

This perspective builds on Casanova's earlier thinking in his seminal book *Public Religions in the Modern World* (1994), where he posits that religions both can and should have a public role in the modern world, especially through entry into the discursive space of civil society. As his general critique of the secularization thesis develops throughout his work, he begins to consider whether secularization became a self-fulfilling prophecy in Europe (2006b: 84). But now, Casanova contends, 'the 'age' of reactive organicism, of secular–religious and clerical–anticlerical cultural and political warfare ... has come to an end' in Western Europe at least, paving the way for a positive public role for religion (1994: 61). Peter Katzenstein concurs in this perspective, suggesting that the growing salience of religion will itself likely lead to demands for new terms of coexistence with secularism (Katzenstein, 2006: 2).

A second important contribution to this trend of thought comes from the engagement of Jürgen Habermas with the ideas of John Rawls and, in particular, with Rawls' 'idea of public reason'. A brief introduction to the latter will be helpful here. Rawls' starting point is the situation of a plurality of conflicting 'comprehensive doctrines' (religious, philosophical and moral) in society. He proposes that in such contexts – as naturally arise in democratic societies with free institutions – 'comprehensive doctrines of truth or right be replaced by an idea of the politically reasonable addressed to citizens as citizens', when citizens engage in public reason[14] (Rawls, 2002: 132). Those who hold comprehensive doctrines are free to introduce these (whether religious or non-religious) into political discussion at any time, 'provided that, in due course, [they] give properly public reasons to support the principles and policies [their] comprehensive doctrine is said to support' (2002: 144). In other words, the person who holds the comprehensive doctrine must, upon entering the public debate or soon thereafter, translate any claims or concerns deriving from the doctrines to which they adhere into a language that is comprehensible – deemable as reasonable – to individuals outside that particular (or outside any) comprehensive doctrine.

Recently and increasingly vocally, Habermas takes issue with this notion, describing it as an 'asymmetric distribution of cognitive burdens':

> Religious citizens, in order to come to terms with the ethical expectations of democratic citizenship, have to learn to adopt new epistemic attitudes toward their secular environment, whereas secular citizens are not

exposed to similar cognitive dissonances in the first place (Habermas, 2005).

This he sees as an imbalance that needs to be rectified. Such strict demands can, in his view, legitimately be placed on politicians, who are obliged to remain neutral within state institutions. But the secular character of the state should not require that *citizens*, too, must personally 'supplement their public statements of religious convictions by equivalents in a generally accessible language' (Habermas, 2006: 9).

Essentially, Habermas speaks of the necessity for secular citizens to learn to live in a postsecular society. A properly functioning public sphere is one in which citizens learn to communicate with one another more substantially, in each other's terms – including religious terms. This requires then a cognitive act on the part of the secular citizen, to transcend a secularist self-understanding of modernity in order to be able to truly accept religious contributions to the political public sphere as having possible cognitive substance (rather than dismissing it from the outset, as an archaic relic of pre-modern society that is bound to become extinct) (Habermas, 2006: 15). Furthermore, it is in the state's interest that such an approach be encouraged: the liberal state should not discourage religious individuals and groups from expressing themselves politically from within their faiths (*as such*), 'for it cannot know whether secular society would not otherwise cut itself off from key resources for the creation of meaning and identity' (Habermas, 2006: 10).

For many, these proposals may come across as fairly radical, normative, and/or highly un-European. Certainly there are many contrary voices (a quick consideration of the popularity in Europe of Richard Dawkins' *The God Delusion* should suffice to make the point). But perspectives that entertain the notion of a postsecular Europe seem to be proliferating, with various mutations, amongst a growing number of scholars in their consideration of the European case, including Charles Taylor, Talal Asad and

Bhikhu Parekh.[15] And they address a very legitimate concern: what are the conditions under which the new pluralism in Europe can be negotiated in a healthy manner? What communicative action is necessary for constructive exchange between Europe's diverse secular and religious groups and individuals? Unequivocally, their responses to these questions call for a legitimate space for religion in the European public sphere.

TOWARDS A POSTSECULAR EUROPE?

As indicated above, theorists continue to debate the virtues – and whether any remaining virtues there be – of the secularization thesis. Peter Berger, himself once one of the strong proponents of the idea, declared himself and fellow secularizationalists mistaken, and suggested that only in Western Europe, and amongst a global secularized elite, did the theory still hold (Berger, 1999, 2000). Recently he has made a different, quite bold claim: 'Modernity does not necessarily lead to a decline of religion. What it does lead to, more or less necessarily, is religious pluralism' (Berger, 2007: 35).

Although there is little agreement on the nature of religiosity versus secularity in Europe, what is indeed certain is that, however strong or weak, religion in Europe (particularly in Western Europe) is marked by a plurality of religious expression. This is most noticeably, but not only, due to the postwar Muslim presence. The proliferation of new religious movements, alternative spiritualities, and the mutating, 'tinkered' Christianities described above (à la Davie, Hervieu-Leger, etc.), all also point to a religious scene which is far from the homogenous (in cases of monopolistic state churches) or even from the neatly pillarized or dual church–state (Netherlands, Belgium, Germany) models that once existed in Europe. Therefore, at this juncture in Europe's religious trajectory, discussion of religion in contemporary Europe will inevitably entail an approach adapted to this situation of plurality. If such an approach necessitates, as Casanova and Habermas suggest, a postsecular mentality, are Europeans likely to achieve it? And if so, what might the implications be?

For the second question, it is interesting to consider the case of Turkey's relation to Europe and to the EU. At a time when scholars have been discussing the potentiality for and desirability of a postsecular Europe, in Turkey there were mass demonstrations *in favour* of secularism in 2007. These demonstrations were provoked by the activities of the current Prime Minister Erdoğan and his ruling Justice and Development (AKP party) *vis-à-vis* the presidential elections (specifically, by Erdoğan's plans to promote a religiously oriented candidate for the presidency).[7] The demonstrations were quite remarkable, and were presented as such by the international media.

But perhaps they are not so striking when considered from the prism – as was the practice above for the cases of the Netherlands, France and Greece – of the specific historical and cultural circumstances underpinning the nation's particular relationship to religion, and the state's place in relation to this. Turkish secularism (or *laïcism*) is one of the key political legacies of Ataturk. It is practically and symbolically tied up with conceptions of Turkey's Westernization and Europeanization process, as envisioned by Ataturk: to be Western and European meant to be modern, and to be modern meant to be secular. Religion was to be rendered a private affair (and downplayed as much as possible – all the more with Islam, given its particular relationship to Europe).

This grand plan of Ataturk's has been the backdrop against which tensions between secularism and Islamism have played out in Turkey since the early twentieth century. Multiple generations of Turks have witnessed limitations set on Islamism, always in the name of Ataturk's 'sacred' causes of Turkish Westernization, democratization, and Europeanization. In other words, this cause became the site of perennial conflicts between the two powerful forces in Turkey of secularism and Islamism. And this has continued to be the case today, with the Turkish military acting as guardians to Ataturk's legacy. The irony in the fact that the military has, itself, at times been a barrier to the EU accession process, precisely in its claimed aim to secure this secular trajectory, is now familiar to most observers. But the situation described here – of simultaneous calls for a postsecular Europe on the one hand, and for a strengthened secularism in Turkey – threatens to introduce an additional irony into a situation (that of Turkey–EU relations) already burdened with ambiguities, contradictions and mixed messages.

To be precise: the irony is not so much in the notion of simultaneous trends in opposite directions (assuming, that is, that such trends are indeed in place). For, also in France, while scholars have been discussing a postsecular Europe, the French were experiencing their own version of a 'pro-secularism fest', in the form of the welcome reception of the Stasi Commission Report. The irony, rather, is in the historical linking by Turkish secular elites of Europeanization with secularization, when seen against the background of Turkey's protracted and difficult integration process, during which time Europe could, theoretically, be detaching itself from secularism and moving towards a postsecular reality. The Turkish case is quite special, but the potential awkwardness suggested here might also apply to newly acceded or other applicant countries.

As for Europe's realistic proximity to a postsecular reality, a return to some general points made in this chapter will aid in consideration of this question. First, scholars continue to be divided on Europe in relation to the secularization thesis: we are still far from a scholarly consensus as to the present religious, or secular, identity of Europe. At the national level, diversity prevails, as Europe represents a broad range of trends and patterns in religiosities and secularities. It seems unlikely that unified trends in one direction or another will develop any time soon at the national level. Meanwhile at the supranational level, the current place of religion in the EU may be described as – at best – ambiguous. The only substantial public discussion on the matter – in the debates on reference to God in the preamble of the Constitutional Treaty – was chaotic and the result unsatisfactory for many participants in the debate.

Furthermore, neither Turks nor (other) Europeans are too sure of whether religion is a factor in Turkey's accession potential. And the channels of communication are open between the European Commission and religious and humanist groups, but the system is far from smooth and balanced. Meanwhile, in some ways religion is stuck in a gridlock between the EU's commitment to both the principles of subsidiarity and of pluralism.

As for the role played by mobility in ushering in significant change to the religious landscape of Europe, this has indeed brought religious issues much more to the fore. But at the current juncture this area of change is heavily dominated by issues related to the Muslim presence and, in most cases, issues to do little with religion, *per se*. It is also dominated by images from the mass media, which hinder rather than help a constructive handling of religious matters and debates in their diverse manifestations across Europe.

From these perspectives then, the dawn of a postsecular Europe along the lines described by Casanova or Habermas is a distant prospect. But the fact that such debates are taking place is, in and of itself, a significant development on the path towards learning what a constructive handling of religion might look like in a European setting.

NOTES

1 Each of these terms, and the relation between them, is the subject of a great deal of academic debate. For our present purposes it will suffice to identify the first term as a process, the second as an ideology, and the third a description, each linked with the notion of the opposition of the worldly to the religious.

2 For a useful account of the historical development of secularization theory, see Swatos and Christiano (1999). For a succinct account of the development of secularism in Europe in comparison with the trajectory of religion in the United States, see Berger *et al.* (forthcoming).

3 Much of the literature is dominated by a focus on the advanced religious market as an important explanatory factor and on rational choice theory as applied to religious preferences. For a useful overview, see Davie (2007).

4 See Talal Asad (2003) for attention to the relation of Islam to the secular.

5 There are certain similarities between the French and Turkish versions of secularism (Turkish laïcism having been influenced by French laïcité), especially in their embeddedness in 'dominant' discourses of national identity in each case.

6 Proposed changes to junior high school history books, designed to present a more 'open' perspective on Greek national history and identity, led to mass protests in 2006, in which the Church was a very vocal participant.

7 More specifically, the Church lost the identity card battle, in the sense that religious affiliation ceased to be printed on newly issued identity cards, but it won part of the struggle *vis-à-vis* the state in demonstrating its ability to influence the electorate in the ensuing municipal and prefectural elections. For more on this subject, see Fokas (2006).

8 Although the European Convention on Human Rights and the European Court of Human Rights are formally under the auspices of the Council of Europe, rather than the EU as such, it is clear that the ECtHR and its rulings play an integral role in the European Union's relations with individual countries.

9 The YOK bill was presented to the Turkish Parliament by the Justice and Development Party (AKP) in May of 2004. The proposed bill introduced significant tension between the AKP and the military (both in the latter's traditional role as guardian of laïcité in Turkey, but also in its disappointment with the new bill's plan to remove military officials from the Higher Education Board). This tension, in turn, provoked a reaction within the EU. The bill was subsequently vetoed by the Turkish President Ahmet Necdet Sezer.

10 The debates on the place of religion in the Constitutional Treaty has been dealt with at length in several texts; for further background information, see Schlesinger and Foret (2006).

11 Such are the preliminary results of the European Commission FP6 research project entitled *Welfare and Values in Europe: Transitions related to Religion, Minorities and Gender* (WaVE). For more information, see www.waveproject.org.

12 The Institute for Jewish Policy Research event, 4 July 2007, with 'Sacralization by Stealth: Demography, Religion and Politics in Europe', presented by Eric Kaufmann, followed by a response by David Voas.

13 A fuller consideration of these developments would need to pay special attention to the factors that provoked these developments in the first place (i.e. in-depth attention to the content of the film *Submission* and to van Gogh's broader attitudes to Islam; attention to the circumstances under which the Mohammed cartoons were printed and reprinted; and attention to Pope Benedict XVI's broader perspectives on and attitudes toward Islam).

14 For an explanation of the notion of public reason, see sections 1 and 2 of Rawls' essay 'The Idea of Public Reason Revisited', (re)published in his monograph *The Law of Peoples* (2002).

15 Parekh prescribes what he calls a 'generous and realistic secularism', though in its content this secularism sounds strikingly like Habermas' postsecularism.

16 Of course, the results of the national elections following these mass protests are especially intriguing, given the AKP's victory with even a greater percentage of the vote than in the previous elections which brought the party to power. The story is somewhat similar to that of the 'identity card issue' in Greece, with the Church losing a battle but winning a war, so to speak, in terms of longer-term consequences. See note ?.

REFERENCES

Al-Azmeh, A. (2007) 'Afterword' in Al-Azmeh, A. and Fokas, E. (eds) *Islam in Europe: Diversity, Identity and Influence.* Cambridge: Cambridge University Press, pp. 208–215.

'After Secularization', *The Hedgehog Review*, 8 (1–2): 5–6, 2006, vol. 8, Nos. 1–2..

Asad, T. (2003) *Formations of the Secular: Christianity, Islam, Modernity.* Stanford: Stanford University Press.

Asad, T. (2006) 'French secularism and the "Islamic Veil Affair"', *The Hedgehog Review*, 8 (1–2): 93–106.

Audard, C. (2007) 'Laicity and the French Republic', paper presented at the Forum for European Philosophy Conference on Secularism, 13 June, London School of Economics, London.

Ayata, S. (1999) 'Une approche de la politique étrangère', *Les Annales de l'Autre Islam*, 6: 221–233.

Berger, P. (1969) *The Social Reality of Religion.* London: Faber & Faber.

Berger, P. (1999) 'The desecularization of the world', in P. Berger (ed.) *The Desecularization of the World: Resurgent Religion and World Politics*. Grand Rapids, Michigan: William B. Eerdmans Publishing Company, pp. 1–18.

Berger, P. (2000) 'Secularism in retreat', in J. Esposito and A. Tamini (eds) *Islam and Secularism in the Middle East*. New York: New York University Press, pp. 38–51.

Berger, P. (2007) 'Pluralism, protestantization, and the voluntary principle' in T. Banchoff (ed.) *Democracy and the New Religious Pluralism*. Oxford: Oxford University Press, pp. 33–48.

Berger, P., Davie, G., and Fokas, E. (2008) *Religious America, Secular Europe? A Theme and Variations*. London: Ashgate Press.

Bruce, S. (2002) *God is Dead: Explaining Secularization*. Oxford: Blackwell.

Cakir, R. (1990) 'Les movements islamistes Turcs et l'Europe', *Cahiers d'Etudes sur la Méditerranée Orientale et le Monde Turco-Iranien*, 10: 15–23.

Cakir, R. (1999) 'The Westernisation process of the Islamists', *Birikim*, (128): 50–51 [in Turkish].

Casanova, J. (1994) *Public Religions in the Modern World*. Chicago and London: University of Chicago Press.

Casanova, J. (2006a) 'Religion, European secular identities and European integration', in M. Krzysztof (ed.) *Religion in the New Europe*. Budapest: Central European University Press.

Casanova, J. (2006b) 'Religion, European secular identities, and European integration', in T. Byrnes and P.J. Katzenstein (eds) *Religion in an Expanding Europe*. New York: Cambridge University Press, pp. 65–92.

Chelini-Pont, B. (2005) 'Religion in the public sphere: challenges and opportunities', *Brigham Young University Law Review*, 3: 611–627.

Crockett, A. and Voas, D. (2006) 'Generations of decline. religious change in 20th-century Britain', *Journal for the Scientific Study of Religion*, 45(4): 567–584.

Davie, G. (2000) *Religion in Modern Europe: A Memory Mutates*. Oxford: Oxford University Press.

Davie, G. (1994) *Religion in Britain since 1945. Believing Without Belonging*. Oxford: Blackwell.

Davie, G. (2007) *The Sociology of Religion*. London: Sage Publications.

Ferrari, S. (2006) 'Religion and religious communities in the EU legal system', in *Proceedings of the Conference on State and Religion in Europe*, 9–10 December, Centre for Islamic Studies, Istanbul, pp. 9–21.

Fokas, E. (2006) 'Greece: religion, nation and European identity', in H. Gulalp (ed.) *Citizenship and Ethnic Conflict: Challenging the Nation-State*. Routledge Press, pp. 39–60.

Fokas, E. (2007) 'Introduction', in Al-Azmeh, A. and Fokas, E. (eds) *Islam in Europe: Diversity, Identity and Influence*. Cambridge: Cambridge University Press, pp. 1–15.

Gorski, P. (2003) 'Historicizing the secularization debate: an agenda for research', in M. Dillon (ed.) *Handbook of the Sociology of Religion*. New York: Cambridge University Press.

Habermas, J. (2005) 'Religion in the public sphere', Lecture presented at the Holberg Prize Seminar, 29 November. Available at: http://www.holbergprisen.no/downloads/diverse/hp/hp_2005/2005_hp_jurgenhabermas_religion-inthepublicsphere.pdf.

Habermas, J. (2006) 'Religion in the public sphere', *European Journal of Philosophy*. 14(1): 1–25.

Habermas, J. and Ratzinger, J. (2006) *The Dialectics of Secularization: On Reason and Religion*. San Fransisco: Ignatius Press.

Hervieu-Léger, D. (2000) *Religion as a Chain of Memory*. Cambridge: Polity Press (*translation of La religion pour mémoire*, 1993).

Hervieu-Léger, D. (2006a) 'The role of religion in establishing social cohesion' in M. Krzysztof (ed.) *Religion in the New Europe*. Budapest: Central European University Press.

Hervieu-Léger, D. (2006b) 'In search of certainties: the paradoxes of religiosity in societies of high modernity', *The Hedgehog Review*, 8 (1–2): 59–68.

Jakelić, S. (2006) 'Secularization, European Identity, and 'The End of the West'', *The Hedgehog Review*, 8 (1–2): 133–139.

Katzenstein, P. (2006) 'Multiple modernities as limits to secular Europeanization?', in T. Byrnes and P.J. Katzenstein (eds) *Religion in and Expanding Europe*. New York: Cambridge University Press, pp. 1–33.

Kaufmann, E. (2007) 'Sacralization by stealth: demography, religion and politics in Europe', working paper, Institute for Jewish Policy Research, 4 July.

Madeley, J. and Enyedi, Z. (2003) *Church and State in Contemporary Europe: The Chimera of Neutrality.* London: Frank Cass.

Marks, G. and Wilson, C. (2000) 'The past in the present: a theory of party response to European integration', *British Journal of Political Science*, 30: 433–459.

Martin, D. (1978) *A General Theory of Secularization.* New York: Harper Colophon Books.

Martin, D. (1994) 'Religion in contemporary Europe', in J. Fulton and P. Gee (eds) *Religion in Contemporary Europe*. New York: Edwin Mellen Press.

Martin, D. (2005) *On Secularization: Towards a Revised General Theory.* Aldershot: Ashgate.

Martin, D. (2006) 'Integration and fragmentation: patterns of religion in Europe' in M. Krzysztof (ed.) *Religion in the New Europe.* Budapest: Central European University Press, pp. 64–84.

Massignon, B. (2007) 'The regulation of religious diversity by the institutions of the European Union: the case of Islam', in eds. Al-Azmeh, A. and Fokas, E. (eds) *Islam in Europe: Diversity, Identity and Influence*, Cambridge: Cambridge University Press, pp. 125–148.

Molokotos-Liederman, L. (2003) 'Identity crisis: Greece, Orthodoxy and the European Union', *Journal of Contemporary Religion*, 18: 291–315.

Molokotos-Liederman, L. (2007) 'The Greek ID cards controversy: A case study on religion and national identity in a changing European Union', *Journal of Contemporary Religion*, 22: 187–203.

Nelsen, B., Guth, J., and Fraser, C. (2001) 'Does religion matter?', *European Union Politics*, 2(2): 191–217.

Norris, P. and Inglehart, R. (2005) *Sacred and Secular Religion and Politics Worldwide.* New York: Cambridge University Press.

Pew Forum (2005) 'Believing Without Belonging: Just How Secular Is Europe?', 5 December.

Ratzinger, J. and Pera, M. (2006) *Without Roots: Europe, Relativism, Christianity and Islam.* New York: Basic Books.

Rawls, J. (2002) *The Law of Peoples.* Cambridge, MA: Harvard University Press.

Rodinson, M. (1991) *Europe and the Mystique of Islam.* Seattle, London: University of Washington Press.

Schlesinger, P. and Foret, F.(2006) 'Political roof and sacred canopy? Religion and the EU Constitution', *European Journal of Social Theory,* 9 (1): 59–81.

Swatos, W. and Christiano, K. (1999) 'Secularization theory: the course of a concept', *Sociology of Religion*, 60 (3): 209–229.

ter Avest, I., Bakker, C., Bertram-Troost, G. and Miedema, S. (2007) 'Religion and education in the Dutch pillarized and post-pillarized educational system', in R. Jackson, S. Miedema, W. Weisse and J.P. Willaime (eds) *Religion and Education in Europe: Developments, Contexts and Debates.* Munster: Waxmann Verlag, pp. 203–219.

24

Welfare State Formation in the Enlarged European Union: Patterns of Reform in Postcommunist States

Susanne Fuchs and Claus Offe

If we allow ourselves to speculate for a moment about the question of how future historians will characterize trends and developments in European political economies during the decades after 1989, a combination of two processes seems plausible as an answer. First, they will point to the slow, halting, and inconclusive process of European integration and the concomitant denationalization (more *de facto* than *de lege*) of policy making in European states, a process which arguably amounts to a secular loss of what has been called 'state capacity'. Second, they will probably also point to the rapid, dramatic, and largely unanticipated demise of state socialism in all European member states of the Soviet Empire, the end of the Cold War, democratic transitions and (largely) consolidations, and the emergence of five new states (excluding an at least equal number of the new-born post-Yugoslav states – and protectorates! – in the Western Balkans).

As the 'New East' becomes Westernized in terms of its regime form as well as its economic and political integration into the EU, the west of Europe underwent changes that made it, as a result of full market integration in the late eighties and the (incomplete) monetary union achieved in the late nineties, increasingly dissimilar with its own postwar patterns of monetarily and fiscally sovereign national welfare states and their various national types, as they were influentially distinguished by Esping-Andersen (1990). According to Esping-Andersen, these postwar welfare states followed, if to different degrees and within contrasting institutional forms, the logic of 'decommodification' of labour – a concept originally proposed by Offe (1972, 1984) to depict the secular decrease of the exposure of employees to market contingencies and the cumulative buffering and protection of workers through *status* (rather than mere *contractual*) rights. With Thatcher's UK playing the role of a fore-runner throughout the eighties, high levels of unemployment on the European Continent, a sharp post-Keynesian turn in hegemonic economic doctrines, and the demise of corporatist and collectivist patterns of compromise and political exchange under the impact of unemployment in a number of European countries all contributed to the rise of market liberal programs and policies and to a trend *reversal* from *de-* to *re-*commodification.

Throughout the 'golden age' of postwar growth, roughly the 30 years after 1945, organized labor could safely assume that wage moderation would be rewarded by political concessions in the form of pension rights, code-termination rights, and employment-friendly monetary policies. But from the eighties on, wage moderation of unions was no longer a price to be paid for *gaining political concessions*. Rather, moderation had now to be considered an imperative to *avoid* further losses of employment and to *ward off negative economic* repercussions. The costs of labour, both in term of wage rates and in terms of social security contributions and benefits, had become the strategic parameter of competitiveness of national economies, their sectors and regions, within an irreversibly supranational economic space. These new realities were very much on the minds of policy makers who set out to design post-socialist welfare state institutions in the prospective new member states of the East. They were aware that the comparatively low costs of their (mostly competitively skilled) labour force provided a major prospect for rebuilding their economies, with the export of labour to some of the old member states even becoming a substantial source of domestic income.

The development of the political economies of the Central and Eastern European countries (CEE), including their welfare systems, has been shaped since the regime change after 1989 – and is likely to be so in the future – by two sets of determinants: the past and the West. 'The past' refers to the material, political, and cultural legacies of the old regime of state

socialism that suffered a definitive collapse in 1989, as well as the collective experience of the circumstances of its breakdown. 'The West' in this context refers to external economic, political, national, and supranational actors in the West, among which one of the most significant has certainly been the European Union and its strategy of Eastern enlargement (EE) and associated efforts to integrate the new member states into the EU. In addition to these two bundles of determinants which have largely shaped the CEE welfare states, a third one consisted of the strategic considerations which entered into the politics of reform by postcommunist political elites who had to cope with the realities of postcommunist economies (all of which have experienced severe economic transformation crises) and a nascent system of democratic politics and policies (with drastically enhanced liberties and other political resources being available to the populations of the postauthoritarian regimes).

Our chapter will address welfare state developments in the eight postsocialist new member states which completed the accession process in 2004 (henceforth termed 'EU-8'): Estonia, Latvia, Lithuania, Poland, the Czech Republic, Slovakia, Hungary, and Slovenia. (The newest round of enlargement, which went into effect on 1 January 2007 and includes Bulgaria and Romania, will largely remain outside the present discussion.) Our discussion will focus upon strategies of external and internal actors concerning welfare state reforms, and on the institutional arrangements as well as performance characteristics of CEE welfare states. We shall also address the controversial issue of whether and in what sense the emerging CEE welfare states diverge from the 'European social model' (ESM) or any of the three well-known welfare state 'regimes', be it because they must be described as a 'new' regime type or be it that they converge with the Anglo-Saxon 'residualist' model, as has been widely suggested in the literature.

Needless to say, Eastern enlargement had already begun long before 2004, when it instead came to its formal completion. The EU-15 (Austria, Belgium, Denmark, Finland, France, Germany, United Kingdom, Greece, Ireland, Italy, Luxemburg, Netherlands, Portugal, Sweden, and Spain) had concluded Association Agreements with all countries of the region as early as 1991 to 1993. In 1993 they decided upon a set of ('Copenhagen') criteria for membership eligibility. The EU received applications for membership between 1994 and 1996, and decided to open accession negotiations at the Luxembourg European Council in 1997. In the early 1990s, once the trade barriers between the CEE region and the EU had been abolished (cf. Clement *et al.*, 2002: table 7, statistical annex), foreign investors began to invest in the postcommunist economies. The total amount of Western foreign direct investment (FDI) in the region is estimated to have reached €150 billion by 2004. Such investment accounted for up to five percent of the GDP for many of the CEE countries and helped in the process of economic recovery (Barysch, 2005: 2 f.). In addition, EU pre-accession programs such as PHARE, ISPA, and SAPARD have assisted the process of conversion to the market economy, with PHARE alone having spent €10 billion in the period from 1990 to 2003, and, from 1990 to 2005, the EU having made payments to all new member states (EU-10, i.e. Cyprus, Czech Republic, Hungary, Estonia, Latvia, Lithuania, Malta, Poland, Slovakia, and Slovenia) totaling nearly €30 billion (EU Commission, 2006: 20 f.) Conversely, exports from the region into the EU-15 boomed throughout the 1990s and led to growth rates in EU-8 (Czech Republic, Hungary, Estonia, Latvia, Lithuania, Poland, Slovakia, and Slovenia) economies, which were well above the EU-15 average (see Table 24.1). Both political and the economic integration (not to forget military integration in the framework of NATO) had a long pre-history anteceding formal enlargement.

Two distinct yet interacting developments have occurred: one is the enlargement of the EU with the economic impacts it has on both the new and the old member states; the other is the formation and reform of the social welfare systems in the new member states. Concerning the impact of Eastern enlargement upon the development of welfare states in the CEE region, the anticipation of one axis of conflict stands out and this has framed political debate: namely, a clear-cut East–West cleavage of interest. Given the labor cost differentials between the EU-15 and the EU-8, the widely feared (though often exaggerated – see below) dynamic is a massive inflow of labor from the latter into the former, and a reverse flow of capital, investment, and jobs. The latter effect is partly mediated through the phenomenon of tax competition, with the lower tax rate and 'flat rate' tax (adopted, for example, by Slovakia) not only having the *consequence* of attracting Western European investors, but also the alleged *precondition* of net transfers flowing as subsidies from EU-15 donors into the EU-8 region, as it is only these transfers that allow for the 'fiscal generosity' of CEE states towards investors in the first place. Many commentators from the continental Western European Union member states fear that the dynamics of this (arguably somewhat distorted) competition might undercut the fiscal viability of the EU-15 welfare states, given the fact that these are plagued anyway by high levels of unemployment and fiscal strain.

But what about the emerging shape of the welfare state among the CEE transition societies, and the forces that determine the outcomes of reform? Three scenarios were distinguished in an influential paper by János Kovács (2002). First, and particularly so in the early 1990s, the prediction was widely shared by Western social policy experts that welfare state transformations in postcommunist countries would undoubtedly emulate none of the continental European or Scandinavian models, but rather that of Thatcher's UK or Reagan's US. The first prognosis thus anticipates the rise of a market-liberal model with means-tested benefits and a moderate system of social insurance targeting a low-income

Table 24.1 Basic indicators for the EU-8 and the EU-15, 2004

			Indicators			
Country	Population (in millions)	GDP 2003 (in billions of euros)	GDP per capita at PPP, EU-25 = 100	Real GDP growth (%) average for 2000–2004	Inflation (%) average for 2000–2004	Current account (in billions of dollars)
Czech Republic	10.2	80.3	70	3.1	2.6	−5.6
Estonia	1.3	8.1	51	7.2	3.5	−1.4
Hungary	10.0	72.6	61	3.9	7.1	−8.8
Latvia	2.3	9.9	43	7.5	3.2	−1.7
Lithuania	3.4	16.3	48	6.7	0.5	−1.6
Poland	38.2	185.2	47	3.1	4.3	−3.6
Slovakia	5.4	29.0	52	4.1	7.7	−1.4
Slovenia	2.0	24.9	79	3.4	6.8	−0.3
EU-8	72.8	426.3	56	4.9	4.5	−24.4
EU-15	383.5	9,373.5	109	2.0	2.0	21.8

Source: Barysch (2005: 2); author's calculations

clientele (Esping-Andersen, 1990: 26); the middle and upper classes, in contrast, would have to rely upon health coverage and pension plans through private means as provided for in the second and third pillars[1] of the social security system. If anything, as will be shown in some detail, this prediction can be rejected as premature and misguided – misguided because the advice recommending social spending austerity had its source in institutions such as the World Bank and the International Monetary Fund, or misguided because it was merely wishful thinking induced by the proponents of such advice (cf. Tomka, 2004: 127–30).

Diametrically opposed, as it were, is a second reading and projection of postcommunist welfare states. This scenario assumes that the long arm of the state-socialist past will hinder any vigorous, consistent, and sustained reform effort. As a consequence, realities will best be described by stagnation and strong path dependency mediated through a mental and political legacy of state protectionism shared by mass electorates and political elites alike. As one of the earliest comparative analyses of postcommunist welfare states concluded, the new political elites have been 'remarkably reluctant' to adopt any fundamental changes of the existing programs, for instance, in the area of old-age pensions (Götting, 1998: 158). In this sense, Kovács speaks of a kind of welfare state that

is part of 'the few relics of the command economy with all its dominant features such as the over-centralization, waste, rationing, shortage, paternalism, rent-seeking and corruption' (Kovács, 2002: 192).

The third position recognizes a mix of the Bismarckian social insurance model (found in conservative corporatist regimes) with additional public–private elements. This mix results from a 'great variety of "small transformations" ' (Kovács, 2002: 193) rather than being the outcome of a great and consistent systemic change in any consistently pursued direction of reform. These transformations are less the consequences of historical legacies or newly adopted ideological attitudes than they are the result of experimentation and the reaction to internal and external pressures. Welfare policies in the Central and Eastern European member states do not follow any consistent pattern that would converge with one of the three (or four) familiar 'welfare regimes' from Western and Southern Europe; nor can the CEE countries be said to have developed a model or 'postsocialist' regime of their own. If anything (as we want to show), they can be described as a bricolage in which both 'social democratic' and 'conservative' elements play a role, while (contrary to widely shared expectations and in defiance of some external pressures) Anglo-Saxon patterns of welfare liberalism can hardly be detected. What prevails is an ideologically 'faceless', as well as arguably economically and politically unstable pot-pourri of policies (Tomka, 2004: 132). Other than that, no uniform trend or pattern can be identified that would remain consistent across countries, time, or sectors of social policy and welfare state institutions. Analysts and commentators appear to largely agree that 'Central and Eastern European welfare systems could be classified by mixed traditional characteristics of the different European models' (EU Commission, 2003: 251).

At the *descriptive* level, the obvious question is: Which of these three trajectories is most consistent with the evidence provided by the data on welfare state reform experienced in the countries of the region since the early 1990s? This question will be at the center of the present paper. At the *explanatory* level, however, the even more challenging question is: What kinds of perceptions, choices, anticipations, and stra-tegic reasoning were the driving forces for the *elite actors* in the *CEE region* when they adopted and implemented welfare state reforms. It is this latter question to which we now turn, mostly relying on the findings and arguments suggested by Vanhuysse (2006), Orenstein (2000), and Cerami (2005, 2006).

An essential feature of Bismarckian social security policies is that they are designed to prevent the outbreak of noninstitutional distributive class conflict. They do so by installing three institutional features into social policy: (a) the selective provision of benefits to those segments of the population (i.e. the core working class) whose economic opposition would be most destructive to the orderly process of economic development; (b) the forging of inter-class alliances (e.g. in the form of social security funding being shared by employers and employees); and (c) the creation of institutional arrange-ments that subdivide the clientele of social security into a number of administrative cat-egories (defined by region, gender, and type of benefits, as well as by such divisions as the employed versus the unemployed, blue collar versus white collar workers, ordinary pensioners versus early retirees, workers in core or 'heavy' industries versus workers engaged in the production of consumer goods and agriculture, etc.), thus shifting the focus of distributive conflict from a conflict between encompassing *class* coalitions to a conflict between *status groups*.

Vanhuysse has persuasively argued in his recent book, *Divide and Pacify* (2006), that an analogous calculus of the preventive man-agement of conflict has been the guiding strategic objective in much of postcommu-nist social policy-making. According to Vanhuysse, given the facts that (a) the work-ing population of the former state socialist societies had never experienced anything but employment security under the old system; (b) it had acquired a mindset according to which both the level of employment and the level of real income is primarily a matter of political decision making; (c) with the transi-tion to political democracy it enjoyed a sub-stantial increase in its political resources after the demise of the monopolistic party dictatorship and, as a result; (d) that it had every reason to engage in vehement distribu-tive struggles because of the high rate and often lengthy duration of unemployment due to the transformation crisis which generated widening economic disparities between the economic 'winners' and the 'losers' of that transformation. The potentially explosive mix of these factors was clearly understood by political elites, and the potential for dis-ruptive distributive conflict anticipated. Responding to these threats, the postcommu-nist elites engaged (largely) successfully in a 'conservative' strategy of pacification through division, thus accomplishing the 'unexpected peacefulness' of the transition process. They managed to defuse the potential for protest through an administrative segregation of the populations affected, thus rendering collec-tive action for distributive conflict more dif-ficult. The main categories in which the working class was divided are those of regu-lar workers, regular pensioners, the unem-ployed and the 'abnormal' (early retired) pensioners, with at least the latter two being strongly reliant on the informal economy.

In a fine-grained analysis of the social reforms that occurred in the Visegrad countries since the early 1990s, Cerami (2005, 2006) concludes that the pattern of reform 'can be described as an ambiguous mix of differentiation and equalization of provisions' (2006: 27) – a pattern that can be alternatively described as a 'recombinant welfare state' or social policy 'hybridization' which, in sharp contrast to the neoliberal precepts proclaimed in the immediate aftermath of the breakdown, remains to a large extent faithful to the Bismarckian tradition of the precommunist era as well as to the egalitarian tradition of the state-socialist period (2006: 32). The absence of a social policy upheaval comparable to that which occurred over the economic and political reorganization of the postcommunist societies is striking. Arguably, it is due to the perceived need to preserve social protection in order to fend off disruptive distributive conflicts (such as the miners' strikes that occurred in Romania in 1998).

Public debate among *non-elites* in the *old* member states, however, has focused on the question of labor migration and wage competition (the French nightmare of the 'Polish plumber'). This is especially true for those countries which share borders with the new member states, such as Austria and Germany. Given the various types of fears, hopes, and anticipations prevalent in the debate in the old and new member states, among elites and the masses alike, the question to be settled is this: How will enlargement affect social welfare in the European Union? That is, will the new member states be the forerunners of 'lean welfare'? Will migration driven by poor economic and social performance in the new member states lead to 'social dumping' and a 'race to the bottom' in some or all of the EU-15 countries? As an overall consequence, will enlargement reshape the social landscape of Europe? In addressing these issues, we start with a comparative analysis of features and trends in the institutional design of the welfare systems in the new member states.

SOCIAL WELFARE SYSTEMS OF THE CENTRAL AND EASTERN EUROPEAN MEMBER STATES – CHALLENGES AND DEVELOPMENTS

We will begin by discussing basic indicators for the EU-8 economies. We then proceed by addressing the most important reforms for the region in health care, pension plans, social exclusion, and the labor market.

Basic indicators

The growth rates among new member states from the CEE exceed those of the EU-15 significantly (see Table 24.1). An important factor determining overall growth in the region was the export boom (e.g. exports rose in Hungary by 380 percent and in the Czech Republic by 280 percent in the ten years before accession) (Barysch, 2005: 2). This boom was fostered by the liberalization of trade among the EU-15 and the CEE. It was additionally fueled by high rates of foreign direct investment (FDI). However, according to a recent report of the European Bank for Reconstruction and Development (EBRD), there are signs that some investors will shift their focus towards southeastern Europe, since privatization in the CEE countries is almost complete and thus attractive objects for investment there are becoming scarce[2] (EBRD, 2005: 29; Vincentz, 2002). However, this is true only for top-down FDI concerning the privatization of formerly state-owned companies. Bottom-up FDI; that is, investment in start-up companies, is less affected by economic privatization being completed, as it continues to be attracted by the low corporate tax rates adopted in the new member states (cf. ZEW and Ernst & Young, 2004; see also section below).

The GDP per capita of the new member states reaches roughly 50 percent of the GDP per capita of the EU-15 (Hönekopp *et al.*, 2004: 1), and even the high growth rates of the past did not significantly diminish this gap.

According to a projection by the German Institut für Arbeitsmarkt-und Berufsforschung (IAB) regarding the development of the GDP per capita in the new member states as a percentage of the average GDP per capita in the EU-15, the overall prosperity gap between the EU-15 and EU-8 will remain significant for a relatively long period of time, even if the more optimistic assumptions about EU-8 growth rates were to turn out true (see Table 24.2).

The shadow economy

Another important economic phenomenon which needs to be taken into account if we want to assess the EU-8 scenario of economic development is the size of the shadow economy (defined as the total of market-based legal production of goods and services that are concealed from public authorities in order to avoid payment of taxes and social security contributions, as well as to avoid compliance

with regulatory standards; cf. Schneider, 2004: 4 f.) as a percentage of the GDP. According to recent estimates, the shadow economy is, on average, twice as high in the Central and East European countries as it is in 21 OECD countries. The average size of the shadow economy in the new member states was almost 30 percent of their official GDP in 2002/2003, as compared to an average of 16 percent in 21 OECD countries for the same period (Schneider, 2004: 30). The respective sizes of shadow economies vary considerably among CEE countries. While those of Latvia and Estonia, for instance, reach almost 40 percent of their respective GDPs, the shadow economies of Slovakia and the Czech Republic are much closer in size (at 20.2 percent and 20.1 percent, respectively, in 2002/2003; see Table 24.3) to those of the OECD average. The relative size of a given shadow economy reflects deficiencies in the administrative capacities of the respective new member states.

Economic activities which are part of a shadow economy are known to harm the real economy in many ways. Losses of tax revenues and social security contributions, for instance, cause a decrease in the quality of public services and may ultimately lead to increased tax rates as a consequence, thus setting in motion a vicious circle. Moreover, no contributions to social security or pension plans are made for persons employed in the shadow economy,

Table 24.2 Prognosis for the development of the GDP per capita in the EU-8 in relation to the average GDP per capita in the EU-15

Country	2003	2010	2020	2030
Assumed annual GDP growth of 2.5% in the EU-8 and 1.5% in the EU-15				
Average EU-8	0.51	0.55	0.60	0.66
Estonia	0.45	0.48	0.53	0.58
Latvia	0.42	0.45	0.49	0.54
Lithuania	0.42	0.45	0.50	0.55
Poland	0.42	0.45	0.50	0.55
Slovakia	0.47	0.50	0.55	0.61
Slovenia	0.71	0.76	0.83	0.92
Czech Republic	0.63	0.67	0.74	0.82
Hungary	0.56	0.60	0.66	0.73
Assumed annual GDP growth of 3.5% in EU-8 and 1.5% in EU-15				
Average EU-8	0.51	0.58	0.71	0.86
Estonia	0.45	0.51	0.62	0.76
Latvia	0.42	0.48	0.58	0.70
Lithuania	0.42	0.48	0.59	0.71
Poland	0.42	0.49	0.59	0.72
Slovakia	0.47	0.54	0.65	0.79
Slovenia	0.71	0.81	0.98	1.19
Czech Republic	0.63	0.72	0.88	1.07
Hungary	0.56	0.64	0.78	0.94

Source: Hönekopp *et al.* (2004: 5); author's compilation, author's calculations.

Table 24.3 Size of the shadow economy in new member states, 1999–2003

Country	Shadow economy (in percentage of official GDP)		
	1999–2000	2001–2002	2002–2003
Czech Republic	19.1	19.6	20.1
Estonia	38.4	39.2	40.1
Hungary	25.1	25.7	26.2
Latvia	39.9	40.7	41.3
Lithuania	30.3	31.4	32.6
Poland	27.6	28.2	28.9
Slovakia	18.9	19.3	20.2
Slovenia	27.1	28.3	29.4
Average	28.3	29.0	29.9
Germany	16.0	16.3	16.8

Source: Schneider (2004: 26, 30); author's compilation and calculations.

thus exposing these individuals to the risk of poverty and reliance on public assistance benefits in old age. This condition applies, for example to Poland and Hungary, where roughly 21 percent of the labor force are engaged in sources of income that belong to the shadow economy.

Taxation and social expenditures

In this section we compare corporate and personal income tax rates, value-added tax (VAT) rates, and payroll taxes for the EU-8 and the EU-15, in order to shed some light on the sources of fiscal revenues and their implications for social policies. Corporate taxes in the new member states are on average much lower than in the EU-15. For instance, Poland reduced its statutory tax rate in 2004 from 27 percent to 19 percent; the Slovak Republic also did so, decreasing taxes from 25 percent to 19 percent; the Czech Republic decreased taxes as well, from 31 percent to 28 percent. In addition, the new member states grant considerable tax incentives to attract foreign investors.[3] Average corporate taxes are not only substantially lower than those levied in EU-15, there is also a great deal of variation among EU-8 states, indicating an intense corporate tax competition unfolding among them. As to the taxation of personal income, the Baltic States and Slovakia implemented a flat income tax rate, with rates ranging between 19 percent in Slovakia and 33 percent in Lithuania. This had the effect of relieving the middle class from the distributive effects of tax progressiveness.

Concerning the welfare-related expenditure side of the national budget, EU-8 levels of social spending are much lower than those to be found in the EU-15 (see Table 24.4). This finding is in line with the well-known tendency for welfare budgets to increase/decrease in direct proportion to per-capita GDPs. While the new EU member states from the CEE region spend on average 19 percent of their GDP on social welfare, the old member states reach a share of about 28 percent. The greatest single factor accounting

for this gap is under-spending by the EU-8 on health care, as compared to EU-15 average expenditures for the same. (EU Commission, 2006: 102).

Not only the level of social expenditures, but also the source of financing differs somewhat between the EU-8 and the EU-15. Concerning the latter, we can observe a broad trend towards shifting contributory systems in the direction of a greater role being played by general tax revenues in financing social welfare insurance and other social expenditures. A similar trend can be found in the emerging EU-8 welfare states, although (and perhaps due to the tradition inherited from the 'Bismarckian' logic of state socialism and its social welfare policies) the shift towards greater financing through tax revenues appears to be somewhat delayed in the CEE region. Total labor costs in Central and Eastern Europe still consist, to a significant extent, of non-wage expenditures (e.g. social insurance contributions). For instance, in Poland social security contributions amount to 47 percent of labor costs, and in Slovakia to more than 50 percent, both countries surpassing even German and Italian expenditure rates. Thus, the new EU member states from the CEE evidently still rely more on contributory financing of social security than is the case for the average EU-15 member state (see Table 24.5). However, the contribution rate determined by government often does not fully cover statutory expenses, so that deficits must be financed out of general tax revenues. The legacies of state socialism mean that the employers' share in contributions is usually higher than that of the employees (see Table 24.5).

To some extent, the EU-8 do seem to stick to the Bismarckian model, regarding the mode of financing the welfare state, which relies on social security contributions shared between employers and employees, and levied against wages, with general tax revenues playing only a marginal role. However, the new member states also suffer from poor labor market performance which is due, in part, to the high non-wage costs of employment (cf. Knogler, 2002).

Table 24.4   Social expenditures[1] (as percentage of GDP) for the EU-15, EU-8, and EU-23

Country	1995	1996	1997	1998	1999	2000	2001	2002
Belgium	28.1	28.6	27.9	27.6	27.3	26.9	27.5	27.8
Denmark	32.2	31.4	30.4	30.2	30.0	29.2	29.4	30.0
Germany	28.9	30.0	29.5	29.3	29.6	29.6	29.8	30.5
Finland	31.7	31.6	29.2	27.2	26.8	25.5	25.7	26.4
France	30.7	31.0	30.8	30.5	30.2	29.8	30.0	30.6
Greece	22.3	22.9	23.3	24.2	25.5	26.3	27.1	26.6
United Kingdom	28.2	28.1	27.5	26.9	26.5	27.1	27.6	27.6
Ireland	18.9	17.8	16.6	15.4	14.7	14.3	15.3	16.0
Italy	24.8	24.8	25.5	25	25.2	25.2	25.6	26.1
Luxemburg	23.7	24.1	22.8	21.7	21.7	20.3	21.3	22.7
Netherlands	30.9	30.1	29.4	28.4	28	27.4	27.5	28.5
Austria	28.9	28.8	28.8	28.5	28.9	28.4	28.6	29.1
Portugal	22.1	21.2	21.4	22.1	22.6	23.0	24.0	25.4
Sweden	34.6	33.8	32.9	32.2	31.8	30.8	31.4	32.5
Spain	22.1	21.9	21.2	20.6	20.3	20.2	20.1	20.2
Estonia	–	–	–	–	–	15.1	14.3	–
Latvia	–	–	–	–	–	15.3	14.3	–
Lithuania	–	–	–	–	–	16.2	15.2	–
Poland	–	–	–	–	–	20.7	22.1[2]	–
Slovakia	18.7	19.8	20	20.2	20.2	19.5	19.1	19.2
Slovenia	–	24.4	24.8	25.0	25.0	25.2	25.5	25.4
Czech Republic	17.0	17.3	18.3	18.3	19.1	19.3	19.2	19.9
Hungary	–	–	–	–	20.7	19.8	19.8	20.9
EU-25	–	–	–	–	–	27.0	27.3	–
EU-15	28.2	28.4	28.0	27.5	27.4	27.3	27.6	28.0
EU-8	–	–	–	–	–	18.9	18.7	21.4

1 Social expenditures as a percentage of the GDP include health, disability, old age, survivor dependent compensation, family benefits, unemployment, housing and public assistance.
2 According to Walwei (2004: 3) the Polish share of social expenditure as per cent of GDP was almost 30%.
Source: Wirtschaftskammer Österreich (2005); author's calculations.

Table 24.5   Social insurance contribution rates of employers and employees, 2002 (%)

Country	Pensions – old age, survivor, and disability	Health	Unemployment	Other – maternity, illness, occupational diseases	Total
	Total (employer/employee), percentages of wages before taxes				
Czech Republic	26 (19.5 + 6.5)	13.5 (9 + 4.5)	3.6 (3.2 + 0.4)	4.4 (3.3 + 1.1)	47.5
Estonia	20 (employer)[1]	13 (employer)[2]	1.5 (0.5 + 1)	–	34.5
Hungary	26 (18 + 8)	14 (11 + 3)[3]	4.5 (3 + 1.5)	–	44.5
Latvia	30.86	general taxes	1.9	2.33	35.09[4]
Lithuania	25 (22.5 + 2.5)	3.0 (employer)[5]	1.5	4.5 (4 + 0,5)	34
Poland	32.52 (16.26 + 16.26)	7.75 (employee)	2.45 (employer)	4.07 (1.62 + 2.45)	46.79
Slovakia	28 (21.6 + 6.4)	14 (10 + 4)	3.75 (2.75 + 1)	4.8 (3.4 + 1.4)[6]	50.55
Slovenia	24.35 (8.85 + 15.5)	12.92 (6.56 + 6.36)	0.2 (0.06 + 0.14)	0.73 (0.63 + 0.1)	38.2

1 Contributions to funded pension scheme as of 1 July 2002: plus 2% of the wage.
2 Including illness cash benefits.
3 The employer pays an additional lump sum of HUF 4500 (approximately 18 euros) per month to the Health Insurance Fund.
4 9% of the overall contribution rate is paid by the employee.
5 No direct employee's contribution, but 30% of the income tax of the employee are transferred to health insurance.
6 The employer pays for occupational risk insurance additionally between 0.2% and 1.2%.
Source: European Commission (2003: 28), own compilation.

Table 24.6   Shift towards the Bismarck model of social health insurance (SHI)

Country	Year SHI law passed	Year contribution collection began	Autonomy of health insurance fund(s)[1]	Contributions and benefits set by the government
Czech Republic	1990	1993	Yes	No
Estonia	1991	1992	Yes	Yes
Hungary	1991	1991	No	Yes
Latvia	1993	1993	Yes	No
Lithuania	1991	1991	No	Yes
Poland	1997	1999	Yes	No
Slovakia	1994	1994	Yes	N/A
Slovenia	1992	1992	Yes	Yes

1 Autonomy is defined as health insurance funds 'that are administered by an agency other than the government itself. This could be through a national health insurance fund which would be in charge of setting and collecting and distributing funds' (European Commission, 2003: 98).
Source: European Commission (2003: 97).

High non-wage labor costs weaken the already imbalanced labor market and shrink the contribution base as a result of increasing incentive to participate in the shadow economy. Therefore, there seems to be at best, also given the size of the informal sector, just very limited room to increase revenues by increasing contribution rates.

SOCIAL PROTECTION SYSTEMS IN THE CENTRAL AND EAST EUROPEAN MEMBER STATES[4]

In the following sections, we try to identify in some detail similarities and differences in the design of social welfare systems in the EU-8. In order to achieve a clearer picture of scope, source, and level of social security in the EU-8, we review the key features of health care, the pension system, measures against social exclusion and poverty, and unemployment insurance and labor market policy. On the basis of this account we shall further discuss the nature and specificity of EU-8 welfare states.

Health care

In the former state-socialist EU-member countries, health care was state controlled and revenues were collected predominantly from state-owned companies. Private contributions existed (if they existed at all) in the

form of informal 'bribes' that were needed to jump the queue. The entitlement to free health care in the CEE was institutionalized as a right of citizenship.

The challenges that postcommunist governments had to cope with pertained to the reorganization of health services and of the mode of financing them. These tasks had to be solved in the context of persistent expectations and demands from a public which continues to regard, in line with state-socialist patterns, the state as provider (rather than mere regulator) of health care (cf. Kornai/Eggleston, 2001). Although the organization of health care diverges from case to case, all of the new EU member states from the CEE have adopted a contributory ('Bismarckian') model of financing parts of health expenses (see Table 24.6). The Czech Republic, Estonia, Hungary, Slovakia, Slovenia, Latvia, and Lithuania, roughly following the German pattern, introduced a system of self-governing, state-regulated regional health insurance funds in the first half of the 1990s, followed by Poland in the late-1990s. The mode of financing health services differs among the new EU member states from the CEE: Latvia and Poland finance a large portion of health expenses through taxation, while the Czech Republic, Estonia, Hungary, Lithuania, Slovakia, and Slovenia rely mostly on contributions. Overall health care expenditures as a percentage of the GDP range from 5.9 per cent in Latvia to 8.9 per cent in Slovenia (data for the year 2000, European Commission, 2003: 122) and is just over one half of the average relative size of health expenditures in the EU-15 (European Commission, 2003: 224).

Governments of the EU-8 approached the problem of reorganizing and financing health care by cutting or privatizing hospital capacities. Also, administrative decentralization of health service facilities to local and non-profit agencies was an important instrument for reforming primary and secondary health care. As a consequence of the downsizing of medical capacities, the provision of services became precarious in some regions. In the EU-15 on average, 96 percent of the citizens need less than one hour to reach a hospital, while this is true for only 87 percent of the CEE citizenry (European Foundation for the Improvement of Living and Working Conditions, 2004: 26 f.).

Health care developments can roughly be summarized as follows. Financing services (and thus the effective demand in the health market) has largely remained a matter of mandatory contributions and taxes, while the actual provision of services (i.e. the supply side) is partly assigned to private and decentralized actors. User fees are common for prescription drugs, dental care, and some rehabilitation services. Private health insurance was introduced in some countries (Estonia, Slovenia, and the Czech Republic), but plays only a minor role in the overall financing of health care (Dietrich, 2003: 99). In addition, all countries introduced mechanisms to enhance the efficiency and control the quality of medical services supplied.

Eastern enlargement has had a significant impact upon the health systems in the EU-8, since it facilitates health-related migration (cf. EU Commission, 2003: 241). In principle, both supply-side actors (e.g. medical doctors) and demand-side actors (patients and their health funds) can seek advantages by crossing member states' borders. To a limited extent, patients who are nationals of new member states are permitted to undergo treatment abroad; they may choose to do so because of the limited availability and/or poor quality of medical treatment that is available at home. As their health funds will have to cover medical costs abroad, these must increase substantially. Conversely, some of the EU-8 member states are expected to profit from the competitively priced health services (such as spa treatments) that they can provide to patients from other EU countries. From the supply-side perspective, there are strong incentives for medical professionals from the new member states to relocate to the old ones – in particular, higher status and income – assuming that professional qualifications and training curricula will be further harmonized throughout the EU. In turn, this development could trigger an outflow of skills and a 'brain drain' among medical professionals in their respective countries of origin.

Social exclusion and poverty

After the political transformation following the collapse of the old regime in 1989, the eight new EU members faced the new challenge of having to fight poverty and social exclusion, which resulted from the steep increase in income inequality and the poor labor market performance that accompanied the economic transition from a socialist to a private market economy. Although not absent under the old regime, poverty was largely a condition experienced by those who were outside of employment; that is, the pensioners, while (open) unemployment was a virtually unknown phenomenon. '[I]n former socialist countries poverty issues were not explicitly on the political agenda' (EU Commission, 2003: 243).

The picture changed dramatically in the early 1990s when a large number of workers lost their jobs, real wage levels decreased under the impact of high inflation rates, and shrinking state-provided transfers and services failed to cope with the kinds and scopes of newly emerging risks; as a consequence, 'poverty became widespread' (EU Commission, 2003: 243). The early retirement age that was characteristic for state socialist regimes inflated the ranks of pensioners in need of social assistance, and the relatively low life-expectancy of men aggravated the problem of financing survivors' pensions. At the same time, company-operated social services and facilities disappeared with the companies or, at any rate, the companies' ability to provide them. States and state-operated companies became unable to care for dependent and highly vulnerable segments of the population such as the elderly, disabled, orphaned, or abandoned children, and the residents of backward, rural areas; vulnerability and marginalization were also tied to the conditions of juvenile delinquency, teenage pregnancy, substance abuse, and prostitution, as well as blatant forms of gender discrimination. (EU Commission, 2003: 245) Women were more strongly affected than men by the new labor market dynamics of rising unemployment, since a comparatively high share of the female labor force was employed in agriculture in rural areas where wages tended to be much lower than in urban areas. Their male counterparts tended to migrate to other areas and usually better paid occupations.

All of these developments exacerbated the pressures that had to be dealt with by families who by default became the ultimate safety net. There are also strong indications that the state socialist system with its paternalistic and authoritarian features had discouraged the rise of 'social capital' and other civil society virtues of caring locally for the rights and wellbeing of fellow citizens, be it within or outside of religious charities and needs-based services, all of which are arguably the most elementary forms of solidarity in social life (cf. Howard, 2003). At the same time, political democratization made the issue of poverty and the policies to alleviate it increasingly salient items on the political agenda. In addition, in some countries the issue of poverty merged with the issue of civil and social rights of minorities, most importantly, the Roma. In Hungary, for instance, this ethnic group made up one-third of the long-term poor,

constituting only about five to six per cent of the overall population. In Slovakia, 80 per cent of the Roma population had to rely on public assistance and disability benefits.

However, early recognition of the existence of poverty issues was rare in the CEE countries, with the notable exceptions of the Czech Republic and Slovenia. These two countries responded timely to the new challenge of poverty in the beginning of early 1990s while, in other countries of the region, poverty and the poor emerged as a policy issue only in the latter half of the decade. This delay in poverty-related policy formation had various causes such as the political priority accorded to pension and unemployment reforms, the poor representational resources and 'voice' of the groups affected by poverty, as well as the widespread belief that poverty is a natural yet transitory side-effect of economic transformation. Not only was poverty for some time disregarded by policy makers, it was also hidden from observation by the failure of official statistics to take account of the phenomenon. If such accounting occurred at all, it was performed by international actors such as the World Bank, ILO, and the UNDP (European Commission, 2003: 176 f.). The Polish government began to respond in the mid-1990s to a poverty report that was submitted by the World Bank; similar responses occurred in Estonia in 1999 and Latvia in 1998. It was only in the course of the accession process that preceded actual enlargement that poverty and social exclusion gained attention due to the EU's emphasis on 'fighting exclusion' and the precondition that new member states had to comply with EU standards and policies. Yet the risk of workers becoming part of the 'working poor' still appears to be considerably higher among the EU-8 than it is in the EU-15.

The institutional means through which the problem of poverty has been addressed in the CEE region are family and child benefits, and means-tested social assistance. In addition, there are housing subsidies for the poor (Slovenia, Poland) and some rudimentary

NGO-operated charitable services and support. As is the case elsewhere, public assistance operates on the basis of an income-level 'poverty line', below which individuals and families are entitled to (cash, in-kind, or service) benefits that will supposedly help to narrow or close the gap. Family and child benefits as well as public assistance are tax-financed and administered at the local level in all countries. Coverage varies but seems nevertheless not quite sufficient.

To summarize, it seems to be fair to say that social exclusion and poverty are issues that were measured, recognized, and addressed only belatedly (in anticipation of accession) in most of the new member states. Poverty in the Central and Eastern European countries is a complex result of the conditions of unemployment, poor health, ethnicity, the breakdown of the safety net of the former state-socialist regime, and administrative and financial deficiencies that prevent anti-poverty schemes from working effectively. Again, no general institutional pattern can be identified across countries and across time, with the only valid generalization being the dysfunction and fiscal constraints which stand in the way of adequate and effective (including preventative) policy measures to alleviate poverty and exclusion.

Pensions

Under the old regime, CEE countries relied on a centralized state-provided pension system. In general, the dominant pension scheme consisted of two tiers, with the first tier being the mandatory public scheme and the second tier being quasi-mandatory (in countries with low flat-rate benefits) or voluntary (in countries with more generous benefits). In addition, the retirement age was (and still is) considerably lower in CEE states (60 years or younger) than in the old member states. Even after raising the retirement age during the last decade, none of the new member states has so far reached the EU-15 standard mandating a 65-year threshold

as the statutory retirement age. Moreover, we must keep in mind that the actual average retirement age is even lower than the statutory retirement age. This is due to early retirement resulting from precarious health conditions or disability of elderly employees, and the high rates of unemployment among older workers. As is the case in some Western European countries, the pension system is effectively used (through arrangements facilitating 'abnormal' retirement, as Vanhuysse, 2006, calls it) to conceal unemployment, and particularly so where effective unemployment insurance is not yet in place. This 'solution,' however, comes at a price: it consists of vast fiscal imbalances between the revenues which the pension system extracts from contributors and the payments which it makes to retired recipients. What this imbalance seems to call for, according to the logic of pay-as-you-go (PAYG) systems, is a *raise* of the statutory retirement age in the public pensions system ('first pillar') – a move, however, which is precluded, because this would only increase the gap between the nominal and the actual retirement ages, given the generally unfavorable labor market situation. As a way out of this dilemma, the burden of providing income to the elderly has partly been shifted to a funded system with mandatory elements, be it in the form of occupational pensions ('second pillar') or private savings ('third pillar'). Thus all countries have devised multitiered models, with the first tier being the basic public pension, the second consisting of supplementary funding (usually provided by public–private or private schemes, e.g. by employers), and the third consisting of additional funding through private savings.

The new member states differ with regard to the time and extent of the introduction of mandatory elements in their respective pension schemes. Only Latvia, Hungary, Poland, and Estonia (and also Bulgaria) have implemented mandatory systems since the late-1990s. Slovakia implemented pension reforms only as of January 2005. Slovakian workers can choose to remain entirely in the PAYG system or to commit a part of their pension savings to investment funds (Tupy, 2006).

Other countries like Slovenia and the Czech Republic decided to reform their first pillar by raising retirement ages and strengthening the contribution–benefits link. The Czech Republic split the first tier into two components; the first includes a citizenship-based flat-rate pension and is complemented by the second, a professional status and earnings-related pension scheme. In addition, a voluntary supplementary pension scheme is available that is run by joint stock companies (Cerami, 2005: 76 f.). Slovenia introduced a comparable system with a mandatory first-pillar scheme (pay-as-you-go) based on citizenship, which is universal in scope and coverage (e.g. contributions for unemployment compensation are also made by the state). Its second pillar is based on an income differentiation scheme managed by the state through the Institute of Pension and Disability Insurance of Slovenia (Cerami, 2005: 84). Thus Slovenia remained closest to the universal and redistributive pension scheme which was typical in the communist regimes. This can be explained as a result of having strong unions which succeeded, for instance, in blocking influence and staving off pressure from the World Bank or the IMF. None of the new member states introduced a privately managed first pillar; thus the Latin American (Chile) model does not seem to have been embraced as a real option.

The collectivist concept of solidarity that was institutionalized in the centralized and universalized system of pensions under state socialism thus gave way to a pluralist and vastly more complex system in which PAYG and funds, and mandatory and voluntary elements all play some role. The new concept of solidarity is less demanding in terms of inter-personal redistribution. What it does emphasize, instead, is a kind of longitudinal solidarity, or the solidarity of present individuals (accumulating savings out of current incomes) with their future selves (receiving capital yields in proportion to those savings).

In order for this liberal (as opposed to its state-socialist counterpart) notion of solidarity and responsibility to become operative, strong institutional underpinnings are needed, for instance, in the form of a well-functioning and adequately regulated banking system which guarantees a link between present savings and future benefits. Similarly, and as far as the remaining public PAYG system is maintained, its adequate operation depends upon the availability of the administrative capacity that is needed to force (primarily) employers to do their duty and to actually make the mandatory social security contributions that are expected of them. 'Contribution evasion' by employers has reportedly become a widespread phenomenon in the region (a 'common and fashionable sport'). Similarly, workers violate norms of solidarity (be it solidarity with fellow workers or be it solidarity with their own future selves) by drawing incomes from the shadow economy, the illegal economy, or by under-reporting their wages (European Commission, 2003: 237 f.).

The problems that policy makers in post-socialist countries must deal with are not just caused by labor market, financial, and demographic conditions. As if that were not already enough of a burden, these problems are also caused by widespread anti-solidarity patterns such as future-discounting or other-disregarding. Unsurprisingly from a sociological point of view, the generalization may not have been entirely oversimplified that as soon as the authoritarian centralist lid was lifted off the pot of state-socialist society, the transition process was marked by symptoms of widespread opportunism, 'short-termism', and the corrosion of loyalties to institutions that are the indispensable underpinnings of any version of solidarity.

Again, as in health care, none of the new EU member states has rejected its general responsibility for social security. All provide basic coverage which is complemented by a second and third pillar, with the former often provided by public–private or private schemes and the latter consisting of private savings.

However, poverty in old age is a problem in many of the new member states. Owing to an absence of indexing in the CEE region, pensions decreased dramatically in value and could fall well below subsistence level. Additional funding schemes like the national pension in Estonia have corrected this problem at least partly, while other countries have granted a flat-rate pension below minimum income levels. Pensioners without substantial savings, other sources of income, or family support thus find it hard to make a living.

Labor market performance and unemployment

All of the transition economies faced a severe recession in the beginning of the 1990s. The bottom was reached for most of them in 1992/1993, but since then the CEE countries have experienced higher average growth rates than the EU-15, as shown above. However, overall economic performance differs considerably among CEE states.

As discussed earlier, there is little reason to expect current growth rates to persist in the medium-term future. But even the high growth rates of the mid-nineties did not lead to anything approaching 'full' employment. Labor market performance varies among the new member states, but unemployment rates are on average higher than those for the EU-15 (with the notable exceptions of Slovenia, the Czech Republic, and Hungary; see Table 24.7). Labor market participation rates, especially for the young and the elderly, are low, and long-term unemployment is a severe problem (see Table 24.7). High unemployment rates among young people reached dramatic dimensions in some countries – almost a third of the 15- to 25-year-olds in CEE countries are jobless (in Poland the level is 40 per cent). Many in this category lack vocational skills and working experience, and thus constitute a pool of largely 'unemployable' labor. (Barysch,

2005: 10). The labor market situation is further aggravated by migration, especially that of highly skilled labor ('brain drain'). Depending on the volume of outward migration, it may well result in a substantial net loss of human capital in the new member states. Thus, migration is likely to be less of a problem for target countries than for the countries from which it originates. In addition, low birth rates and aging societies lead to a shrinking labor force. Demographic change will hit the CEE countries with a time lag, since birth rates were on average higher than in the EU-15 until the 1980s. (Barysch, 2005: 3 f.) The massive material incentives for East–West labor migration (including 'commuter migration') will be further counterbalanced by two constraints: one is the right of EU-15 member states to delay full labor mobility by up to seven years after accession; the other is the presence of linguistic barriers in a Europe with some 20 official languages.

The new member states achieved increasing productivity levels at the expense of jobs and the structure of their respective labor markets which are still dominated by industry and agriculture, and characterized by a largely underdeveloped service sector. These countries face a problem that is well known in the old member states, namely jobless growth (Barysch, 2005: 3 f.). Foreign investment in the mass-production sector cannot cure CEE labor markets in the long run (nor is this the goal of foreign investors), and their future as low-cost production countries is contested by Asian markets. As a consequence of these factors, the new EU member countries face difficulties similar to those plaguing the older member states, albeit on a larger scale.

Since 2001, a slight improvement in labor market performance in the CEE states can be observed. However, since growth rates are predicted to decrease and more restrictive economic policies are expected to be applied in the new member states, a stable and substantial recovery of the labor markets in the countries under study appears unlikely (cf. Knogler, 2002).

Table 24.7 Key labor market indicators for the new member states, 2003

Countries	Labor market participation rate (percentage of population)					Unemployment rate (ILO; percentage of labor force)				Comparative employment structure by sector (percentage of employed labor force)			Employment by type of contract (percentage of employed labor force)			
													Self-employed[1]			
	Total (15–64 years)	Youth (15–24 years)	25–54 years	Elderly (55–64 years)	Woman (15–64 years)	Total	Youth (15–24 yrs)	Women	Long-term unemployed	Service sector	Industry	Agriculture	Total	Without agriculture	Part-time	Limited contracts
Average, new member states	59.9	27.2	77.0	36.0	54.8	–	–	–	–	–	–	–	13.1	8.8	–	–
Estonia	62.9	29.3	77.8	52.3	59.0	10.1	22.9	10.0	4.6	61.5	32.3	6.1	8.1	6.4	8.5	2.5
Latvia	61.8	31.5	77.7	44.1	57.9	10.5	17.6	10.7	4.3	60.8	25.8	13.4	9.5	5.0	10.3	11.1
Lithuania	61.1	22.5	78.9	44.7	58.4	12.7	27.2	13.3	6.1	54.1	28.0	17.8	17.1	6.2	9.6	7.2
Poland	51.2	21.2	67.5	26.9	46.0	19.2	41.1	20.0	10.7	53.0	28.6	18.4	21.7	9.9	10.5	19.4
Slovakia	57.7	27.4	76.0	24.6	52.2	17.1	32.9	17.4	11.1	61.5	34.1	4.4	9.4	9.0	2.4	4.9
Slovenia	62.6	29.1	82.5	23.5	57.6	6.5	15.9	7.1	3.4	52.3	36.9	10.9	9.8	6.6	6.2	13.7
Czech Republic	64.7	30.0	81.7	42.3	56.3	7.8	18.6	9.9	3.8	56.1	39.4	4.5	16.7	15.9	5.0	9.2
Hungary	57.0	26.8	73.7	28.9	50.9	5.8	13.1	5.5	2.4	62.3	31.9	5.8	12.8	11.2	4.4	7.5
Average EU-15	64.4	39.9	77.2	41.7	56.0	8.1	15.6	9.0	3.3	71.0	25.0	4.0	14.2[2]	12.1[2]	18.6	12.8
EU-15 maximum	75.1 (DK)	67.9 (NL)	84.5 (A)	68.6 (S)	71.5 (S)	11.3 (E)	27.0 (I)	15.9 (GR)	5.1 (GR)	80.0 (UK)	33.8 (P)	16.1 (GR)	32.4 (GR)	21.5 (GR)	45.0 (NL)	30.6 (E)
Germany	65.0	44.5	78.1	39.5	59.0	9.6	10.1	9.2	4.6	70.3	27.2	2.4	10.4	9.6	22.3	12.2
EU-15 minimum	56.1 (I)	25.2 (I)	70.7 (I)	28.1 (B)	42.7 (I)	3.7 (L)	6.8 (NL)	4.0	0.9 (L)	53.8 (P)	19.0 (UK)	0.9 (UK)	8.4 (DK)	6.7 (DK)	4.3 (GR)	4.5 (L)

1 Labor force total.
2 Without NL.

Source: Hönekopp (2005: 3); own calculations and compilation.

As a consequence, not a single country in the CEE region fulfills any of the three targets set by the Lisbon Strategy as part of its overall aim to achieve 'full' employment and combat social exclusion within the EU; that is, having 70 percent of the population aged 15 to 64 years, 50 percent of the elderly (aged 55-plus) and 60 percent of women economically active (see Table 24.7).

As unemployment was virtually unknown (at least officially) under the communist regimes, institutions that deal with this feature of capitalist democracies had to be built from scratch. Institutional designs of provisions for the unemployed vary considerably among the new member states. These designs range from an unemployment scheme with flat-rate benefits framed into a comprehensive social security system such as in Latvia's, to a generous contributory and earnings-related unemployment insurance system such as Hungary's, to a tax-financed flat-rate system with strict entitlement rules such as that in Estonia (up to 2002), which comes closer to a form of public assistance. A special case is the Czech Republic, where a generous status-related unemployment scheme is complemented by a policy of active employment promotion. The duration of entitlement is short (six months) and, after that period has elapsed, unemployment benefits are replaced by unemployment assistance which is below the level of minimum subsistence. Employers are legally forced to register job vacancies within five days. Seventy-seven district labor offices administer retraining and qualification schemes and other 'activating' measures. The Slovakian case is similar, although employment policies are more centralized than in the Czech Republic.

Poland changed its unemployment policies after 1994. Before 1994 a contributory, universal, low-level flat-rate system was implemented, which was closer to public assistance than to unemployment insurance. After 1994, the criteria for eligibility were tightened and active employment measures were implemented. In addition, the duration of entitlements differs according to regional labor market performance. In regions with average or above average labor market performance, the period of entitlement can be up to 18 months. In regions with a high unemployment rate, the period of entitlement may be as short as six months – an arrangement which is obviously designed as an incentive to regional mobility.

Slovenia's unemployment compensation system resembles the German model[5] (before the 'Hartz Reforms') with its contributory, earnings-related threefold system: unemployment insurance, unemployment assistance, and ultimately a tax-financed system of public assistance. Benefits are comparatively generous and can amount to up to 70 percent of former net earnings. In sum, the level of real unemployment benefits has decreased in all of the new EU member states. This development is due in part to the absence of indexation to (high) inflation rates, and in part to budgetary constraint and cuts (Knogler, 2002: 42).

As to income inequality within the European Union as a whole, Eastern enlargement increases the Gini-coefficient dramatically (see Table 24.8). Not only did the Gini-coefficient rise, but also the percentage of the low-income population segment jumped from 19.9 (EU-15) to almost 30 percent with the last enlargement. Any further enlargement will increase inequality and poverty even more, and push roughly half of the European population below the poverty threshold.

The variety of institutional designs, levels, scope, and duration of and minimum requirements for benefits are due to different factors. Different strategies of privatization matter, since their structure and their success or failure led to different results in terms of job loss and institutional designs for protection against unemployment (cf. Stark and Bruszt, 1998; Cerami, 2005: 119). Moreover, countries reacted differently to international pressures to reform or implement systems for protection against unemployment; social and political mediation resulted in different policy outcomes.

The implementation of active labor market policies has been only recently enforced in most of the countries under study (with the

Table 24.8   Income, inequality, and poverty in the EU

EU constellation or country	Population[1]	Average income	Median income	Gini-index	Percentage low income[2]
EU-6	222	9,326	7,892	31.0	12.5
EU-9	289	9,343	7,892	32.1	14.2
EU-12	348	8,633	7,166	34.2	19.9
EU-15	370	8,622	7,274	34.2	19.9
EU-25	444	7,685	6,231	38.0	29.6
EU-27[3]	476	7,314	5,959	39.9	33.3
EU-28[4]	535	6,793	5,426	42.3	38.5
EU-28+[5]	550	6,662	4,973	43.0	40.0
EU-28++[6]	620	6,138	4,633	45.4	45.6
USA	258	12,381	9,924	39.4	10.0
Australia	18	9,083	7,600	34.5	10.0
Canada	29	11,716	10,082	31.0	10.0
India	901	521	443	32.8	100.0

1 In millions.
2 Income below 50% median of EU-6.
3 EU-27 = EU-25 + Bulgaria and Romania.
4 EU-28 = EU-25 + Bulgaria, Romania, and Turkey.
5 EU 28+ = EU-28 + Western Balkans.
6 EU 28 ++ = EU-28 + Western Balkans, Belarus, Ukraine, and Moldova.
Source: Boix (2004: 7).

notable exception of Hungary which has coped most successfully with unemployment in the region). This delay is due to two developments. First, public attitudes towards unemployment tended to regard it as a transitional feature or even as 'healthy' for more rapid economic development away from the artificial planned economy under the communist regimes. This attitude was fostered additionally by the neoliberal rhetoric employed by political elites (e.g. in the Czech Republic). Only in very recent years has it been corrected as a result of persisting, high rates of unemployment. Second, as pointed out earlier, social exclusion through a non-inclusive labor market came into the focus of attention in most of the CEE countries only via the process of accession, and the necessity to comply with European standards and take part in European programs. Thus, no consistent unemployment protection and compensation model in the region can be identified.

CONCLUSIONS

After reviewing the major features and developments in CEE social protection systems,

there is no clear indication that a new and distinctive model of postcommunist welfare states has emerged. Only two characteristics are shared by all of the EU-8 new member states. First, corporate and personal income tax rates in the EU-8 region are considerably lower than in the EU-15. The same is true for social expenditure as a percentage of GDP (see Table 24.4). Second, all new member states implemented a Bismarckian type of social insurance system during the 1990s (see Table 24.6), and they accumulate revenues predominantly via social security contributions levied on wages or through direct income tax. As a result, and given the high unemployment rates and poor labor market performance, the burden of non-wage labor costs appears excessive in the CEE countries or, at any rate, far too high to permit a smooth transition to anything approximating 'full' employment. At the same time, none of the new member states in the CEE has abandoned its commitment to state responsibility for social security, or turned to market-liberal models of privatization.

Taking into account the overall picture of the institutional features and related problems of the CEE welfare state, we cannot detect a 'new' social model in this region. As to the three scenarios of CEE welfare state developments that have been suggested by Kovács (2002), the 'muddling through' narrative is by far the most adequate one. The times of consistent 'models' or 'regimes' of European welfare states seem to be over anyway, and pragmatic 'hybridization' (Giddens), or eclectic attempts to balance given internal and external pressures, seems to be the dominant trajectory in the evolution of social protection arrangements. At any rate, portraying the new members from the CEE region as agents of neoliberal welfare state reform is simply wrong. In spite of the neoliberal rhetoric of some segments of the new political elites, no country actually implemented a 'market economy without an adjective' (Vaclav Klaus) nor did (or indeed could) any government stick to the old universal communist welfare regimes. Such mistaken notions have sometimes been used by political elites in EU-15 member states in order to denounce Eastern enlargement and to depict the new member states as threats to continental European welfare states. There is little reason for doubting that such misrepresentations (including the specter of the 'Polish plumber') have contributed to spreading fear regarding the new member states among Western European publics. However (and to the extent that the economies of the new member states display some of the same competitive advantage as those of some of the older member states), this is not due to generally more austere welfare states (and hence lower non-wage costs of labor), but rather to lower wages and lower taxes. But regardless of the truth content of the arguments which are mustered for the spreading of such fears, the result is very unlikely to be more than at best a highly qualified solidarity encompassing all member states of the large EU-27, where 'solidarity' means the readiness to recognize and respect the rights and legitimate pursuit of interests of all fellow Europeans and fellow member states.

In order to model the unfolding conflicts between old and new member states – admittedly in a somewhat speculative manner – we suggest a sequence of three stages of strategic objectives and driving motivational forces. The three stages, which apply unequally to the old and the new member states, are (1) formulation of strategic objectives, (2) awareness of the costs of achieving those objectives, and (3) frustration with the extent to which the objectives may or may not have actually been reached. Starting with the old member states, the original motivation for promoting Eastern enlargement was doubtlessly of a primarily *political* nature, because the priorities of the EU (as well as NATO) around the mid-1990s consisted of helping to consolidate democracy and the rule of law in the CEE region through conditionality, and thereby to 'normalize' the political development of prospective member states through soft forms of outside control. In contrast, the new member states, having just escaped from a tight and authoritarian form of supranational control, were mostly reluctant and skeptical about 'joining Europe'; but this skepticism was consistently trumped by the *economic* prospects of postsocialist reconstruction that were based upon the expectation of free access (of goods and workers) to Western markets, the inflow of FDI into the CEE region, and the claims to modernization subsidies that would come from the EU once full membership status was achieved.

Once the enlargement process was completed (on 1 May 2004 and 1 January 2007 respectively), both sides experienced a wave of 'second thoughts.' Among the new member states, these consisted of the realization of failures and an awareness of necessary sacrifices concerning the respective subordinate objectives. As to the older member states, their intended political aim of having stable and democratic Eastern neighbors was partly offset by the growing *economic* challenges originating from the CEE region. These challenges came in the form of an inflow of goods and labor, and an outflow of investment and funds allocated from EU budgets. Similarly, and in a strictly symmetrical fashion, elites as well as non-elites in the new member states began to perceive the *political* costs of membership – costs that were framed in terms of losses of national autonomy and the need to comply with EU-wide rules and policies. Thus both sides began to perceive reasons for asking themselves, 'Was the price we had to pay for achieving our primary objectives really worth it?'

Finally – and if we read a variety of indicators that emerge in the newly integrated political economy of Europe rightly – a third phase of regret and frustration may well become dominant as the dynamics of the EU-27 unfold. To put it bluntly, both sides will begin to see that what they actually *received* for paying the price they paid is less than what they had anticipated and hoped for. From an EU-15 point of view, this second disappointment relates to the fact that neither regime stability nor the liberal democratic consensus (nor, for that matter, a modern and reasonably corruption-free state structure; not to mention the consistent reluctance that prevails in virtually all CEE member states to join distinctively 'European' initiatives in the area of foreign and international security policies) has taken firm roots in all parts of the region – a disillusion that is all the deeper as it comes with the realization that, after formal enlargement, the leverage of conditionality has practically become inoperative. Conversely, the EU-10 new member states (i.e. growing parts of both their elites and mass constituencies) have also begun to look back on the deal they were drawn into and to see it as a definitely unfavorable one: not only have they sacrificed 'too much' (in terms of national autonomy) but also received 'too little' in return; that is, in terms of the older member states' preparedness to assist them on the road to robust economic prosperity, rather than keeping them in a position of permanent economic dependency.

Time will show whether, or to what extent, the second and third stages of this gloomy model will materialize. Concerning the first stage and the initial patterns of motivation at the beginning of the process that led to Eastern enlargement, it is worth noting that the enthusiasm for 'returning to Europe,' both within the candidate countries as well as in the EU-15 member states was markedly qualified.

Eurobarometer 42 (1994) data show that, at the time of the survey (i.e. shortly before the actual accession of Sweden, Austria, and Finland in 1995), the *least* welcome and least favorably assessed West European candidate country (Norway) was supported by 75 percent of EU-12 citizens, running 20 percentage points ahead in terms of the support for membership compared to the *most* welcome East European candidate country (Hungary), with a 55 percent favorable rating (EU Commission, 2006: 7). In other words, the political divide continues to play a significant role – a legacy of the Iron Curtain as well as other historical, cultural, economic, geographic, linguistic, and religious differences that exist between the EU-15 and the EU-8. Where accession is in fact approved on either side, such 'support for enlargement reflects to a large extent non-altruistic motives' (EU Commission, 2006: 6). At the point of actual accession in May 2004, the supporters of enlargement within the EU-15 just barely outnumbered the opponents by 42 to 39 per cent (Eurobarometer 61). In retrospect, EU-25 citizens express an increasing degree of dissatisfaction with the outcome of Eastern enlargement; negative opinions increased from 35 percent in the fall of 2004 to 39 percent in the fall of 2005 (Eurobarometer 62, 64). After all, among the EU-8, only in Slovenia and Lithuania did an absolute majority of eligible citizens (54 and 58 percent, respectively) support the accession of their countries.

NOTES

1 Traditionally defined, the three pillars are (1) public pensions, (2) occupational pensions, and (3) personal pensions. Redefined, according to the World Bank scheme, the pillars are: (1) non-contributory basic pensions, (2) contributory, forced savings, and (3) voluntary savings.

2 For the old member states, direct investment in the new member states accounts for a relatively small share of total corporate investment (e.g. in Germany, just one to two per cent in recent years) (Barysch, 2005: 2). In 2004, for instance, the old member states invested up to eleven times more in one another's economies (*ibid.*).

3 For an overview on tax incentives in the new member states, see ZEW and Ernst & Young, 2004: 31–5.

4 The flowing sections rely on the European Commission (2003) report on social protection systems in the candidate countries for basic information.

5 The first unemployment legislation in Slovenia (then a republic within Yugoslavia) was passed in 1974; the Slovenian system emulated in fact the German system. http://epp.eurostat.ec.europa.eu/portal/page?_pageid=1153,47169267,1153_47181498&_dad=portal&_schema=PORTAL, accessed 6 August 2006.

REFERENCES

Barysch, K. (2005) 'East versus West? The European economic and social model after enlargement', Essay, Centre for European Reform, London. Available at: http://www.cer.org.uk/pdf/essay_social_model_barysch_oct05.pdf, accessed January 2005.

Boix, C. (2004) 'The institutional accomodation of an enlarged Europe', Working paper, Friedrich-Ebert-Stiftung, Bonn. Available at: http://fesportal.fes.de/pls/portal30/docs/folder/politikanalyse/europpolitikboix.pdf, accessed January 2005.

Cerami, A. (2005) Social Policy in Central and Eastern Europe. The Emergence of a New European Model of Solidarity? PhD dissertation, Universität Erfurt, Staatswissenschaftliche Fakultät. Available at: www.db-thueringen.de/servlets/DerivateServlet/Derivate-4495/cerami.pdf, accessed January 2007.

Cerami, A. (2006) 'The politics of reforms in Bismarckian welfare systems: the cases of Czech Republic, Hungary, Poland, and Slovakia', Unpublished conference paper, Harvard University, Minda de Gunzburg Center for European Studies, Cambridge, MA.

Clement, H., Knogler, M., Quaisser, W. et al. (2002) 'Wachstum in schwierigem Umfeld. Wirtschaftslage und Reformprozesse in Ostmittel- und Südosteuropa sowie der Ukraine 2001/2002', Working paper No. 242, Osteuropa-Institut München.

Dietrich, V. (2003) Auswirkungen einer europaweiten Wahlfreiheit bei Gesundheitsleistungen. Implikationen für das deutsche Gesundheitswesen vor dem Hintergrund einer Ost-Erweiterung der EU. Aachen: Shaker.

Esping-Andersen, G. (1990) The Three Worlds of Welfare Capitalism. Oxford: Oxford University Press.

European Bank for Reconstruction and Development (EBRD) (2005) Building on Success. Annual Report 2004, EBRD, London. Available at: http://www.ebrd.com/pubs/general/ar04.pdf, accessed March 2007.

European Commission (2003) Social Protection in the 13 Candidate Countries – A Comparative Analysis. EC, Directorate for Employment and Social Affairs, Unit E.2. Luxembourg: Office for Official Publications of the European Communities. Available at: http://ec.europa.eu/employment_social/publications/2004/ke5103649_en.pdf, accessed January 2007.

European Commission (2006) 'Enlargement: two years after: an economic evaluation', European Economy Occasional Papers No. 24, Bureau of European Policy Advisers and the Directorate-General for Economic and Financial Affairs. Available at: http://ec.europa.eu/economy_finance/publications/occasional_papers/2006/ocp24en.pdf, accessed March 2007.

European Foundation for the Improvement of Living and Working Conditions (2004) Health and Care in an Enlarged Europe. Luxembourg: Office for Official Publications of the European Communities. Available at: http://eurofound.europa.eu/pubdocs/2003/107/en/1/ef03107en.pdf, accessed March 2007.

Götting, U. (1998) Transformation der Wohlfahrtsstaaten in Mittel- und Osteuropa. Eine Zwischenbilanz. Opladen: Leske und Budrich.

Höhnekopp, E., Langenbücher, K. and Walwei, U. (2004) EU-Osterweiterung – Aufholprozeß mit Chancen und Risiken, IAB Kurzbericht, Ausgabe Nr. 12/12.10.2004, Institut für Arbeitsmarkt- und Berufsforschung der Bundesagentur für Arbeit, Nürnberg. Available at: http://doku.iab.de/kurzber/2004/kb1204.pdf, accessed March 2007.

Howard, M.M. (2003) The Weakness of Civil Society in Post-Communist Europe. Cambridge: Cambridge University Press.

Knogler, M. (2002) 'Arbeitsmarktpolitische Herausforderungen in den EU-Beitrittskandidaten: Abbau der hohen Steuerbelastung der

Arbeitseinkommen', Working paper no. 235, Osteuropa-Institut, München.

Kornai, J. and Eggleston, K. (2001) 'Choice and solidarity: The health sector in Eastern Europe and proposals for reform', *International Journal of Health Finance and Economics*, 1: 59–84.

Kovács, J.M. (2002) 'Approaching the EU and reaching the US? Rival narratives on transforming the welfare regimes in East-Central Europe', in P. Mair and J. Zielonka (eds) *The Enlarged European Union: Diversity and Adaptation*. London/Portland, OR: Frank Cass, pp. 175–204.

Offe, C. (1972) *Strukturprobleme des kapitalistischen Staates*. Frankfurt: Suhrkamp.

Offe, C. (1984) *Contradictions of the Welfare State*. London: Hutchinson.

Orenstein, M.A. (2000) 'How politics and institutions affect pension reform in three post-communist countries', World Bank Policy Research Working Paper 2310. Available from the Social Science Research Network (SSRN) at http://ssrn.com./abstract=630682, accessed March 2007.

Schneider, F. (2004) 'The size of the shadow economies of 145 countries all over the world: first results over the period 1999 to 2003', IZA Discussion Paper No. 1431, Forschungsinstitut zur Zukunft der Arbeit, Bonn. Available at http://www.iza.org, accessed March 2007.

Stark, D. and Bruszt, L. (1998) *Postsocialist Pathways. Transforming Politics and Property in East Central Europe*. Cambridge: Cambridge University Press.

Tomka, B. (2004) 'Wohlfahrtsstaatliche Entwicklung in Ostmitteleuropa und das europäische Sozialmodell', in H. Kaelble und G. Schmid (eds) *Das Europäische Sozialmodel – Auf dem Weg zum transnationalen Sozialstaat*. Berlin: Edition Sigma, pp. 107–139.

Tupy, M.L. (2006) *Slovakia's Pension Reforms*. Washington DC: Cato Institute. Available at: http://www.cato.org/pub_display.php? pub_id=5414.

Vanhuysse, P. (2006) *Divide and Pacify. Strategic Social Policies and Political Protests in Post-Communist Democracies*. Budapest: CEU Press.

Vincentz, V. (2002) 'Deutsche Direktinvestitionen in Osteuropa weiter rückläufig – Arbeitsplatzverlagerungen geringer als befürchet', Kurzanalysen und Informationen Nr. 3, Osteuropa-Institut München. Available at: http://www.oei-muenchen.de/info3.pdf, accessed March 2007.

Zentrum für Europäische Wirtschaftsforschung (ZEW) and Ernst & Young (2004) 'Company taxation in the new EU member states. Survey of the tax regimes and effective tax burdens for multinational investors'. Available at: ftp://ftp.zew.de/pub/zew-docs/gutachten/Studie_ZEW_E&Y_2004.pdf, accessed January 2007.

25

Cities and Territorial Competitiveness

Neil Brenner

The focus of debates on urban governance in Western European cities has been systematically redefined during the last two decades. Whereas Western European urban scholars in the 1970s debated the role of cities as sites of collective consumption, social service provision and income redistribution within the national administrative hierarchies of the Keynesian welfare state, by the early 1980s questions of urban economic development began to occupy center stage. In contrast to the 'old' urban politics, which explored issues such as housing, transportation and public infrastructure, this 'new' urban politics has been focused predominantly on local economic growth, interlocality competition and territorial competitiveness (Eisenschitz and Gough, 1993; Mayer, 1994). According to David Harvey's (1989) paradigmatic analysis, these realignments have signaled the emergence of an 'entrepreneurial' regime of urban governance associated with post-Fordist accumulation strategies, post-Keynesian state forms and the proliferation of new forms of sociospatial polarization throughout the older capitalist world.

In the US, with its institutionally entrenched traditions of local civic boosterism, real estate speculation and urban privatism, the politics of urban entrepreneurialism have a deep historical lineage and have been examined exhaustively, if contentiously, by urban scholars (Logan and Molotch, 1987; Mollenkopf, 1983). However, in Western European states, with their history of municipal welfarism and redistributive forms of territorial regulation, it is far more appropriate to label entrepreneurial urban strategies as 'new', because they are a product of the post-1980s period of geoeconomic restructuring, European integration and national intergovernmental realignments (Jonas and Wilson, 1999; Mayer, 1994). Of course, the new urban politics have crystallized in a range of nationally, regionally and locally specific forms (Harding and Le Galès, 1997; Le Galès and Harding, 1998). However, the basic contours – defined by (a) the proliferation of state-directed local economic initiatives; (b) the institutionalized treatment of urban territorial jurisdictions as potential locations for external capital investment; and (c) the pervasive concern among policy makers to enhance the transnational 'competitiveness' of cities – have been generalized across the European urban system during the post-1980s period (Hall and Hubbard, 1998, 1996; Jewson and MacGregor, 1997).

This chapter situates the consolidation of the new urban politics in Western Europe (to which I shall also refer, following Harvey's [1989] terminology, as 'urban entrepreneurialism') in relation to a series of post-1970s geoeconomic transformations, Europe-wide territorial realignments, national institutional recalibrations and local regulatory strategies. The entrenchment of entrepreneurial forms of urban governance in Western Europe must be understood as the aggregate, unintended outcome of diverse, *ad hoc* political responses to (a) the crisis of North Atlantic Fordism in the 1970s; (b) the acceleration of European integration since the 1980s; and (c) the increasing diffusion of place-based forms of competitiveness policy since the 1990s. From this point of view, urban entrepreneurialism is not a stable, coherent formation of urban governance, but a heterogeneous ensemble of localized crisis-management strategies designed to reignite urban economic development within an increasingly volatile geoeconomic context. However, despite their relatively inchoate, uncoordinated character, a major aggregate consequence of such strategies has been to 'creatively destroy' the politico-institutional infrastructures of Fordist–Keynesian territorial regulation and to entrench a new politics of interlocality competition across the European urban system. Paradoxically, even though this new politics of interlocality competition have proven deeply ineffectual, they have been further consolidated since the 1990s as the risks to individual cities that attempt to 'opt out' from urban entrepreneurialism have intensified.

In order to decipher contemporary transformations of urban governance and territorial development strategies in the European Union (EU), it is necessary first to explore the spatial expressions of geoeconomic restructuring processes and the intensification of European integration during the post-1970s period. On this basis, we can then explore

(a) national and local institutional responses to processes of geoeconomic restructuring and European integration since the 1980s; (b) their implications for urban governance regimes in the 1990s; and (c) their associated contradictions and crisis-tendencies during the last decade. While my emphasis in what follows is on general, pan-European trends, I reject the contention that contemporary forms of 'globalization' are causing a convergence of institutional arrangements in the EU or elsewhere. However, for purposes of this chapter, my concern is less to capture the diversity of forms in which urban entrepreneurialism has been articulated (on which see Savitch and Kantor, 2002) than to elaborate a meso-level analysis of (a) how the core elements of this new urban politics were diffused across the Western European urban system; and (b) the consequences of the latter trend for European territorial development (on this methodological strategy, see Brenner, 2004).

This chapter builds upon and reinterprets a broad, interdisciplinary literature on urban governance restructuring in the post-1980s EU. Interestingly, during the period under discussion here, the remaking of urban governance has attracted increasing analytical and empirical attention across the social sciences, as well as within certain strands of the emergent field of EU studies. Thus, even though discipline-specific epistemologies and research questions continue to inform research on urban governance by, for example, geographers, sociologists, political scientists and political economists, many of the most illuminating studies of this issue, in the European context as elsewhere, now occupy an increasingly postdisciplinary intellectual space (see, for instance, Amin, 1994; Le Galès, 2001). This is not, however, to suggest that any consensus exists regarding the substantive nature of urban governance restructuring in Europe. For, as even a cursory glance at treatments of this topic within the field's key academic journals will reveal, there are still ample theoretical, methodological and empirical disagreements regarding the nature and trajectory of urban governance change in the

European and, indeed, global context (see, for instance, any recent issue of *European Urban and Regional Studies*, *European Planning Studies* or the *International Journal of Urban and Regional Research*). The key point here, therefore, is that our understanding of urban governance within Europe is no longer framed primarily around discipline-specific categories, debates and questions; instead, it is increasingly recognized that an adequate understanding of this multifaceted terrain of political, economic, institutional and spatial transformation requires systematic reliance upon a broad range of intellectual tools drawn from throughout the social sciences, as well as from more applied fields such as architecture, urban planning, administrative science and environmental policy. Accordingly, for purposes of the present discussion, I shall not attempt to demarcate the specific disciplinary, interdisciplinary and/or postdisciplinary legacies of the concepts, methods or arguments elaborated herein. Instead, I take for granted that contemporary studies of the urban question – which encompass yet transcend work on urban governance – are constitutively heterodox, and thus that discipline-specific epistemologies do not illuminate the key debates and developments within this research field. For the most part, however, this chapter focuses on substance rather than epistemology, building upon the heterodox intellectual resources of critical urban and regional studies in order to elaborate a meso-level interpretation of pan-European trends and transformations (for a more detailed account, see Brenner, 2004).

GEOECONOMIC RESTRUCTURING AND TERRITORIAL DEVELOPMENT

During the Fordist epoch, the economic geography of Western Europe was configured as a continental mosaic of national space-economies, each of which was in turn composed of a number of major urbanized zones and development poles in which large-scale, highly capitalized manufacturing industries and their associated labor forces were concentrated. In the Western European context, the geographical heartlands of the Fordist accumulation regime stretched from the industrial triangle of northern Italy through the German Ruhr district to northern France and the English Midlands; but each of these regional production complexes was in turn embedded within a nationally specific system of production and innovation (Nilsson and Schamp, 1996). Throughout the postwar period, these and many other major European urban regions and their surrounding industrial satellites were characterized by consistent demographic growth and industrial expansion as the Fordist system of production reached maturity (Dunford and Perrons, 1994; Rodríguez-Pose, 1998).

As of the early 1970s, however, the breakdown of the Bretton Woods monetary order, the eruption of the oil crisis and the onset of a global economic recession sent shockwaves through this entrenched system of territorial development (Dunford and Perrons, 1994). An accelerated, crisis-induced phase of industrial restructuring ensued which ultimately signaled the dissolution of the Fordist developmental regime not only in Western Europe but throughout the North Atlantic rim (Swyngedouw, 1992). For some time, intense debates have raged throughout the social sciences on the nature of these restructuring processes and their implications for the future trajectory of post-Fordist capitalism both in Western Europe and elsewhere (Amin, 1994). For present purposes, it will suffice to underscore several intertwined tendencies of economic restructuring that have significantly impacted the urban and regional geographies of post-Fordist Europe and contributed to the rise of the new urban politics.

The decline and restructuring of mass production industries

The traditional mass production industries upon which the Fordist growth dynamic was grounded – such as steel, petrochemicals, machine tools, appliances, ship-building and the like – have contracted and declined due to a combination of intensified international competition, market saturation and accelerated technological change. In this context, unemployment rates expanded drastically as a wave of plant closings, layoffs and industrial relocations swept across the European economic landscape (Coriat and Petit, 1991). Although revitalized, neo-Fordist forms of mass production eventually crystallized within these sectors in a number of European manufacturing regions, their industrial output and their share of total employment have diminished markedly relative to the levels associated with the high Fordist period. In the wake of these shifts, many of the boom regions of European Fordism, such as the English Midlands and the German Ruhr district, experienced long-lasting crises that were manifested in mass unemployment, social upheaval, infrastructural decay and advanced ecological destruction. The decline of manufacturing industries has likewise had a profound impact upon more diversified urban agglomerations, such as London, Paris, Hamburg and Milan, which have confronted closely analogous problems within their manufacturing sectors during the last three decades. Whereas Fordist systems of production have in no way disappeared from the Western European economic landscape, they have been profoundly restructured as the socio-institutional conditions for maintaining industrial profitability in the manufacturing sector have been reconstituted under a new geoeconomic configuration (Benko and Dunford, 1991; Martinelli and Schoenberger, 1991).

The rise of flexible production systems

Even as traditional manufacturing sectors have declined, productivity, output and employment have expanded markedly in newer industrial sectors which are grounded upon flexible or 'lean' production systems, characterized by: (a) the use of non-dedicated machinery and multiskilled labor at the firm level; (b) expanding social divisions of labor, dense subcontracting relationships and short-term contracts at the interfirm level; and (c) increasing product differentiation in the sphere of circulation (Storper and Scott, 1989). Although flexible production methods have had a profound impact throughout the advanced industrial economies, they play a particularly important role in three broad sectoral clusters – high-technology industry; advanced producer and financial services; and revitalized craft production (Scott and Storper, 1992). At the same time, flexible production methods have also been introduced into traditional mass production sectors such as automobiles, as large firms develop new strategies to enhance efficiency, to bolster market share and to externalize risks in a turbulent geoeconomic environment. Such strategies generally involve the introduction of new spatial divisions of labor in which (a) command and control functions are centralized at headquarters locations; (b) low-cost production is dispersed outwards through global sourcing arrangements; and (c) other major production functions are subcontracted or outsourced to diverse supplier networks (Nilsson and Schamp, 1996). These fundamental organizational changes have been enabled through the deployment of new information technologies that provide 'new opportunities for increased flexibility in the production process and ... new options to customize products and production' (Nilsson and Schamp, 1996: 122).

The nature of the industrial divide between Fordist production systems and their putative successor(s) remains a matter of considerable academic and political dispute (Amin, 1994). The crucial point here is that the firms and regions associated with these flexibly organized, high-technology sectors have come to account for an increasing proportion of industrial output and employment in Western European economies (Storper, 1996). As in other zones of the world economy, the crystallization of flexible production systems in the Western European context has been particularly apparent in so-called 'neo-Marshallian industrial districts' – for ins-tance, in the M4 corridor, Cambridgeshire, Grenoble, Montpellier, West Jutland, Baden-Württemberg, Emilia-Romagna and Tuscany – where small- and medium-sized firms have traditionally dominated the local economic fabric and where mass production technologies were never widely adopted. However, in addition to these 'new industrial spaces' (Scott, 1988), flexible production systems and high-technology industrial clusters have also come to play important roles within European global cities such as London, Paris, Amsterdam, Copenhagen, Frankfurt, Zürich and Milan. Here, large transnational corporations have come to rely extensively upon local webs of producer and financial services industries that are generally organized in flexible and decentralized forms (Amin and Thrift, 1992 Martinelli and Schoenberger, 1991).

The globalization and integration of European economic space

These sectoral shifts have occurred in close conjunction with an increasing globalization and integration of the European space economy. Particularly since the early 1980s, foreign direct investment flows have massively increased throughout the European economic zone, above all in the United Kingdom, France, the Netherlands and Germany (Amin and Malmberg, 1994; Dicken and Öberg, 1996). Through a combination of mergers and acquisitions, the formation of international strategic alliances and new greenfield investments, North American and Japanese corporations, among others, have become major players in European economies, competing directly with indigenous European firms for national market shares. Dunford (1994: 106) reports that 'direct overseas investment in EU countries reached $98.4 billion compared with $14.8 billion in the 1980s, increasing some three times faster than gross domestic fixed capital formation in most of the large EU economies'. Meanwhile, no longer secure in their established role as 'national champions', major European corporations have likewise internationalized their activities to become an important source of foreign direct investment in North America, in Japan and in Europe itself. Accordingly, cross-border mergers, acquisitions and strategic alliances among European firms have also significantly intensified as of the 1980s. Moreover, above all since the early 1980s, European national economies have been increasingly fused together through the institutions of the European Community and, later, the EU. With the consolidation of the Single European Market (SEM) and the resultant abolition of tariff and non-tariff barriers to trade in 1993, international trade and foreign direct investment among the EU member states' economies accelerated dramatically. These developments, coupled with the deregulation of the financial sector and the process of European monetary integration, have enhanced the mobility of capital within the EU states, reduced transaction costs and intensified interfirm competition for European market shares. Under these conditions, 'companies are increasingly restructuring themselves to serve the European market as a whole rather than a set of national markets. They eliminate national headquarters and have just a European headquarters; they have European-wide marketing strategies; and they streamline their product range and concentrate their production' (Cheshire and Gordon, 1995: 109).

In short, throughout the last two decades, a 'tidal wave of massive organizational and geographical restructuring' (Dicken and Öberg, 1996: 115) has been under way within Western Europe as major European, North American and Japanese firms compete aggressively for market positions within the European economy while struggling to adjust to rapid geoeconomic fluctuations. As a result of these developments, places throughout the EU are being intertwined ever more directly with the 'hyperspace' of transnational corporate capital (Swyngedouw, 1989). Even in the midst of the deepening localization tendencies associated with the rise of flexible production systems (Storper, 1996), the economic vitality of cities and regions has come to hinge more crucially than ever upon their positions within international corporate geographies (Amin and Malmberg, 1994).

TOWARDS A NEW SOCIOSPATIAL MOSAIC

Taken together, the trends outlined above have dramatically transformed the economic geographies of Western Europe. The contemporary 'local–global interplay' has had profound impacts upon disparate locations throughout the European economic landscape, from its core urban centers, regional industrial districts, technopoles and older manufacturing centers to its less developed peripheries, rural zones and margins (Dunford, 1994; Dunford and Kafkalas, 1992). Established economic specializations are being reworked in locations throughout Europe, and at the same time, large corporations have developed new organizational and technological strategies for coordinating increasingly complex production networks across dispersed spaces both within and beyond the EU. At the core of the newly emergent economic jigsaw puzzle, many older European city-regions have experienced simultaneous processes of economic decline and economic rejuvenation as different sectors within their local economies struggle to adjust to a rapidly changing competitive environment. In the resultant see-saw movement of uneven spatial development, formerly dynamic cities and regions are confronted with unforeseen developmental blockages and are forced to reconfigure, or even to create anew, the socio-institutional foundations for industrial expansion (Swyngedouw, 1992).

As these shifts unfold at a range of geographical scales, a new European sociospatial mosaic has crystallized. Although historically

entrenched patterns of sociospatial inequality continue to condition contemporary developmental pathways, the emergent post-Fordist geographical mosaic is characterized by qualitatively new forms of core-periphery polarization, new hierarchies between places and new geographies of social power and marginalization (Dunford, 1994; Moulaert, 1996). In general terms, the emergent economic landscape of post-Fordist Europe can be described with reference to two overarching characteristics.

Centripetal tendencies and increased sociospatial polarization at a European scale

The sectoral transformations of the last three decades have reinforced and intensified the entrenched division between advanced, highly developed urban and regional cores and 'lagging,' less favored or peripheralized zones (Amin and Tomaney, 1995). Likewise, the consolidation of the Single European Market has unleashed powerful centripetal forces that have further concentrated economic capacities, industrial growth, inward investment and labor flows within 'winning regions' at the expense of other less-developed locations (Cheshire, 1999; Dunford, 1994). Leading metropolitan areas have been able to exploit two crucial locational advantages in contemporary restructuring processes. First, they contain large concentrations of highly skilled workers. Second, they are well positioned within advanced communications and transportation networks (Dunford and Perrons, 1994). These tendencies have a engendered a 'self-reinforcing polarization of high-level activities in well-resourced and well-connected nodes' (Dunford and Perrons, 1994: 173).

The resultant grid of macrogeographical inequality may be represented as a 'vital axis' stretching from the southeast of England, Brussels and the Dutch Randstad through the German Rhinelands southwards to Zürich and the northern Italian industrial triangle surrounding Milan (Dunford and Perrons, 1994; Krätke, 1993). The urbanized heartlands of this axis are located, first, in the northwestern urban cores of London, Paris, Brussels, Rotterdam and Amsterdam, and second, in the dynamic cities of southern Germany (Frankfurt, Stuttgart, Munich) and northern Italy (Milan, Turin and Bologna), whose accelerated growth since the 1990s has pulled Europe's economic center of gravity southwards (Dunford and Perrons, 1994: 165). This vast urbanized corridor, whose components are tightly interlinked through advanced communications and transportation infrastructures, is surrounded by a number of important outlying cities, such as Barcelona, Hamburg, Copenhagen, Berlin and Vienna, as well as by various affluent, traditionally corporatist countries, including Switzerland, Austria, Norway, Sweden and Finland. An outer layer of relatively underdeveloped zones and peripheries, characterized by defensive forms of adjustment grounded upon low wages and strong deregulatory tendencies, stretches from the western Atlantic coast to the southern Mediterranean economies and Greece, and now also includes large parts of eastern Germany and East Central Europe (Dunford and Perrons, 1994).

Following the popularization of Brunet's (1989) famous map of the 'blue banana' in the late 1980s, a number of rather fanciful spatial metaphors have been developed to depict this evolving structure of macrogeographical polarization, including the 'blue star', the 'cucumber', the 'European green grape', the 'bowl of fruit', the 'boomerang', and the 'red octopus' (Kunzmann 1998; Kunzmann and Wegener, 1991; Nijkamp, 1993; Taylor and Hoyler, 2000). Such simplistic spatial models have been rightly criticized, however, because they ossify complex networks of relations and interdependencies into a fixed, static territorial grid (Krätke, 1995). Moreover, in so far as they are often developed by public agencies that have a strong interest in depicting particular localities, regions or countries as the 'boom regions' of the future, such models are often

based 'less on empirical evidence than on creative geopolitical imaginations' (Taylor and Hoyler, 2000: 179). For present purposes, the key point is simply that the European economy is now increasingly dominated by a network of interlinked cities that form a broad arc stretching from London, Paris, Brussels and Amsterdam to Frankfurt, Munich, Zürich and Milan, surrounded by several partially superimposed spatial orbits associated with varying levels of peripheralization. This interurban network should be understood as an unevenly articulated, evolving matrix of economic activities, defined by dense concentrations of highly specialized industrial clusters and advanced communications and transportations infrastructures, rather than as a uniform space enclosed with fixed territorial borders. Although this configuration of uneven geographical development has a long lineage within previous historical rounds of capitalist industrialization (Braudel, 1984), its current articulation is a powerful expression of the centripetal forces that have been unleashed during the last three decades of geoeconomic integration and industrial restructuring across the EU.

The rehierarchization of the urban and regional system

Urban hierarchies and interurban sociospatial disparities represent a second, closely related dimension of this newly emergent European mosaic of core-periphery polarization (Budd, 1998). During the Fordist period, each national economy contained an internal hierarchy of cities, suburbs, industrial regions and so-called 'lagging areas' configured according to their specific functions within national, European and global spatial divisions of labor. In the current period of industrial restructuring, such spatial divisions of labor have been profoundly reorganized on a European scale, leading to the production of new forms of interurban polarization (Benko and Dunford, 1991; Krätke, 1993).

First, the forms of Europe-wide sociospatial polarization described above have heavily reinforced the strategic importance of major metropolitan cities within the Western European economy due to their role as concentration points for advanced economic activities and their high levels of connectedness within global and European communications and transportations infrastructures (Dunford, 1994; Veltz, 1996). As foreign direct investment into the EU has increased, a European network of global cities (including London, Paris, Frankfurt, Amsterdam and Zürich) has crystallized in which advanced management, financial and corporate control functions are centralized (Budd, 1998; Kunzmann, 1998; Taylor and Hoyler, 2000). Because such functions are dependent upon an ensemble of specialized producer and financial services, they generate important spillover effects into local economies that reinforce the tendency towards metropolitan polarization (Veltz, 1996).

Second, processes of globalization and European integration have rejigged national urban hierarchies (Sassen, 1993; Taylor and Hoyler, 2000). European global cities now capture many of the economic functions that were previously concentrated within national capitals or major regional centers. Meanwhile, cities in strategically situated border regions or in major transportation hubs (for instance, Lille or Glasgow) have acquired a new strategic importance, while traditional industrial cities and many older port cities (for instance, Sheffield, Oberhausen, Marseilles or Naples) are increasingly peripheralized. Under these conditions, there is an increasing variegation of urban types, configured according to cities' diverse economic specializations within the Single European Market (Kunzmann and Wegener, 1991). As in the US, where processes of industrial restructuring during the 1980s polarized urban development patterns between the declining 'snowbelt' cities of the northeastern manufacturing belt and the 'sunbelt' boomtowns of the south and west, these shifts within the Western European urban system have underpinned nationally specific patterns of interurban polarization, from north/south divides in Germany, the UK and Italy to the crystallization of a new network of 'growth poles' in southern France and the reconcentration of urban development in the Dutch Randstad (Krätke, 1993: 182–3).

Finally, new spatial divisions of labor have been consolidated at a European scale as standardized, low value-added economic functions and back offices have been decentralized into semi-peripheral and peripheral regions of southern Europe and, more recently, into the ascension states of Eastern and Central Europe. From Spain, Portugal, southern Italy and Greece to Poland, the Czech Republic and Hungary, these zones contain significant numbers of cities and towns that lack large clusters of skilled workers and an advanced industrial, transportation and communications infrastructure. Given the centripetal forces and large-scale sociospatial disparities that have been engendered through European integration, it has been extraordinarily difficult for cities and regions located in these marginalized zones to escape from defensive, deregulatory and cost-competitive modes of adjustment.

In sum, the economic geography of post-1970s Western Europe is characterized by: (a) an enhanced concentration of socioeconomic capacities, highly skilled labor and advanced infrastructure investments into major metropolitan areas ('metropolitanization'); (b) a growing differentiation among local and regional economies according to their particular specializations within global and European spatial divisions of labor; (c) enhanced levels of connectivity and interdependence among the most dynamic, globally integrated metropolitan cores; and (d) an increasing functional disarticulation of major urban regions from their surrounding peripheries and from other marginalized areas within the same national territory. In light of these trends, which are exacerbating sociospatial inequalities at all geographical scales, the notion of an 'archipelago economy' introduced by Veltz (1996) provides a vivid, if also disturbing, characterization of the new spatial (dis)order that has emerged in Western Europe during the last three decades.

THE RISE OF THE ENTREPRENEURIAL CITY

It is against the background of these macro-geographical transformations that the consolidation of urban entrepreneurialism in the EU must be investigated. The aforementioned sectoral and geographical transformations have confronted contemporary cities with qualitatively new forms of economic uncertainty, manifested both in new pressures upon existent industrial infrastructures and in new opportunities for future development as they jostle for position within the global and European urban hierarchies (Leitner and Sheppard, 1998). Under these conditions, there are a number of powerful incentives for local politico-territorial alliances to form within cities and to adopt entrepreneurial, competitiveness oriented policies:

- As processes of deindustrialization and reindustrialization unsettle traditional local economic specializations, major local economic actors and institutions may be motivated to develop coordinated policy strategies in order (a) to manage the negative impacts of economic decline, (b) to strengthen those local economic assets that are judged to be a basis for economic renewal and (c) to develop new economic specializations as a basis for future development.
- The intensification of foreign direct investment into the EU may motivate local economic actors and institutions to attempt to construct place-specific locational conditions in the hope of attracting this investment into their jurisdictions. Although shares of inward investment remain less than 10 percent of gross domestic fixed capital formation in most EU countries, this portion has nonetheless significantly increased the dependence of many local economies upon transnational corporations (Dunford, 1994: 107). The resultant local inward investment strategies may entail the introduction of incentives (tax abatements, infrastructural provision) or the development of supply-side policies to build local economic capacities.

- As entrepreneurial strategies diffuse through the urban system, significant economic disadvantages accrue to those local economies in which such strategies have not been deployed (Leitner and Sheppard, 1998). For this reason, major local economic actors and institutions in many European cities have been increasingly constrained to introduce entrepreneurial developmental strategies in order to avoid 'losing ground' to other cities in which such strategies have been deployed more aggressively.

As of the early 1980s, experimental prototypes for entrepreneurial urban policies were being pioneered by local growth coalitions within a relatively small vanguard of Western European city regions. During the subsequent decade, an intensification of local economic development policies was observed in cities throughout the European urban hierarchy (Cheshire and Gordon, 1996; Keating, 1991; Mayer, 1992; Parkinson and Harding, 1995).

Reflecting on patterns of urban governance in the 1980s and early 1990s, Mayer (1994) suggests that the rise of urban entrepreneurialism in Western European cities has been associated with three broad realignments of urban governance: (a) the increasing engagement of local authorities in local economic development projects; (b) the restructuring and subordination of local collective consumption policies; and (c) the crystallization of new local bargaining systems and public–private partnerships. As Mayer (1994) notes, many of these shifts were initiated through 'bottom-up' strategies by local political coalitions struggling to manage the disruptive consequences of economic restructuring through *ad hoc*, uncoordinated local policy adjustments. Crucially, however, Mayer also emphasizes that these local responses have been conditioned by national political institutions and by nationally coordinated projects of state restructuring. Whereas the transformations of European economic space surveyed above undoubtedly provided a critical impetus for the adoption of entrepreneurial urban strategies, it can be argued that the widespread diffusion of the latter throughout the European urban system has been mediated through a number of basic institutional changes within European national states. Thus, as Lovering (1995: 113) explains, 'The major influence leading to "localization" over the past fifteen years has been a series of changes in these [national] political parameters.'

NEOLIBERALIZATION, EUROPEAN INTEGRATION AND THE CRISIS OF KEYNESIAN REGULATORY SPACE

During the course of the 1980s, most European national governments abandoned traditional Keynesian macroeconomic policies in favor of monetarism: a competitive balance of payments replaced full employment as the overarching goal of monetary and fiscal policy (Scharpf, 1999). Meanwhile, the process of European political and economic integration regained momentum as preparations were made under the Delors Commission for the completion of the Single European Market and, subsequently, economic and monetary union (Ross, 1998). By the late 1980s, neoliberal political agendas such as welfare state retrenchment, fiscal discipline, trade liberalization, privatization and deregulation had been adopted not only in the UK under Thatcher and in West Germany under Kohl, but also in many traditionally social democratic, statist or social/Christian-democratic countries, including the Netherlands, Belgium, France, Italy, Spain, Denmark and Sweden (Majone, 1994; Müller and Wright, 1994; Overbeek, 1991; Rhodes *et al.*, 1997; Wright, 1994). While such agendas did not, in most instances, generate Thatcher-style ideological and institutional transformations, they nonetheless entailed what might be termed a 'subversive' neoliberalization of key arenas of socioeconomic policy, as growth-first, anti-welfarist, market-driven logics were increasingly naturalized as the necessary technical parameters within which public policy must be articulated

(Rhodes, 1995). Accordingly, Müller and Wright (1994: 2) contend that a major 'paradigm shift' occurred throughout Western Europe during the 1980s as the character of state intervention shifted 'from Keynesianism to monetarism and neo-liberalism, from *dirigisme* (explicit or gently disguised) to market-driven solutions, from fiscal expansionism to restraint, from mercantilism to free trade'.

During the same period, a variety of international institutions, including the International Monetary Fund (IMF), the World Bank, the Bank for International Settlements, the Organization for Economic Cooperation and Development (OECD) and the General Agreement on Tariffs and Trade (GATT), became important agents of the so-called 'Washington consensus', which attempted to diffuse neoliberal policy agendas such as fiscal discipline, regulatory downgrading, trade liberalization, labor market flexibility, the privatization of public services and unrestrained foreign direct investment on a global scale (Gill, 1998; Tickell and Peck, 2003). In the European context, such market-building, liberalizing and deregulatory policy agendas were further reinforced and generalized through a series of EU-level directives, including, above all, the Single European Act of 1987, which intensified Europe-wide market integration, foreign direct investment and corporate mergers and acquisitions while also contributing to the eventual marginalization of the Social Charter within the 1991 Maastricht Treaty (Röttger, 1997).

During the 1980s, the consolidation of neoliberal state practices at the EU level and their diffusion among Western European national states imposed additional fiscal constraints upon most municipal and metropolitan governments, whose revenues had already been reduced during the preceding decade. Under these conditions, political support for large-scale strategic planning projects waned; welfare state bureaucracies were downsized, not least at metropolitan and municipal levels; and traditional, redistributive approaches to spatial policy were significantly retrenched. The localized relays of the Keynesian welfare national state were attacked as being excessively bureaucratic, expensive and inefficient. Subsequently, new forms of municipal governance, based upon neoliberal principles such as fiscal discipline, lean administration, privatized service provision and the new public management, were introduced (Pickvance and Preteceille, 1991; Wright, 1994). The intensified fiscal squeeze upon public expenditure in cities and regions was among the major localized expressions of the processes of national welfare state retrenchment that began to unfold during the 1980s. As of this decade, the national preconditions for municipal Keynesianism were systematically eroded as local and metropolitan governments were increasingly forced to 'fend for themselves' in securing a fiscal base for their regulatory activities (Mayer, 1994).

The acceleration of European integration during the second half of the 1980s also generated new challenges for cities and regions throughout the continent. For, among all EU member states, the consolidation of the Single European Market in 1993 was widely viewed as a dramatic ratcheting-up of interspatial competition among urban regions on a European scale. With the removal of national barriers to trade and investment, European cities were now seen to compete far more directly with one another than had previously been the case. The much-discussed Cecchini Report, published in 1988, famously articulated this view within a neoclassical framework and interpreted the Single European Market as a means to increase the efficiency of the European economy as a whole (CEC, 1991). By contrast, critics of the Cecchini Report argued that the Single European Market would reinforce centripetal tendencies within the European economy by strengthening the dominant role of large corporations and major urban regions while further marginalizing peripheral cities and regions (Amin and Malmberg, 1994; Dunford and Kafkalas, 1992). While various forms of interspatial competition on a European scale were recognized prior to the 1990s, both defenders and critics of the Cecchini Report concurred that the Single European Market (and, subsequently, the European Monetary Union) would significantly intensify that competition by undermining the ability of national governments to insulate their cities and regions from transnational market forces by means of monetary and fiscal policies. Consequently, since the consolidation of the Single European Market, economic competition within the EU has been widely understood as interurban and interregional competition rather than as a competition among national economies.

INTERLOCALITY COMPETITION AS A (NATIONAL) STATE PROJECT

During the 1980s and 1990s, as cities and regions throughout the EU attempted to adjust to the neoliberalization of key fields of national state policy, and simultaneously, to prepare themselves for the new competitive pressures associated with the Single European Market, qualitatively new forms of state intervention into the urban process were mobilized. Specifically, the shift towards urban entrepreneurialism in Western Europe was animated through the introduction of diverse institutional frameworks and policies oriented towards urban economic rejuvenation and urban competitiveness. The promotion of urban economic growth – particularly within each country's most competitive cities and city-regions – thus became an explicit goal of diverse national, regional and local policies. Across Western European states, independently of inherited administrative structures and political regimes, a number of analogous institutional shifts have underpinned the rise and proliferation of urban entrepreneurialism.

The fiscal squeeze

During the post-1970s recession, national grants to subnational levels were generally reduced and local governments throughout Western Europe became more dependent upon locally collected taxes and non-tax revenues such as charges and user fees (Mouritzen, 1992). In the immediate aftermath of the economic crisis of the 1970s, many Western European local governments delayed capital expenditures, drew upon liquid assets and increased their debts, but these proved to be no more than short-term stopgap measures; additional local revenues were subsequently sought in, among other sources, economic development projects (Fox Przeworski, 1986). With the exception of France, local government spending as a share of GDP declined markedly during this period in most Western European countries (Pickvance and Preteceille, 1991: 203–4). These new constraints upon public expenditure in cities and regions were an important expression and outcome of the processes of welfare state retrenchment that began to unfold throughout the OECD zone during the 1970s. One of the key outcomes of this shift was to pressure localities to seek new sources of revenue through local economic development projects.

The decentralization of intergovernmental relations

In the midst of these new fiscal constraints, central governments throughout the EU began to transfer diverse public policy responsibilities to subnational administrative tiers, in significant part as a strategy to force those levels of public authority to engage more directly in the promotion of local economic development. For instance, even as national fiscal transfers to subnational levels have been diminished during the last three decades, many local governments have been granted new revenue-raising powers and an increased level of authority in determining local tax rates and user fees (Fox Przeworski, 1986). Just as importantly, throughout this period, new responsibilities for economic development, social services and spatial planning were devolved to subnational governments

(Mayer, 1992). In a number of Western European countries, including France, Denmark, Belgium, the Netherlands, Germany, Scandinavia, Spain, Portugal and Italy, local economic development projects have been a key focal point for such devolutionary initiatives, as regional and local state institutions have been increasingly forced to 'fend for themselves' in developing growth strategies for their jurisdictions. Although these trends have been most apparent in traditionally centralized states, such as France and Spain, diverse policies to enhance regional and local autonomy have likewise been enacted in less centralized European states (Parkinson, 1991). In each case, decentralization policies were seen as a means to 'limit the considerable welfare demands of urban areas and to encourage lower-level authorities to assume responsibility for growth policies that might reduce welfare burdens' (Harding, 1994: 370). Even in the UK, where major aspects of local governance were subjected to increasing central control under the Thatcher regime, the problem of local economic governance was among the key issues upon which the restructuring of intergovernmental relations was focused (Duncan and Goodwin, 1989); and it subsequently remained central to the devolutionary agenda of the Blair government.

New national urban policies

Since the economic crises of the 1970s, national governments throughout Western Europe have mobilized a range of policies to address the problems of distressed urban areas and to promote renewed economic growth within major cities and city regions. Initially, national urban policies were oriented primarily towards deindustrializing, distressed cities confronted with social problems such as mass unemployment and the decay of industrial infrastructures. Major examples of such policies include the West German Urban Development Assistance Act, the French Plan of Action for Employment and Industrial Reorganization, the Dutch Big

Cities Bottleneck Program and the British Inner Areas Act. Subsequently, as urban economic restructuring continued in conjunction with processes of globalization and European integration, Western European central governments began to target cities and city regions as the locational keys to national economic competitiveness. In the 'Europe of Regions' – a catchphrase that became increasingly important in national policy discussions as of the mid-1980s – cities were no longer seen merely as containers of socioeconomic problems, but were increasingly viewed as dynamic growth engines through which national prosperity could be assured. With the consolidation of the Single European Market in 1993, this view of the city as an essential economic asset became the dominant one in most Western European national and regional governments (Harding, 1994: 371). Under these conditions, traditional compensatory regional policies were widely abandoned and new national urban policies were mobilized in order to promote a sustained reconcentration of industry and population within major urban regions. The reorientation of Dutch spatial planning towards the Randstad megalopolis in the mid-1980s, the refocusing of Danish regional planning on the Copenhagen region during the early 1990s, the introduction of new national urban growth polities in Italy after 1991 and the adoption of a city-centric approach to spatial planning in post-unification Germany represent prominent instances of this realignment, which is occurring in diverse politico-institutional forms throughout Western Europe.

The construction of territory-specific institutions and development projects

In addition to the intergovernmental shifts discussed above, national governments have also established new institutional forms designed to address concentrated social problems or to promote economic development projects within strategic sites. Such institutions are often autonomous from local state institutions and controlled by unaccountable political and economic elites. Major examples of this trend include enterprise zones, urban development corporations, airport development agencies, training and enterprise councils, inward investment and economic promotion agencies, and other territory-specific forms of public–private partnership that have been introduced in cities throughout Western Europe. The Docklands redevelopment project in London and the Dutch mainports policies in Amsterdam and Rotterdam represent prominent examples from the 1980s and 1990s in which European national governments channeled substantial public subsidies into strategically located economic development projects. Analogous institutional arrangements have been introduced in other major European city regions, as national governments attempt to market their pre-eminent cities as competitive locations for strategic functions – whether for management, production or consumption – in the new global and European spatial divisions of labor.

The redefinition of local state functions

In close conjunction with the aforementioned shifts, the welfarist institutional infrastructures of Western European local states have been systematically transformed since the 1970s (Clark, 1997; Snape, 1995). Whereas postwar Western European local governments had been devoted primarily to various forms of welfare service delivery, collective consumption policies and infrastructure provision, they have been systematically transformed during the last three decades into entrepreneurial agencies oriented towards the promotion of economic development within their jurisdictions. The new entrepreneurial orientation of local state institutions has been articulated in three basic forms. First, confronted with increasing budgetary constraints, local states throughout Western Europe have privatized or contracted out numerous public services and attempted to modernize systems of public administration. In conjunction with these changes, many European local states have more recently embraced the discourses and practices of the 'new public management', with its emphasis on efficiency, flexibility, consumer responsiveness and the 'lean state.' Second, local states have attempted to promote economic regeneration by seeking to acquire subsidies through national and/or European industrial and sectoral programs. In this context, a major goal has been to secure new forms of public aid, whether for firms, households or areas. Third, and most crucially, local states – often in conjunction with regional state governments in federal countries – have introduced a range of new policies designed to promote local growth, including labour market programs, industrial policies, infrastructural investments, place-marketing initiatives and property redevelopment campaigns. Such policies strive to generate endogenous growth potentials and economic capacities within a local or regional economy while also significantly reconfiguring the institutional framework in which urban governance occurs. As noted above with reference to Mayer's (1994) analysis, many local economic development policies have also entailed the establishment of public–private partnerships and other informal governance networks that blur the traditional boundaries between state institutions and the agents of private capital.

These intertwined forms of national and local state restructuring have been essential mechanisms for the rise of entrepreneurial cities across the European urban system. Although the diffusion of urban entrepreneurialism has been highly uneven, the restructuring of national state institutions has arguably been one of its major catalysts throughout the EU zone. To be sure, many localities, cities and regions have articulated place-specific strategies of economic development in response to locally specific problems. The crucial point here, however, is that such strategies have been enabled, animated and

in some cases directly imposed through national politico-institutional shifts that have forced subnational governmental levels to 'fend for themselves' in various policy domains.

This interpretation is borne out in the vast case-study literature on entrepreneurial urban governance in Western European cities. For instance, Harding's (1997) comparative study of Amsterdam, Copenhagen, Edinburgh, Hamburg and Manchester demonstrates the key role of higher levels of government – national states in particular – in encouraging the adoption of local economic development strategies and the formation of development coalitions within each city. In each of these countries, furthermore, the turn towards urban entrepreneurialism has been coupled with a dismantling of traditional regional incentives policies and industrial subsidies in favor of new endogenous growth policies oriented towards regional specialization and clustering in major metropolitan centers. Arguments to the same effect can be gleaned from numerous case studies of post-Fordist urban politics in Western Europe during the 1980s and 1990s (Cheshire and Gordon, 1995; Hall and Hubbard, 1998; Harding et al., 1994; Healey et al., 1995; Heinelt and Mayer. 1993; Jenson-Butler et al., 1997; Moulaert and Demazière, 1995; Parkinson, 1991). In sum, the local economic strategies associated with the rise of urban entrepreneurialism in Western European states must be viewed as key expressions and outcomes of national state projects designed to institutionalize interlocality competition both within and beyond their territorial borders.

The failures of entrepreneurial urban governance

In so far as they institutionalize competitive relations among subnational administrative units, entrepreneurial urban policies are associated with spatially polarizing institutional innovations and regulatory initiatives. In neoliberalized political systems, such policies are justified through the contention that stable macroeconomic growth will be secured as local and regional economies are forced to compete on the basis of their supranational market positions. By contrast, in national and regional contexts in which social- and Christian-democratic traditions have remained more robust, intra-national territorial ine-qualities are usually viewed as an unavoida-ble consequence of global and European economic integration. The polarization of territorial development is seen as an undesir-able but necessary side-effect of political ini-tiatives to maintain national economic competitiveness. In both instances, however, it is assumed that the place-specific competi-tive advantages of city regions will not be threatened by rising levels of intranational sociospatial polarization. More generally, it is assumed that the benefits of urban economic dynamism – both within and beyond the city regions that are targeted for development ini-tiatives – will offset any detrimental political–economic consequences that might flow from the new territorial polarization.

In practice, such assumptions have proven to be thoroughly problematic. For, while uneven spatial development may present cer-tain fractions of capital with new opportuni-ties for profit-making, it may also undermine the socioeconomic and territorial precondi-tions upon which the accumulation process as a whole depends (Harvey, 1982). As numerous urban scholars have suggested, a number of regulatory failures and crisis-ten-dencies have become evident across the Western European urban system during the last two decades, as national, regional and local state institutions have mobilized entre-preneurial forms of urban governance in the absence of a comprehensive regulatory framework for containing their territorially polarizing consequences (see, for instance, Cheshire and Gordon, 1996; Dunford, 1994; Eisenschitz and Gough, 1996; Keating, 1991; Leitner and Sheppard, 1998; Lovering, 1995; Peck and Tickell, 1994, 1995). Such policies have proven contradictory in the sense that, in channeling public resources towards the goal of enhancing urban territorial competitiveness,

they have simultaneously contributed to a destabilization of urban, regional and national economic development. To be sure, the pat-terns of regulatory failure and crisis forma-tion induced by entrepreneurial urban policies have been articulated in nationally, region-ally and locally specific forms. For instance, the macrogeographical impacts of offensive, social-democratic approaches to entrepre-neurial urban policy have been less destruc-tive, destabilizing and polarizing than defensive, neoliberal approaches (Leborgne and Lipietz, 1991). Nonetheless, as Harvey (1989: 10–11) recognized nearly two dec-ades ago, entrepreneurial forms of urban governance cause urban systems to become more 'vulnerable to the uncertainties of rapid change' and thus trigger 'all manner of upward and downward spirals of urban growth and decline' (Harvey, 1989: 10–11). The following are among the major regula-tory failures and crisis tendencies that have been generated through the widespread mobi-lization of entrepreneurial urban policies in post-1980s Western Europe:

- *Inefficiency and waste.* Entrepreneurial urban policies enhance competitive pressures upon sub-national administrative units to offer favorable terms to potential investors. As these policies have been diffused, the potential disadvantages of a failure or refusal to introduce them have escalated (Leitner and Sheppard, 1998). Despite this, there is currently little evidence that such policies generate positive-sum, supply-side gains for local econo-mies, for instance, by upgrading locally embed-ded industrial capacities. More frequently, such initiatives have entailed public subsidies to private firms, leading to a zero-sum redistribution of capi-tal investment among competing locations within the EU (Cheshire and Gordon, 1996; Dunford, 1994). In this manner, entrepreneurial urban poli-cies may induce inefficient allocations of public resources as taxpayer revenues are channeled towards the promotion of private accumulation rather than towards the general conditions of pro-duction or social expenditures. Hence, as Cheshire and Gordon (1995: 122) conclude, 'much territo-rial competition [among cities] is pure waste'.
- *Short-termism.* The proliferation of entrepreneur-ial urban policies has encouraged 'the search

for short-term gains at the expense of more important longer-term investments in the health of cities and the well-being of their residents' (Leitner and Sheppard, 1998: 305). Even though some cities have managed to acquire short-term competitive advantages through the early adoption of entrepreneurial urban policies, such advantages have generally been eroded as analogous policies have been diffused among similarly positioned cities within the European spatial division of labor (Leitner and Sheppard, 1998). In this sense, while entrepreneurial forms of urban governance have helped unleash short-term bursts of economic growth within some cities and regions, they have proven far less effective in sustaining that growth over the medium- or long-term (Peck and Tickell, 1994, 1995).

- *'Glocal enclavization'.* Entrepreneurial urban policies entail the targeting of strategic, globally connected urban regions, or specific locations therein, as the engines of national economic dynamism. Such policies are premised upon the assumption that enhanced urban territorial competitiveness will benefit the broader regional and national space economies in which cities are embedded. In practice, however, entrepreneurial urban policies have contributed to the establishment of technologically advanced, globally connected urban enclaves that generate only limited spillover effects into their surrounding territories. This tendency towards 'glocal enclavization' is being articulated at a local scale, as advanced infrastructural hubs and high-technology production centers are delinked from adjoining neighborhoods, and at supralocal scales, as globally competitive agglomerations are delinked from older industrial regions and other marginalized spaces within the same national territory (Graham and Marvin, 2001). The resultant intensification of national and local sociospatial polarization may undermine macroeconomic stability; it may also breed divisive, disruptive political conflicts.

- *Regulatory undercutting.* Particularly in their defensive, neoliberal forms, entrepreneurial urban policies have encouraged a race to the bottom in social service provision as national, regional and municipal governments attempt to reduce the costs of capital investment within their jurisdictions. This process of regulatory undercutting is dysfunctional on a number of levels: it aggravates municipal fiscal and regulatory problems; it worsens life chances for significant segments of local and national populations; and it exacerbates entrenched inequalities

within national urban hierarchies (Eisenschitz and Gough, 1996; Peck and Tickell, 1995). These outcomes tend to downgrade national economic performance (Cheshire and Gordon, 1996; Hudson, 2001).

- *Uneven spatial development and territorial conflicts.* The aforementioned regulatory problems may assume more moderate forms in conjunction with offensive, social-democratic forms of entrepreneurial urban policy. Nonetheless, offensive forms of urban entrepreneurialism are likewise prone to significant crisis tendencies (Eisenschitz and Gough, 1993, 1996; Leborgne and Lipietz, 1991). First, like defensive approaches to entrepreneurial urban policy, offensive approaches 'operate ... as a strategy for strengthening some territories *vis-à-vis* other territories and other nations' (Leborgne and Lipietz, 1991: 47); they thus 'increase the profitability of strong economies more than the weak' and intensify uneven development beyond the territorial zones in which they are deployed (Eisenschitz and Gough, 1996: 444). The macroeconomic instability that subsequently ensues may undermine the very localized socioeconomic assets upon which offensive forms of urban entrepreneurialism depend (Leborgne and Lipietz, 1991). Second, even more so than defensive forms of urban entrepreneurialism, offensive approaches to urban economic development suffer from serious problems of politicization. Their effectiveness hinges upon being confined to locally delineated areas; yet the apparent successes of such strategies at a local scale generate intense distributional pressures as other localities and regions within the same national territory strive to replicate the 'recipe' or to reap some of its financial benefits (Eisenschitz and Gough, 1996).

- *Problems of interscalar coordination.* The proliferation of place-specific strategies of local economic development exacerbates coordination problems within and among national, regional and local state institutions. First, because entrepreneurial urban policies enhance the geographical differentiation of state regulatory activities without embedding subnational competitive strategies within an encompassing national policy framework, they have undermined the organizational coherence and functional integration of state institutions. For, as Painter and Goodwin (1995: 646) explain, the increasing geographical differentiation of state regulatory activities induced through local economic development policies is 'as much a hindrance as a help to regulation'. Second, this lack of supranational or national regulatory coordination in the field of urban policy may exacerbate the economic crisis tendencies discussed above: it enhances the likelihood that identical or analogous growth strategies may be replicated serially across the European urban system, thus accelerating the diffusion of zero-sum forms of interlocality competition (Amin and Malmberg, 1994).

• *Democratic accountability and legitimation problems.* Finally, the proliferation of entrepreneurial urban policies has generated new conflicts regarding democratic accountability and political legitimation. Many of the new, highly fragmented institutional forms established to implement entrepreneurial urban policies are dominated by non-elected government bureaucrats, technical experts, property developers and corporate elites who are not accountable to the populations that are most directly affected by their activities (Swyngedouw *et al.*, 2002). While this lack of political accountability may enable regulatory agencies to implement entrepreneurial urban policies more efficiently, it systematically undermines their ability to address broader social needs and to maintain territorial cohesion. The institutional fragmentation of political–economic governance induced through entrepreneurial urban policies thus constrains the capacity of state institutions, at various spatial scales, to address many of their dysfunctional side-effects, both within and beyond the cities in which they are deployed. It may also generate serious legitimation deficits if oppositional social forces are able to politicize the negative socioeconomic consequences of entrepreneurial urban policies or their undemocratic character.

However, despite their destabilizing consequences for accumulation and regulation, entrepreneurial forms of urban policy have been further entrenched across Western Europe during the last two decades. The field of urban governance has continued to evolve in the first decade of the twenty-first century, as new institutional and scalar configurations are introduced through diverse forms of regulatory experimentation in neighborhoods, metropolitan regions and intercity networks across the European urban system. Nonetheless, even as this regulatory experimentation

intensifies and still further differentiates the institutional landscape of urban governance, an underlying politics of interspatial competition have been preserved and even strengthened (Brenner, 2004).

This is not to suggest that the multifaceted field of urban governance has been reduced to a narrowly economistic agenda of positioning cities competitively within supranational circuits of capital. The claim here, rather, is that the priority of promoting international territorial competitiveness – which is increasingly understood with reference to both economic *and* extra-economic factors (Jessop, 2002; Messner, 1997) – has come to define the political and institutional parameters within which nearly all other dimensions of urban policy may be articulated. Given the overarching role of redistributive, collective consumption functions at the urban scale within the postwar Fordist–Keynesian framework, the current primacy of entrepreneurial urban agendas represents a striking politicoinstitutional realignment.

SUMMARY AND CONCLUSION

The account of entrepreneurial urban policies developed here suggests a distinctive, postdisciplinary vantage point from which to interpret the vast, case study-based and comparative literature on urban governance in contemporary Europe. While such case studies and comparisons have contributed significantly to our understanding of contemporary European urban development, they have tended to conceive the transition to urban entrepreneurialism as the product of localized, often business-led responses to supranational economic constraints (see, for instance, Jensen-Butler *et al.*, 1997). By contrast, this chapter has emphasized the role of (reconfigured) state institutions in facilitating the mobilization, institutionalization and generalization of entrepreneurial urban policies. To be sure, the proliferation of place-specific economic crises and the intensification of foreign direct investment within urban economies provided local political–economic elites with significant, market-led incentives to form place-based, developmentalist alliances, to embrace the narrative of global and European interlocality competition and, on this basis, to introduce local competitiveness policies (Cheshire and Gordon, 1996). However, in light of the above discussion, the spread of competitiveness-oriented local territorial alliances across Europe must also be understood in relation to the transformed European and national political geographies, intergovernmental configurations and institutional landscapes that were being forged during this same period. For, as Harvey (1989: 15) emphasized over a decade ago, the transition to urban entrepreneurialism 'required a radical reconstruction of central to local state relations and the cutting free of local state activities from the welfare state and the Keynesian compromise'. It was through such national–local recalibrations – alongside a simultaneous intensification of European integration – that localized spaces for regulatory experimentation were opened up across the EU in which aggressively extrospective, yet place-specific, urban development strategies could be mobilized.

The entrepreneurial urban policies described in this chapter were introduced by political alliances rooted within, and articulated across, a variety of spatial scales. In some cases, they involved tangled interscalar articulations among European, national, regional and local political–economic forces, which together attempted to rejig the framework of urban governance and to channel public and private resources into strategic urban locations. In other instances, entrepreneurial urban policies were mobilized by national governments, often by circumventing extant municipal institutions and by establishing centrally controlled forms of local regulation. Under yet other circumstances, locally embedded political–economic alliances played a formative role in the mobilization of entrepreneurial urban policies, often by capitalizing upon strategic opportunities generated through the process of European integration. While activist, entrepreneurial mayors frequently contributed to the formation of such 'local' development regimes – for instance, in cities such as Hamburg, Lille, Lyon, Milan and Barcelona – the restructuring of national state spaces, as described above, was nonetheless almost invariably one of their essential institutional conditions of possibility (Le Galès, 2001; McNeill, 2001). It is crucial to recognize, finally, that entrepreneurial urban policies were promoted by a variety of opposed class forces and political alliances within each national, regional and local context – including neoliberal coalitions concerned to grant new discretionary powers and public subsidies to transnational capital; neocorporatist coalitions concerned to promote cross-class cooperation and to forge 'high-road' developmental pathways; and neostatist coalitions concerned with enhancing the capacity of state institutions to override class-based coalitions (Eisenschitz and Gough 1996; Gough, 2002). Any systematic, comparative study of urban governance restructuring in post-1980s Western Europe would need to examine the contextually specific political, institutional and geographical bases of urban entrepreneurialism within each national territory and their associated projects of urban economic development (Savitch and Kantor, 2002).

This chapter has also underscored the dysfunctional consequences of entrepreneurial forms of urban governance. And yet, despite their polarizing, destabilizing consequences for local, regional and national economies, entrepreneurial approaches to urban governance have been further entrenched. To be sure, a variety of emergent regulatory experiments – from the European Structural Funds and the European Spatial Development Perspective to new forms of metropolitan institutional cooperation, neighborhood-based anti-exclusion policies and interurban networking policies – appear to point beyond the politics of territorial competition that has been outlined in this chapter. Yet, in practice, none of these experiments have succeeded in loosening, much less transcending, the apparent lock-in of competitiveness-oriented approaches to economic governance, either within or beyond cities. Meanwhile, the regulatory deficits and crisis tendencies of entrepreneurial urban policies persist, causing the landscape of economic governance to be still further destabilized throughout the EU.

This is the central paradox of the new forms of urban governance that have been explored in this chapter. In so far as it continually assimilates alternative, opposing political projects, urban entrepreneurialism seems to permit no alternative; it appears to demand compliance to the grim imperative of globalizing, neoliberalizing capitalism – 'compete or die'. And yet, because they exacerbate rather than alleviate the economic dislocations, regulatory failures and territorial inequalities of post-Keynesian urbanization, entrepreneurial forms of urban governance cannot survive in their current institutional and scalar forms. Entrepreneurial cities are thus spaces of conflict, crisis and contradiction; and for this reason, they are also spaces of incessant regulatory experimentation and dynamic institutional searching. The future shape of territorial development in the EU will be molded not only through the legacies of inherited institutional and spatial arrangements, but also through such ongoing regulatory experiments, and the conflicts they will continue to provoke.

REFERENCES

Amin, A. (1994) 'Post-Fordism: models, fantasies and phantoms of transition', in A. Amin (ed.) *Post-Fordism: A Reader*. Cambridge, MA: Blackwell, pp 1–40.

Amin, A. and Malmberg, A. (1994) 'Competing structural and institutional influences on the geography of production in Europe', in A. Amin (ed.) *Post-Fordism: A Reader*. Cambridge, MA: Blackwell, pp. 227–248.

Amin, A. and Thrift, N. (1992) 'Neo-Marshallian nodes in global networks', *International Journal of Urban and Regional Research*, 16 (4): 571–587.

Amin, A. and Tomaney, J. (1995) 'The regional dilemma in a neo-liberal Europe', *European Urban and Regional Studies*, 2 (2): 171–188.

Benko, G. and Dunford, M. (eds) (1991) *Industrial Change and Regional Development: the Transformation of New Industrial Spaces*. London: Belhaven.

Braudel, F. (1984) *The Perspective of the World*. Berkeley: University of California Press.

Brenner, N. (2004) *New State Spaces: Urban Governance and the Rescaling of Statehood*. New York: Oxford University Press.

Brunet, R. (1989) *Les Villes 'Europeennes'*. DATAR: Paris.

Budd, L. (1998) 'Territorial competition and globalisation', *Urban Studies*, 35 (4): 663–685.

CEC, Commission of the European Communities (1991) *The Regions in the 1990s*. Brussels: European Commission.

Cheshire, P. (1999) 'Cities in competition', *Urban Studies*, 36 (4–5): 843–864.

Cheshire, P. and Gordon, I. (eds) (1995) *Territorial Competition in an Integrating Europe*. Aldershot: Avebury.

Cheshire, P. and Gordon, I. (1996) 'Territorial competition and the predictability of collective (in)action', *International Journal of Urban and Regional Research*, 20 (3): 383–399.

Clark, D. (1997) 'Local government in Europe', *West European Politics*, 20 (3): 134–163.

Coriat, B. and Petit, P. (1991) 'Deindustrialization and tertiarization: towards a new economic regime?', in A. Amin and M. Dietrich (eds) *Towards a New Europe?* Aldershot: Edward Elgar, pp. 18–48.

Dicken, P. and Öberg, S. (1996) 'The global context: Europe in a world of dynamic economic and population change', *European Urban and Regional Studies*, 3 (2): 101–120.

Duncan, S. and Goodwin, M. (1989) *The Local State and Uneven Development*. London: Polity.

Dunford, M. (1994) 'Winners and losers: the new map of economic inequality in the European Union', *European Urban and Regional Studies*, 1 (2): 95–114.

Dunford, M. and Kafkalas, G. (1992) 'The global–local interplay, corporate geographies and spatial development strategies in Europe', in M. Dunford and G. Kafkalas (eds)

Cities and Regions in the New Europe. London: Belhaven Press, pp. 3–38.

Dunford, M. and Kafkalas, G. (eds) (1992) *Cities and Regions in the New Europe.* London: Belhaven Press.

Dunford, M. and Perrons, D. (1994) 'Regional inequality, regimes of accumulation and economic development in contemporary Europe', *Transactions of the Institute of British Geographers,* 19 (2): 163–182.

Eisenschitz, A. and Gough, J. (1993) *The Politics of Local Economic Development.* New York: Macmillan.

Eisenschitz, A. and Gough, J. (1996) 'The contradictions of neo-Keynesian local economic strategy', *Review of International Political Economy,* 3 (3): 434–458.

Fox Przeworski, J. (1986) 'Changing intergovernmental relations and urban economic development', *Environment and Planning C: Government and Policy,* 4 (4): 423–439.

Gill, S. (1998) 'European governance and new constitutionalism: economic and monetary union and alternatives to disciplinary neoliberalism in Europe', *New Political Economy,* 3 (1): 5–26.

Gough, J. (2002) 'Neoliberalism and socialisation in the contemporary city: opposites, complements and instabilities', in N. Brenner and N. Theodore (eds) *Spaces of Neoliberalism.* Boston: Blackwell, pp. 58–79.

Graham, S. and Marvin, S. (2001) *Splintering Urbanism.* New York: Routledge.

Hall, T. and Hubbard, P. (1996) 'The entrepreneurial city: new politics, new urban geographies', *Progress in Human Geography,* 20 (2): 153–174.

Hall, T. and Hubbard, P. (eds) (1998) *The Entrepreneurial City.* London: Wiley.

Harding, A. (1994) 'Urban regimes and growth machines: towards a cross-national research agenda', *Urban Affairs Quarterly,* 29 (3): 356–382.

Harding, A. (1997) 'Urban regimes in a Europe of the cities?', *European Urban and Regional Studies,* 4 (4): 291–314.

Harding, A. and Le Galès, P. (1997) 'Globalization, urban change and urban policies in Britain and France'. in A. Scott (ed.) *The Limits of Globalization: Cases and Arguments.* New York: Routledge, pp. 181–201.

Harding, A., Dawson, J., Evans, R., and Parkinson, M. (eds) (1994) *European Cities*

Towards 2000. Manchester: Manchester University Press.

Harvey, D. (1982) *The Limits to Capital.* Chicago: University of Chicago Press.

Harvey, D. (1989) 'From managerialism to entrepreneurialism: the transformation in urban governance in late capitalism', *Geografiska Annaler* B 71 (1) 3–18.

Healey, P., Cameron, S., Davoudi, S., Graham, S. and Madani-Pour, A. (eds) (1995) *Managing Cities: the New Urban Context.* London: Wiley.

Heinelt, H. and Mayer, M. (eds) (1993) *Politik in Europäischen Städten.* Basel: Birkhäuser Verlag.

Hudson, R. (2001) *Producing Places.* New York: Guilford Publishers.

Jensen-Butler, C., Shachar, A. and van Weesep, J. (eds) (1997) *European Cities in Competition.* Aldershot: Avebury.

Jessop, B. (2002) *The Future of the Capitalist State.* London: Polity.

Jewson, N. and MacGregor, S. (eds) (1997) *Transforming Cities.* New York: Routledge.

Jonas, A. and Wilson, D. (eds) (1999) *The Urban Growth Machine: Critical Perspectives, Two Decades Later.* Albany: State University of New York Press.

Keating, M. (1991) *Comparative Urban Politics.* Aldershot: Edward Elgar.

Krätke, S. (1993) 'Stadtsystem im internationalen Kontext und Vergleich', in R. Roth and H. Wollmann (eds) *Kommunalpolitik.* Opladen: Leske Verlag, pp. 176–193.

Krätke, S. (1995) *Stadt, Raum, Ökonomie.* Basel: Birkhäuser Verlag.

Kunzmann, K. (1998) 'World city regions in Europe', in F.C. Lo and Y.M. Yeung (eds) *Globalization and the World of Large Cities.* Tokyo: United Nations University Press.

Kunzmann, K. and Wegener, M. (1991) 'The pattern of urbanization in western Europe', *Ekistics, 58,* 350(1), 282–291.

Le Galès, P. (2001) *European Cities: Social Conflicts and Governance.* New York: Oxford University Press.

Le Galès, P. and Harding, A. (1998) 'Cities and states in Europe', *West European Politics,* 21 (3): 120–145.

Leborgne, D. and Lipietz, A. (1991) 'Two social strategies in the production of new industrial spaces', in G. Benko and M. Dunford (eds) *Industrial Change and Regional Development.* London: Belhaven, pp. 27–49.

Leitner, H. and Sheppard, E. (1998) 'Economic uncertainty, inter-urban competition and the efficacy of entrepreneurialism', in T. Hall and P. Hubbard (eds) *The Entrepreneurial City*. Chichester: Wiley, pp. 285–308.

Logan, J. and Molotch, H. (1987) *Urban Fortunes. The Political Economy of Place*. Berkeley and Los Angeles: University of California Press.

Lovering, J. (1995) 'Creating discourses rather than jobs: the crisis in the cities and the transition fantasies of intellectuals and policy makers', in Patsy Healey *et al.* (eds) *Managing Cities: the New Urban Context*. London: Wiley, pp. 109–126.

McNeill, D. (2001) 'Embodying a Europe of the cities: geographies of mayoral leadership', *Area*, 22 (4): 353–359.

Majone, G. (1994) 'The rise of the regulatory state in Europe', *West European Politics*, 17 (3): 77–102.

Martinelli, F. and Schoenberger, E. (1991) 'Oligopoly is alive and well: notes for a broader discussion of flexible accumulation', in G. Benko and M. Dunford (eds) *Industrial Change and Regional Development*. London: Belhaven Press, pp. 117–133.

Mayer, M. (1992) 'The shifting local political system in European cities', in M. Dunford and G. Kafkalas (eds) *Cities and Regions in the New Europe*. New York: Belhaven Press, pp. 255–276.

Mayer, M. (1994) 'Post-Fordist city politics', in A. Amin (ed.) *Post-Fordism: A Reader*. Cambridge, MA: Blackwell, pp. 316–337.

Messner, D. (1997) *The Network Society*. London: Frank Cass.

Mollenkopf, J. (1983) *The Contested City*. Princeton: Princeton University Press.

Moulaert, F. (1996) 'Rediscovering spatial inequality in Europe: building blocks for an appropriate 'regulationist' analytical framework', *Environment and Planning D: Society and Space*, 14: 155–179.

Moulaert, F. and Demazière, C. (1995) 'Local economic development in post-Fordist Europe', in C. Demazière and P. Wilson (eds) *Local Economic Development in Europe and the Americas*. Mansell: London, pp. 2–28.

Mouritzen, P.E. (ed.) (1992) *Managing Cities in Austerity*. London: Sage.

Müller, W. and Wright, V. (1994) 'Reshaping the state in Western Europe', *West European Politics*, 17 (3): 1–11.

Nijkamp, P. (1993) 'Towards a network of regions', *European Planning Studies*, 1 (2): 149–168.

Nilsson, J.-E. and Schamp, E. (1996) 'Restructuring of the European production system: processes and consequences', *European Urban and Regional Studies*, 3 (2): 121–132.

Overbeek, H. (ed) (1991) *Restructuring Hegemony in the International Political Economy*. New York: Routledge.

Painter, J. and Goodwin, M. (1995) 'Local governance and concrete research: investigating the uneven development of regulation', *Economy and Society*, 24 (3): 334–356.

Parkinson, M. (1991) 'The rise of the entrepreneurial European city: strategic responses to economic changes in the 1980s', *Ekistics*, 58, 350(1), 299–307.

Parkinson, M. and Harding, A. (1995) 'European cities towards 2000', in M. Rhodes (ed.) *The Regions and the New Europe*. Manchester: Manchester University Press, pp. 27–52.

Peck, J. and Tickell, A. (1994) 'Searching for a new institutional fix', in A. Amin (ed.) *Post-Fordism: A Reader*. Cambridge, MA: Blackwell, pp. 280–315.

Peck, J. and Tickell, A. (1995) 'The social regulation of uneven development: "regulatory deficit", England's South East, and the collapse of Thatcherism', *Environment and Planning A* 27 (1): 15–40.

Pickvance, C. and Preteceille, E. (eds) (1991) *State Restructuring and Local Power: A Comparative Perspective*. London: Pinter.

Rhodes, M. (1995) '"Subversive liberalism": market integration, globalization and the European welfare state', *Journal of European Public Policy*, 2 (3): 384–406.

Rhodes, M., Heywood, P. and Wright, V. (eds) (1997) *Developments in West European Politics*. New York: St Martin's Press.

Rodriguez-Pose, A. (1998) *The Dynamics of Regional Growth in Europe*. Oxford: Clarendon Press.

Ross, G. (1998) 'European integration and globalization', in R. Axtmann (ed.) *Globalization and Europe*. London: Pinter, pp. 164–183.

Röttger, B. (1997) *Neoliberale Globalisierung und eurokapitalistische Regulation*. Münster: Westfälisches Dampfboot.

Sassen, S. (1993) *Cities in the World Economy*. London: Sage.

Savitch, H. and Kantor, P. (2002) *Cities in the International Marketplace*. Princeton NJ: Princeton University Press.

Scharpf, F. (1999) *Governing in Europe*. New York: Oxford University Press.

Scott, A.J. (1988) *New Industrial Spaces*. London: Pion.

Scott, A.J. and Storper, M. (1992) 'Industrialization and regional development', in M. Storper and A.J. Scott (eds) *Pathways to Industrialization and Regional Development*. New York: Routledge.

Snape, S. (1995) 'Contracting out local government services in western Europe: lessons from the Netherlands', *Local Government Studies*, 21 (4): 642–658.

Storper, M. (1996) *The Regional World*. New York: Guilford.

Storper, M. and Scott, A.J. (1989) 'The geographical foundations and social regulation of flexible production complexes', in J. Wolch and M. Dear (eds), *The Power of Geography*. Boston: Unwin Hyman, pp. 19–40.

Swyngedouw, E. (1992) 'The Mammon quest: "Glocalisation", interspatial competition and the monetary order', in M. Dunford and G. Kafkalas (eds) *Cities and Regions in the New Europe*. London: Belhaven Press, pp. 39–68.

Swyngedouw, E. (1989) 'The heart of the place: the resurrection of locality in an age of hyperspace', *Geografiska Annaler* B, 71 (1): 31–42.

Swyngedouw, E., Moulaert, F. and Rodriguez, A. (2003) '"The world in a grain of sand": large-scale urban development projects and the dynamics of "glocal" transformations', in F. Moulaert, A. Rodriguez and E. Swyngedouw (eds) *The Globalized City*. Oxford and New York: Oxford University Press, pp. 9–28.

Taylor, P.J. and Hoyler, M. (2000) 'The spatial order of European cities under conditions of contemporary globalization', *Tijdschrift voor Economische en Sociale Geografie*, 91 (2): 176–189.

Tickell, A. and Peck, J. (2003) 'Making global rules: globalization or neoliberalization?', in J. Peck and H.W.C. Yeung (eds), *Remaking the Global Economy*. London: Sage, pp. 163–181.

Veltz, P. (1996) *Mondialisation, Villes et Territoires*. Paris: Presses Universitaires de France.

Wright, V. (1994) 'Reshaping the state: the implications for public administration', *West European Politics*, 17 (3): 102–137.

26

Regions and Regional Dynamics

Anssi Paasi

This chapter will scrutinize regional dynamics in Europe and particularly, how the 'region' is understood in the context of a Europe where region, regionalism and regional identity seem to be currently hugely important ideas, both in the EU and outside it. These categories come together in the popular phrase 'the Europe of regions' that became significant in the EU during the 1990s. This idea implied that nation states were regarded as too small for global economic competition but at the same time too large and remote for cultural identification and participatory, active citizenship (Anderson, 1995, 2000). It also seemed to provide one way to avoid the juxtapositions based on the complicated relations between the ideal of homogeneous nation states and region-bound ethnicities (cf. Hettne, 2001).

The region has also become an important object of research in Europe where many of the expectations regarding the future of political and economic regional dynamics is embedded in this category (Jones and MacLeod, 2004; Keating, 1998, 2004; Keating *et al.*, 2003; Le Galès and Lequesne, 1998). The mushrooming literature on regions worldwide shows that the region has also become significant outside of the European space (Paasi, 2002a). Similarly, regionalism

has generated research worldwide (Calleya, 2000; Hettne *et al.*, 2001; Katz, 2000; Keating and O'Loughlin, 1997; Söderbaum and Shaw, 2003; Wilson, 1998). Even if regionalism as a cultural movement dates back to the nineteenth century (Gilbert and Litt, 1960, the strengthening of regionalism in Europe certainly took place in the 1950s and 1960s. Rhein (2000) associates it with the rise of the European Economic Community (EEC), and its successive constitutional followers, particularly the EU and the Maastricht Treaty (1993). The deepening of the integration has witnessed the fact that the region has become a key category in the EU since the 1990s (Rumford, 2000).

Current academic and practical importance of the region is somewhat paradoxical. The demise of the region (and other particularistic features of social life, such as, community, culture or locality) has been forecasted as part of a strengthening of modernity and the associated state-centric spatiality from the nineteenth century onwards. Indeed, during the nineteenth century many nation states rejected regions. In many states, such as, France, Italy or Spain, governments tried with various degrees of success to wipe out regional or provincial particularities (Keating, 1998). They were regarded as barriers in the construction of national identity and the modern state. On the other hand, in some countries, such as, Finland, provinces have been perpetually regarded as an important mediating scale in the nation-building process but have never gained a democratic political decision-making system in which citizens could vote for their regional representatives. Due to this fact, these units have remained distant to the citizens living in these areas (Paasi, 2002b). In federal states, like Germany and Austria, the power of regions is strong and was established a long time ago. Also, in Spain, Italy and Belgium the regions have gained power. The power of regions has also become stronger in France and the Netherlands. As a recent example, the position of Scotland and Wales has become more prominent in the UK, and hints of the resurgence of regionalism in England, partly following the devolution of institutional power from London in 1997 (cf. Deas and Lord, 2006; Jones and MacLeod, 2004; MacLeod, 1998; Tomaney and Ward, 2000).

A variety of reasons for the current prominence of regions exist. Anderson (2000: 36) recognizes such backgrounds as uneven economic development (and the lack of it!), regional languages and cultures being threatened with decline, federalization as a means of reducing the power of central states or as a means of containing separatist aspirations and conflicts. In the EU, 'region' has become a catchword in the Union's cohesion policy (Rumford, 2000). No wonder then that individuals, social groups, organizations, political parties, states and scientists all use regions to make spatial complexities manageable and to exercise power (Terlouw, 2004).

European regions show today a huge variety in their economic development, cultural and political history, and 'identity', as it is written in various documents and in the collective memory of citizens. Some regions are instruments of the EU or state power that are defined 'from above' and, while they may be important in governance, could be culturally 'thin'. This is particularly the case with new regions developed in EU-level planning rhetoric and practice (Deas and Lord, 2006). Some other regions are recognized as historical and cultural entities whose existence becomes manifested not only in strong identity narratives but also in various institutions, commemorations, and social and cultural movements.

Hence, to scrutinize regional dynamics in Europe is a complicated task, since both 'Europe' and 'region' are contested categories that are constantly redefined by actors operating in the academic world, politics, regional activism, governance or economy. Indeed there are many Europes, depending on our conceptualization of this word (Heffernan, 1998; McNeill, 2004; Mikkeli, 1997; Rietbergen, 2006). Europe itself has at times been represented as a 'cultural region' (Jordan, 1973). However, this is certainly very problematic, knowing the immense cultural heterogeneity of the area (cf. Guibernau, 2001; Paasi, 2001). A major question is how Europeans understand each other, since linguistic diversity is a major cultural feature. At least one thing is obvious in literature: the belief in the central role of Europe in history has been so dominating that even the most brilliant social theorists often take this position for granted (Blaut, 2000). Ironically, this tendency seems to continue in the EU, since the 'Treaty Establishing a Constitution for Europe' includes an implied mission to communicate the Union's values outside of the Union's area to neighbouring countries (Paasi, 2005).

This complexity also holds with the idea of region: there are many kinds of regions for very different purposes. The following citations effectively display this complexity.

A region may have a historic resonance or provide a focus for the identity of its inhabitants. It may represent a landscape, an architecture or a style of cooking. There is often a cultural element, perhaps represented by a distinct language or dialect. Beyond this, a region may sustain a distinct civil society, a range of social institutions. It can be an economic unit, based either on a single type of production or an integrated production system. It may be, and increasingly is, a unit of government and administration. Finally, all these meanings may or may not coincide, to a greater or lesser degree (Keating, 2004: xi).

Regions come in all shapes and sizes, some clearly demarcated by a long history, others little than figments of a central bureaucrat's imagination. Regionalisms likewise range from an almost non-existent sense of regional identity to fully-fledged sub-state nationalisms, a form of identity politics which sees the 'region' as a potentially separate independent country. The terms region and regionalism thus mask a range of quite different phenomena which vary not only from state to state but also within particular states' (Anderson, 2000: 35–6).

The word region refers most typically to substate units but Europe itself is at times understood as a 'region' in area studies, in world regional geography and in regional political economy (cf. Mansfield and Milner, 1997; Terlouw, 2004). As a recent collection of articles confirms, the idea of region has been very significant in Europe in structuring, governing and directing cultural, political and economic interests (Keating, 2004).

Due to the complexity of the topic, this chapter will not just compare given regions in Europe in some regional grid (like formal statistical areas). Rather it aims to problematize the idea of region in the context of Europe. This chapter will lean on an idea that regions, at whatever spatial scale, are social processes that become institutionalized as part of the multiscalar spatial dynamics, and simultaneous interaction of at times contradictory social practices and power relations. The chapter begins with a conceptual discussion on the institutionalization of regions and regional identity. This approach suggests that in the case of each 'region', small or large, the question of the existence of boundaries – open or closed – and symbols, and their use in various institutional practices is crucial. The contested ideas of Europe and European regions will be scrutinized in this framework which will help us to understand the contested meanings of both Europe and the idea of region.

CONCEPTUALIZING REGION AND REGIONAL IDENTITY

While regions and regionalism have often been – and still are (Allen *et al.*, 1998;

Amin *et al.*, 2003) – regarded by many as somehow backwards or reactionary in social science, an opposite tendency has been emerging since the 1980s. Regions at any scale, from local to continental, are today understood as social constructs; they are made by human beings for different purposes (Keating, 2001; MacLeod and Jones, 2001; Murphy, 1991). Regions are simultaneously both products and constituents of social action and always reflect asymmetrical power relations. Some actors normally participate actively in the production of regional space, imagination and consciousness. However, the majority of people only reproduce or 'consume' them and indeed regions may be unimportant to them. Politicians, business people, actors operating in the media and cultural sectors, teachers and researchers, to name some examples, are often activists that hold a key role in defining and shaping meanings and identities to regional spaces. This is certainly the case as far as the definitions of 'Europe' are concerned, but this also holds at lower scales. In the context of political regionalism, activists are key persons in the formation of opinions, and in mobilizing movements and even separatism (della Porta and Diani, 1999; Williams, 1997).

State governance has been and still is the major context for both sub- and suprastate region- and identity-building and maintaining. Gilbert and Litt (1960: 345) wrote almost 50 years ago that

[t]here is no State whose sovereignty extends over only one geographical region. The State is an artificial contrivance by which several, or perhaps many, geographical regions, some natural, some man-made, are welded into one working unit. Nevertheless, if only for the purposes of administration, even the most highly centralized States are split into numerous subdivisions.

A number of scholars argue today that a rescaling of the spatialities of state is taking place and it is increasingly the international markets and regional political responses to global capitalism that generate regionalism and accentuate the significance of regions (Brenner, 1999; Keating, 1998, 2001; Le Galés and Lequesne, 1998; MacLeod, 2001; Scott, 1998; Storper, 1998). Even if their institutional arrangements vary, the EU, NAFTA and APEC, for example, may be regarded as 'regions' and examples of a state-led networked regionalism. They are political results of the globalizing economic competition that has led to the increasing emphasis on regions as part of the restructuring of state. Regionalism in this context is a mirror image of globalization (Hettne *et al.*, 2001; Payne, 2000), and regions and regional identities become important in a new globalizing landscape and multilevel governance.

This has also been the case in the EU. Rumford (2000) has shown that while the region has assumed an increasingly important role in the EU, this has not been merely because of EU politics. Rather, he suggests, region has gained its current role in the EU in the context of globalization, competition and neoliberalism. Indeed, Castells (2002: 234) has suggested that 'Europe is already governed by a network state of shared sovereignty and multiple levels and instances of negotiated decision making'. This complexity and dynamisms of the institutional backgrounds is the core of new regionalism (Keating *et al.*, 2003; MacLeod, 2001). Jessop (2000: 343, cf. 2002: 179) has characterized the globalizing, increasingly complex territorial structures as follows:

[W]e now see a proliferation of discursively constituted and institutionally materialized and embedded spatial scales (whether terrestrial, territorial or telematic), that are related in increasingly complex tangled hierarchies rather than being simply nested one within the other, with different temporalities as well as spatialities ... There is no pre-given set of places, spaces or scales that are simply being reordered. For in addition to the changing significance of old places, spaces, scales and horizons, new places are emerging, new spaces are being created, new scales of organization are being developed and new horizons of action are being imagined.

Even if many scholars have, particularly since the 1990s, suggested that region and the city are crucial for understanding the spatialities of social and economic life (Scott, 1998; Storper, 1998), surprisingly scant attention has been paid to such theoretically challenging questions as what a region is, what regional boundaries means, how to conceptualize these elements and how to study them in practice (Jones and MacLeod, 2004; Paasi, 2002a).

Regions are social processes (Paasi, 1991). These processes, inherent motives and power relations may be based on economy, politics, culture or administration, and may originate from the 'region' in question or from outside it, and they may come together in unique ways in each region-building process. The production of space and associated motives and meanings are also subject to perpetual transformation. Regions are therefore not isolated islands but effectively constituted by networks and processes extending well beyond the borders of each region. Today this context is more often than not the global neoliberal landscape. Regions are also time- and space-specific, having their beginning and end. Nowhere has this become recently as obvious as in the collapse of Yugoslavia, an event that created several new territorial entities. This also shows that new regionalizations may often create fuel for ethnic conflicts.

When regions are understood as contested social processes, not merely flat and passive backgrounds of social action, three simultaneous processes can be conceptualized in their institutionalization (Paasi, 1991, 1996). These processes may occur simultaneously and their order can vary. At first, all regions have some kind of *territorial shape* – boundaries that emerge and exist in various social practices such as culture, governance, politics or economy and that are instrumental in distinguishing one region and identity discourse from others. The functions and meanings of boundaries vary. Respectively, some spatial practices are bounded and exclusive while others are not (Allen *et al.*, 1998; Paasi, 2001). Diverging bordering practices may even occur simultaneously in the same territorial context. Economics, for instance, is normally much more open than administration or politics (Taylor, 1994). The boundaries of many regions in the current EU, for example, are fuzzy and have only heuristic value for planning processes and development projects. Many of these new configurations are in competition with each other and with old administrative regions (Deas and Lord, 2006).

All regions also have a *symbolic shape* manifested in social practice and used to construct narratives of identity and to symbolize a region. The name of the region – often resulting from political or cultural struggle – and numerous other symbols (coat of arms, songs, certain cultural and natural features) may be crucial. Also a specific *institutional shape*, that is a number of institutional practices that are used in maintaining the territorial and symbolic shapes, are needed (Paasi, 1991). While these institutions are often crucial in the production and reproduction of boundaries and distinctions between regions and diverging social groups ('us'/'them'), they may well be located outside of the region. Think, for example, the European Union that is following the logic that has been used by tradition in every nation state. It has a hymn, flag and a flag day, which are, in a way, 'given' to the citizens of individual regions (states) from the outside to create solidarity among them.

A region becomes *established* when it is identified in social practices and regional consciousness, both inside and outside the region – it has an 'identity' (Paasi, 1991). An established region can be used by social actors as a medium in the struggle over resources and power. This is the case with the EU where regions are 'developed' through structural funds to create cohesion and to reduce the problems of uneven development created by globalizing economic competition. This is done, however, by increasing the competitiveness of regions, which in practice means that some regions (or subregions) may develop, while others will not (Rumford, 2000). Regional identity is one keyword in the Union's official policies to promote regional cohesiveness in order to reduce socioeconomic disparities, to harmonize economic spaces and hence to increase regional competitiveness

(Deas and Lord, 2006). At the other extreme, established regions can be used in the struggle against the Other. This typically takes place in such cases where regions and regional identities are strongly associated with ethnicity. Actors involved in these struggles often use 'identity' among their arguments.

Regional identity is an expression mushrooming not only in Europe, but all over the globe (Paasi, 2003). A lot of empirical evidence exist that shows that people's awareness of being involved in open-ended global flows appears to trigger a search for fixed orientation points and action frames. Identity has therefore become one conceptual tool in grasping how globalization reinforces the production of cultural difference by raising very ambivalent tendencies such as individualization and the need for recognition (Beck and Beck-Gernsheim, 2001). Identity refers also to people's attempts to mark boundaries in the ongoing flux of globalization processes (Meyer and Geschiere, 1999). Identity discourses are particularly popular in Europe where the actors in various regions try to promote the 'identity' of their regions, to protect their uniqueness and to accentuate the competitiveness of regions (perhaps partly as a reaction to harmonize the regional planning practices in European space).

The institutionalization of regions thus concomitantly gives rise to – and is conditioned by – the narratives of regional identity. Some further analytical distinctions help to clarify the 'identities' of regions and to understand regional identity narratives in the context of Europe (Paasi 1991, 1996). The *identity of a region* refers to such features of nature, culture and inhabitants that distinguish a region from others. In practice, discussions on the identity of some regions are typically discourses of scientists, politicians, administrators, cultural activists or entrepreneurs that aim to distinguish one region from others. This takes place through the construction of regional divisions, regional marketing, governance and political regionalization. Such classifications are inevitably based on certain choices, where some elements are chosen to constitute an identity narrative and some others are excluded. Thus, they are expressions of power in delimiting, naming and symbolizing space and groups of people. On the other hand, it is possible to distinguish analytically the *regional identity* of the inhabitants; that is, the identification of people with a region. This is what is often labelled as regional consciousness. The people in question may live inside the region (this is the usual presumption in debates on regional consciousness) or outside of it (Paasi, 2002b). Regional consciousness is a hierarchical phenomenon but is not inevitably fixed with certain existing regional levels and this can be based on natural or cultural elements that have been classified, often stereotypically, by regional activists, institutions or organizations as the constituents of the identity of a region. In the European Union regional consciousness is frequently monitored through Eurobarometer surveys and the aim is, of course, to evaluate the European-level identification of the citizens.

NOT ONE BUT MANY REGIONAL EUROPES

Jönsson *et al.* (2000: 1) begin their book, *Organizing European Space,* with a question that one of their colleagues often presents to his students: How many states are there in Europe today? They note how this question invariably triggers certain confusion and prompts diverse answers, depending on how Europe is understood. Europe is a contested space of meanings and dividing lines that define those who belong and who do not belong to Europe and its subregions. To use an expression from art, Europe can be understood as a montage of overlapping modernities that is perpetually transforming (cf. Pred, 1996).

Europe can also be recognized as a set of 'meta-geographies'. Lewis and Wigen (1997) define meta-geography as a set of spatial structures through which people order their knowledge of the world. This idea will be conceived more broadly here so that it includes not only spatial structures but also institutional (economic, political, cultural) practices, discourses and ideologies where these structures are produced and reproduced. Even if the European Union is gradually monopolizing the popular idea of what is Europe, there are still many overlapping Europes. For Sakwa (2006) the EU is the 'official Europe', but he distinguishes also 'pan-Europe' and 'civilizational Europe'. The former is based on the long project of Europe building and its current intergovernmental, rather than supranational, institutions such as the Council of Europe and the Organization for Security and Co-operation in Europe (OSCE). Civilizational Europe is currently the weakest of the three Europes and it emerges from, for example, the long tradition of European art and philosophy, and extends well beyond the existing boundaries of 'official Europe'.

Also Lee (1985) has mapped the metageographies of Europe. He suggests that Europe may be understood as an experience, and an institution and structural body. The experienced Europe may be comprehended in terms of identity. This is an ambiguous idea, since there is no common identity and experience of Europe, even if the EU actively strives to promote this idea. The 'European identity' is on the agenda in many circles and the phrase returns 700,000 web pages in a search with Google (September 2006). These pages display that identities are discussed in many institutional spheres: cultural organizations and discussion forums, academic studies, or education. The topics vary from potential elements of European identity to the problems that immigrants are faced by when entering the Union. Competing discourses on what European identity means have also emerged. This is inevitable, since all collective identities at all spatial scales are political constructs, and include decisions and definitions on behalf of groups of people ('We'). Most cultural traditions seem to embrace dualistic ideas about 'us' and the 'Other' that are used in the construction and representations of identity and difference. These dualisms seem to be particularly important in European tradition and cultural heritage (Paasi, 2001). If there will be a European identity in the future, Castells (2002) argues, the seeds of this identity will be in the realm of values. Castells presents a long list of elements that could be identified as shared feelings, most of them accentuating social solidarity and human rights (cf. Wistricht, 1994). Frankly, this is not dissimilar to the value-based 'civil religion' associated with the dominant US identity narrative. This is based on the fact that people coming from a different context cannot have any common 'primordial' ethnic identity – rather they need common 'values' (Gamoran, 1990).

One background for the lack of common experience is that national states dominate the production and reproduction of the European spaces of identification. States are crucial in the popular politics of place making and in the creation of the apparently naturalized links between places and people. This often takes place through national media and education, which accentuate the importance of language as a medium of identity. More often than not, it is assumed that all individuals should be part of a nation, have a national identity and state citizenship (Gupta and Ferguson, 1992). This accentuates the power of boundaries. More than 60 per cent of the present boundaries in Europe have been drawn during the twentieth century (Foucher, 1998). However, boundaries are not simply lines on maps. Rather they are located everywhere in the practices and discourses of societies: in media, education and identity performances (parades, flag days, commemorations). This makes boundaries particularly significant. However, it is also clear that boundaries are crossed regularly. Indeed border-crossings are part of routine experience in an increasingly dynamic world of flows (things, ideas, people). Moreover, to an increasing degree, borders are differentiated – they are not one and the same; they are increasingly

'networked borders' (Rumford, 2006). Reflecting borders in context provides a perpetual challenge for scholars interested in regional dynamics. This can be done best in comparative projects where scholars scrutinize different case studies and share their knowledge.

Second, Europe can be understood as an institution. The dominant institutional Europe is now certainly based on the EU, a unit constituted by the institutional structures' economic and political–cultural integration. The production of these structures has been a long and complicated process. New layers of legislation and rhetoric have been created along with the expansion and politicization of this unit (Heffernan, 1998; Shore, 2000). During the Cold War period, Europe was very much equated with the West. Europe was seen as consisting of two parts, Atlantic Europe and Eastern Europe, which were linked with the superpowers the US and the Soviet Union (Taylor, 1991). Now most of the former Eastern Europe belongs deeply to the institutional Europe of the EU. Smith (1995) argues that the language of integration has been technocratic and the European unity has been understood as a fact and an unquestioned good. Even if the political dimension has become deeper, the integrationist thinking begins very much from the perspective of economy (and capital). Rumford (2000) observes that, in the context of globalization and neoliberalism, integration is inevitably paralleled with autonomization, a tendency that results in differentation and fragmentation as much as 'harmonization'. This will have serious impacts on regions too. Instead of even development, the current neoliberal economy will more probably produce uneven growth (Rumford, 2000). The EU perpetually develops new practices of territorial and social integration. The ongoing planning practices, for example, aim to create what Jensen and Richardson (2004) call a 'monotopic Europe'. The rise of monotopia is based on the new governmentality of Europe, which aims to create a 'seamless and integrated space within the context of the European project, which is being pursued through the emerging field of European spatial policy' (2004: 3). This puts particular stress on infrastructure that can connect people and places: roads, railways, and so on. The new European polycentric regional system, also echoed by social theorists (cf. Rumford, 2006), is not merely an academic idea on shaping the dynamism of the European regional system but also a practical aim.

In fact, there are many partly overlapping institutional Europes, identified by Sakwa (2006) as pan-European, that help us to think of the boundaries of Europe, and what might be considered in speculation of the possible 'final' boundaries of the EU region. The Council of Europe is an intergovernmental organization (established in 1949) that has 46 member states that have come together with the aim to promote democracy and human rights. The Euro-Atlantic Partnership Council also has 46 members, including 26 NATO members and some non-NATO EU members, together with Russia and many of its surrounding states. The broadest definition of institutional Europe is constituted by the Organization for Security and Co-operation in Europe (OSCE). Its 55 participating countries include not merely traditional European states but also Canada and the US. Further, its current partner states 'stretch' this institutional space even further to encompass such non-European states as Japan, Korea, Thailand, Algeria, Egypt, Israel, Jordan, Morocco and Tunisia (Paasi, 2005). The complicated nature of the previous geographies shows that while the making of the new external border of the EU may help to affirm a 'European identity', the border is divided into many sectors such as the Mediterranean, the Balkans, Central and Eastern Europe (O'Dowd, 2001).

Lee's (1985) third perspective is structural Europe, the perspective of traditional regional geography that has started from Europe's physical and cultural geography, often so that it has ignored the geopolitical realities of Europe. At its extreme Europe has been seen as a peninsula of the Asian continent extending to the Ural Mountains (Guibernau, 2001; Paasi, 2001). One important regional element in the formation of the images of Europe has been, for a long time, regional subdivisions that have been developed to shape the internal social and spatial mosaic of structural Europe. Labels such as Western, Southern, Northern, Eastern and Central Europe became part of the popular terminology in geographical textbooks, maps and atlases, shaping the consciousness of Europe. Some of these terms partly disappeared from the vocabulary during the post-Cold War regional dynamics when the division between West and East collapsed. These representations have been crucial for shaping the consciousness of the territorial shape of Europe but they also have been important for regional actors who have struggled to shape broader European consciousness (Paasi, 2001). A good example of this is the idea of Central Europe, which was revived in many former Eastern European states after the collapse of the Iron Curtain (cf. Bort, 1998; Tägil, 1999). The power of such regionalizations is certainly based on the fact that these geographical ideas are normally reproduced on maps and textbooks used in education. Maps are crucial instruments in shaping the regional consciousness of the citizens (Harley, 1988; Wood, 1992). This fact can also be seen in the EU where new kinds of regions are perpetually developed, named and presented on maps. Some claims have been presented in the EU to implement such new regional representations as part of education taking place in schools (Jensen and Richardson, 2004). Indeed, textbooks are already available on the geography of the European Union (Cole and Cole, 1997).

THE EMERGENCE OF REGIONAL PERSPECTIVE IN EUROPE

Defining any region is an act of power, whether this is academic power to limit and name regions or political power to classify and control citizens at various spatial scales. Any answer to questions such as what Europe is or how many states or regions there are, as well as to name, border and symbolize certain spaces, and suggest a specific regional identity that will distinguish the area in question from others embodies this power. A regional identity and borders are thus two sides of the same coin. Struggles over 'regions' and identities are impregnated with politics and power:

> Struggles over ethnic or regional identity – in other words, over the properties (stigmata or emblems) linked with the *origin* through the *place* of origin and its associated durable marks, such as accent – are a particular case of different struggles over classifications, struggles over the monopoly of the power to make people see and believe, to get them to know and recognize, to impose the legitimate definition of the divisions of the social world, and thereby, to *make and unmake groups* (Bourdieu, 1991: 221)

This implies that discourses on regions or regional identity, in which actors (both individuals and groups) invest their interests and presuppositions in things, may actually create the 'reality' they are describing or suggesting (Bourdieu, 1991: 220); they may provide certain characteristics to these social entities which may, especially if they become institutionalized, effectively provide guidelines for spatial consciousness and social behaviour. Regions are thus significant but ambivalent.

Part of the ambivalence of the European region is, as Harvie suggests, 'awkward: at once vague, specific and spatially intimate' (1994: 9). Nevertheless, after World War II, and especially since the 1960s, regions were recognized in many states as important elements for the modernizing state, especially in spatial planning and regional development policies. Regions gradually became more significant in the economic, political and cultural life of most European states (Harvie, 1994). In France, Italy and the UK, for instance, the region emerged in the 1960s as a space of action for the state. Territorial disparities were recognized as a problem (albeit marginal)

within the otherwise successful macroeconomic policies and the region was chosen as the appropriate level at which to address them (Keating, 1998; Le Galés and Lequesne 1998). Keating (1998: 47) notes how in many states leaning on a Keynesian welfare-state ideology, regions became important to questions of integration. Regional economic problems were actually problems that came to be understood as issues of substate integration, especially in the context of a good employment situation and consistent economic growth. The basic challenge was how to integrate depressed regions into national economies and a particularly important task was to find solutions to lagging industrial development and the management of large reserves of agricultural labour (Keating, 1998).

The 1970s and 1980s witnessed the transfer of power in Europe to regional authorities (Harvie, 1994). Also, many political movements recognized the region as an important unit in spatial pluralism. This occurred both within nationalist and regionalist contexts. The concomitant rise of territorial approaches to politics led to the use of such concepts as 'periphery' and 'centre' in the interpretation of spatial dynamics. Scholars were often looking at the East–West and North–South gradient in Cold War Europe, but they also studied the geo-ethnic dimensions (Rokkan and Urwin, 1983).

From the late 1980s, a new wave of regionalism emerged in Europe, as did the idea of the 'Europe of regions'. Whereas regionalism was originally a national phenomenon (being defensive, integrating or autonomist), since the 1980s regionalism became more economically oriented and often expressed reactions to globalization (Keating, 1998). One of the paradoxes of current times is how globalization is shaping our understanding of spatiality, particularly about the links between territory and function. The neo-modernist utopia accentuating the importance of technology, often associated with the neoliberal ideas of competition, implies how the traditional 'slow geography' of the apparently fixed, territorially based and scaled world will be replaced increasingly with a new 'fast geography', where territory would lose its importance in the process of rescaling.

Agnew (2005: viii) notes how the territorial power based very much on national states since the nineteenth century is giving way to increasingly complex spatialities of power where 'localities, global city regions, regions, and trading blocks connect or network with one another to challenge the primary state-based territorial divisions'. For many, globalization is a process synonymous with deterritorialization – disappearance of boundaries and fixed territorial structures – that would lead to an increasing interdependence of locations, firms, ideas and people. The paradox is that the simultaneous increase in the number of regions and stateless nations that more or less aggressively seek identity, autonomy and influence suggests quite a different tendency, namely a struggle for reterritorialization. These tendencies occur simultaneously.

NEW REGIONALISM IN EUROPE

Along with globalization, a new concept was coined to depict the difference between new tendencies and the old regionalism: 'new regionalism'. Keating (1998) suggests that this was impelled by a functional pressure combined with new forms of political mobilization, and a redefinition of the economic and social meaning of territory. Whereas the state had formerly been the major context for regionalism, now it was the changing continental regime and international market. Concomitantly 'entrepreneurial governance' has gradually replaced the Keynesian welfarist state policy that was popular in Western Europe from World War II until the mid-1970s. A new relationship between the region, the state and the EU has emerged in the new ideological environment characterized by neoliberalism. Rumford (2000: 189) suggests that, in the context of the EU,

regionalism should be understood 'in terms of the region as an economic actor within the framework of neoliberal opportunities and economic governance'. Under these circumstances cohesion works for the market by adding the competitiveness of regions to the global market.

The change of the name of the European Economic Community to the European Union symbolized, Rhein (2002) argues, the increasing importance of suprastate political matters over the economic (cf. Keating, 1998). This deepening and enlarging political Union began to change dramatically the geopolitical vision of what Europe is, and where its external boundaries might be. It also changed the understanding of what are both the traditional regions in Europe, and the new ones that Deas and Lord (2006) label as 'unusual regions' – regions that often seem to transcend, and jar against, established territorially bounded bodies at regional and subnational scale, but which may also cross the existing state borders.

If Europe has become more or less the same as the European Union in popular consciousness and practical international politics (and many states still struggle to get into this specific Europe), to a certain degree this holds with its substate regions too. The European space is divided into regions that are one part of the EU's regional system and logic based on statistical (Nomenclature of Territorial Units for Statistics, NUTS) areas. As to the regional governance, management and the 'harmonization' of the spatial practices in Europe, it is crucial to recognize the power of the NUTS system that was established by Eurostat more than 25 years ago in order to provide a single uniform breakdown of territorial units for the production of regional statistics for the EU. NUTS regions serve as a reference for collection, development and harmonization of Community regional statistics, for the socioeconomic analyses of the regions and for the framing of Community regional policies. Formally, the 'Europe of regions' consists of administrative regions that are represented in official statistics

(Heidenreich, 1998). The importance of the NUTS classification is based on the fact that regional dynamics in the EU are associated very much with the economic development of its regions, and the small- and medium-sized enterprises (SMEs) that are rooted in the regions. The aim of EU research is respectively to maximize regional dynamics and to boost competitiveness for the EU's SMEs.

Statistical information presented in this regional framework is in a crucial position both in the creation of the idea of Europe but also the creation of the practices of cohesion policy. This statistical information also increasingly directs research and our understanding of what European regions generally are. The home page of Eurostat reminds us how '[s]tatistics make news. They are also essential background to many news stories, features, in-depth analyses and TV and radio programmes. Eurostat's Press Office puts out user-friendly news releases on a key selection of data on the EU and Member States and their partners.'[1]

This information may certainly be useful in comparative studies on regional development, voting behaviour and wellbeing, for example, but is not automatically fruitful for the development of social science or area studies. The key problem is that idea of region is often taken for granted in such research. The homogenizing use of statistics easily leads to a situation where the internal differences inside regions are not recognized (Rumford, 2000). Region is thus understood as a given container where social, economic, political or cultural phenomena literally take place, not a dynamic element that both structures and is structured by these phenomena and processes. A critical scholarship must be able to challenge such given regions and scrutinize carefully the contextual and general features of region-building processes: bounding practices, relevant symbols and institutions.

There is also another problem. In spite of the fact that NUTS regions are used in cohesion and structural fund policies, it is very likely that most citizens are not at all aware of the regional political structures of Europe and how their 'own' region is linked with the EU and its programs. Technical Eurobarometer surveys do not give any thorough picture of the regional worlds experienced and shaped by ordinary people. This would require much more sensitive methods and theoretically grounded comparative social science research.

Nevertheless the idea of the 'Europe of regions' draws from this gap between citizens and governance and the perpetual need to fill the democracy deficit of the EU. Strong, self-supporting regions have been part of the basic EU ideology regarding spatial planning and, in particular, structural policy (Keating, 1997; Vartiainen and Kokkonen, 1995). In the EU the claims of regions and of regional autonomy are based on the belief that economic development in regions will depend, above all, upon the capacity of local initiative to exploit local resources (Cappelin, 1995). Regions have been significant in Europe for a long time but the rising importance of subnational regions was institutionalized by the Treaty of Maastricht (1992). Along with the Maastrich Treaty, the EU was to become an ever closer union among the peoples of Europe. The Treaty also established the Committee of the Regions as an advisory body to guarantee that regional development will receive attention among economic and social matters. This formed a background for a major heightening of the salience of the regional question in Europe (Keating and Loughlin, 1997). Accordingly 'regions' have become crucial in the EU's territorial ideologies and this has given rise to activities that tend to harmonize (and arguably, homogenize) not only the administrative and the regional political landscapes of Europe but also to change regions as key competitive units in global neoliberal capitalism, a tendency that has certainly not been restricted to Europe. One factor behind the apparent significance of regions has been the emerging globalization that has curtailed the independent economic power of national states.

Particularly since the late 1990s, regional dynamism and transformations have been associated with accelerating globalization in ways that challenge traditional regions and are still expressions of regionalism. 'Regions' have become global buzzwords in connection with such more dynamic expressions as 'global city regions' or 'global cities' that are identified as motors of global economy on the basis of their capacities and connections with each other. City regions in particular have been seen as part of new regionalism. Scott (2001), for example, interprets city regions as nodes of human labour and communal life scattered across the world. He suggests that these nodes constitute distinctive subnational (or regional) social formations that are currently challenged by globalization. This will lead in many cases to efforts to create new regional political competences, identities and other bases for interterritorial collective action. In some cases city regions cross existing state borders. In the EU, the rise of such new urban–regional complexes has been referred to as an 'infranational revolution' (Scott, 2001: 4). Indeed, a further step has been taken in the EU to identify 'polycentric urban regions', which certainly will require active building of regional organizing capacity, regional coordination, and institutionalize frameworks of cooperation (Meijers and Romein, 2003). It is clear that the ideas of city regions or polycentric urban regions may have both political and academic consequences and raise questions for researchers. Is research increasingly directed to well-doing centres, or 'creative' cities and their success and problems? What will happen in regions that do not fit into to this urban-oriented approach? As Scott *et al.* (2001: 22) have observed, 'Since the incentives to creative intervention are greatest for those wealthy metropolitan areas with the most at stake in global competition, local competitive policies frequently work against equity between regions.'

Globalization has been crucial for regional dynamics in the sense that globalization may be understood as the spread of supraterritorial or transborder relations within the capitalist economy. Special instruments of the new regionalism are the cross-border regions and broader regional alliances ('unusual regions', Deas and Lord, 2006) that operate across the borders between states. These regions have been particularly important in the EU but have also been found significant elsewhere, for instance, East Asia (Jessop, 2002: 184). Cross-border regions can be between two states or pull together several states, as in the Baltic Sea region. The first of them in Europe, the Euroregio, was established between Germany and the Netherlands in 1958, and now there are more than 70 such cross-border regions in operation in Europe (Perkman and Sum, 2002). The intensifying integration process has fuelled their emergence, especially since the 1990s. Deas and Lord (2006) have identified no less than 146 such regional initiatives in the EU, some of them local cross-border projects, some large-scale efforts, crossing the borders of several national states. Many EU programs strive to promote cooperation between regions, in a way creating a small-scale 'foreign policy' for regions and contributing to new forms of regionalization (Keating, 1997, 1998; Rumford, 2000).

Europe possesses no uniform or homogeneous level of regional government in the judicial, political or administrative sense (Keating, 1998:11). There are different kinds of regions and regional action and movements. It is the political, economic and cultural meanings of region that have faced the most important challenges in Europe. As Keating (1998) observes, in some aspects governmental processes, politics and economy are becoming deterritorialized, losing their territorially bounded character, but at the same time a reterritorialization of economic, political and social action is going on. In the new situation there is no new territorial hierarchy to replace the old one but there is a wide variety of new forms of territorial action (Keating, 1998). The role of state as a context of region building is today increasingly understood in relational terms. The state is analysed as a relational set of institutional forms, instead of being associated with the fixed ontology suggested by the old Westphalian state–society perspective (Jessop, 2002; MacLeod, 2001).

The causes and consequences of globalization are bound with the dynamic relations between capitalism and state that manifest themselves in deepening national and regional differences (Hennis, 2001; Scholte, 2005; Telo, 2002). Rumford's (2000) idea of the autonomization that operates in parallel with integration is relevant also as far as regions are concerned. This means, in the context of the EU, that neoliberal economic and ideological forces are crucial for the development of regions, not merely the EU's policies. And often these policies operate in the spirit of neoliberalism by forcing 'regions' into competition. One consequence has been that attention has been given to the local and regional scale where actors struggle to attract investment, as well as educated and skilful workers (Anderson, 2000). These processes have also given rise to a mushrooming interdisciplinary literature that accentuates the importance of knowledge and learning to the competitive advantage of firms, localities, regions and nations, and has motivated the development of such significant concepts as institutional thickness, learning region, social capital, trust, innovativeness and regional identity. All of these concepts place great stress on the dynamism and potential that is embedded in the interaction of economic and cultural factors occurring at various spatial scales. Asheim (1999) has reminded us that Europe is characterized by cultural diversity and that the existence of entrepreneurial and innovative activity is not evenly spread out geographically, which is in stark opposition with the ideal of the European 'cohesion'. This simply means that not all cultural settings offer the same level of social capital and trust. Neither do all regions, especially those on the periphery, always innovate (Morgan 1997). This is in line with Gertler's (2003) suggestion that culture varies from region to region, and not always in a happy way.

Indeed, most regions are not as dynamic Silicon Valley or Baden-Württemberg. In many regions, active institution building has been a way to develop social capital and trust, a development encouraged by the EU. One more problem is that the EU can certainly not monopolize the region under the condition of globalization. The region itself may also be a very heterogeneous and unevenly developed.

According to the currently popular rhetoric, regions are increasingly put into 'competition' with each other to shape their position in the globalizing spatial divisions of labour. This neoliberal idea implies a certain spatial fetishism, since it suggests that regions are 'actors' that are capable of making decisions. However, it is perhaps more correct to think of regions as dynamic social entities that are used by power-holding actors – operating both inside and outside of the region – in their often contested and contradictory practices and discourses. Regions hardly compete, but rather it is the actors and firms operating in a region and outside of the region that create and (potentially destroy) regions. It is therefore important to recognize that regions themselves are not internally homogeneous and do not possess any permanent essence and fixed identity (cf. Raco, 2006; Rumford, 2000).

Regional development is not a constant, of course. The division of Europe into a rich and industrialized 'north' (containing, for example, Germany, Britain, Belgium, France and the Scandinavian countries) and a poor and underdeveloped 'south' (containing countries such as Italy, Greece, Spain and Portugal) has been rapidly changing in the new globalizing context. Guibernau (2001: 15) reminds us how Italy, for instance, has become one of the richest states in the world and a member of G8, and how Spain and Portugal have documented a faster growth in income since their joining the EU. On the other hand, most states have witnessed a deep polarization in their internal regional development. Owing to the fact that a Europe of regions will be a competitive system, there will be both losers and winners. The relationship between centres and peripheries remains ambiguous and mobile at the level of the EU, and new spaces and new distinctions are being created both between and within states (Hassner, 1997: 48). The resulting pattern will be a multidimensional imbalance between places and regions: between states inside the EU, regions in the states, and localities and places inside the regions (Amin and Thrift, 1995; Heidenreich, 1998). This development has long roots and it is not easy to specify the reasons behind this polarization. Systemic forces such as postindustrialization, technological change and globalization have been discussed. On the other hand, it has been suggested that a highly integrated continental market does not solve regional problems (Martin, 2001). In some cases this polarization has been important fuel for the rise of political regionalism. The rise of 'Padanian nationalism' in northern Italy is a case in point. The Lega Nord (the Northern League) has attempted to invent an ethnicity for northern Italy (Padania) and, in this way, justify its political claims for the protection of the economic interests of the region (Agnew, 1995; Giordano, 2000).

LOCATING THE 'REGION TALK' IN THE EU

The European Union thus seems to provide a major context for understanding both the category of Europe *and* region in the current globalizing post-Cold War world. As we saw previously, the expression 'Europe of regions' has become both a popular and an institutional–political slogan associated with the Union. Nowadays this slogan has become so self-evident that Clark (2001) does not include it in his long list of European 'code words'. Some scholars have suggested that since the current EU is a multilevel governance system, it is actually incorrect to speak of a 'Europe of regions', and would perhaps be more correct to speak of a 'Europe with regions' (Vos *et al.*, 2002).

It may be argued that in current debates on Europe, regions are more often than not public representations that exist above all in these discourses and rhetoric – this is particularly the case with those new regions created in planning discourses (Deas and Lord, 2006). This also means that new regions and inherent regional identity narratives in Europe are not so much historical and cultural entities, as products of regionalization processes that take place as part of the Europeanization of the public sector (Shore, 2000). Such regions exist often at first in the naming, strategic definitions and proclamations of politicians, foreign policy experts and academic researchers. As Jensen and Richardson (2004) show, they may then be gradually transformed into representations on maps and texts (administrative areas, various 'circles', 'bananas', 'learning regions', cross-border regions, Euregios, etc.), and into sets of social (political, economic and administrative) institutions, practices and discourses. Even if the expert language of region discourses often remains very distant and abstract for ordinary citizens, these 'regions' may finally have much effect on how people have to operate and how they understand the mosaic of places, regions and boundaries that surrounds them.

The debate on regions and regional identities has been important for decades in the EEC/EU. It became particularly important along with Romano Prodi's Commission's strategic priorities and forms of governance: the rules, processes and practices that affect how powers are exercised at the European level. The European Commission's White Paper (2001) contained a number of recommendations on how to enhance democracy in Europe and to increase the legitimacy of institutions. Local and regional are words that are repeated a number of times in this document, often in such an organic way that these contexts are seen as 'actors' that are capable of making decisions. One obvious strategic aim was to strengthen 'regions' and regional diversity and concomitantly the cultural heritage at the level of the EU, which both would concomitantly lead to a less integrative role of the state.

The links between various spatial scales may thus have strengthened across scales so that the traditional image of the scalar hierarchy (local, regional, state, suprastate) has become much more nuanced. However, the phrase 'Europe of regions' has been very much more a tool of governance 'from above' than a tool of 'regionalism' from below. In practice these perspectives have become – as part of the broader rescaling of governance – fused in different ways and in different contexts, since 'regions' have simply very different meanings in various European states. Painter (2002) suggests critically that the frequent conflation of the different types of region in dominant narratives of European integration is itself a 'regionalist manoeuvre' and it tends to present regions as integrated and coherent wholes. Regional identity is in this context one magic word through which the cohesion and integration of economic, environmental and social activity should occur; for example, with the help of the European Regional Development Fund.

Official arguments regarding the power of regions are thus often strongly rhetorical. Vos *et al.* (2002) have carried out an extensive content analysis of EU documents and found five arguments regarding the added value of European regions. The first suggests that 'regions are agents of efficiency': regions can govern efficiently because of 'local knowledge' and decision making can occur more quickly. The second suggests that 'regions are watchdogs of EU policy'. This argument accentuates regional power in monitoring EU-level decision making. The third argument suggests that 'regions are guardians of cultural diversity'. This harks back to a classical regionalist argumentation that regions are the best medium to promote and protect these cultures. Fourth, 'regions are commercial cultivators'; that is, they can ensure a good socioeconomic climate. Finally, the fifth argument suggests that 'regions are agents of democratization'; that is, since regions are closer to the citizens they

also should narrow the gap between citizens and Euro-politics.

EPILOGUE: REGIONAL FUTURES IN EUROPE

This chapter has analysed regional dynamics in Europe and suggests that Europe itself, as well as regions and regionalizations on whatever spatial scale, are not the result of straightforward evolutionary or autonomous processes. Rather they are contested processes made by individuals and social groups. Regions, their 'boundaries' and the meanings given to them are social constructs. They are expressions of a perpetual struggle over the meanings associated with space, democracy, representation and welfare. Power-holding actors and organizations involved in the production of the territorializations of space may act inside the regions but also outside of them.

The geographies of power are perpetually changing. The enlargement of the EU and the development of the Europe of regions have had a crucial impact on our thinking about regional dynamics in Europe. This development has modified and 'softened' state-based territoriality by creating a more or less standardized substate statistical and administrative level that has direct links to the EU. This may also help to mobilize regionally based human resources in the spirit of new regionalism which starts from an idea that a key source of a region's competitive advantage is embedded in the operation of its local civil society. This accentuates the importance of such elements as regional identity. This has been an important category in the EU politics on regional cohesion, for instance. On this basis, regional actors all around Europe can compare the states of affairs in their respective regions. On the other hand, the EU has motivated the development of new regional spaces that partly compete with these existing regional units and represent utopian regional futures. EU policies are thus crucially shaping the national and regional spatial activities.

Regions thus seem to stay with us. Academic scholars have developed diverging theoretical perspectives to understand the roles of region, devolved and local territories within wider processes of globalization (Tewdwr-Jones and Allmendinger, 2006). New regionalist theories of development in particular have put stress on the transforming relations between territory and function and social construction of regional systems of production (Keating, 2001; MacLeod, 2001). For many economic geographers, regions are key units in the global economy (Florida 1995; Scott, 1998; Storper, 1997). Raco (2006) observes that new regionalism and especially its claims for devolution have been underpinned by three interrelated concepts that see the region as a focus for (1) the formation of common economic strategies in the context of globalization, (2) new forms of cultural identification, and (3) the mediation of co-present social interactions. This means that the new regionalism is characterized by its 'multidimensionality, complexity, fluidity and non-conformity, and by the fact that it involves a variety of state and non-state actors, who often come together in rather informal multi-actor coalitions' (Söderbaum, 2003: 1–2). While there has been a tendency to accentuate the lead and power of some successful regions, such as Silicon Valley, or some German and Italian regions in the EU's Blue Banana corridor, many scholars have warned about making too heroic generalizations of the power of new regionalism on the basis of a few successful cases and have suggested a more careful scrutiny of what a region means in each context (Jones and MacLeod, 2004). This is a perpetual challenge for scholars studying Europe and should be taken seriously.

In spite of the mushrooming interest in regions and regionalism, many authors have been rather sceptical regarding the real power of regions in Europe and offer constant reminders of their weak institutionalization and their relative incapacity to organize economic and social actors (Le Galés, 1998; Le Galés and Lequesne, 1998). One element

of the background for this has been identified by Rumford (2000) who suggests that 'regions' are indeed much more than instruments of EU's structural policies; they are part of the global neoliberal landscape of competition and in fact structural policies touch upon regions only in the EU context. Most scholars are ready to admit that regions will be important functional and institutional elements in the future territorial politics of European states, together with cities and even stateless nations (Keating, 1998). The activities of the EU have very much turned to develop regions that have been part of the NUTS structure, but these activities have been directed towards more ideological 'regional structures' or 'unusual regions' that have become an instrument of making visions and future plans (Deas and Lord, 2006).

There are of course major differences between regions. Vos *et al.* (2002) suggest that it is regions which have a solid institutional basis (e.g. their own legislative assembly, more than purely administrative powers or a degree of financial autonomy) that are best preparing for operating in the world of increasing competition and adapting to new challenges. Downs (2002) observes how the uncertainty generated by the countervailing forces of integration and disintegration prompts contentious questions about shared sovereignty, possibilities for transborder cooperation, the division of citizen loyalties by claimants at local, regional, national, and supranational levels, and democratization via devolution.

Regions and their borders are constituted by and constitutive of social life. Thus they must be central questions to the social theory agenda (cf. Rumford, 2006). The ongoing mobilities and rise of various networks inevitably challenge our fixed and taken-for-granted approaches to these categories (Paasi, 2002b). Entrikin (1999) has reflected the character of places (using the EU as an example) and has argued that a more cosmopolitan view is needed, instead of the established, bounded and exclusive concept of place, a view that would balance the particularistic and universalistic dimensions. This is a challenge in the current Europe, where social processes and identity narratives manifest themselves at different spatial scales and become fused as a consequence of political and institutional transformations, and where the growing flows of refugees and immigrants challenge both the traditional nation (state)-centred identities and narratives of nationally bounded cultures, and local contexts of identity formation.

Regionalism will face the same challenges. Regionalism is a complex phenomenon that draws from culture, economics, politics and policy, and which takes different forms in different contexts that are currently shaped by both the economic tendencies of globalization and local reactions (Keating, 1998). One background for European regionalist separatist movements and demands for devolution has been said to emanate primarily from poorer regions with distinctive cultural identities. Agnew (2006) has recently challenged this idea, often associated with such theoretical notions as 'internal colonialism', and argues that this approach fails to take into account the fact that separatist movements are not inevitably strongly associated with economically disadvantaged regions (think, for example, of 'Padania') and that the prospects for their success are fundamentally affected by existing electoral volatility and the lack of real choice between existing political parties and movements. Political institutional factors may be as or more important than the direct effects of economic and cultural ones in the genesis of and the prospects for regional separatist movements in Europe (Agnew, 2006). On the other hand, Jonas and Pincetl (2006) note, based of their case study in California, that the emerging new civic regionalism in that state draws on long-standing social movements, spearheaded by large-scale business interests and is directed at reorganizing local and State of California government powers in urban areas by rationalizing land use and environmental planning, for instance. In this context, new regionalism has been strongly influenced by the ongoing national and international debates relating to political and economic resurgence of region, and to the neoliberalization and democratization of governance and policy at that scale (see also Katz, 2000).

These examples show that the old phrase coined by geographers is still very much valid: space makes a difference. These examples also suggest that regions and regional dynamics will become an interesting topic in the future for researchers operating in various fields. The best guarantee for the permanent interest of European scholars at least will be the simple fact that much of the social activities occurring at the scale of Europe (a Union) have to do with 'regions' – however we define them.

NOTES

1 http://epp.eurostat.ec.europa.eu/portal/page?_pageid=1153,47169267,1153_47181498&_dad=portal&_schema=PORTAL,6.8.2006

REFERENCES

Agnew, J. (1995) 'The rhetoric of regionalism: the Northern League in Italian politics, 1983–94', Transactions of the Institute of British Geographers, New Series, 20 (4): 156–172.

Agnew, J. (2005) Hegemony. Philadelphia: Temple University Press.

Agnew, J. (2006) 'Open to surprise?', Progress in Human Geography, 30 (1): 1–4.

Allen, J., Massey, D. and Cochrane, A. (1998) Rethinking the Region. London: Routledge.

Amin, A., Massey, D. and Thrift, N. (2003) Decentering the Nation: A Radical Approach to Regional Inequality. London: Catalist.

Amin, A. and Thrift, N. (1995) 'Territoriality in the global political economy', Nordisk Samhällsgeografisk Tidskrift, 20 (1): 3–16.

Anderson, J. (1995) 'The exaggerated death of the nation-state', in J. Anderson, C. Brook and A. Cochrane (eds) A Global World? Re-ordering Political Space. Oxford: The Open University, pp. 65–112.

Anderson, J. (2000) 'The rise of regions and regionalism in Western Europe', in M. Guibernau (ed.) *Governing European Diversity*. London: Sage, pp. 35–64.

Asheim, B.T. (1999) 'Interactive learning and localized knowledge in globalizing learning economies', *Geojournal*, 49 (4): 345–352.

Beck, U. and Beck-Gernsheim, E. (2001) *Individualization*. London: Sage.

Blaut, J.M. (2000) *Eight Eurocentric Historians*. New York: The Guilford Press.

Bort, E. (1998) '*Mitteleuropa*: the difficult frontier', in M. Anderson and E. Bort (eds) *The Frontiers of Europe*. London: Pinter, pp. 91–108.

Bourdieu, P. (1991) *Language and Symbolic Power*. Cambridge: Polity.

Brenner, N. (1999) 'Between fixity and motion: accumulation, territorial organization and historical geography of spatial scales', *Environment and Planning D: Society and Space*, 16 (4): 459–481.

Calleya, S.C. (ed.) (2000) *Regionalism in the Post-Cold War World*. Aldershot: Ashgate.

Cappellin, R. (1995) 'Regional development, federalism and interregional co-operation', in H. Eskelinen and F. Snickars (eds) *Competitive European Peripheries*. Berlin: Springer, pp. 41–57.

Castells, M. (2002) 'The construction of European identity', in B.-Å. Lundvall *et al. The New Knowledge Economy in Europe*. Cheltenham: Edward Elgar, pp. 232–241.

Clark, G.L. (2001) 'Vocabulary of the new Europe: code words for the millennium', *Environment and Planning D: Society and Space* 19 (6): 697–717.

Cole, J. and Cole, F. (1997) *A Geography of the European Union*. London: Routledge.

Deas, I. and Lord, A. (2006) 'From new regionalism to an unusual regionalism? The emergence of non-standard regional spaces and lessons for the territorial reorganization of the state', *Urban Studies*, 43 (10): 1847–1877.

della Porta, D. and Diani, M. (1999) *Social Movements*. Oxford: Blackwell.

Downs, W.M. (2002) 'Regionalism in the European Union: key concepts and project overview', *European Integration*, 24 (3): 171–177.

Entrikin, J.N. (1999) 'Political community, identity and cosmopolitan place', *International Sociology*, 14 (3): 269–282.

Florida, R. (1995) 'Towards the learning region', *Futures*, 27 (5): 527–536.

Foucher, M. (1998) 'The geopolitics of European frontiers', in M. Anderson and E. Bort (eds) *The Frontiers of Europe*. London: Pinter, pp. 235–250.

Gamoran, A. (1990) 'Civil religion in American schools', *Sociological Analysis*, 51 (3): 235–256.

Gertler, M. (2003) 'Cultural economic geography of production', in K. Anderson, M. Domosh, S. Pile and N. Thrift (eds) *Handbook of Cultural Geography*. London: Sage, pp. 131–146.

Gilbert, E.W. and Litt, B. (1960) 'Geography and regionalism', in G. Taylor (ed.) *Geography in the Twentieth Century*. London: Methuen, pp.

Giordano, B. (2000) 'Italian regionalism or 'Padanian' nationalism – the political project of the Lega Nord in Italian politics', *Political Geography*, 19: 445–471.

Guibernau, M. (2001) 'Introduction: unity and diversity in Europe', in M. Guibernau (ed.) *Governing European Diversity*. London: Sage.

Gupta, A. and Ferguson, J. (1992) 'Beyond culture: space, identity, and the politics of difference', *Cultural Anthropology*, 7 (1): 6–23.

Harley, B. (1988) 'Deconstructing the map', *Cartographica*, 26 (1): 1–20.

Harvie, C.T. (1994) *The Rise of Regional Europe*. London: Routledge.

Hassner, P. (1997) 'Obstinate and obsolate: non-territorial transnational forces versus the European territorial state', in O. Tunander, P. Baev and V.I. Einagel (eds) *Geopolitics in Post-Wall Europe*. London: Sage, pp. 45–58.

Heffernan, M. (1998) *The Meaning of Europe*. London: Arnold.

Heidenreich, M. (1998) 'The changing system of European cities and regions', *European Planning Studies*, 6 (3): 315–332.

Hennis, M. (2001) 'Europeanization and globalization: the missing link', *Journal of Common Market Studies*, 39 (5): 829–850.

Hettne, B. (2001) 'The new regionalism: a prologue', in B. Hettne, A. Inotai, A. and O. Sunkel (eds) *Comparing Regionalisms: Implications for Global Development*. London: Palgrave, pp. xxi–xxii.

Jensen, O.B. and Richardson, T. (2004) *Making European Space: Mobility, Power and Territorial Identity*. London: Routledge.

Jessop, B. (2000) 'The crisis of the national spatio-temporal fix and the tendential eco-logical dominance of globalizing capitalism', *International Journal of Urban and Regional Research*, 24 (2): 323–360.

Jessop, B. (2002) *The Future of the Capitalist State*. Cambridge: Polity.

Jonas, A.E.G. and Pincetl, S (2006) 'Rescaling regions in the state: the new regionalism in California', *Political Geography*, 25 (5): 482–505.

Jones, M. and MacLeod, G. (2004) 'Regional spaces, spaces of regionalism: territory, insurgent politics and the English question', *Transactions of the Institute of British Geographers*, 29 (4): 433–452.

Jönsson, C., Tägil, S. and Törnqvist, G. (2000) *Organizing European Space*. London: Sage.

Jordan, T. (1973) *The European Culture Area*. New York: Harper & Row.

Katz, B. (ed.) (2000) *Reflections on Regionalism*. Washington DC: Brookings Institution Press.

Keating, M. (1997) 'The political economy of regionalism', in M. Keating and J. Loughlin (eds) *The Political Economy of Regionalism*. London: Frank Cass, pp. 17–40.

Keating, M. (1998) *The New Regionalism in Western Europe: Territorial Restructuring and Political Change*. Cheltenham: Elgar.

Keating, M. (2001) 'Rethinking the region', *European Urban and Regional Studies*, 8 (3): 217–234.

Keating, M. (ed.) (2004) *Regions and Regionalism in Europe*. Cheltenham: Edward Elgar.

Keating, M. and O'Loughlin, J. (eds) (1997) *The Political Economy of Regionalism*. London: Frank Cass.

Keating, M., Loughlin, J. and Deschouwer, K. (2003) *Culture, Institutions and Economic Development*. Cheltenham: Edward Elgar.

Le Galés, P. (1998) 'Conclusion – government and governance of regions', in P. Le Galés and C. Lequesne (eds) *Regions in Europe*. London: Routledge, pp. 239–267.

Le Galés, P. and Lequesne, C. (eds) (1998) *Regions in Europe*. London: Routledge.

Lee, R. (1985) 'The future of the region: regional geography as education for transformation', in R. King (ed.) *Geographical Futures*. Sheffield: The Geographical Association, pp. 77–91.

Lewis M.W. and Wigen, K.E. (1997) *The Myth of Continents: A Critique of Metageography*. Berkeley: University of California Press.

MacLeod, G. (1998) 'In what sense a region? Place hybridity, symbolic shape, and institutional formation in (post-)modern Scotland', *Political Geography*, 17 (7): 833–863.

MacLeod, G. (2001) 'New regionalism reconsidered: globalization and the remaking of political economic space', *International Journal of Urban and Regional Research*, 25 (4): 804–829.

MacLeod, G. and Jones, M. (2001) 'Renewing the geography of regions', *Environment and Planning D: Society and Space*, 19 (6): 669–695.

Mansfield, E.D. and Milner, H.V. (eds) (1997) *The Political Economy of Regionalism*. New York: Columbia University Press.

Martin, R. (2001) 'EMU versus the regions? Regional convergence and divergence in Euroland', *Journal of Economic Geography*, 1 (1): 51–80.

McNeill, D. (2004) *New Europe: Imagined Spaces*. Oxford: Oxford University Press.

Meijers, E. and Romein, A. (2003) 'Realizing potential: building regional organizing capacity in polycentric urban regions', *European Urban and Regional Studies*, 10 (2): 173–186.

Meyer, B. and Geschiere, P. (eds) (1999) *Globalization and Identity: Dialectics of Flow and Closure*. Oxford: Blackwell.

Mikkeli, H. (1997) *Europe as an Idea and Identity*. London: St. Martins Press.

Morgan, K. (1997) 'The learning region: institutions, innovation and regional renewal', *Regional Studies*, 31 (5): 491–503.

Murphy, A. (1991) Regions as social constructs: the gap between theory and practice. *Progress in Human Geography* 15 (1): 22–35.

O'Dowd, L. (2001) 'State borders, border regions and the construction of European identity', in M. Kohli and M. Novak (eds) *Will Europe Work?* London: Routledge, pp. 95–110.

Paasi, A. (1991) 'Deconstructing regions. Notes on the scales of spatial life', *Environment and Planning A*, 23 (2): 239–254.

Paasi, A. (1996) *Territories, Boundaries and Consciousness*. Chichester: Wiley.

Paasi A. (2001) 'Europe as a social process', *European Urban and Regional Studies*, 8 (1): 7–28.

Paasi, A. (2002a) 'Region and place: regional worlds and words', *Progress in Human Geography*, 26 (6): 802–811.

Paasi A. (2002b) 'Bounded spaces in the mobile world: deconstructing regional identity', *Tijdschrift voor Economische en Sociale Geografie*, 93 (2): 137–148.

Paasi, A. (2003) 'Region and place: regional identity in question', *Progress in Human Geography*, 27 (4): 475–485.

Paasi A. (2005) 'Remarks on Europe's transforming meta-geography', *Geopolitics*, 10 (3): 580–585.

Painter, J (2002) 'Multilevel citizenship, identity and regions in contemporary Europe', in J. Anderson (ed.) *Transnational Democracy: Political Spaces and Border Crossings*. London: Routledge, pp. 93–110.

Payne, A. (2000) 'Globalization and modes of regionalist governance', in J. Pierre (ed.) *Debating Governance*. Oxford: Oxford University Press, pp. 201–218.

Perkman, M. and Sum. N.L. (eds) (2002) *Globalization, Regionalization and Cross-border Regions*. Basingstoke: Palgrave Macmillan.

Pred, A. (1996) *Recognizing European Modernities*. London: Routledge.

Raco, M. (2006) 'Building new subjectivities: devolution, regional identities and the re-scaling of politics', in M. Tewdwr-Jones and P. Allmendinger (eds) (2006) *Territory, Identity and Spatial Planning*. London: Routledge, pp. 320–334.

Rhein, E. (2000) 'European regionalism – where is the European Union heading?', in S.C. Calleya (ed.) *Regionalism in the Post-Cold War World*. Aldershot: Ashgate, pp. 25–44.

Rietbergen, P. (2006) *Europe: A Cultural History*, 2nd edn. London: Routledge.

Rokkan, S. and Urwin D.W. (1983) *Economy, Territory, Identity*. London: Sage.

Rumford, C. (2000) 'European cohesion? Globalization, autonomization, and the dynamics of EU integration', *Innovation*, 13 (2): 183–197.

Rumford, C. (2006) 'Theorizing borders', *European Journal of Social Theory*, 9 (2): 155–169.

Sakwa, R. (2006) 'Introduction: the many dimensions of Europe', in R. Sakwa and A. Stevens, (eds) *Contemporary Europe*. Basingstoke: Palgrave-Macmillan. pp. 1–28.

Sakwa, R. and Stevens, A. (2006) *Contemporary Europe*. Basingstoke: Palgrave-Macmillan.

Scholte J.A. (2005) *Globalization*. London: Palgrave-Macmillan.

Scott, A. (1998) *Regions and the World Economy*. Oxford: Oxford University Press.

Scott, A. (2001) 'Introduction', in A.J. Scott (ed.) *Global City-Regions: Trends, Theory, Policy*. Oxford: Oxford University Press, pp. 1–8.

Scott, A., Agnew, J., Soja, E. and Storper, M. (2001) 'Global city-regions', in A.J. Scott (ed.) *Global City-Regions: Trends, Theory, Policy*. Oxford: Oxford University Press, pp. 11–30.

Shore, C. (2000) *Building Europe*. London: Routledge.

Smith, N. (1995) 'Remaking scale: competitition and cooperation in prenational and postnational Europe', in H. Eskelinen and F. Snickars (eds). *Competitive European Peripheries*. Berlin: Springer, pp. 59–74.

Söderbaum, F. (2003) 'Introduction: theories of new regionalism', in F. Söderbaum and T.M. Shaw (eds.) *Theories of New Regionalism*. Basingstoke: Palgrave-Macmillan, pp. 1–21.

Söderbaum, F. and Shaw, T. (eds) (2003) *Theories of New Regionalism*. London: Palgrave-Macmillan.

Storper, M. (1998) *The Regional World*. New York: Guilford Press.

Tägil, S. (ed.) (1999) *Regions in Central Europe: The Legacy of History*. London: Hurst & Co.

Taylor, P.J. (1991) 'A theory and practice of regions: the case of Europes', *Environment and Planning D: Society and Space*, 9 (2): 183–195.

Taylor, P.J. (1994) 'The state as container: territoriality in the modern state system', *Progress in Human Geography*, 18 (2): 151–162.

Telo, M. (2002) 'Governance and government in the European Union: the open method of coordination', in B.-Å. Lundvall *et al.* (2002) *The New Knowledge Economy in Europe*. Cheltenham: Edward Elgar.

Terlouw, K. (2004) 'Area studies at Utrecht University: a regional geographical approach', *Journal of Contemporary European Studies*, 12 (3): 355–365.

Tewdwr-Jones, M. and Allmendinger, P. (eds) (2006) *Territory, Identity and Spatial Planning*. London: Routledge.

Tomaney, J. and Ward, N. (2000) 'England and the "new regionalism"', *Regional Studies*, 34 (5): 471–478.

Vartiainen, P. and Kokkonen, M. (1995) 'Europe of regions – a Nordic view, in H. Eskelinen and F. Snickars (eds) *Competitive European Peripheries*. Berlin: Springer, pp. 97–114.

Vos, H., Boucke, T. and Devos, C. (2002) 'The *condition sine qua non* of the added value of regions in the EU: upper-level representation as the fundamental precondition', *European Integration*, 24 (3): 201–218.

Williams C.H. (1997) 'Territory, identity and language', in M. Keating and L. Loughlin (eds) *The Political Economy of Regionalism*. London: Frank Cass, pp. 112–138.

Wilson, C.R. (ed.) (1998) *The New Regionalism*. Jackson: University Press of Mississippi.

Wistricht, E. (1994) *The United States of Europe*. London: Routledge.

Wood. D. (1992) *The Power of Maps*. London: Routledge.

27

Europe's Borders

William Walters

It sometimes seems that borders are everywhere in Europe today. Certainly there is an irony here. Not so long ago many commentators were eagerly anticipating a 'borderless' Europe, a unified space open to the movement of people, goods and finance. Yet while the completion of the EU's Single Market project offered institutional confirmation of at least certain powerful debordering tendencies, elsewhere borders, both old and new, have returned to the political scene. For instance, by the end of the 1990s the creation of new states in Central and Eastern Europe had added 8,000 miles of new frontiers to Europe's political map (Foucher, 1998: 235). Montenegro's recent separation from Serbia is only the latest political event to augment this figure. Meanwhile, the politicization and securitization of migration has given rise to the border as 'spectacle' (De Genova, 2002): media coverage relays dramatic images of decrepit boats unloading 'asylum-seekers' (consider how the very term marks its subjects with suspicion) onto the coasts of Europe's Mediterranean islands and its mainland. Politicians only deepen this obsession with borders when they promise 'tougher' controls as a 'solution' to this 'immigration crisis'. Relatedly, and at the same time that it proceeds with schemes to promote cross-border

cooperation to mitigate the legacy of Europe's historical division into myriad nation states, the EU has become the setting for new kinds of border, most notably its moving 'external frontier'. The capacity for effective border control now sits alongside democratic reform and economic stability as a governmental prerequisite for admission into the EU's privileged circle of states. And as the EU moves 'outwards' no discussion of its future composition can take place, it seems, without lengthy and sometimes agonizing debate concerning the present and future 'frontiers' of Europe – 'Where does Europe end?' Meanwhile, academic discourse is rife with borders too. Not only have borders become a central motif for disciplines (once) as different as international relations and cultural studies; there is also the fact that borders and frontiers have become popular metaphors in discussions of identity, power, community and their exclusions. Where once inequality and social struggle was imagined in vertical, sometimes pyramidal shapes (Maier, 2002), today a more horizontal imagination is at work: circles and boundaries demarcate the inside and the out, the included and the excluded. Borders also feature prominently within the political imagination of contestation. Networks as different as Médecins sans Frontières and Noborder reveal how political actors have come to rethink themselves in, across and sometimes against a space of borders. In many ways, borders have become a meta-concept: all manner of social issues now find expression and connection in a language of boundaries, margins and frontiers.

However voluble and ubiquitous, it is important to stress that this veritable explosion of border talk is in many respects quite recent. It is worth recalling that for much of the post-WWII period, the question of borders was relatively marginal within political analysis. The study of borders certainly had a place within the academy but one that was largely confined to certain specialist sub-fields like political geography and international law. Perhaps it was a reflection of the extended period of territorial stability which Europe experienced in the post-WWII period (M. Anderson, 1998: 1), the aspatiality of the social sciences at this time (Soja, 1989), or the fact that as a form of knowledge geopolitics was discredited in many countries by virtue of its association with aggressive nationalism and war (Lacoste, 2001: 132–5). Whatever the specific reasons, the figure of the border had little of the salience it enjoys today.

It is important to acknowledge the relative novelty of border talk in order to avoid a position that takes the contemporary prominence of borders for granted. By this I mean a perspective that posits borders as an essential feature of political order, a necessary feature of state sovereignty, and an obvious topic for any self-respecting volume on European studies. Certainly borders need to be more fully studied and theorized because of the multiple and complex functions they perform within contemporary societies. Certainly bordering offers a useful motif to enrich our understanding of political ordering (van Houtum et al., 2005). At the same time, it is best to approach the topic of borders and bordering in a way that acknowledges the contingency of the present moment. If border talk is everywhere, then it becomes incumbent upon those contributing to such discussions to account for the topicality of borders. However obvious it may seem today, there is perhaps nothing inevitable about our current obsession with borders.

With this point in mind, this chapter surveys some of the main trends and important developments in scholarship relating to Europe's borders. The first section starts from the proposition that we cannot make sense of borders and bordering in Europe without also addressing certain questions about the changing form of political space. Political space is admittedly a somewhat ambiguous concept that invites multiple, potentially contradictory interpretations. However, it is also a useful term enabling us to plot transformations in such key practices as territoriality, political identity and sovereignty. Furthermore, the idea of political space does not commit us in advance to any propositions about the ontology of political order in Europe. Instead, it allows us to work with the understanding that multiple ordering and organizing projects are pertinent and co-exist – the international, the transnational, the network, and so on (Agnew, 1999; Jönsson et al., 2000). Since each implies a different conception of borders, the meaning of borders today becomes quite complex indeed.

A second section examines Europe's borders in relation to the concrete issue of migration. This is apt given that it allows for a more grounded engagement with some of the more abstract questions raised in the discussion of political space. But it is also valid given that the issue of migration has become so central to border talk and border spectacles.

The topic of 'Europe's borders' necessarily raises two questions that should be clarified from the outset. First, there is the matter of *which* borders. We have already noted the current popularity of borders as a metaphor. For practical reasons I shall confine my discussion largely to political, as opposed to, say, social or psychological borders. While a broader, more sociologically informed definition of territory and borders might encompass the space of the home, the neighbourhood, or the terrain of social relations (the borders of class, etc.), I will be limiting my discussion to the borders of states and other political entities and spaces. And while a large literature has examined the subjective, everyday experience of borders (Meinhof, 2002) for the most part I am interested in borders inasmuch as they are institutionalized within regimes of power and governance.

The other preliminary question concerns the meaning of Europe itself. In the wake of important interventions by postmodern geographers, postcolonial critics, historians of ideas and others, the idea that Europe is a stable referent, a geography, civilization or people capable of objectively founding a politics or delimiting a space has been profoundly unsettled (Chakrabarty, 2000; Crowley, 2003; Delanty, 1995; Diez, 1999; Pagden, 2002). If Europe is, in a sense, 'unfamiliar territory' (Delanty and Rumford, 2005: 120), and 'not where it is supposed to be' (R. Walker, 2000), then we cannot point to a place, state or continent called Europe which readily reveals its borders, edges or divisions to an impartial observer. On the contrary, I take the position that debates about the frontiers of Europe are unavoidably political interventions which interject elements of fixture into the fluid and ambiguous space that is Europe. A dynamic and co-constitutive relationship exists between Europe and its borders; whatever their pretensions, analyses of Europe's borders ultimately participate in discursive and political games of European constitution.

BORDERS AND POLITICAL SPACE

A host of developments have combined in recent decades to unsettle what we understand as Europe's borders. Together they can be read as prompting not just a redrawing of borders but a challenge to the modern constitution of political space itself. Any list of such developments would surely include but not confine itself to the following events and transformations: the end of the Cold War and the search for a new security framework at a time when the apparent proliferation of 'non-traditional' and even 'deterritorialized' threats (Ó Tuathail, 1999) makes the meaning of security uncertain; fluid new forms, scales and systems of capitalist accumulation which simultaneously de-privilege the old Fordist spaces of national economy while multiplying and deepening local and transnational economic spaces (Jessop, 1999); the intensification of translocal identities and transnational communities that has arisen from new patterns of migration and settlement and new modes of communication; the rise of regional identities which often pit subnational aspirations for autonomy against centralized political regimes and their cultures. Finally, there has been the political, economic and institutional project of European integration itself. Responding to, catalysing and in some cases regulating the kinds of processes just mentioned, the institutional thickening, and functional and geographical extension of the EU has contributed in powerful ways to unsettle the conventional political map of Europe.

In its encounter with such transformations, much scholarship on the subject of borders and Europe has come to recognize the limitations of state-centric theories, and reject the move which imagines zero-sum relationships between markets and states, globalization and sovereignty, territoriality and virtuality. Recent scholarship has in different ways started with the proposition that an adequate account of borders is not possible without confronting what Agnew (1994) has pithily termed the 'territorial trap'. Accordingly, it has undertaken the difficult task of theorizing configurations of sovereignty, territory and governance that diverge from the deeply ingrained pattern of the modern state system. While this enterprise has taken a number of promising directions, for the purposes of this chapter there are three themes I intend to emphasize: territoriality, sovereignty, and political imagination.

Territoriality

The first line of research orbits the theme of territoriality, and more specifically, the constitution of modern territoriality. A significant body of work has examined different ways in which the territorial state is far from timeless, but in fact the product of institutional dynamics, social constructions, political and geopolitical struggles, and economic forces (Biersteker and Weber, 1996; Spruyt, 1994; Tilly, 1992). By historicizing the political space of the modern state (for instance, typifying it as 'Westphalian' or 'Weberian'), such research has opened a space in which to think more critically and imaginatively about current reconfigurations of power, politics, borders and territory in Europe. A milestone in this respect was Ruggie's hypothesis that with its 'extraterritorial' common market and its 'multiperspectival polity', the EC/EU marks nothing less than the most advanced instance of a wider process in which modern territoriality was becoming 'unbundled' (Ruggie, 1993).

Subsequent research has explored the consequences of this unbundling process for the meaning, location and identity of Europe's borders (J. Anderson, 1996; Hassner, 2002; Maier, 2002). Considerable attention has focused on patterns of cross-border regionalism and region-building (J. Anderson et al., 2003; Kramsch and Hooper, 2004; Perkmann and Sum, 2002). The emergence of subnational and cross-border regions, a process that the EU has sought to instrumentalize as a technology of European integration (for instance, through programmes like INTERREG), is interesting for many reasons. Not the least of these is the pluralization of European space and identity which it effects. But crossborder regionalism also offers a nice illustration of what Diez has called the 'paradoxes of Europe's borders'. 'A basic paradox of European integration', he argues, 'is that the decreasing importance of borders is based on the recognition of those very borders' (Diez, 2006: 237). Crossborder regions and their governmental institutions generate new regional borders, albeit lines that are less dramatic and totalizing than state borders. But in the process of smoothing the historical scars left by the old

borders they turn these borders into objects of policy-making in their own right, changing them from lines into 'two-dimensional space' (Christiansen and Joergensen, 2000: 63)

As the case of regions certainly reveals, European integration has been viewed as a dynamic and contradictory process, one that encourages new patterns of debordering and rebordering and among and across its member states. But when attention turns to the EU itself, understood as an emergent, albeit uncertain polity in its own right, other transformations of borders become apparent. It is here that themes of unbundling and postmodernization have been most emphasized. Typically it is argued that modern political space fostered a certain symmetry of governance and geographical area. Functions of economic regulation, taxation, law, policing, social policy and defence were designed to coincide across the same geographical space. The EU is sometimes regarded as a 'postmodern' polity possessing 'fuzzy borders' precisely because this coincidence of governmental and functional space no longer obtains (M. Anderson and Bigo, 2003; Christiansen and Joergensen, 2000). Membership of the EMU is different from Schengenland which is different from Social Europe. They overlap but each has its own borders. This pattern of course owes much to the pragmatic calculations of states choosing to 'opt' in and out of different areas rather than any grand design. Whatever its genesis, it has been formalized with the legal and conceptual recognition of 'flexibility' as an ethos for the future 'integration' of Europe.

This fuzziness of the Europe's borders only becomes more pronounced once we note that the EU may be the most widely recognized agency to speak in the name of Europe, but it is of course not the only one. Arguing that political institutions offer a more workable and productive way to define 'Europe' than either culture or geography, Wallace (2002) reminds us of the role that organizations like NATO and the Council of Europe have also played in configuring European space. Since each embodies a different idea of Europe, both in terms of geographical scope and identity, then one can say that the boundaries of political Europe are particularly ambiguous.

These kinds of historically informed studies of territoriality have another purpose besides exploring patterns of postmodernization. They have also brought to light other forms of borders and proto-borders that have been eclipsed or marginalized by the idea of the modern state system. By revealing the diverse forms of bordering historically practised by political communities – such spaces as the 'limes' (Rufin, 2001) and the pioneer frontier (M. Anderson, 1996: 4) – these studies have broadened our conceptual repertoire for thinking about new forms of borders. Take the example of the march, an archaic name that in many ways pertains to a premodern territoriality in which states and peoples were not divided by strict lines. The march has been described as 'a neutral strip or belt of severance' (Curzon, 1908), or a frontier 'region' rather than a line (M. Anderson, 1996: 9). But the march could also function not just as barrier but a space of interaction. Ellis has described the Anglo-Gaelic and Anglo-Welsh marches as regions where 'English settlements were often interspersed with native areas, so creating multiple, localized frontiers which were fragmented and fluid, rather than consolidated blocs. Both were zones of interaction and assimilation between peoples of very different cultures' (Ellis, 1995: 683).

Foucher has suggested that, in the period following the Cold War, we see a return of the march in Central Europe. Reminding us that the precise meaning of the word 'Ukraine' is 'march' or 'border area', he observes that 'from the Baltic Sea to the Black Sea, and perhaps part of the shores of the Adriatic Sea, a kind of 'Middle Europe' … an in-between Europe is reviving' (Foucher, 1998: 236).

Since the march can be both a space of interaction and a buffer zone, this concept seems particularly appropriate to the territory designated as the 'Central and Eastern European Countries' (CEEC). A number of studies suggest that EU migration and security policies maintain a complex and contradictory relationship with CEEC (Collinson, 1996; Grabbe, 2000; Lavenex and Uçarer, 2003). On the one hand, a combination of EU membership and partnership agreements has brought this space firmly within the political–economic orbit of the EU. On the other, the terms of enlargement have seen the region accorded the status of a buffer zone, a space which is to insulate the heartland of the EU from what many strategists regard as the turbulent, chaotic spaces of the former Soviet Empire to the east, and more generally global movements of refugees, economic migrants and other mobile 'threats'. Nothing better illustrates this than the patchwork of 'readmission' and 'safe third country' agreements now in place which aim at orchestrating transnational 'flows of expulsion' from the EU area (Rigo, quoted in Mezzadra and Neilson, 2003).

Historical sociologies of the rise of modern territoriality, and its (postmodern) transformation, have certainly deepened our understanding of the meaning and functions of Europe's borders. But they are not without their own shortcomings. I shall briefly make two points in this regard. First, there is often a progressive historiography and sometimes a teleology embedded in the modern/postmodern narrative. Frequently the modern comes to stand for neatness, order and symmetry while the postmodern pole represents fluidity, complexity, diversity, heterogeneity and in certain cases deterritorialization. One problem here is that such a narrative produces (and, it could be argued, requires) an overly simplistic and even mythical view of the modern state. It is worth emphasizing that modern states were not as neatly bounded as the idea of the 'territorial state' suggests. Past as well as present societies had their own forms of 'transnationalism' (Mann, 1993; Paasi, 2005: 25). After all, nearly all the states which first comprised the European Economic Community were, to differing extents, former imperial metropoles. Each state had its national borders, but was simultaneously located within wider, imperial spaces of trade, migration, affiliation and antagonism. Consider, for instance, the way in which migration was relatively unrestricted from the Commonwealth and (former) colonies to Britain until the 1960s, or that it was not until 1981 that Britain adopted a fully national rather than imperial conception of citizenship (Layton-Henry, 2004). Or consider how elementary school textbooks and atlases of the 1950s represented the space of the modern Netherlands, employing colour schemes and ingenious lines to effect a seamless and seemingly natural continuity between the provinces of the Netherlands and various Dutch overseas territories and colonial possessions (Kramsch, 2002). Both cases suggest, at the very least, that the 'fuzzy borders' of the EU are not as unprecedented as scholars sometimes imply. More generally they point to the need to complicate narratives of postmodernization with a greater appreciation of the colonial past and, to use Kramsch's phrase, 'post-colonial present'.

A second problem with the modern/ postmodern narrative about Europe's borders stems from the wider vogue for post-ist labels. As much as these may be useful heuristic devices to plot complex transformations, they tend to inscribe a lack or fragmentation in the heart of the present, characterizing the present largely as an era that comes after a more coherent past. For this reason it could be argued that alongside these post-ism narratives there is a need for other concepts and inquiries that offer what Dean (1999: 179) calls a 'positive account of the present'. Positive is meant here not in a normative sense, but rather in terms of a need to express what is emergent, novel, contingent and irreducible – the domain Foucault has given the name of 'events' (Foucault, 1991).

Fortunately, such a move can be discerned in certain recent studies of Europe's borders. If the tendency in the 1990s was to map changing political space in terms of logics of postmodernization and deterritorialization, current research reveals a greater concern to interrogate the actual constitution of new

spaces and their implications for borders and bordering. For instance, Bialasiewicz et al. (2005) offer a close reading of the recent Draft Constitution, revealing its implications for a process they call the 'constitution of EU territory'. They detect a 'profound ambiguity' with respect to the future of borders. This is because the Constitution harbours an aspiration to advance a European space of shared values and solidarity, expressed through principles of territorial cohesion. At the same time it also reinscribes a 'hard' sense of territory, to be organized through new external border controls as well as a concern with the territorial integrity and sovereign rights of the member states. Other studies have also noted a similar oscillation between 'soft' and 'hard' borders (DeBardeleben, 2005).

In a similar vein, recent scholarship reveals a growing level of interest in the emergence of new legal, political and administrative concepts, such as that of 'neighbourhood' (Delanty and Rumford, 2005: 126–31) or the 'area of freedom, security and justice' (N. Walker, 2004), as well less official identities like 'Schengenland' (Kostakopoulou, 1998; Walters and Haahr, 2005). While I will touch on some of these in the following section, here it is worth noting that a better understanding of Europe's borders will surely require a closer reading of these novel spatialities and configurations, a reading that will doubtless be advanced by comparing them to emergent spaces in other regions. For instance, the literature on borders will surely be enriched by a more sustained comparison of Europe's 'area' with the American system of 'homeland security'.

From sovereignty to sovereign power

If it is now widely observed that territoriality is being transformed, and that borders are becoming more fuzzy, dispersed and ambiguous, then this observation is often paralleled with an argument about the changing nature of sovereignty. One version holds that there is a crisis of state sovereignty, that the exclusive authority of the state to contain and manage movements across its frontier has been irreversibly undone by processes of globalization. Another version emphasizes the political response to globalization. Focusing on the EU, it suggests there has been a reorganization of sovereignty, with political and legal authority being relocated in several directions, including upwards where it is being 'pooled' in supranational authorities. Such accounts capture certain dynamics operating within European integration, not least its intergovernmental dimension. However, they are limited by a somewhat rationalistic and ahistorical conception of sovereignty. Sovereignty is regarded rather like a quantity which can be divided and recombined, or a tradable commodity. But what if sovereignty is subject to qualitative changes? Can we speak of different forms of sovereign power?

If it is possible to discern a move to rethink the nature of sovereign power, especially within international relations, then surely it has been the theme of empire and imperialism where this move has borne most fruit. In examining transformations of sovereignty in the security field in the period 'after' the Cold War, Waever (1997) offers a good example of research that connects themes of empire to the EU and the governance of Europe (but see also Böröcz and Kovács, 2001). Emphasizing that the empires he portrays are 'metaphorical' and not formalized or legal arrangements, Waever suggests that the Europe founded on the 'sovereign equality' of states is giving way to a political space of overlapping authorities. 'The empires metaphor points to a centredness which is not that of the sovereign state; not sovereign equality, but diffuse patterns of centres with power fading off' (Waever, 1997: 61).

While Waever revives a somewhat traditional, territorial understanding of empire, Hardt and Negri (2000) outline a quite novel conception. For Hardt and Negri we are faced not with a revival of imperialism but a new kind of global order they call 'Empire'. Empire is a new form of sovereignty – 'imperial' rather than 'imperialist'. It is not about dividing up and parcelling out territory but the constitution of a single global system based on globalized economic and cultural exchanges. 'Empire is the political subject that effectively regulates these global exchanges, the sovereign power that regulates the world' (2000: xi). 'In contrast to imperialism, Empire establishes no territorial centre of power and does not rely on fixed boundaries or barriers. It is a *decentred* and *deterritorializing* apparatus of rule that progressively incorporates the entire global realm within its open, expanding frontiers' (2000: xii).

Hardt and Negri's emphasis on a new form of sovereignty offers a critical perspective on those arts of governing associated with the fashionable term 'global governance', not to mention the forms of violence perpetrated by political subjects who act in the name of the international community and under the auspices of humanitarian principles. It is a useful way to interpret the modulating networks which weave together national and international, governmental and nongovernmental agencies, since it introduces the question of power into the relationships between these formations and a range of problems associated with 'globalization'. Seen from this perspective, the EU – and arguably the US itself – are not to be equated with empire. Instead, they are but two of the most prominent political agents and institutional sites whose activities are increasingly justified and rationalized by their relationship to this relatively decentred form of authority and the norms and normalization projects it mobilizes.

However, the relationship of this new form of imperial sovereignty to borders is possibly more complicated than Hardt and Negri allow. Under empire, we could hypothesize, borders do not melt into the space of deterritorialized networks and flows. Instead, like trade, literacy, corruption – or any of the other issues that one typically encounters itemized in the international comparisons and periodic country surveys of bodies like the UN, OECD and EU – borders become objects of this imperial authority as well.

Like many other areas of national policy-making, borders are subject to increasingly dense forms of 'reflexive government' (Dean, 1999) by a complex of public and private agencies located both inside and outside the state system. This does not mean that borders cease to 'belong' to particular nations, regions or continents. They retain such historical, political and cultural connections and memories. But it does mean that we can identify a series of new knowledges and practices which now articulate and redeploy the border within the kind of imperial system which Hardt and Negri describe. Consider, for example, how there now exists a series of international agencies both formally within the EU (e.g. FRONTEX) and beyond it (e.g. International Centre for Migration Policy Development) which bring specialist technical knowledge and assistance to bear in the governance of borders, and give practical effect to the new concepts which circulate within their milieu, concepts like 'risk analysis', 'border management' and 'border security'.

There is also the fact of the kind of outlook which this system of authority fosters. Within these agencies the aim is often to encourage an attitude of 'joint responsibility' on the part of neighbouring states (Walters, 2004b: 682). Where once the enemy was stationed on the other side of the border, this new logic of border control identifies a 'transversal' domain of non-state threats as the main locus of intervention (Bigo, 2000, 2002). The system of borders is rethought as an apparatus configured primarily in terms of the policing of 'mobile risks' – a term which, far from being neutral, actively creates a political equivalence between such otherwise heterogeneous identities as refugees, car thieves and illegal weapons-dealers. Meanwhile, there is a particular image of good practice, of effective borders, circulated by this apparatus. It holds that the task of border control is not to enclose nations, or contains societies. Instead, it is to balance 'liberties' with 'security'; to harness all the benefits of economic and cultural 'globalization' while safeguarding civic life from the threatening mobilities that have

also been unleashed by globalization and which, like computer worms and viruses, threaten the integrity of network societies. For this reason, the border as imagined from the perspective of imperial authority is more like a filter (den Boer, 1995) or a firewall (Walters 2004a, 2006) than a fence.

Examining the internationalization, supra-nationalization and governmentalization of Europe's border control from the perspective of imperial sovereignty will surely offer new insights about the nature and topography of borders today. Yet this research may well find it necessary to combine old and new conceptions of empire and imperialism. As Waever notes, there are power gradients and intensities at work here. One does not see a process which transforms all borders equally and in the same way. This transnational expertise about borders does not descend from the sky. Instead, it moves in certain directions, often retracing former patters of imperial power. Put simply, EU policing and immigration experts advise Moroccan state officials of their 'responsibilities' in the management of Europe's borders, not vice versa.

Political imagination

Closely linked to the theme of modern territoriality, as well as the transformation of sovereignty, and increasingly central to recent studies of the changing place of borders in political space, is the theme of political imagination. Van Houtum and Strüver (2002: 141–2) note that, in geography at least, borders are no longer approached as self-evident lines on a map, but 'in terms of socially (re)produced phenomena' which 'differ crucially in their meaning, forms and contents of representations and interpretation from context to context'. Hence the need to grapple with the different imaginations of borders. Similarly, Balibar (2004), following Carlo Galli, argues that a conception of political space cannot analyse only the constitution of power and its control over space(s) but needs to grapple with the 'spatial representations' underlying any concept of power. Neocleous has followed Buck-Morss in adopting an explicitly topographical account of political imagination. This is one that takes seriously the kinds of shapes, icons and figures which populate a given political imagination, giving it a character that is closer to political landscape (Buck-Morss, 2000: 12; Neocleous, 2003: 1–2).

For Neocleous, this understanding of political imagination allows him to query the naturalization of power relations. For instance, he shows how modern practices of territory and borders find a principle of legitimacy in the idea that states are persons inhabiting – and *owning* – 'homes'. When we recall that the Latin word *domus* can refer both to the idea of home but is also related to the practice of subduing and taming the wild, then perhaps it is appropriate to describe as 'domopolitics' those practices which mobilize specifically domestic forms of reason as a way of legitimating authority and rule over territory (Walters, 2004a). One lesson we might draw from the governance of the EU as an 'area of freedom, security and justice' is that domopolitics can operate on multiple scales and spatialities, not just those of the state.

Balibar (2004) offers a particularly insightful discussion of some of the key representations, imaginings and mental patterns that currently underpin discourses about Europe's borders. He discerns four conflicting and largely incompatible patterns of political space, with different implications for the politics of citizenship, security, and mobility. These are the clash-of-civilizations, centre-periphery, global network and borderlands patterns.

The first two patterns underpin a great deal of scholarship on the subject of the 'enlargement' of the European Union and its implications for the meaning and location of its external frontiers. For instance, there are echoes of the civilizational discourse at work in the politics which surrounded the application of Central European states for EU membership. As Kumar (2001: 81) has noted, the case for admission was quite often made by politicians and intellectuals in terms which stressed their nation's possession of quintessential and authentic 'European values'. In the scramble for EU membership Hungary was professed to be more authentically European than neighbouring Romania, and so on. Consequently, as these states jostled to 'rejoin' the European fold, the old borders of Europe took on new relevance as cultural and even civilizational markers.

However, it is Balibar's ideas of global network and borderlands that I want to expand upon here and link to other work on the theme of political imagination. To differing extents, both centre/periphery and civilizational discourses retain a close correspondence with geographical conceptions of space. This is less the case with the global network, invoking as it does the now familiar theme of fluid socioeconomic processes and flows that threaten to escape from territorial control. With the global network there is a 'primacy of circulation processes' over all processes and structures that are fixed and local. The network does not defy geography *per se*. It is often still imagined in geographical terms (for instance, in the *altermondialization* imagery of world forums and mobilizations (Seattle, Porto Alegre, etc.). But these territorializations appear as only a 'mere transitory aspect of a more basic process of 'de-territorialization'. Early readings of the global network saw in it the advent of a new borderless world. Balibar has countered that this discourse does not deprive borders of all meaning but it certainly does 'relativize' them, making them 'transitional' objects and spaces of 'permanent transgression'.

These reflections on the function of borders under globalizing conditions can be deepened if we read them alongside the work of geographers, cultural theorists and anthropologists who are focusing on the material organization and culture of places like the airport, which today function as the nodes and gates of a global mobility system (Cunningham, 2004; Heyman, 2004; Miles, 1999). For instance, Cuttitta argues that we are faced with new borders that are no longer lines marked on the ground but 'elements (even immaterial ones) that permit, hinder or prevent the access to the network flows'. Adapting a term from Ratzel, he notes that in contrast to the 'closed territoriality' of states there now exists the 'new open territoriality of the global *Grenzraum*' (Cuttitta, 2006: 38). The more that border functions aggregate around the major airports and railway stations, moving the border into the inside of the territory (Knippenberg and Markusse, 1999: 11), the more that Europe's major cities rediscover the function they once had as gateways (Virilio, 1987).

Contiguous territories and networks have sometimes been juxtaposed as alternative ways of organizing social relations, politics and much else (Jönsson *et al.*, 2000). However, when we broaden our discussion of networks to include information networks and networked databases, and the non-territorial realm of cyberspace, then the point is brought home that networks are not always processes which transgress borders and undermine the certainties of territory (Bonditti, 2004). On the contrary networks can become spaces of bordering practices in their own right. The EU has certainly championed a benign and largely positive view of networks as symbols and practices of integration, speed and cross-border mobility capable of resculpting European space (Barry, 2001). At the same time it also looks with greater urgency to networks of policing data and surveillance – for example, SIS I and II, Eurodac and now VIS – to underpin its aspirations to be an area of freedom, security and justice. Far from signalling the demise of territory and the limit of borders, it could be argued that such information networks are now deemed vital instruments in securing territory and (certain definitions of) population under conditions where this can no longer be achieved by inspecting people at borders (Bigo, 2000; Huysmans, 2006).

The final image of borders and political space which Balibar discerns is that of borderlands. Connoting a somewhat blurred zone of interchange rather than a rigid line of division, a space of cultural mixing and ambiguous affiliation as much as fixed identity, and subverting the negative value conventionally accorded to the peripheral, the idea of the borderland has proven attractive to certain postmodern theorists of citizenship and space. The borderland has more recently found an audience within EU studies where scholars and policymakers, grappling with the paradoxes and contradictions raised by the drawing of new borders, have found the borderland a rather attractive image and one that is deemed preferable to the hard edge (Batt, 2003).

In a somewhat different vein, Delanty and Rumford (2005) have utilized borderlands as a spatial metaphor for thinking Europe's troubled relationship to global processes. 'If borderlands are seen as spaces within which the EU attempts to accommodate global processes then Europe can be conceived as a continuous borderland perpetually engaged in an attempt to fix its territorial and spatial arrangements into coherent patterns while global processes continually disrupt older geographical certainties' (2005: 133).

Balibar seems to share this creative reading of the borderland as not merely a blurring of geographical borders but a concept capable of applying much more widely to the contemporary condition of the EU. But he goes further in exploring its potential as a motif with democratic possibilities. Following Balibar, to describe Europe as a space of borderlands is to insist on its multiple spatiality and its irreducibly plural social constitution. It is to understand Europe as an open space of intersection and overlapping borderlands. For instance, there is a Euro-Atlantic space, but also a Euro-Mediterranean space. Each borderland exceeds Europe, revealing how the world is folded into Europe and vice versa. Since each can provide the basis for a claim to be the authentic heartland, then the foundational character of such centres and peripheries is made relative, and Europe is decentred. Balibar's minor theory of borderlands indicates how we might move from a real geography to a genuinely political geography of Europe's borders.

If I have dwelt somewhat on Balibar's four political images here, it is not just because they ably demonstrate research that tackles the imaginary dimension of borders and political space. Nor is it because they offer a comprehensive typology of current ways of imagining the meaning of borders. No doubt there are many other political imaginaries that merit further analysis. (Not the least of these is the recurring yet impossible political dream of the border as a wall, an impermeable militarized space of fences, watchtowers and geostrategy. Controversial wall-borders currently defend Spain's enclaves in Morocco, just as they partition large swathes of the borderlands of Israel/Palestine or US/Mexico.) Balibar's intervention is significant in another way: by placing these different imaginations alongside one another he relativizes and de-ontologizes each of them. It is not uncommon that otherwise sophisticated studies become so immersed in their subject matter that their concepts are substantialized and given an ontological depth. For example, rather than seeing networks as one of many ways in which actors have categorized the world for purposes of understanding and acting on it, networks are often interpreted to be the fundamental material and logic of our world, prompting Thompson's (2004) sceptical remark: 'Is all the world a complex network?' Balibar reminds us that debates about borders always contain a performative element. It is always a question of naming the world as this and not that. As such, greater reflexivity about the terms and the function of these debates is merited, and an awareness that borders can be otherwise (Maier, 2002).

MOBILITIES, MIGRATIONS, BORDERS

To this point we have surveyed some of the main trends in the study of Europe's borders, arguing that it is instructive to cluster these around the themes of territoriality, sovereignty and political imagination. Migration provides a prism with which to view some of the above transformations in borders and bordering but in greater empirical and contextual detail. But if research into migration offers certain insights about the meaning and form of Europe's borders today, it does so not merely as one case study among many. For migration has become in many ways one of *the* most central, controversial and politically charged issues confronting discourse and policy about borders. Despite the fact that immigration policy is a multifaceted domain and in no way reducible to the control of borders, it often seems that discussions about migration are almost axiomatically dialogues about borders and vice versa.

Yet as tight as it sometimes appears, it is important to note that this migrations–borders nexus is not self-evident and certainly not timeless. Historically sensitive studies are beginning to reveal that there has been 'significant historical variation in border control priorities' (Andreas, 2003: 78). As Andreas suggests, while the military function of borders has declined, and while economic liberalization and globalization may have lessened the role of the border as a site of customs inspection and foreign exchange control, the function of policing the movement of population has become central to the concept of the border. Historical studies reveal that this latter function is in fact quite recent. In many Western states it was only in the early decades of the twentieth century that immigration control was made a fully national rather than a local or provincial matter, and only at this time that administrative control over the national borders came to be seen as a means to this end (Hammar, 1986; Sassen, 1999). As one study of the English poor law suggests (Feldman, 2003), in the nineteenth century and before, and inasmuch as the movement of people was articulated as a political problem, it was in relation to a space of parish and county borders as much as national frontiers.

While historical perspectives have done much to advance our understanding of the borders–migration nexus, other studies have concentrated upon its contemporary aspects.

I shall briefly survey three of these – research on the political dynamics of bordering, the political economy of borders and capitalism, and finally, analyses of bordering in terms of specific locales and technologies through which it is enacted.

The political dynamics of bordering

One of the most important developments within the interdisciplinary field of border studies is undoubtedly the shift from the study of borders as institutions or lines to border-*ing*, with the latter understood as a verb as much as a noun. Van Houtum characterizes this as a move that pays more attention to the 'human practices that constitute and represent socio-spatial differences in space' (van Houtum, 2005: 672).This shift to examine Europe's borders from the perspective of bordering processes is especially evident in the field of migration politics and policy.

We have seen how political theorists and political geographers have sought to map the changing topography of Europe's borders. But a great deal of research, especially in the area of political science and policy studies, has emphasized the need to understand the political and institutional dynamics underpinning new patterns of bordering. A good example of such research comes from those who have developed Zolberg's insights about 'remote control' immigration policy (Guiraudon, 2003; Guiraudon and Lahav, 2000; Samers, 2004; Zolberg, 1999). Remote control refers to a set of practices and tendencies that are changing what might be called the political geography of migration control, extending border controls away from the wealthiest 'countries of destination' and closer to what official discourse designates as 'countries of transit' and 'origin'. Often precautionary and preventative in their logic, these practices include the widespread use of visa programmes to code risky nationalities and filter out unwanted travellers; carrier liability procedures which seek to enrol airlines and shipping companies into networks of migration control; and policy proposals, as yet unimplemented, to conduct the processing of EU-bound asylum applicants 'offshore', for example in Libya, well before they can reach the 'territory' of Europe. Inasmuch as the EU's accession process has seen hopeful new member states 'importing' Schengen norms and practices of border control so as to demonstrate their fitness for participation in the EU's extended space of free movement and control (Lavenex and Uçarer, 2003), it might also be considered a particular instance of remote control.

One of the strengths of these studies is to suggest ways in which political processes play themselves out in spatializing strategies. Studies of remote control emphasize that border spaces take shape in the midst of policy-making dilemmas. The impulse to relocate controls away from the border needs to be seen as an attempt to mediate between contradictory political objectives. On the one hand political authorities are confronted with public cultures of disquiet about 'immigration'; a media-driven 'governmentality of unease' (Bigo, 2002) that equates 'immigration' with disorder, and enhanced border control with security. But political authorities are also faced with other pressures and concerns. For one thing there is the imperative to maintain open borders for the purposes of trade and tourism. But another is the existence of domestic and international human rights laws that accord migrants and refugees basic protections. In the view of many scholars, these laws and the wider public and legal cultures that support them, constrain governments in their approach to migration. Here, then, we find a powerful motivation to relocate border control away from the border: if the borders of the EU and its close neighbours now demarcate a space of humanitarian protection, new forms of border control aim to regulate access to that space. If the rise of a human rights culture embodies the principle of 'postnational' recognition of claims and even citizenship, then practices of remote control seek to limit access to the territory where such claims might be registered. It is as though the border must now perform an impossible double function hinted at in the notion of becoming an 'area of freedom, security and justice': it must both express the EU's aspiration to be a space of openness and tolerance, and regulate the political liabilities associated with the observance of such principles.

Because of the way that border control is being redistributed across political and virtual space, and is implicating the states of 'sending' and 'transit' countries in the control strategies of European states, a deeper understanding of the phenomenon of remote control will surely require studies of the borders–migration nexus to strengthen their ties with research in geopolitics. Several writers have fruitfully taken up the theme of a geopolitics of migration control (Geddes, 2005; Samers, 2004). Furthering the critical thrust of such work will perhaps involve closer attention to the discursive dimension of this geopolitics. For instance, what politics is at stake in the construction of a regime as a 'transit country'? But it will also be important to recognize that there is now a critical geopolitics that comes 'from below', finding expression in the political and cultural interventions of artists, planners, activists and migrants themselves. For instance, the collective AnArchitektur (2003) has produced what it calls a *Grenzgeografie* of the now defunct refugee camp at Sangatte, near the French entrance to the Eurotunnel. For several years Sangatte had been a significant transit point for unauthorized migration to the UK. Mapping the shifting pathways which migrants created in their confrontation with the fortification of the entrance to the Eurotunnel, AnArchitektur graphically demonstrate how the geopolitics of borders is a deeply contested and dynamic affair.

The political economy of borders

A somewhat different perspective on processes of rebordering in the context of migration comes from scholars working in the tradition of critical political economy. As we have seen, policymaking approaches recognize that economic imperatives impinge powerfully on border policies. However, for those concerned with what we might call the political economy of borders, the socioeconomic dimension is not just one factor amongst several, but pre-eminent. A key observation for such work concerns the constitutive power of bordering projects and the role they play in structuring labour markets, experiences of citizenship and non-citizenship, and social and/or national identity. Certainly this approach highlights how there has been an intensification of border and migration controls across Europe over the past 20 years or so, and how these patterns of securitization and militarization of borders constitute a political response to a number of developments (Huysmans, 2006). Not the least of these are processes associated with globalization, a 'crisis' of mass asylum-seeking, and the fact that the crumbling of the Iron Curtain meant that Western European states could no longer count on state communism to police the movement of people on its eastern flank. But while some rightly stress the way in which these controls make Europe's outer borders a new 'frontier of poverty' (Freudenstein, 2000), and its land borders a new space of suffering and death (Fekete, 2004), others point out that whatever the intensity of these control projects, they do not actually prevent the movement of migrants into Europe, so much as shape the terms under which their movements and subsequent existence takes place (Favell and Hansen, 2002; Mezzadra and Neilson, 2003).

Two points can be made about borders when seen from a critical political economy viewpoint. First, there is a continuity, at least at the level of effects, between the contemporary regime of intensive border and migration controls, and currents of neoliberalization at work within European and global capitalism. While the assertion of political sovereignty and control might appear as antithetical to antistatist, neoliberal logics, it can still be observed that inasmuch as border regimes play an active, constitutive role in criminalizing migrant labour, inasmuch as they give rise to semi-permanent, vulnerable sectors of workers, then Europe's border regime should be seen as a major element in the flexibilization of work (Samers, 2003). This point is underscored by studies of recent changes in labour and immigration law in southern European countries like Italy and Spain. These changes serve to maintain many migrant workers in a state of quasi-permanent deportability (Calavita and Suarez-Navaz, 2003).

The observation that migrant labour is utilized by states and employers as a reserve army is, of course, not new (Castles and Kosack, 1973) cited in Calavita (2003: 400). While its champions highlight its positive relationship to human freedom, critics of capitalism insist that the utilization and reproduction of unfree labour – whether in the form of plantation slavery, transported convicts or today's *sans papiers* – is a recurring and not incidental feature within the history of capitalism (Harvey, 2004; Moulier Boutang, 1998). What changes are the forms in which such unfreedoms are organized and distributed, but at the same time the possibilities which inhere within different practices and regimes of unfreedom – however narrow and circumscribed – for struggles for citizenship.

Second, and following on, there is a point to be made about the border as a site of social struggle. Drawing on studies which stress the autonomous power of struggles from below (Rodriguez, 1996), Mezzadra cautions against the view that sees migrants only as the victims of faceless processes or of organized criminality (Mezzadra, 2004; Mezzadra and Neilson, 2003; see also Koslowski, 2000: 204–5). Without denying that social and economic processes play a profound role in shaping patterns of migration, he insists that the rebordering of Europe be seen as a dynamic, antagonistic process in which the strategic agency of migrants, albeit exercised with varying levels of consciousness and intent, is actually shaping the borders of Europe. In many ways, he suggests, rebordering is not just an assertion of state (or suprastate) sovereignty, but a response to the transgressive practices and rhizomatic pathways, the new social spaces which migrants are fabricating from below. It has often been observed that borders are time frozen in space (O'Dowd and Wilson, 1996: 1–2), expressions of a particular equilibrium of military and diplomatic power between states. At a moment when Europe's borders seem more concerned with the movement of people than politico-military struggles over territory perhaps we can say that it the changing topography and intensity of *social* struggles which they now inscribe.

Border sites and technologies

If studies of remote control migration policy analyse bordering in terms of the logic of states and policy makers, and political economy approaches examine the relationship between forms of capitalism and border regimes, a third set of inquiries should be mentioned. This, in contrast, grapples with the *practical* ways in which bordering is effected. More case-focused in their approach, these projects examine how bordering is enacted at particular sites in terms of particular techniques, strategies and programmes. Utilizing insights and methods drawn from critical anthropology, ethnography and Foucauldian political sociology, such work treats borders as irreducible sites whose functions cannot be read off larger systems but instead require careful analysis of dynamic and contradictory situations. Border control is seen in terms of 'specific routines, technological devices and knowledge that shape a European space of free movement by externalizing and stratifying dangerous, excessive use of freedom' (Huysmans, 2006: 97). Of particular note is the way these studies engage with the question of mobility. Mobility is frequently discussed in unproblematic terms, as a synonym for migration, or symptom of the macroprocesses of globalization.

However, underpinning research into border sites and technologies is an understanding of mobility as a social and cultural value, a political problem, and a sociotechnical accomplishment whose emergence, as such, cannot be assumed but must be explained. As with Lefebvre's notion of space, mobility is seen not as something secondary but always produced under particular historical and cultural circumstances (Cresswell, 2001). Hence it can be asked: what role do borders play in the production, distribution and institutionalization of a range of mobilities and immobilities? What are the technical and practical ways in which bordering is effected?

One site where the intersection of technologies, subjectivities, migrations and markets occurs, giving rise to particular practices of mobility and immobility, is the port. We have already discussed ports in relation to the theme of networks and non-contiguous borders. But they are also relevant to the question of mobilities. Vestraete provides a vivid account of the involvement of private companies in marketing human detection technologies to the Belgian port of Zeebrugge. From the perspective of shipping companies who may be fined for failing to interdict clandestine travellers, refugees are not a human rights issue so much as a cost to production and efficiency. This has given rise to an 'emerging market in the removal of illegal refugees' (Verstraete, 2001: 27). If the rise of human trafficking and smuggling has transformed unauthorized border-crossing into the site of a growing clandestine economy in its own right (Koslowski, 2000), then it would seem that the task of countering these movements is also becoming marketized. Morover, if Europe's borders can be seen as the site of social struggles, then such struggles are producing new economic spaces as well. Further work in this area would add a new dimension to the theme of remote control. For instance, it might consider some of the ways in which private companies are not simply carrying out tasks offloaded by the state, but becoming inventive and strategic sites of border control in their own right. Put differently, and

to connect to an earlier theme in this chapter, if we want to analyse more fully the production of new forms of territoriality, we should not limit our focus to states and their policies but include emerging markets in risk management, security and control.

Other work has focused on airports as spaces of mobile governance (Fuller, 2003; Miles, 1999). Drawing on the literature of surveillance studies, Adey (2004) has applied the idea of 'sorting' to the airport. Given that the redesign and policing of airports has for some time been encoded as an operational norm within the Schengen *acquis*, it is important to note the ways in which airports and other transportation hubs contribute to a stratification of European space. Forming an assemblage with a series of heterogeneous elements that includes passports, European law, security practices, and the economy of cut-price air travel, one sees how airports are helping to create smooth, cross-border, pan-European spaces of business, leisure and tourism. At the same time, these same systems promise to arrest the flow of those subjects who lack the requisite identity or nationality, fit the risk profile, or simply arouse the suspicion of the authorities. For these categories cross-border movement has become ever more difficult. The study of airports as borders offers insights regarding the sifting of population movements, its distribution across different levels, and spaces and scales of mobility.

Sorting techniques stratify European territory, both producing and regulating social access to smooth and striated spaces. But they do not necessarily signal the end of the old borders of Europe. This, at least, is one conclusion to be drawn from van der Ploeg's (1999) careful study of Eurodac. This is an EU initiative to use biometric fingerprint data to control 'illegal immigration' and border crossing by asylum seekers. The political dream of Eurodac is to couple a kind of branding of the mobile subject – a branding which makes the body of the subject bear witness about their status, implicating that body in the 'distribution of benefits, services, rights' (van der Ploeg, 1999: 296) – with an authoritative determination of whether the subject has sought asylum or previously entered territory elsewhere in the EU. Hence Eurodac reveals another paradox of Europe's borders. At the same time that it responds to issues raised by the construction of extended spaces of free movement – and helps to constitute and secure those spaces – it also serves to recognize the old borders of the European state system. In determining, for instance, whether a refugee first entered the EU in France or Italy, Eurodac ensures that the outlines of the national system of borders remain administratively pertinent and politically salient. The case of Eurodac illustrates that we are dealing with new spatial assemblages in which extended trans-European spaces do not displace the old pattern of borders but interconnect with them, in some cases reviving them, in new and unexpected ways.

Eurodac is also interesting from the point of view of changing forms of sovereignty. Foucault introduced his famous study *Discipline and Punish* with a harrowing description of the torture and execution of Damien, a subject convicted of regicide. His point was in part to explore how the sovereign power of the monarchy was performed at the level of the body through gruesome and spectacular practices of life-taking. Could it be that the new kinds of networked sovereignty which Hardt and Negri have theorized are also evident at the level of mobile bodies. In the case of Eurodac, there is a biometrical marking of itinerant bodies not as an expression of a centralized sovereign, but, on the contrary, as a way of governing European space in the absence of a single sovereign centre. It seems that Eurodac has been invented to govern a situation in which political responsibility for governing asylum remains fragmented, decentralized and politically controversial.

CONCLUSION

Charles Maier has suggested that in a very broad sense North America and Europe have been associated with two different kinds of border. A dominant figure within North American thinking is, of course, the frontier. This was a transitional space that appeared within the colonial imagination as dividing 'civilization from nature or from peoples thought to be at a "lower" or less advanced degree of social development' (Maier, 2002: 17). Whereas the North American frontier marks the end, or moving edge of (white) settlement, the idea of a frontier for Europeans is more like a line dividing settlements and populations. The former finds its symbolism in the forest or the prairie, the latter in the border post.

It is tempting to conclude that one of the most interesting features of Europe's borders today is the fact that both these figures appear to be present. On the one hand Europe continues to generate new states and with them, borders that demarcate peoples and territories. Moreover, the politics and programmes of regionalization means that these patterns of state borders are overlaid by a complex space of regional borders which, in certain cases, may anticipate future state borders. Inasmuch as the institutions of the European Union lend support to the viability of new states as well as patterns of region-building, then processes of European integration ensure that Maier's typical European border is far from dead. On the other hand, the practices and programmes known as EU enlargement seem to introduce elements of the North American frontier into European political space. Of course, one should not push the analogy too far. The EU's external frontier is partial and incomplete: a frontier only for some purposes, such as migration control (M. Anderson and Bigo, 2003: 23). Moreover, notwithstanding the attempts of certain commentators to construe it as a civilizational edge, it lacks the explicitly racialized definition associated with the North American frontier. But there are continuities as well: in both cases the frontier operates as a zone where an organized power meets its outside in a relationship of transformation and assimilation. In both cases, one sees the spatialization of asymmetrical relationships in which an expanding power assumes the right to define what is appropriate and just, albeit that this game now plays itself out in the seemingly technical and benign norms and language of political and economic 'governance'.

Yet such a conclusion concerning the co-presence of these two border types in Europe would need to be qualified on at least two counts. First, this is not the first time that these types have been combined. According to Maier, the 'Romans left us an idea of the frontier that shared both elements – the end of their world, but one that had to be fortified against outsiders at a clear border' (Maier, 2002: 18). Second, and this is the more significant point, the frontier and the borderline certainly do not exhaust the possible forms and topographies of borders in Europe today. As we have seen, it is also possible to speak of a third kind of border – a nodal or networked border that is neither a division of population and territory, nor an edge of civilizational order, but a filter or mesh. Most borders allow a certain degree of movement and transgression. But for this nodal border the governance and security of extended spaces of mobility becomes one of, if not *the* principal function(s). Future research could fruitfully examine how the reorganization of political space in Europe – a reconstruction that is associated with the institutional programme of EU enlargement – combines these three types of borders in complex, contradictory and unpredictable ways.

Future research may well uncover other types of border as well. For instance, ethnographic research on the experience of 'trafficked' women is revealing a kind of border-crossing that takes the form of highly dangerous and in some ways epic journeys across rivers and forests (Andrijasevic, 2004). Because they cannot always utilize conventional forms of transit across Europe, the journeys of these subjects are rediscovering a very old kind of border – the 'natural frontier' of the mountain, the coast and the river. The fact that 'natural' frontiers should once again become relevant to the meaning and

experience of borders in Europe suggests that the rebordering of Europe be understood as a complex and relatively open-ended process without a telos.

REFERENCES

Adey, P. (2004) 'Secured and sorted mobilities: examples from the airport', *Surveillance and Society*, 1 (4): 500–519.

Agnew, J. (1994) 'Timeless space and state centrism: the geographical assumptions of international relations theory', in G. Rosow, N. Inayatullah and M. Rupert (eds) *The Global Economy as Political Space*. Boulder, CO: Lynne Rienner, pp. 87–107.

Agnew, J. (1999) 'Mapping political power beyond state boundaries: territory, identity, and movement in world politics', *Millennium*, 28 (3): 499–521.

AnArchitektur (2003) *Grenzgeografie Sangatte*. Berlin. Available at: http://www.anarchitektur.com/aa03_sangatte/aa03_sangatte.pdf.

Anderson, J. (1996) 'The shifting stage of politics: new medieval and postmodern territorialities', *Environment and Planning D: Society and Space*, 14: 133–153.

Anderson, J., O'Dowd, L. and Wilson, T.M. (eds) (2003) *Culture and Cooperation in Europe's Borderlands*. Amsterdam: Rodopi.

Anderson, M. (1996) *Frontiers. Territory and State Formation in the Modern World*. Cambridge: Polity.

Anderson, M. (1998) 'European frontiers at the end of the twentieth century: an introduction', in M. Anderson and E. Bort (eds) *The Frontiers of Europe*. London: Pinter, pp. 1–10.

Anderson, M. and Bigo, D. (2003) 'What are EU frontiers for and what do they mean?' in K. Groenendijk, E. Guild and P. Minderhoud (eds) *In Search of Europe's Borders*. The Hague: Kluwer, pp. 7–26.

Andreas, P. (2003) 'Redrawing the line: borders and security in the twenty-first century', *International Security*, 28 (2): 78–111.

Andrijasevic, R. (2004) *Trafficking in Women and the Politics of Mobility in Europe*. PhD dissertation, University of Utrecht.

Balibar, E. (2004) 'Europe as borderland', Alexander von Humboldt Lectures in Human Geography.

Barry, A. (2001) *Political Machines: Governing a Technological Society*. London: Athlone.

Batt, J. (2003) *The EU's New Borderlands*. London: CER Working Paper.

Bialasiewicz, L., Elden, S. and Painter, J. (2005) 'The constitution of EU territory', *Comparative European Politics*, 3: 333–363.

Biersteker, T.J. and Weber, C. (eds) (1996) *State Sovereignty as Social Construct*. Cambridge: Cambridge University Press.

Bigo, D. (2000) 'When two become one: internal and external securitisations in Europe', in M. Kelstrup and M.C. Williams (eds) *International Relations Theory and the Politics of European Integration*. London: Routledge, pp. 171–204.

Bigo, D. (2002) 'Security and immigration: toward a critique of the governmentality of unease', *Alternatives* 27(Suppl. 1): 63–92.

Bonditti, P. (2004) 'From territorial space to networks: a Foucauldian approach to the implementation of biometry', *Alternatives* 29 (4): 465–482.

Böröcz, J. and Kovács, M. (eds) (2001) *Empire's New Clothes. Unveiling EU Enlargement*. Telford, UK: Central Europe Review.

Buck-Morss, S. (2000) *Dreamworld and Catastrophe*. Cambridge, MA: MIT Press.

Calavita, K. (2003) 'A "reserve army of delinquents": the criminalization and economic punishment of immigrants in Spain', *Punishment and Society*, 5 (4): 399–413.

Calavita, K. and Suarez-Navaz, L. (2003) 'Spanish immigration law and the construction of difference: citizens and "illegals" on Europe's Southern Border', in R.W. Perry and B. Maurer (eds) *Globalization under Construction: Governmentality, Law, and Identity*. Minneapolis: University of Minnesota Press, pp. 99–127.

Castles, S. and Kosack, G. (1973) *Immigrant Workers and Class Structure in Western Europe*. London: Oxford University Press.

Chakrabarty, D. (2000) *Provincializing Europe: Postcolonial Thought and Historical Difference*. Princeton, NJ: Princeton University Press.

Christiansen, T. and Joergensen, K.E. (2000) 'Transnational governance above and below the state: The changing nature of borders in Europe', *Regional and Federal Studies*, 10 (2): 62–77.

Collinson, S. (1996) 'Visa requirements, carrier sanctions, "safe third countries" and "readmission": the development of an asylum "buffer zone" in Europe', *Transactions of the Institute of British Geographers*, 21: 76–90.

Cresswell, T. (2001) 'The production of mobilities', *New Formations*, 43: 11–25.

Crowley, J. (2003) 'Locating Europe', in K. Groenendijk, E. Guild and P. Minderhoud (eds) *In Search of Europe's Borders*. The Hague: Kluwer, pp. 27–44.

Cunningham, H. (2004) 'Nations rebound? Crossing borders in gated globe', *Identities: Global Studies in Culture and Power*, 11: 329–350.

Curzon, Lord (1908) *Frontiers*. Oxford: Clarendon.

Cuttitta, P. (2006) 'Points and lines: a topography of borders in the global space', *Ephemera*, 6 (1): 27–39.

De Genova, N. (2002) 'Migrant "illegality" and deportability in everyday life', *Annual Review of Anthropology*, 31: 419–447.

Dean, M. (1999) *Governmentality: Power and Rule in Modern Society*. London: Sage.

DeBardeleben, J. (ed.) (2005) *Soft or Hard Borders? Managing the Divide in an Enlarged Europe*. Aldershot: Ashgate.

Delanty, G. (1995) *Inventing Europe: Idea, Identity, Reality*. Houndmills, Basingstoke: Macmillan.

Delanty, G. and Rumford, C. (2005) *Rethinking Europe: Social Theory and the Implications of Europeanization*. London: Routledge.

den Boer, M. (1995) 'Moving between bogus and bona fide: the policing of inclusion and exclusion in Europe', in R. Miles and D. Thränhardt (eds) *Migration and European Integration: The Dynamics of Inclusion and Exclusion*. London: Pinter, pp. 92–111.

Diez, T. (1999) 'Speaking 'Europe': The politics of integration discourse', *Journal of European Public Policy*, 6 (4): 598–613.

Diez, T. (2006) 'The paradoxes of Europe's borders', *Comparative European Politics*, 4 (2/3): 235–252.

Ellis, S. (1995) *Tudor Frontiers and Noble Power: The Making of the British State*. Oxford: Clarendon Press.

Favell, A. and Hansen, R. (2002) 'Markets against politics: Migration, EU enlargement and the Idea of Europe', *Journal of Ethnic and Migration Studies*, 29 (4): 581–602.

Fekete, L. (2004) 'Death at Europe's borders', *Race and Class*, 45 (4): 75–83.

Feldman, D. (2003) 'Was the nineteenth century a golden age for immigrants? The changing articulation of national, local and voluntary controls', in A. Fahrmeir, O. Faron and P. Weil (eds) *Migration Control in the North Atlantic World*. New York: Berghahn, pp. 167–177.

Foucault, M. (1991) 'Questions of method', in G. Burchell, C. Gordon and P. Miller (eds) *The Foucault Effect*. Chicago: University of Chicago Press, pp. 73–86.

Foucher, M. (1998) 'The geopolitics of European frontiers', in M. Anderson and E. Bort (eds) *The Frontiers of Europe*. London: Pinter, pp. 235–250.

Freudenstein, R. (2000) 'Río Odra, Río Buh: Poland, Germany, and the borders of twenty-first-century Europe', in P. Andreas and T. Snyder (eds) *The Wall around the West: State Borders and Immigration Controls in North America and Europe*. Lanham, MD: Rowman & Littlefield, 173–184.

Fuller, G. (2003) 'Life in Transit: Between Airport and Camp', *Borderlands e-journal*, 2 (1).

Geddes, A. (2005) 'Europe's border relationships and international migration relations', *Journal of Common Market Studies*, 43 (4): 787–806.

Grabbe, H. (2000) 'The sharp edges of Europe: extending Schengen eastwards', *International Journal*, 76 (3): 519–536.

Guiraudon, V. (2003) 'Before the EU border: remote control of the "huddled masses"', in K. Groenendijk, E. Guild and P. Minderhoud (eds) *In Search of Europe's Borders*. The Hague: Kluwer, pp. 191–214.

Guiraudon, V. and Lahav, G. (2000) 'Comparative perspectives on border control: away from the border and outside the state', in P. Andreas and T. Snyder (eds) *The Wall around the West: State Borders and Immigration Controls in North America and Europe*. Lanham, MD: Rowman & Littlefield, pp. 55–80.

Hammar, T. (1986) 'Citizenship: membership of a nation and of a state', *International Migration*, 24: 735–747.

Hardt, M. and Negri, A. (2000) *Empire*. Cambridge, MA: Harvard University Press.

Harvey, D. (2004) '"The New Imperialism": accumulation by dispossession', in L. Panitch and C. Leys (eds) *The Socialist Register 2004*. London: Merlin, pp. 43–63.

Hassner, P. (2002) 'Fixed borders or moving borderlands?: A new type of border for a new type of entity', in J. Zielonka (ed.) *Europe Unbound. Enlarging and Reshaping the Boundaries of the European Union*. London: New York, 38–50.

Heyman, J.M. (2004) 'Ports of entry as nodes in the world system', *Identities: Global Studies in Culture and Power*, 11: 303–327.

Huysmans, J. (2006) *The Politics of Insecurity*. London: Routledge.

Jessop, B. (1999) 'Narrating the future of the national economy and the national state: remarks on remapping regulation and reinventing governance', in G. Steinmetz (ed.) *State/Culture*. Ithaca, NY: Cornell University Press, pp. 378–406.

Jönsson, C., Tägil, S. and Törnqvist, G. (2000) *Organizing European Space*. London: Sage.

Knippenberg, H. and Markusse, J. (1999) 'Nineteenth and twentieth century borders and border regions in Europe: Some reflections', in H. Knippenberg and J. Markusse (eds) *Nationalising and Denationalising European Border Regions, 1800–2000: Views from Geography and History*. Dordrecht; Boston: Kluwer Academic, pp. 1–19.

Koslowski, R. (2000) 'The mobility money can buy: human smuggling and border control in the EU', in P. Andreas and T. Snyder (eds) *The Wall around the West: State Borders and Immigration Controls in North America and Europe*. Lanham: Rowman & Littlefield, pp. 203–218.

Kostakopoulou, D. (1998) 'Is there an alternative to Schengenland?', *Political Studies*, XLVI (5): 886–902.

Kramsch, O.T. (2002) 'Reimagining the scalar topologies of cross-border governance: Eu(ro)regions in the post-colonial present', *Space and Polity*, 6 (2): 169–196.

Kramsch, O.T. and Hooper, B. (2004) *Cross-border Governance in the European Union*. London; New York: Routledge.

Kumar, K. (2001) *1989: Revolutionary Ideas and Ideals*. Minneapolis: University of Minnesota Press.

Lacoste, Y. (2001) 'Rivalries for territory', in J. Lévy (ed.) *From Geopolitics to Global Politics*. London: Frank Cass, pp. 120–158.

Lavenex, S. and Uçarer, E. (eds) (2003) *Migration and the Externalities of European Integration*. Lanham, MD: Lexington.

Layton-Henry, Z. (2004) 'Britain: from immigration control to migration management', in W. Cornelius, T. Takeyuki, P. Martin and J. Hollifield (eds) *Controlling Immigration: A Global Perspective*. Stanford: Stanford University Press, pp. 297–333.

Maier, C. (2002) 'Does Europe need a frontier?: From territorial to redistributive community', in J. Zielonka (ed.) *Europe Unbound. Enlarging and Reshaping the Boundaries of the European Union*. London: Routledge, pp. 17–37.

Mann, M. (1993) 'Nation-states in Europe and other continents: diversifying, developing, not dying', *Daedalus*, 122 (3): 115–140.

Meinhof, U.H. (2002) *Living (With) Borders: Identity Discourses on East-West Borders in Europe*. Aldershot; Burlington: Ashgate.

Mezzadra, S. (2004) 'The right to escape', *Ephemera*, 4 (3): 267–275.

Mezzadra, S. and Neilson, B. (2003) 'Né qui, né altrove – migration, detention, desertion: a dialogue', *Borderlands e-journal*, 2 (1).

Miles, R. (1999) 'Analysing the political economy of migration: the airport as an «effective» institution of control', in A. Brah, M. Hickman and M. Mac an Ghaill (eds) *Global futures: Migration, Environment, and Globalization*. Basingstoke: Macmillan, pp. 161–184.

Moulier Boutang, Y. (1998) *De L'esclavage au Salariat: Economie Historique du Salariat Bridé*. Paris: Presses Universitaires de France.

Neocleous, M. (2003) *Imagining the State*. Philadelphia: Open University Press.

Ó Tuathail, G. (1999) 'De-territorialised threats and global dangers: geopolitics and risk society', in D. Newman (ed.) *Boundaries, Territory and Postmodernity*. London: Frank Cass.

O'Dowd, L. and Wilson (1996) *Borders, Nations and States: Frontiers of Sovereignty in the New Europe*. Aldershot: Avebury.

Paasi, A. (2005) 'The changing discourses of political boundaries', in H. van Houtum, O. Kramsch and W. Zierhofer (eds) *B/Ordering Space*. Aldershot: Ashgate, 17–32.

Pagden, A. (ed.) (2002) *The Idea of Europe: from Antiquity to the European Union*. Cambridge, New York: Woodrow Wilson Center Press and Cambridge University Press.

Perkmann, M. and Sum, N.-L. (2002) *Globalization, Regionalization, and Cross-border Regions*. Basingstoke; New York: Palgrave Macmillan.

Rodriguez, N. (1996) 'The battle for the border: notes on autonomous migration, transnational communities, and the state', *Social Justice*, 23 (3): 21–37.

Rufin, J.-C. (2001) *L'empire et les Nouveaux Barbares*. JC Lattes.

Ruggie, J.G. (1993) 'Territoriality and beyond: problematizing modernity in international relations', *International Organization*, 47 (1): 139–74.

Samers, M. (2003) 'Invisible capitalism: political economy and the regulation of undocumented immigration in France', *Economy and Society*, 32 (4): 555–583.

Samers, M. (2004) 'An emerging geopolitics of illegal immigration in the European Union', *European Journal of Migration and Law*, 6: 27–45.

Sassen, S. (1999) *Guests and Aliens*. New York: The New Press.

Soja, E. (1989) *Postmodern Geographies*. London: Verso.

Spruyt, H. (1994) *The Sovereign State and its Competitors: an Analysis of Systems Change*. Princeton, NJ: Princeton University Press.

Thompson, G. (2004) 'Is all the World a Complex Network?', *Economy and Society*, 33 (3): 411–424.

Tilly, C. (1992) *Coercion, Capital, and European states, AD 990–1992*, revised paperback edn. Cambridge, MA: Blackwell.

van der Ploeg, I. (1999) 'The illegal body: "Eurodac" and the politics of biometric identification', *Ethics and Information Technology* 1: 295–302.

van Houtum, H. (2005) 'The geopolitics of borders and boundaries', *Geopolitics* 10: 672–679.

van Houtum, H., Kramsch, O. and Zierhofer, W. (eds) (2005) *B/Ordering Space*. Aldershot: Ashgate.

van Houtum, H. and Strüver, A. (2002) 'Borders, strangers, doors and bridges', *Space and Polity*, 6 (2): 141–146.

Verstraete, G. (2001) 'Technological frontiers and the politics of mobility in the European Union', *New Formations*, 43: 26–43.

Virilio, P. (1987) 'The overexposed city', *Zone* 1/2: 14–39.

Waever, O. (1997) 'Imperial metaphors: Emerging European analogies to pre-nation-state imperial systems', in O. Tunander, P. Bayev and V.I. Einagel (eds) *Geopolitics in*

Post-Wall Europe: Security, Territory and Identity. London; Thousand Oaks: Sage, pp. 59–93.

Walker, N. (ed.) (2004) *Europe's Area of Freedom, Security and Justice*. Oxford: Oxford University Press.

Walker, R. (2000) 'Europe is not where it is supposed to be', in M. Kelstrup and M. Williams (eds) *International Relations Theory and the Politics of European Integration*. London: Routledge, pp. 14–32.

Wallace, W. (2002) 'Where does Europe end?: Dilemmas of inclusion and exclusion', in J. Zielonka (ed.) *Europe Unbound. Enlarging and Reshaping the Boundaries of the European Union*. London: Routledge, pp. 78–94.

Walters, W. (2004a) 'Secure borders, safe haven, domopolitics', *Citizenship Studies*, 8 (3): 237–260.

Walters, W. (2004b) 'The frontiers of the European Union: A geostrategic perspective', *Geopolitics*, 9 (2): 674–698.

Walters, W. (2006) 'Rethinking borders beyond the state', *Comparative European Politics*, 4 (2/3): 141–159.

Walters, W. and Haahr, J.H. (2005) *Governing Europe: Discourse, Governmentality and European Integration*. London: Routledge.

Zolberg, A. (1999) 'Matters of state: Theorizing immigration policy', in C. Hirschman, P. Kasinitz and J. DeWind (eds) *The Handbook of International Migration: The American Experience*. New York: Russell Sage, pp. 71–93.

28

An Intellectual Homeland: Governing Mobilities and Space in European Education

Martin Lawn

Education as a policy area has a history in the European Union but it is an indistinct one, especially in its early decades, and it has been transformed in many ways as the overall policy aim of a knowledge economy and the Lisbon form of constant comparison is introduced to it. As it has been changed, moving from patrimony to a space of comparison, so its direction has increased in sophistication and purpose. But the European Union is unable to control its formation by fiat, through personnel policies, political influence and direct funding (in the way that older nation states did with their systems) *and* to overcome multiple players, including powerful 'learning as a commodity' brokers. In the field of education in particular, the governing of education in Europe relies upon a range of old and new public, semi-public, and private actors for its emergence. Networks of actors of many kinds are producing, translating, comparing or imagining a new European education space. Lifelong learning, citizenship and the knowledge economy are shaping

and being shaped together as the determining characteristics of this space. In a way, the idea of an 'intellectual homeland'[1] is being constructed by these actors as well, a process of meaning making which fits the area of education/learning above all.

The chapter has four parts. The first shows the ways in which governance works in the processes of Europeanization have been extended and how it ranges across new key spaces or sites of engagement and involves traditional and, in education, a tighter relation with unfamiliar actors drawn from other spheres of work. The second part shows how an education policy area has come into being over time, indeed from the EU's earliest days, and how in recent years it has become transformed, merging with commerce and policy imperatives on a knowledge economy, into a learning space. The third part focuses on the activities and purposes of European actors, de-territorialized and transnational, and yet producing new forms of entrepreneurial activity in this structured and imagined space.

Finally, the particular attraction between education and new European governance is explored.

A SPACE FOR GOVERNING EDUCATION

Forms of European governance are difficult to disentangle or discover, and this is especially the case with the governance of education. Indeed even the idea of a discernible governing process in the field of education might appear disingenuous. It appears as a footnote to a theory perhaps but not to be part of a shift in thinking about governance and its new forms. The argument here is that at the moment when 'education' has ceased to be invisible as a governed object in European policy, it has been transformed in its scope and governance. The gradual shift from an indiscernible series of activities in the field of culture and education to a regulated space of learning via benchmarks and indicators is also a narrative about a shift in governance in Europe. Early political understandings about the place of education in the creation of the Community may still be in place, but the actuality is that networks of diverse kinds, sectors and actors have been building a European education space for some time. This is a response to the need for new governing strategies and the arrival of a market of mobile private and public agents, working across borders, between institutions and cross-purposes, in the new field of education/learning.

EU governance has become associated with the management of key spaces: regions, cities, networks and borders. Hitherto in European studies spatial considerations have been restricted to the nature of multilevel governance, the challenge of territorial cohesion, and the futurist turn towards speed of communication and flows of objects and people. The advent of the idea of 'network Europe' has demanded a different approach to both the spatiality of Europe and its mechanisms

of governance. The 'governance turn' in EU studies is well documented (Ansell, 2000; Kohler-Koch, 1999, 2002). However, the dynamics of EU forms of governance have proved more difficult to identify. It is argued that the EU, rather than being primarily concerned with state-building or the institutionalization of governance structures, is centrally concerned with the construction of European spaces (Delanty and Rumford, 2005). That is, the EU actively constructs European spaces which it is capable of governing and works to create new policy networks and spaces within which it can deploy European solutions to European problems. The idea of space is much more important to EU governance than suggested by the idea of multilevel governance (Hooghe and Marks, 2001).

The idea of 'network Europe' suggests networks of public, semi-public, and private actors, constructing and enacting European policy in social settings and virtual exchanges, with scientific and discursive trading, extending beyond local, national and even European borders. Networks may be viewed as having the potential to mediate and transform both themselves (Castells, 2006) and the environment in which they operate. However, European spaces are far more complex than even the idea of 'network Europe' would suggest (Borzel, 1997). Recent scholarship on the spatiality of Europe has started to go beyond the idea of Europe as a multilevel or networked polity and into the rescaling of state space (Brenner, 2004), the idea of network society and global connectivity (Castells, 1996) and on societal mobilities (Urry, 2003). Governing is located in a networked, ahistorical space of flows, aiming at imposing its logic over scattered, segmented places (Castells, 1996) and producing a disciplining and enabling space of engagement with state and transnational agencies and elites. Mobilities associated with the single market, interconnectivity, and a single European space (exemplified by Trans-European Networks) point to the transcendence of territorial institutionalization and a transformed subjectivity; a Europeanness.

It is not just that a contemporary focus on network and fluidity is helpful in understanding the education domain but that it only appears visible within a perspective concerned with movement, mobility and contingent ordering (Urry, 2000a, 2000b). It is between space and mobilities that the emergence of a new space of learning and the movement and relations of its networked actors is rendered visible, both to its participants and to its enabling and governing forces. Bricolage is the EU mode of construction of choice but these spaces are created by others as well. New 'spatial entrepreneurs' are responsible for creating new networks and public spaces of communication which later may become appropriated by the EU as spaces of governance (Shore, 2000), in this case for the education domain. They exist in diverse forms and various times and their purposes and logics of actors emerge weakly. They are not necessarily the dominant managerial elites, although these are evident, but technical experts, administrative personnel, academic advisors, evaluators and professional networkers (for institutions and companies). European actors can work – through constructing networks and spaces of cooperation and contestation – in such a way as to further the goal of European integration, but do so by acting independently of the institutions of the EU or in a synergetic and complementary way. This feature of EU governance is under-researched, but is of great relevance to a consideration of both governance and the scope and direction of the Europeanization of education. So, EU governance in education not only involves a mixture of state and non-state agencies, and the coordination of nongovernmental and nonlegislative policy tools, but is being undertaken by independent agencies and actors not formally involved (in the sense of being funded or coordinated) in EU-sponsored projects. Learning operates as a discourse across areas of policy, through its close association with ICT, and it operates as a commodity, marketed across Europe by private companies and entrepreneurial organizations. It is the role of these spatial entrepreneurs in the construction of a European educational policy space, which is the focus of this paper. The term 'spatial entrepreneur' implies an independent actor involved in networking, partnerships, agenda setting, and other forms of soft governance (Lawn, 2006), combining to create a thick tapestry of communication, organizational and network relations, stable and unstable linkages, and career patterns and construction of networked spaces which can subsequently be organized as sites of European governance. These sites of engagement constitute the field of European networking in education, and contain both traditional actors in the field of education (institutional policy makers, university groupings, organized professional interests) and those conventionally considered peripheral to education governance (commercial interests, networks of participation and interest, technological innovators). These 'spatial' entrepreneurs traverse the mobility categorizations used by Urry; that is, global enterprise and global fluidities; they operate in an ordered way across fixed networks and in a heterogeneous and chaotic way as well. As the private and public operations of 'education' are both creating its European field, so a range of participants shift between ordered and ordering behaviours in a mix of network relations.

ASSEMBLING AN EDUCATION AREA

The rise of a Europeanized policy area in education began in the 1950s with ideas of cultural identity and fraternization, and a specialist focus on vocational education, although it always retained a 'semi-clandestine' character (Novoa, 2000). Cultural cooperation was associated with a new identity, 'a European model of culture correlating with European integration' (European Commission, 1971) which in turn acquired pedagogic form. In recent years, detecting education as a policy area is easier, reflecting the rise of international comparisons of educational productivity and performance, and most of all, the growth of education as a key policy area in a knowledge economy perspective. Education has turned from a quiet web of mutual relations within multilevel governance into a field of audit, judgement and action, in which the quality and effectiveness of education and its ability to be benchmarked against world or European standards became the goal. This emergent field was also closely related to knowledge economy discourses in EU policy, which see quality of education as central to a competitive economy. This Europeanization process takes place within a global convergence of communications technologies that reconstitute time and space, spawn the networked flows of transnational, supranational and globalized space, and facilitate the rise of an international commerce in education, and more recently, world agreements in trade in education (Lawn, 2001; Novoa, 2002). While the Europeanizing policy space in education may have appeared opaque, in peripheral, small or accession countries, it is a significant and visible policy practice, appearing as the imposition of a dominant, unified European policy and achieved through funding/policy compliance tradeoffs, often working almost as a sophisticated version of structural adjustment through the imposition *inter alia* of concepts and statistical categories of performance and a 'magistrature of influence' (Lawn and Lingard, 2002; Silova, 2002). Particular elements which drive European governance into existence include: the open method of coordination, post-Lisbon Council (Hingel, 2001; Walters and Haahr, 2005) at the level of national and regional interaction, and supported by scientific commissions on performance and benchmarking (Bos and Schwippert, 2003; EGREES, 2005; Henry, 2001; Scheerens and Hendricks, 2004); a growing academic networking, reflecting a resurgence of cross-border cultural, scientific and associational cooperation in a mixed economy of voluntary, EU-supported and Research Council projects; and the Bologna Process, pushed by networks of universities, adopting a common framework of degree structure and credits.

Nation states constructed education systems with a wide range of executive tools, by means of legislation, system construction, professional training programmes and specialist buildings. Most of all, they were managed through a conceptual discourse in which the purpose and structure of the system and national identity were bound together in building the education service and cultural identity. Attempts to continue the nation-state strategies of developing education and the state together appeared to have influenced the early strategies of the Community in its first decades but jealous partners in state governments impaired the creation of new 'languages of identity', in Anderson's phrase (Anderson, 1983).

Within a short time, following the Treaty of Rome in the late 1950s, the field of education was an interwoven and complex area. To the original idea that Europe was an exceptional source of culture and that education cannot be seen merely as 'a component of economic life' (European Commission, 1971). Corbett (2005: 43) has argued that the early distinction between education and training was 'fast disappearing' and that higher education and education were components of many Community policy sectors including employment, environment, research, consumer protection, overseas development and cooperation, information, industrial affairs and aspects of social policy (2005: 44) and that 'in practice it has been very difficult to make clear distinctions among vocational, professional, and university training, continuing education, and primary and secondary education' (Sprokkereef, 1995). Indeed, although outside observers either assumed a lack of presence for education or confirmed its national role, decision-making mechanisms were being adapted to this particular policy area; there had been a measure of agreement with the Ministers of Education which allowed the Community to enter areas of high national sensitivity (Corbett, 2005). By the late 1990s, the European area of education policy involved a range of system administrators in national agencies, cities and regions

(Beukel, 2001: 129) and a growing range of actions in schools and higher education (exchanges, European dimension, networks, teaching resources, etc.) (Beukel, 2001: 131).

The breadth and scale of the education domain took a significant turn following European Council meetings in Lisbon and Stockholm with the adoption of the target to become the 'most competitive and dynamic knowledge based economy in the world' (Beukel, 2001; Hingel, 2001). For education, this meant a focus on the internal creation of a strengthened area of policy, including the new goals of shared benchmarking and indicators, and a new emphasis on managing the education policy area in Europe under globalization, with its emerging world markets in education services. Intensification involved a wider range of actors. New agents moved freely across Europe (Hiatt, 2000) offering products and opportunities so as to extend their 'influence' and 'brand identity' with new consumers. New 'learning businesses' delivered education as a commodity and searched for new markets. So, when the EU now promoted a new policy on eLearning, it used private–public partnerships to manage project delivery and increase the range of partners and capital in this task (European Commission, 2001c). Its new partners were Nokia, IBM and Cisco. As a commercial group, the European Education Partnership refers to it as the pan-European learning market (EE Partnership, 2002). The EU intends to expand distance learning, double the rate of student and teacher mobility and increase the transferability of qualifications (Kokosalakis, 1998; Slowinski, 1998). Education began to metamorphose into 'lifelong learning systems', connected to the other policy domains of employment, science, technology, and information and communication technologies. This new world trade in education services, often referred to as borderless education, describes distance learning, mobility of students, commercial companies and provider mobility (teachers) and is aimed at providing a 'level playing area' for supply (Hiatt, 2000). The growing

worry inside the Commission is that, in a time of 'borderless frontiers' in education, international corporations and networks are more likely to be delivering education services across Europe than its own state institutions and agencies.

Throughout the last half century the development of projects for comparison, data collection and harmonization was being sustained by projects on cross-institutional collaboration, documentation and statistics, recognition of qualifications and key organizations like EuroStat, EuroBarometer, Eurydice or the European Education Thesaurus. In effect, these agencies provided the standardization processes upon which a more developed process of comparative analysis and action could be built. Under the auspices of the European Statistical System (ESS) a special task force on lifelong learning and statistical data (European Commission, 2001d) was created to bring together all the current demands for numerical information and indicators from within European programmes, and those demanded by new intentions for social and economic development (European Commission, 2001a). In this way, the policy agenda reorganized the process of data accumulation and in turn was able to act more effectively on its lifelong learning agenda.

The 'imagined community' of European education may be discursively bound together by objectives and indicators but it is shaped by constant interaction between groups of linked professionals, managers and experts. This space is formed between state and EU offices, between agencies and subcontractors, between academics and policy managers, between experts and officials, and between voluntary and public sector workers. It is a growing culture, which exists in formal operations, and the interstices between them, in the immaterial world.

Prior to the intensification of the EU internal management, by means of open coordination, the adoption of the goal of a learning society in the Commission's White Paper on Education and Training (Teaching and Learning: Towards the Learning Society)

(European Commission, 1995) signalled a major reworking of its goals for the domain of education. The idea of learning (and not education) has significance as it led to a powerful drive linking lifelong learning and a knowledge economy, combining citizenship and work. Making the link between knowledge and lifelong learning is a necessary solution to the problem of invisibility and the lack of institutional power over the education domain by the EU. In this way, education could be redefined as an individual necessity, rather than as patrimony or as part of community systems. Europeanization could be achieved through this distinctive European way, as a governance strategy and as a mission (European Commission, 1996). The discourse was aimed directly at the individual; it was to offer a vision to them and produce a responsibility for them. The vision made sense of the European project and created a programme in which the citizens of Europe were both appealed to and constructed. Europe was about competitiveness and decisiveness and the individual was the place in which this could be situated. They were to be given the task of managing the future by acquiring the capacity to exercise responsibility for their own education and training choices

The Study Group's vision promised to deliver personal development and social integration in Europe (European Commission, 1996). The idea of producing Europe through learning could not have been more clearly expressed than in a list of oppositions in which the envisioned future was defined. The future Europe was to be constructed by a shift from objective to constructed knowledge; from an industrial to a learning society; from instruction to personal learning; and from formal educational institutions towards new organizational structures for learning. Learning citizens would have to constantly renew their fund of knowledge, extend their citizenship through active solidarity and on a lifelong basis, develop creativity, flexibility, adaptability, the ability to 'learn to learn' and to solve problems. Lifelong learning has emerged as the vision of Europe and in its

governance, the individual is relocated from the nation state into a new space and mobility in which 'learning' is to be situated in them. As the EuroStat Taskforce on lifelong learning pointed out,

At the same time, responsibility for education and learning shifts from the public (state) to non-governmental organizations as well as to the individuals themselves ... While traditional educational institutions have been (and still are) primarily concerned with transmitting knowledge, modern learning opportunities and the LLL approach put the emphasis on the development of individual capabilities and the capacity of the person to learn. At the heart of the LLL concept lies the idea of enabling and encouraging people 'to learn how to learn' (Eurostat, 2001).

Lifelong learning will reconstitute education, widening the field, integrating its functions, centring the individual learner, and stressing performance and comparison. Comparison will be easier after the landscape has been reordered and made transparent (European Commission, 2001a, 2001b).

DIVERSE MOBILITIES

Networking has become an ubiquitous feature in descriptions of modern professional and corporate life and represents, in Castells' words, a 'new organizational paradigm' (1996). The new paradigm has been formed from business networks, telecommunications networking and global competition, with the state a continuing player, and together they constitute a new network enterprise. In this 'space of flows', support has been traditionally offered by the EU in terms of discourse (the role of cooperation), thematic networks and social partner meetings, each provided with limited financial support. The push towards networking has come from the rise of new technologies of communication and the shift in work in education as well.

One of the main ways of discussing networking in Europe is to refer to the policy elites which operate in Brussels and move in and out of national government, directorates and private companies. Described as 'agents of European consciousness' (Shore, 2000), they produce cultural symbols, practices and institutions allowing Europeanization processes to take place. This has been described as a system of 'self representation' (Borneman, 1988), as they act both as producers and analysts of policy, and they connect 'public policies [to] their strategic and institutionalized context' (Kickert and Koppenjan, 1997). They are significant producers of the new European educational space. Their contemporary policy discourse ('globalization', 'society of knowledge', 'modernization', 'accountability', 'democratization'), acts to 'legitimize' certain educational policies in their national settings, even though they may not appear in national policy documents or regulations. It is a constant process of translation and mediation, a privileged system of production of discourse and data (dissemination of studies, reports and statistics). They constitute a new class of deterritorialized, transnational policy actors (Shore, 2000).

In a research project on 'Educational Governance and Social Inclusion and Exclusion' (EGSIE) in the European Union (Lindblad and Popkewitz, 1999, 2000, 2001), interviews with system actors referred to the non-national influences that continued to interrupt the national 'space' of education. The interviews also revealed the actors themselves as bearers of a new policy space in education. On a continuum, German system actors were unaware of European influences (though not of OECD global indicators in education like PISA) while, at the other end, Greek actors saw themselves as modernizing and Europeanizing with the EU having high visibility (Zambeta, 2002). Similarly, Spanish system actors were aware of global market pressures and were concerned that the EU wasn't thinking fast enough about the changed situation and wanted extended analyses and new initiatives (Pereyra, 2002). The complex responses and positioning of these system actors, working on problems of harmonization, competition and exchange in European committees, in task force groups and other supranational bodies, showed them to be simultaneously observers, agents, translators, evaluators and even oppositionalists. They were crucial actors in the construction of this extranational policy sphere. They are aware of the rise of statistical indicators, produced by the EU and the OECD among others, and the way that they are used to 'shape' the education system. Interviewing them revealed the existence of a gradually emerging and distinctive European policy culture in education, constructed through a wide array of committees, exchanges, commissions, networks and regulations, in which they worked to use, shape and imagine a European education of the future. In the intimate work relations of a new Euro education class, a new 'magistracy', translation was their skill and their interest, and yet it was 'ironic' (having elements of warning and mimicry). They turned information into powerful knowledge, reimagining the project of Europe and repositioning the national.

City managers and politicians were acting in a similar way. Europe is now an arena in which the city can work for its own goals of regeneration and social renewal, in which education or learning is often a key element. This was seen clearly in the English case study where a group of city managers, made explicit reference to transnational influence on education policy. For example, in one large Midlands city in the UK, there was a strong concern with maximizing European Union revenue as well as trying to influence EU policy agendas. To achieve this, the city has officers who deal mainly with the EU agenda and directly liaise with their counterparts in other European cities. They collected comparative city data and network for joint funding applications. A reciprocal exchange between city managers was now common, including those working within education.

Student mobility across Europe is also part of this scenario; it is of course a global occurrence (1.8 million students studied outside their country of origin in 2000 and this is projected to rise to 7.2 million by 2025) but with significant European elements. Students travelling across Europe to study are linked by several factors; they are likely to be moving between universities with a strong research mission and encouraged by cosmopolitan and class-based ideas of the values of professional and managerial classes. During the 1990s the Erasmus scheme became increasingly popular across the EU, with total student mobility rising in every year. The gradually increasing flow of students across Europe has changed in character over the years. Its gap year curiosity has been overlaid with a process of shaping and regulating its form and function. The 'Bologna Process, aiming to create a European Higher Education Area (EHEA), although not confined to EU countries, is intended to increase mobility between institutions in Europe, and in so doing, has been designed to improve international *transparency* and to enable academic and professional recognition of qualifications. Mobility effects are intended to be produced locally. A European dimension across the entire range of a university's academic programmes is now part of Erasmus and more emphasis is now placed on teaching staff exchanges, transnational curriculum development and pan-European thematic networks. Universities have shifted from *ad hoc* responses to Europeanization into a central-systematic strategy (where there is a large volume of international work and the international mission is clearly supported) (CHEPS: 10) Institutions now view these mobilities, within Erasmus, as preparing students for the international labour market, and to make themselves known as places that are effective in doing this. A lack of mobility can be read as endangering Europe in its global economy goals and in new institutional goals.

For academics in education, formal networks have appeared in the range of supported networking which reflects the new governance of Europe (regions, trans-national programmes, EU Declarations, etc.) and related funding (through Socrates, Thematic Networks, EU based research projects, etc.).

Professional associations are becoming crucial in the governance of many areas of EU policy, especially ICT (Knill, 2001) where they act to provide expertise in areas where the Commission is weak, and where intervention involves a range of heterogeneous actors. Associations have begun to alter their structures, from federalist and national, to European and individual membership, to cope with the new demands upon them in providing expertise, acting as policy mediators between the national and the transnational, supporting their members and ambitious European goals. European-wide associations now struggle to achieve for their members information and influence, and cope with Commission expectations about their stability and expertise. They engage with a range of supported (partially or wholly funded) networking arising out of the new governance of Europe (regions, transnational programmes, EU Declarations, etc.) and related funding (through Socrates, thematic networks, EU-based research projects, benchmarking work groups, etc.). Other developments which produce networking include: new communications technologies allowing academics to manage information flow easier than in the past; new cross-university agreements and alliances supporting mobility and joint production; education publishing (journals, books, etc.) produced by publishers producing across European markets; creation of cross-Europe 'pressure group' associationism (e.g. European associations for special education or adult education). The rapid pace of formal networking, beyond funding support and onto forms of social partnership, can create difficulties for associations who are unable to manage the degree of stable relations demanded by EU offices (Lawn, 2007). As part of the Lisbon Agenda, academic experts have been on working on European projects to do with equity, quality, investment in education, participation in lifelong learning and private expenditure on education and training, for example, and producing evidence about performance progress on the best use of resources or on the best performers in the five benchmarked areas of policy. This process has connected a range of academic and private experts in quality assurance or benchmarking (Robertson and Dale, 2004); for example, recent projects on benchmarking the quality of education involved seven countries and seventeen experts (Scheerens and Hendricks, 2004), and the 'Equity in European Educational Systems: a set of indicators' project involved six countries and nineteen experts (EGREES, 2005).

Networks are seen as powerful objects, increasingly more powerful than the institutions they grew out of. They are transformatory but also unstable:

> [A] culture of the ephemeral, a culture of each strategic decision, a patchwork of experiences and interests, rather than a charter of rights and obligations, It is a multi faceted, virtual culture … [Yet] it is a material force because it informs, and enforces, powerful economic decisions at every moment in the life of the network (Castells, 1996: 198).

Since networks are based upon trust, are in perpetual circulation and involve asymmetrical relations, they have problems of coordination. They are as strong as their weakest point, they do not respond to centralization or hierarchy and coordination must base itself on the constant 'lubrication' of the social relations inside the network. The social relations of the network are the new relations of production as members, or nodes, can only keep faith with the network if trust is maintained within it and if a useful circulation of information is sustained. Strong networks have high levels of trust which they develop and sustain. So, coordination has to reflect the decentralization of power in the network and the recurring problem of differential responsibility within it.

Does acting like a spatial entrepreneur involve reflexivity about mobility, space and policy? There appears to be a division between networkers who are concerned with a new opportunity space, following their interests, occupation or desires (Mayntz, 1994), and those who are pulled into networks by role, function and task. Institutions

and research actors that are not well connected at the national level are more likely to succeed at the transnational level (Doumas, 2002). In the education domain, there appear to be a number of actors with different responsibilities, purposes and forms of engagement in European networks across voluntary, private and public sectors, namely policy mediators, experts, institutional managers, academics, enablers and learning entrepreneurs (Table 28.1).

As networks are borderless with regard to content, functions and space, they are heterogeneous with regard to membership, involving actors of different interests and skills. The mobilization of voluntary, expert, professional and community groups and associations in Europe, and even their growing collectivity in Europe-wide groupings, can not just be explained by the (limited) financial support offered to them. Their expenditure will always be greater than the support. The appeal of being consulted, advice sought and prospects for discussion proffered is attractive, even when it is not clear if the Commission has much power (Cram, 1998).

The range of actors, their spaces of work and deliberation, and their forms of engagement can no longer be described as an elite of policy makers nor as an extended and distributed form of policy making, nor even as a work within nonbinding policy areas. They may be working to produce a new area of meaning, a regional imaginary in Laïdi's sense (2003), but these actors may not even know they are actors in this Europeanizing process in education. They are attracted to this European space yet vary in their contributions, their expertise, their purposes and their opportunities. As an area of governance, it may not be visible or even disciplining to its members, who are nevertheless creating it. European networking is a soft power tool for the enabling of the governance of Europe, attracting and producing opportunities for the growth of meaning about it, necessary for its production and governance. The informality of their organization, the complexity of their knowledge relations and exchanges, and

Table 28.1   European Networkers in Education

	Responsibility	Purpose	Forms
Policy mediators	Governmental symbolic analysts	Translating and shaping	Committee formal/informal
Experts	Advisory technical and scientific monitoring data harmonization	Construction via supported networks	working group Task groups
Institutional managers	Market share	Market advantage and opportunity Identity management	Alliances
Academics	Evaluation advisory symposia and projects applied research	Professional and knowledge Interest driven	Virtual across borders central meetings conferences
Enablers	Information exchange action review added value	Gateways contact points	Forms of circulation
Learning entrepreneurs	Initiative company	Market organization/market share	All forms – market wikis

the hybridity of their institutional association, combine with their overall interdependence and produce a distinctive form of governance in Europe.

GOVERNING MOBILITIES

It has been argued that the EU actively constructs European spaces which it alone is capable of governing and works to create useful policy networks and spaces within which it can deploy European solutions. In this case, authority cannot be demanded but has to be negotiated so its relation with its partners in civil society is one of steering, guiding and contracting. Significantly in the education domain the EU manages the problem of governing networks by creating a desire for 'Europe' within a political project which aims to attract. This concept of political soft power (Nye, 2004) was used initially to explain the inadequacy of current hard-power American foreign policy. Instead, soft power embraces a whole set of social, cultural and political possibilities, from attractive cultural goods or social policies, to opportunities for engagement or alliance.

The idea is to win cooperation and increase institutional alliances, and its tools are diplomacy, negotiations, patience, the forging of economic ties, political engagement, the use of inducements rather than sanctions, the taking of small steps and tempering ambitions for success. These were the tools of Franco-German rapprochement and hence the tools that made European integration possible (Kagan, 2002).

The creation of meaning is viewed as less deliberate but just as important. It is an attempt to shape a space of meaning in a Europe whose frontiers are fuzzy and with a collective ideal, produced with an element of voluntarism and agreements (Laïdi, 2003). These spaces of meaning are symbolic spaces which transcend national spaces yet they are not 'public transnational spaces' either. The creation of regional meaning, of common European meanings, involves expertise, deliberation, collective actors and regular procedures (Lamy, 2002) and contains governmental logics, civic proposals and expert knowledge. This governance sphere exists in the same space, the same networks and even within the same communications as the knowledge-producing relations of networking in education. Experts work with an expertise which is portable. They act as points of distribution for the ideas of Europeanization, creating, imagining and transmitting within a framing of work and networks that exists within and without kinds of steered partnerships.

Significant system actors act as symbolic analysts (Reich, 1991), dealing with abstract Europeanization ideas in education policy, or building experimental or analytical policy networks. In EGSIE, they appeared to be 'selling' modernization to their countries and their colleagues. Often their language did not seem unique or different to common globalizing discourses (in education – learning skills, knowledge economy and performance, etc.) but their usage appeared in particular ways in the policy space of Europe. It was pedagogic, conceiving and circulating ideas about a 'workable future' in Europe and attempting to manage uncertainty.

ORDERING AND IMAGINING EDUCATION

Education as a policy domain in the EU has shifted over time from policy areas in the minor key, either because of the sensitivities of subsidiarity or lack of political will, into a governing discourse which has merged education with key EU policy areas (economy and competitiveness). This major shift into the goal of a knowledge society, combined with open coordination processes of benchmarking, has altered considerably the quiet field of cooperation and support which prevailed for many years.

Today, the 'European space for education', in all its forms and possibilities, is emerging as a multifaceted web of relations, as commerce, technology-based networks, associations, intergovernmental relations and competition all act to drive it into existence. By its nature, as a transnational flow of information, a disorientation as much as an ordering, it is being created in sharp contrast to the older central roles played by organizations, hard law, statist jurisdictions, rigid borders

and national sites. The apparent indeterminacy of the European space should not disguise its transparency as a hypermodern form of effective governance, taking account new knowledge shifts and rapidly absorbing their possibilities. It is easier to imagine it as multiple spaces, built around function and interest, operating at different intensities and levels, occupying innumerable areas and spheres and constantly emerging into being. Space is reconfigured constantly as the new policy spaces – city to city networks, peripheral countries, northern and southern networks, central and border countries and sites – work with each other via a spider's web of distributed policy-making in multiple centres. System actors try to make sense of the shifting realms in which they are working. Because resources can be captured, at home and in Europe, by increased networking and by a reflexive translation, so the space in which this takes place is also reconfigured. They are not just mobile, they are in a space between, increasingly reimagining policy space, their space of action, its significant elements and personnel, and its purposes. They are taking on the task, for education, of using a Europeanization process and project, to produce new meanings about transnational states and globalization.

It is an attempt to find a space of effective governance, knitting together public and private sectors, and overcoming older national bordered systems. The emerging policy space of education in Europe, a process of complex, network governance, needs actors who take on the functions of governance, import and renew languages of 'external' agencies, become absorbed into policy arenas and act on behalf of hybrid policy agendas. The system actors circulate and translate an explicit language of collection, comparison and evaluation, and of new generic skills and 'learning' which, although of wider international usage than specifically 'European', appeared in particular forms in the Europeanizing space. Europeanization appeared to be the means by which larger visions were projected or demanded and in which a 'workable future' could be conceived. No actor engaging in 'European' education/learning networks is free of the implication that they are both free and networked; that they are constructing and being constructed by their engagement; and that European governance now includes them.

Education may be particularly prone to 'soft governance' methods. Its actors, in different degrees, have histories of involvement in working for national projects and in cooperative networks. State building relied on discursive management of its education actors, for example, just as much as regulatory control. Also, a new internationalism fits closely with normative assumptions about the purposes and practices of education. Imagining a new space may often free them from the tighter and tighter obligations of the old one, of course. At the same time, education can be so closely bound up with the local that it is the case that its actors will be variably involved in trans-European activity. While new actors may come into play, many older ones are less able or willing to engage this way. Yet 'soft governance' can create new possibilities for even the most localized and least cosmopolitan actor. For example, the growth of the European Schoolnet, a school-to-school networking facility across Europe, shows little sign that it was an initiative of European school ministers and was at first intended to share national cultural sites across the web. Schools join daily and work in different ways with each other. Mobilities exist virtually as well. In a discussion of the European higher education space, and the role of the European Commission within it, Keeling (2006) discusses the multiple role of the EC in shaping the discourse, language and priorities of the EHES and tying it into the Bologna process. One of the consequences of this pragmatic series of actions is that 'considerable space for challenges [to it has been] articulated. The Commission is in many ways dominating the discourse, but it has also played a significant part in opening up the discussion of the challenges facing higher education on the European-level' (2006: 222).

Shaping processes, pragmatic action and network governance, all aspects of the creation of a 'workable future', cannot be free of contradiction and opportunity, even in this European form.

The focus on the political, administrative and economic form of the new Europe has obscured this kind of cultural analysis, which emphasizes the processes of production and consumption of policy. The gradual production of the idea of the common European education space is an attempt to build an identity for Europe by creating a form of governance in which lifelong learning, citizenship and the knowledge economy are shaping and being shaped together. The necessity to produce a governing discourse, in which a unity is created and projected into an identified future, is vital to governing Europe, and education/learning is now central to it. While regulation and open coordination methods can intensify and attempt to control European agents of varying kinds, network governance, attracting with different intensities mobile actors who are freely engaged in European processes, allows a soft governance to emerge, none more so than in education/learning. The language of outputs and competences cannot substitute for a collective project, with some end in view, a paradigm of transformation (Laïdi, 1998).

Europe offered the chance to produce meaning and not just results; to generate purpose and not just productivity. At the same time, it was used to 'modernize' and even enforce modernization, a task that the system actors managed, shuttling between sites. The European space is more than an ill-defined space of regulation or flows; it is a space of attraction and meaning, in which soft power is at work, creating a space in which actors are drawn to work within and produce it. It can exist, in ways not originally envisaged, as a kind of intellectual homeland.

The European education space is a condition rather than a system or a place or an object. The key element is that it is created or assembled unobtrusively, and that it is dependent on mobilities. The materiality of the 'education world' – nation states, law, buildings, traditions, design, texts, personnel – have been dissolved in policy terms and replaced by a translucent space. The density of state systems of education is unavailing, and it is bypassed or avoided. Its mass is still mainly left at the political and territorial level of the states. However the lightness of this new policy space hides its conditioning or structuring features. These include

- Production of alternative outlooks. free of direct state compliance measures, it acts as an invitational space, creating visions of new landscapes in education.
- Production of new discursive constructions of 'Europe and education'. attracting interest and possibility by the discourse of shared or new communal spaces of useful work.
- Open source method of construction. Participants are free to use and develop the ideas expressed, to share and exchange them, to construct leading edge versions, and to effect consolidation. Its meanings must be capable of shifting and contain ambiguity.
- Systemless systems. Hidden structures exist within the space, easing and shaping the production of European education – they are networks (of different levels, scale and knowledge capacities); funded programmes, projects, sponsored tasks; communication nets and associations.
- Flexible constructors. Intermittent and virtual mobilities hide contractual relations between constructors, networks and organizations. Intensity of involvement and temporal relations obscure sequences of engagement.
- Data generation. The space is observed and compared by data flow. This allows the space to be envisaged, shaped and steered. New governable policy areas and subjects come into being and into grasp.

This imaginary policy space is also an intellectual homeland. In education, it produces a freedom of attraction and assembly and allows the generation of meaning. Yet, while it appears indistinct, borderless, fluid and fragmentary, this is a space to be governed and education and/or learning is emerging in new forms and created by a complex series of European actors and processes.

ACKNOWLEDGEMENTS

I would like to thank Bob Lingard, Chris Rumford and Terri Seddon for their help with this chapter.

NOTES

1 A term used first in the late 1950s to describe the need for the training of an elite and for a common European intellectual space, a foundational idea within the Community (Corbett, 2005: 38).

REFERENCES

Anderson, B. (1983) *Imagined Communities*. London, Verso.

Ansell, C. (2000) 'The networked polity: regional development in Western Europe', *Governance*, 13: 279–291.

Beukel, E. (2001) Educational policy: institutionalization and multi level governance in S. Andersen and E. Kjell (eds) *Making Policy in Europe*, 2nd edn. London: Sage, pp. 124–139.

Borneman, J.A.F.N. (1988) 'Europeanization', *Annual Review of Anthropology*, 26: 488.

Borzel, T.V.N. (1997) 'What is so special about policy networks?', *European Integration online papers*, 1 (16) 1997-08-25.

Bos, W. and Schwippert, K. (2003) 'The use and abuse of international comparative research on student achievement', *European Educational Research Journal*, 2 (4): 559–573.

Brenner, N. (2004) *New State Spaces. Urban Governance and the Rescaling of Statehood*. Oxford: Oxford University Press.

Castells, M. (1996) *The Rise of the Network Society*. Oxford: Blackwell.

Corbett, A. (2005) *Universities and the Europe of Knowledge: Ideas, Institutions and Policy Entrepreneurship in European Union Higher Education Policy, 1955–2005*. New York; Basingstoke: Palgrave Macmillan.

Cram, L. (1998) 'The EU institutions and collective action; constructing a European interest?', in J. Greenwood and M. Aspinwall (eds) *Collective Action in the European Union*. London: Routledge, pp. 63–80.

Delanty, G and Rumford, C. (2005) *Rethinking Europe: Social Theory and the Implications of Europeanization*. London: Routledge.

Doumas, K. (2002) 'A Short Report on the INNOCULT Project', *European Educational Research Journal*, 1: 141–150.

European Education Partnership (EEP) (2002) *Partnerships in Practice*. Available at: http://www.eep-edu.org/PiP2001.pdf.

EGREES (2005) 'European Group for Research on Equity in Educational Systems. Equity in European Educational Systems: a Set of Indicators', *European Educational Research Journal*, 4: 1–151.

EGREES (2005) 'European Group for Research on Equity in Educational Systems. Equity in European Educational Systems: a Set of Indicators. Part I. Devising Indicators of Equity in Educational Systems: Why and How?', *European Educational Research Journal*, 4: 1–27.

EGREES (2005) 'European Group for Research on Equity in Educational Systems. Equity in European Educational Systems: a Set of Indicators Part II. A Set of 29 Indicators on the Equity of Educational Systems', *European Educational Research Journal*, 4: 33–92.

EGREES (2005) 'European Group for Research on Equity in Educational Systems. Equity in European Educational Systems: a Set of Indicators Part III. Equity in European Educational Systems: an Interpretation of the 29 Indicators'. *European Educational Research Journal*, 4: 1–151.

European Commission (1971) *Resolution of the Ministers of Education*. November 1971. Brussels: European Commission.

European Commission (1995) *White Paper on Education and Training – Teaching and Learning: Towards the Learning Society*. Brussels: Commission of the European Communities.

European Commission (1996) *Accomplishing Europe through Education and Training. In Training*. Luxemburg: Commission of the European Communities.

European Commission (2001a) *Lifelong Learning, Practice and Indicators*. Brussels: European Commission.

European Commission (2001b) *Making a European Area of Lifelong Learning a Reality*. Brussels: European Commission.

European Commission (2001c) *The E-learning Action Plan, Designing Tomorrow's Education*. Brussels: European Commission.

European Commission (2001d) *Report of the Eurostat Task Force on Measuring Lifelong Learning*. Brussels: European Commission.

European Commission (2005) DG EAC Final Report: External evaluation of Erasmus – institutional and national impact. CHEPS/Pricewaterhousecoopers.

Eurostat (2001) *Report of the Eurostat Task Force on Measuring Lifelong Learning*. Brussels: European Commission.

Henry, M., Lingard, B., Rizvi, F. and Taylor, S. (2001) *The OECD, Globalisation and Education Policy*. Oxford: Pergamon Press.

HEFCE (2004) *International Student Mobility*. Report by the Sussex Centre for Migration Research, University of Sussex, and the Centre for Applied Population Research, University of Dundee HEFCE Issues Paper 2004/30.

Hiatt, N. (2000) 'The Millennium Round and the liberalisation of the education market', *Education and Social Justice*, 2: 12–18.

Hingel, A. (2001) *Education Policies and European Governance*. Brussels: Directorate-Generale for Education and Culture.

Hooghe L and Marks, M. (2001) 'Types of multi-level governance', *European Integration online Papers*, 5 (11).

Kagan, R. (2002) 'Power and weakness. Why the United States and Europe see the world differently', *Policy Review Online* 113 (June/July).

Keeling, R (2006) 'The Bologna Process and the Lisbon Agenda: the European Commission's expanding role in higher education discourse', *European Journal of Education*, 4 (2): 203–224.

Kickert W. and Koppenjan J. (1997) *Managing Complex Networks: Strategies for the Public Sector*. London: Sage.

Knill, C. (2001) *The Europeanisation of National Administrations: Patterns of Institutional Change and Persistence*. Cambridge: Cambridge University Press.

Kohler-Koch, B. (ed.) (1999) *The Transformation of Governance in the European Union*. London: Routledge.

Kohler-Koch, B. (2002) European Networks and Changing National Policies. *European Integration Online Papers*, 6 (6). Available at: http://eiop.or.at/eiop/texte/2002-006a.htm.

Kokosalakis, N. (1998) *Non-official Higher Education in the European Union*. Athens: Centre for Social Morphology and Social Policy.

Laïdi, Z. (1998) *World Without Meaning - the Crisis of Meaning in International Politics*. London: Routledge.

Laïdi, Z. (ed.) (2003) *The Delocalization of Meaning*. London/New York: Routledge.

Lamy, P. (2002) 'European approach to global governance', *Progressive Politics*, 1 (1).

Lawn, M. (2001) 'Borderless education: imagining a European education space in a time of brands and networks', in *Discourse*, 22: 173–184.

Lawn, M. and Lingard, R. (2002) 'Constructing a European Policy Space in Educational Governance: the Role of Transnational Policy Actors', EERJ, vol. 1, No. 2.

Lawn, M. (2006) 'Soft governance and the learning spaces of Europe', *Comparative European Politics* 4.

Lawn, M. (2007) 'Governing by Association in Europe ? The problems of the unstable policy network', *Critical Studies in Education [Melbourne Studies in Education]*.

Lindblad, S., and Popkewitz, T. (ed.) (1999) *Education Governance and Social Integration and Exclusion: National Cases of Educational Systems and Recent Reforms*. Uppsala: University of Uppsala Reports on Education.

Lindblad, S. and Popkewitz, T. (ed.) (2000) *Public Discourses on Education Governance and Social Integration and Exclusion: Analyses of Policy Texts in European Contexts*. Uppsala: University of Uppsala Reports on Education.

Lindblad, S., and Popkewitz, T. (ed.) (2001) *Listening to Education Actors on Governance and Social Integration and Exclusion*. Uppsala: University of Uppsala Reports on Education.

Mayntz, R. (1994) *Modernization and the Logic of Interorganizational Networks*. Cologne: Max Planck Institute.

Novoa, A. (2000) The restructuring of the European educational space: Changing relationships among states, citizens and educational communities', in T.E. Popkewitz (ed.) *Educational Knowledge Changing relationships between the State, Civil Society and the Educational Community*. Albany, NY: State University of New York Press, pp. 31–57.

Novoa, A. (ed.) (2002) *Fabricating Europe: the Formation of an Education Space*. Amsterdam: Kluwer.

Nye, J. (2004) *Soft Power – the Means to Success in World Politics*. New York: Public Affairs.

Pereyra, M. (2002) 'Changing educational governance in Spain: decentralisation and control in the autonomous communities', *European Educational Research Journal*, 1: 667–675.

Reich, R.B. (1991) *The Work of Nations*. New York: Vintage Books.

Robertson S and Dale, R. (2004) 'ICT as medium, target, benchmark and outcome for Schooling the Future/Learning Europe', Draft paper, AERA Conference, San Diego.

Scheerens, J. and Hendricks, M (eds) (2004) 'Benchmarking the quality of education', *European Educational Research Journal*, 3: 101–399.

Shore, C. (2000) *Building Europe: the Cultural Politics of European Integration*. London: Routledge.

Silova, I. (2002) 'The manipulated consensus: globalisation, local agency, and cultural legacies in post-Soviet education reform', *European Educational Research Journal*, 1: 308–330.

Slowinski, J. (1998) 'SOCRATES invades Central Europe', *Education Policy Analysis Archives*, 6 (9).

Sprokkereef, A. (1995) 'Developments in European Community education policy'. in J.E. Lodge (ed.). *The European Community and the Challenge of the Future*, 2nd edn. London: Pinter.

Urry, J. (2000a) 'Mobile sociology', *British Journal of Sociology*, 51: 185–203.

Urry, J. (2000b) *Sociology Beyond Societies: Mobilities for the Twenty-First Century*. New York: Routledge.

Urry, J. (2003) *Global Complexity*. Cambridge: Polity.

Walters W and Haahr, J. (2005) *Governing Europe. Discourse, Governmentality and European Integration*. London: Routledge.

Zambeta., E. (2002) 'Modernisation of educational governance in Greece: from state control to state steering', *European Educational Research Journal*, 1: 637–655.

29

Network Europe and the Information Society

Barrie Axford

The idea of 'Network Europe' remains a challenge to much received wisdom about the construction of European spaces of governance and sociality. For as well as promising a 'relativization of scale' through connectivity (Jessop, 2000), arguably, networks constitute a new form of social organization. As Amin has noted, 'The growing routinization of global network practices manifest through mobility and connectivity signals a perforation of scalar and territorial forms of social organization. This subverts any ontology of territorial containment and scalar nesting' (2002: 395). Conventional scales such as the territorial state, as well as other bounded spaces, become links or nodes in wider networks. On the wilder shores of possibility, networks constitute sociospatial forms in which 'neither boundaries nor relations mark the difference between one place and another' (Mol and Law, 1994: 643). Indeed, this may be *the* most potent charge in the idea of 'Network Europe', which concept might otherwise be taken for a convenient summary of routine linkages and transfers, a description of organizational change, a variant on the dynamics of interest group mediation,

or a functional–technical solution to the coordination problems of modern governance. Recourse to these more cautious applications is hardly reprehensible and all have contributed to a deeper understanding of different aspects of Europe-making and especially EU governance. They also serve to temper enthusiasm for more exotic fare which places an 'excessive emphasis on purportedly new features of social life' (Holton, 2005: 210) where networked, circulating entities replace the conventional architectures of borders, territoriality and sovereignty, along with traditional identities.

All of which is salutary since the cautious analyst must qualify talk of transformation with a little down-home realism. Most obviously, a Europe still made up of unified spatiotemporal units (nation-states and societies obviously, but also constructs such as 'fortress' Europe) is unlikely to be unmade completely by the activities of transnational networks of whatever kind. Rather, network links, especially where they cross borders, are more likely to create 'qualitative disjunctures' between different regulatory, sociocultural and political environments at the same time as they enable routine connection between actors separated across time and space (Dicken *et al.*, 2001: 96). Even now, when mobile commodities such as finance capital flow through and around places, states continue to supply key infrastructures for inter and transnational agents and practices. Although states may be increasingly 'denationalized', as Sassen has it, and the national frame of reference deconstructed in some of its signature forms, many European and global networks are constituted in national practice and owe their dynamism to those 'vertebrate' structures which instantiate the modern trinity of identities, borders and orders (Albert *et al.*, 2001; Appadurai, 2006; Lapid, 2001; Sassen, 2006).

The result is a welter of 'mixed spatio-temporal assemblages of territoriality', many produced and networked in the overlapping and intersecting spaces and times of the local, national, regional and global (Sassen, 2006: 397) and, for the analyst, accessible only by careful attention to 'analytic border-lands' (Sassen, 2006: 379–80) where spatial and temporal disruptions or events occur. Indeed, these may be the most obvious emergent properties of an integrating Europe, one that is not simply defined by the expanding borders of the EU. Of course, as part of this dynamic tension the national scale may well lose specific components of the state's formal authority, while other scales – both sub- and supranational – gain strategic clout.

Inevitably there are intriguing variations on this theme and one is very pertinent to this chapter. In Saskia Sassen's recent opus, digital networks sometimes 'confront' state authority (2006: 330), but as she notes, this is only one way of comprehending the complexity of social practices and authority relations revealed in the use of technologies whose key property is a challenge to the very idea of boundaries, but which also enable actors to reinvent the idea of locality, often tied to territory (Axford, 2006). In her terms the European Information Society (EIS) Project and its progeny are just such 'mixed assemblages' of practice and power, part of

a putative transformation which, in time, may prove a paradigm for the shift of capacity from the nation state onto 'global digital assemblages' (Sassen, 2006: 331). These new assemblages are neither national nor global, so they beggar simple analytic dualities and, as Sassen opines, 'master categories'. Because they are not subsumed by, or necessarily predicated on, the existence of national, regional or global scales, institutions and practices, they may well express a new sociological reality. At the very least their existence is a further challenge to the ideology and practices of methodological nationalism which still vitiate our understanding of transnational and global phenomena.

To reiterate: the signal charge in any discussion of networks and European integration is that they enable 'multi-scalar transactions and (in the case of ICT networks) simultaneous interconnectivity among those still largely confined to locality' and thus, 'bypass older hierarchies of scale' (Sassen, 2004: 651). As elements in the imbrication of local, national, European and global they may also constitute what Karin Knorr-Cetina calls *microstructures* – 'forms of connectivity and coordination that combine global reach with microstructural mechanisms that instantiate self-organizing principles and patterns' (2007: 65). She adds that 'global systems based on microstructural principles do not exhibit institutional complexity but rather the asymmetries, unpredictability, and playfulness of complex (and dispersed) interaction patterns, a complexity that results, as Urry says, 'from a situation where order is not the outcome of purified social processes and is always intertwined with chaos' (Knorr-Cetina, 2007: 68; see also Urry, 2003: 106).

Applied specifically to the construction of the European Information Society (EIS) these are radical enough formulations, which as we shall see receive partial endorsement from an analysis of the EIS programme itself. Looked at from a more cautious perspective, the whole EIS project is, in large measure, a perfect mirror of the uncertain character of the integrative project in Europe. At one and the same time it is resolutely statist, intergovernmental and territorial, as well as being a harbinger of a postnational networked polity in Europe or a 'scopic system' replete with Europe-making effects delivered through 'new' media technologies (Knorr-Cetina, 2007). We will return to this theme below.

While much theorizing on European integration still cleaves to a Cartesian model of bounded space (work cited in Pollack, 2005) at the other extreme some commentators have invoked the idea of a borderless, de-territorialized Europe, imparting an almost hyperglobalist feel to the debate about the transformative potential of network connection (*pace* Held *et al.*, 1999; Jensen and Richardson, 2004). Of course, these seeming antinomies simply reflect standard models of twentieth century society and world (dis)order in which the national or transnational, as well as some abstract version of 'global', were, and sometimes still are, treated as discrete or singular scales of social interaction (Mann, 1998: 184). As noted above, these formulations do very little to address the real complexity of the extension of communicative and social relations across European and world space, or allow us to rethink the obdurate though changing nature of existing modalities, including the territorial state and the idea of the national.

By contrast, this chapter will offer a preliminary treatment of Network(ed) Europe in which 'networks, including new media networks of information and communication' – perhaps forms of 'scopic media' – constitute social and technological infrastructures of an increasingly fluid Europe, one expressed through 'relationalities' as much as formal structures (Sassen, 2006; Van Dijk, 1999). Such usage enables an account of European integration which is not bracketed by received models and theories mired in accounts of bounded territoriality or simplistic images of linear, nested scalarity. The upshot is a more textured understanding of processes of 'coordination, complexity, acceleration and control', as well as of those promoting a 'radical interdependence across borders'

(Campbell, 1995: 96), all without making teleological assumptions about particular European endgames or endorsing ideological prescriptions on the demeanour of the emergent European polity. The approach offers the beginnings of a systematic morphological account of polity building in contemporary Europe.

At the same time, we should stress that network models often appear in accounts of European integration, largely stripped of the transformative motif, and this parallels much use of the network 'metaphor' across the social sciences, where the concept is employed with a substantial degree of analytical freedom. At one remove it is used as a 'simple descriptive template laid over a range of empirical phenomena' (Crozier, 2006: 1). At another, it is allowed greater analytical power with some meso-systemic implications, and much of the work of the interest mediation and governance schools falls into this category (Boudourides, 2002). As noted above, only the strongest analytical claims attempt a systematic morphological or social action account of transformative societal and trans-societal change.

We shall begin by looking at just how the concept *network* has been employed across the social sciences, reflecting on network morphologies, and in particular on how certain types of network may promote new forms of connection across scales and new assemblages and microstructures of power. Such an approach is necessary to underline the strengths, but also the weaknesses of the network metaphor. We will then examine network applications that afford insights into a Europe becoming more integrated, but also more pluralistic, decentralized and fluid than is sometimes assumed. Finally, we will address the concept of Network Europe directly, through a consideration of some of the strongest analytical claims, before considering the EIS as a proto-paradigm case of the network polity/society. Following Dicken *et al.* (2001: 96) the argument privileges the idea of Network Europe as a complex of relational processes manifested across a 'multiplicity of geographical and organizational scales' and displaying a complex territoriality. Such a view cannot be limited to official EU information policy strands or see the EU as its sole author. The chapter ends on the scope for future research based on, but not limited by, the network metaphor.

NETWORK METAPHORS AND NETWORK MORPHOLOGIES

A network is an arrangement of nodes tied together by relationships – some instrumental, some affective – that serve as channels of communication, resources, and other coordinating mechanisms. 'Cooperation of various kinds, strategic alliances, exchanges, emotional bonds, kinship ties, personal relations, and forms of grouping and entrenchment can all be seen to work through ties and to instantiate sociality in networks of relationships' (Knorr-Cetina, 2007: 72). The *raison d'être* of networks, and especially communication networks, is to free the agent/user from the bonds of place (Lovink and Schneider, 2004). These are strong claims and, curiously, somewhat at odds with Knorr-Cetina's sense, noted above, that networks are 'sparse' rather than dense social structures. It does, however, bear on some of the vexed issues in discussions of network approaches to social organization and social change.

In many accounts of networks and notably in actor–network theory (Callon, 1999; Latour, 1997) 'hybrid collectives' of individuals, organizations, objects and discourses (Callon, 1999) are seen as exemplars of the fluid and mutable nature of the current global political and cultural economies, constituting new 'architectures of complexity' (Kenis and Schneider, 1991: 25: Podolny, 2001). Even in critical accounts network ontology is often set against the rigidities of hierarchy or the amoral demeanour of markets and found to be a plausible alternative mode of social organization (Thompson, 2003). But with some notable exceptions, network ontology is usually read as 'thin' when set against the 'thick' identities couched in bounded states and societies and various hierarchical solidaries; consisting of only instrumental relationships stretched across, underneath or heedless of borders and geographical space. In the words of a recent reviewer, 'compared to the strong social embeddedness of formal organizations and markets and their institutional and legal ties, networks emerge as nearly devoid of institutional anchoring and social implications' (Kallinikos, 2004: 1). Critically, in terms of polity or state building, network structures and network identities are often cast as too fluid – always on the cusp between dynamism and entropy – to support sound infrastructures of meaning and sustainable rules of resource allocation. In much the same vein, Knorr-Cetina opines that because of this weakness, 'relational connectivity may not be enough to effectively organize complex systems' (2007: 68).

For all that, images of the network are widely employed to capture 'the emergent social and political forms of this inter-connected, technology-driven world' (Appadurai, 2006: 24; Blatter, 2003; Holton, 2005), which morphology is intimated with some panache by Michel Foucault in his treatment of nondisciplinary power (Foucault, 1975). Barry (*pace* Foucault) also reinforces the point that the concept of network crosses the divide between technical and social, and his work offers a view of transnational governance (notably in the EU) in which technologies (especially ICTs) – 'arrangements of artefacts, practices and techniques, instruments and bodies' (2001: 103) – produce a networked infrastructure of governmentality. That he does not provide any real insights into the key notion of 'technical culture' applied to the EIS, or even of culture as the realm of meaning, is a weakness, but does not detract from the main charge in the work, which is to chart the politicization of technology.

So the network metaphor has all the attributes of a late/postmodern *zeitgeist*, exemplifying social process at odds with the organizational practices of boundary maintenance and the hierarchical decision rules through which such practices have been sustained. But as Bulkeley notes, such recognition must not prescribe an either–or model in which scales no longer matter (2005). Rather, it involves 'rejecting the notion of scale as a bounded, territorially complete concept, and of any notion that social relations are contained at particular scales' (2005: 884). As Brenner argues, 'scales evolve relationally within tangled hierarchies and dispersed inter-scalar networks' (2001: 605), and 'the very intelligibility of each scalar articulation of a social process hinges crucially upon its embeddedness within dense webs of relations to other scales and spaces' (2001: 606; see also Painter, 2004). Such insights are necessary and salutary, but the potential for integrating scalar and networked accounts of spatiality in Europe depends very much on how the concept of network is conceived and used.

Undoubtedly, the ubiquity of the network metaphor itself presents difficulties for definitional clarity and use. Robert Holton says that the 'typology of networks now extends to business and trade, policy and advocacy, knowledge and the professions, together with empire and terror, kinship and friendship, religion and migration' (2005: 209) and even this may be too modest a canvass. Painter (2004) offers a nuanced yet permissive typology in which *transmission networks* enable the flows of substances and agents and include the sort of multiscalar commodity chains at the heart of world-systems research, *social networks* comprise the links created through social relations, *actor-networks* involve both the movement of material things and the simultaneous creation of social relations, with the emphasis on practices rather than structures, and *topological networks* describe the complex spatiality of actor-networks.

These are useful distinctions for empirical investigation, and it may be that European networks populate all of these categories. However, actor-network theory (ANT) in particular appears to provide some analytical purchase on the construction of Network Europe and also captures the vagaries of the EIS, not only because it recognizes that more

is happening in networked relationships than transfers between actors – mere connectivity – but through its adherence to relationalities which link social and technological, human and non-human, thus depicting a world 'always in process' (Thrift, 1999: 62). Applied to the idea of Network Europe and the trope of the European Information Society, ANT identifies what Urry terms 'complex, enduring and predictable, networked relationships between people, objects and technologies stretching across multiple and distant spaces and time' (Urry, 2003: 57). These networks may be 'significantly de-territorialized' (2003: 58) but they may well be inserted into territories across all scales (Axford, 2006). Thus do Fligstein and Stone Sweet remind us that '[w]e need to account for how networks emerge in the first place, and we need to understand them more dynamically, as they evolve within the macro-social environments in which they operate'. Put bluntly, 'networks do not spontaneously arise, nor are they self-sustaining. Instead, relationships between producers, consumers, owners, and competitors are, among other things, embedded in relations with government actors, with legislators, administrators, and courts, as these relations are structured by institutions' (Fligstein and Stone Sweet: 2002, 14; Sassen, 2004).

Such complex topologies and structures produce a variety of networked relationships, some relatively contained by geographical and territorial boundaries, others manifestly trans-boundary or global. Europe so configured would be a network of actor networks, each enacting a more Europeanized existence through their dynamism and variable reach. Even if we acknowledge that being 'Europeanized' may be a purely instrumental outcome, it is possible to see how the morphology of networks might facilitate such a shift. First, networks can be intra- and inter- as well as trans-organizational, cutting across more conventional boundaries to establish linkages between different personal, institutional and technological domains. Second, networks can structure social relationships without constraint of place or the need for co-presence. Third, networks promote diverse forms of social mobilization and practice where relationships may be long-distance and involve a mixture of presence and absence (Axford and Huggins, 1999; Knorr-Cetina, 2007).

In short, network analysis allows a looseness and diversity at one with the inchoate character of contemporary Europe and offers a glimpse of the diverse contexts through which a more acute consciousness of it is occurring for many people. But whether it is right to say that political and economic geographies in Europe have now become a matter of association and connectivity, not space, is still open to question (Latour, 1997; Brenner, 1999, 2004). With some caution, we can say that networks and network metaphors are destabilizing Euclidean geometry, rendering conventional borders and institutional orders much less of a 'toplogical presupposition' (Thrift and Olds, 1996; see also Axford, 2006) and showing that what appears to be natural or given in the order of the world, is in fact produced through networks that *enact* quite different kinds of spatiality. Such optimism still leaves questions about the theoretical adequacy and empirical purchase of the network metaphor.

NETWORKS AND EUROPE

Powell and Smith-Doerr (1994) distinguish between the use of network as an analytical tool which aids social research by mapping the topological structures of social interaction, and networks as a form of governance or organizational modality. We might add a further nuance which distinguishes the ontological status of networks as actors from networks as the context or condition for action. These are subtle inflections on what might otherwise appear as a straightforward identification of types allied to a rather more difficult exploration of tactical and strategic power exercised through relational processes

and structures. But the simple fact is that network metaphors are increasingly common in discourses on EU and European integration, notably under one or other versions of the (new) governance motif. Occasionally, as we shall see, far stronger analytical claims are made for a systematic morphological account of contemporary Europe using network concepts. For convenience these different versions will be grouped as *micro, meso and macro* approaches to describe the scope of their systemic implications. We will concentrate upon *meso* and *macro* accounts, but a word is necessary about *micro* analysis in order to identify some particular features of the impact of ICTs and networks on organizational governance and organizational identity in the Europe.

Microsystemic applications are concerned primarily with intraorganizational dynamics and forms and, as a focus of research, currently subject to a good deal of ethnographic investigation. However, microsystemic applications are not always so fine-grained. Take the case of the European Information Society Project (EISP) and its spawn the *e*Europe initiative, now 'one of the dominant models for governing the EU' (Shahin, 2004: 177). Here the intriguing fact is that a policy strand introduced to bolster EU/Europe as a global player in economic terms – with ICTs seen as the technological interface between Europe and its competitors – has also driven profound changes in the conduct of public administration in the Commission and member states. Arguably, it also represents a shift in the demeanour of EU policy development, from 'harder' to 'softer' methods of coordination and control; from an emphasis on regulation to use of the Open Method of Coordination (OMC) between stakeholders (Borras and Jacobssen, 2004. Of course, such an interpretation is not uncontested (Barry, 2001; Radaelli, 2002) and we should beware any form of technological determinism. Nonetheless, the impact of *e*Europe upon institutional change, particularly within the Commission, was and remains a significant aspect of EU governance even though much of the organizational innovation revealed falls into the realm of *e*government, that is, the device of using digital tools to improve the delivery of public services and making public administration more efficient (Shahin, 2004).

As Mark Pollack notes, theories of European integration address ' a variety of topics including *inter alia* the workings of the EU's legislative, executive and judicial processes, [and] the prospects of socialization or deliberation in EU institutions' (2005: 391; see also Schmitter, 1996). We should also note that much of this reflection provides informative, but still largely 'internalist' views of how Europe/EU is being constructed. He also notes the preponderance of middle-range theorizing on the shape and demeanour of EU polity. Mesosystemic accounts reveal a variety of approaches and empirical referents and an increasing number have resort to network models of EU governance (e.g. Barry, 2001; Castells, 1996, 2001; Leonard, 1999; Mann, 1998; Ruggie, 1992; Warleigh, 2000). Fossum tells us that '[g]overnance is not political rule through responsible institutions, such as parliament and bureaucracy – which amounts to government – but innovative practices of networks, or horizontal forms of interaction. It is a method for dealing with political controversies in which actors, political and non-political, arrive at mutually acceptable decisions by deliberating and negotiating with each other' (2006: 119). Pollack also notes that network forms of governance have been extended and intensified during the past decade or so through 'the creation of formal and informal networks of national regulators in areas such as competition policy, utilities regulation, and financial regulation' (2005: 383–5). In contrast to 'most students of legislative politics who emphasize the importance of formal rules in shaping actors' behaviour and polity outcomes, students of policy networks emphasize the informal politics of the EU, in which such networks of private and public actors substantially determine the broad contours of the policies that are eventually brought before the Council and the European Parliament for their formal adoption' (Pollack, 2005: 383–5).

Influenced by both international relations and comparative politics approaches the 'new' governance motif in EU studies employs ideas about nonhierarchical networks, public–private interactions, and governance without government (Bache and Flinders, 2004; Hix, 1998; Jachtenfuchs, 2001; Rosenau and Czempiel, 1992). Other writers have commented on the horizontal dimensions of European integration, using network approaches to describe and explain the workings of transborder networks of relatively closed policy communities populated by public and private actors, as well as the more open networks found in areas such as environmental regulation, the 'open space' ideologies of social forum politics and other third sector or civil society actors (Patomaki and Taiveinen, 2004; Van Audenhove *et al.*, 2005). The relative openness, interdependence and power of these networks invest both the influence of various actors and the substantive content of EU policies (Peterson, 2004).

These insights add considerably to our understanding of the workings of EU policy networks, the transformation of territorial governance, and the prospects for deliberative cosmopolitan democracy at the EU level (Ansell, 2000; Held, 2007; Rumford, 2006, 2007). At the same time much of what they offer is still rooted in forms of methodological nationalism where territory and rationality remain the most powerful constitutive rules. Furthermore, as noted earlier, much work on policy networks in the EU is simply a variant on the study of interest mediation, or sees policy networks mainly as a functional solution to the coordination problems of modern states (Axford and Huggins, 1999; Borzel, 1997). For example, in their study of 'dual networks' in EU regional development policy, Ansell *et al.* (1997) offer a gloss on the standard treatment of multilevel governance (multilevel policy networks) but rely on a basically territorialist model to depict networks built upon the exchange of resources in the form of information and technical assistance across still discrete levels of government (see also Marks, 1993; Rhodes, 1996; Sandholtz and Stone Sweet, 1998).

Even Castells' powerful account of the network state in Europe, to which we shall return later, is informed by these considerations. However, for all its faults, it is easy to misread Castells' concept of the network state in Europe as delineating a European 'state' that is an *uber* version of the national incarnation, albeit in the relatively *stateless* Anglo-American version, rather than the fully institutionalized and centralized model historically more common in continental Europe (Badie and Birnbaum, 1983). In fact he argues that territorial states across Europe are becoming more like the EU in its 'regulatory state' guise (Majone, 1996). In this model, states, including the EU, develop and enhance local and global networks as well as becoming more networked themselves to deal with the vicissitudes of a globalized world visited through environmental risks, agile crime and terror networks, mobility of people, things and flows of capital and information and the diffuse and porous borders that permit them.

This is a key insight and one which underlines the importance of stepping outside the imagery and 'inarticulate major premises' of territoriality (Caparaso, 1996). These premises have acted, and probably still continue to act, as a 'conceptual grid' informing both theoretical and practitioner discourse on European integration (1996). But the processes of globalization and of European integration have relativized identities and territories, by penetrating or dissolving the boundaries around such relatively closed systems, and by creating trans-societal and trans- and post-territorial discursive spaces and networks of relationships. Along the way, important local, national, European and global transformations may be in train; for example, in existing signifiers such as locality, and in the key associations of citizenship and nationality (Axford and Huggins, 1999). Because of these shifts, it is now a matter of dispute as to what constitutes a (political) community in Europe (and elsewhere), and what factors define and legitimate various statuses under it.

Of course, the relative statelessness of EU policy dynamics is also found in many accounts of multilevel governance. But the imagery can be much more dramatic, depicting a Europe 'branching into fractal nets' or 'neo-world orders' (Luke, 1995). Such radical scenarios intimate a more dynamic, more interconnected, yet more fluid milieu for enacting authority and managing flows of influence from multiple sources than can be contained by the Euclidean geometry and identity spaces of territorialized or superterritorialized modernity *pace* much of the MLG literature.

This kind of Network Europe requires a theory of connections (Marcussen and Torfing, 2007; Urry, 2003) and probably a theory of changed borders – to account for both networked and 'cosmopolitan borders' (Rumford, 2007). But it remains very difficult to break out of the territorial/superterritorial trap. Even the intuitively appealing idea of multilevel Europe with its linear metaphor of scales (multiscalar) stretching from micro to macro levels fails to afford such a theory, or to illuminate the difficult conceptual terrain between methodological nationalism and 'spaces of flows' (Pries, 2005).

To be sure, attempts to traverse this terrain are available. Rumford notes that '[i]n the past few years "polycentricity" [the idea that Europe is characterized by multiple centres and diffused growth rather than conventional core-periphery distinctions] has entered the lexicon of EU spatial politics as a useful way of thinking about the decentred, deterritorialized, and "smooth" economic space of the EU (Jensen and Richardson, 2004). On this reading, the EU is not a superstate or suprastate, or even a form of multilevel governance, but a more decentred (or multicentred) spatial arrangement' (Rumford, 2007: 4). Rumford writes convincingly of the tension between a networked Europe thus configured and a Europe (EU) of hard external borders – 'Schengenland', either densely networked within, or bruited as a single, integrated space without internal barriers – a 'monotopia' (Delanty and Rumford, 2005; Jensen and Richardson, 2004). But in a Europe of networked or even 'cosmopolitan borders' conventional scales and notions of territoriality become, if not nugatory, then diffuse; even moot (Balibar, 1999).

Yet, in the kind of cross-border, networked practices and forms already identifiable in what Rumford calls 'postwestern' Europe (2007: 6), scales and territory do not cease to matter. Rather, as the case of cross-border regions (CBRs) in Europe exemplifies, instead of abrogating territoriality *per se*, CBRs actually aim to regenerate particular territories (Christansen *et al.*, 1999) or look to find common ground between them. In this guise they appear as both transnational and intensely local, with 'overlapping areas of institutional authority' (Wallace and Wallace, 1996: 41). Moreover, CBRs are also drivers for building multilevel governance through networks (Kohler-Koch, 2002; Perkmann, 1999). As structures of governance (but also as communicative spaces, where local articulates with national and beyond) they often operate in a network-like fashion to effect cross-border joint action/ cooperation, and produce what Jessop (2002, 34–5) calls 'inter-localization', even 'inter-regionalization'. This consists of horizontal linkages between contiguous localities which are on the same scale (local) but in different national scales (Strihan, 2005). To this extent, locality (as scale) can be seen as an outcome of network interaction at the same time as 'scale fragmentation' (Lissandrello, 2003) means that in such contexts the local is no longer a clearly defined and certainly not a discrete scale for governance purposes. As avatars for a Europe made through connections and flows, rather than bordered grids, CBRs are innovative forms of networked transnationalism (Axford, 2006).

All this promotes a more fine-grained account of network connectivity, but it is some way off a theory of connections, or even of transnationalization. 'Transnationalization' is a generic term for what Pries calls 'the growing quantitative and qualitative importance of pluri-local and trans-national social relations, networks and practices' (2004: 13). He also opines that transnational social spaces offer multilocal frames of reference beyond the social contexts of national societies. As a process, transnationalization may produce 'new and complex frameworks of regulations and institutions, new values, norms and rules and new patterns of behaviour' (2004: 14). Critically, while some forms of transnational practice are no more than movements or exchanges between the container space of one territorial entity and another, other practices intimate at least a transition – and possibly a transformation – to 'post-national scales of political and economic governance in Europe today' (Kramsch, 2003: 214; see also Kastoryano, 2002).

Most meso-level approaches to governance and transnationalization in Europe today shy away from the transformative motif and yet the idea of Network Europe is redolent with such imagery. For example, in his well-known analysis of the 'unbundling' of statist sovereignty in Europe, John Ruggie intimates that the EU may be the world's first post-modern form of transnational governance (1992). Ruggie's interpretation of the EU as a 'space of flows' rather than a territory to be governed or regulated in the conventional sense of these terms was a timely reminder not to confuse the construction of despatial-ized networks and communities or neocommunities with the processes of nation- and state-building characteristic of the transition from premodern to modern societies. A strong reading of Ruggie's account depicts Europe – 'united' Europe – as a space created and reproduced through transnational, regional and local networks of interaction, involving, for example, cultural, commercial, scientific, financial and educational actors and interests.

The same model of complex interdependence across borders is glimpsed in Manuel Castells's allusive discussion of the 'network state' in Europe (1996, 1998, 2001). For Castells, the network state is a product of globalization and his argument about its emergence in Europe is heavily functionalist. He says, '[W]hile most economic activity and most jobs in the world are national, regional, or even local, the core, strategic economic activities are globally integrated in the Information Age through electronically enacted networks of exchange of capital, commodities, and information. It is this global integration that induces and shapes the current process of European unification, on the basis of European institutions historically constituted around predominantly political goals' (2001: 2). So the network state is characterized by the sharing of authority along a network, and a network by definition, has nodes, not a centre. Nodes may be of different sizes, and may be linked by asymmetrical relationships in the network. Yet, 'regardless of these asymmetries, the various nodes of the European network are interdependent on each other, so that no node, even the most powerful, can ignore the others, even the smallest in the decision-making process. If some political nodes do so, the whole political system is called into question. This is the difference between a political network and a centred political structure. Amongst the responses of political systems to the challenge of globalization, the European Union may be the clearest manifestation to date of this emerging form of state, probably characteristic of the Information Age' (2001: 5).

In his challenging account of the politicization of technology, Andrew Barry (2001) explores the proposition that spaces of governance are not simply defined by geographies of territorial and national space. Discussing governance in the EU he argues that much political discourse has become focused on the government of technology, and that key policy initiatives are centred on the development of digitally skilled workforces and citizens. The EIS is a paradigm for these shifts because it grew out of dissatisfaction with received models of EU development – pure market liberalism or state-centred implementation of Community policy. Network models of governance and cross-border connection begun through scientific cooperation and seen as likely to spawn various kinds of 'spillover', were not only conjured as an efficient path to the information society in Europe, but a means of bypassing the national scale.

For all this, Barry is unconvinced by Castells' account of the network state in Europe. Largely his critique is based on the a rejection of Castells' implicit functionalism, which has the network state springing fully armed to protect and promote the EU in the lists of a networked global economy. But he is also exercised by the sense that the EU is not all that well networked in key areas such as harmonization and standardization or through civic association and the realms of public talk. At the same time he is prepared to admit that the EU is 'a political institution in which the model of the network has come to provide a dominant sense of political possibilities' (2001: 101) and this is a signal admission, pointing up the potential for transformation in institutions and practices.

Michael Mann is also exercized by changes/transformations in statist and other infrastructures in a period of multiple globalizations, 'involving the combined strengthening of transnational, international and national networks of interaction' (2006: 541; 1998: 184–207). In this scenario, 'Euro', as he puts it, is just a web of interaction networks, composed of multiple, overlapping and intersecting networks of technical specialists, Euromanagers, businesses, Socrates exchange students, advocacy coalitions, civic associations and financial centres. Euro lacks overall internal cohesion of the sort that is standard in many territorial states and, significantly, it also defies external closure; and this judgement seems as valid in the twenty-first century as in the previous decade.

Of course, Castells' references to a European network state are grounded in a much more encompassing theoretical and empirical account of the emergence of network societies (1996, 1998, 2000, 2001) and rehearse the advantages a network perspective for a systematic understanding of contemporary social development. Although it traffics at the meso-level for much of the empirical detail used, this is really a macromorphological and transformationalist argument. Network morphologies and network logic overtake other forms of social organization, and this logic 'permeates and transforms all realms of social and economic life, initiating a higher level of social determination hitherto unknown' (Crozier, 2006: 17).

The weaknesses in Castells' general argument are legion and have been subjected to a torrent of critique (see e.g., Barney, 2004; Barry, 2001; Thompson, 2003). Suffice to mention here that there is a rather easy acceptance of the one-size-fits-all model of social change, such that networks conceived as technologies are seen as the solution to problems of communication, empowerment, community and democracy; while networks conceived as social and political relations are portrayed as functional responses to globalization and the economic and social problems of national societies. Finally, network forms of governance or state are reflections of the change to the information and knowledge society. In effect, for Castells, networks *become* society whether in national or transnational guise.

Criticism apart, Castells' great contribution to this debate is to allow us to think of Europe/EU as a highly connected space (see also Scott, 2002). Moreover, his perspective stresses the unfinished business of global and European integration. It rejects any sense of ontological closure and regional boundedness largely because of the topologies of network connection. So, even if the notion of a Europe as a network state is counterintuitive, it permits Castells to identify the rescaling of territory (and of state power) being effected through integration processes. If the EU is organized around the dynamics of mobility and interconnection, as an institutional order it is also engaged in the business of managing and regulating movement and flow.

Unlike Castells, writers, such as, Van Djik and Messner are less inclined to treat networks as uncoupled from various social, material, physical and biological contexts (Messner 1997; Van Dijk, 1999; and see Sassen, 2004, on this theme) although Van Djik in particular insists that communication networks (new media) must be treated as part of a theory of modernization involving both time–space distanciation and the disembedding of action

from particular contexts (*pace* Giddens, 1991a, 1991b). Moreover, both authors try to ensure that, unlike Castells, social action is not subsumed by the complexity of network morphology. Again, such cautionary notes have relevance for any discussion of the EIS where it is easy to fall into an unreflective technological determinism.

All three authors canvassed above are interested in how, across the various realms of social life, scale extension and scale reduction are interrelated in contemporary societies, and each privileges the increasing role of new social and media networks. Van Djik has it thus: 'Modern social networks and new media networks of information and communication technology are necessary conditions for the combination of scale extension and scale reduction that currently characterizes all spheres of society. The existence of these networks provides this combination with its social and technological infrastructure' (Van Dijk, 1999: 23) 0 the 'network society'.

Before addressing the EIS directly, let us revisit two other formulations alluded to earlier in the chapter which have novel import for any discussion of spatial politics, Network Europe and the role of ICTs in its construction. In her account of the constitution of different historical assemblages and spatio-temporal frames for social activity, Saskia Sassen develops an argument about the imbrication and mutual constitution of digital and nondigital domains and networked actors by focusing on three key components of the social embeddedness of computer-centred interactive technologies. These are the complex interactions between digital and nondigital domains; the destabilizing of existing hierarchies of scale made possible by such technologies, and the mediating cultures that organize the relations between technologies and users (2006: 325–77). Critically, 'neither territory nor the kind of territoriality that became a key component of the nation-state and of exclusive state authority are at work' in these networks (2006: 326). Digital assemblages operate in what she calls an 'in-between type of spatio-temporal order'

(2006: 379) understood as an 'analytic borderland'. Functionalist accounts notwithstanding, containment by national actors and domains or, by implication, any territorialist conceit, is always likely to be imperfect. Rather, such novel assemblages are likely to be highly disruptive 'insertions' into national and regional scales.

Now, Sassen does not discuss the EIS in this, the fullest statement of her work on global orders. However, the insight afforded into its construction and demeanour by her concept of global digital assemblages is important, suggesting both a 'destabilizing of older hierarchies of scale and the emergence of not fully formalized new ones' (2006: 329). Elsewhere in her previous work on networking in Europe she notes, 'computer-centred interactive technologies facilitate multi-scalar transactions and simultaneous interconnectivity among those largely confined to a locality'. In so doing 'they bypass older hierarchies of scale' (2004: 651). Individual and collective actors connected across conventional scales of political allegiance and activism are no longer confined to domestic roles, but become actors in Europe-wide communication networks, all 'without having to leave their work and roles in their communities'. They may not have become cosmopolitan as a result, let alone 'Europeanized', and yet they are participating in an emergent politics of Europe making (Sassen, 2004, see also Bartolini, 2006).

Sassen's other contributions to the idea of Europe as a network polity are also pertinent to any discussion of the EIS. First is her insistence on the role of private corporate interests and 'informal' activist networks in shaping the activity space of the Internet. Recognizing its segmented, asymmetrical and contested character redresses the vision of the Internet and other digital technologies as functional tools in the service of EU economic competitiveness or as a technical means of promoting a European cultural meta-narrative (Axford and Huggins, 1996). Both of these strands informed the origins of the EIS (Bangemann, 1994, 1997), coupled

to an enduring policy dynamic – partly instrumental, partly expressive – that ICTs are an enabling factor for 'improving public services and democratic processes and (to) strengthen and support public policies (EU Commission, 2003: 7).

In Sassen's version, the Internet and digital networks would not be considered simply as instruments of statism or neostatism in Europe – of system integration, but as relational processes, decentralized, potentially unmanageable and not necessarily predicated on the existence of EU institutions and policies. Her second insight is to identify a specific kind of agency, carried and articulated through multiple localities and connected digitally at scales which include the national, regional and global. In Europe, under the auspices of the EIS, various projects have gone some way to enact this kind of cross-border politics and sociality. These include TELANET, Eris@ and Telecities, all forms of trans-European network (TEN), and all initiated under the EIS programme, while not being entirely contained by its policy agenda. Sassen would argue that none of these projects were predicated on a 'knowing rejection of the national' (2006: 340; Sassen, 2007a, 2007b), but that they may still constitute a 'de facto unbundling' of formal (read state) authority and competence.

Sassen's is both a micro and meso treatment of new, mixed spatial and temporal orders, although with profound macro implications. Karin Knorr-Cetina's discussion of 'global microstructures' (2007) also intimates a novel analytical purchase on the role of digital technologies in the construction of European space, although she does not refer to Europe/EU directly. She argues that 'that genuinely global forms ... fields of practice that link up and stretch across all time zones (or have the potential to do so), need not imply further expansions of social institutional complexity. In fact, they may become feasible only if they avoid complex institutional structures' (2007: 65). These microstructures appear too fast, change too quickly and are too dispersed to be 'contained by institutional orders' (2007: 66). Microstructures are likely to come into play in what has been called 'response-presence-based social forms,' in which participants are capable of responding to one another and common objects in real time without being physically present in the same place. Response-presence-based social forms tend to be bound together by information technologies, the arteries of global and transnational connectedness through which the interactions flow (2007: 66 and Knorr-Cetina and Bruegger, 2002).

Global microstructures share four characteristics. The first is institutional 'lightness', wherein systems are coordinated, but not through hierarchy, formal authority or rationalized procedure. Without being institutionally anchored in these ways, they are nonetheless effective. The second is that while microstructures are 'relational arrangements' (Knorr-Cetina, 2007: 68) they are not, or may not be, simply networks. This distinction, though overstated, seems to turn on the highly 'textured' nature of microstructures which have many elements and practices when set against the allegedly 'sparse' structures of networks. She mentions diasporas and terrorist networks as examples of global microstructures, both infused with spirituality and both intensely local as well as global. Her third feature is that of 'scopic media' which act as mechanisms of coordination on a global scale. Coordination follows from the inter-subjectivity that derives from the nature of these systems as they are 'reflexively observed by participants in temporal continuity, synchronicity, and immediacy' (2007: 69). In scopic systems and via scopic media (especially, but not exclusively, forms of 'new' media), 'the world is informational rather than natural or material (2007: 83) and this is implied by the mediated character of the communities they create'. These worlds are fluid, processual and aterritorial. Finally, using the example of financial markets, she argues that the use of new scopic media is crucial in the transformation of previous spatial systems into 'a temporal stream of sequentially connected activities' (2007: 69).

In the case of currency markets, place-based interests in trading and knowledge about prices have become integrated since the 1980s, into a temporal stream of activities facilitated by electronic information and dealing systems that link participants across locations and time zones. The microstructures so created produce, 'cultures in which interlocking time dimensions and forms of embeddedness in time substitute for the loss of spatial rootedness and stabilization' (2007: 69). These are not stable system structures but 'flow architectures' which realize a kind of 'temporalized complexity' (Luhmann, 1984).

THE EUROPEAN INFORMATION SOCIETY AS A PARADIGM FOR NETWORK EUROPE

Attention to microstructures will tell us a good deal about world-making and Europe-making practices and how these can be advanced through the realms of communication and culture. These realms have assumed a growing significance in recent years in discussions of social and political transformation through media, not just as questions of political display, but as registers of power and interest. From Sassen we learn that the impact of new and especially digital communication technologies is not unmediated, for there is no particular logic or essence in technologies that can be abstracted from their use by actors; to that extent all technologies are embedded in social contexts. At the same time, digital assemblages are 'in between types' of spatio-temporal order and thus not entirely subject to the trammels of particular scales.

In quotidian reality, of course, it is all rather messier. In the most complete statement of Network Europe, Castells has alerted us to the transformative effects of information technologies on 'the organizational arrangements of human relationships of production/consumption, experience, and power, as expressed in meaningful interaction framed by culture.' (2000: 5–6). New communications technologies inform the temper of change in societies, and all processes of transformation – in economy, the reworking of states and state power as well as in culture – are implemented through networks and, more precisely, informational networks. However, the EIS project as an exercise in changing both the political and cultural economies of EU/Europe, as well as its governance structures, is a hybrid construct, or more inchoate, which answers to different and not always congruent imperatives. In one guise it appears resolutely top-down, bureaucratic and rule-driven, albeit heavily reliant on the agency and scale of territorial states to make it work. In another it is mutable, driven by the frames of meaning used by a variety of state and non-state; public and private, human and technological actors and the circumstances in and on which they act. In this latter guise network Europe is being constructed through choices and strategies of social actors (individuals, social groups, perhaps actor-networks) without any necessary reference to locale or hierarchy – bottom up.

For all this irresolution, the European Information Society Project (EISP) and its offshoots such as the *e*Europe initiative, do offer useful insights into the dynamics of the network – and especially the digital network – paradigm applied to Europe and EU integration; if only to underline the complex reflexivity between social actors, material conditions and the implied 'logic' of digital technologies. From its origins in the early 1990s (Bangemann 1994) the EIS was the child of two powerful and apparently contradictory impulses (Axford and Huggins, 1996, 1999). The first impulse has two models of EU development within it. The most powerful in terms of driving EIS policy is the liberalizing credo of the market, embodied in the Single Market process and designed to foster an open, transnational economic space to compete in a networked – and informational – world economy. Jan Servaes (2003: 12) notes the starkly pragmatic origins of the EIS in 'a reaction to Japanese and American initiatives

in information technology'. In this regard the early thrust of EIS policy was to emphasize the liberalization of markets, not least with respect to telecommunications and information technology, and thus appears as a proto-paradigm for a technology and market-driven model of EU political economy (Bangemann, 1994). Consequently, up to 1997, much EIS policy was dominated by 'issues relating to the technological and infrastructure challenges and the regulatory economic environment' (HLGE, 1997; see also Archibugi and Coco, 2005).

Alongside this primary model, although not always at ease with it, sits the related aim of promoting a 're-imagination of community and identity in Europe' (Robins, 1994: 102) through the creation of a Europe-wide communications space and, from the mid 1990s onwards, growing attention to the social impact and promise of information society development (see e.g., CEC, 1997). As part of a concern to 'put people first' (CEC, 1997) the Commission espoused basic aims to 'improve access to information, enhance democracy and social justice, promote employability and lifelong learning, strengthen the capacity of the EU economy to achieve high and sustainable growth and employment, achieve equal opportunity between men and women, promote inclusion, support people with special needs and those lacking opportunities to improve their position and improve quality and efficiency of public administration' (quoted in Servaes, 2003: 13)

Both these strands of policy and the ideological/normative models of EU polity and society that inform them envisage the Europeanization of economic and communicative behaviour and of large areas of social practice – or at least their profound denationalization – through networking. As an implicit corollary, they augur a 'formal devaluation of the vast political resources which have come to be organized in and around the state' (Schmitter and Streeck, 1991: 142). Put another way, these are models of the information society which imply a shift from the 'state of territory and the state of population' to the state of networked Europe, without being evangelical about or directly espousing a particular model of EU polity building (Lovink and Schneider, 2001; and also Sassen, 2006). Thus it is too strong to say that these models of the information society fully countenance the ideal of a borderless Europe, but it is implicit, at least, that scales cease to be a major factor in configuring key elements of the integrative project. In many respects this remains the dominant motif of the Information Society Project, though it is rarely articulated in such radical terms, when the more instrumental language of organizational efficiency, human capital (skills) and good governance will do.

The second major impulse also has two strands. The first envisages European unity as a process akin to nation-state modernization, resulting in the 'isomorphism of people, territory and culture' (Collins, 1990). Scales, and in this case a super-territorialist scale, are at the heart of this conception and national governments are key agents in its delivery. The second traffics a discourse about Europe/ EU in which the key themes have been sustaining cultural diversity and enhancing subsidiarity. Here too the language of scale is pre-eminent but, unlike liberal market discourse, for certain kinds of cultural policy, there is a marked preference for regulation, even Euro-protectionism. (Kaitazi-Whitlock, 2000).

In fact, some accommodation between the two logics has been achieved by promoting the EIS as a major factor in creating, for example, truly Europeanized publics, who in time will 'imagine the new community of Europe' (Robins, 1994: 125). However, the implied accommodation has always been problematic for two reasons. The first is the familiar complaint that it is much too reliant on neofunctionalist spillover between zones of experience as the trigger for radical social change. The second is that it still underwrites a holistic or 'thick' spatial model of European identity, rather than a definition of communities in social or virtual and not spatial terms; as 'networks of interpersonal ties that provide

sociability, support, information, a sense of belonging, and social identity' (Wellman, 2001: 228). Overall, the ways in which the EIS has developed continue to subvent the original principles of accelerated economic integration through interconnectivity and building greater social cohesion along with a sense of European identity (Bangemann, 1994, 1997). The other policy and normative impulse embodies principles now held dear by the Commission and member states, wherein the language of localism, regionalism and multiscalar governance hold sway and only a jobbing transnationalism can be found in the agency of cross-border regions, in trans-city virtual space and in some other forms of trans-European network (TENs). On this reading, the sweep of EIS development can be viewed as the playing out of competing, or at least distinct, narratives of European integration.

Undoubtedly such images have profound macrotheoretical implications for the morphology of networked Europe. But for many practitioners and researchers, at any rate, the burden of much of the EIS policy strand has been couched firmly at the meso level, being exercised by the 'good governance' motif and predicated on a strictly 'internalist' and organizational take on the dynamics of integration (Dai, 2003; Shahin, 2004). Often, particular policy initiatives (e.g., Dialogue, Eris@ and Telecities) have been charged with smoothing out the kinks in the EU politics of scale, notably the still-deficient involvement of subnational actors in EU policy matters and processes. As Barry notes, in such a focus, rather than networks being conceived as the means through which the self-government of populations and the respatializing of affect is constructed via a web of microconnections, the main concern is with a variation on the sovereign power of states in relation to other (subnational) scales of government/governance (2001). This focus is much in line with the burden of a good deal of meso-level research on the contribution of political technologies to the coordination and communication problems of modern states and other 'levels' of governance (Barry, 2001).

Recent work on the idea of communication spaces in Europe, including research on the prospects for a European public sphere through ICT, also displays all the conceptual and analytical tensions noted above (Axford and Huggins, 2007; Rumford, 2007). Very little in the complicated policy strands of the EIS and *e*Europe (European Commission, 2002a), or in key strategic documents (European Commission, 2000a, 2000b, 2001a, 2001b, 2002a, 2002b, 2004a, 2004b, 2006) intimate more than creating enabling conditions within which European-wide public talk can take place. At the same time it is true that the enabling potential of ICT is increasingly invoked by Brussels. In response to the Commission's *e*Participation Initiative under the *i*2010 *e*Government Action Plan (2005 and 2006), the Council of Ministers called upon researchers and member states to 'experiment with innovative *e*participation schemes aiming at increasing participation in democratic processes focusing on tools and addressing citizens' demands' (European Council of Ministers, 2006: 7). Partly, this agenda has been driven by the contribution of valuable research projects launched under Frameworks 5 and 6. Among other things, these projects have explored the information society in Europe from the perspective of the routine use of ICT by people in various facets of everyday life (EMTEL, 2003) and their contribution to transnational civil society building (Van Audenhove *et al.*, 2000). Participation (e-participation) research also carried out under FP5-funded projects to enhance citizens' participation in urban planning explored the practicalities of e-voting and e-deliberation. Under FP6, this agenda was continued with the aim of developing tools and solutions for the use of ICT in legislation, and in political processes at local, regional, national and EU levels (European Commission, 2006). In truth, and as with much of the detailed policy agenda of the EIS, the *e*participation initiative is a support mechanism for the achievement of the *i*2010 agenda for *e*government in

the EU. Primarily, this agenda is to create an entrepreneurial business environment for growth and employment, to support this through attention to e-learning and e-literacy and, through the application of ICT, to contribute to the building of a modern public administration, one that is, to use a well-worn phrase, citizen-facing.

At the same time, other programmes such as Eris@, Telecities and Dialogue have gone some way to intimate the ways in which electronic networks can configure a fluid pattern of European integration. In this fluid Europe there is a complex imbrication of local and European; of communication spaces populated by civic networks, provincial, national and regional networks, as well as functional networks organized around service provision, and which all constitute 'circulating entities' of information exchange and public knowledge (Urry, 2003: 122). None of the programmes listed above look(ed) to enhance the European public sphere *per se*, but many have contributed to the growth of multiscalar communities of communication, at the least. The same is true of the plethora of online and otherwise mediated communications that take place between NGOs, social movements, and other individuals and collectives, as well as via forms of Indymedia, often across borders, to instantiate forms of transnational practice.

LOOKING FORWARD

In this chapter we have examined the idea of Network Europe from a variety of perspectives as a way of addressing wider issues in the complex dialectic of place and space, and as a means of conceptualizing a European polity/society. At its most pristine, the idea of Network Europe prescribes a breadth of analytical vision that confounds the territorial basis of much theorizing on the dynamics of European unity, while not constituting, in itself, *a* theory of European or global integration. At its least radical it subsists in that large but congested zone of research and reflection on the changing governance structures and practices of the EU. The intricacies of these debates may counsel a suitably cautious conclusion in which, following Andrew Barry, we might advert no more than the belief that in the EU and Europe, 'the network has come to provide a dominant sense of political possibilities' (2001: 101). However, while true, this still may be too timid a conclusion and three bolder statements (partly of intent and research prescription) are in order.

The first is that the nature of authority, territoriality and identity (not least of the state) are being rearticulated and rescaled through networks. Use of Sassen's notion of *mixed assemblages* and Knorr-Cetina's insights on *microstructures* will reap dividends when applied to empirical investigation in the EU/Europe context. In this regard the scope of empirical work must venture beyond the confines of much conventional policy network research to engage with the fluid worlds being constructed in Europe and globally in various mediascapes, ethnoscapes and finanscapes (Appadurai, 1999) and in the construction and functioning of networked 'small worlds' and 'second lives' on the Internet, in epistemic communities, among diasporic audiences and networked individuals (Urry, 2003; Knorr-Cetina and Bruegger, 2002). The networks established under the EIS also constitute prime sites for analysis of the transnationalization and, of course, the virtualization of governance and civil society. It may be that, through ethnographic research and research informed by complexity theory, claims that the EIS is a form of 'technical culture' (Barry, 2001) can be better grounded, provided that note is taken of the strictures of Sassen and others that the creation of digital, social worlds is not just a matter of some neat 'interface' between human organisms and hard/soft machines. In general, students of European integration and those concerned with accessing how social worlds are made and remade, should pay more attention to the rigours of network analysis, so that the messy imbrication of social morphologies and social action, digital inclusion and exclusion are better understood (Sarikakis, 2003).

The second is that there is no need to resort to technological determinism to recognize that the networked world is likely to be more informational rather than material. In one sense this simply requires paying more attention to communication networks and spaces in and across Europe and the globe, but perhaps more profoundly, it suggests a greater attention to scopic media as mechanisms which permit 'flow architectures' not limited territorially and which can act – in themselves – as mechanisms of coordination and control; maybe of community. As Knorr-Cetina says this phenomenon can be seen in the operation of electronic markets and the agile networking of terrorists and it is also visible in less charged, or more benign, 'architectures' such as those which sustain communities of music lovers or MS sufferers (Knorr-Cetina, 2005). None of these need be construed as obviously or exclusively European, but that is the whole point. Informational microstructures and the communicative spaces they span enable actors to move 'in and through spaces in ways that transform space and time' (Urry, 2003: 57; for an early treatment of EU as a communicative space, see Deutsch, 1966 and also Schlesinger, 2004).

Finally, the idea of Network Europe opens up the possibility of a critical European and global studies conducted through the dialectic of networks and borders. Borders are now often conceived as mobile, carried, as Sassen notes, in the 'product, the person, the instrument' (2006: 416). Such ideas intimate a fluid Europe in which the 'question of territory as a parameter for authority and rights has entered a new phase' (2006: 416). Communication networks intimate new forms of sociality across scales and new assemblages of power. The task of a critical European studies is to unlock these possibilities and this is no easy task.

REFERENCES

Albert, M., Jacobson, D. and Lapid, Y. (eds) (2001) *Identities, Borders. Orders: Rethinking*

International Relations Theory. Minneapolis: University of Minnesota Press.

Amin, A. (2002) 'Spatialities of globalization', *Environment and Planning*, 34: 385–399.

Ansell, C. (2000) 'The networked polity: regional development in Western Europe,' *Governance: An International Journal of Policy and Administration*, 13 (3): 303–333.

Ansell, C.K., Parsons, C.A. and Darden, K.A. (1997) 'Dual networks in European regional development policy', *Journal of Common Market Studies*, 35 (3): 347–375.

Appadurai, A. (1999) 'Disjuncture and difference in the global cultural economy', in M. Featherstone (ed.) *Global Culture: Nationalism, Globalization and Modernity.* London: Sage.

Appadurai, A. (2006) *Fear of Small Numbers: An Essay on the Geography of Anger.* London: Duke University Press.

Archibugi, D. and Coco, A. (2005) 'Is Europe becoming the most dynamic knowledge economy in the world?', *Journal of Common Market Studies*, 43 (3): 433–459.

Axford, B. (2006) 'The dialectic of borders and networks in Europe: Reviewing "topological presuppositions"', *Comparative European Politics*, 4 (2): 160–182.

Axford, B. and Huggins, R. (1996) 'Media without boundaries: fear and loathing on the road to Eurotrash or transformation in the European cultural economy?', *Innovation: the European Journal of Social Science*, 9 (2): 175–184

Axford, B. and Huggins, R. (1999) 'Towards a post-national polity: the emergence of the network society in Europe', in D. Smith and S. Wright (eds) *Whose Europe? The Turn Towards Democracy.* Oxford: Blackwell, pp. 173–207.

Axford, B. and Huggins, R. (2007) 'The European Information Society: a new public sphere?' in C. Rumford (ed.) *Cosmopolitanism and Europe.* Liverpool: Liverpool University Press.

Bache, I. and Flinders, M. (2004) 'Themes and issues in multi-level governance', in I. Bache and M. Flinders (eds) *Multi-Level Governance.* New York: Oxford University Press, pp. 1–11.

Badie, B. and Birnbaum, P. (1983) *The Sociology of the State.* Chicago: University of Chicago Press.

Balibar, E. (1999) 'At the borders of Europe', *TransEuropeennes*, 17: 9–17.

Bangemann, M. (1994) *Europe and the Global Information Society: Recommendations to the European Council.* Brussels, European Commission, May 26.

Bangemann, M. (1997) 'A new world order for global comunication', Presentation to *Telecom Inter@ctive'97*. International Telecommunications Union, 8 August, Geneva.

Barney, D. (2004) *The Network Society.* Cambridge: Polity Press.

Barry, A. (2001) *Political Machines: Governing a Technological Society.* London: Athlone Press.

Bartolini, S. (2006) 'A comparative political approach to EU formation', Arena Working Paper No. 4, University of Bologna, February. Available at: http://www.arena.uio.no.

Blatter, J. (2003) 'Beyond hierarchies and networks: institutional logics and change in transboundary space', *Governance: An International Journal of Policy, Administration and Institutions*, 16 (4): 503–526.

Borras, S. and Jacobssen, K. (2004) 'The open method of coordination and new governance patterns in the EU', *Journal of European Public Policy*, 11: 185–208.

Borzel, T.A. (1997) 'Organizing Babylon on the different conceptions of policy networks', *Public Administration*, 76 (Summer): 252–273.

Boudourides, M. (2002) 'Governance in science and technology', Contributed paper at the *EASST 2002 Conference Responsibility Under Uncertainty*, 31 July–3 August, University of York.

Brenner, N. (1999) 'Beyond state-centrism? Space, territoriality, and geographical scale in globalization studies', *Theory and Society*, 28: 39–78.

Brenner, N. (2001) 'The limits to scale? Methodological reflections on scalar structuration', *Progress in Human Geography*, 25 (4): 591–614.

Brenner, N. (2004) *New State Spaces: Urban Governance and the Rescaling of Statehood.* Oxford: Oxford University Press.

Bulkeley, H. (2005) 'Reconfiguring environmental governance: Towards a politics of scales and networks', *Political Geography*, 24: 875–902.

Callon, M. (1999) *The Laws of the Markets*. Oxford: Blackwell.

Campbell, D. (1996) 'Political prosaics: transversal politics and the anarchical world', in M. Shapiro and H. Alker (eds) *Challenging Boundaries: Global Flows, Territorial Identities*. Minneapolis: University of Minnesota Press.

Caporaso, J. (1996) 'The European Union and forms of state. Westphalian, regulatory or post-modern?', *Journal of Common Market Studies*, 34: 29–51.

Castells, M. (1996) *The Information Age: The Rise of the Network Society*. Oxford: Blackwell.

Castells, M. (1998) 'The unification of Europe', in *End of the Millennium, Vol 3 The Information Age*. Oxford: Blackwell.

Castells, M. (2000) 'Materials for an exploratory theory of the network society', *British Journal of Sociology*, 51 (1): 5–24.

Castells, M. (2001) 'European unification in the era of the network state', Open Democracy Pilot, 12 December, London.

Christiansen, T. Jorgensen, K.E. and Wiener, A. (1999) 'The social construction of Europe', *Journal of European Public Policy*, 6 (4): 528–544.

Collins, R. (1990) 'National culture: a contradiction in terms?' in R. Collins (ed.) *Television, Policy and Culture*. London: Allen and Unwin.

Crozier, M. (2006) 'The Network Society Thesis: theoretical adequacy and research possibilities', unpublished manuscript, University of Melbourne, Australia.

Dai, X. (2003) 'A new mode of governance? Transnationalisation of European regions and cities in the information age', *Telematics and Informatics*, 20 (3): 193–215.

Delanty, G. and Rumford, C. (2005) *Rethinking Europe: Social Theory and the Implications of Europeanization*. London: Routledge.

Deutsch, K.W. (1966) *Nationalism and Social Communication: An Inquiry into the Foundations of Nationality*. Cambridge MA: MIT Press.

Dicken, P., Kelly, P. and Yeung, H. (2001) 'Chains and networks, territories and scales: towards a relational framework for analysing the global economy', *Global Networks*, 1: 89–112.

EMTEL (2003) *Final Report under 5th Framework*. Grant HPRN ET 2000 00063.

European Commission (1996) *Living and Working in the Information Society: People First*. Luxembourg: Office for Official Publications of the European Communities.

European Commission (1998) *Public Sector Information: a Key Resource for Europe. Green Paper on Public Sector Information in the Information Society*. Luxembourg: Office for Official Publications of the European Communities.

European Commission (2000a) *eEurope: An Information Society for All: Communication on a Commission Initiative for the Special European Council of Lisbon, 23–24 March*. Luxembourg: Office for Official Publications of the European Communities.

European Commission: (2000b) *eEurope 2002 Action Plan: Prepared by the Council and the European Commission for the Feira European Council, 19–20 June*. Luxembourg: Office for Official Publications of the European Communities.

European Commission (2001a) *European Governance: A White Paper*. Luxembourg: Office for Official Publications of the European Communities.

European Commission (2001b) *Towards the e-Commission: Implementation Strategy 2001–2005*. Luxembourg: Office for Official Publications of the European Communities.

European Commission (2002a) *eEurope 2002 Final Report*. Luxembourg: Office for Official Publications of the European Communities.

European Commission (2002b) *eEurope 2005: An Information Society for All*. Prepared for the Seville Council Meeting, 21–22 June. Luxembourg: Office for Official Publications of the European Communities.

European Commission (2003) *The Role of eGovernment for Europe's Future*. Luxembourg: Office for Official Publications of the European Communities

European Commission (2004a) *eEurope 2005 Mid-Term Review*. Luxembourg: Office for Offical Publications of the European Communities.

European Commission (2004b) *Challenges for the European Information Society Beyond 2005*. Luxembourg: Office for Official Publications of the European Communities.

European Commission (2006) *White Paper On A European Communication Policy*. Luxembourg: Office for Official Publications of the European Communities.

European Council of Ministers (2006) *Memorandum on the Commission's eParticipation Initiative under the i2010 eGovernment Action Plan*. Brussels: European Council.

Fligstein, N. and Stone Sweet, A. (2000) 'Constructing polities and markets: an institutionalist account of European integration', paper presented at the Institutionalization of Europe Conference, Robert Schuman Centre for Advanced Study, European University Institute, San Domenico di Fiesole, Italy.

Fossum, J.E. (2006) 'Conceptualizing the EU', *Comparative European Politics*, 4: 94–123.

Foucault, M. (1975) *Discipline and Punish: The Birth of the Prison*. New York: SUNY Press.

Giddens, A. (1991a) *Modernity and Self-Identity*. Cambridge: Polity.

Giddens, A. (1991b) 'Structuration theory: past, present and future', in C, Bryant and D, Jary (eds) *Giddens' Theory of Structuration*. London: Routledge.

Held, D., McGrew, A., Goldblatt, D. and Perraton, J. (1999) *Global Transformations*. Cambridge: Polity.

Held, D. (2007) 'Reframing global governance: apocalypse soon or reform!', in D. Held and A. McGrew (eds) *Globalization Theory: Approaches and Controversies*. Cambridge: Polity, pp. 240–261.

Hix, S. (1998) 'The study of the European Union II: The "New Governance" agenda and its rival', *Journal of European Public Policy*, 5: 38–65.

High Level Group of Experts - HLGE (1997) *Towards a European Information Society For Us All*. Brussels: European Commission.

Holton, R. (2005) ' Network discourses: proliferation, critique and synthesis', *Global Networks*, 5 (2): 209–215.

Jachtenfuchs, M. (2001) 'The governance approach to European integration', *Journal Of Common Market Studies*, 39: 245–264.

Jensen, O. and Richardson, T. (2004) *Making European Space: Mobility, Power and Territorial Identity*. London: Routledge.

Jessop, B. (2000) 'The crisis of the national spatio-temporal fix and the tendential ecological dominance of globalizing capitalism', *International Journal of Urban and Regional Research*, 24: 323–360.

Jessop, B. (2002) 'The political economy of scale', in M. Perkmann and M. Sum (eds) *Globalization, Regionalization and Cross-Border Regions*. Routledge: London, pp. 25–49.

Kaitazi-Whitlock, S. (2000) '"A redundant information society" for the European Union?', *Telematics and Informatics*, 17 (1–2): 39–75.

Kallinikos, J. (2004) 'Networks as alternative forms of organization: some critical remarks', unpublished paper, London School of Economics, London.

Kastoryano, R. (2002) *The Reach of Transnationalism*. New York: Social Science Research Council.

Kenis, P. and Schneider, V. (1991) 'Policy networks and policy analysis: scrutinising a new analytical toolbox', in B. Marin and M. Mayntz (eds) *Policy Networks: Empirical Evidence and Theoretical Considerations*. Frankfurt: Campus Verlag 25–59.

Knorr Cetina, K. (2005) 'Complex global microstructures. The new terrorist societies', *Theory, Culture and Society*, 22 (5): 213–234.

Knorr-Cetina, K (2007) 'Microglobalization', in I. Rossi (ed.) *Frontiers of Globalization Research*. Toronto: Springer, pp. 65–92.

Knorr Cetina, K. and Bruegger, U. (2002) 'Global microstructures: The virtual societies of financial markets', *American Journal of Sociology*, 107 (4): 905–995.

Kohler-Koch, B. (2002) 'European networks and ideas: changing national policies?', *European Integration Online Papers*, 6 (6). Available at: http://eiop.or.at/eiop/texte/2002-006a.htm.

Kramsch, O.T. (2003) 'Re-imagining the "scalar fix" of transborder governance: the case of the Maas-Rheni *Euregio*', in E. Berg and H. van Houtum (eds) *Routing Borders: Between Territories, Discourses and Practices*. Aldershot: Ashgate, pp. 211–237.

Lapid, Y. (2001) 'Identities, borders and orders: nudging international relations theory in a new direction', in M. Albert, D. Jacobsen and Y. Lapid (eds) *Identities, Borders and Orders*. Minneapolis: University of Minnesota Press, pp. 1–20.

Latour, B. (1997) 'On actor-network theory: a few clarifications'. Available at: http://Keele.ac.uk/deps.stt/stt/ant/latour.htm.

Leonard, M. (1999) *Network Europe: the New Case for Europe*. London: Foreign Policy Centre.

Lissandrello, E. (2003) 'Cross-border regions in European context: When "Territoriality" is an outcome of networks interaction. An observation on their "built in" workings', Paper presented at the Third Joint Congress

ACSP-AESOP, 8–12 July, Leven, Belgium, pp. 1–16.

Lovink, G. and Schneider, F. (2001) *A Virtual World is Possible: From Tactical Media to Digital Multitudes*. Available at: http://makeworlds.org/node/22.

Lovink, G. and Schneider, F. (2004) 'Notes on the State of Networking'. Available at http:// www.makeworlds.org/node/102.

Luhmann, N. (1984) *Soziale Systeme. Grundriss einer allgemeinen Theorie*. Frankfurt: Suhrkamp.

Luke, T. (1995) ,World order or neo-world orders: power, politics and ideology in informationalizing glocalities' in M. Featherstone, S. Lash and R. Robertson (eds) *Global Modernities*. London: Sage, pp. 27–62.

Majone, G. (1996) *Regulating Europe*. London: Routledge.

Mann, M. (1998) 'Is there a society called euro?' in R. Axtmann (ed.) *Globalization and Europe*. Pinter: London.

Marcussen, M. and Torfing, H. (2007) *Democratic Network Governance In Europe*. Basingstoke: Palgrave/Macmillan.

Marks, G. (1993) 'Structural policy and multi-level governance in the EC', in A. Cafruny and G. Rosenthal (eds) *The State of the European Community. Vol. 2. The Maastricht Debates and Beyond*. Boulder, CO: Reinner, pp. 391–410.

Messner, D. (1997) *The Network Society: Economic Development and International Competitiveness as Problems of Social Governance*. London: Frank Cass.

Mol, A. and Law, J. (1994) 'Regions, networks and fluids: anaemia and social topology', *Social Studies of Science*, 24: 641–671.

Painter, J. (2004) 'Territory-network', Paper presented at the Social Spatial Theory Workshop A New Spatial Grammar, Durham University, March. Available from the author.

Patomaki, H. and Taiveinen, T. (2004) 'The World Social Forum', *Theory, Culture and Society*, 21 (6): 141–154.

Perkmann, M. (1998) 'Building governance structures across European borders', *Regional Studies*, 33: 657–667.

Peterson, J. (2004) 'Policy networks' in A. Wiener and T. Diez (eds) *European Integration Theory*. New York: Oxford University Press.

Pollack, M.A. (2005) 'Theorizing the European Union: international organisation, domestic polity or experiment in new governance?', *Annual Review of Political Science*, 8: 357–398.

Podolny, J. (2001) 'Networks as the pipes and prisms of the market', *American Journal of Sociology*, 107 (1): 33–36.

Powell, W.W. and Smith-Doerr, L. (1994) Networks and economic life', in N. Smelser and R. Swedberg (eds) *Handbook of Economic Sociology*. Princeton, Princeton University Press, pp. 368–402.

Pries, L. (2004) 'Transnationalism and migration: new challenges for the social sciences and education', in S. Luchtenberg (ed.) *Migration, Education and Change*. New York: Routledge.

Pries, L. (2005) 'Configurations of Geographic and Societal Spaces: a Sociological Proposal between 'Methodological Nationalism' and 'Spaces of Flows'', *Global Networks*, 5 (2): 167–190.

Radaelli, C.M. (2002). 'Democratising expertise?', in J.R. Grote and B. Gbikpi (eds), *Participatory Governance. Political and Societal Implications*. Opladen: Leske and Budrich, pp. 197–212.

Rhodes, R. (1996) 'The new governance: governing without government', *Political Studies*, XLIV: 652–667.

Robins. K. (1994) 'The politics of silence: the meaning of community and the uses of media in the New Europe', *New Formations*, 21: 80–102.

Rosenau, J and E-O. Czempiel (eds) (1992) *Government Without Government: Order And change in World Politics*. Cambridge: Cambridge University Press.

Ruggie, J. (1992) 'Territoriality and beyond: problematising modernity in international relations', *International Organisation*, 47 (1): 149–174.

Rumford, R. (2006) 'Rethinking European spaces: territory, borders, governance', *Comparative European Politics*, 4 (2–3): 127–141.

Rumford, C (2007) 'Does Europe have cosmopolitan borders?', *Globalizations*, 4 (3): 327–339.

Sandholtz, W. and A. Stone Sweet (1998) *European Integration and Supranational Governance*. Oxford: Oxford University Press.

Sarikakis, K. (2003) 'Review of Andrew Barry's *Political Machines: Governing a Technological Society, Culture Machine*'. Available at: http://culturemachine.tees.ac.uk/Reviews/rev28.htm.

Sassen, S. (2004) 'Local actors in global politics', *Current Sociology*, 52 (4): 649–670.

Sassen, S. (2004) 'Electronic markets and activist networks', NEURO-networking Europe, 22 February: pp. 1–12.

Sassen, S. (2006) *Territory, Authority and Rights: from Medieval to Global Assemblages*. Princeton: Princeton University Press.

Sassen, S. (2007a) 'Theoretical and Empirical Elements in the Study of Globalization', in I. Rossi (ed.) *Frontiers of Globalization Research: Theoretical and Methodological Approaches*. New York: Springer, pp. 287–307.

Sassen, S. (2007b) 'The places and spaces of the global: an expanded analytical terrain', in D. Held and A. McGrew (eds) *Globalization Theory: Approaches and Controversies*. Cambridge: Polity, pp. 70–106.

Schlesinger, P. (2004): 'The Babel Of Europe?: An essay on networks and communicative spaces', paper presented at the ESCUS Conference on Cosmopolitanism in Europe, September 13–14, Sheffield.

Schmitter, P.C. (1996) 'Examining the present Euro-polity with the help of past theories', in G. Marks, F.W. Scharpf, P.C. Schmitter and W. Streeck (eds) *Governance in the European Union*. London: Sage, pp. 1–14.

Schmitter, P. and Streeck, M. (1991) 'From national corporatism to transnational pluralism: organised interests in the Single European Market', *Politics and Society*, 20 (2): 133–164.

Scott, J.W. (2002) 'A networked space of meaning? Spatial politics as geostrategies of European integration', *Space and Polity*, 6 (2): 147–167.

Servaes, J. (ed.) (2003) *The European Information Society: A Reality Check*. Bristol: Intellect Books.

Shahin, A (2004) *Virtual Governance? The Relationship Between the Internet and Governance in the European Union*. PhD thesis, University of Hull, December.

Strihan, A. (2005) 'A Network-Based Approach to Regional Borders', Fulbright Seminar, April, Vienna, pp. 1–19.

Thompson, G. (2003) *Between Hierarchies and Markets: the Logic of Network forms of Organisation*. Oxford: Oxford University Press.

Thrift, N. (1999) 'The place of complexity', *Theory, Culture and Society*, 16: 31–70.

Thrift, N. and Olds, K. (1996) 'Reconfiguring the economic in economic geography', *Progress in Human Geography*, 20: 311–337.

Urry, J. (2003). *Global Complexity*. Cambridge: Polity Press.

Van Dijk, J. (1999) *The Network Society: Social Aspects of New Media*. London. Sage.

Van Audenhove, L. and Cammaerts, B. (2004) 'Transnational civil society in the network society', in N. Carpentier, C. Pauwels, and O. Van Oost (eds) *Het on(be)grijpbare publiek/ The ungraspable audience*. Brussels: VUBPress.

Van Audenhove, L., Cammaerts, B., Frissen, V., Engels, L., Ponsioen, A.; Transnational Civil Society in the Networked Society. (2000) *A Study on the Relation Between ICTs and the Rise of a Transnational Civil Society. Final Report*. Terra 2000. Work Package Integration: Story of Terra and Problematique. EU Project under IST 2000. End report for Infonomics.

Van Audenhove, L., Cammaerts, B., Frissen, V., Engels, L. and Ponsioen, A. (2005) *Transnational Civil Society in the Networked Society*. TERRA 2000, Brussels, EU Project under IST 2000.

Wallace, H. and Wallace, W. (1996) *Policy Making in the European Union*. Oxford: Oxford University Press.

Warleigh, A. (2000) 'Beyond the functional – ideational gap: from network governance to network democracy in the European Union?', Civic Paper 2000/2, July. Exeter: University of Exeter.

Wellman, B. (2001), 'Physical space and cyberplace: the rise of personalized networking,' *International Journal of Urban and Regional Research*, 25 (2): 227–252.

Future Directions

30

The Contrasting Fortunes of European Studies and EU Studies: Grounds for Reconciliation?

Francis McGowan

Over the last few years the range of academic activities embraced by European studies has undergone something of a crisis at the same time as the 'subfield' of European Union (EU) studies has flourished. In the US and the UK (and perhaps more broadly), European studies – by which we mean the tradition of teaching and research rooted in broadly based understandings of Europe in its cultural, economic, political and social senses – has experienced some of the more general challenges which have faced interdisciplinary area studies (notably globalization and the 'disciplining' of academic endeavour). By contrast EU studies has apparently gone from strength to strength, effectively identifying itself as a subfield in political science (and possibly the wider social sciences). To some extent the factors which have undermined the broader field have helped to consolidate the more focused activities of EU studies, raising the question whether the two

fields' fortunes are somehow in a zero-sum relationship with one another.

The two fields are clearly intertwined. The study of the EU/EC has been an element in most European studies teaching and research agendas for most of the last 50 years. Indeed, over that period, the heightened profile of the EU has been matched by increased interest in its contribution to Europe's economic and political development. As the EU has grown from 6 to 27 members, with other memberships either on track or at least in prospect, the spatial fit between 'Europe' and the EU has become closer. The widening of the EU has been accompanied by an extension of its competences to embrace a greater range of activities (Pollack, 2000) and a consolidation of its institutional base (Hix, 2005). Inasmuch as these two developments have transformed the profile of the EU, attempts to make sense of the 'nature of the beast' have proliferated (see Pollack, 2005, and Cini and Bourne,

2006, for reviews of the state of the art). It is not, therefore, surprising that an EU of 27 member states with a presence in almost every area of public policy and an ability to provoke political controversy, should increasingly figure in contemporary studies of Europe (or studies of contemporary Europe). Yet, just as the 'EU' and 'Europe' are very far from being equivalent, so the preoccupations of EU studies and European studies might be considered to have distinctive if overlapping agendas. Even a narrowly drawn European studies curriculum or research agenda would tackle a range of historical and cultural issues where the EU contribution was modest or nonexistent and there are aspects of EU studies which would be of at most limited interest to many European studies students and scholars. Indeed there might be more broadly based European studies programmes which would pay only limited attention to the EU and its works while much EU studies teaching and research would make little reference to broader questions of Europe's historical and cultural development. Nonetheless, overall there has been some (often considerable) common ground between the two fields.

In recent years, however, the nature of the relationship between European and EU studies seems to have changed. There appears to have been a certain intellectual sleight of hand which involves an equating of the two or, in some cases, a displacement of the one by the other. Part of the problem, as we will see, is the rather arbitrary way in which the terms are applied in the literature (paralleling the way in which politicians and officials in the EU happily invoke 'Europe' when they are discussing the Union's affairs). But underlying this casual equivalence is perhaps a more fundamental shift in our terms of reference, one which privileges certain aspects of – and approaches to – contemporary Europe at the expense of other broader understandings.

Moreover, for the most part, the emergence of EU studies has coincided with an intensification of particular approaches to making sense of the EU (or any other political institution). As various studies have noted,

EU studies is largely based on political science methods and approaches and it has been affected by the tendency within political science to be defined by particular 'disciplinary' approaches, notably rational choice (Rosamond, 2007b). While this remains only one part of the picture of EU Studies (Jupille, 2006), its growing significance – and the more general turn towards 'disciplinarity' in the field – may be leading to a marginalization of the sort of interdisciplinarity or multidisciplinarity which has informed European studies (as well as some studies of the EU).

Is there a risk that the increased profile of a more 'focused' EU studies has been at the expense of the breadth of analysis? Does the current trend mean that students will be given an unduly narrow perspective on 'Europe' while researchers will plough ever narrower subfields? Are we in danger of losing broader perspectives on the nature of Europe as a region, perspectives which depend upon a more interdisciplinary or multidisciplinary approach?

This trend has been welcomed as a positive development by those inside the tent of EU studies (particularly where they share the core discipline of political science). However if one takes the view that there is more to Europe than the EU and that a bigger toolkit is required to understand Europe, the turn gives cause for concern. While there are undoubtedly insights to be drawn from more focused analyses of the EU as a political system, it is only one part of the picture (arguably in EU studies and certainly in European studies). What is needed, therefore, is a research and teaching agenda which brings EU studies and European studies back into dialogue with one another.

This paper examines how the fields of European studies and European Union studies can be reconciled. It does so by drawing on the insights of 'comparative regionalism' (or regional integration studies). Recent work in this area has been based upon a broader understanding of the idea of region and with that a recognition of the need for a more interdisciplinary approach. We focus particularly on the work of Andrew Hurrell (1995 and 2007), Bjorn Hettne (1994) and William Wallace (1990 and 1994) as scholars trying to make sense of the 'new regionalism', the revival since the 1990s in projects of regional cooperation. While borrowing their attempts to develop a broader notion of 'region', it does so not to contextualize and compare different regional experiences but to understand how Europe as a region has changed over time. Such a historical approach means moving beyond the study of the EU *per se* and drawing upon the insights of a range of disciplines to understand the development of Europe as a region. At the same time, however, it offers an opportunity for dialogue with both the empirical focus of current EU studies and many of the concepts it adopts.

The paper aims to bring together not only the fields of European and EU studies but also to highlight the linkages of each to the more generic fields of area studies and regional integration. Area studies and regional integration studies are approaches to studying the region albeit in different forms: the broad interdisciplinary sweep of area studies covers a variety of aspects of what defines a region while regional integration studies has tended to focus on the institutional frameworks and/or economic linkages which have developed to manage political and economic cooperation. We aim to outline a historically informed synthesis of these different approaches which will give us a better sense of the 'regionness' of Europe over the longer run on the one hand, and, on the other, of the contribution of more or less institutionalized forms of cooperation (of which the EU is the most recent example) to that regionness. In the process, the piece aims to contribute to the broader debate on 'new regionalism' which aims to incorporate the insights of area studies into the study of these regional arrangements (a linkage which has been successfully explored in recent work by Breslin and Higgott, 2000, and Katzenstein, 2005).

We begin by outlining a framework for locating European studies and EU studies according to the vectors of 'scale' and 'scope', or territoriality and disciplinarity. We then focus in on the respective fortunes of our two fields: on the one hand noting European studies as a particular case of the more general problems facing area studies in US and British academia; on the other highlighting EU studies as a particular example of the academic study of regional integration. We explore some of the ways of thinking about 'region' and 'regionness' in the field of comparative regionalism, drawing upon the broader debate on the nature of region as well as the work of Hurrell, Hettne, Wallace and other attempts to put Europe (and European integration) into a historical context. We address some of the possible pitfalls and criticisms such an approach might encounter, recognizing that such an approach risks being considered as teleological (that European unity has been in some sense inevitable) or Eurocentric (that Europe constitutes a superior or dominant pathway of development or civilization). We would argue however that our intention is to make sense of how the region of Europe has developed, with the EU as an important instance of cooperation rather than as the best of all possible Europes and Europe as a space which has over time been characterized by intensive interactions rather than a superior civilization. In the course of sketching how such research might be pursued we hope to reconcile European and EU studies, identifying a possible agenda for research and teaching which draws on the insights of both disciplines; placing the different ideals and practices of integration into a broader context and applying concepts and approaches drawn from current thinking about European integration to inform our understanding of the region in the past.

MAPPING THE FIELDS OF EUROPEAN AND EU STUDIES

If we are to come to terms with the challenges facing European studies and to sort

Table 30.1   Scale and scope in European/EU studies

		Scale of territorial coverage	
		Narrow	Broad
Disciplinary	Focused	European Union/integration studies	The 'wider Europe' in a social science context
Scope	'Holistic'	'Traditional' European studies	The 'wider Europe' in a broader inter-disciplinary context

out its relationship with EU studies we need to have a grasp of what each field seeks to address. That task is not made easy by the looseness with which these and other terms are applied. In one account of the study of 'contemporary Europe' the analysis shifts from a rather general account of the way in which 'Europe' has been researched in the past to a more detailed review of research on the institutions and policies of the EU in more recent times (Wallace, 2000). Others are more explicit in recognizing the problems presented by discussing distinctive but closely related fields (Cini 2006; Rosamond, 2007a).[1]

The nature of the relationship between EU studies and European studies is not as obvious as might be thought. As some accounts would have it, EU studies has historically and institutionally evolved out of European studies (Cini 2006; Calhoun 2003; Wallace 2000; Warleigh-Lack 2006) and it is certainly true that, in terms of training, academic locations and research outlets, there may well have been many students and scholars who encountered the EU in this way. However such accounts do not convey the whole story. It is clear, for example, that much of the North American study of the European Community (arguably the original source of EU studies) originated in mainstream political science (and other 'disciplinary') departments. Closer to home, while many of yesterday and today's EU specialists may have originally taught and been taught in European studies departments, others were located in departments of politics, economics and law where their 'EU' competence was often seen as part of a broader specialism within those disciplines – international organization in the case of politics and international relations, international law in the case of law and trade policy in the case

of economics. These specialisms reflected the extent to which in the early decades of its existence, the EC may have been considered *sui generis* but it also more or less fitted into the existing categories which were used by those interested in the international more than the domestic aspects of their subjects.

There is therefore a relationship between European studies and EU studies, both in the sense of a 'history' as well as in the sense of an 'intersect' or 'overlap' between the two fields, but the fields constitute rather different academic ventures in terms of teaching and research. The above matrix (Table 30.1) attempts to provide a schematic view of these different ventures, and presents a stylized characterization of them according to the dimensions of 'scale' and 'scope'.

By scale we refer to the territorial space addressed by each discipline. This is perhaps more of historical than current importance, being a more important source of differentiation when the European Community comprised six or even 15 states rather than 27. There is a better 'fit' between the EU and Europe in 2008 than there was in 1958. Yet there remain important parts of Europe which remain outside the EU. Moreover there is a sense in which the historical contrast between the EU and Europe defined the original focus of EU studies in terms of politics and policies and those characteristics endure in the current 'discipline' (for example, in analyses of the relationship between the EU institutions and member states). This is apparent when we contrast EU studies with the accounts of Europe in which a more comprehensive approach is adopted or in which a wider range of common themes is explored.

This takes us to our second dimension – 'scope', by which we mean the breadth and depth of the disciplines and perspectives which inform each approach. As we have noted (and will explore more fully later in the paper), EU studies has tended to be dominated by political scientists (IR specialists initially but increasingly comparativists and policy analysts as well) with established contributions from economics, law and history. European studies by contrast lays claim to the spectrum of the humanities and social sciences as its intellectual basis. A relatively early account of European studies as a teaching programme (by the founder of the first 'school' of European studies in the UK, Martin Wight) gives some sense of the ambition of the field: 'The various disciplines, literary, historical, philosophical and social, are so far as possible combined and the connections between them are emphasised' (Wight, 1964: 105).

Looking at our categories it becomes possible to offer a rather stylised view of both European studies and EU studies. We can thus contrast the relatively narrow and focused approach of conventional EU studies (quite focused in terms of territorial and disciplinary scope) with other approaches, most notably its diagonal opposite. (The other two categories entail a more interdisciplinary approach to the EU and a relatively focused view of the wider Europe.) Of course these categories are in a sense extremes and do not take account of the nuances within both disciplines. Few would lay claim to the ambition of the holistic broad approach in a single text. There are perhaps some historians of particular eras of Europe who have approximated this ambition but it is debateable whether they would identify themselves primarily as 'of' European studies (Davies, 1996; Judt, 2005; Mazower, 1998). At the other end of the spectrum our matrix may not give enough recognition of those who claim to be in the field of EU studies but who come from or draw upon a wider range of disciplinary backgrounds (e.g. sociologists like Crouch, 2001, and Favell, 2007, and anthropologists such as Shore, 2000, and Bellier, 1997). Nonetheless the matrix does offer one

way of characterizing some of the key differences between EU studies and European studies in terms of their respective focal points and approaches.

EUROPEAN STUDIES AND THE CRISIS OF AREA STUDIES

Having laid out the characteristics of EU and European studies, how have they fared? As we have indicated, some accounts of the development of EU studies appear to welcome the increased differentiation between the two fields. In a discussion of approaches to the EU, Cini notes how earlier area-studies approaches to the study of EU had suffered 'a loss of credibility', being 'empirically detailed but theoretical(ly) underspecified' (Cini, 2006: 44). Wallace refers to traditional European studies as being 'something of a backwater in terms of scholarship, caught between the social sciences and the humanities and mainly concerned with delivering degree programmes that had a bit of everything and not much depth' (Wallace, 2000: 96) and notes approvingly the fact that the study of the EU has been 'mainstreamed' (2000: 98–9). Such criticisms, moreover, explicitly refer to the problems of European studies as part of the wider problems facing area studies in the last few decades.

Of course it could be questioned whether European studies 'fits' the classic area-studies template. The emergence of European studies was not facilitated by the factors that fostered the study of other areas, or at least not in the same way. Whereas the development of 'non-European' area studies was a function of initially colonialism and subsequently the Cold War (see Worcester and Tarrow, 1994; Rafael, 1994; and Katzenstein, 2001 on the 'diplomatic' roots of area studies), it could be argued that European studies was only possible in the wake of colonialism and the region's changed position as the object rather than the subject of great power politics. Many years ago, Martin Wight argued that European studies emerged as a result of Europe's fall from dominance: after World War II, Europe 'now deposed from world primacy by her American and Russian descendants, could become academically self-aware as one among the several civilizations of the world. University curricula reflect their historical circumstances. The end of European hegemony made the concept of 'European Studies' possible' (Wight, 1964: 100) He also argued that European studies was never as 'vocational' as other area studies and that – at least for European-based scholars – it could not be examined with the same 'detached curiosity' (1964: 103) as other regions. Of course, European studies has moved on from Wight's depiction yet its distinctiveness seems to persist. Writing rather more recently, Calhoun also sees European studies as having a rather ambivalent status *vis-à-vis* area studies as a whole. While arguing that it provided the basic model for area studies, he also recognizes that it has been an odd fit (2003: 5–6) and has followed a rather different trajectory from area studies as a whole (2003: 14–16).

However it is clear that, notwithstanding its allegedly distinctive character *vis-à-vis* other area studies (a claim which would most likely by made by specialists in every area for their own domain), European studies has been susceptible to some of the challenges and critiques which have faced the broader field of area studies. Following on from our earlier discussion of 'scale and scope' the questions of territoriality and disciplinarity have been at the heart of those more general critiques of area studies. These challenges, it should be noted, were not just intellectual and had an impact on the pursuit of 'area-based knowledge' in the way that financial resources were provided for teaching and research.

The challenge of 'globalization' (as a concept) took a variety of forms. In its earliest form, accounts of globalization challenged the actual importance (and conceptual relevance) of nation states as well as certain understandings of 'the region' (e.g. in terms of specificities which were shared by nation states and societies within a particular area). The cultural, economic, political and social effects of globalization diluted or overwhelmed the particularities of nation states while undermining their sovereignty and governing capacity. Academically this rendered the study of particular societies, and the regions in which they were located, less relevant (Horsmann and Marshall 1994; Strange 1996, 1997). While such claims might have seemed interesting grounds for debate, their impact was rather more immediate as research foundations and government agencies appeared to take such claims for the impact of globalization at its word and began to shift funding priorities to the detriment of teaching and research in area studies. Stung perhaps by the practical implications of this particular interpretation of the phenomenon (in the shape of the redeployment of teaching and research funds away from area studies), Hall and Tarrow (1998) provided a robust defence of area studies against simplistic notions of globalization.

Such 'vulgar globalization' has been repudiated in the work of Hirst and Thompson (1996) (who offered an early counter critique of globalization which emphasized the continued importance of the nation state and of the region) and, to some extent, Garrett (1998 and 2000). There is now a recognition that globalization has not meant the end of nations or regions and that there is still a need to understand the characteristics of these in the light of globalization (see Held *et al.*, 1999, and Hay and Marsh, 2000, for reviews of the debate). Katzenstein's (2005) account of 'porous regions' offers just such a balanced sense of the relationship between these phenomena.

Intellectually, therefore, area studies has been able to benefit from more nuanced understandings of the relationship between globalization and the region. However it has faced arguably a more formidable challenge from the 'disciplinary turn' in the social sciences. For nearly two decades, there has been a growing critique of area studies in terms of its credentials as a discipline.

Tessler notes that there has been a conflict between area studies specialists concerned with the particular features of regions on the one hand and social scientists with a disciplinary focus on the other. At the heart of this conflict is 'an important disagreement about social science epistemology, about what constitutes, or should constitute, the paradigm by which scholars construct knowledge about politics, economics and international relations in major world regions' (Tessler, 1999: vii). For such social scientists, area studies has been too 'mushy' and lacking scientific rigour (1999: viii) compared with more 'theoretically grounded' approaches such as rational choice and formal modelling (see Bates, 1997, on the overall critique of area studies and Cini, 2006, and Rosamond, 2007b, on its implications for European – and EU – studies).

While rational choice has informed the orthodox critique of area/European studies, the field has also been subject to a counter-critique from the other emerging strand in social sciences – Tessler argues that the post-modern/reflexive critique of area studies has been as much of a challenge (in some ways rooting its critique in the 'orientalist' and/or 'Cold War' origins of area studies (Tessler, 1999: ix–x). Arguably European studies (and possibly area studies more generally) has responded better to this critique than it has the 'scientific' critique, by recognizing the problematic nature of 'Europe' and incorporating the insights of critical and social theory (Katzenstein, 2005: xi).

THE EMERGENCE OF EU STUDIES AND ITS RELATIONSHIP TO REGIONAL INTEGRATION STUDIES

Like area studies more generally, therefore, European studies has had its share of critiques and challenges since the 1990s. By contrast, the same period has seen the field of EU studies appear to go from strength to strength (Keeler, 2005). As we have seen,

some have seen the consolidation of the study of the EU and its development as a distinctive 'subdiscipline' as something of a 'moving on' from what they perceived to be the limitations and vaguenesses of European studies. Indeed the development of EU studies could be seen as going with the grain of academic debate in rejecting the preoccupations of the broader area studies approach by focusing on the EU as a 'system' and attempting to make the study of the EU more theoretically informed than as the case with the 'thick description' of the past. However, there remains much dispute within EU studies about which direction if should take (even though most would regard these debates as symptomatic of the vitality of the sector rather than of a challenge to its survival). Over the last 20 years there has been a proliferation of approaches which seek to make sense of European integration, in effect a response to both the evolution of the EU itself and the 'sterile debates' which informed earlier debates on the dynamics of its development (Hix, 1994; Pollack, 2005; Rosamond, 2000; Schmidt, 1996). The diversity of approaches has raised questions of disciplinarity, intradisciplinarity and interdisciplinarity.[2]

The disciplinary focus is probably best exemplified by the orthodox (or as Rosamond calls it 'mainstream') political science approach. Arguing that the EU's own institutional development has rendered it more of a system in its own right, proponents of this view consider that it should be analysed by those models which are used to examine political systems. This line of argument is in some ways rather similar to the 'solution' put forward by the disciplinary critics of area studies and entails making the study of the EU more systematic and conforming with social scientific principles. The injection of such 'rigour' into the study of the EU can be seen primarily at the level of the research community (Rosamond, 2007b, provides a critical summary of this debate). It can be also seen in the undergraduate curriculum where proposals for a core-curriculum have been advanced in a way which, while ostensibly interdisciplinary, gives much weight to political science (Umbach and Scholl, 2003). Their views have been criticized by Rumford and Murray, 2003a, as fostering a narrowly defined approach to the study of the EU which would be 'both distorting and limiting').

In contrast to this 'mainstreaming' model are those who want to adopt a more 'pluralist' (in Rosamond's term) approach to understanding the EU, one which is still rooted in political science but which draws upon a wider range of perspectives from across the discipline. This so-called intradisciplinarity (Warleigh-Lack, 2006) in turn shades into yet broader approaches (whether interdisciplinary, multidisciplinary or postdisciplinary – see Cini, 2006, for more details). On the one hand, the intradisciplinary approach draws on the insights of other disciplines as predigested into political science (e.g. rational choice or constructivism) while, on the other hand, other disciplines have begun to focus on the study of the EU from their own vantage points (e.g. the previously noted increased interest in spheres such as anthropology and sociology).

At the same time as researchers and teachers of EU studies have engaged with other disciplines, the study of the EU itself is also being considered in the context of the study of regional integration beyond the European region. This marks in some senses a return to an older preoccupation with 'regionalism' – indeed, historically, the study of what was then the European Community was at the heart of the 'old regionalism' which examined regional cooperation in the developed and developing world in the 1950s and 1960s. In more recent years there has been a revival of interest in comparing developments in the EU with those in North America, Latin America, Asia, and so on. However, just as European studies has been considered as semi-detached from other parts of the area-studies canon, so EU studies has enjoyed – and enjoys – a rather complex relationship with the study of regional integration in other settings. Partly this is to do with the nature of European integration, built upon a particular

set of institutions and apparently more 'successful' than other regional projects, therefore offering more grist to the research mill. Partly it is due to the past experience of regional integration where models originally developed to make sense of European integration in the 1950s and 1960s were applied to other regions but to little effect; whatever the insights generated by regional integration theory on the early European Community it was of little relevance to regional projects elsewhere.[3] In more recent periods some analysts of the 'new regionalism' have tended to focus on regional integration outside of Europe (Grugel and Hout, 1998). There were, however, others who made a link between the revival of the EU and the re-emergence of regionalism (see Gamble and Payne, 1996; Mansfield and Milner, 1997; Payne, 2000), arguing that they were the result of similar forces such as the rise of neoliberalism and globalization (McGowan, 1999). Indeed it is worth contrasting our earlier discussion of the early challenge to area studies from a globalization perspective with the way in which regional integration has been seen by students of globalization – economists as well as political scientists – as a part of the process, whether as a catalyst for it or as a way of mitigating or containing its effects. (Lawrence, 1996; McGowan, 1999).

TOWARDS A RECONCILIATION: 'REGION' AND 'REGIONNESS' IN THE STUDY OF EUROPE

So far we have considered the respective fates of European studies and EU studies and have done so with reference to more general developments in the fields of area studies and regional integration studies. At the risk of oversimplifying, the 'European/EU' cases follow the general trend: area studies has been subject to a mix of material and intellectual challenges whereas regional integration studies has enjoyed something of a revival. If there is a contrast from the general trend it is probably the apparent strength of EU studies; arguably it has been at the vanguard of the regeneration of regional integration studies, as a result of the growing role of – and interest in – the EU. In a tightening academic market (both financially and intellectually) it could be argued that the success of EU studies has been at the expense of the wider European studies agenda. Of more concern is the tendency for the EU studies research and teaching project to redefine European studies in a way where it comes to be considered as the primary component of European studies.

While some protagonists – and maybe some officials – would welcome the equating of the EU and Europe in academic endeavour, others might be uneasy. There is of course no doubt that the EU is a very significant part of the European economy and polity (and to a lesser extent European society and culture – see Shore, 2000, and Medrano, 2003). Any attempt to make sense of contemporary Europe, therefore, cannot ignore the EU. Yet an understanding of Europe which was primarily informed by the development and workings of the EU would be very limited – privileging the activities of actors and institutions over other political (as well as social and cultural) players and spaces and focusing too much on the current developments without a sense of context. Too narrow a definition of EU studies – as proponents of a disciplinary approach might favour – would be even more restrictive. There are of course many active in EU studies who would recognize these dangers and who would argue that their own embrace of interdisciplinarity within EU studies offers a way of avoiding such risks. More valuable still, however, might be to pursue an understanding of the EU which is informed by an understanding of the development of Europe. It is in this context that we argue for the importance of unpicking the elements of European studies and EU studies and considering more closely the issues of region and regionness.

One starting point in reconciling European and EU studies would be to build on the renewed interest in comparing the fortunes of different regional integration projects, including the EU. Warleigh-Lack (2004, 2006) has sought to bring together the insights of EU studies and 'new regionalism' and there has been a more general revival of interest in 'comparative regionalism'. As noted, the return to regional cooperation has, like its predecessor, attracted a good deal of academic attention though the research agenda is much more diverse and has given rise to a more pluralistic approach to comparison. As noted, 'old regionalism' sought to apply models originally applied in an European context, generally unsuccessfully, with the result that the academic interest in regionalism – whether comparative or otherwise – diminished. Current analyses of regionalism are able to make use of a more eclectic range of ideas (drawn not only from the study of the EU but from other disciplines as well), and take into account the rather different circumstances in which integration has taken place as well as a better understanding of the importance of the 'idea of region' (Breslin and Higgot, 2000: 335).

The notion of region has often been taken for granted. As Smouts notes (in a piece which is as much about the subnational aspect of regional as the supranational aspect), '[I]t is characteristic of the region to have neither a definition nor an outline. The empirical criteria which allow the socio-economic entity to be recognised as sufficiently homogenous and distinct are vague and mixed. The 'region' category regroups disparate aggregates and the same term serves to denote subnational formations … intermediaries between the local and the national levels within the state … various cooperation zones including states indeed entire subcontinents … and transborder areas between several subnational regions belonging to different states' (Smouts, 1998: 30–1).

Indeed the region's importance as a focus for research seem to go beyond the specifics of the 'new regionalism'. Emmanuel Adler (1997) talks of the community or cognitive region as increasingly manifest in people's notions of identity. He notes how what is understood as 'home' has grown from the nation state and while the latter is likely to remain as the 'basic reality of international life' he argues that there are other venues. Adapting Karl Deutsch's concept of pluralistic security communities he argues that there is an increasing focus on 'cognitive regions' as integration consolidates. In this context he argues, drawing on Ruggie (1993), that 'territoriality' which had traditionally privileged the nation state becomes unbundled and the relative significance of the region increases.[4]

Wallace, Hettne and Hurrell's approaches to regionalism take on board this broader perspective. While William Wallace focuses upon the contrast between the formal and informal aspects of regions (Wallace, 1990, 1994), the others seek to identify a more multifaceted notion of the region. Hettne outlined his concept of 'regionness' as analogous to ideas of stateness and nation-ness, suggesting five levels or degrees of regionness:

- the region as 'a geographical and ecological unit delimited by natural barriers' (Hettne, 1994: 136);
- the region as a social system implying a mix of 'translocal relations of a social, political, cultural and economic nature' which form a 'security complex';
- the region as 'organized cooperation';
- the region as regional civil society emerging when frameworks promote 'social communication and convergence of values', within which culture and a 'shared civilizational tradition' are important';
- the region as a historical formation with a distinct identity and actor capability, as well as a certain level of legitimacy' (Hettne, 1994: 137)

Hurrell admits that, while some geographical definition is inevitable, there are 'no 'natural' regions'. Instead he argues that 'it is how political actors perceive and interpret the idea of a region and notions of 'regionness' that is critical: all regions are socially constructed and hence politically contested' (Hurrell, 1995: 38–9). He offers five contrasting (but overlapping and potentially cumulative) notions of region:

- *Regionalization.* Referring to 'societal' and undirected processes of social and economic interaction

(Hurrell, 1995: 39) (broadly equivalent to what others consider as informal integration or soft regionalism), Hurrell tends to stress this as referring to a condition of economic relations (including issues of migration). Such regionalism he argues is not necessarily the result of conscious policy (1995: 40)

- *Regional awareness and identity.* Considering this as 'fuzzy' but 'impossible to ignore' (1995: 41), Hurrell explicitly links this notion of the region to Adler's cognitive regions – relying on language, a discourse of regionalism and shared understandings and meanings, which offer various bases for regional awareness including 'the other' (1995: 41). He sees this aspect as a feature of the new regionalism (1995: 41): 'They are framed by historically deep-rooted arguments about the definition of the region and the values and purposes that it represents – although ... as with regionalism, there is a good deal of historical rediscovery, myth making and invented traditions' (1995: 41).
- *Regional interstate cooperation.* By this Hurrell means, 'the negotiation and construction of interstate or intergovernmental agreements or regimes' (1995: 42). Such cooperation could be formal or informal (treaties or looser arrangements).
- *State-promoted regional integration.* He considers this as a process of internal integration along the lines of the European Union 'model' in its economic aspects (1995: 43).
- *Regional cohesion.* Hurrell considers this as a possible 'combination of these first four processes' which '(m)ight lead to the emergence of a cohesive and consolidated regional unit' (1995: 44). Such cohesion might be seen when the region shapes relations between the states of that region and the rest of the world and/ or when the region becomes the focal point for policy making on a range of issues (1995: 44). This arguably could be read as referring to the EU in terms of its broader competences.

Such approaches have generally been deployed to contrast the relative development of regionalism in different parts of the world and in some cases (such as Fawcett and Hurrell, 1995) comparing the EU with other regional projects. However, for our purposes, such approaches could be used for examining the current evolution of integration in the context of the longer term evolution of 'Europe'. Such a historical comparison would not simply focus on the various attempts (through cooperation or conquest) to 'unite' Europe but would look at how 'the regional' and 'integration' have characterized Europe in the past.

Historical perspectives on European integration are not new, ranging from William Henderson's (1959) account of the Zollverein and subsequent work on other forms of cooperation in Europe (1962) to William Wallace's (1990) account of European integration in earlier periods, Walter Mattli's (1999) account of the factors shaping regionalism across time and space and Pagden's (2002) more wide-ranging collection which brings together accounts of the idea of Europe with contemporary understandings of integration. Of particular importance was Deutsch's (1957) attempts to understand processes of integration at the national and regional level. However, as another author of a historically informed approach to integration argued, in seeking to identify generalizations about the necessary conditions for integration, Deutsch 'avoided the questions of whether integration is qualitatively different in different socio-economic formations, why it emerges at some historical periods and … gave no indication of the dynamic that connects or disconnects past and present cases of unification' (Cocks, 1980: 2).

A better approach might be to adapt recent work on defining the region in a comparative context and apply that over time rather than across space. Taking Hurrell and Hettne's characteristics of regions, therefore, we can identify a set of criteria for assessing regionness in Europe over time:

- The extent of actual integration-linkages of trade and migration.
- The extent of values, beliefs, cultures, languages and institutions which are held in common.
- The extent of any shared identity.
- The extent of any shared sense of mission in the form of an idealised sense of region or of proposals for closer cooperation and unity.
- The extent of any formal cooperation, consolidation or other frameworks for integration (whether based on consent or on force)

Addressing the regionness of Europe in these ways cannot really be achieved on the basis of a narrowly defined 'EU studies' agenda (though the latter may still offer important insights – see Mattli, 1999, as well as Dinan's 2006 review of how historians have explored the EU). Instead there has to be an engagement with a much wider range of insights and perspectives of the sort which 'European studies' could provide. The range of factors highlighted here – and the readiness to contextualize historically and culturally – brings into the frame a wider range of understandings of Europe than a narrow account of integration and institutions. At the same time, retaining the concern with integration provides some focus for pooling those insights. As Breslin and Higgot have suggested – with reference to the comparative analysis of regionalism – what is needed 'is a marriage between the disciplinary approaches of the theorist of regionalism and that rich empirical work which recognises the importance of specific historical and political contexts' (Breslin and Higgot, 2000: 341). Arguably what they consider as valuable about the comparative approach – 'a key mechanism for bringing area studies and disciplinary studies together and enhancing both' (Breslin and Higgot, 2000: 341) – would also be relevant for a comparison across time as well as between places.

THE PERILS OF EUROTOPIAS AND EUROCENTRISM

What is proposed is a way of bringing together aspects of studying Europe as a region (whether institutionalized or not) rather than a discipline in its own right (Rumford and Murray, 2003b). Such an approach would entail a fruitful synthesis of the insights of European studies to the study of European integration while also offering the possibility of using concepts and debates derived from the study of the EU to make sense of Europe as a region before 1951 (e.g. the importance of nonstate actors in framing economic cooperation in earlier eras or the possibilities of deploying the insights of the Europeanization debate).

However, it must be recognized that such an approach brings its own problems. The perennial question of the boundaries of Europe as a region is one such problem, though we are inclined to agree with William Wallace who argues that while 'Europe as a region has never had clear boundaries … it has had identifiable core areas, shifting slowly over time in response to internal and external developments' (Wallace 1990: 13). Two more fundamental criticisms need to be considered in more detail, however. At one level, the sort of endeavour envisaged in the last few pages could fall into the trap of prescriptiveness and of teleology; that there has been an 'essence' of Europe over time and that where we are now offers an fulfilment of that essence. At another related level, there is a risk that such a project privileges the development of Europe as a distinctive region, prompting the charge of 'Eurocentrism'.

The relationship between studying Europe and the EU on the one hand and idealizing them on the other is never far from the surface of the academic debate. Calhoun notes the impact of the EU on European studies as 'both part of an analytic project as researchers sought to understand what was happening in Europe and of an ideological–pedagogical project as some European leaders sought to teach students a European self-understanding of the EU' (Calhoun, 2003: 13). Drawing attention to the wave of European histories which explicitly invoke recent steps towards integration, Mitterauer argues that there is 'an obvious synchronicity between a wave of intensive publishing activities and the institutionalization of European history on one hand and the foundation of [European institutions] on the other' (Mitterauer, 2006: 269). He asks whether 'European historiography serve(s) as an ideology to legitimate current European

policies' (2006: 270) and draws parallels with past political movements where nationalism and national historiography have been closely connected (2006: 270). Heffernan (1998) also touches on the 'prescriptive' tendency in much writing about Europe: 'The history of the European idea is … read "backwards" from the present into the past so that recent moves towards European unification appears as an inevitable historical evolution' (1998: 3).

Certainly there is a danger that such an approach falls into the trap of seeing European history, as Delanty notes, 'in quasi teleological terms as a movement towards unity' (Delanty, 2008: 21) Past accounts of the 'emergence of Europe' have been more or less explicit in celebrating European cooperation in the postwar period (in contrast to earlier eras), with de Rougemont's (1966) work a particular example of this. Such tendencies were the target of Delanty's (1995) critique of the 'idea of Europe' where he seeks to deconstruct the 'Platonic-like vision of an immutable European ideal' (1995: 2) and take issue with the largely uncritical nature of the limited existing literature. Others had the opportunity to reconsider their enthusiasm. Hay (1980) repudiates his earlier (1957) writing on Europe as uncritical, claiming that '[w]e were not only assuming a kind of historical inevitability in the notion but trying positively to encourage the process' (1980: 3) and appearing to recognize the need to keep some distance between historical analysis and current affairs.

Yet, as Delanty and others admit, the status quo of nation-state-centric history is not unproblematic either. Blockmans, himself the author of a European Commission-funded history of Europe over the last 1000 years (1997), echoes Le Goff's view that it is impossible to write a truly European history as such nation-state-centric literature dominates the field and 'the national boundaries of modern Europe seem to be indelibly etched into the consciousness of historians' (Blockmans, 2006: 241).

Cutting across the federalist and statist perspectives (in Delanty's terms) might be possible – and the risks of teleology and prescription minimized – by a more detached and critical approach to the EU and Europe, one based on a recognition that the EU does not constitute the end result of past ideals and international conflicts. Instead it marks a particular venture in integration which has its resonances in the ideals and the experience of previous eras. Moreover, such a historically informed perspective does not imply that integration be considered as either a default or a desideratum for it to be of interest and relevance.

It is also important to avoid another sometimes related tendency in previous accounts of Europe's development – Eurocentrism: the slip from explaining what factors might define Europe's 'regionness' – and in the process highlighting certain specificities and shared experiences – to asserting an intrinsic superiority about the European path. Such views are associated with Roberts (1985) and Landes (1998), though Blaut (2000) identifies a much wider range of economic historians and historical sociologists which he considers adopt such a perspective. Moreover the debate on Eurocentrism does raise important questions about how we should consider the development of Europe as a region in a world context over the longer run. However, it is important to recognize, as one critic of the tendency to Eurocentrism appears to, that centring on Europe *per se* is not the same as advocating that Europe has a privileged place in economic and political development (Blaut, 2000).

CONCLUSION

This chapter has sought to explore how European studies and EU studies – and their respective understandings of the region – have developed and interacted over recent years. It has highlighted the ways in which interest in the two fields has evolved and particularly the apparent shift from the more area studies based approach of European studies to the narrower integration agenda of EU studies. The paper has discussed some of the reasons for this shift, placing them in the context of more general debates. While the paper recognizes that some of these reasons relate to the shortcomings of European studies, it also argues that to marginalize that approach in favour of the more focused research programme of EU studies would bring its own problems.

It goes without saying that the EU and Europe are not equivalent and nor are European and EU studies. Of course, it is not possible to understand Europe over the last 50 plus years without taking into account the European Union or its precursors. As one considers the more recent past, moreover, the significance of the EU increases as its shadow casts across a wider territorial space and ever more policy competences. Moreover the EU impacts upon the other parts of Europe that membership has not yet (or might ever) reach. However while arguably a necessary part of anyone's understanding of Europe, the EU is very far from being a sufficient basis for such an understanding.

Moreover, whatever the relationship between 'Europe' and the 'EU' in the public discourse and the political realm, it would be wrong to subsume the agendas of different academic perspectives within a particular approach. It would be even more wrong to marginalize some issues because they did not fit within the research agenda of a particular approach. Instead a better approach is to recognize that there are important questions that each field has to address. Where the two fields overlap, moreover, the research and teaching challenge is not for one approach to displace the other but to bring about an effective synthesis of the two in addressing the nature of Europe as a region. Such an approach has been apparent in some recent scholarship (Katzenstein, 2005) and the paper has sought to identify how the two approaches could be used to inform each other and to understand the ways in which Europe as a region has evolved.

ACKNOWLEDGEMENTS

The principal catalyst for pulling the ideas together was the UACES workshop on inter-disciplinarity organized by Michelle Cini and Alex Warleigh at the University of Bristol in November 2006. Their ideas and comments, along with those of other participants, were of great value in shaping this chapter. I am also grateful to colleagues at the University of Sussex, notably Paul Taggart who has organized numerous discussions on the nature of EU studies and the late Bruce Graham who was responsible for my initial engage-ment with European studies.

NOTES

1 One example of the confusion is to look at how the respective fields are (or are not) addressed by learned associations. Rosamond (2007a) has exam-ined how far particular disciplines dominate the respective national associations. There is an interesting contrast in nomenclatures between the two principal associations. On the one hand, the UK has the University Association for Contemporary European Studies, an organization which has primarily sup-ported research on the EU to the exclusion of most other aspects of European studies (though it has retained a concern about the wider discipline in track-ing the teaching of 'European Studies' – see Smith, 2003). By contrast in the US, the academic community which researches and teaches the EU is organized around the European Union Studies Association while the Council for European Studies (formerly the Council of Europeanists) retains a broader (though not too broad) concern with Europe.

2 The contrast between these different approaches has been at the heart of recent work by Alex Warleigh-Lack (2004, 2006).

3 Some of the early students of regional integration sought to generalise the models which they applied to Europe to other regions. However, fairly quickly, even the most enthusiastic had to recognize that such models were not applicable (shortly before they had to recognise the limited applicability to the European Community itself). See Nye (1969) and Haas (1975).

4 A more critical view of regionalism and the region argues that most accounts 'inevitabilize' the region as a 'particular interpretation of international space' and fail to grasp the changing nature of regions – see Larner and Walters (2002).

REFERENCES

Adler, E. (1997) 'Imagined (security) communi-ties: cognitive regions in international rela-tions', *Millennium*, 26 (2): 249–277.

Bates, R.H. (1997) 'Area Studies and the disci-pline: a useful controversy?', *Political Science and Politics*, 30 (2): 166–169.

Bellier, I. (1997) 'The Commission as an actor: an anthropologist's view', H. in Wallace and A. Young, A. *Participation and Policy Making in the European Union*. Oxford: Clarendon Press, pp. 91–115.

Blaut, J.M. (2000) *Eight Eurocentric Historians*. New York: The Guilford Press,

Blockmans, W. (1997) *A History of Power in Europe: Peoples, Markets, States*. Antwerp: Fonds Mercator Paribas.

Blockmans, W. (2006) 'Europe's history of inte-gration and diversity', *European Review*, 14 (2): 241–256.

Breslin, S. and Higgott, R (2000) 'Studying regions: learning from the old, constructing the new', *New Political Economy*, 5 (3): 333–353.

Calhoun, C. (2003) 'European studies: always already there and still in formation', *Comparative European Politics*, 1 (1): 5–20.

Cini, M (2006) 'The state of the art in EU stud-ies: From politics to interdisciplinarity (and back again?)', *Politics*, 26 (1): 38–46.

Cini, M. and Bourne, A. (eds) (2006) *Palgrave Advances in European Union Studies*. Palgrave.

Cocks, P. (1980) 'Towards a Marxist theory of European integration', *International Organization*, 34 (1): 1–40.

Crouch, C. (2001) 'Breaking open black boxes – the implications for sociological theory of European integration' in A. Menon and V. Wright (eds) *From the Nation State to Europe*. Oxford: Oxford University Press, pp. 195–213.

Davies, N. (1996) *Europe – A History*. Oxford: Oxford University Press.

de Rougemont, D. (1966) *The Idea of Europe*. London: Macmillan.

Delanty, G. (2008) 'The European heritage: his-tory, memory and time' in C. Rumford (ed.) *The Sage Handbook of European Studies*. London: Sage.

Delanty, G. (1995) *Inventing Europe*. Palgrave.

Deutsch, K. (1957) *Political Community and the North Atlantic Area*. Princeton: Princeton University Press.

Dinan, D (2006) 'Interpreting European integration' in D. Dinan (ed.) *Origins and Evolution of the European Union*. Oxford: Oxford University Press, pp. 297–313.

Favell, A. (2007) 'The sociology of EU politics' in K. Jorgensen, M. Pollack and B. Rosamond (eds) *Handbook of European Politics*. London: Sage, pp. 122–138.

Fawcett, L. and Hurrell, A. (eds) (1995) *Regionalism in World Politics: Regional Organization and International Order*. Oxford: Oxford University Press.

Gamble, A. and Payne, A. (eds) (1996) *Regionalism and World Order*. Basingstoke: Macmillan.

Garrett, G. (1998) 'Global markets and national politics: collision course or virtuous circle?', *International Organization*, 52 (4): 149–176.

Garrett, G. (2000) 'The causes of globalization', *Comparative Political Studies*, 33 (6–7): 941–991.

Grugel, J. and Hout, W. (eds) (1998) *Regionalism Across the North South Divide*. Routledge.

Haas, E.B. (1975) *The Obsolescence of Regional Integration Theory*. Berkeley: University of California.

Hall, P.A. and Tarrow, S. (1998) 'Globalization and area studies: when is too broad too narrow?', *Chronicle of Higher Education* 44: 114–115.

Hay, C. and Marsh, D. (eds) (2000) *Demistifying Globalization*. Palgrave.

Hay, D. (1957) *Europe – the Emergence of an Idea*. Edinburgh: Edinburgh University Press.

Hay, D. (1980) 'Europe revisited: 1979', *History of European Ideas*, 1 (2): 11–21.

Heffernan, M. (1998) *The Meaning of Europe: Geography and Geopolitics*. Arnold.

Held, D., McGrew, A., Goldblatt, D. and Perraton, J. (1999) *Global Transformations: Politics, Economics and Culture*. Cambridge: Polity Press.

Henderson, W. (1959) *The Zollverein*. London: Cass.

Henderson, W. (1962) *Genesis of the Common Market*. London: Cass.

Hettne, B (1994) 'The regional factor in the formation of a new world order' in Y. Sakamoto (ed.) *Global Transformation: Challenges to the State System*. Tokyo: United Nations University Press, pp. 134–166.

Hirst, P. and Thompson, G. (1996) *Globalisation in Question*. Cambridge: Polity Press.

Hix, S (1994) ''The study of the European community: The challenge to comparative.

politics', *West European Politics*, 17 (1): 1–30.

Hix, S. (2005) *The Political System of the European Union*. Palgrave.

Horsman, M. and Marshall, A. (1994) *After the Nation-state: Citizens, Tribalism and the New World Disorder*. Harper Collins.

Hurrell, A. (1995) 'Regionalism in theoretical perspective" in L. Fawcett and A. Hurrell (eds) *Regionalism in World Politics: Regional Organization and International Order*. Oxford: Oxford University Press.

Hurrell, A. (2007) 'One world? Many worlds? The place of regions in the study of international society', *International Affairs*, 83 (1): 127–146.

Judt, T. (2005) *Post War – a History of Europe since 1945*. Penguin.

Jupille, J (2006) 'Knowing Europe: Metatheory and methodology in European Union studies' in M. Cini and A. Bourne (eds) (2006) *Palgrave Advances in European Union Studies*. Palgrave, pp. 209–232.

Katzenstein, P. (2001) 'Area and regional studies in the United States' *PS: Political Science and Politics*, 34 (4): 789–791.

Katzenstein, P. (2005) *A World of Regions*. Cornell.

Keeler, J. (2005) 'Mapping EU studies: the evolution from Boutique to Boom Field 1960–2001', *Journal of Common Market Studies*, 43 (3): 551–582.

Landes, D. (1998) *The Wealth and Poverty of Nations*, Little, Brown & Company.

Larner, W. and Walters, W. (2002) 'The political rationality of "new regionalism" Towards a genealogy of the region', *Theory and Society*, 31 (3): 391–432.

Lawrence, R. (1996) *Regionalism, Multilateralism and Deeper Integration*. Washington: Brookings.

Mansfield, E. and Milner, H. (eds) (1997) *The Political Economy of Regionalism*. New York: Columbia University Press.

Mattli, W. (1999) *The Logic of Regional Integration: Europe and Beyond*. Cambridge University Press.

Mazower, M. (1998) *Dark Continent: Europe's Twentieth Century*. Allen Lane.

McGowan, F. (1999) 'Globalisation, regional integration and the state' in M. Shaw (ed.) *Politics and Globalisation*. Routledge, pp. 55–70.

Medrano, J. (2003) *Framing Europe: Attitudes to European Integration in Germany, Spain, and the United Kingdom*. Princeton: Princeton University Press.

Mitterauer, M (2006) 'Exceptionalism? European history in a global context', *European Review*, 14 (2): 269–280.

Nye, J (ed.) (1969) *International Regionalism*. Boston: Little, Brown & Co.

Pagden, A. (ed.) (2002) *The Idea of Europe. From Antiquity to the European Union*. Cambridge University Press.

Payne, A (2000) 'Globalization and Modes of Regionalist Governance', in J. Pierre (ed.) *Debating Governance: Authority, Steering, and Democracy*. Oxford: Oxford University Press, pp. 201–218.

Pollack, M.A. (2000) 'The end of creeping competence? EU policy-making since Maastricht', *Journal of Common Market Studies*, 38 (3): 519–538.

Pollack, M.A. (2005) 'Theorizing the European Union: international organization, domestic polity, or experiment in new governance?', *Annual Review of Political Science*, 8: 357–398.

Rafael, V. (1994) 'The cultures of area studies in the United States', *Social Text* 41: 91–111.

Roberts, J. (1985) *The Triumph of the West*. BBC.

Rosamond, B. (2000) *Theories Of European Integration*. Palgrave.

Rosamond, B. (2007a) 'European integration and the social science of EU studies: the disciplinary politics of a subfield', *International Affairs*, 83 (2): 231–252.

Rosamond, B (2007b) 'The political sciences of European integration: disciplinary history and EU studies' in K. Jorgensen, M. Pollack and B. Rosamond (eds) *Handbook of European Politics*. London: Sage, pp. 7–30.

Ruggie, J. (1993) 'Territoriality and beyond: problematizing modernity in international relations', *International Organization*, 47 (1): 139–174.

Rumford, C. and Murray, P. (2003a) 'Do we need a core curriculum in European studies?' *European Political Science*, 3 (1), 1–8.

Rumford, C. and Murray, P. (2003b) 'Globalization and the limitations of European integration studies: interdisciplinary considerations', *Journal of Contemporary European Studies*, 11 (1), 85–93.

Schmidt, S. (1996) 'Sterile debates and dubious generalisations: European integration theory tested by telecommunications and electricity', *Journal of Public Policy*, 16 (3): 233–271.

Shore, C. (2000) *Building Europe: The Cultural Politics of European Integration*. London: Routledge.

Smith, M. (2003) *The State of European Studies, Report Commissioned by the Standing Conference of Heads of European Studies*. London: SCHES.

Smouts, M.C. (1998) 'The region as the new imagined community' in P. Le Gales and C. Lequesne (eds) *Regions in Europe*. London: Routledge.

Strange, S (1996) *The Retreat of the State*. Cambridge: Cambridge University Press.

Strange, S. (1997) 'The future of global capitalism; or will divergence persist forever?' in C. Crouch and W. Streeck (eds) *Political Economy of Modern Capitalism*. London: Sage, pp. 182–191.

Tessler, M. (1999) 'Introduction: The area studies controversy', in M. Tessler (ed.) *Area Studies and Social Sciences – Strategies for Understanding Middle East Politics*. Bloomington: Indiana University Press, vii–xxi.

Umbach, G. and B. Scholl (2003) 'Towards a core curriculum in EU studies', *European Political Science*, 2 (2): 71–80.

Wallace, H. (2000) 'Studying contemporary Europe', *British Journal of Politics and International Relations*, 2 (1): 95–113.

Wallace, W. (1990) *The Transformation of Western Europe*. London: Royal Institute of International Affairs (RIIA).

Wallace, W. (1994) *Regional Integration: the West European Experience*. Brookings.

Warleigh-Lack, A. (2004) 'In defence of intra-disciplinarity: "European studies", the "new regionalism" and the issue of democratisation', *Cambridge Review of International Affairs*, 17 (2): 301–318.

Warleigh-Lack, A (2006) 'Learning from Europe? EU studies and the re-thinking of international relations', *European Journal of International Relations*, 12 (1): 31–51.

Wight, M. (1964) 'European studies', in D. Daiches (ed.) *The Idea of a University*. Andre Deutsch, pp. 100–119.

Worcester, K. and Tarrow, S. (1994) 'New challenges facing European studies', *PS: Political Science and Politics*, 27 (1): 53–55.

31

Normative Power Europe: A Transdisciplinary Approach to European Studies

Ian Manners

As this book illustrates, the field of European studies is constituted by the need to constantly rethink how best to study contemporary Europe and the transformations which characterize it. European studies is, as Craig Calhoun neatly surmised, 'always already there and still in formation' (Calhoun, 2003a; see also Lindström, 2002; Manners, 2003; Rumford and Murray, 2003a, 2003b; Wallace, 2000; Warleigh, 2004). From my perspective, the field of European studies has been one largely defined by three analytical features. First, it primarily consists of multidisciplinary perspectives on Europe, including language and literature, history, politics, economics, law, geography, sociology, cultural studies, and more (for examples, see Sakwa and Stevens, 2000, or Gowland et al., 2006). Second, the field consists of interdisciplinary foci on Europe as a place, space, and idea (for examples, see Kofman et al., 2000; or Griffin and Braidotti, 2002). And finally a relative absence of transdisciplinary methods for examining Europe (for exceptions, see Passerini, 1998, or Guisan, 2003).

While a discipline can be a community of expertise which considers itself a comparatively self-contained, teachable and knowable domain; 'multidisciplinary study involves employing two or more disciplines, in juxtaposition' (Ellis, 2003). In this respect, multidisciplinary research involves scholars working in a fairly 'self-contained manner' while coming together to work on a shared problem (Denemark, 1999: 53; Lawrence and Després, 2004: 400). In contrast, interdisciplinary study goes beyond (multi) disciplinary comparison towards a more interactive and integrative approach between different disciplines.

Transdisciplinary scholarship is even more demanding, involving research and study around 'complex heterogeneous domains' in order to address complex phenomena (Denemark, 1999: 53; Lawrence and Després, 2004: 400). But whereas, multidisciplinary or interdisciplinary work involves comparison of many perspectives, or cooperation between differing perspectives, transdisciplinary research is like standing on one's head – the reorganization of disciplinary practices in order to transgress and transcend pre-existing frames of knowledge organization:

> Transdisciplinarity, understood as a critical evaluation of terms, concepts, and methods that transgresses disciplinary boundaries can be a means to [a] higher level of reflexivity ... As an epistemological and methodological strategy, transdisciplinarity proceeds from the insight that disciplines are conventionally thought of territorially, as independent domains with clear boundaries. In fact, however, disciplines are characterized by multiple interconnections and shot through with cross-disciplinary pathways. Consequently, the boundaries between them must be understood – much like physical territorial borders – as arbitrary products of social activity (Dölling and Hark, 2000: 1195–6).

Roland Robertson has argued that the complex convergence of disciplines in the processes of globalization demands trans-disciplinary approaches under conditions of globality (Robertson, 1996: 128; see also Hodge, 2002). The emphasis in this chapter will be on this latter approach and will suggest a transdisciplinary approach to European studies I call 'normative power Europe'. At the centre of this approach is an interest in the power of ideas of the common good, and their diffusion in a European context.

Ideas of the common good in Europe have been rarely conceptualized beyond notions of 'national' in European studies. Clearly a means of understanding and analysing contemporary Europe beyond national pre-sumptions is an important but neglected theme in European studies. Although there have been discussions of postnational citizenship (Soysal, 1994) and postnational democracy (Curtin, 1997) in Europe, the analysis of the power of ideas of the common good that are neither merely national nor postnational has received less attention. However, the works of Craig Calhoun, Gerald Delanty and Chris Rumford have addressed the idea of the common good in terms of the 'collective good', 'good society', or 'social solidarity' in ways that seek to go beyond theories of society located solely in terms of national, supranational, postnational, or civil society (Calhoun, 2003b; Delanty and Rumford, 2006).

Calhoun suggests that 'choosing incon-sistency and a plurality of forms of social solidarity and collective identity' is challenging, noting that 'if Europeans choose the course of pluriform social organization ... then they will be sailing in poorly charted waters and in need of serious theoretical work to make sure the taken-for-granted assumptions of nationalist discourse and its intellectual cousins do not close off attractive possibilities' (Calhoun, 2001: 53–4). Delanty and Rumford argue that 'in order to understand the nature of European material, cultural and political realities today a theory of society is needed' (Delanty and Rumford, 2006: 6). They suggest that such a theory is needed in order to get a sense of the notion of the 'good society' that does not presume a link between EU integration and European society; places Europe and the EU within a global frame of reference; and provides a resource for both social theory and contemporary European studies (Delanty and Rumford, 2006: 3–5). The transdisciplinary approach suggested in this chapter is intended to follow these initiatives in order to better grasp the power of ideas of the common good and thus contribute towards theory development in European studies.

The intention in this chapter is to develop a normative power approach to European studies that can be applied across and beyond its con-stitutive disciplines in order to interrogate and transgress the ideas and spaces on/of Europe. Students of European studies should be aware that there are some very good reasons why there has been a relative absence of trans-disciplinary approaches. The participating disciplines of European studies have differing acceptable practices, known as 'normal sci-ence' (Kuhn, 1962), in terms of analytical questions, theories and methods. Furthermore, Ben Rosamond has suggested that concepts, such as, 'normative', 'power', and 'Europe' are among the most contested concepts in the social sciences.[1]

In four parts this chapter will first explore the terms 'normative', 'power', and 'Europe', before applying the approach to an example. In each part I shall explore one of the terms as a means of illustrating how such a transdisciplinary approach may contribute to understanding Europe. Part one examines three different approaches to normative ethics – 'virtues', 'deontology', and 'consequentialism' – in order to make sense of ideas of the common good. Part two looks at three different types of power – 'relational', 'structural', and 'normative' – as a means of understanding the power of ideas of the common good. Part three considers three different means of understanding Europe – 'civilizational', 'categorical', and 'cultural' – to show how the power of ideas of the common good shape our means of comprehending contemporary Europe. Part four will attempt to apply the approach to the question of a European counter-terrorist response. I have chosen this example because of the challenges it presents to contemporary Europe and as a means of illustrating the way a normative power Europe approach opens up transdisciplinary thinking across and beyond disciplinary thinking.

NORMATIVE ETHICS

As a first step towards a more transdisciplinary European studies, I will look at the way different approaches to normative ethics help us make sense of ideas regarding the common good. By the 'common good' I mean the idea of general wellbeing shared by all members of a society. This notion of common good obviously leaves open the discussion of *who* are members of a society and *what* might be their general well being. For example, does the common good apply to local communities, larger 'nations', Europe, or the whole of humanity? Similarly, is the general wellbeing to be found in equality or freedom, for example? The study of normative ethics therefore involves asking what ideas of the common good are considered important, by whom and why. Normative ethics focuses on the impact these ideas have on actions taken by groups and societies, in order to understand which actions are considered right or wrong. In this

respect it is usual to distinguish between three approaches to normative ethics – virtue ethics, deontological ethics, and consequentialist ethics – each of which I shall briefly consider within the context of European studies.

Virtue ethics

Virtue ethics is currently one of the three major approaches in normative ethics. It may, initially, be identified as the one that emphasizes the virtues, or moral character, in contrast to the approach which emphasizes duties or rules (deontology) or that which emphasizes the consequences of actions (Hursthouse, 2003: 3).

Virtue ethicists' such as Philippa Foot and Rosalind Hursthouse draw on Aristotle's notion of virtue in terms of character traits or dispositions (Foot, 1978; Hursthouse, 1999). This tends to put the emphasis on teaching and education as part of the social and personal development of moral virtue. However, as Slote puts it, '[V]arious forms of virtue ethics play down the importance or even deny the existence of generally valid moral rules or principles, and claim that morality is most fundamentally to be understood in terms of inner traits, virtues, that cannot be cashed out in terms of rules or goals' (Slote, 1995: 900). In terms of thinking about transdisciplinary European studies, virtue ethics encourage us to look at the character or traits which guide differing groups and their idea of the common good.

Virtue ethics and their emphasis on the moral character of social groups encourage a focus on the interpretation of virtues such as 'benevolence', 'generosity', or 'justice'. Such an interrogation inevitably involves examining the means through which such virtues become established and the extent to which a group shares them. The establishment of virtues through education, religion, or other social practices clearly form an important part of understanding the shared basis of the common good. General examples of such virtues might include classical merits such as temperance, prudence, fortitude, or justice. More religious virtues, such as, faith and charity entered the catalogue of valued qualities at a latter stage. It is also worth considering the way in which derivations of such virtues entered the discourses of European enlightenment in modern times. Hence, the French revolution championed the virtues of liberty, equality, and 'fraternity' (solidarity), while the European Union (EU) seeks the virtues of unity and diversity.

An example of a virtue ethics approach to ideas of the common good in Europe may be found in the Austrian sanctions crisis in 2000. During the 1990s, the Organization for Security and Cooperation in Europe (OSCE), the Council of Europe (CoE), and the EU had been busily institutionalizing post-Cold War virtues such as human rights and democracy as part of providing moral maps in the 'new Europe' (Manners, 2002: 242–4; Merlingen et al., 2001: 63–4). In February 2000 the creation of a new Austrian coalition government including the neonationalist Freedom Party (FPÖ) led by Jörg Haider directly questioned these virtues. A mixture of reasons, including the role of party groups within EU member states and shared ideas of virtuous politics across the EU, led to the imposition of bilateral sanctions by the 14 other members of the EU between February and September 2000.

The importance given to the virtues of human rights and democracy as ethical reasons for the sanctions is central to understanding the Austrian crisis. Public reasoning and debating of the problems of interfering in the domestic politics of another EU member state were to be increasingly heard throughout the seven-month period, particularly in smaller member states and those that had their own neonationalist concerns (Gingrich 2006: 200–1; Merlingen et al., 2001: 73). Concerns for the counter-productive consequences of the sanctions within Austria were also to be heard, with many commentators pointing to 'widespread anti-EU sentiments' in Austria, and increasingly

beyond (Howard 2001: 26; Merlingen et al., 2001: 73). Despite these concerns with foreign interference and counter-productive consequences, it was the perceived virtues of the principles that held the sanctions in place until September 2000. It was then that the committee of Ahtisaari, Frowein and Oreja, mandated by the European Court of Human Rights (ECHR), whilst criticizing the FPÖ, argued that the Austrian government itself had complied with common European values (Falkner 2001: 11; Merlingen et al., 2001: 72). This decision was made easier by Haider's resignation of the leadership of the FPÖ and the marginalization of the FPÖ by the Christian Democrats within the coalition government (Gingrich 2006: 231; Happold, 2000: 963).

Deontological ethics

The central thought of Kant's account of public reason is that the standards of reason cannot be derivative. Any appeal to other external authorities to buttress our reasoning must fail. Just as a learner cyclist who clutches at passing objects and leans on them for balance thereby fails to balance at all, so a would-be reasoner who leans on some socially or civilly constituted power or authority which lacks reasoned vindication fails to reason (O'Neill, 2000a: 52).

Deontological ethicists, such as, Onora O'Neill draw on Immanuel Kant's notion of public reason in terms of duties and rules governing action (O'Neill, 2000b; Reiss, 1991). As O'Neill's quote illustrates, unlike virtues, a deontological approach involves reasoning the merits of action without reference to, or derivation from an external authority. Roger Crisp clarifies the difference between this approach and that of consequentialism thus – '[D]eontological ethics [are] moral theories according to which certain acts must or must not be done, regardless to some extent of the consequences of their performance or non-performance' (Crisp, 1995: 187). In contrast to virtue ethics, a deontological approach to transdisciplinary European studies emphasizes the rationalization of duties and rules which guide differing groups and their idea of the common good.

Deontological ethics move the focus beyond the character of social groups towards an understanding of group actions and inactions. O'Neill and other neo-Kantians seek to emphasize the progressive and expansive role of public debate and reasoning in creating the rights and duties held to be important within a group. An awareness of the promotion of such rule-governed behaviour through domestic and international law is central to making sense of this shared idea of the common good. Unlike virtue ethics, deontological ethics provides few absolute merits which might be pursued, rather the approach emphasizes the means through which actions are motivated and practised. In this respect, much weight is placed on the establishment of law, including both rights and duties, in the pursuit of the common good. Both advocates and detractors of European integration have argued that Europe has become a 'Kantian paradise' governed by domestic and international law such as the 'acquis communautaire' of the EU (Dalgaard-Nielsen, 2004: 71–3; Menon *et al.*, 2004: 9).

An example of a deontological ethics approach to ideas of the common good can be seen in the genetically modified (GM) food crises from 1998 to date. Since its inclusion in the 1992 Treaty on European Union, the precautionary principle has become an important feature of European international environmental law (Douma, 2000; Welsh, 2006). In February 2000, the European Commission's communication argued that the precautionary principle should be applied when 'preliminary objective scientific evaluation indicates that there are reasonable grounds for concern that the potentially dangerous effects on the environment, human, animal or plant health may be inconsistent with the chosen level of protection' (European Commission, 2000: 3, 10; Baker, 2006: 87; Douma, 2000: 141). The precautionary principle provides a rule-based approach to dealing with uncertainty and risk to life through a reasoned legal principle for action based on the principle that 'prevention is better than cure'. However, the importation of GM maize and soya beans from the US during 1996–1997 raised public concern, particularly following the 1996 BSE crisis, regarding the need for a precautionary approach to the uncertainty and risk associated with genetic modification, production and impact in Europe (Carr 2002: 32; De Marchi and Ravetz, 1999: 748–51; Sicurelli, 2004: 11–12). A mixture of reasons, including the conflicting motivations of international agribusiness and more local organic farming, led to a precautionary moratorium on the importation of GM products into Europe from 1998 to 2004 (Carr, 2002: 33; Karlsson, 2006: 49; GMO Compass, 2006).

The importance given to the role of the precautionary principle as a reason for the moratorium is crucial to making sense of the GM food crisis. The virtues of the precautionary principle and its application to GM food appear contradictory, with advocates of 'freedom' (primarily international agribusinesses such as Monsanto and Syngenta) clashing with supporters of 'justice' and 'prudence' (primarily advocates of local empowerment and international environmental groups such as Greenpeace and Friends of the Earth). Similarly, the consequences of such a precautionary approach are mixed, with concerns about the long-term impact on European bioscience contrasting with the significant consequences for biodiversity of pesticide toleration and transgenic hybridization. Despite these differing virtues and consequences, European support for the precautionary principle in international law ensures that, years after the moratorium ended, most Europeans have a deep suspicion of GM foods with low levels (below 1 per cent) of GM crop plantation in Spain, Portugal, Germany, France, and the Czech Republic. The WTO ruling in September 2006 on the transatlantic trade dispute over GM foods makes clear that high stakes, large uncertainty, and intense normative disputes over GM products cannot and should not be resolved through 'normal' scientific and politics means, prompting a need for extending peer communities, and ensuring the more consistent application of the 2003 Cartagena Protocol on Biosafety which is widely supported in Europe (Bäckstrand, 2003; De Marchi and Ravetz, 1999; Friends of the Earth 2006; Healy, 1999).

Consequentialist ethics

It is a necessary feature of consequentialism that it is a shallow philosophy. For there are always borderline cases in ethics. Now if you are an Aristotelian ... you will deal with a borderline case by considering whether doing such-and-such in such-and-such circumstances is, say, murder, or an act of injustice; and accordingly you decide it is or it isn't, you judge it to be a thing to do or not ... The consequentialist has no footing on which to say 'this would be permissible, this not'; because by [their] own hypothesis, it is the consequences that are to decide (Anscombe, 1958).

Consequentialist ethicists, such as, Elizabeth Anscombe draw on and develop the utilitarianism of Jeremy Bentham and John Stuart Mill in order to argue for normative ethics based on the outcomes of actions (Darwall, 2002; Geach and Gormally, 2006). Unlike the neo-Aristotelian or neo-Kantian approaches, Anscombe argued that a consequentialist approach did not judge ethical cases on their own merit, but looked towards the consequences of action or inaction for guidance. James Griffin clarifies that 'consequentialism [is] a term now used for the view that all actions are right or wrong in virtue of the value of their consequences' (Griffin, 1995: 154). Unlike virtue and deontological ethics which focus on motivations, transdisciplinary European studies using a consequentialist approach involves analysing the consequences of actions and their implications for differing groups and their idea of the common good.

Although consequentialist ethics share an emphasis with deontological ethics on the rights and wrongs of group actions, the focus of this approach is on the interplay between actors and consequences. The implications of this approach are significant for debates regarding the relationships between Europe and the rest of the world, for example raising questions about the merits of European aid and trade. This also introduces the problem of value pluralism and the extent to which the merits of differing consequences may themselves be moral choices (Reader, 2000: 356). This problem has become widespread in debates regarding the relative merits of pursuing the 1992 UNCED Rio and 2002 WSSD Johannesburg sustainable development agenda; the 2000 UN Millennium Development Goals; the 2001 DoHa Declaration; and the 2002 Monterrey Consensus at the same time, with very different consequences (Manners, 2007).

An example of a consequentialist ethics approach to ideas of the common good in Europe might be seen in the Kosovo intervention crisis during 1999. During the 1991–1995 war in Yugoslavia, many European states became convinced that never again would such large-scale massacres of civilians occur while neighbouring states and institutions failed to act (Malmvig, 2006: 64–5). The violence in Yugoslavia did not end with the November 1995 Dayton Accords, and by mid-1998 Europeans were concerned at the escalation of violence by the Kosovo Liberation Army (KLA) and the Serbian security forces (Latawski and Smith, 2002: 216). A ceasefire arranged by Richard Holbrooke with Slobodan Milosovic in October 1998 was soon broken by the KLA, escalating atrocities by Serbian security forces. The EU Forensic Expert Team in Kosovo investigated three sites (Klecka, Volujak, and Racak) involving approximately 200 civilians executed between August 1998 and January 1999, in part contributing to the Rambouillet peace talks in February and March 1999 (Friis and Murphy, 2000; Rainio et al., 2001). The collapse of these talks coincided with a renewed Serbian offensive against the KLA, leading to the launching of NATO's Operation Allied Force in late March 2006, and the fleeing of over 800,000 Kosovar refugees by the time the aerial bombardment ended in early June 2006 (Friis and Murphy, 2000: 767; Huysmans, 2002: 602).

The importance given to the anticipated consequences of military inaction are critical to appreciating the Kosovo crisis (Malmvig, 2006: 76). From June 1998 to March 1999 members of NATO began preparing for direct military involvement in Kosovo, fearful of consequences similar to Bosnia should they not intervene. By the beginning of March 1999 approximately 7,000 personnel (out of a planned 25,000) from the UK, France, Germany, and Italy were deployed in Macedonia in advance of a NATO activation order (House of Commons, 2000). The virtues of 'temperance' in dealing with Milosevic and the warring parties in Kosovo, as well as 'prudence' in taking direct action, were dispensed with in favour of a two-month NATO air campaign. In a similar way, the deontological reasons for non-intervention, including the absence of a UN Security Council mandate and dispensing with questions of sovereignty in international law, did not prevent NATO action, despite opposition from within some member states (particularly Greece and Germany) (Friis and Murphy, 2000: 768–9; Latawski and Smith, 2002: 216). The longer term consequences of the Kosovo crisis were a 'wake-up call for European leaders and European public opinion' emphasizing the need for a 'shared commitment to humanitarian values' in a 'pan-European community of values' (Huysmans 2002: 600; Lavenex, 2001: 856; Solana, 2000: 28).

POWER

As we have just seen, ideas of the common good can be grouped into three different approaches to normative ethics, with diverse affects in the study of contemporary Europe. Similarly, the relative importance of normative ethics can change on a case by case basis, for example in the study of virtue ethics in the European Union it is often the case that 'the most important factor shaping the international role of the EU is not what it does or what it says, but what it is' (Manners, 2002: 252). But the normative ethics motivating differing social groups are not the only factor shaping the power of ideas of the common good – the question of power and how these groups act must also be considered. The notion of power is one of the central, and most contested, concepts in the social sciences. The study of power involves asking how ideas of the common good are acted upon, through what means, and with what effect. Here I will differentiate between three different types of power – relational power, structural power, and normative power – and how they are exercised within the context of European studies.

Relational power

Power corresponds to the human ability not just to act but to act in concert. Power is never the property of an individual; it belongs to a group and remains in existence only so long as the group keeps together. When we say of somebody that [they are] 'in power' we actually refer to [them] being empowered by a certain number of people to act in their name. The moment the group, from which the power originated to begin with, disappears, '[their] power' also vanishes (Arendt, 1969: 44).

As Hannah Arendt observed, relational power is the ability of groups to act in concert. The notion of relational power places the emphasis on concerted action, but it also recognizes the transient nature of such power which can disappear and disperse as quickly as it appeared (Arendt, 1963: 175; Guisan, 2003, 2005: 462–3). In this respect, 'power is to an astonishing degree independent of material factors, either of numbers or means' (Arendt, 1958: 200). Susan Strange suggests that in its most simplistic formulation, 'relational power, as conventionally described by realist writers of textbooks in international relations, is the power of A to get B to do something they would not otherwise do' (Strange, 1988: 24). In transdisciplinary European studies, relational power is to be found wherever such groups are taking concerted action, for example in the rise of 'third way' social democratic governments across Europe during the period 1998 to 2002.

The 'red tidal wave' of the left that swept across Europe during the late 1990s is an interesting example of the strengths and weaknesses of the exercise of relational power (Bell and Shaw, 2003: 1; Ovenden, 1998). The election of the centre/left governments of Romano Prodi (1996), Tony Blair and Lionel Jospin (1997) and Gerhard Schröder (1998) brought widespread expectations that the political parties of the left would, for the first time, be able to act in concert (*Economist*, 1998; Ladrech, 2003; Walker, 1998). Most believed that sharing power in 13 West European governments would allow the use of relational power to pursue the political agenda of the 'third way', 'new centre', or 'democratic socialism' (*Economist*, 1998; Walker, 1999). Such relational power was intended to shape the post-Cold War European agenda of political, economic, social, and foreign policy based on principles such as community, responsibility, accountability, and opportunity (Halpern and Mikosz, 1998; Dickson, 1999).

The relational power of the four social-democratic governments in Germany, France, Britain and Italy, together with the support of the Netherlands, Sweden and Greece (and six others), was hoped to reinvent governance, regulate capitalism, achieve social justice, and pursue liberal internationalism in foreign policy (Halpern and Mikosz, 1998; Judis, 2002; Stiglitz, 2001). Following Strange, the expectation would be that if some of the most powerful states in Europe sought to exercise relational power over these issues, then a leftward agenda should have been achievable. However, as early as 2003 the term 'crisis' was being used by the left after Silvio Berlusconi (2001) and Jean-Pierre Raffarin (2002), as well as Jan Peter Balkenende and Anders Fogh Rasmussen, came to power (Bell and Shaw, 2003: 1). It seems clear that in order to understand the weaknesses of relational power we need to understand the role of structural power in resisting the agenda of the 'third way', as well as the problem which the normative power of social justice has in articulation across Europe and the world.

Structural power

Structural power ... is the power to shape and determine the structures of the global political economy within which other states, their political institutions, their economic enterprises and (not least) their scientists and other professional people, have to operate. ... Structural power, in short, confers the power to decide how things shall be done, the power to shape frameworks within which states relate to each other, relate to people, or relate to corporate enterprises. The relative power of each party in a relationship is more, or less, if one party is also determining the surrounding structure of the relationship (Strange, 1988: 24–5).

In contrast to Arendt, Susan Strange argued that structural power is found in the shaping of the environment within which relations take place. The notion of structural power places the emphasis on determining frameworks, rather than the concerted actions of relational power. In this respect we can distinguish between the importance of the 'agents' in relational power and the role of the 'structures' in structural power (see Giddens, 1979). The emphasis on power structures in areas such as security, production, finance, knowledge and welfare advanced by Strange (1988) is related to Marxist critical theory with its emphasis on structures of production and social relations. Unlike relational power, structural power in transdisciplinary European studies can be found wherever social, economic, and knowledge-based relations are determined by the emerging dominance of transnational media corporations in Europe from 1996 onwards.

In the mid-1920s, a small number of major Hollywood studios controlled film production, and 70 years later the transnational media corporations that own these 'seven sisters' of cinema now dominate the global media industries of film, television, radio, music, newspapers, periodicals, and books (McChesney, 2001). As the Council of Europe's report on 'Transnational media concentrations in Europe' argued in 2004, the rise in media concentration since 1994 had reached new levels through the domination of transnational companies that weakened national regulations and competition rules (Council of Europe, 2004: 7). The deregulation of US media ownership rules in 1996 (the Telecommunications Act), together with the liberalization of the EU market for media (the 1989 Television without Frontiers Directives revised in 1997), prompted a series of mammoth media mergers including Disney and ABC (1995), Time Warner and Turner/CNN (1996), Viacom and CBS (1999), AOL and Time Warner (2000), Vivendi and Seagram (2002) (Jung, 2003; McChesney, 1999). By 2004, the eight globally dominant transnational corporations were Time Warner, News Corp, Viacom, Disney, Bertelsmann, NBC Universal, Sony, and Vivendi Universal, of which only Bertelsmann (Germany) and Vivendi (France) are European (Jung, 2003; Nordicom, 2005a). While some report the relative success of European companies, such as, RTL/ Bertelsmann, Canal+/Vivendi, and the BBC in resisting the power of the non-European corporations to structure European media, this must be considered premature (Council of Europe, 2004; Esser, 2002; Nordicom, 2005b).

Simply looking at traditional, terrestrial broadcast media in Europe tells us very little about the structural power of transnational media, however, for this we have to look at both 'new media' and content (Bondebjerg, 2001; Cohen and Kennedy, 2000). The 'new media' of non-terrestrial communication places an emphasis on cable, satellite and Internet distribution, as demonstrated in the power of four corporations. The world's biggest merger of AOL and Time Warner in 2000, together with the 2006 purchase of Myspace. com by News Corp, illustrate the way in which the old media giants have come to dominate new media space on the Internet. In terms of

cable distribution, the markets of Ireland, the Netherlands, Central and Eastern Europe are dominated by US-owned Liberty Global Europe (Liberty Media have holdings in SBS, News Corp, Time Warner, Vivendi, and Viacom). Similarly, the satellite distribution market in Europe has been largely dominated by just two corporations – News Corp (through the Sky group) and Vivendi (through the Canal+ group until 2003). In terms of content, the European media market is dominated by satellite news from CNN (Time Warner), BBC World, and Fox News (News Corp); infotainment, such as, the Discovery channels (Liberty Media), National Geographic (News Corp); and the History Channel (Disney, Hearst, NBC Universal); children's programmes from Disney, Nickelodeon (Viacom), Fox Kids (News Corp), Cartoon Network (Time Warner); and music channels such as MTV and VH1 (both Viacom).

It becomes clear that European social, economic, and knowledge-based relations are increasingly predetermined by the dominance of a very small number of transnational media corporations who shape what and how we come to know about Europe. As Christopher Marsden argued, when discussing the power of transnational media we need to look beyond the media to ownership: 'Interdependence and the structural power of capital generally is a more holistic explanation of the story than the structural power of the media owner *per se*' (Marsden, 2000: 12). It seems clear that attempts to regulate European markets, in particular media markets and rules of cross-media ownership, as part of the 'third way' agenda of 1998–2002 were on a collision course with the fourth estate of transnational media corporations. The liberalizations of 1996 in the US, the UK, and Germany had already started the concentration of media into the hands of corporations that were resistant to reregulation and unlikely to have programming representing the third way agenda in any fair way. An example might be found in the role of one of the now dominant new media corporations, News Corp, which attempted to overcome European resistance by using sport programming as a 'battering ram' against regulatory and cross-media ownership rules (Robertson, 2004: 293, 298). The case of BSkyB's attempted purchase of Manchester United football club, and merger of News Corp with Canal+, in 1998–1999 illustrated how politics and media ownership mix in News Corp's 'anti-European Union views' (Robertson, 2004: 298). If the relative power of elected governments is constantly weakened by the structural power of transnational capital and its negative effects on democratic pluralism (Council of Europe, 2004: 4–6), we are left with the question of how ideas of the common good might be articulated in a globalized Europe. Here we should turn to the idea of normative power for an understanding of the power of ideas in post-Cold War Europe.

Normative power

> [W]e rely on moral persuasion, the power of argument, and the power on shaming ... Other factors in these circumstances of voluntary compliance are also important, such as the domestic salience of the norm, its legitimacy and coherence, and the extent to which it fits with other prevailing and well-established standards; but norms are expressed through language and the process of argumentation and debate can shape what is said subsequently in both domestic and international venues (Foot, 2000: 9).

If relational power is concerted action and structural power is environment shaping, then normative power presents a third form of power – the power of ideas themselves. As Rosemary Foot suggests, normative power relies on persuasion, argument and shaming rather than action or structure to shape change. In contrast to the action and determination orientations of relational and structural power, normative power is a discursive formation that relies on legitimacy, coherence, and voluntarism for its influence. Although sceptical, Strange had also noted the existence of normative power, suggesting it was 'moral authority, power derived from the proclamation of powerful ideas that have wide appeal, are accepted as valid and give legitimacy to the proclaimers, whether politicians, religious leaders or philosophers' (Strange, 1988: 23). Similarly, in his study of 'Europe in the making' Johan Galtung argued that normative power was one of the 'three classical types of power' and was to be found in 'bad and good conscience' (Galtung, 1989: 14–15, 162 n. 13). In transdisciplinary European studies, normative power is to be found wherever powerful ideas and argumentation are encountered, for example in the constitutionalization of human rights norms in Europe in the post-Cold War era.

The International Bill of Human Rights consists of the 1948 Universal Declaration of Human Rights, the 1966 International Covenant on Civil and Political Rights, and the 1976 International Covenant on Economic, Social and Cultural Rights, together with two protocols. These five accords, together with the 1979 Convention on the Elimination of All Forms of Discrimination Against Women; the 1984 Convention against Torture and Other Cruel, Inhuman or Degrading Treatment or Punishment; the 1989 Convention on the Rights of the Child; the 1990 International Convention on the Protection of the Rights of All Migrant Workers and Members of Their Families; and the four optional protocols, constitute the core international human rights instruments of the United Nations (Office of the United Nations High Commissioner for Human Rights, 2006). Although most Western European states had taken steps towards enshrining these core human rights in law, prior to 1990 the ratification and application of these core instruments was incomplete.

From 1990 onwards the normative power of human rights in Europe illustrates the way in which core rights came to be seen as constitutive of the very idea of the common good across Europe. The end of the Cold War in Europe was marked by the November 1990 Paris Charter of the Conference on Security and Cooperation in Europe (CSCE) which recognized a 'steadfast commitment to democracy based on human rights and fundamental freedoms' (Conference on Security and Cooperation in Europe, 1990: 3). The signing of the European Convention for the Protection of Human Rights and Fundamental Freedoms, and membership of the Council of Europe (CoE) brought nine central European states into the realm of European human rights protection between 1991 and 1993. The June 1993 Copenhagen Criteria for membership of the EU made clear that human rights protection (as well as protection of minorities) was a pre-requisite for accession. It is within this institutional context that 15 European post-Soviet and post-Yugoslav states acceded to most of the seven core international human rights instruments of the UN (the major exception being the 1990 Convention on the Protection of the Rights of Migrant Workers). More specifically, 13 Central and Eastern European states, 17 Western European states, and three Mediterranean states (Malta, Cyprus, and Turkey) acceded to the 1989 Second Optional Protocol to the International Covenant on Civil and Political Rights (abolition of the death penalty) after pressure from the CoE, the EU, and international human rights groups.

This emphasis on the role of the three European institutions of the CSCE/OSCE, CoE, and EU in spreading human rights law overlooks the extent to which it is grassroots human rights movements and advocacy which has led the development of human rights in Europe. Human rights movements for the abolition of slavery, torture, political imprisonment, and the death penalty are all primarily movements of people rather than states, as the work of Anti-Slavery International (founded in 1839 as the Anti-Slavery Society), Amnesty International (founded as the 'Appeal for Amnesty, 1961'), and the Association for the Prevention of Torture (founded in 1977) have illustrated. Chris Brown comments that:

> It is precisely the role of AI [Amnesty International] and similar bodies to 'carp' and 'denounce' without taking on board all the reasons, often quite compelling in nature, for failings in the area of

human rights ... bodies such as AI, which do not possess direct coercive [relational] power, can attempt to promote human rights in a way that is less tied up with Western interests, and are less liable to charges of hypocrisy (Brown, 2001: 29).

It is here that we find the normative power of European civil society activism engaged in persuasion, argumentation and shaming in public, the press, the courts, state institutions, and international organizations 'like water on stone' (Power, 2002) in order to promote ideas of the common good.

EUROPE

Having considered both the reasons why groups act, and means through which groups act on differing ideas of the common good, we can now turn to the question of what are the effects on our understanding of contemporary Europe. This third section involves asking what the consequences are of examining European studies from contrasting analytical perspectives. What we will see is that ideas of the common good are related to the different analytical methods of European studies. The question of what Europe is and how we examine it is the only common analytical focus that European studies shares, and is central to any transdisciplinary study. To illustrate the interrelationship between ideas of the common good, method of analysis and the definition of Europe I will differentiate between three means of understanding Europe – civilizational Europe, categorical Europe, and cultural Europe (see Manners, 2003).

Civilization

There are those who have argued that 11th September initiated a clash between civilizations. Here I disagree, a clash between civilizations requires that there are two civilizations, which there are not. There is only one civilization, and that is ours (Kjærsgaard, 2001).

The opening quote from Pia Kjærsgaard, the leader of the Danish People's Party, suggests a post-11th September understanding of civilizational Europe (Rydgren, 2004; Hervik, 2006; Andersen, 2008). In the post-Cold War era ideas of the common good based on the idea of 'civilization' became popularized by Samuel Huntington (1993). Huntington's argument was that religion became a means of differentiating between groups, and that conflict between these groups was inevitable (Batur-Vanderlippe, 1999; Loomba, 2003; Marfleet, 2003).

The 1980s saw the biological racism of the colonial era adapted to cultural racism for the postcolonial era with 'colour' exchanged for 'religion' (Balibar, 1991: 21; Loomba, 2003: 13). Etienne Balibar argued that

current racism . . . fits into a framework of 'racism without races' . . . It is a racism whose dominant theme is not biological heredity but the insurmountibility of cultural differences, a racism which, at first sight, does not postulate the superiority of certain groups or peoples in relation to others but 'only' the harmfulness of abolishing frontiers, the incompatibility of life-styles and traditions (Balibar, 1991: 21).

It is within this context that other religions rather than other races were increasingly identified as the causes of European problems in the post-Cold War era (Zaslove, 2004: 75).

As cultural racism (neoracism) became popular in Europe during the 1990s, far-right political leaders such as Le Pen (France), Bossi (Italy), Haider (Austria), and Fortuyn (Netherlands) became enthusiasts for a civilizational reading of Europe as predominantly Christian, white and closed to others (Batur-Vanderlippe, 1999: 472; Marfleet, 2003: 84; Quraishy, 2003: 72; Wren, 2004: 153).

The 1990s also saw the growth of neonationalist movements under the banner of 'anti-European' sentiment, including parties such as the French National Front, Italian Northern League (after 1998), Austrian Freedom Party, Danish People's Party, and Swedish Democrats (Chari et al., 2004; Gingrich, 2006: 214–5; Rydgren, 2002: 52; Simonsen, 2004: 361). Andre Gingrich

defines neonationalism as 'nationalism in a globalized period of aggressive postcolonial and post-Cold War readjustment' (Gingrich, 2006: 200). In this respect neonationalists seek to 'enhance negative images of the European Union' and 'oppose the centralized and elite nature of the European Union in the name of the authentic silent majority and the common person' (Gingrich, 2006: 214; Zaslove, 2004: 70).

We should be unsurprised that neonationalist groups dislike the European Union after the Austrian sanctions crisis previously discussed under virtue ethics (above). However, less well known is the resistance to Article 13 of the Treaty of Rome which provides the basis for EU 'action to combat discrimination based on sex, racial or ethnic origin, religion or belief, disability, age or sexual orientation'. Neonationalist opposition to the Constitution for Europe was undoubtedly guaranteed by the new Article II-81 in the Charter of Fundamental Rights of the Union which went further in contending that 'any discrimination based on any ground such as sex, race, colour, ethnic or social origin, genetic features, language, religion or belief, political or any other opinion, membership of a national minority, property, birth, disability, age or sexual orientation shall be prohibited'. The movement from 'action' to 'prohibition' and wider-ranging reference to 'any discrimination' would clearly have been unacceptable to both neonationalists and neoracists.

In this civilizational Europe, some neoracist and neo-nationalist parties have seized the opportunity to invoke the need for 'crusades' of white Christian Europe against the Islamic world, using the war on terror as a pretext – 'This crusade, this war on terrorism is going to take a while' (Bush, 2001a; see also Carroll, 2004; Zaslove, 2004: 75). From this perspective a Europe based on such a civilization would be a very reduced and barren one indeed, excluding almost 60 years of immigration as well as most Eastern European states; of course Greece, Cyprus, Romania, Bulgaria, Macedonia, Turkey,

Bosnia, Serbia, and Albania would also be excluded.

Category

> 'Europe' and 'the European' are also symbolic categories … As such, these symbolic categories are mutually imbricated and craft a field of cultural meanings that produces its own emergent logic. This logic in turn defines the discursive limits of civilization and the relation of differentiated human groupings to that civilization (Lewis, 2006: 88).

As the discussion of civilizational Europe makes clear, our understandings of Europe are symbolic categories created by differing groups to serve political purposes (see Leontidou, 2004; Liotta, 2005). The second perspective looks at Europe as a category in order to escape the ethnic primordialism of the 'civilization'. However, as Gail Lewis illustrates in her discussion of 'imaginaries of Europe', any categories discussed here are themselves the product of cultural meanings, often in opposition to others such as 'the immigrant women' (see also Lutz, 1997). While Lila Leontidou has found that regional narratives of Europe have historically focused on geophysical features such as seas, rivers, and mountains, in the post-Second World War period it is institutional narratives that have dominated (Leontidou, 2004). Similarly, in the post-Cold War world the category of Europe can be found through examining the institutional memberships of those organizations representing and defining what it means to be European – the OSCE, the CoE, and the EU.

The OSCE is primarily a product of the Cold War era, created by the 1975 Helsinki Conference on Security and Cooperation in Europe. The Helsinki Final Act was signed by 35 countries, including the US, the Soviet Union, and Canada, thus creating an East–West understanding of Europe 'from Vancouver to Vladivostok'. By the 1994 Budapest Conference meeting the CSCE had grown to 52 states who agreed to further institutionalization and a name

change to the OSCE. As the world's largest regional security organization, its 56 members must represent the largest understanding of Europe as an institutional category, including the US, Canada, Russia, five central Asian republics, five micro-states, and 43 European countries.

The Council of Europe (CoE) is Europe's oldest political organization, created in the aftermath of the Second World War by the 1949 Treaty of London. The Treaty was signed by ten West European parliamentary democracies with the aim of achieving 'a greater unity between its members' (Article 1). The CoE was thus a Western European organization which initially excluded the dictatorships of southern and eastern Europe because of their absence of individual freedom, political liberty, rule of law, and 'genuine democracy' (preamble to Treaty of London). Fifty years later, by the end of 1989, the CoE had grown to 20 members, including the new democracies of southern Europe. However, the next decade was to be the 'decade which made history' as the Council played a crucial role in guarding democratic security and assisting the transition of Central and Eastern European states to democracy (Huber, 1999). Thus, by 2003 the CoE included 46 European countries, the only major exception being authoritarian Belarus.

The EU is Europe's main integration organization, with its beginnings in the European Coal and Steel Community created by the 1951 Treaty of Paris. As the Treaty was signed by the six Western European states who had been most affected by the Second World War, it was effectively a peace treaty, prompted by the 1950 Schuman Declaration (Fontaine, 2000: 20). After the 1957 Treaty of Rome significantly expanded the integration activities to include economic production and trade, the focus of the newly created European Communities was on the 'pooling of resources' in order to strengthen peace and liberty, including the free movement of persons, services, and capital. By 1989 the EC had enlarged three times and included 12 relatively wealthy Western European parliamentary democracies. The end of the Cold War brought a deluge of applications for membership of the newly restructured EU, resulting in three more rounds of enlargement and a total of 27 members by 2007. Thus membership of the EU currently includes 27 of the 46 CoE member states, excluding Norway and Switzerland in Western Europe.

This brief comparison of institutional categorization illustrates the extent to which 'Europe' is an open category. Whether focused on security (OSCE), democracy (CoE), or integration (EU), Europe as a category can include between 46 and 27 states, stretching from Lisbon to Bucharest, Ankara, or Moscow. But under any categorical definition of Europe a wide range of cultural, ethnic, linguistic, and religious diversity is always included, ensuring that there are no discursive limits to civilization in a neoracist sense.

Culture

In spite of all the difficulties, we are on our way towards building a European Community that cannot be ignored. In this often chaotic European assembly, the voice of France, which sometimes has difficulty making itself heard when it calls for the construction of a 'social Europe', still finds allies in other governments and in the public opinion of various countries. Whilst all of them are deeply attached to their particular cultural traditions, they all implicitly or explicitly share our notion of freedom (Kristeva, 2004: 31).

Moving beyond discussions of civilizational or categorical Europe, it might be more valuable to look at Europe from the perspective of culture where differing cultural traditions across Europe share some common notions such as freedom and a more social Europe. From this third perspective we can acknowledge that geographic, ethnographic, and linguistic categories are primarily cultural constructions. Thus, a better understanding of the power of ideas of the common good will be looked at through culture as a means of comprehending

contemporary Europe. As Maria Todorova suggests, 'It is not symbolic geography that creates politics, but rather the reverse … "Europe" ends where politicians want it to end' (Todorova, 1997: 160; and Liotta, 2005: 67). But we should remind ourselves that politicians and governments are themselves constructed through their particular cultural traditions.

Drawing on the previous discussion of institutional categorization and inspired by Todorova's symbolic geography of the 'Balkans', we can observe how European geography is a cultural production (Paasi, 2001). Because Europe sits at the western end of the Eurasian tectonic plate, any geographical definition of Europe must be topographic rather than geological. Hence geographical discussions of 'continental' Europe are somewhat misplaced, often replaced by discussions of Europe from the Atlantic-to-the-Urals (ATTU). It is worth remarking that while CoE membership may include states from the ATTU, their landmasses stretch from Baffin Bay (Greenland) to the Bering Straits (Russia). Also of interest is the way in which the EU also involves 28 non-European territories around the world, involving the seven 'non-continental and overseas territories of member states' (including French Guiana) and the 21 'overseas countries and territories' listed in the treaties (including Bermuda).

Similar to geography, European ethnography is also a cultural production, consisting of over 100 'nations' or 'peoples' (Fernández-Armesto, 1994; Pedersen, 1992). But any such study of nations or peoples in Europe is highly problematic because of the contested nature of 'ethnicity'. Definitions of ethnicity range from Max Weber's suggestion of 'those human groups that entertain a subjective belief in their common descent because of similarities of physical type or of customs or of both, or because of memories of colonization or migration' (Weber, 1968, in Guibernau and Rex, 1997: 2), to Paul Spoonley's idea of ethnicity representing 'the *positive* feelings of belonging to a cultural group' (Spoonley, 1993, in Guibernau and Rex, 1997: 1). The difficult question arises of who, exactly, are the peoples of Europe? – Filipe Fernández-Armesto's 1994 *Times Guide to the Peoples of Europe* allows space for Ruthenians, Jews and the Roma, but none for the millions of non-indigenous citizens from around the world who are naturalized in Europe.

European linguistics may provide us with a better insight into cultural Europe, but given the Indo-European language roots of much of Europe, we are again presented with the issue of no clear separation within Eurasia. The ten main linguistic subfamilies of the Indo-European language family, together with non-Indo-European Uralic (Finno-Ugric and Samoyedic), Turkic, Basque and Maltese, ensure that languages spoken in Europe are shared with much of the world. The daily presence of semitic Maltese and Finno-Urgic (Finnish, Estonian, and Hungarian) languages in the EU illustrates the extent to which Indo-European languages are not a sufficient identifier of cultural Europe. Similarly, European languages such as English (5.5 per cent of global population), Spanish (4.6 per cent of global population), and Portuguese (2.9 per cent of global population) are widely used as first languages around the world, to the extent that cultural production outside of Europe in these languages has become more dominant within Europe – think of the US or India, Mexico and Brazil for example (Buckley, 1998: 4–5).

Returning to Julia Kristeva's opening quote, it is increasingly the case that, in spite of all the difficulties and resistances, cultural traditions tell us much about social Europe and any European community that might follow. Here it might be more insightful to define cultural Europe by those cultural productions which are widely shared across Europe, for example Europop in the form of the Eurovision song contest and Euro sport in the shape of the UEFA European Football Championship.

The interplay between the EU, television, and entertainment/sporting bodies have produced cultural reconfigurations of Europe. For example, EU media policies such as the 1989 'Television Without Frontiers' Directive and the three MEDIA programmes since 1990 have intertwined with the role of the European Broadcast Union (EBU) to encourage co-productions such as the Eurovision Song Contest. Participation in Eurovision is limited to active members of the EBU, including recent winners from Ukraine, Turkey and Israel, as well as participants from Morocco, Russia and Armenia. Similarly, the combination of EU politics, including the European Court of Justice's 1995 Bosman ruling, and the pro-activity of sporting organizations has broadened definitions of Europe to include Russia, Turkey and Israel, as seen in the Euro 2008 (UEFA European Football Championship) competition. Ahead of the 2008 championships co-hosted by Austria and Switzerland, teams such as Armenia, Azerbaijan and Kazakhstan in group A; and England, Russia and Israel in group B had to play each other in order to qualify.

APPROACHING THE QUESTION OF A EUROPEAN COUNTER-TERRORIST RESPONSE

Throughout this chapter I have argued in favour of a transdisciplinary approach to the study of contemporary Europe that asks a series of questions about the power of ideas of the common good, and their diffusion in a European context. In each part I examined one of these questions: normative, power, and Europe, from three different perspectives. In each response I tried to give an example from contemporary European studies that illustrate the transdisciplinary nature of such an approach. Hence we briefly considered the Austrian sanctions, GMO and Kosovo ethical crises; then the power of the 'third way', transnational media, and human rights; and finally some civilizational, categorical and cultural readings of Europe. Although these examples drew on politics, ecology, economics, sociology, and cultural studies, I did not attempt to weave them together into a single analytical narrative.

To conclude I will briefly look at one question in European studies which demands a transdisciplinary approach because of the challenges it presents to atomistic thinking – how should Europeans conduct a counter-terrorist response? Following the terrorist attacks against civilians in New York in September 2001, and increasingly so since the Istanbul truck bombings of November 2003, the Madrid train bombings in March 2004 and the London public transport bombings in July 2005, Europeans have been asking themselves how to respond to such terrorist threats.

Ethics in counter-terrorism

The first question to ask is what would be an ethically normative way to respond to such attacks? A virtue ethics approach would tend to argue that Europeans should stick to their principles in any counter-terrorist activity, in particular arguing that these terrorist attacks are first and foremost crimes against humanity which require a cosmopolitan approach to security and justice. As commentators from the US, Pakistan, Turkey and the Lebanon acknowledged immediately following the events of 11 September 2001, these were widely seen as 'crimes against humanity' (Bhutto, 2002; Chibli, 2002; Guruz, 2002; Naim, 2002). European commentators were among the first to argue that such crimes must be understood within the wider processes of globalization and dealt with in the context of cosmopolitan politics and law (Beck, 2001; Habermas and Derrida, 2003; Kaldor, 2003; Mégret, 2003). A European virtue ethics approach would be expected to argue along the lines of Mary Robinson, the UN High Commissioner for Human Rights: 'I said very openly and have continued to say

that that's [11th September] a crime against humanity and that it's right and indeed necessary for the whole global community to bring the perpetrators to justice' (Robinson, 2002).

A deontological ethics approach might place greater emphasis on the need for reasoned, legal actions against international terrorism, and would most likely sanction an international 'just war' as was seen in Afghanistan in 2002. A large number of politicians, academics, and commentators around the world supported the US-led war in Afghanistan from 7 October 2001 onwards, with apparent UN Security Council backing in 'supporting international efforts to root out terrorism' (UN Security Council Resolution 1378; see also UN Security Council Resolution 1368). The extent to which the US appeared to work through international law and organizations in order to pursue a 'just war' through operations 'Infinite Justice' and 'Enduring Freedom' seemed a reasoned, legal approach to international justice which could be articulated across the globe (see Elshtain, 2003; Falk, 2001; Holliday 2002; contrast with Chomsky, 2003). Support for a European deontological ethics approach to counter-terrorism was removed when the US began preparing for the invasion of Iraq from October 2002 onwards, despite the lack of UN Security Council support and the largest anti-war protest in history on the 15 February 2003 when millions of demonstrators took to the streets of Rome, London, Madrid, Berlin, and beyond.

A consequentialist ethics approach would seem more likely to place the emphasis on outcomes in terms of defeating terrorists by any means possible, perhaps including a total war on terror. From 11 September 2001 onwards the doctrine of 'total war on terror' was increasingly at the heart of US consequentialist logic which focused on defeating not only terrorists but all enemies, as US Secretary of Defence Donald Rumsfeld noted on 11 September: 'Go massive ... Sweep it all up. Things related and not' (Martin, 2002). Within a year this results-oriented strategy was clarified by the chair of the US Defence Policy Board Advisory Committee, Richard Pearle:

This is total war. We are fighting a variety of enemies. There are lots of them out there. All this talk about first we are going to do Afghanistan, then we will do Iraq ... this is entirely the wrong way to go about it. If we just let our vision of the world go forth, and we embrace it entirely and we don't try to piece together clever diplomacy, but just wage a total war ... our children will sing great songs about us years from now (Pilger, 2002: 13; 2003: 10).

The US invasion of Iraq from the 20 March 2003 onwards divided Europeans between those following a consequentialist ethic (primarily pro-Bush governments in the UK, Italy, Poland, Ukraine, Netherlands, and Spain) and those following a more deontological ethic (e.g., Germany and France). As the disastrous consequences of the invasion became clearer after 2003, European governments in Spain, the Netherlands, Portugal, Hungary, Norway, Ukraine, Bulgaria, and Italy withdrew their military forces from Iraq. In 2006 it was also revealed that the total war on terror's consequentialist ethic involves the illegal extradition and torture of terrorist suspects from Europe (see Amnesty International, 2006; Fava, 2006; Marty, 2006; Mayer, 2005; Priest, 2005). European consequentialist ethics as seen in counter-terrorist activities such as Iraq, extraordinary rendition and other contraventions of civil and human rights thus make it very difficult for virtue ethics and/or deontological ethics to be pursued as well. In their place the counter-terrorist discourses of war on terror and violations of human rights, rather than crimes against humanity and pursuit of international law, ensure that addressing the complex causes of terrorism becomes virtually impossible (Chibli, 2002; von Schorlemer, 2003).

Power in counter-terrorism

The second question to ask is how best to respond to such attacks? Using relational power would tend to involve direct action

with an obvious preference for those resources most ready for action, in particular the armed forces. The use of relational power in counter-terrorism has become the defining feature of the total war on terror with the Philippines, Saudi Arabia, and Jordan also declaring 'total war on terror' (Alexander, 2003; Burns, 2005; Faraj et al., 2004). The US sanctioning of relational power encouraged Russia and China to join the war against their own 'terrorists' in Chechnya and Xinjiang (Hamilton, 2004; Manners, 2007). As Jonathan Stevenson observes:

[A] full-scale Western mobilisation against transnational Islamist terrorism – a total war on terror ... [in which] the West's intelligence, law-enforcement and military assets would be brought to bear against any actual or potential terrorist strongholds or supporters ... would amount ... to furnishing bin Laden with precisely the violent 'clash of civilisations' that is integral to his apocalyptic eschatology (Stevenson, 2006: 96).

During January 2003 the total war on terror through the invasion of Iraq was promoted by US envoy Bruce Jackson (Judis, 2003). This led to the 'Letter of Eight' (signed by eight pro-Bush European leaders) and the 'Vilnus Letter' (signed by ten pro-Bush central European leaders) apparently supporting relational power through the invasion of Iraq (Macmillan, 2003). The division of Europe into 'old Europe' opposing the invasion of Iraq (the popular response across the whole of Europe) and 'new Europe' (the 18 leaders who signed the Jackson letters) was openly encouraged by US Secretary of Defence Donald Rumsfeld as a means of weakening the EU and the UN in order to pursue relational power (Levy *et al.*, 2005).

Exercising structural power would be more longer term and entail addressing the socio-economic and political conditions in which terrorism thrives, in particular through economic and political aid, trade and sanctions (both positive and negative). By the end of 2003, the division of the EU earlier in the year was beginning to be addressed through agreement on the *European Security Strategy* (ESS).

In particular, the ESS clarified the extent to which a common EU counter-terrorist strategy would need to use structural power to address its 'complex causes':

> The most recent wave of terrorism is global in its scope and is linked to violent religious extremism. It arises out of complex causes. These include the pressures of modernization, cultural, social and political crises, and the alienation of young people living in foreign societies. This phenomenon is also a part of our own society (Council of EU, 2003: 4).

Within a year the European Commission had clarified the extent to which structural power would involve taking action to address the root causes of terrorism:

> Action must also be taken to address the root causes of insecurity and the factors which contribute to the emergence of terrorism. Steps aimed at enhancing security must be taken without prejudice to individual rights and freedoms and the openness and tolerance of our societies must be maintained. At the same time EU actions aim to strengthen governance, including the rule of law, and to encourage the development of sound institutions both within the Union and in third countries (European Commission, 2004: 1).

The exercise of structural power by European states has accelerated since the terrorist attacks on civilians in Madrid and London based on a more holistic approach including both domestic and international policies. There emerged a European consensus on the four pillars of an EU counter-terrorism strategy, firstly 'to prevent people turning to terrorism by tackling the factors or root causes which can lead to radicalisation and recruitment, in Europe and internationally' (Council of EU, 2005: 3). Internationally, structural power is being applied through EU Partnership and Co-operation Agreements, including the Cotonou agreement, to 'help address the root causes of insecurity which may contribute to the emergence of terrorism' as well as 'better sequencing of governance, peace and security, linking relief, rehabilitation and development interventions on the basis of a holistic approach to … the prevention of terrorism' (European Commission, 2004: 10, 15).

In contrast to relational or structural power, employing normative power would rely on a much broader approach to transforming the complex causes, radicalization process, and active symptoms of terrorism by engaging with the despair, alienation, grievances, and pressures created by economic, social, cultural, and political change and injustice. This more holistic approach has its origins in the European counter-terrorist strategy discussed above, but the ongoing military failures of the total war on terror in Iraq, together with the rising public awareness and outrage at prisoner abuse, illegal extradition and torture by the US and its European allies is leading to calls for the exercise of normative power to address 'the pressures of modernization, cultural, social, and political crises' (Council of EU, 2003: 4). It is here that the division of Europe created by the invasion of Iraq and accompanying human rights abuses is starting to be healed by a fragile consensus heeding the words of Kofi Annan, the former UN Secretary General:

> The notion of larger freedom also encapsulates the idea that development, security and human rights go hand in hand … This relationship has only been strengthened in our era of rapid technological advances, increasing economic interdependence, globalization and dramatic geopolitical change. While poverty and denial of human rights may not be said to 'cause' civil war, terrorism or organized crime, they all greatly increase the risk of instability and violence … Accordingly, we will not enjoy development without security, we will not enjoy security without development, and we will not enjoy either without respect for human rights. Unless all these causes are advanced, none will succeed (Annan, 2005: 5–6).

Such a consensus increasingly includes an acceptance of using normative power to promote human security as the core of a more holistic counter-terrorist strategy (Liotta and Owen, 2006). For the European Commission, human security means a concern for individuals, not states, and encompasses both freedom from fear (e.g. conflict and human rights abuses) and freedom from want (e.g. poverty and disease) (European Commission, 2005: 2; Ferrero-Waldner, 2006: 103–7). The April 2006 'European Consensus on Development' is an obvious example of this commitment to normative power with its references to promoting human security in order to address the root-causes of violent conflict (European Consensus on Development, 2006: 3, 14) with an emphasis on common normative values:

> EU partnership and dialogue with third countries will promote common values of: respect for human rights, fundamental freedoms, peace, democracy, good governance, gender equality, the rule of law, solidarity, and justice. The EU is strongly committed to effective multilateralism whereby all the world's nations share responsibility for development
>
> (European Consensus on Development, 2006: 3).

Europe in counter-terrorism

The third question to ask is what understanding of Europe emerges as part of this counter-terrorist response? A civilizational Europe would be one fully engaged in a 'clash of civilizations' as part of a total war on terror. As discussed under civilizational Europe earlier, a larger number of groups around Europe have been keen to join with bin Laden and Bush in such a clash, for example with Ari Fleischer (the White House Press Secretary) and Silvio Berlusconi equating Islamic fundamentalism with terrorism (Berlusconi 2004; Fleischer, 2002). For Arundhati Roy this emphasis on civilization involves an 'algebra of infinite justice' where

> the equivocating distinction between civilisation and savagery, between the 'massacre of innocent people' or, if you like, 'a clash of civilisations' and 'collateral damage'. The sophistry and fastidious algebra of infinite justice. How many dead Iraqis will it take to make the world a better place? How many dead Afghans for every dead American? How many dead women and children for every dead man? How many dead mojahedin for each dead investment banker? (Roy, 2001)

In contrast, a categorical Europe would be one where clear-cut categories of good versus evil would be sought and applied, with the argument that 'you are either with us or you are against us' (Bush, 2001b). As discussed earlier, from September 2001 to January 2003, most Europeans were generally with the US in its attempts to counter terrorism,

including the ambiguous sanctioning of torture and extraordinary rendition. However the US invasion of Iraq, as well as the Madrid and London bombings, demonstrated the extent to which there are no such clear-cut categories, with civilians and human rights always being the victims (Guild, 2003). As the EU counter-terrorist strategy from December 2003 onwards makes clear, the phenomena which facilitate terrorist radicalization and recruitment are to be found both within and without Europe, thus blurring any precise distinctions between 'them' and 'us'.

Finally, a cultural Europe would be one in which all such constructions of civilizations, total war, good versus evil, and 'with us' versus 'against us' might be understood as gross simplifications of complex cultural processes. From this perspective it seems clear that the intention of bin Laden and Al-Qaeda was to provoke a response which would strengthen such gross cultural simplifications. Unfortunately the total war on terror in the pursuit of infinite justice is precisely the cultural response which the Salafi jihadists seek. A culturally aware European counter-terrorist response would be one which understood that 'terrorism cannot defeat democracy in a straight fight, but democracy can defeat itself' (Ignatieff, 2004), and that to suspend or abandon human rights, democracy and the rule of law in the name of security 'would be to give the terrorists a victory they could never achieve by themselves' (Ranstorp and Wilkinson, 2005: 7).

CONCLUSION: A TRANSDISCIPLINARY APPROACH

Obviously such a brief and cursory reflection on one of the most demanding questions of our time cannot provide anything other than a casual overview of counter-terrorist policy, but it does help to illustrate how a transdisciplinary approach to almost any issue in contemporary European studies can be opened up for reflection (see Manners

2002 and 2007 for an opening up of human rights and counter-terrorist policies). Similarly, it is worth noting how replies to earlier questions such as 'normative?' and 'power?' tend to predetermine responses to later questions such as Europe?

As I have illustrated through this example, normative power Europe gives us a trans-disciplinary approach to understanding why, how and with what effect differing ideas of the common good constitute, moti-vate and shape Europe. Such ideas of the common good should not be overlooked in European studies for, as Victor Hugo wrote in 1852, 'An invasion of armies can be resisted; an invasion of ideas cannot be resisted' (Hugo, 2004: 441). This transdis-ciplinary approach also suggests a means of developing a theory of society that goes beyond European integration to understand Europe in a global frame of reference, and perhaps thus giving us a better sense of the notion of the 'good society' in contemporary European studies.

ACKNOWLEDGEMENTS

I am very grateful to Catarina Kinnvall, Helle Malmvig, and Chris Rumford for their helpful comments.

NOTES

1 Personal comments to the author.

REFERENCES

Alexander, P. (2003) 'Philippines declare 'total war' on terror after explosion', *Associated Press*, 3 April.

Amnesty International (2006) *Partners in Crime: Europe's Role in US Renditions*. Europe and Central Asia Library, AI Index: EUR 01/008/2006, 14 June.

Andersen, J. (2008) 'Nationalism, new politics, and new cleavages in Danish politics: foreign and security policy of the Danish People's Party', in C. Schori Liang (ed.) *Europe for the Europeans: The Foreign and Security Policy of the Populist Radical Right*. Aldershot: Ashgate Publishing, pp. 103–123.

Annan, K. (2005) *In Larger Freedom: Towards Development, Security and Human Rights for All*. Report of the Secretary General. New York: United Nations.

Anscombe, E. (1958) 'Modern moral philoso-phy', *Philosophy: the Journal of the Royal Institute of Philosophy*, 33 (124): 1–19.

Arendt, H. (1958) *The Human Condition*. Chicago: University of Chicago Press.

Arendt, H. (1963) *On Revolution*. London: Penguin.

Arendt, H. (1969) *On Violence*. New York: Harcourt Brace.

Bäckstrand, K. (2003) 'Civic science for sustainabil-ity: reframing the role of experts, policy-makers and citizens in environmental governance', *Global Environmental Politics*, 3 (4): 24–41.

Baker, S. (2006) 'Environmental values and cli-mate change policy: contrasting the European Union and the United States', in S. Lucarelli and I. Manners (eds) *Values and Principles in European Union Foreign Policy*. London: Routledge, pp. 77–96.

Balibar, E. (1991) 'Is there a 'neo-racism'?', in E. Balibar and I. Wallerstein (eds) *Race, Nation, Class: Ambiguous Identities*. London: Verso, pp. 17–28.

Batur-Vanderlippe, P. (1999) 'Centering on global racism and antiracism: from everyday life to global complexity', *Sociological Spectrum*, 19: 467–484.

Beck, U. (2001) 'The fight for a cosmopolitan future', *New Statesman*, 130 (4562), 33–35.

Bell, D. and Shaw, E. (2003) 'Introduction', special issue on 'What's Left? The Left in Europe Today', *Parliamentary Affairs*, 56 (1): 1–5.

Berlusconi, S. (2004) 'Remarks by President Bush and Prime Minister Berlusconi', Rome, Office of the Press Secretary, The White House, 5 June. Available at: http://www.whitehouse.gov/news/releases/2004/06/20040605-1.html.

Bhutto, B. (2002) 'Pakistan's dilemma', *Harvard International Review*, 24 (1), 14–16.

Bondebjerg, I. (2001) 'European media, cul-tural integration and globalisation', *Nordicom Review*, 22 (1): 53–64.

Brown, C. (2001) 'Ethics, interests and foreign policy', in K. Smith and M. Light (eds) *Ethics and Foreign Policy*. Cambridge: Cambridge University Press, pp. 15–32.

Buckley, R. (1998) *The Global Village: Challenges for a Shrinking Planet*. Cheltenham: Understanding Global Issues.

Burns, F. (2005) 'Jordan's king urges total war on terror', *United Press International*, 24 November.

Bush, G.W. (2001a) 'Remarks by the President upon arrival', Office of the Press Secretary, The White House, 16 September. Available at: http://www.whitehouse.gov/news/releases/2001/09/20010916-2.html.

Bush, G.W. (2001b) 'President welcomes President Chirac to the White House', Office of the Press Secretary, The White House, 6 November. Available at: http://www.whitehouse.gov/news/releases/2001/11/20011106-4.html.

Calhoun, C. (2001) 'The virtues of inconsistency: identity and plurality in the conceptualization of Europe', in L.-E. Cederman (ed.) *Constructing Europe's Identity: The External Dimension*. Boulder: Lynne Rienner, pp. 35–56.

Calhoun, C. (2003a) 'European studies: always already there and still in formation', *Comparative European Politics*, 1 (1): 5–20.

Calhoun, C. (2003b) 'The democratic integration of Europe: Interests, identity and the public sphere', in M. Berezin and M. Schain (eds) *Europe without Border: Remapping Territory, Citizenship, and Identity in a Transnational Age*. Baltimore: Johns Hopkins University Press, pp. 243–274.

Carr, S. (2002) 'Ethical and value-based aspects of the European Commission's precautionary principle', *Journal of Agricultural and Environmental Ethics*, 15 (1), 31–38.

Carroll, J. (2004) 'The Bush crusade', *The Nation*, 279 (8): 14–20.

Chari, R., Iltanen, S., and Kritzinger, S. (2004) 'Examining and explaining the Northern League's 'U-turn' from Europe', *Government and Opposition*, 39 (3): 423–450.

Chibli, M. (2002) 'The Original Sin: 'terrorism' or 'crime against humanity'?', *Case Western Reserve Journal of International Law*, 34 (2): 245–248.

Chomsky, N. (2003) 'Commentary: moral truisms, empirical evidence, and foreign policy', *Review of International Studies*, 29 (4): 605–620.

Cohen, R. and Kennedy, P. (2000) 'Media and communication', in *Global Sociology*. Basingstoke: Palgrave, pp. 248–264.

Conference on Security and Cooperation in Europe (CSCE) (1990) *Charter of Paris for a New Europe*. Paris: CSCE.

Council of Europe (2004) *Transnational Media Concentrations in Europe*. Report prepared by the Advisory Panel to the Media Division. Strasbourg: Council of Europe.

Council of the EU (2003) *A Security Europe in a Better World: European Security Strategy*. 12 December, Brussels.

Council of the EU (2005) *The European Union Counter-Terrorism Strategy: Prevent, Protect, Pursue, Respond*, 14469/4/05, 30 November, Brussels.

Crisp, R. (1995) 'Deontological ethics', in T. Honderich (ed.) *The Oxford Companion to Philosophy*. Oxford: Oxford University Press, pp. 187–188.

Curtin, D. (1997) *Postnational Democracy: The European Union in Search of a Political Philosophy*. The Hague: Kluwer Law International.

Dalgaard-Nielsen, A. (2004) 'Looking to Europe: American perceptions of the old world', *Cooperation and Conflict*, 39 (1): 69–76.

Darwall, S. (ed.) (2002) *Consequentialism*. Oxford: Blackwell.

Delanty, G. an Rumford, C. (2006) *Rethinking Europe: Social Theory and the Implications of Europeanization*. London: Routledge.

De Marchi, B. and Ravetz, J. (1999) 'Risk management and governance: a post-normal science approach', *Futures: the Journal of Policy, Planning and Futures Studies*, 31: 743–757.

Denmark, R. (1999) 'World system history: from traditional international politics to the study of global relations', *International Studies Review*, 1 (2): 43–75.

Dickson, N. (1999) 'What is the Third Way?', *BBC News*, September. Available at: http://news.bbc.co.uk/.

Dölling, I. and Hark, S. (2000) 'She who speaks shadow speaks truth: transdisciplinarity in women's and gender studies', *Signs*, 25 (4): 1195–1198.

Douma, W. Th. (2000) 'The precautionary principle in the European Union', *Review of European Community and International Environmental Law*, 9 (2): 132–143.

Economist (1998) 'Europe: A continental drift – to the left', *The Economist*, 349 (8088), 3 October, pp. 59–60.

Ellis, D. (2003) *Good Practice Guide: Interdisciplinary*. The Higher Education Academy, Subject Centre for Languages, Linguistics and Area Studies. Available at: http://www.lang.ltsn.ac.uk/resources/goodpractice.aspx?resourceid=1430.

Elshtain, J.B. (2003) *Just War Against Terror: Ethics and the Burden of American Power in a Violent World*. New York: Basic Books.

Esser, A. (2002) 'The transnationalization of European television', *Journal of Area Studies*, 10 (1): 13–29.

European Commission (2000) *Communication from the Commission on the Precautionary Principle*. Brussels, 2 February.

European Commission (2004) *European Security Strategy: Fight against Terrorism*. Brussels, 9 November.

European Commission (2005) *Annual Report 2005 on the European Community's Development Policy and the Implementation of External Assistance in 2004*. Brussels: EuropeAid Co-operation Office.

European Consensus on Development (2006) 'Joint statement by the Council and the representatives of the governments of the Member States meeting within the Council, the European Parliament and the Commission on European Union', *Official Journal of the European Union*, C46 (1), 24 February.

Falk, R. (2001) 'A just response', *Nation*, 273 (10): 11–15.

Falkner, G. (2001) 'The Europeanisation of Austria: Misfit, adaptation and controversies', *European Integration online Papers* (EIoP), 5. Available at: http://eiop.or.at/eiop/pdf/2001-013.pdf.

Faraj, C., Schuster, J., and Labott, E. (2004) 'Saudis in 'total war' on terror', *CNN.com*, 22 April.

Fava, G.C. (2006) *Draft Report on the Alleged Use of European Countries by the CIA for the Transportation and Illegal Detention of Prisoners*. Temporary Committee on the alleged use of European countries by the CIA for the transportation and illegal detention of prisoners, European Parliament (2006/2200(INI)), 24 November.

Fernández-Armesto, F. (1994) *The Times Guide to the Peoples of Europe*. London: Harper Collins.

Ferrero-Waldner, B. (2006) 'Human security and aid effectiveness: The EU's challenges', Speech to the Overseas Development Institute, 26 October, London.

Fleischer, A. (2002) Press Briefing by Ari Fleischer, Office of the Press Secretary, 25 November, The White House. Available at: http://www.whitehouse.gov/news/releases/2002/11/20021125-5.html.

Fontaine, P. (2000) *A New Idea for Europe: The Schuman Declaration, 1950–2000*, 2nd edn. Luxembourg: Office for Official Publications of the European Communities.

Foot, P. (1978) *Virtues and Vices and Other Essays in Moral Philosophy*. Oxford: Blackwell.

Foot, R. (2000) *Rights Beyond Borders: The Global Community and the Struggle over Human Rights in China*. Oxford: Oxford University Press.

Friends of the Earth (2006) 'Transatlantic Biotech Trade War: "No Winners" says FoEE as WTO Makes Ruling Public', Friends of the Earth Europe Press Release, 29 September 2006. Available at: http://www.foeEurope.org/press/2006/AB_29_Sept_WTO_GMO_dispute.htm.

Friis, L. and Murphy, A. (2000) 'Turbo-charged negotiations: the EU and the stability pact of South Eastern Europe', *Journal of European Public Policy*, 7 (5): 767–786.

Galtung, J. (1989) *Europe in the Making*. London: Crane Russak.

Geach, M. and Gormally, L. (eds) (2006) *Human Life, Action and Ethics: Essays by G.E.M. Anscombe*. Exeter: Imprint Academic.

Giddens, A. (1979) *Central Problems in Social Theory: Action, Structure and Contradictions in Social Analysis*. London: Macmillan.

Gingrich, A. (2006) 'Neo-nationalism and the reconfiguration of Europe', *Social Anthropology*, 14 (2): 195–217.

GMO Compass (2006) 'GM Maize Growing in Five EU Member States', GMO Compass advocacy website, 29 May 2006. Brussels: European Commission. Available at: http://www.gmo-compass.org/eng/agri_biotechnology/gmo_planting/191.eu_growing_area.html.

Gowland, D., Dunphy, R. and Lythe, C. (2006) *The European Mosaic: Contemporary Politics, Economics and Culture*, 3rd edn. London: Pearson.

Griffin, G. and Braidotti, R. (2002) *Thinking Differently: A Reader in European Women's Studies*. London: Zed Books.

Griffin, J. (1995) 'Consequentialism', in T. Honderich (ed.) *The Oxford Companion to Philosophy*. Oxford: Oxford University Press, pp. 154–156.

Guibernau, M. and Rex, J. (eds) (1997) *The Ethnicity Reader: Nationalism, Multiculturalism and Migration*. Cambridge: Polity.

Guild, E. (2003) 'International terrorism and EU immigration, asylum and borders policy: the unexpected victims of 11 September 2001', *European Foreign Affairs Review*, 8: 331–346.

Guisan, C. (2003) *Un Sens à l'Europe': Gagner la Paix (1950–2003)*. Paris: Éditions Odile Jacob.

Guisan, C. (2005) 'Winning the peace: 'lost treasure' of European integration?', *Rivista Di Studi Politici Internazionali*, 72 (3): 453–470.

Guruz, K. (2002) 'The struggle against terrorism: support from the Turkish academic community', *Vital Speeches of the Day*, 68 (7): 214–216.

Habermas, J. and Derrida, J. (2003) 'February 15, or what binds Europeans together: a plea for a common foreign policy, beginning in the core of Europe', *Constellations: An International Journal of Critical and Democratic Theory*, 12 (3): 291–297.

Halpern, D. and Mikosz, D. (1998) 'The third way: summary of the NEXUS on-line discussion', *Nexus*, May. Available at: http://www.netnexus.org/library/papers/3way.html.

Hamilton, A. (2004) 'Europe must not reject Turkey now', *The Independent*, 9 September.

Happold, M. (2000) 'Fourteen against one: The EU Member States' response to Freedom Party participation in the Austrian government', *International and Comparative Law Quarterly*, 49 (4): 953–963.

Healy, S. (1999) 'Extended peer communities and the ascendance of post-normal politics', *Futures: the Journal of Policy, Planning and Futures Studies*, 31: 655–699.

Hervik, P. (2006) 'The predictable responses to the Danish cartoons', *Global Media and Communication*, 2 (2): 225–230.

Hodge, R. (2002) 'Monsterous knowledge in a world without borders', *Borderlands e-journal*, 1 (1). Available at: http://www.borderlandsejournal.adelaide.edu.au/vol1no1_2002/hodge_monstrous.html.

Holliday, I. (2002) 'When is a cause just?', *Review of International Studies*, 28 (3): 557–575.

Howard, M.M. (2001) 'Can populism be suppressed in a democracy? Austria, Germany, and the European Union', *East European Politics and Societies*, 14 (2): 18–32.

House of Commons (2000) 'Defence – fourteenth report', Defence Committee, UK Parliament, 23 October 2003. Available at: http://www.publications.parliament.uk/pa/cm199900/cmselect/cmdfence/347/34709.htm.

Huber, D. (1999) *A Decade Which Made History – The Council of Europe 1989–1999*. Strasbourg: Council of Europe.

Hugo, V. (2004) *The History of a Crime*. Whitefish MT: Kessinger Publishing.

Huntington, S. (1993) 'The clash of civilizations?', *Foreign Affairs*, 72 (3): 22–49.

Hursthouse, R. (1999) *On Virtue Ethics*. Oxford: Oxford University Press.

Hursthouse, R. (2003) 'Virtue ethics', *Stanford Encyclopaedia of Philosophy*, 18 July 2003. Available at: plato.stanford.edu/entries/ethics-virtue/.

Huysmans, J. (2002) 'Shape-shifting NATO: Humanitarian action and the Kosovo refugee crisis', *Review of International Studies*, 28: 599–618.

Ignatieff, M. (2004) 'Terrorism's other peril is how it transforms us', *The Globe and Mail*, 17 June, p. A23.

Judis, J. (2002) 'Is the third way finished?', *The American Prospect*, 13 (12).

Judis, J. (2003) 'Minster without Portfolio', *The American Prospect*, 14 (5).

Jung, J. (2003) 'The bigger, the better? Measuring the financial health of media firms', *The International Journal of Media Management*, 5 (4): 237–250.

Kaldor, M. (2003) 'American power: from 'compellance' to cosmopolitanism?', *International Affairs*, 79 (1): 1–22.

Karlsson, M. (2006) 'Science and norms in policies for sustainable development: assessing and managing risks of chemical substances and genetically modified organisms in the European Union', *Regulatory Toxicology and Pharmacology*, 44: 49–56.

Kjærsgaard, P. (2001) Speech to the opening of the Danish Parliament, 2 October. Available at: http://www.folketinget.dk/Samling/20011/salen/R1_BEH1_3_4_223.htm.

Kofman, E., Raghuram, P., Phizacklea, A. and Sales, R. (2000) *Gender and International Migration in Europe: Employment, Welfare and Politics*. London: Routledge.

Kristeva, J. (2004) 'Thinking about liberty in dark times', Holberg Prize Laureate 2004, University of Paris. Bergen: Holberg. Available at: http://www.holberg.uib.no/downloads/informasjon/brosjyrer/2004_hp_brosjyre_publikasjonenglish_juliakristeva.pdf.

Kuhn, T. (1962) *The Structure of Scientific Revolutions*. Chicago: University of Chicago Press.

Ladrech, R. (2003) 'The left and the European Union', *Parliamentary Affairs*, 56 (1): 112–124.

Latawski, P. and Smith, M. (2002) 'Plus ça change, plus c'est la meme chose. CESDP since 1998: The view from London, Paris and Warsaw', *Journal of European Area Studies*, 10 (2): 211–228.

Lavenex, S. (2001) 'The Europeanization of refugee policies: normative challenges and institutional legacies', *Journal of Common Market Studies*, 39 (5): 851–874.

Lawrence, R. and Després, C. (2004) 'Introduction: futures of transdisciplinarity', *Futures*, 36: 397–405.

Leontidou, L. (2004) 'The boundaries of Europe: Deconstructing three regional narratives', *Identities: Global Studies in Culture and Power*, 11 (4): 593–617.

Levy, D., Torpey, J., and Pensky, M. (eds) (2005) *Old Europe, New Europe, Core Europe: Transatlantic Relations After The Iraq War*. London: Verso.

Lewis, G. (2006) 'Imaginaries of Europe: technologies of gender, economies of power', *European Journal of Women's Studies*, 13 (2): 87–102.

Lindström, F. (2002) *European Studies as a Field of Knowledge: Theoretical, Methodological and Practical Reflections*. Lund: Studentlitteratur. Available at: http://www.mah.se/upload/IMER/Program/IPES/04.pdf.

Liotta, P. (2005) 'Imagining Europe: symbolic geography and the future', *Mediterranean Quarterly*, 16 (3): 67–85.

Liotta, P. and Owen, T. (2006) 'Sense and symbolism: Europe takes on human security', *Parameters: US Army War College Quarterly*, Autumn: 85–102.

Loomba, A. (2003) 'Remembering said', *Comparative Studies of South Asia, Africa and the Middle East*, 23 (1–2): 12–14.

Lutz, H. (1997) 'The limits of European-ness: immigrant women in Fortress Europe', *Feminist Review*, 57: 93–111.

McChesney, R. (1999) 'The new global media: it's a small world of big conglomerates', *The Nation*, 29 November: 11–15.

McChesney, R. (2001) *Rich Media, Poor Democracy: Communication Politics in Dubious Times*. New York: The New Press.

Macmillan, S. (2003) 'What new Europe?', *Slate*, 19 February. Available at: http://www.slate.com.

Malmvig, H. (2006) *State Sovereignty and Intervention: A Discourse Analysis of Interventionary and Non-interventionary Practices in Kosovo and Algeria*. London: Routledge.

Manners, I. (2002) 'Normative power Europe: A contradiction in terms?', *Journal of Common Market Studies*, 40 (2): 235–258.

Manners, I. (2003) 'Europaian studies', *Journal of Contemporary European Studies*, 11 (1): 67–83.

Manners, I. (2007) 'European Union "Normative Power" and the Security Challenge', in C. Kantner, A. Libertore, and R. Del Sarto (eds) Special Issue: 'Security and Democracy in the European Union', *European Security*, 15 (4): 405–421.

Marfleet, P. (2003) 'The "clash" thesis: war and ethnic boundaries in Europe', *Arab Studies Quarterly*, 25 (1–2): 71–87.

Marsden, C. (2000) 'Not so special? Merging media pluralism with competition and industrial policy', *Inform*, 2 (1): 9–15.

Martin, D. (2002) 'Plans for Iraq attack began on 9/11', *CBS News*, 4 September, Washington. Available at: http://www.cbsnews.com/stories/2002/09/04/september11/main520830.shtml.

Marty, D. (2006) *Alleged Secret Detentions and Unlawful Inter-state Transfers Involving Council of Europe Member States*. Committee on Legal Affairs and Human Rights, Parliamentary Assembly, Council of Europe, 7 June.

Mayer, J. (2005) 'Outsourcing torture: the secret history of America's "Extraordinary Rendition" Programme', *The New Yorker*, 14 February.

Mégret, F. (2003) 'Justice in times of violence', *European Journal of International Law*, 14 (2): 327–345.

Menon, A., Nicolaïdis, K., and Walsh, J. (2004) 'In defence of Europe: A response to Kagan', *Journal of European Affairs*, 2 (3): 5–14.

Merlingen, M., Mudde, C., and Sedelmeier, U. (2001) 'The right and the righteous? European norms, domestic politics and the sanctions against Austria', *Journal of Common Market Studies*, 39 (1): 59–77.

Naim, M. (2002) 'Anti-Americanisms', *Foreign Policy*, 128, 103–104.

Nordicom (2005a) 'The Largest Media Companies in the World by Revenue 2004', Nordicom. Available at: http://www.nordicom.gu.se.

Nordicom (2005b) 'The Largest Media Companies in Europe by Revenue 2004', Nordicom. Available at: http://www.nordicom.gu.se.

Office of the United Nations High Commissioner for Human Rights (UNHCR) (2006) *International Law*. Geneva: UNOG-OHCHR. Available at: http://www.ohchr.org/english/law/.

O'Neill, O. (2000a) 'Bounded and cosmopolitan justice', *Review of International Studies*, 26: 45–60.

O'Neill, O. (2000b) *Bounds of Justice*. Cambridge: Cambridge University Press.

Ovenden, K. (1998) 'The tide turns red?', *Socialist Review*, 224.

Paasi, A. (2001) 'Europe as a social process and discourse: considerations of place, boundaries and identity', *European Urban and Regional Studies*, 8 (1): 7–28.

Passerini, L. (1998) *Europe in Love, Love in Europe: Imagination and Politics in Britain Between the Wars*. London: IB Tauris.

Pedersen, R. (1992) *One Europe, 100 Nations*. Clevedon: Channel View Books.

Pilger, J. (2002) 'America's bid for global dominance', *New Statesman*, 16–30 December: 13–14.

Pilger, J. (2003) *The New Rulers of the World*. London: Verso.

Power, J. (2002) *Like Water on Stone: The Story of Amnesty International*. London: Penguin Books.

Priest, D. (2005) 'CIA holds terror suspects in secret prisons', *Washington Post*, 2 November.

Quraishy, B. (2003) 'Migration, racism and citizenship in Europe', SID On-line Dialogue, *Development*, 46 (3): 71–74.

Rainio, J., Karkola, K., Lalu, K., Ranta, H., Takamaa, K., and Penttila, A. (2001) 'Forensic investigations in Kosovo: Experiences of the European Union forensic expert team', *Journal of Clinical Forensic Medicine*, 8 (4): 218–221.

Ranstorp, M. and Wilkinson, P. (2005) 'Introduction to Special Issue on Terrorism and Human Rights', *Terrorism and Political Violence*, 17 (1–2): 3–8.

Reader, S. (2000) 'New directions in ethics: naturalisms, reasons and virtue', *Ethical Theory and Moral Practice*, 3: 341–364.

Reiss, H. (1991) *Kant: Political Writings*. Cambridge: Cambridge University Press.

Robertson, C. (2004) 'A sporting gesture? BSkyB, Manchester United, Global Media, and Sport', *Television and News Media*, 5 (4): 291–314.

Robertson, R. (1996) 'Globality, globalization and transdisciplinarity', *Theory, Culture and Society*, 13 (4): 127–132.

Robinson, M. (2002) 'BBC Talking Point Special: Mary Robinson, UN Human Rights chief', 21 November. Available at: http://news.bbc.co.uk/2/hi/talking_point/forum/1673034.stm.

Roy, A. (2001) 'The algebra of infinite justice', *The Guardian*, 29 September.

Rydgren, J. (2002) 'Radical right populism in Sweden: Still a failure, but for how long?', *Scandinavian Political Studies*, 25 (1): 27–56.

Rydgren, J. (2004) 'Explaining the emergence of radical right-wing populist parties: the case of Denmark', *West European Politics*, 27 (3): 474–502.

Rumford, C. and Murray, P. (2003a) 'Globalization and the limitations of European integration studies: interdisciplinary considerations', *Journal of Contemporary European Studies*, 11 (1): 85–93.

Rumford, C. and Murray, P. (2003b) 'Do we need a core curriculum in European union Studies?', *European Political Science*, 3 (1): 85–92.

Sakwa, R. and Stevens, A. (eds) (2002) *Contemporary Europe*. Basingstoke: Palgrave.

Sicurelli, D. (2004) 'Transatlantic relations on food safety: international conflict and policy transfer', paper presented to the Second Pan-European Conference of the Standing Group on EU Politics, 24–26 June, Bologna. Available at: http://www.jhubc.it/ecpr-bologna/docs/611.pdf.

Simonsen, K. (2004) '"Europe", national identities and multiple others', 11 (4): 357–62.

Slote, M. (1995) 'Virtues', in T. Honderich (ed.) *The Oxford Companion to Philosophy*. Oxford: Oxford University Press, pp. 900–901.

Solana, J. (2000) 'Europe: defending ourselves', *NPQ: New Political Quarterly*, 17 (2): 27–29.

Soysal, Y. (1994) *Limits of Citizenship: Migration and Postnational Membership in Europe*. London: University of Chicago Press.

Spoonley, P. (1993) *Racism and Ethnicity*. Oxford: Oxford University Press.

Stevenson, J. (2006) 'Outperforming the terrorists', *The Adelphi Papers*, 44 (367): 95–113.

Stiglitz, J. (2001) 'To a third way consensus', *Project Syndicate*, May. Available at: http://www.project-syndicate.org/

Strange, S. (1988) *States and Markets: An Introduction to International Political Economy*. London: Pinter.

Todorova, M.N. (1997) *Imagining the Balkans*. Oxford: Oxford University Press.

von Schorlemer, S. (2003) 'Human rights: the substantive and institutional implications of the war against terrorism', *European Journal of International Law*, 14 (2): 265–282.

Walker, M. (1998) 'EU summit signals shift to keynesian economics', *Europe*, 6 (10).

Walker, M. (1999) 'Third way club gathers members', *The Guardian*, 3 May.

Wallace, H. (2000) 'Studying contemporary Europe', *The British Journal of Politics and International Relations*, 2 (1): 95–113.

Warleigh, A. (2004) 'In defence of intra-disciplinarity: "European studies", the "New Regionalism", and the Issue of Democratisation', *Cambridge Review of International Affairs*, 17 (2): 301–317.

Weber, M. (1968) *Economy and Society*. New York: Academic Press.

Welsh, I. (2006) 'Values, science and the European Union: biotechnology and transatlantic relations', in S. Lucarelli and I. Manners (eds) *Values and Principles in European Union Foreign Policy*. London: Routledge, pp. 59–76.

Wren, K. (2001) 'Cultural racism: something rotten in the state of Denmark?', *Social & Cultural Geography*, 2 (2): 141–161.

Zaslove, A. (2004) 'The dark side of European Politics: unmasking the radical right', *Journal of European Integration*, 26 (1): 61–81.

32

Europe as a Postemotional Idea – or, 'Upon Us All There Still Lies "the Curse of Cromwell"'

Stjepan G. Mestrovic

What is the social meaning of Europe as an idea? What are the social origins, structure, and consequences of this idea, as opposed to discourse concerning the modernist origins, borders, and issues regarding the European Union, European Community, European continent, and European culture? Suppose that one glances at the historical panorama of efforts to establish some sort of idea of Europe ranging from the ancient Greeks (who polarized the distinction between their civilization and barbarians), Roman Emperors through Charlemagne, feudalism, the many religious wars before, during and after Oliver Cromwell, Napoleon, Mussolini, and Hitler, up to and including the contemporary movement to establish a European Union. At first glance, it seems that such discussions are typically framed in *modernist* terms: What were the borders of these various, historical entities that approximated Europe? Anthony Giddens (1987), among others, is adamant in seeking out the borders and their surveillance for various nation-states that are labeled as European. Modernists also seek out 'facts' in

various documents that are regarded as signposts of European civilization, including but not limited to writings by ancient Greeks and Romans, the Magna Carta, edicts drafted by various Christian writers, and classics written by so-called Enlightenment thinkers (Spengler, [1926] 1961; Toynbee, 1978).

In these and related discussions pertaining to Europe, modernists focus upon finding order within chaos (e.g. 'borders' versus 'frontiers'), searching for 'facts', measuring and gauging opinion, faith in science and progress, isolating agendas, and other narratives derived from the Enlightenment (Giddens, 1990). Modernists are frequently accused of taking a Eurocentric perspective and of assuming that modernity itself is a Western European 'project'. Indeed, the Enlightenment and its attendant ideas (democracy, science, civilization, progress, technology, etc.) are regarded as one of the key traits for distinguishing European from 'barbarian' culture. It is a circular argument based upon pre-established ideas concerning the Enlightenment and its attendant ideas: The Enlightenment with a capital 'E' is used as the starting point for discussions which dismiss people who did not have a Renaissance and Enlightenment as non- or less-than-European (such as, the Russians, Turks, Slavic peoples, etc.). In discussions of this sort, and to achieve balance, hardly anybody cites Thorstein Veblen's ([1899] 1965) poignant observations that (1) the Enlightenment was limited geographically to the northwest corner of the European continent and limited in time to a specific century; and (2) the Enlightenment was accompanied by civil and religious wars, witch hunts, and other tendencies that he labels as predatory and frankly barbaric (Mestrovic, 2004). Many other writers have analyzed the barbaric and otherwise dark side of the Enlightenment (Bauman 1991; Mestrovic, 1993; Tocqueville, [1845] 2003; Toulmin, 1992).

But alongside this modernist public discussion, there exists another that is difficult to categorize. One can characterize this other discussion as postmodern, postauratic, posthonorific, carnivalesque, and deconstructionist, but its central features are these: Lyotard (1984) claims that the Enlightenment is really just a story or narrative. More precisely, he refers to the grand narratives of the Enlightenment, which he regards as totalizing and fundamentally oppressive despite the positive ways in which they are typically packaged. Zygmunt Bauman (1991) has traced the origins of nazism, communism, and totalitarianism to tendencies within these narratives to establish extreme 'order' at seemingly any cost. Bauman (1989) portrays Hitler as a modernist, European thinker who wanted to establish an 'orderly garden' of Europe in which Jews and others were regarded as 'weeds'. Akbar Ahmed (1991) has argued that European history and culture are fundamentally anti-Semitic (by which he means anti-Muslim as well as anti-Jewish) in common customs derived from the ancient Greeks and Romans, who, among other traits, sought to display the naked or semi-clad human body in opposition to the Semitic cultural premium put on modesty.

A POSTEMOTIONAL APPROACH TO EUROPE

I propose another approach to the idea of Europe with the concept of postemotionalism. Postemotional society harks back into the distant past in order to create emotional responses in the present, or more precisely, postmotionalism is a cultural development in which synthetic, quasi-emotions become the basis for widespread manipulation by self, others, and the culture industry as a whole (Mestrovic, 1997). Postemotionalism views the rhetorical link between Europe and the Enlightenment as fake. This is because (1) Enlightenment narratives falsely depict the human person and society as excessively rational and generally eschew emotions; and (2) depictions of both Europe and the Enlightenment are actually instances of emotional clinging to *simulations* of both ideas. In reality, persons as well as societies exhibit cognitive as well as passionate qualities, and ideas of both Europe as well as the Enlightenment encompass histories of barbarism. For example, not only did the Enlightened Puritans kill 'witches', they first made sure that the 'witches' were put on trial, had legal counsel, were examined by doctors, and otherwise had access to the most scientific procedures of their day. Thus, postemotionalism involves an obfuscation of facts through the use of displaced emotions from history, and the manipulation of emotionally charged collective representations of reality on the part of individuals as well as the culture industry. 'A working definition of postemotionalism might be that it is a neo-Orwellian mechanism found in Western societies in which the culture industry markets and manipulates dead emotions from history that are selectively and synthetically attached to current events' (Mestrovic, 1997: 11). Postemotionalism always involves confusion, hypocrisies, nostalgia, ironies, paradoxes, and neo-Orwellian manipulation such that 2 + 2 do *not* equal 4. (The main character in Orwell's novel, *1984*, maintains that he is spiritually free so long as he knows that 2 + 2 equal 4.)

Postemotionalism overlaps with postmodern approaches, but is distinct from them. Both postmodernism and postemotionalism as modes of analysis emphasize the importance of simulacra and hyper-reality. However, postmodernism tends to view society as a rootless circulation of fictions (Baudrillard, 1986), and these fictions are mostly cognitive, whereas postemotionalism finds compulsive and emotional (albeit displaced) patterns in the circulating fictions. A postemotional approach to Europe (or any other phenomenon) makes widespread use of what David Riesman ([1950] 1992: 196) called 'fake sincerity', and is itself the outgrowth of what he called other-directed social character. As such, postemotional rituals, politics, and culture in general must be distinguished from more sincere and genuinely emotional responses to European cultural traits in history. In other words, postemotionalism is not like the tradition-directed society's revivification of customs and celebrations that is described by Emile Durkheim ([1912] 1965) and it is not like the inner-directed society's internalization of ideas that were sincere enough to last for at least a lifetime that is described by Riesman.

Examples of political postemotionalism range from the Serbs invoking a grievance from the year 1389 in order to justify their violence in Yugoslavia in the 1990s, Greece using the memory of Alexander the Great in order to block the existence of Macedonia in the 1990s, to France and England still nursing their wounds at losing their empires by reminding the world that they were the founders of civilization and the Enlightenment (Mestrovic, 1995). Similarly, the US used the moral code of the Puritans – who were expelled over 500 years ago from Europe to the North American continent – as the 'beacon of democracy set upon a hill' depicted by Alexis de Tocqueville's *Democracy in America* to justify war against Iraq when the real enemy was Osama Bin Laden. But it seems that few people read the unabridged version of Tocqueville's classic, which deals

with slavery and extermination of Native Americans ([1845] 2003: 370–485). Tocqueville was ambivalent about American society, but most of his academic readers seem to miss this point. Fewer still are concerned with the evil consequences imposed by the Puritans in Europe under the rule of Oliver Cromwell, who has finally come to be regarded by historians as a dictator who perpetrated genocide upon the Irish and persecuted the Scots (see Bennett, 2006; Levene, 2005; Lutz, 2004). Winston Churchill put it well:

'Hell or Connaught' were the terms he [Cromwell] thrust upon the native inhabitants, and they for their part, across three hundred years, have used as their keenest expression of hatred 'The Curse of Cromwell on you'. The consequences of Cromwell's rule in Ireland have distressed and at times distracted English politics down even to the present day. To heal them baffled the skill and loyalties of successive generations. They became for a time a potent obstacle to the harmony of English-speaking people throughout the world. Upon all of us there still lies 'the Curse of Cromwell'. (Churchill, 1957: 9)

As of this writing, the Irish problem has not yet been resolved, and the impoverished Irish who were deported to the US beginning in the 1600s remain a cultural problem. It is not well-known that Cromwell forced tens of thousands of Irish into indentured servitude or white slavery, and sent them to the Americas as punishment (Hoffman, 1993; O'Callaghan, 2001; Walsh, 2007). Many of the descendants of those Irish exiles are labeled as hillbillies, hicks and white trash in the contemporary US, and suffered from prejudice against them (Goad, 1998). In these and other instances, contemporary Europeans (and to some extent, Americans) use ancient European ideas such as civilization and Enlightenment to rationalize seemingly barbaric behaviors and attitudes in their present. More importantly, Cromwell is hailed in England as a hero, but is still despised in Ireland, while Milosevic is revered in Serbia, but perceived as a pariah elsewhere in Europe. Both Cromwell and

Milosevic invoked ideas of European civilization to justify their barbaric acts.

A more in-depth analysis of any of these examples reveals extraordinary connections to ideas surrounding Europe and its meanings. One could argue that Belgrade-sponsored genocide against Bosnian Muslims has little to do with the idea of Europe, because Europeans generally regard the Balkans with the racism captured by Mark Almond's (1994) phrase, 'Europe's backyard'. On the other hand, the postmodernist writer, Jean Baudrillard (1995), has argued that Serbia was doing Western Europe's 'dirty work' on its behalf. Historians generally agree that Europe (and especially the Major government in the United Kingdom) went out of its way not to intervene and not to prevent Belgrade-sponsored genocide against European Muslims, and thereby acquiesced to Serbian intentions (see Cushman and Mestrovic, 1995; Kent, 2006). Were the Serbian or Western European governments who were caught up in this drama sincere in the narratives they presented for public discourse? There is no rational connection between the Ottoman Empire of the fourteenth century and the Bosnian Muslims in the twentieth century, yet this irrational and fake connection was presented and largely accepted by European governments as well as media as justification for aggression and acquiescence to aggression. Genuine principles based upon the ideals of the Enlightenment – which are routinely touted by England and France – should have invoked moral principles as well as constructive action by Europe. It is far more believable that Greece sought a portion of Macedonian territory, divided with Serbia, than that the Greek government was sincerely interested in preserving the memory of Alexander the Great (Michas, 2002).

It is as if the sinister side of American history, found in the unabridged version of Tocqueville's classic, emerged as the Jungian shadow of Puritan ideals in the form of postemotional racism, humiliation, and violence committed against Native Americans,

African-Americans, and other minorities. By Jungian shadow, I am referring to the psychologist Carl Gustav Jung's (1963) theory that individuals as well as social groups keep disagreeable ideas in the 'shadow' or unconscious of public discourse (see Rosen, 1996). Similarly, in Europe, Oliver Cromwell persecuted whole peoples in the so-called British Isles in the name of dichotomous Puritan ideals which amounted to black and white, 'you're with us or against us' thinking that psychologists regard as one of the hallmarks of mental illness. Puritanism created havoc on both sides of the Atlantic, and is increasingly coming to be regarded by historians as a form of religious fundamentalism. To be sure, the postemotional repetition of Puritan severity had been covered up for many decades not only by historians but also by the Thanksgiving holiday in the US. The happy, other-directed (from Riesman) image of the Puritans sitting down to a friendly meal with Native Americans served as a public relations ploy to cover up what latter-day historians regarded as genocidal intentions by the Puritans toward the American aborigines (see Loewen, 1995). The postemotional recycling of Puritan intentions continues to this day in the US war against Iraq that began in 2003. A moral code used to evoke genuine emotions among the Puritans was used at the beginning of the millennium in an attempt to depict US motives in the war against Iraq as a part of an overall plan to bring democracy and freedom to the Middle East. Regarding the cultural legacy of the Puritans, Tocqueville writes:

> Nothing is more peculiar or more instructive than the legislation of this time; there, if anywhere, is the key to the social enigma presented to the world by the United States now ... Blasphemy, sorcery, adultery, and rape are punished by death; a son who outrages his parents is subject to the same penalty. Thus the legislation of a rough, half-civilized people was transported into the midst of an educated society with gentle mores ... I have already said enough to put Anglo-American civilization in its true light. It is the product (and one should continually bear in mind this point of departure) of two perfectly distinct elements which elsewhere have often been at war with one

another but which in America it was somehow possible to incorporate into each other, forming a marvelous combination. I mean the spirit of religion and the spirit of freedom (Tocqueville, [1845] 2003: 41–7).

Tocqueville summarizes: 'The founders of New England were both sectarian fanatics and noble innovators' ([1845] 2003: 55) – a veritable split personality. Tocqueville wrote these words in the year 1845, yet they are still applicable to the US as of this writing, in the year 2007. The US still demands the death penalty for a myriad of offenses, to the surprise of other industrial nations. Blue laws (which refer to laws against buying and selling merchandise on Sundays ranging from alcohol to automobiles, and which are still in effect in most of the US – see Novak, 1996), and puritanical moral codes against drug use, prostitution, sexual matters, and nudity still exist and are enforced with a quasi-religious fervor in the US. Baudrillard (1986) as well as Riesman ([1950] 1992), among other analysts of American culture, have noted the seemingly permanent influence of Puritan culture upon the US. But no major sociological theorist has traced the influence of Puritanism and Calvinism upon the European continent. For example, Adam Hochschild's (1999) brilliant analysis of the Belgian King Leopold's genocide against natives in the Congo fails to confront the sociology of Puritan confrontation with natives who are presumed to be damned. Tocqueville is the only major historian who touches on the issue of how Puritan influence affected English, Dutch, and other northwest European attitudes toward aborigines and others who were not considered as part of the Elect. Even Max Weber ([1904] 1958) concentrates his attention on Puritan influence upon the US, and focuses primarily upon the economic sphere, while he treats Calvinist cultural influence in Europe as an apparent afterthought. Weber writes: 'For the damned to complain of their lot would be much the same as for animals to bemoan the fact they were not born as men … We know only that a part of humanity is saved, the rest damned'

([1904] 1958: 103). Surely this Puritan attitude – that they were saved and everyone else was damned – had an effect on political and other social spheres other than economics. If Tocqueville is correct to depict Puritanism as a sort of collective, split personality, what were its effects on the European continent? This question constitutes a gaping conceptual hole in sociological theorizing on modernity as well as the idea of Europe.

The incessant repetition of past collective traumas – the seemingly endless cycles of civil, religious, genocidal, wars and so-called 'ancient tribal warfare' is reminiscent of the Freudian 'compulsion to repeat', albeit applied to societies and not only to individuals. Freud frequently made analogies between the private obsessions and compulsions of the individual neurotic and societies, but this aspect of his overall thought remains underdeveloped (Mestrovic, 1993). Although he insisted that psychoanalysis was a tool for analyzing individuals as well as groups, societies, and cultures, Freud ([1925] 1959) and psychoanalysis have been absorbed primarily by psychology, which is focused mostly upon the individual. It is beyond the scope of this essay to work out the theoretical scaffolding for how one may comprehend collective compulsions to repeat historical traumas. I have developed such a scaffolding for a sociological reading of Freud on this particular point in my *Barbarian Temperament*, in which I emphasize the importance of Arthur Schopenhauer's ([1818] 1965) philosophy for laying the groundwork for a number of important works in the nineteenth and twentieth centuries in sociology, psychology, literature, and art. There is no intention here to apply a Freudian reading onto history or postemotional theory. Rather, Freud's ideas on the unconscious and the compulsion to repeat were already foreshadowed by Schopenhauer's elaboration of the ideas of the 'will' and the eternal recurrence of the same (which was popularized by his disciple Nietzsche).

Numerous writers in diverse fields have used the theme that history repeats itself. The postemotional concept is a more specific version of this truism in that it focuses upon the synthetic manipulation of the emotional components of history, and upon the disintegrative, dysfunctional consequences of such compulsions. Again, it would take one too far astray from the discussion to analyze whether structural–functionalists, from Parsons and various anthropologists to Durkheim, overemphasize the allegedly integrative functions of deliberate compulsions to repeat holidays, festivals, and other collective representations. Rene Girard (2005) makes a valid point when he asserts that Durkheim's theory can uphold integration through such rites of collective effervescence only at the cost of demonizing, scapegoating, or otherwise inflicting violence on a group that is deemed 'profane' so that the 'sacred' group can feel integrated. In summary, this essay is not concerned with the application of specific theories and theorists who are concerned with compulsions, repetitions, and other revivifications of collective representations, from Schopenhauer through Freud and Durkheim and the functionalists. However, postemotional theory does draw upon and elaborate upon many of these writers. Similarly, it is beyond the scope of this essay to do justice to the history of Europe, even from a sociological point of view, in the manner of Veblen, Marx, or Weber. The aim here is to apply the postemotional concept to the idea of Europe for the sake of gaining a new perspective on existing facts and theories.

For example, I have already touched upon Tocqueville's powerful indictment of the Puritans for understanding American cultural compulsions, and pointed out that the Puritan impact on European cultural compulsions has been neglected. But the very idea of Europe as a sort of United States of Europe bespeaks a postemotional repetition of Tocqueville's desire to teach the Europeans how to establish democracy. It also points to similar problems encountered by the Europeans in managing regional differences (the Mediterranean region is regarded by

the UK, Germany, and France with much the same sense of superiority and contempt that the American North viewed and continues to view the American South). The Muslims of Europe are the rough equivalent of African-Americans in terms of chronic racism and ethnic tensions that boiled over into genocide in the Balkans in the 1990s. If Tocqueville is correct that the stain of slavery will never be washed out of the American cultural fabric, it seems that the stain of the Ottoman Empire's conquest of a portion of Europe will never be forgotten by Europe. It is the collective narcissistic injury that is repeated in a myriad of Puritanical orgies against Semitic peoples in Europe, from the Crusades through the many wars prior to World War I, the Holocaust, and through the genocide against the Bosnian Muslims in the 1990s. The Puritans are not just the cultural descendants of Cromwell and Calvin, but all those who sought and continue to seek out the 'weeds' in the orderly garden that is supposed to be Europe, including Napoleon and Hitler. And the 'weeds' are not just the Muslims and the Jews, but all those who are deemed as threatening to the neat and tidy European garden, including Slavs, Sicilians, Albanians, Turks, and others. One of the most important postemotional connections is the one between the Puritans and their goal of establishing a 'pure' and perfect society with the Serbs and their similar goal of ethnic purity or 'ethnic cleansing.' One could argue that the idea of ethnic cleansing is ancient, and distinctly European.

REBECCA WEST'S CLASSIC STATEMENT ON EUROPE REVISITED

Which European writer and book may be regarded as the rough equivalent of Tocqueville's *Democracy in America*? I believe a good reply to this question is Rebecca West's ([1940] 1982) classic *Black Lamb and Gray Falcon*. It is tempting to dismiss Tocqueville, West and others, such as, Baudrillard, as writing 'travel journals'. In fact, West achieves something that no sociological writer on Europe has achieved: she writes of the Balkans in constant interplay with European history and European ideas, such as, the Enlightenment, Nazism, Mussolini, the Manichean heresy, the Roman Empire, English civilization, and other matters pertaining to Europe. For example, the Manichean heresy – as it was regarded by Christians in Europe – refers to pre-Christian beliefs that the world is divided into descendants of the good 'light' versus the evil 'dark'. Manicheans held to extreme dualisms, which preceded the Puritans, and whose beliefs were never entirely eradicated from European thought. For example, the important Catholic theologian, St. Augustine, converted from Manicheanism to Catholicism, but many of his teachings maintain elements of Manichean heresy (e.g. the belief that the 'body' is evil, so that sex should never be enjoyed, and one should engage in sex only out of a sense of duty to procreate), which were revived by Calvin (see Melchert, 2002). More importantly, West unifies this diverse and far-reaching discussion with reference to a compulsive repetition of cultural differences with Islam. I propose to undertake a rereading of West's classic in reference to postemotionalism. The fulcrum of West's analysis is to be found in the following passage:

> These people of Dalmatia gave the bread out of their mouths to save us of Western Europe from Islam; and it is ironical that so successfully did they protect us that those among us who would be broad-minded, who will in pursuit of that end stretch their minds till they fall apart in idiocy, would blithely tell us that perhaps the Dalmatians need not have gone to that trouble, than an Islamized West could not have been worse than what we are today. Their folly is certified for what it is by the mere sound of the word 'Balkan' with its suggestion of a disorder that defies human virtue and intelligence to accomplish its complete correction. I could confirm that certificate by my own memories: I had only to shut my eyes to smell the dust, the lethargy, the rage and hopelessness of a Macedonian town, once a glory to Europe, that had been too long Turkish. The West has done much that is ill, it is vulgar and superficial and economically sadist; but it has not known that

death in life which was suffered by the Christian provinces under the Ottoman Empire ([1940] 1982: 148)

From the outset, West displays her racist attitude by reminding the reader that the word 'Balkan' is a 'term of abuse, meaning a *rastaquoere* [social intruder] type of barbarian' (p. 21). But she attributes this barbarism to Turkish influence, not the Balkans *per se*. Thus her favorite Balkan people are the Serbs and the Dalmatians, who were, in her view, least influenced by the Turks. Her journey begins on a train to Zagreb, which is full of German tourists who are taking holidays that are approved by the Nazi regime. 'The Germans have always hated the Slavs,' she observes (p. 51), as if to find something good about the Germans.

While visiting the ruins of the Roman Emperor Diocletian's place in Split, Croatia, she muses on connections among St. Augustine, the Manicheans, and the peoples of Europe who preceded and succeeded the Romans:

> We have no real evidence that the peoples on which the Roman Empire imposed its civilization had not pretty good civilizations of their own, better adapted to local conditions. The Romans said they had not; but posterity might doubt the existence of our contemporary French and English culture if the Nazis destroyed all records of them' (p. 164).

What are the connections? St. Augustine and St. Jerome 'declared that [they] valued marriage only because it produced virgins' (p. 168). She continues:

> They would have felt amazement had they known that, some few centuries later, the Church would have persecuted them, even to death, for such wedded chastity. For over this coast there was to spread from the hinterland of the Balkan Peninsula the Puritan heresy known as Paulicianism or Patarenism or Bogomilism or Catharism, knowing certain local and temporal variations under these names, but all impassioned over the necessity of disentangling the human spirit from the evilness of matter' (p. 168).

Note that in an irrational and racist manner, West manages to blame even the origins of Puritanism on the Balkans! The real Puritans valued virginity slightly less than Augustine, the Bogomils, and others, but the common strand is a fanatical, fundamentalist hatred of 'dirty' materialism in favor of some highly idealized and unreal 'purity' of spirit. Note that she does not isolate the Puritans as a unique band of European religious fundamentalists, but treats them instead as one of several refractions of European fanaticism. It would be an interesting and important task to undertake a rereading of Europe's history as the postemotional repetition of various persecutions of individuals and peoples in the name of such Puritanical–Manichean dualisms. For example, Cromwell, Hitler, Mussolini, and Milosevic – among other European dictators – were obsessed with establishing 'pure' societies and persecuting the ones they regarded as 'dirty' – in other words, with ethnic cleansing. She writes: 'The whole of modern history could be deduced from the popularity of this heresy in Western Europe: its inner sourness, its preference for hate over love and for war over peace, its courage in dying, its cowardice about living' (p. 173). One wonders why Max Weber did not delve further into the roots of Calvinism, as far back as West travels conceptually, to the early Church fathers and earliest heresies. Arguably, Augustine was more Calvinist in his hatred of the body and its pleasures than Calvin. West writes that

> according to this early Christian doctrine, some peoples are wholly of the darkness, Jews and Turks and pagans. It is put forward solidly and without sense of any embarrassment that there are those who are predestined to pain, contrary to the principles of human justice. Calvin admitted this with agony, but there is none here; and Dostoevsky never complains against the God who created the disordered universe he describes (p. 176).

I agree with the elective affinities among collective representations across many centuries of European history and thought that West uncovers. From early Christian doctrine to Calvin through Dostoevsky and after him – these are all postemotional repetitions of an early and collective narcissistic injury to the 'civilized European' by the imagined insult caused by the 'barbarian's' very existence.

But for all her insight, she does not display any embarrassment either at her own racism toward Turks. And it does not seem to occur to her that Puritanism had an effect on English civilization which she idealizes in contrast to the alleged barbarism of the Balkans.

West's discussion of Napoleon is set in similar terms of a Manichean dualism between purity and lust, light and darkness:

> There was a time in Napoleon's life when the whole of Europe appeared to be suffering defeat before France only in order to rise again and put on an immortal brightness. But in a few months the prospects changed. It was as if there had been an eclipse; the Manicheans would have recognized its nature. In Napoleon there seemed now to be nothing but darkness (p. 185).

She again connects this compulsive repetition in European history to the conflict with the Ottomans by quoting an elderly gentleman from Dalmatia: 'We are in some respects all barbarous simply because we spent so much of our time defending the West. We fought the Turk, and then we fought the Turk, and then we fought the Turk' (p. 214).

When she turns to the Archduke Franz Ferdinand and the period of Austro-Hungarian rule in Europe, she again connects the discussion to these same, fundamental traumas. In her view, Ferdinand arranged his own assassination in a way because he picked the holy day of the Battle of Kosovo (St. Vitus Day) to visit Sarajevo:

> Franz Ferdinand must have been well aware that he was known as an enemy of Serbia. He must known that if he went to Bosnia and conducted maneuvers on the Serbian frontier just before St. Vitus's Day and on the actual anniversary paid a state visit to Sarajevo, he would be understood to be mocking the South Slav world, to be telling them that though the Serbs might have freed themselves from the Turks there were still many Slavs under the Austrian's yoke (p. 343)

In these and other ways, according to West, Ferdinand 'had placed at their posts the beaters who should drive him down through a narrowing world to the spot where Princip's bullet would find him' (p. 336). I shall not challenge here West's intriguing analysis of an assassination that helped spark World

War I. Of greater importance is her almost Freudian-like description of a European leader's personal trauma as related to many collective traumas that again reopen the wound that is perceived to be caused by 'the Turk'. In my reading of West's analysis of this important event in European history, the postemotional wounds of the Battle of Kosovo from the year 1389 are treated as if they were still fresh wounds in the year 1914. And these same artificial wounds would be resurrected by Slobodan Milosevic on the same feast day in Kosovo in 1989, triggering the Balkan Wars of the 1990s. Would European history have been different had Ferdinand chosen a different date to visit Sarajevo? Or would this same trauma have found another outlet and led to a similar result?

One of the apparent reasons that West does not sympathize with Ferdinand or the Austro-Hungarians is because 'in 1739 by a hideously treacherous agreement the Austrians handed Belgrade and its Serb inhabitants to Turkey' (p. 467). In her view, the Europeans had again brought future darkness on themselves by this and similar acts. In her view, the Serbs are the heroes of European history because they consistently despised 'the Turks'.

And what is her view of the Serbian dictator, King Alexander? She rationalizes his use of torture by noting that 'a bad penal tradition has been inherited both from Turkey and from Austria' (p. 478). In her view, all the Serbian kings were 'fighting against the Turks, the practitioners of pagan luxury' (p. 522). This fact alone made them noble in her eyes. Confronted by the fact that Alexander was a failed dictator who could not preserve Yugoslavia, and who was eventually assassinated, she writes:

> He could not secure unity among the Croats and Slovenes and Serbs, but he himself had never wished to include the Croats and Slevenes in his kingdom. He had hoped, at the beginning of the war, not for a Yugoslavia, not for a union of all South Slavs, but for a Greater Serbia that should add to the kingdom of Serbia all the Austro-Hungarian territories in which the majority of the inhabitants were Serbs (p. 590)

West is honest in her assessment of Alexander's mendacity and aims, but does not condemn them. Interestingly, the quest for a Greater Serbia reappeared postemotionally in the 1990s under the dictatorship of Milosevic. This collective quest is justified by Serbian culture as well by West on the basis of Kosovo: Serbia somehow earned the right to territorial self-aggrandizement, and eventually to ethnic cleansing, because of its martyr-like suffering at the hands of the Turks on behalf of the rest of Europe. What is more interesting is that a similar argument was used by the Milosevic regime, and was accepted, for the most part, by Western Europe in the 1990s, and especially by Great Britain. As Gregory Kent (2006) demonstrates in his recent assessment of the Balkan Wars of the 1990s, Great Britain was Belgrade's most important defender during Serbia's aggression against its neighbors. This postemotional affinity between 'Great' Britain and 'Greater' Serbia bespeaks a sociological 'mirroring' of collective intentions, akin to how mentally disordered individuals often find partners who 'mirror' them psychologically. One ought to ask the same question concerning London's motives *vis-à-vis* other peoples in the British Isles that West asks regarding Belgrade's motives *vis-à-vis* the South Slavs, namely: whose interests were most served by the various establishments of Great Britain followed by United Kingdom, and at whose expense? It is certain that the Scots, Irish, and Welsh have expressed discontent over the course of many years at these arrangements that are similar in some ways to the disgruntled Yugoslav peoples (Croats, Slovenes, Bosnians). What is the postemotional energy that drove English expansionism? After all, Alexander sought to be Emperor of all the Russias in addition to being King of the Serbs, and England at one time 'ruled the world'. West does not try to conceal her disgust at the 'filth' she claims she encounters in every town and region that she regards as properly Muslim. Her attitude is not that different from similar sentiments expressed by Anglo-Saxon racists toward all people of color.

LINKS TO CONTEMPORARY ISSUES IN EUROPE

The postemotional energy of the tensions that West uncovered continue to animate contemporary Europe, especially its relations with Turkey, the Muslim minorities living in Europe, and its alliance with the US in the conflict that goes by the vague title of 'war against terror'. I agree with West that the 'original' template of ideas that is being compulsively reproduced is the Manichean splitting between pure and dirty, light and darkness, good and evil. The idea of Europe relies upon the nucleus of this radical splitting, either–or thinking, black or white categorization. Ultimately, when people call themselves European, they seem to mean that they are 'civilized' in opposition to the 'barbarians' at their gate or in their midst. Postemotionalism dictates that Europeans compulsively repeat various programs to impose 'light' through violent means and ethnic cleansing against the 'dark' peoples. It is possible to read the history of Europe from this postemotional perspective, from Diocletian through the various heresies, Crusades, Puritanical regimes, Inquisitions, fascisms, Quisling regimes, and ethnic cleansings. The cultural refractions of this heresy include the rise and continued dominance of Puritan thinking in the US as well as Europe in constant opposition to 'dark' people, from African-Americans to Gypsies, Jews, Muslims, and others.

Contrast Max Weber and Alexis de Tocqueville on the broad issues being discussed in this chapter. In *The Protestant Ethic and the Spirit of Capitalism*, Weber does not scrutinize the European origins of Puritanism or its affinities with earlier heresies; he assumes the dominance, uniqueness, and special nature of Puritan culture without defending these assumptions; and he neglects completely the consequences of Puritan culture on Europe in an analysis that is mostly America-centric. His reference to the 'Iron Cage' takes up one page of his analysis, even though it has been overemphasized by sociologists. It is little wonder that

in *The McDonaldization of Society*, George Ritzer (1995) could and did popularize the 'nice' version of Puritanism, distilled from Weber, that it promotes efficiency, control, rationality, and production. This is precisely the reading of Weber that appeals to and supports the ruling elites who continue to make use of the collective representations derived from Puritanism on both sides of the Atlantic. Weber and Ritzer never bother to question or deconstruct the typical traits that are attributed to the idea of Europe, and by extension, the United States: Enlightenment, rationality, and progress, are depicted as exclusively benign phenomena. The key point, missed by Ritzer and scores of contemporary theorists, is Tocqueville's ironic description of the cultural style that Puritans used to destroy people they regarded as already damned:

> The Spanish, using unparalleled atrocities, which bring an indelible shame upon themselves, have not succeeded in exterminating the Indian race, nor even in preventing them from sharing their rights; the Americans of the United States have attained both these results with amazing ease, quietly, legally, and generously, with no spilling of blood, with no violation to the great moral principles in the eyes of the world. *Men could not be destroyed with more respect for the laws of humanity*. (Tocqueville [1845] 2003: 397, my emphasis).

In other words, Puritan culture McDonaldizes genocide in the same manner that it McDonaldizes the economic sphere. On the other hand, Tocqueville notes that the Spanish preceded the Puritans in settling the US, but that Spanish cultural influence was eclipsed by the Puritans. Tocqueville noted that a shrine was erected to Plymouth Rock – and the shrine stands at Plymouth to this day – but that most Americans did not (and still do not) think of the Spanish when thinking of the origins of America. Similarly, and to this day, the territorial war against Mexico that created the state of Texas and other Western states is not part of the routine cultural history taught in the US. The real history – which includes genocide against aborigines – is found in works such as *Lies My Teacher Told Me* (Loewen, 1995) and books by Howard Zinn (2005). Similar approaches to the history of Europe would be helpful. Tocqueville also treats the many wars American fought internally, against Native Americans, the French, and even the American South in cultural terms, as refractions of Puritan beliefs that it set the standard for the New Jerusalem, against all others who were considered damned and therefore expendable. Despite the historical accuracy and complexity of Tocqueville's account, his stature in the social sciences does not compare with the iconic status of Weber. Weber is listed in every sociological theory textbook, while Tocqueville is conspicuously absent.

The current war against terror is confusing and seemingly irrational in the explanations that are offered by the government as well as the information media. If it began by the United States attacking Afghanistan because of the terrorist attack that has come to be known at 9/11, it must be noted that as of this writing, Osama bin laden is still at large. The US waged war on Iraq even though Saddam Hussein had no connection of any sort to either 9/11 or Al-Qaeda. These discrepancies were swept away with the Puritanical and postemotional rhetoric that the US was waging wars against specific Islamic nations in order to promote democracy, spread the 'cause of freedom,' and to advance the cause of the Enlightenment. As of this writing, the net effect has been very similar to that of the real Enlightenment, and is far from the stated goals: civil war in Iraq, abuse and killing of Iraqi civilians, the heightening of cultural schisms in Iraq and the exacerbation of religious fanaticism (Galbraith, 2007; Ricks, 2007). The real Enlightenment in Europe was marked by similar ethnic, civil, and religious wars and persecution, alongside the rhetoric of science and progress.

A divided Europe joined the US in this global war on terror as the 'Coalition of the Willing.' Even though this coalition has dwindled over the years, and even though the population in much of Europe opposed the war, most European governments, and especially the Blair government, supported the war (Serfaty, 2007). Despite a rhetoric of European democracy and standards for human rights, most European governments knew of and aided the US in the controversial program known as 'rendition', in which terrorist suspects were flown via European airports and into some European nations to be tortured (Grey, 2007). In many ways, Baudrillard's (1995) indictment of the Europeans as being happy to let the Serbs do their dirty work for them in the Balkan Wars of the 1990s still applies to Europe *vis-à-vis* the War on Terror, only this time they are happy to let the US do their dirty work for them:

> The fine point of the story is the following: in carrying out ethnic cleansing, the Serbs are Europe's cutting edge. The 'real' Europe in the making is a white Europe, a bleached Europe that is morally, economically, and ethnically integrated and cleansed. In Sarajevo, this Europe is victoriously in the making ... The scenario is the same as with Saddam Hussein: in our battle against him, we deployed a great deal of media and technology. In the final analysis, however, he was, and is, our objective ally. Reviled, denounced, and discredited in the name of human rights, he remains our objective ally against Iran, against the Kurds, and against the Shiites. This is why the Gulf War never really took place: Saddam was never our true enemy. This is also the case with the Serbs. By banishing them from the human community, we are actually protecting them and continuing to let them carry out their work (Baudrillard, 1995: 82–5).

Baudrillard's (1994) claim that the Gulf War never really took place remains controversial. Analysts who are locked into the straitjacket of postmodernism as an analysis of cognitive simulacra try to explain that he meant that the Gulf War was apprehended mainly as imagery on television, and therefore was not real. I am not concerned with resolving this debate on these overly rational terms. Note that when his comments on the Gulf War are read in the context of the passage above, in which he conjoins issues of racism, the idea of Europe, the Gulf War, the Balkan War of the 1990s, Iran, the Kurds, and Shiites – a new and postemotional interpretation is possible. With uncanny prophecy, Baudrillard managed to suggest that the first and second Gulf Wars, the Balkan War, and the looming wars against

Iran, the Kurds, and Shiites are all conjoined. Since 1990 to the present, Europe and the US have been waging one long, protracted war against various Muslim societies for reasons that do not seem to make sense, and in that sense, are 'unreal'. If Saddam Hussein was the problem, why was the problem not resolved with the defeat of Iraq in 2003 and his execution? Why was the Balkan War not resolved with the Dayton Peace Accords that established a dismembered Bosnia-Herzegovina? The obvious answer seems to be that the real problem lies elsewhere – in the compulsive repetition of the 'curse of Cromwell,' which encompasses Tocqueville's depiction of the Puritan extermination of Native Americans and of slavery.

It is important to note that Great Britain played a prominent role in both wars against primarily Muslim people: the Major government was the most responsible for allowing the Milosevic regime to persecute Bosnian Muslims, and the Blair government was most responsible in Europe for perpetuating America's war against Iraq. There also exist British parallels to the abuse of Iraqis at Abu Ghraib, at the British-run Camp Breadbasket and elsewhere in Iraq.

A reading of these events and alliances using the concept of postemotionalism does not focus on the rationalizations that European governments offer for their support. Most of these rationalizations turn out to be baseless: there were no WMDs in Iraq, it is doubtful that the 7/7 attacks in London had any links to Iraq. Rather, postemotionalism shifts the focus onto the compulsive rhetoric used in Europe that is eerily similar to the rhetoric that was used in history to justify its wars against the 'dark' people. Europe, as the 'civilized' and 'Enlightened' entity in the world, will bring democracy, freedom, and progress to the 'barbarians' who live in 'darkness' – even if this means that democracy will be delivered at the point of a gun or missile. This widespread rhetoric of the Enlightenment 'narrative' falls on deaf ears among Europe's Muslim minorities.

For example, in the year 2006, much of France was in flames due to riots by French Muslims. In February of 2006, Danish cartoonists reissued 'cartoons' of Muhamed that had already offended many Muslims in the winter of 2005. The Danish government defended the publication of these cartoons as an example of the Enlightenment-derived right to free speech. Many Muslims linked the Danish problem to US and European intentions in general as being anti-Muslim. Riots spilled over the borders of Europe as far away as Indonesia and Malaysia.

It seems to be the case that the more that European governments support the US position on terrorism and uphold a similar rhetoric of transplanted Puritanism in the new millennium, the more terrorism, insurgency, and opposition to Europe and the US grows. The war on terror is built upon a counter-productive, which is to say, postemotional and irrational basis. It is not a war for territory, colonization, expansionism or other modernist goals as much as it is a war to repeat past European traumas, and 'this time', to 'get it right'. A war on 'terror' is as metaphysical and irrational as many previous wars waged by Europe in the name of pure ideals. There have always been terrorists in history, from Northern Ireland to Bulgaria in recent history, to the terrorists on both sides in the clash between the Austro-Hungarians and Ottomans, and beyond. Stopping terrorists is one thing, but waging an unwinnable war on the idea of terror itself is another. The latter is a postemotional component of the idea of Europe.

Tradition-directed societies were and still are severe in their response to such postemotional arguments and onslaughts. The traditionalist is socialized to regard abusive behavior of this sort as a loss of *honor*, and to interpret it in terms of *shame*. Akbar Ahmed (2005) points out in his analysis of what he calls the 'post-honor world' that following the disclosure of the abuse at Abu Ghraib and Guantanamo Bay, Muslims concluded that the US president lacked a sense of honor, and reinterpreted his actions against Saddam Hussein and other Muslims accordingly. The execution of Hussein in 2006 did nothing to resolve seemingly endless wars that began in Sarajevo and Baghdad, and that are poised to spread against Iran and much of the Islamic world. Similarly, the 'clash of civilizations' invoked by Samuel Huntington (1998) may be reformulated as the clash of a postemotional, posthonor society with tradition-directed, honor-bound society. The tragic result is that the postemotional type seems not to notice the grievous sense of humiliation and shame that the abuse evokes in the tradition-directed type (Mestrovic, 2007). Humiliation breeds revenge (see Boehm, 1984) and leads to 'insurgency' – but the postemotional type is incredulous at the Iraqi insurgency against Americans and Europeans who conceive of themselves as liberators.

POSTEMOTIONAL MANIPULATION IN CONTEMPORARY EUROPE

The Balkan Wars of the 1990s were a severe embarrassment to the European Community, which was eventually replaced with the European Union. After all, genocide was occurring on the European continent and Europe seemed impotent or unwilling to stop it, despite its usual rhetoric of human rights, freedom, and so on derived from Enlightenment narratives. The Balkan Wars were a reminder to Europe that it has not overcome its postemotional compulsions from history. Similarly, the ongoing war against terror is likely to have severe consequences not only for the European Union but for the idea of Europe. If and when this particular war on terror comes to an end, critics will wonder out loud why and how Europe, with all its lofty ideals, stood idly by and allowed Iraq to be dismembered – literally Balkanized, complete with ethnic cleansing – and for Muslims to be tortured and imprisoned without due process – and on European soil. Will this latest war and Europe's collusion in it go down in history as yet another refraction of the Inquisition, the Crusades and other Puritanical or Manichean episodes from Europe's history?

To keep this stark reality at bay, in postemotional society, public relations have become an absolutely essential ingredient of all social life. Hence, European governments hire veritable armies of public relations experts whose job is to filter raw reality into something palatable for the masses, who are socialized into believing in the sincerity of Enlightenment narratives. This reality must exhibit what Herbert Marcuse (1964) called the 'happy consciousness'. Talking points become essential. Thus, European governments respond to reports of torture by parroting the American line that the civilized West does not engage in torture. Opposition is thereby neutralized because it seems anti-European to suspect that Europe could condone torture in the new millennium (even though it condoned genocide at the end of the previous millennium on its own soil). The EU reports that found that European governments participated in rendition and torture of terrorist suspects is neutralized with a plethora of hair-splitting rationalizations: that some of the European countries that allowed their prisons to be used for torture were not 'real' members of the EU at the time, that Europe simply allowed the flights and transfers, but not the torture, and so on. The postemotional type cannot tolerate the cognitive dissonance that a European, as an exemplar of idealized values supposedly derived from the Enlightenment, could engage in torture or abuse. The public is quickly distracted by the governments and media to fear the Muslims in their midst as potential terrorists, and the whole postemotional cycle repeats itself anew.

Spokespersons for European governments stress that the idea of Europe stands for and seeks democracy, human rights, and peace in general, and in Iraq in particular. Nevertheless, alongside the US, Europe engages in or tacitly supports behavior that some human rights groups have labeled as torture. The message of democracy is not perceived to be out of sync with undemocratic behaviors that violate the Geneva Conventions and other more recent European codes of human rights. The situation is analogous to Rebecca West's inability to see her own racism even though she brilliantly analyzes racism and hatred throughout European history. I argue that the penultimate reason for this hypocrisy is the belief in the back of the European mind – or elsewhere beneath the surface – that Muslims and other minorities are truly children of darkness, and deserve to suffer. This is the ancient compulsion that Europe must overcome if it is to achieve a genuine Enlightenment. Against the many glib depictions of the European Enlightenment as an exclusively benign phenomenon, found in most academic texts, one would do well to remember Winston Churchill's poignant observation: Upon all of us there still lies 'the Curse of Cromwell'.

REFERENCES

Ahmed, A. (1991) *Postmodernism and Islam*. London: Routledge.

Ahmed, A. (2005) *Islam Under Siege*. Cambridge: Polity.

Almond, M. (1994) *Europe's Backyard War*. London: Mandarin.

Baudrillard, J. (1986) *America*. London: Verso.

Baudrillard, J. (1994) *The Gulf War did not take place*. New York: Power Publications.

Baudrillard, J. (1995) 'No pity for Sarajevo','in T. Cushman and S. Mestrovic (eds), *This Time We Knew: Western Responses to Genocide in Bosnia*. New York: New York University Press, pp. 79–89.

Bauman, Z. (1989) *Modernity and the Holocaust*. Ithaca: Cornell University Press.

Bauman, Z. (1991) *Modernity and Ambivalence*. Ithaca: Cornell University Press.

Bennett, M. (2006) *Oliver Cromwell*. London: Francis & Taylor.

Boehm, C. (1984) *Blood Revenge*. Philadelphia: University of Pennsylvania Press.

Cushman, T. and Mestrovic, S. (1995) *This Time We Knew: Western Responses to Genocide in Bosnia*. New York: New York University Press.

Churchill, W. (1957) *A History of the English Speaking Peoples: the Age of Revolution*. New York: Dodd, Mead & Co.

Durkheim, E. [1912] (1965) *The Elementary Forms of the Religious Life*. New York: Free Press.

Freud, S. [1925] (1959) *An Autobiographical Study*. New York: W.W. Norton.

Galbraith, P. (2007) *The End of Iraq: How American Incompetence Created a War Without End*. New York: Simon & Schuster.

Giddens, A. (1987) *Nation-state and Violence*. Stanford: Stanford University Press.

Giddens, A. (1990) *Consequences of Modernity*. Stanford: Stanford University Press.

Girard, R. (2005) *Violence and the Sacred*. New York: Continuum.

Goad, J. (1998) *The Redneck Manifesto: How Hillbillies, Hicks, and White Trash Became America's Scapegoats*. New York: Touchstone.

Grey, S. (2007) *Ghost Plane: The True Story of the CIA Rendition and Torture Program*. New York: St Martin's Press.

Hochschild, A. (1999) *King Leopold's Ghost: a Story of Greed, Terror, and Heroism in Colonial Africa*. New York: Mariner.

Hoffman, M. (1993) *They Were White and They Were Slaves: the Untold History of the Enslavement of Whites in Early America*. London: Ruffin House.

Huntington, S. (1998) *Clash of Civilizations and the Remaking of World Order*. New York: Simon & Schuster.

Jung, C. (1963) *Memories, Dreams, and Reflections*. New York: Pantheon.

Kent, G. (2006) *Framing War and Genocide: British Policy and News Media Reaction to the War in Bosnia*. Cresskill: Hampton Press.

Levene, M. (2005) *Genocide in the Age of the Nation-State*. London: Tauris.

Loewen, J. (1995) *Lies My Teacher Told Me: Everything Your American History Textbook Got Wrong*. New York: Touchstone.

Lutz, J. (2004) *Global Terrorism*. London: Routledge.

Lyotard, J. (1984) *The Postmodern Condition*. Minneapolis: University of Minnesota Press.

Marcuse, H. (1964) *One-Dimensional Man*. Boston: Beacon.

Melchert, N. (2002) The Great Conversation: A Historical Introduction to Philosophy. New York: McGraw-Hill.

Mestrovic, S. (1993) *Barbarian Temperament*. London: Routledge.

Mestrovic, S. (1995) *Genocide After Emotion: the Postemotional Balkan War*. London: Routledge.

Mestrovic, S. (1997) *Postemotional Society*. London: Sage.

Mestrovic, S. (2004) *Veblen on Culture and Society*. London: Sage.

Mestrovic, S. (2007) *The Trials of Abu Ghraib: an Expert Witness Account of Shame and Honor*. Boulder: Paradigm.

Michas, T. (2002) *Unholy Alliance: Greece and Serbia in the Nineties*. College Station: Texas A&M University Press.

Novak, W. (1996) *The People's Welfare Law and Regulation in Nineteenth Century America*. Chapel Hill: University of North Carolina Press.

O'Callaghan, S. (2001) *To Hell or Barbados: the Ethnic Cleansing of Ireland*. New York: Brandon.

Orwell, G. (1949) *1984*. London: Penguin.

Riesman, D. [1950] (1992) *The Lonely Crowd*. New Haven: Yale University Press.

Ricks, T. (2007) *Fiasco: The American Military Adventure in Iraq*. New York: Penguin.

Ritzer, G. (1995) *The McDonaldization of Society*. Thousand Oaks: Pine Forge Press.

Rosen, D. (1996) *The Tao of Jung*. New York: Viking.

Schopenhauer, A [1818] (1965) *The World as Will and Idea*. New York: Dover.

Serfaty, S. (2007) *Architects of Delusion: Europe, America, and the Iraq War*. Philadelphia: University of Pennsylvania Press.

Spengler, O. [1926] (1961) *Decline of the West*. New York: Vintage.

Tocqueville, A. [1845] (2003) *Democracy in America*. New York: Penguin.

Toulmin, S. (1992) *Cosmopolis: the Hidden Agenda of Modernity*. Chigaco: University of Chicago Press.

Toynbee, A. (1978) *Arnold Toynbee: a Selection from his Works*. Oxford: Oxford University Press.

Veblen, T. [1899] (1965) *Theory of the Leisure Class*. London: Penguin.

Walsh M. (2007) *White Cargo: the Forgotten History of Britain's White Slaves*. New York: Mainstream.

Weber, M. [1904] (1958) *The Protestant Ethic and the Spirit of Capitalism*. New York: Scribner's.

West, R. [1940] (1982) *Black Lamb and Grey Falcon: A Journey Through Yugoslavia*. London: Penguin.

Zinn, H. (2005) *People's History of the United States: 1492 to Present*. New York: Harper.

33

Understanding the Real Europe: A Cosmopolitan Vision

Ulrich Beck

One of the most vital international debates in the social sciences today is focused on redefining cosmopolitanism in order to understand the dynamics of the cultural, the social and the political at the beginning of the twenty-first century.[1] The most expansive and interesting field for both exploring and deploying the new cosmopolitanism is Europe (Balibar, 1998; Beck, 2003; Beck and Grande, 2007; Delanty and Rumford, 2005; Kaldor, 1995). This cosmopolitan vision means that the EU can become neither a state nor a nation. Hence it cannot be thought of in terms of the nation state. The path to the unification of Europe leads not through uniformity but rather through acknowledgement of its national differences. Diversity is the very source of Europe's identity and creativity. Even the solution to national problems lies in European interaction.

Europe has a novel and empirical reality that all its critics fundamentally skip over. The reason anti-integrationists cannot imagine a future for Europe is that they cannot image its present. They are trapped in the contradictions of EU member nations' misunderstanding of themselves. And this false picture of Europe's present is blocking its future development. The Eurosceptics have it the wrong way round. The solution to the EU's problems is not more nationalistic realism. Rather, it is more Europe, more of the reality we are already experiencing – a cosmopolitan Europe (Beck, 2002; Beck and Grande, 2007; Delanty and Rumford, 2005). National categories of thought have created this impasse. National 'irrealism' is Europe's problem. I wish to develop this argument by discussing six key questions: (1) What is cosmopolitanism? (2) How does it relate to the identity of Europe? (3) How does it relate to the history of Europe? (4) Why do national categories of thought make Europe impossible? (5) How does cosmopolitanism relate to the concept of state? (6) What could be the impact of cosmopolitan Europe on world politics?

WHAT IS COSMOPOLITANISM?

What does the concept of cosmopolitanism mean precisely? How does cosmopolitanism differ from similar concepts situated beyond the particular, such as the concepts of universalism, multiculturalism and postnationalism? How is it related to modern society and its transformation? And what does the concept of cosmopolitanism contribute to our understanding of Europeanization? These questions are urgently in need of clarification because the concept of cosmopolitanism is currently in vogue and is made to serve as a synonym for many things: globalization, globality, glocalism, globalism, universalism, multiculturalism, pluralism, imperialism. All of these, so it is claimed, contain a cosmopolitan element; nevertheless, their adherents also leave no doubt that there is a world of difference between these concepts. What exactly does that difference consist of?

The concept of cosmopolitanism has both a time-honoured and a future-oriented meaning. Indeed, what makes it so interesting for a theory of modern societies is that it is both *pre*-national and *post*-national. It can be traced back to the Cynics and Stoics of antiquity, who in fact invented the word. Subsequently, it played a role in European societies whenever they found themselves confronted with fundamental upheavals. It acquired central importance in the philosophy of the Enlightenment (in Germany, in Kant, Fichte, Schelling, Wieland, Forster, Herder, Goethe, Schiller, Heine and others) (cf. Kleingeld, 1999; Schlereth, 1977; Thielking 2000; Toulmin, 1990); it was taken up again in the nationalistically oriented, culturally critical philosophy of the late nineteenth century (e.g. Meinecke, 1907); and, finally, the current debates on globalization rediscovered it as a positive counterweight to the organizing power of the market in the nation state (cf. Archibugi, 2003b; Archibughi and Held, 1995; Archibugi *et al.*, 1998; Beck, 2005, 2006; Cheah and Robbins, 1998; Held, 1995; Kaldor, 2000; Kaldor *et al.*, 2003; Levy and Sznaider, 2001; Linklater, 1998; Pogge, 1992; Vertovec and Cohen, 2002).

In light of this long prehistory, it would be presumptuous to expect that this concept would have a consistent meaning. However, we can nevertheless identify two premises that form the core of the cosmopolitan project. Cosmopolitanism combines appreciation of difference and alterity with efforts to conceive of new democratic forms of political rule beyond the nation state (cf. Brennan, 1997). Daniele Archibugi has summarized this normative core of cosmopolitanism in three principles: tolerance, democratic legitimacy, and effectiveness (Archibugi, 2003a: 11).

With my understanding of cosmopolitanism, I draw expressly on this strand of tradition. However, I also want to use the concept in a quite specific way – namely, as a *social scientific* concept – and for a quite specific social state of affairs, namely, a specific way of *socially dealing with cultural difference*. The concept of cosmopolitanism can thereby be distinguished in an ideal-typical manner from a number of other social ways of dealing with difference, in particular hierarchical subordination, universalistic and nationalistic sameness, and postmodern particularism (for a detailed account of the social scientific concept of cosmopolitanism and its counter-concepts, see Beck, 2006, chapter 2). In the present context it is important that the concept of cosmopolitanism, whose specific point resides in overcoming the dualities of the global and the local, the national and the international, is not specified in *spatial* terms; specifically, it is not bound to the 'cosmos' or to the 'globe'. The principle of cosmopolitanism can be located and applied everywhere, and hence also to regional geographical units such as Europe. Indeed, to understand Europe in cosmopolitan terms means defining the European concept of society as a regionally and historically particular case of global interdependence.

In the first place, cosmopolitanism differs fundamentally from all forms of vertical differentiation that seek to bring social difference into a hierarchical relation of *superiority and subordination*. This principle can be applied, on the one hand, within societies in so far as they form, in part, highly differentiated caste and class systems. However, it was also used to define relations to other societies. Typical here is that one denies 'the others' the status of sameness and equality and perceives them in a relation of hierarchical subordination or inferiority. At the extreme, the others count as 'barbarians' devoid of rights. Not only premodern societies tried to deal with difference in this way; the modern construction of colonial empires from the sixteenth century onwards also followed this principle. Moreover, as Huntington's (1996) concepts of civilization and the clash of civilizations show, even the postmodern constellation itself is susceptible to a hierarchy of difference.

The *dissolution of differences* represents the countervailing principle to hierarchical subordination. It presupposes the development and recognition of *universal* norms that facilitate the justification and institutionalization of the equal treatment of others. The universalistic approach replaces the multitude of different norms, classes, ethnic identities and religions with one unified norm. We can distinguish between at least two variants of universalism: a *substantial universalism* that advocates the equality and equal value of externally different others on the basis of substantive norms; and a *procedural universalism* that is primarily geared to fair rules in dealing with otherness and to formal justice. Universalism in both of these forms is a typically modern way of dealing with difference, though not the only one. There are a number of other modes of dealing with difference, among others, the principles of nationalism and of cosmopolitanism.

Nationalism standardizes differences while at the same time demarcating them in accordance with national oppositions. As a strategy of dealing with difference, it too follows an either/or logic, though instead of the distinction between higher and lower it operates with the distinction between internal and external. Nationalism has two sides, one directed inwards, the other outwards. Towards the inside, nationalism aims to dissolve differences and promote uniform norms. It has this in common with universalism. However, because of its limited territorial scope, the dissolution of differences must always remain incomplete and difference is emphasized towards the outside.

In this sense, nationalism dissolves differences internally while at the same time producing and stabilizing it towards the outside.

Here it is important that nationalism lacks a regulator of its own for dealing with difference in its external environment. It is as likely to tend towards enlightened tolerance as towards nationalistic excess (cf. Dann, 1993). In its most extreme form, therefore, nationalism not only exhibits commonalities with universalism but also with premodern forms of hierarchical subordination. For it also has a tendency to reject the entitlement of other nations and to stigmatize them as 'barbarians' – and thereby, itself assume barbaric traits. Thus, we can safely assume that nationalism is the typical mode of dealing with difference in the *first* modernity. With the distinction between first and second modernity I seek to capture how late twentieth century societies underwent an epochal shift. But I reject the idea that this is a move from the modern to the postmodern. These are all not postmodern, but 'more modern' societies. The first modernity was 'nation-state centred', the second modernity is 'non-nation-state centred'. In the latter the indissoluble link of society and nation-state is broken. This is why the European 'society of societies' is a model of second modernity (Beck and Grande 2007; Beck and Lau, 2005).

Cosmopolitanism differs from all of the previously mentioned forms in that here the *recognition of difference* becomes a maxim of thought, social life and practice, both internally and towards the outside. It neither orders differences hierarchically nor dissolves them, but accepts them as such, indeed invests them with a positive value. Cosmopolitanism affirms what is excluded both by hierarchical difference and by universal equality, namely preceding others as different *and* at the same time equal. Whereas universalism and nationalism (and premodern, essentialistic particularism) are based on the either/or principle, cosmopolitanism rests on the 'both/and' principle. The foreign is not experienced and assessed as dangerous, disintegrating and fragmenting but as enriching. My curiosity about myself and about difference makes others irreplaceable for me. There is also an egoism of cosmopolitan interest. Those who integrate the perspective of others into their own lives learn more about themselves *as well as* others.

The cosmopolitan principle of regarding others as both equal and different admits of two interpretations: the recognition of the distinctiveness of others may refer to *collectives* or to *individuals*. Both interpretations are constitutive for the principle of cosmopolitanism. On the former, collective reading, it becomes difficult to distinguish from the principle of *multiculturalism*. However, the principle of multiculturalism refers exclusively to collective categories of difference; it is geared, first, to (more or less) homogeneous groups and, second, locates the latter within the nation-state framework. In this respect, multiculturalism is antagonistic both to transnationalization and to individualization. By contrast, this is *not* the case for cosmopolitanism but the precise opposite: the cosmopolitan principle heightens awareness of the fact that the apparently sharp ethnic boundaries and territorial bonds are becoming blurred and intermingling at both the national and the transnational levels. As a result, under conditions of radical global insecurity, all are equal and everyone is different.[2]

Hence cosmopolitan calls for new concepts of integration and identity that facilitate and affirm coexistence across borders, without requiring that distinctiveness and difference be sacrificed on the altar of supposed (national) equality. 'Identity' and 'integration' are then nothing more than different words for hegemony over the other or others, of the majority over minorities. Cosmopolitanism accepts difference but does not absolutize it; rather, it seeks out ways for rendering it universally tolerable. In this, it relies on a framework of uniting and universally binding norms that should prevent deviation into postmodern particularism.[3]

In the philosophy of the Enlightenment, this is particularly apparent in the cultural cosmopolitanism of Georg Forster. Forster's defence of cultural difference does not imply a pure form of pluralism but is based rather on the universal norm of human equality (cf. Kleingeld, 1999: 516). Although cosmopolitanism is not an invention of the *second* modernity, I believe that it is the typical mode of dealing with difference within second modernity. A cosmopolitan Europe would thereby be, in the first instance, a *Europe of difference*, of accepted and recognized difference.

From this perspective, diversity, be it of language, of lifestyles, of economic systems, or of forms of state and democracy, would be primarily conceived as an inexhaustible source, perhaps *the* source, of Europe's cosmopolitan self-understanding, and not as a hindrance to integration (cf. Landfried, 2002). However, European cosmopolitanism also signifies the restriction and regulation of difference. Thus, a cosmopolitan Europe means simultaneously both difference *and* integration. It thereby opens up an alternative to the existing programs of European integration, which either locate Europe above the nation states and combat national particularities as hindrances to European unification or want to subordinate Europe to the nation states and national interests and regard every step towards further integration with scepticism.

Of the approaches to dealing with difference and sketched here, three – universalism, nationalism and cosmopolitanism – represent, heuristically speaking, *modern* variants. Universalism has one thing in common with each of the other two principles. With nationalism it shares the idea of equality and of the equal treatment of difference, and hence the goal of unity and uniformity. With cosmopolitanism, it shares the conception of the universal validity of norms. For this reason, cosmopolitanism was originally long identified with universalism since both sought to overcome particularism, the local restriction of norms (cf. Kleingeld, 1999: 516). Later, however, cosmopolitanism succeeded in allying itself also with nationalism and in aiming to realize notions of equality within a nationally circumscribed space or among several such spaces.[4]

There are two radical counterproposals to these modern ways of dealing with difference. They are, on the one hand, the essentialistic hierarchy of difference, which is by no means restricted to the premodern period, and, on the other, the postmodern incommensurability of difference.[5] Cosmopolitanism should not be confused with postmodernism or interpreted as a variant of the latter. The postmodern strategy of tolerating difference consists in absolutizing otherness without a supportive framework of substantive and procedural norms. This approach absolutizes relativism to such a point that shared ideals of order and selection criteria are completely lacking. That upon which cosmopolitanism places so much value, namely, internalized and institutionalized mutual perspective taking with others, is ultimately illusionary in postmodern particularism, even to the point of being culturally excluded and always ideologically suspect. Although here equality among others no longer rests on essential differences, it does rest on the incommensurability of perspectives.[6]

In order to clarify the social scientific concept of cosmopolitanism, it is not only important to differentiate it analytically and heuristically from other premodern, modern and postmodern conceptions of how to deal with difference; is equally important to recognize that the various modern strategies for dealing with difference not only differ from each other but also, when conceived in terms of cosmopolitanism, also in a certain sense condition each other, indeed even complement each other. On the one hand, cosmopolitanism requires a certain fund of universal norms in order to regulate the treatment of difference and to direct the 'struggle for recognition' (Honneth, 1992) into socially acceptable channels. Here the question of how comprehensive this fund of shared norms must be, of whether it can be restricted to procedural norms, or whether it must in addition include substantial norms (however they are established), can remain open. However, one thing is certain: if these norms are missing, if there are no universally

accepted criteria and there is no rule-governed procedure for dealing with difference, then there is a danger that cosmopolitanism will degenerate into postmodern particularism and/or into open violence.

However, this is not the end of the problem. If cosmopolitanism wants to guarantee collective in addition to individual rights and identities, then it also needs a political mechanism for institutionally producing and stabilizing *collective* difference. But this is precisely the strength of nationalism, which represents the historically most successful way of underpinning and stabilizing collective difference with universalistic norms. Where such *stabilizers of difference* are missing, cosmopolitanism is in danger of degenerating into substantial universalism.

This is of cardinal importance for the idea of a cosmopolitan Europe. Cosmopolitan Europe is not only the antithesis of, but also presupposes, national Europe. It cannot transcend national Europe but must cosmopolitanize it from within. In this sense, I speak of a nationally rooted cosmopolitanism. Hence, it would be utterly false to think of the national and the cosmopolitan as two autonomous levels, or as two mutually exclusive political principles, and to play them off against one another. Rather, the cosmopolitan must be conceived as the *integral* of the national and must be developed and empirically investigated as such. In other words, the cosmopolitan changes, preserves and *opens* the past, the present and the future of particular national societies and the relations among national societies.

Viewed in this way, cosmopolitanism must not only integrate different national traditions and norms, it must at the same time offset various modern modes of dealing with difference. Its characteristic relation between the various modern forms of dealing with cultural difference is determined not by the either/or principle but by the both/and principle. We must discover cosmopolitanism as an at least partially effective real utopia and *bring it to awareness* in a two-fold sense. In short, cosmopolitanism must become aware of its own conditions of possibility if it wants to be effective in the long run. If cosmopolitanism becomes aware of its ability to connect and offset the various modes of dealing with otherness and difference, then it can be understood, and theoretically and empirically developed, as *reflexive* cosmopolitanism. Reflexive cosmopolitanism, sociologically defined, would thereby become the regulative principle through which the interaction between universalistic, national and cosmopolitan principles in the second modernity must be conceived and regulated. But this doesn't answer the question: who are the agents of cosmopolitanism in all of this? Who identifies with cosmopolitanism apart from theorists of cosmopolitanism? This, of course, is an open question. There might be a 'thick cosmopolitanism from below' which can be found in all kinds of global civil society movements; actors and experts in international and transnational organizations; groups, movements and networks of transnational migrants. But most important is that we are confronted with a kind of *enforced* cosmopolitanism: in a world of global risk nobody can exclude the other any longer (Beck, 2006).

HOW DOES COSMOPOLITANISM RELATE TO THE IDENTITY OF EUROPE?

Those who would reinvent the Christian West in order to build walls around Europe are turning the project of the European Enlightenment on its head. There is nothing more convincing than an example to illustrate this thesis: Imagine that at a party you encounter a dark-skinned woman who speaks perfect Swedish or German or Italian or Polish. I bet that at the earliest opportunity you will want to involve this woman in an exchange, which we sociologists call the 'dialogue of origin':

– May I ask, where you come from?

– From Stockholm.

– No, I mean, where do you come from *originally*?

– Yes, from Stockholm.

– Ok, but where do your parents come from?

– My mother comes from Stockholm.

– But where does your father come from?

– My father was American.

– Aha ...

This 'Where do you come from originally?' question is a tough one. It is still part of the way many Europeans see themselves. Of course, the Germans are originally German. It is the territorial ontology of identity, according to which every person has one homeland, where he or she comes from and ultimately belongs. Accordingly conclusions can be drawn from the colour of a person's skin about language, passport, and about the person themselves.

'Guest workers', 'deportation', 'asylum seekers' – that is the horizon of language, values and action against which Europe's dealings with immigrants take place and are reflected. The results are evident, for example, in the *banlieus* of France, where setting cars alight has become an everyday experience. Everywhere in Europe one meets with disappointed, alienated immigrants, whose anger can easily turn to violence. Certainly, the immigrant communities have to take a share of the blame. But really what is in operation here is cycle of exclusion: European societies exclude the migrants, and their anger and violence is directed against the society in which they want to arrive, but never can.

Immigrants are the disappointed lovers of Europe. To become German, even if one speaks the language, has a passport and a job, is a never-ending journey. A German scientist with dark skin was beaten unconscious in Potsdam near Berlin. He has everything it takes to be a good German: a passport, a family, a job, even a doctoral thesis on the subject of 'The development of shower nozzles for more effective washing of vegetables and potatoes'. Could he be more German? He was German in every respect bar the colour of his skin, which remained dark. Turkey is of course the looming question that has brought this long-buried discourse of origins out of hiding. People who want to keep the Turks out have suddenly discovered that the roots of Europe lie in its Christian heritage. Those who share our continent, but do not share this Christian heritage, are seen as Europe's Other.

But this is taking the idea of an ethnic nation – that you have an identity you get from your parents and which cannot be changed by option or learning – and reapplying it at the level of Europe. It is about conceiving national and cultural identities as inherently and mutually *exclusive*: that you can't have two of them in the same logical space. This is not only empirically wrong, it is totally at odds with the idea of Europe. If identities are mutually exclusive, Europe is an impossible project. The whole idea of the EU was based on the idea that you could be German and French or Swedish and European, or British and German at the same time.

Dangerous traces of this exclusivist idea exist even in the seemingly benign idea of cultural 'dialogue.' The picture normally evoked by 'dialogue' is of two separate entities, 'Islam' and the 'West', each occupying their own territory, who then need to reach out to each other in order to have contact. But in fact, both entities already interpenetrate each other. And what's more, they are both full of internal differences as large as any they have with each other. Where can you find room in 'Islam' and the 'West' for all the second- and third-generation Muslim immigrants that are now an integral part of every country in Europe? Or for that matter for 'Westernized' Muslims, if culture is what tells? Or for the Arab bourgeoisie, the Oriental Christians, the Israeli Arabs? The list of exceptions goes on until it swamps the rule. The closer we look at empirical reality, the clearer it becomes that the presumption of cultural homogeneity is really a *denial* of reality. You can homogenize milk, but not modern society and never, by no means, Europe.

But it gets worse. Those who would reinvent the Christian West in order to build walls around Europe are turning the project of the European Enlightenment on its head. They are turning Europe into a religion. Indeed, they are virtually turning it back into a race. There could be nothing more anti-Western and anti-Enlightenment than that.

The true standards for 'Europeanness' lie in the answer to the question 'What will make Europe *more* European?' And the answer is a more cosmopolitan Europe, where national identities become less and less exclusive and more and more inclusive. 'Europeanness' means being able to combine in one existence things that only appear to be mutually exclusive in the small-mindedness of ethnic thinking. It is, of course, perfectly possible to be a Muslim and a democrat, just as one can be a socialist and a small businessperson – or less pleasantly, a Danish global businessman and the founder of an anti-foreigner organization. The European conception of humanity doesn't contain any concrete definition of what it means to be human. It can't. It is of its essence that it be anti-essentialist. It is not an accident that Europeanness is mostly defined procedurally. Only a pragmatic political definition can express this anti-essential essence. The flipside of this substantial emptiness is radical tolerance and radical openness. It is this that is the secret of Europe's success.

HOW DOES COSMOPOLITANISM RELATE TO THE HISTORY OF EUROPE?

Cosmopolitan Europe was consciously conceived and launched after the Second World War as the political antithesis to a nationalistic Europe and the physical and moral devastation that had emerged from it. It was in this spirit that Winston Churchill, standing amidst the ruins of a destroyed continent in 1946, enthused: 'If Europe were once united … there would be no limit to the happiness, to the prosperity and the glory which its four hundred million people would enjoy.' It was the charismatic statesmen of the Western democracies, who experienced the war – and specifically the individuals and groups most identified with resistance against the Nazis – who reinvented Europe. And they consciously sought to reach past the mass graves and national cemeteries back into the European history of ideas.

Cosmopolitan Europe is thus a project born of resistance. It is important to remember what this means because two things come together in it. In the first place, resistance was not the automatic result of collapse. It was a reaction against the traumatic experience of European values being perverted. Cosmopolitan Europe was born in bitter realization that the idea of what constitutes the 'truly human' implies the subhuman. And that when 'truly human' becomes the basis of a nation state, the result is a totalitarian regime that seeks to exclude, to separate out, to remodel, or to annihilate all people who can't or don't want to fit its ideal.

This brings us to the second point: if we no longer base ourselves on some transcendent human substance that needs to be saved, then what is it I am trying to nurture and preserve? If we are now dealing with decentred subjects of which no one can definitely say what they are or what they ought or want to be, then what is the inviolate essence our institutions should be set up to protect? On what grounds can we guarantee that it won't be hauled off, tortured, and killed? The resistance that built Europe was motivated by clear ideas of inviolable human dignity, and of the moral duty to relieve the suffering others. The basis of common humanity was the feeling of sympathy – a structurally empty feeling that draws its content from outside. These cosmopolitan ideals then became the foundations of the postwar European project.

Cosmopolitan Europe was founded as something that struggles morally, politically, historically, and economically for reconciliation. It was intended as a decisive break with all previous political history, and it accomplished it. With it, 1,500 years of intra-European warfare came definitively to a close. This ideal of reconciliation was not so much preached idealistically as practiced materialistically. The first step towards the 'limitless happiness' that Churchill foresaw was a limitless market. Reconciliation was accomplished by being encoded into institutions, through the creation of profane interdependence in the economy, in politics, in security matters, in science, and in culture. Cosmopolitanism was created consciously, but it was created first as a reality, not as a theory.

If we want to excavate the original consciousness of cosmopolitanism that lies at the basis of the European project, it is the collective memory of the Holocaust that provides our clearest archive – as Daniel Levy and Natan Sznaider argue in their book on 'cosmopolitan memory' (Levy and Sznaider, 2004, 2005) The founding set of documents of European cosmopolitanism, written when the war was still warm, as it were, were those of the Nuremberg Trials. Here we can see clearly how a cosmopolitan institutional logic was the first thing the builders of Europe reached for in trying to make a break with the past. The Nuremberg court created both legal categories and a trial procedure that went way beyond the sovereignty of the nation state. It did so for practical reasons. It was the only way to capture in legal concepts and court procedures the historical monstrosity that was the systematic and state-organized extermination of the Jews.

Article 6 of the Charter of the International Military Tribunal delineates three categories of crime: crimes against peace, war crimes, and crimes against humanity. It was in terms of these new categories that Nazi crimes were judged and Nazi criminals were tried and sentenced. Crimes against peace and war crimes both still presuppose the sovereignty of the nation state. They presuppose the laws of a nation-state system of which they are violations. The concept of crimes against humanity, on the other hand, suspends the nation-state presumption. It is the embodiment of the cosmopolitan vision in legal form.

It was in many ways ahead of its time. The lawyers and judges who participated in the Nuremberg Tribunal were ultimately unable to get to grips with this new category. But of the three, it is this category that has endured in the European imagination. Today, even when we speak of 'war criminals', what we really mean, as if it were now obvious, is people who have committed 'crimes against humanity'. What was being introduced here was not a new law or an even a new legal principle but rather a new legal logic, a new legal grammar that broke with the previous nation-state logic of international law.

Here is the definition of Article 6c:

Crimes against humanity: namely, murder, extermination, enslavement, deportation and other inhumane acts committed against any civilian population, before or during the war; or persecutions on political, racial or religious grounds in execution of or in connection with any crime within the jurisdiction of the Tribunal, whether or not in violation of domestic law of the country were perpetrated.

The first key formulation is 'before and during the war' – this is what distinguishes crimes against humanity from war crimes: there may be no war. And a second is that such crimes exist 'whether or not in violation of domestic law of the country where perpetrated'.

These enormous breaks with nationally based legal concepts were necessary to prosecute the persecution of the Jews, because much of it had been legal according to the laws of Nazi Germany and had happened before the war took place. But taken together they change everything. They posit an individual responsibility for all perpetrators that is based outside the national legal context and based in the community of nations. What had been crimes against the state now become crimes against humanity. So if the state becomes a criminal state, the individual who serves it must still reckon with being charged and sentenced for his deeds before an international court of law.

It is at this point that cosmopolitan Europe generates a *genuinely European inner contradiction*, legally, morally, and politically. The traditions from which colonial, nationalist and genocidal horror originated were clearly European. But so were the new legal standards against which these acts were condemned as crimes against humanity and tried in the spotlight of world publicity. At this formative moment in its history, Europe mobilized its traditions to produce something historically new. It took the idea of the recognition of humanity of the Other, and made this the foundation of a historically new counter-logic. It specifically designed this logic to counteract the ethnic perversion of the European tradition to which the nation-based form of European modernity had just shown itself so horribly liable. It was an attempt to distil a European antidote to Europe.

It is a mass grave upon which the new Europe made an oath and chose a different path. Europe's collective memory of the Holocaust recalls the basis of the EU. It is a warning sign that when modernity develops exclusively in the grooves of the nation state, it builds the potential for a moral, political, economic, and technological catastrophe without limit, without mercy, and without even any consideration for its own survival.

In its elevation of pessimism to permanent despair postmodernity joins hands with nationalistic Europe. Both deny the possibility of struggling against the horror of European history by radicalizing the idea of Europe. And both ignore the institutionalization of this struggle at the very centre of what it means to be Europe. And both ignore the attempt to make Europe more European by making it more cosmopolitan. In this sense, present-day European pessimism reverses the old rule: it remembers the past in order to forget the present. And I believe there is a deep continuity between European pessimism and postmodernity. Both have in common a critique of modernity, an antimodernity, that offers no alternative but the past. By contrast, cosmopolitan Europe is the European tradition's institutionalized internal critique. This process is not complete; it cannot be completed.

Indeed, the sequence of enlightenment, postmodernity and cosmopolitan modernity represent its beginning stages.

WHY DO NATIONAL CATEGORIES OF THOUGHT MAKE THE THOUGHT OF EUROPE IMPOSSIBLE?

The national point of view sees two ways and two ways only of reading contemporary European politics and integration. It sees it either as federalism, leading to a federal superstate; or as intergovernmentalism, leading to a federation of states. Both models are empirically inadequate. They fail to grasp essential things both about present-day Europe and about the nations that make it up. But they are both also, in a deep-structural sense, anti-European. They deny the goal most worth attaining: a Europe of diversity, a Europe that helps diversity to flourish. This is obvious when it comes to the idea of a federation of states which are seen as defending their sovereignty against the expansion of European power. From that perspective, European integration can only be seen as European self-colonization. But it's just as true in the conception of a federal superstate. That is how Europe looks when it is filtered through the exclusive categories of national thought, which can only understand it in one way: as a huge ethnocultural nation state. This makes no sense, as its opponents point out. Such a nation is improbable, unwanted and un-European. But rather than faulting their conception, they fault reality. It never occurs to them that maybe Europe isn't properly conceived of as a nation state writ large.

Both the federation of states and the federal superstate describe the same zero-sum game from different angles. Either there is one single state of Europe (federalism), in which case there are no national member states; or else the national member states remain Europe's rulers, in which case there is no Europe (intergovernmentalism). Within this framework of thought, whatever Europe gains, the individual nations lose. And this is true whether one is for a given option or against it. This is what it means to say that national categories of thought make the thought of Europe impossible. Caught up in the false alternatives of the national viewpoint, we are given the choice between no Europe – or no Europe! The same two sides of one dead-end are as prominent as they have ever been in the current debate about the Constitution.

Methodological nationalism denies the empirical reality of Europe, which is that it is already a unity of diversity. And it misses that this is already also true of the nations that make it up. 'The time is out of joint: O cursed spite that ever I was born to set it right' – that could be the motto of the 'Hamlet generation', which sees itself obliged to redefine and reshape the future of Europe. Let us remind ourselves: The ghost of his father commands Hamlet to restore justice in the rotten state of Denmark – long before the controversy over the cartoons. Worldwide religious militancy as reaction to the publication of cartoons in Denmark. That would have been beyond our imagination until now.

The world has become cosmopolitan not by option but by condition. And this enforced cosmopolitan condition is laden with conflict. Despite the ever-increasing perfection of border surveillance, neither Denmark nor Germany nor Sweden nor Europe can be sealed off from the rest of the world any more. The Other, the stranger, whether of another nationality or religion can no longer be excluded. Anyone who still believes they can barricade themselves in their own house has been deceived by limited national views and reflexes. Such a viewpoint suggests something that no longer exists, but which has become a widespread illusion in a globalized world: the backward-looking fiction of the national gaze.

But there is a cosmopolitan alternative. Just as the Peace of Westphalia ended the religious wars by separating state from religion, we might consider it the ultimate goal of the European project to separate state and nation. Cosmopolitanism does not mean an abolition of nation, any more than Westphalia meant an abolition of religion. Rather, it means the constitutional enshrinement of the principle of national and cultural and ethnic and religious tolerance. Many people consider the Peace of Westphalia the foundation of the modern European state system. If that is true, then the principle of tolerance was Europe's founding principle, the basis of its unwritten constitution. And on this argument, the essence of the postwar European project has been to deepen this principle of tolerance and to extend it. The areligious state did not abolish religion. Rather it allowed it to flourish. It allowed there to be more than one; it allowed true religious diversity. And the same is true of the anational state. The goal is not to abolish national identities, but to save them from their own perversion, just as Westphalia saved religion from its perversion into religious war.

The concept of a cosmopolitan Europe opens our eyes to what has already long been here, which now needs to be affirmed and radicalized against the narrow-minded tendencies of the national viewpoint. A logic of inclusive oppositions is the only way to finally attain a Europe of national diversity. The concept of the anational, cosmopolitan state both mirrors the reality of Europe and furthers the realization of its norms. The legal realities of the EU already express this new kind of both/and reality that is gradually replacing the old either/or of national homogeneity. National and European legal and political cultures have coexisted now for decades and are continuing to coevolve. They have merged into a European legal culture without abolishing national political cultures. They present a domain of continuous overlap that expresses political and social reality. The problem is that our ideas of the nation state that have failed to keep up with this reality.

The creation of interdependencies in every field of politics – the politics of mutual imbrication that makes Europeanization such a ubiquitous feature of our lives – is not a one-off form of cooperation that ultimately leaves the nation states involved untouched. Rather, Europeanization seizes and transforms national sovereignty in the core of its being. This is where the intergovernmental perspective fails to grasp reality. Nation states have already turned into transnational states, not only socially, but administratively, in the heart of their *raison d'état*. Europe has already changed from a nation-state system into a transnational state system. The point is to make it a better one, in pragmatic and practical terms.

The question has often been asked, if the nations of Europe are so discontented, why do they not leave the EU? And the answer is because they follow their own national interests. But without intending it, each following its own interests pulls all of them further and further into the same cooperative system. Each nation limits its right to go off on its own because it expects the others to combine together – and if they do not, it will be disadvantaged. When repeated over time, these expectations of each other's expectations creates in each country a new national core. Each nation now has the expectations of all the others encoded within it. This is how European interests emerge as a nation's own interests. This is how the national zero-sum game can be gradually replaced by a European plus-sum game. And this is how national interests become Europeanized. They become reflexive national interests by following repeated joint strategies of self-limitation. And they follow these strategies because they work. So it is not only the social fabric that has become thoroughly cosmopolitanized. It is even true of the pure national interests themselves. Nations don't follow cosmopolitan realism out of altruism, but rather out of egoism, out of realism.

The decline of the nation state is really a decline of the national content of the state and an opportunity to create a cosmopolitan state system that is better able to deal with the problems that all nations face in the world today. Economic globalization, transnational terrorism, global warming: the litany is familiar and daunting. There are a host of problems that are clearly beyond the power of the old order of nation states to cope. The answer to global problems that are gathering ominously all around and which refuse to yield to nation state solutions is for politics to take a quantum leap from the nation-state system to the cosmopolitan state system. Politics needs to regain credibility in order to craft real solutions. More than anywhere else in the world, Europe shows that this step is possible. Europe teaches the modern world that the political evolution of states and state systems is by no means at an end. National *realpolitik* is becoming unreal, not only in Europe, but throughout the world. It is turning into a lose–lose game. Europeanization means creating a new politics.

HOW DOES COSMOPOLITANISM RELATE TO THE CONCEPT OF THE STATE?

One political response to globalization is the 'cosmopolitan state'. This is grounded in the principle of the state's neutrality towards nationality and allows national identities to exist side by side through the principle of constitutional tolerance (Beck, 2005). This is exactly what understanding the real Europe is about. Just as the Westphalian Peace put an end to the religion-based civil wars of the sixteenth century by separating religion and the state, a response to the nation-based world wars of the twentieth century – so the theory goes – could be to separate the state from the nation. Just as the areligious state enables different religions to be practised, so the cosmopolitan state of Europe ought to guarantee the coexistence of national identities via the *principle of constitutional tolerance*. Just as the scope and context for political action were redefined at the beginning of the modern era by forcing Christian theology into a secondary role, so today national theologies and teleologies need to be

tamed to the same end. And just as this was utterly out of the question for the theological outlook in the middle of the sixteenth century – indeed, it effectively spelt the end of the world – so today such a thing is just as unthinkable for the 'theologians of the national', signalling as it does a break with the basic premise of politics, namely the friend-or-foe system. And yet if we take our cue from the ideas bequeathed to us by Jean Bodin and Johann Althusius, who demarcated state sovereignty from the encroachments of religion and opened it up to history and politics, it becomes possible to reground this *cosmopolitan sovereignty* theoretically and develop it politically, in opposition to the historically discredited premise of national homogeneity, so that it enables real diversity to flourish.

But what does the ancient and suddenly revitalized adjective '*cosmopolitan*' mean when placed in relation to the weighty noun '*state*' to make the 'cosmopolitan state'? For one thing, it marks itself off from *constitutionalism* and establishes the fact that a purely constitutional transnational order; that is, one based on general or constitutional law, will remain internally unstable as long as it is not supported by a corresponding consciousness in the population, by a *transnational identity, culture and statehood*. What is cosmopolitan about the cosmopolitan state, then, is that the creation of a transnational order depends on a genuinely cosmopolitan community whose influence profoundly shapes the politics of its member states. For this to occur, though, it is necessary to overcome the notion of a *single*, homogenous, territorially bounded home nation fenced off from those deemed to be culturally different, and to replace it with the notion of a *dual homeland*. Both elements are possible and necessary: cosmopolitan state entities are reliant on nationally rooted cosmopolitanisms. The adjective *national* insists on self-determination. The cosmopolitan question in response, however, is self-determination – *against whom*? How are the victims of (national) self-determination integrated into society? In what terms are the impacts of self-determination on those deemed to be culturally different spoken about within a 'national' community? How can the 'barbaric freedom' of sovereign communities (Kant) be transformed into a cosmopolitan freedom in which the voice of the other is present in the experiential and cultural spaces of the national self?

In an era of cultural globalization and ethnic–national plurality, this can only become possible through a postnational, plural-national state that is neutral towards and tolerant of nationality, one that acquires its legitimacy from the traditions of nationalities that have been opened up and reformed in line with cosmopolitan values. It can only be achieved by a cosmopolitan sovereignty which

- takes account of rapidly accelerating global interdependency;
- explores and develops the cooperative sovereignty of states for purposes of solving global-national problems; and
- establishes peace amidst the diversity and rivalry between ethnic groups and nations while also protecting this diversity.

Being cosmopolitan, then, means acknowledging both equality and difference at the same time and feeling committed to the planet as a whole. The global problems faced by those deemed to be culturally different must be present, they must be heard, they must have a voice – culturally as well as politically – in the political community.

To nationally trained ears this sounds like a completely unrealistic utopia, and yet in many of its basic elements it is already a reality. The path towards a cosmopolitan state is followed every time a country puts democracy and human rights above autocracy and nationalism; where efforts are made to incorporate firmly within the decision-making process itself the impacts of decisions on those deemed to be culturally different; where attempts are made to harmonize and make a new connection between the rights of minorities and majorities,

between universalistic and particularistic rights. The process by which international law has been relativized in relation to the new prominence of human rights (with all the maddening developments and confusions this entails) also points in this direction. In this context Europe can really only be thought of as a new variety of transnational, cosmopolitan state entity that draws its political strength from the act of affirming and taming European national diversity, with all its endearing parochialisms.

Imagine Europe as a cosmopolitan confederation of states which work together to curb the excesses of economic globalization and which demonstrate respect for difference – especially the difference of their fellow European nations – rather than denying it or bureaucratically negating: this could be, or become, a thoroughly realistic utopia. The theory and concept of the cosmopolitan state are distinct from three positions: the dangerous illusion of a nation state that fends for itself; the neoliberal idea of a minimal, deregulated business-led state; and the unreal temptations of a unified world state. The concept of the cosmopolitan state represents an appropriate response to the twentieth-century history of right-wing and left-wing regimes of terror, as well as to the endless history of colonial and imperial violence. Bodin conceived of state sovereignty as an authority that creates order amidst the tumult of a postreligious world. He could not know what we know today, namely that the antidote to the anarchy he so feared – state sovereignty – has infinitely increased and perfected the potential for horror, hatred, and anti-human violence.

Of course, *the* example of the concept of the cosmopolitan state in action is the *struggle for a political Europe*, one that is more than just a conglomeration of nation states that jump at each other's throats at regular intervals. It is a matter of overcoming ethnic nationalism and the nation state, not by condemning them, but rather by protecting them within a constitutional scheme that affirms different cultures and facilitates peaceful coexistence. In order to achieve this, the European continental ethos of democracy, the rule of law and political freedom needs to be renewed and cultivated for the transnational era (as outlined in the work of Held *et al.*, 1999). Metaphorically speaking, Europe must absorb the 'American dream' that says: you can be whoever you want to be. You are not determined by your origin, class, skin colour, nation, religion, or gender!

A cosmopolitan Europe of national differences – what does that mean, say, in relation to Britain? In my view, the islanders' Euroscepticism does not warrant critique on account of their desire to hold fast to their own national civilization, but rather because of their inability to understand that a cosmopolitan Europe, far from dismantling it, actually safeguards it. A Europe without the British version of civilization would not be Europe. The most important historical event of the twentieth century, the overthrow of the national socialist regime of horror, would have been unthinkable without British determination to defend European values in Europe against a German people incited to fascism. This was a product of British history, an example of *British cosmopolitanism*, which needs to be preserved as the founding act of a new Europe rather than overcome. In similar fashion, now is the time to discover a cosmopolitan France, a cosmopolitan Germany, a cosmopolitan Italy, Poland, Spain, Greece and so on, and to encourage them to be partners in a cosmopolitan Europe.

WHAT COULD BE THE IMPACT OF COSMOPOLITAN EUROPE ON WORLD POLITICS?

The architecture of a cosmopolitan union of states might also point the way out of a politics of false alternatives in other regions of the world, especially in regions where chronic ethnic-national conflicts rage. This possibility becomes clear when I compare the political architecture of the transnational cooperation state with that of national federalism. Both demand a highly differentiated yet balanced power structure in which *functional spheres of sovereignty*, such as law and order and education, as well as cultural autonomy and local government authority, are organized in a decentralized way – within nation states in the case of federalism, and between different states or quasi-state organizations in the case of transnationality. Likewise, it is also possible to conceive of in-between, hybrid forms of a transnational or cosmopolitan architecture of state confederation, which, in both small and large steps, would successively do away with the apparently solid unity of nation and state by means of the plus-sum game of transnationalization, without generating a power vacuum in the process.

In many contexts, there have only been two alternatives until now: *either* national – and therefore state – self-determination *or* subordination to national – and therefore majority-dominated – apparatuses of state institutional power. In these instances, a new option has now emerged, that of *cosmopolitan state federalism*. In zones and regions of the world, for example, where there is chronic ethnic-national conflict, such as the endlessly complicated and intractable dispute between the Israelis and the Palestinians; or again, in the face of impending annexation, as in the case of Hong Kong or Taiwan by China, such an option makes it possible to pursue a 'third way' that is neither exclusive nation statehood nor annexation.

Initially, of course, this is *a purely intellectual possibility* and one that seems utterly unrealistic given the very real conditions of violence, expulsion, terrorism, war, hatred, and exclusive territorial claims that exist. Nonetheless, the idea of cosmopolitan coexistence between states in the global age alone may be capable of unblocking people's minds and opening up new paths for action and negotiation.

Perhaps the idea of the cosmopolitanization of nation states can generate a new strategy for finding peaceful solutions to chronic conflicts over nationality and imperial dependencies, since two things can be achieved by it at the same time. First, the loss of nation-state autonomy can be compensated by extending the pooled sovereignty of participating governments and countries; this in turn makes it possible, second, to create bridges of prosperity and legal frameworks that foster the coexistence of mutually exclusive cultural claims, certainties, and traditions. This new cosmopolitan extension of state authority, conceived as a response to globalization, creates and reinforces economic and legal interdependencies and to this extent is able to operate as a strategy of prevention. Especially after the failure of the second Iraq war the catchphrase for the future might be: 'Move over America, Europe is back!'

Let me finish by anticipating the future of Europe in three scenarios.

The decay scenario

The decay scenario assumes that the EU is collapsing under its internal and external contradictions. On this scenario, the EU would not succeed in integrating the new Eastern European member countries economically, in advancing the 'positive', market-correcting integration of the Community and in reforming and democratizing the European institutions. The result would be that the neo-liberal market logic would hollow out the national welfare-state transfer systems and that the political forces which advocate a renationalization of politics would gain new adherents in both the 'old' and the 'new' member states.

European politics would thereby become trapped in a *nationalistic vicious circle*. Strong nationalistic parties and movements would paralyse the European institutions and block supranational decisions. Moreover, this would be taken at the national level as an excuse to restore more powers to the member states. As a result of these internal conflicts,

the EU would ultimately fragment into a larger number of strategic state alliances and regional regimes with at best modest supranational powers.

The stagnation scenario

The stagnation scenario assumes that the EU will succeed in integrating the Eastern European countries into the Community economically and in maintaining a (more or less) functioning internal market. However, the greater heterogeneity in the ranks of the member states will make it impossible to agree on market-correcting policies at the European level. Any further deepening of integration as well as any extension of the competences of the Community in the area of foreign and security policy would be blocked by the member states because of their divergent interests. The EU would be frozen in the condition of a neoliberal economic zone lacking any farther-reaching political claims and with dubious democratic legitimation.

The cosmopolitanization scenario

Finally, the cosmopolitanization scenario begins from the assumption that Europe has arrived at a turning point at which conflicts over fundamental questions are becoming imperative. What holds a postnational Europe together and what contribution is it able and willing to make to creating what global system? One concern of cosmopolitan Europe will be to integrate the EU economically in the wake of Eastern enlargement and to liberate it from the fetters of the neoliberal internal market project. A further concern will be to lend it a distinctive profile and to strengthen it in the domain of foreign and security policy and transform it into a second global centre of power that succeeds in committing its ally, the US, to a cosmopolitan global order; that is, one based on the recognition of difference. Such a cosmopolitan Europe will not be free from contradictions but it will find ways and means of dealing with these tensions and of preventing the Community from being fragmented and politically stymied by the unavoidable ambivalences of the second European modernity. However, this scenario presupposes that Europeans recreate and politically reconstitute Europe at the beginning of the twenty-first century. European renewal is based on four pillars:

- First, strengthening a *European civil society* on the basis of universally shared constitutional norms.
- Second, the transition to a new *postnational model of democracy* that, instead of discouraging the European citizens, accords them an active role in the European decision-making process.
- Third, introducing a new *cosmopolitan approach to integration* no longer geared to 'harmonizing' rules and overcoming (national) differences but to acknowledging them.
- Fourth, establishing Europe as the driving force of a global cosmopolitanism and as a member of the new transatlantic security community.

NOTES

1 For examples of such work see: Appadurai (1991); Appiah (1998); Archibugi *et al.* (1998); Beck (2000, 2006; Beck and Sznaider (2006); Brighouse and Brocks (2005); Burawoy *et al.* (2000); Cheah and Robbins (1998); Cohen and Vertovic (2002); Delanty (2001, 2006); Dirlik (1997); Fine (2003, 2006); Grande (2006); Held *et al.* (1999); Huntington (2004); Kaldor (2002); Kaldor *et al.* (1999); Levy and Sznaider (2005); McRobbie (2006); Mertens (1996); Sassen (2006); Shaw (2000); Stevenson (2002); Szerszyinsky and Urry (2006); Turner (2006), Van der Veer (2002); Wimmer and Glick Schiller (2002); Zubaida (2002).

2 On the critique of multiculturalism, see Beck (2006).

3 Needless to say, here the devil is in the details. Who lays down the procedures in accordance with which these minima are determined? Who imposes them in the face of opposition? How are conflicts resolved in which one or both sides are not ready to renounce the use of organized violence which violates the minimal norms of civilization? These questions already make clear that cosmopolitanism does not provide any pat answers but is replete with dilemmas.

4 For this reason, orthodox Marxist philosophy does not regard cosmopolitanism as opposed to, but rather as the 'reverse side of bourgeois nationalism and chauvinism'. According to Marxist doctrine, it is 'the reactionary response to socialist internationalism' (Klaus and Buhr, 1975: 667).

5 The distinction between the premodern period and modernity is intended here only in a heuristic sense and in full awareness that it is encumbered by an extremely problematic distinction between tradition and modernity. It is also true that the hierarchy of difference was *integral* to the process of European nation-state formation in the eighteenth and nineteenth centuries in the shape of colonialism. The terrorist attacks of September 11 2001 are also being used to replace the lost 'communist enemy' with an 'Islamic enemy'.

6 This involves a strange irony. Postmodernity, which developed to unmask and overcome essentialism, in fact revives it in the guise of a postmodern quasi-essentialism of the incommensurability of others. This shares with the premodern 'natural' essentialism of difference the notion that one must accept things as they are.

REFERENCES

Appadurai, A. (1991) 'Global ethnoscapes. Notes and queries for a transnational anthropology', in R.G. Fox (ed.) *Recapturing Anthropology: Working in the Present*. Santa Fe: School of American Research Press.

Appiah, K.A. (1998) 'Cosmopolitan patriots', in P. Cheah and B. Robbins (eds) *Cosmopolitics. Thinking and Feeling Beyond the Nation*. Minneapolis, London: University of Minnesota Press.

Archibugi, D. (2003a) 'Cosmopolitical democracy', in D. Archibugi (ed.) *Debating Cosmopolitics*. London: Verso.

Archibugi, D. (ed.) (2003b) *Debating Cosmopolitics*. London: Verso.

Archibugi, D. and Held, D. (eds) (1995) *Cosmopolitan Democracy: An Agenda for a New World Order*. Cambridge: Polity Press.

Archibugi, D., Held, D. and Köhler M. (eds) (1998) *Re-imagining Political Community. Studies in Cosmopolitan Democracy*. Cambridge: Polity Press.

Balibar, E. (1998) 'The borders of Europe', in P. Cheah and B. Robbins (eds) *Cosmopolitics*. Minneapolis: University Press of Minnesota Press.

Beck, U. (2000) 'The cosmopolitan perspective. Sociology in the second age of modernity', *The British Journal of Sociology*, 51 (1): 79–105.

Beck, U. (2002) The terrorist threat: World risk society revisited, *Theory, Culture & Society*, 19 (4): 39–55.

Beck, U. (2003) 'Cosmopolitan Europe', in S. Stern and E. Seligmann (eds): *Desperately Seeking Europe*. London: Archetype Publications.

Beck, U. (2004) 'The Truth of Others: A Cosmopolitan Approach', *Common Knowledge*, 10 (3): 430–449.

Beck, U. (2005) *Power in the Global Age*. Cambridge: Polity Press.

Beck, U. (2006) *The Cosmopolitan Vision*. Cambridge: Polity Press.

Beck, U. and Grande, E. (2007) *Cosmopolitan Europe*. Cambridge: Polity Press.

Beck, U. and Lau, C. (2005) 'Second modernity as a research agenda: theoretical and empirical explorations in the 'meta-change' of modern society', *The British Journal of Sociology*, 56 (4): 525–557.

Beck, U. and Sznaider, N. (2006) 'Unpacking cosmopolitanism for the social sciences: a research agenda', *The British Journal of Sociology*, 57 (1): 1–23.

Brennan, T. (1997) *At Home in the World: Cosmopolitanism Now*. Cambridge, MA: Harvard University Press.

Brighouse, H, and Brock, G. (2005) *The Political Philosophy of Cosmopolitanism*. Cambridge: Polity Press.

Burawoy, M., Blum, J.A., George, S., Gille, Z., Gowan, T., Haney, L., Klawiter, M., Lopez, S.H., Riain, S.Ó. and Thayer, M. (2000) *Global Ethnography: Forces, Connections and Imaginations in a Postmodern World*. Berkeley: University of California Press.

Cheah, P. and Robbins, B. (eds) (1998) *Cosmopolitics. Thinking and Feeling Beyond the Nation*. Minneapolis: University of Minnesota Press.

Cohen, R. and Vertovic, S. (eds) (2002) *Conceiving Cosmopolitanism. Theory, Context and Practice*. Oxford: Oxford University Press.

Dann, O. (1993) *Nation und Nationalismus in Deutschland. 1770–1990*. München: Beck.

Delanty, G. (2001) 'Cosmopolitanism and violence', *European Journal of Social Theory*, 4 (1): 41–52.

Delanty, G. (2006) 'The cosmopolitan imagination: critical cosmopolitanism and social theory', *The British Journal of Sociology*, 57 (1): 25–47.

Delanty, G. and Rumford, C. (2005) *Rethinking Europe. Social Theory and the Implications of Europeanization*. London/New York: Routledge.

Dirlik, A. (1997) *The Postcolonial Aura: Third World Criticism in the Age of Global Capitalism*. Boulder: Westview Press.

Fine, R. (2003) 'Taking the 'Islam' out of cosmopolitanism. An essay in reconstruction', *European Journal of Social Theory*, 6 (4): 451–470.

Fine, R. (2006) 'Cosmopolitanism and violence: difficulties of judgment', *The British Journal of Sociology*, 57 (1): 49–67.

Grande, E. (2006) 'Cosmopolitan political science', *The British Journal of Sociology*, 57 (1): 87–111.

Held, D. (1995) *Democracy and the Global Order: From the Modern State to Cosmopolitan Governance*. Cambridge: Polity Press.

Held, D., McGrew, A., Goldblatt, D., and Perraton, J. (1999) *Global Transformations*. Cambridge: Polity Press.

Honneth, A. (1992) *Kampf um Anerkennung. Zur moralischen Grammatik sozialer Konflikte*. Frankfurt a. M.: Suhrkamp.

Huntington, S.P. (1996) *The Clash of Civilisations and the Remaking of World Order*. New York: Simon & Schuster.

Huntington, S.P. (2004) *Who Are We? The Challenges to America's National Identity*. New York: Simon & Schuster.

Kaldor, M. (1995) 'European institutions. Nation-states and nationalism', in D. Archibugi and D. Held (eds) *Cosmopolitan Democracy. An Agenda for a New World Order*. Cambridge: Polity Press.

Kaldor, M. (2000) *Neue und alte Kriege*. Frankfurt a. M.: Suhrkamp.

Kaldor, M. (2002) 'Cosmopolitanism and organized violence', in S. Vertovic and R. Cohen (eds) *Conceiving Cosmopolitanism*. Oxford: Oxford University Press.

Kaldor, M., Fellman, N., Joenniemi, P., Lodenius, L. and Øberg, J. (1999) 'From peace movements to cosmopolitan networks', in R. Jansson (ed.) *Peace Work for the Next Millennium*. Aland Islands Peace Institute.

Kaldor, M., Anheier, H. and Glasius, M. (2003) *Global Civil Society. Yearbook 2003*. Oxford: Oxford University Press.

Klaus, G. and Buhr, M. (eds) (1975) *Philosophisches Wörterbuch. 11. Auflage*. Leipzig: VEB Bibliographisches Institut.

Kleingeld, P. (1999) 'Six Varieties of Cosmopolitanism in Late Eighteenth-Century Germany', *Journal of the History of Ideas*, 60 (3): 505–524.

Landfried, C (2002) *Das politische Europa. Differenz als Potential der Europäischen Union*. Baden-Baden: Nomos.

Levy, D. and Sznaider, N, (2001) *Erinnerung im globalen Zeitalter: Der Holocaust*. Frankfurt a. M.: Suhrkamp.

Levy, D. and Sznaider, N. (2004) 'The institutionalization of cosmopolitan memory: the Holocaust and human rights', *Journal of Human Rights*, 3 (2): 143–157.

Levy, D. and Sznaider, N. (2005) *The Holocaust and Memory in the Global Age*. Philadelphia: Philadelphia Temple University Press.

Linklater, A. (1998) *The Transformation of Political Community. Ethical Foundations of Post-Westphalian Era*. Columbia: University of South Carolina Press.

McRobbie, A. (2006) 'Vulnerability, violence and (cosmopolitan) ethics: Butler's Precarious Life', *The British Journal of Sociology*, 57 (1): 69–86.

Meinecke, F. (1907) *Weltbürgertum und Nationalstaat. Studien zur Genesis des deutschen Nationalstaats*. München: Oldenbourg.

Mertens, T. (1996) 'Cosmopolitanism and Citizenship: Kant Against Habermas', *European Journal of Philosophy*, 4 (3): 328– 347.

Pogge, T.W. (1992) 'Cosmopolitanism and sovereignty', *Ethics*, 103 (1): 48–75.

Sassen, S. (2006) *Denationalisation: Territory, Authority and Rights in a Global Digital Age*. Princeton: University Press.

Schlereth, T. (1997) *The Cosmopolitan Ideal in Enlightenment Thought*. Notre Dame: University of Notre Dame Press.

Shaw, M. (2000) *Theory of the Global State. Globality as Unfinished Revolution*. Cambridge: Cambridge University Press.

Smith, A.D. (2002) *Nations and Nationalism in a Global Era*. Cambridge: Polity Press.

Stevenson, N. (2002) 'Cosmopolitanism and the future of democracy. Culture and the self', *New Political Economy*, 7 (2): 251– 267.

Szerszynski, B. and Urry, J. (2006) 'Vulnerability, mobility and the cosmopolitan: inhabiting the world from afar', *The British Journal of Sociology*, 57 (1): 113–131.

Thielking, S. (2000) *Weltbürgertum. Kosmopolitische Ideen in Literatur und politischer Publizistik seit dem achtzehnten Jahrhundert*. München: Fink.

Toulmin, S. (1990) *Cosmopolis: The Hidden Agenda of Modernity*. New York: Free Press.

Turner, B.S. (2006) 'Classical sociology and cosmopolitanism: a critical defence of the social', *The British Journal of Sociology*, 57 (1): 133–151.

Van der Veer, P. (2002) 'Colonial cosmopolitanism', in S. Vertovic and R. Cohen (eds) *Conceiving Cosmopolitanism*. Oxford: Oxford University Press.

Vertovec, S. and Cohen, R. (2002) *Conceiving Cosmopolitanism. Theory, Context, and Practice*. New York: Oxford University Press.

Wimmer, A. and Glick Schiller, N. (2002) 'Methodological nationalism and beyond: nation-state building, migration and the social sciences', *Global Networks*, 2 (4): 301–334.

Zubaida, S. (2002) 'Middle Eastern experiences of cosmopolitanism', in: S. Vertovic and R. Cohen (eds) *Conceiving Cosmopolitanism. Theory, Context, and Practice*. New York: Oxford University Press.

34

The Mountain Comes to Muhammad: Global Islam in Provincial Europe

Faisal Devji

In 1989, Muslims around the world protested against Salman Rushdie's portrayal of the Prophet Muhammad in his novel *The Satanic Verses*. In addition to forcing the novel's British–Indian author into hiding, these protests also signaled the emergence of a global Muslim politics on the European continent. Since 1989, the world has been swept by periodic waves of Muslim protest, all of which are invariably concerned with demonstrations against some European insult to the Prophet. My objective in this essay is to ask what political meaning these protests represent in the context of European liberalism.

Despite appearances these global events by no means represent the fanatical fringe of an otherwise familiar politics of protest, since Muslims protesting what they consider to be insults to Muhammad's person are not interested in proposing some alternative vision for the world. Rather than making an argument or backing some cause, we shall see that these men and women protest so as to exhibit their suffering and call for its recognition. Their only demand is that such

recognition be followed by a symbolic withdrawal of the hurtful insult. No claims are made for compensation and few for retribution, since the threats and violence of the protesters are intended, at least rhetorically, to compel only the global recognition of their suffering, and lead therefore to the removal of its entirely symbolic cause – whether this be a book, a set of images or some comments in a speech.

In other words, protest here is not about some popular interest staking its claim to political life, but instead represents the offer of a stark moral choice to the world by a display of suffering. Indeed the Muslim abandonment of politics in its traditional form is matched by the adoption of sacrificial practices that go beyond the mere exhibition of suffering to deliberately produce it. Thus, the routine spectacle of injury and even death among so many protestors, from the Rushdie affair of 1988 to the papal controversy of 2006, transforms protest itself into a practice of sacrifice. Yet these protests are concerned more with the creation of a global Muslim constituency than with the actions of non-Muslims or apostates, since they work according to an internal dynamic that is rarely affected by the reaction of outsiders. Drawing inspiration from each other as much as from the would-be insult that is apparently their cause, these protests sweep the globe according to an internal calendar and rhythm.

BURNING BOOKS

The massive protests occasioned in 1988 by the publication of Salman Rushdie's novel, *The Satanic Verses* (Rushdie, 1988), arguably provided the non-Muslim world with its first demonstration of Islam's globalization. This differed from an international Islam in that more than any such incident in the past, the protests over Rushdie's novel referred neither to a particular interest being threatened, nor to a particular cause being fought. Rather their apparently idealistic concern with the Prophet Muhammad's portrayal meant that these protests were defined in terms of equal relevance for Muslims everywhere. More than pilgrimage, holy war or the kind of pan-Islamism that would mobilize Muslims internationally in support of Bosnians or Kashmiris or Chechens, in other words, the Rushdie affair was global because it concentrated Muslim attention on an issue completely detached from persons and places.

Of course, protests against *The Satanic Verses* did have particular meaning at every point in their trajectory, from Bradford to Srinagar, Islamabad, Tehran and beyond. But what made these events global was their lack of fixed location, geographic and political, a phenomenon rendered possible in large part by the unprecedented media exposure within which they occurred, such events being made available instantaneously and repeatedly in the virtual space of television. Given the highly publicized refusal by Muslims to read *The Satanic Verses* or deal with issues like its author's freedom of expression and interpretation, it is even possible to say that Muhammad's portrayal became the site of a global debate for which Rushdie was himself incidental.

Early protests against the novel used it almost randomly as a kind of weapon at hand. A weapon, for example, that allowed Muslims in Bradford to find a voice that could be heard outside the cloisters of state-funded race-relations programs, in this way ironically fulfilling the novel's attempt to give British Asians their own voice. Or one that allowed Indian Muslims to agitate against the bigotry of Hindu nationalists, who delighted in the novel, by asking for a ban on the book. In this preglobal phase of the Rushdie affair, when *The Satanic Verses* represented British or Indian bigots in almost random fashion, the rest of the Muslim world remained unfazed. Even the Ayatollah Khomeini dismissed the novel as yet another petty irritant in the eye of Islam. But somehow, with the media blitz in Britain and riots in the Indian subcontinent, the Rushdie affair catapulted, again randomly, into a global event.

My point here is twofold: that the author and his novel were incidental to the Rushdie affair, and that randomness was essential to its globalization. So attempts by certain Muslim groups to stage a repeat performance of this event, in concert with sections of the media in Europe and America, have not been successful. For instance efforts to make the Bangladeshi author Taslima Nasreen into another Rushdie seem to have been believed only by her and Rushdie himself. One imagines the local Islamists and global media that promoted Nasreen for this role being concerned more with their advertising and sales than with her freedom of expression or anything else. But then for many Muslims the real subject of the Rushdie affair was not Salman Rushdie but the Prophet Muhammad. It was the interpretation of his life and work that constituted the stuff of their debate, one which I believe was so passionate because it radicalized the portrayal of Muhammad in a more thoroughgoing fashion than *The Satanic Verses,* itself.

The title of Rushdie's novel refers to an obscure event in the life of the Prophet, a case of satanic interpolation in the revelation he was vouchsafed, which ostensibly puts both Muhammad's integrity and that of this revelation in doubt. Yet Muslim reaction to the novel, including Ayatollah Khomeini's *fatwa* against it, did not deal with any of the theological issues raised by the book. It consisted instead of objections to Rushdie's unflattering portrayal of the Prophet as leader, friend and family man, in the process putting aside a whole polemic tradition that would demonstrate Muhammad's veracity by textual interpretation and theological reasoning. Muslim reaction to the novel was not concerned with demonstrations of veracity, only those of offence and injury.[1] This is particularly true for the Shia branch of Islam, to which Khomeini belonged, since it refuses to acknowledge the occurrence, and so the theological status, of any satanic attempt to interfere with scripture.

The Prophet was not a properly religious figure in this debate but rather a model of civic virtue, in keeping with the long-standing efforts of Muslims to conceive a new social order by rethinking the idea of citizenship on the model of Muhammad's Medina. The Prophet's properly religious position was even undermined by this debate, in which he no longer related to his followers by way of miracles, saintly figures, sacred texts or even theological reasoning, but simply by representing a civic ideal. And Muhammad as the model citizen of a virtual state becomes the sign of a new social order in part because he is deprived of any real particularity, having been transformed simply into the ideal of this order. A virtual order that is both everywhere and nowhere, like an afterimage of the historical state. Naturally I am exaggerating the distinction between the old Prophet and the new, but only to point out the implications of liberating Muhammad from the chains of theological reasoning and mystical emanation that had once bound him to believers. The chief such implication being that the Prophet comes to represent

a certain kind of civic ideal calling for a very different sort of allegiance from his followers.

Such an image of the Prophet Muhammad began to emerge during the nineteenth century in places like British India, where influential movements were working to reform or purify Islam. These movements, whether liberal or fundamentalist, attacked what they saw as superstitious belief in mysteries and miracles of all kinds. Distancing the prophet from these superstitions, they held him up as a great historical figure and a model of civic virtue. But the more Muhammad was stripped of miraculous attributes, the more vulnerable he became to insult and attack, for he was, after all, only human. It was the Prophet's humanity that required the protection of his followers and made him so dear to them. This explains why a diminution of the Prophet's religious status during this period was matched by a corresponding elevation of his status as a figure of love and reverence. Thus both liberals and fundamentalists in the nineteenth century began to disapprove of the European usage 'Muhammadan' for them, decrying this supposed attempt to make Muslims out to be like Christians, the worshippers of their Prophet. Yet at the same time they spilt more ink on glorifying Muhammad and writing biographies of him then perhaps all the Muslims who had gone before. And if insulting the Prophet had been a grave enough offence for the Muslims of earlier times, it became a far more volatile issue now that Muhammad had become in some sense the ward of his community.

BACK TO THE FUTURE

In the nineteenth century, however, the Prophet was not yet a global figure, in the sense that he did not bring together Muslims in the same way as he did during the Rushdie affair. How has the political order that served to define Muhammad as a model of civic virtue during the nineteenth century changed in the twentieth century and beyond? What role does the Prophet Muhammad play in this process? Sixteen years after the Rushdie affair, insulting depictions of the prophet provided occasion for another grand manifestation of Islam's globalization, in which the answers to all these questions became evident.

In September 2005, the Danish newspaper *Jyllands-Posten* published a number of caricatures on the subject of Islam, Muslims and the Prophet Muhammad. It had solicited these as part of a competition in which cartoonists were asked to address the supposed fear that Danes and other Europeans felt in depicting Islam critically. In response to the publication, Muslims in Denmark protested against some of the cartoons, especially that portraying Muhammad as a terrorist, with one group of protestors actively trying to gain the support of Muslim leaders in the Middle East (Devji, 2006). The series of diplomatic and other representations made by Muslims to the Danish government during this period all resulted in the latter invoking the liberal principle of freedom of expression in defence of *Jyllands-Posten*'s right to print such material.

By the end of the year this obscure event had snowballed into a global controversy, with Muslims the world over protesting, often violently, against Danish and other Western interests in countries from Indonesia to Lebanon. In their nonviolent aspect these demonstrations included a widespread boycott of Danish goods that was unprecedented in its extent. Such events kept the cartoon controversy at the centre of global attention for many weeks, even pushing news from the war in Iraq off the front pages. But despite the extraordinary passions unleashed among the protestors as much as among their opponents, Muslim demonstrations had completely dissipated by March 2006, leaving in their wake a state of universal confusion about what the crisis had all been about.

Both controversies, that of 1988 and of 2006, revolved around the portrayal of Islam's Prophet, and both were discussed in the West as threats to freedom of expression. The debate on freedom of expression goes back to the origins of liberalism – or rather to the origins of the nation state that is its political body. Sadly the terms of this debate also go back to the beginnings of liberalism, and are unable to encompass the radical novelty of the challenge that confronts it. Unlike the weight of tradition that loads down such debate, the illiberal character of Muslim protest is astonishingly modern in form. After all, freedom of expression only has meaning within old-fashioned national states, because it protects the speech of one section of citizens against another, and even against the state itself. Muslim protests, on the other hand, have meaning in an absolutely new global context.

The cartoon protests, like those over Rushdie's novel, were remarkably dispersed geographically, and unconcerned for the most part with the rights of states or the responsibilities of citizenship. If this unconcern were due only to ignorance or irrationality among them, such protesting Muslims might eventually be educated to become the good citizens of a liberal democracy. Unfortunately this was not the case. Muslim protests, which moved so far beyond the bounds of state and citizenship, were informed by the new rationality of a global arena. Within this arena freedom of expression's more restricted realm had been rendered irrelevant. For at the global level there is no common citizenship and no government to make freedom of expression meaningful even as an expression. Liberalism was being challenged here not by its past but by its future.

Muslim protesters did not represent some religious tradition that needs to be schooled in the lessons of modern citizenship. Rather their protests brought into being a hypermodern global community whose connections occur by way of mass media alone. From the Philippines to Niger, these men and women communicated with each other only indirectly, neither by plan nor organization, but through the media itself. And just as during the Rushdie affair of 1988, most Muslims in 2006 were hurt not by the offending item, a book read or an image seen, but by its global circulation as a media report. Yet it was this very circulation of the offending item as news that also allowed Muslims to represent themselves as a global community in, through and as the news. Moreover they could only do so by way of English as a global language. It is no accident that the cartoon controversy took the Muslim world by storm only when it was reported on the BBC and CNN, for English and not Arabic is the source language of global Islam.

In this hypermodern community traditional distinctions of belief and practice have ceased to be relevant, as indeed has religion itself in an old-fashioned sense. For the generic Muslim protester who was displayed on television screens across the world could not be marked by any specifically theological concern. Indeed only the first global controversy surrounding the Prophet involved a specifically theological issue, the charge of apostasy levelled at Salman Rushdie, but even this was marginal when compared with the secular rhetoric of Muslim hurt. And if in the Rushdie affair the explicitly religious issue of scriptural interpolation was never taken up as a cause for offence even in the Ayatollah Khomeini's fatwa, Muslims protesting nearly 20 years later also made nothing of Islam's supposed proscription of the Prophet's image. In any case there is a long if contested history of Muslims depicting their Prophet. Such images continue to proliferate among Shiites, for example, without in any way dampening the outcry over the cartoons in Baghdad or Tehran.

These theological concerns are in fact interesting only to the defenders of liberal democracy, who think of challenges to its freedoms in terms that are a few centuries out of date. That it should be a religious group demonstrating its globalization here was in any case consonant with liberalism's past. The nation state, after all, was founded to subdue religion, seen as the only entity capable of providing an alternative foundation for political life. So it is only natural if today

Islam seems to confront the liberal state with its own founding myth, having become the Frankenstein's monster of its history. Liberal democracy appears doomed to repeat its own past by the way in which it prefigures its enemies – always understood as offering politics alternative foundations like that of religion. If not religion, then anarchism, fascism or some other historical rival of the liberal state comes to occupy this role in the long-running drama of its founding. But this is not true of global Islam, which should be defined in terms of liberalism's future instead of its past.

As in the Rushdie affair, the Prophet insulted by these Danish cartoons is not a religious figure of any traditional sort. In 1988 it was Muhammad as husband and family man who stood impugned in the eyes of protesters. Many protesters in the new century continued to express their hurt by comparing the Prophet to members of their 'family', hardly a religious role for him to play and one of dubious orthodoxy in any case. This is a language that belongs more in the Christian than the Muslim tradition. In fact, Muhammad as father, husband and family man has become a role model of the most modern kind, one representing the ideal Muslim not as the citizen or even the leader of a state, as he did for yesterday's fundamentalists, including even Ayatollah Khomeini, but as a properly global figure instead. And the Prophet as a global figure manifests himself in domestic rather than political ways. It is his very particularity as father, husband and family man that has been universalized beyond the language of state and citizenship, giving Muhammad a mythic countenance as part of a global family.

Muslim protests over the caricatures of Muhammad published in the Danish newspaper *Jyllands-Posten* did not pose any threat to the freedom of expression in liberal democracies. They presented a challenge to liberal democracy itself as a political form that is being made parochial within a new global arena. Liberalism, after all, has no presence outside the nation state, which is why the international order these states operate in has never itself been liberal. Indeed such an order is not even meant to operate in a liberal way, since this would render the liberalism of its constituent units irrelevant. Whether we look to the theorists of liberalism or at the international order itself, all we see are general prescriptions for peace and particular compacts between states. In many respects the international arena remains a Hobbesian state of nature for liberal theory, which can only conceive of it otherwise by invoking the idea of a universal state.

However suspicious they may be of the universal state as an idea, liberals depend upon it to imagine as well as to create an international order. The idea of a universal state is deeply embedded within organizations like the United Nations, which operates according to the analogy that states in an international order are like individuals in a national one. But what happens when individuals and groups themselves, rather than the nations and states that would represent them, come to occupy a space that is no longer international but global? Liberalism's unwillingness as well as inability to manage the global arena in its own terms leaves the latter open to challenge from without. And if this challenge by no means spells the doom of nation states, it does force them into new shapes that put liberalism's premises and foundations into question. What could be more indicative of this than the erosion of civil liberties in such states as part of the global war on terror? Liberal democracies today are increasingly shot through with new global vectors, running the gamut from immigrants to multinational corporations. Islam provides only one, though perhaps the most interesting one, of these vectors.

While Islam is certainly not the only global movement around, nor the only one to issue challenges to liberal democracy, its geopolitical situation has made of this populous religion the most volatile phenomenon of our times. Islam's globalization is possible because it is anchored neither in an institutionalized religious authority like a church,

nor in an institutionalized political authority like a state. Indeed, it is the continuing fragmentation and thus democratization of authority in the world of Islam that might account for the militancy of its globalization. What did the global protests over a few Danish cartoons demonstrate if not the splintering of Islamic authority, since these expressions of Muslim outrage were rarely organized by any seminary or political party, to say nothing of any state?

In fact, it was the media that allowed Muslims to organize themselves as a global community without political institutions, since their protests as seen on television inspired and even competed with each other. The media therefore functioned like a gigantic mirror, permitting Muslims to recognize themselves as a global community without any institutional form. Indeed it was this global community whose support states, parties and other political bodies in the Muslim world rushed to claim by joining in the cartoons fray. But in the absence of any significant religious or political authority in today's Muslim world, it is precisely unseen figures like Al-Qaeda or the Danish cartoons that have the ability to mobilize Muslims globally, though of course in different and even opposing ways. For example, the cartoon protests by and large eschewed the rhetoric of holy war, though they did invoke the same themes of hurt and respect as Al-Qaeda does.

Islam no longer serves merely to voice reactions against colonialism or democracy, capitalism or modernity, but increasingly sets the terms for politics globally. So the unexpected escalation of the cartoon controversy moved it well ahead of any demonstrations over Iraq, Afghanistan or Guantanamo Bay. Of course these and other more local issues certainly informed Muslim anger. But they did so by providing global Islam an opportunity to manifest itself in the most arcane and therefore autonomous way: through a set of caricatures. By chancing in seemingly arbitrary fashion upon the Danish cartoons as a cause, Muslim protesters were only proving global Islam to be relatively unhampered by the political traditions proper to liberalism. Like other global movements, from environmentalism to pacifism, the Muslim one we are looking at is free to map its own trajectory and will not follow the dictates of someone else's idea of political rationality.

It was left for liberal democrats to puzzle over the meaning of this movement, coming up with explanations for it like American imperialism, economic exploitation or Third World dictatorship. Meanwhile the protesters themselves, who must have been more than familiar with such shibboleths, were content to ignore them altogether. The Danish cartoons did not simply disguise the political or economic causes of Muslim anger in religious terms, for we have seen that their anger had little or no religious substance. Rather they allowed Muslims to set the terms for global politics precisely by fixing on an issue that national states are unable to address. Yet this very issue, of personal hurt, insult and offence, is more than familiar to liberal democracy. It is as if Muslim protesters were hesitantly feeling around the global arena they had occupied by extending to it the familiar practices of the nation state, though outside its geographical and juridical boundaries. Their recourse to legal language and categories, like calling for states to ban offensive publications, also illustrates the paradoxical way in which Muslims inhabited the global arena, for such calls became meaningless the moment they were made outside state borders. In so far as they were global subjects, then, Muslims and their Prophet were hurt because they had been denuded of the protection that states and citizenship have to offer. Their hurt was nakedly felt and nakedly expressed, existing outside the cosseted debate on freedom of expression.

It is because global Islam comes to us from the future that it exposes so clearly the limits of liberal democracy. Such limits are evident in the circular definition that has marked liberalism from its founding days: only those will be tolerated who are themselves tolerant. Such a definition deprives tolerance of any moral content by making it completely dependent on the behaviour of others. Tolerance therefore becomes a process of exclusion in which it is always the other person who is being judged. Even at its most agreeable, however, the definition is severely limited, because its circularity works only within the bounds of a national state. It is unable to deal with real differences at all and certainly not with difference at a global level. As important as it undoubtedly is, we should remember that liberal tolerance was never meant to replace every other ethics in a civil society, but is instead a procedural and legalistic form specific to the functioning of the nation state.

There are many other kinds of tolerance possible, including the Christian one called charity, which would convert others or foster good relations with them by forbearance and example. But moral rather than legal definitions of tolerance, like the Christian one, tended not to be invoked in this controversy, with commentators abandoning the claims of civil society altogether to become ventriloquists for the state. Yet it is surely within civil society that the problem lies, and statesmen from Gandhi to Mandela have in the recent past mobilized precisely such nonlegal conceptions of tolerance to effect great social transformations. For tolerance can have no moral content if it exists only as the legal provision of mutual indifference. Indeed this kind of respect is not even amenable to legislation, which only recognizes it in the act of proscription. It occurs outside the law as a moral principle, and can be grasped only by sinking below the negative universality of liberal tolerance, tied as it is to the state's neutrality and indifference, to reach the positive if particular tolerance of Hindus, Christians, or indeed atheists. The paradox of this particularity is that it is far more expansive than the universality of liberal tolerance, because it cannot be confined within the borders of a nation state.

It was this particularity of respect, and even the positive tolerance of Christian charity, that

so many Muslim protesters had been demanding, in no matter how frightening a manner.
Their fulsome expressions of hurt, after all,
were not derived from the cartoons in any
direct way, since these remained unseen for
the most part, but from the absence of respect
for Muslim feeling. Unlike the photographs of
American soldiers abusing Iraqi prisoners at
Abu Ghraib, these images had not been globally circulated to spur Muslim anger. Like
Rushdie's novel before them the cartoons
were in fact not supposed to be seen at all,
which explains popular actions against newspapers in the Muslim world that did try to
incite protests by printing them. Indeed the
rumour of disrespect has proven a greater
incitement to protest than any evidence of
desecration. Thus the violent protests of 2005
in some parts of the Muslim world over
unconfirmed media reports that American
soldiers in Afghanistan had flushed pages of
the Quran down toilets. The hurt experienced
by such acts has to do not with their materiality so much as with the disrespect that such
materiality only brings to light.

That a few invisible caricatures should
cause more offence globally than large numbers of photographs depicting torture in the
most real way is an important fact, and one
that has little to do with the outrage of any
specifically religious feeling. Given the invisibility of the cartoons in the Muslim world,
there was no real outrage to religious feeling
there but only the report of European disrespect. In other words the materiality of the
images themselves had nothing to do with
the protests they inspired, only the apparent
injury done to Muslim feeling by the report
of their circulation, which made the experience of hurt one of hearing rather than of
sight. It was not the public act of blasphemy
or desecration that was seen to be criminal, in
legalistic terms, but rather the private contempt it betrayed. More than an offence
experienced, therefore, Muslims were protesting at the violation of a moral principle.
This was the non-juridical principle of respect
within a global civil society made possible
by media, markets and migration.

Yet the initial demand by Danish Muslims
to have their own prejudices protected did
not threaten freedom of expression in any
way. Nor did Muslims in Denmark or elsewhere in Europe and North America make
their demands in a criminally violent manner.
Such demands are in fact made all the time in
liberal democracies, whose boundaries of
free expression are therefore constantly shifting. From state secrets to racial discrimination, libel and copyright to sexual harassment,
proscriptions on expression are being put in
place by the very defenders of its freedom.
Indeed today's global war on terror has led
to the most concerted reduction of such
freedom in decades.

In the meantime, Muslims are inventing
new forms of moral and political practice for
a global arena, such were the remarkable
boycotts of Danish goods in many parts of
the Islamic world. However unfair or unjust
they might have been, these peaceful and
individualized boycotts of unprecedented
extent were, like the controversial cartoons,
perfectly legal and even democratic. Indeed
they derived from a tradition of nonstate or
civil society boycotts that include the movement to divest from apartheid-era South
Africa. Both these boycotts operated through
transnational capitalism to create a global
politics outside the cognizance of states. We
have already moved a step beyond the banning and burning of the Rushdie affair here.

More important, however, is the fact that
this global mobilization of Muslims should
have represented itself neither in the old language of imperialism and oppression, nor
indeed in that of resistance and jihad. Instead
it took its rhetoric from the arsenal of liberalism itself, merely extending categories like
democracy and civil society into a global
arena (Devji, 2005). But this extension also
transforms such categories, which seem
finally to have achieved the universality that
liberalism invested them with, if only outside
the nation state and its legal forms. What
resulted from these protests and boycotts,
then, was not simply damage to the Danish
economy, but rather a complete reversal of

the primal scene of liberal freedom as it was staged by *Jyllands-Posten*.

The scenario envisioned by *Jyllands-Posten* was of a poor immigrant minority being 'tested' for its tolerance by an entrenched and wealthy majority. But isn't the classical doctrine of liberal tolerance meant to protect minorities from majorities and not the other way around? Having gone on to fulfil the newspaper's prediction by failing its test, this wretched minority could then be accused of threatening the majority's liberal constitution. I will not go into the unpleasant task of speculating about the newspaper's motives in creating its own news by scooping itself in this way, nor ask about the rise in its sales afterwards. The denouement was a sudden implosion of the paper's national audience into a global Muslim one, within which the unfortunate Danish majority unexpectedly became a minority. Did these boycotts, then, signal the slow movement of democratic practices from a national to a global arena – one in which there exist as yet no institutions to anchor them?

LONGING FOR CHRISTIANITY

On 12 September 2006, a day after the fifth anniversary of the 9/11 attacks was commemorated around the world, Pope Benedict, the Sixteenth spoke about the relationship of faith and reason to an audience of academics at Regensburg University. The pontiff began his argument by citing a medieval text disparaging the Prophet Muhammad as someone who had brought to the world 'things only evil and inhuman, such as his command to spread by the sword the faith he preached'.[2] The Pope did not explicitly condone these words, which for him illustrated one way in which the relationship of violence and religion had been thought about in the past. And it is worth noting that the words were quoted from a volume edited by an eminent Arab priest who had translated the Quran and was a champion of Christian–Muslim understanding.

For Benedict XVI the importance of the words he was quoting lay in the fact that the Byzantine emperor who spoke them condemned such violence because it was unreasonable. What followed was a wide-ranging meditation upon the role of reason in religion whose depths I will not attempt to sound, being concerned here by the views of those Muslims who protested at the speech, not least in order to uphold their own ideas of Christian virtue and papal dignity.

Whatever his intention in mentioning the Prophet and his revelation, the Pope's citation of this medieval text was broadcast around the world in the form of a soundbite, thus provoking an almost immediate reaction, violent in places, among Muslims who called for Benedict XVI to apologise for the hurt his words had caused them. And while the Vatican was quick to issue retractions and clarifications that assuaged some of Muhammad's followers, many others pronounced their dissatisfaction at these guarded and diplomatic statements, with a few even calling for the pontiff's abdication or conversion to Islam. The controversy allowed Muslims across the world to mount yet another spectacle of their religion's globalization, although the statements, demonstrations and acts of violence fuelling it did not match the scale of those protesting the Danish caricatures of Islam's founder earlier that year. But the fact that they should have occurred so soon afterwards, and so much more rapidly, is telling given that nearly 20 years separated the cartoon controversy from the first spectacle of Islam's globalization, which had as its cause protests over the publication of *The Satanic Verses* in 1988.

When authors like Rushdie or the Pope are made responsible for the offensive portrayals of Muhammad circulated in the media, they are attacked not as individuals but the media-enhanced representatives of abstractions like the West, Christendom or Zionism. Unlike those who criticize them, in other words, Muslim protesters are concerned not with the individual intentions behind these media statements but with their global dissemination as collective products of the West, Christendom, and so on. They are entirely taken up by the attempt to anchor these geographically dispersed and institutionally unmoored abstractions by holding specific persons accountable for them. And it is this specification of culpability that makes Muslim protest a form of address rather than interpretation. While their critics let 'militants' or 'extremists' remain abstractions by speaking of them indirectly and in the third person, the protesters addressed specific persons in the most direct way, and demanded equally specific responses of them. Such addresses were indeed the only invitations to dialogue to emerge from these controversies.

As with the previous spectacles of Islam's globalization, demonstrations against the Pope's words had secular rather than religious meaning, because they were occasioned only by the 'hurt' caused to Muslim feeling and made no claims about the truth of Muhammad's revelation. By recognizing this hurt and responding to it in as secular a manner, the Pope undercut his own speech on the relationship of faith and reason at Regensburg University by showing how difficult it is to use religious language outside sectarian borders. On the other hand the more violently Muslims protested, the less secular their hurt became, since its expression now damaged the very image of Muhammad's character that his followers sought to defend. In other words by damaging their own cause these Muslims took leave of secular reason without adopting a particularly religious reasoning in the process. Maybe this is how the relationship of faith and reason that Benedict XVI had addressed at Regensburg University manifests itself outside the academic institutions of European democracies.

More interesting about the secularization of Muslim protest was its overwhelming rejection of the language of law. Whether marked as sacred or profane, the vocabulary of legal transgression and punishment was left unpronounced, and there were no important *fatwas* issued as in the Rushdie affair.

It is also significant that jihad, which the pontiff had referred to in his speech, was not by and large declared against him, thus illustrating the multiple ways in which Muslim protest is manifested globally. As with the Danish cartoon controversy, Muslim anger at the Pope's comments did not follow the Al-Qaeda line, and in fact put it quite in the shade by setting another kind of agenda for Islam's globalization. After all, the Pope was asked for an apology so that forgiveness might be extended him. However coercive in its violence, this Muslim demand can be taken as an invitation to the kind of dialogue that Benedict XVI called for in his speech, and it was indeed seized upon as an opportunity by the Pope himself as well as a number of Muslim leaders.

At the very moment that Christian and Muslim leaders determined to engage in a dialogue, however, it became evident that such a thing was no longer possible in a global arena. How could dialogue, in its traditional form, hope to interrupt the fractious and fragmented exchanges of this controversy without itself becoming a media spectacle? In any case the Pope had nobody to talk to, since there exists no ecclesiastical authority in Islam. The only thing that Benedict XVI could do was speak to a more or less random selection of Muslim representatives, the first of whom were the ambassadors of Muslim countries to the Vatican. Yet these men were sometimes themselves Christian, and unlikely to be religious leaders in any case. As representatives of the international order, furthermore, they were incapable of managing the global community within which the controversy had occurred. It was because they had all realized the impossibility of dialogue in this new arena that the meetings convened and statements issued by these leaders assumed a distinctly theatrical countenance. Indeed the controversy ended by providing both 'moderate' and 'extremist' Muslims with a lot of free advertising, very little of which had anything to do with dialogue. For at the end of the day the only exchange possible in the controversy's global arena was that between repentance and absolution.

Contrition and forgiveness are of course religious acts, which is why their entirely secular deployment in this controversy becomes significant. If it was not before God but Muslims worldwide that the Pope was meant to repent, and not from God but these Muslims that he was to receive forgiveness, then nothing separates such contrition from that which had recently been expressed by the Hollywood actor Mel Gibson, amidst much media attention, for anti-Semitic remarks he had made. Yet there is a difference here that goes beyond the fact of Muslim violence, which is that moral categories provide the only vocabulary for dialogue in a global arena whose lack of political institutions stands in contradiction to humanity's increasing inter-dependency. How else was the head of the world's largest religious organization to communicate with Muslims belonging to many organizations or none at all? Certainly not by way of international institutions like the United Nations, which exists only to give voice to its member states.

If Muslim anger appeared to be so raw, this is because it voiced a global presence that remains as yet unmediated by any institution or authority. And if Muslim hurt appeared so intensely felt, this is because it expressed disappointment at the supposed lapse of a religious leader who had otherwise enjoyed considerable respect in the world of Islam. Indeed given the absence of a priestly hierarchy in Islam, and the invisibility of iconic Muslim figures like Osama bin Laden, Benedict XVI may even have represented his missing equivalent in the Islamic tradition, by standing in for this non-existent figure in the curious respect paid him by Muslims. If not the Pope himself, then certainly his title evokes for many Muslims as well as Hindus and others a specifically Christian aura of otherworldliness and sanctity, one that leads them to expect a different kind of language from him. This is why Benedict's alleged lapse into what seemed to be common

prejudice was so shocking for Muslims who, as it were, accidentally overheard the Pope speak of their Prophet, since he did not choose to address them while doing so. The pontiff's initial refusal to recognize that Muslims might be part of his audience was unlikely to have been malicious in its intent, for it is still possible in the West to pretend that the world is not in fact interconnected in such a way as to give even the most arcane utterance a global audience. This had also been Salman Rushdie's mistake.

While the Pope called for a global dialogue in Regensburg, he nevertheless addressed this call to a parochial audience, as if it was their duty alone to spread this new gospel among those, Christian as well as Muslim, who were assumed incapable of initiating it. And so it took the strong and unexpected Muslim reaction to his speech to make the Pope's wish a reality. That such a reaction had not even been afforded the far more demonized figure of the American President George W. Bush, despite his much-resented talk of a crusade in the immediate aftermath of 9/11, bears testimony to the specificity of Muslim disappointment in Benedict XVI. It is as if the protesters were acknowledging, with sadness as much as anger, that the Pope, too, had to be included in the ranks of those who would defame their religion. What is extraordinary, of course, is that Muslims should have expected anything different, given the steady diet they are fed by the militants among them of Christianity's crusading spirit. So it is in fact a hopeful sign that Muslims did not expect a description of Islam's violence from the head of a church that has contributed the words 'crusade' and 'inquisition' to our vocabulary.

Presiding as he does over an immense and venerable apostolic hierarchy, the Pope possesses the kind of reputation and respect among the world's peoples, and especially among those who are not themselves Christians, that other religious leaders can only dream of. And however unrealistic or even absurd the expectations spawned by such respect, they have informed the world's reactions to Rome's doings for a considerable length of time. Writing in the wake of the Second World War, for example, Hannah Arendt commented on the Vatican's silence at the doings of Nazi Germany, a state with which Rome had signed a concordat (Arendt, 2003: 214–26). Breaking this silence, claimed Arendt, may have done little to effect the course of war or even the behaviour of German Catholics, silence therefore being one way in which the Vatican hid its impotence from the sight of the world (Arendt, 2003: 218). And unlike those who would find the Church as a whole culpable of collaborating with fascism, Arendt not only pointed to the priests who risked and lost their lives defending its victims, she also made it clear that the Vatican behaved in no way differently than any other state when it came to protesting the extermination of the Jews (Arendt, 2003: 217). But this precisely was Rome's greatest betrayal, to behave in a secular rather than a religious way by placing political considerations over moral ones, a betrayal that Arendt claimed lost the Church an opportunity to renew its own mission, as much as that of religion in general, for a humanity sorely in need of it (Arendt, 2003: 225).

It is this very betrayal of what they saw as the Church's mission that Muslims were protesting in 2006, just as they had done before in celebrated instances like the Ayatollah Khomeini's address to Pope John Paul II, who in 1979 tried to mediate between Iran and the US and have American hostages in Tehran released. The pontiff had been asked by President Carter to mediate in this matter precisely because of the respect he enjoyed among Muslims, something the ayatollah acknowledged in his response, saying that people expected more from a religious leader of the Pope's eminence than from a politician like the American president. While appreciating John Paul's concern for the fate of US embassy staff whom the Iranians accused of being spies, Khomeini wondered if any Pope had ever offered to intercede on behalf of those oppressed by dictators like the Shah:

> The ears of thirty-five million Iranians, who suffered for fifty years beneath the yoke of imperialism and repression … as well as the ears of millions of oppressed people throughout the world, have constantly been straining to hear some expression of sympathy on the part of the Pope, or at least some indication of paternal concern for the state of the oppressed, coupled with an admonishment of the tyrants and oppressors, or a desire to mediate between the oppressed peoples and those superpowers that profess to be Christian. But our ears have never heard any such expression of sympathy or concern (Khomeini, 1981: 278).

Incorporating Hannah Arendt's indictment of the Vatican's secularism, Khomeini's comments add to it the disappointment of Muslim expectations, which, the ayatollah warned the Pope, will tarnish the name of Christianity. By posing as a friend solicitous of the Church's spiritual mission, Khomeini allowed himself to become more Catholic than the Pope, even offering to join the latter in a common religious endeavour at the end of his address:

> Please convey my greetings to the Pope and tell him that he and I both, as men of religion, have a responsibility to give moral counsel. We ask that he assist our weak people by giving all the superpowers fatherly advice or by summoning them to account for their deeds (Khomeini, 1981: 285).

However disingenuous such a statement, it demonstrates that the ayatollah's dialogue with the Pope was premised upon his identification with Christianity. It was also one premised upon the recognition that Muslims entertained certain hopes of the Church. Indeed the rhetorical effect of Khomeini's address is premised entirely upon the very real hope that even unbaptized populations have of the world's largest religious organization. It is the disappointment of this expectation that also gives rhetorical force to Muslim dissatisfaction with the speedy retractions and clarifications that proceeded from the Vatican in response to their protests. For what appeared to dissatisfy these protesters were precisely the secular remnants in the pontiff's carefully couched apologies. Yet if for all their rage, protesting

Muslims had the audacity to expect Christian humility of the Pope, this in no way contradicted Benedict's own audacity in asserting the role of faith within a secular dispensation. Such indeed was the import of his speech at Regensburg University.

While a great deal has already been written about the complex role that Islam and its prophet play in the pontiff's now notorious address, to say nothing of the position that Jews and Protestants also occupy in it, what has so far gone unremarked is the Pope's use of violence as a criterion to decide upon the truth of religion. On the surface this is an extraordinary argument for Benedict XVI to make, not only because it goes against centuries of Catholic tradition, but also because it is secular to the core. During the Inquisition violence had been justified by describing it as an act of love, since the Church was committed to saving the souls of its victims and not their bodies. Whatever else it might have been, such reasoning was religious rather than secular, because it prized the soul's salvation over the body's comfort. To abjure violence for the sake of the body is to adopt a secular form of reasoning, even if the soul's salvation remains the final goal. Nonviolence can therefore provide the criterion of religious truth only if it is separated from the reasoning of secular betterment. And this is a promise the Church does indeed possess in doctrines like the sanctity of life – though to be fulfilled it needs to be extended from abortion and euthanasia to the death penalty and war.

The point of this controversy was not that Muslims had misunderstood the Pope, that Benedict XVI had misunderstood the Prophet, or that either party had acted out of hatred and prejudice. However true or false any of these points may be, the controversy's great irony was that the pontiff's Muslim protesters should have engaged so fully with the argument of his speech. They did so not by providing an illustration of what happens when faith and reason are separated, but rather by demonstrating how difficult it is for anyone, including the Pope himself, to move beyond the language of secularism. This indeed is the crisis of religion to whose resolution Benedict XVI had dedicated his papacy. It is telling in this respect that the leader of a venerable church, the world's largest religious organization, should broach the subject of religion's crisis by referring to Christianity's old rival Islam, which by posing as the very embodiment of faith's fervency has pushed Christianity in a secular direction and so into crisis. Whatever his intent in doing so, the Pope's invocation of Muhammad was remarkable for the importance it accorded the Prophet, as if it was from the fire of Islam's faith alone that Christianity could now light its own lamp, though only look upon its own crisis of faith. For it was to describe the crisis of Christian faith that Benedict XVI delivered his speech at Regensburg, something he could only do by invoking the name of Muhammad.

Has not Islam taken control of the language of faith on a global scale, by posing as faith's most fervent exemplar in the sacrificial spectacles of its globalization? And was not this position held, not so long ago, by the Roman Catholic Church, which gloried in the mystery of doctrines that surpassed reason? Yet today these mysteries, of transubstantiation and consubstantialism, to say nothing of saintly miracles and papal infallibility, have fallen beneath the fervid star of Islam in Catholicism's very homeland. Even more interesting is the fact that Muslim fanaticism has provided a home for precisely the vices that were for centuries seen as character traits of the Roman Church. Was it not Catholicism that was accused by Protestants as well as secularists of being a worldwide movement dedicated to subverting the freedom of nation states? And were not its adherents said to profess loyalty to a foreign leader who gave religious sanction to the breaking of all agreements with those he deemed heretics and apostates, up to and including approving their assassination?

While Western commentators on the controversy tended to neglect these strange parallels, those in the Muslim world were well aware of them, to the degree that Ayman al-Zawahiri hastened to add Al-Qaeda's voice to a dispute not of its making by pointing out that Roman Catholicism might even hold the copyright on the kind of faith that surpassed reason, referring in particular to its doctrines of original sin, incarnation, the Trinity, and papal infallibility.[3] But it is precisely this situation that makes the kind of dialogue Benedict XVI called for at all possible, if only by showing us how intertwined these religions are with each other as well as with secularism. This dialogue can even be seen occurring in the extraordinary importance that the pontiff's address accorded the Prophet and his revelation, as well as in the corresponding importance that Muslims accorded the speech at Regensburg. But given that it is occurring among large masses of people in an uneven global arena lacking any institutions of its own, it would be foolish to expect such dialogue to be conducted in parliamentary or academic fashion. Indeed the Pope himself has made it very clear that he attaches little value to interfaith dialogue of this kind.

In his address at Regensburg University, the pontiff described Europe as Christianity's spiritual homeland, though he knew of course that the majority of Christians, and indeed Catholics, live outside this partial continent. By explicitly forsaking the desire to return to Christianity's Asian origins, and even to 'the God of Abraham and Isaac', Benedict XVI could not have been so crude as to reject his religion's Jewish heritage. Like the reference to Muhammad, this reference to Abraham's sacrifice of Isaac was literally and metaphorically 'put in quotation marks' by being cited from another text, in this case that of a Protestant theologian, thus allowing the Pope to distance himself from its radical implications. It seems clear, nevertheless, that Benedict XVI rejected the violent sacrifice demanded by a transcendent God for the immanence of one who sacrificed Himself for mankind. God's incarnation in Jesus, therefore, means finishing with the religion of violence, whose transcendent God has

been sacrificed to man and may now be found manifested in the church as well as in the papacy itself. This is certainly a striking argument to make, though it does not at any point leave the closed circle of Roman Catholic doctrine, which means that the only form of dialogue it initiates is a proselytizing one.

Yet by criticizing Muslim and Protestant attempts to recover the moral transcendence of Judaism's heritage, as signified in the story of Abraham's willingness to sacrifice his son at the command of an unknown God, the pontiff was also asking Christian Europe to remain true to its own past. And this Hellenistic past, the Pope well knew, was common to Judaism and Islam as much as it was to Christianity. Indeed this largely pagan heritage could be possessed by none of these religions because it was external to all three, and even to Europe itself within its current geographical boundaries. Might the pontiff's speech be heard as an invitation for Europe to contribute her own history to the dialogue of faith and reason, one in which all Europeans, however defined, could participate? Perhaps this is too charitable a reading, but whatever the case, his boldness in turning to Europe's pagan past requires more attention than has been given the pontiff's address even by his staunchest supporters. In yet another irony, then, the only people to acknowledge the Pope's radical agenda and even take it seriously were its Muslim detractors, whom Benedict XVI had to thank for the unprecedented interest that his speech evoked among Roman Catholics themselves, though it was clear that they were neither to be aroused nor united in the Pope's name as Muslims were in that of their Prophet. The impotence concealed by the Vatican's silence at the doings of Nazi Germany was here made evident to all, even if dressed up in the garb of tolerance and civilization.

Was it then the secularism of his own flock that prompted the pontiff to retract his denial of Abraham's sacrifice by invoking this very prophet in responding to Muslim protest? Mentioning Abraham as the common ancestor of Arabs and Jews, as well as the common patriarch of all three monotheisms, Benedict XVI lapsed back into one of the great clichés of interfaith dialogue, whose latitudinarian ways he professes to dislike. Moreover the God of the so-called Abrahamic religions is precisely the God of Abraham and Isaac, whose sacrificial transcendence the Pope had already rejected. Far from constituting the benign community of interfaith dialogue, in other words, the kinship of the three monotheisms is based on Abraham's violation and sacrifice of kinship itself. For if anything, the story of Abraham and Isaac tells us that there is no violence greater than that of kinship, and that violence is itself a form of kinship in the physical and emotional intimacy it makes possible between enemies. The task of interfaith dialogue, as the Pope himself might agree, is not merely to recognize kinship but instead to deal with its violent consequences. In any case the Abrahamic kinship of monotheistic religions is of less historical importance for Islam than it is for Judaism and Christianity. While Europe and the Middle East might well have functioned as monotheistic cloisters, the vast bulk of the Muslim world has historically bordered not Jewish or Christian societies but Hindu, Buddhist and Zoroastrian ones. For the overwhelming majority of Muslims, therefore, Christians and Jews were mythical kin who have only achieved some reality through colonialism and migration.

The universal interconnectedness that globalization makes possible means that the dialogue called for by the Pope has already begun. But despite the fact that it has the whole world as its stage, this dialogue possesses no space of its own, for being global in dimension it can be conducted neither in the seminary nor the madrassa, to say nothing of the university. This is also a dialogue that finds no place in the national and international politics of our time. So it occurs on the street and in the media, in demonstrations and soundbites rather than in treatises and contracts. It is easy to find examples of such dialogue outside Europe, where this controversy had received some of its most acute analysis. Indian and Pakistani Muslims, for example, were prominent by their presence in the global protests against the Pope. And while both countries have a long record of contributing to international Islamic causes, this is by no means a uniform phenomenon. Pakistani Muslims, for instance, entered the Danish cartoon protests very late in the day, and certainly much after their Indian neighbours had lost interest in them. On the other hand the latter have never joined the global jihad movements that preoccupy Pakistani militants in any significant way. Both countries have a history of anti-Christian feeling, though in India it is Hindu militants who are involved in attacks on this minority. In both countries, moreover, it is mostly Protestant Evangelicals in rural areas, both missionaries and converts, who come under fire, and not the long-established Catholic communities who live in urban settings.

Missionary activity and licentiousness are generally the causes, actual or ostensible, of prejudice or violence against Christians in India and Pakistan, though even on these grounds they are targeted far less than other religious groups, mostly Muslims of one sort or another. In the immediate aftermath of the Danish cartoon protests, Catholics around the world, but especially in India and Pakistan, began their own much more peaceable demonstrations against the showing of a Hollywood film called *The Da Vinci Code*, which retold Christian history by claiming that Jesus and Mary Magdalene had married and produced a line of descendants who survive to this day. The villain of the piece is the Roman Catholic Church, which according to the film has spent more then two millennia tracking down and killing Christ's descendants.

These Catholic demonstrations were clearly and explicitly inspired by Muslim protests over the Danish cartoons, in a startling illustration of how Islam has come to occupy the language of faith globally. Like Muslim as well as Hindu protests in the subcontinent, Catholic demonstrations expressed themselves using the secular vocabulary of hurt, making no claims to the religious veracity of their feelings. What is more, these demonstrations were joined by numbers of Muslims in both countries, with prominent Muslim clerics rallying their followers to support a cause they saw as being foreign to themselves. This support, in other words, was premised not on the fact that Muslims, too, were offended by the film's portrayal of Jesus, who is one of Islam's prophets, but on their sympathy for the hurt felt by their Christians compatriots. This form of support is not at all unusual in the subcontinent, despite the routine forms of religious violence to be found there, for whether they are granted it or not, such sympathy is just as routinely invoked by Hindu or Muslim groups making their own demands. These demands are voiced in ethical rather than juridical terms, being widely understood and appreciated as such.

While it was obvious that the Muslims who supported Catholic protesters in India and Pakistan, often against their own governments, did so for a complex set of reasons that might have included the assertion as much as the abnegation of self-interest, it is also true that in doing so they participated in a dialogue with their Christian neighbours. One part of this dialogue was to show that unlike many Christians in the West, who had refused to acknowledge Muslim hurt during the cartoon controversy, they were entirely capable of sympathizing with the followers of other religions. In the end the offending film was banned in Pakistan as well as in a number of Indian states, without, it seems, endangering freedom of speech more generally. Abstract rights were sacrificed to concrete feelings in a way that was constitutionally troubling while being ethical at the same time.

Indeed ethical considerations were paramount in the film's banning, since Christians in the subcontinent are a minority so small as to be incapable of compelling their governments to do anything by putting pressure upon them. In other words it is precisely the relative insignificance of Christians in India and Pakistan that made these countries' capitulation to their demands so significant. For banning or censoring *The Da Vinci Code* was clearly an act of principle rather than the result of pressure, and as such it worked to redeem the far more controversial concessions that Pakistan and India make to more important religious groups like Hindus or Muslims. However good or bad such concessions may be on constitutional grounds, those made to Christians in particular permit social life in the subcontinent to be marked by an explicitly ethical instead of a merely juridical character. And this is only possible because of the presence of minorities in these societies.

None of this meant, of course, that Christians and Muslims during the *Da Vinci Code* controversy had suddenly become allies or even friends, only that a kind of dialogue made up of media statements and spectacles had been set in motion between them. So when the Pope became a target for Muslim ire, Catholics in India and Pakistan had to tread very carefully. However they responded in exactly the ethical way that was demanded of them, though I do not mean by this that Roman Catholics apologized to Muslims out of fear. In India at least, where there is no history of Muslim–Christian violence, the pontiff's flock announced its determination to endure the consequences of the controversy with fortitude, blaming neither Pope nor Prophet for their travails. Did not this expression of Christian spirit illustrate in the most striking way the unity of faith and reason that Benedict XVI had called for?

NOTES

1 There were a few exceptions to this rule, among the most interesting being an analysis of *The Satanic Verses* by Iran's minister of culture. See Sayyid Ataullah Mohajerani, *Naqd-e Tuteyeh-e Ayat-e Shaytani*. Tehran: Entesharat-e Ettela'at, p. 1378.

2 'Ayman Al-Zawahiri reacts to Bush, Pope; urges Muslims to support mujahidin.' Available at: http://www.centcom.mil/sites/uscentcom1/What%20Extremists%20Say/Ayman%20Al-Zawahiri%20Reacts%20to%20Bush,%20Pope;%20Urges%20Muslims%20to%20Support%20Mujahidin.aspx?PageView=Shared

REFERENCES

Arendt, H. (2003) '*The Deputy*: guilt by silence?' in *Responsibility and Judgement*. New York: Schocken Books, pp. 214–226.

Devji, F. (2005) *Landscapes of the Jihad: Militancy, Morality, Modernity*. London: Hurst.

Devji, F. (2006) 'Back to the future: the cartoons, liberalism, and global Islam'. Open Democracy. Available at: http://www.openemocracy.net/conflict-terrorism/liberalism_3451.jsp.

Khomeini, I. (1981) 'Address to Monsignor Bugnini, Papal Nuncio' in *Islam and Revolution: Writings and Declarations of Imam Khomeini*, Vol. 1 (translated and annotated by H. Algar). Berkeley, CA: Mizan Press, pp. 78–85.

Rushdie, S. (1988) *The Satanic Verses*. London: Viking Penguin.

35

Cosmopolitan Europe and European Studies

Craig Calhoun

Europe is an object of aspirations – and anxieties – on the European continent. It is as exciting and controversial in Britain. And it is also an object of global interest. At the moment, each of these is focused largely on the notion of a more cosmopolitan Europe. This idea of cosmopolitan Europe is developed in a range of academic analyses. But it is rooted in an amalgam of three different sets of intellectual and popular images.

Europe has long been seen as sophisticated, worldly wise, the continent of independent cinema *auteurs* and profound philosophers, Gaulloises cigarettes, Italian suits, and German music. This continues. Cosmopolitanism is in considerable part a name for sophistication. The cocktail is actually an American invention, but the sensibility has a European copyright. Of course, Europeans exemplified this sophistication not just on the continent, but in their colonial outposts, writing and drinking at Raffles in Singapore, playing dangerous sexual games in Alexandria; painting and partying in Morocco. It is the Europe, American, Irish, and British artists and writers sought to experience between the wars. It is the decadence

that informed their accounts. But this is also a key aspect of Europe that joined elites (even while the connections of ordinary folk remained more often national). It is the Europe of which Paris was the nineteenth-century capital for Benjamin, and which seemed only more sophisticated in the twentieth century as war gave it an air of tragedy and then existentialist melancholy. This image of sophisticated Europe persists, reinforced by contrasts between French presidents with mistresses and American presidents who pray. But it has to be said English seems more and more cool in some sophisticated European quarters, partly because business has a new glamour and partly because of global media. And the English doesn't all come from England (or even Ireland).

Europe is newly exciting because of the project of integration. This is one of the most important political experiments undertaken anywhere in the last half century. Just as Europe was pivotal to imagining the nation state as the primary unit of politics from the seventeenth century forward – and making this substantially if imperfectly so – it is now pivotal to discussions of whether the nation state can be transcended. The nation state sometimes seems inherited from time immemorial, but it is really a project of the last 350 years. And it has been a project of integration at least as much as division, probably more. This is hard to remember with its history marked so heavily by warfare (not to mention genocide and ethnic cleansing). But national integration – albeit always imperfect – was also a condition of Europe's achievement of the modern welfare state and closely tied to the development of capitalism. So from the first steps of economic community to proposals to integrate the European Union still further, Europeans have embarked on transforming but continuing a long-term integration, not overcoming nearly natural ethnolinguistic or political divisions. And the basic questions about European integration are not merely whether nation states can be transcended and what sorts of identities they retain within a union, but precisely the same questions that were basic for nation states before: will the structures of integration radically privilege capital or will inequality and accumulation be tempered by redistribution, high levels of public service, and strong rights for labor? Will liberal democracy provide wide enough participation and benefits to maintain a social peace or will there be disenfranchisement and discontent severe enough to nurture revolutionary movements or insurgent violence? As old elites struggle to maintain their power and to do so incorporate some new elites, will they resort to mechanisms of policing and social control that make contentious politics (and perhaps progressive change) much harder and riskier?

Not least, Europe is at the center of imagining (and sometimes trying to act on) a cosmopolitan understanding of the world as a whole and itself as part. This is mostly an ethical perspective, rooted in Europe's old traditions of philosophical and religious universalism. It offers a hint of transcendence to a continent many think of (perhaps misleadingly) as postreligious. This is the European cosmopolitanism that informs high levels of foreign assistance and enthusiasm for careers in human rights advocacy and humanitarian action. It is shaped by a sense of being in a global as well as a continental community of fate – notably in regard to looming environmental catastrophe. It also informed some of the European opposition to American-led war in Iraq (though perhaps not as much of the popular opposition as elite commentators assumed, since there were a variety of reasons to think that invasion was a bad idea). It informs European efforts to work through or in cooperation with the United Nations. And in more academic settings, this cosmopolitanism informs an effort to grasp global political challenges in terms rooted in terms of ethical universalism. Intertwined with this universalistic stance on global ethics is an effort to think through the diversity globalization has brought to Europe itself. Being a part of the globe is not (as at least some Europeans may wish) simply a matter of relations to people off the continent. Europeans have had to recognize that global diversity is an internal European matter – and cosmopolitan arguments have been posed to address this in similar ways. But this is full of ambiguities, for universalism and embrace of diversity do not automatically go together. Yet 'people of color' (other than white) and 'people of religion' (including especially Muslims) are now integrally a part of Europe – even if they remind some Europeans of the 'others' Europe used to be defined against.

COSMOPOLITAN EUROPEAN STUDIES

European studies has never been simply a field of European self-study. It has been importantly shaped by views from Europe's periphery – notably Britain – and Europe's former colonies. That pattern is partially reproduced in the present volume. Most authors are British; Americans outnumber continental Europeans. This is partly a fluke of language, of course, but not entirely. It is also a reflection of some of the 'knowledge-forming interests' constitutive of European studies.

European studies was also shaped by continental European engagements in self-understanding. These were always also matters of self-creation. Catholic Christendom's networks of priestly knowledge and early universities shaped an idea of Latinate Europe. This influenced not only religious identity but political legitimacy, and the two together informed the Crusades as a pan-European project. The Crusades were also pivotal in a history of defining Europe by its others, including not only Islam but Orthodox Christianity. The Protestant Reformation contested Catholicism but also convulsed Europe's politics, though along with catastrophic conflicts it also brought a new level of popular involvement in politics. Symbolized by vernacular Bibles, this also brought discussion of both transnationally European and national identities.

Of course, the Reformation also brought war (though not without other influences). Growing literacy and new religious engagement mobilized citizens in new ways. Religious differentiation challenged the maintenance of political integration. Some princes saw opportunities in defying the Pope, others in challenging the heresies of the first group. And the polities involved were highly heterogeneous, from tiny German principalities and electorates to massive transnational empires. Indeed, the 1648 Congress of Westphalia ended not only wars of religion but wars over the place of empire as a form of European integration. Even more consequentially, perhaps, it marked the marginalization of the transnational Catholic institutions and diplomatic missions that had previously been prominent. Before the Reformation, after all, it had been Church institutions above all that connected different parts of Europe. At the Congress of Westphalia, the parties accepted a definition of secular political authority that excluded these institutions, emphasizing instead the singularity of sovereignty over each territory.

The Treaty of Westphalia was among other things pivotal to a series of efforts to construct a European peace based on agreement among rulers – and a conviction that at least in principle rulers reflected nationally defined and legitimated states. Nation-building was itself transnational as all European countries took on a common approach to identity and political legitimacy. Universities and educational systems more broadly became a prominent feature of this transnational model of nation-building. Each engaged, among other things, in situating a national self-understanding in relation to the larger web of European self-understandings. Prominently, each involved claims to Europe's classical heritage – the grandeur that was Greece and the glory that was Rome as symbolic resources for eighteenth and nineteenth century France and Germany, for example. And each engaged European Christendom, and Europe's histories of conflicts and connections.

In this context, European studies grew as nationally differentiated engagements with a partially common ideals and history. But it might not have gained so strong a sense of European identity without racial, religious, and imperial distinctions from global others. For European empires expanded at the same time that European states integrated. Europeans established colonial universities and secondary schools. In these – and well beyond them – they both taught aspects of the European intellectual tradition and formed an account of Europeanness. This was sometimes tacitly, sometimes explicitly racial. The development of the category of the métis, for example, was racial not national but the construction of whiteness was European. The point is not simply that Europe was racist; it is, rather, that this specific form of racism was produced in significant part by intellectual work – the work of anthropologists, doctors, and lawyers (Saada, 2007). And if this intellectual work was informed first and foremost by inquiry into the biology and culture of those dominated by colonialism it was also informed by reflection on Europeanness.

As important as the demarcation of Europeans from 'natives' was the construction of a common identity among Europeans and people of European descent. This was prominent in trading cities and in the 'gentle-manly' relations prevailing among Europeans in colonies – even when their home countries were at war. Above all, it was a crucial feature of many immigrant societies. As Tom Paine wrote, 'Europe, not England is the parent country of America.' And of course Tom Paine was not simply an American but also an Englishman and at least an honorific Frenchman. In usage, such as, Paine's, Europe appeared as a source of high cultural resources to be claimed by Americans and to be claimed as a common inheritance, across class lines by upwardly mobile autodidacts such as himself as well as across national lines. Partly racial, partly civilizational, this was different from the mainly national identities dominant on the European continent.

In the English-language world, British imperial dominance shaped European studies (and America's rising power shaped it further). The ambiguous relationship of island Britain to continental Europe was long-standing. It was at once able to maintain a discrete sense of itself that projected Europe as 'over there' and ruled by a succession of continental European monarchs. Britishness was always constructed in relationship to the continent as well as to other specific nations (and of course the colonies). And as a trading, seafaring power, Britain was also a mediator among Europeans and between Europeans and others. But above all, as the dominant world power in the late eighteenth and nineteenth centuries, Britain situated its self-understanding in relation to Europe on the one hand and the rest of the world on the other.

Colonies also posed the challenge of teaching European civilization – to the colonized, of course, but equally to the colonizers. As has been remarked recently (but not always recognized), for example, the first chair of English was in India. In contexts like India, Europeans needed to learn how to understand and reproduce civilizational identities that were less problematic at home. In a different way, this was also an issue for settler colonies,

like Australia, where the production of Europeanness was both a claim to connection with 'mother countries' – not just Britain but a range of societies sent migrants – and like whiteness a bond among occupiers. I will discuss the American example but it is hardly the only one.

AMERICA'S EUROPE

America played a distinctive role in the production of Europe (and European studies). All the settler colonies – Australia, New Zealand, and South Africa, among others – had special relationships with Europe. In most cases, though, this was strongly a relationship to particular European nation states (even if, as in South Africa, two in succession). In Canada, Britain and France were distinct poles of identity; other Europeans were relatively marginal. But in the US the colonial tie was severed earlier than in other settler colonies and nineteenth-century immigration was diversely multinational, though overwhelmingly European.

Different immigrant groups maintained strong ties to European homelands, constructing 'hyphenated' identities, and the WASP elite remained Anglophile. Nonetheless, as the higher educational system developed it produced a distinctive preliminary education in European high culture. 'Western civilization' was constructed out of a mix of classical antiquity, European history, and great works of modern European thought, art, and literature. Europe anchored an Atlantic civilization as well as a broader occidental one (see in general Bailyn, 2005, and specifically on the black Atlantic, Gilroy, 1993).

Much of the intellectual background lay in the close relationship between eighteenth- and nineteenth-century European thought and classical antiquity. Europeans simultaneously celebrated the glory that was Greece, the grandeur that was Rome, and the sense that they were progressing beyond bounds the ancients had never breeched, at least in some fields. John Stuart Mill's fiercely modernizing father taught him Latin and Greek almost as soon as he could walk. Thinkers like Tocqueville, Hegel and indeed Marx all exemplified the nineteenth century's simultaneous appreciation of the ancients and desire for progress. These thinkers were required reading for elites in nearly every European country (and indeed for many working class autodidacts). These participated in a common European intellectual world, though most were always intensely conscious of national differences as well. They engaged each other and drew on a common 'conversation' with the ancients. But it was a distinctive feature of American universities and colleges not only to demand grounding in the classics, but to marry this to systematic and cross-national teaching of European 'culture'.

Even as American universities and colleges gradually gave up the classical curriculum after the 1870s, they continued to embrace aspects of it – rethought as the roots of European civilization. And even as they took up the curricular structure of the 'major' patterned after the research fields of the PhD degree (itself a European, specifically German, import), they continued to consecrate the study of Western civilization as a necessary preliminary. Indeed, this was in part the homage paid to classics, history, and philosophy when the curriculum was redesigned to emphasize the sciences (including social sciences). And it is significant how little American thought or history the Western civilization courses incorporated, how much they remained European until their 1960s crisis.

But though the consecration of European studies as the necessary foundation for higher education ensured it a place, it also tended to ossify it. This quickly became a course that everyone had taken – and thought their descendants should take in the same form. At its most trivial, it was the canonical course that prepared gentlemen to make appropriate allusions in after-dinner speeches and political debates. Even when developed with the most depth and thought, though, it remained

rooted in appreciation for the heritage of a seemingly already established tradition rather than the production of new knowledge. It was also an introduction to an enormously broad range of thought, cultural production, and history and thus did not reflect any specific field. Growing specialization in academia reduced its connection to current scholarship. With the rise of analytic philosophy, for example, philosophers tended increasingly to withdraw from teaching Western civilization (or even the history of European philosophy; their lower-level undergraduate teaching centered more on courses like logic, each abstracted from attention to any particular cultural context). Historians continued to teach Western civilization, and some, especially intellectual historians, continued to champion the course and the intellectual tradition it reflected. Textbook authors and teachers tried to draw in the results of new research and intellectual perspectives. But while the Western civilization approach remained prominent background, the twentieth century saw the rise of a new perspective centered in social science.

The new social science disciplines all claimed European roots and their early American leaders appropriated European theoretical foundations. Some were immigrants and others studied in Europe. If social Darwinism was an American invention, it nonetheless clearly built on Spencer and Darwin. From Boas to DuBois, Sorokin to Parsons, Schumpeter to Veblen, social scientists were engaged in a transatlantic conversation. But social science was engaged not only in the appropriation of disciplinary identities and histories; it was engaged in the production of new knowledge and new intellectual orientations. Indeed, the transformation of social philosophy into empirical research agendas – often linked to social reform – was especially prominent in the US.

The distinctiveness of the US from Europe was a prominent topic. Many American economists and political scientists were keen to stress the distinctiveness of American institutions but attention to European ones was basic to the comparison. Sociologists sought to understand European immigrants to the US by looking at their social and cultural contexts on each side of the Atlantic. And if the field of comparative politics would eventually attend broadly to states around the world, it grew out of the comparisons of European states to each other and Europe to America – as for example in Gabriel Almond's and Sidney Verba's famous studies of civic culture (1963). Much the same was true more generally for the research on 'modernization' so influential in the postwar era. Though this became mainly an approach to studying the less developed world, its base lay in historical studies of development in Europe. See, for example, the classic volume edited by Charles Tilly, *The Formation of National States in Western Europe*. This was the capstone to the remarkably influential series of books sponsored by the Committee on Comparative Politics of the Social Science Research Council – one of the centers of 'modernization theory'. In his foreword, Lucien Pye described it as a 'return to Europe'. After the committee's more than 20 years of exploring political change in the developing world, it turned its attention back to the continent that yielded that very contrast of developed and developing.

DECENTERED EUROPE

In many of these studies, Europe became something of an unmarked category, simply 'the modern'. This would set the stage for later critiques and efforts to 'provincialize Europe', to borrow a phrase from Dipesh Chakrabarty (2000). More generally, social scientists struggled to disengage the specifically European from putatively more universal accounts. While some would focus on the critique of 'Eurocentrism' others (including many of the authors in Tilly, 1975) would emphasize that the canonical accounts did not do justice to Europe either, and needed to be revised on the basis of new research.

Attention to the colonial and postcolonial world also offered another kind of challenge to the conventional approach to Europe. If the critique of Eurocentrism emphasized the fallacy of treating Europe as the world, this second critique emphasized the fallacy of treating European identity, culture, and politics as internal developments of Europe itself. Rather, new work stressed, European ventures outside of Europe made and remade the notion of Europe itself. This was already an important issue in the era of the Crusades and the recovery of Greek classics by way of Arab scholars. It became still more important in the context of voyages of exploration, the development of colonial empires, migrations, and global capitalism.

European self-understanding was heavily shaped by the rise of nationalism and especially the nineteenth-century organization of academic history as national history. While nationalist imaginaries recognized the situation of each nation amid a cluster of comparable others, they encouraged an account of the sources of each as essentially internal. This tended to obscure the nature of conquest and immigration and also early projects of 'ethnic cleansing'. The famous 1066 invasion of England, thus, involved Normans – only ambiguously 'French' – and the English, who were hardly ethnically homogeneous. Yet the Normans became a part of English history and culture, not simply foreign to it (Anderson, 1991). Indeed, only a few years before the Battle of Hastings, England's King Ethelred (wonderfully known as 'the unredy' or more politely 'the ill-advised') had issued a proclamation ordering all Danes out of his kingdom; many who had resided in Oxford were killed in the St. Frideswide's Massacre (which the king found just and honorable, even though it involved the murder of men, women, and children who had taken refuge in the sanctuary of a church). Similar events took place in all European countries, partially undoing earlier mixtures but also creating new ones. The repression of Muslims and Jews in Spain is perhaps the most dramatic early modern case, but obviously the complicated project and horrific results have continued throughout the modern era, afflicting different countries at different times.

This restructuring of European ideas of who belongs where involved a construction of Europe as a collection of nations with putatively rightful claims to specific territories and governed by discretely sovereign states. This was the Westphalian model of 1648 – though it named a project only partly realized over the next 300 years, not an actual fact. In any case, the idea of a Europe of the nations is not simply a new way of thinking about European integration in the context of the EU. It is a renewal of an old – but for the most part modern – understanding of Europe. This built on earlier use of 'nations' as a term for people of different culture, language, and descent, but the older 'nations' represented for example in medieval universities and church assemblies (e.g. Lombardy, Piedmont) were not constructed as integral political units and do not map neatly on the new state order. They suggested the residues of vernacular differences within the common culture of Latinate Christendom, but not the construction of peoples putatively bound together by history and culture and constituting the bases for evaluating the legitimacy of states. This older meaning was transformed as nations were associated with states and states produced more coherent internal communication, institutions, and administration. Scholars produced accounts of ostensibly national history, writers and critics produced national literatures, and so forth. If the histories and cultural claims were more integral than simple empirical reality justified, European nations were nonetheless structures for integrating populations across lines of difference – regional, ethnic, religious and sometimes class. This new notion gave Europe clear standing as a location in the world, as constituted internally by symmetrical but discrete states. These were sometimes at war but nonetheless distinctive as a group. And in their colonies, Europeans knew each other both as members of the same racialized dominant group, and as

citizens of different European states – and their legal systems commonly provided distinctively for other Europeans.

This new notion also implied the self-production of Europe (just as it did the self-production of each nation within Europe). And thus it suggested the treatment of exploration, colonization, and globalization of markets as something active Europeans did to the passive rest of the world. Much can be (and has been) said about this, but the point I want to make here is that much of the production of modern Europe has involved borrowings and appropriations from non-European sources – from Arabic numerals, to South Asian pajamas, and Chinese habits of cleaning teeth. Moreover, much of the production of modern Europe comes specifically from the colonial venture. Techniques of European state-making were developed in colonial administration and extended into the domestic affairs of national states. The rise of standing armies as part of the conquest and domination of colonies became also a part of domestic life and both in military service and in its representation in the media a source of some integration among different localities within nations. The rise of capitalism and modern industry was not simply a discrete event within Europe but an event in the relationship of Europe to international trade.

Not least of all, the cultural traditions of Europe were enriched by production from outside the European homelands and metropolitan centers. Predictably, this is most true for French, Spanish, Portuguese and English, made world languages partly by colonial projects. Paris is a center for world music and French a vital language for African literature (even as it otherwise declines as a *lingua franca*). Latin American literary production now outstrips Iberian in fame and vitality. Prominent exemplars of English literature and drama have come surprisingly often from Ireland, from colonial outposts in Asia, and even from those for whom English is a second language. From Joyce and Beckett to Stoppard, Rushdie, and Achebe, English literature is far more than the product of native

English authors. Some of this is simply writing elsewhere in originally European languages, but most of it is also an enrichment and transformation of literary traditions initially more narrowly European. And it has wrought transformation as well in humanities fields focused on European studies.

CHANGING CONCEPTUALIZATIONS

The conceptualization of Europe has shifted over time. From centering on the notion of Western Christendom (vis-à-vis Eastern Orthodoxy as well as Islam) it reflected increasingly a field of competition among strengthening states (as well as the continent that housed the metropoles of competing empires). Though migrations, long-distance trade, and cultural flows characterized Europe from ancient times, the rewriting of European history in terms of the nation state emphasized the internal production of each country and a notion of Europe as the aggregate of these ostensible separate processes. At the same time, claims to the common inheritance of classical antiquity reinforced a sense of commonalty among Europeans, especially elites. And projects of modernization reflected a commonality within the competitive project: the partially shared vision (and stakes) of modernization, prosperity, and political legitimacy. These intertwined stories provided the main framework for the conceptualization of Europe in relation to lands beyond the Austro-Hungarian Empire as well as those around the world. Though deeply challenged by the twentieth century world wars they were not completely dislodged. Indeed, they were renewed in the years of reconstruction after World War II with their development of modern welfare states – *Les Trente Glorieuse* as the French call them. The period from 1945 to 1973 was the 'Golden Age of Western Europe' according to Eric Hobsbawm (1993). Europe suggested a Western model distinct from America as well as the communist past.

Even projects that reached beyond this framework – like colonialism and migration and eventually the European Union – were largely addressed in ways that reproduced it. The story of migration to America, for example, was analyzed as a story of modernization that brought some Europeans to a new country where their old national and religious traditions bore new fruit. It was sometimes a morality tale suggesting that Europe needed to modernize more, sometimes one that stressed the importance of claims to European heritage for American status groups. But it was not taken until recently as a basis for problematizing the very idea of Europe.

In the late twentieth century, the study of Europe was revitalized and the traditional idea(s) of Europe rethought. One impetus came from the perspective of 'postcolonies' trying to establish the meaning of Europe in their histories. Another came from efforts to reconsider the entanglement of Europe with ideas of civilization and progress. This was shaped notably by efforts to come to terms with the Holocaust and the twentieth century's legacy of wars. It was also influenced by a range of social movements that generated interests in 'identities' and 'differences' – gender and ethnicity among others – that had been subordinated in the dominant accounts of European history (and indeed, contemporary politics, culture, and social life). Not least, the construction of welfare states seemed a culmination of many modern European ideas, projects, and struggles. Though these provided enormous benefits they also generated new and largely unexpected dissatisfactions. 'New social movements' reflected some of these. Indeed, the idea of new social movements was distinctively European in both provenance and reference (though appropriated occasionally for studies elsewhere). It reflected a sense of the end of the great social democratic narrative of the integration of different social needs in a single overarching movement and the development of welfare states in response (see, for example, Melucci, 1989). Finally, the project of European Union generated both growing interest in itself and a new interest in conceptualizing Europe. This was both part of an analytic project as researchers sought to understand what was happening in Europe, and part of an ideological–pedagogical project as some European leaders sought to teach students a European self-understanding supportive of the EU (and particular visions of the EU).

EU-CENTERED EUROPE

After 1989, European integration was both strengthened and challenged. At the institutional (or 'functional') level, a host of new projects and connections knit Europeans of different nationalities more closely together. Opening of interior borders and the introduction of the euro were perhaps most prominent. A long economic boom stimulated trade and consolidation of enterprises (including some media). But at the same time, migration to Europe from less developed countries grew and became more of a public issue. Some of the less developed countries were in Eastern Europe and these produced their own migrants (as Southern Europe had earlier) and then candidates for enlargement of the Union.

In the 1990s, the EU approached some of the challenges with an effort to constitute a new common understanding of Europe. Projects ranged from rewriting history books to sponsoring academic linkages among European countries to funding centers for 'EU studies' in America and elsewhere.

During the 1990s, 'cosmopolitanism' became a more and more important dimension of European self-understanding. Sources for this ranged from sociological theories of 'reflexive modernization' to growing emphasis on the development of international law to renewal of mostly neo-Kantian ethical universalism to the prominence of human rights activism and humanitarian assistance. Europe was in the forefront of all of these. And each informed understanding of a distinctively European role in the world.

Indeed, most of these various different sorts of 'cosmopolitan' concerns and theories applied in principle to the world as a whole. But they were not only developed disproportionately in Europe; Europe was also understood as a primary example (e.g. Beck and Grande, 2006; Rumford, 2007). Britain perhaps led the way in applying the term 'cosmopolitanism' itself, but a range of Europeans participated in this as in all the others and each flourished more in Europe than in most other regions. There are large academic literatures associated with each of these. Cosmopolitanism became part of European self-understanding.

Humanitarian assistance is indicative. There was an old history: the Red Cross was a European invention. In the wake of the 1960s disillusionment with more direct political engagement, Médecins sans Frontiers (MSF) became the most influential of a new range of humanitarian organizations which combined service with an implicit political challenge in the form of witness to the world's atrocities. The European Community Humanitarian Aid Department (ECHO) was founded in 1992 and quickly became very influential. The EU came by the end of the decade to account for about half of all global humanitarian assistance. Not only the EU but European national donors were prominent, both in total amounts of financing and in pioneering a 'good donor' initiative. European youth flocked to work in humanitarian assistance.

International humanitarian assistance was understood as a distinctively ethical way of engaging problems in the larger world – different from what many Europeans understood as the hegemonic stance of the US. It reflected not only personal ethics, but a sense that Europe itself was particularly ethical. This was of a piece the idea of reflexive modernization as well as the spread of neo-Kantian ethics. It fit with the notion of a Europe that since World War II and the Holocaust had taken special pains not only to produce peace but to learn from and correct for previous moral failings (some associated with nationalism).

This dovetailed with European abolition of the death penalty. Jean-Pierre Faye offered this as a defining motto: 'Europe is where there is no death penalty' (quoted in Savater, 2005: 43). It simultaneously marked an ethical stance and an understanding of this ethical stance as a measure of being 'more civilized' (*pace* Adolf Muschg, 2005: 24, who equated the achievements of Western Europe with a 'civilizing of politics').

It is typical to date this European divergence from the US to the invasion of Iraq in 2003. This certainly sharpened the split dramatically – and made it a source of division within the EU – but it didn't create it. This is a reminder, among other things, that the divergence is not an artifact of the Bush administration which has sometimes symbolized and often exacerbated it. Indeed, the growing divergence from the US was publicly prominent in widespread public concern over the US vote against the 1998 Rome Statute that would authorize the International Criminal Court. The US seemed often to argue for a 'realist' foreign policy focused simply on its national interests while Europeans (if not always the EU as such or all national governments) called for an 'idealist' engagement with values and higher purposes.

Another arena in which this was particularly pronounced was thinking about the environment. Ulrich Beck's notion of a world risk society – a society in which a sense of collective risks was pivotal for self-consciousness and attempts at collective action – reflected a widespread European sense of being in a community of fate (Beck, 1992, 1997; Giddens, 1990). And fate looked far too likely to be set by environmental catastrophe. Other possible collective risks – from genetically modified foods to nuclear meltdowns – seemed also especially to galvanize European attention. Some of these seemed open to national or continental solutions but many were necessarily global. So again, a growing dimension of European self-awareness was that of being situated in a problematic world.

At the same time, the EU struggled to develop a foreign policy – notably with regard to the breakup of Yugoslavia and eventual military involvements there. The cosmopolitan orientation that informed humanitarian assistance and environmental consciousness was less help here. On the one hand, some European national governments helped to hasten the dissolution of Yugoslavia by a surprising rush to recognize secessionist states. On the other hand, the wars that followed were troubling on many dimensions. At the simplest, they involved the first wars on European soil in decades. Second, ethnic cleansing made them reminiscent of some of the horrors of the Holocaust. Third, under NATO auspices, EU member states – including Germany – were called to send militaries into combat.

The 2001 attacks on the US and subsequent attacks in Britain and Spain heightened security concerns and provoked a dramatic reorientation of foreign policy. Most immediately, they resulted in war in Afghanistan. European troops were prominent and members of national militaries were this time sent explicitly in the name of the EU. In January 2001 the EU and NATO had already begun a 'strategic partnership' but now this was put to new tests.

Perhaps most influentially the terrorist attacks focused the already growing European anxiety about immigrants, and about Muslims in particular. Controversy over Muslim immigrants became a widespread theme in European politics and public debates. On the one hand there were fears over security, cultural identity, and economic competition. On the other hand there were accusations that government policies were creating a 'Fortress Europe'. The prominence of the immigration issue continued into academic European studies where it was perhaps the dominant topic (both on its own and linked to broader questions about the development of 'postnational citizenship'). It was remarkable to what extent academics took the immigration issue as simply a matter of clashes between cultural difference and universalistic ethics, without for example very much critical attention to issues like the aging and low birth rate of European populations that helped to ensure jobs for migrants.

But the reframing also had a further effect, presenting the issue of immigration as also a question about the place of religion on a largely secular continent. Neither public nor policy makers were prepared. Nor were academic experts on Europe, most of whom subscribed uncritically to an understanding of secularization as inevitable in modernity and a matter of simple decline and the subtraction of religion out of public life (Taylor, 2007). Moreover, this question coincided with the fact that some of the new members of the EU were dramatically more religious – and publicly invested in religion – than was normative among the old members. Poland was the main symbolic example.

These concerns came to a head with the drafting of a proposed Basic Law for the EU. Popularly dubbed a 'constitution' this was subject to widespread controversy. Not the least controversial were proposals backed by German, Italian, Polish, and Slovakian delegates to add mention of 'God' and Europe's Christian heritage. But the aristocratic leadership of former French president Valéry Giscard d'Estaing was almost as controversial.

In all of these dimensions, academic studies of Europe and academic participation in public debates about the nature and identity of Europe was prominent. This was perhaps most sharply focused in 2003 after the US led a coalition including Britain, Spain and some 'new European' countries into war in Iraq. Protests were widespread in Europe. Somewhat surprisingly, Jürgen Habermas (in an essay co-signed by Jacques Derrida and published simultaneously in German and French) suggested that 'The simultaneity of these overwhelming demonstrations – the largest since the end of the Second World War – may well, in hindsight, go down in history as a sign of the birth of a European public sphere' (Habermas and Derrida, 2005: 4). As Levy *et al.* (2005) point out, Habermas's claim echoed Dominique Strauss-Kahn's assertion that 'On Saturday, February 15, 2003, a nation was born on the streets. This nation is

the European nation'. It is no accident, of course, that where Strauss-Kahn saw a nation Habermas saw a public sphere. The idea that Europe is becoming a nation (or national state) is still nearly taboo among academic Europeanists – though it is an entirely plausible argument. And in any case, for Habermas the idea of nation is associated too indelibly with bad nationalism of the past.

Habermas and many others responded specifically to the failure of Europe to develop a common foreign policy. The American Secretary of Defense followed on various American academics in making an invidious distinction between 'new' and 'old' Europe. To respond effectively would require a level of cohesion the EU had not achieved. The EU was easily incapacitated in controversial but important matters, Habermas (2006) argued, because of old assumptions that EU affairs were entirely matters for interstate negotiation and especially that a minority of states should be able to exercise a veto over policies desired by a majority. And here Habermas was prepared to go beyond his previous advocacy of mere 'constitutional patriotism' to call for a more substantive European identity. 'A transformative politics, which would demand that member states not just overcome obstacles for competitiveness, but form a common will, must connect with the motives and the attitudes of the citizens themselves ... The population must so to speak 'build up' their national identities, and add to them a European dimension' (Habermas and Derrida, 2005: 7). The Habermas/Derrida essay was controversial partly because it went beyond seeking common denominators to identifying a 'core' Europe and charging it with leadership of the rest.

Habermas and Derrida offered an explicit account of what they regarded as the essence of existing European identity:

> In European societies, secularization is relatively developed. Citizens here regard transgressions of the border between politics and religion with suspicion. Europeans have a relatively large amount of trust in the organizational and steering capacities of the state, while remaining skeptical toward the

achievements of markets. They possess a keen sense of the 'dialectic of enlightenment'; they have no naively optimistic expectations about technological progress. They maintain a preference for the welfare state's guarantees of social security and for regulations on the basis of solidarity. The threshold of tolerance for the use of force against persons is relatively low. The desire for a multilateral and legally regulated international order is connected with the hope for an effective global domestic policy, within the framework of a reformed United Nations (2005: 9).

This is an account that academic Europeanists would find largely familiar, though most would likely find it incomplete: emphasizing politics and policy, making its point about skepticism towards markets one-sidedly and neglecting actual engagement in market capitalism and attendant consumption practices (on which see Victoria de Grazia's 2005 reminder that this involves features that bring Europe together with America as well as some which separate). One might also remark on music and style, or on questions of openness, to immigrants and to social mobility.

Habermas and Derrida point, indeed, to many features American specialists on Europe would take to be evidence of 'civilizing' tendencies America would do well to emulate. By and large, specialists in European studies are sympathetic to the EU or are even open advocates for increasing integration – as though their scholarly investment in Europe called for clearer ascendancy of the whole over constituent nations. Habermas hoped that this identity would grow stronger, and not least, that it would lead Europeans to constitute a stronger EU by ratifying the proposed Basic Law in 2005. But French and Dutch electorates would come to surprise both Habermas and the academic Europeanists by rejecting the Basic Law.

EUROPEAN INTEGRATION AND THE POLITICS OF FEAR (AND HOPE)

In 2005, just before the first series of referenda on the proposed European Basic Law,

observers noted a perplexing trend: European Jews voting for far-right-wing political parties. In Antwerp, for example, at least 65 percent of those registered as Jews during World War II died during the Holocaust yet at least 5 percent of the Jewish population 60 years later has voted for Vlaams Belang, the xenophobic far-right Flemish party that focuses on Muslims but was founded by Nazi collaborators (Smith, 2005).

Most Belgian – and more generally European – Jews are probably outraged by *Vlaams Belang*. There may be a long-term drift of Jewish voting from more leftist to rightist parties, but that isn't really the issue. The issue has nothing to do with generalizing about Jews, nor simply with left or right. It has to do with fear making for strange alliances, since after all the party the surprising 5 percent of Jews have voted for is not simply rightist, it is extreme nationalist. It is, in an ironic way, a party of unity, for some, a party that says one particular common bond should trump certain internal differences and at the same time create a wall against 'foreign' incursions.

It is no accident that such nationalism could play on anxieties raised simultaneously by Muslim immigration and European integration. But this is not just a Belgian or European phenomenon. Versions of the same thing are happening in many places in the world. People are seeking protective solidarities against a variety of real or perceived threats. They seek different kinds of solidarities: ethnic, nationalist, religious, regional, corporate, and others. In general, none feels adequate and fears remain powerful, which may help turn any of the defensive solidarities into something offensive.

The strange juxtaposition of Jews voting for the descendants of Nazis because they fear Muslims is not merely an ironic reflection of how difficult it is to make sense of the multiple identities by which each is located in the modern world. It is a challenge to the notion that 'thin' identities, those grounded in the common procedures of a constitution or an entirely civic nationalism, are ascendant in Europe. The very language of civic nationalism is ironically deployed in articulating what amounts to an ethnic identity. A group of immigrants is described as undesirable because of the 'thickness' of its cultural traditions, which resist assimilation, and the undesirable character of some of its alleged cultural practices. The charges are framed in the language of civic nationalism and Enlightenment. That a not insignificant number of European Jews join in reflects not only how widespread the phenomenon is, but also the power of this rhetorical formation.

This involves a peculiar form of 'culturalism' which is widespread in European debates about immigration (Schinkel, 2008). Informed, ironically, by modern anthropological relativism, it suggests that the immigrants need to return to their 'own cultures' which must follow their own paths of development. This culturalism is paradoxically coupled with claims to universalistic ethics – as what Europeans have and others lack. Indeed, many in the Netherlands implicitly, if paradoxically, claim the heritage of the Enlightenment as a sort of ethnic attribute. Their main insistence is not on race but culture, on having absorbed the Enlightenment into their culture in a way that Muslim immigrants could not or would not. This sort of view is widespread in a range of European countries where a liberal immigration policy has been juxtaposed to a strong sense of national identity with the result that the grandchildren of immigrants, themselves citizens and often children of citizens, are not recognized as nationals. And it is analogous to Samuel Huntington's (2004) arguments about the gulf between the democratic–capitalist culture of the US and the inescapable alienness of Hispanics.

Cosmopolitanism becomes, ironically, the language of rejection of immigrants who are inadequately cosmopolitan. Therefore, the immigrants are accused of not respecting human rights or other universal values, as well as of not learning the local language. European struggles over the relationship of cosmopolitanism to belonging reflect a particular history of nationalism and a particular

project of transnational integration. They have influenced the development of cosmopolitanism as a core theme in both political theory and global politics. This has sometimes brought problematic assumptions. For example, the 300 years after the Peace of Westphalia are sometimes treated as an era of global order based on national states. The nation-state project was indeed one powerful force between 1648 and the current period. But to call this an era of global order requires some sense of irony, since nation states engineered such massive violence. It was in the context of these wars, indeed, that the very cosmopolitan idea of humanitarian actions to reduce the suffering wars entailed took root, with the founding of the International Committee for the Red Cross in 1863 and the Geneva Conventions of 1864 as its symbols. But the fact of these wars, and the fact that refugees were hardly greeted with open arms in all instances, remind us that Kant's effort to renew commitments to the ancient idea of political asylum were efforts in theory that did not immediately define practice.

Likewise, the Peace of Westphalia ended Europe's main religious wars, but ushered in an era of new struggles to define, unify, and strengthen national states. It was not simply an era of actual nation states, and therefore the present era is hardly simply the end of the era of nation states. After Westphalia, national projects – and states – benefited from the international understanding of nations as crucial to the legitimacy of states, but they also confronted challenges including the integration of populations that didn't necessarily speak a common language let alone share a fully common culture. Most were in fact confessional states – perhaps ironically a long-term reason for European secularism and suspicion of religion, but in the short-run part of the pursuit of national integration (Casanova, 1994). European nationalism, moreover, was almost always intimately connected to European imperialism. At its most republican, revolutionary France never ceased being actively imperial – not when the Revolutionary Assembly confronted the

Haitian revolution and not when the Third Republic faced the Algerian drive for independence.

Over decades, the project of European integration has itself become a response to the fact that no European country is a superpower. This encourages cooperation as much as the threat of war any one of them might pose to the others. Europe needs to unite, Europeans are told, in order to compete effectively in global markets. This is made possible, Europeans are told, by a common European civilization. And moreover, Europeans still have a *mission civilisatrice* to the rest of the world. Not least of all, as Jurgen Habermas and Jacques Derrida (2003) argued in their joint letter after the US invasion of Iraq (published simultaneously in *Frankfurter Allgemeine Zeitung* and *Libération* on 31 May 2003), Europeans have an opportunity and a responsibility to 'balance out the hegemonic unilateralism of the United States'. Europe's solidarity is not simply intra-European, but also counterposed to the US and the non-West. And here again, the assertion of cosmopolitanism figures as among other things an answer to perceived excesses of nationalism.

Global projections of US state power are at the same time imperialist, nationalist, and neoliberal. They combine attempts to reshape ostensibly sovereign nation states, to derive national advantages for the US, and to promote global capitalism. Some US leaders express ambitions to spread democracy – and indeed claim the language of human rights as an object rather than (as often) a criticism of US policy. When hegemonic powers use the language of democracy and popular will it is easy to be cynical. The neoconservative advocates of 'democracy promotion' in fact renewed an older US tradition (Guilhot, 2005). But promoting democracy by imperial domination is problematic. At the same time, it is important to recognize that a new assertion of imperial power is not simply a return to some 'pre-Westphalian' order, as though for 350 years the world has been neatly and peacefully ordered by nation states.

Nationalism and imperialism have been more mutually connected and interdependent than that. And finally, it is important to recognize that cosmopolitanism can be as much the project of neoliberalism as of cultural creativity or human rights, that global citizenship is extremely inegalitarian, and that national and local structures of belonging still matter a great deal (Calhoun, 2003a). We need not embrace nationalism uncritically to see that nation states still provide the contexts of everyday solidarities and most people's life projects; they still are they primary arenas for democratic public life; and they are focal points for resistance to imperialism.

A key question was whether Europe could begin to play these roles as well – offering its citizens a meaningful sense of shared belonging and capacity to plan an effective international role counterbalancing imperialism. Cosmopolitan democracy seemed not only an attractive possibility but the clear direction of progress, borne ineluctably on the tide of globalization (Held, 1995, offered one of the most important statements). But of course tides have a way of turning, and globalization brought resistances as well as embraces. Theories that made cosmopolitanism seem too easy left many cosmopolitan liberals unprepared for new challenges symbolized by September 11th, and more generally for a world in which suspicions and cultural divisions were powerful, in which a struggle over solidarities and identities was by no means consistently 'liberal', and in which a hegemonic global superpower claimed to be cosmopolitan and advance democracy – though hardly without dissent. Even in Europe, the politics of fear flourished.

The proposed 'Constitution' of 2005 seemed to embody the cosmopolitan ideals of European integration. It fared no better than the dream of a common foreign policy faced with US-led war and struggles against terrorist tactics. Indeed, the so-called Constitution illustrated not only a weak point of the European Union but also the weakness of approaches to transnational unity grounded only in formal legal arrangements not social solidarity. It was a document only techno-crats could love, and which some technocrats loved partly because it was designed to empower them at the expense of democratic public participation. It was too long to be read, let alone memorized; too complicated to be incorporated in a meaningful way into the collective consciousness of Europeans. It was a manifestation of a process that thought of a constitution as simply a basic law and not as a process of constituting political relations among citizens. That the writing was overseen by Valéry Giscard d'Estaing, a quintessential 'Énarch' (gradu-ate of France's super-elite national school of administration), was apt and that he showed no comprehension of the depth of doubt and distrust his document inspired was telling.

Ironically, the debate over the constitution may have been the most meaningful demon-stration of a European public sphere yet seen. It involved much more active public debate and discussion, though fewer protests in the streets than the opposition to the US-led invasion of Iraq in 2003 which Habermas, Derrida, and others identified as the birth of this public sphere. But the opposition was as strong as it was (and still is) partly because the process of 'constituting' Europe had not included the nurturing of a strong pan-European public sphere (Calhoun, 2003b; Nash, 2007). This contributed to suspicions of the technocratic constitution and indeed to fear of the European project itself, at least as currently led.

Moreover, just as the domination of national states and large-scale markets achieved in the nineteenth century over local communities and other groupings like craft unions or provincial cultures was hardly a one-sided blessing, so too would it be a mis-take to think transcending the national is only and entirely a path of progress. Europe, for example, is perhaps less 'neoliberal' in policy than the US (though at points Britain and some of the new European countries would rival the US). But it is just as embedded in global capitalism. Who wins and who loses is in every historical recurrence an open ques-tion, decided in significant part by how the process plays out – and by struggles over its terms. In such struggles, power is typically lopsided. As Pierre Bourdieu (2002) sug-gested, unification usually benefits the dominant.

This was true in the forging of national states, but the process nonetheless created openings for new groups and occasions for struggle to increase democracy and public services. There are similar opportunities in European and indeed global integration. But the advance of democracy is far from a simple or guaranteed byproduct of such inte-gration. It still takes struggle fought with very unequal resources.

In such struggles, seemingly anti-cosmopolitan resistance is often a weapon of those in danger of intensified exploitation by domi-nant interests; it may shape a better interna-tional order and eventually better terms for cosmopolitan transcendence of parts of the nation-state system. But equally, extensions of transnational power and capitalist markets can also inform fears that fuel populist reactions against immigrants. These are fears not merely from the ethnically prejudiced – though they may also be that – but fears as well from citizens who feel that their citizenship buys them less and less protection from global threats and less and less partici-patory democracy.

European integration and non-Western immigration put enormous pressures on the solidarity and self-understanding of European societies. Much cosmopolitanism speaks only poorly to this predicament. By insisting on the language of liberal universalism as a basis for European integration or global rights, by relying one-sidedly on notions like constitutional patriotism, and by imaging that larger solidarities are always produced by escape from narrower ones, rather than by transformations of these, it loses purchase on reality. In particular, it loses purchase on the possibility of actual historical production of larger and better but still incomplete and imperfect projects of integration.

Crucially, as Claus Offe (2006) has argued, even when discussions of the EU invoke a potential European identity, they seldom offer any suggestion that the completion of European integration would be a process of *liberation*. Integration may be practically useful. It may strengthen economic competitiveness. It may enable Europeans to act with more effect on the world stage. But it does not seem to offer liberation from either illegitimate government or external domination. In invoking American imperialism, Habermas suggests that (at least 'core') Europeans are being dominated. But this is domination in setting policy towards other parts of the world, not in governing Europe itself. By contrast, nationalism has often captured emotional commitment by its integration with projects that promised liberation, from colonial rule, for example, or from aristocracies at home that abused the people.

The defeat of Europe's new constitutional treaty in French and Dutch referenda sent the European Union – and the European public sphere – into crisis. Defeat was greeted with shock by many European elites, even though the discontent behind the votes had been brewing for years and been manifestly boiling for months. As the referenda approached, opinion polls sounded the alarm for pro-European intellectuals. Jurgen Habermas (2005) famously wrote to French voters – and in general called on the European left to vote in favor of the Constitution. 'In my view,' he said, 'a Left which aims to tame and civilise capitalism with a "No" to the European constitution would be deciding for the wrong side at the wrong time.'

Backing Europe, however, meant in this case backing the 'basic law', described widely as a constitution. Habermas grasped that the document was flawed and that there was widespread impatience with the elites driving European integration. He did not seem to grasp equally how elitist and offensive the document itself was, how perfectly it symbolized the notion that a cosmopolitan Europe would be democratic only in form, not in egalitarian participation. Habermas

hoped Europe would be enabled to act with greater agency when bolstered by the legal unity of the Constitution. 'We can only meet the challenges and risks of a world in upheaval in an offensive way by strengthening Europe,' he wrote, 'not by exploiting the understandable fears of the people in a populist manner.'

A politics of fear was very prominent in the European constitutional referenda. It seized in large part on immigrants and European Muslims. But it also reflected the notion that democratic participation in public affairs was to be diluted precisely at a time when powerful global forces were undermining social benefits which citizens of different countries felt they had gained by centuries of struggle – and when their states were engineering neoliberal reforms rather than protecting important institutions from the leveling effects of either global capitalism or the power of an 'American model' and military. Immigrants became readily available and relatively easy to name targets for fears aroused by other sources.

The results are sometimes saddening as well as perplexing – as in the case of Antwerp Jews who voted for *Vlaams Belang*. Fear – a widespread basic insecurity – is a central issue, and a challenge to which global cosmopolitanism has not yet faced up. People do not always name the sources of their fears very accurately. They say they are afraid of immigrants when they are most afraid of losing their jobs. They say they are afraid of European integration when they are most afraid that their children will fail to find careers and not be there for them in their old age. Politicians may manipulate their fears by playing on the most visible foci, those easiest for them to articulate. But the pervasiveness of the fear and anxiety are clues that they transcend these causes. They come from global neoliberal capitalism and its destruction of stable economic institutions. They come from new technologies that change social relations, even inside families, and thereby fundamental human relations to the world. They come from aging – both individually and in whole generations – with its attendant worries over sickness and death and in the meantime where to find care and money a safe place to live. They come from natural disasters like tsunamis and from such not completely natural disasters as the AIDS pandemic or avoidable famines and such humanly wrought disasters as civil wars and genocides, terrorism and counterterrorist projects that seem only to breed more terrorism. And the fears and anxieties are magnified by the media because they produce audiences as well as political extremists.

There are many and realistic reasons for fear and anxiety – indeed, there are enough that we should be impressed that we are not afraid all the time. We take public transport despite terrorist attacks. We approach most strangers with an optimism that we will find good ways to get along and maybe find pleasure in our very differences. We have children, despite the world they will face. But we are able to do these things precisely because we do not face the frightening and anxiety-provoking world alone. Ironically, the liberal individualist underpinnings of much cosmopolitan thought suggest in essence that we should. That is, they suggest that we start from individual moral subjects abstracted out of particular social relations and cultural traditions and ask what obligations they owe to each other. This is a mistake, for the antidotes to insecurity and the capacity for democracy alike lie not simply in individual reason but in social solidarity. This starts at the very personal and the very local, but matters also for communities, cities, and nations. An integrating Europe needs to be experienced as providing, not removing, such webs of solidarity.

dominions. It was the central focus of world wars that brought death and destruction to every continent. It was the site from which the idea and ideal and ideology of the West were carried to a range of 'Easts' from Russia to India to the Middle East and the Far East (both comprehensibly named only in relation to Europe). It was the birthplace of capitalism. And it is now the world's most interesting experiment in transnational integration.

So too, European studies – as a loose collection of inquiries and as a more or less organized field of study – have important roots in views of Europe from off the continent. They are also the product of transnational institutions and connections that predated nationalism. European studies have long been and still are important parts of the making of Europe. This means both imagining culture and society at the level of the continent, and using scholarly and research-based knowledge of Europe as a basis for practical policy.

European history and contemporary European affairs are shaped by both cosmopolitanism and nationalism at the same time, not just serially. Europe is indeed one of the best natural laboratories for studying cosmopolitanism, whether by this one means an elite style and ethnical universalism, or an engagement with difference. Such studies reveal tensions among these versions of cosmopolitanism, and between each and nationalism (as well as religious and other commitments or structures of belonging). European studies is likely to thrive because these challenges make Europe interesting – not because it is obvious what Europe means as a historical category, how integrated it is today, or what it will be in the future.

CONCLUSION

Europe has always mattered beyond Europe. It was a curious and sometimes threatening northern frontier to the Roman Empire. It was a collection of alluring, frustrating, and exploitative metropoles to Europe's colonial

REFERENCES

Almond, G. and Verba, S. (1963) *The Civic Culture*. Princeton: Princeton University Press.

Anderson, B. (1991) *Imagined Communities*, revised edn. London: Verso.

Bailyn, B. (2005) *Atlantic History*. Cambridge, MA: Harvard University Press.

Beck, U. (1992) *Risk Society: Towards a New Modernity*. Cambridge: Polity.

Beck, U. (1997) *World Risk Society*. Cambridge: Polity.

Beck, U. and Grande, E. (2006) *Cosmopolitan Europe*. Cambridge, Polity.

Bourdieu, P. (2002) 'Unifying to better dominate,' in *Firing Back*. New York: New Press.

Calhoun, C. (2003a) 'The class consciousness of frequent travelers: toward a critique of actually existing cosmopolitanism,' *South Atlantic Quarterly*, 101 (4): 869–897.

Calhoun, C. (2003b) 'The democratic integration of Europe: interests, identity, and the public sphere,' in M. Berezin and M. Schain (eds) *Europe Without Borders: Re-Mapping Territory, Citizenship and Identity in a Transnational Age*. Baltimore: Johns Hopkins University Press, pp. 243–274.

Casanova, J. (1994) *Public Religions in the Modern World*. Chicago: University of Chicago Press.

Chakrabarty, D. (2000) *Provincializing Europe*. Princeton: Princeton University Press.

de Grazia, V. (2005) *Irresistible Empire: America's Advance through Twentieth-Century Europe*. Cambridge, MA: Harvard University Press.

Giddens, A. (1990) *Consequences of Modernity*. Cambridge: Polity.

Gilroy, P. (1990) *The Black Atlantic*. London: Verso.

Guilhot, N. (2005) *The Democracy Makers: Human Rights and the Politics of Global Order*. New York: Columbia University Press.

Habermas, J. (2005) 'The illusionary 'Leftist No': Adopting the constitution to strengthen Europe's power to act', *Nouvel Observateur*, 7 May.

Habermas, J. (2006) 'The development of a European identity', in J. Habermas (ed.) *The Divided West*. Cambridge: Polity, pp. 67–82.

Habermas, J. and Derrida, J. (2003) 'February 15, or, what binds Europeans Together: Please for a common foreign policy, beginning in core Europe', in D. Levy, M. Pensky and J. Torpey (eds) *Old Europe, New Europe, Core Europe*. London: Verso, pp. 3–13.

Habermas, J. and Derrida, J. (2005) 'After the war: the rebirth of Europe,' in D. Levy, M. Pensky and J. Torpey (eds) *Old Europe, New Europe, Core Europe*. London: Verso, pp. 71–97.

Held, D. (1995) *Democracy and Global Order*. Cambridge: Polity.

Hobsbawm, E. (1993) *The Age of Extremes: The Short Twentieth Century 1914–1991*. New York: Pantheon.

Huntington, S. (2004) *Who Are We? The Challenges to America's National Identity*. New York: Simon & Schuster.

Levy, D., Pensky, M. and Torpey, J. (2005) 'Introduction' in D. Levy, M. Pensky and J. Torpey (eds) *Old Europe, New Europe, Core Europe*. London: Verso, pp. 1–23.

Melucci, A. (1989) *Nomads of the Present: Social Movements and Individual Needs in Contemporary Society*. Philadelphia: Temple University Press.

Muschg, A. (2005) 'Core Europe: Thoughts about the European identity,' in D. Levy, M. Pensky and J. Torpey (eds) *Old Europe, New Europe, Core Europe*. London: Verso, pp. 21–27.

Nash, K. (2007) 'Out of Europe: Human rights and prospects for cosmopolitan democracy', in C. Rumsford (ed.) *Cosmopolitan Europe*. Liverpool: Liverpool University Press, pp 89–104.

Offe, C. (2006) 'Social protection in a supranational context: European integration and the fates of the European social model', in P.K. Bardhan, S. Bowles and M. Wallerstein (eds) *Globalization and Egalitarian Redistribution*. Princeton: Princeton University Press, pp. 306–319.

Rumford, C. (ed.) (2005) *Cosmopolitanism and Europe*. Liverpool: Liverpool University Press.

Rumsford, C.(ed.) (2007) *Cosmopolitan Europe*. Liverpool: Liverpool University Press.

Saada, E. (2007) *Les enfants de la colonie: les métis de l'Empire français entre sujétion et citoyenneté*. Paris: Découverte.

Savater, F. (2005) 'Europe, both needed and in need', in D. Levy, M. Pensky and J. Torpey (eds) *Old Europe, New Europe, Core Europe*. London: Verso, pp. 41–43.

Schinckel, W. (2008) 'On culturalism,' in W. Schinkel (ed.) *The State of the State*. London: Palgrave/Macmillan.

Smith, C.R. (2005) 'Europe's Jews seek solace on the right', *New York Times*, February 20.

Taylor, C. (2007) *A Secular Age*. Cambridge, MA: Harvard University Press.

Tilly, C. (1975) *The Formation of National States in Western Europe*. Princeton: Princeton University Press.

Index